the HARVARD GUIDE to MODERN PSYCHIATRY

the HARVARD GUIDE to MODERN PSYCHIATRY

EDITED BY Armand M. Nicholi, Jr., M.D.

The Belknap Press of Harvard University Press

Cambridge, Massachusetts, and London, England · 1978

Library of Congress Cataloging in Publication Data

Main entry under title:
The Harvard guide to modern psychiatry.

    Includes bibliographical references and index.
    1. Psychiatry.   I. Nicholi, Armand M., 1928-
[DNLM: 1. Psychiatry.   WM100 H337]
RC454.H36   616.8'9   77-11036
ISBN 0-674-37566-1

To my wife, Ingrid, and my teacher, the late Elvin Semrad

CONTRIBUTORS

Ross J. Baldessarini, M.D.
Associate Professor of Psychiatry, Harvard Medical School
Associate Director, Mailman Laboratories for Psychiatric Research, McLean Hospital

Morton Beiser, M.D.
Professor of Psychiatry, University of British Columbia
Director of Research, University of British Columbia–World Health Organization Center for Research and Training

Martin A. Berezin, M.D.
Associate Clinical Professor of Psychiatry, Harvard Medical School
Training and Supervising Analyst, The Boston Psychoanalytic Institute

Norman R. Bernstein, M.D.
Assistant Professor of Psychiatry, Harvard Medical School
Director of Child Psychiatry, Massachusetts General Hospital

Ann W. Birk, PH.D.
Clinical Consultant, Learning Therapies, Inc., Newton, Massachusetts

Lee Birk, M.D.
Associate Clinical Professor of Psychiatry, Harvard Medical School
Clinical Director, Learning Therapies, Inc., Newton, Massachusetts

Ned H. Cassem, M.D.
Associate Professor of Psychiatry, Harvard Medical School
Chief, Psychiatric Consultation-Liaison Service, Massachusetts General Hospital

Max Day, M.D.
Assistant Clinical Professor of Psychiatry, Harvard Medical School
Clinical Associate in Psychiatry, Massachusetts General Hospital

T. Corwin Fleming, M.D.
Assistant Clinical Professor of Neurology, Harvard Medical School

Shervert H. Frazier, M.D.
Professor of Psychiatry, Harvard Medical School
Psychiatrist-in-Chief, McLean Hospital

Norman Geschwind, M.D.
James Jackson Putnam Professor of Neurology, Harvard Medical School
Director, Neurological Unit, Beth Israel Hospital, Boston, Massachusetts

Thomas P. Hackett, M.D.
Eben S. Draper Professor of Psychiatry, Harvard Medical School
Chief of Psychiatry, Massachusetts General Hospital

Ernest Hartmann, M.D.
Professor of Psychiatry, Tufts University School of Medicine
Director, Sleep and Dream Laboratory, Boston State Hospital

Seymour S. Kety, M.D.
Professor of Psychiatry, Harvard Medical School
Director, Mailman Research Center, McLean Hospital

Gerald L. Klerman, M.D.
Professor of Psychiatry, Harvard Medical School
Director, Stanley Cobb Research Laboratories, Massachusetts General Hospital

Lee B. Macht, M.D.
Associate Professor of Psychiatry, Harvard Medical School
Director, Clinical Services, Cambridge-Somerville Mental Health and Retardation Center, and Department of Psychiatry, The Cambridge Hospital

John E. Mack, M.D.
Professor of Psychiatry, Harvard Medical School
Head, Department of Psychiatry, The Cambridge
Hospital

William W. Meissner, M.D.
Associate Clinical Professor of Psychiatry, Harvard
Medical School
Chairman of the Faculty, The Boston Psycho-
analytic Institute

John C. Nemiah, M.D.
Professor of Psychiatry, Harvard Medical School
Psychiatrist-in-Chief, Beth Israel Hospital, Boston,
Massachusetts

Armand M. Nicholi, Jr., M.D.
Instructor in Psychiatry, Harvard Medical School

Carl Salzman, M.D.
Assistant Professor of Psychiatry, Harvard Medical
School
Codirector, Somatic Therapies Unit and Psycho-
pharmacology Research Laboratory, Massachu-
setts Mental Health Center

Joseph J. Schildkraut, M.D.
Professor of Psychiatry, Harvard Medical School
Director, Neuropsychopharmacology Laboratory,
Massachusetts Mental Health Center

Benjamin Seltzer, M.D.
Instructor in Neurology, Harvard Medical School
Associate in Neurology, Beth Israel Hospital,
Boston, Massachusetts

Elvin V. Semrad, M.D.
Late Professor of Psychiatry, Harvard Medical
School
*Late Senior Clinical Consultant and Director of
Psychotherapy*, Massachusetts Mental Health
Center

David V. Sheehan, M.B., B.CH., B.A.O.
Instructor in Psychiatry, Harvard Medical School
Director, Hypnosis and Psychosomatic Medicine
Clinic, Massachusetts General Hospital

Ira Sherwin, M.D.
Assistant Professor of Neurology, Harvard Medical
School
*Associate Chief of Staff for Research and Develop-
ment*, Veterans Administration Hospital, Bedford,
Massachusetts

Peter E. Sifneos, M.D.
Professor of Psychiatry, Harvard Medical School
Associate Director, Department of Psychiatry,
Beth Israel Hospital, Boston, Massachusetts

Alfred H. Stanton, M.D.
Professor of Psychiatry, Harvard Medical School
Director, Psychosocial Research Unit, McLean
Hospital

Alan A. Stone, M.D.
*Professor of Law and Psychiatry in the Faculty
of Law and the Faculty of Medicine*, Harvard
University

George E. Vaillant, M.D.
Professor of Psychiatry, Harvard Medical School
Codirector, Cambridge-Somerville Alcohol Pro-
gram, The Cambridge Hospital

Elinor Weeks, M.D.
Clinical Instructor in Psychiatry, Harvard Medical
School
Child Psychiatrist, Cambridge-Somerville Mental
Health and Retardation Center, The Cambridge
Hospital

Justin L. Weiss, PH.D.
Assistant Professor of Psychiatry, Harvard Medical
School
Director of Psychological Services, Massachusetts
Mental Health Center

Contents

Foreword

AS TWENTIETH-CENTURY psychiatry encompasses knowledge from an increasing number of related disciplines, the boundaries of psychiatry become difficult to define. Consequently, students, professionals, and interested laymen have come to realize the need for a clear and concise presentation of the relevant psychiatric information now available. This volume meets that need and is a tribute both to the excellence of the Harvard medical community and to the success of Armand M. Nicholi's efforts to organize a definitive and useful statement of knowledge in the field. The authors demonstrate their impressive experience and expertise in the many branches of psychiatry that now prevail. They have obviously engaged in intensive discussion and interchange during the years required for the fruition of this volume. We now have a concentrated, authoritative summary of the area we call "psychiatry"—as fine as any we have seen in several decades.

The present generation of Harvard scientists has organized a volume of discourses that ought to be *the* book to read and the first book to study. The authors are well-known contributors in their fields and eminently qualified to communicate without jargon. In addition to being regarded as experts and fine teachers, many have assumed significant responsibilities as heads of services, departments, or institutions. As such, they are aware of the practical as well as the theoretical aspects of clinical care and treatment. Their presentations have both the clarity and organizational elegance that characterize good teachers and the down-to-earth qualities derived from day-to-day service to people in trouble.

It is apparent that considerable thought and care went into the organization and validation of details, thus giving primary consideration to the volume's usefulness as an educational tool. This has been a thorough, careful, and painstaking collaboration. Truly, the years spent in preparing this book have been a dedicated public service to the whole field of mental health and behavioral science.

All essential branches of this field are well considered. Many chapters have excellent historical summaries of particular areas of psychiatry. I would strongly recommend this text to scholars, trainees, and educators—indeed, to anyone interested in continued education and certification. The American Board of Psychiatry and Neurology and those serving on its several committees have consulted these authors or their publications often in making up examinations for candidates seeking specialty rating in psychiatry and neurology.

The Harvard Guide to Modern Psychiatry should be the basic text for anyone interested in mastery of essentials. It will also introduce the reader to the particular viewpoints of eminent clinicians and scientists who will continue to make contributions to the literature for many years to come.

Milton Greenblatt, M.D.

President, American Board of
    Psychiatry and Neurology, 1976
Professor of Psychiatry, University
    of California–Los Angeles

Preface

THIS BOOK BEGAN in the fall of 1973 when, over dinner, Shervert Frazier and I discussed the need among busy students and professionals for a brief, technically sound book on psychiatry. I had become aware of this need through my contacts with students, residents, and candidates for board exams. Dr. Frazier, who had just completed several years with the American Board of Psychiatry and Neurology, suggested that with recertification imminent, the usefulness of such a volume would increase. The following winter I began to map out a general format and table of contents based on what Dr. Frazier and I considered core material.

Throughout the preparation of this book, certain goals have been kept in mind. To attain precision and technical accuracy, authors who had contributed to and written extensively in their fields were invited to discuss their specialties; to minimize overlap and discontinuity, the number of authors was limited to about thirty; to keep the book focused and to avoid irrelevant detail, the authors attempted to restrict their discussion to what they considered essential for their chapters; to attain clarity and to avoid the common stylistic criticisms directed against medical writing generally, the authors were encouraged to focus on style as well as content. We struggled throughout to attain brevity without sacrificing completeness and to produce not simply a guide to the significant literature but a guide to the detailed knowledge necessary for the practice of modern psychiatry.

Three years ago the contributing authors met for the first time in Cambridge and thus began a series of informal meetings that continued throughout the preparation of the book. In addition, authors exchanged chapters and a formal network of readers was set up. Each chapter was read critically by the editor, an outside authority, a medical student, and a resident. Thus many chapters were revised at least a half-dozen times before reaching the publisher, where they underwent a meticulous process of further editing. (We have, incidentally, followed the standard English practice of using the pronoun *he* or *his* whenever the sex of an individual is not specified.)

Because we considered the history of psychiatry too vast and too significant to individual fields to be covered within a single chapter, historical summaries have been included in several chapters. For more detailed coverage of this subject, we refer the reader to one of the many excellent works on the history of psychiatry.

Although rigorously scientific in its approach and reflecting the major research developments made possible by new technology, the book remains focused on the patient, not as an object of research but as a person. Perhaps this emphasis comes through most clearly in Max Day and Elvin Semrad's statement that the therapist who treats the severely ill must "love the patient."

When Dr. Semrad died in 1976, during the preparation of this book, the world lost one of its most gifted psychiatrists. I believe his chapter on schizophrenic reactions, written with his close associate Max Day, captures his uniquely sensitive and humane approach to the patient. As a student, I had the good fortune to observe his enormous clinical skills at first hand and to witness his remarkable and often startling ability to make immediate, effective contact with the most seriously withdrawn patients. Some students were puzzled by his injunction to "love the patient." In our era of modern technology, it seemed anachronistic, unscientific, and, if not downright mawkish, at least impracticable considering the unkempt and extremely regressed patients he interviewed during his seminars. Nevertheless, his injunction seemed to me the key to understanding his psychotherapeutic approach.

In time I realized that Dr. Semrad's approach was based on a quality essential to all effective patient care: the capacity to step out of one's own conflicts sufficiently to become acutely aware of the patient's needs and to convey a strong willingness to help. English usage of *love* is so broad that it has little meaning; Greek provides helpful refinements. The word that I believe comes close to Dr. Semrad's meaning is *agape*—a disinterested, objective willing of the best for a person regardless of how one feels toward him. Other forms of love in the Greek lexicon—*storge* (affection), *eros* (involving passion), or *philia* (friendship)—involve primarily positive feelings, whereas *agape* involves primarily one's will and one's actions. The therapist-patient interaction is too complex and the therapist's feelings subject to too many uncontrollable variables for him to feel positive toward all of his patients all of the time. Yet he must always act in the patient's best interest, regardless of how he feels toward the patient at the moment. Biblical usage of *agape* denotes love between creature and creator, as in the first great commandment ("Thou shalt love the Lord thy God . . ."), and also love for another person, as in the second great commandment ("Thou shalt love thy neighbor as thyself"). *Agape*, it seems to me, is essential in all mature human relationships and epitomizes the ideal attitude of the therapist toward his patient.

Dr. Semrad demonstrated this concept clearly in his interaction with his patients and students. Both sensed instinctively that he was strongly *for* them, that he genuinely wanted the best for them. We hope this book serves as a testimonial to the clinical competence and the compassion he manifested as a teacher and clinician.

When the planning, writing, and publication of a book extend over several years, it becomes difficult to acknowledge everyone who has helped. I am indebted to Shervert Frazier for helping to map out the general format; to the authors for their patience, cooperation, and warm friendship; to John Nemiah for his encouragement and criticism of several chapters; to Patricia Gerbarg, who read each chapter meticulously and gave valuable insights from a student's perspective; to W. Glenn Jamison, who read and commented on each chapter from a resident's point of view; to M. Robert Gardiner, Randolph Catlin, Roy Grinker, and Sissela Ann Bok for reading and commenting on specific chapters. I would also like to express my gratitude to Vernon Grounds for his unwavering encouragement; to Joyce Olesen for her constructive, substantive editing of many chapters; to Barbara Gale for her copy editing; to William E. Walker, Jr., Vester Hughes, and Kenton and Nancy McGee for helping to make the book's preparation possible.

A. M. N.
Concord, Massachusetts
August 1977

Introduction

The Therapist-Patient Relationship

CHAPTER 1

Armand M. Nicholi, Jr.

T HE QUALITY of the doctor-patient relationship, important in all medical specialties,
becomes absolutely crucial in the practice of psychiatry.* In no other branch of medicine does
the course and outcome of treatment rest so
heavily on the highly complex and extremely
sensitive interaction between doctor and patient.
From the first moment of contact, the doctor or
therapist initiates a process that involves a multiplicity of factors within himself as well as within
the patient and determines in large measure
whether or not the patient recovers. In this
process, the patient's personality becomes the
primary therapeutic focus; the therapist's personality (the vehicle for his skills, sensitivity, and
experience), the primary therapeutic instrument;
and the interaction between the two, the matrix
in which all psychotherapy either succeeds or
fails. Even before therapy actually begins, the
quality of the initial encounter facilitates or impedes the therapist's attempt to complete a successful evaluation. The lack of initial rapport
hinders his efforts to establish an accurate diag-

nosis, to determine the indications for treatment, and to choose the appropriate treatment
modality.

Though systematic study and controlled research on the therapist-patient relationship remains surprisingly limited, some recent studies
shed light on the reasons why many of these relationships fail (Hill, 1969; Kline Adrian, and
Spevak, 1974; Salzman et al., 1970). These studies investigate patients who left therapy against
medical advice either after an initial interview or
after a few sessions. They point out that one component of the therapist-patient relationship supersedes all others in determining whether the
patient continues with therapy: the therapist's
ability to convey an intrinsic interest in the patient has been found to be more important than
his position, appearance, reputation, clinical experience, training, and technical or theoretical
knowledge. Though this finding, like many significant research findings on human behavior,
appears obvious once we become aware of it,†
the practical application of this knowledge is by

---

* The principles discussed here apply to all therapist-
patient relationships, regardless of their duration or the form
and intensity of the therapy. Physicians in other specialties
aver that these principles indeed apply, by and large, to all
doctor-patient relationships.

† "It seems to be my fate," said Freud, "to discover only
the obvious: that children have sexual feelings, which
every nursemaid knows; and that night dreams are just as
much a wish-fulfillment as day dreams" (Jones, 1953, vol. 1,
p. 350).

no means obvious. Close, detailed attention must therefore be given to how, within the confines of a professional relationship and without patronizing or condescending, the therapist conveys genuine interest to the patient.

This question can best be considered by focusing particularly on what happens between therapist and patient during the initial evaluation. This chapter will describe not only the basic principles and dynamics of an effective therapist-patient relationship but also its tone or emotional ambience; it will emphasize specific details of the initial encounter that are often taken for granted, seldom discussed, and frequently unheeded but nevertheless crucial.*

The major elements of this initial encounter are these: (1) the therapist's attitude toward the patient; (2) the therapist's emotional resources and standard of conduct; (3) the professional versus the social relationship; (4) the concepts of resistance and therapeutic alliance; (5) obstacles in the patient; (6) feelings toward the therapist: reality and transference; (7) obstacles in the therapist: impediments to listening; (8) feelings toward the patient: reality and countertransference; (9) jargon and humor as obstacles; and (10) ethical considerations: sexual relations within therapy.

The Therapist's Attitude toward the Patient

The therapist's approach to the patient sets the tone for the initial interview. Whether the patient is young or old, neatly groomed or disheveled, outgoing or withdrawn, articulate or inarticulate, highly integrated or totally disintegrated, of high or low socioeconomic status, the skilled clinician realizes that the patient, as a fellow human being, is considerably more like himself than he is different and that even if he understands only a fraction of a patient's mental functioning, that patient will contribute significantly to the therapist's understanding of himself and of every other patient. The therapist also

realizes that each patient, regardless of how prosaic in appearance and background, is considerably more complex than can be grasped or described, no matter how brilliantly detailed the therapist's dynamic and genetic formulation; that each patient offers the therapist the potential for increasing his own professional skills and understanding, as well as for contributing to the body of knowledge in this relatively new specialty he practices. These realizations motivate the skilled and sensitive therapist to approach each patient with no little degree of humility, care, and respect.

The Therapist's Emotional Resources and Standard of Conduct

When a therapist first introduces himself to a patient—whether in a hospital ward, outpatient clinic, or private office—he brings to that first contact a reservoir of feelings, attitudes, and past experiences. His confidence in his clinical skills, his tolerance of the perplexity inherent in the diagnostic process, his ability to step out of his own needs and conflicts sufficiently to become aware of those of the patient, his attitude toward sickness, his sensitivity to suffering, his ability to recognize and to confront directly intense feelings of anxiety, depression, anger, dependency, and sexuality both in his patients and in himself, his intrinsic desire to help, his awareness of nuances of what people feel and subtleties in the expression of feelings, his ability to relate warmly, his respect for himself and for others, his value for human life, indeed, his very philosophy of life—all influence his approach to the patient and his capacity for establishing an effective therapist-patient relationship. In essence, the therapist must draw upon those resources within himself and observe the same courtesies he uses in his social and family relationships. The therapist must guard against the widespread tendency to neglect these common courtesies or to allow traditional scientific and medical formalities to supersede them in his relationship with his patients.

A patient consulting any doctor suffers stress, not only because of conflicts prompting the consultation but also because of conditions inherent in the doctor-patient relationship. The patient,

* We will view the therapist-patient relationship from a psychodynamic perspective, not because this perspective surpasses others, but because most training centers teach psychotherapy from this perspective and because psychoanalytic theory currently is more richly developed.

for example, is usually confused about the significance of his symptoms, unaware of their cause, apprehensive about what the doctor will recommend, and he often feels embarrassed or humiliated at exposing what he considers exceedingly personal details of his life. Under such circumstances he is particularly vulnerable, and for this reason he deserves even more consideration than in ordinary social interactions. Too often, however, he receives less. Even the simple introductory handshake is often neglected—perhaps because of the doctor's hectic schedule, because the doctor shares a common human tendency to withdraw from emotional illness, because he adheres to a distorted concept of the psychoanalytic model wherein the doctor never touches the patient (see chapter 17, "The Psychotherapies"), or, more likely, because he has never been formally taught to heed such issues.

The mundane yet often neglected practice of shaking hands helps set the tone for the initial relationship between therapist and patient. Shaking hands firmly with a patient brings to the first moments of contact an element of personal warmth and respect. This simple gesture eases the tension preceding the initial interview and reassures the patient, who almost always approaches the doctor with a degree of apprehension. To the patient, the doctor represents not only an awesome stranger who will probe the most intimate aspects of his life but also a highly knowledgeable authority with the power to make life and death decisions—or, in the case of a psychiatrist, what may be even more anxiety provoking, decisions concerning sanity and soundness of mind. Because so many people harbor this threatening image, a simple handshake at the beginning and at the end of the first session helps make the doctor seem more human. The following illustrates this point:

After presenting the history of a patient to the staff of a large teaching hospital, a resident doctor attempted to bring the patient from the ward to the conference to be interviewed. The patient, somewhat suspicious and fearful of confronting a large group, refused to enter the conference room. Another resident then went to persuade the patient. Again he refused. A third and fourth resident also tried unsuccessfully. Then a fifth resident spoke briefly to the patient, who immediately followed him into the conference room. When the staff reviewed the incident later, the only difference in approach appeared to be that the successful resident had taken the time to introduce himself and to shake the patient's hand.

The therapist's general attitude sets the stage for the development of initial rapport and for the establishment of a constructive working relationship, even as he meets the patient and asks him to be seated in his office. How does the therapist, for example, address the patient? Does he use the first or last name only, dispensing with the title of Mr., Miss, or Mrs. before the patient has granted that liberty? Does the doctor dismiss these common courtesies as stuffy formality? Or does he use them to express respect for the patient as a fellow human being? Is the therapist relaxed and at ease? Does he sit comfortably in his chair—close enough to hear a soft-spoken person but far enough away to avoid causing discomfort to those sensitive to physical closeness? Or is he tense and on edge, giving the impression of being more interested in obtaining the necessary facts and moving on quickly to the next patient than in the patient as a person? The skillful clinician carefully observes the impact of his words and behavior, realizing that all he says and does conveys his attitude toward his patient.

In essence, all that takes place in the initial stages of the therapist-patient relationship can be measured against a single, simple standard: is the therapist, in his exchange of initial courtesies, as warm and respectful to the patient as he would be to a dignitary visiting his home? Meeting such a visitor for the first time, the therapist would introduce himself, offer his hand, and take pains to make the visitor welcome and comfortable. The therapist would honor the visitor's title until given permission to dispense with it. He would strive to be relaxed and composed without being aloof or stilted and to be warm and responsive without being familiar or effusive. He should do the same in his first meeting with the patient.

The Professional versus the Social Relationship

If the therapist follows this standard of conduct, is there a risk of blurring the lines between a professional and a social relationship? How does the doctor-patient relationship differ from others? Although a doctor is expected to have a clear understanding of the differences, his medical school experience seldom helps him achieve this understanding. Though he may express the same amenities in both his professional and social relationships, the skilled clinician seldom confuses one with the other. He realizes that as long as his patient remains his patient, the therapist-patient interaction must, for the benefit of the patient, remain within the context of a professional relationship; this relationship differs from the social one in that it exists to perform a unique task—namely, to evaluate and treat the conflicts prompting the patient to seek psychiatric help.

The professional relationship is therefore a somewhat constrained, though nevertheless spontaneous, relationship in which the therapist directs his clinical skills and experience toward this evaluation and treatment. Whereas a social relationship focuses on the needs of both parties, a professional relationship focuses solely on the needs of the patient—never on the needs of the therapist. This helps him maintain objectivity and develop an acute sensitivity to the ways the patient's emotional conflicts manifest themselves in the interaction with the therapist. The therapist keeps his input into the relationship as stable and consistent as possible to help gauge subtle changes in the patient's reaction to him. He carefully directs his words and behavior to what he judges to be, in both the short and the long term, the best interests of the patient. This imposes limitations on the relationship, providing a degree of frustration for both parties. The patient becomes frustrated because his emotional conflicts and his tendency to regress often create expectations and demands that cannot be met. The therapist experiences frustration and a degree of loneliness as well because some of his patient's needs, and all of his own, must by and large be filled elsewhere. It cannot be emphasized too strongly, however, that although a professional relationship sets clearly defined limits and demands a degree of restraint and reserve, it by no means precludes warmth and kindness. Furthermore, to the extent that most patients need to see the therapist as a friend, as someone strongly *for* them, and to the extent that they consider a friend to be "a person with whom one is allied in a common struggle" or "a person whom one knows and trusts," as *The American Heritage Dictionary* defines the term, then to that extent a professional relationship also does not preclude friendship.*

The Concepts of Resistance and Therapeutic Alliance

Once the patient is seated, the therapist focuses his attention on facilitating in every way possible the patient's efforts to tell his story, which comprises the events and conflicts in the patient's life leading to his consulting a psychiatrist or other professional. More than in any other branch of medicine, the diagnostic formulation leans heavily on the patient's description of his symptoms and his explanation of the reasons for his visit. Though the patient may be eager to tell his story, partly to find relief from inner stress, and though the therapist may be eager to hear this story, realizing its indispensable contribution to his evaluation, the process of communication often runs into obstacles in both patient and therapist.

Dynamic psychiatry has focused considerable attention on understanding the manifestations and sources of obstacles in the patient. These observations have led to the clinical concept of *resistance*—those forces within the patient, conscious and unconscious, that oppose the purpose of the evaluation and the goals of the therapeutic process and that may be expressed in behavior, feelings, attitudes, ideas, impulses, and fantasies. This concept is fundamental to understanding the puzzling complexities of the interaction between therapist and patient. Close scrutiny of the therapist-patient relationship has revealed, paradoxically, that although patients come seeking relief from pain, they overtly or covertly oppose the therapist's efforts to effect that relief. A part of the patient strongly opposes not only the therapist but also the part of himself that seeks help.

The concepts of resistance, transference, and countertransference represent the most basic elements of dynamic psychiatry and illuminate many confusing and paradoxical aspects of the

* Both ancient Romans and ancient Greeks described the doctor-patient relationship in terms of friendship (see Seneca *De beneficiis* 6. 16 and Hippocratic *Praecepta* 50. 9. 258).

therapist-patient relationship. Though observed primarily in the context of intensive therapy, they often occur early in the therapist-patient interaction (see chapter 17, "The Psychotherapies").

The clinical manifestations of resistance are myriad. The patient may be several minutes late for his sessions; he may stare at the floor and avoid looking at the therapist, slouch in his chair or hide behind his hands, sit stiffly and not move at all or move incessantly, announce that he has nothing to say, that his symptoms have disappeared (the so-called flight into health), that he sees no reason for his being there, or that he refuses to discuss what prompted him to make an appointment. He may use jargon to avoid expressing what he feels, assume ignorance or stupidity, automatically reject every comment made by the therapist, joke incessantly, express his utter hopelessness of ever being helped, attempt to talk about the psychiatrist, express overt hostility and uncooperativeness, excessive compliance, or an overeagerness to please. He may be seductive; he may stutter, stammer, or become mute; or he may speak in one- or two-word sentences, as in the following:

"What brings you to see me?"
"My wife."
"You called for an appointment because your wife suggested it?"
"Yes."
"How do you understand her suggesting you see a psychiatrist?"
"I don't."
"Did you ask her?"
"No."

The skilled clinician learns to recognize the many forms of resistance in the patient, for he realizes that their detection and resolution determine whether his relationship with the patient will progress or founder.

The *therapeutic alliance* refers to those aspects of the therapist-patient relationship based on the patient's conscious and unconscious desires to cooperate with the therapist's efforts to help him. Whereas resistance represents all those forces in the patient opposing help from the therapist, the treatment alliance represents all the rational, nonneurotic parts of the patient desiring help.

Conceptually, the notion of the therapeutic alliance developed from theories of ego psychology and involves those ego functions relatively independent of the instinctual drives—the autonomous ego functions (Hartmann, 1964; A. Freud, 1966). The concept has received considerable attention in the literature of psychodynamics under such terms as *treatment alliance*, *working alliance*, and *therapeutic contract* (Zetzel, 1956; Menninger, 1958; Greenson, 1965; Stone, 1967; Friedman, 1969; Sandler, Dare, and Holder, 1973).

Obstacles in the Patient: Manifestations of Resistance

Tension and anxiety may interfere with the patient's ability to think and speak clearly and thus provide resistance to free expression. This tension arises not only from the stresses inherent in the therapist-patient relationship but, to a greater extent, from the repression of unconscious material underlying the psychological symptoms. The most superficial probing of this repressed, emotionally charged material may arouse intense anxiety and cause the most articulate person to stammer, grope for the right word, misuse or mispronounce words, or make grammatical errors he would seldom otherwise make.

Furthermore, subjective experience often defies easy verbalization. Physicians who become patients attest to the difficulty of translating their own symptoms into words, their extensive medical vocabulary notwithstanding, even when their symptoms are physical, localized to one part of the body, and acute in onset. Patients find that psychological symptoms, with their frequently irrational, unconscious determinants, and with their onset usually extending over months or years, are extremely difficult to verbalize or describe clearly.

When a patient struggles with such difficulties, the therapist must take steps not only to reduce this initial tension in every way possible but also to avoid intensifying it, deliberately or unthinkingly. If the patient at first refuses to talk about a topic, it is best merely to make note of it and go on to some other area. The therapist may explore briefly what makes the patient reticent, but the all-important issues of trust and confidentiality can be discussed with the patient at a later moment (see chapter 2, "History and Mental Status"). Some therapists deliberately increase anxiety for the avowed purpose of observing how the patient reacts under stress. Because most patients already suffer enormous stress, however, such measures are uncalled for and usually counterproductive. Other therapists, influenced by a distorted notion of the analytic model, may be aloof, distant, and distressingly unresponsive during the initial interview. To refuse to answer a patient's question, for example, without first explaining the reason why this and other customary modes of communication must be modified during the interview, unnecessarily increases the discomfort of the patient and reflects insensitivity on the part of the therapist. To express impatience by looking at the clock or moving restlessly as the patient struggles to express himself, to attempt to hurry the interview by offering alternate words or phrases as a patient gropes for the right one, to correct a patient's mispronunciation, misuse of a word, or grammatical error (a temptation, for example, when the therapist is insecure and the patient a learned professor) are all ways therapists may unthinkingly increase the tension and discomfort of the patient, impede the history-taking process, and thereby make the evaluation more difficult.

Whatever steps the therapist takes to mitigate this initial anxiety, on the other hand, facilitate both the patient's efforts to communicate and ultimately his own evaluation. A brief comment as the patient is being seated, for example, may help ease initial tension: "Did you have trouble finding the office?" "Has it stopped raining?" To the inexperienced therapist this banter may seem unprofessional, a waste of time. But the skilled clinician begins his evaluation from the first moment of contact with the patient. During this initial exchange of amenities, the therapist can observe a great deal about the patient's demeanor and his interaction with people. He can avoid any risk of the patient's using these friendly comments to carry on a lengthy social conversation (and thus delay confronting the emotionally charged issues) by focusing immediately on the basic information needed for his evaluation: birth date, marital status, previous psychiatric

help, and other information the patient knows well and can relate with ease. This makes possible a gradual transition from the initial exchange of amenities to the more difficult but central question, "What brings you to see me?" Whatever steps the therapist takes to help the patient confront this question with a minimum of inner fear and anxiety will set the stage for the establishment of further rapport and for a successful first interview.

The therapist's mannerisms can cause negative reactions in certain patients, and it is important that he be sensitive to these reactions when they occur. For example, the sixty-year-old president of a large corporation requested consultation with a university psychiatrist to help resolve some long-standing difficulties with his son, who was attending that institution. During the second interview, the executive stormed out of the office and failed to return. "What bothered me more than anything else," he said later, "was that every other word the psychiatrist used was a four-letter word. Perhaps he does this to show he is 'with it,' but I found it insulting and disrespectful. I left with the impression that he had more maturing to do and needed more help than I."

This incident points to the tendency of some clinicians who work with adolescents and young adults to tailor their dress and speech to that of their patients to help establish rapport. Such efforts usually fall short of success, the adolescent's dress and speech being an effort to establish distance from the adult world and to find his own identity. The important issue, however, is that the therapist be alert to the effects of his dress, speech, and other mannerisms on particular patients so he can deal with barriers that emerge. Most of the errors the therapist makes, however, are far less obvious than mistakes in scheduling or offensive mannerisms. More often they result from his inability to listen sympathetically, an insensitive comment, premature reassurance, a judgmental tone ("Why did you do that?"), or a patronizing air ("Come into the office, dear"). All may evoke negative feelings in the patient that interfere with the establishment of rapport.

Other obstacles the therapist may encounter early on may arise from the patient's *misconceptions* about psychotherapy, gains from illness,

displaced motivation, or the use of psychological defenses to avoid meaningful material. A
common misconception arises from the fear that
the doctor will pass on information about the patient to others or compile a record of the patient
to which future employers or other agencies will
have access. The therapist must assure the patient that standards of the utmost confidentiality
will be followed, even when discussing clinical
material with supervisors or other clinicians; the
name of the patient must be revealed only with
the patient's consent. Erosion of confidentiality
inevitably erodes the relationship with the patient. Another misconception is that the therapist will "brainwash" an individual or influence
the patient against his will to give up a certain
philosophy or lifestyle—for example, a member
of the women's liberation movement may fear
that the therapist will influence her to settle for a
traditional role she views as that of a second-class
citizen; a devout person may fear that the therapist will ridicule or destroy his faith; or a homosexual seeking help for nonsexual problems may
fear that the therapist will attempt to change his
sexual orientation. Direct reassurance and clarification of the goals of evaluation and therapy
will help remove such barriers.

Secondary gain (as opposed to "primary
gain") refers to certain benefits the patient
enjoys in being ill that cause him to take advantage of his illness and to prolong it. Such benefits
include increased personal attention, disability
compensation, and decreased responsibility, as
well as more subtle gratifications such as the satisfaction of the need for self-punishment or the
vengeful punishment of others who are forced to
take responsibility for the patient or to share his
suffering. Such secondary satisfactions from
illness may cause the patient to refuse to cooperate with therapy and must be detected and dealt
with at the outset of treatment.

Displaced motivation may also be a barrier.
Not infrequently a patient comes to the therapist
only because a parent, a spouse, or a family physician sends him. If the patient sees no need for
help, the first task of the therapist is to shift motivation from the referring person to the patient
himself. By carefully exploring the patient's conflicts, the therapist can help the patient understand how these conflicts impair functioning in

important areas of the patient's life. This understanding will often help the patient realize his
need for therapy. (Sometimes, of course, the patient may not in fact need help, and the therapist
can be immeasurably reassuring by conveying
this to the family or other referring person.)

Among the psychological defenses, in addition
to repression, that become obstacles is the use of
intellectual reasoning to avoid painful feelings.*
This kind of *intellectualization* involves expressing complaints with the use of jargon: "I
seem to be suffering from severe ego diffusion,"
or "I think I have a number of unresolved
pregenital conflicts." This obstacle occurs frequently in patients who work or study in hospital
or university communities. The therapist must
halt this tendency immediately by explaining
that the patient's task is to express what he feels
and experiences in his own words.

Feelings toward the Therapist:
Reality and Transference

The sources of resistance providing the most
powerful obstacles to diagnostic and therapeutic
efforts are the patient's feelings toward the therapist. All feelings in relationships as we now
understand them run on a double track. We
react and relate to another person not only on
the basis of how we consciously experience that
person in reality, but also on the basis of our
unconscious experience of him in reference to
experiences with significant people in infancy
and childhood—especially parents and other
family members. We tend to displace feelings
and attitudes from these past figures onto people
in the present, especially if the person in the
present has features similar to the person in the
past. An individual may, therefore, evoke intense feelings in us—strong attraction or strong
aversion—totally inappropriate to our knowledge of or experience with that person. This
process may, to varying degrees, influence our

---

* Recent attempts to categorize obstacles or resistance according to source have led to terms such as (1) *defense resistance*, including repression and intellectualization; (2) *transference resistance*, in which feelings displaced onto the
doctor act as resistance; (3) *secondary gain resistance*,
wherein gratifications of being ill outweigh the distress of the
illness; and (4) *superego resistance*, stemming from the patient's sense of guilt and need for punishment.

choice of a friend, roommate, spouse, or employer.

Feelings toward the therapist also have this twofold basis. They arise first from reactions to what the therapist is in reality—how he treats the patient, his manner, his dress, the length of his hair, the tone of his voice, the warmth or coldness of his personality, the firmness of his handshake—to all that he says and does in his interaction with the patient. Secondly, they arise from what he represents to the patient's unconscious. Feelings toward the therapist, therefore, stem not only from the real, factual aspects of the therapist-patient interaction but also from feelings displaced onto the therapist from unconscious representation of people important to the patient early in his childhood experiences. These displaced or transferred feelings tend to distort the therapist, making him appear to be an important figure in the patient's past; they create, in one sense, an illusion (Sandler, Dare, and Holder, 1973). This phenomenon of "transference," of displacing feelings from a person in the past to a person in the present, gives rise to some of the most intense, colorful, complex, perplexing, potentially destructive, and eventually most therapeutically useful aspects of the entire therapist-patient relationship.

Although transference reactions occur in all relationships, they occur most frequently and most intensely in relationships with authority. This happens especially in doctor-patient relationships, partly because patients often view the doctor as an authority figure and tend to displace onto him feelings once directed toward their parents, the first authorities in their lives. In addition, illness fosters regression to childlike patterns of response, which in turn lead to a strong passive dependence on the doctor. While doctors have been aware of transference phenomena for centuries, they failed to appreciate their complexity and therapeutic value until Freud studied and described them in detail (S. Freud, 1895, 1905, 1912).

Not all feelings toward the therapist, of course, interfere with the patient's telling his story. Positive feelings, because they evoke a desire to please the therapist, usually facilitate the patient's efforts to communicate. Such feelings may cause a sudden, marked improvement in the patient when the disappearance of symptoms results primarily from a desire to please the therapist. These so-called transference cures (not to be confused with "flight into health," a form of resistance) may be temporary, disappearing as soon as the intensity of the positive feelings toward the therapist diminishes. When positive feelings become too intense, however, when the need to please and to win approval becomes excessive, positive feelings may have the reverse effect, causing the patient to withhold information he feels may provoke the therapist's disapproval. In addition to the excessive need to please, positive feelings may also give rise to strong erotic feelings toward the therapist, which may in turn increase the patient's anxiety and interfere with easy communication. Negative feelings toward the therapist, on the other hand, almost always pose a barrier to easy communication. Anger and hostility evoke a reluctance to confide in the therapist and a tendency consciously or unconsciously to withhold significant details.

Transference feelings that become barriers to communication (whether the feelings are positive or negative) usually become manifest during the course of intensive therapy and will be discussed in greater detail in chapter 17, "The Psychotherapies." Sometimes, however, such barriers manifest themselves early in the therapist-patient relationship and seriously interfere with its progression. Because the therapist and patient have not yet established a therapeutic alliance, this obstacle may not only impede the therapist's evaluation but may also, unless resolved, abruptly and prematurely terminate the relationship.

During the first few sessions of an evaluation, a thirty-three-year-old woman experienced great difficulty speaking to the doctor. She entered the office and immediately began to cry. When she apologized for her loss of control, the doctor waited patiently for her to regain her composure and encouraged her to express all of her feelings. The intensity of the crying, however, continued throughout several sessions and made it impossible for the patient to speak. The doctor's efforts to explore the cause of her crying only increased her sobbing. She would feel fine until she entered the waiting room, then be overcome with fear and remorse. She expressed confusion over her fear of the doctor and her inability to talk to him. Entering the office, she would burst into tears, clench her fists, and press her arms against her body as though protecting herself. Her face would twitch, her hands tremble, and her whole body shake uncontrollably. Out of desperation, she consulted another doctor. The consultant suggested she return to her doctor, make one more effort to resolve the impasse and, if that proved unsuccessful, he would find another therapist for her. When she returned to her doctor and discussed in detail her session with the consultant, it became clear that her description of her doctor to the consultant paralleled word for word her description of her father given during the initial interview. When the doctor pointed this out to her, she said she had often noticed that the doctor's eyes were "exactly the same" as her father's. The doctor then explored with the patient her early and current relationship with her father, described by her as "a very special relationship." As a child, she had been his favorite and held him in awe. She spoke in glowing terms of his intelligence, his handsome appearance, and his strength. She mentioned also that he was cold, highly critical, somewhat cruel, and much hated by the rest of the family. Though she loved him, she feared him, and as a child she had found it impossible to talk with him. She recalled that her older, eleven-year-old sister had failed to respond quickly when her father called and had been "beaten by him with a belt until she bled." Even as an adult, she trembled when speaking with him on the phone. As she explored her relationship with her father, she realized how much her feelings toward the doctor paralleled those feelings experienced repeatedly as a small child toward her father. Once recognized and explored with the patient, the obstacle was overcome, the evaluation completed, and the relationship continued into a prolonged, constructive therapeutic experience.

Transference resistance, because it poses such a powerful obstacle, must be recognized early and dealt with immediately by the therapist, especially when it occurs during the initial evaluation or during the early stages of therapy. The therapist may recognize that a barrier exists and that it obviously relates to how the patient feels toward him, but how does he diagnose such feelings as transference reactions? His ability to distinguish between transferred and "reality" aspects of the patient's reactions may prove vital to

a continuation of the therapist-patient relationship.

Transference reactions have characteristics that the skilled clinician readily recognizes. First, transference is essentially an unconscious process. Though the patient may be aware of what he feels and perceive that his feelings are somewhat strange or bizarre, he has little or no awareness at the beginning of therapy of the source of these feelings or of their displacement from that source to the therapist. In the case described above, the patient was acutely aware of her own anxiety and realized she feared the doctor, but she had no idea of what caused these fears or of their relation to an early figure in her life whom she loved and at the same time feared intensely. Second, transference feelings are inappropriate in time and in intensity to the circumstances in which they occur. The patient may underreact or overreact—and may be fully aware that the reaction is inappropriate; the patient in the illustration expressed confusion because her fear of the therapist was out of keeping with what she described as his warmth and compassion. Third, transference reactions are characterized by ambivalence, that is, by the coexistence of opposing feelings or emotions toward the same person. In this case, the patient felt fear and a degree of hostility toward the doctor but also feelings of respect, admiration, and sexual attraction.

Because transference reactions are so prevalent, so colorful in their intensity, and so helpful in understanding the patient's dynamics, the therapist may become entranced by them and neglect the reality aspects of his relationship with the patient. Although his patient may be hypersensitive, may struggle with impaired self-esteem, may be insatiably dependent, and may manifest other conflicts causing frequent interpersonal difficulty, the therapist must not be lulled into neglecting the part he may be playing in provoking barriers within the patient.

If the therapist mistakenly treats feelings based on the reality of the relationship as transference feelings, he may permanently destroy the possibility of a good working relationship with the patient. If, for example, he makes a mistake in scheduling the initial interview and the patient arrives only to be told to come at some other time, or if he is late for the patient's first appointment, the patient may be furious with the therapist, even before making contact with him. If the therapist then treats the patient's anger as transference, ignoring the reality on which the anger is based, he may never see that patient again. Once the anger is recognized, the therapist must explore the anger with the patient to help to determine its source. Anger and other negative feelings may stem from transference or reality aspects of the relationship or both, and neither can be ignored.

Obstacles in the Therapist: Impediments to Listening

Just as serious obstacles to the diagnostic and therapeutic process arise within the patient, they also arise within the therapist. The latter become especially destructive to the therapist-patient relationship when they interfere with the therapist's capacity to listen. The therapist's ability to convey a genuine interest in his patient, to facilitate the patient's communication, and to establish a solid therapeutic alliance depends in large measure on his capacity to listen effectively. Before discussing obstacles that interfere with listening, this section will attempt to define it.

How can one describe the all-important, seemingly simple, yet enormously complex process of effective listening? Listening effectively involves first and foremost keeping out of the patient's way as he attempts to tell his history. To keep from obtruding, to keep quiet, to keep the spotlight focused completely on the patient—these are among the therapist's most difficult tasks. Effective listening involves several elements: having sufficient awareness and resolution of one's own conflicts to avoid reacting in a way that interferes with the patient's free expression of thoughts and feelings; avoiding subtle verbal or nonverbal expressions of disdain or judgment toward the content of the patient's story, even when that content offends the therapist's sensibilities; waiting patiently through periods of silence or tears as the patient summons up courage to delve into painful material or pauses to collect his thoughts or his composure; hearing not only what the patient says but what he is trying to say and what he leaves

unsaid; using both ears and eyes to detect confirming or conflicting messages in verbal content and affect (from tone of voice, posture, and other nonverbal clues); scanning one's own reactions to the patient; avoiding looking away from the patient as he speaks; sitting still; limiting the number of mental excursions into one's own fantasies; controlling those feelings toward the patient that interfere with an accepting, sympathetic, nonjudgmental attitude; realizing that full acceptance of the patient is possible without condoning or sanctioning attitudes and behavior destructive to him or to others.

Although it takes place in a setting of physical inactivity, listening involves an intensely active emotional and intellectual process. The therapist absorbs a vast array of complex, often confusing, and conflicting data. He then sifts what he considers relevant from irrelevant detail and uses this detail continuously to refine his diagnostic impression. Effective listening provides the key to moving beyond the crude and often dehumanizing method of diagnosing by attaching labels and makes it possible for the therapist to formulate his diagnosis on conflicts specific to the patient and eventually to use this information to make appropriate therapeutic intervention. In essence, effective listening is the focus of all of one's mental and physical processes onto the patient, so that for that span of time between the patient's entrance into the office and his departure, he has the therapist's unwavering attention.

Just as anxiety within the patient may interfere with his efforts to communicate, *anxiety within the therapist* may erect barriers to communication. Though usually less intense and more subtle, anxiety within the therapist may impede not only the patient's telling his history but also the therapist's ability to hear that history. Tension and anxiety within the therapist may have many sources, the most common being the nature of the material explored in the psychiatric interview. Unconscious thoughts and feelings are highly charged emotionally and whether overtly manifest, as in a psychotic patient, or carefully defended against, as in a less disturbed patient, they may create considerable tension in both patient and therapist. Extreme anxiety in the patient may arouse anxiety in the therapist, and the contagious quality of depression may cause the therapist to feel despondent and emotionally drained. The absence of the usual verbal responses in a schizophrenic patient may cause the therapist to feel uneasy or apprehensive.

If the patient's conflicts parallel unresolved conflicts in the therapist, the anxiety aroused in the therapist may cause "blind spots," making it difficult for him to hear or to understand aspects of the patient's story. For example, a first-year resident experienced unusual discomfort working with patients whose problems were primarily sexual. The resident's own background and conflicts severely inhibited him sexually so that he dated little and found it necessary to avoid even plays and movies with sexual scenes. During his own analysis, he discovered that when his patients focused on sexual problems, his intense anxiety not only made it difficult for him to hear what they were saying but also caused him to interrupt them frequently and change the subject. In another instance, a resident became pregnant unexpectedly. Her ambivalence toward this unplanned pregnancy caused her to deny it and to avoid thinking or talking about it. As her pregnancy became increasingly evident, she reported to her supervisor that her patients "all seemed suddenly to be falling apart." On further exploration with her supervisor, she realized she had failed to mention her pregnancy to her patients and to tell them that she would soon be leaving them. She had not previously seen that the recurrence of symptoms in many of these patients accompanied expressions of dissatisfaction with her and of anger toward earlier figures who had left them. Once she recognized this blind spot, she discussed these issues with her patients and observed an immediate lessening of their agitation and discontent. (For more on pregnant therapists, see Nadelson et al., 1974; Baum and Herring, 1975.)

The therapist's professional insecurity may also add to his tension, making it difficult for him to tolerate a patient's hostility or criticism, especially if it stems from the intuitive ability many disturbed patients display for detecting specific weaknesses and insecurities in others. Confidence in his own clinical skills, gained through training and experience, helps the therapist tolerate these attacks quietly, with a minimum of anxiety, anger, or other defensive reactions. Another source of anxiety in the therapist is the confusion inherent in the early phases of every evaluation. The interviewer must, for varying degrees of time, tolerate working in the dark. As is not the case with medical and surgical patients, causes of the psychiatric patient's symptoms are rarely discoverable through physical examination, X rays, and laboratory procedures. Each patient presents a complex puzzle that may take considerable time and effort to solve.

How a therapist handles his anxiety determines whether or not the anxiety becomes an obstacle. People handle anxiety in different ways—some by talking excessively, others by becoming excessively quiet. If a therapist characteristically handles anxiety by becoming quiet, he may run some risk of appearing distant and withdrawn from the patient. This is by far the lesser of two evils, however, for if he handles anxiety by talking excessively, he will inevitably obstruct progress. It is axiomatic that when a therapist is talking he cannot be listening. He may, for example, give premature reassurance, conveying the impression that he doesn't really understand the seriousness of the patient's symptoms. A patient may reveal thoughts of killing himself or of killing others. The therapist, made anxious by this, may respond that many people have such thoughts, or that thinking is not the same as acting, then quickly change the subject and thus fail to explore conflicts underlying such thoughts and the possibility of their being expressed in action.

One young woman with metastatic carcinoma searched in vain for a doctor or a member of her family who would discuss her illness with her or acknowledge it seriously. Even a therapist she consulted found confronting a young, dying person so anxiety-provoking that he would not at first allow her to discuss her illness. When he realized this, he struggled for words that would recognize her grave condition and yet not contribute to her despair. When he told her that he realized the seriousness of her illness but also realized that she, like everyone else, did not know whether tomorrow she would live or die, she found relief, some degree of hope, and freedom to express her feelings.

Fatigue may act as another obstacle to effective listening. Being battered by anxiety-provoking, emotionally charged material hour after hour while physically immobile can be emotionally exhausting and physically debilitating for even the most experienced clinician. Perhaps for this reason, Freud expressed horror that a doctor was seeing ten patients a day and called it a concealed attempt at suicide. It betrays no professional secret to acknowledge that many patients have observed their therapists falling asleep—not only those sitting behind a couch but also those in face-to-face confrontation. Such experiences, though humorous on one level, do little to convince the patient of the therapist's intrinsic interest. Regular physical exercise, a well-ventilated office, proper spacing of patients, and light lunches to minimize postprandial drowsiness can help reduce fatigue and its influence on the difficult task of listening effectively. Again, it is axiomatic that if a therapist sleeps he cannot listen.

Impatience is still another obstacle to listening, involving excessive eagerness to make the diagnosis. This may be particularly prevalent when the therapist plans to present his material to a supervisor or at a case conference. The diagnostic process ought to be continuous throughout the evaluation and refined during the various stages of therapy. If the therapist arrives at a diagnosis prematurely, he risks hearing only material confirming his diagnosis. This kind of overeagerness may also lead to impatience. Rather than waiting calmly for the patient to express in words the circumstances and the complexity of the feelings prompting him to seek help, the therapist may attempt to hurry the process by asking several questions at once: "How did your father die, where were you when it happened, and how did you feel when you heard about it?" Or, if the patient pauses to answer one question, the therapist may ask a second question before the first is answered. Such attempts to accelerate the process—even if the therapist has only one session to complete his evaluation—usually confuse the patient, make him more tense, and impede his efforts to tell his story.

Another obstacle—*inattentiveness*—results from the failure of the therapist to use both ears and eyes for the acute perception that is part of effective listening. The clinician must listen attentively to what the patient says, to what he avoids saying, and to subtle changes in tone that may point to important areas to explore. In one instance, a thirty-nine-year-old woman, relating some of her family history during an initial interview, mentioned the name of a young man she knew as a teenager. The therapist noticed a slight change in the tone of her voice when she spoke his name and asked her if this young man had any special significance. She burst into tears as she explained he was the first and only man she really loved, that he had rejected her, and that she had never completely resolved her grief. That particular loss and its many ramifications proved to be a central issue in a consequent successful course of psychotherapy.

Though some therapists find it difficult to confront patients face to face, to look at them openly and directly, the listening process does nevertheless involve looking at and observing the patient. (One reason Freud used a couch involved difficulties he had in looking at patients and having patients look at him.) A patient feels he does not have the therapist's full attention if the therapist keeps looking away. A patient may become openly hostile if, when speaking, he notices the therapist shift his gaze to his fingernails, to papers on the desk, or to the window. Though an unblinking stare obviously distracts, an attentive, level gaze reassures the patient and helps focus the therapist's attention on signs easily overlooked; the twitch of an eyelid, the slight watering of an eye, a transient flush, the almost imperceptible tremble of the chin, and subtle, fleeting facial expressions may all provide clues to emotionally charged areas. Though the therapist may, of course, look away when he comments or when the patient pauses, his eye contact with the patient helps both him and the patient to communicate.

Restlessness, the inability to sit still, may also impede communication. A fidgety, restless therapist may appear impatient, inattentive, and disinterested. The clinician should realize that his time with the patient belongs totally to the patient and attempt to settle down comfortably to give the patient his full attention. The stresses peculiar to the psychiatric interview make it difficult for the therapist to settle down and sustain a composed demeanor. This difficulty can be minimized if the clinician, in developing his potential as a therapist, comes to terms with what he considers the passive, receptive aspects of his character.

Daydreaming erects still another barrier, since listening effectively requires focusing the therapist's full mental faculties. Keeping the mind focused on the patient for a sustained period of time is the most important and often the most difficult aspect of effective listening. The emotionally charged content of the patient's history, the unmet physical and emotional needs of the therapist, and the combination of all other obstacles interfere with this aspect of listening. The therapist must limit his natural tendency to take brief mental excursions into his own thoughts and daydreams. The more frustrated the therapist is in his extraprofessional life, the more frequent will be these excursions and the greater the tendency to use, in fantasy, details of the patient's life to satisfy vicariously the therapist's own unmet needs. When the therapist's attention wanes, when he leaves on one of these mental excursions, the patient senses his absence; a vacant stare or a brief glance away from the patient may telegraph this departure. Not infrequently, the patient's suspicion that the therapist has left is confirmed by the therapist's asking a question the patient has just answered. Though it may be unrealistic to expect these excursions to cease entirely, the skilled clinician limits them by continually refocusing his mind on the patient. The ideal is to work toward "session-tight compartments," wherein the therapist shuts out his own concerns, needs, and preoccupations and focuses entirely on those of the patient.

Feelings toward the Patient: Reality and Countertransference

The therapist's feelings toward the patient may also impose a barrier. As is the case with the feelings of the patient toward the therapist, the feelings of the therapist toward the patient have a twofold basis. First, they are based on the reality of the patient's appearance, personality, character, and conflicts; second, they are based on what the patient represents to the therapist's unconscious in terms of early significant figures. The tendency of the therapist to displace feelings from these earlier figures onto the patient is referred to as countertransference. (The "counter" in *countertransference* means "parallel to" or "complementary to," as in *counterpart*, and not "opposite" or "contrary to," as in *counterphobic*.)

If a therapist feels strongly negative toward a patient, he must determine whether these negative feelings arise from the reality or from the transferred aspects of the relationship. Some therapists feel it is unfair to the patient and to themselves to begin therapy with a patient they do not like. It must be kept in mind, however, that most patients have some unlikable quality —defects of character, pockets of immaturity, regressive, dependent, and manipulative features of their illness. These features have created difficulties in their relationships with people generally and will eventually manifest themselves in their relationship with the therapist. The therapist, therefore, will probably encounter in most patients some qualities he does not like. The sensitive clinician, however, makes careful distinctions between the symptoms of the patient, on the one hand, and the patient as a person, on the other, and will not permit the negative feelings provoked by the symptoms to interfere with his desire to understand and to help the person.

If the negative feelings of the therapist, however, stem from countertransference feelings, he may have considerably more difficulty understanding and controlling them. Early in the therapist-patient relationship, for example, a therapist may find himself experiencing intense feelings toward a patient that appear to have no basis in reality.

A resident found himself curiously depressed and upset after evaluating a young woman for therapy. The interview had gone well. The patient was intelligent, personable, and articulate; she had classical symptoms, appeared to be psychologically minded, was well motivated, and readily accepted the doctor's suggestion for therapy. Although the doctor had time to see the patient in therapy, he decided to refer her to another doctor. After the interview, the doctor found himself struggling with a sadness that persisted throughout the day. Only when reviewing his notes that evening did he realize that during the course of the interview the patient had mentioned that she was pregnant and discussed the necessity of her leaving her proposed therapy briefly for her confinement. This led the doctor to recall a recent experience of his own, when his wife had left him to enter the hospital to give birth to their first child; this recollection in turn flooded him with early memories of the desertion he had felt when his mother had left him as a small boy to deliver his younger brother.

As with transference, countertransference involves inappropriately intense feelings and the unconscious displacement of such feelings from a person in the past to one in the present.

Jargon and Humor as Obstacles

The counterproductivity of the patient's use of psychological jargon in describing his symptoms or giving his history has already been mentioned. The therapist must also avoid this tendency in his communication with the patient. Technical terms purportedly facilitate communication within a specialized field. In psychiatry, where the terms often lack precise and standardized definitions, they confuse more often than they clarify. An inexperienced therapist with an uncertain grasp of psychiatry may become entranced with this language and use it freely with both his peers and his patients. Because one tends to fear what one does not understand, such terms may unnecessarily frighten the patient.

Technical terms not only confuse; they also dehumanize, oversimplify, and, when used pejoratively, express veiled hostility. Bruch (1974) writes that "young psychiatrists are apt to acquire an extensive psychoanalytic vocabulary, and this excess verbiage may act like shining but distorting glasses . . . Instead of sympathetically observing and responding to his patient . . . he will label him with accusing, punitive, and essentially invalidating epitaphs—'passive-aggressive,' 'masochistic,' 'compulsive.'" Such terms often convey "badness" as well as sickness, and no therapist would tolerate others' using them to refer to his own family. Bruch continues, "The less secure a therapist is, the more likely he will cling to stereotyped concepts and a cliché-ridden vocabulary" (p. 25). Insecurity, however, does

not always fade with experience, and the tendency to use obsolete and confusing terms is not limited to young therapists.

The ability to describe human behavior with psychodynamic understanding but without psychoanalytic jargon requires a good grasp of basic concepts. As a therapist grows in understanding, he ought to be able to express himself to both colleagues and patients without jargon. Observers sitting in on the workshops of Anna Freud, for example, have been impressed at the almost complete absence of psychoanalytic terms.

Humor can exert a wonderful humanizing influence in interpersonal relationships, easing tension and facilitating communication. Often during the arduous process of psychotherapy, a hearty laugh between therapist and patient underscores Addison's comment that "mirth is like a flash of lightning, that breaks through a gloom of clouds." Yet humor also has destructive potential in the therapist-patient relationship and can become an obstacle to progress.

To avoid the destructive aspects of humor, the therapist must be alert to what the patient actually feels from moment to moment. A patient may smile, laugh, or giggle not because he feels amused but because he feels anxious. A twenty-eight-year-old woman, for no apparent reason, would suddenly flush crimson during her therapy sessions and begin to giggle uncontrollably. As she explored these reactions she realized that erotic thoughts and feelings toward the therapist precipitated this anxious giggling and paralleled childhood and adolescent feelings experienced when her nude father entered her room each night to lock her windows. A twenty-six-year-old man would giggle suddenly and uncontrollably while experiencing toward his therapist the same apprehension he experienced as a child toward a harsh, punitive father. Both patients expressed embarrassment and annoyance at these episodes.

Joking and other forms of humor may be a form of resistance. A witty, intelligent graduate student, for example, announced suddenly to the interviewer that he had been out with a beautiful girl the night before. He said, "She had long black hair flowing down her back; none on her head, just down her back," and laughed uproariously. The sudden, unexpected joke and the contagiousness of his laugh caused the therapist to join in. Several such episodes later, when the therapist focused on the process as well as the content of the interview, he realized the patient told a joke whenever he approached emotionally charged topics. The joke served to release anxiety and to change the subject quickly. Patients may use humor to deal with painful topics or to screen feelings that would overwhelm them if confronted directly. A young woman, recently notified that her father was dying, introduced this subject by laughingly describing a number of his amusing idiosyncrasies.

Anxiety in the therapist may cause him to smile inappropriately or otherwise to use humor destructively. The anxiety aroused by an enraged patient threatening violence may cause the therapist to smile and to provoke the patient's rage further. Explicitly sexual material may also make an inexperienced therapist smile anxiously, giving the patient the impression of being laughed at. Even the simple rule of smiling with and not at the patient (Kubie, 1971) needs to be followed judiciously. If the therapist had joined in the uncontrollable giggling of the two patients mentioned above, he would have increased their discomfort, and if he had continued to laugh with the graduate student, he would have encouraged the student's resistance. Realizing the dangers of humor must not, however, preclude a warm smile or appropriate spontaneous laughter. A dour therapist who makes no response to a patient's humorous overtures can be a tedious bore and may increase the patient's discomfort.

The key to using humor appropriately is being tuned in to the patient's feelings, to his mood as it changes from session to session and from topic to topic. The therapist must remember that most psychiatric patients are extremely sensitive to being laughed at, that although others may have found the patients' symptoms and irrational behavior amusing, the patients find them painful. Sometimes a patient will suddenly see a ludicrous aspect to his behavior and burst into laughter. The therapist can, of course, join in the laughter; but laughing at the patient or making fun of his symptoms through mockery, sarcasm, or irony will inevitably set a discordant tone and become an obstacle to the relationship.

Ethical Considerations: Sexual Relations within Therapy

No discussion of the therapist-patient relationship would be adequate without mention of the ethical and moral issues involved—an area of increasing interest in the psychiatric literature. All the aspects discussed so far imply that this relationship must be focused completely on the welfare of the patient and conducted within the framework of high ethical standards. The lowering of these standards, many believe, has impaired the quality of the relationship, provoked widespread concern over patients' rights, and contributed to passage of recent laws that attempt not only to protect these rights but to define and regulate the therapist's conduct (see chapter 31, "Psychiatry and the Law"). These laws reflect society's insistence that high standards be maintained.

The striking increase in interest in medical and psychiatric ethics during the past decade has centered on a number of ethical issues. In this chapter, only the issue of sexual activity between patient and therapist will be considered—an issue that concerns the ethics of the professional relationship itself. (For discussion of other ethical issues, the reader is referred to the references at the end of this chapter and to chapter 17, "The Psychotherapies," chapter 31, "Psychiatry and the Law," and chapter 28, "Treating the Person Confronting Death.")

Sexual relations between therapist and patient have recently become a topic of open discussion not only in the lay press but also in the most recent medical literature. Although changes in sexual mores and other aspects of our culture have contributed to this discussion, the Hippocratic oath—the traditional ethical guideline for physicians—proscribes sexual relationships with patients, indicating that this subject has been a concern of the profession for centuries.

Until the 1970s, doctors discussed this topic *sotto voce*. The evidence consisted primarily of anecdotes, and the general impression was that only a tiny percentage of highly disturbed individuals practiced such behavior. Since 1970, a few documented studies have been published. Kardener (1974) surveyed 460 physicians and reported that "between 5 and 13 percent . . . engaged in erotic behaviors, including and excluding sexual intercourse, with a limited number of patients" and that the psychiatrists in this sample were "least likely to engage in erotic acts, particularly compared with obstetrician-gynecologists and general practitioners" (p. 1134).

Yet psychiatrists, and other therapists, for reasons discussed throughout this chapter, may be most vulnerable. As already discussed, the therapist-patient relationship, especially when carried out over an extensive period of time, fosters complex, intense, and often confusing feelings in both patient and therapist. These may include romantic and sexual feelings that the patient insists on expressing physically and demands that the therapist reciprocate. Though this situation occurs less frequently than novels and movies imply, its occurrence presents a delicate problem for the therapist. While he must encourage the free expression of all thoughts, feelings, and wishes, he must limit the patient to expressing them verbally. He must reject the patient's physical expression of such feelings but must be exceedingly careful never to reject the patient. Because these intensely positive feelings create unfulfilled yearnings and are therefore often stressful for the patient, the therapist must not dismiss them lightly or insensitively.

Sometimes the patient's demands are overt. But as Freud wisely observed, "It is not a patient's crudely sensuous desires which constitute the temptation. These are more likely to repel . . . It is rather, perhaps, a woman's subtler and aim-inhibited wishes which bring with them the danger of making a man forget his technique and medical task for the sake of a fine experience" (1915, p. 170). The patient may convey these "subtler wishes" by expressing an inability to confide fully in a person without being close physically, or by expressing sexual dreams or fantasies about the therapist in a manner calculated more to arouse than to explore or enlighten. As a first step, the patient may attempt to change the restrained, formal relationship into a more familiar one by asking the therapist personal questions concerning his age, his marital status, and his residence. The therapist will do well to remember that although patients may press to make the relationship more intimate, they often become extremely uncom-fortable when they succeed. Motives for changing the relationship are at best mixed, and a part of the patient is usually greatly relieved to keep the relationship a professional one. Because romantic and sexual feelings may be a form of resistance and impede therapeutic progress, they must be confronted, explored, and resolved so that therapy can proceed. Such exploration soon makes clear that these feelings have little to do with the personal charm of the therapist but would be directed toward anyone sitting in his chair. Thus, analyzing these feelings not only reduces their intensity in the patient but also reduces the tendency of the therapist to be flattered by them.

The issue of a physical relationship becomes more complicated if the therapist experiences romantic and sexual feelings toward the patient. Until the late 1950s, erotic feelings toward the patient were seldom discussed in the literature except to state they must never be tolerated (Tower, 1956). In 1959, however, Searles described such feelings in the therapist as a frequent and normal occurrence during the course of intensive therapy. Current authors agree with Searles and it no longer seems necessary to view these feelings in the therapist as an intolerable aberration in themselves. By and large, however, the psychiatric profession considers acting on these feelings to be an expression of pathology in the therapist (Davidson, 1976). Though recognizing sexual love as one of the most fulfilling pleasures, medical and psychiatric organizations have traditionally taken an unequivocal stand against sexual activity within the therapeutic relationship.

As part of the recent widespread discussion of medical ethics, some therapists have recently questioned this traditional moral stance. And if Wagner's findings (1972) are representative— that 25 percent of freshman medical students he studied thought that physical expressions of feelings were acceptable if both parties' feelings were genuine—we may expect students and young clinicians to question this traditional stance with increasing frequency. Do sufficient reasons exist to justify this standard or have present-day mores made it passé? The following, based on a review of recent literature, on clinical observations of a few who transgressed this standard, and on interviews with colleagues serving on national and local ethics committees, are some reasons why wisdom dictates that the therapist adhere to the traditional standard.

Perhaps most important, a breach of this standard may be destructive to the patient. First, erotic feelings in the patient are usually a source of resistance, and physical expression of them with the therapist impedes their resolution and obstructs therapeutic progress. Acting out feelings interferes with their verbal expression and thus with the work of therapy. Second, a large percentage of patients come to psychiatrists today seeking help in controlling impulses (in contrast to overcoming inhibition of impulses, as occurred more frequently in the past). The physical expression of sexual impulses in therapy not only indicates that the therapist also lacks this control but may also exacerbate the very problem —the patient's lack of control—for which the patient seeks help.

A physical relationship may also be destructive to the therapist-patient relationship. Sexual activity changes the professional relationship to an intimate social one and thereby reduces or destroys its therapeutic effectiveness. The therapist can no longer function as an objective, caring source of healing. To find a therapist to whom one can relate effectively, whose qualities of character one can respect, in whose integrity and competence one can have confidence, and to whom one can entrust one's life is indeed a rare experience. A patient may travel great distances and make considerable sacrifices to consult such a therapist. To deprive a patient of this source of professional help and healing is, as Kardener states, "psychologically a frighteningly high price the patient must pay" (1974, p. 1135).

Such a relationship may be destructive to the therapist. When a therapist has sexual relations with a patient, the experience often exerts a negative influence on the way he sees himself and the ways others see him. The concern that he may have harmed a patient or lowered his professional standards may lead to a loss of confidence. In addition, the sexual activity almost inevitably becomes known to colleagues and to others in the community (Grunebaum, Nadelson, and Macht, 1976). Although the therapist may choose to ignore traditional moral

standards in the conduct of his personal life, society and his professional colleagues expect, and indeed demand, that he heed them in his professional life (Redlich and Mollica, 1976). When a therapist fails to do so, he compromises his integrity and his reputation. Even when the therapist follows the questionable recommendation (Marmor, 1972) that those who cannot control their countertransference feelings should terminate treatment and marry the patient, difficulties persist. Davidson raises several cogent questions: "What is to be done when the therapist enters into the same situation with another patient in the future? . . . Is it possible for the psychiatrist ever to terminate his moral and ethical obligations to the patient? . . . There is some legal precedent for believing that duties of a physician toward a patient continue after termination of the contractual agreement" (1976). One might also ask what effect this marriage will have on other patients in the therapist's practice and in his community.

The sexual relationship may be a source of potential legal liabilities. Alan Stone (1976) writes that sexual activity between therapist and patient creates the possibility of "malpractice liability" if the patient claims some psychological harm as a result. Courts have construed the doctor-patient relationship as comparable to a fiduciary relationship, or the relationship between guardian and ward. Thus the legal validity of consent from the patient becomes dubious as a legal defense.

The therapist's own breach of the traditional moral code represents a departure from the ethics of his profession. If a therapist belongs to the American Medical Association, the American Psychiatric Association, or the American Psychological Association, he swears to uphold its canon of ethics, which proscribes sexual activity between therapist and patient. Some authors (Jonsen and Hellegers, 1974; Redlich and Mollica, 1976) criticize this canon for lack of moral substance and for failing to define professional character, virtue, right action, or duty. Others, however, argue that laws and codes can only define the lowest acceptable standards and that virtue, character, and right action can never be legislated; instead, they must ultimately reflect an individual's personal ethics, view of man, philosophy of life, professional integrity, and commitment to the welfare of his patients.

Although Freud worried that "those who are still youngish and not yet bound by strong ties" may find it particularly difficult "to keep within the limits prescribed by ethics and technique" (1915, p. 169), ethics committees have found that complaints of sexual activity with patients have been primarily against older therapists—perhaps those who have had close ties and lost them. Whether young or old, the therapist must be careful to avoid using the patient to fulfill needs that otherwise would be met in his extraprofessional life.

The silence previously accorded the subject of sexual activity between doctor and patient may have been due partly to the fact that any discussion of it inevitably risks sounding moralistic and judgmental. Nevertheless, as the literature continues to focus on this issue in the future, we may find it helpful to keep in mind the following: although sexual feelings may arise naturally within the therapeutic relationship, because of the nature of that relationship, sexual activity, regardless of the circumstances, is considered by law and by the profession an exploitation of the patient; although mores change, basic moral principles endure; and the wise therapist adheres closely to these principles—in the best interest of his patient, of himself, and of his profession.

Perhaps because of the dehumanizing effects of modern medical technology, the physician-patient relationship has been receiving increasing attention in the medical literature. The more we understand this interaction, the more we realize its complexities and the ways in which it differs from what we expect.

The importance of the attitude of the psychiatrist in setting the tone for his relationship with the patient has already been stressed. The therapist may approach the patient merely as a "case," whose character structure, symptoms, and defenses must be assessed in order to attach the appropriate diagnostic label. Or he may look beyond the patient's pathology to see a fellow human being with unique characteristics, and with the same hopes, fears, aspirations, feelings, and perhaps, except for differences in degree, the same conflicts as his own—a suffering human being who may have skills and areas of knowledge superior to those of the therapist but whose illness has made him dependent on the therapist and particularly vulnerable. The latter approach will ensure a degree of humility in the therapist and prevent the patronizing arrogance afflicting some who hold a degree of power over others. It will also facilitate giving the patient the same warmth and courtesy accorded a respected guest, a cherished relative, or, one would hope, the therapist himself should he become a patient. More important, the therapist will more likely have a desire to help the patient—to give him hope, to allay his fears, and to alleviate his pain.

Wanting to help the patient, wanting the best for the patient and acting accordingly—whether a particular patient evokes positive or negative feelings—necessitates no little degree of maturity on the part of the therapist. It requires him, regardless of feelings he may have to the contrary and regardless of the particular status of the patient, always to act in the best interest of that patient. Perhaps this indiscriminate, unbiased concern—the Greeks called it *agape*—encompasses all that we mean when we speak of sympathy, empathy, and compassion.

Although the therapist has a moral obligation to attain and to maintain his maximum clinical competence, no theoretical knowledge or technical skill can ever compensate for the absence of this quality of sensitive concern. Its presence, however, will not only convey that intangible but clearly perceived "intrinsic interest" in the patient but will also help the relationship weather the multitude of errors and ignorance that is the lot of every psychotherapist.

In psychiatry, unlike other branches of medicine, therapeutic progress rests entirely on the therapist's ability to relate effectively to his patient. Once a therapist makes contact with his patient, he begins a journey strewn with obstacles arising both within himself and within his patient. An understanding of these obstacles helps the therapist avoid the usual pitfalls and snags that bog down his diagnostic and therapeutic efforts, and, more important, helps him know what to do once these barriers arise. This understanding necessitates an acute sensitivity to the needs and reactions of his patients, as well as an acute self-awareness that provides him ready access to his own emotional resources and limitations. If the therapist fails to gain this understanding, he may find the arduous task of psychotherapy frustrating and ultimately intolerable. If, on the other hand, he strives consciously and continuously throughout his professional life to increase this understanding, if he uses his teaching, research, administrative and other experiences, not to escape from his patients but to enhance his understanding of them, he will in time—despite the loneliness and isolation of his work—be recognized as a competent clinician. This recognition will come not only from increasing numbers who need and seek his help but also from the other skilled craftsmen in his field—those who do the work for which psychiatry exists and who are responsible for whatever respect the profession enjoys. More important, as the therapist increases his understanding of his relationship with his patients and uses this understanding to relieve their suffering, he will find few endeavors in life more deeply gratifying.

References

Baum, E. O., and C. Herring. 1975. The pregnant psychotherapist in training: some preliminary findings. *Am. J. Psychiatry* 132:419–422.

Bruch, H. 1974. *Learning psychotherapy: rationale and ground rules*. Cambridge, Mass.: Harvard University Press.

Davidson, V. 1976. Psychiatry's problem with no name: therapist-patient sex. Paper presented at the 129th Annual Meeting of the American Psychiatric Association, Miami, Florida.

Freud, A. 1966. *Normality and pathology in childhood*. London: Hogarth Press.

Freud, S. 1895. Studies on hysteria. In *Standard edition*, ed. J. Strachey. Vol. 2. London: Hogarth Press, 1955.

—— 1905. Fragment of an analysis of a case of hysteria. In *Standard edition*, ed. J. Strachey. Vol. 7. London: Hogarth Press, 1953.

—— 1912. The dynamics of transference. In *Standard edition*, ed. J. Strachey. Vol. 12. London: Hogarth Press, 1958.

—— 1915. Observations on transference-love. In *Standard edition*, ed. J. Strachey. Vol. 12. London: Hogarth Press, 1958.

Friedman, L. 1969. The therapeutic alliance. *Int. J. Psychoanal.* 50:139–153.

Greenson, R. R. 1965. The problem of working through. In *Drives, affects, behavior*, ed. M. Schur. New York: International Universities Press.

—— 1967. *The technique and practice of psychoanalysis*. Vol. 1. New York: International Universities Press.

Grunebaum, H., C. Nadelson, and L. Macht. 1976. Sexual activity with the psychiatrist: a district branch dilemma. Paper presented at the 129th Annual Meeting of the American Psychiatric Association, Miami, Florida.

Hartmann, H. 1964. *Essays on ego psychology*. London: Hogarth Press.

Heimann, P. 1960. Counter-transference. *Br. J. Med. Psychol.* 33:9–15.

Hill, J. A. 1969. Therapist's goals, patient aims and patient satisfaction in psychotherapy. *J. Clin. Psychol.* 25:455–459.

Jones, E. 1953. *The life and work of Sigmund Freud*. Vol. 1. New York: Basic Books.

Jonsen, A. R., and A. E. Hellegers. 1974. Conceptual foundations for an ethics of medical care. In *Ethics of health care*, ed. L. Tancredi. Washington, D.C.: National Academy of Sciences.

Kardener, S. H. 1974. Sex and the physician-patient relationship. *Am. J. Psychiatry* 131:1134–36.

Kardener, S. H., M. Fuller, and I. N. Mensh. 1973. A survey of physicians' attitudes and practices regarding erotic and non-erotic contact with patients. *Am. J. Psychiatry* 130:1077–81.

Kernberg, O. 1965. Notes on countertransference. *J. Am. Psychoanal. Assoc.* 13:38–56.

Kline, F., A. Adrian, and M. Spevak. 1974. Patients evaluate therapists. *Arch. Gen. Psychiatry* 31:113–116.

Kubie, L. 1971. The destructive potential of humor in psychotherapy. *Am. J. Psychiatry* 127:861–866.

Marmor, J. 1972. Sexual acting out in psychotherapy. *Am. J. Psychoanal.* 22:3–8.

Menninger, K. A. 1958. *Theory of psychoanalytic technique*. New York: Basic Books.

Nadelson, C., M. Notman, E. Arons, and J. Feldman. 1974. The pregnant therapist. *Am. J. Psychiatry* 131:1107–11.

Osler, Sir William. 1963. *Aequanimitas and other papers that have stood the test of time*. New York: Norton.

Redlich, F., and R. F. Mollica. 1976. Ethical issues in contemporary psychiatry. *Am. J. Psychiatry*, 133:125–141.

Salzman, C., R. I. Shader, D. A. Scott, and W. Binstock. 1970. Interviewer anger and patient dropout in walk-in clinic. *Compr. Psychiatry* 11:267–273.

Sandler, J., C. Dare, and A. Holder. 1970. Basic psychoanalytic concepts: VIII, Special Forms of Transference. *Br. J. Psychiatry* 117:561–568.

——— 1973. *The patient and the analyst.* New York:
International Universities Press.

Searles, H. F. 1959. Oedipal love in the countertransference. *Int. J. Psychoanal.* 40:180–190.

Stone, A. A. 1976. Legal implications of sexual activity
between psychiatrist and patient. *Am. J. Psychiatry*
133:1138–41.

Stone, L. 1967. The psychoanalytic situation and
transference: postscript to an earlier communication. *J. Am. Psychoanal. Assoc.* 15:3–58.

Tower, L. E. 1956. Countertransference. *J. Am. Psychoanal. Assoc.* 4:224–255.

Wagner, N. 1972. Ethical concerns of medical stu-
dents. Paper read at the Western Workshop of the
Center for the Study of Sex Education in Medicine,
Santa Barbara, California.

Zetzel, E. R. 1956. Current concepts of transference.
Int. J. Psychoanal. 37:369–376.

Recommended Reading

Entralgo, P. L. 1969. *Doctor and patient.* New York:
McGraw-Hill.

Fromm-Reichman, F. 1950. *Principles of intensive
psychotherapy.* Chicago: Chicago University Press.

Kernberg, O. 1965. Notes on countertransference.
J. Am. Psychoanal. Assoc. 13:38–56.

Rawls, J. 1971. *A theory of justice.* Cambridge, Mass.:
Harvard University Press.

Sollitto, S., and R. M. Veatch, eds. 1974. *Bibliography
of society, ethics and life sciences.* Hastings-on-
Hudson, N.Y.: Hastings Institute of Health and
Human Values.

PART ONE

Examination and Evaluation

History and Mental Status

CHAPTER 2

Armand M. Nicholi, Jr.

T HE PREVIOUS CHAPTER described the influence of the therapist-patient relationship on the success or failure of the psychiatric interview, especially those interviews directed toward the initial evaluation. During the evaluation, the therapist not only interacts with the patient but also simultaneously observes this interaction carefully and critically. The information obtained through this observation, together with biographical and other data from the psychiatric interview and psychological tests, provides the basis for assessing the patient's emotional status.

Just as the assessment of physical illness is based on a history, a physical examination, and indicated laboratory tests, psychiatric assessment includes a history (the anamnesis), a psychiatric (mental status) examination, and, when indicated, psychological tests. This chapter will deal with the psychiatric history and examination; psychological testing will be covered in the following chapter.

Because the psychiatric evaluation involves answering questions critical to the patient's welfare (is he suicidal? does he need hospitalization? are his symptoms psychogenic or organic in origin?), the evaluation ought to be conducted or at least supervised by an experienced psychiatrist.

Some psychiatric hospitals now have their most experienced staff members perform or supervise the initial evaluation of patients. An individual may come to the clinic or hospital or to a psychiatrist's private office on his own, or he may be referred by his family, a friend, or his family physician. On the basis of the evaluation, the examiner must decide whether or not the patient is ill, the nature of his illness, and the treatment most appropriate for that illness and must relate his findings to the referring source.

A psychiatric evaluation requires the examiner to perform the challenging task of grasping in a limited amount of time the past and present difficulties that prompt the patient to consult a psychiatrist. Its goal is to discover the nature and intensity of the patient's inner conflicts, the extent to which they interfere with important areas of functioning, and whether or not they warrant therapeutic intervention. In addition to considering differential diagnosis among the psychogenic disorders, the interviewer must be especially alert to the possibility of organic illness, particularly organic mental disorder, and must determine whether and to what extent such disease contributes to the patient's psychological symptoms. Some psychiatric symptoms may be direct expressions of certain organic disorders—brain tumors, uremia, or drug reactions. for example—and not just emotional reactions to their physically incapacitating effects. Such conditions demand immediate medical or surgical intervention and must be diagnosed promptly.

Evaluation of the psychiatric patient may take one or several interviews to complete. However many sessions are needed, the interviewer will make optimal use of his time if he has a clear idea of the general areas to explore and the specific kinds of information needed for an accurate assessment. The traditional approach to the evaluation derives from the older, descriptive psychiatry and follows the structured, systematic method of history taking and physical examination used in general medicine. With the arrival of the newer, dynamic psychiatry, many psychiatrists found the traditional approach rigid, confining, and incompatible with their efforts to explore the human personality. Consequently, several modifications of the traditional approach have been introduced, notably by Deutsch (1955), Sullivan (1954), Finesinger (1948), Menninger (1963), and Scheflen (1963). Although a structured question-and-answer approach to the psychiatric patient may yield a wealth of objective facts, analytically-oriented psychiatrists have stressed that this approach interferes with obtaining the kinds of information they find essential to an accurate psychiatric assessment—an empathic understanding of the patient's inner conflicts, some indication of the unconscious determinants of these conflicts, and an awareness of how these conflicts manifest themselves in the therapist-patient relationship.

This emphasis on the limitations of the structured question-and-answer approach has led some psychiatrists to the extreme stance of using no structure at all, approaching the patient in a haphazard, disorganized way, and collecting incomplete psychiatric records. As in other medical disciplines, the key to accurate assessment is thoroughness. The skilled clinician often makes a diagnosis others have missed simply on the basis of having looked carefully where others have neglected to look. Thoroughness demands that the diagnostician have in his mind a clear outline of the important areas to cover and the

specific details to elicit within these areas. In this way he will be less likely to make serious omissions. His approach to the patient, however, must never be rigid or routine but must be tailored to the specific needs, conflicts, and personality of the individual patient.

The Psychiatric History

Although the psychiatrist must be flexible and spontaneous in his approach to the patient, he must nevertheless record the historical data obtained during the evaluation in a meaningful and organized form. Good record keeping makes it possible for not only the interviewer but also others to read and understand the record at a later date. If the interviewer has clearly in mind an outline of the specific categories of information to ascertain, he can readily check his notes at the end of an interview to see what types of information have been omitted and cover those areas during the next interview.

Format for the Psychiatric History

Attention to the topics suggested below may contribute to the interviewer's thoroughness and help him to organize and record data without imposing a rigid question-and-answer approach. The psychiatric history ought to include the categories described below.

1. *Identifying data.* The psychiatrist needs to know the patient's name, address, phone number, date and place of birth, sex, marital status, and education, the referring source, and the name and address of the patient's closest relative.

2. *Chief complaint.* A brief statement of the patient's current difficulty—the "presenting problem"—is usually given in reply to the question "What brings you to see me?" or "What brings you to the hospital?" More than any other, this part of the patient's history ought to be quoted verbatim, even when the information comes from a relative or other informant.

3. *Present illness.* Once a patient describes his main complaint, he will usually, with the encouragement of the doctor, describe other complaints, both recent and long-standing. Though this information may be presented in a disorganized and haphazard way, the doctor must form-

ulate and record an orderly chronological summary of the development of the patient's signs and symptoms, the nature and intensity of his conflicts, previous episodes of illness and their outcome, and past psychiatric treatment and hospitalization. The patient's awareness of and attitude toward his illness—the tendency to deny, minimize, or exaggerate as well as evidence of primary and secondary gains—should be noted.

4. *Personal history*. The record should include a summary of the patient's life with emphasis on events in his past not covered in the preceding category but pertinent to understanding his present illness. If the patient's symptoms point to certain diagnostic possibilities, the clinician's knowledge of etiological factors will indicate areas to be explored in depth. If, for instance, the examination reveals that the patient has lost the ability to pronounce words or to name common objects (amnestic aphasia), the interviewer will focus his attention on questions confirming or ruling out organic mental disorder (see chapter 15, "Organic Mental Disorders"). The interviewer's knowledge of predictable crises in an individual's development—the beginning of school, the birth of a sibling, the loss of a parent through death or divorce, the onset of puberty, departure from home for boarding school or college—also provides clues to areas that may prove helpful to explore. Recording this information in chronological order will help give an overview of the emotionally significant aspects of the patient's life. Some potentially fruitful categories of information are suggested below.

Infancy. Among the facts that should be noted carefully are the place and condition of birth; whether the patient was breast- or bottle-fed; whether the pregnancy was planned and the child wanted; the emotional climate of the home; illness and hospitalizations; age at toilet training, of sitting, walking, and talking; any unusual circumstances of birth; and any discontinuities in the infant-mother relationship. Much of this information must be obtained, of course, by the patient from his parents or older siblings.

Childhood. Important information about this period includes childhood diseases and hospitalizations; the patient's relationship with each parent and that between parents; the emotional climate of the home; any discontinuities in relationships with either parent through divorce, death, or other causes; the patient's relationships with other members of the family; temper tantrums, stuttering, nightmares, phobias, bedwetting, or other psychological difficulties; earliest memories, daydreams, and repetitive dreams; childhood personality traits; his reaction to discipline; any tendency to excessive dependence or independence.

Adolescence. It is important for the psychiatrist to explore the patient's preparation for and reaction to onset of puberty; his degree of impulse control (how did patient express aggression and the intensification of sexual interests and desires?); his adaptation to parental demands; his relationship with members of the family; peer relationships—the number of friends and the quality of friendships with both sexes; the physical and emotional accessibility of each parent; his reaction to sexual experience; his adoption or rejection of parental moral standards; and any special gifts or talents.

Adulthood. The important facts about the adult's establishment of emotional and financial independence and his career planning and career identity themselves fall into several categories. All the types of information discussed below are important in the patient's adult life and ought to be explored in this part of the history-taking process; some aspects of the patient's adult life, however, grow naturally out of its earlier phases and thus may overlap with other sections of the history.

Educational and occupational history. Difficulties in starting school, school phobias; academic and emotional adjustment throughout the school and college years; relationship with classmates and especially with teachers; unusual experiences in school or in college; successes and failures. Job experiences, reasons for changing jobs, conflicts with peers, repetitive conflicts with superiors, and job performance and satisfaction.

Social history. Relationships with peers of both sexes; community activities; hobbies, religious interests, philosophy of life; cultural interests; ethical standards and concerns; attitudes toward aging and death.

Sexual and marital history. How and from whom first sexual information was obtained; sexual experiences in childhood and adolescence; control of sexual impulses as an adult; onset and history of menses; reactions to wet dreams; premarital sexual experiences and emotional reactions to them; courtship and marriage; sexual relationship with spouse—frequency, satisfaction, climax, conflicts; birth control, pregnancies, abortions; sexual deviations; extramarital relationships; conflicts in marriage; feelings and attitudes toward menopause.

Medical history. All illnesses, accidents, hospitalizations, and operations, in chronological order; attitudes toward illness, hospitalization, and treatment; past medications, drugs now being ingested—especially abuses of alcohol, nicotine, tranquilizers, amphetamines, and other drugs.

Family history. A detailed record of the parents, siblings, grandparents, and other relatives important to the patient, especially during his early years; the dominant parent and the parent with whom the patient has identified most; which parent enforced discipline and how; family values; ethnic, economic, social, and religious background; age of parents at death, divorce, or separation; any family history of physical and emotional illnesses, suicides, or alcoholism; description of patient's own family (spouse and children).

Technique

While the evaluating psychiatrist's general approach to the patient will be similar to any other initial therapist-patient relationship (see chapter 1, "The Therapist-Patient Relationship"), a few additional techniques are particularly useful in taking the psychiatric history. When asked why he has come to the hospital or the doctor's office, the patient may not only describe his chief complaint but also provide considerable information concerning his history. The doctor ought to explore specifically and in detail the events that immediately precipitated the patient's seeking help. Such exploration will often reveal details not at first mentioned by the patient. At first, for example, the patient may give com-

plaints he has had for months or years as reasons for his seeking help. If, however, the interviewer asks, "But what led you to seek help at this particular time?" and follows up with, "Can you think of any other reasons why you sought help now?" the patient may recall a whole series of precipitating events that influenced his decision to consult a psychiatrist.

The doctor can help make the interview more spontaneous and free-flowing by using clues from the patient to broach the various subjects he wishes to explore. If, for example, the patient mentions his parents while describing his chief complaint, the doctor may say, "You mentioned your parents a few minutes ago; can you tell me more about them?" It is usually most fruitful to ask a general question like this one and then to focus on specific details—"Do your parents live together?" "How old are they?" In this way—and in a spontaneous manner—the doctor obtains the details of the family history.

Obtaining historical information by this method rather than by following a rigid outline may present some difficulty in organization, but the interviewer can arrange the material later when he enters it into the patient's permanent record or prepares it for presentation to a supervisor or staff conference. The interviewer ought to feel free to take notes during the initial evaluation to help him recall specific dates and other details accurately. If he uses his own shorthand to make his notes brief, he can usually take them unobtrusively. Patients sometimes wait until the interviewer stops writing in order to have his full attention. If this situation occurs, the doctor can encourage the patient not to wait, reassuring him that the doctor will continue to listen even while jotting down notes. Some patients may find the doctor's writing too great a distraction. In such cases, the doctor must limit himself to taking down a date or a key word and write more extensive notes at the end of the hour. Still other patients may object to note taking out of fear that the notes will become accessible to those who will use them against the patient. Such an objection may offer the doctor his first opportunity to discuss the important issue of confidentiality (see chapter 1, "The Therapist-Patient Relationship," and chapter 31, "Psychiatry and the Law").

Because most psychiatric patients suffer from emotional conflicts, the interviewer will find it helpful—not only while taking the history but throughout his contact with the patient—to focus on the patient's feelings. Questions to the patient ought therefore to begin with the phrase "how do you feel . . ." rather than "what do you think . . ."

Although the interviewer ought to refrain from making interpretations during the evaluation, he may indicate areas that will be fruitful for the patient to explore further if therapy is indicated. He might say, for example, "You may find it helpful to explore the possibility of a relationship between the angry feelings you described toward your father and your reactions to your many different employers over the years." Though not an interpretation, such statements help clarify issues and point to areas of conflict for the patient to work on later.

The first person mentioned by the patient during the initial interview may give the interviewer a clue to his most significant current relationship. Exploring this relationship may open the door to a great deal of information concerning the present difficulty.

When a patient answers "I don't know" to a question, the interviewer can sometimes help him by not going on to another question immediately. If the interviewer responds, instead, with "What comes to mind?" the patient may reveal a great deal about the topic not at first readily accessible to him. In this way, the patient will begin a process of exploring his own thoughts and feelings through free association. This method will prove especially helpful to him if at the end of the evaluation he is referred for psychoanalytically oriented psychotherapy.

When the patient relates information that appears illogical, confusing, or contradictory or that seems to have no basis in reality, the doctor may find it helpful to give him the benefit of the doubt and say, "I don't understand," rather than, "You aren't being clear," or, "You don't make sense." The doctor may also help establish rapport by reminding the patient that although the interview will focus on the part the patient plays in the difficulty he encounters, the doctor realizes that other people may have contributed to these difficulties. Sometimes patients feel the

doctor thinks they are to blame for all of the difficulty described in their history, when they know that spouses or parents or employers play a predominant role. Focusing solely on the patient's conflicts may also give him the impression that he has no strengths and is more severely ill than he really is. The doctor can reassure a highly sensitive patient by acknowledging, when possible, the part others play in the patient's problems as well as the patient's own strengths and assets; he must nevertheless remind the patient that their primary task is to understand the patient's conflicts and the part, however major or minor, these conflicts play in his impaired functioning.

Throughout the evaluation, the interviewer should encourage the patient to express all of his thoughts and feelings freely. The doctor should not hesitate to point out that an accurate evaluation necessitates knowing as much as possible about the patient. He can encourage this free flow of expression by being responsive. He may nod or say, "I understand," or acknowledge the patient's feelings by saying, "That must have been difficult for you." If the patient suddenly stops talking, the interviewer may encourage him to continue by repeating his last phrase. This particular method of eliciting information encourages the patient to use free association as a means of eliciting information from his unconscious. Felix Deutsch called this method of history taking the "associative anamnesis" and found it especially effective in patients with psychosomatic complaints. Deutsch writes:

If the examiner allows [the patient] to talk without asking leading questions the patient will usually give a detailed account of his complaints and ideas about his illness. When he has exhausted his ideas and recollections about his disturbances he will stop and wait to be asked a question. The examiner waits until it is clear that the patient will not continue spontaneously, then he repeats one of the points of the patient's last sentences in an interrogative form. Usually the examiner repeats one of the . . . complaints last mentioned, being careful to use the same words as the patient. The patient then usually gives new information centering around his symptoms and is stimulated to further associations. (1939, p. 357)

Though the doctor ought to encourage the patient to speak freely, he must guard against obviously irrelevant chatter, and ought not to hesitate to ask a question directing the patient to more relevant material. Free association is used primarily by psychoanalytically oriented psychiatrists as a means of obtaining historical data during the evaluation. For a comparison of this method with others, the reader is referred to L. H. Havens's paper "Clinical Methods in Psychiatry" (1972).

The skillful clinician may use the patient's associations and references to elicit a rather complete history, the patient elaborating on what he himself has introduced. Toward the end of the evaluation, however, the doctor may see gaps in the information he has obtained; he must pursue this material by direct questioning. He will usually find it more productive even when eliciting specific details to avoid questions that can be answered simply yes or no and to make his questions open-ended. "Tell me about your relationship with your brother" will usually yield more information than "Do you have a good relationship with your brother?" Furthermore, questions ought always to be couched in terms and asked in a context that the patient finds least humiliating and embarrassing. If a patient says she experiences great anxiety when physically close to men, the doctor may suspect from this and similar comments that the patient may be struggling with homosexual feelings. He would err, however, if he approached this subject directly. Instead he might ask the patient to tell him more about her discomfort with men. She might state that her close relationships had always been with women. If the doctor then asked, "Has this closeness included a physical relationship?" she might reply, "No, but I have thought about it often." In this gradual and non-threatening way, the doctor can open the door for the patient to discuss her homosexual feelings and fantasies—a topic she might never discuss with a stranger if his approach were less tactful and less appropriately timed. Patients seldom speak of their difficulties in terms of "homosexuality," "frigidity," or "impotence," and the doctor's sensitivity to the comfort of the patient will usually preclude his use of such terms.

The technique of history taking can be refined by observing skilled clinicians and by taping interviews and listening to them with supervisors. A tape recorder ought never to be used, how-ever, without the permission of the patient and without informing him explicitly how and by whom the tape will be used. The presence of a recorder may make it difficult for some patients to speak freely. The doctor's efforts to be tactful and to make the patient comfortable must be natural and unobtrusive. Like that of a good musical accompanist, the better the doctor's technique is in taking a history the less noticeable it will be to both interviewer and patient. But tact must never be used as an excuse for avoiding sensitive areas and thus failing to explore pertinent subjects. For example, failure to rule out suicidal thoughts whenever they might possibly be present may have disastrous consequences. "Have you had thoughts of injuring yourself?" ought to be asked whenever the doctor has the slightest suspicion that the patient may be suicidal.

The Psychiatric Examination

The purpose of the psychiatric or mental status examination is to observe and record in a systematic way the current emotional state and the specific mental functions of the patient.

Prior to the nineteenth century, physicians recorded their observations on psychological disorders in a highly personalized narrative style. Then, beginning with Pinel, Esquirol, and Falret in the early 1800s and culminating in Kraepelin's classification, published in 1899, psychiatrists began to stress a more scientific and objective clinical approach. Not until 1918, however, was there a systematic form for reporting the psychiatric examination; in that year Adolf Meyer (who first referred to such an exam as the *mental status*) published his "Outlines of Examinations" (see Meyer, 1951). His structured format, with slight modifications, has been taught to psychiatrists in the United States for the past fifty years (Donnelly, Rosenbert, and Fleeson, 1970).

Dynamic psychiatrists have long resisted and criticized the use of any standard form for recording the mental status examination, considering it timeworn, rigid, stereotyped, dehumanizing, offensive to sensitive patients, and an impediment to observing unique characteristics of the patient. They have also pointed to widespread inconsistencies in the categories and definitions of terms on which standardized forms rest (Weitzel et al., 1973). Rather than the standardized descriptive format, they have advocated a free-form, narrative approach. Other psychiatrists, however, have argued that the free-form method has produced a generation of psychiatrists with no idea of how to conduct a mental status examination (Weitzel et al., 1973) and has resulted in hospital records that are disorganized, incomplete, and useless for statistical analysis and carefully controlled research (Donnelly, Rosenbert, and Fleeson, 1970). Because recent studies have found the free-form style of recording to be less efficient and less thorough, especially in providing information for data-processing equipment now used in many hospitals, there is a great deal of interest in developing a form with widespread acceptance (Weitzel et al., 1973; Donnelly, Rosenbert, and Fleeson, 1970).

Format for the Psychiatric Examination

The format proposed here is based on a consensus among professors of psychiatry from medical schools across the country on what is essential in a mental status examination (Weitzel et al., 1973). Such a form ought never to be used like a physical examination form; rather, it is intended primarily to help organize and record data. The examiner can explore most of the categories while taking the psychiatric history; indeed, the history will give him clues to which items he needs to focus on and which he can ignore. A graduate student currently doing honors work in mathematics, for example, need not be given IQ tests. The mental status examination, therefore, varies with each patient. (Terms are based primarily on the 1975 edition of the American Psychiatric Association's *Psychiatric Glossary.*)

1. *General appearance.* Specific idiosyncratic characteristics of dress and grooming ought to be noted as well as posture, gait, facial expression, and gestures. The interviewer should note any distinctive feature that would identify the individual immediately.

2. *Attitude.* What is the patient's attitude toward his illness, toward the interview, and toward the doctor? If ill, is he aware that he is ill? Is he cooperative or evasive, arrogant or ingratiating, aggressive or submissive, outgoing or withdrawn? Does he express feelings freely or does he avoid them obviously? These observations give clues to the patient's main defense mechanisms as well as to patterns of relating to people generally.

3. *Motor behavior.* The posture and gait of the patient should be noted as well as tics, tremors, posturing, pacing, grimaces, and other abnormal bodily movements. Nail biting, wringing of the hands, tapping of the foot, chewing movements, and other manifestations of anxiety may appear or intensify during the interview and give clues to emotionally charged content. Some types of abnormal motor behavior point to specific disorders—the psychomotor excitement of a manic patient, for instance, or the psychomotor retardation of the depressed patient.

4. *Speech.* Tone of voice, pitch, rate of speech (very fast and pressured as in a manic state or very slow as in a depressed state), affectations, and mutism or other abnormalities should be noted. These disturbances characterize the patient's form of speech, that is, the way he speaks, rather than what he says. What the patient says, that is, the content of his speech, will be mentioned under thought processes.

5. *Affective states.* The term *affect* refers to what the patient is feeling at the moment, to the feeling tone or emotional state and its outward manifestations. The feeling tone (affect) may be flat or blunted with little emotion expressed. Anger, fear, euphoria, elation, ecstasy, depression, irritability, and other emotional states should be noted. Affect that appears to be inappropriate to the patient's circumstances or thought content has important diagnostic implications. The patient's subjective description of his feeling tone over time, that is, his *mood*, ought to be noted and recorded.

6. *Thought processes.* From attending to the content of the patient's speech, the interviewer can observe disturbances in thought processes, in the structure and rate of associations, and in the flow of ideas. Does one thought logically follow another or are the patient's thoughts loosely connected?

7. *Thought content.* The content of a patient's

thinking can be assessed by listening to his history. The patient's preoccupations, ambitions, repetitive dreams, and daydreams will give some idea of this content. Pathological content must be noted carefully (for example, unusual suspiciousness, depressive ideas, expressions of worthlessness, hypochondriacal ideas, ideas of unreality, obsessions, phobias, and delusions).

8. *Perception*. Perception is the capacity to be aware of objects and to discriminate among them. The interviewer must observe and record any distortions in the patient's perceptions of reality; illusions and hallucinations constitute the more serious forms of perceptual distortion.

9. *Intellectual functioning*. A general impression of the patient's intellectual capacity will be gained from listening to his history. His general level of knowledge must be measured against the years of formal education he has completed and his particular family and cultural background. If the interviewer suspects certain forms of schizophrenia or certain kinds of organic mental disorder, he ought to look for disturbances in abstract thinking. This disturbance can be measured by asking the patient the meaning of some of the more common proverbs.

10. *Orientation*. Disorientation in terms of person, place, or time must be noted. Disturbances in orientation occur primarily, though not exclusively, in organic mental disorders.

11. *Memory*. Disorders of memory can usually be detected while taking the patient's history. His ability to recall past and recent events can be tested as the doctor elicits dates and other details of his life. If there appear to be gaps in his memory or if the dates he gives conflict, the doctor can explore this possibility in more detail.

12. *Judgment*. The examiner must evaluate the patient's ability to compare and assess alternatives in deciding on a course of action. (The patient's ability to make and carry out plans, to take the initiative, to discriminate accurately, and to behave appropriately in social and other situations reflect his judgment.) His ability to compare facts or ideas and to draw correct conclusions from facts is also a reflection of his judgment, as are his capacity to carry out his responsibilities appropriately, and his ability to meet academic, business, and family obligations adequately. All may be assessed in the course of the psychiatric history.

The Significance of Abnormalities

Observation of abnormalities in any of these twelve general categories will guide the clinician toward ruling in or out a particular diagnosis or conclusion about the patient's mental status. Some signs and symptoms will indicate the necessity for psychological or neurological tests. The clinician must always keep in mind the possibility of organic illness as he reviews the various areas of the psychiatric evaluation, since such disorders must be diagnosed and treated promptly.

Abnormal appearance. If a patient appears disheveled and unkempt, the examiner ought to determine from family or friends whether he was neat in appearance before the onset of his present difficulties. A deterioration in dress and grooming sometimes marks the onset of schizophrenia or depression. The examiner should also be aware of the seductive dress and manner of some patients with hysterical character disorders, the exhibitionistic dress of some male homosexuals, the drab, excessively loose clothing worn by some sexually inhibited women, and the dark glasses worn continuously by some paranoid patients. Overly fastidious dress and grooming may indicate obsessive-compulsive traits. Although most individuals fall between the extremes of dress, appearance must never serve as a basis for diagnosis but only as an indicator of conflicts worthy of further exploration.

Abnormal attitude. Certain disturbances in attitude will alert the examiner to specific diagnostic possibilities. The doctor ought to be aware of the suspiciousness, evasiveness, and arrogance that characterize some paranoid patients; the uncooperativeness or impatience of severely manic patients; the reserved, remote, and unfeeling attitude of the schizophrenic; the resistant, uncooperative attitude of the passive-aggressive patient; the apprehensive attitude of the patient suffering from acute anxiety neurosis; the apathetic, helpless attitude of the depressed patient; and the easily distracted, seemingly indifferent attitude of the patient suffering from an acute brain disorder.

Abnormal motor behavior. A number of disorders may show themselves in motor abnormalities. A

few are discussed here. *Echopraxia* is the patho-
logic repetition, by imitation, of the movements
of another person; this motor disturbance is
often seen in catatonic schizophrenics. In *cerea
flexibilitas* ("waxy flexibility") a patient maintains his body position for long periods of time;
the patient's arm or leg will remain passively in
the position in which it is placed. This motor disturbance is characteristic of catatonic schizophrenia but may also occur in organic mental
disorders. *Catalepsy*, a generalized condition of
diminished responsiveness usually characterized
by trancelike states and immobility, occurs in
various organic and psychological disorders. *Cataplexy*, a temporary loss of muscle tone and
weakness, may be precipitated by laughter,
anger, or surprise. The term *automatism* refers
to automatic and apparently undirected motor
behavior that is not consciously controlled and is
seen often in psychomotor epilepsy. *Stereotypy*,
the persistent, mechanical repetition of speech
or motor activity, is observed in some schizophrenics.

Hyperactivity in an adult suggests the possibility of a manic condition. *Hyperkinesia*, a state of
restless, destructive and assaultive activity, may
occur in a child during periods of great emotional stress or following encephalitis and other
forms of organic mental disorder. Chronic
restless activity in an adult may be a manifestation of anxiety or of an agitated depression.
Akathisia refers to the particular type of restlessness and uncontrolled motor activity associated
with certain psychotropic drugs such as the
phenothiazines. A *compulsion* is an insistent,
repetitive, intrusive, and unwanted urge to perform an act that is contrary to the person's ordinary wishes or standards; failure to perform the
compulsive act leads to overt anxiety. A person
with an obsessive-compulsive neurosis manifests
obsessive ideas, pervasive doubts, and compulsive rituals such as repeated hand washing or
checking to see that the gas or lights have been
turned off. The suffix *-mania* is used with a
number of Greek roots to indicate a morbid
preoccupation with certain kinds of activity or a
compulsive need to behave abnormally. Some
examples follow:

dipsomania: the compulsion to drink alcoholic beverages

egomania: the pathological preoccupation with self
erotomania: the pathological preoccupation with erotic fantasies or
activities
kleptomania: the compulsion to steal
megalomania: the pathological preoccupation with delusions of power or
wealth
monomania: the pathological preoccupation with one subject or idea
necromania: the pathological preoccupation with death or dead bodies
nymphomania: the abnormal and excessive
need for sexual intercourse,
used to describe women*
pyromania: the morbid compulsion to set
fires
trichotillomania: the compulsion to pull out
one's hair

Manic patients may be in constant motion with
an apparent inexhaustible supply of energy.
Catatonic excitement also involves extreme
overactivity. Decreased activity is seen in some
depressed patients (*psychomotor retardation*)
and some catatonic patients (*catatonic stupor*).
Paralysis or muscular weakness (*asthenia*) may
be present as a hysterical symptom. *Hysterical
aphonia* is the loss of speech and *astasia-abasia*,
the inability to walk or stand; both are associated
with hysterical conversion.

Abnormal speech. Like abnormalities in motor
activity, abnormalities in speech are associated
with particular disorders. *Mutism* is the refusal
to speak for conscious or unconscious reasons
and is often present in severely psychotic patients. *Punning* and *rhyming* occur in manic
states and in schizophrenic disorders. *Verbigeration*, the stereotyped and seemingly meaningless
repetition of words or sentences, is seen in certain types of schizophrenia. *Aphasia* refers to a
loss of previously possessed facility of language
comprehension or production caused by lesions
located in specific regions of the brain. *Amnestic*
(or *anomic*) *aphasia* is the loss of the ability to
name objects; *Broca's aphasia*, the loss of the
ability to produce spoken and (usually) written

* *Satyromania*, excessive sexual excitement in the male, is
more often referred to as *satyriasis*.

language, with comprehension retained; and *Wernicke's aphasia*, the loss of ability to comprehend language, with the ability to produce it retained.

Abnormal affect. A broad range of mental disorders manifest disturbances of affect. Rage, anger, or hostility may characterize the paranoid schizophrenic; tension and apprehension, one with acute anxiety reaction or with a phobia; and extreme anxiety associated with personality disorganization, patients with homosexual or other states of panic. The examiner should also be aware of the feeling of unreality concerning the environment or the self (*depersonalization*) and the ambivalence seen in certain schizophrenic patients and of the inappropriate giggling and silliness seen in hebephrenic schizophrenia. Other disturbances in affect are *euphoria*, an exaggerated feeling of physical and emotional well-being not consonant with outward events, which occurs in organic mental disorders and toxic or drug-induced states; *elation*, a feeling of confidence and enjoyment associated with increased motor activity; *exultation*, an intense elation with feelings of grandeur; and *ecstasy*, a feeling of intense rapture and joy. All of them may occur under inappropriate circumstances in acute manic states in patients suffering from manic-depressive psychosis or schizophrenia. *Anxiety*, the apprehension or uneasiness that results from the anticipation of danger, usually of intrapsychic origin and therefore unconscious, is often distinguished from *fear*, the apprehension resulting from a consciously recognized, usually external, threat or danger. Anxiety is ordinarily present in all neurotic illness.

Abnormal thought processes. Abnormalities observed in patients' thought processes may indicate the presence of particular disorders. *Circumstantiality* is a disturbance in the associative thought processes in which a patient digresses into unnecessary detail and inappropriate thoughts before communicating the central idea; it is observed in schizophrenia, in obsessional disorders, and in some cases of epileptic dementia. *Neologisms*, seen in some schizophrenic patients, are new words or condensations of several words formed in an effort to express a highly complex idea. Neologisms may also occur in patients with organic mental disorders. *Word salad* is an incoherent mixture of words and phrases that is commonly seen in advanced states of schizophrenia. *Perseveration* is the pathological repetition of the same response to different questions. This repetition results from the patient's clinging to a specific thought or idea and is observed in some patients with organic mental disorders, in catatonic schizophrenics, in patients suffering from senile dementia, and in those who have suffered an injury to the speech centers of the brain. *Incoherence*, a type of disjointed, confusing speech, results when one idea runs into another so that both thought and speech disregard the laws of logic. Incoherence is seen in severely disturbed psychotic patients, usually those suffering from schizophrenia. *Echolalia* is the pathological repetition of one person's words by another and sometimes represents a regression to childlike forms of mocking behavior in a patient expressing hostility and resentment. Some clinicians, however, believe that this behavior represents a neurological deficit and is an attempt to maintain a continuity of thought processes. Echolalia occurs in certain cases of schizophrenia, particularly in catatonic schizophrenics.

Condensation refers to a thinking process in which one symbol stands for a number of others and results in the fusion of various ideas or concepts into one; it is observed primarily in schizophrenics. *Flight of ideas* describes a succession of thoughts without logical connections and with a rapid shifting from one idea to another. Ideas follow in quick succession but do not progress, so that the point of the conversation is never reached. Flight of ideas may occur in the early stages of schizophrenia and in patients in the manic phase of a manic-depressive psychosis. *Retardation* of thought involves a slowing of the thought processes reflected in slow speech; the patient often comments that his thoughts come slowly and with great difficulty. It may be observed in depressed patients and in certain schizophrenic patients. *Blocking* is another obstruction to the flow of thought or speech where the thought processes suddenly appear to cease entirely. The blockage appears to be related to strong feelings such as anger or terror that accompany certain thoughts and interrupt their progression. Whatever the interruption in the train of thinking, it appears to be totally unconscious. Blocking occurs primarily in schizophrenia, though it may occur to a lesser degree in acute anxiety.

Abnormal thought content. Abnormalities in thought content may appear as delusions, hypochondriacal ideas, obsessions, or phobias. A *delusion* is a firm, false, fixed idea or belief that is inconsistent with the patient's educational and cultural background. The important aspect of a delusion is its fixed nature; the patient adheres to the false belief against all reason, logic, and evidence to the contrary. Delusions of grandeur arise from feelings of inadequacy or inferiority and involve an exaggerated idea of one's own importance. Delusions of persecution involve a false belief that one is being harassed or oppressed; delusions or ideas of reference, a false belief that the remarks or actions of others have special meaning for oneself; and delusions of self-accusation, false ideas of self-blame and remorse. Delusions of control involve false feelings that one is being controlled by others. Delusions of infidelity derive from pathological jealousy that one's spouse is unfaithful. Paranoid delusions involve an intense oversuspiciousness leading to persecutory delusions. The presence of a delusion in a patient is of great diagnostic significance, since it indicates that a patient is psychotic. Therefore, delusions are pathognomonic of the psychoses, although they do not, of course, occur in all psychotics. Delusions occur primarily in schizophrenia but may appear in any of the psychoses, including those associated with organic mental disorders.

Hypochondriasis, or hypochondria, is an exaggerated concern for one's own health that is not based on any physical illness, although the patient feels ill. A patient may be preoccupied with a particular organ of his body or with an idea that he is incurably ill with a specific physical disease. Hypochondriasis may occur during the involutional period of life (that is, after age forty-five), during depressions, and in certain schizophrenics.

An *obsession* is a pathological persistence of a thought, feeling, or impulse that can neither be dispelled by conscious processes nor be influenced by logical reasoning. The obsessive thought is usually unwanted by the patient and consciously distasteful to him, but it is often unconsciously desired. Obsessive thoughts frequently occur in combination with compulsive acts. Both occur in obsessive-compulsive neurosis.

Phobia is the persistent, obsessive, unrealistic fear or pathological dread of an object or situation; it is believed to arise through a process of displacing an unconscious conflict onto a symbolically related external object. Some of the more common phobias are acrophobia (fear of heights), agoraphobia (fear of open places), ailurophobia (fear of cats), algophobia (fear of pain), claustrophobia (fear of closed spaces), erythrophobia (fear of blushing), hematophobia (fear of the sight of blood), mysophobia (fear of dirt and germs), pathophobia (fear of disease or suffering), panophobia (fear of everything), and xenophobia (fear of strangers).

Abnormal perception. A number of disorders characterized by abnormalities in perception are described here. An *illusion* is a disorder of perception defined as the misinterpretation of a real experience—hearing one's name in the distant sound of a train, for instance, or seeing shadows of trees as animals. Illusions occur frequently in toxic states and in schizophrenia. In contrast, a *hallucination* is a false sensory perception in the absence of external stimuli. Hallucinations may be induced by factors such as drugs, alcohol, and stress and may involve taste, touch, sound, sight, or smell. *Hypnagogic hallucinations* are false sensory perceptions occurring in healthy people midway between falling asleep and being awake. (Both hallucinations and illusions may be induced in healthy people by prolonged isolation or by the influence of certain drugs such as mescaline.) *Auditory hallucinations* (those involving hearing) are the most frequent forms of perceptual disturbance; they are common in schizophrenic patients, who often will speak to or quarrel with the "voices" they hear. *Visual hallucinations* (involving sight) occur much less frequently than auditory hallucinations but are seen occasionally in the deliria of acute infectious diseases and toxic psychoses. *Olfactory hallucinations* (involving smell) sometimes occur in schizophrenic reactions and with organic lesions of the temporal lobe. *Gustatory hallucinations* (involving taste) are rare false perceptions of taste; when they occur, they are usually associated with hallucinations of smell. Both occur in uncinate fits. *Tactile hallucinations* (involving touch) occur principally in toxic states and in certain drug addictions. The sensation that insects are crawling under the skin (*formication*) occurs commonly in delirium tremens and cocainism. *Kinesthetic hallucinations* are false perceptions of movement or sensation and commonly occur after the loss of a limb ("phantom limb"), in toxic states, and in certain schizophrenic reactions. Atropine and its derivatives may cause a patient to see people in miniature (*Lilliputian hallucinations*), and other drugs such as alcohol, marijuana, and phenothiazines may evoke hallucinations in some people. Withdrawal of drugs such as alcohol, barbiturates, and tranquilizers may precipitate visual hallucinations in people addicted to them.

Agnosia is the inability to recognize objects. This disturbance in perception is caused by organic mental disorders and not by a defect in elementary sensation or a reduced level of consciousness.

Abnormal intellectual functioning. Intelligence, an extremely difficult quality to define, usually refers to the ability to understand, recall, and mobilize previous experience in adapting to new situations; it encompasses a number of mental processes such as accuracy of thinking, the capacity for complex thought, and the ability to manipulate ideas in a constructive way. The examiner can obtain a fairly good estimate of the patient's intelligence in taking the history. The patient's vocabulary and general fund of information, interpreted in light of his educational and cultural background, will give the examiner some idea of the patient's intelligence. If a question of serious impairment exists, intelligence may be more accurately assessed by means of one of several standardized intelligence tests (see chapter 3, "The Clinical Use of Psychological Tests"). *Mental retardation* is usually defined as an organically caused lack of intelligence to a degree that interferes with social and vocational performance, although not all authorities agree

with this definition (see chapter 26, "Mental Retardation"). *Dementia* may be considered an irreversible loss of mental functioning due to organic causes (see chapter 15, "Organic Mental Disorders").

Abnormal orientation. In certain severe psychiatric disorders, orientation is impaired. Disorientation to time consists of a loss of awareness of the hour, the day, the date, the month, the season, or the year; disorientation to person, a lack of awareness of one's identity; disorientation to place, a lack of awareness of one's location and spatial orientation; and disorientation to situation, a lack of awareness of why one is in a particular place. Disorientation may occur in any psychiatric disorder where impairment of memory or disturbance of perception or attention exists. Disorientation may therefore be present in organic mental disorders as well as in acute episodes of the affective disorders and of schizophrenia.

Abnormal memory. Memory may be defined as the ability to recall to consciousness previously registered experiences and information. The examiner can attain from the history a fairly good assessment of the patient's ability to recall both recent and remote events. *Amnesia*, absence of memory, may be complete or partial and may have either an emotional or an organic basis. Some patients may recall very little before an emotionally traumatic event such as the death of a significant figure in their lives, even when that event has occurred relatively late in childhood or early adolescence. *Hysterical amnesia* is a highly selective loss of memory involving emotionally charged events. *Anterograde amnesia* is loss of memory for recent events and is usually progressive; it occurs frequently in arteriosclerotic cerebral degeneration. *Retrograde amnesia* involves past events and is not usually progressive. Brain trauma may sometimes give rise to amnesia for events immediately before or immediately after the accident. Delirium, epilepsy, and certain dissociative reactions such as fugues often give rise to memory disorders. A *fugue* is a personality dissociation characterized by amnesia and involving actual physical flight from the area of conflict.

Hypermnesia, the excessive retention of memories, occurs in certain disorders such as paranoia and hypomania. *Paramnesia* is the falsification of memory by distortion of recall. Types of paramnesia include *retrospective falsification*, a recollection of the true memory to which the patient adds false details; *confabulation*, an unconscious filling in of gaps in memory with experiences that the patient believes to be true but that have no basis in fact; and *déjà vu*, an illusion of visual recognition in which a new situation is incorrectly regarded as a repetition of a previous memory. The patient may feel that a new scene is familiar or that he has previously lived through a current experience. *Déjà vu* usually occurs when the present situation has a link in the patient's mind with some past experience that he can no longer remember. In *jamais vu*, the patient experiences a false unfamiliarity with situations that he has actually experienced. *Déjà vu* and *jamais vu* may occur in schizophrenics, in patients suffering from certain psychoneuroses, in those with lesions of the temporal lobe including epilepsy, with patients in states of fatigue or intoxication, and sometimes in normal individuals. The examiner must therefore be especially alert for defects in memory when examining patients suffering from fugues or other dissociative reactions, from head trauma and delirium, or from epilepsy.

Abnormal judgment. A patient's judgment is impaired if his thoughts and actions are inconsistent with reality. Judgment is impaired in various organic mental disorders as well as in certain psychogenic disorders—for example, in the manic phase of a manic-depressive psychosis.

Technique

It has already been stressed that the examiner can conduct most of the mental status examination while taking the history and that neither the history nor the examination should follow a rigid, stereotyped format. If the interviewer is skillful and a keen observer, he will be able to tailor his approach to the specific needs of the patient and, in a relaxed natural manner and without embarrassment to the patient, obtain all the information needed for the examination.

Through keen observation and careful listening, the examiner can note the patient's general appearance, his speech, his attitude during the interview, his behavior, his affective state, as well as thought processes and thought content. While taking the history the interviewer can also note whether or not the patient is oriented and can assess the state of his memory by noting his ability to recall recent and remote experiences. How the patient relates to people and whether or not he handles social and other affairs appropriately and with discernment can also be observed while taking a history and used to assess the patient's judgment.

The techniques to be followed in the examination depend in large part on what the interviewer has observed while taking the history. If the content of the interview raises the possibility of defects in the patient's judgment, for instance, the doctor may say, "You mentioned that your family complained of your suddenly spending too much money. Can you tell me more about this complaint?" Later, the doctor may ask, "Has your family had other complaints?" Similarly, the doctor may use a clue from the patient to test the patient's memory: "You said earlier that you had difficulty remembering things lately. Can you remember my name?" "Can you remember the name of this hospital?" "Can you tell me today's date? What year it is?" (Forgetting the day may have little significance, but forgetting the year will always be significant.)

If the examiner has doubts about the patient's thought processes or content, he can focus on these areas with specific questions. "Do you have difficulty concentrating?" "Do you have difficulty controlling your thoughts?" "Can you tell me what you daydream about most?" These and similar questions may help focus on specific difficulties that the doctor may feel it necessary to explore. If the patient gives evidence of disturbances in perception, the doctor ought to guide the patient toward this area in a conversational and indirect manner. If the patient alludes to people controlling his thoughts or telling him what to do, the doctor may ask, "Can you tell me more about these people?" or, "Who are these voices that you hear?" and then explore them in detail.

With experience, the examiner will learn to

use specific kinds of questions to explore various areas of the mental status examination. If the interviewer thinks it necessary to test the patient's span of attention or the speed of his thought processes, he may ask him to subtract seven from one hundred and to keep subtracting by sevens. If the interviewer suspects that the patient has difficulty with abstract thinking, he may ask the patient to interpret a number of proverbs: "What is the meaning of 'a stitch in time saves nine'?"

Whatever questions the examiner uses to test specific functions, his manner in asking them and his judgment of whether or not they are appropriate for a given patient determines, in large measure, their effectiveness. If the questions are inappropriate or asked in a stilted, unnatural manner, the patient may consider them insulting, crude, or humiliating. Though a complete psychiatric examination is vitally important for the evaluation of the patient, the doctor must be careful to conduct the examination with respect for the patient and his comfort. A friendly and tactful manner will make the patient's cooperation more likely and thus assure a thorough and accurate assessment.

A patient who is unwilling or unable to speak poses a difficult problem in evaluation. The doctor's observational and descriptive powers must come into full play here. He should note whether the patient will shake hands, say hello, speak spontaneously, answer questions, or be willing to write even if he is unwilling to speak. Does he talk to himself, appear to be listening to voices, or appear suspicious, preoccupied, or inattentive? Does he exhibit abnormal facial expressions, posture, or bodily movements? Every unusual detail of the patient's general appearance and emotional reaction ought to be noted and recorded. This information may be extremely helpful in understanding the patient, especially when his inaccessibility is the first stage of a gradually developing emotional disorder.

The Physical Examination

Every evaluation of a psychiatric patient ought to include a complete physical examination. The neurological aspects of such an examination are often of great significance, especially in patients with intellectual deficit or disturbances of memory and attention and those with aphasias, agnosias, and apraxias. If any of these symptoms is present, the psychiatrist may choose to refer the patient to a neurologist for a thorough neurological workup. In hospital practice, a psychiatrist will usually give a physical examination as part of the patient's general workup. In private practice, some psychiatrists refer their patients to internists and general practitioners for the physical examination. Regardless of who performs the physical examination, the doctor evaluating the psychiatric patient must assume responsibility for seeing that it gets done.

Diagnostic Formulation and Assessment for Treatment

The diagnostic formulation includes a summary of the patient's history and of the examination and a provisional diagnosis based on these findings. It also includes a clear description of the present symptoms and emotional conflicts, of the genetic factors involved (that is, of the constitutional and early life experiences contributing to the disorder), and of the dynamic or psychological processes resulting in the conflicts. A diagnostic classification from the *Diagnostic and Statistical Manual of Mental Disorders* (DSM-II) may also be included.

After formulating the diagnosis, the examiner confronts the most important part of the evaluation—determining whether treatment is indicated and what type of treatment will be most effective. A competent examiner will strive to avoid bias toward any one form of therapy and will be sufficiently informed to determine the most effective therapeutic modality for each patient. To refer a patient for behavior therapy, for short-term psychotherapy, for electroconvulsive therapy, for psychoanalysis, or for other forms of therapy without specific and clear indications for such a referral is irresponsible. Like unnecessary surgery, unnecessary therapy ought to be discouraged. Often, therapy is prescribed even when the indications for it are unclear because the doctor feels it can do no harm. It can. In addition to wasting time, effort, and financial resources, it may result in a number of untoward complications.

To determine whether treatment is indicated, the doctor must assess the degree to which the patient's conflicts seriously interfere with his functioning in important areas of his life. If they do not interfere, or if they interfere in an area of functioning not currently important to the patient, they do not warrant therapeutic intervention. A doctor may be enormously reassuring to such a patient simply by helping him understand that he does not need treatment. (For a more detailed discussion of various therapies, see chapter 17, "The Psychotherapies.")

Concluding the Interview

In bringing the initial session to a close, the examiner must avoid cutting the patient off in the middle of an important part of his history or making him feel that he is being summarily dismissed. Terminating a session smoothly is not always easy—particularly if either the patient or the doctor has conflicts over leaving people or being left—and a degree of firmness and technical skill is often necessary in the examiner. If he will see the patient again, of course, the interviewer can close by saying, "Let's continue here the next time." In this way, he notifies the patient that the hour is up, expresses interest in the patient's history by saying he would like to hear more about it, and encourages the patient to maintain continuity with the next session.

At the end of an evaluation, the examiner should ask whether the patient has any questions about the therapist's impressions or recommendations. Information about the nature of the evaluation, about a particular type of therapy recommended, or about the qualifications of the clinic or therapist to whom the patient is being referred will reduce the patient's anxiety and help him to follow through with the examiner's recommendations.

The evaluation of a psychiatric patient comprises a thorough history, a detailed psychiatric examination, and, when indicated, psychological tests. The examiner's primary purpose is to assess within a limited number of sessions the nature and intensity of the patient's emotional conflicts and to determine the most effective treatment for their alleviation or resolution. Because a misdiagnosis may have untoward consequences for the patient, the evaluation ought to be conducted by therapists still in training only under the supervision of senior and experienced staff members. In addition to his experience and knowledge, an examiner's thoroughness determines in large measure, the accuracy and effectiveness of his evaluation; the clinician's ability to be thorough will be enhanced if he has clearly in mind the important areas to cover in both the history and the examination. Finally, though tact and sensitivity must always characterize his questioning, they must never interfere with the completeness and accuracy of his evaluation.

References

American Psychiatric Association. 1968. *Diagnostic and statistical manual of mental disorders*. 2nd ed. Washington, D.C.

—— 1975. *A Psychiatric Glossary*. Washington, D.C.

Deutsch, F. 1939. The associative anamnesis. *Psychoanal. Q*. 8:354–381.

Deutsch, F., and N. F. Murphy. 1955. *The clinical interview*. New York: International Universities Press.

Donnelly, J., M. Rosenbert, and W. Fleeson. 1970. The evolution of the mental status—past and future. *Am. J. Psychiatry* 125:997–1002.

Finesinger, J. E. 1948. Psychiatric interviewing I. Some principles and procedures in insight therapy. *Am. J. Psychiatry* 105:187–195.

Havens, L. H. 1972. Clinical methods in psychiatry. *Int. J. Psychiatry* 10, no. 2:7–28.

Menninger, K. A. 1963. *The vital balance*. New York: Viking Press.

Meyer, A. 1951. *The collected papers of Adolf Meyer*, ed. E. E. Winters. Vol. 3. Baltimore: Johns Hopkins University Press.

Scheflen, A. E. 1963. Communication and regulation in psychotherapy. *Psychiatry* 26:126–136.

Sullivan, H. S. 1954. *The psychiatric interview*. New York: Norton.

Weitzel, W., D. Morgan, T. Guyden, and J. Robinson. 1973. Toward a more efficient mental status examination. *Arch. Gen. Psychiatry* 128:215–218.

Recommended Reading

Beckett, P. G. S., and R. Senf. 1962. Methodological problems in the electronic processing of psychiatric data with examples from a follow-up study. *Psychiatr. Res. Rep.* 15:133–145.

Climent, E. C., R. Plutchik, H. Estrada, L. Gaviria, and W. Arevalo. 1975. A comparison of traditional and symptom-checklist based histories. *Am. J. Psychiatry* 132, no. 4:450–453.

Fowler, R. D., Jr., and C. F. Stroebel. 1969. The computer and the clinical decision process. *Am. J. Psychiatry* suppl. 125:21–27.

—— 1960. *The anatomy of judgment.* New York: Basic Books.

Johnson, A. M. L. 1955. Observer error: its bearing on teaching. *Lancet* 2:442–424.

Katz, M. M., J. O. Cole, and H. A. Lowery. 1969. Studies of the diagnostic process. *Am. J. Psychiatry* 125, no. 7:937–947.

Kilpatrick, S. S. 1963. Observer error in medicine. *J. Med. Educ.* 38:38–43.

Laska, E., D. Morrill, N. S. Kline, E. Hackett, and G. M. Simpson. 1967. Scribe—a method for producing automated narrative psychiatric case histories. *Am. J. Psychiatry* 124:82–84.

Mayer-Gross, W., E. Slater, and M. Roth. 1960. Examination of the psychiatric patient. In *Clinical psychiatry*, ed. E. Slater and M. Roth. 2nd ed. London: Balliére, Tindall & Cassell.

McIntyre, H. D. and A. P. 1942. The problem of brain tumor in psychiatric diagnosis. *Am. J. Psychiatry* 98:720–726.

Meikle, S., and R. Gerritse. 1970. A comparison of psychiatric symptom frequency under narrative and checklist conditions. *Am. J. Psychiatry* 127:379–382.

Menninger, K. A., M. Mayman, and P. W. Pruyser. 1962. The psychological examination. In *A manual for psychiatric case study.* 2nd ed. New York: Grune & Stratton.

Pool, J. L., and J. W. Correll. 1958. Psychiatric symptoms masking brain tumor. *J. Med. Soc. N.J.* 55:4–9.

Rubert, S. L., and F. B. Remington. 1963. Why patients with brain tumors come to a psychiatric hospital: a 30-year survey. *Psychiat. Q.* 37:253–263.

Shader, R. I., W. A. Binstock, J. I. Ohly, and D. Scott. 1969. Biasing factors in diagnosis and disposition. *Compr. Psychiatry* 10:81–89.

Slack, W. V., G. Hicks, C. Reed, and L. Van Cura. 1966. The computer-based medical history system. *N. Engl. J. Med.* 274:194–198.

Soniat, T. L. L. 1951. Psychiatric symptoms as associated with intracranial neoplasms. *Am. J. Psychiatry* 108:19–22.

Spitzer, R. L., J. Endicott, J. L. Fleiss, and J. Cohen. 1972. The psychiatric status schedule and technique for evaluating psychopathology and impairment in role functioning. *Arch. Gen. Psychiatry* 23:41–55.

Spitzer, R. L., J. L. Fleiss, E. I. Burdock, and A. S. Hardestry. 1964. The mental status schedule: ratinale, reliability, and validity. *Compr. Psychiatry* 5:384–395.

Stevenson, I. 1968. *The psychiatric examination.* Boston: Little, Brown.

Stillman, R., W. T. Roth, K. M. Colby, and C. P. Rosenbaum. 1969. An on-line computer system for initial psychiatric inventory. *Am. J. Psychiatry* suppl. 125:8–11.

Temerlin, M. K. 1969. Suggestion effects in psychiatric diagnosis. *J. Nerv. Ment. Dis.* 147:349–353.

Waggoner, R. W., and B. K. Bagchi. 1954. Initial masking of organic brain changes by psychic symptoms. *Am. J. Psychiatry* 110:904–910.

Whitehorn, J. C. 1944. Guide to interviewing and clinical personality study. *Arch. Neurol. Psychiatr.* 52:197–216.

The Clinical Use of Psychological Tests

CHAPTER 3

Justin L. Weiss

IN THE MOST general sense, psychological tests are used in psychiatry to provide a dynamic and descriptive understanding of the patient. Factors important in understanding each patient may include his cognitive processes, such as thinking, perception, and memory; his experience and expression of emotions; significant inner conflicts; prominent defensive and coping mechanisms; recurrent interpersonal themes and orientations; and vulnerability and resources in response to stress. The psychologist ordinarily employs a battery of tests (discussed in some detail in this chapter) in order to obtain an appropriate range of information and observations. The test report provides an integrative interpretation of the data focused on diagnostic, planning, and treatment issues.

Fundamentals of Test Construction and Use

The term *test* implies a more or less systematic approach to the development and use of some set of tasks, questions, or other stimuli. While tests vary considerably in the degree to which they have been systematically derived, they gen-

erally arise from a context of controlled experimentation, in contrast to the usual clinical investigative stance for observation or interview in psychiatry. A standardized test, such as one of the widely used intelligence tests, is likely to have the following characteristics: items or questions selected on the basis of empirical studies; directions for administration and scoring; norms based on the performance of identified samples of subjects; and quantitative estimates of the reliability, validity, and utility of the test. Less standardized tests will normally have some of these attributes.

Test Construction and Administration

Test items are selected in many different ways. Hermann Rorschach selected his final series of ten inkblots from a much larger number; in the process of developing his technique, he found it helpful to include inkblots with certain properties and not others on a purely empirical basis. Intelligence and personality tests of today represent a blend of items taken from earlier tests, modified items, and new concepts and operations. Sophisticated techniques are used in order to determine the combination of items and procedures that will best sample the behaviors of interest and meet a variety of other needs.

Another aspect of the systematic character of tests is that administration and scoring is usually done in accordance with specific directions. These procedures are intended to insure that test results are comparable even when they involve different individuals and situations. The most important such comparison makes use of normative data. Some tests—again the standardized intelligence test is the model—are used with normative tables based on the scores of groups of subjects who have been carefully selected in accordance with sampling procedures. These sampling procedures must take into account the intended applications of the test. For example, standardization of an intelligence test requires sampling a sufficiently large group of subjects in each age group to be covered by the test, since intellectual performance is known to vary with age. Similarly, if the norms are to be applicable to a given population—to American adolescents and adults, for instance—the sampling procedures should provide appropriate representation of such variables as education, occupation, race, urban versus rural residence, and, so far as possible, any other factors that could bias the data if not taken into account.

The *reliability* of a test refers to its consistency and stability. Split-half, test-retest, and interjudge agreement are the most common methods of determining the reliability of a test. The reliability of a long spelling test, for example, may be estimated by splitting the test in half; one correlates the number of correct responses to odd-numbered and even-numbered items. Correlating scores on such a test obtained from the same individuals on two occasions one week apart would be an appropriate means of assessing reliability on a test-retest basis. This method, however, would be less reliable when applied to the scores of psychiatric patients on a scale measuring depressive mood, which is likely to fluctuate over time. Interjudge agreement would be the method of choice if one wished to develop a scoring system for the content of thematic stories; here we need to know that two or more scorers can apply the concepts and rules of the system in the same ways.

The *validity* of a test refers to the degree to which it measures what it is supposed to measure. Three types of validity are usually delineated: content, predictive, and construct. Content validity is concerned with how well the test samples the behaviors of interest. Predictive validity refers to the accuracy of the test in measuring relevant characteristics or events. Predictive validity need not be limited to future events; concurrent and postdictive validity are self-explanatory terms for other kinds of "predictions." However, certain concepts that one wishes to measure lack simple or agreed-upon criteria. Tests of anxiety or ego strength, for example, cannot be easily validated by reference to external events. Their construct validity is established by the gradual accumulation of evidence that they correlate with a variety of other measures or behaviors commonly accepted to be manifestations of the construct in question.

The *utility* of a test refers to how useful it is for a particular purpose. In clinical practice, one should be concerned with what a test will add to that which could be known easily, quickly, or inexpensively from previously available sources. Tests are unlikely to have great utility in predicting outcomes with either very high or very low base rates of occurrence in the population of interest.

Clinical versus Actuarial Approaches

In the past twenty years, much has been written about the controversy between clinical and actuarial or statistical approaches to assessment in psychiatry (Meehl, 1954). These terms refer to different ways of handling data. The clinical approach is more familiar, traditional, and widely used; it leaves to the psychologist the task of determining the meaning and importance of various aspects of the data as he considers the total picture with some degree of subjectivity and intuitive skill based on experience. The actuarial approach may also use any kind of data, but the information must be coded, usually in quantitative terms. The processes of inference are entirely prescribed by rules applied rigorously to all cases; these rules are derived from known relationships between test data and other variables. In general, the actuarial method of handling data is less subject to error and usually more accurate in making specific predictions based on measurable criteria, while the clinical method is more likely to yield a meaningful understanding of an individual.

The Typical Test Battery in Clinical Practice

Clinical psychologists in the United States most often obtain a sampling of the patient's personality, resources, and difficulties by means of a battery of different types of tests. The Rorschach technique, the Thematic Apperception Test (TAT), and the Wechsler Adult Intelligence Scale are the three tests most often employed in the clinical evaluation of patients above the age of fifteen. The Children's Apperception Test (CAT) and the appropriate age level of intelligence test are used together with the Rorschach for children. The Minnesota Multiphasic Personality Inventory (MMPI), an objective measure of personality and psychopathology, is also used widely with adolescents and adults. The standard battery is supplemented by various special purpose tests, such as instruments for the systematic assessment of neurological deficit or difficulties in learning or memory. The integration of results from a battery of tests allows the clinician to assemble a complete psychological study.

Projective Tests

When a visual stimulus with some degree of ambiguity is presented to an individual and an appropriate response set is established, the assumption is made that to some degree the responses will reflect the individual's particular ways of organizing and describing experience. Depending upon the specific characteristics of the stimuli and the task, such basic psychological processes as associative thinking, imagination, cognitive style, conflicts, defense mechanisms, adaptive techniques, and modes of interpersonal relationships may be brought into play.

A common attribute of projective tests is that there is no "right" answer. In describing what an inkblot suggests to him or making up a story in response to a picture, the subject is given minimal guidelines concerning expected or typical performance. This situation in itself often

arouses anxiety; for this reason, many clinicians believe that analysis and interpretation of projective tests are especially useful in understanding how an individual is likely to react under stress. Since the psychologist in clinical practice often examines patients when they are already under considerable stress from external or internal pressures of their own, it is important to recognize the special nature of the projective test. While it may provide especially transparent windows on psychopathological modes of perceiving, thinking, feeling, and behaving, it may not enlighten the examiner sufficiently concerning the patient's typical level of functioning under clear and structured conditions with minimal anxiety.

The value and utility in interpreting an individual's responses to projective tests are highly dependent upon the examiner's experience and knowledge of personality and psychopathology within a theoretical framework. The psychologist's inferences from projective tests emerge from the same general set of concepts used to observe the development and functioning of people in general and people with psychiatric difficulties in particular.

The Rorschach Technique

Hermann Rorschach, a Swiss psychiatrist, discovered that the specially prepared series of inkblots he had been using to study perceptual processes could be helpful in differential diagnosis. His *Psychodiagnostics*, published in 1921 and translated into English in 1942, marked the beginning of projective testing. The technique was brought to the United States in the early 1930s, and by the next decade it had become the favorite clinical instrument of the psychologists who ventured into the growing field of psychiatry during and following World War II. American psychologists such as Beck (1944, 1945, 1952) and Klopfer and his colleagues (1942, 1954, 1956) published important guides to the administration, scoring, and interpretation of the Rorschach inkblots. Rapaport, Gill, and Schafer (1945) and Schafer (1948, 1954) had tremendous impact on subsequent use of the Rorschach through detailed studies of response patterns in various psychiatric diagnostic groups and especially by proposing a framework for Rorschach interpretation based on psychoanalytic ego psychology.

The Rorschach stimuli consist of ten symmetrical "inkblots," each on a piece of white cardboard; five of the blots are entirely in shades of black and gray, two include areas of red, and the last three are entirely multicolored. They are presented to all subjects in a standard sequence with instructions to "say what it might look like." No further guidance is provided. The examiner records accurately not only the patient's words but also relevant aspects of his behavior. After the free associations, the examiner conducts a nonleading inquiry in order to determine where and how the various percepts were seen and what aspects of the blot suggested them (the "determinants," such as form, color, shading, and movement).

The recorded Rorschach protocol provides three sources of data for interpretation: (1) formal aspects of the response process, most of which are represented in scoring categories devised by Rorschach, (2) the dynamic content and sequence of the responses, and (3) the patient's interpersonal behavior in the test situation. The most important formal qualities are those of location, determinants, form level, content categories, and organization of thought and language. The experienced psychologist examines trends in the scoring summary (called a "psychogram") against the backdrop of his own experience, which includes knowledge of normative data from published studies. For example, one patient may show a strong tendency to use tiny and unusual areas of the blots while another may tend to organize major elements into coherent wholes. It is a short inferential leap to suggesting that the first individual usually organizes his experience in a fragmented fashion, attending to details at the expense of the larger view, and that the second is more able to integrate and to generalize.

Each of the determinants is associated with interpretive characteristics. To oversimplify considerably, the degree to which color in the blots is represented in the individual's responses is related to reactivity to emotional stimulation; the frequency of responses involving humans in motion may be indicative of the relationship

between fantasy or anticipation and action; and responses to the shading or textural aspects may suggest the quality and intensity of anxiety. The patient's reality testing—the capacity to perceive the experiential world as it is and as others perceive it—is inferred primarily from the "form level" of the Rorschach responses. Using both published norms and subjective judgment, the examiner scores each percept as a plus or a minus on the basis of the general correspondence between the inkblot area used and the actual shape of what the patient has seen. The percentage of plus responses is the form level. Content categories may indicate emphasis on particular themes and provide a crude estimate of the breadth or narrowness of the patient's available interests. Finally, Rorschach scoring systems include notations for describing clinically significant aspects of thought and language disturbance.

The content of the Rorschach protocol is interpreted in accordance with the psychologist's understanding of the implications of images and symbols and the sequential manner in which they are given by the patient. Schafer (1954) has formulated the most extensive guide for the interpretation of Rorschach content, deriving his meanings from psychoanalytic theory. Dependent, sadomasochistic, or authoritarian orientations, for example, may be suggested by images of food, a person being torn apart, or Napoleon, respectively. Sexual identity, guilt, different emotional states, and other themes may be inferred from the content of responses. Content interpretation is not a simplistic "dreambook" process; major trends of the personality cannot be identified merely by equating them with symbols. Valid and meaningful interpretations of content depend upon the convergence of evidence and the integration of content hypotheses with inferences from the formal and behavioral data.

Since the Rorschach technique provides a special kind of transaction between two people, the patient's behavior is carefully recorded so that predominant modes of interaction may be included in the analysis. One may note submissive, challenging, evasive, seductive, euphoric, passive-aggressive, or suspicious tendencies—the possibilities are endless, and it is the psychologist's task to study them objectively and weave them into the interpretive tapestry.

The Thematic Apperception Test

The TAT had its origins in the studies of normal personalities conducted by Henry A. Murray and his colleagues at Harvard. First described in the mid-1930s (Morgan and Murray, 1935), it was published and marketed as a test in 1943 and has since been a part of the typical clinical psychological examination and a major instrument in personality research.

The TAT consists of a series of black-and-white pictures, chiefly drawings or woodcuts, most of which portray one or more people in situations designed to elicit themes of psychological significance. The subject is asked to make up a story for each picture and to specify what led to the situation, what is happening, what the characters are thinking and feeling, and how the story ends. The stimuli are sufficiently ambiguous to allow the subject to project individual fantasies, feelings, patterns of relationship, needs, and conflicts.

There are thirty pictures in the complete set, including some alternative versions for males and females or for adults and adolescents. Twenty pictures were intended to be shown to each subject, but, because of the length of time involved, most clinicians tend to use a shorter subset of ten to twelve cards.

Formal scoring systems are not widely employed in analysis of the TAT, although a number of clinicians have described their procedures, and the reader may find it of interest to compare independent interpretations of the same TAT by a group of experts (Shneidman, 1951). Clinical analysis is a matter of carefully developing hypotheses from each story, taking into account the nature of the subject's identification with the characters, the feelings expressed, the conflicts and resolutions presented, and the defensive and adaptive activities. The clinician uses his experience, aided by published accounts of the prominent themes brought out by each picture (Henry, 1956), to determine whether a particular story deserves special emphasis because of its idiosyncratic quality.

One TAT card, for example, depicts a young man reclining with eyes closed while an older man stands over him with one arm raised. The patient may see the young man as asleep, ill, or dead; the older man, as praying, hypnotizing, caring, curing, or attacking. The figures may be strangers or in an intense relationship; the antecedent and consequent elements may be logically and emotionally congruent with the scene described or they may be magical or arbitrary; the narrative may be coherent or it may reflect blocking or disorganization of thought. As with the Rorschach, sophisticated interpretation depends on the clinician's thoroughness and skill in assigning appropriate weight and meaning to the various aspects of the data and in drawing a psychological portrait that is both valid and useful.

Other Projective Tests

Space permits only the briefest mention of other projective tests with some importance in clinical practice. *The Sentence Completion Test*, which has been modified or redesigned by various clinicians (Rohde, 1957; Rotter and Rafferty, 1950) consists of a list of sentence beginnings for the subject to complete, such as "My mother . . ." and "My greatest mistake was . . ." There are typically four or five such items relevant to each of a number of personality dimensions. Interpretation focuses on two aspects of response—the level of adjustment or disturbance, and the personal meaning of the content.

The Blacky Pictures (Blum, 1950) were originally developed in a study that tested certain psychoanalytic propositions concerning psychosexual development (Blum, 1949). The subject is presented with a series of thirteen cartoons featuring a dog named Blacky in situations designed to evoke stories and themes relevant to the purpose of the test—Blacky nursing from Mama, or Blacky blindfolded with his tail on a chopping block toward which a huge knife is descending through the air. The subject is asked to provide stories, which are supplemented by structured questions; Blum has devised detailed scoring systems and ingenious procedures for research use. In clinical practice today the test is given primarily to children and interpreted without formal scoring.

Human figure drawings are considered to be

another projective device. Typically the subject is asked to draw a person (almost always a whole person), after which another sheet is provided for a drawing of a person of the opposite sex. There are variations, one of the earliest of which was the House-Tree-Person technique of Buck (1948). Figure drawings may be stylized or highly expressive of one's individuality. Most interpreters place emphasis on the portrayal of "body image" and its disturbance. Size, stance, facial expression, dress, and emphasis on particular body parts are among the characteristics to be noted. Some examiners supplement the drawings with a few open-ended questions, such as "What kind of person is this?"

Extended discussions and reviews of these and other secondary projective tests are available in a volume edited by Rabin (1968).

Objective Tests

In contrast to projective tests, which elicit the individual's response patterns in an open-ended and relatively unstructured fashion, objective tests typically consist of standard items in response to which the subject answers true or false or expresses preference or agreement-disagreement. Objective inventories or tests may be classified as either direct or indirect.

Direct inventories consist of items relevant to a particular variable, and the score obtained by the subject is taken to be a measure of that variable. For example, the first personality inventory, developed by Woodworth as an aid in the psychiatric screening of World War I recruits, asked 116 questions pertaining to common mental and physical symptoms. The score was used as an index of maladjustment, and those whose scores exceeded a certain "cutting point" were interviewed by psychiatrists. This approach is efficient for its purposes, and its validity depends considerably on the honesty and self-awareness of the respondent.

An indirect objective test includes a wider variety of items; many of them are direct in the sense that they ask in straightforward fashion about relevant content. Other items, however, are less obviously related, and they are included because they have empirical rather than face validity —that is, they have a demonstrated correla-

tion with nontest variables of interest. Some indirect inventories such as the MMPI also include scales that measure defensive behavior on the part of the subject.

The Minnesota Multiphasic Personality Inventory

By far the most widely used objective test in clinical practice and research is the MMPI, published by Hathaway and McKinley (1943). Designed as an aid to psychiatric diagnosis, the MMPI began as a pool of more than a thousand true-false items taken from case reports, texts, and similar sources. The responses of groups of patients with confirmed psychiatric diagnoses of various kinds were compared with those of a sizable group of presumably normal people (visitors to a hospital). Eight "clinical" scales were developed on an entirely empirical basis. For example, the schizophrenia scale consists of items on which schizophrenics and normals differed significantly in the proportion of true and false answers. Items were eliminated for various statistical reasons but never because their content seemed unrelated to schizophrenia; the criterion was whether the item discriminated schizophrenics from normals.

The authors intended the MMPI to render accurate diagnostic judgments very simply— schizophrenics were expected to have their highest score on that scale; depressives would peak on the depression scale. Two things very soon became apparent: (1) quite a few individuals with no psychiatric history scored high on one or more scales, and (2) interpretation through a more complex analysis of configurations would permit not only more accurate diagnosis but personality description as well.

There are several forms and modes of presentation for the MMPI. Most popular is the booklet form that is used to administer a 550-item true-false questionnaire to groups of patients. The patient is encouraged to try to answer each item, although a "cannot say" category is available. The answers may be scored with hand templates but machine-scored forms are used almost exclusively today. The score for each scale is the sum of all responses to its particular items that are scored in the "keyed" direction. For example, a subject's raw score on the schizophrenia scale would be the sum of true and false responses that matched those distinguishing the original schizophrenic sample from the normals. The raw score is converted to a T-score—a statistical device that makes it possible to compare the elevations on different scales with the score distributions of the original Minnesota sample of normals; the resulting common scale has a mean of 50 and a standard deviation of 10.

The published profile sheet lists three validity scales and ten clinical scales. The validity scales were designed to aid in estimating response predispositions that might alter the patient's scores. The L (lie) scale consists of fifteen items referring to socially desirable but rather unlikely behaviors, such as "I always read every editorial in the newspapers every day." Thus a higher than normal score on this scale suggests a naive individual who cannot be frank about himself, at least in the context in which the test is taken. The F (deviant response) scale was developed to detect random or otherwise invalid records. The K (defensiveness) scale, derived from items endorsed by a group of psychiatric patients who obtained unusually low profiles, measures "test-taking" attitude and is also used to improve the validity of five of the clinical scales by adding to their raw scores all or part of K before the T-score conversion.

The clinical scales are as follows:

1. *hypochondriasis* (Hs)—exaggerated concern with physical symptoms, with or without organic basis
2. *depression* (D)—sadness, low morale, apathy, lethargy, and lack of hope
3. *hysteria* (Hy)—blandness, emotional displays, naiveté, and bodily symptoms
4. *psychopathic deviate* (Pd)—characterological difficulties in social adjustment, with delinquent or antisocial behavior
5. *masculinity-femininity* (Mf)—empirically derived from a small group of male homosexuals with no other pathology
6. *paranoia* (Pa)—suspiciousness, sensitivity, delusions of persecution and grandeur, and ideas of reference
7. *psychasthenia* (Pt)—anxiety, phobias, obsessive rumination, compulsive behavior, and guilt

8. *schizophrenia* (Sc)—social withdrawal, inappropriate behavior, bizarre ideas, hallucinations, and delusions
9. *hypomania* (Ma)—overactivity, elevated mood, excitement, distractibility, and denial of distress
0. *social introversion* (Si)—a measure of introversion-extroversion

Hundreds of additional scales have been developed from the MMPI item pool for special research or clinical purposes. The Ego Strength Scale (Es), empirically derived by Barron (1953) as a predictor of response to outpatient psychotherapy, is often used clinically.

Translation of MMPI scales into meaningful statements about personality and psychopathology begins with an examination of the validity scales. If the F or K scales are unduly elevated, the psychologist will either qualify his interpretations or, in extreme cases, judge the entire test to be invalid on the basis of deviant response (F) or massive defensiveness (K). Assuming that the validity is within acceptable limits, one then considers the two or three scales with the highest elevations. Clinical significance is usually attached to scores of 70 or above, since these are at least two standard deviations above the original mean for normals. Most systems for classifying MMPI profiles utilize this method; the different categories of profiles are usually called code types. This example compares the two highest scales on hypothetical MMPI profiles given by three male psychiatric inpatients in their early twenties.

	Highest scale	*Second highest scale*
Mr. A	2. Depression	7. Psychasthenia
Mr. B	4. Psychopathic deviate	9. Hypomania
Mr. C	6. Paranoia	8. Schizophrenia

Assuming that the hospital population includes a substantial number of patients with neurotic and characterological disorders as well as psychoses, both logic and empirical evidence would suggest that Mr. A's symptoms and complaints involve primarily depression and anxiety, probably in the neurotic range; that Mr. B is likely to deal with his anxiety through action, some of which may bring him into conflict with authority; and that

Mr. C would show a clinical picture of strange behavior and thoughts and hostile, suspicious, withdrawn interaction, with a probable diagnosis of paranoid schizophrenia. Confidence in these judgments would be greatest if the two scales in question had high elevations and stood out considerably above the others.

These statements are fairly elementary. However, much more is known about patients with these and other code types as a result of both accumulated clinical experience and more systematic investigations. Marks and Seeman (1963, 1974) have provided the most extensive descriptions of correlates and clinical sketches of adult and adolescent patients with different code types. Their earlier efforts had two basic limitations: (1) attempts to apply their rules for code typing to other clinical samples showed that between 30 and 70 percent of patients could not be classified, and (2) the validity of their diagnoses and other findings was not really examined widely. In my own work, I have found that these and other published diagnostic correlates of MMPI code types have limited validity with different clinical populations; because of this, the development of local normative data seems necessary.

In the 1960s efforts to describe the uses of the MMPI culminated in what was an inevitable development, given the test's objective properties and the ease with which it lends itself to actuarial analysis. The thinking of expert MMPI clinical interpreters, supplemented by empirical studies, was translated into computer programs which produced automated interpretations of machine-scored MMPIs. Four such programs are commercially available at this writing, and others are under development. Excellent reviews of these automated testing services are available (Manning, 1971; Dahlstrom, Welsh, and Dahlstrom, 1972).

Other Objective Tests

While tests of interests, aptitudes, values, and achievement are objective in nature, they are beyond the scope of this chapter. These as well as several infrequently used scales of personality adjustment are described and reviewed in Lanyon and Goodstein (1971) and Cronbach (1960).

Standardized Intelligence Tests

The Stanford-Binet Scales

Intelligence has been defined in many ways. A general definition—the ability to learn from experience—is most widely accepted today, but it clarifies little. The progenitor of today's tests of intelligence was developed specifically for the purpose of measuring that ability when, in 1904, Alfred Binet, a psychologist who had been studying individual differences in "higher" mental abilities, was asked to devise a method of identifying those schoolchildren of Paris who might and might not be expected to learn at a satisfactory level. Binet collaborated with Theodore Simon in assembling thirty different tasks or problems, arranged in ascending order of difficulty. Further revisions led to the development of an age-scale format. The various tasks were grouped according to the percentage of children able to complete them, and the concept of mental age was introduced by comparing the score attained by an individual child with the score expected for the average normal child of the same chronological age.

Like other early scientists who studied individual differences, Binet initially took a logical approach to deciding which abilities were most important in predicting school performance. He made use of empirical data as well, however. Having selected his tests, he tried them out on a few children labeled "intelligent" or "not intelligent" by school directors and teachers and was guided in his definition of intelligence and his decisions about the tasks to be used in measuring it by the differences he observed between the two groups of children.

A number of American psychologists began to experiment with the Binet-Simon scales. They were used primarily in evaluating mental retardation until Lewis Terman of Stanford University standardized his revision of the scales by testing 1000 native-born California children and 400 adults and published the first edition of the Stanford-Binet in 1916. The concept of the intelligence quotient (IQ = mental age ÷ chronological age) was introduced at that time.

The 1916 Stanford-Binet became the standard measure of intelligence. It was used primarily in schools and in evaluating retardation, though Terman also used it to select a number of intellectually gifted children who were studied longitudinally. It consisted of ninety short tests arranged at age levels ranging from three years to "Superior Adult." In 1937, Terman and Maud Merrill published a revision (Form L), which, among other advantages, was much better standardized and included an alternate form (Form M) that could be used for retesting. There were now 129 tests with age levels ranging from two years to Superior Adult III. The most recent revision (Form L-M), published by the same authors in 1960, incorporated the best items from the existing two forms into a single scale. It also attempted to correct for differences among age groups in the distribution of IQs by substituting a deviation IQ for the empirically obtained mental age (MA) to chronological age (CA) ratio.

The basic procedure for arriving at an IQ involves establishing the basal and ceiling levels for the individual being tested and giving credit for the intervening age levels in proportion to the items passed. For example, if a child exactly 8 years old passes all of the items at the VII year (basal) level, half of the items at age levels VIII and IX, and none at age X (the ceiling level), the mental age is calculated by crediting 84 months for age VII and adding 6 months each for ages VIII and IX, for a total of 96 months or 8 years. In this instance mental age (8) divided by chronological age (8) is equal to 1; the IQ is obtained by multiplying this value by 100.

It was the Stanford-Binet that brought psychologists into the field of psychiatry through the need of the first child guidance clinics to obtain standardized measures of intelligence. As experience in the use of this instrument grew, it became apparent that observations of the patterning of different abilities and of the ways in which problems were solved were valuable supplements to the measurement of the IQ; this recognition marked the beginning of the intelligence test as a clinical tool.

The shortcomings of the Stanford-Binet, especially in evaluating adults, were many. Its age conversion tables stopped at age 16 because Terman had found no increase in the average number of tests passed beyond that age. One therefore had to make the assumption that the various mental abilities remained constant through the rest of life, which not only was un-

warranted but made the test of limited clinical use with adults. The scales were also too heavily weighted with verbal items at the upper age levels, which weakened them as discriminators of differences in perceptual-motor development and impairment. Furthermore, clinicians were accustomed to thinking in terms of the intactness or degree of impairment of specific intellectual functions for diagnostic purposes, and the Stanford-Binet format could render only a crude approximation of specific abilities.

The Wechsler Scales

David Wechsler, working on the adult psychiatric wards of New York City's Bellevue Hospital, developed and carefully standardized a different kind of intelligence test. Published in 1939 and known as the *Wechsler-Bellevue Scale*, it consisted of eleven different subtests, each made up of items in ascending order of difficulty and selected to assess some particular aspect of intellectual functioning. Wechsler grouped six of the subtests into a Verbal Scale and the other five into a Performance Scale. This structure permitted the following statistical procedures: (1) the points credited on each subtest could be converted into standard scores with a mean of 10, facilitating comparisons among different aspects of intelligence reflected in the subtests; (2) these standard or weighted scores could be summed separately for the verbal and performance subtests in order to provide a Verbal and a Performance IQ in addition to the Full Scale IQ; (3) each of these IQs located the individual statistically within his own age group; and (4) these IQs had the same meaning at all ages because for each group a mean IQ of 100 and a standard deviation of 15 were established.

The standardization of the Wechsler-Bellevue was an improvement on that of the Stanford-Binet; the sample was representative of American English-speaking adults with respect to education and occupation. For practical reasons, race and socioeconomic level could not be appropriately controlled for, and the Wechsler-Bellevue norms could be applied only to whites sixteen years of age or older.

The *Wechsler Adult Intelligence Scale* (WAIS), published in 1955, was a much needed revision of the Wechsler-Bellevue and it stands today as the major adult intelligence test in clinical use. The changes included improvement in item content and order and upward extension of item difficulties, but the principal revision was a much more adequate standardization that reflected 1950 U.S. Census data and represented the population from ages sixteen through sixty-four as accurately as possible in terms of geographic region, urban-rural residence patterns, race, occupation, and education. The standardization sample comprised 1700 subjects, equally divided by sex and subdivided into seven age groups.

The WAIS includes the following eleven subtests: Information, Comprehension, Arithmetic, Similarities, Digit Span, and Vocabulary in the Verbal Scale; and Digit Symbol, Picture Completion, Block Design, Picture Arrangement, and Object Assembly in the Performance Scale. Factor-analytic studies have demonstrated that these do not represent eleven different components of intelligence. However, for clinical purposes they do provide a range of varied tasks that allow the clinician to describe and interpret not only the patient's general level of attainment but also the specific patterning of different kinds of intellectual functioning as suggested by subtest comparisons and observations of the manner in which the problems are approached and solved. Extensive rationales and guides for the clinical interpretation of the WAIS are available (see Allison, Blatt, and Zimet, 1968).

Wechsler had hoped that profile analysis—the comparison of subtest scores—would be a fruitful diagnostic tool, especially for organic damage, since his normative data led him to believe that differential decreases in subtest scores with increasing age would be a valuable key to the early detection of neurological deficit. Most experts now agree, however, that his sampling, which was necessarily cross-sectional, led to an erroneous conclusion about intellectual abilities over the life span and that a longitudinal study of the same individuals would demonstrate later peaks in some abilities and much less decrement in others than he found. In any event, diagnosis by profile analysis has generally not been well supported by controlled investigations, and most clinicians today use subtest differences and patterns primarily as a source of hypotheses—and

then only when the magnitude of the differences is substantial.

Optimal use of the WAIS or any other standardized test of intelligence in clinical practice requires that the psychologist take many factors into account. The motivational state of the patient is of importance for at least two reasons: first, because the level of test performance may be lowered by ongoing depressive, anxious, or hostile states, or by particular wishes, concerns, or fears about the testing or its consequences and, second, because recommendations for treatment, schooling, or special training based on the IQ and pattern of intellectual functioning should take into account the capacity of the patient to mobilize his resources in these directions. Furthermore, the patient may have talents, especially in creative or technical pursuits, that are not adequately evaluated by an intelligence test. The effects of educational and cultural deprivation upon intellectual achievement must also be considered if realistic and helpful planning is to be provided.

The *Wechsler Intelligence Scale for Children* (WISC), published in 1949, was an extension of the Wechsler-Bellevue (W-B) Scales. New items were combined with some of the easier W-B items to cover the age range from 5 to 15 years. The Digit Symbol subtest was replaced with a simpler Coding test; Digit Span and an added series of Mazes were to be used optionally. The WISC was standardized on 2200 white American boys and girls, and the 1940 census was utilized to determine representativeness with respect to geographical area, urban-rural residence patterns, and parental occupation.

The WISC was readily accepted by most psychologists as an improvement over the Stanford-Binet. Its ease of administration and scoring, the interest of children in the materials, the comparable meaning of IQs at any age, and the available rationales for subtest interpretation and verbal-performance differences were some of its major assets (Sattler, 1974). Its limitations included the lack of nonwhite children in the standardization group; the restricted range of IQs (46 to 154), which made assessment of the severely retarded and the gifted imprecise; and certain problems in scoring some verbal responses.

The WISC-R (Wechsler, 1974) is a recent revision that retains much of the WISC with the following changes: modification or elimination of items felt to be ambiguous, obsolete, or unfair to particular groups of children; lengthening of some subtests to increase reliability; shift in the age range (which had been 5 to 15) to 6 to 16; representation of nonwhite children based on the 1970 census; and the administration of verbal and performance subtests in alternating sequence.

The *Wechsler Preschool and Primary Scale of Intelligence* (WPPSI) appeared in 1967. It covers ages 4 to 6½ and substitutes three new subtests —Sentences, Animal House, and Geometric Design—for the Digit Span, Picture Arrangement, Object Assembly, and Coding tests of the WISC. The structure and the IQ derivations are exactly like the other Wechsler scales, and the standardization group consisted of 1200 boys and girls, 200 in each half-year age group included in the norms. Nonwhite children are proportionately represented. The WPPSI appears to have many of the advantages noted for the WISC. It tends to have a somewhat higher level of difficulty than the Stanford-Binet, particularly at the upper intelligence levels, so that IQs are not interchangeable between the two tests.

Sattler (1974) is the most complete and authoritative source for discussion of the uses and limitations of intelligence testing with children, and his chapter on testing minority group children is a gold mine of clinical and research information.

Assessment of Neurological Deficit

The use of psychological tests in the assessment of brain damage or disease depends on the basic assumption that the behavioral manifestations of cerebral lesions (1) will be apparent on testing and (2) may be reliably differentiated from performance deficits due to other causes. Two general approaches to the study of neurological deficit by means of psychological procedures have been employed: the clinical and the neuropsychological.

The Clinical Approach

The first approach, commonly used by clinical psychologists working in a psychiatric setting, employs a standard test battery and seeks to identify aspects of the patient's performance that are especially suggestive of cerebral impairment. Not infrequently, the clinician will use supplementary tests for brain damage when a more extensive and detailed study is warranted by the patient's history, neurological examination, or performance on the regular battery. This clinical approach maintains a dichotomy between patients with and without brain damage. Thus there is a tendency to regard brain damage as a unitary concept in spite of the fact that test performance will vary considerably in accordance with the nature and locus of the lesion.

The Neuropsychological Approach

The second approach is that of the neuropsychologists, who work closely with neurologists and neurosurgeons rather than in psychiatric settings. Halstead's laboratory at the University of Chicago Medical School, opened in 1935, was the pioneer effort in this movement. Halstead set out to study what he called "biological intelligence" rather than brain damage. He utilized an extensive battery of procedures that he believed would reflect more closely the state of the brain than did standard intelligence tests.

Halstead settled on a series of ten separate tests, which yielded an "index of impairment," and showed that this index was accurate in predicting the presence of frontal lobe damage. Reitan, the leading contemporary neuropsychologist, opened his laboratory at the University of Indiana Medical School in 1951 and was able to demonstrate that Halstead's index was a valid discriminator of many types of brain damage. The best single test was Halstead's Category Test, which correctly identified forty-seven of fifty brain-damaged patients in a study with carefully matched, medically hospitalized control patients.

Reitan's more recent work has been concerned with validating the differential test behaviors associated with left- versus right-hemisphere lesions, with focal versus diffuse damage, and with recent versus long-standing impairment. He has established, for example, that in patients with brain damage, the left hemisphere is almost always implicated in the presence of aphasic

bran domage, left hemisphere

aphasic symptoms (naming, reading, spelling, writing, and calculating), impaired right-handed performance on various tactile and motor tests, and lower Verbal than Performance scores on the WAIS. Conversely, right-sided lesions are likely in the presence of construction dyspraxia (impaired copying of designs), lower Performance than Verbal WAIS scores, and impaired left-handed speed on tactile and motor tests. Reitan has also used decrement in unilateral and bilateral tasks involving touch, hearing, and vision as aids in localization (Reitan, 1973).

While the neuropsychological approach has been much more carefully studied and validated than has the clinical, it is one thing to demonstrate differences between groups of subjects and quite another to make accurate diagnostic decisions in individual cases. This is especially difficult in cases of subtle, early, or slowly developing deficit. (The same, of course, is true of the neurological examination and the EEG.) Nevertheless, the neuropsychological approach appears to rest on a sound foundation, and its application to psychological testing in psychiatric settings is likely to increase.

Clinical Interpretation

The clinical use of psychological tests in the discrimination of brain damage ordinarily relies upon a functional approach. The psychologist has in mind certain aspects of mental functioning which are especially likely to be impaired in the presence of damage, and these functions are assessed with particular care. This discussion will focus on illustrative uses of tests for each of these primary functional areas.

Formation and flexibility of concepts. Goldstein's observations of the behavior of traumatically brain-injured patients led to his formulation of impaired conceptual thinking as the cornerstone of neurological deficit. He posited a "loss of the abstract attitude," by which he meant that the impaired patient found it difficult to perceive, organize, or integrate objects or events by abstracting their common properties and was much more likely to deal with them in terms of their concrete or functional elements (Goldstein, 1939). For example, the Similarities subtest of the WAIS begins with the question "How are orange and banana alike?" The following responses illustrate abstract, functional, and concrete levels of conceptualization, respectively: "both fruit"; "can eat them both"; "different colors and don't look the same." Goldstein also noted the inflexibility of concept formation—that is, once the brain-damaged patient has arrived at a concept that relates a group of objects, he is often unable to shift his set and perceive a second organizing principle. Patients with neurological deficit also may show decrement in their ability to analyze a complex stimulus into its elements and then synthesize them into a meaningful whole. Finally, these patients may exhibit confusion and sometimes disorganization when they must keep in mind two or more aspects of a complex task simultaneously, even though they may do well enough on each aspect separately.

The Rorschach technique lends itself well to qualitative evaluation of these conceptual difficulties. The patient may respond to the Rorschach cards, for example, as though they were real pictures or drawings rather than ambiguous inkblots; this concrete approach makes it hard for him to give other interpretations to the same blot area once he has seen "what it really is." In extreme cases, the brain-damaged patient will give the same response almost indiscriminately to several blots and will have a severely restricted capacity to project different images. Some "organics" have great difficulty in using the brightly colored blots perceptually and will merely name the colors.

The Similarities subtest of the WAIS has been mentioned as useful in identifying impaired conceptual thinking. Asked to say how two things are alike, the patient runs into trouble as the similarities become the least bit subtle or abstract. He may, for example, know that a dog and a lion are both animals, but the differences may prevent him from making the abstraction. Neurological impairment often tends to simplify and polarize thought processes in this way; things are either the same or they are different, and it is difficult to deal with the possibility that both can be true. The proverbs on the Comprehension subtest of the WAIS may also reveal concreteness of thought.

Goldstein and Scheerer (1941) developed a series of clinical tests for use in the diagnosis of brain damage. Only one, the *Object Sorting Test*, sees much contemporary clinical use, largely because of its inclusion in the Menninger battery. In this test of concept formation, the patient is presented with a large group of familiar objects spread on a table. In the first part of the test, he is asked to put with an item selected by the examiner "all the other things that go with it" and then to say why he put them all together. In response to a series of such items in this "active" part of the test, the signs of neurological deficit are likely to be expressed in very limited conceptual groupings and in concrete or simple functional definitions. Given one red poker chip as the stimulus, for example, the patient may add only the other chip (yellow), and explain his grouping by saying, "They're the same." The nonimpaired person is more likely to make a larger grouping, using objects that, by virtue of being round (or red, or playthings) share that attribute with the red chip.

On the second, or "passive," part of the test, the patient is given a series of predetermined groups of objects, and his task is merely to state the concept that unites them. Here one looks for failure to find an explanation, for concepts that explain only part of the group, and for highly concrete responses. This test is also useful in distinguishing the "restrictive" errors of the neurologically impaired patient from the "expansive" errors often made by schizophrenics with thought disorder.

Learning and memory. Impairment of memory and especially of the ability to learn efficiently is a second important aspect of many organic brain syndromes. The Digit Span subtest of the WAIS provides a brief test of immediate memory, but it is highly subject to anxiety. Not infrequently, patients with brain damage will show a disproportionate loss in the ability to recall digits backward. Some clinical psychologists follow Rapaport's practice of inserting into the WAIS a test of immediate and delayed recall of an emotionally charged paragraph. On a more general level, the clinician is also sensitive to the patient's lapses of memory or failure to retain the task orientation during any part of the examination.

For more extensive exploration of memory and learning ability, the *Wechsler Memory Scale* (Wechsler, 1945) is often used in clinical practice. It consists of seven sections: (1) Personal and Current Information ("Who is President of the United States?"), (2) Orientation ("What day of the month is it?"), (3) Mental Control (counting backward from twenty to one), (4) Logical Memory (reproducing the content of two paragraphs read aloud to the patient), (5) Memory Span (recalling digits forward and backward, from the Wechsler-Bellevue), (6) Visual Reproduction (copying four geometric figures from memory), and (7) Associate Learning (learning pairs of words, some of which are commonly associated and some of which are not meaningfully related and therefore much harder to learn). Wechsler devised a Memory Quotient (MQ) for comparison with his IQ, based on his data showing a decline in memory functions after age twenty-five. Because of the relatively poor standardization of this scale, however, most clinicians use the MQ only as an estimate of gross memory impairment and interpret the decrement in specific functions clinically.

Visual-motor organization. The third major function that is especially vulnerable to neurological deficit is that of visual-motor organization, where impairment may be revealed through the patient's coordination of hand and eye in complex perceptual, analytic, and synthetic tasks. The *Bender Visual Motor Gestalt Test* (Bender, 1938) is widely used for this aspect of assessment. The patient is presented with a series of simple geometric designs, which he is to copy on a blank sheet of paper. Dots, circles, loops, sinusoidal curves, and touching and overlapping figures are among the design elements involved; the patient must copy them and organize the nine reproductions in some coherent and planned fashion on the blank paper. Decrement in fine motor control may be apparent on this test. The patient may also rotate the figures toward a more favorable axis or simplify complex elements in an attempt to compensate for his deficit. In extreme cases, one finds perseveration (arbitrary repetition) and gross inability to reproduce design elements higher on the developmental scale, such as diamonds and acute angles

angles. Special additional procedures using the Bender, such as having the patient draw the designs either from memory afterward or on a paper specially prepared with interfering background lines, have been found useful by some clinicians.

The Block Design subtest of the WAIS is regarded as a good brief test of visual-motor organization. Here the patient is shown a series of red and white design patterns, which he must reproduce with square colored blocks. The designs become more complex as the patterns must be mentally broken up in order to see how, for example, diagonal red stripes may be constructed by contiguous placement of blocks. Earlier designs can be made with four blocks in a two-by-two pattern, while the later ones require nine blocks in a three-by-three arrangement. The mode of approach may be significant diagnostically; many brain-damaged patients tend to proceed primarily on a trial-and-error basis, to show little evidence of learning, and to become disorganized when the task becomes frustrating. The *Grassi Block Substitution Test* is a valuable adjunct for more extensive exploration of this aspect of visual-motor difficulty (Grassi, 1953).

Controversial Issues

A considerable degree of controversy has arisen concerning the use and possible abuse of various psychological tests. Two main issues, each involving a different type of test, may be identified.

Cultural-Racial Bias

Standardized tests of intelligence such as the Stanford-Binet and the Wechsler scales, because of their heavy weighting of previously learned verbal knowledge and skills, discriminate to some degree against the educationally disadvantaged. A related issue was brought to the fore when Jensen (1969) attempted to demonstrate—through longitudinal studies using IQ data—the existence of genetic black-white differences in intelligence. "Culture-fair" tests have been developed but not widely used. In clinical practice, the psychologist takes the subject's background into account and is careful to interpret test results in terms of specific measured

abilities rather than general intellectual potential. Jensen's critics have taken him to task on both methodological and sociopolitical grounds, and the matter is far from resolved.

Invasion of Privacy

As a consequence of its use in personnel selection, the MMPI has come under fire because some of its items ask about sensitive personal matters such as sexual behavior and attitudes and religious beliefs. A further concern is that applicants for jobs in government or industry may be discriminated against on the basis of their answers to such questions. The MMPI was intended to be used in psychiatric settings where the disclosure of personal feelings is part of a help-seeking and help-providing contract. It was not developed for use in personnel selection, where its application is often coercive and irrelevant to legitimate employment criteria.

Suggested Referral Practices

The psychiatrist's understanding of the functions and limitations of testing and his open communication with both the psychologist and the patient are major determinants of how useful the test report will be. A thoughtful referral includes carefully formulated questions and appropriate discussion with the patient and the psychologist both before and after the testing.

Indications for Psychological Testing

Some clinical situations require less than a full battery of tests; generally this is the case when the objectives of the assessment are specific and circumscribed. For instance, if the planning for the patient requires only an evaluation of intellectual functioning, the psychologist may find it sufficient to administer a WAIS or WISC, supplemented by one or more special-purpose tests if more definitive judgments are required. Such assessments will often be helpful in evaluating learning disabilities or neurological deficit. Occasions arise when specific diagnostic questions (such as determining presence of a psychotic state) may be handled quite adequately by administration of a single objective or projective test; sometimes the results will be clear, and sometimes further investigation will be needed.

More often than not, the psychiatrist has somewhat more complex objectives in mind, and the full test battery is used in order to increase the range of data. To the degree that the patient has been able and willing to enter into the examination process, the major patterns of personality functioning and the nature and degree of psychopathological processes may be elicited and described. The evaluation of more circumscribed problems can easily be part of this comprehensive examination.

Formulating the Questions

The psychiatrist will find it helpful to formulate questions as specifically as possible, consulting first with the psychologist about the applicability of testing to the issues at hand. Testing can be helpful when the question is one of differential diagnosis. Assessment of the presence of thought disorder in an acutely disturbed patient, for example, or of the relative importance of depressive and schizoid features can ordinarily be done profitably. Retesting after a period of treatment can be especially illuminating. The psychologist cannot say what treatment will be best for the patient, but he can make relevant observations. For example, the patient's ability to withstand stress without decompensating in the testing situation may help the therapist judge whether supportive treatment with a disturbed individual might safely move toward an emphasis on uncovering.

Preparing the Patient

The psychiatrist should always discuss the testing with the patient before the psychologist is seen. If this is done in a perfunctory and evasive manner, the patient's feelings of anxiety or resentment will reduce the value of the examination and hinder the establishment of a working alliance. The patient's previous experience with testing, either in clinical settings or in school or business, should be explored in order to discover and assist with negative feelings and unrealistic expectations. The psychiatrist should have an idea of what the testing is like and should make clear but not exaggerate its importance in his

study of and planning for the patient. Finally, the therapist should be prepared to discuss the testing with the patient afterward. The patient expects that his time and effort will have been put to productive use, and he will often also be worried about negative evaluations or implications based on his performance; these are the main things to which the sensitive psychiatrist will attend in a post-testing discussion.

Understanding the Psychological Report

The psychological report is the formal, detailed statement of the psychologist's understanding of the patient as interpreted from the test data. A give-and-take discussion between the referring therapist and the tester will clarify discrepancies and ambiguities that may arise from the report, permit the raising of additional questions, and add to the psychiatrist's understanding of how testing can help him in his work.

The most enlightening reports tend to be person- rather than test-oriented. While some of the raw data may be included for illustrative purposes, it is neither necessary nor helpful for the psychologist to justify every interpretation by citing the evidence or to submit a laboratory report full of figures. The psychiatrist will naturally find most useful the reports of psychologists who share the same theoretical and diagnostic frame of reference. Schafer (1954) has made the important point that when the psychologist suggests a diagnosis that differs from the one made by the psychiatrist, discussion of the observations leading to the diagnosis will often reveal that the disagreement lies in dissimilar diagnostic rules of inference rather than in conflicting interpretations of the patient's behavior.

Most psychiatrists and psychologists collaborate with mutual respect and understanding, and it is under these conditions that the psychiatrist is able to make optimal use of the psychologist's skill and experience for the benefit of the patient.

References

Allison, J., S. J. Blatt, and C. N. Zimet. 1968. *The interpretation of psychological tests.* New York: Harper & Row.

Barron, F. 1953. An ego-strength scale which predicts response to psychotherapy. *J. Consult. Clin. Psychol.* 17:327–333.

Beck, S. J. 1944. *Rorschach's test*. Vol. 1. New York: Grune & Stratton.

—— 1945. *Rorschach's test*. Vol. 2. New York: Grune & Stratton.

—— 1952. *Rorschach's test*. Vol. 3. New York: Grune & Stratton.

Bender, L. 1938. *A visual motor gestalt test and its clinical use*. American Orthopsychiatric Association research monographs, no. 3.

Blum, G. S. 1949. *A study of the psychoanalytic theory of psychosexual development. Genet. Psychol.* monographs 39:3–99.

—— 1950. *The Blacky pictures*. New York: Psychological Corp.

Buck, J. N. 1948. The H-T-P test. *J. Clin. Psychol.* 4:151–159.

Cronbach, L. J. 1960. *Essentials of psychological testing*. 2nd ed. New York: Harper & Row.

Dahlstrom, W. G., G. S. Welsh, and L. E. Dahlstrom. 1972. *An MMPI handbook: clinical interpretation*, vol. 1. Minneapolis: University of Minnesota Press.

Goldstein, K. 1939. *The organism*. New York: American Book.

Goldstein, K., and M. L. Scheerer. 1941. *Abstract and concrete behavior: an experimental study with special tests. Psychol. Monogr.* 53, no. 2. Evanston, Ill.: American Psychological Association, Northwestern University.

Grassi, J. R. 1953. *The Grassi block substitution test for measuring organic brain pathology*. Springfield, Ill.: Thomas.

Hathaway, S. R., and J. C. McKinley. 1943. *The Minnesota multiphasic personality inventory*. New York: Psychological Corp.

Henry, W. E. 1956. *The analysis of fantasy*. New York: Wiley.

Jensen, A. R. 1969. How much can we boost IQ and scholastic achievement? *Harvard Educ. R.* 39:1–123.

Klopfer, B., ed. 1956. *Developments in the Rorschach technique*. Vol. 2. Yonkers-on-Hudson, N.Y.: World Book.

Klopfer, B., M. D. Ainsworth, W. G. Klopfer, and R. R. Holt. 1954. *Developments in the Rorschach technique*. Vol. 1. Yonkers-on-Hudson, N.Y.: World Book.

Klopfer, B., and D. M. Kelley. 1942. *The Rorschach technique*. Yonkers-on-Hudson, N.Y.: World Book.

Lanyon, R. I., and L. D. Goodstein. 1971. *Personality assessment*. New York: Wiley.

Manning, H. M. 1971. Programmed interpretation of the MMPI. *J. Pers. Assess.* 35:162–176.

Marks, P. A., and W. Seeman. 1963. *The actuarial description of abnormal personality*. Baltimore: Williams & Wilkins.

Marks, P. A., W. Seeman, and D. L. Haller. 1974. *The actuarial use of the MMPI with adolescents and adults*. Baltimore: Williams & Wilkins.

Meehl, P. F. 1954. *Clinical versus statistical prediction*. Minneapolis: University of Minnesota Press.

Morgan, C. D., and H. A. Murray. 1935. A method for investigating fantasies: the thematic apperception test. *Arch. Neurol. Psychiatry* 34:289–306.

Rabin, A. I., ed. 1968. *Projective techniques in personality assessment*. New York: Springer.

Rapaport, D., M. M. Gill, and R. Schafer. 1945. *Diagnostic psychological testing*. Vols. 1 and 2. Rev. ed., ed. R. R. Holt. New York: International Universities Press, 1968.

Reitan, R. M. 1973. Psychological testing of neurological patients. In *Neurosurgery: a comprehensive reference guide to the diagnosis and management of neurosurgical problems*, ed. J. R. Youmans. Philadelphia: Saunders.

Rohde, A. R. 1957. *The sentence completion method: its diagnostic and clinical application to mental disorders*. New York: Ronald Press.

Rorschach, H. 1942. *Psychodiagnostics: a diagnostic tool based on perception*. Berne: Hans Huber.

Rotter, J. B., and J. E. Rafferty. 1950. *Manual: the Rotter incomplete sentences blank*. New York: Psychological Corp.

Sattler, J. M. 1974. *Assessment of children's intelligence*. Philadelphia: Saunders.

Schafer, R. 1948. *The clinical application of psychological tests*. New York: International Universities Press.

—— 1954. *Psychoanalytic interpretation in Rorschach testing*. New York: Grune & Stratton.

Shneidman, E. S. 1951. *Thematic test analysis*. New York: Grune & Stratton.

Terman, L., and M. Merrill. 1960. *Stanford-Binet intelligence scale*. Boston: Houghton Mifflin.

Wechsler, D. 1945. A standardized memory scale for clinical use. *J. Psychol.* 19:87–95.

—— 1958. *The measurement and appraisal of adult intelligence*. 4th ed. Baltimore: Williams & Wilkins.

—— 1967. *Manual for the Wechsler preschool and primary scale of intelligence*. New York: Psychological Corp.

—— 1974. *Manual for the Wechsler intelligence scale for children—revised*. New York: Psychological Corp.

Brain and Behavior

Neural Substrates of Behavior

CHAPTER 4

Ira Sherwin
Norman Geschwind

AFTER MUCH WORK on his "project for a scientific psychology" (1895) Freud abandoned the attempt to construct an anatomico-physiological model of the mind and instead turned his attention to his now famous psychological model. He predicted, nevertheless, that a time would come when neurophysiology would be sufficiently developed to allow for the construction of such a model. Today a considerable body of knowledge exists regarding the function and anatomy of the central nervous system that can be related to specific patterns of behavior.

Much of what is known about the neurological basis of human behavior derives from the study of patients with trauma, vascular accidents, neoplasms, infections, and degenerative disorders, as well as therapeutically intended lesions created by the neurosurgeon. As a result of the neuropathological, neuroradiological and electrophysiological studies of such patients, a rich and fascinating literature exists, which indicates that certain specific disturbances of behavior may be understood in terms of focal brain lesions. Those alterations in behavior characterized primarily by elementary deficits (paralysis and sensory loss) have usually been the concern of the neurologist and neurosurgeon. Some

brain lesions, on the other hand, produce specific alterations in behavior that are characteristically psychiatric in nature.

Despite this specificity, psychiatrists have shown a tendency to group all such cases under a single rubric in the *Diagnostic and Statistical Manual of Mental Disorders*, that of "organic brain syndrome." This simplification occurs because of the erroneous assumption that a single syndrome, albeit of varied etiology, characterizes all such patients. Indeed, the most recent edition of the *American Handbook of Psychiatry* states, "On the psychic level *an* organic syndrome has been identified . . . This group is the least controversial one in the classification, but this is based on the relative ease with which *the* syndromes can be defined and not on a real understanding of pathogenesis" (italics added). The editors add, "This classification is logical, flexible, and comprehensible" (Brill, 1975, p. 1129). This chapter will attempt to demonstrate that such a unitary grouping of the various behavioral disturbances that arise from lesions involving diverse portions of the brain is not at all logical and that it is, in addition, neither truly flexible nor comprehensible. On the contrary, a number of clinical syndromes become compre-

59

hensible when they are considered as relatively specific derangements of brain physiology and anatomy.

Electrical Activity of the Brain

Since the majority of cases of behavior disorder, even those of neurological origin, do not come to necropsy, and because of the inherent dangers in certain radiographic (contrast) studies, electrophysiological recordings have been heavily relied on to document the existence and location of a focal lesion when neurological and psychiatric examinations suggest its presence. From these data, supplemented by those derived from electrical stimulation of the brain in man and animals, the concept of electroclinical correlation has evolved. Before proceeding to an analysis of some of these data, we shall present a brief review of the fundamentals of electrogenesis in the nervous system.

Fundamentals of Electrogenesis

Nervous tissue basically consists of two types of cells, glial cells and neurons. Although glial cells have important electrophysiological properties of their own, only the electrophysiological properties of the neuron are considered here.

The neuron consists of three components: (1) the cell body or soma; (2) a single, relatively long process or axon; and (3) usually multiple, shorter processes arising from the soma, called the dendrites. Although the dendrites tend to be short, generally less than a few millimeters in length, the axons may be extremely long. A single axon originating in the motor cortex and ending in the lumbosacral portion of the spinal cord may be over one meter in length. The neurons of the central nervous system are linked at specialized membrane junctions called synapses. The most typical arrangement is for the axon terminals of one neuron to impinge on the dendrites of another, forming axodendritic synapses. The cell membrane of the neuron consists of a double layer of complex lipoproteins. The membrane of the axonal portion is wrapped in concentric layers of myelin, and even the finest, seemingly unmyelinated fibers may be surrounded by at least a single layer of myelin. The myelin may be thought of as an insulator surrounding the axon.

In the steady state, the concentration of potassium is greater inside the cell than in the surrounding extracellular fluid. Sodium, on the other hand, is at a higher concentration outside the cell than inside. The cell membrane may be thought of as containing tiny openings called pores, which are sufficiently large to allow potassium ions to move through the membrane but too small for the passage of negatively charged organic anions. As a result, when the potassium ions diffuse through the membrane from the area of high to the area of low concentration, an electrostatic charge is built up that impedes and finally halts further outward flow of potassium.

In this steady state, an adequate stimulus (ordinarily an excitatory synaptic input) will cause the difference in potential to reverse its polarity, resulting in the generation of an action potential. The sequence of events may be summarized in the following way. When a nerve impulse (action potential) arrives in the axon terminals at an excitatory synapse, it causes the presynaptic membrane to depolarize, resulting in an influx of calcium ions. This influx, in turn, causes the synaptic vesicles inside the presynaptic membrane to release an excitatory transmitter substance (such as acetylcholine) into the synaptic cleft between the presynaptic membrane of one neuron and the postsynaptic membrane of its neighbor. A change in the ionic permeability of the postsynaptic membrane results, leading to a reduction in the electrical potential difference across the membrane (depolarization). This change in potential has been termed the *excitatory postsynaptic potential* (EPSP). The EPSP decays exponentially over about four milliseconds, after which the postsynaptic membrane resting potential is restored. If, as a result of a large number of simultaneously occurring EPSPs (spatial summation) or a large number of sequential but overlapping EPSPs (temporal summation), the membrane potential is sufficiently depolarized, an avalanche-like change in the sodium conductance ensues. The net effect of all these changes is the generation of the so-called all-or-none, or action, potential (see fig. 4.1).

In contrast to the sequence described above, when incoming presynaptic impulses arrive at an inhibitory synapse, the released inhibitory trans-

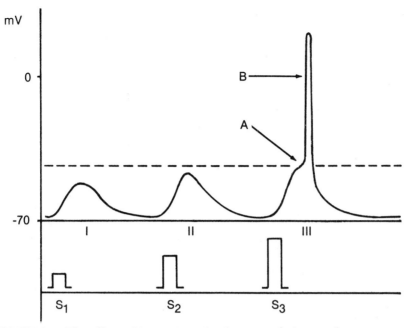

FIGURE 4.1. The effect of increasing stimulus strength (summed synaptic input) on the transmembrane potential of a neuron. S_1–S_3 are stimuli of increasing intensity. Evoked EPSPs are shown in I and II; note the change in amplitude. In III, the EPSP reaches the depolarization threshold for the generation of action potentials (dotted line). Note the change in slope on the rising phase of the action potential; A is the contribution of the initial segment, and B represents the soma's contribution to the all-or-none potential. The ordinate is in millivolts and the abscissa, in arbitrary units.

mitter moves the transmembrane potential from its resting level to a higher level (hyperpolarization). The resulting transmembrane potential change is termed an *inhibitory postsynaptic potential* (IPSP). The IPSP, in contrast to the EPSP, moves the resting membrane potential of the neuron away from its all-or-none potential firing threshold.

In summary, then, the EPSPs, which may sum with one another, are graded potentials in that they may be either larger or smaller, depending upon the nature of the summation. The action potential is a threshold phenomenon that either does not occur or, if it does, is of uniform amplitude, that is, the maximum size that the change in ionic conductance can produce.

Ordinarily the site of all-or-none potential generation is that portion of the axon close to the soma, the initial segment. Along the course of the axon, the myelin is periodically interrupted, and the points of discontinuity are known as the nodes of Ranvier. Regeneration of the action po-

tential at each node along the axon results in saltatory conduction (jumping from node to node). If, as a result of experimental electrical stimulation, an action potential is initiated in the axon itself, this saltatory conduction will take place both in the normal direction (orthodromic manner) and in the retrograde direction (antidromic manner) back toward the cell body.

Animal studies have shown that antidromic conduction occurs in experimental epilepsy when the electrical fields generated by multiple neuron discharges directly excite axons as they pass through an aggregate of epileptic neurons (epileptogenic focus). As a result, abnormal patterns of neuronal propagation occur that might account for many of the bizarre hallucinatory experiences of some epileptic patients. Similarly, such abnormal propagation might account for the failure of fiber-sectioning operations (commissurotomy, for example) in the treatment of epilepsy.

Although much of the foregoing synaptic

physiology is based on data derived from experiments on the peripheral nervous system, essentially the same events occur at central nervous system (CNS) synapses. However, while acetylcholine is the transmitter substance at some CNS synapses, possible transmitters at others include glutamate, catecholamines, serotonin, glycine, and GABA (γ-aminobutyric acid).

Cerebral Electrical Activity

In 1875, during his successful search for the cerebral counterpart of the action potential in peripheral nerves, Richard Caton noted spontaneous electrical oscillations of the exposed cortex in unstimulated animals. In 1929, Hans Berger reported recording these same spontaneous oscillations in brain potential through the intact skull in humans, thus introducing the technique of electroencephalography.

Initially, attempts were made to explain these slow oscillations in terms of envelopes of action potentials arising synchronously from large numbers of single neurons. More recently investigators have come to regard these brain waves as summed EPSPs and IPSPs generated in the apical dendrites of the cortex.

The spontaneous electroencephalogram (EEG) of the awake but relaxed (with his eyes closed) adult human consists of oscillating electrical potentials with a bandwidth of approximately 0.5 to 30 cycles per second and an amplitude that varies from about 2 to as many as 200 microvolts. Activity in the frequency band from 0.5 to approximately 3.5 cycles per second (hertz or Hz) has been termed delta rhythm; from 4 to 6 Hz, theta rhythm; from 7 to 12 Hz, alpha rhythm; and from 13 to 30 Hz, beta rhythm. The most abundant component, often considered the fundamental frequency, of the waking adult human EEG is the alpha rhythm. Opening the eyes normally causes the alpha rhythm to disappear and be replaced by a lower-voltage, faster rhythm. This phenomenon has been termed the arousal response. Of all electrical brain activity, the alpha rhythm has been studied most intensively. Nevertheless its origin—that is, the nature of its electrical generators—is still poorly understood. Perhaps the most widely accepted theory of the origin of alpha activity is that of the so-

called facultative pacemaker, described by Andersen and Andersson (1968). According to this theory, the 10-Hz alpha rhythm arises from the long, recurrent inhibition that characterizes thalamic electrical activity. Thus alpha rhythm is seen as a cortical potential reflecting excitatory and recurrent inhibitory barrages from the thalamus; these barrages have an overall period of 100 milliseconds and thus a frequency of 10 cycles per second.

Although many problems remain to be solved before the genesis of brain waves is completely understood, the electroencephalogram has become a useful tool in both the research laboratory and the clinic. Its early promise for studying deranged cerebral activity has been realized most fully in the area of epilepsy. In the case of petit mal epilepsy, one of the few nearly pathognomonic waveforms may be seen in the so-called 3-per-second spike and wave discharges. In patients with petit mal epilepsy, this EEG pattern, like clinical seizures, may be provoked by hyperventilation.

In structural lesions of the brain, the EEG is characterized by slow waves in both the theta and the delta ranges. Although normal in sleeping adults and in children, delta activity is always abnormal for the waking adult. The spatial distribution of the delta waves is of localizing value but does not provide information regarding the etiology of the lesions.

Although Berger's description of the human EEG aroused great hope that this technique would provide valuable insights into psychiatric disorders, this promise has gone largely unfulfilled. Various abnormalities have been described in the EEG of psychiatric patients, but the EEG has been of extremely limited value in the assessment of functional psychiatric disorders.

With the introduction of small laboratory computers, however, new methods of analyzing the EEG have become possible. One of the most commonly used techniques is signal averaging, which permits the extraction of waveforms not discernible in unprocessed EEG data. By presenting various types of stimuli in varied paradigms, average evoked response (AER) excitability cycles and the contingent negative variation

(CNV) or expectancy wave (E) may be obtained. Both hold promise as useful tools in the investigation of some forms of neurosis and psychosis. The EEG has also shown itself to be of value in the analysis of sleep disorders (see chapter 7, "Sleep").

Mental Syndromes Related to Localized Brain Pathology

The very title of this chapter implies that at least some aspects of behavior may be related to physiological events occurring in localized neural systems. The alternative concept—that behavior is dependent upon the function of the brain as a whole—would make the further analysis of specific mind-brain relationships impossible. Several examples of such relationships that have been established by sufficient evidence are discussed below. They are grouped according to the part of the brain involved in the disorder of behavior.

The Role of the Reticular Formation

The reticular formation is a system of nerve fibers and cells occupying the medial portion of the brainstem from the medulla to the thalamus. Its behavioral correlates have been investigated in detail, and it appears to play a major role in consciousness, wakefulness, and attention.

Consciousness and its underlying neural systems. While consciousness is clearly dependent on the function of localized neural systems, unfortunately no good definition of consciousness exists. Indeed, it is much easier to delineate the unconscious state than to define consciousness itself, and the problem of definition is too complex to be handled within the limited scope of this presentation. We will therefore adopt as a working definition a paraphrase of one suggested by Bremer and Terzuolo (1953): consciousness is a singular quality of cerebral functioning characterized by a differential and selective reactivity and giving rise to the harmonious integration and organization of behavior that ensures the appropriate response in a given situation.

More than a century ago in his *Principles of Human Physiology* (1842), Carpenter suggested a subcortical locus (the thalamus) as the seat of consciousness. His formulation, however, clearly implies the necessity of a cortical-subcortical integration for the expression of this function. By the beginning of this century the emphasis had shifted, and consciousness was generally held to be a function of the cerebral cortex. The role of brainstem mechanisms in the maintenance of consciousness gained new importance, however, as a result of clinicopathological studies of sleep disturbances.

With the introduction of the EEG, Berger was able to correlate changes in the electrical activity of the brain with cycles of wakefulness and sleep in normal persons. Not long thereafter, Bremer conducted his now classical experiments in brainstem-sectioned animals (the *encéphale isolé* and the *cerveau isolé* preparations). In essence, these studies suggested that sleep resulted from an interruption of the sensory input to the cortex. Inherent in this view was the notion that a deficiency of stimulation was the cause of sleep. Unconsciousness was thus regarded as a passive process resulting from an elimination of the sensory inputs necessary to maintain the conscious state. Later work by Ranson (1939) and Hess (1957), on the other hand, suggested the possibility that unconsciousness was an active process resulting from the activity of a specific hypothalamic center.

These suggestions of a major role for various subcortical structures in the maintenance of consciousness may be considered the immediate antecedents of the modern theory of the brainstem reticular formation (Moruzzi and Magoun, 1949). They observed that electrical stimulation of the brainstem reticular formation in the cat produced an EEG pattern of desynchronization (activation) that was associated with behavioral arousal. This observation led them to recognize a second (nonspecific) sensory system, the ascending reticular activating system (ARAS), which parallels the classical (lemniscal) sensory system. They found that the lemniscal system projects in a restricted manner to the primary sensory areas of the cortex. The nonspecific system, on the other hand, has diffuse, widespread connections with the other portions of the cortical mantle, that is, the association cortex. The ARAS also differs from the lemniscal system in the nature of its input, since it receives connections not only from the peripheral receptors but from most portions of the central nervous system. Ultimately Moruzzi and Magoun showed that interrupting the lemniscal pathways by surgical means while sparing the reticular formation did not affect wakefulness. If, on the other hand, the reticular formation was damaged, even though the lesion spared the classical lemniscal pathway, the animal became comatose and remained in that state until the time of death.

Attention. The brainstem reticular activating system (BRAS) has direct connections with the association cortex, probably by way of the internal capsule. Brief, high-frequency electrical stimulation of this system leads to long-lasting (tonic) EEG and behavioral arousal. In addition, the BRAS has connections with the group of nonspecific thalamic nuclei, which in turn give rise to a set of indirect, diffuse projections to the association cortex. Low-frequency electrical stimulation of this diffuse thalamic projection system leads to synchrony of the EEG and sleep. High-frequency stimulation leads to brief (phasic) EEG and behavioral arousal. It appears, therefore, that the direct pathway from the BRAS to the cortex provides a means for generalized and prolonged arousal, while the indirect pathway (through the diffuse thalamic projection system) provides a means for brief and selective shifts of attention. The foregoing indicates an important role for the BRAS and the diffuse thalamic projection system in the maintenance of the attentive-conscious state. It is well known, however, that unconsciousness may ensue in the absence of a lesion in this location, as in cases of extensive widespread damage to the cortex (decortication), for example. Unilateral functional decortication produced by the intracarotid injection of sodium amytal (Wada test) may also cause unconsciousness. According to some but not all researchers, this occurs more frequently when the sodium amytal is injected into the left than into the right hemisphere. It seems obvious, therefore, that the cerebral cortex, like the reticular-thalamic system, exerts a critical if not crucial influence in maintaining the state of consciousness.

In summary, the state of discriminative awareness that we call consciousness is maintained by the anatomical and functional continuity of an integrated neural system composed of the cerebral cortex, the medial thalamic nuclei, and the brainstem reticular formation. Interruption of this integrated system anywhere along its pathway may be expected to lead to some disturbance of consciousness, the nature of which need not be identical in each instance. In this way, different levels of consciousness (including sleep) differ from each other not only quantitatively but also qualitatively. Similarly, clinical states of disturbed consciousness may be regarded as more or less distinct syndromes. The differences between these syndromes depend not so much upon the exact anatomical site of the lesions as they do upon which functional component of the cortical-subcortical system is involved.

The most profound depression of consciousness, resulting in a vegetative state, may be produced equally well by a complete disruption of the ascending and descending pathways of this system, extensive decortication, or destruction of the brainstem reticular formation.

Both selective (bilateral mesiofrontal) cerebral decortication and partial interruption of the diffuse thalamic projection system may result in a unique disturbance of consciousness, coma vigil ("wakeful coma") or akinetic mutism. Lesions in either of these anatomical areas eliminate the phasic while sparing the tonic component of consciousness. Since the tonic component is spared, the clinical appearance of the patient is one of wakefulness, the eyes tending to follow the examiner as he moves about the room. The patient, however, makes no response to auditory, visual, or tactile stimuli. On the one hand, he appears to be vigilant, yet on the other, by his lack of response, he appears to be comatose. This clinical picture must be differentiated from the "locked-in syndrome" resulting from an infarction of the pons, in which lack of responsiveness is due not to impaired consciousness but rather to a diffuse upper-motor neuron paralysis sparing only the extraocular muscles.

The foregoing clearly demonstrates that consciousness depends on the integrity of a localizable neural substrate. To conceive of this cortical-subcortical system as a seat or center of consciousness, however, would be equivalent to a Cartesian view of the pineal gland. Rather, it must be considered an integrated system that provides a critical physiological background against which multiple interacting mental processes give rise to consciousness. By what mechanism the integration of these processes gives rise to consciousness remains obscure, as much an enigma today as when Huxley wrote, "But what consciousness is, we know not; and how it is that anything so remarkable as a state of consciousness comes about as the result of irritating nervous tissue, is just as unaccountable as the appearance of the Djin when Aladdin rubbed his lamp in the story" (1866, p. 193).

Limbic System Syndromes

Phylogenetically, the limbic system comprises some of the oldest components of man's brain —the hippocampus, the hippocampal gyrus, the septal nuclei, the pyriform (entorhinal) cortex, the amygdala, the fornix, portions of the hypothalamus, certain thalamic nuclei (anterior, dorsomedial, and intralaminar), the cingulate gyrus, and parts of the orbitofrontal cortex. The primitive cortex of the limbic system appears first in mammals; it is found in a large convolution that Broca named the Great Limbic Lobe, since it surrounds the brainstem in the form of a border. Because of its close relationship to olfactory structures, this old mammalian brain was formerly believed to serve a purely olfactory function. The now classical work of Papez (1937) has led to the view that these neural circuits were usurped to subsume memory and to elaborate certain emotional states, including those that guide behavior according to the two basic principles of life, self-preservation and preservation of the species.

MacLean (1959) suggested the term *limbic system* to encompass the limbic cortex per se and those structures with which it has direct connections (see fig. 4.2 for a stylized depiction of the limbic system). The olfactory pathways and the medial forebrain bundle may be represented as

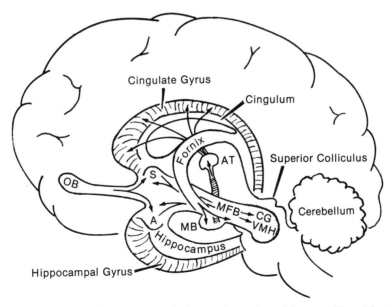

FIGURE 4.2. The limbic system, right hemisphere viewed from midline. The olfactory structures and medial forebrain bundle divide the limbic ring into the upper crescent, driven by the septum, and the lower, driven by the amygdala. A, amygdala; AT, anterior nucleus of the thalamus; CG, central gray matter; MB, mamillary bodies; MFB, medial forebrain bundle; OB, olfactory bulb; S, septal region; VMH, ventromedial hypothalamic nucleus.

dividing the limbic ring into upper and lower crescents. Clinical and experimental findings suggest that the lower (amygdala-driven) crescent is primarily concerned with emotional states and behaviors that ensure self-preservation. Evidence derived primarily from patients with limbic epilepsy (temporal lobe epilepsy) reveals that in man these circuits serve the activities of feeding, fighting, and self-protection. The upper (septum-driven) crescent of the limbic ring, on the other hand, appears to be involved in the elaboration of feeling states concerned with preliminaries to copulation and reproduction. The outflow from both of these limbic subdivisions commingles in the medial forebrain bundle and thence converges upon certain hypothalamic regions. A third portion of the limbic system, including the hippocampal formation, fornix, and mammillary bodies, comprises a critical circuit for memory, in particular for the ability to memorize or lay down new memory traces.

In man, lesions of the limbic system give rise to several characteristic clinical syndromes. Disorders of the limbic function may be grouped into two categories: (1) those due to destructive lesions and (2) those resulting from irritative lesions. Destructive lesions of the limbic system, like destructive lesions elsewhere, produce symptoms by one of two mechanisms. First, loss of neural tissue may give rise to negative signs, that is, to the loss of a function that depends upon the integrity of the destroyed brain region. Second, destructive lesions may give rise to positive signs that represent the release of functions subserved by other structures normally under the control of the destroyed area. In the case of the limbic system, this process frequently involves a release of hypothalamic functions. Irritative lesions of the limbic system express themselves as temporal lobe seizures. A single lesion, however (such as a brain tumor), may be both destructive and irritative.

Temporal lobe epilepsy. In no other disorder do the disciplines of psychiatry and neurology overlap so extensively as in temporal lobe epilepsy (TLE). Its high incidence, resistance to treatment, and difficult differential diagnosis make it the most troublesome variety of seizure disorder. The seizures in other forms of focal epilepsy are characterized by elementary neurological signs and symptoms, such as paresthesia and myoclonic movements. Temporal lobe seizures tend, however, to be characterized by complex sensorimotor and autonomic disturbances superimposed on a background of altered consciousness. The following list, adapted from *Gastaut's Clinical Electroencephalographic Classification of Epileptic Seizures* (1970), presents some of the more common seizure patterns in this form of epilepsy.

TLE with impaired consciousness only

TLE with cognitive symptomatology
1. with dysmnesic disturbances (*déjà vu, jamais vu*, amnesia)
2. with ideational disturbances (including "forced thinking" and dreamy state)

TLE with affective symptomatology (depression, elation)

TLE with psychosensory symptomatology
1. with illusions (macropsia, micropsia)
2. with hallucinations (see below)

TLE with psychomotor symptomatology (automatisms)

Compound forms of TLE
1. with motor symptoms
   a. versive (generally contraversive, that is, turning toward the side opposite the epileptic focus; head and eye deviation)
   b. posturing
   c. phonatory (vocalization and speech arrest)
2. with special sensory or somatosensory hallucinations
   a. somatosensory
   b. visual
   c. auditory
   d. olfactory
   e. gustatory
   f. vertiginous
3. with autonomic symptoms
   a. flushing
   b. pallor
   c. diaphoresis
   d. piloerection

The neurological examination in patients with TLE is usually completely normal. An infrequent but important sign is homonymous superior quadrantanopsia due to injury of the Meyer's loop portion of the optic radiation. Formerly, the automatisms common to this form of epilepsy had suggested the term *psychomotor seizures*. With the advent of electroencephalography and the finding that in the bulk of such cases the initial electrical abnormalities occurred in the temporal lobe, the term *temporal lobe epilepsy* has come to be preferred (other forms of epilepsy are considered in chapter 15, "Organic Mental Disorders").

Situated in the middle fossa of the skull, the temporal lobe—especially its anterior pole and inferior surface—is vulnerable to injury, particularly in the acceleration-deceleration type of head trauma. The most common lesion found in patients with TLE is mesial temporal sclerosis (MTS). A commonly held view is that this lesion results from a period in intrauterine hypoxia resulting in brain swelling and herniation, compromising the blood supply to this portion of the temporal lobe. According to this theory, the seizures, which usually begin in late childhood or early adult life, are the result of this prenatal lesion. An alternative theory holds that MTS results from postnatal hypoxia caused by a prolonged febrile convulsion in early childhood. According to the second theory, therefore, the temporal lobe seizure focus develops as a consequence of a preexisting seizure diathesis. The determination of which theory is correct has important pathophysiological and therapeutic implications, but these are beyond the scope of the present discussion.

Clinical seizure patterns vary markedly from case to case. In the simplest form, there may be a momentary absence, which on clinical grounds may be very similar to a petit mal attack except for its longer duration (exceeding 15 seconds). Similarly, temporal lobe seizures may be indistinguishable, on clinical grounds, from the major motor seizures characteristic of grand mal epilepsy. More typically, however, temporal lobe seizures are characterized by one or more of the phenomena outlined in the list above. If the seizure is not witnessed by a trained observer, diagnosis may be extremely difficult since temporal lobe seizures frequently produce a retrograde amnesia, thus making it impossible for the patient to give an adequate description of his seizures. Distortions of perception and frank

hallucinations are common. One of the most characteristic is the olfactory hallucination or "uncinate fit," the hallucinated smell typically having a stenchlike quality. Seizure foci in the posterior portion of the temporal lobe may produce both auditory and visual hallucinations. Unlike the simple light flashes occurring with seizure discharges that arise in the occipital lobe, the visual hallucinations in TLE tend to be complicated "formed visions." This sort of hallucination is probably more common with right-sided than left-sided temporal lobe foci.

A common misperception occurring in TLE is *déjà vu*—the feeling that an episode occurring in the present has occurred in exactly the same manner in the past. The opposite effect, *jamais vu*, is less common. In some instances temporal lobe seizures are characterized by affective changes. Typically, there is a vague sensation of uneasiness, depression, or fear. Most striking, but also most unusual, is a feeling of exhilaration, at times approaching ecstasy.

Up to this point we have considered symptoms of a psychiatric nature that are essentially a part of the seizure (ictus) itself. Other psychiatric findings in patients with TLE do not appear to be part of the seizure but, rather, appear between seizures (interictally). This presents something of a tautology, however, if we define the seizure solely in behavioral terms. The adoption of electrophysiological criteria would provide only an incomplete solution to this dilemma. This is so because discharges deep in the temporal lobe may not be apparent in the scalp-recorded EEG.

This ictal-interictal distinction is not purely academic; it has important medicolegal implications in acts of violence. Feelings of anger accompanied by aggressive acts are a serious feature of this disorder. Based on a detailed analysis of the histories of a large number of epileptics in English prisons, complex automatisms and altered states of consciousness seem incompatible with the carefully planned and skillfully executed acts of violence described as committed by some patients with TLE. This discrepancy is confirmed by the findings at surgery for temporal lobe epilepsy. Electrical stimulation of an epileptogenic focus that effectively reproduces the characteristic clinical aspects of the patient's seizure rarely if ever evokes aggressive assaultive behavior, even when the EEG shows evidence that a seizure has been provoked.

The aggressive behavior in patients with TLE differs from that of the usual psychopath in that the aggressive or violent acts are not a way of life. They do not, however, appear in a completely paroxysmal fashion; usually a precipitant is present, and the temporal lobe epileptic often goes to great pains to justify his overreaction to a seemingly minor provocation. Characteristically, the patient gives a long-winded roundabout explanation for his behavior. This feature, like the tendency of temporal lobe epileptics to harbor grudges, distinguishes the aggressive-assaultive behavior of temporal lobe epileptics from that seen in patients with frontal lobe lesions.

In addition to aggressiveness, certain other behavioral features seen in temporal lobe epileptics have given rise to the notion of a "temporal lobe personality," notably a deepening of emotional responsiveness characterized by religious fervor and cosmic concerns. A day-to-day variability in temperament occurs in which aggressiveness alternates with an unctuous good-naturedness; temporal lobe epileptics also show a tendency toward overly detailed analysis of trivial events and verboseness in both speaking and writing. Clinically, this behavior is described as "sticky" or "adhesive."

Another very serious possible result of temporal lobe epilepsy is the development of a schizophreniform psychosis. Described in detail by Slater and Beard (1963) and confirmed by many other investigators, this disorder occurs in long-standing TLE and is characterized by paranoid and rarely catatonic features. As is not the case with true schizophrenia, affective responses are preserved and deterioration to a hebephrenic state is unusual. Although some authors deny a special relationship between temporal lobe epilepsy and severe psychopathy, their data in fact reveal a higher incidence of psychotic reactions among temporal lobe epileptics than among other epileptics. Although the mechanisms involved are not clear, data from many studies suggest that the severe behavioral disturbances characterizing temporal lobe epilepsy are more likely to occur when the epileptogenic focus is in the dominant rather than in the nondominant hemisphere.

Alterations in sexual behavior may appear in temporal lobe epilepsy. The most common disturbance is hyposexuality, although heightened sexual drive has also been noted. In surgical series in the United States and in England, patients have been described in whom sexual drive returned following the surgical cure of temporal lobe epilepsy. Other sexual patterns that arise in patients with TLE are homosexuality, lesbianism, transvestism, and bizarre fetishism.

One of the most serious complications of TLE is the appearance of a so-called mirror focus. In this situation the epileptogenic focus in one temporal lobe produces a secondary contralateral focus by electrical bombardment across the anterior commissure. Experimental data suggest that initially this secondary (mirror) focus is dependent upon the primary focus—that is, if the primary focus is surgically extirpated, the secondary focus will disappear. After some time, however, the secondary focus may become independent and will persist even if the primary focus is removed; this situation may result in a severe memory disturbance similar to that seen in Korsakoff's psychosis.

Surgical treatment may be considered for a patient whose TLE does not respond to anticonvulsant therapy. In such a case, the timing of surgery becomes critical with respect to the establishment of an independent mirror focus; once an independent mirror focus develops, surgery may aggravate rather than ameliorate the intellectual impairment. In general, surgery in TLE has had an encouraging degree of success in reducing the seizures themselves. Aggressive behavior, however, when present, is less likely to be eliminated, and the schizophreniform psychosis appears to be totally resistant to surgery. Although this discussion has concentrated on the surgical treatment of intractable TLE, surgery is indicated only in a small minority of patients. The majority of patients with TLE respond favorably to anticonvulsant therapy, in particular to primidone and carbamazepine.

The Wernicke-Korsakoff syndrome. Memory functions governed by the limbic system may be divided into three temporal categories: immediate (short-term) memory, recent (short-term) memory, and remote memory. The boundaries between these categories are not sharp; in particular, the use of *short-term memory* to indicate both recent and immediate memory function has been a continuing source of confusion. The term *immediate recall* designates the function that is clinically tested by asking patients to repeat a series of numbers, letters, or other items; the ability to recall immediately is more a measure of attentiveness than of memory. *Remote memory* is the term used to indicate the memory function concerned with the ability to retrieve and recall the store of old information, much of which has been subject to overlearning. Between these two lies *recent memory*—the ability to memorize. It is this component of memory that is most vulnerable to the effects of electroconvulsive therapy (ECT). A relatively selective disturbance of recent memory characterizes the Wernicke-Korsakoff syndrome.

In 1887 S. S. Korsakoff described an amnestic syndrome in patients with alcoholic peripheral neuropathy to which he gave the name polyneuritic psychosis. Korsakoff's psychosis, as this disorder is now known, is often referred to as the amnestic confabulatory syndrome. The hallmark of this disorder is a disturbance of recent memory, with relative preservation of remote memory and usually complete sparing of immediate recall. Confabulation (the replacement of fact with fantasy in memory), on the other hand, is a variable, although more dramatic, feature of this disorder. Since it is often absent even in the early stages and almost invariably disappears in the later ones, the simpler term *amnestic syndrome* is more appropriate. The most consistent pathological findings include lesions involving the gray matter surrounding the third ventricle and aqueduct, mammillary bodies, brainstem, and medial dorsal nuclei of the thalamus.

After some time it was recognized that these changes were similar to those previously reported in 1881 by Wernicke in an acute encephalopathy accompanying malnutrition. If patients survived the acute phase of their illness, Korsakoff's psychosis would result. While the majority of the reported cases have suffered from chronic alcoholism resulting in thiamine deficiency, Korsakoff's syndrome may also be caused by malnutrition, vascular disease, and trauma. Posttraumatic Korsakoff's psychosis, unlike the vitamin-deficiency form, is likely to be followed by nearly complete recovery. While the lesions involving the mammillary bodies have generally been considered of greatest importance in accounting for recent memory disturbance, Victor, Adams, and Collins (1971) ascribe this disorder to lesions found in the medial dorsal nuclei. Both bilateral fornicotomy for the treatment of third ventricle tumors and bilateral anterior temporal lobectomy for the treatment of epilepsy have been reported to produce Korsakoff's syndrome. This evidence strongly suggests that the circuit made up of the hippocampal formation, the fornix, and the mammillary bodies and probably the medial dorsal nuclei constitute a critical neural network for recent memory function.

Transient global amnesia. The condition known as transient global amnesia involves a curious, circumscribed loss of memory and occurs in elderly patients, usually those past sixty years of age. It is characterized by the sudden inability to recall or record memory traces of recent events. Elementary neurological deficits are not a feature of the disorder. The attacks, lasting from a few hours to a full day, are generally followed by a complete recovery of memory, except for the time covered by the attack itself and a brief antecedent period of several minutes or several hours. The transitory nature of the episode and its occurrence in the elderly has led to the suggestion that it represents a transient ischemic attack. Unlike other transient ischemic attacks in which repeated episodes are the rule, second attacks are quite rare in the transient global amnesia syndrome. Because of the similarity between the circumscribed recent memory loss in these patients and the memory disturbance seen in Korsakoff's syndrome, bilateral involvement of the hippocampal-mammillary body circuit of the limbic system has been suspected. Some support for this notion comes from EEG findings during an attack. Bitemporal paroxysmal slow and sharp wave activity has been observed in three reported cases. In some cases the attack may represent a seizure.

The Klüver-Bucy syndrome. Klüver and Bucy (1939) found that bilateral ablation of the anterior portions of the temporal lobe in the monkey produced a striking set of behavioral changes, including a taming effect, psychic blindness, oral tendencies, and hypermetamorphosis, a type of heightened distractability. The monkeys act as though they can no longer discriminate visually among objects; instead, they explore all objects (such as food and feces) by mouthing (tasting) and smelling. In addition, they show sexual disturbances, including indiscriminate mounting of partners of either sex and excessive masturbation.

Subsequent studies have indicated that bilateral damage to limbic structures of the temporal lobe—in particular the amygdaloid complex, the hippocampus, and the pyriform cortex—is essential for the appearance of this syndrome. Most cases reported in man show only portions of the full syndrome observed in monkeys, but the complete syndrome does occasionally occur. In man, apathy is more characteristic than is the placidity seen in monkeys. Apathy, or flattened affect, may cause patients with limbic neoplasms to be mistakenly diagnosed as schizophrenic.

Limbic encephalitis. Rabies virus and herpes simplex are neurotropic viruses with a special affinity for the temporal lobes. Herpes encephalitis often causes an acute or subacute onset of irritability and personality and memory disturbance that may bring the patient to the attention of a psychiatrist. Headache is a common feature, and seizures usually appear at some point in the course of the disease. The diagnosis may be confirmed by the presence of a fourfold rise in anti-herpes simplex antibodies. Some cases have been treated with pooled gamma globulin or iododeoxyuridine (an antagonist of DNA synthesis), but disagreement persists as to the effectiveness of these therapies.

Rabies often presents subacute symptoms after a long incubation period of perhaps several months. The antecedent animal bite may thus be forgotten and early diagnosis made difficult. Early symptoms include difficulty in concentrating, irritability, hyperactivity, and personality changes. Headache, when present, is usually not severe. Ragelike behavior ultimately appears, with the patient cursing and striking out at those about him (the French word for rabies is *rage*). Alternating with this hyperactivity are quiescent periods in which the patient lies in bed appearing mentally alert but terrified. Agonizing pharyngeal spasms occur, triggered at first by attempts to drink and ultimately by the mere sight of water (hydrophobia). Generalized convulsions ensue, the patient ultimately lapses into coma, and death occurs within hours. Once symptoms have appeared, only supportive treatment is possible. Prior to the appearance of symptoms, rabies antiserum and duck-embryo vaccine prophylaxis are indicated.

Discussion so far has focused primarily on the involvement of the temporal lobe components in behavioral disorders. Attention will now focus on an examination of the hypothalamic portion of the limbic system.

Kleine-Levin syndrome. Occurring most often in adolescent males, the Kleine-Levin syndrome is characterized by episodes of hypersomnia followed by hyperactivity, overeating, excessive masturbation, outbursts of abusive behavior, shouting, laughing, singing, and hallucinations. Polydipsia, hyperhidrosis, and elevated blood sugar may be additional features. These episodes recur every 3 to 6 months and last 2 to 3 days. EEGs recorded during the attack have, in a few cases, revealed bilateral quasi-paroxysmal bursts of slow waves. This syndrome has been reported in association with brain tumors and trauma and as a sequela of encephalitis. Usually, however, no specific etiology can be determined.

Pleasure and rage reactions. Electrical stimulation of the septal region in animals may elicit grooming behavior and phallic erection. Animals with electrodes implanted in the septal and ventrolateral portions of the hypothalamus will, when given the opportunity, repeatedly stimulate themselves, suggesting that these brain regions are involved in the elaboration of pleasurable feelings. Others have interpreted this behavior as representing a repetition compulsion (see Freud, 1920). Observations of patients whose septal regions have been electrically stimulated and who report a "good feeling" suggest that the former interpretation may be more correct. Dostoyevsky, a temporal lobe epileptic, described a feeling of ecstacy accompanying some seizures, a report that suggests electrical spread to the hypothalamus.

Rage reactions and aggressive behavior accompanied by excessive food intake (hyperphagia) have been reported in man and animals following lesions involving the ventromedial region (VM) of the hypothalamus. These studies suggest that the VM ordinarily serves to inhibit feeding activity and aggressive behavior, which are normally elaborated by the more lateral portions of the hypothalamus. The issue of ragelike behavior has already been considered in some detail.

Frontal Lobe Syndromes

Because of the proximity of the posterior frontal cortex to the motor and sensory strips, elementary motor and sensory findings commonly accompany frontal lobe syndromes. From the viewpoint of the psychiatrist, the most interesting and perhaps most significant features of the frontal lobe syndromes are behavior and personality disturbances. Frequently a reduction in drive occurs, demonstrated by lack of initiative and spontaneity and accompanied by a kind of agitated apathy in which the patient frequently shows decreased psychomotor activity punctuated by brief bursts of inappropriate overactivity. Lack of productive thinking and incapacity to make decisions are often seen. The affect is frequently euphoric, although apathy is also common. Lesions involving primarily the orbital surface of the frontal lobes are characterized by more severe personality changes with less involvement of intellect. Patients with such lesions demonstrate a rather shallow affect and may become angry and aggressive with only trivial provocation. Aggressive behavior in frontal lobe disorders tends to be short-lived and, unlike the aggressiveness seen in temporal lobe epilepsy, lacks the depth of affect and ruminating or grudgelike quality seen in TLE. Patients with frontal lobe disorders frequently show lack of inhibition characterized by poor insight and judgment, leading to such behavior as exhibitionism, urination in public, and coprolalic speech. Euphoria, when present, is often characterized by inappropriate facetiousness and jocularity (*Witzelsucht*).

Although clinical features overlap to some degree, depending on the extent of the underlying lesion, several important clinical entities deserve individual comment; they may be grouped together under the rubric of frontal dementia.

Treatable frontal dementias. The classical frontal dementia is *general paresis*. Although now relatively rare, it has considerable importance because it is one of the forms of dementia that can be treated. More than 80 percent of patients may be cured when treated early with penicillin. The disease is characterized by the insidious onset of intellectual deterioration and marked changes in personality. While less common, perhaps the most striking feature is delusions of grandeur, which differentiates this disorder from true mania. More commonly, the patient may show a blunting of affect difficult to distinguish from a true depression.

Another treatable frontal dementia is *normal-pressure hydrocephalus*, a nonabsorptive (communicating) type of hydrocephalus that develops in the absence of a demonstrable lesion. The disorder is characterized by disturbance of gait, dementia, and incontinence. The diagnosis, when suspected, may be confirmed by specialized X-ray studies such as computerized axial tomography (CAT scan), pneumoencephalography, intrathecal radioisotope scan, and cerebrospinal fluid (CSF) infusion-absorption tests. Ventriculoatrial shunting may result in a dramatic recovery. *Space-occupying lesions* involving the frontal lobe, particularly meningiomas, may respond to neurosurgical intervention. Clinically, onset of the disease is insidious and headache is a common feature.

Untreatable frontal dementias. The disorders described in this section have, in actuality, a widespread pathology. They are considered here because symptoms referable to the frontal lobes are predominant.

Unlike the early biparietal symptoms characteristic of Alzheimer's disease, the more common presenile dementia (discussed in the section on occipital and parietal lobe syndromes), *Pick's disease* often causes prominent early changes related to the frontal lobes. The dementia of Pick's disease is often characterized by apathy and asocial behavior, with a relative preservation of intellect. In contrast, patients with Alzheimer's disease usually show much less marked changes in personality structure early in the course of their illness and more prominent changes in intellectual function. In a small number of patients with Alzheimer's disease, however, the frontal lobes may become affected early in the course, and in some cases of Pick's disease early intellectual changes occur. As a result, clinical distinction of these disorders is often uncertain.

While pathological changes in the caudate nucleus are the hallmark of *Huntington's chorea*, other cerebral lesions are always present. The dementia of Huntington's chorea is of the frontal type, producing an insidious change in personality. Some cases develop little or no chorea, making diagnosis difficult. On the other hand, numerous case reports indicate that the chorea may sometimes be quite prominent with little or no dementia. When both occur together, diagnosis is usually not difficult, but this condition must occasionally be distinguished from chronic schizophrenia complicated by phenothiazine-induced tardive dyskinesia (see chapter 18, "Chemotherapy"). A careful history is usually sufficient to make the distinction.

Another type of frontal lobe dementia, *Marchiafava-Bignami disease*, is among the serious neurological sequelae of chronic alcoholism. Originally thought to be a disease of Italian wine-drinkers, the disorder has been reported in almost all ethnic groups and in all types of alcoholics from beer- to scotch-drinkers. Although the pathological hallmark is atrophy of the corpus callosum, the clinical picture is that of a frontal dementia, usually with incontinence and gait disturbance.

Variations on the surgical theme of *frontal lobotomy* have produced controversial results. Certain behavioral changes, however, are shared by all of them to a greater or lesser degree, and may be summarized as: (1) reduction in drive; (2) reduced self-concern; (3) superficial, shallow affect; and (4) stimulus-bound responses to environmental cues. In short, behavioral changes following frontal lobotomy are characteristic of those occurring in frontal lobe syndromes, although they may be more or less severe depending on the operation.

Patients with *pseudobulbar palsies* are frequently misdiagnosed as demented. Their tendency to laugh or cry excessively, usually in response to a trivial, albeit appropriate, stimulus, coupled with dysarthric, indistinct speech, often leads the uninitiated to assume a diagnosis of dementia. The pseudobulbar palsies are so called to indicate that bilateral upper-motor neuron paresis gives a false impression of lower-motor neuron pathology. The neurological picture includes a flattened, expressionless face, wide palpebral fissures with diminished eye blinking, hoarseness, dysphagia, drooling, and dysarthria. Just as the paresis represents a sham bulbar paralysis, so the emotional responses represent sham affect. Despite the excessive laughing or crying, interrogation of the patient reveals that he does not experience a degree of happiness or sadness commensurate with his behavior; rather, inappropriate emotional behavior represents the loss of the modulating influence of the upper-motor neurons. The situation is analogous to the loss of modulation of motor activity—that is, to hyperreflexia and impairment of voluntary movement resulting from an upper-motor neuron lesion. While drooling and expressionless facies contribute to the impression that the patient may be demented, the tendency to tearfulness may also lead to the incorrect diagnosis of depression. Both of these misdiagnoses may frequently be avoided by interrogating the patient about his feelings and by closely observing his spontaneous behavior over a period of time. Pseudobulbar states arise most commonly as a result of bilateral cerebrovascular disease and as a part of the picture of motor neuron disease (amyotrophic lateral sclerosis).

Parietal and Occipital Lobe Syndromes

The calcarine cortex of the occipital lobe and the postrolandic cortex of the parietal lobe contain the primary analyzers subserving visual and somatesthetic functions. They receive direct projections from the lateral and medial ventroposterior nuclei of the thalamus and the lateral geniculate bodies, respectively. The largest portion of the parietal and occipital lobes—the primary association areas—receive projections from the nonspecific thalamic nuclei. That portion of the cortex at the confluence of the temporal, parietal, and occipital lobes (the angular gyrus) constitutes a secondary association area receiving projections from the primary association cortexes. In summary, sensory information in the lemniscal and visual systems arrives via the specific thalamic nuclei at the primary sensory cortexes. These regions, in turn, project to the primary association cortex, which also receives projections from the nonspecific thalamic system. The primary association cortex, in turn, projects to the secondary association cortex. Associations from one sensory sphere to another (cross-modal) are thought to occur in the angular gyrus.

Destructive and irritative (epileptogenic) lesions of the primary sensory cortexes lead to elementary sensory deficits and simple hallucinatory experiences such as flashes of light or formication. Epileptogenic lesions of the secondary association cortex may lead to more complex hallucinatory experiences that mimic psychiatric disturbances.

Disturbances of body image. Self-awareness of the body image derives from a complicated integration of various sensory inputs. The most severe disturbance of body image is the *denial* or unawareness of deficits in bodily integrity seen in right hemisphere disorders. The *Gerstmann syndrome* is often cited as a special example of a more general disturbance of body image. The four principal components of this syndrome are finger agnosia, right-left disorientation, acalculia, and agraphia. A fifth component (not originally described by Gerstmann but since suggested by Schilder) is constructional disturbance, that is, the inability to draw. While some argument has ensued as to whether these features constitute a definite clinical entity, most investigators agree that this symptom complex reflects a disturbance involving the dominant (usually left) parietal lobe.

Topographagnosia. Related to the more general problem of constructional disturbance is that of topographical disorientation. This dysfunction (topographagnosia) is manifested by difficulty in maze learning and route finding. Clinically it may be tested for by asking the patient to draw or locate significant features on a diagram of his home or hospital room.

Visual hallucinations. Although less common than auditory hallucinations, visual hallucinations are an important feature of schizophrenic reactions. When they occur as a result of focal brain pathology, the concomitant appearance of neurological deficits, such as field defects, changes in the sensorium, or other elementary findings, aids in the differential diagnosis. Visual hallucinations may occur in many nonfocal brain diseases such as delirium tremens, drug intoxication, acute and chronic alcoholism, febrile states, metabolic encephalopathies, and encephalitis.

When visual hallucinations result from focal brain pathology, the type of hallucination often gives a clue to the anatomical structures involved. When the primary visual cortex or the primary visual association cortex is involved, hallucinations tend to be similar to those perceived by blind persons—flashes of colored or white light forming discrete points or spots or moving lines and swirls of light (phosphenes). Formed hallucinations arise only when the secondary association cortex is involved. Occasionally, formed hallucinations occur with occipital lobe lesions if the right hemisphere is involved. Numerous reports have been made of tumors of the temporal lobe causing visual hallucinations. A review of these case reports suggests that the hallucinations probably represent seizure activity. Complex visual and auditory hallucinations are common phenomena in temporal lobe epilepsy.

A particular form of visual hallucination likely to produce a confusing diagnostic picture is *peduncular hallucinosis*, a condition arising from lesions involving the mesencephalon and the interpeduncular fossa (such as pituitary or hypothalamic tumors). Pressure from such lesions on the optic tracts may account for the diminished visual acuity that is a common feature of this syndrome. The hallucinations themselves, however, may represent calcarine region ischemia secondary to bilateral obstruction of the posterior cerebral arteries. Whatever the precise mechanism, the clinical features are fairly uniform and consist of mild confusion, diminution in visual acuity, and the frequent complaint of giddiness or vertigo. The hallucinations are characterized by well-defined, brightly colored images of miniature people and miniature animals in rapid motion; they are uniformly ego-dystonic and frequently arouse a sensation of pleasure, interest, and curiosity in the patient.

While hallucinations accompanying focal brain lesions are of particular interest because of their value in localizing the lesion, they are, in fact, much less common than the visual hallucinations experienced in diffuse neurological disorders such as the toxometabolic states.

Alzheimer's disease. The Alzheimer's form of presenile dementia (see also the discussion of Pick's disease) is considered here because of the prominent early involvement of the parietal lobes, although temporal and later frontal lobe involvement are usual. The pathological hallmarks of the disease, as in senile dementia, are the neurofibrillary tangles and plaques, the latter often most prominent in the temporal lobes. The dementia begins between the ages of forty-five and sixty-five in 80 percent of all cases. Unlike the frontal dementias, the usual early clinical picture is one of intellectual impairment with relative preservation of personality structure. Elementary focal neurological signs, like the disorganization of personality, are late features of the illness. Aphasia is a common later feature of Alzheimer's disease, and one that is rarely, if ever, seen in other forms of dementia such as general paresis, Huntington's chorea, or multiple sclerosis.

Mental Syndromes Related to Lateralized Pathology

Up to this point we have considered highly circumscribed (focal) lesions. The mental syndromes described below are of "lateralizing value," that is, they are valuable in determining which side (hemisphere) of the brain is abnormal.

Left (Dominant) Hemisphere Syndromes

In most persons, including left-handers, the left hemisphere is dominant for speech. A number of fairly specific clinical syndromes can be delineated in which the causative pathology resides in the left hemisphere.

Disturbances of consciousness. An individual's overall level of discriminative awareness (consciousness) apparently depends on the interaction of several systems. These include the association cortex, the reticular activating system, and the diffuse thalamic system. As pointed out earlier, the association cortex projects reciprocally to the reticular activating system and the diffuse thalamic projection system. Data obtained by Serafetinides, Hoare, and Driver (1965) in the performance of the Wada test suggest that abolition of electrical activity (electrocerebral silence) in the left hemisphere frequently results in unconsciousness. A similar injection of sodium amytal into the right carotid artery results less frequently in unconsciousness. Similarly, Dandy's data from patients undergoing surgery for aneurysm of the anterior cerebral artery suggest that coma is more frequently a complication of ligation of the left anterior cerebral artery than of the right (1930). The mechanisms accounting for this lateralized effect are not known.

Language disorders. Perhaps the most fully studied and easily demonstrable specialized function of the left hemisphere is language. For most people the left hemisphere is essential for verbal tasks, including speech and comprehension of spoken language, reading, and writing. Loss of these functions is referred to as aphasia, alexia, and agraphia, respectively. In over 99 percent of right-handed individuals, the left hemisphere is dominant for speech. The situation for left-handers is not quite as clear; increasing evidence suggests that language function may be represented to some extent in each hemisphere. Regardless of handedness, the presence of aphasia indicates a lesion of the left hemisphere in at least 95 percent of all cases. Impairment of a related function, the ability to carry out skilled motor tasks in response to verbal commands or other cues, is referred to as apraxia.

Numerous schemata have been developed over the years to classify the various aphasic syndromes. For the clinician, the classification devised by members of the aphasia unit of the Boston Veterans Administration Hospital is perhaps the most useful. In this scheme, the aphasias are divided according to whether repetition of verbal material is normal or abnormal. The aphasias characterized by abnormal repetition are Broca's aphasia, sometimes referred to as "expressive" aphasia; Wernicke's aphasia, sometimes referred to as "receptive" aphasia; conduction aphasia; pure word deafness; and global aphasia. The terms *expressive* and *receptive* should be avoided because they are used in many different senses and therefore lead to confusion. Aphasias in which repetition remains normal are transcortical motor aphasia, transcortical sensory aphasia, isolated speech center disorders, and anomic aphasia. Reading and writing ability are disturbed in the case of alexia with agraphia. In a related syndrome, alexia without agraphia, only reading ability is disturbed.

Broca's aphasia is characterized by conversational speech that is nonfluent, effortful, and dysarthric. Comprehension of spoken language, however, may be essentially normal; repetition is impaired but often somewhat better preserved than spontaneous speech. Similarly, comprehension of written language is generally preserved, while writing is invariably abnormal. Cases that have come to postmortem examination and brain scan studies *in vivo* have shown a high correlation of this aphasic syndrome with lesions involving the posterior inferior portion of the third frontal convolution (Broca's area). Paralysis of the right extremities (hemiplegia) and apraxia of the left extremities are common attendant findings.

In contrast to those with Broca's aphasia, patients suffering from *Wernicke's aphasia* characteristically have fluent conversational speech with only minimal dysarthria; spontaneous speech often reveals word-finding difficulty and paraphasias (substitutions within language). Literal paraphasias involve phonemes, while verbal paraphasias involve words; occasionally patients with Wernicke's aphasia make completely incorrect utterances (neologisms). When multiple paraphasias occur, the patients' speech is frequently incomprehensible and is sometimes referred to as *jargon aphasia*. Repetition, as indicated above, is abnormal, as is the comprehension of spoken language; reading and writing are generally also impaired. The focal brain lesion in this syndrome involves the posterior

superior portion of the first temporal gyrus. The language disturbance often occurs in isolation without evidence of other neurological involvement such as hemiplegia. Because the patient's speech is fluent (though in jargon), cursory examination may result in the misdiagnoses of confusion or psychosis.

Clinically, *conduction aphasia* is characterized by fluent speech, frequently contaminated by paraphasic errors, with good preservation of comprehension. Repetition and naming, on the other hand, are seriously impaired, as is writing. Although reading aloud is poorly performed, comprehension of written material is often preserved. In this disorder the lesion is found lying in the white matter of the supramarginal gyrus. Damage to the underlying arcuate fasciculus disconnects the temporoparietal language area (Wernicke's area) from the frontal language area (Broca's area). In some instances, the lesion has been located in the first temporal gyrus. The former location, however, is more common and may be suspected by the presence of cortical sensory loss (deficits in stereognosis, two-point discrimination, and so forth) involving the right half of the body.

The second group of aphasias—those in which repetition tends to be preserved—presents a more complicated clinical and pathological picture. Although most often the result of focal brain disease, diffuse encephalopathies from a variety of causes may produce similar clinical findings. Because of the peculiar and unusual nature of these findings, such patients are often referred to a psychiatrist.

Isolated speech center disorders, while rarely encountered as the full-blown syndrome, are not uncommon as *formes frustes* or arrested conditions. In this disorder, speech is even less fluent than in Broca's aphasia; indeed patients will often not speak at all unless spoken to. When the patient does speak, the language is characterized by parrotlike repetition (echolalia). While the patient may repeat what is said to him with good articulation, no comprehension of speech is demonstrated. This situation holds true for written as well as spoken language. Given the first part of a familiar phrase, the patient may repeat it and complete the phrase. Given the phrase "My country, 'tis of thee," for example, the patient will repeat it and often add, "Sweet land of liberty." The underlying lesion in this disorder is one of extensive involvement of the cerebral hemisphere with sparing of the peri-Sylvian region containing Broca's area, Wernicke's area, and the connecting arcuate fasciculus. The most common cause is an infarct in the border zone between the anterior and the middle cerebral artery circulations, an area selectively vulnerable to oxygen insufficiency (hypoxia). The clinical picture results from the fact that the speech areas have been disconnected from the entire association cortex, making it impossible for the patient to make any associations in terms of either behavioral response or language response to language stimuli. More restricted isolations result in motor and sensory transcortical aphasia.

Like Broca's aphasia, *motor transcortical aphasia* is characterized by nonfluent speech with relatively good preservation of comprehension. As is not the case with Broca's aphasia, however, the patient repeats normally, reading and writing are undisturbed, and the speech is not dysarthric. The responsible lesion is limited to the more anterior portion of the selectively vulnerable border zone, involving primarily the frontal association cortex anterior and superior to Broca's area.

While motor transcortical aphasia corresponds to the anterior part of the isolated speech center syndrome, *sensory transcortical aphasia* corresponds to its posterior portion. Thus the patient speaks fluently but incoherently. Since repetition is remarkably preserved, he frequently responds to queries by echolalic speech. If a response is made to a question, it is generally totally unrelated. As might be anticipated from the discussion of the isolated speech syndrome, the patient will show alexia and agraphia and possibly a cortical sensory disturbance, but no paresis. Here the causative lesion involves the border zone of the dominant parietal lobe.

Anomia, or word-finding difficulty, is among the most common components of the various aphasic syndromes. When present in its mildest form, it may be associated with only slight difficulty in comprehension and mildly paraphasic

speech. Repetition is normal, and elementary neurological signs are usually absent. The word-finding difficulty is not limited to spoken language but is manifest in writing as well. This clinical constellation may be due to a focal lesion, usually vascular in nature, involving the posterior portion of the border zone area (angular gyrus). Anomic aphasia may also occur in the absence of a demonstrable lesion in this area. Metabolic encephalopathies and tumors remote from this site, even tumors in the opposite hemisphere causing cerebral edema, may give rise to this syndrome, although the mechanism by which this occurs is unclear.

Global aphasia refers to the aphasic syndrome produced by large lesions involving both Broca's and Wernicke's speech areas, as well as the bridging cortical and subcortical structures. Depending on the extent and nature of the damage, the aphasia may resemble Broca's aphasia with components of Wernicke's aphasia or, conversely, Wernicke's type with some of the components of Broca's aphasia. Even in its most severe form, mutism is extremely rare.

Pure word deafness is a rare syndrome characterized by an isolated difficulty in the comprehension of speech, with moderately impaired repetition. The cause is either a large subcortical lesion of the dominant temporal lobe or bilateral cortical lesions of the superior temporal gyrus with sparing of Wernicke's area.

Pure alexia without agraphia is an isolated difficulty in the comprehension of written language. The underlying lesion is a complex one in which there is destruction of the left visual cortex and the splenium (the posterior one-fifth) of the corpus callosum. This is nearly always produced by an infarct in the distribution of the posterior cerebral artery. As a result, the intact right visual cortex is cut off from Wernicke's speech area. The patient is unable to read because the written word no longer arouses the spoken form of the word.

Pure alexia with agraphia is an isolated difficulty in reading and writing. The lesion usually involves part of the angular gyrus and acts to disconnect the visual association cortex from the speech area. Thus written words fail to elicit written forms.

The symptom complexes of the left hemisphere are not infrequently accompanied by significant psychiatric symptoms. As indicated above, patients with an aphasia may be mistakenly diagnosed as suffering from mental disorders such as confusional states or dementia. Similarly, a patient whose speech is characterized by many paraphasic errors and neologisms may be mistaken for a schizophrenic. It is important, too, to recognize that the development of focal brain lesions producing aphasia in patients with schizophrenia may be overlooked. Tragically, some patients with a fluent paraphasic type of aphasia have been hospitalized with a misdiagnosis of psychotic reaction.

As in the case of many chronic illnesses, depression may become a feature in aphasic patients. Because of the patient's language disorder, however, assessing affect and mood may be difficult. It cannot be overemphasized that behavioral observations by themselves may be grossly misleading. For example, anterior frontal lobe damage, which may be present in Broca's aphasia, may lead to psychomotor retardation and a diminished sphere of interests. When questioned, however, patients with this disorder frequently do not express feelings of depression; in this circumstance, apathy is mistaken for depression. In some patients with Broca's aphasia, the depression may be a reactive depression of the type seen in any chronic illness and may be unrelated to the specific cerebral lesion. In Wernicke's aphasia, depression is rare and patients frequently appear euphoric and unconcerned about their disability.

Some patients with Broca's aphasia demonstrate a keen awareness of their deficit and often exhibit marked frustration at their inability to speak correctly. Goldstein (1963) described an extreme degree of frustration, characterized by weeping, anger, and withdrawal, for which he used the term *catastrophic reaction*. The characteristics of the aphasias, arranged to indicate differential diagnosis, are listed below.

Aphasias with normal repetition
1. comprehension impaired
   a. fluent—transcortical sensory aphasia
   b. nonfluent—isolated speech area disorder

2. comprehension preserved
   a. fluent—anomic aphasia
   b. nonfluent—transcortical motor aphasia

Aphasias with impaired repetition
1. comprehension impaired
   a. fluent—Wernicke's aphasia
   b. nonfluent—global aphasia
2. comprehension preserved
   a. fluent—conduction aphasia
   b. nonfluent—Broca's aphasia

Right (Nondominant) Hemisphere Syndromes

Compared with the left hemisphere, the right hemisphere has a more restricted repertoire of exclusive functions. This difference may be more apparent than real, and in recent years activity specialization within the right hemisphere has been increasingly recognized. Many of these activities may be special examples of the more general function of visual-spatial orientation and integration. However, while deficits in spatial and visual orientation and integration may be strikingly apparent following damage to the right hemisphere, such deficits are also seen, to a lesser degree, as a result of lesions involving the left hemisphere. This relative preponderance of function is similar to that for the deficits in language function previously described. While language is predominantly a function of one hemisphere (usually the left), a language disturbance, although a less serious one, may occur when the other hemisphere is damaged. Several more or less distinct examples of this breakdown in visual-spatial orientation and integration—forms of the *apraxias* and *neglect*—deserve particular comment.

Constructional apraxia denotes a difficulty in drawing, copying, and the manipulation of spatial patterns for design. Lesions involving the right hemisphere that cause constructional apraxia generally produce marked difficulty in recall of spatial orientation. Patients with this condition will frequently get lost and not be able to find their own hospital rooms. When constructional apraxia results from a left hemispheric lesion, the principal difficulty involves execution, that is, drawing or copying. In the absence of any other neurological findings, an isolated constructional apraxia strongly suggests the possibility of a right hemispheric lesion.

The term *prosopagnosia* is used to denote difficulty in recognizing faces of well-known individuals. As with constructional apraxia, there is only a relatively greater likehood of this deficit appearing with right hemispheric than with left hemispheric lesions. The syndrome is actually quite rare, and some investigators claim, on the basis of postmortem findings, that bilateral hemispheric lesions must be present for its appearance.

Dressing apraxia must be distinguished from *unilateral neglect*, in which the patient ignores one side of the body while attending to and grooming the opposite side normally. In a true dressing apraxia, the deficit appears to be a visual-spatial disturbance; the patient is unable to orient the garment in space in an appropriate manner to permit correct dressing. If, for example, the patient is handed a shirt with one sleeve turned inside out, he will twist it helplessly and be unable to orient the sleeve so that he can correctly don the garment. The dressing difficulty that occurs as part of the more general phenomenon of neglect is—like other examples of unilateral neglect—more commonly but not exclusively associated with right hemisphere damage. The visual-spatial type of dressing apraxia occurs in patients with severe right hemispheric lesions or bilateral posterior cerebral lesions.

Neglect can and does occur after damage to either hemisphere, but it is more frequent with lesions involving the right hemisphere. In its mildest form, neglect is characterized by inattention and usually requires some maneuver on the part of the examiner, such as double simultaneous stimulation, to elicit the phenomenon. In a more severe form of *unilateral neglect*, the patient appears to be unaware of one side of his body; observation reveals that he tends to use the limbs on one side of the body more than those on the opposite side. When confronted with these observations, patients will acknowledge that they have the demonstrated difficulty and also admit concern about their disability, but usually their concern is not expressed unless the

examiner deliberately attempts to elicit it. In a still more severe form, the patient is manifestly unconcerned and appears indifferent to his disability even when confronted with it. In its most severe form, the patient overtly denies his illness. Even such striking deficits as blindness (Anton's syndrome) and hemiplegia (Babinski's agnosia) may be denied. When confronted with his deficit the blind patient, for example, may state that he is unable to perform a given task because he doesn't have his eyeglasses or because the room lighting is inadequate. An aphasic patient may state that he speaks poorly because he does not have his dentures in his mouth.

The mechanism underlying unilateral neglect is far from clear. Denny-Brown and his associates (1952) have suggested that the disorder may result from an imbalance of the normally finely integrated functions of the two hemispheres, to which they apply the term *amorphosynthesis*. They maintain that through years of practice the nervous system comes to respond to equally balanced sensory inputs reaching both hemispheres. When, however, one hemisphere begins to malfunction, the central nervous system responds to stimuli arriving in the normal hemisphere but "neglects" weaker signals arriving in the damaged hemisphere. This suggestion, unfortunately, provides no explanation for the preponderance of right-sided lesions in the disorder. It is tempting to speculate, however, that—in a manner analogous to the specialization of the left hemisphere for language function—the right hemisphere has become specialized to perform the postulated integration of competing sensory inputs. Unlike the situation in aphasia, however, in which good clinical-pathological correlation exists between restricted focal lesions and specific disturbances in language, no such data are available to support this intriguing notion. Denial of illness, manifest in the most severe form of neglect disorders, has been studied in detail by Weinstein and Kahn (1955). They maintain that such denial is commonly accompanied by a tendency toward short-lived outbursts of anger and a facetious euphoric affect. These features, as we have noted, are also common in the frontal lobe syndrome. Speculation can reasonably follow that a combination of pathological changes giving rise to such frontal signs and those responsible for amorpho-synthesis may be present in patients with denial of illness.

Denial of illness caused by focal cerebral pathology must necessarily be distinguished from denial arising from purely psychological causes. The psychogenic type of denial is usually intel-lectualized, rationalized, and presented in a quasi-logical manner. In contrast, the denial oc-curring in brain-injured patients tends to be ex-pressed in crude and concrete terms, as in the case of the aphasic patient who blames his den-tures for inability to speak or the blind person who blames the poor illumination of the exam-ining room for his inability to see.

Early formulations concerning musicality con-sidered it a function of the right hemisphere. More recent evaluation of musical ability in mu-sicians and nonmusicians suggests that the left hemisphere is dominant for analytic processing of musical stimuli while the right hemisphere is specialized for holistic processing.

This chapter has attempted to demonstrate that localizable neural systems exist that, if dam-aged, express morphological or physiological dis-continuity, or both, as relatively specific alter-ations of behavior. These findings should not, however, be interpreted as having established the existence of centers for certain patterns of behavior. Rather, they demonstrate that the integrity of certain neural systems is essential if particular aspects of behavior are to continue in a normal fashion. These findings thus provide a first step that may lead us to an understanding of the ways in which local brain regions interact to produce the integrated activity we call behavior.

References

American Psychiatric Association. 1968. *Diagnostic and statistical manual of mental disorders*. 2nd ed. Washington, D.C.

Andersen, P., and S. A. Andersson. 1968. *Physio-logical basis of the alpha rhythm*. New York: Appleton-Century-Crofts.

Bremer, F., and C. Terzuolo. 1953. Interaction de l'écorce cérébrale et de la formation réticulée du tronc cérébrale dans le mécanisme de l'éveil et du maintien de l'activité vigile. *J. Physiol.* (Paris) 45: 56–57.

Brill, H. 1975. Classification and assessment of psy-chiatric conditions. *American handbook of psychi-atry*, ed. S. Arieti. Vol. 1. 2nd ed. New York: Basic Books.

Carpenter, W. B. 1842. *Principles of human physiol-ogy*. London: Churchill.

Dandy, W. E. 1930. Changes in our conception of localization of certain functions in the brain. *Am. J. Physiol.* 93:643.

Denny-Brown, D., J. S. Meyer, and S. Horenstein. 1952. The significance of perceptual rivalry resulting from parietal lesions. *Brain* 75:429–471.

Freud, S. 1920. Beyond the pleasure principle. In *Standard edition*, ed. J. Strachey. Vol. 18. London: Hogarth Press, 1955.

Gastaut, H. 1970. Clinical electroencephalographic classification of epileptic seizures. *Epilepsia* 11: 102–113.

Goldstein, K. 1963. *The organism: a holistic approach to biology derived from pathological data in man*. Boston: Beacon Press.

Hess, W. R. 1957. *The functional organization of the diencephalon*. New York: Grune & Stratton.

Huxley, T. H. 1866. *Lessons in elementary physiol-ogy*. London: Macmillan.

Klüver, H., and P. C. Bucy. 1939. Preliminary analysis of functions of temporal lobes in monkeys. *Arch. Neurol. Psychiatr.* 42:979–1000.

MacLean, P. D. 1959. The limbic system with respect to two basic life principles. In *The central nervous system and behavior*, ed. M. A. B. Brazier. New York: Josiah Macy Foundation.

Moruzzi, G., and H. W. Magoun. 1949. Brain stem re-ticular formation and activation of EEG. *Electroen-cephalogr. Clin. Neurophysiol.* 1:455–473.

Papez, J. W. 1937. A proposed mechanism of emo-tion. *Arch. Neurol. Psychiatr.* 38:725–743.

Ranson, S. W. 1939. Somnolence caused by hypotha-lamic lesions in monkey. *Arch. Neurol. Psychiatr.* 41:1–23.

Serafetinides, E. A., R. D. Hoare, and M. V. Driver. 1965. Intracarotid sodium amylo barbitone and cerebral dominance for speech and consciousness. *Brain* 88:107–130.

Slater, E., and A. W. Beard. 1963. The schizophrenia-like psychosis of epilepsy. *Br. J. Psychiatry* 109: 95–150.

Victor, M., R. D. Adams, and G. H. Collins. 1971. *The Wernicke-Korsakoff syndrome*. Philadelphia: Davis.

Weinstein, E. A., and R. L. Kahn, 1955. *Denial of*

illness: symbolic and physiological aspects. Spring-field, Ill.: Thomas.

Wernicke, C. 1881. *Lehrbuch der Gehirnkrankenheiten fur Artze und Studirende*. Vol. 2. Kassel: Fisher.

Recommended Reading

Critchley, M. 1953. *The parietal lobes*. London: Edward Arnold.

Eccles, J. C. 1959. Neuron physiology—introduction. In *Handbook of physiology*, section 1, *Neurophysiology*, ed. J. Field, H. W. Magoun, and V. E. Hall, vol. 1. Washington, D.C.: American Physiological Society.

Egger, M. D., and J. P. Flynn. 1967. Further studies on the effects of amygdala stimulation and ablation on hypothalamically elicited attack behavior in cats. In *Structure and function of the limbic system*, ed. W. R. Adey and T. Tokizane. Progress in Brain Research, *vol. 27. Amsterdam: Elsevier*.

Evans, J. H. 1966. Transient loss of memory, an organic mental syndrome. *Brain* 89:539–548.

Fisher, C. M., and R. D. Adams. 1964. Transient global amnesia. *Acta Neurol. Scand.* suppl. 9, 7–83.

Flor-Henry, P. 1969. Psychosis and temporal lobe epilepsy. *Epilepsia* 10:363–395.

Fredericks, J. A. M. 1969. Disorders of body schema. In *Handbook of clinical neurology*, ed. P. J. Vinken and G. W. Bruyn. Vol. 4. Amsterdam: North Holland.

Freud, S. 1895. Project for a scientific psychology. In *The origins of psychoanalysis*, ed. M. Bonaparte, A. Freud, and E. Kris. New York: Basic Books, 1954.

Geschwind, N. 1965. Disconnexion syndromes in animals and man. *Brain* 88:237–295, 585–644.

Goodglass, H., and E. Kaplan. 1972. *The assessment of aphasia and related disorders*. Philadelphia: Lea and Febiger.

Green, L. N., and R. Q. Cracco. 1970. Kleine-Levin syndrome: a case with EEG evidence of periodic brain dysfunction. *Arch. Neurol.* 22:166–175.

Hamlin, R. M. 1970. Intellectual functions 14 years after frontal lobe surgery. *Cortex* 6:299–307.

Herrington, R. N., ed. 1969. *Current problems in neuropsychiatry, schizophrenia, epilepsy, and the temporal lobe. Br. J. Psychiatry* special publication, no. 4. Ashford, Kent: Headley Brothers.

Kiloh, L. G., and J. W. Osselton. 1966. *Clinical electroencephalography*. 2nd ed. London: Butterworth.

Kinsbourne, M. 1971. The minor cerebral hemisphere as a source of aphasic speech. *Arch. Neurol.* 25:302–306.

Klüver, H., and P. C. Bucy. 1937. Psychic blindness and other symptoms following bilateral temporal lobectomy in rhesus monkeys. *Am. J. Physiol.* 119:352–353.

Lishman, W. A. 1968. Brain damage in relation to psychiatric disability after head injury. *Br. J. Psychiatry* 114:373–410.

Magoun, H. W. 1963. *The waking brain*. Springfield, Ill.: Thomas.

Poeck, K. 1969. Pathophysiology of emotional disorders associated with brain damage. In *Handbook of clinical neurology*, ed. P. J. Vinken and G. W. Bruyn. Vol. 3. Amsterdam: North Holland.

Reeves, A. G., and F. Plum. 1969. Hyperphagia, rage, and dementia accompanying a ventromedial hypothalamic neoplasm. *Arch. Neurol.* 20:616–624.

Segarra, J. M. 1970. Cerebral vascular disease and behavior: I. The syndrome of the mesencephalic artery. *Arch. Neurol.* 22:408–418.

Shagass, C. 1972. *Evoked brain potentials in psychiatry*. New York: Plenum Press.

Sherwin, I. 1976. Temporal lobe epilepsy: neurological and behavioral aspects. *Annu. Rev. Med.* 27:37–47.

The Biochemistry of Affective Disorders: A Brief Summary

CHAPTER 5

Joseph J. Schildkraut

THE INTRODUCTION OF drugs effective in the treatment of depressions and manias (the affective disorders) has had a major impact not only on clinical psychiatric practice but also on biological research in psychiatry. These drugs include the monoamine oxidase inhibitor antidepressants, the tricyclic antidepressants, and lithium salts. Extensive study of the neuropharmacology of these drugs has suggested that their action on the metabolism of biogenic amines (norepinephrine, dopamine, and serotonin) may be important in their clinical effects.

Research on the metabolism of biogenic amines in depressive and manic patients has uncovered many clues to the underlying biochemical pathophysiology of affective disorders. Moreover, recent findings suggest that certain measurements of biogenic amine metabolism may provide a biochemical basis for classifying depressive disorders and possibly for predicting differential response to antidepressant drugs. Studies of endocrine changes and electrolyte metabolism have also been a part of research

This work was supported in part by Grant MH 15413 from the National Institute of Mental Health.

on affective disorders. (See Schildkraut, 1974b; Schildkraut, Sachar, and Baer, 1976, for further information on these topics.)

Biogenic Amines

A Summary of Basic Neuropsychopharmacology

The term *biogenic amine* generally refers to three compounds—norepinephrine and dopamine, which are catecholamines, and serotonin, an indoleamine. All have a single amine group on the side chain and are consequently also called monoamines. In the brain these compounds function as biochemical neurotransmitters.

The neuroanatomy of specific monoamine-containing neurons has recently been mapped using histochemical fluorescence microscopy. While these studies have provided evidence for discrete monoaminergic neuronal systems within the brain, they have also indicated that these systems may be neuroanatomically and physiologically interconnected. However, these monoaminergic neuronal systems account for only a small fraction of the neurons within the central nervous system. Although pharmacological and clinical studies have often focused on individual monoamines, interactions among the monoaminergic neuronal systems and between them and other neurotransmitter systems do occur, with biochemical and physiological processes involving one neurotransmitter modulated or regulated by another.

Catecholamine biosynthesis in noradrenergic neurons proceeds along the pathway shown in figure 5.1. In dopaminergic neurons the synthesis of catecholamines proceeds only up to dopamine because these neurons lack the enzyme dopamine-β-hydroxylase, which converts dopamine to norepinephrine. In the adrenal medulla and possibly some areas of the brain, norepinephrine can be methylated to form epinephrine.

As figure 5.2 indicates, norepinephrine stored in the presynaptic neuron is discharged into the synaptic cleft by nerve impulses. Most of the discharged norepinephrine is thought to be removed from the synaptic cleft by reuptake into the presynaptic neuron; there it is retained by storage granules or undergoes deamination by monoamine oxidase. A small fraction of the discharged norepinephrine is inactivated in the

region of the postsynaptic neuron by the enzyme catechol-O-methyltransferase (COMT), which converts it to normetanephrine. This O-methylated metabolite may then be deaminated. In brain, the major metabolite of normetanephrine is thought to be 3-methoxy-4-hydroxyphenylglycol (MHPG).

Within the presynaptic neuron, some norepinephrine may diffuse or "leak" from storage granules into the cytoplasm and onto mitochondrial monoamine oxidase without producing extraneuronal physiological effects at receptors. Monoamine oxidase converts norepinephrine into deaminated catechol metabolites (dihydroxymandelic acid and dihydroxyphenylglycol). These metabolites may be subsequently O-methylated to form 3-methoxy-4-hydroxymandelic acid (vanillylmandelic acid or VMA) and 3-methoxy-4-hydroxyphenylglycol (MHPG). As noted above, MHPG is also a metabolite of normetanephrine in the brain. Considerable interest has recently focused on MHPG, since it is the major final metabolite of norepinephrine originating in the central nervous system; some fraction of urinary MHPG, however, derives from norepinephrine in the peripheral sympathetic nervous system (fig. 5.3).

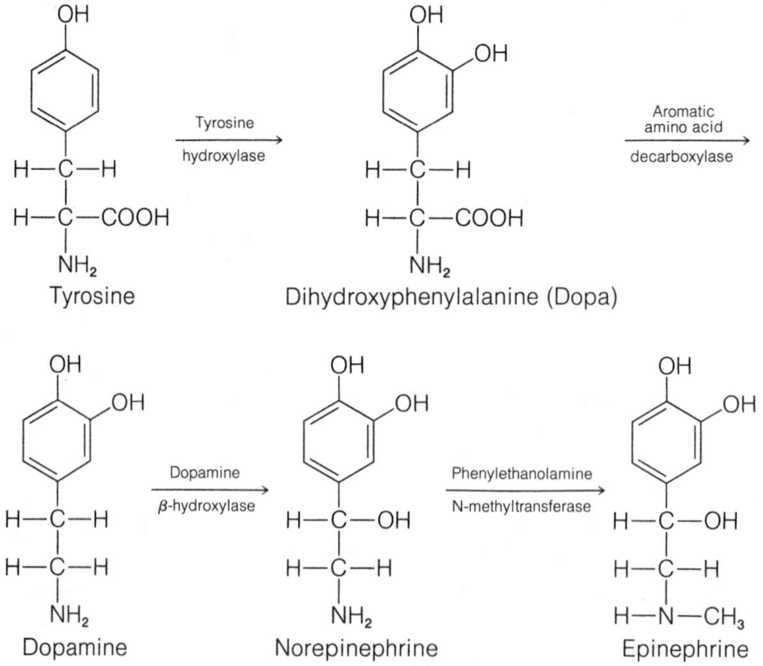

FIGURE 5.1. The biosynthesis of catecholamines.

NORADRENERGIC NEURON AND RECEPTOR

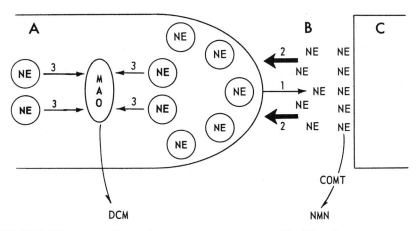

FIGURE 5.2. A noradrenergic neuron and receptor. In this schematic representation of a noradrenergic nerve ending (A), synaptic cleft (B), and receptor (C), NE
indicates norepinephrine; NMN, normetanephrine; DCM, deaminated catechol metabolites; COMT, catechol-O-methyltransferase; MAO, monoamine oxidase (within
a mitochondrion); 1, discharge of norepinephrine into the synaptic cleft and onto receptor; 2, reuptake of norepinephrine from the synaptic cleft; and 3, intracellular release of norepinephrine from storage granules into cytoplasm and onto mitochondrial monoamine oxidase. (Adapted from Schildkraut and Kety, 1967. Copyright
1967 by the American Association for the Advancement of Science.)

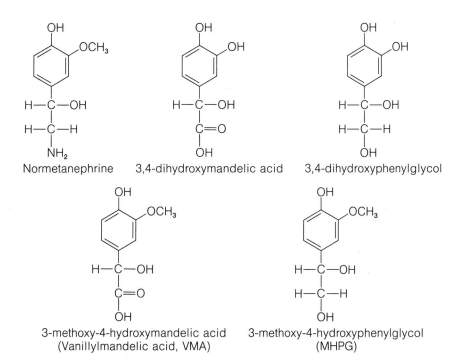

FIGURE 5.3. Metabolites of norepinephrine.

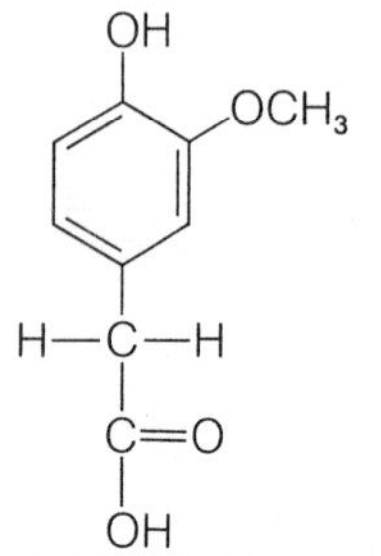

FIGURE 5.4. Homovanillic acid (HVA), a major metabolite of dopamine.

Like norepinephrine, dopamine may be metabolized by O-methylation and deamination. The major dopamine metabolite of interest in clinical studies is the deaminated, O-methylated metabolite homovanillic acid (HVA), shown in figure 5.4.

The biosynthesis and metabolism of serotonin are shown in figure 5.5. Serotonin is metabolized by monoamine oxidase; the serotonin metabolite of most interest in clinical research is 5-hydroxyindoleacetic acid (5-HIAA).

Psychoactive drugs may alter the physiological activity of monoamines by interfering with any of the processes involved in synthesis, storage, release, or metabolism, as well as by altering the sensitivity of receptors to one or another monoamine. In general, the drugs used in the treatment of depressive and manic disorders alter the metabolism or physiological disposition of one or another of the monoamines. These biochemical effects, described below, may be related to the effects of these drugs on affective states in man.

Approximately twenty years ago it was recognized that in some patients *reserpine*, a drug used as an antihypertensive, could cause depressions that were clinically indistinguishable from certain naturally occurring depressions. Concurrent studies in animals indicated that reserpine impaired the capacity of neurons to retain monoamines in storage granules, causing intraneuronal deamination, and that brain levels of all three biogenic amines (norepinephrine, dopamine, and serotonin) were lowered significantly after administration of reserpine.

At about the same time, it was observed that *monoamine oxidase inhibitors* (initially used in the treatment of tuberculosis) could cause euphoria and possessed antidepressant properties when administered to some patients. Studies in animals showed that drugs of this class prevented the deamination of monoamines by inhibiting the enzyme monoamine oxidase, thus producing an increase in the levels of norepinephrine, dopamine, and serotonin in the brain.

Tricyclic antidepressants increase the physiological effects of monoamines at synapses and potentiate the effects of norepinephrine and serotonin in a number of physiological systems. Their potentiation of norepinephrine was explained by the discovery that imipramine interferes with the reuptake of norepinephrine in peripheral and central neurons. Inhibition of norepinephrine reuptake by presynaptic neurons prevents the physiological inactivation of norepinephrine at the synapse and increases levels of norepinephrine at receptors. Several additional

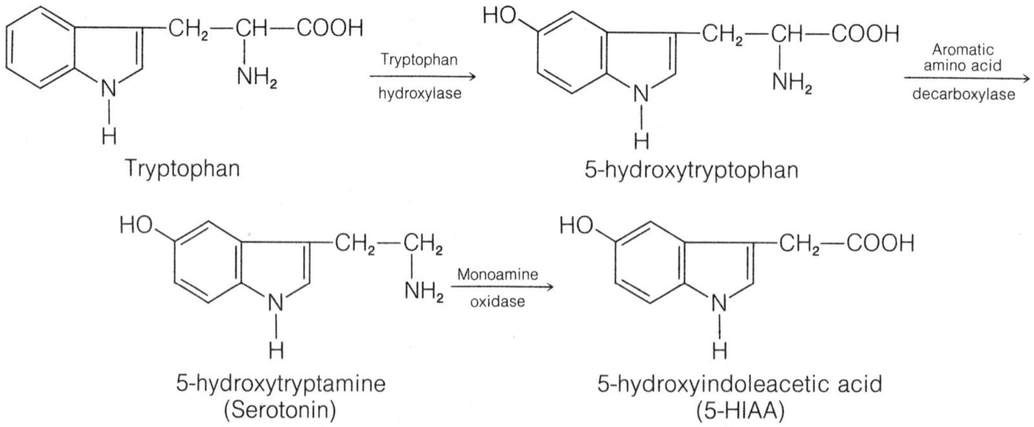

FIGURE 5.5. The biosynthesis and metabolism of serotonin.

tricyclic antidepressant drugs (among them desmethylimipramine, nortriptyline, and protriptyline) inhibit the uptake of norepinephrine in presynaptic neurons, but others, like amitriptyline, are considerably weaker. Amitriptyline, however, is a more potent inhibitor of serotonin uptake than drugs such as desmethylimipramine. These differences may account for some of the variations in clinical properties among the tricyclic antidepressants.

Tricyclic antidepressants also prevent the deamination of norepinephrine and other monoamines by mitochondrial monoamine oxidase. The mechanism of action has not yet been clarified. While *in vitro* studies indicate that high concentrations of tricyclic antidepressants inhibit the enzyme monoamine oxidase, these drugs may also act at intraneuronal membranes (such as the mitochondrial membranes) to prevent norepinephrine from interacting with monoamine oxidase, just as they act at neuronal membranes to prevent the reuptake of norepinephrine into presynaptic neurons.

Inhibition of monoamine uptake and decrease in monoamine deamination occur after acute administration of tricyclic antidepressants. Clinical antidepressant effects, however, generally require chronic rather than acute administration. Recent studies of the effects of chronic administration of tricyclic antidepressants on norepinephrine turnover and metabolism have shown that further changes in turnover occur with prolonged administration of tricyclic antidepressants. Such chronic changes, in conjunction with acute effects, may contribute to the drugs' clinical antidepressant properties.

Amphetamine exerts a stimulant and euphoriant effect by releasing norepinephrine and dopamine from neurons in the brain and possibly by inhibiting the neuronal reuptake of norepinephrine. It also decreases the deamination of norepinephrine in the brain. The central effects of amphetamine may be due to both increased release and decreased reuptake of catecholamines at central synapses. Tachyphylaxis occurs clinically with amphetamine, and amphetamine-induced psychomotor stimulation is often followed by a "rebound" depression and fatigue. These changes may reflect the temporary depletion of catecholamines available for continued release.

Like the antidepressant drugs, *electroconvulsive therapy* (ECT) may also alter the turnover and metabolism of biogenic amines in the brain. In animal studies, single electroconvulsive treatments increased the turnover of norepinephrine, dopamine, and serotonin in the brain. After a series of electroconvulsive treatments, the increased turnover of norepinephrine persists for at least one day after the last electroconvulsion. Other forms of prolonged stress, however, cause similar changes in the turnover of monoamines in the brain.

Numerous studies have examined the effects of *lithium* on the turnover and metabolism of biogenic amines in the brain, but it is difficult to draw simple generalizations from their findings. Evidence from research in animals and man suggests that lithium produces alterations in catecholamine disposition and metabolism that decrease the amount of norepinephrine available for discharge onto receptors. Thus lithium appears to affect norepinephrine metabolism in a manner opposite to that of many antidepressant and stimulant, euphoriant drugs. (For further discussion of the material covered in this section, see Schildkraut, 1970, 1973.)

Catecholamines and Related Substances

Catecholamines and normetanephrine. In patients with bipolar manic-depressive disorders,[*] the urinary excretion of norepinephrine and dopamine (and, less consistently, of epinephrine) is relatively lower during periods of depression than during periods of mania or after recovery. In several studies, the changes in norepinephrine excretion appeared to precede changes in clinical state. Some patients with agitated or anxious depressions show increased catecholamine excretion.

The excretion of normetanephrine, the O-methylated metabolite of norepinephrine, is higher during manias or hypomanias than during depressions. In some studies of manic or hypomanic patients the magnitude of the normeta-

---

[*] Throughout this chapter, the terms *manic-depressive* and *bipolar* are used synonymously to refer to patients with disorders characterized both by at least one hypomanic or manic episode and by one or more depressive episodes. These are to be differentiated from unipolar depressions, in which there is no history of a prior hypomanic or manic episode.

nephrine elevation reflected clinical severity. A gradual rise in the excretion of normetanephrine has been observed during clinical improvement in patients with endogenous depressions treated with the tricyclic antidepressant imipramine.

Further studies will be required to determine whether these changes are primary manifestations of the underlying pathophysiology or secondary to changes in behavior and posture that occur during depressions or manias. In any event, urinary norepinephrine, normetanephrine, epinephrine, and metanephrine derive mainly from the peripheral sympathetic nervous system and the adrenal medulla rather than from the brain, since the brain-blood barrier prevents catecholamines and their O-methylated amine metabolites from leaving the brain without further metabolism. At best, therefore, urinary measurements of these substances reflect events in the brain only indirectly.

MHPG. Several lines of evidence suggest that 3-methoxy-4-hydroxyphenylglycol (MHPG) or its sulfate conjugate is the major metabolite of norepinephrine in the human brain, as it is in a number of other species. MHPG is also synthesized from norepinephrine originating in the peripheral sympathetic nervous system, however, and the exact fraction of urinary MHPG that does in fact come from norepinephrine in the brain is not known. Recent studies have suggested, however, that in man, as in the subhuman primates, the contribution from the brain may be substantial.

Some longitudinal studies of patients with amphetamine-induced and naturally occurring bipolar manic-depressive episodes indicate that levels of urinary MHPG are lower during depressions and higher during manic or hypomanic episodes than after clinical remissions. It is unlikely that alterations in motor activity or levels of stress can account for these changes in MHPG excretion; rather, it appears that the changes are more closely related to the changes in clinical state per se.

All depressions are not clinically or biologically homogeneous, and all depressed patients do not excrete comparably low levels of MHPG. Recent studies have accordingly examined MHPG excretion as a possible biological crite-

rion for classifying the depressive disorders and for predicting responses to specific forms of antidepressant pharmacotherapy.

Several investigators recently noted that MHPG excretion was lower in patients with bipolar depressions than in patients with unipolar, chronic characterological depressions (that is, with unipolar dysphoric depressive syndromes) or certain other types of unipolar depressive disorders. These findings suggest that there may be a biologically related group of depressive disorders with relatively low MHPG excretion (of which bipolar manic-depressive depressions represent a clinically identifiable subgroup) and another group of depressive disorders with relatively higher MHPG excretion (of which unipolar chronic characterological depressions represent a clinically identifiable subgroup). Further studies are needed to explore this hypothesis.

It has also been suggested that MHPG excretion may provide a biochemical criterion for predicting differential responses to treatment with antidepressant drugs. Preliminary findings suggest that depressed patients who excrete low levels of MHPG prior to treatment with imipramine or desmethylimipramine respond better to treatment with these antidepressants than do patients who excrete relatively higher levels of MHPG. In contrast, depressed patients with higher levels of urinary MHPG may respond more favorably to treatment with amitriptyline than patients with lower levels of MHPG. These findings, which require further confirmation, thus imply that urinary MHPG might provide a biochemical criterion for choosing between amitriptyline and imipramine in the treatment of patients with depressive disorders.

Several groups of investigators have recently examined the levels of MHPG in the lumbar cerebrospinal fluid (CSF) of patients with affective disorders. Such data do not, however, necessarily provide a better index of norepinephrine turnover and metabolism in the brain than does urinary MHPG—first, since MHPG measured in lumbar CSF probably reflects norepinephrine metabolism in the spinal cord as well as in the brain and, second, since CSF levels of MHPG are determined both by the rate of MHPG efflux from the CSF and by its rate of production in the central nervous system. Several studies have found a poor correlation between measures of CSF and urinary MHPG.

While one group of investigators reports that MHPG levels in the CSF were significantly lower in a series of depressed patients than in control subjects, other investigators have not confirmed this finding. Differences in the types of depressed patients, in experimental procedures or techniques for obtaining lumbar CSF, and in the control group might account for these discrepant findings. Moreover, since the level of MHPG in the CSF may reflect changes in the rate of efflux of MHPG from the CSF as well as in its rate of formation, and since there is no available technique for blocking the efflux of MHPG from the CSF, these factors remain confounded and the interpretation of CSF levels of MHPG remains problematic.

In summary, urinary excretion of MHPG appears to vary in relation to clinical state in patients with manic-depressive disorders. Urinary MHPG may provide a biochemical criterion for classifying some types of depressive disorders and possibly for predicting differential responses to pharmacotherapy with tricyclic antidepressant drugs. Further studies, however, must reproduce and extend these observations before they can be regarded as definitive.

Homovanillic acid. Homovanillic acid (HVA), a deaminated, O-methylated metabolite of dopamine, can be measured in lumbar CSF and may provide information about the cerebral metabolism of dopamine. The concentration of HVA in lumbar CSF is considerably lower than that in ventricular CSF, reflecting the existence of a transport system for the removal of HVA in the region of the fourth ventricle. As with measures of MHPG in the CSF, the level of HVA in the CSF at any given time does not necessarily reflect the rate of production of this metabolite, since the rate of efflux may vary over time and among subjects. Information on the production rate of HVA may be obtained by blocking efflux from the cerebrospinal fluid with probenecid, a drug that inhibits the transport of acid metabolites of biogenic amines (such as HVA and 5-HIAA, a deaminated metabolite of serotonin).

Many investigators have reported that base-line levels of HVA in the CSF were lower in de-

pressed patients than in control subjects.* Several have studied base-line levels of HVA in lumbar CSF in relation to subtypes of depressive disorders or specific clinical characteristics. Clear-cut findings have not yet emerged from such studies. Similarly, the data on base-line levels of HVA in the CSF of hypomanic and manic patients are equivocal.

The accumulation of HVA in lumbar CSF following probenecid administration is lower in at least some depressed patients when compared with controls. Preliminary findings suggest that reduced accumulation of HVA in depressed patients may be specific to certain diagnostic subtypes or may be associated with particular clinical characteristics such as motor retardation. Further studies will be required to confirm this.

It is clear, over all, that at least some patients with depressive disorders have reduced base-line levels of HVA in the CSF and reduced accumulation of HVA in the CSF after probenecid administration. The possibility that measures of HVA in the CSF may be of value in differentiating subtypes of depressive disorders is currently under investigation. (For further information about the catecholamines and related substances, the reader is referred to Bunney and Davis, 1965; Goodwin and Post, 1975; Maas, 1975; Maas, Dekirmenjian, and Fawcett, 1974; Schildkraut, 1965, 1974a, 1974b; Schildkraut, Sachar, and Baer, 1976; Van Praag, 1974.)

Indoleamines and Related Substances

The measurement of *5-hydroxyindoleacetic acid* (5-HIAA), a deaminated metabolite of serotonin, in lumbar cerebrospinal fluid (CSF) may yield information about the metabolism of serotonin in the brain, although some of the 5-HIAA in lumbar CSF may come from the spinal cord. Many investigators have reported that base-line levels of 5-HIAA in the CSF are lower in depressed patients than in controls, and in some studies the decrease in CSF levels of 5-HIAA in depressed patients persisted after recovery. However, other investigators have found normal

---

* The term *base-line level* of HVA (or 5-HIAA) in the CSF is used to distinguish this measurement from the accumulation of HVA (or 5-HIAA) in the CSF after administration of probenecid.

base-line levels of 5-HIAA in the CSF of depressed patients. Decreased base-line CSF levels of 5-HIAA also occur in other psychiatric conditions, including schizophrenic disorders. Conclusive data have not emerged from studies of base-line levels of 5-HIAA in the CSF of hypomanic or manic patients.

The total accumulation of 5-HIAA in the CSF following probenecid was lower in depressed patients than in control subjects in a number of recent studies, but not in all. Evidence suggests that decreased accumulation of 5-HIAA after probenecid administration may occur in a subgroup of patients with depressive disorders not otherwise distinguishable on the basis of psychopathological or other clinical characteristics. Further studies are needed to determine whether 5-HIAA levels in the CSF will be of clinical value in distinguishing biological subtypes of depressive disorders.

Several studies have reported a reduction in the levels of serotonin or 5-HIAA in the hindbrain or brainstem of depressed patients after suicide, but the data from these studies are not fully consistent. Moreover, interpretation of these data is exceedingly difficult because of the uncontrolled variables inherent in such studies.

Several groups of investigators recently examined aspects of *tryptophan* metabolism including the levels of tryptophan in the CSF and other body fluids in patients with affective disorders. Because of the complex physiology and biochemistry involved, these findings do not permit simple generalizations and a detailed review of this work is beyond the scope of this chapter. (The indoleamines are discussed at greater length in Coppen, 1974; Goodwin and Post, 1975; Maas, 1975; Schildkraut, 1974b; Schildkraut, Sachar, and Baer, 1976; Van Praag, 1974.)

Enzymes in Biogenic Amine Metabolism

Some investigators have recently reported that platelet monoamine oxidase activity was lower in bipolar depressed patients than in unipolar depressed patients or normal controls. In a small number of bipolar patients studied longitudinally through both depressive and manic episodes, platelet monoamine oxidase activity did not vary with the phase of the illness. Another group of investigators has reported that platelet monoamine oxidase activity was higher in a heterogeneous sample of depressed patients (predominantly unipolar) than in normal subjects matched for age; in still another study, plasma monoamine oxidase activity was significantly higher in premenopausal depressed women than in control subjects.

It is difficult to compare these findings, since different substrates were used in determining monoamine oxidase activity. Moreover, it is uncertain whether platelet (or plasma) monoamine oxidase activity provides a reliable index of monoamine oxidase activity in other tissues—particularly in the brain, which may have different isoenzymes. Nevertheless, these findings raise the possibility that measures of platelet monoamine oxidase activity may offer a biochemical criterion for differentiating subtypes of depressive disorders.

Initial studies suggest that red blood cell catechol-O-methyltransferase activity may be reduced in women—but not men—with primary unipolar depressive disorders. All studies, however, have not confirmed these findings. In several studies, no differences in dopamine-β-hydroxylase activity were observed in manic or depressed patients when compared to control values.

Another recent study examined the activities of tyrosine hydroxylase, dopamine-β-hydroxylase, monoamine oxidase, and catechol-O-methyltransferase in tissue from various regions of brain obtained from depressive suicides, alcoholic suicides, and persons dying of natural causes. No significant differences were found between enzyme activities in the brain regions of controls and in those of suicides, with the possible exception of tyrosine hydroxylase in the substantia nigra, where depressive (but not alcoholic) suicides showed greater activity. (For further discussion of the material in this section, see Murphy and Wyatt, 1975; Schildkraut, 1974b; Schildkraut, Sachar, and Baer, 1976.)

Neuroendocrine Studies

The secretion of anterior pituitary hormones is controlled by hypothalamic neuroendocrine cells that release specific stimulating and, in some instances, inhibiting factors. The activity of hypothalamic neuroendocrine cells is regulated by a variety of neurotransmitters including the biogenic amines. It appears probable that any given endocrine response is under the simultaneous control of several neurotransmitter systems.

The synthesis and secretion of adrenal corticosteroids is controlled by *adrenocorticotropin* (ACTH) from the pituitary. Secretion of ACTH, is regulated, in turn, by corticotropin-releasing factor (CRF) from the hypothalamus. Secretion of adrenal corticosteroids in depressed patients has been studied more extensively than any other hormone system. Hypersecretion of cortisol occurs in many severely depressed patients, particularly those experiencing severe anxiety, active suicidal impulses, or psychotic decompensation. After clinical recovery, cortisol secretion approaches normal. Hypersecretion of cortisol occurs more frequently in patients with unipolar depressions than in patients with bipolar depressive disorders.

While it has been suggested that nonspecific psychological stress may contribute to the hypersecretion of cortisol in depressed patients, recent findings suggest that cortisol hypersecretion reflects a more fundamental and specific neuroendocrine abnormality in depressive disorders. In addition to the increase in total cortisol secretion, the pattern of secretion is also altered; in many depressed patients, cortisol secretion fails to turn off from the late evening through the early morning hours as it does in normal subjects. In at least some depressed patients, the hypersecretion of cortisol, particularly in the late evening, is resistant to suppression by dexamethosone.

Growth hormone (GH) is normally secreted from the anterior pituitary in response to falling blood sugar, among other stimuli; the response to insulin-induced hypoglycemia is commonly used to test for the adequacy of GH secretion. Several investigators have reported that some depressed patients show relatively deficient GH responses to hypoglycemia when compared with control subjects; one group has observed deficient GH responses to orally administered L-5-hydroxytryptophan in depressions. While de-

pressed patients were also initially reported to show diminished GH responses to orally administered L-dihydroxyphenylalanine (L-dopa), this decrease was not observed in a subsequent study when the possible effects of menopause were controlled. Clarification of the neuroendocrine basis for these findings awaits further research.

In postmenopausal women the secretion of *luteinizing hormone* (LH) from the anterior pituitary rises markedly. In one recent study, postmenopausal women with primary unipolar depressions had significantly lower plasma LH concentrations than did normal postmenopausal women. The specific neuroendocrine basis for these changes remains to be elucidated, although there is some evidence that brain catecholamines may be involved.

Base-line measures of pituitary-thyroid function are generally normal in depressed patients. However, several groups of investigators recently observed a diminished secretion of *thyroid-stimulating hormone* (TSH) in response to the administration of *thyrotropin-releasing hormone* (TRH) in depressed patients. Exploration of the physiological basis of this finding will require further study. (Neuroendocrine studies are discussed in more detail in Carroll and Mendels, 1976; Sachar, 1975, 1976; Schildkraut, Sachar, and Baer, 1976.)

Electrolyte Metabolism

Many investigators have studied electrolyte metabolism in patients with affective disorders. Sodium metabolism has been examined most extensively, and it is now fairly clear that sodium retention (measured by a number of different techniques) is greater during depression than after recovery, although the physiological basis for this phenomenon is unknown. Changes in sodium metabolism during mania or hypomania have been studied less extensively, and the findings have been inconsistent.

Consistent findings have not yet emerged from studies of the metabolism and distribution of potassium in depressive disorders, although abnormalities have been reported by some investigators. Studies of the metabolism of calcium and magnesium in depressive disorders have not yet produced a consistent body of data, although the findings of one group of investigators suggest that urinary excretion of calcium decreases during recovery from depression. Further research will be required in this area. (For further discussion of the topics, see Baer, 1973; Durell, 1974; Schildkraut, Sachar, and Baer, 1976.)

Overview

The clinical and biological heterogeneity of the affective disorders has long been recognized in psychiatry. This heterogeneity has been evidenced in recent years by the differential responses of various types of depressions to different treatments. Recent studies of biogenic amine metabolism in patients with affective disorders have revealed important clues to the pathophysiological substrates underlying this heterogeneity and support the hypothesis that specific subgroups of patients with depressive disorders may exhibit specific abnormalities in the metabolism of one or another of the biogenic amines. Moreover, these findings appear compatible with the possibility that, in patients with affective disorders, some changes in biogenic amine metabolism may occur in association with changes in affective state; other abnormalities in monoamine metabolism may represent enduring constitutional factors.

It is important, however, to avoid simplistic interpretations; measurements of the levels of monoamines and their metabolites in various tissues (including the brain) and body fluids (including the CSF) do not enable us to distinguish among the underlying physiological processes. Low levels of a monoamine or metabolite, for example, might occur either with a primary deficiency in synthesis leading to a decrease of the monoamine at receptors or with a feedback-induced decrease in synthesis secondary to an excess of the monoamine at receptors. Similarly, high levels of a monoamine metabolite could occur either with a primary increase in synthesis leading to a greater quantity of the monoamine at receptors or with a feedback-induced rise in synthesis secondary to a functional deficiency of the monoamine at receptors; such a deficiency might be due to increased inactivation of the monoamine or to decreased receptor sensitivity to the monoamine. Clarification of the underlying pathophysiological processes in patients with depressions and manias may come with further understanding of the neurochemical effects of drugs used in their treatment.

While individual studies have focused on one or another of the monoamines, physiological interactions between monoaminergic neuronal systems (noradrenergic, dopaminergic, and serotonergic) are well documented. It appears that biochemical and physiological processes involving one monoamine may be modulated by another. Alterations in cholinergic activity also may be involved in the pathophysiology of the affective disorders, and recent findings suggest that physostigmine, an acetylcholinesterase inhibitor, can transiently decrease manic symptoms as well as precipitate depressions (see Janowsky, El-Yousef, and Davis, 1974).

Heuristic hypotheses relating the affective disorders to alterations in biogenic amine metabolism are at best reductionistic oversimplifications of complex biological states involving many other biochemical, physiological, and psychological factors. Included among these are abnormalities in neuroendocrine regulation and electrolyte metabolism. Current evidence does not permit the meaningful integration of these diverse findings. Some of the endocrine changes associated with depressive disorders, however, may reflect abnormalities in monoaminergic neuronal systems within the brain, particularly the hypothalamus.

Investigators have recently undertaken to examine biochemical variables in relation to existing clinical categories such as endogenous and nonendogenous depressions, chronic characterological depressions, bipolar manic-depressive depressions, and unipolar depressions. However, these clinical categories are not defined in identical terms by all investigators and comparing findings from different studies is therefore difficult. Furthermore, since it is generally agreed that these clinically defined categories do not necessarily represent biologically homogeneous entities, it may be strategically more useful to examine the possibility that biochemical criteria, perhaps in combination with specific clinical criteria, could serve as independent variables for classifying subtypes of depressive disorders. Such an approach could lead to new categories that are biologically more meaningful and therapeutically more relevant than those defined under any currently available system of clinical classification.

Following the advances in other areas of medical nosology, many investigators now envision the development of a psychiatric nosology based not only on the clinical phenomenology of affective disorders but also on knowledge of the biochemical mechanisms underlying these phenomena. It now seems likely that biochemical tests may become as routine in the diagnostic workup of patients with affective disorders as they are currently in the evaluation of patients with other types of metabolic disorders.

References

Baer, L. 1973. Electrolyte metabolism in psychiatric disorders. In *Biological Psychiatry*, ed. J. Mendels. New York: Wiley-Interscience.

Bunney, W. E., Jr., and J. M. Davis. 1965. Norepinephrine in depressive reactions. *Arch. Gen. Psychiatry* 13:483–494.

Carroll, B. J., and J. Mendels. 1976. Neuroendocrine regulation in affective disorders. In *Hormones, behavior and psychopathology*, ed. E. J. Sachar. New York: Raven Press.

Coppen, A. 1974. Serotonin in the affective disorders. In *Factors in depression*, ed. N. S. Kline. New York: Raven Press.

Durell, J. 1974. Sodium and potassium metabolism: lithium salts and affective disorders. In *Factors in depression*, ed. N. S. Kline. New York: Raven Press.

Goodwin, F. K., and R. M. Post. 1975. Studies of amine metabolites in affective illness and in schizophrenia: a comparative analysis. In *Biology of the major psychoses*, ed. D. X. Freedman. Res. Publ. Assoc. Res. Nerv. Ment. Dis., vol. 54. New York: Raven Press.

Janowsky, D. S., M. Khaled El-Yousef, and J. M. Davis. 1974. Acetylcholine and depression. *Psychosom. Med.* 36:248–257.

Maas, J. W. 1975. Biogenic amines and depression. *Arch. Gen. Psychiatry* 32:1357–61.

Maas, J. W., H. Dekirmenjian, and J. A. Fawcett. 1974. MHPG excretion by patients with affective disorders. *Int. Pharmacopsychiatry* 9:14–26.

Murphy, D. L., and R. J. Wyatt. 1975. Neurotransmitter-related enzymes in the major psychiatric disorders: 1. catechol-O-methyl transferase, monoamine oxidase in the affective disorders, and factors affecting some behaviorally correlated enzyme activities. In *Biology of the major psychoses*, ed. D. X. Freedman. Res. Publ. Assoc. Res. Nerv. Ment. Dis., vol. 54. New York: Raven Press.

Sachar, E. J. 1975. Evidence for neuroendocrine abnormalities in the major mental illnesses. In *Biology of the major psychoses*, ed. D. X. Freedman. Res. Publ. Assoc. Res. Nerv. Ment. Dis., vol. 54. New York: Raven Press.

——— 1976. Neuroendocrine dysfunction in depressive illness. *Annu. Rev. Med.* 27:389–396.

Schildkraut, J. J. 1965. The catecholamine hypothesis of affective disorders: a review of supporting evidence. *Am. J. Psychiatry* 122:509–522.

——— 1970. *Neuropsychopharmacology and the affective disorders*. Boston: Little, Brown.

——— 1973. The effects of lithium on biogenic amines. In *Lithium: its role in psychiatric research and treatment*, ed. S. Gershon and B. Shopsin. New York: Plenum Press.

——— 1974a. Biochemical criteria for classifying depressive disorders and predicting responses to pharmacotherapy: preliminary findings from studies of norepinephrine metabolism. *Pharmakopsychiatr. Neuropsychopharmakol.* 7:98–107.

——— 1974b. Biogenic amines and affective disorders. *Annu. Rev. Med.* 25:333–348.

Schildkraut, J. J., and S. S. Kety. 1967. Biogenic amines and emotion. *Science* 156:21–30.

Schildkraut, J. J., E. J. Sachar, and L. Baer. 1976. Biochemistry of affective disorders. In *Psychotherapeutic drugs*, ed. E. Usdin and I. A. Forrest. New York: Dekker.

Van Praag, H. M. 1974. Towards a biochemical typology of depression? *Pharmakopsychiatrie* 7:281–292.

Genetic and Biochemical Aspects of Schizophrenia

CHAPTER 6

Seymour S. Kety

T HE MODERN SCIENCE of genetics has revolutionized cell biology and contributed significantly to the understanding of a large number of medical diseases. It has only recently begun to have an impact on psychiatry. A large number of problems peculiar to psychiatry have contributed to this lag. Human behavior, which is the special concern of psychiatry, is particularly sensitive to scientific scrutiny. Because of its real or assumed theological, social, and political implications—about which there are powerful divisions and polarizations—the study of genetic factors in normal and abnormal human behavior is sometimes seen as a threat to deeply held convictions.

Psychiatric genetics also encounters other difficulties of interpretation. The phenomena that constitute its data are more complex, more subjective, more difficult to quantify and objectify than those that are the province of other branches of medicine, and the major mental illnesses have yet to be clearly delineated and classified. At this time, genetic factors have been elucidated and their mode of transmission clearly specified only in mental disorders such as the mental deficiencies in which a specific, pathognomonic biochemical defect has been estab-

lished and serves as a genetic marker. Of the several hundred such disorders that have been characterized, a few representative ones will be discussed here.

Gregor Mendel, from careful naturalistic observations and experiments more than a hundred years ago, deduced the fundamental principle of genetics—that hereditary traits are transmitted from parents to offspring in the form of paired units, one derived from each parent. These we now recognize as the genes representing specific nucleotide sequences in the long DNA strand that forms the genetic skeleton of a chromosome. In the human species there are twenty-three pairs of chromosomes, one of each pair coming from each parent. One pair represents the sex chromosomes; the remaining twenty-two are called autosomes. Genetic male characteristics are transmitted as a modified form of the X or female chromosome; this modification is called the Y chromosome. The sex chromosome pair is XX in female offspring and XY in male offspring. In the male the X member is derived from the mother and the Y member, from the father.

Each gene determines the synthesis of a specific type of RNA that, in turn, determines the synthesis of a specific protein, which may be a structural component or an enzyme. If one gene of a pair is absent or defective, the individual will suffer a reduction in that particular protein of roughly 50 percent. If both genes are affected, the amount will be reduced to a negligible value. Where a 50-percent reduction in the protein is enough to interfere with its normal function, a dominant disorder will result, since one defective gene will produce the defect in spite of the presence of one normal gene. If a 50-percent reduction still permits normal function, both members of the pair will have to be defective to produce a disorder, which will then be a recessive disorder.

In the course of the cell divisions necessary to form an ovum or spermatozoon, the paired chromosomes are separated so that the final sperm or egg cell contains only one member of each chromosome pair. New pairs are established in fertilization. Sometimes this separation of the pairs does not occur, so that a germ cell may result that has one of its chromosomes paired, and the resulting fertilized egg will contain three representatives of that chromosome. In most cases the resulting individual will be defective by virtue of an excess of certain gene products, the characteristics of the disorder depending upon the chromosome that is triplicated. Down's syndrome (mongolism) results from a trisomy or triplication of chromosome 21. In a much rarer form of Down's syndrome, the gene excess is produced by an abnormal chromosome 15 containing a supernumerary fragment of a chromosome 21. In contrast to trisomy of autosomes, disturbances in the number of sex chromosomes (XXX, XXY, XYY, and XO) are associated with relatively mild somatic and mental defects.

A large number of single-gene defects leading to mental retardation have been identified. Some are associated with psychosis. The first of these to be described was phenylketonuria (PKU), an autosomal recessive deficiency of phenylalanine hydroxylase. The intellectual deficit can be minimized by a low-phenylalanine diet during the first few years of life. Galactosemia, also an autosomal recessive defect, can similarly be effectively treated by excluding milk from the diet. A third genetic disorder in which early recognition and intervention may prevent mental retardation is maple syrup disease, in which there is a failure to decarboxylate the branched-chain amino acids (leucine, isoleucine, and valine). A diet very low in these amino acids has been used with encouraging results.

In Hartnup disease, another autosomal recessive defect, there is disordered tryptophan transport with manifestations very similar to those of pellagra. Transient personality changes, dementia, or psychosis may be the only manifestation of the disease. Lesch-Nyhan syndrome is an X-linked recessive defect in purine metabolism leading to severe mental retardation and also to a characteristic type of self-mutilating behavior.

Genetic Factors in Schizophrenia

In schizophrenia there are as yet no specific and pathognomonic genetic markers. Evidence for the significant operation of genetic factors in schizophrenia has been difficult to obtain, and their mode of transmission has yet to be established.

Schizophrenia and the affective disorders are at present phenomenological syndromes, and there is little reason to insist that they represent single diseases. The ascertainment of their presence in the population, their characterization and nomenclature are often quite arbitrary, strongly influenced by social and cultural factors, by schools of psychiatric thought, and by subjective biases that can be minimized only with great care. If more patients suffer from schizophrenic illness than are seen by psychiatrists, as total population surveys indicate, then a family with two schizophrenic members will have a greater chance of being discovered than a family with only one. Thus a selective bias favors familial patterns in such mental illnesses. In addition, since diagnosis depends upon a subjective evaluation that, though very sensitive, is susceptible to bias from preconceived hypotheses, a diagnosis of schizophrenia in one member of a family is apt to increase the probability of a similar diagnosis for other family members who show psychiatric disorder. Finally there is the epistemological problem of the nature of the conclusions permissible from the data available. The tendency to infer proof of a hypothesis from observations that are simply compatible with it has often led to premature conclusions regarding the overriding importance of either genetic or environmental factors.

The finding that a disorder runs in families is usually the first evidence suggesting that genetic factors may be important, and this has been the case in schizophrenia. A number of epidemiological studies confirm the experience of individual psychiatrists that the close relatives of schizophrenics show a considerably elevated incidence of the disorder. Whereas the incidence in the general population is somewhat less than 1 percent, the incidence in parents of schizophrenics is 5 percent, and in their siblings and children, approximately 10 percent (Slater and Cowie, 1971). The incidence figure for parents of schizophrenics is probably misleadingly low and can be accounted for by the attenuation of information from older records and especially by the selective factors that operate in mating and marriage to reduce the probability that an overt schizophrenic will become a parent. Leaving aside ascertainment and diagnostic biases discussed previously and accepting the higher risk of schizophrenia in the relatives of schizophrenic patients at its face value, it does not necessarily constitute strong evidence for the operation of genetic factors since families share both their genetic endowment and their environmental influences. Pellagra, which also shows a strong familial tendency, was at one time erroneously regarded by some on that basis as a simple genetic disease.

More compelling evidence has come from studies of the incidence of schizophrenia in the monozygotic and dizygotic twins of schizophrenics. Since the former are practically identical genetically while the latter share no more of their genetic constitution than do siblings, a disorder in which genetic factors played an important role would be expected to have a high concordance (or coincidence) rate in monozygotic twins and a concordance rate in dizygotic twins not significantly different from its coincidence in siblings. Studies of schizophrenia in twins over the past fifty years have found with remarkable consistency that the concordance rate in dizygotic twins is similar to that in siblings, whereas in monozygotic twins it may be two to six times as high (Gottesman and Shields, 1972). It has been argued that these differences may be inflated to some extent by virtue of selective and subjective biases as well as by the fact that monozygotic twins share more of their environment than do dizygotic twins even of the same sex (Kety, 1959; Rosenthal, 1962). It is not likely, however, that this fact can account for the entire difference, since dizygotic twins in turn share considerably more of their environment than do siblings of different ages; yet the concordance rate in both types of relationship is remarkably close.

The most definitive twin study and one that took great pains to avoid these sources of error was described recently by Gottesman and Shields (1972). The study was based upon fifty-seven twin pairs in which at least one member of each pair was schizophrenic. There were twenty-four monozygotic and thirty-three dizygotic pairs, and these were discovered systematically in a total of 45,000 patients treated at the Maudsley Hospital over a period of sixteen years. Subjective bias and the effect of different psychiatric acculturation and persuasion were ingeniously minimized by presenting six judges of different backgrounds and orientation (from England, the United States, and Japan) with case summaries of the 114 individuals. Each made his own diagnosis on every case record independently and without knowledge of the relationship of one case to another. In contradiction to claims that psychiatrists cannot distinguish the insane from the sane, the six raters showed a good degree of agreement in their diagnoses of schizophrenia and normality. Each found a higher concordance of schizophrenia in the monozygotic than in the dizygotic twins, and their consensus yielded a concordance of 40 to 50 percent in the monozygotic and 9 to 10 percent in the dizygotic pairs. Although this study laid to rest the notions that schizophrenia is a myth and that it cannot be recognized reliably, environmental variables could not be controlled; their contribution to the difference in concordance rates between monozygotic and dizygotic twins cannot be ruled out.

A recent device for disentangling genetic from environmental variables has been the study of adopted individuals and their biological and adoptive relatives since, unlike naturally reared individuals, an adopted person receives his genetic endowment from one family but shares his environment with another (Kety, 1959).

Using this concept, several groups have reported observations or conducted studies of the incidence of schizophrenia in individuals related either genetically or environmentally to schizophrenic probands—that is, to schizophrenic family members who brought the family under study. In examining the pedigrees of schizophrenics in Iceland, Karlsson (1966) discovered a number of individuals closely related genetically to schizophrenics but who had lived apart from them. They showed a high incidence of schizophrenia in contrast to the general population and even in contrast to a group of people reared with schizophrenics to whom they were not genetically related. Heston (1966), in a survey of Oregon state psychiatric hospitals, identified forty-seven individuals, with a mean age of thirty-six, born to known schizophrenic mothers but reared apart from them. Of these, five had become schizophrenic; of fifty controls born to nonschizophrenic mothers but reared by others, none had become schizophrenic. Both types of individual in Heston's study were fairly evenly divided between those reared in institutions and those brought up in foster or adoptive families. Comparing the incidence of schizophrenia and other forms of psychopathology in the two groups with different types of rearing, he found no significant differences.

In 1963 a group of American and Danish investigators began to compile a total sample of adults in Denmark who had been legally adopted at an early age by people not biologically related to them. The compilation began with those adopted in the city or county of Copenhagen and was used as the basis of several different investigations of the genetic and environmental influences of schizophrenia (Kety et al., 1968; Rosenthal et al., 1971; Wender et al., 1974; Kety et al., 1975). It has since been extended to all of Denmark and used in the study of other mental and behavioral disorders.

One of the studies in schizophrenia examined the type and prevalence of mental illness in the biological and adoptive relatives of adoptees who had become schizophrenic (Kety et al., 1975). Thirty-three schizophrenic adoptees (called "index" adoptees) were selected by independent re-

view of the abstracts of the institutional records of adoptees who had been admitted to a mental institution at some time. Unanimous agreement on a diagnosis of chronic, latent, or acute schizophrenia was arrived at among four raters. A control group of adoptees who had not been admitted to a psychiatric facility was selected by matching with each index case on the basis of age, sex, socioeconomic class of the rearing family, time spent with biological relatives, periods in child-care institutions, or placement in a foster home before transfer to the adopting family.

A total of 512 relatives of the 33 schizophrenic adoptees and their controls were identified through population records. Of these, 119 had died and 29 had emigrated or disappeared. Of the remaining 364 relatives, more than 90 percent participated in an exhaustive interview conducted by a psychiatrist who had not been informed about the relationship of any subject to a proband. Extensive summaries of these interviews were then prepared, edited to remove any clues regarding the relationship of the subject to a proband, and read independently by each of three raters. These raters independently recorded their best psychiatric diagnoses for each subject from a list of possible diagnoses—covering the entire range of the American Psychiatric Association's *Diagnostic and Statistical Manual of Mental Disorders*—from no mental disorder to chronic schizophrenia. After a consensus was arrived at among the three raters, the code was broken and the subjects were allocated to their respective four groups: biological or adoptive relatives of schizophrenic index adoptees and biological or adoptive relatives of control adoptees.

Of these four populations, the biological relatives of the schizophrenic adoptees differed from the rest in being genetically related to a schizophrenic with whom they had not lived. With regard to mental illness other than schizophrenia, these relatives did not differ from the three types of relatives unrelated genetically to a schizophrenic adoptee. In the case of schizophrenia, however, there was a higher prevalence in the biological relatives of index cases than among persons who were not genetically related to a schizophrenic. For chronic schizophrenia, prevalence in the biological relatives of index cases was 2.9 percent compared with 0.6 percent in the others; for latent schizophrenia, it was 3.5 percent compared with 1.2 percent; and for uncertain schizophrenia, it was 7.5 percent compared with 2 percent. Overall, 13.9 percent of those genetically related to the schizophrenic index cases received one of these diagnoses, compared with 2.7 percent of the adoptive relatives of schizophrenics. The difference between the group genetically related to the schizophrenic index cases and those not so related is highly significant statistically and speaks for the operation of genetic factors in the transmission of schizophrenia. Little evidence of schizophrenic illness was found in the biological relatives of probands diagnosed as having "acute schizophrenic reaction."

These findings are compatible with a genetic transmission in schizophrenia, but they are not entirely conclusive, since possible environmental factors such as *in utero* influences, birth trauma, and early mothering experiences were not ruled out. The study included, however, biological paternal half siblings of index cases and controls who had only a genetic relationship to their proband; they shared the same father but not the same mother, neonatal mothering experience, or *in utero* or postnatal environment with their adopted half siblings. A significant concentration of schizophrenia and of uncertain schizophrenia was found in the paternal half siblings of the schizophrenic index cases with whom they had shared no prenatal or postnatal environment.

Although these observations indicate that genetic factors are important in schizophrenia, they do not exclude the operation of environmental factors on a genetically transmitted predisposition to schizophrenia, as indicated by the 50 percent discordance for schizophrenia in monozygotic twins. The nature of the crucial environmental factors has not been established. They may depend upon interaction with other members of the family or on other social influences. They may also be related to birth trauma, diet, or infection.

These observations do not permit the conclusion that schizophrenia is a unitary disorder, since they are equally compatible with a syndrome of multiple etiologies and different modes of genetic transmission. A number of clearly defined genetic disorders may be associated at some time in their course with behavioral states closely resembling or indistinguishable from schizophrenia. Huntington's chorea often begins with schizophrenialike manifestations, as does Wilson's disease. Metachromatic leukodystrophy is an autosomal recessive deficiency of cerebroside sulfatase leading to mental retardation and early death. This disorder has an adult form of which more than twenty cases have been reported, and each of these was first diagnosed and institutionalized as schizophrenic before the development of neurological symptoms. One case has been reported of schizophrenia associated with homocystinuria. The metabolic defect was shown to be genetic and to result from a deficiency of the enzyme methylene tetrahydrofolate reductase. The patient was also mentally retarded. Treatment with folic acid, which was expected to bypass the enzymatic defect, resulted in a disappearance of the schizophrenic manifestation in each of several trials. It is possible that schizophrenia will some day be found to consist of several different disorders with a final common path.

Evidence that genetic factors are important in the etiology of schizophrenia has some implications in regard to the advice that psychiatrists can give to patients and their families. The feeling of guilt that commonly exists in the parents of schizophrenics derives from the widely promulgated but unproven hypothesis that the parents' interaction with and rearing of the child plays a crucial role in the development of the disorder. Knowledge that genetic factors are important, although we do not know their mode of expression, and that environmental factors are equally important, although we do not know specifically what they are, should diminish both the complacency of the psychiatrist and the guilt of the parents.

Newly acquired information about the etiology of schizophrenia complements the body of knowledge that already exists to provide the basis for genetic counseling. Even in the absence of an accepted theory of genetic transmission and without the ability to ascribe etiological significance to particular environmental variables, it is still possible to estimate the risk of the occurrence of schizophrenia in the relative of a schizophrenic person on the basis of empirical information. Certain caveats, however, should be given serious consideration.

First, the empirical risk figures for the development of schizophrenia in relatives of a schizophrenic patient (10 percent in full siblings and children) were obtained from and hold for classical chronic schizophrenic illness. For the recent accretions to the syndrome such as latent schizophrenia and especially acute schizophrenic reaction, comparable risk data do not exist; in any case the risk is likely to be considerably less. The certainty of the diagnosis and the severity of illness in the affected relative is therefore of crucial importance in predicting the probability of occurrence in other members of the family.

Second, the empirical risk figure for a relative is the risk over a normal lifetime and is most appropriately applicable to children not yet born. A thirty-year-old adult who has not developed schizophrenia has a considerably smaller chance of developing the disorder (approximately 50 percent of the risk he had at birth), and in one who had reached the age of forty-five or fifty the remaining risk of schizophrenia would be small indeed.

Third, the risk in an individual should increase with the number of his relatives who evidence definite schizophrenia and with the closeness of their relationship to him. Thus the risk in the offspring of two schizophrenics is not 10 percent but closer to 40 percent. The best estimate of risk would take these factors into account along with the age of the respective relatives and the number without any indications of schizophrenia. Adoption randomizes the unknown environmental variables but does not remove them. Studies using adopted individuals, already described, indicate that the risks for schizophrenia in biological relatives are not appreciably altered by the process of adoption.

Biochemical Factors in Schizophrenia

If genetic factors play a significant role in the etiology of schizophrenia, then biochemical factors must do so as well, since the genes can only operate through biochemical mechanisms. The idea that schizophrenia has a biochemical basis is not new. The Hippocratic physicians postulated that insanity resided in the brain and was the result of chemical disturbances there. In the last century, Thudichum restated that hypothesis, though he wisely decided that it was important first to understand the normal chemistry of the brain. Until recently, biochemical attacks on schizophrenia were premature and simplistic, elaborated without substantive knowledge. The optimistic results reported were often the consequence of dietary, pharmacological, or other nondisease variables (see Kety, 1959). Such studies were inadequately controlled and could not be confirmed.

Meanwhile, there has been a remarkable increase in fundamental knowledge about the biochemistry of the brain, the physiology and pharmacology of the synapse, and the relationships between these and behavior. A few cautious hypotheses are emerging. These represent not great leaps from insufficient basic information but rather short and logical steps. Two hypotheses relating to the biological substrates of schizophrenia that have stimulated considerable research activity are discussed below.

Transmethylation

In 1952, Harley-Mason speculated that biological transmethylation might be involved in schizophrenia (see Osmond and Smythies, 1952). He was impressed that many hallucinogens were methylated substances and that one of these, mescaline, would result from the O-methylation of dopamine at the 3, 4, and 5 positions. Although O-methylation of catecholamines had not yet been described, he postulated that this might occur and that in schizophrenia there might be an accumulation of hallucinogenic methylated metabolites. He singled out 3,4-dimethoxyphenylethylamine as being of special interest since it had been reported to produce catatonic behavior in animals.

This hypothesis received its first test in the administration of niacin or niacinamide in large doses to schizophrenics based on the thesis that these substances would be methylated and competitively divert the biological transmethylation process away from the production of hallucinogenic substances. The striking therapeutic results that were at first reported have not been confirmed in more recent controlled trials. The administration of niacinamide to animals does not significantly depress brain levels of S-adenosylmethionine. Therefore, niacinamide is not an effective methyl acceptor in the brain and its administration did not constitute a test of the transmethylation hypothesis. The hypothesis was later tested in another manner by Pollin and his associates (1961), who administered methionine to schizophrenic patients in conjunction with a monoamine oxidase inhibitor. Methionine can increase S-adenosylmethionine levels and enhance transmethylation. In approximately one-third of the patients, psychosis was briefly exacerbated, and this phenomenon has been reported in subsequent studies. Methionine alone, without monoamine oxidase inhibition, can produce the same manifestation in schizophrenic patients. Although it is difficult to exclude the possibility that methionine produces a toxic psychosis superimposed on schizophrenia, normal subjects who receive the same dose of methionine experience no such effect. Thus the results in schizophrenia are compatible with the hypothesis, although alternative possibilities have not been ruled out.

Evidence for the existence of an enzyme, indoleamine-N-methyltransferase, in several tissues including the brain (Saavedra, Coyle, and Axelrod, 1973) has been obtained. This enzyme is capable of methylating tryptamine to dimethyltryptamine, although it does not methylate serotonin. Several studies report finding methylated indoleamines in the blood or urine of schizophrenics, and some suggest a correlation with the intensity of psychosis occurring either spontaneously or in association with the ingestion of methyl donors. Since one of these, dimethyltryptamine, is known to be a potent hallucinogen, such observations are quite provocative. They have not, however, been confirmed by unassailable analytical techniques.

The recent finding of a significantly diminished level of monoamine oxidase in the platelets of schizophrenic patients (Wyatt et al., 1973) has aroused considerable interest; it has been confirmed by several but not all groups. Low monoamine oxidase levels are found in the biological relatives of schizophrenics including monozygotic twins who may themselves not be schizophrenic. This finding—which should be free of the artifacts introduced by drugs, institutionalization, and other nondisease variables—suggests that a reduced level of monoamine oxidase in some schizophrenic patients is a genetic characteristic. If hallucinogenic methylated amines are formed in normal individuals but detoxified by monoamine oxidase, then a diminution of this enzyme in schizophrenia could account for an abnormal accumulation of such amines in those affected.

The Dopamine Hypothesis

Pharmacology offers two approaches to the pathogenesis of a disorder. One is to investigate the mechanism of action of drugs that ameliorate the disorder; the other, to examine the actions of drugs that produce or mimic the disorder. In the case of schizophrenia, both of these approaches have been pursued.

Since the discovery in 1951 that chlorpromazine was beneficial in the treatment of schizophrenic patients, a number of phenothiazine derivatives have been prepared, many of which have antipsychotic properties. Later, haloperidol, a butyrophenone not chemically related to the phenothiazines, was also found to be effective in the treatment of schizophrenia. As both groups of drugs came into wide use, it became evident that an important side effect of both was the development of symptoms like those of Parkinson's disease, in which the nigrostriatal system of the brain was known to be involved. With the elucidation of dopamine as the transmitter in the nigrostriatal pathway and the discovery that this amine is deficient in the caudate nucleus of patients suffering from Parkinson's disease, it became possible to explain the extrapyramidal effects of the antipsychotic drugs as an action on dopamine. Carlsson and Lindqvist (1963) first suggested that antipsychotic drugs acted by blockade of dopamine receptors. They found that chlorpromazine and haloperidol increased the levels of dopamine metabolites in the brain while promethazine, a phenothiazine drug not effective in schizophrenia, did not.

They speculated that an increased release of dopamine in the case of the active antipsychotic drugs was brought about by a feedback mechanism in response to the blockade of dopamine receptors. Since that observation, evidence has accumulated to establish that such a blockade of dopamine does occur. Several pharmacological studies have confirmed the increased synthesis and turnover of dopamine in the brain in response to psychoactive congeners. Blockade of dopamine receptors has been demonstrated physiologically by microelectrode recording techniques and biochemically on dopamine-sensitive adenylate cyclase of the brain. Matthysse (1973) has pointed out that the phenothiazines have a notoriously wide spectrum of actions from effects on protozoan motility to the pecking behavior of pigeons and that a criterion for the mechanism involved in antipsychotic activity would be the ability of the effect to discriminate between effective and ineffective phenothiazines and butyrophenones. To a considerable extent, that criterion has been met in the case of dopamine receptor blockade. In the case of two exceptions, thioridazine and clozapine, potent antipsychotic drugs without parkinsonian side effects, Snyder has suggested that their anticholinergic properties may prevent the extrapyramidal effects and has demonstrated that these two drugs have the greatest anticholinergic effects of any of the antipsychotic agents.

Although the phenothiazines were at first thought to be useful merely as "tranquilizers" of disturbed behavior, it became apparent that they had specific effects on the cardinal features of schizophrenia. In contrast to sedative agents like the barbiturates or antianxiety drugs like diazepam, which were no more effective than placebo in the treatment of schizophrenics, chlorpromazine in large-scale controlled studies produced significant improvement in thought disorder, blunted affect, withdrawal, and autistic behavior, all characteristics of schizophrenia as described by Bleuler. The ability of these agents to activate some withdrawn patients and to modify their flat affect toward normal is in no way a sedative or tranquilizing effect.

Although lysergic acid diethylamide (LSD) commands considerable interest because of its ability to produce a toxic psychosis thought to resemble schizophrenia, the psychosis induced by amphetamine overdose is in fact much closer to schizophrenia and has often been confused with that disorder even by experienced clinicians. Chronic amphetamine toxicity is characterized by a paranoid psychosis, auditory hallucinations, and stereotyped behavior with little delirium or confusion. Schizophrenic patients have reportedly been able to recognize an LSD psychosis as different from their usual symptoms but have been unable to differentiate an amphetamine psychosis. Furthermore, amphetamine, methylphenidate, and L-dopa can precipitate active schizophrenia in schizophrenic patients during remission.

There is evidence to suggest that amphetamine psychosis is mediated through release and potentiation of dopamine at specific receptors in the brain. The stereotyped behavior induced in animals by amphetamine can be prevented by lesions of the dopamine pathways. Dopamine itself or apomorphine, which is known to stimulate dopamine receptors, will produce stereotypy when injected in the brain.

In summary, several types of agents show a remarkable convergence on dopamine synapses in the brain (Matthysse and Kety, 1975). Amphetamine, the drug that produces a psychosis most closely resembling schizophrenia, appears to act by potentiating dopamine at its synapses in the brain. A large number of drugs in different chemical classes are able to block dopamine receptors and have specific beneficial effects on the cardinal features of schizophrenia. This effect has led to the hypothesis that an overactivity of dopamine synapses may play a crucial role in the pathogenesis of schizophrenia, although no evidence for an increased turnover of dopamine in schizophrenic patients has been found.

Although hyperactivity of dopamine synapses could explain certain features of schizophrenia such as stereotyped behavior, paranoid delusions, and auditory hallucinations, it would not in itself account for other characteristics of schizophrenia, such as anhedonia, withdrawal, autism, and flatness of affect. These manifestations involve behavioral components that in animals appear to be related to the activity of norepinephrine. Thus considerable indirect evidence indicates that norephinephrine pathways are involved in appetitive or reward behavior, in exploratory activity, and in elevated mood. In schizophrenia, then, it is possible that anhedonia, withdrawal, and flatness of affect represent an insufficiency of norepinephrine at its synapses. A parsimonious mechanism exists that could produce both the increase in dopamine activity and the decrease in norepinephrine activity required by the more complete explanation of the symptoms. That mechanism may be the enzyme dopamine-β-hydroxylase, which converts dopamine to norepinephrine at noradrenergic endings in the brain. A throttling of that enzyme could conceivably result in the release of dopamine at the expense of norepinephrine. Wise and Stein (1973) have reported significant diminution in dopamine-β-hydroxylase in post mortem studies of the brains of schizophrenics. A replicatory study by another group found a diminution that was not significant.

Other biochemical findings in schizophrenia involve serotonin, histamine, and acetylcholine, although they are few and their significance remains to be explored. A reciprocal relationship between cholinergic and catecholamine pathways is suggested by the ability of physostigmine to prevent the acute exacerbation of psychosis that can be precipitated by methylphenidate in schizophrenics during remission. The insensitivity of schizophrenics to histamine, as evidenced by a diminution in the wheal ordinarily produced by histamine, has not yet been explained.

Although the synapse is crucial to higher nervous activity and is likely to be the important site of action of drugs, hormones, and metabolic derangements that affect the mind, the number of neurotransmitters and other modulators of synaptic activity is legion. For example, γ-aminobutyric acid (GABA) is a ubiquitous neurotransmitter that has important interactions with the catecholamine system. A number of polypeptides discovered in the hypothalamus where they regulate the release of pituitary hormones are now known to have a wide distribution in the brain and to exert more general actions. Even though the antipsychotic drugs may act by blocking dopamine receptors, their effectiveness in schizophrenia need not imply a primary deficit

there and would be equally compatible with disturbances in other systems that interact with dopamine synapses.

Although biochemistry hardly offers an adequate explanation of behavior, mood, cognition, or their disturbances in the major psychoses, it is apparent that considerable progress has been made. The relevance of certain areas of research, notably investigations of the synaptic functions of the biogenic amines and other modulators of synaptic activity, has become more clearly established. The effectiveness of certain drugs in controlling psychotic manifestations of schizophrenia, recent demonstrations of the chemical nature of the synapse, and indications of the significant role that genetic factors play in the genesis of schizophrenia offer persuasive evidence of the existence of biochemical disturbances within schizophrenia; newly developed techniques should enhance the opportunities for elucidating the nature and function of these disturbances.

References

Carlsson, A., and M. Lindqvist. 1963. Effect of chlorpromazine or haloperidol on formation of 3-methoxytyramine and normetanephrine in mouse brain. *Acta Pharmacol.* 20:140–144.

Gottesman, I. I., and J. Shields. 1972. *Schizophrenia and genetics: a twin study vantage point*. New York: Academic Press.

Heston, L. L. 1966. Psychiatric disorders in foster home reared children of schizophrenic mothers. *Br. J. Psychiatry* 112:819–825.

Karlsson, J. L. 1966. *The biologic base of schizophrenia*. Springfield, Ill.: Thomas.

Kety, S. S. 1959. Biochemical theories of schizophrenia. *Science* 129:1528–1532, 1590–1596.

Kety, S. S., D. Rosenthal, P. H. Wender, and F. Schulsinger. 1968. The types and prevalence of mental illness in the biological and adoptive families of adopted schizophrenics. In *The transmission of schizophrenia*, ed. D. Rosenthal and S. S. Kety. Oxford: Pergamon Press.

Kety, S. S., D. Rosenthal, P. H. Wender, F. Schulsinger, and B. Jacobsen. 1975. Mental illness in the biological and adoptive families of adopted individuals who have become schizophrenic: a preliminary report based upon psychiatric interviews. In *Genetic research in psychiatry*, ed. R. Fieve, D. Rosenthal, and H. Brill. Baltimore: Johns Hopkins University Press.

Matthysse, S. 1973. Antipsychotic drug actions: a clue to the neuropathology of schizophrenia? *Fed. Proc.* 32:200–205.

Matthysse, S., and S. S. Kety, eds. 1975. *Catecholamines and schizophrenia.* Oxford: Pergamon Press.

Osmond, H., and J. Smythies. 1952. Schizophrenia: a new approach. *J. Ment. Sci.* 98:309–315.

Pollin, W., P. V. Cardon, and S. S. Kety. 1961. Effects of amino acid feedings in schizophrenic patients treated with iproniazid. *Science* 133:104–105.

Rosenthal, D. 1962. Problems of sampling and diagnosis in the major twin studies of schizophrenia. *J. Psychiatr. Res.* 1:116–134.

Rosenthal, D., P. H. Wender, S. S. Kety, J. Welner, and F. Schulsinger. 1971. The adopted away offspring of schizophrenics. *Am. J. Psychiatry* 128, no. 3:307–311.

Saavedra, J. M., J. T. Coyle, and J. Axelrod. 1973. The distribution and properties of the non-specific N-methyltransferase in brain. *J. Neurochem.* 20:743–752.

Slater, E., and V. A. Cowie. 1971. *The genetics of mental disorders.* London: Oxford University Press.

Wender, P. H., D. Rosenthal, S. S. Kety, F. Schulsinger, and J. Welner. 1974. Crossfostering: a research strategy for clarifying the role of genetic and experiential factors in the etiology of schizophrenia. *Arch. Gen. Psychiatry* 30:121–128.

Wise, C. D., and L. Stein. 1973. Dopamine-β-hydroxylase deficits in the brains of schizophrenic patients. *Science* 181:344–347.

Wyatt, R. J., D. L. Murphy, R. Belmaker, S. Cohen, C. H. Donnelly, and W. Pollin. 1973. Reduced monoamine oxidase activity in platelets: a possible genetic marker for vulnerability to schizophrenia. *Science* 179:916–918.

Sleep

CHAPTER 7

Ernest Hartmann

THERE ARE a number of reasons why physicians and psychiatrists should be interested in sleep. First of all, complaints of sleep disturbance are among the most common of all symptoms; it is important to know when they may signal a specific serious and treatable illness and when they are nonspecific and part of a general malaise or anxiety. Complaints of poor sleep are not the only clues to sleep pathology—too much sleep and daytime tiredness turn out to be important clues to serious and treatable illnesses such as narcolepsy and sleep apnea. For the psychiatrist, the nature of a sleep disturbance can also help in the diagnosis of certain depressions that may present few other symptoms or none at all. Finally, many researchers believe, despite some initial disappointments, that in studying the biology of sleep and especially the biology of dreaming we are studying the biology of mental illness as well.

Although the term *sleep research* summons up visions of complex polygraphic apparatus, sleep is basically a behavioral state. Sleep is a regular, recurrent, easily reversible state of the organism characterized by relative quiescence and by a great increase in threshold of response to external stimuli, relative to the waking state.

Thus the basic definition of sleep is behavioral. Certain electroencephalographic (EEG) and polygraphic characteristics can now be accepted as part of a definition of sleep, however, because of their regular and constant association with the behavior of sleep. It is worth emphasizing that EEG changes often considered characteristic of sleep may be deceptive. The deep, slow waves usually associated with sleep, for instance, can be found in the waking state under certain pharmacological conditions and also during certain phases of anesthesia or coma. Thus, when and if the EEG tracing is used to make the "diagnosis" of sleep, it is the regular patterning, rather than any single characteristic wave form, that is most important.

Methods of Studying Sleep

For a great many years, researchers have been interested in studying the amount, depth, and "goodness" of sleep; the results of this work are useful from the clinical point of view, both in evaluating the course of a mental or physical illness and in evaluating sleeping medication. A variety of techniques has been employed to study sleep. One classic method is the subjective report; the doctor, for instance, simply asks the patient how he has been sleeping and whether he is sleeping better or worse than usual. This is a straightforward and inexpensive way of evaluating sleep, widely used and not to be denigrated; it can be refined to a certain extent by the use of questionnaires that ask specific questions of interest. Although the information obtained from subjective reports is sensitive to many sources of bias, it nonetheless supplies information not obtainable by any other means. It is obvious, for example, that a sleeping medication that looked perfect based on various objective studies but that left the patient feeling miserable in the morning would be a poor medication indeed.

The sometimes biased subjective reports may be supplemented by the use of an observer, who looks in on the patient or subject at stated intervals, perhaps every fifteen or thirty minutes during the night, and records his observations—"awake," "asleep," "not certain." This method has the advantage of being able to be applied to a large number of sleeping persons at the same time at relatively low expense, and such observations have been found to correlate fairly closely with EEG measures of sleep, except in certain problematic situations such as the case of depressed patients in the early morning hours.

During the 1930s and 1940s, a popular technique for measuring length and depth of sleep was to attach a simple movement-sensitive device to the bedsprings and record the amount of bed movement during the night. This method is based on the somewhat oversimplified notion that sleep can be gauged by diminution of movement and that the deepest sleep is the sleep with least movement. Still, these studies did lead to rough estimates of changes in the length of sleep and to a general notion that the early hours of sleep were the deepest, at least in the sense of containing the least motion—an observation that, so far as it goes, is still valid.

More recently, EEG and polygraphic studies of sleep have become commonplace. These involve continuous measurement of variables of interest—most commonly the occipital and parietal EEG, eye movement, muscle potential, and, in certain cases, the electrocardiogram (EKG) and measures of respiration. This method

has the obvious advantage of providing a minute-by-minute record of the entire night's sleep. Among its disadvantages are its cost and the fact that application of the electrodes necessary for recording may disturb sleep somewhat and necessitate one, two, or sometimes more nights of adaptation to the sleep laboratory before a proper evaluation can be made.

A Typical Night of Sleep

The following is a brief summary of the phenomenology of sleep, that is, of what occurs during a typical night of sleep, in a young adult. A great deal of the information is derived from recent polygraphic studies, but many of the findings are amenable to study by other techniques, including visual observation.

As the subject falls asleep, his brain waves go through certain characteristic changes, classified as stages 1–4. Waking EEG is characterized by alpha waves (8–12 cycles per second) and low-voltage activity of mixed frequency. As the subject falls asleep, he begins to show a disappearance of alpha activity. Stage 1, considered the lightest stage of sleep, is characterized by low-voltage, desynchronized activity and sometimes, by low-voltage, regular activity at 4–6 cycles per second as well. After a few seconds or minutes, this gives way to stage 2, a pattern showing frequent spindle-shaped tracings at 13–15 cycles per second (sleep spindles) and certain high-voltage spikes known as K-complexes. In a few more minutes, delta waves, high voltage activity at 0.5–2.5 cycles per second, make their appearance (stage 3); eventually, in stage 4, these delta waves occupy the major part of the record (see fig. 7.1).

Sleep is cyclical, with four or five periods of "emergence" from stages 2, 3, and 4 to a stage similar to stage 1. Subjects awakened during these periods frequently report that they have been dreaming (60 to 90 percent of the time); such periods are characterized not only by stage 1 EEG patterns and by rapid conjugate eye movements but by a host of other distinguishing factors. Among these factors are a great irregularity in pulse rate, respiratory rate, and blood pressure; the presence of full or partial penile erections in the male; and general muscular atony interrupted only by sporadic move-

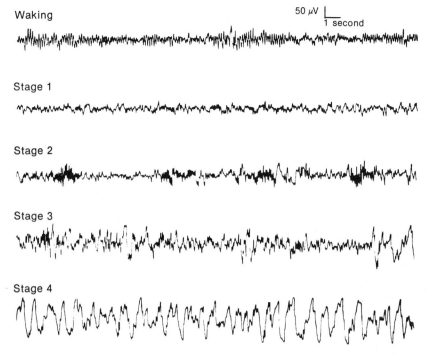

FIGURE 7.1. The EEG of sleep in a human adult. Shown for each stage of sleep is a single-channel, monopolar recording from the left parietal area, with the ears as a neutral reference point.

ments in small muscle groups. These periods of emergence differ markedly from typical stage 1 sleep as well as from the other three stages. Because of the distinguishing characteristics described above and because of their neurophysiological and chemical nature, these periods are now almost universally seen as constituting a separate state of sleep. This view is reinforced by the fact that similar periods differing from the remainder of sleep are found in nearly all mammals and birds studied. These periods are referred to as D (desynchronized or dreaming) sleep and the remainder of sleep as S (synchronized) sleep. These two states are also known as REM (rapid eye movement) sleep and NREM (non-rapid eye movement) sleep; as paradoxical sleep and orthodox sleep; or as active sleep and quiet sleep.

Several important characteristics of the typical night's sleep should be noted (see fig. 7.2). First of all, there are four or five D-periods during the night, and the total time taken up by the periods (D-time) is about 1½ hours, a little over 20 percent of total sleep time. There is some variation,

of course, but it is striking that all of the many hundreds of human subjects studied have such D-periods and that these almost always take up 20 to 25 percent of the total night's sleep. The first D-period occurs about 90 to 100 minutes after the onset of sleep; this interval may be longer in some normal subjects, but it is significantly shorter only in a few abnormal clinical and experimental conditions.

The cyclical nature of sleep is quite regular; a D-period occurs approximately every 90 to 100 minutes during the night. The first D-period tends to be the shortest, usually lasting 5 to 10 minutes, while the later D-periods may last 20 to 40 minutes each. Most D-time occurs in the last third of the night, whereas most stage 4 sleep occurs in the first third of the night.

S-sleep can be neatly organized according to depth: stage 1 is the lightest and stage 4 the deepest stage, measured by arousal threshold as well as by the appearance of the EEG. Unfortunately, D-sleep does not fit into this continuum. Human electroencephalographic data alone might indicate that D-sleep is a light sleep. The

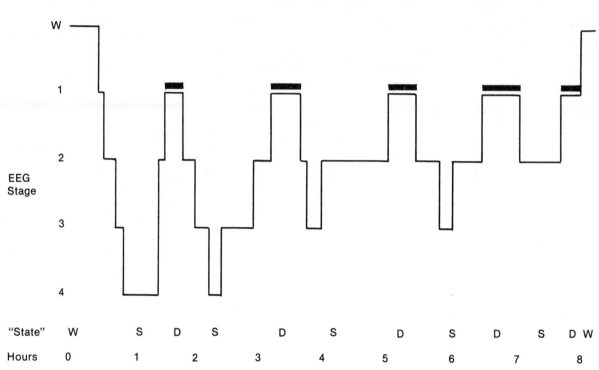

FIGURE 7.2. A typical night of sleep in a young adult. The diagram represents the mean derived from many all-night recordings. The heavy lines indicate D-periods, which are characterized by stage 1 EEG patterns and the presence of rapid conjugate eye movements (shown as x's). W, waking periods; S, synchronized sleep; D, desynchronized sleep.

arousal threshold in animals is higher in D- than in S-sleep, however, and resting muscle potential is lowest during D-sleep. Thus, D-sleep is neither truly light sleep nor deep sleep but a qualitatively different kind of sleep.

The constant and very regular characteristics of a night of normal sleep are sensitive indicators of disturbance; they can be used to study alterations associated with various forms of pathology or produced by various drugs.

The Phylogeny of Sleep

According to our behavioral definition of sleep, most vertebrates—certainly reptiles, birds, and mammals—may be said to display some form of sleep. Reptiles show behavioral sleep and recordings somewhat similar to mammalian S-sleep; in a few instances, brief episodes of a state

very much resembling D-sleep have been recorded as well. Birds have definite periods of both S- and D-sleep, although the D-periods are generally very short and account for a small percentage of total sleep time.

Within the class Mammalia, the two states of sleep have been studied in a wide variety of species. It is likely that almost all mammals have S- and D-sleep. D-sleep appears to be absent, however, in a single very primitive mammal, the spiny anteater. If this lack of D-sleep is verified, it could have important implications for scientists in helping to determine when the differentiation of the two states of sleep arose phylogenetically.

No very obvious relationships have yet emerged among species in terms of amounts of S- or D-sleep. The so-called higher mammals, such as humans and apes, show neither more or less sleep nor more or less D-time than the lower forms. Within a closely related group like the rodents, the animals that are usually preyed upon (the rabbit, for example) have less D-time than the predators (such as the rat). To some extent this distinction holds true across many groups of mammals—carnivores tend to have more D-time than herbivores, while the amount of D-time recorded in omnivores falls between the two—and makes sense from the point of view of adaptation and selection, since the muscular relaxation of the D-state would make an

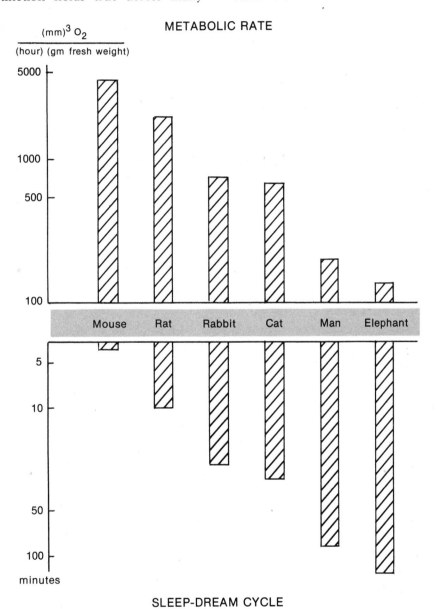

FIGURE 7.3. Basal metabolic rate and length of the sleep-dream cycle for six mammalian species. Metabolic rate is roughly in inverse proportion to the length of the sleep-dream cycle. The ordinate is a logarithmic scale in both cases to allow values of very different magnitudes to be represented. Metabolic rate is expressed in terms of cubic millimeters of oxygen consumed each hour per gram fresh weight of body tissue. The sleep-dream cycle is measured in minutes.

animal especially vulnerable, and long D-periods would be especially disadvantageous to herbivores and to preyed-upon animals.

Even though the relationship of D- and S-sleep among species is not entirely clear, a definite relationship can be seen between the basal metabolic rate of a species and the length of its sleep-dream cycle (usually defined as the time from the end of one D-period to the end of the next). Smaller mammals with higher metabolic rates have shorter sleep-dream cycles than larger ones; there is an inverse relationship between the metabolic rate of a species and its sleep-dream cycle length (see fig. 7.3). Indeed, the same relationship can be found between metabolic rate and the length of the pulse cycle, the respiratory cycle, the gestation period, and the life span. This similarity helps to establish the fact that the sleep-dream cycle is one of the basic bodily cycles in mammals.

The Ontogeny of Sleep

One of the most consistent findings in recent sleep studies is that the young of any species always have more sleep time and considerably more D-time than the adults. The young adult human, as we know, spends 16 to 17 hours awake and 7 to 8 hours asleep, of which perhaps 6 hours are spent in S-sleep and 1½ hours in D-sleep. Both S- and D-sleep, on the average, decrease slightly with increasing age. The newborn child sleeps 16 to 18 hours, at least half of it in D-sleep. Although exact definition and scoring of S- and D-sleep are somewhat problematic in very young children, this finding has been repeatedly confirmed and suggests that D-sleep is developmentally a very primitive state. The same ontogenetic relationship appears to hold for other mammalian species. The young mammal always sleeps more than the adult and has an especially high percentage of D-time. In addition, the sleep-dream cycle is clearly present at birth and is generally shorter in the newborn of any species than in the adult.

The Neurophysiology and Neurochemistry of Sleep

It is impossible in a brief discussion to do justice to the complex and very important neurophys-

iological and neurochemical aspects of sleep; the interested reader is referred to the work of Moruzzi (1972) and Hobson (1969a, 1969b) for further information. Maintenance of the waking state depends on the activity of the ascending reticular activating system (ARAS), which sends impulses to the forebrain. For some time after discovery of the ARAS, it was assumed that sleep supervened whenever ARAS activity fell below a certain level (the passive theory of sleep). It now appears that several active processes subserve sleep. Synchronized sleep in animals probably depends on activity of certain centers in the brainstem, especially the raphe nuclei, as well as certain areas in the medial forebrain; other areas in the hypothalamus and the thalamus cannot be entirely excluded. It is possible but not certain that all these regions eventually exert an influence on ARAS activity. In addition, a brainstem system is necessary for the initiation and maintenance of D-sleep; several pontine areas may be involved, including the locus ceruleus and the giant-cell tegmental fields found in the brainstem tegmentum.

The chemistry of sleep is also being rapidly elucidated. Evidence indicates that chemical factors found in the cerebrospinal fluid or even the blood of sleep-deprived animals can put normal animals to sleep. It is not certain, however, that these factors are involved in the normal physiological initiation or maintenance of sleep. Normal sleep involves the serotonin-containing raphe nuclei of the brainstem; in experiments with cats, destruction of these nuclei eliminates sleep and inhibition of serotonin synthesis diminishes or eliminates sleep for a period of days. Catecholamine (norepinephrine or dopamine) mechanisms appear to be involved in the maintenance of waking or arousal, and it has been suggested that norepinephrine systems may be restored or replenished during sleep.

Sleep Deprivation

Literally hundreds of investigators have studied sleep deprivation in recent years, but overall results have been somewhat disappointing.

Physiologically, a sleep-deprived subject shows a central (brain) hypoarousal, combined, at least in certain stages, with an autonomic hyperarousal. After several days of sleep deprivation, the waking EEG shifts away from alpha and in the direction of lower frequencies; pulse and respiratory rates are frequently increased. Recovery sleep after a period of sleep deprivation involves a great deal of slow-wave sleep (stage 3 and 4 sleep) in the first hours and an increase in D-time in subsequent hours or days.

The psychological effects of sleep deprivation have not always been easy to determine and obviously depend a great deal on social and environmental factors. Thus a period of sleep deprivation undergone in an army group where sleep deprivation is seen as a challenge to be overcome will have very different effects from sleep deprivation in a 24-hour "marathon" group, where the emphasis is on increasing self-awareness. Many studies have investigated what tasks are especially sensitive to sleep deprivation; overall, the conclusion has been that the difficulty of a task —to a small extent—and its length and its dullness—to a far greater extent—make it susceptible to disruption by sleep deprivation. Thus the only tasks that have reliably picked up differences between rested subjects and subjects who have experienced half a night's sleep loss involve hours of monitoring a television display, with responses required when certain symbols are seen. Unfortunately, such results can be interpreted as showing merely that a sleep-deprived subject is more likely to fall asleep, since the tasks sensitive to sleep deprivation are exactly those during which one might be expected to doze off at least briefly. Although it has been hard to establish sleep-deprivation effects with such objective psychological tests, there is no doubt that a subjective effect results and can be measured "objectively" as an effect on mood-rating forms. Various studies involving adjective check lists have found decreases in scales such as alertness and vigor and increases in scales such as confusion and fatigue; these results are hardly surprising.

Prolonged periods of sleep deprivation have sometimes led to increasing ego disorganization, hallucinations, and delusions. It has been widely assumed that a long enough period of sleep deprivation would produce a psychosis in normal subjects, but this cannot be stated with certainty, both because of obvious ethical considerations in conducting research and because the occasional subjects who either deprive themselves of sleep for long periods or who volunteer for long-term sleep-deprivation studies must be considered somewhat atypical.

Since the advent of EEG techniques, it has become possible to deprive persons selectively of D-sleep, or of the deeper portions of S-sleep (it is not possible to deprive someone completely of synchronized sleep without producing total sleep deprivation). Selective D-deprivation produces two unquestioned effects. First, during the night when the subject is being awakened at the beginning of each D-period, he makes an increasing number of beginnings, or attempts to have a D-period; thus, while four or five awakenings are sufficient for total D-sleep deprivation on the first night, twenty to thirty awakenings are often required by the fifth night, and it is often impossible to continue the study much longer than that. Second, the recovery sleep is usually characterized by greatly increased D-sleep (rebound increase). Psychological effects are less certain. Although it was first reported that D-deprivation produced disorganization and would eventually produce psychosis (in line with suggestions by Freud and others), recent results have not been conclusive. It has been possible to differentiate only to a limited extent psychological changes produced by D-sleep deprivation from those produced by stage 4 deprivation. A careful study in this area by Agnew, Webb, and Williams did describe greater physical lethargy in subjects deprived of stage 4 sleep and more irritability and social difficulties in the D-deprived group.

The Pharmacology of Sleep

A wide variety of sleeping medications and other drugs is known to reduce D-time. The reduced D-time has come to be regarded almost as a general, nonspecific indication of chemically or physically disturbed sleep. Very few drugs produce an increase in D-sleep, usually only those like reserpine, which reduces brain amine levels or activity.

The reduction of D-sleep and the distortion of other stages of sleep sometimes brought about by alcohol, sleeping medications, and many other drugs has led to some concern that normal sleep is not occurring, even though it has been difficult to demonstrate any change in waking performance after such disruptions. The barbiturates are typical of a large number of sleep-inducing and other medications. They produce a decrease in D-time when first given, followed on continued administration by a return almost to normal levels, and then a rebound increase in D-time after discontinuation. During continued administration, it is hard to notice subjective or objective signs of disturbed sleep, but it has also been difficult to show that these drugs continue to have a beneficial effect on sleep. Thus, an initial clear-cut reduction of sleep latency (the time required to fall asleep) is often followed, on continued administration, by a return of sleep latency to predrug levels. The period after discontinuation, however, is clearly associated with subjective and objective disturbance and irritability, many body movements, and increased reports of poor sleep and nightmares. The danger, still insufficiently appreciated, is that a patient who may have required sleeping medication for some transient problem may discontinue the medication, find himself afflicted with disturbing symptoms, and, if he has not been warned about predictable withdrawal effects, conclude that he obviously requires sleeping medication; he may then resume taking such drugs on a long-term basis.

Sleep researchers have been seeking a more "natural" sleeping medication, one that would reduce both sleep latency and awakenings without reducing D-time or producing other sleep distortions. Some recent studies suggest that the amino acid L-tryptophan may have these properties.

Requirements for Sleep

The exact functions of sleep are not yet known. Some groups have proposed that sleep can be seen chiefly as a time of nonbehaving that can be adaptive for an animal, but most investigators believe that sleep has some basic restorative function. The relative constancy of the sleep requirement supports this view. Sleep time in young adult humans averages about 7 hours and 45 minutes and varies surprisingly little across differences in culture or geographical area. Changes within individuals are also fairly small. Norwegians living above the Arctic circle, for instance, who live under the extreme conditions of the "midnight sun" in summer and the "noon moon" in winter nonetheless sleep an average of only 40 to 50 minutes longer in winter.

It is likely then that a certain amount of sleep is generally required even though the amount may be hard to determine precisely. In one study, a number of normal subjects attempted to reduce their nightly average of sleep time by 15 minutes each week; they were relatively successful until they reached levels of 5 to 6 hours per night, when continuation became very difficult and the subjects suddenly found one excuse or another to drop out of the study. Another study, attempting to differentiate persons who appeared to require a great deal of sleep (over 9 hours a day) from those who required very little sleep (less than 6 hours a day), concluded that the long sleepers were generally "worriers" who took things very seriously, had many complaints and anxieties about themselves and the world, and could be seen as "reprogramming" themselves frequently during the day; the short sleepers, on the other hand, tended to be nonworriers who were relatively "preprogrammed," that is, who had a way of running their lives that satisfied them and that they altered relatively little.

Sleep in Mental Illness

Despite expectations based on associations between dreaming and psychosis, the laboratory sleep of a hospitalized schizophrenic patient—considered as a whole—is relatively normal. During acute episodes, sleep is often disturbed and D-time is low, but it is not likely that this change is intrinsic to the schizophrenic process; it is more probably an effect of extreme anxiety. Some chronic schizophrenic patients will show perfectly normal sleep patterns. In others, slow-wave sleep (stage 3 and 4) decreases, but this may be related to the postulated central hyperarousal of certain schizophrenic patients.

Mania and depression are associated with unusual sleep patterns. EEG studies have confirmed the very short sleep time usually found in manic patients; all stages of sleep appear to be reduced to a certain extent, although there is some disagreement among studies. In our investigations, D-sleep especially was reduced, while stage 4 sleep remained close to normal levels.

Sleep is usually abnormal in depression, and several distinct patterns can be described. The most frequent sleep pattern in severe depression involves insomnia—more often difficulty in remaining asleep than difficulty in falling asleep. Laboratory sleep studies have confirmed that some depressed patients have frequent awakenings during the night as well as early morning awakenings, reduced slow-wave sleep time, reduced D-latency, and sometimes reduced D-sleep as well. Other depressed patients have hypersomnia—increased total sleep time—without dramatic alterations in sleep stages and usually with increased D-time. In fact, most depressed patients demonstrate an increased tendency to have D-sleep; some have increased D-time, but almost all manifest decreased D-latency, a lengthened initial D-period, and increased eye movements during D-periods. There is no general agreement about the relationship between sleep and depression. Possibly there are two factors: (1) an increased requirement for sleep and for D-sleep, present in most or all depression, and (2) the inability to remain asleep, which is present in some severely depressed patients.

Sleep Pathology

Sleep disorders can be divided into a number of classes, briefly described here. First, some medical and psychosomatic disorders are exacerbated during sleep; anginal attacks, for instance, appear to be frequent during D-sleep, and extrasystoles (premature ventricular beats), more frequent during both D-sleep and stage 4 sleep. Second, there are episodic occurrences during sleep; these include enuresis (bed-wetting), sleepwalking, and pavor nocturnus (night terrors), which occur chiefly during arousals from slow-wave sleep, and tooth grinding and head banging, which may occur in children during almost any stage of sleep. Third, sleep pathology in the stricter sense of "primary sleep disorders" involves defects in the sleep-waking mechanisms. Narcolepsy is a special condition characterized by short sleep attacks in the daytime and frequently by cataplexy (sudden collapse with lowered muscle tone), sleep paralysis, and hypnagogic hallucinations. Laboratory studies reveal that narcoleptics have an abnormally short D-

latency at night, and cataplectic attacks consist of an almost immediate change from waking to D-sleep. Thus this condition can be seen as a failure of the normal mechanism inhibiting D-periods. In addition to narcolepsy, several distinct varieties of hypersomnia have been described.

Sleep apnea is a recently described condition in which the patient may complain either of frequent awakenings or of increased sleep with daytime tiredness. Polygraphic recordings demonstrate multiple periods of complete apnea (cessation of breathing) lasting 15 seconds or more and terminating in an awakening. The pathology may be either local (involving respiratory muscles and airway tissues) or central (involving brainstem areas controlling respiration).

By far the most common sleep complaint is insomnia. In my view, insomnia can best be seen as a symptom or a final common pathway that can be produced by a number of antecedent causes; there may also be a "primary" insomnia, however. In young patients, insomnia is most frequently "sleep-onset insomnia" (inability to fall asleep), often related to anxiety and particularly to anxiety about "letting go." A frequent cause of inability to remain asleep (characterized by frequent awakenings during the night or by early morning awakenings) is depression. Insomnia is also frequently produced by any medical condition in which pain or discomfort plays a role. Insomnia lasting for several weeks frequently occurs during withdrawal from sleeping medication or tranquilizers.

Treatment of any sleep disorder should involve a careful medical-psychiatric history and physical examination so that a specific diagnosis can be made. A simple diagnosis of insomnia followed by prescription of a sleeping pill is seldom in the best interests of the patient.

Recommended Reading

Agnew, H. W., Jr., W. B. Webb, and R. L. Williams. 1967. Comparison of stage four and 1-REM sleep deprivation. *Percept. Mot. Skills* 24:851–858.

Chase, M. H., W. C. Stern, and P. L. Walter, eds. 1972. *Sleep research*. Vol. 1. Los Angeles: University of California, Brain Information Service, Brain Research Institute.

—— 1973. *Sleep research*. Vol. 2. Los Angeles: University of California, Brain Information Service, Brain Research Institute.

—— 1974. *Sleep research*. Vol. 3. Los Angeles: University of California, Brain Information Service, Brain Research Institute.

Foulkes, D. 1966. *The psychology of sleep*. New York: Scribner's.

Freemon, F. 1972. *Sleep research: a critical review*. Springfield, Ill.: Thomas.

Hartmann, E. 1967. *The biology of dreaming*. Springfield, Ill.: Thomas.

—— 1973. *The functions of sleep*. New Haven: Yale University Press.

Hartmann, E., J. Cravens, and S. List. 1974. Hypnotic effects of L-tryptophan. *Arch. Gen. Psychiatry* 31:394–397.

Hobson, J. A. 1969a. Sleep: physiologic aspects. *N. Engl. J. Med.* 281:1343–1345.

—— 1969b. Sleep: biochemical aspects. *N. Engl. J. Med.* 281:1468–1470.

Kales, A., ed. 1969. *Sleep: physiology and pathology*. Philadelphia: Lippincott.

Kales, A. and J. D. 1974. Sleep disorders: recent findings in the diagnosis and treatment of disturbed sleep. *N. Engl. J. Med.* 290:487–499.

Kleitman, N. 1963. *Sleep and wakefulness*. Chicago: University of Chicago Press.

Moruzzi, G. 1972. The sleep-waking cycle. *Ergeb. Physiol.* 64:1–165.

Weitzmann, E. 1973. *Advances in sleep research*. Vol. 1. Flushing, N.Y.: Spectrum.

Psychopathology

Theories of Personality

CHAPTER 8

William W. Meissner

S INCE THE ROLE of psychoanalytic concepts in clinical psychiatric thinking has been major and central, it is useful to begin any consideration of the major theories of personality in the development of modern psychiatry with the development of Freud's ideas and then move to discussion of their modification and enrichment by his successors. In this chapter, these complex and interrelated ideas will be organized systematically within a more or less historical perspective, with later portions of the material building on and amplifying earlier ideas. The discussion of later, nonanalytic theorists will be more succinct, since their contributions have entered the stream of psychiatric thinking in more specific or confined ways and, to this point in the development of psychiatric thinking, have served more as modifications of existing paradigms than as independent bases for clinical theory.

Classic Psychoanalytic Theory

Sigmund Freud (1856–1939), the founder of psychoanalysis, revolutionized psychiatric thinking and laid the groundwork for the psychodynamic approach to mental disorders. Although recent contributions have in many respects superseded Freud's original formulations, basic Freudian concepts still provide the foundation of psychoanalytic understanding.

The Concept of Hysteria

Freud based his earliest theories on observations of the relation between hysteria and hypnosis. His study of hypnotic and posthypnotic suggestion indicated that unconscious ideas persisted in the mind and continued to influence the patient's actions and behavior, even though the patient remained totally unaware of such influence. From these observations, Freud theorized that persistent unconscious ideas in the hysterical patient give rise to hysterical symptoms.

In Freud's early collaboration with Josef Breuer, Breuer explained hysterical phenomena on the basis of "hypnoid states"—spontaneous dissociations by the patient resembling those dissociations produced by hypnotic suggestion. Breuer observed that amnesia followed these states of autohypnotic dissociation and suggested that hysteria occurred more readily in such states than in waking states.

Freud disagreed. He observed that hysterical symptoms disappeared when the memory of specific traumatic events surrounding the onset of the symptom was brought into conscious awareness. The further crucial observation followed that powerful mental forces excluded such traumatic ideas from consciousness and that these pathogenic ideas could only be brought into consciousness by means of forceful psychical work.

From these interlinked notions, Freud derived his concepts of *repression* and *resistance*. Although he found that the conscious expression of the pathogenic idea and its associated affect helped alleviate the hysterical symptoms, he also noted that powerful repressive forces had expelled the pathogenic idea from consciousness. These same forces later resisted therapeutic attempts to bring the idea back into connection with the rest of the patient's conscious mental life.

Freud found that the pathogenic ideas usually involved the patient's conflicts over sexuality. He postulated that such pathogenic ideas were specifically related to concrete traumatizing sexual events that had occurred in earlier childhood experiences. At first, Freud thought that the trauma was an actual physical seduction, practiced on or by the child at some early point in infancy, which had so overwhelmed and threatened the child that powerful repressive forces had to be mobilized to prevent the memory of the trauma from emerging into awareness. He based his "seduction hypothesis" on the recollection of such experiences and the intense affects of agitation, moral conflict, self-reproach, fear of punishment, and guilt associated with them in a large number of his patients.

Freud's early theory of hysteria was specifically a theory of defense, based on repression, resistance, and the seduction hypothesis. The concept of repression and the related notion of defense constitute basic notions in psychoanalytic theory and rest on the assumption that there are basic dynamic forces in the human mind that are the source of powerful motivations as well as their correlative defenses, either of which can work against the other in situations of conflict.

The seduction hypothesis was central to Freud's thinking for many years. As his clinical experience grew, however, and as his own self-analysis deepened, he began to wonder whether the confirmation of his hypothesis by his patients was more the result of his suggestion than reality. He gradually realized that his patients' accounts of seduction were not actual historical events but, rather, expressions of deep sexual wishes and fantasies from the infantile period. This realization was a turning point. His focus on the actual historical experience of the child diminished as he recognized the greater importance of the child's inner motivations, wishes, and fantasies.

On the ruins of the seduction hypothesis, however, Freud built the theoretical foundation of the psychology of dynamic mental forces expressed in repression, resistance, and conflict. From these conceptualizations, he developed the theory of psychoneurosis related to the vicissitudes of infantile sexuality, according to which infantile wishes escape the control of repressing forces and erupt into consciousness in a distorted form—the neurotic symptom. His attention next focused on the functions of these dynamic inner forces and their relationship to sexual drives.

Dream Theory

Freud then studied the operation of dynamic inner forces and their manifestations in dreams. During this period, he also evolved the technique of free association, during which his patients frequently reported dreams and their related material. He discovered little by little that dreams had definite meanings, which could be deciphered through the patient's associations. Patients often reported material related to repressed memories and ideas of which they were otherwise unaware.

The study of dreams became for Freud the "royal road of the unconscious," and his development of dream theory paralleled his analysis of psychoneurotic symptoms. According to Freud, the dream is a conscious expression of an unconscious fantasy or wish. The *dream work* (the process by which the dream is formed) produces the material of the dream (manifest content), which expresses the underlying unconscious ideas (latent content) in a distorted, masked form. Associations reveal the hidden links between the dream symbols and the disguised repressed ideas.

Freud postulated that the dream censor opsee p. 123

poses the admission of unconscious ideas to conscious awareness during the waking state, but, during the regressive relaxation of sleep, it allows some of the unconscious content to be incorporated into dream material. The dream work consists of four transforming mental processes —displacement, condensation, symbolism, and projection—which modify the latent dream ideas. The latent ideas are sufficiently disguised to be tolerable to the patient's ego and to pass the restrictive control of the censor. This relaxation of repression, which allows unconscious content to come to the surface, is analogous to the release of repression which Freud had previously found to be involved in the production of hysterical symptoms.

In all of these areas, Freud gradually conceptualized two basic forces of the mind—those which bring repressed material out of the unconscious to the level of conscious awareness and those which force material back into the unconscious or maintain a barrier against its escape from the unconscious. These two basic mental forces, the repressed and the repressing, and the nature of the conflicts between them, became a central focus of his thinking.

Freud gained an understanding of the repressing agencies of the mind through the study of hysteria, dreams, and related manifestations. He envisioned two opposed psychic systems, one that produces a rational organization of dream thoughts similar to normal thinking and another that creates bewildering and irrational dream thoughts. The latter system, called *primary process*, serves as a pathway for the discharge of psychic tension. The rational system, called *secondary process*, involves inhibition and delay and serves to correct and regulate the primary system. All psychic operations, all thoughts, partake of these modalities in varying degrees.

The Topographic Model: Early Formulations of Instinct Theory

During the quarter-century after the abandonment of the seduction hypothesis, the topographic model dominated Freud's thinking. This model delineates the relationships of various elements in the psychic apparatus to consciousness.

The model is based on four assumptions. The first, psychological determinism, posits that symptoms and dream phenomena have specific, detectable, demonstrable meaning within a causal psychological network. The second assumption, unconscious psychological processes, holds that unconscious repressed material influences present experience and is regulated by the pleasure principle and by primary process. The third assumption, that unconscious psychological conflicts exist, forms the basis of a theory of psychoneurosis as expressed in resistance and repression. The fourth assumes that unconscious processes, forces, and conflicts derive from basic psychological energies originating in instinctual drives. Repression of such energies and their subsequent distortions and transformations give rise to neurotic symptoms and anxiety.

The conscious system is the region of the mind in which perceptions derived from extrinsic stimuli are integrated and brought into awareness. Such perceptions include awareness of bodily processes as well as mental processes, thoughts, or affects. At this stage of Freud's thinking, objective consciousness and its associated mental content were assumed to be roughly equivalent to the ego.

The preconscious system consists of mental events, processes, and contents that enter conscious awareness relatively easily by focusing of attention. Preconscious thought organization ranges from relatively reality-based or problem-solving thought sequences (secondary process) to more primitive fantasies, daydreams, or dreamlike images, which reflect primary process organization. The preconscious is subject to both conscious and unconscious influences. However, one function of the preconscious is to maintain the repressive barrier or censorship against unconscious wishes and desires. The transformation of unconscious processes to preconscious or conscious levels takes place only with great difficulty and by the expenditure of considerable energy to overcome the repressive barrier.

The unconscious can be defined in descriptive terms—that is, as mental events that are not conscious. In more strictly dynamic terms, the unconscious refers to mental contents and processes excluded from consciousness by the force of repression. In this dynamic sense, uncon-

UNC scious contents consist of drive representations or wishes that are in some sense unacceptable, threatening, or incongruous with the intellectual or ethical standards of the individual. Nonetheless, the drives constantly strive for discharge and thus give rise to the intrapsychic conflict between the repressed and the repressing forces of the mind.

The systematic unconscious represents the region of the mind in which unconscious dynamic processes operate and within which memory traces are organized by primitive modes of association (primary process). The elements of the systematic unconscious are subject to the repressive barrier and to primary process thought organization. As in the dream process, these elements are relatively divorced from verbal symbols. They tend to express unconscious wishes and derive from instinctual forces, particularly the sexual instincts.

Freud struggled to achieve an adequate formulation of the instincts. One of his best-known definitions of the term *instinct* is a "concept on the frontier between the mental and the somatic, as the psychical representative of the stimuli originating from within the organism and reaching the mind, as a measure of the demands made upon the mind for work in consequence of its connections with the body" (1915, pp. 121–122). The nature of the connection here between the biological and psychological factors is still a basic problem in analytic thinking. Analysts tend to emphasize one or the other aspect of this definition, variously stressing biological or psychological features.

The influence of sexuality played a primary role in Freud's thinking, but his ideas were not clearly articulated until 1905 in his *Three Essays on the Theory of Sexuality*. At that time, he presented a schema based on the stages of the development of sexual drives that has become the classic paradigm of analytic theory. Although he had freed himself from the seduction hypothesis and the conviction that early sexual trauma was the cause of neurosis, he remained convinced that neurotic disturbances had their roots in disturbances of the sexual drive. This conviction and his attempts to build a theory to support it would eventually yield to the appreciation of the roles of narcissism and aggression—but at this point he saw the energy of the psychic apparatus

almost exclusively in libidinal terms. The relation of the energies involved in narcissism and aggression, as well as those involved in ego functions, to the sexual energy of libido was an issue that emerged gradually and remained problematic.

Freud described four characteristics of instincts: source, impetus, aim, and object. The source is the part of the body from which the instinctual drive arises; thus libidinal drives arise from specific erotogenic zones—the mucous membranes of the mouth, anus, and genitalia. The impetus is the amount or intensity of the demand made by the instinctual drive. The aim of the instinct is the action by which it achieves satisfaction and reduces the intensity of stimulation at the source. Finally, the object is the person or thing that satisfies the instinctual drive and that allows the instinct to discharge its tension by serving as the target of the action. Freud thought that the object was the most variable and interchangeable characteristic of the instinct, but our increasing understanding of the importance of specific objects (such as parents) in the infant's experience has considerably modified this point of view.

During infancy and early childhood, stimulation of the mucous membranes of the mouth, anus, or external genitalia causes erotic sensations. These pregenital instincts are integrated under the domination of the genital zone during normal development. Nonetheless, the pregenital erotic components from the oral and anal zones retain a place in adult sexual activity, particularly in foreplay or in forms of perversion. The young infant's sexuality is polymorphous-perverse and gradually undergoes selective repression. These component instincts may thus undergo a variety of transformations, distortions, and fixations and become the basis for various forms of psychopathology.

The emergence and predominance of specific erotogenic zones and their respective erotic component instincts (drives) are organized into a sequence of progressive phases that follow a biologically determined pattern. Thus, a developmental sequence of phases can be traced: in earliest infancy the oral phase, followed by the anal phase, which then gives way to a phallic or oedipal phase.

In the earliest months of life, the *oral phase*,

the infant cannot survive unless he gains relief from painful inner physiological states, and he depends on external care-taking objects to accomplish this. The oral zone gains satisfaction of hunger needs by feeding. The experience of unsatisfied need and frustration in the absence of the breast, followed by the need-satisfying release of tension in the presence of the breast, provides the infant's first awareness of external objects. The mother's capacity to respond empathically to the infant's needs permits the homeostatic balancing of physiological needs within the child, insofar as relief from hunger is provided before the hunger becomes excessively intense or frustrated.

The oral zone maintains its dominant role in the organization of behavior through approximately the first eighteen months of life. Oral drives are both libidinal and aggressive. Oral erotic needs—to take in, suck, swallow, and thus achieve quiescence—dominate in the early portion of the oral phase but become mixed with more aggressive components (oral sadism) later. Oral aggression can be expressed in biting, chewing, spitting, or crying.

The *anal phase* of psychosexual development extends roughly from one and a half to three years of age. The maturation of neuromuscular control over the sphincters, particularly the anal sphincters, permits greater voluntary control over the retention and expulsion of feces. At the same time, parents demand that the child relinquish some of this control and accede to toilet training. Voluntary sphincter control is part of the increasing shift from the relative passivity of the oral phase to greater activity. Conflicts arise over issues of control, particularly in the struggle with the parents over the retaining or expelling of feces.

Anal eroticism refers to the sexual pleasure in anal functioning, both in retaining the precious feces and in presenting them as a gift to the parent. Anal sadism is the expression of more aggressive wishes connected with the discharging feces as powerful and destructive weapons. The child can exert power over the parent by control of evacuative functions; he can yield and give up the fecal mass or he can refuse to yield and withhold it. The child's sense of sphincter control is fragile and easily threatened. If his attempts to withhold stubbornly are excessively punished

or his loss of control excessively shamed, the child may regress to more primitive, oral patterns of behavior, such as thumb-sucking, mouthing, and so forth.

In the transition to the *phallic* or *genital phase*, the pregenital components (oral and anal) are integrated into a new configuration in which the primary focus of sexual interest and stimulation is in the genital area. This phase begins in the third year and continues to the end of the fifth year. The child becomes aware of sexual differences, and the penis becomes the organ of principal interest to children of both sexes. This period is critical in the early formations of the child's gender identity. The genital character of the libidinal organization at this phase justifies calling it a "genital" or "phallic" phase, but the quality of genital drive organization remains infantile and differs radically from the genital reorganization that takes a more mature and decisive form in adolescence (puberty).

In the pregenital period, the child's relationships primarily involve one-to-one interactions with each parent separately. In the phallic period, the child achieves a new level of complexity in object relationships. His interaction now involves both parents at once, and this triadic relationship is referred to as the oedipal situation. The Oedipus complex, involving a loving (sexual) attachment to the parent of the opposite sex and ambivalent rivalry with the parent of the same sex, derives from this situation as the final stage in the development of infantile sexuality. The resolution of this situation, involving both loving attachment and rivalrous hostility, is one of the basic achievements of personality development.

The oedipal involvement is less complicated for boys than for girls since the boy remains attached to his first love object, the mother. But the boy's interest in the mother takes a strong erotic turn, such that he desires to possess her exclusively and sexually. From the beginning of his oedipal involvement, the boy expresses his wishes toward the mother by wanting to touch her, by trying to get into bed with her, and by expressing wishes to replace his father. Competition from siblings for the mother's affection is intolerable, but primarily the little lover wants to eliminate his arch-rival, mother's husband—his father.

Such destructive wishes evoke a fear of retaliation that often gives rise to severe anxiety. Freud postulated that the punishment fits the crime and that the basic anxiety for the male child in this period is the fear of castration. He suggested that castration anxiety arouses a fear of narcissistic injury that is stronger than the erotic attachment to the mother. Under the pressure of castration anxiety, the boy must renounce his oedipal love for the mother and must identify with the father by internalizing paternal prohibitions and restraints. The picture cannot be this simple, however, since the child also loves his father and at times feels anger or hatred toward his mother. He seeks approval and affection from the father, and this homosexual component may have a powerful influence in the shaping of the child's personality.

The oedipal situation is considerably more involved for girls, who must shift their primary attachment from the mother to the father under the pressures of oedipal involvement and prepare for their future sexual role. Freud thought that the anatomical difference between the sexes, specifically the little girl's lack of a penis, precipitated the oedipal situation, positing that the lack of a penis provokes an intense sense of loss and narcissistic injury, as well as envy of the larger male organ. Freud believed that once the young girl realizes that she does not have a penis, her attitude toward the mother changes, since she holds the mother responsible for bringing her into the world with inferior genital equipment. This hostility can be intense and may color the child's future relationship to the mother. The further discovery that the mother also lacks a penis increases the child's hatred and devaluation of the mother, so that she turns to her father in the vain hope that he will give her a baby in place of the missing penis.

According to Freud, the girl's sexual love and ambitions toward her father meet continuing disappointment and frustration. The wish to be loved by the father fosters identification with the mother, whom father loves and with whom he sleeps. The threat to the little girl is not castration or loss of a physical organ, but, rather, the loss of love—at one level, loss of father's love in competition with mother, but at a deeper and more infantile level, loss of mother's love as well. Conse-

quently, resolution of the oedipal attachment involves a renunciation of her father in order to gain a more suitable, nonincestuous love object.

Freud regarded the Oedipus complex as the nucleus for the development of the child's personality and the genesis of neuroses and symptom formations. He further held that *introjections*—the internalizations and concomitant psychic activity of libidinal fixations, object attachments, and identifications—that the child derives from the oedipal situation profoundly influence the development of character. These introjections, by which parental standards and prohibitions are internalized, are the means by which oedipal conflicts and the tensions in the child's relationship to his parents are resolved so that the child can assimilate aspects of parental personalities. By this process, they form the core of the child's emerging superego.

Narcissism

The notion of narcissism led to important modifications in Freud's instinct theory. In a number of clinical states—including schizophrenic withdrawal, states of physical illness and hypochondriasis, deep sleep, and certain forms of object choice, particularly homosexuality—Freud thought that libido was withdrawn from outside objects and turned in toward the patient's own ego. This occurred dramatically in certain megalomaniacal delusions characterized by grandiosity (an enormously inflated sense of one's importance).

Freud ascribed these conditions to *primary narcissism*, a state existing at birth in which the infant's libidinal energies seek only the satisfaction of physiological needs and the preservation of inner equilibrium and well-being. Involvement with significant objects in the environment is necessary for survival and draws the infant's libido outward from this initial state. The infant's libido attaches to external objects and becomes object libido. But in traumatic situations, which may be physical or psychological (physical injury or threat of injury, object loss, excessive deprivation or frustration), object libido may detach from objects and reinvest in the ego as narcissistic libido. Freud referred to this regressive reinvestment in the person's own ego as *secondary narcissism*.

The concept of narcissism created a dilemma for Freud's instinct theory, which was based on the distinction between sexual-libidinal instincts and ego (self-preservative) instincts. Narcissism seemed to Freud a form of libidinal investment in the ego, but it also appeared to overlap both sexual-libidinal and ego instincts. Conflict would therefore occur between different parts of the sexual instinct—between that part directed to the ego (narcissistic libido) and that part directed to objects (object libido)—rather than between sexual and ego instincts. This assumed dualism was further questionable since it seemed that although the component instincts (oral, anal, phallic) were derived from a single sexual instinct, they could come into opposition. How can conflicting forces come from a single instinct? The whole question of narcissism and its place in the understanding of human instinctual and libidinal structure remains an important area of psychoanalytic investigation. The question of whether narcissistic libido is derived from object libido or whether it has an independent derivation and development is a subject of current debate.

Aggression

Originally Freud regarded aggressive manifestations as related to libidinal factors expressed in the perversion of sadism. To relate aggressive aspects to sexual instincts was difficult, however, because their aims were different: the sexual aim was pleasure or gratification; the aim of aggression was the infliction or avoidance of pain. The one seeks to preserve the object as a source of pleasure, the other to destroy the object as a source of pain. Eventually, Freud saw the aggressive component as independent of libido. He then attributed aggressiveness to the ego instincts but thought that sadism had some libidinal components. The basic dualism of libidinal versus ego instincts was further contradicted when evidence of self-destructive tendencies in depressed and masochistic patients made it clear that sadistic or aggressive impulses are not always self-preserving. This led Freud to remove aggressiveness from the ego instincts and to consider it

a separate instinct, on an equal footing with libidinal instincts.

The Life and Death Instincts

When Freud formulated the notions of life and death instincts in *Beyond the Pleasure Principle* (1920), he returned to the basic dualism in his instinct theory that had been challenged by the intermediate theories regarding narcissism and aggression. The life and death instincts represent his attempt to link the theory of instincts to a biological framework. The essential frame of reference came from Freud's earliest attempts to provide a physiological model as the basis for explaining mental phenomena. The model proposed that the tendency of the nervous system to rid itself of stimuli and reduce levels of tension (constancy principle) was the basis for gaining pleasure and minimizing pain. Thus Freud did not divorce his understanding of the instincts from tenets of the underlying "economic principle" with which he had started his theoretical career—entropy and constancy.

Freud postulated that the death instinct (*thanatos*) was the tendency of all living organisms to return to a state of total quiescence. This was an extension of the constancy principle, which proposed that all organisms tend to return to a state of minimal stimulation. Freud felt that the death instinct was the dominant force in biological organisms. In opposition to this force, he posited the life instinct (*eros*), the tendency for organisms to reunite, reorganize, and form greater and more complex forms of organization. Arguments over the validity of the basic instincts, which tend to preoccupy themselves with the death instinct, often lose sight of the importance of the life instinct, which stands in opposition to the closed-system "economics" of the death instinct (based on principles of entropy and constancy) and provides a basis for an open-system concept of instinctual motivation.

Freud's final formulations of the dualistic instinct theory were essentially concerned with a general biological speculation. The relevance of this speculation to clinical observation or practice has been a matter of considerable question and controversy. Freud pointed to the clinical phenomena of the repetition compulsion (the general tendency in human behavior to repeat painful experiences) and masochism (the tendency to accept suffering and pain) as the strongest supportive evidence for the death instinct, but even these phenomena can be understood on other grounds and without appeal to such ultimate instinctual tendencies.

From the Topographic to the Structural Viewpoint

The topographic model served an important function in providing a framework for the development of Freud's instinct theory, but it had deficiencies. The main difficulty was its inability to account for certain clinical findings. First, the defense mechanisms that Freud's patients employed appeared as unconscious resistances during treatment and were themselves not easily made conscious. Freud concluded from this that the agency of repression could not be identical with the preconscious, since it was unconscious. Second, Freud's patients frequently exhibited an unconscious need for punishment or an unconscious sense of guilt. But, in terms of the topographical model, the guilt-inducing moral agency making this demand was allied with the antiinstinctual repressive forces which should have been readily available to consciousness in the preconscious level of the mind.

Because of these difficulties, the topographic model gave way to the structural model proposed in The Ego and the Id (1923). This initiated a new era in the theory of psychoanalysis, dominated by the theory of the three structures—the id, the ego, and the superego—which explain all mental phenomena.

The Development of the Ego Concept

The ego concept evolved through the various phases of Freud's thinking as well as post-Freudian developments. The first phase, ending in 1897, saw the ego as a dominant mass of conscious ideas and values distinct from the impulses and wishes of the repressed unconscious. This ego was primarily concerned with defense, which was synonymous in this phase with repression.

The second phase of the concept of the ego, from 1897 to 1923, was influenced by Freud's abandonment of the seduction hypothesis and his concern with the instinctual drives, their representations, and their transformations. The concept of the ego was closely linked to the ego instinct, which Freud was struggling to clarify. Defense was limited primarily to repression and consisted of an instinctual force directed against unconscious derivatives. The ego's activities followed the reality principle and secondary process and included the capacity for delay of gratification.

During the third phase, from 1923 to 1937, the structural theory emerged in which the ego was defined as a structural entity and was definitively separated from the instinctual drives. Within the structural framework, the ego was a coherent organization of mental processes and functions oriented toward the perceptual-conscious system, and it included mechanisms responsible for resistance and unconscious defense.

This ego was still relatively passive and weak, responding to pressures from id, superego, and reality. Soon, however, the position of the ego was strengthened in Freud's reanalysis of anxiety in Inhibitions, Symptoms, and Anxiety (1926). Freud no longer saw the ego as merely passively responding with defensive repression to the turbulent demands of the id; rather, he viewed it as actively regulating the drive derivatives to produce a signal anxiety, an anticipation of danger, which set the defensive processes in motion. Signal anxiety became, for Freud, an autonomous ego function for the initiation of defense. In this way, the ego could turn passively experienced anxiety into active mastery; that is, the anxiety signal triggered a defensive response in the ego that overcame or avoided the threatening danger. The danger here was taken as coming from instinctual impulses, such as incestuous wishes, castration fears, and fears of separation and loss. Toward the end of this period, Freud introduced the notion that the ego evolved from sources independent of inherited instinctual drives. The ego was no longer seen as deriving from the instincts by way of confrontations with reality; rather, it was seen as having its own autonomous genetic roots.

The fourth phase of ego concept began with

Anna Freud's *The Ego and the Mechanisms of Defense* (1936) and culminated in the systematizing elaborations of Heinz Hartmann and David Rapaport. Hartmann's key contributions were the development of a theory of ego autonomy and emphasis on the principle of adaptation. *Ego autonomy* refers to the innate or acquired capacity of the ego to function independently of instinctual impulses and the influence of drive derivatives. *Adaptation* refers to the capacity of the organism to fit in and adjust harmoniously to the environment. The adaptational approach not only linked psychoanalytic theory with biological thinking but also laid the groundwork for elaboration of analytic principles into the framework for a general psychology of behavior.

Metapsychological Assumptions

Five metapsychological assumptions stated in part explicitly and in part implicitly by Freud express the minimum assumptions within which psychoanalytic theory is articulated. All statements of the theory express the respective points of view of these five assumptions or principles, and no psychoanalytic formulation is complete without taking all of these perspectives into account. The five assumptions are: First, the economic (energic) principle: psychological energies exist which follow the laws of conservation and entropy and are subject to specific transformations. Second, the dynamic (motivational) principle: psychological forces exist which are defined by direction and magnitude. Third, the structural point of view: abiding psychological configurations (structures) exist that are hierarchically ordered and subject to a slow rate of change. Fourth, the genetic (developmental) point of view: psychoanalytic explanation must include propositions concerning psychological origins and development. All psychological phenomena originate in innate givens (maturational factors) that develop according to an epigenetic plan; the totality of earlier forms codetermines all subsequent psychological phenomena. Fifth, the adaptive point of view: psychoanalytic explanation concerns relationships to the real environment. Adaptive processes are either autoplastic, in which the self is modified to adapt to environ-

mental demands, or alloplastic, in which the self restructures and modifies the environment to meet its own demands and needs, or both. These processes serve to maintain, restore, or improve existing states of adaptiveness, thereby ensuring a fit with the environment and survival.

The Tripartite Theory

In the structural theory, Freud placed the sexual and aggressive instincts in a special part of the mind called the *id*, which he believed to be a completely unorganized, primordial reservoir of instinctual energies under the domination of primary process. The id is, therefore, part of the unconscious, although not coextensive with it. The instinctual drives are biologically given, hereditary, and concerned only with seeking immediate discharge. These drives, however, are not simply random sources of energy but are specifically ordered by primary process organization. The presence or degree of structure in the id remains a question of theoretical debate.

The *ego* in the tripartite theory is closely related to consciousness and to external reality, and yet has unconscious operations in relation to the drives and their regulation. Freud provided a comprehensive definition of the ego:

> Here are the principal characteristics of the ego. In consequence of the pre-established connection between sense perception and muscular action, the ego has voluntary movement at its command. It has the task of self-preservation. As regards external events, it performs that task by becoming aware of stimuli, by storing up experiences about them (in the memory), by avoiding excessively strong stimuli (through flight), by dealing with moderate stimuli (through adaptation), and finally by learning to bring about expedient changes in the external world to its own advantage (through activity). As regards internal events in relation to the id, it performs that task by gaining control over the demands of the instinct, by deciding whether they are to be allowed satisfaction, by postponing that satisfaction to times and circumstances favorable in the external world, or by suppressing their excitations entirely. It is guided in its activity by consideration of the tension produced by stimuli, whether these tensions are present in it or introduced into it. (1940, pp. 145–146)

The ego serves as an intrapsychic agency with a variety of functions. First, it controls and regulates instinctual drives. To assure the integrity of the individual and to mediate between the id and the outside world, the ego must be able to delay immediate discharge of urgent wishes and impulses. This involves progression from domination by the pleasure principle to domination by the more adaptive reality principle, as well as a shift from primary process to secondary process cognitive organization. The ego also concerns itself with the relationship to reality, particularly in maintaining the sense of reality and the capacity for adaptive reality testing (the capacity to evaluate the external world and its meanings correctly).

The ego also carries out a variety of defensive functions. At first the concept of defense was synonymous with repression, but later the notion of defense became more differentiated and was linked to the signal theory of anxiety. Signal anxiety enables the ego to bring into operation a variety of defense mechanisms in response to specific signals of instinctual danger.

Another primary function of the ego is the function of synthesis—uniting, organizing, and binding together various drives, tendencies, and functions so that the individual is able to think, feel, and act in an organized and integrated manner. The synthetic function is concerned with the organization of ego functions into a consistent and coherent adaptive pattern.

The *superego* is the structural modification of the ego responsible for unconscious guilt, masochism, and negative therapeutic reactions. The concept of the superego supersedes the old censor of Freud's early dream theories. It arises from the internalization of parental prohibitions and prescriptions (ideals) in the resolution of the oedipal involvement. Thus the oedipal boy internalizes the potentially castrating father to avoid the oedipal guilt associated with incestuous sexual wishes toward his mother and murderous wishes against his father. The superego results from this identification with the punishing father, an identification based on the parental superego, which prohibits ("Thou shalt not") and prescribes ("Thou shalt").

Freud derived the mechanisms for internalization of the superego from his analysis of mourning and melancholia (1917), both of which result from object loss. In mourning, the ego gradually withdraws its libidinal attachment to the lost ob-

ject; the detached libido then directs itself to other substitute objects. In melancholia (depression), the libido cannot free itself from the object and instead takes the object into the ego, where it becomes a split-off part of the ego. As Freud put it, "the shadow of the object fell upon the ego," so that the original ambivalence toward the object—love and hate—is redirected toward the self (p. 249). He called this mechanism introjection or "narcissistic identification." In the case of superego formation, to which Freud applies this analysis, love and hate of the parental objects are thus internalized or introjected.

The internalized superego and the ego structures are the basis of the personality development of the child. While the superego originates in parental internalization, it also involves the internalization of social ethical standards, moral ideals, values, and prohibitions of conscience. The superego includes both protective, rewarding functions associated with ideals and values (ego ideal) and punitive, critical functions related to the unconscious sense of guilt and moral conscience (superego aggression).

While Freud's analysis of the superego derived from his experience with depressed, obsessional, and paranoid patients, significant areas of superego-ego integration remain that require further exploration. The formation and integration of value systems is one such area. The further understanding of adaptive superego functions has implications for the evolution of human culture.

Rebellious Disciples

The group that Freud gathered around him consisted of both devoted followers, the first generation of adherents to psychoanalysis, and men and women of independent mind and considerable creative capacity who disagreed with some of his formulations. The history of the psychoanalytic movement is a fascinating study in the interplay of personality conflicts and the genesis of revolutionary ideas. Not only was this a period of ferment in Freud's own psychoanalytic thinking, but the deviating viewpoints of some of his followers served as nodal points in the development of his own thinking and in the history of the movement.

For some of these disciples it was difficult to accept without question or rebellion the powerful hegemony of Freud's thinking. Freud's emphases on the role of libido in the etiology of neurosis and on the vicissitudes of sexual drives were impervious to other viewpoints. But the scope and complexity of psychoanalytic theory enlarged over the years, some of the differing viewpoints contributed to the larger body of analytic thinking. This is particularly true of the work of Alfred Adler (1870–1937), the first of the rebellious disciples.

Turning against the biological emphasis of Freud's ideas and particularly the role of sexuality in the neuroses, Adler left the ranks of Freud's disciples in 1911. His own work then focused on issues of inferiority versus superiority. His original ideas were concerned with organ inferiority but were then expanded to the general issue of human inferiority. Adler thought that inferiority as a universal human feeling originates in the child's feelings of inferiority because of his smallness and helplessness and that inferiority is countered by the need to seek a dominating or superior position. He further held that striving for power was essentially masculine in character, while passivity and inferiority were more feminine. Striving for superiority was therefore described as "masculine protest."

The struggle for superiority expressed the "will to power," and Adler reinterpreted the role of the oedipal complex in terms of its inherent power relationships, that is, the need to subjugate the mother and compete successfully with the father. For Adler, the will to power was the guiding force in human behavior, and his formulation forced Freud to deal more explicitly with aggression and the nature of defense.

Adler later emphasized the social aspects of human involvement, particularly what he termed "social interest," which could channel and restrain the will to power. He recognized the importance of the child's experience with important caretakers in the development of mutual dependency, but he diverged from Freud's intrapsychic and biological orientation. He also regarded education as an important means to achieve and amplify social interest. Recent developments in psychoanalysis have broadened the mainstream of psychoanalytic thought to include Adler's viewpoints. Adler's psychology was the equivalent of an ego psychology before its time.

Carl Jung (1875–1961) was an independent thinker. Though Freud at first designated him as his successor, the tension between the two men intensified through the years of their collaboration. Jung split with Freud in 1916 by publishing his *Psychology of the Unconscious*, in which he attacked Freud's notion of libido and reformulated the libido theory. He suggested that sexual libido was only a variant of a more primal libido, synonymous with an undifferentiated form of energy. For Jung, such energy emerged in the prepuberty period and only then began to play its predominant role.

Jung had more clinical experience with psychotic patients than did Freud. Furthermore, his writings reflected his deep immersion in the rich mythic and symbolic lore of many cultures, particularly those of the Orient. He gave symbols a broader and deeper interpretation than the restrictively sexual interpretation inherent in Freud's view. Jung was more sensitive to the transmission of neurotic difficulties from parents to children and emphasized the role of the mother. Only late in his career did Freud begin to appreciate the importance of the child's early interaction with the mother—an important area of interest for contemporary psychoanalysts.

Jung's notion of the collective unconscious (the deepest level of the unconscious mind, which contains psychic elements common to mankind in general and derived from phylogenetic experience) influenced Freud's thinking, particularly his idea of the "primal horde" as the origin of social structures. Although Freud thought that the taboo against incest was the result of racial memory of primal experiences, the notion of the collective unconscious never became a functional part of his theory. For Jung, the collective unconscious was a vital resource inherent in the patient's individual psyche, manifested through dreams and symbols and serving as a source of great therapeutic potential. Thus the dream was interpreted as an expression of archetypes or primordial images from the unconscious.

Jung differed from Freud in his theory of libido

and in his conception of the nature and function of the unconscious. Jung's libido theory postulated a more general form of psychic energy which tended to play down Freud's emphasis on sexual instincts and the sexual derivation of the neuroses. Moreover, Jung saw the unconscious as the repository of phylogenetic or racial experience, in contrast to Freud's more ontogenetic view of the unconscious as related to infantile experience and repression. In his later work, Jung's ideas took a pseudomystical and religious direction which became increasingly remote from clinical experience and seemed to have limited clinical applicability.

Otto Rank (1884–1939) was for many years Freud's devoted follower and secretary; only gradually did he define his own ideas and begin to diverge from Freud's. Rank did not accept Freud's formulations of the Oedipus complex. He presented instead a theory that related all neurotic anxiety to the birth trauma, which in his view produced a primal anxiety, expressed in neurotic manifestations, that slowly diminished throughout life. Separation anxiety was thus essential to his theory, since he felt that all later forms of separation reactivated the primal anxiety of the birth trauma.

Freud entertained some of these ideas and tried to relate them to his own notions of anxiety. But Rank saw his theory as the basis for a method of therapy that he felt could abbreviate the long, laborious course of analysis by actively emphasizing the birth trauma from the inception of therapy. Freud objected to this increased activity by the analyst and to focusing the analytic process in such a narrow way.

Rank interpreted the response of his patients to his active interventions in terms of conflicts over dependency and independence. He concluded that the basic problem was really the patient's difficulty in asserting his own will—another form of birth trauma, the birth of individuality. He began to view Freud's technique as one that fostered the tendency of the patient to submit, thus undermining his will. Rank stressed the present interaction with the analyst, and rather than emphasizing past relationships, he focused on issues of separation from the mother. He set a definite time limit for the treatment in order to intensify and precipitate separation is-

sues. Rank's will therapy has reverberations with Adler's and Jung's ideas and considerable influence on later experimentation by Ferenczi, Alexander, and others attempting to modify and shorten analytic treatment.

The Post-Freudians

In contrast to the rebellious disciples, the post-Freudians were more faithful followers who did not break with the master but extended and deepened his ideas. This group is the core of more orthodox psychoanalytic thinking after Freud.

Karl Abraham (1877–1925) was one of Freud's first disciples. He founded the Berlin Institute and enjoyed a prolific career as psychoanalyst and psychiatrist. His work in applying psychoanalytic insights to the psychoses, particularly in differentiating between hysteria and dementia praecox, is classic. Abraham's observation that psychotic patients lack the capacity for meaningful libidinal involvement with other human beings contributed significantly to Freud's views on narcissism. Abraham elaborated Freud's instinct theory, helped to crystallize the stages of infantile libidinal development and to relate them to forms of adult character pathology, and presented detailed descriptions of oral, anal, and genital character types. Moreover, starting from Freud's views on mourning and melancholia, Abraham developed the psychoanalytic understanding of depression, particularly the role of introjection in such pathological states.

Melanie Klein (1882–1960) trained under Abraham in Berlin and then moved to London. Her research and teachings became a source of germinal inspiration and sharp controversy that still profoundly influence psychoanalytic thinking. Klein took her point of departure from Freud's later instinct theory, particularly the death instinct. Working primarily with very young children, she described the operation of instinctual dynamics in the first years of life.

She held that the child, driven by the death instinct, is compelled to rid himself of intolerable, destructive impulses (predominantly oral) and to project them externally. The earliest recipient of these projected impulses is the mother's breast, which provides the need-satisfying nourishment and satiation (good breast) but also often deprives and fails to satisfy (bad breast). At this stage, the images of the breast are part-objects that the infant has yet to combine into a single whole object—the mother. Early frustration of oral needs, even in the first year of life, reinforces these trends so that the bad breast becomes a persecutory object. The experience of the bad breast and its associated persecutory anxiety form the earliest developmental stage in Klein's theory—the paranoid position.

The bad breast withholds gratification and thus stimulates the child's primitive oral envy. This envy and the sadistic wishes it provokes take the form of wishes to penetrate and destroy the mother's breasts and body. In boys, these primitive destructive impulses give rise to the fear of retaliation (based in part on projection), which takes the form of castration anxiety; in girls, the primitive envy is expressed in envy of the mother's breast during the oral developmental phase and is later transformed into penis envy during the genital phase. Klein held that by the time of weaning, the child is capable of recognizing the mother as a whole object possessing good and bad qualities. However, combination of good and bad qualities in a single object—previously separated in part-objects—creates a dilemma: destructive attacks on the bad object will also destroy the good and needed object. This prevents the child from unleashing aggressive impulses against the object and lays the basis for the depressive position in which aggression is directed against the self rather than the object. The guilt associated with destructive wishes against the object is the precursor of conscience.

Even at this early level of development, Klein postulated the formulation of a primitive superego. Particularly in the anal-sadistic phase, this primitive superego directs aggression against the self so that the child seeks to eject it. Projection of superego elements permits acceptance of good introjects (internalization of good objects), which alleviates the underlying paranoid anxiety. The superego elements are later reintrojected to become the agency of guilt and early forms of obsessional behavior. The Kleinian emphasis on good and bad introjects, following Abraham's lead, concentrates on the vital relationships to objects at the earliest level of child

development. This aspect of Klein's thinking has been the point of departure for later object-relations theories.

Sandor Ferenczi (1873–1935) was another of the early circle who influenced later psychoanalysis. He experimented with the psychoanalytic method, and it was on these grounds that he finally deviated from Freud. Ferenczi tried to shorten the course of analytic treatment by intensifying the patient's emotional experiences—a procedure he called "active therapy," which was frowned on by the more orthodox analysts. He attempted a variety of forms of suggestion and behavioral modification, using a technique of forced fantasies which antedated certain contemporary therapeutic developments. His work emphasized the emotional rather than the intellectual-interpretive aspects of analysis and was the precursor of more flexible, active approaches to treatment that adapt the therapeutic process to the patient's special needs and personality organization.

Wilhelm Reich (1897–1957), one of the later followers of Freud, rose to prominence in the 1920s as a creative contributor to psychoanalysis. Regrettably, later in his career, his quest for the biological roots of the libido theory led him to formulate the orgone theory, an unfortunate pseudoscientific aberration.

Reich's contributions to psychoanalytic thinking were his ideas of character structure and character analysis. He viewed character as a defensive structure, an armor for the ego against both internal instinctual pressures and external environmental stimuli. He held that character armor becomes an automatic pattern of reaction, which retains a certain flexibility in healthier characters but becomes rigid and unyielding in the neurotic personality. He saw character formation as an attempt to resolve conflicts over incestuous wishes.

Reich's character analysis derived from his hypothesis that resistances are inherent in the character structure of neurotic patients. Resistances reveal themselves in the patient's characteristic ways of acting and reacting, exemplified by traits such as passivity, arrogance, and argumentativeness. He felt that character traits and character resistance had to be distinguished by repeatedly confronting the patient with these traits until the patient began to experience them as foreign bodies requiring removal. This undermining of character resistance would then open the way for revival of repressed infantile material and its analysis along more strictly Freudian lines.

Anna Freud (1895–) has become the leading interpreter of orthodox analytic views. Her work *The Ego and the Mechanisms of Defense* (1936) brought the ego and its defenses into the center of clinical interest and work. In her view, attention to and analysis of the patient's defenses are mandatory, along with the analysis of instinctual components.

Anna Freud has also been a major contributor and guide in the development of child analysis. She was one of the first to adapt analytic techniques to the treatment of children, using play techniques particularly. Later, she became the central figure in the more orthodox reaction to Melanie Klein's views about child analysis and development. She insisted on the need to modify analytic techniques in work with children, especially in view of the immaturity of the child's psychic structures and the child's relative inability to distinguish reality from fantasy. She disagreed with Klein's views of early superego formation and the Kleinian attempts to use direct interpretation in therapy with young children.

Franz Alexander (1891–1964), one of the younger generation of analysts whom Freud himself thought promising, spent most of his career in the United States. His contributions to psychosomatic medicine, particularly his theory of psychosomatic specificity and specific organ vulnerability, strongly influenced psychosomatic research of the 1940s and 1950s. The specificity hypothesis suggested that some organic diseases have not only a specific pathophysiology but also a specific psychopathology.

Another contribution involved his attempts to apply analytic principles to dynamic psychotherapy. He adopted a more flexible position, questioning traditional psychoanalytic dogmas about therapy such as whether length and intensity of therapy necessarily imply depth of therapeutic effect, or whether a small number of interviews necessarily precludes more stable and profound therapeutic effects. Alexander focused on what he considered the essence of the psychoanalytic process—the bringing into awareness of unconscious motivations and feelings, thus extending conscious control over behavior.

He experimented with several parameters of therapy, including deliberate interruptions of treatment as a way of increasing the emotional intensity and efficacy of the therapeutic process. Such artificial separations confronted the patient with his dependency and were intended to enable the patient to recognize and accept his independence.

Alexander emphasized the emotional aspects of therapy in his concept of the "corrective emotional experience." Under the favorable conditions of therapy, he attempted to expose the patient to emotional conflicts handled unsuccessfully in the past. Rather than stressing the repetitive aspects of infantile conflicts in the transference relationship, Alexander emphasized the differences between the infantile conflict situation and the current therapy situation. He thought that these emotional aspects of the treatment process were necessary for therapeutic results, and, consequently, he underplayed the therapeutic effects of insight gained through interpretation—the more traditional analytic view. Alexander's formulations have profoundly influenced the technique of analytically oriented psychotherapy.

The Neo-Freudians

The neo-Freudians gained recognition in the 1930s, taking their point of departure from later Freudian ideas. They rebelled against basic analytic orientations, particularly the instinct theory, and put greater emphasis on social and cultural factors. At the time, this development took the form of a rejection of more orthodox analytic concepts, since analytic theory had not matured sufficiently to assimilate these new directions. This divergence is no longer so striking or radical because contemporary psychoanalytic theories have developed to the extent that they now experience greater rapprochement with and awareness of overlap and complementarity between more orthodox and later neo-Freudian positions.

Although Karen Horney (1885–1952) was trained in the orthodox psychoanalytic tradition, her early contributions not only stamped her as a distinguished contributor to psychoanalytic thinking but also presaged the direction of her later thinking. Early in her career, she challenged Freud's ideas on feminine psychology, on the nature of the neurotic process, on the concept of the death instinct, and particularly on the role of cultural factors in neurosis.

Many of her ideas had an Adlerian quality, although her thinking was strikingly original. She formulated a holistic notion of the personality as an individual unit functioning within a social framework and continually caught up in interaction and mutual influence with its environment. While she recognized the role of biological needs and drives, she shifted the emphasis in her theory of personality and neurosis to the dynamic influences of cultural and social factors. She found it necessary to reject Freud's structural theory and his theory based on the "economics" of psychic energy. She emphasized current interactions and motivations rather than infantile libidinal derivatives operating through the repetition compulsion.

At the center of her theory was the concept of the self. She postulated an actual self, a real self, and an idealized self as the main facets of the personality. The actual self was the sum total of the individual's experience. The real self was a more central force or principle, unique within each individual and equivalent to a sense of healthy integration or harmonious wholeness. The idealized self, however, was a manifestation of neurosis and served as a means of avoiding psychic conflict by adopting an attitude of superiority or self-sufficiency or by demanding special consideration. The idealized self is, in Horney's terms, a form of glorified self-image that can progressively encompass more aspects of the personality and, when relatively or totally unconscious, provide the source of neurotic claims and demands. Fears, inhibitions, and feelings of deprivation can thus be transformed into unbalanced demands for and expectations of attention or support that can control the individual's inner life and external behavior. Horney referred to this imbalance as the "pride system," which manifests itself in excessive standards and expectations, on the one hand, and excessive self-hatred and self-contempt, on the other. This system produces a condition of alienation from the self and characteristically neurotic solutions of inner tension. Horney's ideas concerning the idealized self and the pride system come close to current psychoanalytic ideas concerning narcissism.

In regard to therapy, Horney rejected symptom relief or social adjustment as adequate therapeutic goals. Rather, she emphasized self-realization and self-actualization, dealing with the here and now in contradistinction to the derivatives of past experience. Further, she emphasized the activity of the analyst in the therapeutic process rather than the stereotype of the analyst as a detached, unfeeling, unresponding mirror. She felt that the emotional involvement between therapist and patient was an important aspect of the therapeutic process.

Harry Stack Sullivan (1892–1949) was the first of the neo-Freudians to receive his psychoanalytic experience and training entirely in the United States. Following men like Adolf Meyer and William Alanson White, Sullivan turned away from the biological and instinctual bias of classic psychoanalytic theories and concentrated on interpersonal relations as the central concept of his thinking.

His theory of development did not altogether abandon basic biological drives or needs. But rather than seeing bodily zones as the determining source of developmental changes, he regarded them as the critical areas through which the child established interpersonal contact with the significant figures in his environment. Sullivan highlighted the need for security, which he felt could only be satisfied through meaningful, gratifying interpersonal relationships. According to Sullivan, the confidence derived from these relationships creates a sense of self-esteem that overcomes the feelings of powerlessness and helplessness that are part of the human condition. The lack of a sense of security or self-esteem, exacerbated by an abiding sense of disapproval by the significant figures (parents), becomes a source of anxiety.

Sullivan saw anxiety as the propelling force for personality development and the central element in the etiology of neuroses, psychoses, and other forms of psychopathology. The "self-system" discharges tension in acceptable ways, prevents the individual from being overwhelmed by anxiety, and maintains the personality as an effectively functioning entity. When the anxiety-containing resources of the self-system are exceeded, clinical symptoms result. Both neuroses and psychoses stem from disturbances in interpersonal relationships. Freud regarded psychosis as the result of conflict between the ego and reality and viewed neurosis as an intrapsychic conflict among the id, ego, and superego. For Sullivan, however, the basic conflict was between the individual and the human environment of significant others. Sullivan believed that intrapsychic conflicts were derived from interpersonal conflicts by the internalization of external objects and conflicted relationships.

Sullivan's approach to therapy did not differ radically from more analytic approaches, but he focused specifically on anxiety and the interpersonal context in which it occurred. He saw the therapist as an active participant-observer in an exploratory process. Correspondingly, he emphasized current patterns of interpersonal interaction rather than genetic aspects of the individual's behavior.

Erich Fromm (1900–) received some of his training at the Berlin Psychoanalytic Institute, but his orientation was that of a social psychologist primarily interested in the role of cultural and social processes in producing mental disorder. The chief focus of Fromm's attack on Freud was his criticism of the theories of libido and psychic energy.

Fromm saw neurotic devices as mechanisms for escaping from tensions arising from the basic dichotomies of human existence. The need to escape results in irrational methods of relating to the social group, which Fromm describes as sadomasochism, destructiveness, and automaton conformity. The sadomasochistic mechanism of escape allows the individual to lean on another for support; that other, in turn, represents a power or authority whose resources can be exploited. The destructive mechanism attempts to cope with the feeling of powerlessness by trying to destroy or eliminate the other, perceived as an object of potential threat. Alternatively, the individual may try to escape by automaton conformity, in which he blindly adopts and becomes dependent on cultural patterns.

Fromm described some character patterns re-lated to the specific mechanism of escape used by an individual. His character types are the receptive, the exploitative, the hoarding, the marketing, and, finally, the productive character. The receptive character is one who becomes dependent on a magic helper. The exploitative character exercises power over others, exploiting and using them. The hoarding character's underlying insecurity and fear of loss are salved by hoarding and possessiveness. The marketing character has a predilection for automaton conformity; the self is sold like a commodity and worth is defined in terms of success. Fromm's productive character, roughly equivalent to the genital character of Freud and Abraham, has achieved the capacity for love and creative work. The emphasis in Fromm's characterology is not on the internal determinants of character but, rather, on the shaping of character by extrinsic social forces and cultural influences.

Object-Relations Theorists

Historically, the impetus for the theory of object relations came from Melanie Klein, particularly from her notion of intrapsychic introjects representing the internalization of significant object relations. This trend has been reinforced by the increasing proportion of patients with severe character problems or personality disorders in which major patterns of living in relation to other people are fundamentally disturbed. Analytic attempts to treat such patients have led to explorations of their personality organization as well as problems of early object relations and their effect on personality development.

Michael Balint (1896–1970) focused on the earliest stages of mother-child involvement. He rejected Freud's formulation of primary narcissism, in which the infant's attachment to objects derives from a primary state of self-contained libidinal investment. He substituted a stage of primary love in which the infant begins life in a condition of relatedness to the maternal object and is libidinally invested in her. He accepted the lack of differentiation between self and object so characteristic of this early stage and emphasized the need for a harmonious fitting together of mother and child, especially at the beginning of the child's life.

From this early symbiotic matrix, two basic life

attitudes develop as the infant's perceptions of himself and the mother differentiate. These polar tendencies in the way the child structures the object world take shape in the course of individuation. One is the tendency to feel safe and secure by maintaining close, clinging attachments to objects (ocnophilic) so that separation becomes the central anxiety. The opposite tendency seeks safety and security through the exercise of ego capacities in exploring the world away from objects. A corollary of the latter tendency is the sense of danger by engulfment. This motivates the development of skills in dealing with people without getting deeply involved or attached (philobatic). These extreme tendencies are usually mixed to varying degrees in individual personalities.

Balint concerned himself with the manifestation of developmental failures in the therapeutic process. He distinguished between phases of benign and malignant regression. During benign regression in analysis, the analyst provides a form of empathic recognition which enables the patient to bear the unstructured experience with at least manageable anxiety. Lost infantile objects can then be mourned and the patient's assumptions about the object world recast. In malignant regression, the ego is overwhelmed by unmanageable anxiety, which prevents the patient from doing the work of therapy. Balint referred to this level of the analysis as the basic fault, a fundamental disturbance in object relations prior to the acquisition of language. He felt that the basic fault could not be repaired by verbal techniques and interpretation but required something that was nonverbal, yet specifically derived from the object relationship between patient and analyst.

If Melanie Klein's theory was an instinctual theory without an ego, the theory of object relations developed by Ronald Fairbairn (1889–1964) was an ego theory without instincts. Fairbairn's approach has been elaborated and articulated by Harry Guntrip (1901–) in recent years.

Fairbairn tried to separate psychological science from its biological roots and thereby to dissociate his theory of the ego from the theory of instincts as biological drives. He stressed that instincts are inherently object-seeking, rather than concerned with energy reduction or tension discharge. Therefore, he postulated that the mental

apparatus consists of inherently dynamic structures from the beginning of life and that the ego likewise is integrated, whole, and object-related from the first. These aspects of dynamic functioning and structure are for Freud the outcome of a developmental process, but for Fairbairn they are unexplained givens of his theory. Consequently, his theory bypasses any real concept of ego development or of the development of object relations; it also bypasses the problems of self-object differentiation by simply postulating that the ego is related to its objects from the beginning.

Fairbairn's theory predicates an initially undivided ego. Consequently, all psychic structures evolve as ego substructures by a process of splitting (a defensive mechanism by which good and bad impulses and objects are separated) and introjection (a defense in which a representation of a loved or hated object is internalized and serves as a quasi-autonomous source of psychic activity); the two processes involve parallel splitting of objects and of the ego. These formulations reflect Fairbairn's preoccupation with schizoid patients in whom the inner splitting of the ego and the withdrawal from object-relatedness is the central pathology.

Fairbairn, Guntrip, and other object-relations theorists address themselves to the ambiguities regarding the personal ego in classic analytic structural theory. As long as the ego is regarded as an organization of functions, as in the structural theory, there is no place in it for the personal, subjectively apprehended, and sensed ego as a source of inner activity (the subjective sense of "I"). Fairbairn's object-relations theory challenges the structural viewpoint by postulating a personal (subjectively perceived) ego, but does not resolve the inherent ambiguity between the personal and the structural ego, that is, a subjective source of personal activity versus an organization of functions.

Donald Winnicott (1897–1971), a gifted pediatrician who became a psychoanalyst, contributed ingeniously to the study of early object relations and character pathology by focusing on the earliest stages of mother-child interaction.

Winnicott described the emergence of what he called transitional objects, the infant's first object possession that is perceived as separate from the infant's self. Winnicott argued from close study of infant behavior in using transitional objects that the object stands for the maternal breast, or the first external object to which the infant relates. The emergence of the transitional object antedates capacities for reality testing. Winnicott held that the transitional object could become a fetish object and persist as a part of adult sexual adjustment. It could also influence later anal erotic organization, in which case feces could become a transitional object.

The transitional object exists in the realm of illusion, which is contributed to by both the external reality of the object (the mother's breast) and the internal object (the introjected breast) yet is distinct from both. This intermediate area of experience, shared by both inner and external reality, absorbs the greater part of the infant's experience and is retained in areas of adult creativity and imagination. The transitional object itself is usually decathected—that is, it becomes less and less an object of emotional investment—and its importance thus diminishes as it is replaced by emerging cultural interests.

The mother's participation in this intermediate realm of illusion, which the transitional object inhabits, depends on her responsiveness to the infant's need to create her as a good mother. In this responsiveness she functions as a "good-enough mother." Her failure to provide good-enough mothering results in the emergence of a false self in the child, a condition that represents a failure in developmental experience and results in a variety of character pathologies. Winnicott's notions of the formation of the false self are similar to Balint's formulations regarding the basic fault and to Fairbairn's notion of the schizoid personality. Such patients are neither neurotic nor psychotic, but they relate to the world through a compliant shell that is not quite real to them or to us. These disturbed personality types reflect deficits in very early object relations, specifically in the mutuality and reciprocal responsiveness of the early mother-child object relationship. Winnicott, along with the other object-relations theorists, has been intensely concerned with the modifications of the analytic process that may be required to meet the needs of such defective personalities. The model for such modifications in Winnicott's approach is good-enough mothering.

Contemporary Psychoanalytic Ego Psychology

Contemporary ego psychology began with the work of Anna Freud and Heinz Hartmann (1894–1970). Miss Freud's work on the ego appeared in German in 1936 and Hartmann's monograph, *Ego Psychology and the Problem of Adaptation*, in 1939. Anna Freud's work completed the ego psychology of her father, which viewed the ego primarily as preoccupied with the work of defense and reaction to instinctual pressures. Hartmann's work opened the way to a new set of problems and concepts that turned the ego's face more explicitly to the outside world. Hartmann's insistence on ego autonomy and adaptive capacities initiated the systematic elaboration of a more powerful ego psychology and the development of broader psychosocial understanding of the ego's activity and involvement in the external environment.

Hartmann's outstanding contribution was the clarification and elaboration of Freud's theory of ego psychology. Freud had suggested that the ego was formed by gradual modification of the id by the impact of external reality on instinctual drives, as a result of which the pleasure principle was gradually replaced by the reality principle. Freud thus emphasized the effect of instincts on ego development.

Hartmann introduced some important modifications to this theory by postulating primary autonomous ego functions that develop independently of the drives and of conflicts. Together with Kris and Loewenstein, he suggested that the ego does not differentiate from the id, as Freud had suggested, but that both id and ego develop from a common undifferentiated matrix. Furthermore, the rudimentary apparatuses that underlie primary autonomous ego functions (perception, motility, memory, and intellect) are present from birth and may undergo congenital or genetically determined variations. These rudimentary ego apparatuses work to enable the infant to fit in with the object and the environment to gain satisfaction of instinctual needs and drives. The balance of controlling forces—ego autonomy from the demands of the id, as well as ego autonomy from the demands of the environment—required for optimal functioning of the organism forms the basis for Hartmann's theory of the adaptive functions of the ego in mediating between external reality and the demands of internal psychic systems. Hartmann introduced the adaptational point of view as one of the basic assumptions of psychoanalytic theory and linked it to the concept of the autonomy of the ego.

Hartmann designated an area in which the ego functions without intrapsychic conflict, which he called "conflict-free." This area of ego functioning includes the capacities for perception, intuition, comprehension, thinking, language, certain aspects of motor development, learning, and intelligence. When any of these functions becomes secondarily involved in conflict, the conflict-free operation may be impeded. The guarantee of conflict-free functioning depends on the primary autonomous structure of the ego as an independent realm of psychic organization that is not totally dependent on or derived from the instincts. The emergence of primary autonomous factors requires stimulation by an "average expectable environment" that guarantees and supports their autonomous development and functioning.

The ego may also retrieve certain functions from the domination of drive influences. Hartmann referred to this aspect of ego autonomy as secondary autonomy. Thus, a mechanism that arises in the service of defense may become an independent structure such that the drive impulse merely triggers the "automatized" function. For example, reaction formations (such as emphasizing cleanliness to defend against anal impulses related to filth and dirt) may lose their defensive quality and become nonconflicted and adaptive aspects of character. This change of function requires a different form of energy. Hartmann related the conflict-free area of functioning to neutralized energies derived from libidinal or aggressive energy by the desexualization of libidinal drives or the deaggressivization of aggressive drives. This provides the autonomous ego functions with energies whose drive interference or dependence is minimal.

Hartmann's ego psychology dealt primarily with ego mechanisms and structures and only incidentally with instinctual drives and derivatives. It concerned itself primarily with ego mechanisms and structures and the formal aspects of their organization. Hartmann tried to shift the focus of psychoanalysis from a clinically oriented, content-based theory to a more general theory of the psychic apparatus and human behavior.

The major architect of this domain of ego psychology was David Rapaport (1911–1960), the great systematizer of ego psychology, who developed Hartmann's ideas about the functioning of the ego, with particular attention to the ego's cognitive functioning. Rapaport's work has given rise to a number of hypotheses that have stimulated major efforts to test psychoanalytic theories by extra-analytic experimental designs. Rapaport, more than any other analytic thinker, has spurred the effort by which psychoanalysis can evolve into a general theory of psychological behavior.

Erik Erikson (1902–) made two important contributions to psychoanalytic thinking with his modification of instinct theory and his epigenetic theory. Erikson's modification of instinct theory suggests a relationship between the instinctual zones as formulated by Freud and the development of specific modalities of ego functioning. Erikson links aspects of ego development with the genetic timetable of instinctual development, whereby particular erotogenic zones become the loci of stimulation for the development of particular modalities of ego functioning.

The first mode of ego development—the oral-incorporative or "taking-in" mode—relates to the oral phase. The subsequent oral-retentive mode consists of taking and holding on to things. These elements of getting, getting what is given, or getting to be a giver lay the groundwork for a basic sense of trust, which is a primary psychosocial attainment. Similarly, in the later anal-urethral muscular stage, retentive and eliminative modes operate through the capacity for self-control over impulses of letting go and holding on. These modalities of retention and elimination underlie the second nuclear psychosocial conflict, the establishment of basic autonomy or, conversely, the laying down of the basis for a sense of shame or doubt.

Erikson proposes an epigenetic schema that spans the entire life cycle. At each stage of his schema, basic psychosocial crises must be resolved. The resolution of each crisis provides the basis and starting point for the resolution of succeeding crises. Erikson designates eight psychosocial crises: (1) basic trust versus basic mistrust, (2) autonomy versus shame and doubt, (3) initiative versus guilt, (4) industry versus inferiority, (5) identity versus role confusion, (6) intimacy versus isolation, (7) generativity versus stagnation, and (8) ego integrity versus despair.

Erikson's notion of identity has had great impact on contemporary thinking, but difficulties arise in integrating this elusive notion with the traditional psychoanalytic framework. Erikson describes identity in the following terms: "At one time, then, it will appear to refer to a conscious sense of individual identity; at another to an unconscious striving for a continuity of personal character; at a third, as a criterion for the silent doings of ego synthesis; and finally as a maintenance for an inner solidarity with a group's ideals and identity" (1959, p. 102). Thus identity seems to have at one and the same time an internal and an external frame of reference. Internally, it relates to the integration of the self; externally, it relates to those aspects of social and cultural organization by which the individual is accepted into and becomes a functioning part of his society and culture.

The notion of identity has served as an integrating concept at a point in the history of psychoanalysis when attempts are being made to integrate psychoanalytic theory with broader aspects of social and cultural influence. Such theoretical integration remains a serious problem, however. One could view identity as an aspect of the integration of the self-concept, but the status of the self-concept itself in psychoanalytic theory is by no means secure. Nevertheless, with his concept of identity and the epigenetic schema of psychosocial crises, Erikson has opened up a rich and provocative area for future exploration.

Psychological Theories of Personality

The theories discussed in this section present a variety of models of the personality that derive from psychological investigation rather than from clinical experience. Although these theories have not arisen within a clinical context

and thus lack the broad relevance and immediate application to clinical concerns of primarily psychoanalytic theories, their importance for psychiatric thinking cannot be underestimated. They have stimulated a considerable body of research, and some have provided a basis for understanding more specific areas of psychiatric work (the theories of Piaget on development and Lewin on group dynamics, for example). Finally, they provide perspectives on human experience and behavior that often reach beyond the limited psychopathological view of more specifically clinical theories. An important work of the future is the integration of these psychological approaches with more explicitly clinical theories. These psychological approaches have been subdivided here into six theoretical categories: humanistic (Allport, Maslow), factor (Cattell), field (Lewin), systems-information (von Bertalanffy, Ruesch), phenomenological (Rogers, existentialist), and learning theories (Piaget, Gestalt, stimulus-response, cognitive control).

Humanistic Theories

Humanistic theories approach behavior in relatively holistic and dynamic terms. They are primarily concerned with what is unique and distinctive about human behavior and experience.

Gordon Allport (1897–1967) was for years the dean of American personality theorists. Impressed by the complexity and uniqueness of the individual human personality, he envisioned personality as an open system in constant interaction with its environment, not subject to the laws of entropy, as are closed, physical systems. Allport distinguished between the historical roots of motives and their current functioning. He held that motivation may be, and in healthy individuals usually is, independent of its origins. He termed this the *functional autonomy* of motives, a formulation very close to, if not identical with, Hartmann's notion of secondary autonomy.

Central to Allport's theory of personality is the trait, by which he meant a determining tendency or predisposition to action resulting from the integration of several habits. These combinations are never exactly the same in different individuals, but they do show certain biological and cultural similarities that form comparable modes of adjustment. Traits, then, are generalized predispositions to behavior that provide the basis for personality description.

Allport took a staunch position against scientific reductionism in psychology, particularly regarding personality. He saw two contrasting orientations toward the study of personality. The first came from a Lockean tradition, the second from a Leibnitzian or Kantian position. In the Lockean position, the mind begins as a *tabula rasa*, and its development is determined by environmental influences. By contrast, the Leibnitzian or Kantian tradition postulates a perpetually self-activating mind whose development comes from its own inner potentiality and spontaneous dynamisms. Allport thought that a dynamic synthesis was required to integrate the respective contributions of these orientations and thus provide an adequate understanding of personality.

The theory of personality developed by Abraham Maslow (1908–1970) is a theory of psychic health rather than of sickness. It postulates a hierarchy of needs underlying human motivation; when the needs with the greatest potency are satisfied, the next level of needs presses for fulfillment. The hierarchy reaches from the most basic physiological needs to the highest order of esthetic and spiritual needs.

For Maslow, man is essentially good. The development and behavior of the individual can only be subverted by the interference of society, which places impediments to the fulfillment of man's inner needs. Particularly important are the needs for esteem, knowledge, and beauty. But social institutions and processes can also help in the process of self-actualization. The self-actualized man, who makes full use of his capacities and potentialities, is the central and idealized prototype of Maslow's theory. Such individuals are able to use their capacities and potentialities fully and are characterized by high levels of objectivity, humility, and creativity, lack of inner conflict, and a capacity for joy.

The notion of peak experiences is important in Maslow's theory. These are experiences in which an individual feels especially fulfilled, intensely satisfied, and functions to the full limits of his potentiality. Such moments are found in the lives of ordinary people, but they are particularly characteristic of self-actualized individuals.

In therapy, Maslow aimed at increasing self-knowledge and understanding and mobilizing the potentialities and resources of individuals toward greater self-actualization. He stressed man's inherent goodness and capacity for love, and he made therapeutic efforts to mobilize these capacities by generating intense, emotional peak experiences. He felt positively about the sensitivity movement and the development of growth centers, since he thought that they might prove to be a vehicle for unleashing such experiences.

Factor Theories

The mathematical approach to personality relies on objective methods of personality measurement and the application of mathematical techniques, particularly forms of analysis of variance and covariance and factor analysis, to assess the role of personality factors in an individual and unique personality. These factors are similar to the traits defined by humanistic theories. Quantitative methods of personality study, particularly the method of multivariate design, derive from the work of Francis Galton, Carl Spearman, and L. L. Thurstone. This approach involves the simultaneous measure and correlation of multiple variables, which can be reduced to a limited set of underlying functional unities and then used to predicate particular patterns of personality.

The underlying factors or source traits give rise to surface traits, that is, to behaviors that appear and disappear in combination with each other. Functional psychological testing tries to discover the inherent dynamic, temperamental, or functional capacities of the human personality. A specific act expresses the total personality, which is evaluated by the profile of source trait scores. The act therefore represents an intersection of a multidimensional personality functioning within a multidimensional context.

The multivariate factor analyst attempts to make a diagnosis similar to that of the clinician. The difference is that the factor analyst actually measures the changing strength of symptoms and calculates their covariation to elucidate the interconnection of symptoms, rather than assessing them on a relatively intuitive basis, as does the clinician. For example, R. B. Cattell

(1905–) developed a personality factor test involving sixteen quantitatively determined factors which provide a profile of the functioning personality. Cattell's sixteen factors include warmth of affect, intelligence, ego strength, excitability, dominance, superego strength, shrewdness, guilt proneness, and self-sufficiency. Further efforts are needed to apply sophisticated quantitative techniques to clinical work. The advent of computer scoring will, one hopes, facilitate this development.

Field Theory

The dominant figure in field theory was Kurt Lewin (1890–1947), who was trained in phenomenology, mathematics, and Gestalt psychology. He saw personality as a composite of forces and vectors operating in a field of forces—like iron filings in a magnetic field. The data were essentially observational and intuitive, but the theory tried to express these more or less intuitive psychological elements in mathematical terms. The field approach has had little impact on individual personality study, but it has influenced the study of group and social processes. Lewin's approach to behavior presumes that a systematic psychology can be based on experience and a common-sense approach to reality, that behavior means goal-directed action, and that the proper language of psychological theory is geometry, specifically topology.

The fundamental concept in Lewin's system is the "life space," the sum of all facts that determine the person's behavior at a given point in time. The life space includes two primary dimensions: the psychological environment and the person himself. The psychological environment is the external or physical environment, insofar as it determines the person's behavior. The emphasis on causal determination and on behavior distinguishes the psychological environment from more strictly phenomenological considerations. The emphasis, therefore, is not on the person's subjective perception or understanding of external influences, but on the causal action of these elements in determining behavior. Behavior is not simply activity but is defined specifically as a change in the psychological environment. Activity qualifies as behavior only to

the extent that it brings about changes in the psychological environment. This broadened concept of behavior includes dimensions not directly related to external behavior, such as loyalty, aspirations, and hopes, all of which are defined as behavior because they affect the psychological environment.

Lewin used geometry to represent the psychological environment. He assumed that behavior is goal directed and can be represented as movement within a geometric space. Topology (rubber-sheet geometry) offers an analogy for human interactions in that topological properties do not change when the spatial configurations are stretched or distorted. Within this topological representation, the environment is composed of discrete regions equivalent to significant psychological events.

Within the topological field, motivation and movement are depicted as psychological forces, having vectors (direction) and strength or intensity. This manner of representation has commonsense validity, even though the explanation of vector forces is more or less intuitive. Forces are directed toward goals. When the goal attracts, it possesses positive valence; the goal is equivalently a psychological region of positive valence. Similarly, unpleasant or dangerous regions in the psychological space have negative valence. These valences and their combinations constitute the force field within which the psychological forces interact.

The second dimension of the life space in Lewin's analysis is the person. The person's motivation comes from need states. The need system is in a state of tension or "hunger." The state of need tension (thirst) gives a specific region of the environment (water) a positive valence. Achievement of the goal provides satisfaction of the need state and consequently need reduction. When the need state is unsatisfied and the tension persists, the person tends to think about or become preoccupied with the need-satisfying object or situation. The classic experiment was that of Zeigarnik, who showed that subjects were preoccupied more about unfinished than finished problems (the Zeigarnik effect).

In general, Lewin's field theory has a commonsense foundation and a certain degree of commonsense validity. However, the concepts are purely operational, such that the links between theoretical terms and concrete observation can be made only by commonsense assumption or intuition. Moreover, topology tends to be primarily descriptive and does not permit the systematic derivation of testable hypotheses. It has no place for personality traits or internal structural modifications that might influence the direction of the behaviors. Similarly, there is no place for internal dispositional states, such as anxiety, depression, and other states of emotional arousal. The most fruitful application of Lewin's concepts has been to areas of social psychology and group process, where it has been used with considerable ingenuity in describing the operational forces within group psychological environments.

Systems-Information Theory

Stimulated by the mathematical concepts of servomechanisms and cybernetics in the work of Norbert Wiener (1894–1964) and by information theory, the general systems approach developed in areas foreign to psychiatry, such as engineering. Only within the past few years has it found application within psychiatry in the work of Jürgen Ruesch (1909–) and others.

The crucial mechanism in the cybernetic process is the feedback circuit, along which the output of the system sends a modifying feedback signal that modulates the ongoing activity of the system. Positive feedback increases the level of output by the system, while negative feedback reduces the output. The biological organism consists of aggregates of interacting feedback circuits that maintain internal homeostasis. Homeostasis is the basic steady state of the organism; it depends on the operation of interlocking regulations that maintain certain variables within a constant range and direct the organism toward specific goals. The system is constantly monitored by feedback mechanisms to maintain its internal stability or its target direction.

Living organisms are open systems with continual input from and output to the environment. Feedback mechanisms maintain this open system in a steady state, but this homeostasis requires the continuous exchange and flow of material. Such systems may maintain themselves in a state of negative entropy, that is, in a condition of greater improbability, order, and complexity. Such systems increase their level of order, complexity, and differentiation through development and adaptation.

Within this framework, the human personality has the properties of a system with a dynamic ordering of parts and processes involved in mutual interaction and regulation. Psychopathology is a disruption of the system rather than a loss of single functions. Personality itself is an integration of subsystems that are, at the lowest level, biological or physiological. These subsystems are integrated into the functioning personality system, which in turn is a subsystem of broader social and cultural systems, in relation to which the individual is involved in continuous mutual regulation and adaptation. At each level of system integration, the feedback mechanisms and homeostatic regulations are qualitatively different. However, the system perspective provides an overall integrating schema by which the various parts can be studied and understood in relation to one another.

A subvariant of the systems approach is the application of communications theory to psychiatry (Ruesch, 1957). Communication is a process of social interchange determined by the organs of communication, the social environment with which the individual interacts and communicates, and the manner in which the individual's knowledge, skills, and capacities for adaptation are influenced by his experience.

The message is the basic unit in this communication system. Various parts of social systems regulate each other by the exchange of messages. Communication of messages can be disturbed or disrupted when messages are given or perceived in a distorted way, when they are not perceived at all, when they are poorly timed, arriving too early or too late, or when they are inappropriate to the situation. Disruption in the communication system may occur in any of the components of the process: in the communicator, in the message, or in the environment in which the communication is given.

Therapeutic interventions within this framework try to determine the causes of disordered communication and to correct them. These functions do not consist of energy transformations but rather of the transformation of information in the form of messages, a process that involves encoding and decoding, coordination, and combination of messages. In the therapeutic setting, the focus on processes of communication helps to increase the individual's awareness of his own disordered communications and the ways in which they affect other people. This may lead to the abandonment of unnecessary assumptions and distorted beliefs and to the modification of certain attitudes that may distort communications to and from others.

Phenomenological Theories

Phenomenological theories focus on the uniqueness of the human individual and his self-actualizing potential. They explicitly oppose the reductionism of behaviorist approaches. On this point, they concur with humanistic approaches to personality. They differ, however, in their emphasis on the individual's present experience in defining the psychological field.

The theory of Carl Rogers (1902–) is unique among psychological theories in that it derives from a primary concern with therapy, specifically from his client-centered psychotherapy. Within Rogers's phenomenological and organismic theory, the phenomenological field is equivalent to the totality of the individual's experience. The self is a differentiated portion of the phenomenological field consisting of the individual's image and evaluation of himself.

Rogers postulates and makes the basis of his therapy an inherent self-actualizing tendency and an innate valuing process. Conflict arises when the need for approval comes into conflict with the self-actualizing tendency. Rogers's nondirective, client-centered approach stresses the attitudes of the therapist as they are communicated to the client.

The critical attitudes include the therapist's genuineness and openness in dealing with the client, his attitude of unconditional positive regard for the client, and, finally, the therapist's accurate, empathic understanding of the client's feelings, sentiments, and attitudes. The therapist's empathic and understanding acceptance allows the client to express his thoughts and feelings and increasingly to be able to listen to his own communications. Slowly he accepts and integrates the therapist's attitudes toward himself, and thus he is able to express himself more openly and to become increasingly free to grow in more natural and self-actualizing directions.

Philosophical and phenomenological in orientation, the existential approach to human behavior stands in diametrical opposition to reductionistic or behavioristic orientations toward the human personality. In the existential perspective, man's self-awareness is his most basic experience. Existential psychiatrists emphasize the uniqueness and individuality of each human being, of each human existence. They look to the phenomenological aspects of the individual's experience of himself and the world in which he exists. Similarly, existential psychotherapy examines the actual encounter between two concrete human beings and tries to describe and to understand it in terms of current, actual experience. In this respect, the psychiatric existential approach attempts to describe the unique communication of the human dyad in terms formulated by existential philosophers—what Heidegger called *Mitsein*, or being-with-others, and what Buber referred to as the *I-Thou relationship*. Existential approaches emphasize actual, immediate, usually emotional experience as opposed to historical (developmental) determinants. In this regard, existential psychiatry approximates the self-actualizing tendencies characteristic of a number of psychological theories.

Learning Theories

Theories of learning deal more or less exclusively with cognitive aspects of the personality. However, their influence on psychiatric thinking has been profound, particularly Piaget's work on studies of child development; and behavioral learning theories have been implemented in behavioral therapy and behavior modification (see chapter 19, "Behavior Therapy and Behavioral Psychotherapy," for a more detailed discussion). Learning theories have proliferated and developed, particularly through experimental studies of behavior and development. At this writing, we are entering a period of active investigation of the role of these theories in the development of clinical theory and techniques.

Piaget. Throughout his long and productive career, Jean Piaget (1896–) has generated a series of studies that has made his work a dominant influence in the study of child development. Because Piaget's work has focused almost exclusively on the child's cognitive development, its application to clinical practice has been somewhat limited, but his ingenious empirical observations and heuristic approach have stimulated much important research.

Piaget's approach rests on a biological foundation. He is concerned with the development and adaptation of biological structures in the growing organism. His theory thus concerns itself with the processes by which structural modifications take place in relation to the organism's need to perform specific adaptive functions. New structures are needed to adapt older persistent patterns of functioning to new conditions of environmental stimulation. The organism must have the capacity to adapt to environmental demands and to modify those demands in the interest of adaptation. Piaget applies this biological orientation to human behavior. He tries to identify the age-specific structures at each level of development and to show how they adapt to environmental demands and, alternatively, how they modify the environment itself and its demands. The former orientation is autoplastic, and the latter is alloplastic.

The central term in Piaget's thinking is the *schema*, the pattern of behavioral organization that corresponds roughly to the biological notion of structure. Schemata may be simple or complex and apply to all aspects of the organism's functioning. The knee-jerk reflex, for example, is a simple level of behavioral organization; other reflexes, such as the sucking reflex, also represent low-level schemata. It becomes immediately obvious, however, that the schema is not simply equivalent to the behavioral response to a specific stimulus. The sucking reflex is in fact considerably more complex and rapidly becomes part of a more elaborate pattern of behavioral adaptation, which includes the child's searching for the breast, the performance of sucking movements while the child watches the mother's prep-

arations for feeding, and such nonnutritive sucking behaviors as sucking the thumb and spoons.

The schema is not locked to specific stimuli but is relatively mobile. Once the schema is elicited and the pattern developed, it can apply to a variety of objects. The grasping schema, for example, can apply to all forms of graspable objects. Such mobility allows the evolving schema to be placed in the service of goal-directed activity; the schema thus becomes instrumental and can be used more adaptively in sequences of behaviors governed by goal intentionality.

Piaget focuses for the most part on sensorimotor schemata, which are concerned primarily with overt behavioral activities. But he also describes cognitive schemata, such as the number system, the concept of space, and the laws of logic. Such cognitive schemata are forms of internal activity and derive from sensorimotor schemata by internalization. Thus the visual image is an internalized form of looking activity. Similarly, thinking is a more complex cognitive schema that involves a series of mental acts, such as adding and making inferences or judgments; when these internal actions are integrated into a coherent logical system, they become concrete or formal logical operations. The concept of the schema is thus a complex notion involving both overt motor behavior patterns and internalized thought processes, spanning a spectrum of behaviors from predictable reflex behaviors to the highly complex organizations of conceptual understanding.

The schema is also adaptive. Piaget describes the process of adaptation in terms of the complementary processes of assimilation and accommodation. Assimilation refers to the capacity of the organism to deal with new situations and problems by the application of old, previously established mechanisms. Accommodation refers to the organism's capacity to change and modify itself in order to manage specific situations or problems that may at first exceed its capacity. The adaptive function is most clearly elicited in situations where assimilation is incomplete. Such incomplete assimilation stimulates the schemata to change, develop, and thus undergo accommodation. Piaget refers to such a situation as one of stimulus-nutriment, in which continuing stimulation "nourishes" the schema. Such nutriment is essential not only for maintaining the integrity of the schema but also for eliciting its inherent potentiality for development.

Piaget envisions the enlargement of early, relatively primitive cognitive schemata into more elaborate forms which are integrated into what he calls *groupings*. Piaget uses this mathematical term to refer to a system of logical operations that enjoys a certain coherence, closure, and reversibility. Such groupings provide the cognitive stability that allows the individual to achieve a degree of cognitive equilibrium with his environment. Such stability and equilibrium of cognitive functioning are necessary for effective adaptation.

Perhaps Piaget's most important contribution is his description of the child's cognitive development. He describes four developmental periods: the *sensorimotor* period, the *preoperational* period, the period of *concrete operations*, and finally the period of *formal operations*.

The sensorimotor period extends from the time of birth to about two years of age. The child is born with certain reflexes that are gradually integrated into more elaborate sensorimotor schemata. These schemata develop under internal maturational pressures and under the influence of sensory experience. The schemata organize sensory input and contribute to the child's adaptive behavior. The child gradually develops the capacity to coordinate information from the various sensory modalities, which leads to the integration of sensory schemata and consequently to gradual attainment of a more consistent degree of behavioral equilibrium. The integration of sensory schemata also lays the foundation for the child's increasing appreciation of the external world as having permanence and constancy in its own right.

In the beginning, for example, the child responds only to objects immediately present in his visual field. But with time, the child begins to appreciate that the object has a persistence and permanence even when it is removed from the visual field. By the age of eight to twelve months, the child will undertake active search for such vanished objects. In addition to achieving a sense of the reality and constancy of objects, the child also begins to elaborate new schemata and to integrate preexisting schemata into sequences

of goal-directed behavior that are governed by specific intentions. Such integrations are motivated by the need to achieve the endpoint of the behavioral sequence. The child gradually develops the capacity to evolve new sequences of behavior under the direction of such motivation and thus can elaborate increasingly complex schemata to apply to new objects and situations.

Schemata are behaviorally adaptive and concretely follow sequences of cause and effect, but the child lacks conceptual schemata that correspond with those in the behavioral realm. Consequently, the child's behavior is concrete, limiting the extent to which adaptive activity can be planned and organized. Only in the latter stages of the sensorimotor period does the child develop a capacity for mental representation and the accompanying capacity to construct imaginative representations of behavioral sequences. Mental representations can be detected, for example, in the child's ability to search for objects that have disappeared from view and in his growing understanding of and ability to manipulate spatial relations.

The preoperational period extends from about the second to the seventh year of age. During this period, the earlier mental representations develop into an emerging cognitive picture of the external world, its many relationships, and the laws governing its processes. The first primitive conceptual schemata are merely internal copies of the sensorimotor schemata already developed. Gradually, these become organized and integrated into interrelated conceptual systems that Piaget calls "operational," implying that the elements of the system are related by the laws of groupings. The period of preoperational development is thus essentially transitional.

The child's conceptual thinking during this period is relatively unintegrated, falling into frequent contradictions and inconsistencies. For example, the child can classify a given man as a father or a repairman, but he may not be able to see that the same man can be both father and repairman. Nonetheless, on the level of everyday behavior, the child's activity is reasonably stable and integrated. Where his use of language is closely linked to behavioral schemata, it may show many signs of logical thinking, but the child is still incapable of performing simple logical problems. It is easy to overestimate his capacities on the basis of such behavioral attainments; nonetheless, during this period his concepts remain piecemeal acquisitions that lack coherent organization. Thus he does not behave consistently when he is required to integrate temporally separate events. For example, judgments of size may use height at one point and width at another. If asked to compare between objects of such different, inconsistent series, the child may not consistently apply criteria. Before the emergence of more coherent logical structures, there is a relatively concrete intuitive stage during which the child's mental imagery allows him to imagine and predict the effect of behavioral sequences or environmental events. But the conceptual fragmentation limits his capacity for organization and prediction. Moreover, certain essential logical qualities, such as the concepts of invariance and conservation, have not yet been achieved.

The period of concrete operations extends from about the seventh to the eleventh year. At this stage, the child's thought processes become more organized and function with greater stability, reasonability, and consistency. The child acquires a basic understanding of a variety of groupings, but Piaget emphasizes that this understanding is essentially concrete, that is, oriented toward the actual observation and manipulation of concrete events in the child's environment. Consolidation of schemata serves as the basis of a higher-order equilibrium that permits a greater degree of adaptiveness. The achievements of the sensorimotor period represent a more strictly behavioral level of equilibrium and adaptation, but by the time the child reaches the period of concrete operations, he begins to achieve a level of conceptual integration which allows for higher-order adaptability.

The child acquires an understanding of the relationships of size, the equality of number sets, the distinction between numbers of objects and spatial arrangements, and the simple relationship between classes of objects. Concepts of time, space, the number system, and laws of logic are still relatively rudimentary. Logical groupings remain relatively isolated, and the child is unable to relate them to one another or to see them in terms of their relation to the universe of possibilities.

The child of this age has only an incomplete understanding of the relationships that exist among classes of concepts. Some concepts seem beyond his grasp—volume as the product of quantity and density, for example. He may be able to perceive relationships between certain factors, but it is more difficult for him to arrange situations to reveal a given relationship between factors. Thus the scientific logic of experimentally controlling and manipulating variables still exceeds his understanding even on an intuitive basis. The child's problem at this stage is one of understanding the relationships among concrete operational groupings that he has already grasped separately.

In the period of formal operations, the child masters these problems and achieves a higher level of cognitive organization and conceptual capacity. This stage extends from about the eleventh year through preadolescence and into the adolescent years. At this stage, the child begins to understand the principles of causal thinking and scientific experimentation. He is able to plan and execute experiments and to draw logical inferences from the results. He also becomes capable of combinatorial thinking, of understanding the implications of propositional logic, and of comprehending and resolving equilibrium problems. At this stage, then, the child's conceptual schemata reach their highest degree of organization and capacity for adaptation and control of environmental stimuli. He is capable of analyzing and using complex logical sequences, inductive and deductive reasoning, and complex conceptual integrations, and of planning sequences of concepts and behaviors to attain specific objectives.

Piaget's formulations come from empirical observation and have a high heuristic value. His work, however, has been criticized for its lack of experimental controls and systematic organization. Piaget's method is essentially anecdotal, based on empirical naturalistic observation. Moreover, his reports have been incomplete and selective and do not account for variability among different groups of children. We are left with little idea of the degree of validity of his observations or of the range of responses of different children to experimental situations.

Piaget's theories, nonetheless, highlight important areas of investigation. In general, he has put psychological insight ahead of operational formulation or systematic theory; his theories represent valuable hypotheses but do not provide a rigorous theory of cognitive development. Though his work provides no clear connection between specific observations about thought processes and the more abstract level of theoretical formulation, he has nonetheless effectively opened vast areas for further exploration and more systematic validation.

Gestalt theory. Gestalt psychology arose in the early years of the present century in reaction to experimental psychology, particularly in the form developed by Wilhelm Wundt (1832–1920). Wundt attempted to understand complex processes by breaking them down into component elements. Complex conscious states were envisioned as nothing but combinations of simple, stable perceptual and cognitive elements, associated or bound together in a variety of ways.

The Gestalt viewpoint was initially proposed by Christian von Ehrenfels (1859–1932), for whom the form of the whole (square) was independent of its component parts (lines). This form-of-the-whole or form-quality (*Gestaltsqualität*) was not simply equivalent to the sum of its parts.

Gestalt experimental work was advanced by Max Wertheimer (1880–1943) and later by his students Kurt Koffka (1886–1941) and Wolfgang Köhler (1887–1967). Wertheimer investigated the sensation of motion and discovered that the impression of motion could be created by two separate stimuli perceived in rapid succession. He insisted that the perception of movement is essentially different from the perception of a series of static visual stimuli. This phi phenomenon, as he called it, was unexplained by Wundt's atomistic approach.

Wertheimer examined more closely the relationship of part and whole. He believed that organized wholes are perceived directly and that the understanding of parts results from a process of subsequent analysis. Thus he arrived at one basic law of Gestalt psychology, the law of membership character, which states that the elements (the notes in a musical melody) of a given event or form (Gestalt) are definable only in terms of their relationships within that given event. Further, wholes or forms can be experienced as

such, even when specific elements are missing or distorted. This gave rise to a second important law of Gestalt psychology, the law of *prägnanz*, according to which the form (Gestalt) or organized entity tends to be perceived in a structured, orderly, closed, and stable way.

Gestalt psychology regards the relations among parts as a secondary result of an analysis of the total Gestalt, which is itself primary, primitive, and inherent in the process of sensory perception. Consequently, this perception is not dependent on learning or experience. The theory minimizes association and denies the existence of a mosaic stage in the process of perception, that is, perception of component elements that are then combined into a percept. Instead, it uses the concept of a dynamic field whose parts are interacting at the very moment of perception. The perceiver's task is not to create but to apprehend the order and meaning contained in the structure of the world.

Objects of perception are related to their field as figure to ground. The object (figure) has definite form, unity, and power of organization that set it off from the indefinite, unstructured background. Perceptual groupings are possible because their similarity is greater than that of other parts of the perceptual field, making the group stand out in structural relief from the field.

Gestalt psychology emphasizes the innate aspects of perceptual experience and behavior and the intuitional rather than the analytic aspects of cognitive processing. Köhler's famous experiments on problem solving by monkeys by means of "insight," as opposed to trial and error, is a striking example. Gestalt theory has had little impact on modern psychiatry, but it has been indirectly revived in recent years in Gestalt therapy, which bases its approach on the structured unity of experience, on the dynamic unity of the organism-environment field, on an emphasis on figure-ground formations as expressing transactions between environment and subject, and on the flow of emotions as caught up in the actual experience and action patterns in the group therapy context.

Stimulus-response theories. These theories are concerned with the application to personality theory of concepts drawn from behavioristic learning models. These learning concepts are not concerned primarily or specifically with clinical issues; rather they focus on the definition and measurement of specific experimental variables. Learning theories do not delve into inner psychic processes but are content to examine extrinsic stimulus conditions and external behaviors. This experimental concern biases learning theories toward an emphasis on behavior rather than on object relations or intrinsic motivations.

Such theories tend to be reductionist rather than synthetic or integrative. They attempt to bridge the gaps among different species by the presumption that learning variables are consistent among them. The only admissible evidences are those that are observable or measurable. Explanations are based on intervening variable paradigms in which stimulus and response variables are defined and codified as independent and dependent variables and intervening variables are postulated to explain their functional relations. There are few or no commitments as to the nature of the internal changes that take place through learning.

There are two main varieties of behavioral learning theories, one based on reinforcement and the other on contiguity. According to reinforcement theory, the probability that a random response will recur under similar stimulus conditions is increased when the response is associated with a reduction of motivation or drive. This reduction of drive or satisfaction of need is called the law of effect or reinforcement. Reinforcement theorists include Clark Hull (1884–1952), B. F. Skinner (1904–), and Kenneth Spence (1907–). In contrast, contiguity theory explains learning in terms of the contiguity in experience of stimulus conditions. Contiguity theorists such as E. R. Guthrie (1886–1959) see the learning process as a strengthening of connections between stimulus and response or between associated stimuli, not as a by-product of reinforcement but as an inherent effect of the action on the organism of any stimulus pattern. Recurrence of the pattern will tend to evoke its correlative response. New (learned) connections are established on the basis of temporal simultaneity of cues and responses.

A subvariant of these positions, developed under the influence of Gestalt formulations, is Edward C. Tolman's purposive behaviorism. For Tolman (1886–1959), learning is the acquisition of information about the environment, which he designates as "sign-Gestalt expectations" or "sign-significate relations." The organism acquires cognitions to the effect that a given stimulus (sign), if responded to, will lead to another stimulus (significate), and these together constitute a "cognitive map." Cognitive maps are acquired through the experienced spatial and temporal patterning of stimulus events that relate sign and significate. Tolman envisions this process as inherently purposive, so that immediate rewards are not necessary for learning to occur. Behavior is rather a consequence of expectations of reward and the organism's readiness to respond.

Perhaps the most significant development in this area is the application of learning theories to social learning. The application of learning theories to the socialization of the child was begun by Neal Miller (1909–) and John Dollard (1900–), was advanced by Robert Sears (1908–), and more recently has been enlarged by the contributions of Albert Bandura (1925–) on questions of modeling.

The basic theory is that children learn to become human beings only through contacts with other people in society. Individuals must learn to regulate behavior in accordance with social norms and standards. The principal agents of this teaching are the parents. Learning is accomplished by rewarding social behaviors, thus reinforcing them, and by punishing behaviors which violate social rules. Generally, the actions that require protracted socialization involve sex, aggression, dependency, status seeking, power, and striving for affection. Punishment of these responses associates anxiety with these basic impulses. Punishment may be physical, or it may be symbolic—the threat of loss of parental love and approval. This may establish a link between the anticipation of punishment and the punished impulses, so that the child comes to fear his own desires and has to find ways of dealing with this fear.

Within the family context, since parents both punish and reward, they are both loved and hated. The loving and protecting, on the one hand, and the fear and dislike, on the other, lay the basis for the ambivalence of children toward their parents in our culture. The necessity for regulating and dealing with these emotions generates certain mechanisms calculated to reduce anxiety and fear. The child uses repression and the other mechanisms of defense to minimize these feelings. The diminution of anxiety reinforces such defenses, as well as other defense mechanisms or neurotic symptoms that may develop.

The influence of imitation, especially imitation of parental models, is particularly important in social learning, and it holds a central place in the work of Miller and Dollard. Imitative behavior can be reinforced either extrinsically, as when the mother praises a child for copying desirable behavior or scolds or punishes him for copying undesirable behavior, or intrinsically, as when imitation achieves rewards similar to those granted the copied behavior. Imitative behavior may also be self-reinforcing, and social behavior can also be acquired vicariously by observation of a model's behavior. In modeling, the behavior of the copier approximates that of a model. The potentialities of vicarious learning through the experience of modeled behavior have been explored by Bandura, and the importance of this avenue for the acquisition and development of social behaviors cannot be underestimated.

Warm interaction with and affectionate attachment to a model increase the likelihood of imitation and copying. Imitative behavior, thus reinforced, tends to generalize into a tendency to behave like the care-taking model. Such generalized imitation, which copies multiple aspects of the model's behavior, is the behavioral equivalent of identification. Thus, the child's socialization involves internalization not only of specific behavioral patterns but also of the beliefs, attitudes, and values of the care-taking object.

Cognitive controls and cognitive styles. The examination of cognitive structure in the last few decades is primarily a result of the work of Herman Witkin (1916–), Jerome Kagan (1929–), and George Klein (1918–1971). Witkin and Kagan have focused on the notion of cognitive style (the consistency of individual differences in the organization of cognitive functions and the experi-

ence of the perceptual field). Witkin developed the Rod-and-Frame Test and the Embedded Figures Test, from which he defined the characteristics of field dependence and field independence, that is, the extent to which the subject's perception is influenced by background factors, or the extent to which the subject has difficulty in keeping an object or item separate from its surroundings. Field-independent subjects are better able to overcome the specific context in which information is embedded. Kagan later formulated global versus articulate extremes of style, as a further development of these ideas. These extremes define a continuum of varying degrees of differentiation of experience: at one extreme, there is a consistent tendency for experience to be global and diffuse, with the organization of the field as a whole dictating the way in which parts are perceived; at the opposite extreme, experience tends to be more articulated and structured, so that parts are experienced as discrete and organized within the total field.

Klein's studies of cognitive controls took their point of departure from Rapaport's psychoanalytic formulations. Klein postulated stable individual differences in cognitive functioning that represent specific ego controls operating within the conflict-free sphere. Ego controls organize and manage information input and thus coordinate ego functions with environmental demands and internal impulses and drives.

The main cognitive control principles are: focal attention (scanning behavior, diffuse versus focal); field articulation (adaptive processing of information from a stimulus field, field dependence versus independence, and inclusion versus exclusion of irrelevant information); leveling-sharpening (integration of sequentially experienced stimuli—levelers tend to assimilate new experiences with old; sharpeners tend to maintain discrete impressions of sequential stimuli); and equivalence range (the breadth and number of categories used to relate objects and their properties, that is, few categories and exact standards for inclusion versus broad categories and less concern with differences between informational units).

These approaches have stimulated active research on the development and functioning of cognitive capacities. One potentially useful area for investigation is the relationship between defense mechanisms and principles of cognitive control, as, for example, the connection between repression and leveling.

The above survey can hardly be complete or sufficiently detailed, but it does suggest the rich complexity and diversity of the clinical and psychological theoretical approaches that impinge on our attempts to understand human behavior and experience. Too often in the history of psychiatry, such theories have been approached with a closed mind, as though one theory had an exclusive claim on a valid view of the human mind to the exclusion of others. The intention of this survey has been to advance the view that these theories do not stand in opposition but, rather, that each has grasped its own fragment and perspective of the overall reality. I hope that this review has at least stimulated the reader in the interest of further theoretical integration and deepening clinical understanding. It is only in this direction that we can hope ultimately to help our patients understand themselves and thus direct their lives more adaptively and creatively.

References

Erikson, E. H. 1959. *Identity and the life cycle: selected papers. Psychol. Issues* 1, monograph no. 1. New York: International Universities Press.

Freud, S. 1915. Instincts and their vicissitudes. In *Standard edition*, ed. J. Strachey. Vol. 14. London: Hogarth Press, 1957.

——— 1940. An outline of psychoanalysis. In *Standard edition*, ed. J. Strachey. Vol. 23. London: Hogarth Press, 1964.

Recommended Reading

Abraham, K. 1953. *Selected papers on psychoanalysis*. New York: Basic Books.

Alexander, F., M. Grotjahn, and S. Eisenstein, eds. 1966. *Psychoanalytic pioneers*. New York: Basic Books.

Alexander, F., and S. Selesnick. 1966. *The history of psychiatry*. New York: Harper & Row.

Allport, G. W. 1955. *Becoming*. New Haven: Yale University Press.

——— 1960. *Personality and social encounter*. Boston: Beacon Press.

Ansbacher, H. and R., eds. 1965. *The individual psychology of Alfred Adler*. New York: Basic Books.

Baldwin, A. I. 1968. *Theories of child development*. New York: Wiley.

Balint, M. 1965. *Primary love and psychoanalytic technique*. New York: Liveright.

——— 1968. *The basic fault*. London: Tavistock.

Brenner, C. 1973. *Elementary textbook of psychoanalysis*. Rev. ed. New York: International Universities Press.

Burton, A., ed. 1974. *Operational theories of personality*. New York: Brunner/Mazel.

Campbell, J., ed. 1971. *The portable Jung*. New York: Viking Press.

Cattell, R. B. 1950. *Personality: a systematic, theoretical, and factual study*. New York: McGraw-Hill.

Dollard, J., and N. E. Miller. 1950. *Personality and psychotherapy*. New York: McGraw-Hill.

Ellenberger, H. F. 1970. *The discovery of the unconscious*. New York: Basic Books.

Erikson, E. H. 1963. *Childhood and society*. Rev. ed. New York: Norton.

Fairbairn, W. R. D. 1952. *Psychoanalytic studies of the personality*. London: Tavistock.

——— 1954. *An object-relations theory of the personality*. New York: Basic Books.

Flavell, J. H. 1965. *The developmental psychology of Jean Piaget*. Princeton, N.J.: Van Nostrand.

Freud, A. 1936. *The ego and the mechanisms of defense*. New York: International Universities Press, 1946.

Freud, S. 1905. Three essays on the theory of sexuality. In *Standard edition*, ed. J. Strachey. Vol. 7. London: Hogarth Press, 1953.

——— 1917. Mourning and melancholia. In *Standard edition*, ed. J. Strachey. Vol. 14. London: Hogarth Press, 1958.

——— 1920. Beyond the pleasure principle. In *Standard edition*, ed. J. Strachey. Vol. 18. London: Hogarth Press, 1955.

——— 1923. The ego and the id. In *Standard edition*, ed. J. Strachey. Vol. 19. London: Hogarth Press, 1961.

——— 1926. Inhibitions, symptoms, and anxiety. In *Standard edition*, ed. J. Strachey. Vol. 20. London: Hogarth Press, 1959.

Fromm, E. 1947. *Man for himself*. New York: Rinehart.

——— 1955. *The sane society*. New York: Rinehart.

Gardner, R., P. S. Holzman, G. S. Klein, H. B. Linton, and D. P. Spence. 1959. *Cognitive controls. Psychol. Issues* 1, monograph no. 4. New York: International Universities Press.

Gardner, R., D. N. Jackson, and S. J. Messick. 1960. *Personality organization in cognitive controls and intellectual abilities. Psychol. Issues* 2, monograph no. 8. New York: International Universities Press.

Gill, M. M., ed. 1967. *The collected papers of David Rapaport*. New York: Basic Books.

Guntrip, H. 1961. *Personality structure and human interaction*. New York: International Universities Press.

—— 1969. *Schizoid phenomena, object-relations, and the self*. New York: International Universities Press.

—— 1973. *Psychoanalytic theory, therapy, and the self*. New York: Basic Books.

Guthrie, E. R. 1935. *The psychology of learning*. New York: Harper.

Hartmann, H. 1939. *Ego psychology and the problem of adaptation*. Trans. D. Rapaport. *J. Am. Psychoanal. Assoc.* monograph series, no. 1. New York: International Universities Press, 1958.

—— 1964. *Essays on ego psychology*. New York: International Universities Press.

Horney, K. 1939. *New ways in psychoanalysis*. New York: Norton.

—— 1950. *Neurosis and human growth*. New York: Norton.

Hull, C. L. 1943. *Principles of behavior*. New York: Appleton-Century-Crofts.

—— 1951. *Essentials of behavior*. New Haven: Yale University Press.

Jacobson, E. 1964. *The self and the object world*. New York: International Universities Press.

Jung, C. G. 1916. *Psychology of the unconscious: a study of the transformations and symbolisms of the libido, a contribution to the history of the evolution of thought*. Trans. B. M. Hinkle. New York: Moffat, Yard.

Koffka, K. 1935. *Principles of gestalt psychology*. London: Kegan Paul.

Köhler, W. 1947. *Gestalt psychology*. New York: Liveright.

—— 1966. *The place of value in a world of facts*. New York: Liveright.

Lewin, K. 1935. *A dynamic theory of personality*. New York: McGraw-Hill.

—— 1951. *Field theory in social science*. New York: Harper & Row.

Maslow, A. 1954. *Motivation and personality*. New York: Harper & Row.

May, R., E. Angel, and H. F. Ellenberger, eds. 1958. *Existence: a new dimension in psychiatry and psychology*. New York: Basic Books.

Meissner, W. W., J. Mack, and E. V. Semrad. 1975. Classical psychoanalysis. In *Comprehensive textbook of psychiatry*, ed. A. M. Freedman, H. I. Kaplan, and B. J. Sadock. 2nd ed. Baltimore: Williams & Wilkins.

Miller, N. E., and J. Dollard, 1941. *Social learning and imitation*. New Haven: Yale University Press.

Mullahy, P. 1955. *Oedipus: myth and complex*. New York: Grove Press.

Munroe, R. L. 1955. *Schools of psychoanalytic thought*. New York: Dryden.

Pavlov, I. P. 1941. *Conditioned reflexes and psychiatry*. New York: International Publications.

—— 1960. *Conditioned reflexes*. New York: Dover.

Piaget, J. 1951a. *The child's conception of the world*. London: Routledge and Kegan Paul.

—— 1951b. *Judgment and reasoning in the child*. London: Routledge and Kegan Paul.

—— 1952a. *The language and thought of the child*. London: Routledge and Kegan Paul.

—— 1952b. *The origins of intelligence in children*. New York: International Universities Press.

—— 1954. *The construction of reality in the child*. New York: Basic Books.

—— 1967. *Six psychological studies*. New York: Random House.

—— 1970. *Structuralism*. New York: Basic Books.

Rogers, C. R. 1951. *Client-centered therapy*. Boston: Houghton Mifflin.

—— 1961. *On becoming a person*. Boston: Houghton Mifflin.

Ruesch, J. 1957. *Disturbed communication*. New York: Norton.

Segal, H. 1964. *Introduction to the work of Melanie Klein*. New York: Basic Books.

Spence, K. W. 1956. *Behavior theory and conditioning*. New Haven: Yale University Press.

Sullivan, H. S. 1953. *The interpersonal theory of psychiatry*. New York: Norton.

Thompson, C. 1957. *Psychoanalysis: evolution and development*. New York: Grove Press.

Tolman, E. C. 1932. *Purposive behavior in animals and men*. New York: Century.

von Bertalanffy, L. 1968. *General system theory*. New York: Braziller.

Winnicott, D. W. 1965. *The maturational process and the facilitating environment*. New York: International Universities Press.

—— 1971. *Playing and reality*. New York: Basic Books.

Woodworth, R. 1948. *Contemporary schools of psychology*. New York: Ronald Press.

Zetzel, E. R., and W. W. Meissner. 1973. *Basic concepts of psychoanalytic psychiatry*. New York: Basic Books.

The Dynamic Bases of Psychopathology

CHAPTER 9

John C. Nemiah

PSYCHOPATHOLOGY may be viewed from two basic aspects, the phenomenological and the explanatory. In its phenomenological aspect, psychopathology is concerned with pathological distortions of psychic functions as these may be seen and described either by the individual experiencing them or by an external observer. Self-observation is private and subjective and deals with consciously experienced events such as feelings, sensations, and perceptions; observations made by others are public and objective and are primarily concerned with the behavior of the individual being observed. Phenomenological psychopathology is a descriptive discipline and is not concerned with explanations. It attempts to delineate, define, and categorize symptoms and behavior and to ascertain how they are related to one another in the various pathological syndromes that constitute psychiatric illness.

The psychopathologist, however, commonly moves beyond pure description and endeavors to explain the genesis of the phenomena he observes. His explanations may be in terms of neuropathological states that he correlates with psychological and behavioral abnormalities, or he may remain conceptually within the sphere of psychology, viewing psychopathological phenomena as the result of underlying psychic processes. The nature of these explanations depends on the theoretical models used to frame them, and it is the variety of such models that has led to the confusion and frequent lack of communication among those concerned with understanding mental disorders.

The phenomenological approach to psychopathology will receive fuller treatment elsewhere in this volume in those sections dealing with the description of clinical syndromes and with mental status. The central concern in what follows here is the psychological explanation of the observed phenomena. Our attention will be focused on the psychodynamic mental mechanisms derived from psychoanalysis, which for the modern clinician, especially in America, has proved to be the most useful and widely employed theoretical approach.

Mental Mechanisms

Basic to the understanding of mental mechanisms are two key concepts, unconscious mental processes and psychological conflict, which can best be understood by viewing them through their historical development.

The Unconscious: Development of the Concept

"There is no explanation . . . of this fact," wrote Coleridge as he puzzled over the sudden, unbidden return to his consciousness of a forgotten name, "but by a full sharp distinction of mind from Consciousness—the Consciousness being the narrow *Neck* of the Bottle" (Coburn, 1951, p. 31). Borrowed in part from his reading of contemporary German philosophers and in part derived from his own intuition, Coleridge's comment reveals an awareness of unconscious mental processes long antedating modern dynamic psychology. Indeed, throughout the nineteenth century, at first among poets, novelists, and philosophers and then gradually among psychologists, a growing concern with the phenomena related to these processes played a dominant role in the development of social and intellectual thought.

Mesmer and animal magnetism. Although he did not directly conceive of the unconscious, Franz Anton Mesmer (1734–1815) during the last quarter of the eighteenth century first focused scientific attention on the observations that led ultimately to the formulations of dynamic psychology (Mesmer, 1781). At first in Vienna and then in Paris, he practiced a form of therapy that alienated his fellow physicians but attracted patients by the thousands. Mesmer's basic therapeutic maneuver was the magnetic pass. Patient and therapist sat opposite one another, knees touching, while the latter moved his hands downward from the patient's head to his groin in repeated sweeping movements. In response, the patient would feel warmth spreading over his body and would at length succumb to the therapeutic "crisis," a convulsion having all the earmarks of what is called a hysterical seizure, from which he would awake symptom-free. Equally effective crises could be produced by the touching of objects over which the mesmerist had made magnetic passes, the most common of these being the *baquet*, a large covered tub full of water, bits of glass, and iron filings. The drama that pervaded Mesmer's treatment rooms is evident in an early nineteenth-century eyewitness account of the spectacle of patients clustered around the *baquet*:

A very long cord extended from the circular cover of the baquet, which the patients wound around their limbs without tying it. Disagreeable lesions, such as wounds, tumors and deformities, were not exposed to view. At length, the patients drew near to each other, touching hands, arms, knees or feet. The handsomest, youngest and most robust magnetisers held also an iron rod with which they touched dilatory or stubborn patients. When the baquet, the rods and the cords were ready, the patients soon entered into the crisis. The women, being the most easily affected, were almost at once seized with fits of yawning and stretching: their eyes closed, their legs gave way and they seemed to suffocate. It was in vain that they were exposed to the sounds of the harmonium or the soothing strains of the piano or of songs; these measures seemed only to increase the patients' convulsions. Sardonic laughter, piteous moans and torrents of tears burst forth on all sides. Bodies were thrown back in spasmodic jerks, respiration became rasping, and the most terrifying symptoms were visible. At this point the actors in this strange drama ran in front of one another, distracted and delirious; they congratulated one another, kissed one another with joy or started back in horror.

Another room was padded and presented a different spectacle. There women beat their heads against padded walls or rolled on the cushion-covered floor, feeling as though they were choking. In the midst of this panting, quivering throng, Mesmer, dressed in a lilac coat, moved about, extending toward the less disturbed a magic wand, stopping in front of the more agitated and gazing steadily into their eyes, while he held both their hands in his, bringing the middle fingers into immediate contact in order to establish rapport. Now he would execute movements from a distance with his hands and fingers spread apart to stimulate a massive current of fluid; at other times he would cross and recross his arms with extraordinary rapidity in order to produce a more localized movement of fluid.

Although flummery was clearly a staple of Mesmer's therapeutic armamentarium, his procedures were sufficiently effective to draw the ire of his professional colleagues, who found his therapeutic successes a threat to their practices; ultimately in 1784 a Royal Commission was appointed by Louis XVI to investigate his activities. In its brief and measured report, the Commission confirmed the existence of the phenomena Mesmer claimed to produce, but they denied the validity of the theory by which Mesmer explained the pathogenesis of illness and his cure of it through the inducement of a convulsion (*Rapport des commissaires*, 1784).

Mesmer's theoretical formulations were borrowed from the ideas of scientific and philosophical predecessors who saw in the movement of the planets evidence of a universal magnetic attraction. Mesmer adapted this notion to his own needs, proposing that in a state of health the universal magnetic fluid flowed freely through animal bodies; that disease was the result of the pathological blocking of the fluid's passage through human organs; and that cure resulted when the therapist, by means of his magnetic passes, caused fluid to enter the body of his patient and to flow within it with sufficient force to break through the pathological blockages, thus restoring a normal balance. Animal magnetism, as Mesmer termed it, was a universal fact that underlay both illness and its cure.

For the Royal Commissioners, animal magnetism was a chimera. By a series of controlled experiments they showed that patients were cured if they merely thought they had been magnetized when, in fact, magnetic procedures had not been carried out. The effects of the alleged animal magnetic fluid, they concluded, were merely the result of imagination. Having damned the theory, they proceeded to derogate the facts and urged the banning of magnetic therapy as a dangerous and immoral practice.

Puységur and somnambulism. Although Mesmer ultimately departed from Paris in disgust, he left behind him many enthusiastic disciples, mostly laymen, who carried on his work and ideas. Foremost among them was the Marquis de Puységur (1751–1825), an artillery officer, who after learning the techniques of magnetism (or mesmerism, as it also came to be called) returned to his country estates to apply it to the sick among the farmers who worked his fields. Not only were his initial attempts crowned with success, but he found that patients could be relieved of their symptoms without undergoing the dramatic, often violent convulsion central to Mesmer's technique. Even more striking was his discovery of artificial somnambulism in the response of a young peasant named Victor to the magnetic treatment of a febrile "inflammation of

the lungs." After a short period of exposure to Puységur's passes, Victor fell into an apparent sleep and then began talking with an animation unusual for him in his ordinary waking state. Puységur was surprised to find that when his patient reverted once more to his normal personality at the conclusion of the therapeutic session, he had no recollection of what had transpired during the mesmeric trance (Puységur, 1809).

Today we recognize these phenomena as typical of both spontaneously occurring hysterical somnambulism and induced hypnotic trance. For Puységur it was a startling novelty, but thereafter it became a commonplace in magnetic therapy. In the decades that followed, it was repeatedly studied and described in treatises on magnetism and in monographs devoted more specifically to somnambulism. Puységur and most of those who followed him attributed not only the phenomena of somnambulism but all the varied effects of magnetic passes to the same magnetic fluid that Mesmer postulated. There were exceptions, notably Abbé Faria and Bertrand in France, both of whom championed psychological causes, but the swelling crowd of magnetists (or mesmerists) at work in France, Germany, and England during the early decades of the nineteenth century believed that they were inducing physical changes in their subjects by directing animal magnetic fluid into their bodies.

Braid and hypnotism. In the 1840s a Manchester surgeon swung popular opinion from its predilection for magnetic fluid to an acceptance of the paramount role of subjective, psychological factors in the behavior manifested by mesmerized patients. Like his many clinical predecessors, James Braid (1795–1860) found hypnotism (or neurohypnotism), as he renamed magnetism, a useful therapeutic measure for a variety of somatic ailments and an effective analgesic for surgical procedures. After a brief flirtation with a physiological explanation of the phenomenon (Braid, 1843), he ultimately proposed that hypnotism produced its effects through the operation of an idea implanted in the subject's mind by the suggestion of the hypnotist (Braid, 1852).

The introduction of Braid's ideas into France sparked a revival of interest in phenomena that, as presented by the mesmerists, had lost their lustre. The view that these phenomena were a result of suggestion rather than of magnetic fluid was widely adopted by clinicians and investigators, and hypnotism regained the ground that magnetism had lost. The School of Nancy, notably represented by Ambroise-Auguste Liébault (1823–1904) and Hippolyte Bernheim (1840–1919), developed the psychological concept of suggestion to the point where the use of hypnotism almost disappeared. The rival camp of Jean Martin Charcot (1835–1893) and his colleagues at the Salpêtrière in Paris, maintaining a more physiological orientation in their adaptation of Braid's psychological notions, forced hypnosis into a rigid conceptual scheme that fitted their preconceived ideas better than the clinical facts. It was, however, in Charcot's clinic that hypnosis followed the path that led to dynamic psychiatry.

Charcot, the Salpêtrière school, and hysteria. Charcot was a neurologist whose clinical activities brought him into contact with a number of patients, mainly young women, with sensorimotor manifestations of major hysteria for which, as he early recognized, no neuropathological lesions could be demonstrated. In the course of their investigations, Charcot and his colleagues developed a theoretical framework to explain the phenomena, employing concepts that were partly physiological and partly psychological. They soon recognized that specific mental functions related to the hysterically disturbed sensations and muscular movements were lost to conscious awareness and to voluntary recall and control. At the same time, however, the apparently lost mental functions remained operative beneath the level of full consciousness. If, for example, a totally anesthetic hand were touched three times out of the patient's sight, he would suddenly—and seemingly spontaneously—think of the number three, even though he had felt nothing in his extremity.

From a variety of clinical observations, as well as a number of experiments designed to elucidate the nature of hysterical symptoms, the concept of dissociation arose. According to this concept, specific mental functions become separated (or dissociated) from the mainstream of consciousness and, as a consequence, are lost to voluntary control. The loss of these mental operations

then leads to the appearance of hysterical symptoms. If, for example, the mental elements related to the arm (sensations, ideas of movements, and the like) are dissociated, anesthesia and paralysis of that limb ensue. Similarly, the dissociation of visual perceptions is followed by hysterical blindness, and loss of memory for specific past events is manifested clinically as amnesia. When large clusters of associations and memories are dissociated, the patient develops the condition of multiple personality, a disorder that fascinated clinicians in the latter half of the nineteenth century.

The phenomenon of dissociation formed the point of articulation with the interest in hypnosis central to Charcot and his school. They soon discovered not only that hysterical patients were generally highly hypnotizable but also that, under hypnosis, the dissociated functions and memories could be brought into consciousness, with a resulting return of the sensations, movements, and memories whose loss underlay the various hysterical symptoms. Moreover, the paralyses, anesthesias, and amnesias occurring spontaneously in hysteria could be artificially produced by the suggestion of the hypnotizer, without the subject's conscious awareness that the disturbances had been suggested to him. Such clinical and experimental findings resulted in the concept of unconscious mental processes and led to an awareness of the role of such processes in the production of symptoms.

Of particular importance among the pathogenic subconscious elements were dissociated memories of traumatic events. A patient described by Pierre Janet, for example, suffered from a fear of the color red. In her usual state of consciousness she could not explain this phobia. Under hypnosis, however, she recalled and relived, as if she were actually experiencing it, the emotionally painful memory of her father's death and burial many years before. In particular she revived, with intense emotion, the image of a bouquet of red flowers placed on his casket, an image totally forgotten and inaccessible to her conscious memory (Janet, 1898). In many patients, unconscious memories of past, emotionally traumatic events, such as loss or frightening accidents, could be uncovered by clinical investigation that provided an understanding and explanation of the genesis and specific nature of their symptoms—findings that led to the traumatic theory of the genesis of neurotic illness.

It is evident from this brief review that psychological concepts and theories were an important element in the approach of Charcot and his colleagues at the Salpêtrière to the problem of psychiatric illness, reaching their apogee of sophistication in the work of one of Charcot's most famous pupils, Pierre Janet (1858–1947). At the same time, however, the Salpêtrière School never departed from a basic conviction that the genesis of the clinical phenomena lay in the realm of disordered brain function. This was particularly evident in the explanation of dissociation, especially as developed by Janet.

In Janet's view, each individual was born with a certain quantum of nervous energy as his hereditary endowment. In the normal person this energy serves to bind together all the neural processes and their associated mental functions into a unified whole under the dominance of conscious awareness, the central feature of which is the experience of oneself as an integrated, individual personality. In certain people, however, a hereditary deficiency of nervous energy occurs that leads (either spontaneously or as the result of the expenditure of energy in experiencing strong emotions) to a loosening of the normal synthesis of the personality and a falling away of mental elements from the control of conscious awareness. This falling away results in the dissociation of memories and mental functions that then form the pathogenic source of symptoms. In this scheme, hypnotizability was considered a pathological trait, since it gave evidence of a weak integration of the personality secondary to an inadequate quantity of binding nervous energy. Normal people, the Charcot School believed, were not suggestible and could not be hypnotized (Janet, 1903, 1907).

This was the state of clinical theory regarding mental processes when Sigmund Freud (1856–1939) came to Paris in the 1880s to study neuropathology under Charcot at the Salpêtrière. He soon found himself swept up by the enthusiasm of those around him for the study of hysterical patients, and he was rapidly diverted from working in the laboratory as he learned to recognize the clinical characteristics that distinguished hysteria from neurological illnesses, as he became acquainted with the techniques and phenomena of hypnosis, and as he absorbed the concept of dissociation and the traumatic theory of hysterical symptom formation. After several intellectually stimulating months he returned to Vienna primed to turn his clinical attention in new directions.

Breuer and Freud. The way was opened for Freud to exploit his recently gained knowledge through his association with Josef Breuer (1842–1925), an older, established, and respected Viennese neurologist. In 1880 Breuer had undertaken the case of Anna O., a well-to-do young woman suffering from a host of incapacitating hysterical symptoms (Breuer and Freud, 1895). Breuer planned to treat her with hypnosis, using it in the then traditional fashion as a means of removing symptoms by direct suggestion. He discovered, however, that his patient responded in an unorthodox manner. Under the influence of hypnosis, and at times spontaneously, she lapsed into somnambulistic states of altered consciousness in which she appeared to experience vivid hallucinations, which she described at length. As Breuer listened to her recitals, he realized she was reliving past traumatic events, which were often represented symbolically in her symptoms; furthermore, he discovered that when she had recounted such an episode, giving vent to all the emotions associated with it, the hysterical symptom disappeared. On one occasion, for example, when she was suffering from a hysterical inability to drink, she recounted seeing a colleague's dog drinking from a water glass. At the time she had been disgusted and angered but had said nothing, only to develop her hysterical hydrophobia shortly thereafter. In the hypnotic treatment session with Breuer she recalled this episode, expressed aloud the anger she had felt but suppressed at the time of the event, asked for a glass of water, and awoke from the hypnotic trance in the act of drinking. From that point on she was free of the symptom.

Breuer capitalized on his chance finding and, over a series of hypnotic sessions, actively directed the patient's recall to the events and emotions behind a variety of her symptoms, which disappeared as a result. In his subsequent collaboration with Freud, Breuer reported his experiences, and together they applied what they called their "cathartic treatment" to several other hysterical patients, ultimately publishing their results in *Studies on Hysteria* (Breuer and Freud, 1895), a monograph presenting their clinical findings and theoretical speculations.

The work of Breuer and Freud carried the use of hypnosis a step beyond the practice of the Salpêtrière school by recognizing the importance of "catharsis." Hypnosis, as has been mentioned, had till then been employed therapeutically to remove and suppress symptoms through the authoritative suggestion of the hypnotizer. To this Breuer and Freud added the important technical innovation of raising to consciousness the memories and related emotions deriving from the traumatic events immediately responsible for producing the symptoms—a technique based on the traumatic theory of neurosis. Theirs was the first move toward a truly dynamic psychology, which Freud was shortly to formulate in his theoretical considerations of dissociation.

Psychological Conflict: Emergence of a Basic Model

The French school had explained dissociation as the result of a pathological lowering of nervous energy, which weakened the normal synthesis of brain and mental functions so that certain elements escaped from voluntary control and from consciousness. In his theoretical formulations in *Studies on Hysteria* (1895), Breuer followed the French in the importance he ascribed to the hypnoid state in producing dissociation. According to Breuer, an individual who underwent an emotionally traumatic experience while in a "spontaneously occurring" hypnoid state of altered consciousness would fail to carry the memories of the event into consciousness when he returned to his normal state. The memories and the related emotions would remain behind in a condition of dissociation, acting as a pathogenic focus for the formation of symptoms. In this explanation dissociation was viewed as the result

of the passive falling away of mental elements from the totality of the ego.

Defense hysteria. Initially Freud concurred in Breuer's formulation, at least publicly, only briefly alluding in the initial chapter of *Studies on Hysteria* to "defense hysteria" as opposed to "hypnoid hysteria." This small phrase was the leading edge of a theoretical explanation of dissociation that led to a radically new concept of the functioning of the human mind. As he developed his ideas in subsequent papers, it became clear that Freud had laid the foundation for dynamic psychology.

Certain mental elements (ideas, emotions, desires), Freud proposed, were unacceptable to the individual's ego because they were frightening, unethical, disgusting, or otherwise undesirable. Accordingly, the ego actively forced these unpalatable elements from consciousness and held them beyond voluntary recall in an unconscious, dissociated state. Dissociation, in this theoretical model, was the result of active mental processes as one part of the mind came into conflict with another. Although the concept of dissociation was shared by all, the passive, static explanatory model of Breuer and the Salpêtrière school was replaced in Freud's theory by a dynamic view of the mind that led ultimately to the sophisticated psychoanalytic formulations of normal and pathological psychic functioning.

Freud's subsequent clinical work led to alterations in his therapeutic techniques and to further additions to his theory. For a variety of reasons he gave up formal hypnosis and adopted instead the method of free association, which required the patient to report every thought that crossed his mind during therapeutic sessions, however trivial or unpleasant it seemed. It soon became evident that this was an impossible task and that, however motivated he might be to comply, the patient exhibited involuntary gaps and hesitations in his associations or consciously withheld information—a "resistance" that Freud recognized as the outward effect of the inner mental repressing and censoring processes he had postulated as causing dissociation. At the same time, as he worked with his patients over an extended period of time, he found them developing unrealistic feelings and attitudes about him that appeared to be more appropriate to, and to result from, relationships formed in the early years of their lives—a phenomenon that he termed and we know now as "transference."

Early etiological formulations. Such was the state of Freud's thinking when he advanced his first etiological formulations of the neuroses (1894, 1895, 1896). The traumatic theory of neurosis was basic to these early explanations, and in particular he learned from his patients that sexual traumata were involved in almost every incidence. In the face of such a trauma, as Freud viewed it, the individual initially protected himself from the painful emotions it aroused by repressing them. As a result, the undischarged emotional energy associated with memories of the trauma had to be processed further to prevent it from forcing its way back into consciousness. This was accomplished, in the hysterical neurosis, by converting the excess psychic energy into a somatic symptom or, in the case of obsessions and phobias, by displacing it to other seemingly harmless ideas. The choice of process—and hence of symptom—was determined by the patient's constitutional predisposition, although Freud strongly disagreed with the French insistence that neuroses resulted from hereditary degeneracy. In Freud's view, neurotic symptoms could occur in people with sound heredity when confronted by a sufficiently painful trauma. Furthermore, as the number of his hysterical patients, most of them women, increased, he discovered that though the outbreak of neurotic symptoms might follow an adult sexual trauma, his patients invariably reported an earlier painful sexual experience in childhood involving an adult, usually the patients' fathers. These clinical observations led him to propose that the cause of hysteria lay in a sexual assault suffered passively in childhood at the hands of the father, or, less commonly, of another older relative.

Freud's tidy explanation of the genesis of hysteria soon met a sudden and, for its author, a painful death. Before reviewing the circumstances of its demise, however, it is useful to look briefly at Freud's views on the nature of anxiety. In an early paper (1895), he proposed that anxi-ety neurosis should be separated as a clinical entity from neurasthenia, the name then commonly given to an amorphous clinical syndrome encompassing the symptoms of depression, anxiety, and multiple somatic complaints. The genesis of anxiety, he posited, was quite different from that of other psychiatric symptoms. It arose in normal individuals who were unable for one reason or another to discharge sexual libido in natural sexual intercourse and in whom, as a consequence, sexual excitation was transformed into somatic anxiety. Unlike hysterical, phobic, and obsessional symptoms (in the production of which complex psychological processes were at work), anxiety was seen as a direct physiological transformation of energy without psychic elaboration, and Freud accordingly termed anxiety an "actual" neurosis as opposed to a psychoneurosis, the category to which the other syndromes belonged.

In this early phase of his clinical work, Freud had defined and delimited four of the five major neuroses in modern nosological use, only neurotic depression being absent from his list. These survived the catastrophe that befell his explanatory theories as he put them to the test in further investigations. He had found that all of his hysterical patients reported a sexual assault in childhood; when he attempted to confirm the truth of their accounts, however, Freud discovered that independent witnesses to his patients' lives could not corroborate them. The traumatic theory of the etiology of hysteria could not be substantiated, however attractive it was as an intellectual edifice.

Freud was initially in despair, as we learn from his letters to his friend Fliess (Bonaparte, Freud, and Kris, 1954), but further observations soon provided the impetus for revising and extending his theory. Partly from his continued clinical examination of patients, and apparently in part from his self-analysis and the exploration of his own dreams, he became aware that what his patients reported as memories of real sexual seductions were in fact memories of childhood sexual fantasies. From this flowed his recognition that human sexuality, contrary to general belief, antedated the appearance of puberty and that early in life the child normally experienced vivid sexual feelings and fantasies, referable to a variety of bodily zones and directed at the significant people in his life. From this realization the concept of an orderly development of the child's libidinal drives from their earliest oral manifestations to their final stage of genital primacy gradually emerged. Concurrently, the child's personal relationships ran their course from the initial dyadic tie to the mother, through the triangular oedipal situation involving both parents, and then beyond to adult genital relationships with a member of the opposite sex (see chapter 8, "Theories of Personality"). In individuals who suffered distortions and arrests during these normal developmental stages, conflicts arose over unresolved infantile sexual drives and relationships—conflicts leading in adult life to neurotic symptoms (Freud, 1905).

The topographic model. In the light of his observations, Freud fashioned a psychodynamic scheme of the human psyche and of symptom formation that guided his thinking and his practice during the early years of this century (Freud, 1910). In this theoretical framework, which came to be known as the topographic model of the mind, two important forces, the libidinal and the life-preserving instincts, were in conflict. The latter were viewed as a function of the ego, which controlled the libidinal instincts and regulated their discharge in such a way as to preserve the individual's physic and social integrity. An important element in the ego's control of the libido was the mechanism of repression, which rendered unconscious the dangerous and unacceptable sexual drives, along with the emotions and fantasies deriving from them. The psyche was seen as made up of a conscious portion, the ego, and an unconscious portion containing the repressed elements. To this "topography" of the mind Freud ultimately added yet another region, the preconscious, containing those mental elements neither forcibly contained in the unconscious nor in consciousness at any given time, but readily available to the ego through voluntary recall.

Though relegated to the unconscious by the ego's repression, the banished drives were not necessarily rendered inactive, and indeed they tended to maintain a steady pressure for reemergence into consciousness and for expression.

The psychic tension thus engendered was often unpleasant, and alternate means of discharging libidinal energy were required to reduce the discomfort in conformity with Freud's principle of constancy, according to which the nervous system operated to keep its total energy at a minimum. The quantity of repressed libidinal energy could thus be reduced in three ways: through its discharge in socially acceptable but not overtly sexual modes of behavior (sublimation); in psychoneurotic symptoms, as the result of its pathological distortion by defense mechanisms; or as anxiety, through its direct physiological transformation into somatic symptoms.

The structural model. The topographic model functioned well as a guide for the early psychoanalytic investigators and clinicians when their interest was focused on psychoneurotic disorders. With the application of psychoanalytic techniques and formulations to a wider sphere of emotional illnesses, however, it was found to be inadequate to encompass all the facts. When Freud turned his attention to depression, he began to recognize a need to revise his theoretical conceptions. First, it became apparent from the observations of the vagaries of self-esteem in depression (and equally in megalomania), that narcissism or "self-love," of which self-esteem and self-preservation were important elements, was a function of libido investing the self. If self-preservation was in fact a manifestation of libidinal instincts, then the topographic model's view of libidinal and self-preservative instincts as separate and conflicting could not be maintained (Freud, 1914, 1920).

Furthermore, it became evident that aggression had not been adequately dealt with in the earlier theoretical structure, where it had been considered an integral part of the masochistic and sadistic forms of libidinal drive. From his exploration of the nature of aggression in the form of suicidal, self-mutilating, and self-castigating behavior in depressed patients (and perhaps, too, from the magnitude of the aggression evident in the horror of the world war that was then raging), Freud was forced to the conclusion that aggression was more than a shading of libido; it was a full-fledged drive in itself (Freud, 1917, 1920). His further discoveries of unconscious ego functions, especially the defenses, and of the role of conscience—a mental agency neither clearly part of the ego nor an instinct—in depressed patients led Freud at length to recognize the inadequacy of the topographic model to encompass these facts. The consequent necessity for refashioning his theoretical structure led him to propose a new map of the mind—the so-called structural model.

With the transition from the topographic to the structural model we come into the familiar territory of the id, ego, and superego, that troika of mental agencies into which the mind is divided in modern psychoanalytic theory. The focus of attention is no longer on topographically locating a mental event in the conscious or unconscious parts of the psyche but on the functional aspects of the three structural elements composing the mental apparatus. The nature of these agencies is described in greater detail elsewhere (see chapter 8, "Theories of Personality") and their functions will only be summarized here.

The id is viewed as the source of the instincts, or drives, which are experienced in consciousness by the ego as emotions and as fantasies, the nature of which is determined by the drive; such fantasies represent in imagination the discharge of the drive. According to analytic theory, the sexual (libidinal) and aggressive drives provide the basic motivation for human behavior, normal and abnormal, and are the source of psychological conflict. Theoreticians are not in universal agreement that aggression has a biological origin similar to that of libido, however; in the view of many, aggression is a reaction to the blocking of the discharge and gratification of drives.

The ego is conceived of as a set of functions that enables the organism to adapt to its internal and external environment. Sensation, perception, logical thought, control of the motor apparatus, the use of language, and the testing of reality are all ego functions that underlie the purposeful behavior and survival of the individual in his universe. In particular, the ego controls the id drives and channels their discharge in ways that bring gratification through behavior that is socially acceptable and physically harmless to the individual. Central to this controlling func-

tion are the ego defenses, which will shortly be described at greater length.

The superego, a developmental offshoot of the ego, is the locus of the ego ideals, the individual's set of images of the kind of person he would like to be. Vested in the superego is the capacity to observe oneself and one's behavior and to judge whether that behavior accords with one's ideals. Finally, in its role as judge, the superego causes the ego to experience a rising or lowering of self-esteem as the individual does or does not live up to those ideals—the phenomenon known commonly as conscience.

In the structural model, the unconscious is no longer seen as one of the component parts of the psyche. Rather, the term *unconscious* is now used to describe a quality of each of the three major divisions of the mental apparatus. The whole of the id and its drives is viewed as being unconscious, whereas the various elements of the ego and superego may be either conscious or unconscious. Anxiety is also conceived of differently in the structural model. In the topographic model, as mentioned earlier, anxiety was thought to be a direct somatic translation of undischarged libido into physiological processes. In the structural model, anxiety becomes the property of the ego; as an ego affect, it acts as a signal of a forbidden id drive that is threatening to escape from control. Depression, the ego's response to the loss of either an important object or an ideal, is also an ego affect important to psychic equilibrium. Both anxiety and depression are painful affects and motivate the ego to undertake defensive operations to prevent or remove the conscious experience of psychic pain. Thus psychological conflict may be created among the various psychic agencies that interact in a more or less stable psychodynamic equilibrium.

Before discussing the role of psychological conflict in the production of psychiatric disorders, it will be helpful to review in more detail the nature and variety of the ego defenses.

Ego Defense Mechanisms

Repression. The fundamental mechanism of ego defense, repression, involves forcing thoughts, memories, and feelings into the unconscious, followed by an active and continued exclusion of them from conscious awareness. Repression occurs automatically, outside the sphere of conscious awareness. It thus differs from suppression, which is the volitional exclusion of thoughts and feelings from conscious attention. Repression is a universal and normal human mental mechanism. It occurs notably in the course of growth and development as the phase of latency begins at the end of the oedipal period, rendering unconscious much of what has gone on before in the individual's life and resulting in the phenomenon of infantile amnesia—the universal inability of adults to remember their early childhood in any but the most fragmentary manner. Repression, however, continues to be employed in later life as a mechanism of defense against specific, anxiety-provoking thoughts and feelings aroused both by the pressure of inner drives and by the stimuli of external events.

The effect of repression may be observed by most of us in the common occurrence of forgetting a well-known name or being unable to recall a dream upon awakening. We *know* that we know the name, or that we have dreamed vividly during the night just passed, but no amount of mental effort enables us to recall the forgotten material. Indeed, in the attempt to recall it, we catch repression in the act of excluding it from our consciousness. It becomes evident that the memory or image is not permanently erased from our minds when, at some later point in time, the "forgotten" name or dream suddenly flashes quite unbidden into consciousness.

In a more clinical setting, repression is responsible for the gaps in patients' memory for significant events in their lives. It is most strikingly manifested in the clinical condition of amnesia (more fully elaborated in chapter 10, "Psychoneurotic Disorders"), in which the memory of whole segments of life is lost to the patient.

Susan H., a young woman of eighteen, was brought to the hospital in a state of confusion. Her mental clouding rapidly cleared after admission, but it was then evident that her mind was completely blank for the events of the seven hours prior to coming to the hospital. She had no idea where she had been or what she had been doing and was surprised to find herself on a psychiatric ward. By no amount of struggling to remember could she recall what had happened,

and it was only when she was put into a state of light hypnosis that her memory was restored. It was then discovered that the period covered by the amnesia had been one in which she had suffered an intolerable disappointment—abandonment by her boy friend at a time when she desperately needed his help. Through the defense of repression, she was able to protect herself against the emotional pain aroused by this event.

Denial. In its strict sense, denial refers to denying the existence of an external fact of reality. Its universality is evident in the immediate response of most people to an unexpected personal catastrophe—"It's not true!" Ordinarily, reality rapidly reasserts itself, and the individual confronts the painful fact with appropriate emotions and actions, but in some cases denial continues as a prolonged reaction of varying degrees of severity.

A young widow complained of headaches and an inability to grieve for her husband, who had hanged himself in the cellar some weeks before. In the initial interviews, the patient described how she could not bring herself to believe that her husband was dead. She kept everything in the house as it had been when he was alive, preserving his personal effects in the living room and his clothes in the closet, and each night she found herself setting his place at the dinner table and listening for the noise of his car in the driveway as she anticipated his return from work. Her sense of reality was not entirely shattered, however, for even while she was quite involuntarily behaving as if he were alive, intellectually she knew he was dead, though she could not feel it emotionally.

In other patients denial leads to a delusional conviction that nothing has changed and to an adamant rejection of facts that prove the contrary. Denial is commonly seen also in patients suffering from a physical illness who refuse to recognize the significance of their symptoms despite having information that should lead them to know better. Thus individuals frequently delay consulting their physician about the signs and symptoms of cancer, even though they have repeatedly been exposed to information on cancer detection in the popular press. Or patients will ignore chest pains indicating a myocardial infarction despite the fact that a close relative has recently died of a heart attack after suffering similar symptoms.

In repression and denial, both the cognitive and the emotional aspects of the mental content are banished from consciousness. If these defensive operations were entirely effective, that would be an end of the matter. But, as we have seen, the process of rendering something unconscious does not necessarily make it inoperative. On the contrary, an equilibrium of forces is set up, with the excluded material, especially the drives, constantly pressing for conscious expression and discharge. Repression and denial cannot, therefore, be simply isolated, single acts of defense; rather, they must constantly exert a countering energy against the material they have initially pushed from consciousness. In addition to repression and denial, a number of other ego defenses allow a partial representation in consciousness of the unacceptable mental contents in ways that make them tolerable to the ego; these may constitute the primary defensive operation in themselves, or they may be employed as defenses auxiliary to repression when the repressed material exerts an unusual degree of pressure to break through into consciousness.

Isolation. Isolation involves the separation of an idea from its associated affect, usually with the disappearance of the latter from conscious awareness. It is seen particularly in the ego's attempt to defend itself against the aggressive drive and is a common and widespread mental mechanism in those whose approach to the world is more thoughtful and intellectual than emotional. If not overdone, it is a useful psychological maneuver for professional people like physicians who must deal with human misery and pain with sufficient detachment to be able to apply effective and rational therapy. Isolation, when carried to an extreme, compromises the full development of the human personality and leads to characterological abnormalities or overt psychiatric symptoms.

One patient with an obsessional character well beyond the limits of normality was almost totally devoid of feelings, especially those of anger and aggression. During one therapeutic session he reported having a "fantasy" that he had seen the therapist struck down by a truck on the street,

and he described in almost too vivid detail his imagery of the therapist lying crumpled, bleeding, and broken on the street. He would infer from his fantasy, commented the patient, that he was angry at the therapist. "Do you feel it?" asked the latter, to which the patient replied, "No," in an emotionless, dry, matter-of-fact tone of voice. His response demonstrated the effect of the defense of isolation, which had excluded all feeling from consciousness but had permitted the patient to remain comfortably aware of a gory tapestry of destructive thoughts.

Isolation also less commonly refers to a process whereby the individual is prevented from seeing the connection between emotionally or causally related events. He may, for example, object to something the therapist has said or done and then shortly thereafter report a hostile fantasy about the therapist with no recognition of the relation of the one event to the other, despite the fact that their close association in time would suggest a significant connection.

Displacement. In displacement, a drive or emotion is severed from its original connection with a person or event and is attached to a substitute person or object. With its origin thus disguised, the drive or emotion may more safely be expressed. Anger that cannot be shown to a superior at work is commonly unleashed on someone lower in the hierarchy or on the individual's family. The sexual fantasies of an adolescent for a teacher or for the parent of a friend reveal the displacement of forbidden, if thinly disguised, libidinal desires for a parent. Displacement also forms an element in the transference that routinely develops in the doctor-patient relationship. Anxiety, along with the drive that arouses it, is particularly subject to displacement, especially in the phobic symptom.

In a young woman with a severe phobia of boats, it was discovered in the course of analytic psychotherapy that her first serious sexual encounter had taken place in the cockpit of a sailboat—an event that had aroused in her simultaneously great sexual excitement and tremendous anxiety over feelings and behavior that she felt were taboo. From that point on, as the result of the displacement of sexual feelings and anxiety to the incidental setting associated with her sexual arousal, boats came symbolically to represent the forbidden affects and thereafter were a source of neurotic phobic anxiety.

One might, in the language of learning theory, say that boats had become a conditioned stimulus, and, indeed, in the mechanism of displacement are to be found ego processes that provide a link between the concepts of psychoanalysis and learning theory (see chapter 8, "Theories of Personality").

Turning against the self. Similar to displacement, in that the drive or emotion remains in consciousness but is deflected from its initial object, turning against the self is a defense mechanism most commonly employed against anger and aggression, particularly as these feelings are related to depression and some forms of masochistic behavior.

A young woman came to the psychiatric clinic complaining of depression. It was discovered in the course of her evaluation that her depression was related to a recent move to a new house that had caused her to lose contact with several neighbors and friends and especially with her mother, with whom she had an unusually close relationship. Furthermore, as it turned out, she had made the move not because she herself had wanted to but because she thought it would be better for her children in the new home. In the attempt to discover what she felt about the move, including possible elements of resentment toward her children for being in large part the reason for her own deprivations, it became apparent that not only was there no conscious resentment toward them, but, as we shall see in more detail in the discussion of reaction formation, she had never experienced any anger whatsoever at them in any situation. When questioned as to whether she had ever punished her children, she replied that she never had, that she never could harm them, that "rather than hurt them, I'd rather hurt myself." Here one could see openly and literally a turning inward on herself of the anger that would appropriately have been felt toward her children.

Negation. In negation the underlying, anxiety-provoking drive or emotion is evident, but it is stated in terms opposite to what is meant. This occurs through the simple expedient of prefixing a negative to the expression of the feeling, im-

pulse, or fantasy. A middle-aged man, for instance, had spent six months in a hospital for chronic, incapacitating back pain. He seemed on the surface quite unperturbed at the absence of significant relief or improvement from his physician's therapeutic efforts. When asked what he felt about this, he replied, "Do you mean did I want to take my doctor and punch his nose all bloody and out of shape? Oh, no, Doc, I never had any thoughts like that!"

Undoing. Undoing is generally associated with the obsessive-compulsive neurosis. With this defense, the patient attempts to reduce the anxiety accompanying frightening impulses or fantasies, usually aggressive in nature, by retracting them in thought or action. A young man, for example, would think each time he turned off a light switch, "My father is going to die"; then, overcome with concern at this idea, he would say to himself, "I take back that thought," and his anxiety would be quieted. A patient described by Freud moved the limb of a tree he had found in the street, fearing it would upset his lady friend's carriage to her injury. Shortly thereafter he was overcome with concern lest in its new position it might bring harm to someone else, returned to the spot, and replaced the limb where he had originally found it. It should be noted that both initial thought or action and the countering move of undoing have no relation to reality. They are a form of magical thinking stemming from inner psychological processes.

Reaction formation. The defenses that have been discussed thus far are mental mechanisms that play a central part in the formation of discrete psychiatric symptoms. Reaction formation, however, is a defense mechanism that results in the creation of enduring behavior patterns that help to determine the nature and quality of the individual's character structure and personality.

Reaction formation is characteristically a defense against aggression, against dependency, and against passivity. In protecting himself against the anxiety aroused by these drives, an individual adopts and exhibits attitudes and patterns of behavior that are the exact opposite of the drive, feeling, or idea and that exclude it from conscious awareness and expression.

Reaction formation against aggression leads to behavior characterized by excessive concern for other people (especially those toward whom there is underlying aggression), by a marked, unrealistic altruism, and by an undue tolerance of unpleasantness in other people that one would expect to evoke resentment or anger. In the patient who turned the anger initially directed toward her children against herself, reaction formation played a major part in determining the quality of her relationship toward them. The mother of three youngsters aged six years to three months, she had never once left them with a family member or baby sitter, for fear that something terrible would happen to them if she were not in constant attendance. She reported that she had never been able to spank or otherwise punish any of her children and that whenever she took them with her to do the family shopping, she felt compelled to buy them a toy. She was, as she herself commented, "too good to them," a judgment corroborated by her husband and sisters. In the course of her therapeutic work, however, there emerged from behind her concern a degree of resentment at the demands of motherhood that reached, in her fantasies, the intensity of killing her sons.

Reaction formation against dependency needs (counterdependence) is perhaps best seen in those patients who deny a serious physical illness, or who, when incapacitated by an illness or injury, fight against assuming the sick role. (This pattern of behavior is elaborated later in this chapter in the discussion of dependency as a source of conflict.) Closely related to counterdependency, reaction formation against passivity is most commonly found in men, especially in those who have doubts about their masculinity or who cannot tolerate a conscious awareness of any kind of feminine or homosexual tendencies. Such individuals are bluff, tough, and rugged in their manner and their pursuits; they enjoy work demanding physical prowess and strength, will seek out tasks that present danger and challenge, and like to attempt problems that have defeated other men. A patient, for example, who was hospitalized for a back injury sustained at work described his life-long enjoyment of construction work that required him to operate huge cranes and powerful earth-movers. He had always vol-

unteered for dangerous assignments refused by his fellow workers and boasted about his bravery in the face of physical hazards or personal injury. On one occasion, he reported proudly, he had continued working all day after the terminal portion of his little finger had been torn off by a conveyor belt.

Counterphobia. Related to, if not a special form of, reaction formation, the counterphobic defense is aimed specifically at the anxiety associated with phobias. As such it represents an attempt by the individual affected to turn passive sufferance of a phobic situation into active mastery in such a way that he now experiences pleasure in an activity or situation that formerly caused him pain. Thus a person with a plane phobia may learn to pilot an airplane himself, or one suffering from a fear of heights will take up rock climbing as a hobby.

Identification. The mechanism of identification is employed to protect the individual against both anxiety and the pain of loss. Unlike imitation, in which there is a conscious attempt to mimic the behavior of others, identification involves unconscious processes that lead to the adoption of attitudes, attributes, and behavior patterns of another person with whom one has had a significant relationship. The pain deriving from the loss of an important person can be stilled or postponed by identification with him. A common form of such identification is seen in the appearance in a bereaved person of the somatic symptoms of the illness that killed the deceased. A woman, for example, whose mother had died of myocardial infarction consulted her physician shortly thereafter because of chest pain and breathlessness. Identification may affect the individual's entire life style, as in the case of a wife who takes over her husband's business after his death—a defense that is not only financially profitable but allows her to preserve internally the treasured image of the person she has lost.

In identification with the aggressor, the individual can master the anxiety produced by a person he fears. One commonly sees this defense in a child who, after a visit to the doctor or a trip to the hospital for surgery, subjects a doll or sibling or companion to a playful reproduction of the shots he has received or the operation he has undergone.

Projection. A mechanism of defense that leads to both neurotic and psychotic phenomena, projection is most commonly found in that universal if unpleasant human propensity for creating scapegoats. One can relieve one's sense of guilt by blaming other people or external circumstances for events that are primarily of one's own doing. The projection of anxiety-provoking impulses is more serious, for it often leads to paranoid delusions.

A young man began to feel that strangers talking to each other across the car from him in the subway were calling him a homosexual. Not long after, when a man pressed against him in a subway rush-hour crowd, he was convinced that this was a homosexual advance. A few days later an acquaintance held a lighted match to his mouth, requesting him to blow it out in order, he thought, to indicate his homosexuality to others. Thereafter he was tortured by the conviction that everyone where he worked knew and talked constantly about his sexual leanings. These conclusions were, of course, false; they arose from his own consciously unrecognized homosexual drives, projected and played out in the world of people external to him.

Projection, it should be noted, unlike most of the other defenses discussed so far, causes a distortion in perception and interpretation of the environment. In the projection of guilt, the distortion may be incomplete, since there are frequently real, external events conspiring with personal deficiencies to bring about guilt-producing failures, and it is possible to emphasize the role of the former in preference to the latter with only a partial falsification of the facts. In the projection of an impulse, however, external circumstances generally have little or no congruence with the individual's interpretations of them. The subjective distortion alone, however, does not make for a full-blown delusion, for the individual may be intellectually aware that his perceptions, however vivid and compelling, are not "really" true. It is only when he loses his capacity to distinguish inner fantasy from outer reality—that is, when he loses his reality testing—that he develops a delusional conviction that his perceptions are accurate—a conviction that no amount of argument, fact, or evidence to the contrary can shake.

Regression. The term regression is used in a general sense to refer to the retreat from a later developmental level of personality organization to behavior and thinking characteristic of an earlier phase. Regression is employed in a defensive way to avoid the anxiety associated with oedipal, genital conflicts by returning to more primitive, pregenital stages of organization; it is a primary defense in the production of the obsessive-compulsive neurosis (see chap 10, "Psychoneurotic Disorders"). Probably equally common is defensive regression in the face of oedipal anxiety from a position of adult, heterosexual object love to a level of childish dependency.

A young woman undertook psychotherapy because of an incapacity to form a lasting tie with a man. She would repeatedly enter upon a relationship with hope and enthusiasm, only to find her ardor cooling after a few weeks, leading to a breaking off of the liaison. Early in the course of therapy she approached the subject of her strong sexual feelings for men, a topic that made her visibly anxious. She reported in her next visit that she had been anxious for a day or two following her previous session and then began talking spontaneously, freely, and easily about her close attachment to and dependency on her mother. Finally toward the end of the hour her therapist asked her about the sexual feelings she had described the time before. Immediately the patient became anxious and was unable to talk about the subject. Her spontaneous (and comfortable) preoccupation with her relationship to her mother was a defensive response to anxiety over heterosexuality, manifested in a regressive flowing of her associations away from the anxiety-producing sexual feelings to memories and material having to do with her preoedipal, dependent, little-girl ties to her mother.

Conversion and sublimation. Before leaving the subject of defense mechanisms, it is necessary briefly to consider two mental processes that, though not universally considered defenses, are theoretically important in processing mental energies and in helping the ego in its attempts to remain free of anxiety. The processes are conversion and sublimation.

The term *conversion* appeared early in Freud's theoretical conceptions and represented for him the means by which repressed psychic excitation could be transformed into a somatic expression of the energies involved—a transformation that was seen clinically as a sensory or motor hysterical symptom. This concept provided him with an explanation of the differences among neurotic symptoms. In the phobia, for example, the psychic excitation associated with a pathogenic idea remained in the psychic sphere and was merely displaced to another, originally neutral idea, rather than being transformed by conversion into a hysterical disorder of bodily functions. The term soon became, and remains today, indissolubly linked with hysteria to designate that form of the disorder manifested by sensorimotor symptoms, and much has been made of the "mysterious leap from mind to body" involved in this transformation (Deutsch, 1959). Conversion is a useful concept in explaining the processes involved in the constellation of neurotic symptoms evidenced by an individual, but it confuses the issue to dwell on the mystery of the transformation of a mental event into a somatic event as a process uniquely associated with hysteria, for the same mysterious transformation exists in the translation of a conscious volitional idea into action, for example, the idea of raising one's arm into the actual physical movement of the limb. The difference lies in the fact that in hysteria the transformation occurs outside of the sphere of conscious volition and control—that is, in a state of dissociation.

Sublimation is another psychoanalytic concept introduced early into the theoretical structure and, though much has been written about it since, it remains neither clearly defined nor completely understood. Sublimation is considered to involve the neutralization of instinctual energy (particularly that deriving from pregenital drives) in such a manner as to render it conflict-free and available for the socially acceptable and useful activities—notably those involved in scientific and artistic pursuits—on which civilization rests. The concept is more relevant to psychoanalytic theory as a general system of psychology applicable to all of human behavior than to psychoanalytic explanations of psychopathology.

Psychodynamic Aspects of Psychiatric Disorders

Having reviewed the structural elements of the psyche and the conflicts that exist among them, we are now in a position to examine in greater detail the ways in which disturbances in the functioning of these elements lead to psychiatric disorders.

Normal Psychological Equilibrium

In the psychologically normal human being (a mythical figure, perhaps, but one that many persons approximate) the conflicting forces of the various psychic elements result in a stable equilibrium that permits the individual to function in a mature, adaptive, and self-fulfilling way. Realistic about and responsive to the world around him, he is capable of experiencing a wide range of feelings, of entering into lasting and satisfying human relationships, and of working creatively and effectively. His drives, though controlled by the ego, find ready avenues to expression in constructive activities without being warped, stunted, or constricted. In such individuals a balance among the various psychic elements and a flexibility in their interaction maintain equilibrium or facilitate a prompt restitution if it is temporarily disrupted by emotional stress.

Distortions in Psychological Equilibrium

Permanent distortions in many people's psychic structure lead to constrictions in their lives (often visible in their behavior and relationships), even though, within limitations, they may function for long periods of time with a measure of success. The individual, for example, in whom isolation is a central ego defense mechanism against strong, underlying affects may appear to his acquaintances to be emotionally distant and reserved and to favor his head over his heart in most situations. Although constricted in his emotional life, he may, in fact, be very effective at a job requiring intelligence, reason, and logical thought. Such distortions, however, though often compatible with living a conventional and successful life, render the individual vulnerable to the outbreak of psychiatric symptoms in the face of environmental stresses to which his emotional conflicts make him specifically sensitive. One or two examples will make this clearer.

Dependency as a source of conflict. In many people dependency needs are a source of conflict since they run counter to the person's ideal image of himself as independent and self-sufficient. In addition, he may be anxious that if he relies on others, they will disappoint him by failing to help and support him. As a result, dependency needs are controlled and pushed from conscious awareness by a specific form of reaction formation known as counterdependence. Externally, such persons are independent and self-sufficient to an extreme degree. They have often begun to work early in adolescence, since they disliked being dependent on their parents, and their adult life is geared to hard work for long hours; not infrequently they hold two jobs and do not allow themselves to take leisurely, relaxing holidays or vacations, finding work around the house to keep them active during such periods away from their regular employment. They ask for nothing, accept no help, insist on doing things for themselves, and will not allow themselves to borrow even the smallest item, preferring to do without if they cannot obtain it by themselves. At the same time they are unusually generous and helpful and are consequently often taken advantage of. As one patient expressed it, "I want to make my own way. I want to be here and I want the other guy to be there. I want to stand on my own two feet, and if anybody has got to have anybody to lean on, I want him to lean on me, not me lean on him."

As one observes such behavior (and it is often quite obvious to family and friends, who frequently comment that the individual is "too independent"), it is evident that individuals evincing this behavior in extreme forms are leaning over backward to avoid any appearance of being dependent, vehemently denying that they have any such tendencies. If, however, such an individual suffers an incapacitating accident or a serious illness, for example, a myocardial infarction, which forces him into the role of a dependent invalid, one notices a specific pattern of behavior. At first, the patient (for such he now is)

becomes both anxious and depressed over his enforced inactivity, and tries to deny or minimize the severity of his physical condition, often to the point of refusing to comply with medical orders for rest or medication or other procedures that are indicated for the treatment of his condition. At length, however, if the physical illness and resulting incapacity continue, a change occurs in his behavior. Gradually he becomes more and more demanding of help, more vocal in his complaints of pain and discomfort, and more dependent on others around him. His behavior, in other words, has shifted 180 degrees from his stance of excessive independence to a position of equally excessive dependence. Indeed, one not infrequently discovers that long after the disappearance of the physical disorder that set the process in motion, the patient remains vociferous in his complaints (usually of pain), totally incapacitated, and aggressively dependent on others for help, money, and support. The symptoms, initially resulting from the tissue damage of injury or illness, are now prolonged by psychological factors.

Upon psychological examination of such patients, one finds that behind the premorbid pattern of excessive independence and self-sufficiency are strong, underlying dependency needs, controlled and kept unconscious by the defensive reaction formation of counterdependency. The counterdependency, it should be pointed out, has in many ways been a valuable and effective pattern of behavior. Not only has it kept the underlying undesirable drive at bay, but it has also enabled the individual to be a highly effective and productive worker and a stable, reliable source of support to his family. At the same time, however, the psychological equilibrium resulting from the conflict over dependency needs is a rigid and inflexible one. Unlike most people, who can occasionally—when the situation is appropriate—permit themselves to rely on and take help from others, individuals with this psychological constellation can tolerate no show of dependence whatsoever, and their underlying needs in this regard ordinarily find no outlet for discharge or gratification.

When an incapacitating injury or illness forces such patients into a situation of passive dependency on others, their psychological equilibrium is put under a severe stress. On the one hand, their characteristic defense of excessive activity is removed from them by their physical incapacitation; on the other, their dependency needs are invited into open expression by the solicitousness and concern of family, friends, doctors, and other caregivers, as well as by the expectation and requirement of those concerned with the patient's welfare that he remain inactive. Furthermore, it is easier in this new situation for the individual —after the initial period of protest—to tolerate his dependency and inactivity, since he can view these as forced upon him by circumstances beyond his control; the injury or illness was not of his own doing but an unbidden, unwanted, external accident. He can, and does, maintain his image of himself as a person who wants to be active and independent but who is involuntarily kept from being so by his symptoms. In this setting a new psychological equilibrium emerges in which the symptoms play a central role. They now provide an avenue of discharge for the formerly hidden dependency needs and permit the gratification of these needs, while simultaneously allowing the patient to maintain his self-esteem, since he does not have to admit responsibility for his dependency or for wishes to be dependent. From a clinical point of view the patient has developed chronic psychological invalidism.

Sexuality as a source of conflict. Before discussing the significance of these observations for the nature of psychological functioning, let us look at another example of a change in psychological equilibrium resulting from environmental stress. The sexual instinct, as we have seen, is a common source of anxiety and conflict. In its pressure to find an outlet for discharge in overt sexual behavior, it is met by the countering force of defensive repression, which renders the instinct largely unconscious. A relatively stable psychological equilibrium results, enabling the individual to function effectively and comfortably in many areas of his life so long as he is not subjected to situations that unduly arouse the underlying instinct. If, however, the latter occurs— if an environmental stimulus increases the pressure of the repressed libido and threatens to overwhelm the defensive repression—the

individual experiences mounting anxiety that leads the ego to erect auxiliary defenses to keep the libido under control. If the process of defensive repression is successful, a new psychological equilibrium is established that may find the individual more restricted in his behavior than before as a result of symptoms representing external manifestations of the auxiliary defenses that have been brought into play.

The young woman with a phobia of boats, mentioned in the earlier discussion of displacement, had functioned reasonably well in her daily life at school and home during the greater part of her adolescence. She was, however, unusually naive and ignorant about sexual matters that were commonplace knowledge among her friends. Her virginal innocence was matched by an absence of curiosity about sex and a lack of interest in the usual adolescent exploratory sexual behavior. Her behavior and the quality of her human relationships, in other words, appeared to be the result of a repression of libido that brought about an exaggerated inhibition and constriction of normal adolescent sexuality.

The patient's defense functioned effectively for a number of years, and her psychological equilibrium remained stable and unshifting until her later teens. It was then that she met a young man of more than passing interest, who put increasing pressure on her to engage with him in sexual activity. Though anxious, she controlled herself until one day, when they were out sailing, her own desires were aroused to the point where she gave in to him and indulged in extensive foreplay short of intercourse. Thereafter, for a brief period of days, she was overcome by deep guilt and mounting anxiety, in the course of which she developed a severe and lasting phobia of boats.

In psychological terms these developments can be understood in the following way. For several years the patient's psychological equilibrium allowed her to function reasonably comfortably, although it caused a constriction in her sexual life and activities. As the relationship with her boy friend developed, however, a stress was imposed on the equilibrium as the repressed libido was stimulated to more open expression. The effect of the stress was seen in her anxiety, but no major shifting or change in the equilibrium occurred until the episode on the boat. At that point the defense of repression was momentarily overpowered, resulting in the experience of acute anxiety and guilt. The ego was motivated by these emotions to bring forth the auxiliary defenses first of displacing the libido and associated anxiety to the image of boats and then of projecting them outward onto real, external boats. These now became the primary source of anxiety, which could be controlled by the further defense of avoiding the anxiety-provoking phobic object. A new equilibrium was thus established that enabled the ego to regain its control over the instinctual impulse and the related anxiety. It was, however, an equilibrium different in structure from the one that had existed before—one that was manifested clinically by the emergence of a psychiatric symptom, the phobia, and that imposed greater restrictions on the patient's life and freedom of movement than she had suffered before the shift in equilibrium took place. Now, in addition to her difficulties with sexual activity, she could not venture near the ocean front of the town in which she lived for fear of seeing a boat, nor could she look at television, attend the movies, or read the daily paper or current magazines without an acute fear that she might run across the picture of one—a state of affairs that was as incapacitating as a severe physical illness.

Symptom Formation

On the basis of the concepts discussed so far, it is possible to explain the process of symptom formation and the onset of psychiatric illness in more general terms. From what has been said of the nature of psychological equilibrium, it is evident that behind the personality that uniquely characterizes each human being is a stable balance of psychic elements that persists over time and determines the quality of his behavior and his relationships as these are known by other people. When the individual is subjected to stress, the balance of forces making up the stable equilibrium is acutely altered through changes in the instinctual components or in the ego structure that controls them, or in both.

Stress may be the result of internal or external factors. The latter are commonly the precipitants of psychoneurotic syndromes, as well as of some of the more serious psychotic disorders.

The loss of an important person, a disabling injury or illness, situations that stimulate the aggressive or libidinal drive, major changes imposed on one's customary pattern of living—all serve as potential emotional crises that alter the balance of forces in the psychological equilibrium. The same result may also be effected by inner changes: damage to the brain through injury or illness, the ingestion of substances (amphetamines or LSD, for example) that radically alter ego functions, or the as yet poorly understood alterations in brain metabolism that lead to changes in mood and drives as well as in ego functions. All of these factors may seriously upset the balance previously existing among the various psychic elements. The initial period of stress may be manifested only by symptoms of anxiety and depression, but as the stress continues and changes occur in the psychic structure, the external signs and symptoms of a psychiatric disorder appear, evidence that a new and pathological psychological equilibrium has replaced the old—an equilibrium that persists even though the precipitating distress has ceased to exist.

Categories of Symptoms

The model of psychic structure reviewed here not only enables us to understand the processes entering into the production of psychiatric disorders but allows us as well to make a logical classification of psychiatric symptoms and signs based on their origins in that structure. Symptoms and signs fall into three major categories: (1) those representing ego affects; (2) those resulting from the operation of ego defenses; and (3) those stemming from ego defects that arise from the destruction or distortion of basic ego functions.

Ego affects. Anxiety and depression are the two primary ego affects and, as symptoms, are components of almost all psychiatric disorders. They are, as we have seen, indicators of strain in the psychic structure when it is under the stress of precipitating events that upset the balance between instinctual drives and ego-controlling mechanisms.

Ego defenses. The emergence of auxiliary defenses in response to stress leads to the appearance of a variety of symptoms and signs that are determined by the nature of the defense that helps to produce them. This aspect of symptom formation is particularly prominent in the onset of psychoneurotic syndromes (see chapter 10, "Psychoneurotic Disorders," for a more detailed review of these clinical disorders).

Ego defects. Symptoms and signs that result from defects in ego functions are most commonly found in the more serious psychiatric disorders and comprise two major classes: (1) Many clinical manifestations represent the direct effect of the destruction of specific ego functions; included in this category are the loss of reality testing central to many psychotic illnesses, the memory loss found in brain disease, and the confusion and delirium of the toxic psychoses. (2) Other clinical signs and symptoms result from the release of mental processes ordinarily partially or completely controlled by the intact ego but now emerging into view as ego functions are compromised; this class includes such phenomena as the irruption of partial, deviant sexual drives or the appearance of autistic, primary process thinking.

The Concept of Abnormality

Before concluding this review of the processes involved in the appearance of psychiatric disorders, we must briefly consider the concept of abnormality. This discussion of psychopathology has tacitly assumed that the phenomena resulting from disturbances in the psychic structure fall into the category of the abnormal—that is, that they are the signs and symptoms of psychiatric disease. If, however, we try to define what we mean by "abnormal" or "psychopathological," it becomes apparent that this is no simple task, for no single definition will suffice, and disagreement often exists as to what is and what is not a manifestation of emotional disorder.

In general, the phenomena of psychiatric illness fall into three categories: (1) those that cause the individual pain and about which, consequently, he complains; (2) those considered unusual and abnormal by others or by society at large; and (3) those that deviate from a theoretical concept of normal functioning.

The subjective criterion. Painful affects like anxiety and depression or other symptoms that hamper the individual's life and well-being motivate him to seek out a physician, to complain of his difficulties, and to ask for help in removing what troubles him. Many phenomena ordinarily included in the realm of psychopathology, however, are not considered abnormal by the individual who manifests them; the paranoid patient, for example, who assaults another person whom he views in his delusions as a dangerous persecutor, does not see himself as sick or in need of treatment. It is only in the judgment of others that he is considered irrationally dangerous and abnormal.

The normative criterion. Many aspects of behavior are so obviously bizarre, unreasonable, and outré that consensus on their abnormality is easy to achieve. Unfortunately for a rigorous definition of psychopathology, more often than not agreement cannot be reached. For example, patterns of behavior considered psychopathological in one society may be viewed by another as being within the cultural norms. Furthermore, within our own society it is particularly difficult to reach a consensus on the normality or abnormality of certain forms of sexual behavior, especially in the current climate of opinion about sexual mores. Homosexuality, for example, once considered a psychiatric disorder, is now seen by many as an expression of the sexual drive that is a normal alternate to heterosexuality, and by a recent vote of the American Psychiatric Association it has been banished from the official classification of mental illnesses.

The theoretical criterion. By certain normative standards the common cold or minor skin blemishes might be considered normal since they occur almost universally among human beings. At the same time, when viewed against knowledge of physiological processes that leads to concepts of health, they are seen to be the result of processes that, if hardly serious or life-endangering, are nonetheless pathophysiological. The same principle can be applied to psychological phenomena, which can be judged by theoretical norms of behavior derived from observations of the process of human growth and development. In this view, each individual is born with a potential for the full development of his psyche to a level of adult maturity. The process of development occurs in phases and stages, at any one of which environmental stress may cause distortions in psychic growth that are carried into adulthood as disturbances in psychic function and restrict the individual's inner freedom, making him vulnerable to the outbreak of psychiatric disorders. Thus, for example, within this conceptual framework, homosexuality and other forms of sexual behavior deviating from full genital heterosexuality are viewed as being the persistent remains of earlier stages of the sexual drive that have failed to follow the usual pattern of growth and development. The details of the developmental process are extensively presented elsewhere in this volume (see chapter 8, "Theories of Personality"); this examination will be limited to the specific aspects that have a bearing on the emergence of adult psychiatric disorders.

Psychogenetic Aspects of Psychiatric Disorders

Thus far we have been concerned primarily with the dynamic aspects of psychopathology—that is, we have viewed psychiatric disorders as resulting from the interplay of psychological forces that make up the psychic structure as it exists in the adult patient under examination. We have, so to speak, focused on that structure in a temporal cross-section. The psychic structure of the adult, however, is the result of a long period of development—it has a history that includes an infinitude of shaping experiences in childhood that have helped to determine the adult personality. The roots of psychiatric disorders lie in disturbances during these early formative influences, and it is as important (if often more difficult) for the psychiatrist to uncover and understand these psychogenetic factors in illness as it is for him to dissect the dynamic forces involved (Hartmann and Kris, 1945).

The Formation of Developmental Arrests

Environmental stresses may, of course, lead to distortions in the psyche at any point in time, but it is the stresses that occur in early life that produce the most profound and long-lasting pathological changes. These may occur at any phase in the child's development and affect his instinctual life, his ego structure, and the character and quality of his relationships. There are usually indications in the behavior of the child that the developmental process is not progressing smoothly. Transient symptoms such as phobias or nightmares, undue attachment to a parent, disturbances in basic functions such as bowel and feeding problems or enuresis, temper tantrums—all point to the possibility of disturbances that may lead to developmental arrests and fixations of greater or lesser degree. Ordinarily, as the oedipal phase is completed, many of the indications of earlier psychic disequilibrium disappear under the mantle of repression that ushers in the latency period. As the latency child turns to the tasks of schooling and of broadening his social horizons beyond his immediate family, he may appear, superficially at least, to function fairly normally. But he carries with him the scars of the earlier developmental difficulties that later determine the nature of his relationships and act as pathogenic foci for the outbreak of psychiatric disorders in the face of the stresses of adolescence and adulthood.

It should be emphasized that these foci are unconscious. The memories and feelings associated with the stresses that have produced the developmental distortions are deeply repressed and return to consciousness only in the course of psychotherapy or other special circumstance. However, although they are unconscious, the effect of these earliest formative experiences persists throughout life, as the following cases illustrate.

Developmental Arrests and Adult Symptoms

George M., a married man of thirty-four, consulted a doctor because of increasing anxiety over an obsessional thought that he had bumped into people he passed, especially "older people," causing them to fall and injure themselves. He was particularly concerned that he had knocked bystanders on subway platforms onto the tracks, where they had been run over by a train and killed. He grew so alarmed over this possibility that he had given up traveling by subway and had called the public transportation company several times to make sure that no one had met his death in this fashion. In direct association to these symptoms, he reported that when he was three and a half, his father had shot himself in a state of depression following an incapacitating fall at work. As the patient, over thirty years later, recounted the facts of his father's death, he burst into deep sobs, lamenting his loss and the fact that he had never had the chance really to know his father.

From a dynamic point of view it was evident that the patient was in serious conflict over aggression, the destructiveness and intensity of which was indicated by the violent nature of his obsessional fantasies and fears and the anxiety they aroused in him. Further evidence of the importance of this conflict lay in the fact that throughout his life he had always been concerned about being aggressive. He could remember only one occasion in his life when he had been angry and described himself as a person who had consistently tried to be friendly, agreeable, and "easy-going," no matter what provocation he might have had to anger—reaction formation, in other words, had been a significant ego defense throughout his adult life.

In the search for the psychogenic roots of the patient's neurosis, two observations are helpful: (1) the marked similarity between the patient's obsessional concern that he would harm others by causing them to fall and the circumstances of the father's suicide in a state of depression that had its inception in an incapacitating fall; and (2) the fact that thirty years after the event, the patient cried about his father's death as if the tragedy were recent. The normal process of mourning that would ordinarily have attenuated his grief appeared to have been blocked, leaving the emotion alive and poignantly fresh over the many years that had elapsed since the tragic event.

Let us reflect for a moment on the psychological state of a little boy of three and a half years in the normal course of his growth and development. At that age he is emerging from the anal phase, with all of the attendant ambivalence, aggression, and concern over control of emotions and body functions; he is gradually entering the early stage of the oedipal period, characterized not only by erotic fantasies and longings for the mother but by a highly ambivalent relationship with the father—a mixture of admiration and love, and of intense rivalry and aggression accompanied by destructively hostile fantasies. At the same time, the ego's perception of reality is not firmly established; the child believes that his thoughts are omnipotent and that he can effect changes in the physical world merely by thinking that they will happen.

It is not surprising that, falling on this mental set, the death of his father should have had a profound effect on the patient when he was a little boy. The magical conviction of the omnipotence of his thought was confirmed as reality matched his fantasy. As a result he experienced a strong sense of guilty responsibility for his father's demise and developed fearful respect for the power of his aggressive drive. From then on it was necessary to keep aggression under strict control. Reinforced by the fateful events in his environment, the mental constellation characteristic of that age remained fixed, impervious to the forces of normal development that would otherwise have tempered his aggressive drive and modified his ego functions in the direction of more mature and rational thinking. The distortion in his psyche that was thus created persisted as a fixation point into his adult years, to reemerge in a neurotic illness that had many of the qualities characteristic of the childhood stage of development in effect at the time of the original trauma.

Much of the reconstruction of the psychogenesis of George M.'s illness is inferential, based upon general knowledge of the sequential phases of human psychological development, not upon his own memories of that period of his life and the sad occurrence that disrupted it. In Mary K., however, a married woman of twenty-six, we can see directly and convincingly the connection between adult symptoms and traumatic childhood events.

Mary K. was admitted to the psychiatric ward of a general hospital because of severe anxiety mixed with depression. Her symptoms had started some six months before in response to the abrupt appearance of a phenomenon that puzzled and shocked her. One morning, for no apparent reason and without forewarning, she suddenly thought of herself and her father clinging naked together in a sexual embrace. From that time on the thought recurred, against her will and despite her attempts to banish it from her mind, and she found herself repeatedly preoccupied with imagined visions of the scene. It was the mounting anxiety and despair in the face of this unshakable phantom that caused her to seek medical help.

As her history unfolded over a series of interviews, several additional facts of importance emerged. The imagined scene had initially appeared at a time when the patient's father, after a long period in which they had had no communication, had generously offered to help her over some financial difficulties. She was surprised and troubled at his overtures, since, as she vehemently insisted, she and her father had nothing in common. Indeed, she elaborated, in a lengthy protest, on the fact that, far from being close to him, she had always hated him, had always felt tense and uncomfortable in his presence, and had consistently avoided him.

Confronted by the interviewer with the passionate (and suspicious) urgency of her denial of closeness to her father, she at length reported that they had not always been so distant. As a little girl she had, in fact, been his favorite, and he had regularly showered affection and attention upon her, at times going so far as to take her into his bed in innocent but affectionate play. One day when she was eleven and was hanging on the arm of his chair as he read the paper, she suddenly had the image of the two of them locked in a naked embrace. Shocked and terrified, she ran to her mother. Though the image had not recurred, she had kept emotional and physical distance from her father thereafter.

As the patient revealed this information in a therapeutic session, her anxiety became intense, and she was for a time unable to talk. At length, however, as the interview came to an end, she brought forth a new fact: she had slept in a crib in her parents' bedroom until she was nearly six. The following day she reported yet a further fact: the night before her distressing symptom had

suddenly appeared she had had a nightmare about animals noisily mating in a zoo. In direct association to her dream she recaptured a long-lost memory of having waked in the middle of the night at the age of five to observe her parents having sexual intercourse. When they noticed her watching, they sprang apart and her father angrily ordered her to go back to sleep. Once again the patient was consumed by almost paralyzing anxiety as she described this event. It was, however, followed by an immediate and complete relief from her symptoms—a relief still present on a follow-up visit several months later.

Even in this condensed history, the psychogenic roots of the patient's adult neurosis are clear. As a part of her normal growth and development she was, at the age of five, in the midst of an oedipal attachment to her father with all its attendant erotic fantasies and wishes. Occurring at this phase of her psychosexual evolution, witnessing her parents' sexual activity (not only on the occasion recounted but quite possibly on others as well, in view of the fact that she slept regularly in their bedroom) intensified her libidinal attachment to her father to an abnormal degree. As a result the process of normal development, which would ordinarily bring about an attenuation of this attachment, was distorted, and the patient remained fixated in her incestuous ties. Subjected to the repression that accompanied the onset of latency, the whole complex went underground. It emerged from its unconscious state in the transient initial outbreak of her symptom when the patient was eleven, following which she redoubled her defensive efforts against the dangerous incestuous impulse through her angry avoidance of any relationship with her father. Thus protected, she was able to move through adolescence to adulthood, marriage, and motherhood, but the unresolved oedipal tie rendered her liable to further neurotic difficulty, which irrupted under the stress of her father's attempt to help her—an approach that activated the underlying incestuous libidinal impulse and intensified it to the point where it once again emerged in the form of a neurotic illness.

Developmental Arrests
and the Pattern
of Adult Relationships

The final patient considered here is of interest, not so much because of her symptoms (which were numerous and severe) but because the pattern of her adult relationships to men can be traced to its origin in her early childhood. In 1910 Cecile V., a spinster schoolteacher in her middle forties, consulted Dr. Theodore Flournoy, the Professor of Psychology at the University of Geneva, because of a deeply troubling and recurrent pattern of behavior. Although most of the time she lived the sedate, proper life of a schoolmistress, she would on occasion suddenly find herself invaded by lewd sexual fantasies and dreams, accompanied by an overpowering libidinal drive that led her to masturbation and, she hinted, more rarely to sexual encounters with men. After a week or so the storm would pass, and she would return to her usual prim self, troubled, guilty, and filled with remorse at her loss of control.

Flournoy saw the patient over a considerable period of time, during which he obtained a detailed history of her life, in part directly from her and in part from the frequent letters she sent him and from a journal she kept of the course of her difficulties (Flournoy, 1915). From these various sources the unusually virginal and sexually innocent quality of her adolescence becomes apparent. She had been, as she reported to Flournoy, aware that her sisters and her school classmates had had their "secrets," but she had remained ignorant of their substance and had had no curiosity or desire to learn about them.

During her eighteenth year she was seduced by a man considerably her senior, who, as she put it, precipitated her "into the furnace of sexual emotions and of brutal, filthy revelations" (p. 21). Panic-stricken and sick at heart, she consulted a textbook in her father's library to seek enlightenment about what had happened but succeeded only in becoming terrified that she was pregnant. From then on, however, she led an active social life, with numerous male friends and suitors until the death of her father some ten or twelve years later. His demise coincided with her experience of a religious conversion, which gave her a measure of control over her passionate feelings, broken only by the periodic irruptions of libidinal desire for which she eventually consulted Flournoy.

Of particular interest was the nature of the relationships she experienced with men. She would repeatedly be attracted to men much older than herself, who often were married and frequently quite openly reminded her of her father. Initially the friendship would be based on common intellectual and artistic interests, but invariably sexual passions would emerge, producing a crisis of conscience of such turbulence that the patient would be forced at length to break off the liaison, only to start the process all over again with another man. As a result, the patient had reached middle age without having married and without having allowed herself the human satisfaction of lasting love.

The dynamic aspects of the patient's disorder are clear. Central to her difficulty is a profound conflict over her sexual drive. During the greater part of her adolescence it was controlled by the defense of repression—so tightly controlled that the patient not only had none of the libidinal strivings and fantasies normal for girls of her age but lived in total ignorance of all things sexual. After her rude awakening at the age of eighteen, the full force of her libido was unleashed and the conflict became overt, not only causing her deep mental anguish but determining the course of her repeatedly frustrated relationships with men.

It is in her journals and letters to Flournoy that we discover the psychogenetic roots of her adult conflict, for there she reveals for us two important facts. First, she describes her emotional isolation in childhood from all the members of her family save her father. He, she reported, "was alone able to win my heart," and from her earliest years there existed between them "a delicious intimacy." She developed for him "an affection that was exclusive, passionate and jealous"—an affection that continued through the first decade of her life into the early part of her adolescence (p. 19). The second psychogenetic element rose from events in her seventh year; at that time she was taught to masturbate by one of the maids in the family ménage, a practice that she adopted with wild abandon, mixed from the start with intense guilt, shame, and emotional conflict. Although she is not explicit in her written account, she apparently soon gained control over her sexual activity and during her latency and adolescence had no memory of this behavior, which like everything else associated with sexuality was subjected to the massive repression noted earlier. Only with the reappearance of her libidinal drive after the seduction at eighteen did she recall these experiences, feelings, and practices of her childhood, a recollection colored by the same guilty horror that attended and blighted her adult sexual life.

Despite the differences in their adult behavior and neurotic disorders, a central feature is common to Cecile V. and Mary K.—the failure in each to resolve their oedipal ties to their fathers. In the period of Cecile V.'s early childhood before the latency phase, an intense attachment to her father and a marked conflict over genital sexuality were present. The disappearance of much of this conflict during her adolescence is more apparent than real; it was merely rendered unconscious by a pathological degree of repression that prevented any awareness whatsoever of her libidinal strivings. With this degree of inhibition she was unable to engage in the usual adolescent exploration of heterosexual behavior and relationships that normally attenuates the childhood ties to the father and opens up new channels for an eventual mature, adult experience of love and marriage with a suitable man. In Cecile V. the normal processes of growth and development had been blocked, and her sexual drive remained fixated at the oedipal phase. When it reemerged into consciousness at eighteen, it was unchanged. With its incestuous coloring unmodified, it not only determined her repeated choice of paternal men in relationships that bore the stamp of her unresolved tie to her father, but in each instance, as sexual feelings grew for her partner, their unmodified oedipal character made them a source of intense anxiety and conflict. As a consequence, the patient was forced to reject such forbidden desires and to break off the relationship. Imprisoned by her past, she could only repeat it endlessly in her future.

Preoedipal Fixations and Borderline Characteristics

In these three patients the psychogenetic origins of their adult disorders were to be found in fixations along the oedipal phase of their development. In each of them a potential capacity for forming a positive, adult relationship with other human beings existed—a capacity inhibited and distorted by conflicts arising from these fixations that set the stage for the emergence in adulthood of neurotic illness.

In many individuals, however, the potential for such relationships is severely limited or does not seem to exist at all. Instead of reaching out to others with a love (however inhibited by conflicts) that altruistically recognizes the other's needs and attempts to satisfy them, they form relationships that are based on a narcissistic dependency that seeks only to gratify their own wants without regard for the needs of others. Hand in hand with such dependency goes a potential for violent and destructive aggression if the dependent needs are not gratified. The relationships established by such individuals are characterized by a profound ambivalence, by repeated attempts to manipulate others to gain their ends, by a tendency to see others as either completely good or totally bad, by a propensity for experiencing slights and rejections where none has occurred, and by distortions in ego functions, manifested particularly by the use of projective defense mechanisms and by difficulties in distinguishing fantasy from reality.

In this large group of borderline individuals (see chapter 14, "Personality Disorders") the psychogenesis of the disorder lies in the preoedipal phases of their development. Inadequacies in parental care during these earliest stages of psychological growth, when the child's needs for nurturing are paramount, lead to fixations at the level of oral dependency, primitive aggression, and immature ego functions that are carried on into adult life. Of particular importance is the fact that such individuals do not develop the capacity for a basic trust in the good will, concern, and caring qualities of other people (Erikson, 1963). They approach every relationship with the conviction that it will bring them pain and harm, and until they are certain of their ground, they maintain a guarded distance from emotional ties.

This fundamental suspiciousness of others has an important bearing on the psychotherapy of such patients, as contrasted with those whose neurotic disorders stem primarily from oedipal conflicts. The latter enter into therapy with the expectation that the physician is there to help them. They at once form a therapeutic alliance with the therapist, within the framework of which they are enabled from the start to examine their inner conflicts with an emotional distance from their feelings and fantasies that leads to therapeutic insight. With the borderline patient, on the other hand, the initial phases of treatment must be devoted to establishing his sense of trust and to creating the therapeutic alliance without which insight psychotherapy cannot be carried on. Indeed, in many borderline patients, the capacity to develop insight may be severely limited if not absent, and the improvement they achieve in therapy is based mainly on the positive relationship they are gradually able to form with their physician. In such patients, furthermore, the attempt of the therapist to focus on the patient's dependency needs and primitive aggression may overwhelm the patient with unmanageable emotions and fantasies—a situation that will preclude his forming a therapeutic relationship. Too often thoughtless and uncritical attempts to probe the emotional depths of the borderline patient will make him worse rather than better.

In view of these clinical facts, it is evident that as one assesses each new patient, it is important to distinguish between those whose problems arise primarily out of oedipal conflicts and those whose disorder is mainly preoedipal in origin. The planning of appropriate treatment must rest on a careful evaluation not only of the patient's symptoms but of his personality characteristics and patterns of relationships as well, in both their dynamic and their psychogenetic aspects. This is often a difficult task, in good part because our knowledge in these areas is as yet incomplete, and much of current clinical research (Gunderson and Singer, 1975) is aimed at elucidating and refining the details of the psychopathology of the borderline patient.

The fact that the vocabulary used throughout this discussion of dynamic psychopathology has been psychological in nature should not be construed to mean that the function of the brain is irrelevant to psychopathological phenomena. On the contrary, one assumes that neurological processes underlie psychodynamic mechanisms, even though in our current state of ignorance these are unknown to us. One may anticipate, however, that with an increasing knowledge of neurochemistry and neurophysiology, significant correlations between the physical and psychological aspects of behavior will become evident and that the frustrated hopes of Freud's "Project for a Scientific Psychology" (1895–6) will ultimately be realized.

References

Bonaparte, M., A. Freud, and E. Kris, eds. 1954. *The origins of psychoanalysis*. London: Imago.

Braid, J. 1843. *Neurypnology, or the rationale of nervous sleep*. Rev. ed., ed. A. E. Waite. New York: Julian Press, 1960.

——— 1852. *Magic, witchcraft, animal magnetism, hypnotism, and electrobiology*. 3rd ed. London: John Churchill.

Breuer, J., and S. Freud. 1895. Studies on hysteria. In *Standard edition*, ed. J. Strachey. Vol. 2. London: Hogarth Press, 1955.

Coburn, K. 1951. *Inquiring spirit*. London: Routledge and Kegan Paul.

Deleuze, J. 1819. *Histoire critique du magnétisme animal*. 2nd ed., 2 vols. Paris: Belin-Leprieur.

Deutsch, F. 1959. *On the mysterious leap from the mind to the body*. New York: International Universities Press.

Ellenberger, H. F. 1970. *The discovery of the unconscious*. New York: Basic Books.

Erikson, E. 1963. *Childhood and society*. 2nd ed. New York: Norton.

Flournoy, T. 1915. Une mystique moderne. *Arch. Psychol.* 15:1–224.

Freud, S. 1894. The neuro-psychoses of defence. In *Standard edition*, ed. J. Strachey. Vol. 3. London: Hogarth Press, 1962.

——— 1895. On the grounds for detaching a particular syndrome from neurasthenia under the description "anxiety neurosis." In *Standard edition*, ed. J. Strachey. Vol. 3. London: Hogarth Press, 1962.

——— 1895–6. Project for a scientific psychology. In *The origins of psychoanalysis*, ed. M. Bonaparte, A. Freud, and E. Kris. New York: Basic Books, 1954.

—— 1896. The aetiology of hysteria. In *Standard edition*, ed. J. Strachey. Vol. 3. London: Hogarth Press, 1962.

—— 1905. Three essays on sexuality. In *Standard edition*, ed. J. Strachey. Vol. 7. London: Hogarth Press, 1953.

—— 1910. Five lectures on psychoanalysis. In *Standard edition*, ed. J. Strachey. Vol. 11. London: Hogarth Press, 1957.

—— 1914. On narcissism: an introduction. In *Standard edition*, ed. J. Strachey. Vol. 14. London: Hogarth Press, 1958.

—— 1917. Mourning and melancholia. In *Standard edition*, ed. J. Strachey. Vol. 14. London: Hogarth Press, 1958.

—— 1920. Beyond the pleasure principle. In *Standard Edition*, ed. J. Strachey. Vol. 18. London: Hogarth Press, 1955.

—— 1923. The ego and the id. In *Standard edition*, ed. J. Strachey. Vol. 19. London: Hogarth Press, 1961.

Gunderson, J. G., and M. T. Singer. 1975. Defining borderline patients. *Am. J. Psychiatry* 132:1–10.

Hartmann, H., and E. Kris. 1945. The genetic approach in psychoanalysis. *Psychoanal. Study Child* 1:11–30.

Janet, P. 1898. *Névroses et idées fixes*. 2 vols. Paris: Félix Alcan.

—— 1903. *Les obsessions et la psychasthénie*. 2 vols. Paris: Félix Alcan.

—— 1907. *The major symptoms of hysteria*. New York: Macmillan.

Mesmer, F. A. 1781. *Le magnétisme animal*. Paris: Payot, 1971.

Nemiah, J. C. 1961. *Foundations of psychopathology*. New York: Oxford University Press.

Puységur, A. M. J. C. de. 1809. *Mémoires pour servir a l'histoire et à l'établissement du magnétisme animal*. 2nd ed. Paris: Cellot.

Rapport des commissaires chargés par le Roi de l'examen du magnétisme animal. 1784. Paris: L'imprimerie Royale.

Psychoneurotic Disorders

CHAPTER 10

John C. Nemiah

T HE PSYCHONEUROTIC disorders are syndromes, not well-defined diseases like
physical illnesses, which can be traced to visible,
specific pathological lesions in discrete organs.
Although the physiological bases for the major
mental illnesses (notably psychotic depression
and possibly schizophrenia) are approaching
clarification, few if any clues currently exist as to
the pathophysiology of the neuroses. Their definition rests on a loose clinical grouping of
symptoms that cluster together with a fair degree
of regularity; as syndromes, however, they
exhibit considerable overlapping of phenomena.
The strict, conceptual definition of any psychoneurosis is an ideal. In the world of patients the
ideal is rarely found; individuals with hysterical
symptoms may also be anxious or depressed,
or a person with a phobia may also manifest
obsessive-compulsive symptoms. In choosing a
diagnosis for any given patient, the clinician is
usually guided by the predominant symptoms,
and it is sometimes necessary to be content with
the diagnostic label of "mixed psychoneurosis."

Furthermore, neurotic syndromes are fluid;
though some patients are consistent in the kind
of symptoms they exhibit over long periods of
time, in others one syndrome will give place to

another. A classic example of this is to be found
in *Grace Abounding*, John Bunyan's spiritual
autobiography (1666), in which he describes suffering as a young man from a classical phobic
neurosis; as his spiritual turmoil mounts in intensity, the phobic symptoms are replaced by a
crippling obsessive-compulsive neurosis, which
in turn eventually yields to a severe and typical
depression.

The lack of definitional sharpness inherent in
the syndromatic nature of neuroses is further
compounded by the sparseness of clinical facts
and studies concerning their incidence and natural history. In the United States during the past
several decades, clinical interest has focused
more on the psychodynamic understanding of
specific symptoms than on the form and course
of neurotic syndromes. Although foreign clinicians have given greater attention to the latter
aspect, their studies have not as yet provided sufficient data to permit real clarity in clinical diagnosis and description. The incidence of the various neuroses in any given population is not
accurately known; patients often do not consult
a physician for neurotic problems, or, if they do
go to their general practitioner, the diagnosis
may not be accurately made. Even among psy-

chiatrists, the absence of universally accepted diagnostic criteria leads to inexact categorization, so that in surveys of the incidence of neurotic problems, looseness of definitions precludes exact statements about the frequency of specific neuroses. Thus little is known with certainty about the epidemiology of the psychoneuroses, and in the discussion that follows, epidemiological factors will be mentioned only when relevant data exist.

It must also be kept in mind that because very few long-term studies have been conducted of the course and outcome of neurotic disorders, it is not possible to speak with confidence of their natural history. It is evident from clinical contact with individual patients that in some the symptoms run a chronic, unremitting course; in others, the outbreak of the disorder may be an isolated, limited event; in still others there may be a fluctuating pattern of remissions and exacerbations, sometimes clearly reactions to environmental pressures, sometimes alternating for no apparent reason. Studies of the course of specific syndromes in a large series of patients are rare, however, and this lack of information often makes it difficult to determine whether changes concomitant with therapeutic procedures are the result of those procedures or whether they arise from unknown causes.

Dynamic and Psychogenetic Aspects of Psychoneurosis

Although certain neurotic symptoms, notably those of anxiety, may often be related to neural and biochemical processes, the appearance and manifestations of psychoneurotic syndromes cannot, as has been mentioned, be traced to discrete neuropathological lesions. Etiological explanations have, therefore, generally made use of psychological rather than physiological terms and concepts. Such psychological explanations fall into two major categories, the dynamic and the psychogenetic; these concepts have been reviewed more fully elsewhere (see chapter 9, "The Dynamic Bases of Psychopathology") and will be only summarized briefly here.

Dynamic constructs are concerned with the factors in the patient's current disorder and the ways they interact to produce the clinical symptoms. Thus stresses in the patient's environment, his instinctual and emotional response to these stresses, his internal defenses, and other aspects of his ego functioning are all taken into account as elements in a dynamic equilibrium resulting, through a combination of the various conflicting forces involved, in the external manifestations of the neurotic disorder. The inner workings of the patient are viewed in a temporal cross-section.

There is, however, more to the human being in both his physiological and his psychological aspects than appears at any given point in time. He is an organism with a past that includes specific developmental phases—characterizing his growth from infancy to maturity—and an idiosyncratic history of personal events and experiences that, through learning, help to determine who and what he is. The kinds of environmental stresses to which he is sensitive, the nature and strength of his drives and emotions, the defenses he characteristically employs to protect himself from emotional pain—all these are shaped and determined in large part by his past. By the same token, the origins of the individual's adult neurotic disorders are to be found in such earlier experiences and processes of growth and development (see chapter 8, "Theories of Personality"). In attempting to understand and help his patient, the clinician must explore these psychogenetic determinants of his patient's disorder as well as the dynamic elements in his psychic conflict.

In clinical work with patients, the dynamic elements in an individual's disorder are generally determined more easily, and with a greater degree of accuracy, than the psychogenetic factors involved. The latter are more deeply buried in the individual's past and subject to deeper repressions and distortions; it is often difficult to document their specific nature through the independent evidence of external witnesses. Psychogenetic formulations for any given patient are, therefore, frequently more inferential and uncertain than those that describe the dynamic aspects of his disorder. In the discussion of specific neurotic syndromes that follows, more attention will be paid to dynamic than to psychogenetic features.

In most physical illnesses symptoms and the pathophysiological mechanisms behind them suggest the therapeutic techniques needed to restore the patient to health. In psychoneurotic disorders, symptoms and the psychopathological processes producing them are less reliable as guides to treatment. Although the clinician frequently employs palliative measures aimed at symptom removal and suppression (often all that is available to help the patient), the decision to use psychotherapy that aims at uncovering and changing the underlying psychopathological processes cannot be based only on an assessment of the patient's symptoms and the syndromes they compose. More important indications for such insight psychotherapy are to be found in the nature of the individual's ego functions and personality structure, regardless of the kind of symptoms from which he suffers. (The general rationale for treatment of neurotic disorders is discussed in chapter 17, "The Psychotherapies.") In the consideration of the separate syndromes that follow, comments on treatment will be restricted to techniques that have a specific bearing on the symptoms themselves.

Psychoneurotic Syndromes

Anxiety Neurosis

While anxiety may appear as a symptom in almost all psychiatric disorders, it characteristically appears as the predominant or sole manifestation of illness in anxiety neurosis. In an acute or chronic form of the disorder, anxiety is experienced both as a subjective emotion and as a variety of physical symptoms representing the effects of muscular tension and autonomic nervous system activity. Frequently this anxiety is unrelated to specific events or situations, or to obvious precipitating stimuli in the environment; it is then referred to as "free-floating anxiety."

Clinical features. The subjective, emotional experience of anxiety is the most compelling aspect of the syndrome and, when present in the form of acute attacks, rapidly drives the sufferer to seek help. Most of us know from our own experience what anxiety is like, at least in its milder forms, and without the capacity to draw

upon introspection, it would not be possible really to understand the qualitative aspects of the emotion. In many ways similar to fear, especially in its somatic accompaniments, anxiety differs from fear in two important ways: it is a response to a frightening inner impulse rather than to an external danger, and it has a central quality of eerie dread. In some individuals the dread may have a specific content (that one is dying of a heart attack, for example), or it may be a nameless terror.

The somatic symptoms of anxiety are numerous and appear clinically in varying combinations. Cardiac manifestations are common and include tachycardia, which rarely rises over 140 beats per minute when anxiety alone is involved. Palpitations and extrasystoles are frequent complaints along with "sharp" and "sticking" pains in the anterior chest wall to the left of the sternum. Often the patient experiences breathlessness and a sense of "air hunger," sometimes severe enough to make him loosen his clothes or run to an open window. Sweating, especially of the palms and axillae, chilly feelings, flushing in the face, and goose pimples may add to his distress, which is compounded by an uneasiness in his stomach. Dizziness and lightheadedness are common, and the patient may feel himself atremble, partly from a fine tremor of his extremities, but partly too from a subjective inner sense of "trembling inside his skin."

To these symptoms characteristic of the acute variety of anxiety are added a number of somatic sensations that accompany the subacute form of the syndrome. Heartburn, epigastric fullness, and belching are matched in the lower reaches by flatulence, loose stools, diarrhea, and constipation, the latter two often occurring alternately. Chronic muscular tension may lead to a variety of musculoskeletal aches and pains, especially backache, pains across the shoulders and neck, and headache. The latter is commonly complained of in the occipital region or on the top of the head and is usually found, on careful questioning, to be a sense of tightness or pressure. In patients with chronic anxiety these somatic symptoms may overshadow the more subjective emotional aspects of anxiety, and the existence of subjective anxiety may be missed if it is not specifically inquired about.

The onset of anxiety neurosis may be sudden or gradual. In some patients it is ushered in by an unexpected, mysterious outbreak of acute anxiety; in others the appearance of subacute, somatic symptoms heralds its arrival. The acute attack may last for only a moment or two or may continue for minutes on end, the patient experiencing waves of anxiety that reach the intensity of incapacitating panic and leave him, when the episode dies away, feeling limp and exhausted. In some patients there may be only a few isolated attacks, with relative well-being in between; in others the acute form occurs against a background of chronic, subacute symptoms, and in some there may be repeated attacks of acute anxiety for days on end. Except in the cases of patients in whom the attacks are few in number and limited to brief periods, anxiety neurosis in both its acute and subacute forms can be an incapacitating, demoralizing disorder, not only painful to experience but leading to difficulties in thinking and in focusing attention that often severely disrupt the capacity for intellectual and occupational pursuits.

Behavorial observations. The examination of patients with anxiety neurosis shows what one would expect to find in persons suffering from the symptoms already described. In those with subacute anxiety one sees a restlessness, a quickness and jerky awkwardness of movements, and a fine tremor of the outstretched hands secondary to general muscular tension and inner uneasiness. The pulse may be elevated, the hands cold and sweaty, and as one observes the patient, one may notice an irregular, sighing respiration; the patient may experience difficulty in talking because of dryness in the mouth or a "frog in the throat" that necessitates frequent guttural clearing. The external effect of acute anxiety is readily apparent, for the sufferer is highly agitated, with despair and terror in his facial expression as he discloses his fear of dying and begs for help and relief from the torment of his panic.

Etiology. As is evident from the earlier consideration of psychodynamic processes (see chapter 9, "The Dynamic Bases of Psychopathology"), anxiety is a sign of psychological conflict resulting from the threatened emergence into con-

sciousness of forbidden repressed mental contents. In searching for the meaning of anxiety, one must ask what unconscious material the patient is afraid of, and what consequences he fears, should it emerge into conscious discharge and expression.

What he fears is the escape from the prison house of the unconscious of aggressive and libidinal drives and their derivative emotions and fantasies. The quality and intensity of the aggressive drive may vary from simple competition with another person all the way to destructive, murderous impulses. The libidinal drive is feared in all its developmental modalities (oral, anal, and genital) and in its more complex or partial manifestations, such as voyeurism, masochism, and sadism. A particularly important aspect of libido in the production of anxiety, especially in men, is that related to homosexuality. Homosexual panic is a common and violent form of anxiety, seen most frequently in younger men, in particular when they have been subjected for the first time to a concentratedly male environment such as living in army barracks.

Fear of expressing and discharging the forbidden impulses appears in four forms, labeled according to the nature of their consequences. In superego anxiety, the individual suffers from an anxious expectation of the sharp pricking of his conscience if he transgresses his inner code of behavior. Castration anxiety is characterized by a fear of retributive physical punishment and injury and is so named because it is associated with fantasies, deriving from the oedipal phase of development, of being castrated or otherwise subjected to genital mutilation. Separation anxiety refers to the fearful anticipation of losing the esteem, love, and caring of important and necessary people. And, finally, id or impulse anxiety involves the fear, often mounting to sheer panic, of the dissolution of one's total being as an individual if the impulse pushing for discharge escapes the controls stringently imposed upon it.

Thus far the etiology of anxiety has been considered only in its more psychological aspects. It is evident that physiological factors are at work as well, from the less well-understood functioning of the limbic system and hypothalamus to the more completely delineated processes of the peripheral autonomic nervous system. These, as we have seen, result in changes in the end organs involved, the conscious perception of which constitutes an integral part of the total experience of anxiety. The relation of these physical processes to the experience of anxiety has not yet been completely elucidated, but it is clear that earlier theories—notably that of William James (1907)—defining emotion as only the perception of peripheral discharges are in conflict with more recent observations that central nervous system discharges are accompanied by the conscious experience of anxiety even in the absence of peripheral activity (Davison, 1966). Mention must also be made of the role of excessive blood lactate levels in the production of the symptoms of anxiety (Grosz and Farmer, 1969), although the exact relevance of this observation to the etiology of anxiety neurosis has not been entirely clarified.

Differential diagnosis. It is usually possible to distinguish anxiety neurosis from other psychiatric conditions. Although, as has been pointed out, anxiety is found as a symptom in most psychiatric syndromes, the presence or absence of the specific identifying characteristics of other disorders (such as phobias, obsessive-compulsive phenomena, and the thought disorder of schizophrenia) will enable the clinician to apply the proper diagnostic label. Occasionally a psychiatric illness will be ushered in by anxiety as the leading and only symptom, but a short period of observation will reveal the emergence of other symptoms giving the clue to the diagnosis. Perhaps the most difficult diagnostic situation is found in the case of patients in whom anxiety and depression are mixed; it must be left to the clinician to judge which of the symptoms predominates or whether their equal mixture justifies a diagnosis of "mixed neurosis with anxiety and depression."

Anxiety neurosis may on occasion be confounded with illnesses having a well-defined physical pathology. In hyperthyroidism, nervousness and tremor are prominent elements, but the characteristic endocrine changes and the findings on physical examination, such as exophthalmus, establish the diagnosis. It must be remembered, however, that many patients manifest symptoms of anxiety, even after they have been rendered euthyroid, and that this anxiety may in its own right be an important ingredient of the disease. Similarly, Ménière's disease and pheochromocytoma may be mistakenly diagnosed as anxiety neurosis; here too, as with hyperthyroidism, a careful history and physical examination and appropriate laboratory studies will point to the underlying cause of the symptoms. Finally, the symptoms of anxiety, especially in the dramatic form of an acute attack that drives the patient to an emergency ward for help, may be mistaken for an acute myocardial infarction. More than one patient who has been rushed to a medical intensive care unit has been found, in the course of an extended and careful study of his coronary circulation, to have no abnormalities other than the functional disorders of an anxiety neurosis.

Treatment. Certain specific psychotherapeutic techniques are useful for controlling both acute and chronic anxiety. Progressive relaxation exercises, first proposed by Jacobson (1938), transcendental meditation, and hypnotic suggestion (in susceptible patients) help to quiet symptoms, possibly because each in its own way activates the relaxation response mediated centrally by the hypothalamus (Benson, Beary, and Carol, 1974). Nor must one overlook the almost universally beneficial effect of a supportive relationship with a stable, encouraging, and sustaining therapist to whom the patient can complain of his symptoms and confide his inmost concerns and conflicts.

Medication, though not a substitute for psychological measures, is often an essential adjunct to the management of individuals suffering from anxiety. The minor tranquilizers (such as meprobamate, chlordiazepoxide, and diazepam) are particularly useful not only in diminishing muscular tension and subjective anxiety but in inducing sleep in those patients afflicted with insomnia as a part of their disorder. Whenever possible, these medications should be employed as a soporific in preference to the barbiturates because of the possibility of habituation to the latter drugs. As might be expected from their mechanism of action, adrenergic blocking agents such as propranolol (Granville-Grossman and Turner, 1966) have been effective in treating the symptom of anxiety in a few experimental series of patients; their general clinical use must await more extensive clinical study.

Hysterical Neurosis, Dissociative Type

The central feature of the dissociative form of hysterical neurosis is a sudden alteration in mental functioning leading either to an altered state of consciousness or to a change in identity, manifested in somnambulism, amnesia, fugue states, and multiple personalities.

Clinical features. Somnambulism is an episodic alteration in the individual's state of consciousness, lasting for minutes or hours, during which the patient may experience vivid hallucinations, often recreating traumatic events in his past of which he usually has no conscious memory in his normal state. The patient is generally but not always amnestic for the period of somnambulism and is apparently out of touch with people and objects in his surroundings during the course of it. Janet has described a number of such patients, among them a young man called Ch.

Almost daily, mainly in the morning, [he] may be surprised alone in his room in strange attitudes. He stands before a mirror and appears to scowl and simper at himself. He smiles, half closes his eyes, throws sidelong looks, bends down and gives little tosses of his head or makes beckoning gestures with his hand. Then he walks about the room, but not at all with his ordinary gait: he moves with mincing steps, his body swaying to and fro with brusque sideways movements. He balances his hips as if to swish a dress from side to side, and in fact runs his hands over an imaginary skirt, accompanying this with grimaces and little tosses of his head. From time to time he stops in the middle of these acts and changes his pose: now he assumes a grave and majestic mien; his eyes are half closed with an air of modesty and dignity, but he maintains his womanly bearing and the undulation of his skirts, chattering under his breath as he bends right and left. This performance is prolonged for several hours with many variations in grimaces and poses. (Raymond and Janet, 1904, pp. 28–29)

When questioned, the patient described his experience during these episodes as follows:

"It is not my fault if I grimace in this way. It is one of those girls who has eclipsed me. You cannot imagine the mischief they do to me. They are little girls whom I have met every day for the past two years in this miserable district where I am obliged to live. I feel driven

to stand on the street when they go to work; they have gained tremendous power over me, they penetrate me with their glances, and eclipse me. There are moments in the day when I am alone when I am no longer myself. The image of one of these young girls appears to me so vividly that I see her talking, gesticulating . . . It is so clear and precise that I follow the movements of her head and imitate them without being aware of it. I try in vain to find myself, for it seems to me that I disappear, I lose my ego, my real existence; it is as if I no longer existed, as if they had taken my place. My body takes on the manners of one of them, her funny little ways, the constant shaking of her bird-like little head. When another one of them invades me, she produces a different impression, for she makes me carry my head high and proudly; others give me erotic ideas or oblige me to chatter like themselves; at length they transform me completely . . . I feel such self-disgust that I even beat myself; I have put up genuine struggles against this other self, but in vain. I spend hours at a time searching for myself in the midst of the impressions left upon me by these girls, but against my will I disappear more and more." (p. 29)

In this poignant and remarkably self-perceptive account there appears (in addition to a striking instance of the process of identification) a major alteration of Ch.'s state of awareness. Although, unlike many somnambulistic patients, he is not amnestic for the episode, he is at the time completely absorbed by images and feelings that hold him in their grip and rivet his attention to the exclusion of all else in the real world around him.

Amnesia is the most common form of dissociative hysteria and is not infrequently seen in large general hospital emergency wards. It is usually precipitated by a minor physical accident or an emotionally traumatic event. The patient complains of having totally lost his memory for the events of a period of time that may cover only a few hours or may include his entire past life. The Reverend Mr. Hanna described by Sidis and Goodhart (1905), for example, could remember nothing of his past life after a trivial carriage accident; he had forgotten how to read, write, talk, and walk, and appeared during the initial phase of his disorder to have the mental state of an infant. By contrast, when brought to an emergency ward by the police, Susan H. (see chapter 9, "The Dynamic Bases of Psychopathology") had a circumscribed loss of memory that covered only seven hours of her life; her recovery of memory revealed that those seven hours centered around an intensely painful disappointment that was blotted out by the amnesia. In some patients fragmentary images related to the forgotten events return as ego-alien symptoms. The Reverend Mr. Hanna, for example, had vivid "dreams" of places that were unfamiliar to him but were recognized by his parents as scenes from his past life; Susan H. described a recurrent visual hallucination of a parking lot, which proved to be the stage for the disappointment that precipitated her disorder.

Finally, it should be noted that amnesia may appear in other patterns than the most common form just described. In some patients the loss of memory is limited to those elements associated with a specific person or object, the memory for other simultaneously experienced events remaining intact. In addition to such systematic amnesia, one may occasionally find a continuous (or anterograde) amnesia in which the patient forgets each event as it occurs, living as if he were a mere point of consciousness moving through time without registering memories for any of the events that are taking place.

The individual suffering from a fugue state suddenly loses his identity, gives up his customary life and habits, and characteristically wanders far from home, where he sets up a new life as a seemingly different person. After a period of weeks or months, he abruptly "wakes up," mystified and distressed to find himself in a foreign place in alien circumstances, and with a total amnesia for all that has gone on during the time of the fugue. One of the most striking examples of a fugue state has been bequeathed to us by William James (1907; see also Hodgson, 1891) in his account of Ansel Bourne, a minister who disappeared from Providence, Rhode Island, and lived in Philadelphia for some weeks as the proprietor of a small store before waking suddenly one morning, wondering in panic where he was and what he was doing in such strange surroundings.

The most arresting form of dissociative hysteria is that of the multiple personality. Its exact incidence is unknown, but it must be rare, for only a hundred-odd cases have been described in the psychiatric literature of the past two centuries, the great majority being reported between 1890 and 1920. Many of these reports, however, compensate in length for their smallness in number and some have achieved the proportions and quality of novels.

The typical patient manifests one or more secondary personalities, which alternate with the primary personality in controlling the individual's conscious awareness and behavior. Usually the principal secondary personality is fully aware of the existence and thoughts of the primary personality, whereas the latter has a more restricted range of awareness, knows nothing of the former, and has an amnesia for those periods in which the secondary personality is in control. The primary personality, furthermore, is usually restricted in emotional and social life as compared with its secondary counterpart. Typically, the former is as proper, "good," conventional, and moralistic as the latter is gay, carefree, mischievous, and irresponsible, and the secondary personality often heaps scorn and plays annoying tricks on the primary.

Margaret B.,* a woman of thirty-eight, was brought to the hospital with a paralysis of her legs following a minor car accident that had occurred some six months before. She reported that until three years before her admission to the hospital she had enjoyed smoking, drinking, visiting night clubs, and otherwise indulging in parties and social activities. At that point, however, she and her husband, who was an alcoholic, were converted to a small, evangelical religious sect. Her husband achieved control of his drinking, she gave up her prior social indulgences, and the two of them became completely immersed in the activities of the church, activities that for the patient included extensive practical nursing among the sick of the congregation.

Soon after her admission it was determined that the patient's paralysis was hysterical, and further history revealed that she often "heard a voice telling her to say things and do things." It was, she said, "a terrible voice" that sometimes threatened to "take over completely." When it was finally suggested to the patient that she let the voice "take over," she closed her eyes, clenched her fists, and grimaced for a few moments during which she was out of contact with those around her. Suddenly she opened her eyes

---

* I am indebted to Dr. F. H. Frankel for permission to use these observations.

and one was in the presence of another person. Her name, she said, was "Harriet." Whereas Margaret had been paralyzed, and complained of fatigue, headache, and backache, Harriet felt well, and she at once proceeded to walk unaided around the interviewing room. She spoke scornfully of Margaret's religiousness, her invalidism, and her puritanical life, professing that she herself liked to drink and "go partying" but that Margaret was always going to church and reading the Bible, "But," she said impishly and proudly, "I make her miserable—I make her say things and do things she doesn't want to." At length, at the interviewer's suggestion, Harriet reluctantly agreed to "bring Margaret back," and after more grimacing and fist clenching, Margaret reappeared, paralyzed, complaining of her headache and backache, and completely amnestic for the brief period of Harriet's release from her prison.

Behavioral observations. Except in the case of the patient in the midst of a somnambulistic episode, little that is remarkable occurs in the behavior of those suffering from dissociative hysteria. The somnambulist is out of contact with the observer and his environment and may often be seen engaging in the complex, seemingly purposeful patterns of behavior that are the outward manifestation of his inner vivid experience of hallucinatory memories. It is occasionally possible by talking quietly and persistently to a person in this state to penetrate the barrier of his indifference and to gain control of his behavior—in other words, to change a spontaneous episode of somnambulism into one that has all the earmarks of an induced hypnotic trance.

Except possibly for evidence of emotional distress, amnestic patients appear normal during the period of time for which they later develop amnesia. At the point of transition from one state to the other, the patient may undergo a brief, somnambulistic alteration of consciousness visible to the observer; on recovery, however, his behavior and mental status are normal, save for the obvious gap in memory.

Similarly, nothing is obviously abnormal in patients during a fugue state or in the grip of a secondary personality. They are alert and in contact with their surroundings, appear to have their wits about them, and are able to function quite adequately for long stretches of time. As with amnestic patients, there may be a brief transitory period of somnambulistic behavior in the passage from one state to another, and, of course, those who are familiar with the patient's normal personality are able to detect a marked change in character and behavior, both in the midst of a fugue and in the phase of a secondary personality.

Etiology. The conditions under consideration are among the most dramatic of all psychiatric disorders, and they have captured the imagination of laymen and psychiatrists alike. Indeed, they provided psychopathologists of an earlier generation with the observations that enabled them to develop and refine the concepts of dissociation and the unconscious. In these disorders one sees dissociation in pure culture—great complexes of associated mental elements temporarily flung out of conscious awareness beyond the powers of voluntary recall, or suddenly invading and dominating consciousness in the form of rich, intricately woven personalities.

From a psychodynamic point of view, as seen earlier, dissociation is only a part of the process, for it represents the end result of the force of repression acting upon mental elements. It is not always clear in patients with dissociative hysteria why repression has been set in motion, but two different factors can be found in many of the cases that have been studied. In some patients, repression protects the ego against a painful affect associated with the memories of an emotional trauma. This appeared to be the situation with Susan H., who was shielded by her memory loss from the pain of disappointment when she thought herself abandoned by her boy friend. In other patients, the repression and resulting dissociations provide a defense against undesirable drives over which the individual is in conflict. In Margaret B., for example, repression removed from conscious awareness all of her inclinations to indulge herself in pleasures that, from the point of view of her religious ideals, were sinfully improper.

While repression is clearly the major mechanism of defense in dissociative hysteria, other psychological processes may contribute to the final clinical picture. Of particular note is the role of identification in the fashioning of a secondary personality. Margaret B., for example, had as a little girl had a playmate, Harriet, to whom she was devoted. When they both were six, Harriet had suddenly been taken ill with an acute infectious disease and died in three days. Margaret had been deeply upset at the time and had wanted to die in her friend's place. At some undetermined time after that event, Harriet had gone "inside Margaret," as Harriet reported when she held sway in consciousness, and she had lived there quite happily up until the point when Margaret "got religious" and their tastes for entertainment and pleasure diverged. Internalizing the image of her dead friend appeared to have protected Margaret from despair and sorrow at her loss—despair and sorrow that emerged unspent and unabated when, under hypnosis, the adult patient was directed to revive these memories of an event then thirty years in the past.

Finally, a word must be said about the relation of hypnosis to the phenomena of dissociative hysteria. The production of artificial somnambulism by hypnotic procedures has already been mentioned. The same techniques can be used to bring about amnesia for events occurring under hypnosis and to create temporary changes in personality. Posthypnotic suggestion can also cause the hypnotic subject to undertake specific actions or to experience hallucinations after his return to a normal waking state; the resulting actions appear quite spontaneously and unbidden, and the patient has no memory of having been given instructions to carry them out. This process is paralleled in the patient with dissociative hysteria by the "return of the repressed" in the form of hallucinatory, ego-alien fragments of the underlying, unconscious mental complex —such as Susan H.'s vision of a parking lot or the voice that spoke to Margaret B. Hypnosis, then, is a tool for the experimental production of many hysterical symptoms, and it has been repeatedly used in this way to explore the nature of dissociation.

Differential diagnosis. Dissociative hysteria is not likely to be confused with other psychiatric syndromes, with the possible exception of schizophrenia. Although the individual manifesting multiple personalities may loosely be said to have a "split personality," the disturbance is quite different from the fragmentation of ego structure and loss of major ego functions found in schizo-

phrenia. In the patient with a multiple personality, the ego splits into two or more parts, but in well-developed cases, each portion of the ego has a set of intact ego functions that allow the individual to cope with daily living without evidence of a thought disorder or the other abnormalities in mental processes characteristic of schizophrenia. Sometimes somnambulistic trance may be confused with a catatonic stupor, but the somnambulistic state is generally short-lived, and when the patient returns to normal consciousness, there is no evidence of the disturbances in thinking that characterize schizophrenia. Somnambulism must also be distinguished from sleepwalking, which occurs most commonly in children and is associated with electroencephalographic patterns of deep sleep.

Somnambulistic episodes occasionally resemble the automatisms found in temporal lobe epilepsy. An absence of other hysterical symptoms and electroencephalographic evidence of temporal lobe dysfunction point to a diagnosis of epilepsy and are indications for further neurological studies. Postconcussional amnesia may be distinguished from hysterical amnesia by the fact that the recovery of memory in the hysterical variety is usually rapid and total, in contrast to the gradual and often incomplete return of memory following head injury.

Treatment. In patients with amnesia and the less frequently occurring fugue states, it is important to uncover the dissociated memories as rapidly and as completely as possible and thereafter to help the individual to face and deal more directly with any painful affects or environmental difficulties associated with them. Otherwise he will be more likely to resort to dissociation in the face of future emotional stress. Often the patient will recover his lost memories in the course of an interview in which he is encouraged to talk and associate freely. If more direct and vigorous measures are required, hypnosis or a sodium amytal interview may be employed.

Hysterical Neurosis, Conversion Type

Hysterical neurosis, conversion type (or conversion hysteria, as it is generally called in current psychiatric parlance) has been recognized as a clinical entity for centuries. From the "wandering uterus" concept of the early Greeks, through the medieval theory of demon possession, to the nosological preoccupation with "major hysteria" in the last century, and on into modern psychodynamic formulations, hysteria has been viewed, as Sydenham stated three hundred years ago, as a condition that could mimic all the physical diseases to which man is heir. As this implies, hysteria is characterized by a diversity of somatic symptoms mediated primarily by the sensorimotor nervous system, without evidence of localized pathological lesions. Although predominantly a disorder of women, it may be found in men when the symptoms follow an accidental injury that is the subject of litigation.

Clinical features. A wide variety of abnormal movements may be found in hysterical patients, ranging from tremors of the limbs, head, and trunk, through bizarre, often complex and stereotyped choreiform tics and jerks, to massive spasms affecting the whole body, such as those seen in the *arc de cercle* or in hysterical seizures. The tremors are loose, unrelated to motion, and often become worse when attention is directed to them. The *arc de cercle* looks like the spasm of full-blown tetanus, the patient forming a convex arc with his body, so that only his head and heels touch the bed. In other forms of spasm (labeled *attitudes passionelles* by the French clinicians of the last century), the patient assumes and maintains a fixed posture like that of prayer or frozen terror. In the hysterical seizure, the patient manifests wild, aimless twistings and flailings of arms and legs, as he throws himself from one side of the bed to the other, usually, however, without bruising or hurting himself. A particularly dramatic form of abnormal movement is seen in astasia-abasia, a gait disturbance in which the patient staggers and stumbles, his trunk wobbling wildly from his hips, as he clutches at the air or the walls for support.

More common in modern hysterical individuals are the pareses and paralyses that affect one limb or another. Paresis characteristically involves an arm or a leg, either singly or in combinations such as hemiparesis or paraparesis, in a distribution that follows the common perception of the limb rather than one determined by peripheral or central nervous system pathways. Thus an arm will be affected from the shoulder girdle or wrist down (the so-called glove or sleeve distribution); unlike the paralysis secondary to brain injury, this paresis is more marked proximally than distally. There is often, furthermore, a dissociation of function. For example, a patient may be quite capable of standing or moving his legs when lying or sitting but be totally unable to walk. Hysterical paralysis is found on closer inspection to be a tonic contracture of antagonist muscles around a joint, rendering the limb immobile in either a flexed or extended position. Usually when one attempts to move the affected extremity, one finds the patient exerting a contraction in his musculature proportional to the force applied by the examiner: the harder the latter tries to flex or extend the limb, the harder the patient resists. It should be remembered, however, that these responses occur without the patient's conscious volition.

Finally, among the hysterical disorders of movement are aphonia and aphagia. In aphagia the patient is unable to make the movements necessary for swallowing food or water. In aphonia he cannot tense his vocal cords for vocalization, although he is perfectly able to whisper, and there is no other disturbance of language functions.

Like the movement disorders, sensory disturbances, though protean in their possible manifestations, are usually found in a small number of common patterns. The organs of special sense may be affected, especially vision and hearing, with resulting hysterical blindness and deafness; constrictions of the visual fields may be found ranging from a symmetrical partial loss in the periphery to a retention of central vision only —the so-called gun-barrel vision. Both visual and auditory hallucinations occur in hysterical patients, the visual being more common. They are generally stereotyped, well-structured little vignettes of a scene, or a brief spoken sentence, unassociated with any characteristic signs and symptoms of schizophrenia. Upon further exploration these hallucinations are frequently found to be consciously experienced fragments of a more extensive unconscious complex of mental associations—such, for example, as those seen in Susan H. and Margaret B.

The most common sensory disturbances are those involving the perception of touch, pain, and position. They are almost invariably found in a limb affected by hysterical paralysis, although they can frequently exist alone without any accompanying motor disturbance. Like the pareses and paralyses, the location of hysterical anesthesia and analgesia follows a pattern conforming to the common concept of a limb in the typical "glove" and "stocking" distribution. Hemianesthesia is also common, the sensory loss stopping exactly in the midline and frequently involving the entire half of the body. In some patients there may be irregular, idiosyncratic areas of sensory loss—a phenomenon known to witch hunters in the past who diagnosed their victims by the presence of these "devil's patches." Localization of anesthesia in the genital region of women contributes to the frigidity so common in hysterical females; when accompanied by spasm in the neighboring musculature, it leads to hysterical dyspareunia. The sensory disturbances are usually complete, and the loss of pain sensation permits the patient to endure all manner of noxious and potentially damaging stimuli (deep pricking with a needle, for example) without any conscious awareness of discomfort. Finally, it should be noted that for a patient with a hysterically paralyzed limb accompanied by loss of touch, pain perception, or position sense, there is no conscious awareness of having a limb at all. As Margaret B. said of her useless legs. "My legs—they're not there. I have no legs at all."

A particularly prevalent form of sensory disturbance in the modern hysterical patient is that of pain. Most often situated in the abdomen in women, the disturbance frequently leads to a mistaken diagnosis of intraabdominal disease, especially of the generative organs, which is too often followed by surgery and the mutilating removal of ovaries or the freeing up of "adhesions." The readiness to operate of some surgeons unfamiliar with hysteria is met by the avidity of many of these patients for surgery—some of them undergo repeated procedures and have the tell-tale "checkerboard" abdomen as a witness to their neurotic need. Hysterical pain may not infrequently follow the pattern of a fatal illness suffered by a person close to the patient, who, through a process of identification, com-

plains of the same symptoms manifested by the departed.

Finally, hysterical symptoms may supersede those that first resulted from a physical illness or injury, enduring long after the physical disorder has healed. Back and leg pain resulting from an injury, especially when industrial compensation is involved, is particularly liable to psychological complications of this sort, and the course of idiopathic epilepsy may be confused by seizures that are hysterical in origin rather than neurogenic. Patients who present such a mixture of physically and emotionally induced symptoms offer a difficult diagnostic and therapeutic challenge to the practicing clinician.

Behavioral observations. One of the most striking and perhaps most classical features of hysterical patients is their *belle indifférence*, a term coined by French investigators to designate the lack of anxiety manifested by these patients concerning symptoms that would appear to be highly inconvenient or even catastrophic. Thus a patient with hysterical blindness or a totally incapacitating paraplegia may be completely unconcerned about his loss of function and show no interest in its cause or implications. Such a state of indifference, however, usually exists only in regard to the hysterical symptoms themselves; the patient may suffer from overt anxiety, worry, and concern about other aspects of his life.

Apart from the pathognomonic features already mentioned, hysterical patients generally show little that is grossly abnormal in their mental status. Much has been made of the behavioral lineaments of the hysterical character —perhaps too much, since modern clinicians are hardly unanimous about the exact criteria for the diagnosis, let alone its etiology or its relation to the hysterical neurosis. In general (and in contrast to the obsessional character, which will be described later), individuals with hysterical character traits are graced with a richness of emotions, personal warmth, creative imagination, and well-developed intuition. These are not in themselves pathological characteristics; indeed, they may well be assets to their possessors, especially if they are balanced by an equal capacity for logical, orderly thought. When carried to an extreme, however, certain elements of hysterical behavior—observed and described in some, if not all, patients with conversion hysteria—may create difficulties in clinical management. Some patients are prone to be unusually free and open in their emotional expression, at times to the point of dramatic exaggeration, and they may often be openly sexually seductive, needlessly exposing their bodies during professional examinations or making suggestive, coy, inviting remarks to their physicians and others caring for them. At the same time, they show a narcissistic preoccupation and concern with themselves and, behind the seductiveness, an underlying passive-dependent need for help, protection, and nurturance. Motivated by these various needs, these patients attempt to obtain gratification from others through threats of suicide or other measures that play upon the guilt of those around them. Although it is easy to respond to this behavior with a variety of judgmental or otherwise harmful attitudes, it should be remembered that no matter how exaggerated, dramatic, or contrived the patient's behavior may appear, it is, like the accompanying symptoms, the expression of underlying psychological conflicts.

Finally, a brief word must be said about the behavior of patients in the midst of a hysterical seizure. To superficial observation they appear to be out of contact with their environment and quite unresponsive to what is going on around them. Careful examination, however, reveals that this is not the case; when held, restrained, or manipulated by those in attendance, they will respond quite obviously to the movements of others, resisting strongly, for example, the attempt to move one of their limbs or to open their eyelids. They are able, furthermore, to perceive and register more complex stimuli. A young woman seen in an emergency ward during a violent hysterical seizure, for instance, suddenly went rigid, held her breath, and turned blue from apnea. A young resident, alarmed by this turn of events, slapped her face to stimulate breathing, which returned to normal at once, though the patient remained apparently unconscious throughout. A few days later, however, on the psychiatric ward where she had been admitted, she spoke vehemently and angrily about "that doctor" who had slapped her face. Without in-

dicating it at the time, she had obviously been acutely aware of what had been going on around her.

Etiology. In conversion hysteria, as in the dissociative form, repression is the basic mechanism of defense; it leads to the splitting off from consciousness of an unacceptable drive and its related emotions and fantasies. Unlike dissociative hysteria, however, in which major disruptions of memory or personality follow upon the process of dissociation, in conversion hysteria unconscious mental elements are manifested in a return of the repressed material in the form of restricted, localized somatic symptoms that often symbolize what has been excluded from consciousness. It is this translation of mental energies into a somatic discharge to which Freud gave the name of *conversion* (1894). Some of the conceptual difficulties inherent in this theoretical process have already been noted, but the term remains a useful one, if only because it points to a difference in the mechanisms that produce clinical symptoms in dissociative and conversion hysteria.

In the classical psychodynamic formulation of conversion hysteria, the sexual drive is repressed, having become a source of potential anxiety to the adult patient because of unresolved oedipal conflicts originating in childhood. Indeed, hysteria has become the paradigm of the sexual neurosis, and the term *conversion hysteria* has for many clinicians the automatic implication that oedipal genital libidinal conflicts will be found behind the symptoms. In recent decades, however, it has become apparent that pregenital drives, notably aggression and dependency needs, may be the prime motivating factors in the production of hysterical symptoms; the traditional notion of hysteria as based only on sexual conflicts must therefore be viewed with caution.

A further dynamic factor must be considered, which, if not primary in the chain of causation, clearly plays a part in the prolongation and intractability of hysterical symptoms. A patient who is incapacitated by hysterical paralyses or major sensory disturbances such as blindness finds that secondary gains result from his disability. His illness may, for example, permit him to avoid unpleasant situations that he would have to face if he were well; often, too, he is the center of solicitous attention from others because of his invalid state, enabling him to gratify dependency needs. The element of secondary gain in hysterical symptoms has led behavioral psychologists to propose that hysterical symptoms are learned responses—that is, when the patient discovers that a symptom reduces his anxiety over difficult situations and brings the gratification of dependency needs, the symptom becomes positively reinforced and will be reproduced on future occasions of stress. The behaviorist approach, though helpful in understanding the often stubborn fixity of hysterical symptoms once they have appeared, does not adequately explain their initial production—an explanation more adequately supplied by the concepts of a psychodynamic conflict psychology.

Differential diagnosis. Because they so commonly affect the sensory and neuromuscular systems, the symptoms of conversion hysteria may be confused with those of neurological disease, especially idiopathic epilepsy and multiple sclerosis. The transient pareses without definite neurological signs that may appear early in the course of multiple sclerosis are hard to distinguish from the monopareses of hysteria. In such cases it may be necessary to reserve judgment until the diagnostic neurological signs of central nervous system involvement appear. In hysterical seizures, as noted earlier, the movements are random and diffuse, usually without the regular tonic and clonic muscular contractions of idiopathic epilepsy. The recovery of consciousness after hysterical seizures is rapid, without the period of obtunded awareness and mentation that follows an epileptic attack, and the pathognomonic brain wave changes of idiopathic epilepsy establish that diagnosis with certainty.

It is impossible here to review the differential diagnosis between hysteria and all the multitude of physical diseases that it may imitate. The differentiation is particularly difficult and important when pain, especially in the abdomen, is the presenting symptom. Proper diagnosis must be established through the judicious use of physical and laboratory examinations and a careful psychological assessment of the patient's personality and conflicts, as well as from a thorough history

aimed at eliciting the existence of other past or concurrent hysterical symptoms.

Treatment. As noted earlier (see chapter 9, "The Dynamic Bases of Psychopathology"), the study of patients with symptoms of conversion hysteria led first to the method of cathartic therapy and then to the techniques of psychoanalysis. For a number of years these techniques were thought by many psychiatrists to be the treatments of choice. In recent years, however, there has been increased recognition that a large number of those suffering from conversion hysteria do not respond favorably to analytic measures, because of the nature of both their personality structures and the underlying psychological conflicts. In such cases, the disorder tends to be chronic and leads to varying degrees of disability and disturbance in personal relationships. Temporary relief from specific symptoms may often be effected through direct suppression by hypnotic suggestion or through cathartic methods, but the symptom thus removed tends to recur, or to be replaced by a new one affecting another part of the body. In many patients, supportive therapy is the best one has to offer.

Phobic Neurosis

The phobic neurosis, as contrasted with hysterical disorders, is a condition in which, as with anxiety neurosis, anxiety forms a central part of the syndrome. Unlike the free-floating affect of anxiety neurosis, however, the anxiety of phobic neurosis is restricted to certain specific conditions, a circumstance that gives the patient some measure of control over it. Characteristic of phobic neurosis is the fact that the patient experiences irrational, overwhelming, and at times crippling anxiety in the face of a variety of objects or situations that present, realistically speaking, little or no actual danger.

Clinical features. If one had any doubts about the luxuriant profusion of phobias, a simple consultation with any medical dictionary would dispel them; there one finds lists of literally dozens upon dozens of irrational fears. There seems to be almost nothing on earth that has not at some time and in some place inspired terror in some timid breast. Fortunately for the nosologist the teeming multitude may be classified in three major categories proposed by Janet (1903): (1) phobias of objects, (2) phobias of situations, and (3) phobias of functions. Furthermore, although there are potentially thousands of different phobias, in clinical practice the great majority of patients manifest only a small number of common forms.

The largest numbers of irrational fears fall into the category of phobias of objects, the most common probably being those of familiar animals (such as cats, dogs, snakes, or mice) and of vehicles of transportation, the fear of airplanes currently holding first place. Phobias of situations include fear of heights, of being in crowds, or of closed spaces, and the familiar agoraphobia, or fear of open spaces. The last is one of the most incapacitating of phobias and is not quite accurately named in the Greek-derived term, for on closer inspection it becomes apparent that what the patient usually fears is venturing alone away from the shelter of his home. Simply being on the street even a block or two away is sufficient to arouse a degree of anxiety that prevents him from going further. If, however, he is accompanied by others (often a specific person known as the "obligatory companion"), he can travel long distances without concern. Phobias of function refer to a variety of bodily processes such as eating, voiding, or blushing (erythrophobia), the latter occurring especially when the patient feels he is observed by other people.

Many phobic objects are actually a source of danger about which a certain degree of fear is appropriate. Planes do crash, snakes do bite, and a fall from a height can have serious consequences, but these eventualities are statistically very unlikely. People may normally have a small amount of apprehension and tension in the face of such objects or situations, but the apprehension does not reach the intensity of panic found in phobic patients; it does not have the quality of eerie dread characteristic of neurotic anxiety, nor does it cause one to avoid the situation at all costs, as is the case with those suffering from phobic neurosis. In patients with this disorder, avoidance is mandatory if they are to escape being overwhelmed by anxiety; as a result, their capacity to lead a normal, freely active life is often severely compromised.

Although the phobia is the cardinal and often the only manifestation of the phobic neurosis, other symptoms may be present. Feelings of depersonalization are present in a number of phobic patients—a combination of symptoms to which Roth has called particular attention (1959a). Patients may also experience periods of mild to moderate depression secondary to lowered self-esteem at having to give up an activity because of phobic avoidance. An individual, for example, who cancels a trip or drives rather than flies because of a plane phobia, may see this as a personal defeat and as evidence that he is not the strong, effective person he would ideally like to be. By the same token, an individual who carries out an activity despite the phobic anxiety attached to it may experience a feeling of mild euphoria and heightened self-esteem because of his inner victory over his fears. It is also possible for a phobia to be hidden behind a counterphobic attitude or behavior pattern (see chapter 9, "The Dynamic Bases of Psychopathology").

Behavioral observations. There is little that is remarkable in the mental status and behavior of patients with phobic neurosis, especially when they are not confronted with the phobic situation or object. In the face of the phobic stimulus, especially if there is no escape from it, the classical manifestations of anxiety will be evident, particularly as anxiety mounts to the intensity of panic. Although the phobic neurosis has been viewed by many analysts as resulting from the same underlying oedipal conflicts as hysteria (hence the common designation *anxiety hysteria*), patients do not necessarily show hysterical personality traits; many, in fact, are much more likely to be obsessional than hysterical in their character structure and behavior.

Etiology. In conversion hysteria, as noted earlier, the anxiety-provoking impulses and their associated emotions and mental contents (fantasies and related memories) are repressed from conscious awareness. The energy of the repressed impulse is then discharged through a physical symptom that symbolically represents the underlying conflict and allows the discharge of the impulse without anxiety, since the expression occurs in a disguised form that masks the true aim of the originally feared impulse. In the phobic patient, after the initial process of repression, there is no such disguised, modifying avenue for the discharge of the impulse. Its continued push for direct conscious discharge arouses anxiety that necessitates the ego's calling up auxiliary defenses to control the drive—defenses that result in the phobic symptom.

As a first step, the anxiety and its associated impulse are displaced from the primary stimulus arousing the drive to an associatively related but in itself innocuous element in the mental complex. Thus in the patient with a phobia of boats, mentioned earlier, the anxiety associated with the memory of a pleasant but forbidden sexual encounter was displaced onto the memory of the boat on which it occurred—the boat itself being an emotionally neutral and insignificant fragment of the entire complex of memories of the experience. The process of displacement was incapable by itself, however, of protecting the patient from anxiety, since there was no easy way for her to avoid recalling the image of the now frightening boat. An added mechanism was needed to allow her to put further distance between herself and the stimulus; this was accomplished by projecting the anxiety from the inner mental image of a boat to real boats in the external world. The patient could now physically avoid boats in her environment and thus defend herself from experiencing anxiety. Her self-protection occurred, however, at the expense of a considerable degree of freedom of action, for she was now forced to shun places where she might encounter boats, and she feared looking at the newspapers or television lest she see a picture of one.

The phobia, then, represents the end product of a series of ego defense mechanisms—repression, displacement, projection, and avoidance. In early theoretical formulations of the disorder, repressed oedipal conflicts were viewed by clinicians as being the pathogenic material underlying the phobic neurosis—that is, incestuous genital libidinal impulses were responsible for the ego's response of anxiety, which in turn was essentially a fear of castration. In the light of recent clinical experience, however, these views have been broadened, and it is now recognized that not only genital sexuality but pregenital drives as well (especially aggression and dependency needs) are a source of anxiety in the phobic

neurosis and, in addition, that separation anxiety, particularly in agoraphobia, has equal importance with castration anxiety in motivating the ego to employ the defensive measures that lead to the formation of the phobic symptom.

A further contribution to the understanding of phobia formation comes from the concepts of learning theory. The mechanism of displacement may be viewed as a specific case of the general phenomenon of classical conditioning; an unconditioned response (instinctual anxiety, for example) can, through learning, be elicited by a previously neutral stimulus linked by association with the unconditioned anxiety-provoking stimulus. This model alone, however, does not fully explain phobic phenomena. In laboratory experiments, the repetition of conditioned stimuli without reinforcement by the unconditioned stimulus rapidly leads to the extinction and ineffectiveness of the former. This finding is at variance with the clinical fact that the phobic (conditioned) stimulus, without reinforcement by the unconditioned stimulus, maintains its power to rouse phobic anxiety despite repeated exposure to it over many years. Additional help in explaining these clinical observations comes from the newer concepts of operant conditioning (see chapter 19, "Behavior Therapy and Behavioral Psychotherapy"), which has shown experimentally that behavior which reduces the experience of pain tends to be maintained as long as it is effective—that is, behavior may be learned. This concept is applicable to many neurotic symptoms resulting from ego defenses, in addition to phobias; since defenses reduce the pain of anxiety, they (and the symptoms resulting from them) will persist as long as they remain effective in protecting the individual from painful affects.

Differential diagnosis. Phobic neurosis is not likely to be confused with other illnesses. The phobia may occur as a symptom, however, in the early phases of a schizophrenic psychosis or it may be part of a fully established schizophrenic illness. The diagnosis of schizophrenia will, of course, be determined by the presence of the characteristic signs and symptoms indicating a major disturbance in ego functioning.

Treatment. Mention has already been made of the stubbornness of phobic symptoms, which

often persist in the face of prolonged psychotherapy that has effected beneficial changes in
other areas of the patient's emotional life. The
findings of learning theory, which are complementary to psychodynamic explanations of
symptom formation, help us to understand the
reasons for this persistence and have provided
therapeutic measures that are clinically effective
where other treatment modalities have failed.
The techniques of reciprocal inhibition and
flooding (see chapter 19, "Behavior Therapy and
Behavioral Psychotherapy") have been found to
be particularly useful; the effectiveness of reciprocal inhibition is often enhanced by employing
hypnosis in hypnotizable patients to induce the
relaxation that is integral to the treatment
process.

Obsessive-Compulsive Neurosis

Among the more striking and bizarre manifestations in the panorama of neurotic symptoms are
the obsessions and compulsions that characterize the obsessive-compulsive neurosis. Most people have transient, minor episodes of obsessive
or compulsive behavior (such as feeling compelled to make sure one has turned off the stove
or locked the front door of the house), but in the
obsessive-compulsive neurosis these take center
stage and often form the major preoccupation of
the individual's waking attention.

Clinical features. Central to the disorder is the
obsession in which a thought, a word or phrase,
or a mental image obtrudes on the individual's
conscious awareness, an image upon which he is
forced to dwell, often for hours on end, against
his will and better judgment. The obsession may
have no meaning to its victim, or it may refer to
the consequences, past or future, that the individual fears as the result of some act he has committed.

A young man suddenly had the thought after
leaving for work that he had left a cigarette
burning at home. He tried to dismiss the idea
from his mind as a needless worry, but it returned repeatedly despite his attempts to dispel
it. As the morning wore on, he found himself
dwelling with an unpleasantly mounting anxiety
on images of the cigarette falling from the ash-

tray, setting fire to the papers on his desk, and
engulfing his house in flames. The stubborn persistence of these thoughts interfered with his
work even though he was rationally convinced
that he had actually crushed out his cigarette and
that even if he had not no serious harm could
come from it.

Many of the features that characterize the obsession are present in this brief vignette: (1) it is ego-
alien, seemingly coming to the individual's mind
from outside himself; (2) it forces itself upon its
victim's attention against his will; (3) it is accompanied by a sense of anxious dread, often of vividly anticipated harmful events; (4) although
helplessly preoccupied with the obsession, the
individual recognizes that both it and the feared
consequences are absurd, irrational, and in all
likelihood without foundation in external fact;
and finally (5) the individual struggles to resist
the intrusion of the obsession into his consciousness.

Obsessional rumination, a more intellectual
form of the symptom, forces the individual into
long, pseudophilosophic cogitation over unan-
swerable and often trivial questions, such as why
two and two make four. Doubting, a related phenomenon prominent in many patients, involves
them in long internal questionings of the truth of
matters of fact or of the conclusions of their
rational, logical thinking.

In the compulsion, the individual is beset by
an impulse to action. Like the obsession, the
compulsion is ego-alien, compelling, accompanied by dread, known intellectually to be non-
sense, and resisted by its victim. George M., for
example (see chapter 9, "The Dynamic Bases of
Psychopathology"), was obsessed with the notion
that he had injured bystanders by jostling them
and causing them to fall. His anxiety over the obsession usually induced in him an overwhelming
compulsion to retrace his steps to observe for
himself that he had caused no damage. In such
cases, the compulsion represents a means of preventing or neutralizing the harmful effects of an
obsessional thought; in others, it may directly
express an aggressive or harmful impulse, as in
the case of the individual who feels compelled to
shout out obscenities during a solemn public ceremony.

In compulsive acts the compulsion is overtly

put into action. These acts frequently appear strange and senseless to the observer and may at times lead to complex, unintelligible rituals. Boswell has captured for eternity the paradigm of the compulsive act in Johnson's

anxious care to go out or in at a door or passage by a certain number of steps from a certain point, or at least so as that either his right or his left foot (I am not certain which), should constantly make the first actual movement when he came close to the door or passage. Thus I conjecture: for I have, upon innumerable occasions, observed him suddenly stop, and then seem to count his steps with a deep earnestness; and when he had neglected or gone wrong in this sort of magical movement, I have seen him go back again, put himself in a proper posture to begin the ceremony, and, having gone through it, break from his abstraction, walk briskly on, and join his companion. (*Life of Johnson*, vol. 1, p. 232)

It was, as Boswell comments, a "superstitious habit, which he had contracted early, and from which he had never called upon his reason to disentangle him."

Behavioral observations. As in most neurotic syndromes, little is generally notable in the behavior of patients with obsessive-compulsive neurosis; despite the occasional bizarreness of some of the characteristic symptoms—in which primary process thinking can be observed (see chapter 11, "Schizophrenic Reactions")—no other evidence of schizophrenic thought disorder occurs. In particular, the patient maintains reality testing and is fully cognizant of the fact that his obsessions and compulsions are in actuality absurd. Only when the patient is engaging in a compulsive act can anything truly abnormal be observed; at these times the oddness of his behavior cannot be missed. He is often so utterly absorbed in what he is doing that he appears oblivious of his surroundings until he has completed the full measure of his ritual to his own satisfaction. Indeed, forcing him to break off in the middle will usually produce visible signs of anxiety.

In addition to these episodic and clearly unusual actions, one may notice the subtler and not always obviously abnormal characteristics of the obsessional personality. In a clinical interview the patient is seen to be stiff and formal in bearing and posture. He shows little emotion and tends to be intellectual, thoughtful, and rational in his conversation. He will often discourse at length and in detail about a subject and may persist in his train of thought with a tenacity that makes it hard for the interviewer to break in or to direct the conversation to other topics. His speech is commonly stilted, with convoluted sentence structures and qualifying phrases ("sort of," "kind of," "somewhat") that enable him to avoid making a statement that sounds too assertive or challenging, or one with which the listener can take issue. He appears generally cooperative if not frankly deferential to the interviewer and sets great store by being punctual for appointments and by otherwise complying with the rules and requirements of the social structure.

Etiology. The primary defense mechanism in the obsessive-compulsive neurosis is regression. In the face of stimuli that arouse anxiety-provoking oedipal libido, instead of repressing the drive and converting the energy into somatic symptoms as in hysteria, or displacing and projecting it as in the phobic neurosis, the patient with an obsessive-compulsive neurosis retreats from the oedipal position and regresses along the path of psychosexual development to the anal phase, a regression often aided by the presence of anal fixations resulting from disturbances in the patient's initial passage through that developmental stage during early childhood. The defensive regression thus set in motion secondarily brings about changes in the elements of the psychic structure that lead to new psychological problems requiring further defensive maneuvers.

Changes in the id are seen in the reemergence of drives characteristic of the anal phase of development. In the normal process of early psychological growth, anal-sadistic and anal-libidinal drives are superseded during the oedipal period by genital libido that, in a partial fusion of the two, tempers the sadism to a gentler, more constructive form of aggression and redirects the libido from anal to genital aims. With regression the fusion is undone, and the recurring sadistic and anal-libidinal drives must be dealt with by the ego. The direct effect of this defusion is seen in the ambivalence that characterizes many obsessional patients, who quite consciously experience both love and hatred toward those who are close to them. The ambivalence is further manifested, though more indirectly, in the obsessional individual's incessant doubting and his often paralyzing indecision when faced with making a choice.

Perhaps the most important of the changes that occur in the ego are the defenses that it erects to control the archaic drives unleashed by regression, for it is these that determine the nature of the symptoms that characterize the obsessive-compulsive neurosis. Central to these defenses are isolation, the maneuver that renders the emotional component of the drive unconscious but allows the related fantasies to remain in the individual's consciousness, and reaction formation, the character defense that controls aggression and anal impulses through patterns of behavior that are qualitatively the opposite of the underlying drives. When the defenses of isolation and reaction formation are functioning successfully, they lead to the intellectual, emotionless, unaggressive, and perfectionistic cast of the obsessional personality; the individual, though his emotional life is restricted and stunted, remains relatively free of anxiety and is able to function proficiently for long periods of time. When, however, the strength of the drive is increased or the effectiveness of the defenses is weakened, or when both occur, the drive itself threatens to emerge into consciousness. Because of the increment of energy that they receive from the strengthened drive, anal-aggressive and anal-erotic fantasies, once pale, lifeless, and undemanding, are now infused with that compelling quality that characterizes obsessions and compulsions. Anxiety, furthermore, increases as the drives come closer to the surface, and auxiliary defenses are marshaled to aid in their containment. Foremost among these secondary defenses is undoing, a mechanism that is seen most patently in the compulsive acts and rituals with which the obsessive-compulsive patient tries to reverse the effects he fears from the operation of the drive.

The frequently bizarre quality of obsessions and compulsions results from a regression of the ego to developmentally earlier forms of thought and perception characteristic of the mental operations of young children and savages. Of particular importance in this respect is the magical thinking that colors obsessional thoughts

and compulsive rituals. Thoughts appear to be omnipotent—the individual feels that they can directly effect changes in the physical environment—and the paralogical processes of primary thinking predominate, particularly in regard to the obsessive ideas and compulsive urges. At the same time, as has been pointed out, the ego's function of reality testing remains intact and the patient is fully aware of the absurdity of his magical notions.

Finally, it must be noted that regression leads to a reemergence of a developmentally earlier superego, characterized by the loftiness and exacting demands of its ideals and the harshness of its punishment for ideals unfulfilled and injunctions transgressed. This feature underlies the prominent sense of guilt and anxious dread that so strongly affects the patient suffering from the obsessive-compulsive neurosis.

Differential diagnosis. The obsessive-compulsive neurosis is easily distinguished from other neurotic disorders when the patient manifests the classical symptoms of obsessions and compulsions. There are, however, some areas of overlap with the symptoms of other psychiatric illnesses, especially the phobic neurosis. In their pure and typical form, phobias and obsessions are clearly distinct: the phobia is a fear of harm coming to the individual from an external object; in an obsession the patient fears that through his own actions harm will occur to someone else, but the distinction is often not so clear-cut. In a phobia of knives or scissors, for example, the individual fears harming others with the instrument, and, as in the typical phobia, he can control his anxiety by avoidance. Or in a phobia of germs, though the individual fears harm from an external source, he is unable to avoid what he senses as a ubiquitous threat and will often attempt to counter his anxiety by elaborate compulsive rituals of handwashing. There is, in other words, a region between the pure phenomena at the ends of the spectrum where the boundaries between the syndromes are blurred and where the diagnosis must be established from observations concerning the patient's personality, basic underlying conflicts, and ego defenses.

Obsessive-compulsive neurosis is less likely to be confused with the major mental illnesses than with other psychoneurotic disorders. Nonetheless, 20 percent of patients with depression are reported to have obsessive-compulsive symptoms and 30 percent manifest obsessional character traits, these being particularly common in the history of those who develop depression in middle life. Finally, as with the symptom of phobia, obsessive-compulsive phenomena may appear suddenly as the leading edge of a schizophrenic episode. As has been pointed out, however, the bizarreness of many obsessions and compulsions, although reflecting the irruption of primary process thinking, does not signify the presence of a psychosis if reality testing remains intact.

Treatment. Patients with severe and long-standing obsessive-compulsive symptoms are notoriously refractory to treatment by traditional psychotherapeutic measures. Good results have been reported with analytically oriented therapy, however, with individuals whose defensive structure is flexible enough to permit them to gain conscious access to the drives—particularly aggression—underlying the symptoms. Recent reports of the use of behavior techniques aimed specifically at symptom control, particularly response prevention and modeling (see chapter 19, "Behavior Therapy and Behavioral Psychotherapy"), suggest that they may be effective even in chronic cases of long duration. Successful results have also been reported recently with the use of imipramine (Tofranil) for obsessional patients who have an affective component in their illness, but further clinical studies are needed to document the more general effectiveness of the somatic therapies in this group of patients.

Depressive Neurosis

Any discussion of depression is complicated by two facts. First, the word *depression* is used to refer both to an almost universally experienced affect and to a psychiatric disorder. Second, the psychiatric disorder, in which the affect of depression is a central symptom, is probably not a unitary illness, since from a clinical point of view depressed patients fall into three major diagnostic categories—depressive neurosis, manic-

depressive disease, and agitated depression. In depressive neurosis, the onset is precipitated by the loss of an important person, object, or position. The affect, though qualitatively appropriate for the precipitating event, is either more intense or of longer duration than normal, without evidence of accompanying psychotic mental processes.

Clinical features. The cardinal symptom of depressive neurosis is, not surprisingly, depressive affect, a subjective experience hard to define. To describe it as a state of being sad, unhappy, melancholy, gloomy, lugubrious, woeful, dismal, and low in spirits is merely to give synonyms for an emotional experience that can be recognized and appreciated only by those who have felt it. Like anxiety, it is an ego affect, with this difference: whereas anxiety anticipates a dreaded event in the future, depression looks backward to a saddening event in the past.

Closely related to and usually accompanying depression is a lowered sense of self-esteem, a diminution of self-confidence, and a tendency to harsh self-criticism, which, especially in psychotic depressive illnesses, may lead to serious suicide attempts. In addition, the depressed patient notices a variety of other associated feelings: apathy and emotional deadness lead him to lose interest in what were formerly important and absorbing pursuits; he becomes emotionally isolated from those around him and no longer has feelings for those he formerly loved, unless it is an irritable resentment at their presence and their concern for him, which he feels intrudes upon his lonely withdrawal; his perceptions of the external world are changed and colored by his inner desolation—what once were gay, vibrant, meaningful surroundings become bleak, sunless, and lifeless.

Somatic symptoms also form an important part of the depressive neurosis. Prominent among these are fatigue, lassitude, and a general sense of heaviness and lack of energy. Headaches and backaches are common, as are a variety of poorly described gastrointestinal complaints, such as epigastric fullness, belching, and anorexia. Sleep is frequently disturbed; usually there is either difficulty in getting to sleep or early waking that leads to fatigue and lassitude in the morning, a condition that improves as the day progresses. Some patients may, paradoxically, complain of excessive sleepiness. Although in most individuals the depressive affect is prominent, it must be remembered that in some the somatic complaints overshadow the emotional, leading the unwary physician to a mistaken diagnosis of physical illness.

Behavioral observations. As might be expected, the patient with depressive neurosis appears depressed. Slumped posture; despairing sighs; easy tearing of the eyes; a sad, glum face across which a smile rarely passes; a flat, lifeless voice—all bespeak the underlying melancholy mood. Although the neurotically depressed patient is usually not retarded in speech or movement and remains in contact with the observer, he may appear preoccupied with his troubles and may find it hard to carry on a lengthy or animated conversation. A degree of irritability may be apparent, and when the loss or other precipitating event behind the depression is touched upon, his depressed affect will deepen, often to the point of tears.

Etiology. First and foremost in the production of neurotic depression is an external precipitant. This is commonly the loss through death, desertion, or withdrawal of affection of someone to whom the patient is attached. Other forms of loss may likewise precipitate a neurotic depression—the loss of a job, for example, financial reverses, or a move from familiar surroundings to a new home and strange circumstances.

Central to depression is a fall in self-esteem. As Bibring has pointed out (1953), an individual's sense of worth as a person depends on his perceiving himself as strong and effective, as conforming to his ideals of what is right, and as being valued by other people. The lowering of self-esteem when any one of these conditions is absent is accompanied by a feeling of depression.

The depressive affect resulting either from loss or from lowered self-esteem, of course, is not in itself abnormal. Indeed, when an individual fails to experience sadness in such situations, the absence of affect is in itself strong evidence of psychopathology. This is the case, for example, in persons who fail to grieve following the death of

an individual with whom they have had a close, loving relationship. It is only when the depression is disproportionate to the severity of the precipitant or when it lasts abnormally long that it is to be viewed as a neurotic disorder. Persons who manifest such abnormal responses frequently have personality structures that make them particularly sensitive to loss and prone to a lowering of self-esteem. These personality features, which are considered briefly below, constitute a further element in the production of neurotic depression.

The human relationships of many people are characterized by a marked degree of dependence on another person for love, support, guidance, and encouragement. Two factors enter into this type of relationship: (1) a direct, passive dependent need and (2) a tendency to lowered self-esteem resulting partly from a sense of helplessness and weakness and partly from an overly strict and punitive superego, particularly in respect to the manifestations of the aggressive drive. To combat this tendency toward lowered self-esteem, such people require an unusual amount of reassurance from others that they are loved, appreciated, and respected. Individuals with this form of personality organization (in which narcissism plays an important role) react to a frustration of their dependent needs with intense aggression toward those who disappoint them.

It is apparent that the narcissistic person is especially sensitive to loss. Because his need for love is imperative, he reacts with feelings of intense despair and hurt to disappointment by the individual on whom he depends. He is especially sensitive to minor indications of withdrawal on the part of others; a slight degree of disapproval, of no real concern to a more mature person, is experienced by the narcissistic person as a serious, potentially catastrophic loss of the support he so desperately needs. He is, in other words, particularly liable to develop neurotic depression in situations that in mature individuals produce either no significant response or only the normal, self-limited grief that is the natural aftermath of a serious loss.

Finally a word must be said about the role of the aggressive drive in depression. Anger and aggression, as Lindemann has shown (1944), are probably normal, nearly universal elements in the process of natural grief. In the narcissistic individual, the arousal of the aggressive drive is particularly dangerous and threatening. Not only does it arouse his sense of guilt and painfully lower his self-esteem because of his superego's strong disapproval of angry feelings and fantasies and their expression, but, in addition, such an individual fears that his being angry will cause an even greater withdrawal and rejection on the part of the person on whom he deeply relies for love and support. As a result, he erects defenses that control the aggressive drive and deflect it from its primary target. Prominent among these defenses is turning against the self (see chapter 9, "The Dynamic Bases of Psychopathology"). The effect of this defensive maneuver is to reinforce the tendency of the superego to self-criticism and to direct aggressive feelings, thoughts, and even actions against the self—a mechanism that plays an important role in suicidal impulses and acts.

In summary, then, the disorder of neurotic depression, in contrast to the affect of depression and normal grief, occurs in individuals with a personality structure that enhances their sensitivity to loss and brings into play specific mechanisms of defense against aggression that deflect it from its primary object onto the person himself.

Differential diagnosis. Faced with a depressed patient, the clinician must determine to which of the major depressive syndromes his illness belongs. The depressive neurosis may be distinguished from manic-depressive disease by several significant characteristics. In the case of the manic-depressive patient, often no obvious precipitant is present; the affective disturbance is more profound than in depressive neurosis and the accompanying somatic symptoms are more intense; suicidal ideas are prominent and suicide itself is common; self-denigrating delusions may be present; and the disability resulting from the disorder is generally much greater than in depressive neurosis. Manic-depressive disease is, furthermore, a recurrent condition, returning over the years in repeated episodes and not infrequently interspersed with periods of mania. The agitated depression, on the other hand, is a disorder that tends to occur in middle or later life in

a person without a prior history of depression; it is particularly characterized by the high degree of anxiety and motor agitation manifested by the patient. As in patients with manic-depressive disease, psychotic delusions may be present in those manifesting agitated depression, and the drive toward suicide or self-injury is particularly strong and dangerous.

Although in a system of diagnostic classification it is necessary to make sharp distinctions among the various types of depression, such distinctions may well be more conceptual than phenomenological. Clinical investigators do, in fact, disagree about the nature of depressive disorders—some adhere to the view that neurotic depression is clearly differentiated from psychotic depression; others see the one blending into the other along a spectrum of increasing severity without well-defined boundaries. The battle between the monists and the dualists, now of some fifty years' duration, is still being waged without signs of any imminent resolution (see chapter 13, "Affective Disorders"). One may hope, however, that the current investigations of the neurochemistry of depressive states (see chapter 5, "The Biochemistry of Affective Disorders") will provide new information leading to a reconciliation of the two points of view.

Treatment. In addition to the variety of useful psychotherapeutic approaches, drug therapy may prove helpful in relieving the symptoms of depressive neurosis in patients who do not respond to psychological measures. Generally speaking, lithium and the monoamine oxidase inhibitors should be reserved for patients with the more severe depressive illnesses, and the drug treatment of depressive neurosis should be restricted to the use of tricyclic antidepressants. It is essential with all patients in this category, however, to establish a solid therapeutic relationship; the employment of medication should be viewed as an adjunct to, not a replacement of, psychotherapy.

Other Neuroses

Primarily of historical interest, several other psychoneurotic syndromes have been resurrected from a quiet grave by the editors of the second edition of the American Psychiatric Association's *Diagnostic and Statistical Manual of Mental Disorders* (1968) in order to bring that classification more into line with the *International Classification of Diseases* adopted by the World Health Organization in 1967. Although these syndromes have little practical, clinical usefulness and in most instances dignify with a syndromic name symptoms that are generally a part of other, more common, psychiatric disorders, they will for the sake of completeness be briefly reviewed here.

Neurasthenic neurosis. Named by the American psychiatrist, George M. Beard, in the latter half of the nineteenth century, neurasthenic neurosis encompassed in his definition a panorama of loosely related symptoms including anxiety, phobias, fatigue, insomnia, and muscular aches and pains (Beard, 1880). After a brief period of popularity with continental clinicians, it was more carefully examined by clinical investigators, notably by Freud, who separated from it more sharply and narrowly defined conditions such as anxiety neurosis and phobic neurosis, ultimately leaving the term denuded of most of its symptoms (Freud, 1895). As currently defined in the *Diagnostic and Statistical Manual* (DSM-II), its usage is restricted to a disorder characterized by muscular weakness and easy fatigability that often reaches a state of exhaustion.

A chronic, often highly debilitating disorder, neurasthenia may be sudden or gradual in onset. Once begun, the symptoms may run a remitting course or may persist without letup. They frequently begin or are intensified during a period of emotional stress and can reach peaks of severity sufficient completely to incapacitate the patient, whose behavior shows little that is unusual except for a degree of listlessness and apathy consistent with the severity of the fatigue of which he complains.

Janet (1903) saw in the weakness of neurasthenia the direct manifestation of the lowered quantum of nervous energy that was for him the central factor in all emotional illness. In Freud's early formulations neurasthenia was, like anxiety neurosis, an "actual" neurosis, but instead of resulting from an accumulation of libido, as did anxiety, it reflected an excessive loss of libido—especially when libidinal energy was ex-

pended in masturbation. In subsequent analytic theory, neurasthenia was seen as the result of neurotic conflicts (especially those involving the aggressive drive) in which mental energy was expended in maintaining ego defenses to such a degree that little remained available for the individual's other mental functions or for his daily activities.

Neurasthenia should be differentiated from the fatigue that accompanies chronic infectious diseases such as brucellosis or that follows viral infections, and from the weakness found in endocrine disorders involving the thyroid, adrenal cortex, and pituitary. As suggested earlier, neurasthenia does not often occur in pure culture, and when it is found as a presenting complaint, the clinician should search carefully for evidence of other neurotic symptoms, especially anxiety and depression, which may indicate that the neurasthenia is merely one manifestation of one of the more common neurotic disorders.

Depersonalization neurosis. Depersonalization is usually seen as one of the symptoms of the more common psychiatric disorders, especially depression and schizophrenia. In some patients, however, it may be the predominant disturbance, and in that event it is diagnostic of depersonalization neurosis. As an isolated or merely occasional phenomenon, depersonalization is not only common but should not be viewed as evidence of emotional illness. In those instances, however, when it persists for long periods of time or recurs in frequent attacks, it can become incapacitating. The disorder usually begins suddenly, without warning, and is almost entirely limited to people between the ages of fifteen and thirty.

In depersonalization the individual experiences himself, his body, or his mental operations as alien, strange, and unfamiliar, and he may complain of a drying-up of his emotions. There may be specific distortions of the body image —hands or feet, for example, may feel enlarged out of proportion to the rest of the body. In a special form of depersonalization, doubling, the individual senses himself as being entirely out of his body and observes himself as if he were another person. In addition to these perceptions involving the physical and psychological self, there may be similar distortions of the external world; things, settings, and people may be experienced with the same sense of their unreality and unfamiliarity. (Although these latter phenomena are included in the official nomenclature under the heading of depersonalization, they are more accurately to be termed *derealization*, the term *depersonalization* being restricted to distortions in the individual's perceptions of his person.) These disturbances in the sense of reality can be very painful and are often accompanied by anxiety and dizziness.

Little that is abnormal is observed in patients with depersonalization neurosis. They are in contact with others, show no disorder in their thinking, and, except for being anxious, manifest no unusual affect. In particular, the patient is fully aware of his symptoms as alien to him, unpleasant, abnormal, and undesirable.

The etiology of depersonalization is not well understood. It is frequently produced by a variety of physiological factors, such as the ingestion of psychotomimetic drugs, electrical stimulation of the cortex, and sensory deprivation; it may also be found in patients suffering from lesions affecting the brain. Psychological explanations have focused either on its function as a defense in psychological conflicts or on the theoretical concept of shifts in the libidinal cathexis of the boundaries of the ego (Federn, 1953). 9 v

Patients with the symptom of depersonalization should be carefully examined for indications of schizophrenia and depression, and in view of its association with intracranial lesions and its occurrence in epileptic auras, thorough neurological studies are indicated. There is no specific treatment for depersonalization neurosis. Although some investigators have reported an improvement in the symptoms with dexedrine and sodium amytal (Cattell, 1966), the addictive and other dangerous attributes of the amphetamines should generally preclude their use.

Hypochondriacal neurosis. Hypochondriasis, like hysteria, has a long and venerable history, but unlike hysteria it is not a diagnostic term commonly used in modern clinical psychiatry. Despite the fact that it has been restored to the canon of official psychiatric illnesses in DSM-II, no consensus exists among clinicians as to whether it should in fact be considered a psychi-

atric entity. As defined by DSM-II, it is a chronic disorder characterized by a persistent preoccupation with the functions of one's body and intractable fears that one is suffering from physical illness.

Hypochondriasis may appear at any age but most commonly begins in the fourth or fifth decade of life; in one-third of all cases it arises in patients with a physical illness that provides a basis for their complaints.

Although patients may complain of mental symptoms that they interpret as the signs of approaching insanity, in most instances the complaints are physical in nature. These are generally diffuse and widespread throughout the body and rarely follow a pattern recognizable as the result of pathophysiological processes. Complaints are often based on the individual's awareness of a mild, insignificant bodily sensation, and at times, among the mélange of poorly defined generalized symptoms, the patient may present highly specific, minutely detailed and localized, and often unusual complaints, such as those of a woman who informed her physician that every time she touched the inside of her right nostril with her index finger her head would be drawn in a spasm down to her right shoulder, following which her entire body would be subject to gross, jerking tremors.

Despite the frequent bizarreness of their symptoms, patients exhibit no evidence of a thought disorder, and their complaints, though often fixed and refractory to reassurance, are not delusional. The patient describes his difficulties in great detail, often demonstrating them graphically to the observer and using medical terminology he has learned in his many previous contacts with physicians. He is almost totally preoccupied with his bodily complaints, and it is difficult to get him to discuss personal difficulties or disturbing life events. His affect of worried concern, though perhaps inappropriate in view of the medical insignificance of his symptoms, is nonetheless quite consistent with his emotional concern over his bodily state.

Most theorists stress the narcissistic nature of hypochondriacal symptoms and view them as reflecting the investment of the body and its organs with narcissistic libido. Prominent among the psychological formulations is the concept that by eliciting concern, attention, and help from others in response to their somatic complaints, patients are able to gratify their oral-dependent needs. The defensive function of symptoms—protecting the patient from the lowered self-esteem and depression that would result from an underlying destructive drive if he did not punish himself through his hypochondriacal suffering—has also been proposed.

Hypochondriacal complaints may mask symptoms of anxiety and depression that will be missed if the physician does not specifically ask about them. Hypochondriacal individuals may also develop genuine physical illnesses, the recognition of which may often be extremely difficult through the fog of neurotic complaints. The appearance of new symptoms in the familiar medley of the old should alert the clinician to this possibility and constitutes grounds for examinations and laboratory studies that he might otherwise be inclined to forgo.

There is no specific treatment for hypochondriacal symptoms, which are well known for their refractoriness to all therapeutic approaches. If they are part of an underlying depression, they may improve when the depression itself is properly treated, but, as Roth has pointed out (1959b), depressions in which hypochondriacal symptoms are prominent respond less favorably to therapy than depressions without such a complication.

Having surveyed the panorama of the neuroses, we must remind ourselves once again that they are only syndromes—clusterings of symptoms and signs that, though sometimes sharply differentiated from one another, more often than not have unclear boundaries, frequently so blurred as to be almost undetectable. While they are useful as a rough means of classifying neurotic illness, the diagnostic categories alone cannot be employed as a guide to determining the proper treatment. Of far more importance in this regard is an assessment of the ego functions and relationships of the patient manifesting neurotic symptoms. Although this compounds the difficulty of our diagnostic task, it greatly increases our effectiveness as therapists.

References

American Psychiatric Association. 1968. *Diagnostic and statistical manual of mental disorders.* 2nd ed. Washington, D.C.

Beard, G. M. 1880. *A practical treatise on nervous exhaustion (neurasthenia).* New York: Wood.

Benson, H., J. F. Beary, and M. P. Carol. 1974. The relaxation response. *Psychiatry* 37:37–46.

Bibring, E. 1953. The mechanism of depression. In *Affective disorders,* ed. P. Greenacre. New York: International Universities Press.

Boswell, J. 1791. *Life of Johnson.* New York: Oxford University Press, 1933.

Bunyan, J. 1666. *Grace abounding to the chief of sinners.* London: J. M. Dent, 1956.

Cattell, J. P. 1966. Depersonalization phenomena. In *American handbook of psychiatry,* ed. S. Arieti. New York: Basic Books.

Davison, G. C. 1966. Anxiety under total curarization: implications for the role of muscular relaxation in the desensitization of neurotic fears. *J. Nerv. Ment. Dis.* 143:443–448.

Federn, P. 1953. *Ego psychology and the psychoses.* London: Imago.

Freud, S. 1894. The neuro-psychoses of defence. In *Standard edition,* ed. J. Strachey. Vol. 3. London: Hogarth Press, 1962.

——— 1895. On the grounds for detaching a particular syndrome from neurasthenia under the description "anxiety neurosis." In *Standard edition,* ed. J. Strachey. Vol. 3. London: Hogarth Press, 1962.

Granville-Grossman, K. L., and P. Turner. 1966. The effect of propranolol on anxiety. *Lancet* 1:788–790.

Grosz, H. J., and B. B. Farmer. 1969. Blood lactate in the development of anxiety symptoms. *Arch. Gen. Psychiatry* 21:611–619.

Hodgson, R. 1891. A case of double consciousness. *Proc. Soc. Psychic. Res.* 7:221–257.

Jacobson, E. 1938. *Progressive relaxation.* Chicago: University of Chicago Press.

James, W. 1907. *The principles of psychology.* 2 vols. New York: Holt.

Janet, P. 1903. *Les obsessions et la psychasthénie.* 2 vols. Paris: Félix Alcan.

Lindemann, E. 1944. Symptomatology and management of acute grief. *Am. J. Psychiatry* 101:141–148.

Raymond, F., and P. Janet. 1904. Dépersonnalisation et possession chez un psychasthénique. *J. psychol. norm. pathol.* 1:28–37.

Roth, M. 1959a. The phobic anxiety-depersonalization syndrome. *Proc. R. Soc. Med.* 52:587–595.

——— 1959b. The phenomenology of depressive states. *Can. Psychiatr. Assoc. J.* spec. suppl. 4:32–54.

Sidis, B., and S. P. Goodhart. 1905. *Multiple personality: an experimental investigation into the nature of human individuality*. New York: Appleton.

World Health Organization. 1967. *International classification of diseases*. 8th rev. ed. Washington, D.C.: National Center for Health Statistics.

Recommended Reading

Breuer, J., and S. Freud. 1895. Studies on hysteria. In *Standard edition*, ed. J. Strachey. Vol. 2. London: Hogarth Press, 1955.

Dugas, L., and F. Moutier. 1911. *La dépersonnalisation*. Paris: Félix Alcan.

Fenichel, O. 1939. The counterphobic attitude. *Int. J. Psychoanal*. 20:263–274.

Freud, S. 1909a. Analysis of a phobia in a five-year-old boy. In *Standard edition*, ed. J. Strachey. Vol. 10. London: Hogarth Press, 1955.

—— 1909b. Notes upon a case of obsessional neurosis. In *Standard edition*, ed. J. Strachey. Vol. 10. London: Hogarth Press, 1955.

—— 1914. Mourning and melancholia. In *Standard edition*, ed. J. Strachey. Vol. 14. London: Hogarth Press, 1958.

Gillespie, R. D. 1928. Hypochondria: its definition, nosology and psychopathology. *Guy's Hosp. Rep*. 78:408–460.

Hill, D. 1968. Depression: disease, reaction, or posture? *Am. J. Psychiatry* 125:445–457.

Janet, P. 1907. *The major symptoms of hysteria*. New York: Macmillan.

Kiersch, T. A. 1962. Amnesia: a clinical study of ninety-eight cases. *Am. J. Psychiatry* 119:57–60.

Lewis, A. J. 1934. Melancholia: a clinical survey of depressive states. *J. Ment. Sci*. 80:277–378.

May, R. 1950. *The meaning of anxiety*. New York: Ronald Press.

Nemiah, J. C. 1975. The neuroses. In *Comprehensive textbook of psychiatry*, ed. A. M. Freedman and H. I. Kaplan. 2nd ed. Baltimore: Williams & Wilkins.

Prince, M. 1906. *The dissociation of a personality*. New York: Longmans, Green.

Salzman, L. 1968. *The obsessive personality*. New York: Science House.

Schizophrenic Reactions

CHAPTER 11

Max Day
Elvin V. Semrad

The schizophrenic reactions are a group of diseases that cause massive disruptions of thinking, mood, sensorimotor functioning, and behavior; they lie at the most severe end of the spectrum of psychopathology. Schizophrenics show a greater degree of disturbance in intrapsychic function, character structure, and interpersonal relationships than patients suffering from any other mental disorder. Intrapsychic problems are reflected in thought, speech, mood, and sensory perception; character pathology, in the nature of superego and ego functions; and interpersonal problems, in attitudes toward and relationships with other people. Because character structure develops from particular intrapsychic modes of responding to early interpersonal relationships, an individual's past is reflected in his current functioning. In both past and present, the schizophrenic shows extreme disturbance in every sphere of functioning.

During decompensation—the clinical breakdown of the personality—the schizophrenic appears to relinquish control of himself in essential areas of his life. Throughout history, man's reaction to this violation of "humanness" has been correspondingly extreme—fear of this loss of control, horror at what happens to the individual schizophrenic, contempt for such self-abandonment, and, finally, resignation at being unable to understand or alleviate the illness. Each new investigator must master his own reactions toward the patient before he is able to study and treat schizophrenia objectively. Such reactions account, in part, for the many harsh, though often well-rationalized, approaches to the schizophrenic throughout history. Even modern approaches intended to help the patient, including chemotherapy or milieu efforts, are as likely to result in increased patient neglect as merely custodial hospital approaches. The choice of such approaches stems partly from our reaction to the awesomeness of the disease, which causes us to distance ourselves from those who manifest it. At times, however, emphasis has been placed on confronting rather than avoiding the extreme aberrations of schizophrenic behavior. Practices in the Hippocratic period in Greece, the Arab enlightenment, the nineteenth-century moral treatment movement in the West, and attempts during the last thirty-five years to understand and deal with the psychotic as an individual have all reflected this treatment emphasis.

Historical Summary

What we term *schizophrenia* has been known for at least 3400 years. Sanskrit writings described it as early as 1400 B.C. The Greek physicians of the Hippocratic school in the fifth century B.C. called it "dementia" and distinguished it from mania and melancholia. During the second century and for more than a thousand years thereafter, schizophrenia was considered a form of possession by the devil and was dealt with accordingly in religious courts, jails, and asylums.

During the nineteenth century, modern psychiatry progressed from observing symptoms to defining specific illnesses with common manifestations, focusing on related groups of illnesses and, eventually, studying their underlying somatic and psychological factors. Classificatory efforts in the late eighteenth and early nineteenth centuries led to descriptions of symptoms, illness groups, and patterns of recovery. Jean Etienne Esquirol described "hallucinations" and "monomania," while Heinrich Neumann first used the term *recovery with defect*. Joseph Guislain, Karl Ludwig Kahlbaum, and Arndt stressed the interrelatedness of different psychoses. Benedict Augustin Morel introduced the term *demence précoce*, thus making a distinction between the mental state of the generally young schizophrenic and the apparently similar mental state of the senile, demented patient. The term *idiocy* was used to describe the results of congenital defects or those acquired very early in life, while *dementia* connoted acquired or reversible defects. By 1868, Kahlbaum had described catatonia; Ewald Hecker's descriptions of hebephrenia followed in 1871. Attempts to understand the illness focused increasingly on the patient's age at onset, his ability to recover, and the degree of remaining defect. Theoreticians disagreed about whether the etiology of schizophrenia was somatic or emotional and about whether diseases should be viewed as distinct clinical entities or as degrees of a single mental illness.

In the late 1890s, Emil Kraepelin (1898) classified symptoms, symptom complexes, and isolated illnesses within two broad categories based on outcome; dementia praecox resulted in de-

terioration, while manic-depressive psychosis showed exacerbations and remissions but not deterioration. However, the fact that 13 percent of patients with a diagnosis of dementia praecox recovered without defect raised doubts about the inevitability of deterioration.

Sigmund Freud (1911) believed the content of schizophrenics' speech confirmed his theories of the unconscious motivation of human behavior and the stages of psychosexual development. He ultimately concluded, however, that schizophrenia represented such a degree of narcissistic regression that treatment was impossible. Despite his pessimism concerning treatment of schizophrenics, Freud's formulations have enabled subsequent theorists and therapists to develop a more comprehensive understanding of the etiology and treatment of this illness.

Eugen Bleuler (1911) used Kraepelin's systematic classification of psychoses and Freud's dynamic understanding of the unconscious to redefine the disorder as schizophrenia (splitting of the mind). He described the fundamental symptoms as disturbances of association and affect, a preference for fantasy over reality, and an inclination to draw away from reality (autism). Blocking and systematic splitting of thoughts, feelings, associations, and acts were secondary. The very symptoms that had been described earlier as essential—hallucinations, delusions, negativism, and stupor—were no longer considered crucial for diagnosis.

Carl Jung (1906) was also influenced by Freud's concepts of unconscious motivation in human behavior and used word associations to explore networks of related memories, events, interactions, and feelings. Jung saw these unconscious complexes as powerful forces in individuals' lives. His formulations of introverted and extroverted personalities, developed subsequent to his break with Freud, have proved useful in understanding the emotional life of the schizophrenic.

Adolf Meyer (1950), working during the first quarter of this century, considered schizophrenia a reaction to a traumatic life situation, a view basic to his psychobiological approach to all mental illness. Referring to schizophrenia as a group of "reaction" disorders, Meyer viewed them as the outcome of habitual patterns of mal-adaptive responses based on organic, psychological, and sociocultural factors. He considered clinical symptoms less basic to conceptualizing mental disturbance than the nature of the stress and the individual's reaction to it. This approach contributed to a unitary view of all mental and emotional illness as points along a continuum extending from neurosis to psychosis.

The trend toward a concept of schizophrenia as a single disorder was counterbalanced by further classificatory efforts. By 1904 O. Diem had added the subtype *simple schizophrenia*, still one of four recognized forms of the disease. Jacob Kasanin added the subtype *schizoaffective psychosis* in 1933. In 1939, G. Langfeldt introduced the concept of *reactive schizophrenia*, or schizophreniform psychosis; this disorder appears in individuals with good work and social adjustment, who are not characteristically schizoid, apparently in response to a traumatic, external event. In contrast to reactive schizophrenia, *process schizophrenia* (a revival of the concept of dementia praecox) was considered to arise without external trauma and eventually to lead to deterioration. In 1949, Paul Hoch and P. Polatin added *pseudoneurotic schizophrenia*, in which the patient shows pervasive anxiety, a constant preoccupation with sexual problems, and a rigid nonresponse to prolonged psychotherapy; closer examination reveals schizophrenic abnormalities of thinking and emotional reaction. This subtype has not been widely accepted as diagnostically or nosologically useful.

In the 1920s and 1930s, Harry Stack Sullivan (1953a, 1953b) noted the importance of interpersonal relationships in the development of schizophrenia. He stressed that striving for security or self-esteem and for the fulfillment of physiological drives, impaired in most mentally ill persons, is particularly damaged in the schizophrenic.

More recently, other theoreticians have stated their belief that an ontological concept of schizophrenia is not justifiable. Thomas Szasz (1957, 1961) has contended that behavioral symptoms deviating from the norm are not necessarily signs of pathology. Ronald Laing (Laing and Esterson, 1964) regards a schizophrenic episode as a necessary break from a destructive family or sick society. Thus diverse views regarding the nature of the illness continue to appear.

Toward a Unitary View of Mental Illness

Several perplexing factors impede our ability to understand schizophrenia. Although the illness is characterized by recognizable behavioral manifestations, the overt clinical picture may vary sharply at critical points in the individual's life. This variation helps to explain the fact that different observers often describe the same schizophrenic patient in apparently contradictory ways. Furthermore, psychotic and neurotic manifestations cannot always be clearly separated. Some schizophrenic patients show evidence of neurosis, while some neurotics demonstrate apparently psychotic thinking and behavior. When borderline personalities regress, they too show signs of psychosis (Kernberg, 1967).

The nature of regression further complicates the picture. Some psychotics regress only once, apparently "get things out of their systems," and seem not to need to regress again. This fact embarrassed Kraepelin and may be one of Laing's considerations in his focus on the crucial and potentially healthy nature of a psychotic break. Some schizophrenics may regress repeatedly to the same level of disorganization. Others may regress to deeper levels after repeated illnesses and may in time remain severely catatonic. These various courses and outcomes appear to represent many different types of schizophrenia; the essential personal problems are similar, however, regardless of clinical picture. Furthermore, these underlying problems are not, in our view, fundamentally different from those found in the affective and borderline disorders. The difference is one of degree.

The history of psychiatry during the last hundred years has supported this unitary view in important ways. Psychiatrists joined the search for a toxic cause of schizophrenia after the influenza epidemic of 1889–91. Freud's theory that regression was based on unconscious motivation and Meyer's view of schizophrenia as a reaction to stress led to a more thoughtful study of the psychiatric concomitants of the influenza epidemic of 1918–19. Karl Menninger's studies in 1919, 1922, 1928, and 1930 (1959) indicated that influenza could trigger schizophrenic reactions that varied in kind and degree; from this evidence, Menninger postulated the existence of a toxin as a mediator. The specifics of the psychotic picture were found to depend at least in part on preexisting mental substructure, rather than on the presumed toxin. In addition to schizophrenic reactions to influenza, Menninger observed manic-depressive and psychoneurotic illnesses. His findings provided further evidence that a single, nonspecific catalyst could release a series of regressions in people across a broad range of pathology, even in the absence of demonstrable genetic, family, or personality pathology and previous indications of illness. These reactions, however serious, were reversible. Thus Menninger's clinical and statistical data imply that mental illness is a progressive series of related disturbances, a concept that has had wide influence on the diagnosis and treatment of mental disorders.

Further evidence for locating schizophrenia at one end of a spectrum of progressive disturbances was supplied by a neurologist, Bartolomé Llopis (1946), who studied the effects of severe pellagra during the Spanish Civil War. He found every degree of disturbance, from neurasthenic through depressive, manic, paranoid, and schizophrenic states to states of clouded consciousness that often led to death. These different psychic states "passed by imperceptible stages of transition from one to another, in a determined order, and in correspondence with the gravity of the situation as a whole" (p. 85). With recovery, the process was observed in reverse order. This natural nutritional experiment convinced Llopis of the existence of an "axial syndrome common to all psychoses," that is, of a continuous series of related psychic disturbances.

Along with the evidence from these naturally occurring disease phenomena, our own clinical experience convinces us of the inconstancy and mutability of diagnostic categories. Long-term observation, often in the form of continuing psychotherapy, can help distinguish a manic with delusions from a grandiose paranoid schizophrenic. In addition, our observations of regression and improvement in patients in contact with community mental health facilities complement those of Menninger and Llopis, even though the changes they noted were due to the action of a nonspecific disease or dietary factor and those we noted were emotionally induced. During a patient's first visit to the outpatient department he would be given a diagnosis of phobia or neurotic depression; this condition might be followed in time by a deeper depression, then a psychotic depression, then a manic episode, and, finally, a paranoid state or catatonia. Recovery might also proceed through these various states in reverse order. Furthermore, when patients suffered the humiliation of chronic hospitalization, they often regressed from one clinical state to another. When involved in interaction with an interested, caring person, a chronic, bitter, paranoid patient, for example, could advance to the level of a florid manic. The importance of human contact and interest as a prime factor in clinical improvement cannot, in our view, be overestimated.

In our own experience with patients with different formal diagnoses (the final diagnostic picture being in part a result of either chronic hospitalization or the patient's total reaction to accumulated insult), we have been struck by the basic similarity of their underlying problems. Schizophrenia, like all psychosis, is experienced as a life-and-death struggle for emotional survival. What distinguishes the different clinical pictures are the particular defense mechanisms employed to deal with inner tension. Although symptomatology and particular constellations of defenses differ, neither symptoms nor defenses are specifically related to severity of illness, outcome of illness, or outcome of therapy.

Etiological and Conceptual Approaches to Schizophrenia

Numerous theories have been advanced to explain the development of schizophrenia. Because the study of the illness is necessarily based on theories of its etiology, some discussion of theoretical frameworks is necessary to a thorough presentation of its clinical features and treatment approaches.

The five basic approaches to the study of

schizophrenia are often listed as descriptive, biological, psychoanalytic, behavioral, and sociocultural; while this categorization is formally useful, we prefer to discuss theories of the etiology of the disease in terms of two basic subject areas: the biological, including genetic, biochemical, and physiological theories and research, and the psychological and social, encompassing behavioral, psychoanalytic, and socioepidemiological theories.

Description, of course, is a necessary tool in all investigative endeavors, although it is not explicitly listed in either of our two categories. In formulating conceptual schemes for approaching schizophrenia phenomenologically, for example, descriptions of symptoms were followed by description and classification of diseases. These nosological emphases, in turn, were broadened to include description of natural history, or reaction patterns in time. More recently, more sophisticated techniques based on factor analysis and cluster analysis of schizophrenics' behavior patterns have been used to revise nosological categories.

Each theoretical approach is incomplete separately, and few bridges exist among hypotheses and findings that are often mutually contradictory. Thus knowledge of schizophrenia remains fragmentary, and the need for an eclectic approach, one that could explore the usefulness of diverse conceptual frameworks and integrate their contributions, becomes increasingly apparent.

Biological theories of the etiology of schizophrenia are discussed in detail elsewhere in this volume (see chapter 6, "Genetic and Biochemical Aspects of Schizophrenia," and chapter 18, "Chemotherapy"); we shall therefore concentrate on the nonbiological theories in our review. In contrast to theories that postulate a demonstrable biological basis for schizophrenia, psychological and social theories attempt to specify nonorganic bases for the illness. Focused on the individual's emotions and behavior, these theoretical frameworks are used to explore the dynamics of discrete psychological functions, complex intrapsychic and psychosexual mechanisms, family interaction, and social environment. We shall discuss these approaches as they have been developed by behavioral, psycho-

analytic, and social and epidemiological theorists and researchers.

Behavioral Theories

The behavioral approach to schizophrenia began in the 1920s with Ivan Pavlov's work on learned behavior and conditioned responses (1941). Pavlov saw schizophrenia as a generalized inhibition or chronic hypnotic state arising from excessive stimulation of a nervous system weakened by hereditary or acquired damage. His studies of experimentally induced "neuroses" in animals provided the impetus for extensive theoretical formulation and experimental research in various forms of conditioning and for a resurgence of interest in the treatment of psychosomatic disorders (see chapter 19, "Behavior Therapy and Behavioral Psychotherapy," and chapter 16, "Psychosomatic Disorders"). From these early principles of classical conditioning, W. Horsley Gantt (1944) developed the concepts of schizokinesis and autokinesis, which may be seen as having analogues in both the psychodynamic and psychosomatic manifestations of schizophrenia. He described schizokinesis as a built-in, unacquired response mechanism—part of the functioning of the normal organism. This mechanism is based on a split in response between the emotions and the visceral systems, on the one hand, and the emotions and the skeletal musculature on the other hand. In the heart, for example, responses form more quickly, are of greater intensity, and are more resistant to extinction than they are in the skeletal muscles. Gantt used autokinesis to refer to the internal development of responses on the basis of old stimulation.

In recent years behaviorists have viewed schizophrenia as a chronic condition of nonadaptive response; early disturbed reinforcement patterns lead to faulty generalizations of response that interfere with perceptual and cognitive behavior. Behavioral therapy based on operant conditioning (see chapter 19, "Behavior Therapy and Behavioral Psychotherapy") has been used to change behavior by reinforcement experience, particularly with autistic children and chronic adult schizophrenics (Cohen et al., 1972; Liberman, 1972).

Behavioral formulations of abnormal perception combine concepts from theories of formal thought disorder with others from learning theory in an effort to understand schizophrenia as a developing process. Jung (1906) was one of the first to trace formal thought disturbances and symptoms from patients' diminished attention and perception. McReynolds (1960) found that the schizophrenic patient was "flooded" by unassimilable perceptions against which he defended himself by apathy and withdrawal. Shakow (1963) studied reaction time and found that patients distracted by irrelevant aspects of a stimulus were unable to concentrate on the relevant aspects; they could not maintain what he called a "major set," that is, readiness to respond to a stimulus and to organize the response in time.

Mednick and Schulsinger (1968) studied matched children of schizophrenic and normal mothers over several years. The schizophrenic mothers' labor and delivery were difficult, perhaps revealing their affective response to childbirth, and their children had more fragmented and idiosyncratic responses on cognitive tests than the children of the normal mothers. These children's adjustment was poor; their home life was less harmonious than that of the normal mothers' children; they perceived their mothers as unreliable and scolding, and they were lonely. When upset, they withdrew. Maladjustment became severe following the mother's psychiatric hospitalization.

From genetic, learning, and family data on schizophrenic children, McReynolds (1960) has theorized the existence of a predisposition, possibly genetic, leading to great anxiety and slow adjustment under stress. Schizophrenic children show a strong physiological response to mild stress, rapid acquisition of conditioned responses, slow recovery from autonomic imbalance, and excessive generalization of responses to stimuli.

Psychoanalytic Theories

Each successive layer of psychoanalytic theory has added a new dimension to our understanding of schizophrenia. Although some of the older theories diminish in importance in the light of more current formulations, for the most part the total effort contributes to our understanding of the illness. In this section we shall focus on psychoanalytic concepts and theories as they have contributed to the general body of psychodynamic theory. We shall examine the contributions of workers who have emphasized therapeutic techniques in our discussion of treatment.

Although Freud's theories did not focus directly on schizophrenia, his earliest concepts of "defense neuropsychoses" (1894) are helpful in understanding both psychosis and neurosis as modes of dealing with unbearable psychic pain; his concept of ego libido extended our knowledge of mental mechanisms by providing increased understanding of the disorganized ego in a state of conflict. Freud applied his theory of the role of sexual regression in the development of illness in his explication of paranoid breakdown in the Schreber case (1911). In response to stress, Freud believed, Schreber regressed to a state of earlier, unintegrated homosexual attachment to his father and dealt with the unacceptable threat of homosexuality by denying his impulses and projecting them onto others in a delusional thought system (see chapter 12, "Paranoia and Paranoid States").

Working in England in the 1920s, Melanie Klein (1932) emphasized the importance of the early mother-child relationship and the primitive defense mechanisms for dealing with the pain of psychosis as well as of early childhood. Her theory of object relations—based on aspects of Freud's theory of the death instinct and on her own clinical work with children, psychotics, and borderline cases—described crucial battles as occurring within the developing psyche during normal infant development. Klein described these as critical phases mirrored in adult psychotic states—a *paranoid-schizoid* phase during the first six months of life and a *depressive* phase beginning at six to nine months.

During the first phase the infant realizes his dependence on his mother, is overcome with anxiety, rage, and frustration, and uses the defense mechanisms of splitting, introjection, and projection in dealing with her as a satisfier of his needs, or "part object" (see chapter 8, "Theories of Personality"). When good experiences with his mother predominate, the child dreads losing her. He then passes through the second phase, in which he must come to terms with this possi-

depressive

bility of loss. His dread is heightened by premature involvement in conflicts of the oedipal period—fantasies of the mother's sexuality as well as of her relationship with his father and siblings.

The work of Harry Stack Sullivan (1953a, 1953b) spanned the 1920s, 1930s, and 1940s. He stressed deeply disturbed interpersonal relationship as the basis for schizophrenia, rather than the intrapsychic mechanisms emphasized by the followers of Freud and Klein. Related approaches were developed by Frieda Fromm-Reichmann, Silvano Arieti, and others from the Washington school of psychiatry, by Edith Jacobson (1967) in New York, and by Elvin Semrad in Boston.

Heinz Hartmann (1953) related schizophrenic psychopathology to severe conflicts, over uncontrolled aggression, which can interfere with the development of autonomous ego functions and thus disturb perception and disrupt logical thought and human relationships. Frustration, the danger of threatened or actual separation, and interference with achievement of aims may all lead to outbursts of aggression. Dependent people who dread separation and loss are particularly vulnerable to such events. Hartmann viewed aggression and its consequences as crucial issues in schizophrenia as well as in other psychoses and borderline states and held that both the amount of aggression and the nature of the defenses used to deal with it determine diagnosis; this view is consistent with a unitary theory of psychosis.

William and Karl Menninger, who worked in many areas of psychiatric research, treatment, and education from World War I to the present, and who derived their theoretical bases from Meyer and Freud, were instrumental in changing the view of the American psychiatric community toward schizophrenia. Partly as a result of Karl Menninger's data on the influenza epidemic of 1918–19, described earlier, schizophrenia has come to be regarded less as an illness than as a reaction to stress. William Menninger helped to introduce this new attitude into the official nomenclature of the American Psychiatric Association; the classification system he developed for the Veterans' Administration became the basis for the *Diagnostic and Statistical Man-*

ual of Mental Disorders (DSM-I) published by the A.P.A. in 1952. In 1958, Karl Menninger formulated a unitary theory of the progression of mental illnesses, from "simple nervousness" through neurotic illness, undisguised aggression, psychotic disorganization, and repudiation of reality to malignant anxiety and depression ending in death.

In the 1940s, psychoanalytic theorists turned their attention to object relations in general, focusing particularly on the earliest form, the mother-child relationship. Margaret Mahler (1963, 1968) noted that schizophrenic children's inordinate attachment to their mothers stunted their psychosocial abilities; from this observation, she developed the concept of "separation-individuation." This process occurs within the first three years of life, beginning with normal symbiosis with the mother, and culminates in the child's recognition of himself as a separate individual. The schizophrenic child and the psychotic adult fail to negotiate this process and are both severely dependent on a valued person for sustenance and support.

More recently, analytic theory has focused on the importance of the ability to bear anxiety and depression for normal development (Zetzel, 1949, 1965). Schizophrenics lack both capacities, and part of the therapeutic strategy is to help patients face psychic situations they have avoided because of their incapacity to heed warning signals: anxiety for closeness and depression for loss. The ability to experience anxiety and sadness appropriately is thus a sign of increasing strength in patients (Klein, 1960; Segal, 1956).

The influence of object-relations theory and of Sullivan's focus on interpersonal relations has led other theorists to apply psychoanalytic theory to disturbed family communication; family interaction can then be used as a conceptual framework for the study of schizophrenia. Ruth and Theodore Lidz (1952) studied the mothers of schizophrenic patients and found that they had nurtured a parasitic attitude in their children. The patients, feeling that they were important to their mothers, complied with parental expectations in order to receive support. Observations that the irrationality of the family is transmitted directly to the child led the investigators to conceptualize two forms of family interaction or bonding patterns (Lidz et al., 1957a, 1957b; Lidz et al., 1958). In "marital skew," one partner dominates the emotional life of the family. Such families usually consist of either a domineering, hostile wife and a passive, dependent husband or a tyrannical, narcissistic husband and a fearful, acquiescent wife. In either case, the weaker partner diverts hatred of the spouse toward the spouse's favored child. In "marital schism," each partner is disappointed and disillusioned with the other and relies on the children for support and comfort. The partners live together in mutual isolation, the family splits into warring camps, and the children bear the guilt of allying themselves with one parent against the other. By 1965, the Lidzes' investigations had led them to conclude that parents of schizophrenics are fundamentally unable to nurture offspring (Lidz, Fleck, and Cornelison, 1965). The schizophrenic's family fails to transmit modes of behavioral reciprocity and accommodation and thus fails as a social institution.

By 1973, Theodore Lidz placed more emphasis than he had previously on schizophrenic thinking as a basis for the illness and suggested that the patient develops his own egocentric overinclusiveness in order to adapt to that of his parents. Lidz and his school had consistently described important patterns in the families of schizophrenics, ascribing the illness more specifically to the direct impact of these patterns than to the role of the patient's intrapsychic and ego reactions and adaptations.

Gregory Bateson and his associates (1956) studied another form of family bonding and developed the concept of the "double bind," a special form of ambivalence in which mother, father, or siblings make overt requests or imply demands for a strong reaction that conflicts with the one required by the situation (such as telling a child with a brutal, hateful father, "Your father loves you"). Failure to acknowledge or accede to the irrational demand incurs either a threat to inner equilibrium or the possibility of punishment; thus there is no acceptable response. The child cannot flee the conflict, and feelings of paralysis, anger, anxiety, and helplessness result. In Bateson's view, psychosis develops to deal with such situations. The child eventually learns to use the double bind (a means of identifying

with the aggressor) against other people. Bateson holds that these situations occur repeatedly in the childhood of the schizophrenic. Although double-bind patterns are frequently discernible in disturbed families, we note that they are found in many apparently normal families as well and are, in fact, an ordinary aspect of life. The psychosis-vulnerable individual, however, never learns to deal with them successfully, as others do.

Lyman Wynne and his associates (1958) describe the bond of "pseudomutuality," wherein constricted roles are assigned to family members at the expense of their individuality. Even when these roles are interchanged, their shared rigidity and narrowness maintain a superficial togetherness. Like Lidz, Wynne believes that the child learns irrationality, which becomes a pattern of living for him; his internalization of the pathological aspects of the family leads to disturbances such as fragmentation of experience, identity diffusion, and disturbed perception and communication (Wynne and Singer, 1963). Once internalized, however, this system of mutuality cannot break down without leading to overt schizophrenia. According to Wynne and Singer, the style of interpersonal relations in the family is also tied to cognitive development; inappropriate cognitive and affective distance or closeness among family members leads to a sense of purposelessness. These findings are compatible with the fragmentation and amorphousness witnessed in schizophrenic thinking, echoing the "looseness of associations" that Bleuler described.

Don Jackson (1967) was struck by the underlying order in the apparent disorder, coldness, and cruelty of the schizophrenic's family and held that such families are in fact not at all disorganized. On the contrary, they are structured to allow family members little access to the wide repertoire of behavior available to most people; the bizarre behavior observed in such families is a sign of the restrictions they impose. Within this framework, the patient learns irrational behavior directly from his family. Our clinical experience reveals, however, that the patient learns selectively, within his own need system; the lessons he learns depend on his particular intrapsychic and accommodative defenses. He rejects what he cannot use, even in a disturbed family. He does not, in our view, become psychotic by directly learning bizarre behavior.

Social Theories

Because schizophrenia is not only a severe but a widespread disorder—affecting roughly one of every one hundred people at some time in their lives, social theories of its cause must take account of what is known about its frequency and about what parts of the population are at the greatest risk of developing the disease. Before discussing socioepidemiological theories of its etiology, therefore, we shall briefly review the major epidemiological data on schizophrenia.

Epidemiological factors. Determining the frequency of schizophrenia is more difficult than for many other diseases because of discrepancies in diagnosis and methodological weaknesses in gathering and validating data. Disagreement about the diagnosis of schizophrenia is widespread. European psychiatrists limit the term to patients fitting Kraepelin's classical description, while psychiatrists in the United States make the diagnosis more frequently. The conviction of many psychiatrists in the United States that "once a schizophrenic, always a schizophrenic" has automatically increased the rate of existing cases (prevalence). However, the growing number who feel that patients who recover from the illness should no longer be labeled schizophrenics in remission has recently brought about a reduction in prevalence. Measurements of the frequency of any disease depend not only on diagnostic standards but also on data sources and collection methods; differences in these factors lead to widely varying statistical results.

Some difficulties in obtaining consistent measurements are readily apparent. Because not all schizophrenics are admitted to treatment facilities, sources other than hospital admissions records must be used. The psychiatric case register, a longitudinal record of all the people in a geographically defined community who receive care in its mental health facilities, is common overseas; adequate safeguards are required to assure privacy and make its use practical in the United States. Occasionally a field survey is made of all cases in a given geographical or cultural community. Clearly, consistent methods of evaluating sources and collecting data are hard to achieve. Until they are developed, statistics on the frequency of the disease cannot be considered totally reliable.

The incidence of schizophrenia—that is, the number of new cases in a given population during the course of a year—has ranged from 0.043 to 0.069 percent in the United States over the last twenty-five years, yielding 92,450 to 148,350 new cases each year. Its prevalence—the fraction of the population defined as schizophrenic during a year—is between 0.23 and 0.47 percent. Between 494,500 and 1,010,500 people therefore need treatment annually in the United States. Lifetime prevalence—the percentage of those now living who have had or are likely to have schizophrenia at some point in their lives—is 1 percent in the United States, yielding a total of about 2,150,000. The United States incidence is somewhat lower than that shown in European and Asiatic studies: 0.085 percent in large communities no matter what the social structure (Slater and Cowie, 1971). Projection on a worldwide basis results in an incidence between 1,500,000 and 3,000,000, a prevalence between 6,900,000 and 14,100,000 at any given time, and a lifetime prevalence of 30,000,000. The total direct and indirect cost of schizophrenia to the United States is estimated to be $14 billion annually. (See chapter 29, "Psychiatric Epidemiology," for further discussion of the incidence and prevalence of psychiatric disorders.)

Among the factors affecting the development of schizophrenia, *age, sex, and marital status* appear to be particularly important. Most schizophrenia begins in the mid-teens and continues at a high level of incidence until the mid-fifties. Incidence decreases with each successive decade for men but starts high for women aged fifteen to twenty-four, increases between twenty-five and thirty-four, and levels off at a slightly lower level until age fifty-five. More women than men become schizophrenic. Farina and his colleagues (1963) found the rate of schizophrenia to be identical for men and women who remained married. The rate was much higher, however, among women who were separated or divorced than for married women. Among schizophrenics or schizophrenics-to-be, men appeared to remain single more frequently, while women married and then separated and divorced. The meaning of these sexual differences in the pattern of incidence is not clear. What is certain is that the illness affects the individual in his most productive period. Except for two studies (Schooler, 1961; Rao, 1964), the results of which may have been influenced by other factors, no relationship has been found between schizophrenia and *birth order*.

Differences also appear among *ethnic and religious groups*. Incidence of schizophrenia among Jews in the United States is slightly lower than among Protestants and Catholics (Malzberg, 1930, 1931, 1959). Blacks and Puerto Ricans are two to two and one-half times as likely to be schizophrenic as whites (Malzberg, 1956, 1959).

Geographical mobility is an important factor in the incidence of mental disorders including schizophrenia (see chapter 13, "Affective Disorders"). In general, the more extreme the change, the more pronounced the effect will be. Transition from one culture or country to another is more important than the mere distance traveled (see Astrup and Ødegård, 1960; Cade and Krupinski, 1962; Leacock, 1957; Malzberg, 1962; Ødegård, 1936; Tietze, Lemkau, and Cooper, 1942). There are, however, some interesting exceptions to this rule. European Jews emigrating to Israel, for example, had a lower rate of schizophrenia than the indigenous Jewish population in Israel (Halevi, 1963); perhaps in this instance the motive and emotional meaning of migration outweighed its stresses. At the other extreme, some isolated towns in northern Sweden have an incidence of schizophrenia three times the world rate of 0.085 percent.

The epidemiological picture of schizophrenia has changed recently in one important respect: the number of hospitalized schizophrenics in the United States has been decreasing since 1955. This population fell from 223,000 in 1966 to 163,000 in 1970 and continues to decrease. At the same time, the annual rate of discharge has risen from 3.4 percent in 1967 to 9.4 percent in 1970 (Gunderson et al., 1974). Among the causes of this reduction in the number of hospitalized schizophrenics are increased use of drugs, a less stigmatizing attitude toward mental illness, open-door policies, the use of night and day hospital care, and the trend toward increased treatment in community mental health centers (see chapter 18, "Chemotherapy"). These optimistic statistics are in some sense misleading, however, since regardless of the total number in hospitals, half of all hospitalized mental patients are schizophrenics. The disease is tenacious, and annual readmission rates have doubled at the same time as the proportion of patients hospitalized has decreased. Thus, despite many encouraging developments, incidence and prevalence remain the same as before the more recent treatment settings and modalities were introduced.

Socioepidemiological theories. Investigations of the relationship between social factors and schizophrenia have, for the most part, focused on social class and residence patterns. Landis and Page (1938) found that the rate of schizophrenia varied with the size of United States cities; Arieti (1975) pointed out similar relationships for different parts of Italy. Faris and Dunham (1939), working in the United States, noted a high density of schizophrenics in urban ghettos and other underprivileged parts of the city. This finding led to two contradictory views: first, that schizophrenics drift to such areas because they are socially and economically incompetent and can more easily be absorbed in a disorganized environment, and, second, that such areas "breed" schizophrenics because they are populated by people laden with severe socioeconomic problems (see chapter 29, "Psychiatric Epidemiology"). Clark (1948, 1949) attempted to broaden this concept of "drift" to encompass movement from higher to lower status occupations. Faris himself (1955) considers high degrees of social isolation and disintegration—conditions that are intensified in the central city—as powerful causal factors in schizophrenia.

Leighton (1959) has suggested that rapid social change results in social disequilibrium and accentuates poverty, cultural confusion, secularization, family strife, and fragmented communications networks. This social disorganization may, in turn, result in individual alienation, unmet personal needs, and higher rates of mental illness. Leighton believes that as societies have evolved from close-knit villages to urban and industrial systems, vulnerability to psychiatric disease has increased. Yet the few methodologically sound cross-cultural epidemiological studies show that the incidence of the most common psychosis, schizophrenia, is the same in all societies. Leighton's theory, then, does not fully account for the incidence of psychosis.

Mishler and Scotch (1963) have reviewed cross-cultural and epidemiological studies from the preceding twenty-five years and have found that the highest incidence of schizophrenia was consistently in the lowest socioeconomic class (measured by occupation), while the lowest rate was found almost as consistently in the managerial class. No conclusions were drawn about the relationship of migration and social mobility to the incidence of schizophrenia, and no consistent evidence is presented on variations in rates of schizophrenia in different cultures or the impact of changing one's culture on the incidence of schizophrenia.

In reviewing a large number of studies, Kohn (1968) notes that rates of all mental disorders, particularly schizophrenia, are highest at the lowest socioeconomic levels of society. This correlation is most dramatic in cities with populations greater than 500,000, although it is also seen in cities of between 100,000 and 500,000 people; it is not noted in small towns or in rural areas. Kohn contends that the notion of downward mobility, implying a "drift" from a higher to a lower status, is not relevant to schizophrenics; because the schizophrenic has never experienced achievement, his mobility along an occupational axis is negligible. Kohn notes the direct relationship between stress and mental disturbance found in the Midtown Manhattan study (Srole et al., 1962). Furthermore, Rogler and Hollingshead's study of lower-class schizophrenics in San Juan, Puerto Rico (1965) indicates that during the year prior to the onset of illness, schizophrenics-to-be suffer more significant stress in their families than others in lower-class or working-class strata. These findings raise the possibility that patterns of family relationships may contribute to stress precipitating schizophrenia.

Waxler (1974) holds that societies neither cause different rates of mental disorder nor tolerate different degrees of deviance but that they do respond in different ways to psychiatric illness once it occurs. Because social labeling is an indicator of social expectations (telling the patient what he is and what he can and cannot expect of himself), the responses of helpers and others in the society may actually prolong the patient's sickness. Waxler sees the relative power of the patient in the treatment system as crucial to the maintenance or abandonment of his role as a patient. If his family supports him, the patient also does better in dealing with his illness.

The "antipsychiatry" movement represents an attempt to redefine psychosis as a social and interpersonal situation rather than as a disease. In part, it has arisen from psychiatry's increasing emphasis on the importance of interpersonal relationships in producing, maintaining, and treating the disease. This movement is a protest against the longstanding tendency of psychiatrists to react to schizophrenia as something to be actively dealt with by the therapist and endured passively by the patient. Certainly the thoughtless and neglectful care of many patients has provided understandable impetus for movements that seek to refocus study and treatment on more humane bases. We ourselves do not believe, however, that viewing the illness solely as an interpersonal phenomenon acknowledges the importance of individual inner dynamics; such a view may even exacerbate the patient's pathology.

Both of the psychiatrist's roles—that of father confessor and that of prison warden—have led to excesses. The "anti-" school is part of the recurrent protest movement in psychiatry that sensitizes us both to the difficulty of seeing the schizophrenic as a suffering human being and to the ease with which psychiatrists slip into the comfortable roles of diagnostician, researcher, or caregiver. Siirala (1961, 1963), for example, sees schizophrenia as emerging from a common sickness—in his delusions the schizophrenic delivers prophecies, which psychiatrists should reveal, to explain society's collective guilt for crimes committed and concealed through the centuries. Laing (1960, 1967) sees schizophrenia as a way of dealing with an impossible, persecuting family; in his view, it is not a disease but the result of a diseased relationship and, consequently, the only sane way to live with sick people. For Szasz (1961), the term *schizophrenia* is a dangerous diagnostic category; he questions its use on several grounds: (1) only symptoms with demonstrable physical lesions qualify as manifestations of disease; (2) mental symptoms are subjective in nature and depend on sociocultural and ethical norms; (3) mental symptoms are expressions of problems in living; and (4) psychiatric problems are not illnesses but conflicts over ways of achieving social values and are distorted by psychiatrists' use of medical terminology.

Clinical Features

Although it is not yet clear what causes schizophrenia, and although opinions differ on objective criteria for diagnosing the disorder, characteristic groups of symptoms can be described with considerable accuracy. Four major factors contribute to each individual's clinical picture: (1) inherited factors, which are still poorly understood, (2) early deprivation, frustration, pain, and trauma endured by the patient; (3) the character structure derived from the patient's mode of dealing with early trauma; and, especially, (4) the availability or lack of a sustaining figure who has ministered to the patient's needs and helped him maintain psychic equilibrium, albeit with psychotic defenses. An individual's pattern of psychotic regression may be as personal as his fingerprints yet no more significant in predicting onset, course, or outcome of his illness. Nevertheless, because of the need to note progression and regression, to evaluate the effects of therapy, and to compare individuals and populations, we will discuss the signs of the illness and its major subtypes.

Signs and Symptoms

Eugen Bleuler (1911) believed the essential disease process to be the splitting of the personality, shown in four main ways: disturbance of associations, disturbance of affect, autism, and heightened ambivalence, often called the "four A's." When associative links between thoughts are loosened or destroyed, looseness of associations occurs and bizarre, illogical, and chaotic thinking results. When affect is split, it becomes inappropriate and mood is exaggerated, indifferent, shallow, or flattened. Autism is the absorption in private, subjective ideas, including daydreams, delusions, and hallucinations; as these increase, the patient loses contact with reality. Ambivalence is expressed in uncertain, hesitant affect. The combined result of these four disturbances is that the patient is unable to organize meaningful, logical, consistent thoughts, behavior, or interactions.

Kurt Schneider's list of the first-rank signs and symptoms of schizophrenia (1957, 1971) includes delusions; hearing one's thoughts spoken aloud; auditory hallucinations concerning one's behavior (giving orders, describing or mocking the prescribed behavior); somatic hallucinations; feeling that one's thoughts are controlled; feeling that one's thoughts spread to other people and affect their behavior; and feeling that one's actions are controlled or influenced from the outside. Some clinicians believe these signs and symptoms primarily describe paranoid people and are therefore too narrow; others find them broad enough to apply to illnesses other than schizophrenia as well.

Schizophrenia may affect the patient's perceptions, thoughts, affect, will, speech, motor control, and social behavior. Disturbances in each of these areas are discussed below.

Perceptual disorders. Hallucinations, sense perceptions without related external stimuli, are most frequently auditory but may be visual, olfactory, or gustatory. Patients may also experience coenesthetic hallucinations, or perceptions of altered states in body organs with no known psychological mechanism to account for them ("My brain is throbbing," "My liver is rotting"). In present-day clinical situations, however, such complaints may be masked by involving the patient too quickly in milieu and drug therapy.

Patients with perceptual disorders may also experience *déjà vu* and feelings of unfamiliarity with their environment. Light may look brighter or dimmer; people may seem larger (macropsia) or smaller (micropsia), closer or further away; and time may seem to pass too slowly or too quickly.

Cognitive disorders. Schizophrenic delusions are false beliefs not amenable to change by reason or experience. Although their source is personal, their content has a cultural context. In Mesmer's day, patients spoke of being influenced by magnetism; now they may speak of being influenced by atomic radiation. Delusions of persecution—feelings of being tortured by unknown forces—are the chief symptom in paranoid schizophrenia and often have an unconscious sexual meaning (Tausk, 1919). Their counterparts, delusions of grandeur, indicate that the individual considers himself important enough to be persecuted. In both instances, the patient derives some comfort from these delusions, since he is the focus of attention, even if malevolent.

Periods of fright may be followed by a sense of revelation, of suddenly understanding the true meaning of one's life. End of the world (*Weltuntergang*) fantasies also occur (Conrad, 1958), as do ideas of reference, in which hidden, mystical meanings that point to issues in the individual's private life are ascribed to everyday events; songs on the radio, for example, may indicate to the patient that his sad state is appreciated. In noting the mystical-magical thinking of schizophrenics, Storch (1924) related it to primary process thinking in dreams; both use mechanisms of distortion, condensation, reversal, and substitution. Goldstein (1946) has interpreted these cognitive disorders as a tendency toward concrete thinking accompanied by loss of the ability to think abstractly or decreased ability to generalize from specific examples. Cancro (1968) has found that, although patients retained the ability to think abstractly, they also showed autistic thinking.

Von Dormarus (1946) observes that schizophrenics' reasoning is based on identifying an insignificant quality shared by unlike objects. Thus patients may connect objects on the basis of spatial or temporal proximity or even similarity of sound (*Klang*), in associations such as marriage/carriage/disparage. Schizophrenic thinking also includes a teleological view of events as dependent on the will of others.

Cameron (1938) notes a tendency toward overinclusiveness, or focusing on irrelevant details, which results from the loosening of associations. Payne (1966) attributes overinclusiveness to a central impairment of the process of filtering incoming stimuli, usually occuring during a delusional mood. Shakow (1971) describes neophobia, an intense fear of anything new and an exaggerated need to cling to old patterns. In addition, the schizophrenic may suffer from blocked thoughts and speech; he may suddenly stop responding, may respond after a pause of even minutes, or may simply become perplexed.

These distortions of thinking creep into every aspect of the schizophrenic's life—his speech, work, and art—and they all follow highly personal, autistic, and unconventional rules. Such expressions differ from the consciously unconventional approaches of a style like cubism, which, although highly symbolic, has a basis in generally accepted organized thinking and thus appeals to people other than the artist. The schizophrenic's symbolism is private and bizarre, in part self-expressive and in part defensive.

Disorders of affect. Most schizophrenics express their feelings less frequently and less intensely than normal people, so that they appear indifferent or apathetic. The most clearly pathognomonic sign is emotional shallowness. Judgments about appropriate emotions must, however, be measured against cultural norms and considered in the light of the individual's testimony that he has lost empathy with others. The schizophrenic may be unable to experience pleasure (anhedonia), and the responses of hebephrenics, in particular, may be unsuitable to the situation; the patient may, for example, laugh on hearing of the death of a loved one. Inappropriate affect (parathymia) may result from the breakthrough of private feelings or from the patient's inability to express his mood exactly. Emotions described by the patient as "strange" are experienced during both the acute breakdown and exacerbations of the illness; they may include exaltation of mood, an oceanic feeling of oneness with the universe, ecstasy, religiosity, and apprehension about the destruction of one's body and the world. These disorders of affect occur in extremes of catatonic frenzy and catatonic stupor. Frenzy takes the form of ceaseless excitement and loud, incoherent talking and shouting. Catatonic stupor is apparent in the patient's lack of spontaneity as well as in muteness, negativism, imitation of the movements and gestures of the person the patient is observing (echopraxia), and repetition of complicated acts regardless of context (stereotypy).

Volitional disorders. The schizophrenic's ambivalence and negativism and his fear of the destructiveness of his negative wishes impair or paralyze his will. Although ambivalence, the simultaneous experience of opposite feelings or desires, is present in nearly everyone, it is more intense in the schizophrenic than in normal people; it serves him as a mechanism to deny pain and to avoid dealing with conflicts. Ambivalence is dramatically evident in the case of a patient observed hitting his mother's right cheek with one hand while caressing her left cheek with the other. Some patients express negativism by refusing to carry out any request or doing the opposite; others obey automatically and mechanically.

Verbal disorders. The schizophrenic's language tends to be excessively concrete yet privately symbolic. His speech or writing may be incoherent, a form of self-expression rather than communication, and often contains made-up words (neologisms) related to his personal dilemma. Some patients become monosyllabic or mute. Others repeat words and phrases spoken by the interviewer (echolalia) in what may be a desperate effort to contact the interviewer, but the effect of which is to push him away. Regressed schizophrenics may repeat words and phrases senselessly (verbigeration). Such disturbances of normal speech, once observed frequently in state hospitals, are rarely seen in community practice today because patients are engaged in therapy sooner. Some chronic patients show stilted and grotesquely quaint use of language, a compromise between expressing thoughts and scrambling their inner, hidden meaning.

Motor disorders. Although motor activity is generally reduced in schizophrenics, extreme excitement may occur or motion may become awkward. Mannerisms are seen in speech and

movement. Grimaces may be grotesque or ticlike; when they appear as gestures of disapproval, they indicate that the patient is censoring his own thoughts. Echopraxia occurs in motorically disturbed (catatonic) patients; this and other forms of imitation may represent the patient's attempt to get close to another person by being like him, while submerging all disagreement in the process. Requests may be carried out in robotlike fashion (automatism), as if the patient were saying, "I satisfy you, so don't bother me." In chronic schizophrenics, stereotypy is seen. The extremes of stupor and catalepsy, including waxy flexibility (in which a limb placed in a particular position is allowed to remain there for long periods), occur in neglected chronic schizophrenics.

Disorders of social behavior. Psychiatry's increasing emphasis on interpersonal relationships in recent years has been reflected in the study of disturbances of social behavior. In the case of schizophrenics, withdrawal ranging from intense shyness to outright reclusiveness has been noted. Grinker and Holzman (1973) identified five independent areas of disturbance in the schizophrenic, the first of which, cognitive disorder, we have already discussed. The other four emerge from disturbed interpersonal relationships; they are a disturbance of the capacity to experience pleasure, especially pleasure with other people; a strong tendency to be dependent on others; an impairment in social competence; and a particularly vulnerable self-image.

As regression continues, especially in neglected patients, patterns of behavior deteriorate to the extent that the patient no longer performs the usual social amenities, takes care of his appearance, or keeps himself clean. The deeply regressed patient may have fits of screaming, hoard worthless articles, put things into his mouth, and smear or eat feces; women may hide things in the vagina. Self-mutilation occurs in fewer than 1 percent of cases (Panteleev, Yanatchkova, and Pashkova, 1972). Nineteen percent of schizophrenics attempt suicide, and between 2 and 3 percent succeed (Niskanen and Achté, 1972)—a remarkably low figure, considering the nature of their life-and-death struggle. Suicide attempts are often made during the onset of the first episode, when the patient senses something terrible happening to his mind and feels there is no one to whom he can turn for help. Attempts at suicide also occur during periods of depression in chronic schizophrenia. Although catatonics and enraged paranoids may be violent, homicide is rare. Lehmann (1975) reports one homicide a year among 10,000 patients in the community over a period of thirty years and attributes both suicide and homicide to the schizophrenic's profound sensitivity to rejection by a figure on whom he relies.

The Major Syndromes

In 1898 Kraepelin organized the signs and symptoms of dementia praecox into three clinical syndromes, now known as catatonic, hebephrenic, and paranoid schizophrenia. Bleuler (1911) redefined schizophrenia as a single psychopathological reaction with varying outcomes and added simple schizophrenia to Kraepelin's list. In addition to these four classical syndromes, we shall consider less common, less well-defined syndromes such as childhood schizophrenia, schizoaffective schizophrenia, and postpartum schizophrenia.

Simple schizophrenia. Simple schizophrenia appears during or after puberty and is characterized both by an insidious loss of ambition and interest in life and by a progressive deterioration of the personality. The patient may experience transient hallucinations and delusions and may withdraw increasingly from friends and family. He may drop out of school or quit work, sleep during the daytime and stay awake at night, or wander impulsively and purposelessly in the neighborhood or across the country. The simple schizophrenic's intense denial and refusal to consider anything important defends him against the pain that characterizes his life.

A nineteen-year-old woman was admitted to the hospital after deteriorating in personality over several years. She had been close to her mother, who fought constantly with the patient's alcoholic father. A plain girl, she complained in high school that boys did not like her. She avoided her classmates and family, stayed up at night, showered for long periods, and took

long walks; on some of these walks she was promiscuous. She complained that the neighbors were talking about her, calling her a whore. After graduating from high school with failing grades, she took a secretarial course and obtained an office job. She refused to work after becoming convinced that the other employees were talking about her. She talked of going to Hollywood to become a movie star but stayed in her room except for her nightly walks. At the same time, she stopped washing herself or combing her hair, complained of semen in her milk, refused to eat, and lost weight. She developed a grimace of disapproval and blinked her eyes. Finally, unable to deal with her, her mother brought her to the hospital.

This case represents a typical history of the regressive course of a simple schizophrenic. The patient, faced with an embattled family situation, withdraws from the challenges of the end of adolescence. She censures her own sexuality, by turns acting out her fantasies and projecting her disapproval of them. Similarly, her alternate preoccupation with and avoidance of bathing and grooming reflect her view of herself as dirty and her consequent judgment of herself as immoral.

Hebephrenic schizophrenia. Hebephrenic patients, whose disorder appears during late adolescence, regress to primitive, disorganized behavior, exhibit marked thought disorder and limited social contact, and appear disheveled and unconcerned about themselves. They may seem stubbornly unresponsive, or their emotional responses may be inappropriate, characteristically marked by silly grins and outbursts of laughter.

A twenty-two-year-old seamstress was admitted to the hospital after becoming reclusive at home and neglecting herself. She had been a shy, quiet, compliant girl, who had brought her pay home, keeping only a small amount for personal expenses. The family arranged for her to date several men, but she made no effort to engage them socially. She began to make mistakes at work, combining inappropriate colors and threads and sewing sleeves to waistbands. When she was fired, she feared telling her mother and locked herself in the bathroom, laughing and singing at the top of her voice. When the family brought her to the hospital, she withdrew further, walked barefoot or with one slipper on, and wrapped herself in a blanket like a toga. She wiped her lips repeatedly and fastidiously until a callus appeared. She replied yes or no randomly to all questions and continued pacing and smiling to herself.

The hebephrenic reaction of this patient to her inability to face her own identity and independence at the beginning of adulthood was an extreme continuation of her previous shyness and compliance. Rather than confront her terror of adulthood, she withdrew into bizarre behavior socially and at work and, finally, in the hospital.

Catatonic schizophrenia. The essential feature of catatonic schizophrenia is abnormal motor behavior. It appears in late adolescence or early adulthood. Spontaneous activity is reduced sometimes to the point of catatonic stupor. In this state, the patient may demonstrate muteness, negativism, stereotypy, echopraxia, or automatic obedience; intermittent outbursts of excitement or, in rare cases, waxy flexibility may occur. Intravenous injections of barbiturates can allay the symptoms of stupor for a few hours so that the patient can respond normally. Recovered patients and those in therapy report that they were frozen in immobility as a solution to their intense ambivalence. In catatonic excitement, the patient may talk and shout to the point of incoherence or become overactive and destructive or assaultive. Without medical help some patients exhaust themselves and die. In these instances modern drug therapy (usually with one of the major tranquilizers) may save the patient's life.

In catatonic patients, extremes of incoherence, overactivity, and underactivity are forms of intense denial.

A twenty-seven-year-old coal heaver lost his father and, within six months, became withdrawn, gestured inappropriately, and frequently fell to his knees to pray and crossed himself at home, in the street, and at work. He also, uncharacteristically, took lessons in ballroom dancing. He was admitted to the hospital in a state of excitement, complaining that voices called him a queer and that cars came by the house, flashing their lights on and off as signals. He became

negativistic, then blocked in speech and thought to the point of muteness. His bouts of demonstrative silent prayer often ended in an attack on one of the staff or other patients. After he had been subdued by several attendants and sedated, he would be silent and withdrawn for an indeterminate period, which would be followed by renewed prayers and violence. Finally, after he had attacked and hurt several people, he was lobotomized. (These events occurred before modern drug treatments were available.)

Catatonia is an attempt to deal with massive rage by the extremes of muscular immobility and outbursts of destructive behavior. To control his explosive, "masculine" rage following the death of his father, this patient turned to what were for him "feminine" interests, such as dancing; when this change was insufficient to contain or assuage his rage, he resorted to extreme religiosity. Since neither approach dealt successfully with his loss, he would erupt intermittently in catatonic excitement.

Paranoid schizophrenia. The paranoid schizophrenic has delusions of persecution and of grandeur. He is tense, suspicious, guarded, and reserved to the point of being vague or even mute, like a catatonic. He may be hostile or aggressive yet can conduct himself well socially. In some patients, suspiciousness leads to litigiousness. Intelligence is well preserved, in contrast to other subtypes of the disease, and can be used freely in areas not affected by pathological ideas. Paranoid schizophrenics tend to become symptomatic later than catatonics and hebephrenics— that is, in their late twenties and early thirties. The paranoid patient's use of projection as his main defense reveals ego resources greater than those of other schizophrenics because it reduces inner tension more effectively than the defenses of denial, distortion, and other primary process mechanisms used by catatonic and hebephrenic patients.

A twenty-five-year-old college graduate stopped working as a secretary upon hearing of her mother's impending operation for glaucoma. She became fearful and began sleeping in her mother's bed at night. After she stopped eating for fear of being poisoned, she was admitted to the hospital, where she stood in corners or walked about smiling knowingly. She had many delusions: people were out to hurt her; the radio mocked her thoughts and commented on her every act; if she sat down, a penis in the chair would enter her vagina against her will, and she wanted to remain a virgin until she was married. She thought a television camera was concealed in the shower head, so she refused to take showers; at night she thought the bed vibrated and that everyone therefore knew she was having intercourse. After a strong disagreement with her therapist, she felt that he was two different people, one good and one bad. She tried to explain herself and her sufferings endlessly and helplessly.

This patient reacted to the threatened loss of her mother by resorting to a paranoid delusional thought system. She acted out her need for infantile comfort by getting into bed with her mother and dealt with increased tension by projecting her impulses onto others, hoping that they would share responsibility for them. She disapproved of her sexual impulses and projected them onto her surroundings—the shower head, the chair, and the bed. She also projected her self-disapproval onto the people around her, who she thought were whispering about her. She could tolerate little frustration from the therapist without resorting to splitting him into two people.

Other Syndromes

Childhood schizophrenia, or infantile autism, a rare disease that affects 0.03 percent of children at any given time (one tenth the prevalence of adult schizophrenia), appears before puberty. In the first year of life, the childhood schizophrenic shows abnormalities in motor behavior and muscular control that lead to poor motor coordination and result in spinning and twirling. He stares, unable to communicate normally or make eye contact with people, and the interviewer or parent feels the absence of emotional contact. The child may have normal intelligence but may not speak until the age of five or six, or he may lose developed speech. Sleep patterns are disturbed, and the child does not respond to ma-

ternal affection, does not distinguish between animate and inanimate objects, takes no interest in pets, and shows repetitive, stereotyped behavior. Islands of normal behavior may nonetheless remain. *Schizoaffective schizophrenia* is dominated by schizophrenic signs—thought disorders or reports of feeling controlled by outside forces, for instance—with the addition of an affective abnormality. When blatant enough, the euphoria (playful and overactive behavior) or depression (depressed demeanor and behavior, often with suicidal ideas) of schizoaffective schizophrenia can be distinguished from the usual inappropriateness of affect seen in schizophrenics. The schizoaffective type has a better prognosis than other schizophrenics but a poorer one than the manic-depressive. *Postpartum schizophrenia* occurs after childbirth and may be due to endocrine changes, changes in body image, or activation of unconscious psychological conflicts related to pregnancy and the intrapsychic reorganization required to become a mother. Zilboorg (1929) and other authors have focused on the role of hostility during pregnancy and after delivery in the appearance of the disorder.

Differential Diagnosis

The first step in the differential diagnosis of schizophrenia is to rule out circulatory or metabolic diseases such as cerebral arteriosclerosis, hyperthyroidism, or hypothyroidism, which could account for the schizophrenialike symptoms. Toxic psychosis caused by alcohol or street drugs (amphetamines, LSD, or other hallucinogens) must also be eliminated as causes. The patient's own history of drug use is notoriously unreliable because patients are often both ashamed of their use of drugs and defiant about it. A drug psychosis resolves within a few days, however, making it clear that the patient is not schizophrenic.

It is important to distinguish schizophrenic behavior from that of the adolescent, who also is typically preoccupied with abstract philosophical ideas, has changes in mood, is shy and introspective, and spends his time daydreaming. The patient's history and the details of his current disturbance, together with a careful study of his thought processes, affect, and method of meeting developmental hurdles, help to clarify the diagnosis (see chapter 24, "The Adolescent").

The counterculture, once strictly an adolescent phenomenon, poses problems in the diagnosis of schizophrenia now that it affects older age groups. Many of its attitudes and jargon ("I'm getting bad vibes from you") are reminiscent of those of the schizophrenic. These aspects include (1) interest in Eastern philosophic concepts that might strike Westerners as bizarre, (2) unexpected dramatic behavior, and (3) suspicion and defiance toward conventional, scientific, and analytic thinking. Such behavior may be seen among normal people in the counterculture, as well as among eccentrics, psychopaths, or schizophrenics-to-be. The individual whose traits reflect his allegiance to the counterculture can be distinguished from the schizophrenic, through continuing observation, by the stability of his thinking and emotional life and by the consistency of his active goals.

Neurotic symptoms may overlie schizophrenia and make the diagnosis difficult. The schizophrenic may exhibit hysterical features, including conversion, and obsessive-compulsive behavior in dealing with neurotic conflicts over love and competition. A patient who appears hysterical or severely obsessive may actually be a borderline schizophrenic and go on to develop full-blown schizophrenia. The presence of extreme neurotic symptoms, therefore, does not rule out schizophrenia.

The distinction between schizophrenia and affective psychosis is sometimes problematic. The frenzied catatonic's essential disturbance is thought disorder, to which his hyperactivity is a reaction; his acts are consequently unpredictable and senseless; his affect, difficult to understand; and his speech, irrational. His attention may not be easy to engage, since he is preoccupied with bizarre, fragmented, autistic thoughts. The primary disturbance of the manic-depressive, on the other hand, is his high or low mood and overactivity or underactivity; his easy distractibility reflects his need to avoid inner pain. Depressive psychoses may resemble catatonic pictures, but disturbed thinking is crucial to a schizophrenic diagnosis. In contrast, gloomy thoughts,

depressed mood, and disturbed sleep will predominate in a depressed schizoaffective patient.

Psychological testing alone cannot yield a definitive diagnosis of schizophrenia, although it may be useful in predicting outcome. In general, the clinical experience of the tester may be more useful than the tests themselves. In the Rorschach test, the schizophrenic's confabulation or contaminated responses (for example, mixtures of sexual and geographic imagery) are reminiscent of the juxtapositions in his art. Some of the more common responses to the Rorschach cards, such as human content and movement, are lacking. The TAT (Thematic Apperception Test) is not so useful as a diagnostic indicator as it is in specifying issues that are important to the patient. In drawing tests, the schizophrenic reveals regressive trends and disturbances in his own body image through his mannered, grotesque representations of people and objects. Intelligence tests show greatly divergent levels of achievement; verbal, vocabulary, and information scores are generally high while performance scores are low. Yet responses are overinclusive, focusing on irrelevant details; on the other hand, because of his preoccupation, the patient is unable to complete missing details. The Minnesota Multiphasic Personality Inventory (MMPI), a standardized self-report inventory based on 550 statements to be answered true or false, can be useful in corroborating the presence of thought disturbance in doubtful cases but is unreliable when used alone.

All diagnostic signs for schizophrenia notwithstanding, the experienced observer's intuitive recognition of the essential nature of the illness proves invaluable in making the diagnosis. Rümke (1959) described the "praecox feeling," the observer's reaction when empathy with the patient is so difficult to achieve that the observer *knows* he is dealing with a schizophrenic.

The Dynamics of Intrapsychic and Psychosocial Development

During the last thirty years, as interest in studying schizophrenia has grown, focus on the family has also increased. Initial observations emphasized the mother. Sullivan (1953a, 1953b) saw her as anxious; Fromm-Reichmann (1959) defined the "schizophrenogenic mother" as either overprotective or hostile, overtly or subtly rejecting, and distant. That mothers of schizophrenics had deep-seated problems of their own, in addition to those that arose in reaction to the patient, seemed undeniable. Observations of fathers revealed them to be either weak and ineffectual or authoritarian and paranoid. By the late 1950s, the role of the patient's entire family in his development of schizophrenia was recognized. Clinicians now realize that the interplay of family members as a unit is more important than the particular qualities of any one of them. Whether its behavior patterns are based on anxiety, coldness, aloofness, or aggression, the family is nonetheless highly organized for the single goal of staying together.

These observations have led to formulations of family interaction and bonding patterns by Lidz, Wynne and Singer, Bateson, and Jackson (discussed earlier in this chapter). In the view of these theoreticians, family patterns of interaction provide a significant part of the background as well as the substance for the child's development of schizophrenia. That is, growing up disarms the child, making him less capable of coping, and also provides the issues that go on to preoccupy him. Each parent's personality and behavior, the couple's interaction, and their particular form of bonding are independent variables affecting the child's condition. The cost of the parents' modes of dealing with inner turmoil is paid by the child, who becomes schizophrenic. His development of the disorder is tied to characteristic attitudes and difficulties at various stages.

Infancy and Early Childhood

The normal child receives sufficient physical and emotional satisfaction from the mother in early life to develop feelings of basic trust in both the mother and himself and basic optimism toward life so that he feels he can grow up and become an autonomous human being. The child's self-image includes both qualities he views as desirable and others he considers noxious; it is made up of his body image (itself partly physiological and partly emotional), his sense of his own identity apart from his parents, and his impressions of his parents' view of him. Accumu-

lated feelings about himself and memories of interactions with the parents are assimilated as internal images (introjects) of the self and the parents. If these images and memories derive from primarily positive and satisfying interactions, they help the child sustain lonely moments and give him strength to face problems, even the difficult parts of the relationship with the mother. The introjects govern the child's attitudes toward himself and others and his behavior in interpersonal relationships; thus they determine whether his negotiation of early developmental stages will be successful or not.

The child interprets these internalized psychic events according to the mode of thinking available to him at each developmental stage. In infancy he becomes accustomed to his mother. At the same time he begins to think teleologically; he believes, sometimes inappropriately, that events depend on the will of others—a form of early universal thinking revived by the adult schizophrenic, particularly the paranoid. Although some schizophrenics seem to have been cared for adequately as infants (Arieti, 1975), difficulties arise when they begin to show signs of gaining individuality and separating from the mother at the age of about nine months (Mahler, 1963). The Kleinians feel that the basic damage is done earlier, within the first six to nine months of life. A small proportion of children (perhaps those who become hyperkinetic or who have minimal brain damage, which they outgrow) show that something is terribly wrong within themselves by persistent crying and restlessness; the mother's anxiety may precipitate or increase this reaction.

Nonlogical primary process thinking predominates during the first three years of life in normal people and remains in their dream life; remnants of primary process thinking are seen in schizophrenics' defensive patterns of denial, projection, and distortion (Semrad, 1966). This mode of thinking is gradually replaced by secondary process thinking—that is, by conventional logic.

According to the Freudians, the nucleus of the growing child's ego is formed by complementary inner experiences, including introjects of mother (all the infant knows about the mother as well as his emotional reaction to her) and self-images (inherited images, growing sexual feelings, body image, identity, and the sense of pleasing or displeasing the parents). In Kleinian terms, these inner experiences form internal objects; in Arieti's terms, the child's self-image. More recent psychoanalysts have described them as self-and-object representations.

When the preschizophrenic's mother is anxious, angry, guilty, or withdrawn, the child experiences frustration and—in the absence of counterbalancing positive experiences—his self-image is distorted. The mother recognizes the child's negative self-image and responds by feeling even more guilty, hostile, or detached; her reaction, in turn, increases the child's frustration. Thus both contribute to the self-perpetuating cycle. The child's lack of a preponderance of good experiences with his mother makes it difficult for him to separate from her completely and gain sufficient individuality. He understands his suffering in terms of primary process thinking and blames himself. When this feeling cannot be successfully repressed, the next solution available is to project the conflict onto the external world. The father is experienced in the same way as the mother. The situation becomes even more complicated in cases in which the usual parental roles are reversed and the father is too weak to be able to counteract the mother's effects on the child.

The interplay between the preschizophrenic child's self-image and the parents' projection of their affective state onto that child has crucial ramifications for his development. Because his body image is stunted, the child feels weak or monstrous and has doubts about his sexual identity. Basically, he is aware of this situation, but he may feel it is advantageous to identify with the more threatening parent (perceived as an aggressor) in order to be able to deal with him or her. This identification makes him feel more aggressive himself and further distorts his self-image. If the child feels rejected by both parents, his sexual identity is still further weakened; any sexual identity feels dangerous and he may refuse to identify with either parent. Such children may become autistic and refuse to learn the parents' language, using neologisms instead.

Girls may prematurely turn to their fathers for comfort, but this clinging raises incest fears and represents an unworkable solution; because of the girl's basic identification with the mother, she cannot tolerate incestuous feelings. The boy who turns to his father to escape from his mother is threatened by homosexual concerns and may protect himself against them by a stormy relationship with the father.

Within this psychic context, self-esteem is poisoned by frustration, bitterness, anger, guilt, and withdrawal. Rather than face his introjected images of his mother as a dangerous person, the child may change these into merely distressing images of her, so that he settles for a chronically dissatisfying, though less painful, relationship both with her and with people generally. Another solution is to tell himself that he is intrinsically bad. Thus he maintains the fiction that his mother is after all good, since she is his main source of sustenance. This attempt to transform the image of the dangerous mother into a good one cannot, however, be carried out successfully, and the patient retains a weak and helpless self-image.

Later Childhood

At latency, particularly at school, the child enters the larger world. For the preschizophrenic child, the intellect, now reinforced by secondary process thinking and the defenses of intellectualization and rationalization, helps submerge much early turmoil. He still feels, however, no basic trust, no dependable sense of acceptance, and no ease of communication. The child enters latency having had to deny a large part of his inner life, a necessity that already deprives him of crucial inner resources and distorts his view of himself as both a separate and a sexual being.

Arieti (1975) sees two general patterns of prepsychotic behavior at this point in development, the schizoid type and the stormy type. The *schizoid personality* is aloof, detached, and less involved than normal people. He has learned that his parents do not respond favorably either to his attempts to please them by compliance or to his aggressive approaches. By avoiding both techniques, he minimizes assaults on his self-esteem and on his weak, superficial self-image. To achieve this detachment, he denies his emotions and distances himself physically from situations that arouse emotion, avoiding even eye contact with others. Yet the parents exert subtle pressures; the child goes through the motions of compliance to avoid displeasing them, but he remains uncommitted. This solution is unsatisfactory since the child's resentment, though deeply buried, grows. His isolation is never complete enough to protect him, and he longs to connect himself to people. Beneath his denial and even his lies is an intense yearning for life and people. Yet his introjects continue to force him to see others as a danger, a view that reinforces his isolation.

The *stormy prepsychotic*, according to Arieti, must be observed for relatively long periods of time to see that his behavior can change unexpectedly from compliance to aggression or detachment, without his being aware of its fluctuations; short periods of observation reveal one or two types of reaction but not their interrelationship. These behavior patterns develop in response to a mother and an immediate family who evince violent and unpredictable swings of mood and response. The inconsistent family interaction, the child's overwhelming sense of rejection, and his weak sense of sexual identity all reinforce his negative self-image. His sense of being "bad" is so devastating to his self-esteem that he tries to deny it by being "good." Vacillations between these extremes save some self-esteem, but at the expense of a stable identity. In later childhood, both stormy and schizoid types adjust to their families, and their families adjust to them. If these children are able to learn that not everyone is like their own mothers and fathers, they may be able to negotiate the future more effectively.

Adolescence

The schizoid type enters adolescence markedly detached and sensitive to defeat and aggression (even to the mild and pleasurable sadism inherent in joking). The battle is always that of the self against the parents. Some enter a religious order or the Army in an attempt to find good parents, to defy or outdo their own, or to submit to authority without responsibility. Others may join groups on the fringes of society, becoming bohemians, hippies, or street people. The schizoid

person may decrease his need for satisfaction to an absolute minimum and work in isolation on abstract projects. Because he perceives himself as having no feelings about his personal, immediate life, he may pretend to have emotions. When he attempts to choose a life course, his indifference makes it difficult for him to assert himself. If he does, old anxieties and memories of early experiences return to plague him so that he feels he is in the grip of criticizing authorities. His educational and work records deteriorate progressively, and his effectiveness is nullified.

During adolescence the stormy personality is unable to build a stable self-image, since the questions pertinent to this period (who he is, what he expects of himself, what society expects of him) increase self-doubts that are already intense. He may become continuously aggressive or pseudocompliant or may use alcohol and drugs excessively. Love affairs, marriage, and jobs increase his anxiety and concomitant strange behavior. His attempts to engage life and people fail because they are inadequate and shallow, and he appears bizarre.

The preschizophrenic leaves latency with increased ability to rely on his intellectual defenses, which give him some hope for a better future. The psychological task of adolescence—clarifying his own identity and giving up his parents as sustaining and supporting figures—poses too great a threat for him, however. Because the preschizophrenic's relationship with his parents has been primarily bad, he cannot give them up. His attempts to relinquish dependence on his parents and to establish a separate identity for himself as an adult are thwarted by his inability to deal with the rage, disappointment, sadness, and self-devaluation that loss comprises; he cannot grieve successfully. The preschizophrenic senses that his life will be unsatisfactory and sees himself as inadequate, worthless, and unlovable. Thus the elements of loss and grief inherent in adolescent development present further obstacles to his emotional maturation.

The sexual urges of puberty confront the preschizophrenic with the incompleteness of his sexual identity and the flimsiness of his total personality. Either latent or conscious homosexual yearnings increase his anxiety about himself as a sexual being. If he acts out his compulsive homo-sexual wishes, he may come into conflict with society; if, however, he tries consciously to suppress his yearnings, his symptoms will increase under the pressure of sexual urges. Sexual indifference, a component of his general indifference, may provide an apparent solution to his dilemma. Above all, the preschizophrenic feels inadequate as a love object, and the conviction that he can never elicit love or sexual desire is devastating.

The Natural History of Schizophrenia

Before the onset of psychosis, the patient-to-be experiences panic; he has reached the end of his rope emotionally and sees no hope for the future. He is terrified and disorganized, foresees a danger, and tries to escape. Arieti (1975) notes two more elements in this panic. First, the catastrophe in adult life recalls the earliest failures in their primary process form; second, regressive thinking magnifies the hideous form of the defeat, so that everything seems useless. Feelings seem clear yet are unverbalized; the prepsychotic is afraid to put his feelings into words or ask for help.

In our view, the psychosis is a voluntary act on the part of the patient, a flight or avoidance mechanism in the face of unbearable pain. The patient tries to obliterate a powerful affect by forgetting the experience and the ideas or feelings that aroused it. The ego's rejection of both the disturbing affect and its cause precipitates the psychosis, since in choosing to treat the painful experience as if it had never taken place, the individual has rejected a portion of the reality crucial to his functioning. This rejection may lead to hallucinatory confusion; the content of the hallucinations is an accentuation of the thoughts aroused by the initial threatening experience. Obsessions may also result; if they are sufficiently intense, they may overwhelm the ego's capacity for critical judgment, and he may regress to using primitive defenses to diminish pain.

Onset

Schizophrenia may be acute or chronic in onset or may appear in response to life-cycle stress.

Acute onset is triggered by an event with critical intrapsychic meaning for the patient. In our experience, this catalyst is most often a loss, especially that of a person to whom the patient has been close and with whom he has had a mutually dependent relationship; this "compliant object" satisfies the patient's needs and uses him symbiotically so that he lives in false equilibrium until the loss.

When onset is acute, the patient is faced with three alternatives for dealing with his unbearable pain: homicide, suicide, or psychosis. He chooses psychosis and withdraws from a reality he can no longer endure. Illness emerges as the only option available for the survival of a particular individual, given his genetic background, his early developmental history, and his current environment of pain and frustration. This compromise between the patient's unbearable pain and the related rage and his need to survive contains an element of choice that is crucial to understanding the development of the psychosis-vulnerable individual, the psychosis itself, and especially its treatment (Semrad, 1966).

As the patient-to-be regresses from secondary process thinking and the use of intellectual defenses to primary process thinking and the use of the primitive defenses of denial, distortion, and projection, he reinterprets the event that precipitated his panic in terms of the earliest injuries to the self and experiences a growing sense of failure. For example, the paranoid schizophrenic who once felt that others were justified in looking down on him hints at a plot against him; just as be feels unjustly accused, he accuses the accuser. By blaming the FBI or the homosexuals for plotting against him, he can deny his original feelings that his parents were malevolent. The delusion of persecution, however, revives the psychotic's original terrifying view of his parents and his abject picture of himself. Some patients regress to intense denial ("I don't care") to mask their feelings of defeat; others distort reality with delusions to assuage pain.

As primary process thinking takes over, perception, cognition, and memory become contaminated with delusional thinking, and the sense of reality grows hazy. Because the patient's most severe problem is his enormous rage, he regresses in order to avoid dealing with both his anger and the loss that aroused it. Additional problems develop because present external reality is confused with memories of infantile psychological reality; the result is a state described by Federn as "loss of ego boundaries" (1952). The patient's uncertainty about his identity makes him afraid that he is coming apart physically, that his reactions and fate are magically interconnected with others', or that he is in control of all about him. At this point the acute psychosis is fully established.

Acute schizophrenia may also appear under the stress of important events in the life cycle—menarche in the female, for example, or (as Morel noted as early as 1860) erections and ejaculations in the adolescent male. Other critical events are graduating from high school or college or leaving graduate school; getting a job; an engagement, marriage, childbirth, the birth of a particular child; promotions; menopause in women and mid-life crisis in men; children's departure from home; the illness or death of parents, a spouse, or friends; and the general weakening that occurs in the senium.

Many of these events, at least some of which all individuals must face, are especially threatening to the psychosis-vulnerable person because of his reaction to the mixed loss and gain that they imply. Each successive developmental step threatens to remove this individual from the apparent safety of early dependence on his mother; this is a loss he cannot sustain, even when this crucial relationship has been out of balance as well as nurturing. The increased responsibility that comes with new stages in life therefore heightens his anxiety. The further along the individual is in the life cycle, the greater difficulty he experiences in negotiating these developmental changes; themes of failure and disillusionment come to predominate in his thinking about them.

The third major type of onset is a prolonged slide into chronic schizophrenia. Cumulative frustration from recurrent life failures converts an existing, occult illness into overt schizophrenia. Individuals with a history of such frustration may have remained in the community for many years, sustained by a valued person who eventually becomes unavailable because of illness, a shift in responsibilities, departure, or death. The patient's gradual slide into failure and illness, which has previously been masked by this relationship, then becomes clear.

Course

The course of schizophrenia varies with each individual's life circumstances and consists of advances, halts, remissions, and exacerbations. The meaning of each of these stages may be overlooked in superficial history taking or obscured by the use of insufficiently refined nosological categories. Improvements or regressions, for example, may occur in reaction to seemingly trivial external events, such as transfer to another location, illness, medical procedures, or even a visitor. In order to comprehend the significance of such changes, the therapist must understand the intrapsychic meaning of each event.

Individuals with acute reactions to obvious external stresses may recover quickly. The course of other patients, however, is characterized either by progression of the disease or by remissions and exacerbations leading eventually to a chronic state. Even when the patient has recovered, residual symptoms may alter thought, capacity for empathy, and behavior sufficiently to make full vocational, social, and sexual development impossible; thus the outlook for many schizophrenics remains bleak.

Much of the regressed behavior of chronic schizophrenics was formerly thought to be due to "hospitalosis," defined as a clinical result of impersonal, custodial care in mental hospitals. A constant factor in the chronic nature of the schizophrenic's illness, however, is his ability to evoke hostility and, consequently, neglect in all who come into contact with him. Although hospitalosis is a particular manifestation of humanity's general fear and dislike of the patient, therapists, relatives, and staff members of community service centers respond to unhospitalized patients with similar attitudes.

Untreated Schizophrenia

Arieti (1975) describes four stages of increasing regression observed in hospitalized patients during the preceding three decades. *Stage one* consists of three phases during which the psychosis is full-blown. In the first phase, primary process takes over functions of secondary process thinking, and anxiety is either present or easily provoked. In the second phase, the patient undergoes a period of confusion, when everything seems strange and "crazy" to him. In the third phase, psychotic insight emerges; the patient understands the world according to a new system of autistic thinking. The catatonic seeks to deny this new psychotic insight by his immobility or excitement. The hebephrenic resorts to primary process thinking. The paranoid, with his heightened tendency to project, avoids and denies his conflicts by mobilizing his remaining conscious and logical forces in the service of his unconscious. Stage one may last for several weeks or months.

During *stage two*, the struggle between the illness and reality ceases and the patient regresses. Anxiety is apparently reduced, and the patient's behavior becomes increasingly asocial and stereotyped as he attempts to avoid the catastrophic reactions of murder, suicide, or giving up completely. Three general reactions are observed in hospitalized patients during this stage: intransigent challenges to the institution and refusal to cooperate, withdrawal, and apparent adoption of the institution's official view of him in order to get along. These responses lead to antisocial and asocial behavior, as patients argue, withdraw, or pretend compliance. Although modern use of drugs reduces antisocial behavior, asocial behavior remains unchanged.

Stage three, which Arieti calls the preterminal stage, begins five to fifteen years after onset of the psychosis; by this time signs of the disease have disappeared. Hallucinations or delusions are not present or, if they are, they have no emotional charge. Patients show little overt illness and are often described as "burnt out." In fact, they have learned to hide the signs of their sickness and now pick their skin, pull out their hair, perform rhythmic movements, decorate themselves, and hoard things with no practical or symbolic value.

Stage four, the terminal stage, begins seven to forty years after the onset of the psychosis, according to Arieti, and appears as the transition from a psychological to a neurological state. Patients who showed inactivity in the preterminal

stage become more active, although not so much so as normal people. They may become violent, assaultive, and destructive but have no hallucinations or delusions. Patients become obese, grabbing food and eating it quickly; they typically gorge themselves on preferred foods first, then all food, then all small objects. Their intent is not suicidal; rather, they seem compulsively to insert all available objects into their mouths. Such patients will smear themselves with their feces and eat their own feces with pleasure. They experience a gross decrease in responsiveness to physical pain or discomfort—pinpricks, suturing, cold, burns, and normally unpleasant tastes—as if the affective meaning of pain has been reduced or lost. Reaction to smell remains strong, however, and seems stronger as other sense reactions decline; this fact attests to the extreme regression taking place in this stage, since olfaction belongs to the most primitive part of the brain's limbic system.

Arieti believes that these manifestations signify regression to increasingly primitive levels of psychological and neurological organization. When higher levels fail to function properly, several lower levels are simultaneously disinhibited, interfere with each other, and increase confusion. Reorganization at any level of integration therefore becomes impossible.

Prognosis in Schizophrenia

Patients who suffer acute breakdowns have a better prognosis than patients with chronic illness. The type of clinical syndrome also affects prognosis. Without milieu and drug therapy, paranoids have the best prognosis; catatonics, an intermediate prognosis; and hebephrenics and simple schizophrenics, the worst. With drugs, catatonics do as well as paranoids; hebephrenics do better than without such treatment, while simple schizophrenics are least responsive.

Each exacerbation of the illness increases the danger of further personality damage. In 1898, Kraepelin found that 13 percent of his patients recovered from the first attack, although most of these relapsed; only 15 percent of these had a passable social remission (appeared to the superficial eye to be managing their everyday lives adequately). Today, with good follow-up treatment and well-controlled maintenance drug therapy, 85 to 90 percent will continue in their particular states of social recovery. Thirty to 40 percent of these patients are stable but chronic; they are now more often released into the community than formerly. Some patients show remission with defects, such as increased aloofness, selfishness, or reduced ambition or spontaneity, that may be so subtle that only close friends or the family may be aware of them.

Many patients, however, have to work at a level requiring less responsibility or initiative than before their illness; they often prefer to work away from human contact, alone, or at night. Fifty years ago the chances for complete recovery were 2 to 4 percent; they are no better today. After five years of illness, 60 percent of schizophrenic patients will be socially recovered, 30 percent will be socially handicapped but still living in the community, and 10 percent will be hospitalized.

The three most important elements determining the prognosis for a schizophrenic patient are the presence of supportive family members, especially a mate, to whom the patient can return; the patient's own capacity to bear depression; and continuing contact with a caring therapist. Support may be lost through the death of a parent (Nicholi and Watt, 1977) or through moving to a new neighborhood or even a new apartment; such occurrences account for 60 percent of relapses (Brown and Birley, 1968). Other relapses may follow from ceasing medication. Fifty percent of institutionalized patients freed from symptoms by the use of drugs discontinue medication after discharge because the lack of continuing therapeutic contact makes them feel uncared for (Gunderson et al., 1974). Routinely issued prescriptions cannot substitute for the therapist's careful attention to the meaning of drugs for the individual patient and to their place in his general life situation.

Treatment

The main focus and goal of all treatment is the understanding of the individual patient as a human being, regardless of whether the therapeutic emphasis is on individual or group therapy, milieu therapy, therapeutic communities, chemotherapy, ECT, or other organic approaches. Before discussing our own approach to psychotherapy with schizophrenics, we shall review the work of others whose techniques and experience, specifically in the realm of psychotherapy, have been based on such an understanding of the patient.

Modern Psychoanalytic Psychotherapy

As Sigmund Freud deepened his study of narcissism, he despaired of the schizophrenic's ability to develop a true transference relationship in psychoanalysis and therefore doubted the possibility of treating the schizophrenic by this means. We now know that, just as neurotics develop a neurotic transference, schizophrenics develop a psychotic transference that can be productively used and studied in treatment.

While Freud held that the schizophrenic patient narcissistically withdrew his emotional investment from others onto himself, Paul Federn (1952) saw the patient as deficient in feelings for himself, consequently viewing himself as worthless and unlovable ("negative narcissism"). Unlike Freud, Federn believed that the schizophrenic could develop a transference to the therapist and worked at helping the patient undo regression by strengthening his ego, thus reducing his dependence on primary process thinking. Federn often used a woman helper (the patient's mother or sister or a female nurse) to provide care between sessions. This figure provided warmth and served both as an outlet for positive transference and as an anchor during a state of negative transference. Federn relied on the healthy part of the patient to combat the sick part—a necessary approach during recompensation, or the process of discharging his unbearable affects and going back to his former and usual way of dealing with people and life.

Melanie Klein's psychoanalysis of children (1932) led her to explore the development of the child's mind and the importance of primitive defenses in forming both the child's mental structure and his object relations with others. In her psychoanalysis of adult schizophrenics, she recognized paranoid anxieties, arising from the very young child's paranoid-schizoid position, and the dread of loss, arising from his early depressive position. Theorizing that the superego was formed by the age of nine months, she analyzed its primitive aspects early in treatment in order to humanize its strong influence and make that influence benevolent. Klein believed that interpersonal relationships are externalizations and symbolizations of inner unconscious fantasies. In her psychoanalysis of both adult schizophrenics and children, she explored childhood fantasies of parental intercourse and focused on the patient's use of primitive defenses (splitting, fragmentation, projection, and introjection) to deal with these fantasies. Her therapeutic technique was based on the conviction that the analyst's consistency in understanding the patient's unconscious, including his difficulties while at the mercy of his fantasies, provides the main source of strength in the patient's analytic experience.

Klein's followers—principally Rosenfeld, Bion, and Segal—further developed her understanding of schizophrenia while effecting some degree of rapprochement with other analysts' ideas about psychoanalysis. The influence of this school is great in England, on the Continent, and in South America. Herbert Rosenfeld (1965) based his treatment of schizophrenia on four assumptions: 1) withdrawal may be used as a defense against paranoid anxieties as well as against closeness; (2) the unconscious can be interpreted to the patient in a way he can understand; (3) the patient develops a psychotic transference that can be analyzed; and (4) projective identification may be used as a defense to deal with other people, to jettison unacceptable impulses such as envy, and to control the analyst, thus satisfying the patient's guiding fantasy of leading his life parasitically at the analyst's expense (see chapter 8, "Theories of Personality"). In his own clinical work, Rosenfeld, like Federn, used the healthy portions of the patient's ego to overcome those engaged in psychotic defenses. W. R. Bion (1961) made major contributions to the field of group therapy by analyzing psychotic as well as neurotic elements of group behavior. He stressed that in individual therapy the psychotic resorts to projective identification since, unlike the neurotic, he cannot repress painful material. Hannah Segal (1950) interpreted unconscious material to

the patient at the level of greatest anxiety, thus engaging the patient's trust in the therapist's courage in facing the psychosis.

During the 1940s, John Rosen (1963), following Federn's approach, used a helper to care for the patient between sessions and relied heavily on the force of his own personality in effecting change in therapy. His primary contribution was the technique of "direct analysis," introduced when many still felt hopeless about the possibility of psychotherapy for schizophrenics. To increase therapeutic impact, Rosen arranged 8- to 16-hour therapy sessions in front of an audience. At first his interventions consisted of interpretations of the patient's unconscious sexual and aggressive drives and conflicts, delivered without preparatory analytic work. Although unconscious sexual conflicts have now been shown to be the least important of the schizophrenic's difficulties, Rosen's approach worked. His success demonstrates that anything that lightens the patient's burden helps him. In Rosen's case, his belief in the effectiveness of a coherent, organized system was a major factor in engaging the patient in therapy and speeding recompensation. His discovery that patients who were helped to recover by his approach regressed without follow-up treatment confirmed the need for further therapy to stabilize recovery. Rosen recognized the importance of the early mother-child relationship as background for the illness and described it as a "perversion of maternal love"; he also noted the patient's tendency to project the childhood world of the nagging, seductive, bribing, depriving mother onto his current situation, thus distorting the present by making it resemble the past. Rosen's notion that the patient views his mother as extremely malevolent is reminiscent of Fromm-Reichman's description of the "schizophrenogenic mother" and of the views of Lidz, Wynne and Singer, Bateson, and Jackson on the crucial role of mother-child interaction in the precipitation of the illness. To a certain degree, however, we believe, Rosen overlooked the role played by the mechanisms of the patient's own ego in forming a view of the actual mother. He stressed the importance of the therapist as a good foster parent, and his extensive sessions with the patient, together with the coherence of his system, communicated concern, sincerity, and competence to the patient.

Working within a psychoanalytic framework, Marguerite Sechehaye (1951), a Swiss psychologist, treated a schizophrenic girl many hours a day in her home over a number of years. She understood the patient's primitive needs and fears and tried to satisfy them symbolically, referring to the treatment approach as "symbolic realization." This warm relationship permitted the patient to relive her earliest traumas and resolve them magically. While it is not likely that many therapists who work with schizophrenics can duplicate this approach, Sechehaye's empathy and dedication in engaging the patient in the therapeutic process of recovery are impressive.

Various therapists have combined Freud's theories of the unconscious and Sullivan's emphasis on interpersonal relations in their formulations of the development, onset, course, and treatment of schizophrenia. Frieda Fromm-Reichmann (1948, 1959) applied psychoanalysis to the treatment of psychotics, developing what we now know as psychoanalytically oriented psychotherapy. Early in her career she taught that the therapist must accept the patient as he is; later she revised this view in favor of appealing to the adult part of the patient. (This change mirrors the intellectual shifts of Federn, Rosen, and many others and perhaps reflects each individual therapist's necessary development rather than a coherent view of treating schizophrenia.) Fromm-Reichman conducted daily sessions with the patient and used interpretation cautiously. Although sessions were as frequent as in psychoanalysis, the patient sat up. Primary emphasis was placed on the patient's present relationship to the therapist and to others; this issue was investigated in the light of the past, but treatment did not focus essentially on the development of the illness.

Fromm-Reichmann relied on the growing value of the therapeutic relationship to the patient to help him accept the loneliness implicit in his withdrawal, his continued yearning for contact, and his need to be met with adult expectations rather than coddled or exploited. By viewing symptoms as a reformulation of old, frustrating interpersonal relationships, she helped the patient accept earlier losses without resorting to distortions to avoid pain; the more the patient could accept, the more he could integrate his life. Fromm-Reichmann was impressive as a therapist and as a teacher of many who are now leaders in this field.

Otto Will (1967), one of Fromm-Reichmann's students, stressed the importance of the therapist's defining the relationship with the patient and refusing all the patient's desires to deny it by withdrawing, by protesting his inability to change, or by claiming indifference. The therapist achieves this relatedness by regular meetings during which he attempts to engage the patient's senses and emotions as fully as possible. The therapist becomes a model with whom the patient can identify; within this role, he interprets life for the patient with less distortion than the patient's parents and helps the patient to identify and correct his own distortions. Gradually the patient becomes aware of how he came to be the person he is; he learns to accept members of his family as they are and to emancipate himself from them without denying their meaning to him or isolating himself.

In his extensive writings on the psychodynamics of schizophrenia and the transference, Harold Searles (1960, 1965), another of Fromm-Reichmann's pupils, has emphasized the inclusion of the external environment in his treatment of the patient. According to Searles, the patient fights the transference in order to fight acknowledging his dependency, since yielding to transference would mean giving up omnipotence. Because the transference leads to increased use of projection, the therapist gains access to views of the patient's world; he can then give the patient glimpses of the therapist's world, so that the two alternate. The therapist must therefore maintain a fundamental concern for both psychic freedom and situational latitude, respecting the privilege of looking into the patient's private, inner world by not forcing himself into it. He offers himself as a larger-than-life model with whom the patient can identify and against whom he can test his projections. The patient can then deal with the issue he has projected by facing his own feelings toward it.

Silvano Arieti (1975), another member of this school, began his work with formal studies of schizophrenic thinking and, in his present clinical work, links formal thought disturbances with psychodynamic disorders. He holds that establishing a sense of relatedness between the patient and the therapist is the first therapeutic task. Symptoms will then diminish, but they may recur with further stress, particularly that due to loss and separation. The patient cannot control symptoms until he understands the psychological truth of his past and present life, his own low estimate of himself, and his conversion of this low self-esteem into hallucinations and ideas of reference by means of primary process thinking. Because feeling like a victim is more palatable to the patient than recognizing his active disapproval of himself, therapy consists of helping him endure suffering based on his failures. The patient grows stronger because he sees how he can produce (and therefore reduce) his own symptoms; he is thus not merely a passive victim. According to Arieti, the patient's delusions contain a "punctiform insight"—a minute but accurate appreciation of others' attitudes toward him—hidden in his distorted perception and experience. The therapist must therefore respect and attempt to expand the patient's ability for accurate perception and comprehension of his interpersonal situation; at the same time, the patient's use of rationalization and other self-consoling devices must be analyzed.

John Whitehorn (1944), a student of Adolf Meyer, preferred active, personal participation to passivity in his approach to schizophrenics. He emphasized the importance of engaging the patient during the evaluation process and developed a method for conducting the initial interview, which he taught his students. Whitehorn stressed the value of studying the schizophrenic's personality trends—the strong as well as the weak. His concern with the therapist's impact on the patient led him to compare the attitudes of therapists and the effect of their different attitudes on treatment. He designated Type A therapists, who were active and firm, especially in setting limits and expressing personal attitudes, and Type B therapists, who were passively permissive and instructional. Whitehorn found that schizophrenics treated by Type A therapists showed immediate and persistent improvement, while patients treated by the Type B therapists showed less immediate improvement; a five-year follow-up of this second group of patients showed gradual progress that reached the same level as those treated by the Type A therapists.

Elvin Semrad developed his therapeutic approach from Whitehorn's concept of personality trends and Freud's theories of human motivation. Up to his death in 1976, he encouraged individual and group therapy with schizophrenics and stimulated many students to develop both treatment modalities. He held that the therapist begins by respecting the psychological dilemma of the patient; continuing study of the patient's situation then leads the therapist to share the patient's emotional burden and the process of recompensation from his psychosis. Semrad subsequently studied the role of unmastered aggression in the predisposition to psychosis and in its onset and maintenance. He saw schizophrenia as a psychosomatic illness in which the patient gives in early and in extreme ways to the universal tendency to substitute physical sensations and symptoms for painful emotions ("conversion process"). Losses upset this precarious balance, which lacks the cushion of a good mother-child relationship. Because the schizophrenic is overwhelmed by panic at his loss and because his immature ego is incapable of dealing with its two important warning signals, anxiety and depression, the conversion process no longer functions adequately; the schizophrenic must then resort to the primitive techniques of denial, projection, and distortion to deal with anxiety. Semrad's view of the processes of therapy and recovery in schizophrenia is an integral part of the following discussion of our psychotherapy with schizophrenics.

Psychotherapy with Schizophrenics

The discussion that follows presents our own views of the nature of psychotherapy with schizophrenics and describes the interactive treatment techniques that have evolved from our clinical experience. Although terminology may differ, our basic tenets are similar to those of many of the authors we have already discussed.

The principal themes and concepts discussed in this section have emerged from our clinical experience with patients during the turmoil of acute decompensation and the course of therapy. We focus on these patterns as they appear in patients' ongoing relationships with people who are emotionally significant to them; as they have emerged in relationships with similar people in the past; and, in particular, as they reappear in relation to the therapist.

The essence of therapy with the schizophrenic is the interaction between the creative resources of both therapist and patient. The therapist must rely on his own life experiences and translate his knowledge of therapeutic principles into meaningful interaction with the patient while recognizing, evoking, and expanding the patient's experience and creativity; both then learn and grow from this experience.

In order to engage a schizophrenic patient in therapy, the therapist's basic attitude must be an acceptance of the patient as he is—of his aims in life, his values, and his modes of operating, even when they are different from and very often at odds with his own. Loving the patient as he is, in his state of decompensation, is the therapist's primary concern in approaching the patient. As a result, the therapist must find his personal satisfactions elsewhere. His job is extremely taxing in its contradictions, for he must love the patient, expect him to change, and yet derive his affectional satisfactions elsewhere and tolerate frustration.

The schizophrenic needs a person who will comply with his infantile needs and aims by replacing the valued person he has lost. This need is supplied by the therapist, who may partly gratify some of the patient's infantile needs while consistently pressing him to acknowledge, bear, and put into perspective the current reality he dreads. At first the emphasis is on the factor precipitating the psychosis; accepting the disavowed feelings related to onset of psychosis releases the rage, anxiety, and pain of abreaction, which, in turn, releases energy for further work in therapy and for activities in life. The focus shifts to the burdensome introjects within the patient; examining the inner images in detail exposes the patient's need for the very infantile avoidance mechanisms that have led him both to emotional disaster and to the doctor's attention.

The therapist must provide the patient with additional figures who can engage him therapeutically (Federn, 1952; Rosen, 1963), since the therapist's own relationship with the patient cannot always provide sufficient sustenance. These people are often the ward administrator, ward staff members, ancillary personnel, and others involved in special approaches to the family through casework or family therapy (Semrad, 1966; Semrad and Day, 1959). During crises, the therapist will need their help to tide the patient over; hospitalization may also be necessary to save the patient from errors in judgment or from temporary destructive impulses.

When the patient is overwhelmed by the pain of psychotic thinking, medication may be helpful by reducing anxiety so that he can begin once again to manage his own life. The active participation of both patient and therapist in the use of medication is necessary and may, in fact, be the most therapeutic aspect of the use of drugs. Because exploration and understanding of psychotic thinking are crucial to helping the patient minimize his pain, we do not advocate masking its manifestations. Nor do we aim for temporary comfort, convenience for the ward or family, or surface calm at the cost of the patient's continuing effort to bear his psychotic pain and put it in perspective in order ultimately to strengthen himself (Semrad, 1966); medication, rather, should be used only during crises and for short periods of time (Havens, 1963). This approach to medication, though not generally popular, is the one we believe has the best chance of benefiting the patient psychotherapeutically.

During hospitalization the therapist must keep himself and the others who have therapeutic contact with the patient minimally punitive, minimally intellectual, and minimally seductive. Yet each of these elements has some role in the treatment approach. Sometimes a small amount of punishment is useful in setting limits; at other times, a slightly seductive attitude is useful in engaging the patient and showing him that one can enjoy life, as long as it is clear that the overture is for the patient's sake and not for the therapist's gratification. Sometimes an intellectual clarification can help the patient sense and explore emotional relationships.

Overall, the therapist's aim is to provide what Anna Freud calls a "corrective ego experience" (1951) to help relieve his suffering and equip him to live in some state of peace with himself. This goal implies providing the patient with a series of experiences with people who will help him to differentiate impulses arising within him from those stimulated by others. These sensations and interactions lead to real relationships, which should be emotionally gratifying and stimulating in order to help the patient experience physical and emotional comfort in the presence of other people. This is a difficult task because the patient's psychotic mechanisms keep him constantly on the run from physical as well as emotional pain. He must be helped to share the pain in order to acknowledge it and thus limit its traumatic aspects. People on the ward show him ways of dealing with his life that are not presently available to him and that he can imitate in his attempt to deal with everyday events.

At some point early in therapy, the therapist must explore in a respectful way what hurts the patient. It is important to find out how the patient expects to be helped, to clarify what help the therapist can actually provide, and to establish a mutually acceptable agreement about the aims of therapy. Defining what is and is not possible in therapy is important from the beginning so that expectations and frustrations will not grow disproportionately. The therapist's expectations of the patient can be just as much a problem as the patient's expectations of the therapist.

The basic techniques of all dynamic psychotherapy—suggestion, abreaction, manipulation, clarification, and interpretation (Bibring, 1954)—are used in therapy with schizophrenics. The first three place the patient in a psychological position to use the therapist's help. Clarification is used much more frequently than interpretation because too little is known about what goes on in the patient's unconscious to be able to interpret it. The therapist must listen to and organize the patient's emotional and interpersonal communication—particularly what he has avoided saying—in order to collect clues about what precipitated the decompensation.

In order to engage the patient in the truest therapeutic sense, the therapist must enter actively into his psychic life as if he were a new symptom. The patient, in turn, must become part of the therapist's life; the therapist must sense the patient's emotions within himself. Only by such an affective experience can the therapist become aware of the depth of the turmoil the patient is experiencing. For this reason, the therapist will find it difficult to treat only psychotics.

Identifying the emotional impasse. In treating a schizophrenic in an acute psychotic state, identifying the emotional impasse the patient faces is more important than making a formal diagnosis because of its implications for proceeding with further work. Determining what kind of person the patient is and how he came to be a patient is crucial; the quality of each patient's ways of functioning and way of life is unique and must be fully understood. We are interested in what caused the patient to resort to a psychosis—that is, what led to the decompensation. As discussed earlier, the emotional precipitant is usually the loss of someone highly valued, one of the normal but stressful stages of the life cycle, or chronic frustration. The nature of the precipitant alerts the therapist to investigate related areas so that he is aware of affects and pains the patient is avoiding.

Making a personal diagnostic summary. The therapist's first concern is to be available to the patient as a person who has assets he lacks, on whom he can depend, and from whom he can borrow ego techniques by imitation. The therapist's repeated, consistent presence is extremely supportive, more so than anything he can say. The second priority is formulating a personal diagnostic summary that focuses not on symptoms but on the patient's habitual ego techniques, or the patterns of interaction by which he negotiates his relationship with the therapist and with significant people in past and present.

The therapist can use his own physical

responses to assess whether the patient is inviting him into his life or pushing him away. Ego techniques serve as clues to the patient's needs. The patient may use the defense of denial to avoid his own yearnings for love; he may use distortion (hallucinations and delusions) as an appeal to the therapist to help him think clearly; or he may use projection, asking the therapist to share responsibility for his own impulses.

The patient's personality is consistent (Whitehorn, 1944) and may be classified according to clusters of repetitive behavior; each behavioral pattern is based on an excessive need for a sustaining person, a defensive device to deal with the need, and an adaptive mechanism for negotiating the continued flow of sustenance. The inappropriate persistence of childhood patterns into adult life leads to pathology and may be observed by the therapist and others who deal with the patient during the course of therapy. To aid in making administrative clinical judgments, suggesting therapeutic interventions, and evaluating progress and regression, a forty-five-item Ego Profile Scale has been devised to categorize and measure the patient's habitual techniques for dealing with his needs and with people regarding important life issues (Semrad, Grinspoon, and Fienberg, 1973). Each item on this continuum is rated between 0 and 6; the scale is based on indices of the patient's psychological functioning. Patient responses are then categorized according to nine general types of defensive-adaptive ego technique, which are arranged in gradations from most primitive to most mature.

Because the ego is overwhelmed by pain and frustration during the catastrophe of acute psychosis, it resorts to patterns of denial, distortion, and projection to preserve itself. As the ego becomes stronger, it begins to use obsessive-compulsive, hypochondriacal, and neurasthenic patterns to elicit help, support, and encouragement from other people. Only as the patient recovers does the ego turn to the neurotic patterns of dissociation, somatization, and anxiety. While these ego techniques do not represent optimal mental functioning, they help the patient in two ways. On an interpersonal level, they permit him to attain a degree of mutual gratification with another person and willingly to accept accommodations and make sacrifices in order to achieve a degree of inner constancy and a sense of relating equitably with others. On an intrapsychic level, these techniques also lessen unconscious conflicts over instinctual impulses.

Supplying the need. On the basis of his awareness of the patient's ego techniques, the therapist must supply what the patient needs, either directly, through his own candid, respectful interaction, or indirectly through the other people whom he provides for the patient for this purpose. He helps the patient to talk feelingly in facing painful issues, with the expectation that he can learn to bear the pain—the essence of the "corrective ego experience" (A. Freud, 1951).

While accepting the patient at his level of functioning, the therapist must have the strength to disapprove of the patient's psychotic thinking and behavior. The trick is to accept the patient but to reject his psychosis. Otherwise, the patient may feel that he has hoodwinked the therapist or that the therapist does not care about the truth of his emotional life.

The catatonic's way of life is to forget what is important and what hurts (Semrad, 1966). Regardless of personal style, the therapist must help the patient confront what he wants to forget: the concrete, mundane details of his loss. The therapist may use manipulation, reconstructing the specific details of the traumatic experience, along with the attendant physical and emotional reactions, in order to revive the chain of events leading to chronic frustration. The patient's anxiety and protests confirm that the therapist is on the right track. The therapist then encourages the patient's uncritical emotional release of the avoided pain (abreaction). He returns repeatedly to the important issues until they are part of the patient's everyday life; thus he teaches the patient that relief from pain comes only from remembering, reliving, and acknowledging its reality. Before this experience, the patient has split off part of his ego and wasted energy on the psychic job of avoiding pain. His denial during therapy therefore signals the need to recall the pain. As the therapist shares responsibility with the patient for the pain, without seduction or criticism, the patient learns to bear and respect the feelings in his own body (Khantzian, Dalsimer, and Semrad, 1969). Often the confirming reaction is an outburst of tears and sadness as the painful item is accepted.

The paranoid patient may quickly move to reject the therapist. In this case, the therapist must not attempt closeness to the patient precipitately but, rather, must explore what feelings—especially in the patient's body—make him uncomfortable and must help him to understand them. The patient can relax only as he accepts responsibility for his feelings.

With the hallucinated and deluded patient more than with any other, the therapist must listen for what is not being said. The patient evades the truth of his situation, is unable to accept the reality of his defeats and failures, and toys with the irrelevant explanations he offers for his predicament. The therapist must scan the details of the patient's real life to find the source of his dissatisfaction and help the patient see what he omits. The therapist's ability to face the pain of this reality without distortion strengthens the patient.

In all of these therapeutic encounters, the therapist forces himself on the patient, who then tends to identify with the therapist as an aggressor. This form of identification is a normal defense applied to the therapeutic situation in order to help the patient use new techniques in facing painful issues directly. These techniques enhance the beneficial effects of the therapist's constant scrutiny of the relationship between him and the patient and permit the patient to remain as open as possible to trust, support, and confidence. A patient who lives in reciprocal, loving trust with another person does not need to be psychotic and can return to his level of optimal functioning on the strength of his own successful interpersonal experience. At first he may learn to be nonpsychotic only during therapy hours. If the patient regresses from projection to denial, the change points to unacknowledged feelings in the relationship, which must be worked out before therapy can continue. As stated earlier, the therapist gets his clue to the level at which the patient is functioning from the hierarchy of defenses (Semrad, Grinspoon, and Fienberg, 1973).

The three major functions of the therapist in treating the regressed psychotic patient are making a personal diagnostic summary, supplying what the patient needs, and helping the patient to give up infantile behavior (even if only by relying on techniques he learns from the therapist); together, these steps may take three to four months. After the acute phase of the psychosis, recovery takes place in several phases, the first of which is the neurasthenic.

The neurasthenic phase. The neurasthenic phase in recovery from psychotic regression is the patient's island of security in his task of integrating the sadness of his real life (Semrad and Madow, 1974). In the therapeutic alliance, he no longer uses his narcissistic defenses, yet he needs his therapist's help to solve the dilemma of his life with dignity and self-respect. Because lack of success is so threatening during this phase, the patient magnifies difficulties to excuse failure. If the therapist loses patience, he may threaten the patient's self-esteem by expecting performance and not respecting the patient's need to plan for himself; the patient may then resort to excusing his failures rather than risking more. The therapist must make it clear to the patient that he cares, shares responsibility, and is willing to try again.

The depressive phase. Initial emergence from acute psychotic turmoil and transition to recovery are often followed by a depressive phase (Roth, 1970). When this phase ends, either remission or exacerbation of illness takes place. During the depressive phase, the patient, who has only recently—in the neurasthenic phase—shown a return of old ego strengths, begins to relinquish signs of resocialization, wants to reduce therapy hours or stop therapy altogether, and begins to stay in bed longer. The therapist, who has felt in touch with the case until this time, begins to feel the hours are unfocused. Depression varies from neurotic to psychotic in character, with all vegetative signs present except insomnia (since the patient retreats to bed). Suicidal ideas, impulses, and attempts are common.

A patient is often treated with ECT or drugs to help relieve the depression, but these efforts miss the point of his dilemma: he needs to be helped to face the sadness of his plight rather than to be deprived of the affect necessary for this sadness. Sometimes the therapist dreads confronting this misery. Fragmentation of therapy is particularly counterproductive during this phase; one therapist may treat the patient in the hospital during the acute, florid psychotic phase; another, in the community after discharge, when he becomes dull and depressed. Treatment by the same therapist through all these phases is optimal and often necessary for the patient's recompensation, since the therapist who is involved with the acutely sick patient is aware of his needs and typical defensive patterns.

If the neurasthenic phase is the patient's way of dealing with the family's or the therapist's unrealistic expectations for performance, whether they are real or projected, then the depressive phase is a somewhat more mature, though still defensive, way of dealing with the underlying sadness of his life situation. Such depressive reactions are more marked in "reactive" schizophrenia than in chronic states; they last an average of about three months.

The return of optimal social functioning. If the patient successfully negotiates the depressive phase, he can hope for a return of optimal social functioning. Before the patient can realistically investigate the psychotic aspects of his personality, he must mend fences with family members. Psychosis is often experienced as a gigantic tantrum by the patient's relatives, who rarely forgive his psychotic aggressiveness. The period of recompensation is not a time for great intrapsychic or psychogenetic understanding, and both therapist and patient may be frustrated if the therapist moves in that direction. The patient must regain social functioning with people in his immediate environment in order to return to his life with them, and another nine or ten months may be needed after initial recompensation before he can restore this equilibrium. The patient may also decide to give up people with whom his relationship is especially painful and endure the resulting grief for them. He must also recognize that the skewed solutions for problems often offered at home contrast greatly with the truer,

more reality-oriented solutions he may encounter outside the home. In any case, he must have time and energy for this kind of reorganization before being able to look inward.

Problems in therapy. At some point in the midst of apparently productive therapy, the patient may experience *separation anxiety;* he may regress or talk about ending therapy. This occurrence is often mistaken for a sign of general improvement and may be misinterpreted by the therapist as an appropriate signal to reduce contact. In fact, the patient may be reacting to his growing dependence on the therapist. His recognition of this dependence, and of the possibility of not needing the therapist some day, increases his anxiety. Again, all disturbances in relationships are reflected by changes in the patient's use of ego techniques. The possibility of being able to leave the therapist at some point is reassuring, as well as distressing, however, and brings up the next and most important issue—the matter of the psychosis itself.

Investigating the psychotic episode is of paramount importance for the preceding work to remain useful. Most painful for the patient is discussion of the things the therapist did to help him: prescribing drugs; causing him to feel defeated and abandoned because he felt the therapist had given up on him; disagreeing in regard to his best interest; and so on through the whole range of interactions of the initial relationship. Once the patient has dealt with the therapist's role during the psychotic episode, he can begin to explore his own. Another two years are generally required to integrate the psychotic episode into the meaning of his life. In the very course of investigating the details of the decompensation, the patient learns from this and other decompensations what the habitual pitfalls in his life are; he discovers the nature of the series of interpersonal relationships and impasses that has led to the psychotic episodes. Only by integrating all the affects for each of these decompensations and understanding their most frightening aspects in detail can he feel strong enough to use this understanding for further growth. Many patients and therapists regard accomplishment of these tasks as sufficient until the patient is motivated to undertake further therapeutic work (Semrad, 1966). Since much psychotherapy stops at this point, we know little about the essence of psychosis.

The analysis of the psychosis-vulnerable ego. Understanding the sources of the schizophrenic's individual historical development requires an analysis of the psychosis-vulnerable ego. In practice, this analysis is made only with selected patients, and only after the work already described has been accomplished. If this investigation is undertaken, unanswered questions remain. Should the same therapist who treated the decompensated patient attempt to analyze that patient's ego? Or should a new therapist serve more specifically as a transference object? Our own inclination is to build on past work, continue the therapy with the same therapist, and analyze past therapist-patient interactions that may affect the emerging transference.

Infantile transference needs interfere with the patient's optimal ego functioning. By interpreting these needs, at the same time that he provides measures to sustain and gratify the patient so that he can achieve some integrative capacity, the therapist helps the patient deal with these needs as well as with his present reality situation. Delusional transference may appear as a sign of the patient's dissatisfaction with the therapist in the current relationship. When the patient suffers too much pain in the presence of the therapist, he may again resort to the conversion process (Deutsch and Semrad, 1959) by the usual techniques of distortion, projection, and denial. Supporting the patient's conscious awareness of his libidinal and aggressive identifications is the procedure of choice at such a juncture, especially in the case of patients with paranoid, blaming tendencies. Contradiction replaces potentially dangerous needs, wishes, and anxieties with a totally different order of experience, disguised by distortions, and leads to changes that maintain infantile patterns of adaptation (Rycroft, 1960). Transference may appear to be lacking when it is masked by strong anxiety; this anxiety should accordingly be interpreted as a defense against unconscious transference feelings. The transference is thus brought into open awareness as a resistance that can be analyzed.

Although transference is present from the beginning of contact, the patient may not be able to acknowledge the human side of his relationship with the therapist for a long time. If the therapist has interpreted the transference from the beginning, together with the patient's defensive fantasies of the therapist as persecutor, and demonstrated that these fantasies are the consequence of anticipated punishment for the aggression, it may be possible to avoid damming up anxiety in the patient.

Projective identification is a typical transference phenomenon in the schizophrenic and a secondary defense mechanism for alleviating depressive anxiety. The patient splits off painful parts of the self relating to the people he has lost and projects them onto the available person. The split-off state of his ego and projection of these aspects onto others then leads to alterations in his ego boundaries; this process increases anxiety, which fosters regressive dependence and counteractive aggression.

The wish to possess the parents by fusion underlies all the relationships of the psychosis-vulnerable individual; it is the patient's mode of dealing with the despair and rage of his empty ego. The therapist must understand this state of affairs and the patient's defense against it in order to help him, in the context of a trusting relationship, to analyze his emptiness, despair, and rage. As the patient becomes aware of depressive anxiety in relation to growing sadness, he may try to project the depression. This process accounts for many psychiatrists' concerns about depression during recovery from schizophrenia. Each time, the anxiety must be interpreted to the patient, for with increased tolerance of this sadness comes increased ego strength. When stress goes beyond the sum of emotional support available to the patient, the interactions may become disorganized and primitive—a state of "transference psychosis."

The therapist studies the patient's inadequate postponements and repressions and then helps him postpone and repress more effectively, thereby building ego structure. At all times, concern over real-life problems, such as work and dealings with others, should take precedence over inner problems; lack of awareness of such difficulties will lead to regressions. Cautiously, the therapist deprives the patient of immediate satisfactions and helps him to acknowledge, accept, and be continually aware of his needs. As the patient distinguishes between the real and the transferred relationship with the therapist, he can reabsorb aspects of himself that he has projected by distinguishing between himself and the therapist.

As the patient gradually begins to change, the therapist experiences anxiety about these changes (Searles, 1961); he must acknowledge the changes to the patient without demanding further growth. Neutral responses are essential in dealing with the patient's basic ambivalence about individuation; a neutral attitude frees the patient to change for his own reasons rather than to cling to autism or change to please the therapist. The purpose of the close relationship is to help the patient form and absorb a clear image of another person with whom he can identify (Hoedemaker, 1955), an inner image necessary for effective ego functioning; it also serves as a tool for dealing with his overwhelming aggression and masochism. The patient is eager for normal aggressiveness in another person in order to deal with as many divergent situations as possible. His false positive attitude, which masks the hatred and self-hatred that has choked the ego, must be exposed and analyzed without endangering the patient's ego or people he values (Spotnitz, 1961–62). The therapist may need to become the focus of this hatred, for only in this way can the patient learn to accept his early introjects of his parents and his murderous feelings toward them and refrain from acting out his feelings. Thus the patient can mobilize his aggression, master it, and begin to use it creatively.

The main goal of analysis is not so much to relieve symptoms (except, of course, for the earlier and intermittent relief of anxiety) as to lay bare ego defects, expose artificial emotions, and encourage the patient to confront dreaded situations and thereby to test his fearful assumptions about the world. Thus the patient builds new ego structures and lessens his need to behave as an automaton.

Group Psychotherapy

While group approaches have been used with schizophrenics for centuries, group psycho-therapy with these patients began in the early part of this century. Its main impetus came from the advent of dynamic psychiatry in the late 1940s. Until the 1960s, most group therapy with schizophrenics took place on an inpatient basis. The recent trend toward caring for patients in the community places a demand for performance on therapy groups without providing them with a physical institution to support and foster the group envelope (Day, 1964). Although not as economical a treatment for psychotics as initially expected, group therapy has proved useful for the study and treatment of the process of recompensation from psychosis.

Standish and Semrad (1951) have described the process of "group formation" with hospitalized psychotics and the process of ego recompensation, without calling it by that name. In forming a group with psychotics, the leader evaluates eight or ten patients to orient himself and them to the nature of their problems. He then obtains their agreement to participate in a therapy group with the privilege of interacting spontaneously and the responsibility of doing so appropriately. At first the members test him to see if he really expects them to assume responsibility for what happens in the group. As he consistently pursues this course, they become aware of their yearnings to depend on him, their maneuvers to defend against this dependency, their wishes to compete with him, and their defenses against these wishes. These conflicts manifest themselves in further testing: patients ask questions, demand guidance, are silent, come late or not at all, sleep, fight, or are bored. They express their frustrations by cautiously criticizing outside authorities, such as the government, the President, the superintendent, the nurse on the ward, and finally criticize the leader himself. The leader offers himself as a focus for such criticism without retaliating and, at the same time, as a model of someone who accepts, tolerates, and even encourages verbal expression of aggression. By identifying with the leader as an aggressor, the patients take in his strength and use it, in turn, to face some of their own anxiety-laden experiences. By discussing their hallucinations, delusions, and misinterpretations, they find that they are accepted by the leader and other patients and that all of them have had similar experiences. Simple relief is obtained by airing these problems in the group. The recognition of common difficulties is also comforting, and the patient finds some relief from the loneliness of his frightful experiences.

Gradually patients accept dependence on the leader as natural and interdependence on one another as useful in learning about themselves and others. This interdependence prepares them for mutual and self-exploration under the persistent encouragement of the leader. As they feel safer in relation to the leader, patients begin to explore their relationships with each other; this stage usually coincides with the recompensation of their egos and the concomitant discussion of situations at home and at work and plans for the future. Group therapy has proved to be most useful when the consolidation of the group and the recompensation of the ego coincide.

The story is quite different, however, when the patient is ready to leave the hospital. In 1954, Blau and Zilbach showed that many patients could be maintained at home with the support of regular, continuing group therapy begun in the hospital; many of these patients had formerly had frequent relapses. Group therapy might thus begin to counteract the perils of the neurasthenic and depressive phases of recovery, but therapists have most often been content to let patients go their own way once they are discharged. Patients who are vulnerable to issues of loss are commonly exposed to repeated loss in clinic settings, where therapists in training regularly leave for another facility (Day and Semrad, 1971). With the current emphasis on quick recompensation by the suppression of psychosis with drugs, even group coalescence may not be achieved.

In private practice, psychotics are part of therapy groups—generally only one or two psychotics in a group of neurotics and borderline patients. The neurotics generally fear them and hold back from extending themselves for the psychotics, while borderline patients tend to be more understanding of the psychotics' plight. The leader's implicit acceptance of the psychotic helps him find a place in the group. The essential factor is the therapist's insistence that the patient come to the group, whether recovered or regressed. Gradually, the group process begins to deal with the psychosis so that the patient will

slowly acknowledge some of the pain in his life. Progress is slow, but some gains can be made.

Group therapy is a practical means of helping psychotics recover. Underlying details of the disease process and the process of recovery, on the other hand, can probably be ascertained more readily in individual therapy. The consensus of authors from 1956 to 1966 concerning group therapy for schizophrenics is "that task-oriented, goal-directed synthetic group work aimed at adaptation is more useful with this particular type of patient than the strictly analytic approach" (Schniewind, Day, and Semrad, 1969, p. 651).

Family Therapy

Treating the schizophrenic and his family as a unit can be useful from several points of view. Some workers even view this as the essential approach. The relatives, who feel guilty for causing or contributing to the patient's illness and who feel they are being talked about in his therapy, have a chance to observe the therapist in action and to recognize that he is not malevolent or blaming. They see how he operates and why treatment may take a long time, overcome their feelings of being left out, and benefit from treatment themselves. The family can be helped to face impasses or unresolved major conflicts; skewed relationships can be seen in action and analyzed, and the patient can be encouraged to communicate material necessary to begin the resolution of certain issues. Symbiotic ties, family distortions, and nonacceptance of the patient's illness can be identified, and distortions can then be worked on as they develop. Finally, the patient learns that the family is not omnipotent in relation to the therapist or, by extension, to the patient (Rabiner, Molinsky, and Gralnick, 1962).

Milieu Therapy

Group approaches on the larger scale of the ward and the hospital began over forty years ago. Simmel (1929) had seen the necessity for a hospital atmosphere that would provide the schizophrenic with a different reality than the one he had experienced at home. Sullivan (1953a,

1953b) attempted to set up such a therapeutic environment in Baltimore in 1931. The full impact of the trend toward milieu therapy and the therapeutic community was not felt until after World War II, however. At that time, experiments with group therapy and investigations into the treatability of schizophrenia and the importance of the milieu in such treatment were undertaken, partly as a reaction against the accumulated neglect perceived in the state hospital system.

Various investigators have contributed to this field. Caudill (1958) described the impact of dehumanization of the patient on the ward but failed to consider the patient's active role in this process. Stanton and Schwartz (1949) noted the importance of openly airing disagreements among those with power over the patient; covert disagreement led the patient to regress and to an increase in his symptoms. Maxwell Jones (1953), working in an open hospital with borderline patients and those with acting-out character disorders, adapted the kangaroo-court meetings the patients had been holding on their own to larger therapeutic purposes, involving the whole community of patients and staff. This device was useful in helping the individual and larger groups to assume responsibility for issues that involved them all (Edelson, 1964); the meetings raised important issues of responsibility, for the group, and of conscience, for those with superego defects. Hospital wards began the open-door policy, giving privileges to most patients who could manage them.

Community meetings, at which patients bring up all kinds of issues, have become common in hospitals. Although many of these efforts are humane and even democratic, the atmosphere they create poses a problem for the acute schizophrenic who is trying to recompensate. It focuses too much attention on the patient, blowing up each minor incident into a major brouhaha. Insufficient time is available for isolation, thinking over issues, or just letting things settle. The schizophrenic needs calm and quiet in order to recover. He must be able to attach himself to a ward aide or nurse, for example, to pour out his feelings, identify with the staff member, and recompensate. Milieu and group approaches may suit the needs of teen-agers, borderline patients

who are acting out, and middle-class mental health professionals more than they suit the needs of the acute schizophrenic. After the experience of his home life, however, the chronic schizophrenic can often adapt to a milieu approach and remain untouched.

Artiss (1962) feels that education in the rudiments of social behavior should be part of the treatment regimen. The patient should be able to interact regularly with healthy people and should be required to do so. In this way, ward personnel become active psychotherapists by being available to the patient for discussion of his feelings. Despite some serious drawbacks, the overall effect of this method has been beneficial in providing the patient with various treatment approaches, including occupational therapy, attitude therapy, vocational rehabilitation, education, work therapy, recreation, resocialization, and remotivation therapy. No single approach, however, is a sure cure or even necessary for every patient. Each approach is useful insofar as the professional devotes himself to it as a way of engaging the patient in a meaningful relationship. Secondarily, it supplies specific knowledge or experience that the patient lacks (Semrad and Day, 1959).

All of the treatment strategies discussed so far are based on psychotherapeutic or behavioral techniques. Schizophrenia has also been treated with various therapies. Because chemotherapy is by far the most widely used of the nonpsychological treatments, it is discussed at length in the following section. *Electroconvulsive therapy* (ECT), accepted as effective in treating depression, has been reported by some investigators to reduce or eliminate schizophrenic symptoms such as delusions, hallucinations, ideas of reference, and catatonic postures. Its usefulness in treating schizophrenic reactions, however, remains open to question. (See chapter 21, "Electroconvulsive Therapy," for a more detailed discussion of ECT.)

Chemotherapy

Since the mid-1950s, major tranquilizers or neuroleptics have become popular in the treatment of schizophrenia (see chapter 18, "Chemotherapy," for a discussion of their development, effects, and side effects). Where psychotherapy is unavailable, in some parts of the United States and in many other parts of the world, chemotherapy is the only reasonable approach. Certain advantages of the drugs—most commonly the phenothiazines (Thorazine) and butyrophenones (Haldol)—are apparent. Chronicity has been reduced to 75 percent of its former rate in the United States (Brill and Patton, 1964), largely by the use of drugs; chronic patients can take care of their physical needs, show almost no violence, and are quieter and more tractable. Antisocial symptoms are reduced, but asocial symptoms are not affected (Arieti, 1975).

In many cases, however, the use of drugs serves the needs of society for a quieter, more manageable person but does not free the patient to understand himself and take over responsibility for his own fate. In fact, these drugs, acclaimed as increasing the patient's accessibility to psychotherapy, often have the opposite effect. In our view, the essential factor in engaging the patient in therapy—the impact of two interacting personalities—can be lost in a chemical haze, and the therapeutic interaction risks being reduced to hostile negotiations over taking, increasing, or doing away with medication.

Since patients in general are eager to deny their need for the hospital and the therapist, the diminution of anxiety experienced by some patients on drug therapy decreases the meaning and usefulness of this anxiety in motivating recovery. After discharge patients may discontinue the use of drugs, regress, return to the hospital with less hope of being understood or helped, and become part of the category known as "chronic." Some patients prefer drugs as a way to avoid facing their dependence on the therapist or any other human being. In such cases, the drug program may be successful, but the patient uses the drug to avoid confronting his need for others and to satisfy his fantasy of omnipotent independence.

Other patients, fearing drugs, see them either as a sign of dependence or as some dangerous food that will control, change, or poison them. Such fantasies must be identified, traced to their sources, and analyzed if the patient is to be able to use the drugs reasonably. Merely mentioning these fantasies or elaborating on possible side effects does not help the patient; the unconscious, dynamic meaning of the drug to the patient must be understood. Above all, when drugs are used, it is important that the patient be helped to assume responsibility, with the psychiatrist, for taking them, continuing their use, increasing or decreasing the dosage, and discontinuing them, as appropriate, so that he continues to determine his own fate in sickness and health. Thus the use, abuse, and disuse of drugs become important parts of the doctor-patient relationship. Certainly, a sudden flare-up in symptoms should not necessarily be dealt with by increasing dosage, since it may stem from unrecognized feelings in the relationship. Quickly turning to drugs convinces the patient that his needs will not be recognized and creates a feeling of hopelessness.

Seclusion and Restraint

Seclusion and restraint are useful adjuncts in the treatment of the acutely disturbed patient. When patients are flooded with hallucinations and delusions, they are easily overstimulated by the activity of the ward and may react with disturbed, abusive, and violent behavior. The seclusion room (or "quiet room") diminishes overstimulation until the patient can regain control of himself. Some patients resort to being alone or asking for the quiet room when they suffer an excess of delusional thinking. For others, seclusion provides a useful point from which to negotiate for ward privileges, which are predicated on assuming responsibility for their behavior, regardless of their inner feelings. Sometimes a ward aide sits at the door and talks with the patient so that he can express his concerns. The presence of the aide, with whom the patient must deal and reason, helps force human interaction and the slow establishment of a working agreement before new privileges are achieved. The patient gains a sense of comfort and safety when he sees that he is not all-powerful and all-dangerous to the rest of humanity, that he can be safely contained in the quiet room.

Physical restraint is less frequent now than before the advent of tranquilizers, when its injudicious use added to the patient's sense of helplessness. In current practice, the implied restraint from a person in attendance is offered as a stimulus to work for varying degrees of privileges on the ward, in the hospital, and off the grounds. These devices are useful in increasing patients' responsibility for their behavior. At all times a fine line must be drawn between controlling the patient because we fear him and his primitive demands on and aversion from life and helping him fulfill his genuine need to learn self-mastery.

Our understanding of the biological, intrapsychic, familial, and social origins of schizophrenia is at best fragmentary, and evidence is often contradictory. Nevertheless, the general outlines of this complex condition are apparent to the experienced observer. Understanding of the patient's impact on others and of the therapist's harmful and healthy impact on the patient has grown in the last five decades. As a result, the patient can be understood, treated humanely, and helped to understand himself, to recover his usual state of functioning, and to rehabilitate himself.

The study of schizophrenia also confirms the importance of helping the human being deal with emotional pain, frustration, and failure—during normal development as well as in treatment—and emphasizes the effect of these stresses on character structure and way of life. Research on schizophrenia consequently has important implications not only for the treatment of the individual schizophrenic but also for our understanding of the complex and critical nature of early childhood development, child rearing, and the educative process.

References

Arieti, S. 1975. *Interpretation of schizophrenia*. New York: Basic Books.

Artiss, K. L. 1962. *Milieu therapy in schizophrenia*. New York: Grune & Stratton.

Astrup, C., and Ø. Ødegård. 1960. Internal migration and disease in Norway. *Psychiatr. Q.*, suppl. 34:116–130.

Bateson, G., D. D. Jackson, J. Haley, and J. Weakland. 1956. Towards a theory of schizophrenia. *Behav. Sci.* 1:251–264.

Bibring, E. 1954. Psychoanalysis and the dynamic psychotherapies. *J. Am. Psychoanal. Assoc.* 2, no. 4:745–770.

Bion, W. R. 1961. *Experiences in groups*. London: Tavistock.

Blau, D., and J. J. Zilbach. 1954. The use of group psychotherapy in post-hospitalization treatment. A clinical report. *Am. J. Psychiatry* 111, no. 4:244–247.

Bleuler, E. 1911. *Dementia praecox or the group of schizophrenias*. New York: International Universities Press, 1950.

Brill, H., and R. E. Patton. 1964. The impact of modern chemotherapy on hospital organization, psychiatric care and public health policies: its scope and its limits. In *Proceedings of the third world congress of psychiatry*. Vol. 3.

Brown, G. W., and J. L. T. Birley. 1968. Crises and life changes and the onset of schizophrenia. *J. Health Soc. Behav.* 9:203–214.

Cade, J. F., and F. Krupinski. 1962. Incidence of psychiatric disorders in Victoria in relation to country of birth. *Med. J. Aust.* 49:400–404.

Cameron, N. 1938. Reasoning, regression and communication in schizophrenia. *Psychol. Monogr.* 50:1–34.

Cancro, R. 1968. Thought disorder and schizophrenia. *Dis. Nerv. Syst.* 29:846–849.

Caudill, W. A. 1958. *The psychiatric hospital as a small society*. Cambridge, Mass.: Harvard University Press.

Clark, R. E. 1948. The relationship of schizophrenia to occupational income and occupational prestige. *Am. Sociol. Rev.* 13:325–330.

———— 1949. Psychoses, income, and occupational prestige. *Am. J. Sociol.* 54:433–440.

Cohen, R., I. Florin, A. Grusche, S. Meyer-Osterkamp, and H. Sell. 1972. The introduction of a token economy in a psychiatric ward with extremely withdrawn chronic schizophrenics. *Behav. Res. Ther.* 10:69–74.

Conrad, K. 1958. *Die Beginnende Schizophrenie*. Stuttgart: Thieme.

Day, M. 1964. The therapeutic envelope. Paper presented at the annual meeting of the American Group Psychotherapy Association, January 1964.

Day, M., and E. V. Semrad. 1971. Group therapy with neurotics and psychotics. In *Comprehensive group psychotherapy*, ed. H. I. Kaplan and B. J. Sadock. Baltimore: Williams & Wilkins.

Deutsch, F., and E. V. Semrad. 1959. Survey of Freud's writings on the conversion process. In *On *the mysterious leap from the mind to the body*, ed. F. Deutsch. New York: International Universities Press.

Diem, O. 1904. Die einfach dememte Form der Dementia praecox (Dementia simplex). *Arch. Psychiatr.* 37:111–187.

Edelson, M. 1964. *Group dynamics and the therapeutic community*. New York: Grune & Stratton.

Farina, A., N. Garmezy, and H. Barry. 1963. Relationship of marital status to incidence and prognosis of schizophrenia. *J. Abnorm. Soc. Psychol.* 67:624–630.

Faris, R. E. L. 1955. *Social disorganization*. New York: Ronald Press.

Faris, R. E. L., and H. W. Dunham. 1939. *Mental disorders in urban areas*. Chicago: University of Chicago Press.

Federn, P. 1952. *Ego psychology and the psychoses*. New York: Basic Books.

Freud, A. 1951. An obituary: August Aichorn. *Int. J. Psychoanal.* 32:51–56.

Freud, S. 1894. The neuro-psychoses of defence. In *Standard edition*, ed. J. Strachey. Vol. 3. London: Hogarth Press, 1962.

—— 1911. Psycho-analytic notes on an autobiographical account of a case of paranoia (dementia paranoides). In *Standard edition*, ed. J. Strachey. Vol. 12. London: Hogarth Press, 1958.

Fromm-Reichmann, F. 1948. Notes on the development of treatment of schizophrenics by psychoanalytic therapy. *Psychiatry* 11:263–273.

—— 1959. *Psychoanalysis and psychotherapy: selected papers of Frieda Fromm-Reichmann*, ed. D. M. Bullard and E. V. Weigert. Chicago: University of Chicago Press.

Gantt, W. H. 1944. Experimental basis for neurotic behavior. *Psychosom. Med.* monogr. 3, nos. 3, 4. New York: Harper, Hoeber.

Goldstein, K. 1946. Methodological approach to the study of schizophrenia. In *Language and thought in schizophrenia*, ed. J. S. Kasanin. Berkeley: University of California Press.

Grinker, R. R., and P. S. Holzman. 1973. Schizophrenic pathology in young adults. *Arch. Gen. Psychiatry* 28:168–175.

Gunderson, J. G., J. H. Autry, L. R. Mosher, and S. Buchsbaum. 1974. Special report: schizophrenia, 1973. *Schiz. Bull.* 9:15–54.

Halevi, H. S. 1963. Frequency of mental illness among Jews in Israel. *Int. J. Soc. Psychiatry* 9:268–282.

Hartmann, H. 1953. Contribution to the metapsychology of schizophrenia. *Psychoanal. Study Child* 8:177–198.

Havens, L. H. 1963. Problems with the use of drugs in the psychotherapy of psychotic patients. *Psychiatry* 26:289–296.

Hoch, P. H., and P. Polatin. 1949. Pseudoneurotic forms of schizophrenia. *Psychiatr. Q.* 23:248–276.

Hoedemaker, E. 1955. The therapeutic process in the treatment of schizophrenia. *J. Am. Psychoanal. Assoc.* 3:89–109.

Jackson, D. D. 1967. Schizophrenia. The nosological nexus. In *The origins of schizophrenia*, ed. J. Romano. Amsterdam: Excerpta Medica Foundation, 1968.

Jacobson, E. 1967. *Psychotic conflict and reality*. New York: International Universities Press.

Jones, M. 1953. *The therapeutic community: a new treatment method in psychiatry*. New York: Basic Books.

Jung, C. G. 1906. *The psychology of dementia praecox*. Nervous and Mental Disease monograph series, no. 3. New York, 1936.

Kasanin, J. 1933. The acute schizoaffective psychoses. *Am. J. Psychiatry* 13:97–126.

Kernberg, O. 1967. Borderline personality organization. *J. Am. Psychoanal. Assoc.* 15:641–685.

Khantzian, E. J., J. S. Dalsimer, and E. V. Semrad. 1969. The use of interpretation in the psychotherapy of schizophrenia. *Am. J. Psychother.* 23, no. 2:182–197.

Klein, M. 1932. The significance of early anxiety situations in the development of the ego. In *The psychoanalysis of children*, trans. A. Strachey. 3rd ed. London: Hogarth Press, 1948.

—— 1960. A note on depression in the schizophrenic. *Int. J. Psychoanal.* 41:509–511.

Kohn, M. L. 1968. Social class and schizophrenia: a critical review. In *The transmission of schizophrenia*, ed. D. Rosenthal and S. S. Kety. Oxford: Pergamon Press.

Kraepelin, E. 1898. *Dementia praecox*. London: Livingstone, 1918.

Laing, R. D. 1960. *The divided self*. London: Tavistock.

—— 1967. *The politics of experience*. London: Penguin.

Laing, R. D., and A. Esterson. 1964. *Sanity, madness, and the family: families of schizophrenics*. 2nd ed. London: Tavistock.

Landis, C., and J. D. Page. 1938. *Society and mental disease*. New York: Rinehart.

Langfeldt, G. 1939. *The schizophreniform states*. Copenhagen: Munksgaard.

Leacock, E. 1957. Three social variables and the occurrence of mental disorder. In *Explorations in social psychiatry*, ed. A. H. Leighton, J. A. Clausen, and R. N. Wilson. New York: Basic Books.

Lehmann, H. E. 1975. Schizophrenia: clinical features. In *Comprehensive textbook of psychiatry*, ed. A. M. Freedman, H. I. Kaplan, and B. J. Sadock. 2nd ed. Baltimore: Williams & Wilkins.

Leighton, A. H. 1959. *My name is legion*. New York: Basic Books.

Liberman, R. P. 1972. Behavioral modification of schizophrenia: a review. *Schiz. Bull.* 6:37–48.

Lidz, R. W. and T. 1952. Therapeutic considerations arising from the intense symbiotic needs of schizophrenic patients. In *Psychotherapy with schizophrenics*, ed. M. W. Brody and F. Redlich. New York: International Universities Press.

Lidz, T. 1973. *The origin and treatment of schizophrenic disorders*. New York: Basic Books.

Lidz, T., A. R. Cornelison, S. Fleck, and D. Terry. 1957a. The intrafamilial environment of the schizophrenic patient: I. The father. *Psychiatry* 20:329–342.

——— 1957b. The intrafamilial environment of schizophrenic patients: II. Marital schism and marital skew. *Am. J. Psychiatry* 114:241–248.

Lidz, T., A. R. Cornelison, D. Terry, and S. Fleck. 1958. Intrafamilial environment of the schizophrenic patient: the transmission of family irrationality. *A. M. A. Arch. Neurol. Psychiatr.* 79:305–316.

Lidz, T., S. Fleck, and A. R. Cornelison. 1965. *Schizophrenia and the family*. New York: International Universities Press.

Llopis, B. 1946. The axial syndrome common to all psychoses. *Psychoanal. Rev.* 46, no. 3:85–110.

Mahler, M. S. 1968. *On human symbiosis and the vicissitudes of individuation*. New York: International Universities Press.

Mahler, M. S., and M. Furer. 1963. Certain aspects of the separation-individuation phase. *Psychoanal. Q.* 32:1–14.

Malzberg, B. 1930. The prevalence of mental disease among Jews. *M. H.* 14:926–946.

——— 1931. Mental disease among Jews. *M. H.* 15:766–774.

——— 1956. Mental disease among Puerto Ricans in New York City. *J. Nerv. Ment. Dis.* 123:262–269.

——— 1959. Important statistical data about mental illness. In *American handbook of psychiatry*, ed. S. Arieti. Vol. 1. New York: Basic Books.

——— 1962. Migration and mental disease among the white population of New York State: 1949–1951. *Hum. Biol.* 34:89–98.

McReynolds, P. 1960. Anxiety, perception and schizophrenia. In *The etiology of schizophrenia*, ed. D. D. Jackson. New York: Basic Books.

Mednick, S. A., and F. Schulsinger. 1968. Some pre-morbid characteristics related to breakdown in children with schizophrenic mothers. In *The transmission of schizophrenia*, ed. D. Rosenthal and S. S. Kety. London: Pergamon Press.

Menninger, K. 1958. Toward a unitary concept of mental illness. In *A psychiatrist's world: the selected papers of Karl Menninger, M.D.*, ed. B. H. Hall. New York: Viking Press, 1959.

——— 1959. *A psychiatrist's world: the selected papers of Karl Menninger, M.D.*, ed. B. H. Hall. New York: Viking Press.

Meyer, A. 1950. Fundamental conceptions of dementia praecox. In *Collected papers of Adolf Meyer*. Vol. 2. Baltimore: Johns Hopkins University Press.

Mishler, E. G., and N. A. Scotch. 1963. Sociocultural factors in the epidemiology of schizophrenia. *Psychiatry* 26:258–294.

Nicholi, A. M., II, and N. F. Watt. 1977. The death of a parent in the etiology of schizophrenia. *Am. J. Psychiatry*, in press.

Niskanen, P., and K. Achté. 1972. *The course and prognosis of schizophrenic psychoses in Helsinki: a comparative study of first admissions in 1950, 1960 and 1965*. Helsinki: Helsinki University Central Hospital Psychiatric Clinic, monograph no. 4.

Ødegård, Ø. 1936. Emigration and mental health. *M. H.* 20:546–553.

Pantaleev, D., M. Yanatchkova, and R. Pashkova. 1972. Dysmorphophobic delusions and the Van Gogh syndrome in schizophrenic patients. *Nevrol. Psikhiatr. Nevrokhir.* 11:48.

Pavlov, I. P. 1941. *Conditioned reflexes and psychiatry*. New York: International Publishers.

Payne, R. W. 1966. The measurement and significance of overinclusive thinking and retardation in schizophrenic patients. In *Psychopathology of schizophrenia*, ed. H. Hoch and I. Zubin. New York: Grune & Stratton.

Rabiner, E. L., H. Molinsky, and A. Gralnick. 1962. Conjoint family therapy in the in-patient setting. *Am. J. Psychother.* 16:618–631.

Rao, S. 1964. Birth order and schizophrenia. *J. Nerv. Ment. Dis.* 138:87–89.

Rogler, L. H., and A. B. Hollingshead. 1965. *Trapped: families and schizophrenia*. New York: Wiley.

Rosen, J. N. 1963. *The concept of early maternal environment in direct psychoanalysis*. Doylestown, Pa.: Doylestown Foundation.

Rosenfeld, H. A. 1965. *Psychotic states: a psychoanalytic approach*. New York: International Universities Press.

Roth, S. S. 1970. The seemingly ubiquitous depression following acute schizophrenic episodes, a neglected area of clinical discussion. *Am. J. Psychiatry* 127:51–58.

Rümke, H. C. 1959. The chemical differentiation within the group of the schizophrenias. In *Proceedings of the second international congress for psychiatry*, ed. W. A. Stoll. Zurich: Orell Füssli Arts Graphiques.

Rycroft, C. 1960. The analysis of a paranoid personality. *Int. J. Psychoanal.* 41:59–69.

Schneider, K. 1957. Primare und sekundare Symptome bei Schizophrenie. *Fortschr. Neurol. Psychiatr.* 25:487–491.

—— 1971. *Klinische Psychopathologie.* 9th ed. Stuttgart: Thieme.

Schniewind, H. E., M. Day, and E. V. Semrad. 1969. Group psychotherapy of schizophrenia. In *The schizophrenic syndrome*, ed. L. Bellak and L. Loeb. New York: Grune & Stratton.

Schooler, C. 1961. Birth order and schizophrenia. *Arch. Gen. Psychiatry* 4:91–97.

Searles, H. F. 1960. *The nonhuman environment in normal development and in schizophrenia.* New York: International Universities Press.

—— 1961. Anxiety concerning change as seen in the psychotherapy of schizophrenic patients with particular reference to the sense of personal identity. *Int. J. Psychoanal.* 2:74–85.

—— 1965. *Collected papers on schizophrenia and related subjects.* New York: International Universities Press.

Sechehaye, M. A. 1951. *Symbolic realization.* New York: International Universities Press.

Segal, H. 1950. Some aspects of the analysis of a schizophrenic. *Int. J. Psychoanal.* 31:268–278.

—— 1956. Depression in the schizophrenic. *Int. J. Psychoanal.* 38:339–343.

Semrad, E. V. 1966. Long-term therapy of schizophrenia. In *Psychoneurosis and schizophrenia*, ed. G. L. Usdin. Philadelphia: Lippincott.

Semrad, E. V., and M. Day. 1959. Techniques and procedures used in the treatment and activity program for psychiatric patients. In *Psychiatric occupational therapy*, ed. W. L. West. Dubuque, Iowa: Boone.

Semrad, E. V., L. Grinspoon, and S. B. Fienberg. 1973. Development of an ego profile scale. *Arch. Gen. Psychiatry* 28:70–77.

Semrad, E. V., and M. Madow. 1974. A frequently encountered troublesome problem (neurasthenic phase) in the recovery from a regressive period (psychosis). Paper presented at Conference on Narcissistic Neurosis, Schizophrenia and Psychoanalysis, 2 November 1974, Boston.

Shakow, D. 1963. Psychological deficit in schizophrenia. *Behav. Sci.* 8:275–305.

—— 1971. Some observations on the psychology (and some fewer, on the biology) of schizophrenia. *J. Nerv. Ment. Dis.* 153:300–330.

Siirala, Martii. 1961. *Die Schizophrenie—des Einzeln und der Allgemeinheit.* Göttingen: Vandenhoeck und Ruprecht.

—— 1963. Schizophrenia: a known situation. *Am. J. Psychoanal.* 23:39–66.

Simmel, Ernst. 1929. Psychoanalytic treatment in sanatorium. *Int. J. Psychoanal.* 10:70–89.

Slater, E. T. O., and V. Cowie. 1971. *The genetics of mental disorders.* London: Oxford University Press.

Spotnitz, H. 1961–2. The narcissistic defense in schizophrenia. *Psychoanal. Rev.* 48, no. 4:24–43.

Srole, L., T. S. Langner, S. T. Michael, M. K. Opler, and T. A. C. Rennie. 1962. *Mental health in the metropolis.* The Midtown Manhattan Study, vol. 1. New York: McGraw-Hill.

Standish, C., and E. V. Semrad. 1951. Group psychotherapy with psychotics. *J. Psychiatr. Soc. Work* 20:143–150.

Stanton, A. H., and M. S. Schwartz. 1949. The management of a type of institutional participation in mental illness. *Psychiatry* 12:13–26.

Storch, Alfred. 1924. *The primitive archaic forms of inner experiences and thought in schizophrenia.* New York: Nervous and Mental Disease Publishing Co.

Sullivan, H. S. 1953a. *The interpersonal theory of psychiatry.* New York: Norton.

—— 1953b. *Conceptions of modern psychiatry.* New York: Norton.

Szasz, T. S. 1957. The problem of psychiatric nosology. *Am. J. Psychiatry* 114:405–413.

—— 1961. *The myth of mental illness.* New York: Harper & Row.

Tausk, V. 1919. On the origin of the influencing machine in schizophrenia. *Psychoanal. Q.* 2(1933):519–556.

Tietze, C., P. Lemkau, and M. Cooper. 1942. Personality disorder and spatial mobility. *Am. J. Sociol.* 48:29–39.

Von Domarus, E. 1946. The specific laws of logic in schizophrenia. In *Language and thought in schizophrenia*, ed. J. S. Kasanin. Berkeley: University of California Press.

Waxler, N. E. 1974. Culture and mental illness: a social labeling perspective. *J. Nerv. Ment. Dis.* 159, no. 6:379–395.

Whitehorn, J. C. 1944. Guide to interviewing and clinical personality study. *Arch. Neurol. Psychiatr.* 52:197–216.

Will, O. A. 1967. Schizophrenia: psychological treatment. In *Comprehensive textbook of psychiatry*, ed. A. M. Freedman and H. I. Kaplan. Baltimore: Williams & Wilkins.

Wynne, L. C., I. Ryckoff, J. Day, and S. Hirsch. 1958. Pseudomutuality in the family relations of schizophrenics. *Psychiatry* 21:205–220.

Wynne, L. C., and M. T. Singer. 1963. Thought disorder and family relations of schizophrenics. I. A research strategy. II. A classification of forms of thinking. *Arch. Gen. Psychiatry* 9:191–206.

Zetzel, E. 1949. Anxiety and the capacity to bear it. *Int. J. Psychoanal.* 30:1–12.

——— 1965. Depression and the incapacity to bear it. In *Drives, affects and behavior*, ed. M. Schur. Vol. 2. New York: International Universities Press.

Zilboorg, G. 1929. The dynamics of schizophrenic reactions related to pregnancy and childbirth. *Am. J. Psychiatry* 85:733–766.

Paranoia and Paranoid States

CHAPTER 12

Max Day
Elvin V. Semrad

I N ANCIENT GREECE, *paranoia* was a nonspecific term that referred to a distracted mind. During the eighteenth century it was applied to any disorder characterized by delusional thinking. The French alienists described *la folie raisonnante* or *la folie lucide* in the early 1800s. Esquirol, emphasizing a particular aspect of the disorder, called it "monomania." In 1871, Lasègue described persecutory delirium or delusion. The phenomenology of paranoia was detailed by German psychiatrists. Griesinger classed it among his "primary deliria"; Meynert called it "amentia." In 1863, Kahlbaum limited the term to delusions of a grandiose or persecutory nature. Yet in the 1880s, Emanuel Mendel, sensing a deeper relationship between paranoia and repetitive illnesses such as manic-depressive psychoses, described "periodic paranoia."

Toward the end of the nineteenth century, Kraepelin (1919), adopting the terminology of those who preceded him, categorized paranoia separately from dementia praecox because of its different nature, course, and outcome. He defined true paranoia, a rare condition, as a syndrome characterized by well-systematized delusions with little or no tendency to regression, remission, or recovery and only rare hallucina-tions. He thus distinguished true paranoia from paraphrenia, or the paranoid states, in which the delusions are not as well systematized or as logically organized. Kraepelin placed paranoia and paranoid schizophrenia at the ends of a diagnostic spectrum representing degrees of logical or delusional thinking. Although paranoid schizophrenics also show delusions of persecution or grandeur, these delusions are less well organized or rationalized than those of paranoid patients, and more signs of regression may be present.

Kraepelin located the paranoid states or conditions between these two extremes. The delusional systems of patients with these conditions are fairly well systematized (that is, not bizarre), but they are not as logically constructed as those of the paranoiac. Emotional response is appropriate to belief, and social behavior is well mannered. Delusions are usually characterized by ideas of reference; mistaken notions of personal influence, megalomaniacal grandeur, or persecution; or unshakable, unreasonable jealousy regarding marital infidelity—all without associated hallucinations.

Within the strict Kraepelinian definition, the diseases are rare and no remission or recovery is possible. Modern approaches, however, have tended to broaden both definition and diagnosis; paranoid patients may be regarded as erratic or fanatic rather than psychotic. Paranoid reactions and recovery from them appear more frequently than in Kraepelin's time.

In 1911, Bleuler described a delusional structure in paranoia similar to that seen in schizophrenia. Freud, using a dynamic approach, also observed the underlying relationship between paranoia and schizophrenia. He held that the fixation point for paranoia was narcissistic, while that for schizophrenia was autoerotic and therefore developmentally earlier. During the theoretical elaboration of the second major stage in his libido theory—the theory of narcissism (see chapter 8, "Theories of Personality")—Freud (1911) analyzed the autobiography of Schreber, a distinguished judge, who wrote of his paranoid breakdown.

Freud saw Schreber's paranoia as an expression of projected, unconscious homosexuality and explained the phenomenon developmentally. During childhood, Freud believed, the incipient paranoiac lingers for an unusually long time (is fixated) at the narcissistic level of development; the point of fixation is not exact, lying somewhere near autoeroticism (gaining pleasure from one's own body), narcissism (libido invested in the self, particularly the genitals), and homosexuality. Because the homosexual love for the father is forbidden, what is disavowed by consciousness is welcomed by the unconscious and leads to active repression—a covert death for these wishes. The onset of illness occurs with a disappointment in love or a mishap in social relations with other men, leading to a wave of libido that finds no outlet and sweeps back regressively to the point of fixation. Impulses from this point return to consciousness in disguised form—a noisy attempt to recover the lost love. In Freud's view, however, these distortions are not the foundation of the illness; rather, they represent the mode by which the repressed homosexual love returns. The illness itself consists of the individual's libidinal regression from concern with the internal images of the love object (decathexis) to narcissistic concern. The delusions are the patient's attempt to reinvest libidinal interest in the love object and to deal with this forbidden love ("return of the repressed").

Although in Freud's analysis of Schreber's paranoia the illness is an expression of projected, unconscious homosexuality, the defense mechanisms of projection and contradiction, rather than the homosexuality itself, are of paramount importance. For the paranoid, projection is a mechanism by which guilt-producing, unacceptable, aggressive heterosexual or homosexual impulses are ascribed to a persecutor (usually the figure of a former love object) who either displays these unacceptable wishes or accuses the paranoid of having them. Paradoxically, the very impulses that the patient has strenuously avoided return to haunt him in disguised form. Contradiction is a means of vehemently denying the dangerous and forbidden wish—"I, a man, love him."

Within Freud's scheme, denial of this wish can be contradicted in one of four ways, each addressing itself to a particular clinical picture of paranoia. In pure paranoia, the statement is, "I do not love him; I hate him because he persecutes me." In erotomania, "I do not love him; I love her, because she loves me." In paranoid jealousy, "It is not I who love the man; she loves him"; for a woman the statement is, "It is not I who love women; he loves them." In megalomania, "I do not love at all—I do not love anyone—only myself." In describing the four modes by which the defense of contradiction operates to nullify the dangerous homosexual wish, Freud thus presents a theme unifying the major clinical paranoid pictures.

In recent years, with greater understanding of the importance of the mother-child relationship, some doubt has been cast on unconscious repressed and projected homosexuality as the main basis for paranoia. Macalpine and Hunter (1955) have reviewed Schreber's original memoirs and ascribe the state to a basic uncertainty concerning his identity, occurring after many disappointments in his personal and marital life at the time of his wife's menopause. They find that Schreber basically dreaded feminization, rather than castration, as Freud held. Stoller (1975) holds that Freud's view of paranoia as rooted in early homosexual yearning still has merit if the notion of "transsexuality" (primitive yearning to merge with the mother) is substituted for "homosexuality." Stoller sees Schreber's dread as fear of merging with a mother figure, with whom the paranoiac is basically yet conflictually identified.

Rycroft has extended the meaning of contradiction as a defense mechanism in the paranoid personality, defining it as "an organized pattern of behavior and thought designed to replace repressed wishes, feelings, and anxieties by a totally different order of experience" (1960, p. 69). This capacity to cover an unconscious layer of misery and suffering with a conscious layer of organized and often vindictive activity—which can assume adversary, political, or religious forms—can account for the various clinical presentations of paranoia and the paranoid states.

Classification and Symptoms

Paranoia and paranoid states are a group of psychoses characterized by delusions of influence, reference, grandiosity, jealousy, or persecution that occur without hallucinations. The delusions are logically organized and systematized in paranoia and less logical in paranoid states. Pure paranoia is rarely diagnosed in modern times because it is so narrowly defined. Many more marginal cases occur than were originally conceived, and most recover, or don't recover, without contact with a psychiatrist.

Paranoia

In pure paranoia, a chronic delusional state, logical and well systematized, develops gradually. Hallucinations are rare and exacerbations and remissions occur, but the personality remains essentially intact and can function well in relation to the environment. The delusions may become increasingly complex as more energy and logic are applied to their elaboration. The three major variants are erotomania, paranoid jealousy, and megalomania.

Erotomania. Although Freud referred to a male in his formulation of the concept of erotomania, women most frequently manifest this particular type of paranoia. The patient fancies that a famous man is in love with her and therefore she with him. She feels that for reasons known only to the two of them, the loved one cannot acknowledge this love openly. She may pursue

him but then be shocked by his sexual advances, since sexual reality does not usually fit into the fantasied scheme.

Paranoid jealousy. Following engagement, marriage, or a narcissistic injury, a pathological jealousy may arise; the patient constructs an elaborate rationale whereby trivial incidents or casual events are seized upon as confirmatory evidence and misinterpreted. In conjugal paranoia (Revitch, 1954; Revitch and Hayden, 1960), the patient inflicts a humiliating relationship of long duration on the spouse. With the exception of this relationship, however, he maintains good contact with the environment and conducts his affairs well; he may in fact conceal his paranoid attitudes so well that the spouse is considered abnormal. The spouse, however, is usually collusive in strengthening the paranoid attitudes and may excite the patient's suspicious attitudes by making secret phone calls or opening the patient's mail. A general feeling of inadequacy, homosexual conflicts, and the mutually destructive aspects of the marital relationship are exacerbating factors. The relationship with the spouse thus not only keeps the illness alive and flourishing but builds on preexisting pathology. Often only an interview with both patient and spouse reveals the true state of affairs to the psychiatrist.

Megalomania. The patient may feel omnipotent or extremely important from early childhood and be convinced that he has unusual talents as a scientist, artist, inventor, or prophet, with no objective evidence of these talents. He may work hard for certain social movements that seem to express and satisfy his ambitions, but he usually does so on the fringes in a fanatic manner. Some patients invest all their efforts in litigation with little or no foundation in recognizable fact. Megalomaniacal patients neglect whatever actual talents they may have and fail to develop the personal, professional, social, and sexual aspects of their lives.

Paranoid States

The paranoid states lie symptomatically between paranoia and paranoid schizophrenia; paranoid delusions occur without hallucinations, and the delusional system is logical but neither as well systematized as that seen in paranoia nor as bizarre as that of paranoid schizophrenia. A tendency to hypersensitivity, exaggeration, and misinterpretation is seen; when compounded with tenaciously inflexible demands and expectations, an abrupt and tyrannical manner results.

In an individual who has adequately managed the vicissitudes of his life prior to the involutional period—albeit with defensiveness and a tendency to feel hurt and to blame others for failures—the involutional state is characterized by the growth of new paranoid delusions. Depression and agitation may also occur. The sensorium is clear, intellectual functions are not affected, and thought disorder does not occur. The prognosis is less favorable than in involutional melancholia.

Diagnosis

The essential diagnostic feature of paranoid reactions is a marked delusional system. Lack of trust is evident, rooted in an absence of trust in the parent-child relationship. The patient also manifests defensiveness and suspiciousness during examination. Suspiciousness may actually coexist with naiveté—a lack of normal guardedness—with regard to the actions and expectations of others (Grunebaum and Perlman, 1973). The patient suffering from this form of social skills deficit thus often feels he is being taken advantage of, a situation that may heighten the inflexibility of his demands, his tendency to rationalize and blame, and his feeling of general inadequacy, particularly sexual inadequacy.

Some patients may be polite during the initial phase of the examination. Others quickly express their hostility and suspiciousness. In addition to manifesting a defensive posture, the patient directs attention to small details, questions the meaning of the interviewer, manifests irritability to external stimuli, and takes inordinate measures to "set the record straight." Finally, frank delusions occur; their degree of organization varies depending upon the specific syndrome involved.

Intelligence tests may or may not be helpful in the diagnosis of the paranoiac. Paranoid patients

cooperate with testing and perform well verbally, but discrepancies appear in subtests. As the tests grow more difficult, the patient becomes more tense and suspicious. The Rorschach test may reveal very little if the paranoia is mild or has abated; it may demonstrate a great deal with a frankly paranoid patient. Test behavior may include total rejection of the test materials, prolonged reaction time, or a limited number of responses. Side comments, in addition to the content of the responses, reveal suspicious reactions to a dangerous environment (seen in emphasis on malevolent eyes and masks) and confusion of sexual identity. The total impression from the Rorschach of a paranoid patient communicates external threat, a need for self-protection, and problems of impulse control. The Thematic Apperception Test (TAT) reveals doubts concerning people's motives, confusion of sexuality, manipulation of the main figure by others, and a tendency to moralize.

The nature of the delusions differentiates the specific paranoid syndromes. As described earlier, the delusional system in paranoia is well systematized and logical; it is less well systematized in paranoid states and is frankly bizarre in paranoid schizophrenia. In the involutional paranoid state, the age of onset is later than in the other paranoid syndromes. Frank depression and agitation may occur, and delusions concern death, destruction, and persecution.

Occasionally a manic with paranoid delusions must be differentiated from a paranoid patient. The affective state is more labile in the manic and can easily turn to mania or tears during the interview; the paranoiac, however, will maintain a steady mood. There is little empathy in the paranoid patient and little likelihood of his accepting comfort from the interviewer. The manic will be expansive, while the paranoid will be cautious, reserved, and constricted in his approach.

Drug states and organic states usually present symptoms that contrast dramatically with those manifest in paranoia. In drug states, frightening hallucinations with bizarre, poorly systematized delusions occur; in organic states, such as the organic mental disorders, marked forgetfulness, poor memory, disorientation, and defects in judgment and affect are apparent (see chapter 15,

"Organic Mental Disorders"). Nonetheless, the particular paranoid syndrome must be distinguished from drug and other organic states because both may present delusional systems resembling paranoia.

Epidemiology

The statistics for paranoid illnesses are obscure for three general reasons: because of the suspicious nature of the patient population (which keeps its secrets to itself); because of a tendency to view many of these people as merely cranks; and because paranoid people do not come to official attention, especially in nonurban communities. Although Kraepelin found that paranoia was more common in men, certain forms, like erotomania, are more common in women. A recent study of only fifty-two patients (Johanson, 1964) revealed equal male and female distribution.

Paranoid schizophrenics become ill later in life than hebephrenics and catatonics, usually in their late twenties and early thirties. Paranoid states appear in persons in their thirties, and paranoia is more common after age thirty-five or forty. In addition to the age difference among these related illnesses, a shift occurs from the use of primary process thinking in paranoid schizophrenia to secondary process thinking in paranoia.

Some relationship has been noted between paranoid reactions and immigrant or migrant status; individuals moving to a foreign country may experience a paranoid or schizophrenic reaction, which may abate when they return home (Johanson, 1964); these responses may be primitive reactions to loss. On the other hand, while paranoid schizophrenia is the most common form of schizophrenia among native-born Americans, as a group they are less susceptible to paranoid states than immigrants; the meaning of this difference is not clear (Polatin, 1975). Paranoid reactions also appear to occur more frequently in urban areas, perhaps because paranoids are more likely to come into contact with others than other disturbed persons and because less densely populated rural areas can tolerate a greater degree of paranoid behavior than crowded urban centers.

Paranoid reactions also appear to occur more frequently among those with hearing loss. This correlation may reflect more than the suspiciousness arising from being unable to hear what is being said about one. Paranoia may also be a defense against loss; feeling that one is plotted against may be easier to acknowledge than loss of a necessary sense organ on what seems to be the road to final dissolution.

Pathogenesis

These psychiatric illnesses appear to have no genetic or neuropathological etiology; psychological mechanisms play the major role. We will discuss these mechanisms as currently understood within a psychoanalytic framework.

Vulnerability to paranoia begins in the earliest months of the child's relationship to the mother. Many factors in different combinations play important roles, including coldness and strife between the parents; the pain of frustrated instinctual needs; subsequent intrapsychic maneuvers of the child to deal with the aggression mobilized by this frustration; and insufficient or excessive perceptual stimulation, which may occur at any point in the child's early development. Later on in childhood, the defensive sexual sequelae to these early infantile factors result in feelings of danger to one's stability and self-defeat.

A background of fear, bitterness, frustration, callousness, and occasional open warfare exists in many families of paranoids, resulting in frustration of the child's instinctual needs and an attitude of basic mistrust. A pervasive yearning for the mother in a special close way leads to an abnormally intense primitive identification with her. This identification is heightened when minimal gratification is denied. The child then has to defend himself against both the need for gratification and the fear of its frustration.

If perceptual deprivation (by inadequate parental contact) or overload (by family strife) is maintained for a sufficient length of time with sufficient severity, it can provide a climate for a paranoid reaction (Sarvis, 1962). Susceptibility to a paranoid reaction varies with the availability of defenses and escape mechanisms, such as sleep, unconscious fantasy, and identification with the aggressor.

For a child to thrive and grow normally, he must obtain a basic minimum of satisfaction for his needs. In addition, he must experience an external reality in which his parents live their lives in a reasonable manner. Both of these factors are lacking in the paranoid-to-be. Since the child cannot change his environment, he changes himself (his ego) to console himself. He manufactures a "reality" that explains to him why he is immobilized and terrified in his surroundings and resorts to three chief mechanisms of defense—denial, distortion, and projection. Denial is used to nullify the effects of painful reality but, in fact, is an aversion to this painful reality, which is nonetheless always close to the surface of his awareness. Distortion occurs not only in the form of comforting daydreams and unconscious fantasies but also in the form of contradiction—a coherent, manufactured fabric to explain his misery. Projection in particular is used to deal with massive aggression for which there is no outlet. The child projects his aggression onto the parent because the hatred is too painful to bear and identifies with the image of that hateful parent—mechanisms referred to as "projective identification" by Melanie Klein (1932) and "identification with the aggressor" by Anna Freud (1936). The child attempts to resolve this painful situation by a process of repression that leads to the formation of a hostile, demanding set of values (primitive superego). This new psychic apparatus then becomes the vigilant detector of dangerous aggressive and sexual impulses.

Entry into the oedipal period involves differing patterns for the male and the female. The male looks to the father for strength in dealing with the unsatisfied and dangerous primitive yearnings for oneness with the mother and must then often deal with homosexual anxieties. (While Freud began his investigation of paranoia with the homosexual factors of the oedipal period, subsequent investigators have focused on the earliest infantile factors.) Identification with the mother relieves the female of the homosexual anxieties experienced by the male. She must nevertheless defend herself against yearnings for primitive closeness with the mother because she is not sufficiently individuated and looks to the

father for salvation from these yearnings. But closeness to the father is more than the oedipal situation can provide because of incest fears, and her delusions then become preoccupied with heterosexual dangers. These delusions cloak the primal tug toward oneness with the mother and salvation by the father and negate necessary separateness and search for selfhood.

With the exception of sexual features, postoedipal developmental patterns are similar for males and females. The paranoid-vulnerable child emerges from the oedipal period defending himself with an air of rigidity, pride, haughtiness, suspiciousness, and disdain (Meyer, Jelliffe, and Hoch, 1911) that distances him from his peers by his attitude either of positive omnipotence (megalomania) or of negative omnipotence ("They're all against me"). During adolescence his intellectual defenses gain him some recognition, although his aloofness still precludes active interpersonal involvement. He shows little interest in sex and, unlike other adolescents and young adults, does not attempt to find a partner. He may have particular friends on whom he pins all his hopes, but his relationships lack reciprocity of feeling and sharing. If he marries, he finds it difficult to enjoy a warm, sexual relationship. In fact, it is with marriage that the first paranoid suspicions often emerge against the fiancée or spouse.

Some paranoid-vulnerable males show signs of latent or overt homosexuality. Some workers see homosexuality as a defense against the primitive mother-child relationship (Klein, 1932; Rosenfeld, 1949). Male homosexuality itself, which springs from the son's distorted relationship to the father, is traceable to an earlier disturbance in the mother-son relationship (Bieber et al., 1962; Socarides, 1968; White, 1961). Various workers (Arieti, 1975; Macalpine and Hunter, 1955; Stoller, 1975) have not found homosexuality to be the crucial issue; rather, they note a confusion in sexual identification (a much earlier disturbance), which Stoller calls "transsexualism" (an intense, unrelinquished early identification with the mother). The fear of changing sex is ubiquitous in male paranoiacs, as in all male psychotics. In contrast, the delusional-hallucinatory system in female paranoid patients most often concerns a heterosexual attack with no dread of changing sex (Greenspan and Myers, 1961; Klaf, 1961; Klein and Horwitz, 1949).

In summary, the disparate symptomatology apparent in male and female paranoids can be explained by the nature of their premature leap into the oedipal situation. Precocity in this developmental sphere enables the child to escape the accumulated frustrations of the early mother-child relationship. For the male, this escape carries the threat of homosexuality; for the female, the threat of incest. In resolving the oedipal conflict, these threats are repressed. After the psychotic break, however, the homosexual and incestuous fantasies return to haunt the male and female paranoiac in different forms.

Psychodynamics

Onset of the illness may be acute or chronic. In the acute type, the appearance of paranoid delusions is sudden, as in patients with involutional disorders who, though ineffective in many areas of life, showed no paranoid ideas before. Often the delusions are an acute reaction to a loss. More common, however, is chronic onset, wherein paranoid delusions increase, with exacerbations and remissions but no overall disappearance of symptoms.

The precipitant of the overt psychosis may be either significant or trivial, such as an accident, a misunderstanding, an injustice that most people would deal with, or a particular attitude of the spouse. However, the intrapsychic meaning of the precipitating event accounts for an intensity of reaction out of proportion to the event itself. Psychodynamically, the precipitant often has the significance of the loss of a sustaining and supporting figure or carries the danger of increased closeness, gratification, and responsibility—as in a crucial life event such as marriage, childbirth, or personal advancement. The event revives the affective memories of old childhood miseries and unleashes rage from old frustrations; the individual thus experiences current and past stress simultaneously. The pain is more than he can bear, and he projects his unacceptable sexual and aggressive impulses onto available figures, as if they were the causes of his suffering.

His deeper hope is that they will share responsibility for his impulses and not merely criticize him for them. At the same time, he fabricates a delusional story of varying degrees of plausibility, depending upon the amount of logical (secondary process) thinking available to him, to account for his suffering and contradict actual circumstances. The route to the paranoid psychosis has been taken, with all former friends turned into persecutors.

At the beginning of his psychosis the paranoiac may be aware of the strength and inappropriateness of his delusions and may try to conceal them, but sudden outbursts occur that he cannot mask or rationalize. He may even move to a new environment where he feels temporarily safe, but soon the old delusions reassert themselves, excluding the reality of his circumstances. At such a juncture, hopelessness may lead to a suicidal attempt to escape the torment, or an attempt to turn on one of his imagined tormentors and murder him.

Just as the schizophrenic has a period—as the breakdown begins—during which he believes he finally understands his whole life, so the paranoiac experiences the phenomenon of "pseudo-community" (Cameron, 1943). Formerly vague, ominous threats of persecution form a coherent system wherein the persecutors become known and organized as a definite group—the FBI, the Mafia, the communists, the capitalists, and so on. Because the delusional system is now clear to him, he has a relation to the pseudocommunity of his delusions; "knowing" his persecutors gives him comfort.

Since the underlying precipitants for paranoid reactions are losses of or cumulative frustrations at the hands of sustaining figures, these reactions may in fact be self-limiting, like reaction to any other loss. After the patient completes the process of his distorted grieving, albeit with a paranoid superstructure, he may then recover and his symptoms will seemingly disappear. For this reason, and because contemporary society tolerates more divergence in life styles and attitudes, many such people will recover their former state in time without seeing a psychiatrist. In situations where the paranoid runs afoul of the law, an employer, or an institution, however, or where the spouse insists, he may be forced to see a psychiatrist.

Treatment

Although the outlook for successful treatment of paranoids has been bleak for a number of reasons, Retterstöl (1966) feels that two-thirds of patients improve with a combination of therapy and medication. The biggest obstacle in the treatment of paranoid patients may be the therapist's preoccupation with the details of the patient's particular system of delusional contradiction, his projections, and his homosexual stories, rather than with his emotional plight, his interpersonal relations, his frustrations and failures. If the therapist recognizes and responds to the patient's dilemma—his loss or frustration—the patient will haltingly respond by becoming involved with the psychiatrist in therapy. Treatment can then proceed as with the psychotherapy of the schizophrenic (see chapter 11, "Schizophrenic Reactions").

Individual Therapy

In our therapeutic approach, the first task is to diagnose the nature of the current emotional impasse. Once the issues contributing to this impasse are surmised, the therapist helps the patient face them, detail by detail, against his overt wishes, until the misery is laid bare. As this occurs, the intensity of the patient's concern about the delusional system fades. A resurgence of characteristic paranoid feelings is indicative of feelings toward the therapist that have not been faced.

Many therapeutic attempts have been sabotaged by premature discussion of the patient's homosexual fears and wishes. They are, in our view, as irrelevant to the nature of his emotional impasse as any other delusional system of contradictory thinking. The therapist must be ever alert to the patient's feelings toward the therapist—not to interpret sexual feelings but to help him face yearnings for closeness, dread of loss, and defense against the primal parental involvement.

In addition, the therapist shares the burden of the patient's pain regarding aggression or for-

bidden sexuality by letting him project freely onto his persecutors, or even onto the therapist. Unfortunately, many therapists rebel at the prospect of being a whipping boy, but it is a necessary psychological position if therapy is to be successful. It may take two to three years for the patient to begin to accept responsibility for some of these issues. To force him to face up to them prematurely merely increases his emotional pain without providing him with any possibility of relief. Projection is a useful device for unburdening himself of painful matters without acknowledging direct responsibility. This process at least permits discussion of the issues in detail; their ramifications then become more complete and, consequently, more human and meaningful. As the patient witnesses the therapist calmly accepting the projected issues, he can, by identification, receive the strength to accept them as well.

The essential ego techniques used by the paranoid patient are denial, projection, and contradiction, a special form of distortion. These techniques are used by the therapist as a base line for the patient's level of functioning. As his defenses change with regard to the same issues, progress is noted along a continuum—the patient's "ego profile scale" (Semrad, Grinspoon, and Fienberg, 1973). We observe improvement as the patient shifts from projecting his performance failures to making excuses for them ("neurasthenic patterns"). Further shifts that allow him to feel anxious ("anxiety alerts") are signs of growing strength (see chapter 11, "Schizophrenic Reactions").

Pursuing the patient's current and past misery will lead to a depressive reaction—a hopeful sign. Some of the depression may occur because of missed meetings, vacations, and illness. Depression will also arise as the patient faces details of his failure in life or as he realizes the damage he has inflicted on his life during his psychotic episodes. These depressions are useful because they imply recognition and acceptance of responsibility for self-inflicted failure—a momentous step for an individual accustomed to using projection, denial, and contradiction. The therapist helps the patient welcome his sadness at such junctures rather than masking this sadness with kind words, consolation, or drugs.

Feeling responsible for self-inflicted failures helps the patient grow. *by responding at gentle ?*

Paranoid patients must also be helped to mend their fences with relatives. As they recognize how they have destroyed the continuity of their family life, patients can be encouraged to see what they can do to reestablish it, as well as what can never be reestablished. In trying to keep the patient in the old relationship, the spouse may behave in ways that are collusive with the psychosis. The patient must realize which of these patterns, although familiar to him, are now antithetical to his well-being. He must see that he can deal with his loved ones, as with the outside world, in ways other than the old ones.

Family or individual therapy to help the spouse face the loss of the old relationship with the paranoid patient can be useful. Patients also become aware of their dread of separating from the therapist and, finally, of wanting to enjoy such separation at some point.

Although analysis of the psychosis-vulnerable ego would be time-consuming, this method could teach us more about the development of the various forms of paranoid psychosis. Many more case studies of this sort are needed before we can understand in any depth the meaning of the specific contradictory delusional systems inherent in these illnesses that have so long harassed and fascinated us.

Group Therapy

Therapy for paranoid conditions in groups that include patients with various disorders is a very useful approach. The patient can safely hide in the group until he is ready to begin to divulge the intensity of his hatred and distrust; at times of stress, he can resubmerge in the group. The entry of newer members, the departure of older ones, and the loss of the therapist at intervals for vacations, illnesses, or professional reasons gradually force the patient to face the intensity of his need and yearning for people. This realization leads him to talk more of the frustrations in his current and past life, and facing this suffering strengthens him.

One of the biggest problems with this therapeutic mode is to ensure the patient a place in the group. The therapist must love the patient enough to retain that place, since most of the members will not want the patient there. Paranoid patients require opportunities for outbursts of bitterness and anger that frighten other members. The therapist must be ready to allow them to leave the group after an outburst, only insisting that they return to say good-bye, in order to understand the meaning of their leaving. Affection for the group and particular appreciation of aspects of each member's personality often coexist with the rage prompting peremptory leave-taking. Gradually other members learn to bear some of the rage, rather than collusively inciting other pathological behavior, and to deal with the patient's misery and suffering rather than his system of contradicting delusions. A steady hand is required to keep such a group on an even course.

All in all, this is a knotty group of psychoses. Although not far removed from the schizophrenias, they differ from them in their specific psychodynamic mechanisms rather than in early developmental background. The similarity of intrapsychic history among paranoid and schizophrenic patients perhaps accounts for some of the current diagnostic difficulty.

Any human endeavor that encourages outlets for blaming, for an adversary view of life, or for seeing oneself as the suffering victim can attract individuals of a paranoid predisposition, providing them with rationalized outlets for their pent-up frustrations and aspirations. Some of these individuals may become leaders of religious or political movements. They may then be regarded as charismatic and above reproach or understanding; their psychological problems are overlooked and they are sanctioned as special humans.

Paranoid reactions have been defined as a group of illnesses for only a little over a century. Only in the last forty years have scholars and psychiatrists begun to discuss the possibilities of their role in global politics, mass movements, and large-scale violence and suffering. Mankind has had to distinguish—probably more often than has been acknowledged—between the paranoid psychotic and the truly inspired leader fighting against oppression for social justice. In addition to helping individuals who seem to be preoccupied with baseless litigious ends, fanciful or dangerous schemes, and projected rationales for inner turmoil, we can attempt to decrease the prevalence of the disorders they signal by increasing our knowledge of their interrelation with other psychoses and borderline states and by addressing future efforts to earlier case identification and treatment.

References

Arieti, S. 1975. *Interpretation of schizophrenia*. New York: Basic Books.

Bieber, I., H. J. Dain, P. R. Dince, M. G. Drelich, H. G. Grand, R. H. Gundlach, M. W. Kremer, A. H. Rifkin, C. B. Wilbur, and T. B. Bieber. 1962. *Homosexuality*. New York: Basic Books.

Bleuler, E. 1911. *Dementia praecox or the group of schizophrenias*. New York: International Universities Press, 1950.

Cameron, N. A. 1943. The paranoid pseudo-community. *Am. J. Sociol.* 49:32–38.

Freud, A. 1936. *The ego and the mechanisms of defense*. New York: International Universities Press.

Freud, S. 1911. Psycho-analytic notes on an autobiographical account of a case of paranoia (dementia paranoides). In *Standard edition*, ed. J. Strachey. Vol. 12. London: Hogarth Press, 1958.

Greenspan, J., and J. M. Myers, Jr. 1961. A review of the theoretical concepts of paranoid delusions with special reference to women. *Penn. Psychiatr. Q.* 1:11–28.

Grunebaum, H., and M. S. Perlman. 1973. Paranoia and naïveté. *Arch. Gen. Psychiatry* 28:30–35.

Johanson, E. 1964. Mild paranoia: description and analysis of fifty-two in-patients from an open department for mental diseases. *Acta Psychiatr. Scand.* suppl. 177, 40:1–100.

Klaf, F. S. 1961. Female sexuality and paranoid schizophrenia. *Arch. Gen. Psychiatry* 1:84–86.

Klein, H. R., and W. A. Horwitz. 1949. Psychosexual factors in the paranoid phenomena. *Am. J. Psychiatry* 105:697–701.

Klein, M. 1932. *The psychoanalysis of children*. London: Hogarth Press.

Kraepelin, E. 1919. *Psychiatrie: ein Lehrbuch für Studierende und Aertzte*. 8th ed. Leipzig: Barth.

Macalpine, I., and R. A. Hunter. 1955. *Daniel Paul Schreber: memoirs of my nervous illness*. London: William Dawson.

Meyer, A., S. E. Jelliffe, and A. Hoch. 1911. *Dementia praecox, a monograph*. Boston: Badger.

Polatin, P. 1975. Psychotic disorders: paranoid states. In *Comprehensive textbook of psychiatry*, ed. A. M. Freedman, H. I. Kaplan, and B. J. Sadock. Vol. 2. Baltimore: Williams & Wilkins.

Retterstöl, N. 1966. *Paranoid and paranoiac psychoses*. Springfield, Ill.: Thomas.

Revitch, E. 1954. The problem of conjugal paranoia. *Dis. Nerv. Syst.* 15:2–8.

Revitch, E., and J. W. Hayden. 1960. The paranoid marital partner: counselor's client, psychiatrist's problem. *Rutgers Law R.* 9:512–527.

Rosenfeld, H. 1949. Remarks on the relation of male homosexuality to paranoia, paranoid anxiety and narcissism. *Int. J. Psychoanal.* 30:36–47.

Rycroft, C. 1960. The analysis of a paranoid personality. *Int. J. Psychoanal.* 41:59–69.

Sarvis, M. A. 1962. Paranoid reactions: perceptual distortion as an etiological agent. *Arch. Gen. Psychiatry* 6:157–162.

Semrad, E. V., L. Grinspoon, and S. E. Fienberg. 1973. Development of an ego profile scale. *Arch. Gen. Psychiatry* 28:70–77.

Socarides, C. W. 1968. *The overt homosexual*. New York: Grune & Stratton.

Stoller, R. J. 1975. *Perversion: the erotic form of hatred*. New York: Pantheon Books.

White, R. B. 1961. The mother-conflict in Schreber's psychosis. *Int. J. Psychoanal.* 42:55–73.

Recommended Reading

Money, J. 1969. Sex reassignment as related to hermaphroditism and transsexualism. In *Transsexualism and sex reassignment*, ed. R. Green and J. Money. Baltimore: Johns Hopkins University Press.

Searles, H. F. 1961. Sexual processes in schizophrenia. *Psychiatry* 24:87–95.

Winnicott, D. W. 1960. Ego distortion in terms of true or false self. In *The maturational processes and the facilitating environment: studies in the theory of emotional development*. New York: International Universities Press, 1972.

Affective Disorders

Gerald L. Klerman

I N CONTRAST TO the "age of anxiety" that followed World War II, we may now be entering an "age of melancholy," precipitated in part by recent global events and consequent "doomsday" prophecies concerning nuclear warfare, overpopulation, and ecological destruction. Public attention to and acknowledgment of depressions and other affective states have increased during the 1970s. Coverage of mental illness by the media has reduced the stigma attached to depressive states, and a number of political leaders, astronauts, and figures in the arts and entertainment fields have publicly acknowledged that they have suffered from depressions.

Since the early part of this century, clinicians and investigators have grouped together a variety of psychiatric states and syndromes under the rubric "affective disorders." The dominant features common to these disorders are disturbances of the patient's mood and affect, most often depression but also elation and mania. Impressive progress has been made in research related to these disorders. Rapid improvements have been made in the effectiveness of drug therapies (detailed in chapter 18, "Chemotherapy"), especially the use of the neuroleptics, the tricyclic antidepressants, the monoamine oxidase (MAO) inhibitors, and lithium. The efficacy of these new treatments has improved the prognosis for affective disorders, and new forms of psychotherapy—family, group, behavioral, and cognitive—have increased the diversity and availability of community-based mental health services. Growing numbers of individuals with depressive symptoms are seeking psychiatric attention, attesting to the public's increased confidence in psychiatry.

This chapter will describe the clinical, diagnostic, etiological, epidemiological, and treatment aspects of affective disorders. Although these disordered states are now diagnosed by symptomatic and behavioral criteria, clinicians and researchers seek to establish etiological bases for diagnosis. This ideal is far from being realized either in psychiatry in general or in the diagnosis of affective disorders in particular. Multiple etiological factors are involved—genetic, biochemical, psychodynamic, and socioenvironmental—and these processes may interact in any given patient in complex ways. In the majority of affective states, etiology is uncertain and clinicians suspect varying combinations of stress, personality, central nervous system (CNS) changes, and other factors. Since knowledge of most of these factors is limited, and at best relies on evidence removed from the immediate clinical situation, this chapter will emphasize the symptomatic and behavioral features of the adult disorders.

Epidemiological studies in Scandinavia (Essen-Möller and Hagnell, 1961), the United Kingdom (Brown, Bhrolchain, and Harris, 1975), New Haven (Weissman and Myers, 1976), and New York (Srole et al., 1962) indicate that perhaps 15 to 30 percent of adults in the general population experience depressive episodes, often of moderate severity, at some point in their lives. However, only 10 to 25 percent of individuals with depressive symptoms and behaviors seek professional attention. Thus a vast reservoir of clinically distressed individuals exists, but because of inability to gain access to treatment, financial disadvantage, stigma and shame, or other reasons, most of them do not receive treatment for their depression. This group poses a challenge to the mental health profession and an opportunity for clinical psychiatry.

The Clinical States

The term *depression* has many different meanings. For the neurophysiologist, depression refers to any decrease in the electrophysiological activity of an organ or system, as in "cortical depression." The pharmacologist uses the term to refer to drug actions that decrease the activity of an organ or system; thus the CNS depressants include the barbiturates and the anesthetics, related neither clinically nor pharmacologically to "antidepressant" drugs. The psychologist classifies as depression any decrement in optimal performance, such as slowing of psychomotor activity or reduction of intellectual functioning. For the clinical psychiatrist, however, depression covers a wide range of changes in affective state, ranging in severity from the normal mood fluctuations of everyday life, sometimes called sadness or despondency, to severe melancholic psychotic episodes related to psychodynamic mechanisms of loss and repression.

Until recently, clinical depressive states have been classified according to alteration in psychomotor activity, with manic excitements associated with excessive CNS activity and depressive symptoms caused by inhibition of CNS functioning. Therapy based on this model uses drugs (either stimulants and depressants) whose actions oppose the direction of presumed abnormal CNS activity. This classification and therapeutic approach, viewed along a "stimulant-depressant continuum," provided the classical model for neuropharmacology, an approach partially valid for situations in which amphetamines and barbiturates were the major CNS agents.

Recent proposals relating catecholamines—a group of amines in the central nervous system that act as neurotransmitters in subcortical centers, particularly the limbic and the diencephalic—to affective disorders parallel this older view. The "catecholamine hypothesis" is the latest version of a series of hypotheses relating affective behavior to changes in brain chemistry and physiology. Whereas dopamine is currently the center of attention for investigating the action of neuroleptic drugs and the pathogenesis of schizophrenia, investigation has associated norepinephrine with affective disorders; excess levels are hypothesized as being involved in the development of mania and decreased levels, in that of depression.

While the catecholamine hypothesis has had great heuristic value for research, it has not as yet produced biochemical measures useful in diagnosis or treatment. Moreover, the complex actions of newer psychotropic drugs, particularly the phenothiazines and tricyclic antidepressants, make the more simplistic notion of a stimulant-depressant continuum obsolete. Lithium's ability to prevent the recurrence of both manic and depressed episodes suggests neurochemical processes common to both elations and depressions or to their predisposition.

The neurochemical hypotheses discussed briefly here illustrate the current ferment in etiological research and theory and the tentative nature of current knowledge of causation. In the absence of established neurophysiological, biochemical, or psychodynamic mechanisms to explain the etiology or pathophysiology of affective disorders, assessment and therapeutic decisions continue to be based primarily on clinical criteria.

Distinguishing Normal Mood from Clinical Psychopathology

Feelings of sadness, disappointment, and frustration are a normal part of the human condition.

The distinction between normal mood and abnormal depression is not always clear, and psychiatrists disagree about what affective phenomena should be diagnosed as pathological.

Affective disorders involve an accentuation in the intensity or duration of otherwise normal emotions. Because almost all human beings experience unhappy, sad, depressed, and discouraged states, patients' distress readily gains the empathic understanding of clinicians and family members. This very familiarity sometimes renders clinical assessment and differential diagnosis difficult, however, because it obscures the boundary between normality and abnormality; family and friends tend to minimize the severity of the patient's difficulties because the manifestations may seem like a normal emotional state.

In severe forms, most affective states are clearly seen as pathological by virtue of intensity, pervasiveness, persistence, and interference with usual social and physiological functioning. The difficult problems arise in the milder cases. A number of features distinguish clinically ill patients from those with normal mood. In addition to disturbances of mood, the psychopathological state involves a combination of the following features:

1. impairments of body functioning, indicated by disturbances in sleep, appetite, sexual interest, and autonomic nervous system and gastrointestinal activity
2. reduced desire and ability to perform the usual, expected social roles in the family, at work, in marriage, or in school
3. suicidal thoughts or acts
4. disturbances in reality testing, manifested in delusions, hallucinations, or confusion

When suicidal thoughts and acts and impairment of reality testing occur, they usually indicate a need for psychiatric attention.

Symptoms of Depression

Clinically, patients with depressions most often experience one or more emotional, cognitive, physiological, and social symptoms and behaviors; some of the most important are listed below and discussed in the following section.

1. depressed mood characterized by reports of feeling sad, low, blue, despondent, hopeless, gloomy, and so on
2. inability to experience pleasure (anhedonia)
3. change in appetite, usually weight loss
4. sleep disturbance, usually insomnia
5. loss of energy, fatigue, lethargy, anergy
6. agitation (increased motor activity experienced as restlessness)
7. retardation of speech, thought, and movement
8. decrease in sexual interest and activity
9. loss of interest in work and usual activities
10. feelings of worthlessness, self-reproach, guilt, and shame
11. diminished ability to think or concentrate, with complaints of "slowed thinking" or "mixed-up thoughts"
12. lowered self-esteem
13. feelings of helplessness
14. pessimism and hopelessness
15. thoughts of death or suicide attempts
16. anxiety
17. bodily complaints

Depressed mood is a characteristic symptom, reported by over 90 percent of patients. The patient usually describes himself as feeling "sad," "low," "blue," "despondent," "hopeless," "gloomy," or "down in the dumps." Along with this state of inner distress, the physician often observes changes in posture, speech, facial expression, dress, and grooming consistent with the patient's self-report. A small percentage of patients do not report the mood disturbance, perhaps because of denial or repression. These patients manifest other symptoms, sometimes called "masked depressions" or even "smiling depressions," that cause the physician to suspect depression. Although the patient denies conscious awareness of depression, the clinician's empathic response may lead him to infer the presence of a depressive state. This conclusion may, in turn, be supported by the patient's life circumstances, which may involve recent loss and the report of other symptoms.

An inability to experience pleasurable events is almost universal among depressed patients. Patients report that previous sources of gratification, such as food, sex, hobbies, sports, social events, or time spent with family, children, or friends, no longer provide pleasure. In severe forms, the patient is described as *anhedonic*.

About 70 to 80 percent of patients experience *loss of appetite* with accompanying weight loss.

A minority, usually younger patients with milder forms of depression, experience a compensatory increase in food ingestion, often in the evening and at night.

The majority of depressed patients (80 to 90 percent) experience some form of insomnia. A small percentage, however, increase their sleep, often as a way of avoiding stressful situations. *Sleep disturbance* may involve difficulty falling asleep, with ruminations and reexamination of details of life circumstances; being awakened in the middle of the night by frightening dreams or uncomfortable body sensations; early morning awakening; and a feeling of poor sleep.

Related to the inability to experience pleasure are patients' reports of *fatigue and lethargy*. Sometimes diagnosed as neurasthenia or anergy, these symptoms are associated with reduced social, familial, occupational, and sexual activity, feelings of "being run-down," "heaviness in arms and legs," and "energy being drained from my body." Patients will often interpret these feeling states as indicative of nervous exhaustion, overwork, nervous breakdown, or vitamin or nutritional deficiency. In severe forms, the patient may believe, sometimes with delusional intensity, that he is suffering from some serious malady such as cancer or tuberculosis.

Agitation refers to increased psychomotor activity experienced by the patient as ego-alien and reported as restlessness or tension. The patient complains of being unable to relax, unable to sit still, "fidgety," or "jittery." In contrast to the overactivity of the elated patient, which involves socially purposeful acts (albeit often poorly timed, socially inappropriate, or grandiose), the activity of the agitated patient involves tension-releasing efforts such as pacing, wringing of hands, nail biting, finger tapping, or increased smoking. Some of these behaviors are within the range of the normal "tensions" of everyday psychopathology, and many, if not most, of the individuals labeled "tense" and "high-strung" are probably manifesting mild to moderate agitation. Although anxiety and agitation frequently occur together, distinguishing the two is clinically useful, particularly since moderate to severe agitation responds well to phenothiazines and other neuroleptic drugs but not to benzodiazepines.

During the clinical interview, the psychiatrist may observe generally slowed movement, decreased facial expression, fixed gaze, and reduced eye scanning. All these physical manifestations are characteristic of the *psychomotor retardation* of depression and are usually correlated with the patient's subjective report of lethargy and decreased activity. The speech of the psychomotorically retarded depressive is slower and reduced in volume, at times to the point of inaudibility. Answers to questions will be delayed and the lag between stimulus and response will be prolonged. The content of the response itself will often be sparse; in severe forms, the patient's response may be only a few words or incomplete sentences. In the rarely seen but serious syndrome of "depressive stupor," the patient may be completely inactive, mute, and incontinent and may refuse to eat. Differentiating depressive stupor from catatonic states requires careful history taking and close observation that may be facilitated by amytal interview.

Reduced sexual interest is common during depression and may go unrecognized if the psychiatrist does not make detailed inquiries. In men, impotence is a frequent distressing symptom that may aggravate existing marital tensions and further diminish the patient's self-esteem.

The depressed patient will complain of a loss of the "zest of life" and a decrease in his usual level of interest in work, social activities, sports, leisure and recreational activities, family life, and hobbies. Although *loss of interest* may occur, the patient's actual level of performance may not fall. In mild to moderate states, the patient overestimates his difficulties, but in severe states, he may be unable to assume his ordinary responsibilities or family roles, claiming "nervous exhaustion" or "inability to cope."

In his classic paper "Mourning and Melancholia" (1917), Freud postulated that *guilt and self-reproach* were characteristic of melancholia (depression) but not of normal grief. Subsequent clinical research has revealed the inaccuracy of both parts of this formulation; many grieving persons feel shameful and guilt-ridden, while many depressed people do not consciously experience, acknowledge, or report guilt. Guilt seems to be associated in Western societies with conflicts generated by the prescriptions and proscriptions of child-rearing practices and religious beliefs, internalized as superego and conscience. Cross-cultural studies indicate that guilt and feelings of worthlessness are far less common in African and Asian societies, while shame and complaints of bodily dysfunction and loss of energy are more prevalent. In severe forms of depression, the patient's feelings of worthlessness may reach delusional proportions and be associated with condemning and critical auditory hallucinations. Whereas the paranoid patient experiences these ideas and voices as false accusations and sees himself as the victim of persecution and malevolent intent, the psychotic depressive feels that the criticisms are accurate and justified.

Depressed patients complain of *difficulty in concentration*, "slowed thinking," "mind being blank," "poor memory," and similar symptoms. Inhibition of thought and obsessional ruminations on self-doubts, worries over the future, self-reproach, and suicidal urges may cause these patients to be preoccupied by inner thoughts and less attentive to environmental demands. On formal psychological testing, accuracy is usually retained but speed and performance are slowed. In severe forms, particularly among the elderly, differential diagnosis from early stages of dementia may be difficult.

Low self-esteem and feelings of inadequacy and despondency are personality traits considered part of the psychodynamics of those predisposed to recurrent depression. Although controversy exists over the evidence supporting these psychodynamic predispositions, clinicians and investigators generally agree that during the acute depressive state the patient feels "inadequate," "incompetent," and "a failure" and believes that family, friends, and work associates regard him similarly. Beck (1969) emphasized this cognitive impairment among depressives, pointing out the depressed patient's decreased ability to assess his own performance and others' views of him. Furthermore, these difficulties may persist even after remission of the acute depression. The self-esteem of patients who experience recurrent or chronic depressions falls even further as the illness progresses or recurs.

Closely related to the depressed patient's difficulties in sustaining self-esteem are *feelings of helplessness*. Patients complain that they cannot cope even with small tasks of dress, self-care, or grooming; parental, household, or occupational responsibilities are even more difficult to negotiate. Feelings of helplessness relate less to actual levels of performance than to failure to meet expectations. Cultural patterns, child-rearing practices, and family values condition many depressives to be perfectionist, achievement-oriented, and self-critical and to have high ethical and moral standards. Internalization of such expectations renders these patients sensitive to the gap between wish and reality and therefore prone to admonish themselves as weak, inadequate, and helpless during depressive episodes.

Handicapped by low self-esteem and feelings of helplessness, many depressives also report being *pessimistic and hopeless*. Fears and worries about health, finances, family affairs, and career also concern many patients; they anticipate misfortune, experience gloom, and forecast doom. In severe forms, despair may be all-encompassing and may be associated with suicidal thoughts and acts.

Every physician should be aware of the risk of suicide in depressed patients. Death by suicide occurs at the rate of about 1 percent during the year of the acute episode and 15 percent over the lifetime of a patient with recurrent depressions. By sympathetic but systematic interviewing, the clinician can elicit the patient's thoughts, impulses, and possible intentions. Many patients have *suicidal thoughts*, but only a few have suicidal intent. The period of risk extends from the acute episode into the weeks and months after symptomatic remission; the highest suicidal mortality occurs during the six- to nine-month period after symptomatic improvement has occurred.

Approximately 60 to 70 percent of depressed patients report *anxiety*. It may be difficult to assess these rates since the term is often used in a casual sense to describe any unpleasant inner state, rather than in its precise sense—that is, a subjective state of inner distress with thoughts of dread, fear, foreboding, or anticipation of danger or harm, accompanied by autonomic nervous system dysfunctions such as sweating, palpitations, rapid pulse, or "butterflies in the stomach." Because of the frequent association of anxiety with depression, differential diagnosis may be difficult—a problem that will be discussed in detail later in this chapter.

Depressed patients frequently suffer multiple *bodily complaints*; almost every organ system may be involved. Complaints include headache, neck ache, back pain, muscle cramps, nausea, vomiting, lump in the throat, sour taste in the mouth, dry mouth, constipation, heartburn, indigestion, flatulence, blurred vision, and pain on urination. General physicians, internists, and other medical specialists often prescribe extensive and at times expensive diagnostic workups for these patients.

Very rarely does the patient experience only one of the somatic or psychological symptoms described above. Because depressed mood and a significant number of other associated symptoms (four or five) occur together with greater than random frequency, clinical subgroups such as "agitated" and "motorically retarded" types have been proposed. Terms such as *symptom configuration, cluster, constellation,* or *syndrome* refer to the coexistence of associated symptoms and behaviors.

There is no one depressive syndrome and no agreement about how to delineate the different elations and depressions. Most clinicians and investigators accept the existence of heterogeneity within the affective disorders.

Clinical Course and Outcome of Depressions

Comprehensive information concerning the clinical course of depressions is necessary to the clinician as well as to public health planners and agencies. Prognostic factors are helpful in clinical assessment, diagnosis, and treatment decisions for individual patients, particularly those with chronic or recurrent forms of depression, as well as for those with high suicide risk. In public health psychiatry, outcome data aids in planning programs and facilities for the long-term treatment of chronic and recurrent patients, particularly in community mental health settings. Reliable information exists on certain aspects of depression, particularly the likelihood of remission, recurrence, and suicide for large heterogeneous groups.

Remission of the acute episode. Most depressive states are self-limiting. Acute depressed episodes have relatively good prognoses even without specific therapy. Most patients with acute depressions have remissions with almost complete symptomatic relief and return to previous levels of intellectual, interpersonal, and occupational functioning. Alexander (1953), reviewing the experience of the 1920s and 1930s, found recovery or social improvement rates of 44 percent for hospitalized patients within the first year and more than 50 percent over longer periods. These rates applied to hospitalized patients with severe disorders, often psychotic in form, who were treated before the advent of electroconvulsive therapy (ECT). The introduction of ECT improved rates of recovery and reduced symptomatic distress and social disability.

Outpatients and neurotic depressives, who often have milder illnesses and may not require hospitalization, have better "spontaneous" improvement rates. Such improvements may represent placebo responses, the impact of psychosocial forces and family support, the pathophysiology of the illness, genetic determinants, or responses to the emotional support implicit in all treatment settings. Somatic therapies decrease the intensity of symptoms, hastening recovery rather than producing a "cure." Spontaneous improvement rates approximate the rates reported in uncontrolled clinical drug trials (drug trials without control groups for comparison) and in placebo groups, in which 50 to 60 percent of the patients were considered improved. With intensive treatment, however, the duration of depressive episodes is markedly shortened. With current treatment, especially drug therapy, as many as 70 to 85 percent of patients have marked to complete remission of acute episodes.

Duration of the acute episode. Studies of acute depressive episodes (usually in hospitalized patients) were conducted before 1950 and reviewed by Beck (1969) and Robins and Guze (1972). These early studies reported a mean duration of six to eight months. However, recent changes in diagnostic criteria, which now include milder cases of depression, and the widespread use of ECT and psychopharmacological treatments have reduced the reported duration of acute episodes to weeks rather than months.

Chronicity. About 15 percent of patients have depressions with a chronic course and do not return to previous levels of social functioning. They experience persistent bodily complaints, irritability, sleep disturbance, fatigue, and pessimism. Although we cannot predict which acutely depressed patients will become chronic, many clinicians report that as patients age they have an increased tendency toward chronicity. Family history, lack of social supports, and long-standing personality maladaptations also contribute to chronicity.

Probability of recurrence. The high rate of recurrence poses one of the major problems in long-term treatment. Although most patients have only a single episode of depression, 40 to 50 percent have one or more recurrences. Maintenance treatment with lithium or tricyclic antidepressants has reduced the rate of recurrence, thereby reducing the personal misery and social distress of the patient. Because patients with recurrent episodes require special treatment planning, the ability to predict high probability of recurrence would be of great clinical value.

Change in diagnosis. American psychiatrists continue to debate the validity of the distinction between schizophrenia and the affective disorders. One criterion for judging the validity of the diagnosis of depression is whether the symptom pattern holds up over time. However, studies investigating change in diagnosis from affective disorder to schizophrenia found the percentage of change to be only about 7 percent. Clinically, this finding implies that except for a small percentage of cases, the features of the recurrent illness will be similar to those of the original disorder.

Suicide. Suicide attempts and deaths from suicide constitute a major public health concern. The suicide rate among patients with chronic and reactive depressions is 29 to 35 percent; patients with involutional reactions or manic depressive disorders have suicide rates as low as 13 to 30 percent, indicating that the diagnostic groups are predictive. Overall, in long-term follow-up, the death rate by suicide is about 15 to 25 percent.

Elations and Manias

Although manic episodes occur far less frequently than depressions, their dramatic character continues to fascinate psychiatrists and laymen. *Mania*, the most widely used term, stems from earlier experience with psychotic states. More recent clinical experience, however, indicates a spectrum of elations. Use of the term *elations* is therefore recommended to encompass the spectrum of heightened mood from normal states of happiness, joy, and pleasure to extremes of delirious mania in which the patient may be "maniacal," markedly excited, hostile and assaultive, or paranoid and delusional. The spectrum of elations is outlined below.
1. normal states: happiness, pleasure, joy
2. neurotic elations: cyclothymic personality, hypomanic personality
3. hypomania (nonpsychotic)
4. mania (psychotic): delusions or other manifestations of impaired reality testing
5. "delirious" mania: severe overactivity, hostile attitude toward others, destruction of property, assaultiveness toward others, paranoid delusions

The distinction between hypomania and mania is conventionally based on signs of loss of reality testing. Manic patients usually manifest delusions of grandeur, poor judgment, and other signs of impaired reality testing.

Insufficient attention has been paid to patients with mild or neurotic elations. Although a number of clinicians and psychoanalysts, especially Lewin (1950) and Deutsch (1965) have described these patients, the diagnosis of neurotic elation has not entered the official nomenclature. Many individuals experience short-lived episodes of heightened self-esteem, increased work ability, decreased need for sleep, buying sprees, and distractability. Since the patient regards the episode as ego-syntonic and socially adaptive, he seldom consults a psychiatrist. These experiences in neurotic patients may be similar to enduring patterns in hypomanic personalities (people with relatively consistent base-line patterns of increased activity, good mood, and sociability) and cyclothymic personalities (those with recurring, alternating periods of mild depression and elation). The recognition of such states is important, not only in understanding the patient's personality problems but also in diagnosing forms of affective disorders responsive to lithium treatment.

Elated states occur much less frequently than depressions. Among patients with recurrent manic-depressive illness (now called "bipolar" illness), only 10 to 20 percent present with a manic episode or a history of previous manic episodes. By and large, clinicians agree on the major clinical characteristics of elations, including hypomania and mania; they are listed below.

1. elevated mood (high, elated, euphoric, ecstatic)
2. irritability, hostility, and belligerence
3. increased self-esteem
4. grandiosity
5. poor judgment
6. overactivity (motor, social, sexual)
7. flight of ideas
8. decreased sleep
9. distractability
10. shopping sprees
11. social intrusiveness
12. collecting of clothes, possessions, or other objects

Manic patients manifest distinctly impaired social and familial behavior patterns. In the hospital setting, they appear headstrong, intrusive, manipulative of the self-esteem of others, sensitive to vulnerabilities and conflicts within the group, irresponsible, and frequently compelled to test limits. They tend to alienate family members and to experience a high divorce rate.

Considerable disagreement exists about diagnosing the manic syndrome when delusions, hallucinations, and thought disturbance are present. Between 15 and 25 percent of manic patients have hallucinations or delusions and excitement, a symptom pattern described in nineteenth-century literature as "delirious mania." As the clinical course progresses, the stage of euphoria and sociability may gradually subside, and a stage of hostility and irritability with paranoid trends may become predominant. Occa-

sionally the excitation becomes so severe that the patient may be destructive, hostile, and aggressive. Some clinicians regard these clinical variations as atypical forms, suggesting that the boundaries of the manic diagnosis should be enlarged (in part to justify a trial of lithium).

Manic episodes have a high tendency to recur (Pollock, 1931); follow-up studies reveal that before the introduction of lithium only about 25 percent of manic patients had one episode (Rennie, 1942). Almost all patients with manic episodes also have depressive episodes. Variation occurs, however, in the duration and severity of the manic episode and in the intervals between recurrence. The variations of these intervals have major implications for treatment, especially in the selection of patients for lithium to prevent recurrence. Before 1940, the duration of episodes averaged about three months, but since 1950 a marked tendency toward shorter episodes has been noted with the use of phenothiazines, butyrophenones, electroconvulsive therapy, and lithium. In general, the first episode tends to occur in young adulthood. Manic episodes in people over fifty should alert the clinician to possible CNS illness, such as tumor, or the effects of drugs such as amphetamines, alcohol, or steroids.

New diagnostic criteria and the availability of effective treatments for the acute episode (phenothiazines, butyrophenones, lithium) and for prevention of recurrences (lithium) have increased research and clinical interest in mania and elations. In addition, treatment of a broader range of phenomena increases the likelihood of expanding understanding of affective illness and developing more effective treatment efforts.

Approaches to Diagnosis and Classification

The diagnosis and classification of the affective disorders is currently in the process of revision. The traditional psychotic-neurotic distinction and endogenous-reactive dichotomy have been critically reexamined and two new classifications have been proposed: the primary-secondary distinction of Robins and Guze (1972) and Robins et al. (1972), and the unipolar-bipolar dichotomy first described by Leonhard, Korff, and Schulz

(1962) and subsequently developed by Perris (1966) in the United States and by Angst (1966) in Switzerland. These new groupings have been advocated to resolve uncertainties derived from the concept of manic-depressive insanity initially described by Kraepelin.

Ideally in modern scientific medicine, diagnostic assessment of individual patients and nosological classification of disease in patient groups would be based on knowledge of etiology, pathophysiology, psychodynamics, and epidemiology. Unfortunately, knowledge in these areas for the affective disorders, while progressing rapidly, has not reached a level necessary for either comprehensiveness or certainty. Therefore, current diagnostic assessment of individual patients must be based predominantly on clinical and psychopathological information, supplemented by other sources. Nosological classifications, similarly, are based almost exclusively on clinical and psychopathological criteria.

The current research strategy is to define nosological groups as precisely as possible, using consistently applied criteria that are not confounded by etiological or therapeutic assumptions. It is hoped that the delineation of new, "pluralistic" groups according to these criteria will facilitate better communication among clinicians and lead to categories capable of generating research that will, in turn, yield knowledge for sound etiological classification.

Before reviewing the historical bases for various controversies surrounding the etiology and diagnostic classification of depression, it is desirable to make explicit the pluralistic point of view. With regard to etiology, a pluralistic view maintains that no single cause, in itself, can explain depression. Genetics, early life experience, environmental stress, and personality combine in various complex ways in the etiology and pathogenesis of depression; in individual patients these factors may operate to different degrees. For groups of patients with various subtypes of depression, one or another factor may predominate, but it is unlikely that the "necessary and sufficient" etiological bases for the classificatory model that has prevailed in classical medicine is applicable to the depressions described here.

A pluralistic view also informs diagnostic classification; depression is regarded as a syndrome or, rather, a group of syndromes. New nosological groupings have been proposed to resolve the ambiguities and inconsistencies of previous classifications.

Early Formulations

Theories of the etiology of depression underlie nosological classification; they may be described in terms of unitary, dualistic, and pluralistic approaches. The unitary approach, proposed in the United States by Adolf Meyer and his students and in Great Britain by Sir Aubrey Lewis, Meyer's most influential student and disciple, emphasizes the similarities that characterize all depressive episodes. This approach evolved at the end of World War I from Meyer's extensive critique of Kraepelin's concept of dementia praecox as a "disease entity" (Dana et al., 1905). This critique was an important step in the development of Meyer's theory of "psychobiology," which viewed all mental illness as a mode of adaptation to life's vicissitudes rather than as a series of separate disease entities. Within this framework, followers of the unitary approach acknowledge gradations in depression from minor to major disturbance, but they repudiate the classifications implied in the psychosis-neurosis distinction or the endogenous-reactive dichotomy.

The dualistic approach embodied in these traditional dichotomies—psychotic-neurotic and endogenous-reactive—tends to divide patients according to the degree to which they manifest loss of higher mental faculties. The psychotic-neurotic dichotomy places patients along a continuum based on the extent to which disturbances are associated with impaired reality testing, manifested by delusions, hallucinations, impaired memory, and confusion. In actuality, however, manifestation of these features determines where patients are located at the "psychotic" end of this continuum; by exclusion, the "neurotic" end of the continuum is associated with the absence of these psychotic manifestations, rather than with any clearly delineated or defined symptom pattern or psychological function.

The most influential dualistic formulation is derived from Gillespie's widely quoted paper

"The Clinical Differentiation of Types of Depression" (1929), which proposed a distinction between "reactive" depression and "endogenous" or "autonomous" depression; this division subsequently attained wide acceptance in western Europe, Great Britain, and Canada. Gillespie's formulation united two sets of observations, those focused on a symptom complex (vegetative signs such as sleep disturbance and weight gain) and those concerned with the "autonomous" nature of the symptom course. Rather than emphasizing the role of environmental stress as a precipitant for the onset of the illness as did Meyer and his followers, Gillespie noted the apparent nonresponsiveness of the patient's symptoms to the environment once the depressive episode had begun. He regarded severe depressive conditions as "driven from within"—autonomous and unreactive to the immediate environment—and thus endogenous. This formulation presupposes a continuum and, as in the case of the psychotic-neurotic dichotomy, emphasis has been placed on the characteristics at the most severe end of that continuum. The assumption has been that patients at the "reactive" end are defined by relative absence of "endogenous" characteristics—an assumption not subjected to empirical testing until recently.

Discussions concerning both the psychotic-neurotic and endogenous-reactive formulations have tended to equate the two in order to support etiological formulations that see the psychotic and endogenous forms of depression as having biological or constitutional bases, while the neurotic and reactive forms are psychological or developmental in origin. Close clinical scrutiny reveals, however, that these conceptualizations are not necessarily interchangeable. Although in American settings "psychotic depression" is a commonly employed diagnosis, psychosis is not one of the criteria for diagnosis of the endogenous depressive pattern. This diagnostic usage does not limit "psychotic" to its strict meaning of break with reality, manifested by hallucinations, delusions, and ideas of reference (by these characteristics, fewer than 15 percent of depressed patients in large samples will have psychotic features). Rather, psychotic depression as a clinical entity is used more broadly to emphasize severity of symptoms, degree of functional and social impairment, and level of psychosexual or ego regression.

During the 1930s and 1940s, considerable acrimony was generated over theories concerning the unity or heterogeneity of depression and affective disorders. By World War II, however, the debate between advocates of unitary and dualistic approaches appeared to have been settled by Lewis's extensive and important work (1934), which broadened and deepened Meyer's psychobiological explorations. In Britain, western Europe, and the United States, the unitary approach was predominant until the mid-1950s.

Many American clinicians have adopted this point of view. They hold that psychotic depressions differ from neurotic depressions only by severity of symptoms, indications for hospitalization, and legal requirements for commitment or certification. They also tend to reject nosological schemes and to emphasize social factors and personal experience in the genesis of depression, while deemphasizing organic, constitutional, or genetic factors.

Although earlier approaches made significant contributions to our theoretical understanding of depression and helped broaden assessment and treatment capabilities, they lack clarity and completeness in important areas. The more recent pluralistic approach regards both the Meyerian unitary concept of illness and the dualistic approaches of traditional dichotomies as too broad, on the one hand, to specify differences among symptoms and symptom clusters that often overlap, and too narrow, on the other, to describe in sufficient detail differences among and within patient groups.

Theoreticians and clinicians subscribing to a pluralistic approach regard depression and other affective disorders as a group of multiple symptom complexes or syndromes, like anemias, arthritic diseases, or heart disorders, rather than as a single disease. Research is underway to develop diagnostic criteria and nosological classifications that will define multiple subgroups of homogeneous patients and thereby facilitate the identification and verification of multiple etiological factors.

Primary and Secondary Affective Disorders

New classifications of the affective disorders have a strong research orientation. The main goal of recent classificatory endeavors is to develop categories that allow for testing of possible etiological principles rather than incorporating these principles into the categories themselves. Categorizations amenable to replication and evaluation will ideally help promote and ensure consistent application of diagnostic groupings in clinical settings. Toward these ends, categories should be as simple as those in other medical fields and should be able to gain validity from research data.

Robins et al. (1972) propose a distinction between primary and secondary affective disorders—an initial separation based on two criteria: the chronology of onset in relation to the patient's psychiatric history and the presence of associated illnesses. Within this classification, primary affective disorders occur in the group of patients who have previously been well or whose only previous psychiatric disease was mania or depression; secondary affective disorders occur in mentally ill persons with previous psychiatric illness. Diagnosis is thus possible without reference to immediately apparent life stress, and the knotty etiological questions posed by the endogenous-reactive distinction can be averted. Diagnosis is also independent of severity, again circumventing etiological issues implicit in the psychotic-neurotic diagnostic classification. To say that criteria for primary and secondary affective disorders do not include the presence or absence of a life event as a precipitant or of psychotic features is not to say that these features are not important in the assessment of depressed patients, decisions about treatment, or prognosis at outcome. Rather, the Robins group proposes that the diagnostic criteria for primary-secondary affective disorders not include these features as necessary or sufficient for assignment to a diagnostic classification. (See figure 13.1 for a summary of the primary-secondary scheme of classification.)

Exact data on the prevalence of affective dis-

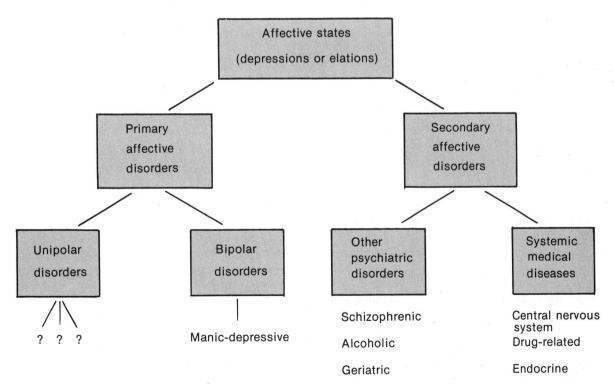

FIGURE 13.1. The nosology of affective disorders (adapted from Klerman, 1975).

orders characterized as primary and secondary are not available. In a large sample of patients with depression seen in emergency rooms of general hospitals, 55 percent were found to have primary affective disorders and 33 percent, secondary affective disorders; for approximately 10 percent of the patients, diagnostic assignment could not be made (Robins et al., 1972).

Depressive states also occur that are secondary in temporal sequence but that are associated with other psychiatric disorders. In order to apply primary-secondary diagnostic criteria, therefore, diagnostic criteria for the alternative, nonaffective psychiatric disorders must be specified. Toward this end, it is to the credit of Robins and his associates that they have published their criteria for a number of disorders, such as schizophrenia, hysteria, and alcoholism. The association of depression with alcoholism and schizophrenia, for example, has been well documented. Secondary manic states also occur; elated mood and overactive behavior may be secondary to organic states or the effects of drugs. In patients with schizophrenic symptoms or with histories of a previous schizophrenic episode, an elated or manic episode would be considered part of the schizophrenic syndrome according to the Robins criteria. For other psychiatric investigators, however, such an episode would be labeled schizoaffective.

Secondary affective disorders are also often associated with general medical illness or drug reactions. Affective states, particularly depressions, often occur in patients with pneumonia, infectious hepatitis, or mononucleosis. Endocrine disorders, particularly those of the thyroid, adrenal, and pituitary glands, are often associated with mood dysfunction. Another important group of affective disorders is the consequence of drug effects, especially those of the Rauwolfias, amphetamines, and steroids. Secondary affective disorders therefore include affective states secondary in time to other well-defined psychiatric syndromes and secondary to, or associated with, concomitant systemic medical diseases or drug reactions.

The primary-secondary distinction is not a definitive diagnostic tool. Rather, it is intended as an initial step toward classifying multiple diagnostic groups.

Unipolar and Bipolar Disorders

The value of distinguishing those depressed patients with a history of manic episodes (the bipolar group) from those with recurrent episodes of depression only (the unipolar group) was initially suggested by Leonhard, Korff, and Schulz (1962) as an elaboration of Kraepelin's concept of manic-depressive illness. Their proposal was adopted by Angst, Perris, Winokur, Robins, and others involved in familial and psychopathological studies of affective disorders in the 1950s and 1960s.

Since then, considerable evidence of genetic, familial, personality, biochemical, physiological, and pharmacological differences between bipolar and unipolar patients has accumulated. For example, genetic studies have shown that the families of patients with bipolar illness have a far higher frequency of previous psychiatric disorders than patients with depressions alone. Psychopharmacological studies indicate differences in the response of bipolar and unipolar patients to many psychoactive drugs, especially lithium.

Endogenous and Reactive Depressions

During the 1950s, after the introduction of tricyclic antidepressants, interest revived in aspects of the endogenous-reactive dichotomy useful in searching for predictors of subgroups responsive to ECT and to drug treatment. The current concept of an endogenous depressive pattern rests on four principal hypotheses.

1. covariation of symptom clusters, with the central group of symptoms—including slowing down, early morning awakening, weight loss, guilt, and unreactivity—occurring together
2. negative correlation with life stress and with history of recent precipitating events, depressions without a recent history of external stress presumably resulting from some intrinsic biological process, hence the label "endogenous"
3. correlation with age: older patients more likely to be endogenous; younger patients more likely to be reactive
4. correlation with personality, endogenous patients showing more stable and nonneurotic

premorbid personality patterns than reactive depressives

Although research has partially verified these four hypotheses, a number of unsettled issues contribute to a decline of interest in the endogenous-reactive typology for establishing clear patient groups. First, diagnostic criteria for the endogenous type vary. Some clinicians use the syndromal or symptom cluster criteria and minimize the importance of life events; others emphasize the history of observed life events in making the diagnosis, even in the absence of the characteristic symptom complex. Some clinicians require both criteria, while others are flexible, shifting their criteria between symptom pattern and reactive events in different patients, in accordance with clinical judgment. To add further to the confusion, many psychiatrists insist that if the clinician persevered in searching for the history of stress, all depression would prove to be reactive. In addition, investigations of patients categorized according to the endogenous-reactive typology may not have ensured that research samples included only patients with primary affective disorders; that is, samples may have included those with secondary conditions such as schizophrenia or alcoholism.

In clinical practice, the endogenous-reactive dichotomy as a diagnostic tool arranges patients along a continuum rather than establishing clearly defined groups; most patients appear to lie at midpoints on the continuum, few at the extremes. Therefore, although endogenous symptom features do predict positive patient response to ECT and tricyclics, the statistical distribution is insufficient to distinguish clear patient groups.

Moreover, classification of patients into endogenous and reactive groups based on the presence or absence of stressful events has not proved useful. This is not to say that environmental stress, particularly that due to crucial life events, is not important in determining a patient's vulnerability to depression, in the overall assessment of a depressed patient's resources, or in decisions about treatment with psychotherapy, drugs, or combinations. Because the importance of life events may vary, however, and because they may appear in combination with other factors, they should not be used as a crite-

rion for assigning patients to the endogenous group nor taken as designating a clear-cut nosological category.

Clinical experience and research findings indicate that the utility of the endogenous concept lies mainly in drawing attention to the symptom cluster composed of vegetative signs—particularly early morning awakening, psychomotor retardation, and weight loss. These symptoms do occur together in statistical association and predict positive response to ECT and tricyclic antidepressant treatment.

Gillespie's endogenous-reactive proposal has once again stimulated considerable important research and has aided the clarification of issues regarding symptom clustering, the role of life events, type of treatment, and prediction of outcome. It is unlikely, however, to lead to criteria for discrete diagnostic patient groupings that will contribute to sound etiological knowledge.

Psychotic and Neurotic Depressions

In the late nineteenth century and the first decade of the twentieth century, "psychotic" came to indicate the disturbance of higher-level mental functions—memory, language, orientation, perception, and thinking. Freud and other psychoanalysts believed that psychoses involved the "loss of reality testing," one of the functions of the ego. Although the classic meaning of the term *psychotic* emphasized loss of reality testing or impairment of "higher" mental functioning, manifested by delusions, hallucinations, confusion, and impaired memory, two other meanings or criteria have evolved during the past fifty years. The most common meaning of the term has become synonymous with severity or impairment of social and personal functioning, manifested by social withdrawal and inability to perform the usual tasks of household and occupation. The third use of the term is derived from psychoanalytic theory and employs degree of ego regression, as formulated by Fenichel in his influential work *The Psychoanalytic Theory of Neurosis* (1945), as the criterion for illness. In current practice, the term has lost its precision and is synonymous with severe impairment of social and ego functions. Furthermore, attempts to separate psychotic and neurotic patients into distinct, statistically verifiable nosological groups have been unsuccessful. Current evidence indicates that psychotic-neurotic distinctions, like those within the endogenous-reactive dichotomy, occur on a continuum, along which patients can be placed.

Psychotic depressions are relatively infrequent in current clinical practice. Only 10 percent of large samples show delusions, hallucinations, confusion, and other manifestations of impaired reality testing. With better diagnostic criteria, more mental health facilities, greater willingness of patients to seek psychiatric help, and new psychopharmacological agents, treatment is being initiated earlier in the clinical course, before psychotic stages develop.

Etiological assumptions have also confused the distinctions that characterize this dichotomy. Biological causes and disturbances of brain function are presumed to account for psychotic forms of depression. Neurotic forms, on the other hand, have been ascribed to social and psychological causes that lead to impairment of personality function. Evidence for these presumed etiological correlations is at best minimal.

In clinical practice, the endogenous-reactive dichotomy has, unfortunately, been used interchangeably with the psychotic-neurotic distinction. This usage is not valid, since psychotic states may also often follow reactions to life stress, such as loss and grief. Furthermore, individuals with endogenous features, particularly sleep disturbance and weight loss, may not have other endogenous symptoms such as delusions or hallucinations.

The psychotic-neurotic continuum thus has limited clinical utility. The diagnosis of psychotic depression implies severe impairment, higher suicidal risk, and possibly the need for hospitalization. Moreover, patients with psychotic depressions do not respond to tricyclic antidepressants alone, and may require combined tricyclic and phenothiazine treatment or ECT. Pending further research, the psychotic-neurotic distinction should be regarded as a descriptive continuum of some value in clinical judgment, rather than a means for distinguishing clear-cut nosological groupings with established etiological differences.

Similar ambiguities arise with the concept

"neurotic." For the most part, neurotic depressions refer to "nonpsychotic" forms of depression. Although little evidence exists that precipitating events are highly correlated with nonpsychotic symptom states, in many instances the term *neurotic depression* is used synonymously with *reactive depression*. Other clinicians use the term *neurotic* to refer to those depressions that arise in people with long-standing character problems or chronic maladaptive personality patterns.

Many older classifications and textbooks separated neurotic depressions from other forms of affective disorders, particularly affective psychoses (including manic-depressive illness). These were treated as psychoses, often together with schizophrenia, whereas neurotic depressions were treated in the same category as other neuroses. This discussion has attempted to examine all forms of affective disturbance, independent of whether or not they have previously been categorized as neurotic or psychotic with regard to symptoms, degree of severity, or impairment of social functioning.

Recent evidence indicates that neurotic depressives respond well to tricyclics. The efficacy of tricyclics, particularly imipramine and amitriptyline, for psychotic forms of depression was established in the 1950s and 1960s, even when samples included admixtures of patients today diagnosed as bipolar. The VA-NIMH studies (Prien, Klett, and Caffey, 1973) indicate that bipolar depressives treated with tricyclics do less well than those treated with placebo. For unipolar, mainly nonpsychotic patients, however, tricyclics were slightly more effective than lithium, and both were more effective than placebo. The Boston–New Haven studies (Klerman et al., 1974) showed a rapid symptomatic improvement in neurotic depressed patients during the acute phase with amitriptylene; over two-thirds of the patients had a 50 percent reduction in depressive ratings in four to six weeks, and most were asymptomatic, or only mildly ill, when the maintenance phase began. The tricyclic antidepressants are especially valuable in the outpatient treatment of neurotic depressive states. If response to treatment is regarded as a means of validating criteria for nosology, substantial evidence now exists for including depressed patients usually diagnosed as neurotic in the group designated as having primary affective disorders.

Neurotic Depression and Anxiety Neurosis

The practical as well as theoretical importance of accurate diagnosis is most evident in treating neurotic outpatients with affective states. Differentiation between anxiety states and depressive reactions has diagnostic, theoretical, and therapeutic implications, and symptom overlap for the two conditions is considerable. Many studies report, for example, that the most common types of depression show mixed anxiety-depression symptoms. In clinical practice, therefore, the physician is often unclear whether a given patient should be classified as suffering from "depression with secondary anxiety" or as "anxious neurotic with associated depression." Moreover, some theorists have argued for including anxiety states within the affective disorders and for a single continuum from anxiety to depression.

Recent findings, summarized in figure 13.2, demonstrate that patients diagnosed as depressed reported themselves to be more severely impaired on most items overall; anxious patients rated themselves as most anxious, while the depressed patients rated themselves as most depressed. When levels of depression were held statistically constant, the anxious patients reported significantly more somatic symptoms. About 35 percent of the patients could not be assigned to one group or another. These findings demonstrate the need to separate anxious and depressed states within the larger group of neurotic disorders (Derogatis, Klerman, and Lipman, 1972; Prusoff and Klerman, 1974).

The Schizoaffective States

The schizoaffective states also pose theoretical and practical nosological problems. Theoretically, these states challenge the separation of the affective disorders from other "functional" states, especially the schizophrenias. The problem as-

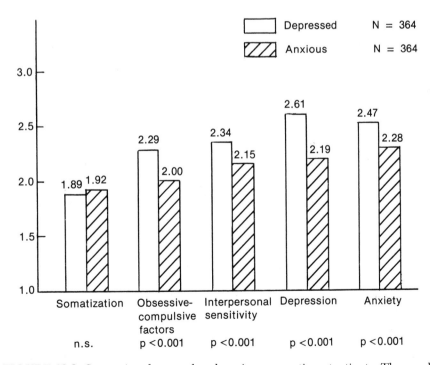

FIGURE 13.2. Separating depressed and anxious neurotic outpatients. The graph shows the mean ratings for depressed and anxious patients on five symptom factor scales; *n.s.*, not statistically significant. (From Prusoff and Klerman, 1974.)

sumes practical importance because of claims that patients with schizoaffective states respond to lithium. Although lithium has well-established efficacy for pure manic episodes, less clear-cut results are obtained in patients with an admixture of schizoaffective symptoms. Here the lack of criteria causes problems. Diagnostic studies have found that patients diagnosed as having affective disorders in British centers would be diagnosed as schizophrenic in the United States. In addition, many clinicians and research studies report changes in the clinical picture and diagnosis over time. The general range for the shift from manic-depressive to schizophrenic diagnoses is low—about 7 percent (Robins and Guze, 1972).

When Kasanin introduced the term *schizoaffective* in 1933, he was attempting to present clinical evidence to counter Kraepelin's postulate that emotional expression was absent in schizophrenia, since at that time absence or flatness of affect was considered a necessary diagnostic criterion. The schizoaffective diagnosis appeared in the United States and international nomenclatures in the 1950s and has been a source of considerable disagreement ever since. Some clinicians consider it a form of affective disorder while others regard it as a variant of schizophrenia, in keeping with the American tendency to regard a "touch of schizophrenia" (or psychosis) as schizophrenia. Still others (Perris, 1966) regard it as an independent disorder. The diagnostic situation is further confused, however, by findings from recent genetic studies that place the schizoaffective group closer to the affective disorders than to the schizophrenic psychoses. Most American psychiatrists place schizoaffective patients within the schizophrenic group, while only a few recommend that they be considered a separate group. Pending clarification of all relevant etiological issues by further research, clinicians and investigators should carefully describe their patient groups and their diagnostic terms before delineating definitive nosological categories.

Epidemiological Factors

Interest in the epidemiology of the affective disorders has grown in recent years. Investigation in this area focuses on the incidence and prevalence of the disorders in total populations and in subgroups defined by sociodemographic factors such as age, sex, and social class.

Incidence and Prevalence

The affective disorders, particularly depression, are thought to be the most frequently occurring or prevalent psychiatric disorders in adults. The meaning of such statements can vary, however, and statistics and reports of the frequency of occurrence are derived from a variety of measures.

Incidence (new cases per year) and prevalence (total cases per year) are the basic epidemiological rates. Attaining the most complete information on these rates, however, requires community surveys. Although the cases under treatment (treated prevalence) reflect true incidence and prevalence, in addition to providing information on the use of mental health facilities, only a minority of persons with affective disorders seek or receive medical or psychiatric attention, that is, become patients.

Prevalence and incidence rates will, of necessity, vary with the individual country's mortality rate—both the general mortality and that specifically associated with affective disorders. However, the lifetime expectancy measure allows for an age-corrected expression of morbidity, independent of the mortality rate. This measure is therefore useful for international and historical comparisons.

The lifetime expectancy of developing an affective illness of any type ranges from 8 percent to 20 percent. For Western nations, if attention is limited to manic-depressive illness, lifetime expectancy is about 1 to 2 percent. If broadly defined neurotic depressions are included, however, lifetime expectancy rates increase markedly, going as high as 20 to 30 percent in some estimates (Essen-Möller and Hagnell, 1961). These higher rates are determined not only by broadened diagnostic criteria but also by contemporary social forces—the public's expanding expectation of relief from distressing symptoms such as anxiety, tension, and depression; the weakening of traditional psychosocial supports, such as the extended family, the neighborhood, and religious institutions; and the expectation that the health system, especially psychiatry, can, should, and will respond to these forms of distress.

A wide variety of data about the incidence and prevalence of affective disorders comes from studies of admissions to psychiatric facilities, usually public mental hospitals. Figures for manic-depressive illness, expressed as annual admission rate per 1,000,000 population, range from 30 to 40 percent. The reported rates show wide variation because admissions are influenced by a number of factors: differences in the availability of mental hospitals; the presence of other facilities for the care of the mentally ill; changes in diagnostic practices; the severity of the patient's illness; demographic characteristics of the communities from which patients are drawn and to which they return; and attitudes of the patient's family and the community toward the mentally ill.

Many authors comment that a considerable proportion of individuals with depressive illness never see a physician. Considering all categories of depressive illness, only 20 to 25 percent of depressed people receive treatment. The proportion of depressed patients seen by psychiatrists is highest for psychotic illness: one-third of patients considered to have had a depressive psychosis were admitted to mental hospitals; the proportion of those suffering from manic psychosis admitted to hospitals is higher. Reported prevalence and incidence figures, however, particularly those based on hospital admissions, must be viewed as minimum estimates (Klerman and Barrett, 1973). Milder cases are now being treated, further reducing the duration of treatment reported for incidence and improvement rates of acute cases.

Sex and Age

An almost universal trend, independent of country, is the greater prevalence of depressive disorders among women than among men. Regardless of the measure used—annual incidence, hospitalization rate, point prevalence, or lifetime expectancy—there is a fairly consistent female-to-male ratio of 2:1 when all depressive disorders are considered. This difference is most marked for neurotic depression, for which it is as great as 4:1 or 5:1. The sex difference is less marked for manic-depressive illness, where the ratio of females to males is 1.5:1 or 2:1. Silverman sums up the sex role difference in this way: "There appear to be no exceptions to the generalization that depression is more common in women than in men, whether it is the feeling of depression, neurotic depression, or depressive psychosis" (1968).

The peak admission rate for manic-depressive and involutional depressive reactions occurs in patients aged forty-five to sixty-four. For neurotic depressive reactions, peaks occur between twenty-five and forty-four and between forty-five and sixty-four years of age. The lifetime expectancy for moderate to severe affective disorders is 8 to 10 percent for men and twice that, or 16 to 20 percent, for women. When only well-defined manic-depressive illness is considered, however, the figures drop to around 1 percent for men and 2 percent for women. Using hospital admission data for manic-depressive illness, the annual first admission rate for males is 8 to 10 per 100,000, with peak incidence occurring at age fifty-five to sixty-four. Comparable data for women reveal an annual first admission rate for manic-depressive illness of about 15 to 20 per 100,000, with peak incidence at age sixty to sixty-nine.

Social Class

Social class, occupation, and education are related to type, duration, and treatment of psychiatric illnesses. An almost universal finding, for example, is the increased incidence and prevalence of schizophrenia in lower-class groups. In contrast, manic-depressive illness was first reported to be a disorder of the upper and middle classes by Faris and Dunham (1939) on the basis of data from public mental hospitals alone. Subsequent investigators, however, have found no relationship between social class and manic-depressive disorders.

When educational achievement and occupational level are used as indices of social status, the findings show some relationship between social class and type of illness, summarized by Odegaard: "The relative incidence of affective psychosis as compared to schizophrenia tends to be somewhat higher in higher social strata, but this trend is neither strong nor constant" (1956).

Marital Status

Marital status is another social variable related to the incidence of certain mental disorders, especially to schizophrenia, with a much higher rate of disorder among people who are single, widowed, and divorced. With affective disorders, this relationship either does not exist or is very weak. Hospital admission rates for affective illness are practically the same in single and married groups. Though researchers (Pearlin, 1962) have reported increased incidence rates of depressive neuroses and reactive or situational depressions among separated and divorced individuals, they conclude that marital status shows a much less significant relationship to the broad spectrum of depressive disorders than it does to schizophrenia and that the relationship is negligible for manic-depressive illness alone. Even though schizophrenics are less apt to marry and though manic-depressives marry at the same rate as their healthy, age-matched peers, the relationship between marriage and manic-depressive illness remains insignificant.

Etiological Factors

In addition to descriptions of behavior, diagnosis, classification, and epidemiology, a comprehensive understanding of the affective disorders must include investigations of causation and pathogenesis. In addition to providing crucial assumptions for the validation of diagnostic and nosological approaches, knowledge concerning the etiological bases of pathology is also the goal to which critical aspects of psychiatric inquiry aspire.

Genetic Factors

The possibility of a genetic factor in the etiology of depression has been investigated in Scandinavia, Germany, the United Kingdom, and, recently, the United States. Four basic techniques of genetic investigation are used.
1. familial aggregation studies, comparing illness rates within and between generations of a particular family
2. twin studies, comparing illness rates in monozygotic (MZ) and dizygotic (DZ) twins

3. general population surveys, comparing illness rates of relatives of depressed patients with those of the general population
4. linkage studies using known genetic markers such as blood type or color blindness

Evidence from such investigations supporting genetic transmission includes an increased frequency of the illness in relatives of the proband (patient) compared to the general population; a greater concordance rate for the disease in MZ twins than in DZ twins; an increased frequency of psychiatric abnormality in relatives of the affective illness proband than in the general population; and onset of the illness at a characteristic age without any evidence of a precipitating event.

Family studies. There is virtually unanimous agreement that the frequency of affective illness, particularly manic-depressive disease, increases in the relatives of diagnosed patients. The prevalence is in the range of 10 to 25 percent for first-degree relatives of ill probands. Although the categories of depressive illness vary from study to study, a similar morbidity risk occurs among parents, siblings, and children of affected probands. The morbidity risk among first-degree relatives is 15 percent, in comparison to the general population's risk of 1 to 2 percent for manic-depressive disease. All studies have found that patients in the manic-depressive subgroup of the primary affective disorders have a high family incidence rate.

Twin studies. Twin studies show that concordance rates for manic-depressive psychosis are 68 percent for MZ twins and 23 percent for same-sexed DZ twins. These clearly different rates support the hypothesis of genetic etiology.

If the operation of a genetic factor is accepted, what is the mode of transmission? Some investigators propose an autosomal dominant gene with incomplete penetrance—autosomal dominant because of the similar morbidity risk (15 percent) among parents, children, and siblings, but incomplete penetrance to explain the less than 100-percent concordance in MZ twins. Other genetic hypotheses, heterogeneity of genes or polygenic models, for example, do not have an advantage over the dominant, single-gene model, which has the greatest predictive power.

Good evidence exists for a genetic factor in affective illness. Furthermore, the genetic evidence supports the use of bipolar-unipolar classifications of patients with affective illness.

Other Biological Factors

In addition to genetic transmission, other biological factors may be significant in the cause and pathogenesis of affective disorders. These factors include electrolyte disturbances, especially of sodium or potassium; neurophysiological alterations based on findings from electrophysiological studies using electroencephalography (EEG) and evoked potential methods; dysfunction and faulty regulation of autonomic nervous system activity; neuroendocrine abnormalities, including hypothalamic, pituitary, adrenal cortical, thyroid, and gonadal changes; and neurochemical alterations, especially in the biogenic amines, which serve as CNS and peripheral neurotransmitters (including norepinephrine, serotonin, dopamine, and acetylcholines).

The research in support of these hypotheses has been extensive and of high quality. Neurochemical hypotheses, particularly those involving the catecholamines, have received the greatest attention, because of the function of these monoamines as neurotransmitters involved in the actions of psychoactive drugs (see chapter 18, "Chemotherapy," and chapter 5, "The Biochemistry of Affective Disorders").

Life Events and Environmental Stress

Most American clinicians and some investigators have long been convinced that a relationship exists between stressful life events and clinical depression. Clinical case discussions often include statements relating stress, especially from life events, to the onset of depressive episodes. In such discussions, life events are thought to play an important role in the etiology of depression, at least its precipitation, as evidenced by statements such as "The depression arose in relation to . . ." or "The depression was precipitated by . . ." Some clinicians even believe that life

events play the primary or major role in depressions, while others are more conservative, limiting the role of life events to contributing to onset and timing of the acute episode.

The theory of an environmental etiology of affective disorders has multiple sources: Meyer's general psychobiological approach, psychological observations on reactions to loss, and psychopathological studies relating the presence or absence of precipitating events to the assignment of patients along the endogenous-reactive continuum.

While empirical studies supporting the relationship of life events to the entire range of psychiatric illnesses are inconsistent in quality and inconclusive, the same is not true for studies focusing on affective disorders. Here the quality of research design and experimental methods is good, if not excellent, and the findings are positive and internally consistent.

In general, the research confirms the existence of a relationship between life events and depression. Recently the more refined hypothesis that particular events or classes of events may be associated with the onset of depressive illness has been studied. For example, the New Haven group characterized life events as either "exits from" or "entrances into" the social field and found that exits such as deaths and losses are more frequently associated with depression. In addition, when life events are classified as desirable or undesirable, a greater number of undesirable events are associated with depression (Paykel, 1974).

In any review of this evidence, a few cautionary notes are in order. Specific events can contribute only partially to the onset or development of depression. Wender (1967) notes that when the incidence of a single event to account for the disease is low (as with affective disorders), the power of a single event to account for the disease is relatively limited. Thus in analyzing loss in relation to depression, exits from the social field occurred to 25 percent of depressives and 5 percent of controls. Exits precede depression in only a small (though substantial) number of depressive cases. Furthermore, less than 20 percent of any population experiencing exits becomes clinically depressed. This evidence suggests that a significant factor in the depression must be some predisposition, whether genetic, psychosocial, or characterological.

Personality and Psychodynamic Factors

Clinicians since the time of Hippocrates have noted that certain "temperaments" are related to depressions and elations, but only in the twentieth century, following the observations of Freud (1917), Abraham (1927), Rado (1929), Bibring (1953), and other psychoanalysts, have these relationships been explored in depth. It is widely believed that persons prone to depression are characterized by low self-esteem, strong superego, clinging and dependent interpersonal relations, and limited capacity for mature and enduring object relations. While these traits are common among depressives, no single personality trait, constellation, or type has been established as uniquely predisposed to depression. All humans, of whatever personality pattern, can and do become depressed under appropriate circumstances, although certain personality types—the oral-dependent, the obsessive-compulsive, and the hysterical—may be at greater risk of depression than the antisocial, the paranoid, or certain other types who utilize projection and other externalizing modes of defense.

Similarly, efforts have been made to identify a single psychodynamic factor or mechanism, such as loss or hostility turned against self, as central and unique to the psychogenesis of depression. While these factors have gained wide clinical emphasis, especially in guiding psychotherapy, the research evidence supporting their etiological basis is still being developed. (The theories and psychodynamics of these intrapsychic and interpersonal concepts are elaborated in chapter 8, "Theories of Personality," chapter 9, "The Dynamic Bases of Psychopathology," and chapter 10, "Psychoneurotic Disorders.")

Psychodynamic formulations are concerned not only with ongoing dynamic conflicts, evident in guilt, reactions to loss, or hostility turned against the self, which may be involved in the manifest depressive episode, but also with features that may antedate the acute depressive episode and therefore may be regarded as etiological. Some of these are rooted in personality, since a major psychodynamic hypothesis focuses on the predisposition of certain personality types to depression.

More basic in psychodynamic thinking is the belief that the most crucial etiological forces are those that operate in childhood. Regarding depression and mania, emphasis on infancy and early childhood has focused on possible impairments of ego function and sensitivities to separation and loss that arise from the vicissitudes of the early mother-child relationship. Attempts to test this hypothesis have relied on direct observation of infants and young children, particularly those in institutions who develop the "anaclitic" depressions described by Spitz (1946) and Bowlby (1969). Another line of investigation has focused on the frequency of parental loss and other kinds of psychic trauma in the childhood of depressives. While these studies indicate that, as a group, depressives seem to experience more parental loss from death, separation, or other causes than normal or other diagnostic groups, this factor alone does not seem sufficiently universal to account for all forms of depression. At the present time, the psychodynamic hypotheses are primarily of great heuristic value, contributing to case formulation, guidance of psychotherapeutic practice, and the design of future research.

Treatment Considerations

For the most part, the treatment of depressions and related affective disorders is a gratifying experience for patients, their families, and psychiatrists. Because of the range of biological and psychological treatments available, patient response is generally good, particularly during the acute episode. Special problems arise in planning long-term treatment because some depressions and most manias tend to become chronic or to recur.

Given the availability of multiple effective treatments—drugs, ECT, and various types of psychotherapy (including cognitive, behavioral, family, and psychoanalytic)—the skillful psychiatrist is urged to adopt a pluralistic view. The therapist should ask himself this question about each patient: "What treatment would be most appropriate for this patient at this point in his clinical illness and personal life?" The flexible pluralistic approach is called for, without commitment to theoretical schools or treatment ideologies.

Treatment of Acute Depressions

Table 13.1 presents the different classes of drugs used in the treatment of acute depressions. These include tricyclic antidepressants, MAO inhibitors, psychomotor stimulants, and various sedatives and tranquilizers.

Tricyclic antidepressants. Currently, the most widely used and generally the most effective antidepressants are the tricyclic antidepressants, which include three chemical subseries. Imipramine is the original compound of the prototypic subseries, which also includes desipramine. Another related series is derived from the dibenzocycloheptene nucleus and includes amitriptyline, nortriptyline, and protriptyline. Recently, a third series of tricyclic derivatives, including doxepin, has been marketed; these drugs' structure

is similar to the nuclei of the phenothiazines and thioxanthenes. All three chemical series share similar pharmacological and clinical actions. In normal human subjects, the tricyclic drugs induce mildly sedative effects similar to those of the phenothiazines. Their clinical antidepressant effect is probably related to their capacity to potentiate the CNS actions of norepinephrine.

The dose range of the tricyclic compounds is wide. It is possible to start patients at low dose—20–40 mg/day of imipramine or its equivalent—and gradually build up to 200–300 mg/day. The initial therapeutic response may require from one to two weeks of treatment and may not become maximal until the third or fourth week. In controlled trials, differences between drugs and placebo first appeared at about two weeks and became maximal at about three to four weeks. If some clinical response has not occurred within four to six weeks at an adequate and individualized dose, continuation of the drug is usually not worthwhile and an alternate treatment should be considered. The adequate dose is ar-

TABLE 13.1. Drugs used in treating depressions.

Main group and chemical type	Generic name	Trade name
Tricyclic antidepressants		
Iminodibenzyls	Desipramine	Norpramin, Pertofrane
	Imipramine	Tofranil
	Trimepramine	Not available in U.S.
Dibenzocycloheptenes	Amitriptyline	Elavil, Endep
	Nortriptyline	Aventyl
	Protriptyline	Vivactil
Dibenzoxepin	Doxepin	Sinequan
Monoamine oxidase inhibitors		
Hydrazines	Isocarboxazid	Marplan
	Nialamide	Not available in U.S.
	Phenelzine	Nardil
Nonhydrazines	Pargyline	Eutonyl
	Tranylcypromine	Parnate
Psychomotor stimulants		
Amphetamines	Amphetamine	Many brands
	Dextroamphetamine	Many brands
	Amphetamine in combination with barbiturate	Dexamyl
Nonamphetamines	Methylphenidate	Ritalin

rived at by gradually raising the total daily dose until the patient develops the therapeutically desired response; although disconcerting autonomic effects sometimes occur, the desired response most frequently emerges first.

The optimal duration of treatment for the acute episode has not been fully determined. Current clinical practice is to reduce the dosage slowly in an attempt to withdraw the drug approximately three months after remission and to observe the patient's reactions. Tricyclic drugs should not be discontinued rapidly. Some period of gradual withdrawal is desirable, since symptoms of nausea, vomiting, malaise, and muscular pains occasionally occur as manifestations of a mild withdrawal reaction.

Although the tricyclic drugs are relatively safe, a variety of adverse effects, mostly minor, occur—particularly with doses above 200–300 mg/day. The most common are due to autonomic actions: dry mouth, increased sweating, difficulty in visual accommodation, postural hypotension, memory difficulty, and urinary retention. The most serious adverse effects are possible induction of cardiac arrhythmia in patients with known EKG or cardiac abnormalities. These effects are related to dosage and are more common in the elderly. Rare instances of jaundice and blood dyscrasia also have been observed.

Monoamine oxidase inhibitors. Based on chemical structure, the MAO inhibitors are divided into two subgroups: the hydrazines, of which phenelzine and isocarboxazid are presently marketed in the United States; the nonhydrazines include tranylcypromine and pargyline, which is also used for hypertension.

All of these drugs inhibit MAO in animal brains. In depressed patients, pharmacologically induced reduction in MAO activity correlates with improvement in the patient's mood and clinical symptoms. While their pharmacological actions are of continuing research importance, controlled comparisons indicate that the MAO inhibitors are generally less effective than the tricyclic derivatives but more effective than placebo. A number of clinicians maintain that certain patients respond specifically to MAO inhibitors. Before concluding that a patient is unresponsive to drug treatment, a trial with an MAO inhibitor is therefore indicated.

Adverse reactions are more common with the MAO inhibitors than with the tricyclic series. Dry mouth and other anticholinergic effects occur, and hypotension is common with higher doses. With tranylcypromine, amphetaminelike CNS stimulation effects may occur. A serious problem with the MAO inhibitors is the risk of acute hepatic damage (which led to the withdrawal of iproniazid and pheniprazine from the market). The most serious effect, hypertensive encephalopathy, has resulted from toxic interactions with other drugs and certain foods, including yeast, certain beans, pickled herring, chocolate, milk and cream products, and various wines and cheeses.

Combinations of MAO inhibitors with a tricyclic antidepressant, or the use of MAO inhibitors less than one week after the tricyclic has been discontinued, may result in restlessness, hypertension, and even coma. Because of these adverse effects and the limited range of efficacy, MAO inhibitors are used mainly for patients who have not responded to tricyclic antidepressants.

MAO inhibitors are prescribed less frequently today than they were a decade ago because of their adverse effects. However, the pendulum may have swung too far, and many patients who might benefit from MAO inhibitors do not receive them.

Psychomotor stimulants. Psychomotor stimulants, of which the amphetamines were the prototype, are currently much less important in the treatment of depression than they were in the past. Amphetamine, dextroamphetamine, methylphenidate, and related drugs increase alertness and produce elevation of mood, but these effects are transient, often disappearing after a few days. Controlled trials of amphetamines do not demonstrate more effectiveness than placebo for the majority of patients.

Because many patients also experienced increases in anxiety, tension, irritability, and cardiovascular stimulation with amphetamines, barbiturates were often prescribed as adjunctive treatment in the past, and several amphetamine-barbiturate combinations were marketed. Pharmacological studies in animals and in normal humans indicate that amphetamines and barbiturates in combination have synergistic effects that, in humans, produce greater elation and less interference with normal performance than either drug alone. These effects, however, are of limited clinical therapeutic value in most depressions.

The principal objection to the use of amphetamines is the tendency toward abuse and dependence. Because the dose is often increased by the patient to maintain the initial benefits, tolerance develops rapidly, and toxic psychoses resembling paranoid states may occur. A withdrawal syndrome, which includes fatigue, hyposomnalism, and increased rapid eye movement (REM) sleep, has been documented.

Sedatives and tranquilizers. In clinical practice, many depressive patients receive tranquilizing or sedating compounds such as phenothiazines, meprobamate, or benzodiazepines, either alone or in combination with antidepressant agents. This therapeutic regimen is usually aimed at relieving symptoms such as anxiety, insomnia, restlessness, agitation, irritability, and tension —frequent components of the depressive state. When such symptoms are the predominant manifestations or presenting complaints, a depressive diagnosis may be obscured and tranquilizers alone are often prescribed.

Patients with schizophrenic, delusional, or paranoid features and those with previous history of psychosis often respond poorly to tricyclic antidepressants alone. Combined treatment with a phenothiazine, however, may be effective. This is not true for all antipsychotic drugs, since Rauwolfia derivatives (such as reserpine) precipitate depression.

Controlled trials have documented the efficacy of the phenothiazines in certain depressed patients. Imipramine and the tricyclics are superior in emotionally retarded depressives, while thioridazine and the phenothiazines may be of greater value in psychotic depressions. There is considerable overlap, however, among the actions of phenothiazines, thioxanthenes, and tricyclic drugs.

Electroconvulsive therapy. Electroconvulsive therapy (ECT) has been used to treat depression for thirty years. A carefully controlled pulse of electrical energy is passed through the head, causing an initial tonic contraction followed rapidly by a generalized convulsion. The preferred technique today is to anesthetize the patient with a rapid-acting barbiturate and modify the muscular effects by giving short-acting muscle relaxants. (It has been shown that the convulsion is necessary for therapeutic effect.) The immediate posttreatment effects are confusion, headache, and muscular pains. Although the treatment is relatively safe, with a risk no greater than that of minor anesthesia, it should be prescribed with care. While it is usually given in a hospital setting with an anesthesiologist in attendance, it can be given to selected outpatients.

The major adverse effect is memory loss, and although rarely severe, it may distress the patient. The memory loss usually lasts only a week or two and can be ameliorated by restricting the frequency of ECT treatments to not more than three per week and by limiting the total number of treatments in any course to twelve or fifteen. In those who respond, some brightening of mood is obvious after four treatments. ECT tends to act more rapidly than drugs and is also more effective, good response having been demonstrated in about 80 percent of appropriately selected patients.

Absolute contraindications for ECT are few, but the possibility of memory impairment must be carefully considered when the patient's occupation depends upon mental agility. The danger of memory loss also severely limits the reuse of ECT for patients who have had a relapse. An interval of at least four months between courses is recommended, and an even longer interval is wise if repeated courses have already been given.

While it is impossible to predict accurately which patients will respond, experience indicates favorable results with middle-aged and older patients, with those who have had a previously stable personality adjustment, or with those with a psychotic or endogenous depression. ECT remains the treatment of choice for the severely symptomatic, the actively suicidal, and those patients whose medical condition contraindicates the use of drugs.

Long-term Treatment of Affective Disorders

Long-term chemotherapeutic treatment of affective disorders has received increased attention in the past decade. Soon after demonstration of the effectiveness of treatment of the acute episode, early clinical experience showed that relapse and recurrence could be prevented in many patients by continuing treatment beyond the acute episode. Well-controlled clinical trials were subsequently conducted using lithium carbonate, imipramine, and amitriptyline for effective maintenance treatment of manic patients, bipolar manic-depressives, recurrent unipolar depressives, and neurotic depressives with a tendency toward chronicity and recurrence. These controlled trials demonstrated the value of long-term drug treatment of affective disorders. In addition, a few trials support the efficacy of combined psychotherapy and chemotherapy.

Whereas the goals of treatment in the acute episode are to reduce the symptoms of depression and to facilitate the patient's return to his premorbid state, the goal in long-term treatment is usually to prevent relapse, which is often manifested by impairment of the patient's social and vocational performance. In addition, maintenance therapy aims to relieve chronic, low-grade disturbing symptoms, enhance the patient's personal adjustment, and increase his satisfaction with life.

Four groups of patients are most suitable for maintenance therapy: (1) patients with recurrent depressions of both the bipolar and unipolar types (the best demonstrated results have been with these patients); (2) patients with a chronic depressive disorder, often manifested by long-standing depressive, hypochondriacal, neurasthenic, and neurotic symptoms (these chronic depressions often represent partial resolutions of acute episodes that occurred months or years previously); (3) neurotic patients with tendencies toward fluctuations of their depressive symptoms related to long-standing personality maladjustments and impaired interpersonal relations; and (4) schizoaffective patients with depressive symptoms. Two types of drugs with demonstrated efficacy in clinical drug trials are used for maintenance therapy—lithium carbonate and tricyclic antidepressants, particularly imipramine and amitriptyline.

There is excellent evidence that lithium is effective in preventing recurrences of chronic and recurrent mania and in the treatment of bipolar manic-depressive patients. Lithium has been used successfully since the late 1950s for the treatment of acute manic episodes. Its use to prevent recurrent mania is a widely accepted practice. Experience with maintenance treatment with lithium now indicates that recurrent depressive episodes will also be prevented in the bipolar type of manic-depressive disorder. Evidence for its utility in the treatment of unipolar recurrent depressive illness is still incomplete, although many clinicians utilize it for this purpose. While there are some preliminary reports of the value of lithium for the treatment of acute depressive episodes, the findings are inconsistent and this use of lithium cannot be recommended. The main value of lithium at the present time still appears to be in the maintenance treatment of affective disorders. In addition to the use of lithium for maintenance therapy, there is evidence of the value of tricyclic treatment, particularly for unipolar depressions and recurrent neurotic depressions.

Hospitalization

Hospitalization of depressed patients is required much less frequently now than in the past. In current practice, the majority of patients with depressions, and even many with mild to moderate elations or hypomanic states, can be treated effectively on an ambulatory basis. Hospitalization is of particular value for overactive manic patients, suicidal patients, severe depressives for whom problems of weight gain, insomnia, or severe agitation predominate, and patients with associated medical conditions requiring special diagnostic and treatment facilities.

The average hospital stay is usually less than one month. During the hospitalization, the patient's family is often involved in the treatment program through either conjoint or collaborative family therapy. Early in the course of hospitalization, plans for rehabilitation and aftercare should be instituted, particularly for those patients with recurrent or chronic depressions for whom maintenance therapy with drugs and psychotherapy is likely to be necessary.

Psychotherapy

The psychotherapy of depression has three distinct aspects:

Psychotherapeutic management. The development of rapport, empathy, and understanding is basic to all psychiatry and is in fact involved in all doctor-patient transactions. Special problems arise, however, in relating to depressed patients for optimum psychotherapeutic management; they are discussed below.

Specific psychotherapeutic techniques. A number of psychotherapies may be used as the major treatment modality with depressed patients during the acute episode or in long-term treatment; these include psychoanalysis, individual psychodynamic psychotherapy, behavior modification techniques, group therapy, and family therapy.

Combined psychotherapeutic and chemotherapeutic treatment. This is probably the most widely used therapy in clinical practice.

Psychotherapeutic management. During the acute depressive episode, the therapist should be active, available, and flexible in his approach to the depressed patient. Nondirective psychotherapy is contraindicated since patients may interpret this approach as rejection, with negative effects. During diagnostic interviews, the psychiatrist should be active in eliciting information, particularly concerning possible suicidal trends, thoughts, and impulses; other vital information includes sexual fantasies and performance, sleep changes, appetite and weight changes, bodily functions, and various fears and apprehensions. This information can and should be sought in a friendly but persistent manner—in an interview rather than an interrogation. The psychiatrist should be flexible with regard to his appointment schedule. Patients need not always be seen for fifty minutes, and it may be useful to see the patient more frequently than once each week for brief periods. If the patient has episodes of anxiety and panic, he should feel comfortable about calling the psychiatrist on the telephone to obtain temporary support. The psychiatrist should not hesitate to see the relatives, both to elicit background information and, particularly in suicidal patients, to obtain their understanding, cooperation, and assistance.

Particular problems arise for patients who ask for reassurance—"Tell me I'm not losing my mind," "Tell me I'm going to get better." It is not always therapeutically useful to reassure the patient automatically; members of the family have been attempting reassurance for weeks. Rather, the patient should be asked, "What do you mean by losing your mind?" The response may be, "I feel like jumping out the window," or, "I may want to divorce my husband." Before providing simple reassurance, the psychiatrist should attempt to probe the patient's fears and anxieties; the source may not be self-evident or even conscious.

Another related, general management problem concerns the response to complaints of bodily dysfunction. Depressed patients frequently complain of difficulty in sleeping, appetite loss, fatigue, headache, backache, intestinal cramps, constipation, and other problems. Too often these patients are told by physicians, "It's all in your mind." The research evidence is to the contrary; depression is a total body state with psychosomatic interrelationship. The depressed patient is not "imagining" his bodily symptoms. Dysfunctions of the neuroendocrine and autonomic nervous systems in fact exist in depression, and patients perceive alterations in their bodily functions that are reversible as the depression is alleviated. Consequently, physicians who tell the patient, "It's all in the mind," are doing themselves and their patients a disservice. The psychiatrist who inquires carefully about bodily dysfunctions and attempts to explain the nature of psychosomatic relationships will often strengthen his therapeutic alliance with the patient.

Specific psychotherapeutic techniques. A number of specific forms of psychotherapy are useful during the acute depressive episode. These include psychoanalysis, behavior modification, group therapy, family therapy, and psychodynamically oriented individual psychotherapy.

The usefulness of psychoanalysis in acute depressions remains a source of controversy. No systematic or controlled studies of the outcome of psychoanalysis in the treatment of depression exist, but on the basis of clinical observations, psychoanalysis seems indicated for neurotic depressions in individuals with long-standing personality disorders. It is less clearly indicated as primary treatment for patients with bipolar manic-depressive illness or those who have had severe, recurrent depressions.

Individual psychotherapy based on psychodynamic principles remains the most widely used form of psychotherapy. Although systematic, controlled clinical studies do not exist, clinical observations strongly support the value of this form of psychotherapy during both acute and long-term treatments. Indirect support for its efficacy can be found in the literature on cognitive behavioral therapy, group therapy, and the studies of therapy aimed at interpersonal relations. In practice, most individual psychotherapy conducted once, twice, or three times a week uses combinations of cognitive, behavioral, interpersonal, and exploratory techniques. Cognitive behavioral psychotherapy developed recently as a specific technique for dealing with patients with problems of self-esteem and misperception, who often blame themselves unduly and underestimate their ability to perform. This form of psychotherapy is often justified on empirical as well as theoretical grounds; research has demonstrated that depressed patients suffer from low self-esteem and difficulties in interpersonal relations, particularly in the context of social situations, families, and small groups. Beck (1969), Seligman (1972), and Lewinsohn (1974) have developed new forms of individual, family, and group therapies derived from studies of cognitive, behavioral, and social learning aspects of the depressed patient's psychological functioning.

Group therapy that assists patients in their social roles and facilitates the development of social skills has proved useful, particularly where patients receive a mirror image or feedback of the impact of their interpersonal behavior on others. This form of group therapy often reverses the social skills deficit of depressed patients. Research indicates that many depressed patients are unable to obtain the social rewards that other people elicit in group situations (Lewinsohn, 1974).

The effect of psychotherapy aimed at improving the patient's interpersonal relations on patients with affective disorders has been evaluated by studies in Boston and New Haven (Weissman et al., 1974) and in Philadelphia (Friedman, 1975). Whether conducted by psychiatrists or social workers, the evidence suggests that the patient's coping ability in interpersonal difficul-

ties—particularly in marriage, family relations, and child rearing—can be improved by psychotherapy. At the present time, little research evidence exists for patients with affective disorders to support or refute the efficacy of psychotherapies whose goals are resolution of personality conflicts originating in childhood.

Marital issues and their treatment are a particular problem for women in today's culture. Epidemiological research has shown a rapid increase of depressions in young women, particularly well-educated women. Their depression seems related to the conflictful position of women in contemporary society and their wish to redress what they feel to be inequities in the conventional marriage relationship. Current forms of marital therapy do not merely treat the depressed woman who complains of symptoms; rather, group or couples methods are employed to improve the modes of communication and the transaction between patient and spouse.

It is important to distinguish between psychotherapeutic techniques useful in the management of the acute symptomatic episode from those most helpful in long-term treatment. During the symptomatic acute stage, emphasis is on relief of symptoms to facilitate the patient's return to some form of premorbid social and occupational adjustment. It is questionable whether techniques such as psychoanalysis or other uncovering techniques are most effective here.

On the other hand, as the patient's acute symptomatic state subsides, exploration of current interpersonal relations, intrapsychic conflicts, and antecedent developmental experiences is indicated. This form of long-term therapy seems most appropriate for patients with problems of self-esteem, interpersonal difficulties, and conflicts involving guilt, hostility, and sexuality.

Combined chemotherapy and psychotherapy. In practice, large numbers of patients are treated with drugs in combination with psychotherapy. There are three groups of patients for whom this regimen is indicated. The first includes patients who have been on maintenance treatment with lithium or tricyclics. As mood symptoms subside with the aid of drugs, problems of irritability appear, and issues previously ignored, such as child rearing and marriage, become the focus of family attention. These concomitant problems are well addressed by psychotherapeutic intervention. Patients with neurotic character problems and other long-standing personality maladjustments form the second group. These patients do not seem to do well on drugs alone and may benefit from the drug-psychotherapy treatment combination by exploring the developmental antecedents of the problems while simultaneously receiving support and alleviation of mood and somatic symptoms. Finally, combined therapy is useful for patients with depressions that arise in the context of marital conflicts. Numerous controlled trials of drugs and psychotherapy indicate that the combination is almost always more effective than either component alone, particularly with more severely ill patients, such as manic-depressive and severely impaired neurotic patients.

The rationale for combining drugs and psychotherapy is that each appears to act on different targets. Psychotherapy is most beneficial in enhancing social effectiveness and personality functioning, whereas drugs are most effective in influencing the pathophysiology of symptom formation, such as sleep disturbance, loss of energy, and loss of sexual libido.

The majority of depressive patients can be treated on an ambulatory basis with the use of alternative treatments, both chemotherapeutic and psychotherapeutic. The psychiatrist should be familiar with the range of treatments available and skilled in the use of the standard drugs, alone or combined with specific forms of psychotherapy. Just as important as specific therapeutic techniques is the psychiatrist's development of a general psychotherapeutic approach toward the patient—a process emphasizing support, empathy, and a positive attitude while offering substantive amelioration and longer-term growth possibilities rather than simple reassurances.

The unifying theme of this chapter—the concept of pluralism in the study and treatment of affective disorders—has been developed in three main areas. First, a pluralistic approach recognizes the multiplicity of etiological factors—genetic and intrapsychic factors, crucial life events, and social stress—currently under investigation in the pathogenesis of affective disorders. Second, in diagnostic assessment and nosological classification, a pluralistic emphasis rejects unitary or dualistic approaches. Rather, it attempts to construct a classificatory system that will meet four objectives: to acknowledge the existence of multiple types of disorder; to provide reliable and valid groupings of relatively homogeneous patients; to inform clinical judgment regarding treatment decisions; and to enhance research strategies to generate information concerning etiology and pathogenesis. Third, as applied to treatment, pluralism accepts the efficacy of many treatments—pharmacological, psychotherapeutic, and electroconvulsive—and provides the psychiatrist with both the challenge and the opportunity to tailor treatment decisions to the individual patient and to combine humanistic skills with flexibility and pragmatism.

References

Abraham, K. 1927. *Selected papers of Karl Abraham, M.D.* London: Hogarth Press.

Alexander, L. 1953. *Treatment of mental disorder.* Philadelphia: Saunders.

Angst, J. 1966. Zur Atiologie und Nosologie endogener depressiver Psychosen. *Monogr. Gesamtgeb. Neurol. Psychiatr.* 112:1–118.

Beck, A. T. 1969. *Depression: clinical, experimental and theoretical aspects.* New York: Harper & Row.

Bibring, E. 1953. The mechanism of depression. In *Affective disorders*, ed. P. Greenacre. New York: International Universities Press.

Bowlby, J. 1969. *Attachment and loss.* Vol. I. London: Hogarth Press.

Brown, G., M. Bhrolchain, and T. Harris. 1975. Social class and psychiatric disturbance among women in an urban population. *Sociology* 9:225–254.

Dana, C. L., A. Starr, A. Meyer, et al. 1905. A discussion on the classification of the melancholias. *J. Nerv. Ment. Dis.* 32:112–118.

Derogatis, L. R., G. L. Klerman, and R. S. Lipman. 1972. Anxiety states and depressive neuroses. *J. Nerv. Ment. Dis.* 155:392–403.

Deutsch, H. 1965. *Neuroses and character types: clinical psychoanalytic studies.* New York: International Universities Press.

Essen-Möller, E., and O. Hagnell. 1961. The frequency and risk of depression within a rural population group in Scandinavia. *Acta Psychiatr. Scand.* suppl. 162, 37:28–32.

Faris, R. E., and H. W. Dunham. 1939. *Mental disorders in urban areas*. Chicago: University of Chicago Press.

Fenichel, O. 1945. *The psychoanalytic theory of neurosis*. New York: Norton.

Freud, S. 1917. Mourning and melancholia. In *Standard edition*, ed. J. Strachey. Vol. 14. London: Hogarth Press, 1958.

Friedman, A. S. 1975. Interaction of drug therapy with marital therapy in depressive patients. *Arch. Gen. Psychiatry* 32:619–637.

Gillespie, R. D. 1929. The clinical differentiation of types of depression. *Guy's Hosp. Rep.* 79:306–344.

Kasanin, J. 1933. Acute schizo-affective psychoses. *Am. J. Psychiatry* 90:97–126.

Klerman, G. L. 1975. Overview of depression. In *Comprehensive textbook of psychiatry*, ed. A. M. Freedman, H. I. Kaplan, and B. J. Sadock. 2nd ed. Vol. 1. Baltimore: Williams & Wilkins.

Klerman, G. L., and J. E. Barrett. 1973. The affective disorders: clinical and epidemiological aspects. In *Lithium: its role in psychiatric treatment and research*, ed. S. Gershon and B. Shopsin. New York: Plenum Press.

Klerman, G. L., A. DiMascio, M. M. Weissman, B. Prusoff, and E. S. Paykel. 1974. Treatment of depression by drugs and psychotherapy. *Am. J. Psychiatry* 131:186–191.

Kraepelin, E. 1921. *Manic-depressive insanity and paranoia*. Trans. M. Barclay. Edinburgh: Livingstone.

Leonhard, K., I. Korff, and H. Schulz. 1962. Temperament in families with monopolar and bipolar phasic psychoses. *Psychiat. Neurol.* 143:416–434.

Lewin, B. 1950. *The Psychoanalysis of elation*. New York: Norton.

Lewinsohn, P. M. 1974. A behavioral approach to depression. In *The psychology of depression*, ed. R. J. Friedman and M. M. Katz. Washington, D.C.: Winston-Wiley.

Lewis, A. J. 1934. Melancholia: a clinical survey of depressive states. *J. Ment. Sci.* 80:277–378.

Odegaard, O. 1956. The incidence of psychoses in various occupations. *Int. J. Soc. Psychiatry* 2:85–104.

Paykel, E. A. 1974. Recent life events and clinical depression. In *Life stress and illness*, ed. E. K. Gunderson and R. H. Rahe. Springfield, Ill.: Thomas.

Pearlin, L. I. 1962. Treatment values and enthusiasm for drugs in a mental hospital. *Psychiatry* 25:170–179.

Perris, C. 1966. A study of bipolar (manic-depressive) and unipolar recurrent depressive psychoses. *Acta Psychiatr. Scand.* suppl. 194:1–189.

Pollock, H. M. 1931. Recurrence of attacks in manic-depressive psychoses. *Am. J. Psychiatry* 11:567–574.

Prien, R. G., C. J. Klett, and E. M. Caffey, Jr. 1973. A comparison of lithium carbonate and imipramine in the prevention of affective disorders in recurrent affective illness. Cooperative Studies in Psychiatry, prepublication report no. 94. Perry Point, Maryland: Veterans Administration, Central Neuropsychiatric Research Laboratory.

Prusoff, B., and G. L. Klerman. 1974. Differentiating depressed from anxious neurotic outpatients. *Arch. Gen. Psychiatry* 30:302–309.

Rado, S. 1929. The problem of melancholia. *Int. J. Psychoanal.* 9:420–438.

Rennie, T. A. C. 1942. Prognosis in manic-depressive psychoses. *Am. J. Psychiatry* 98:801–814.

Robins, E., and S. B. Guze. 1972. Classification of affective disorders. In *Recent advances in the psychobiology of the depressive illnesses*, ed. T. A. Williams, M. M. Katz, and J. A. Shield, Jr. Washington, D.C.: Government Printing Office.

Robins, E., R. A. Munoz, S. Martin, and K. A. Gentry. 1972. Primary and secondary affective disorders. In *Disorders of mood*, ed. J. Zubin and F. A. Freyhan. Baltimore: Johns Hopkins University Press.

Seligman, M. E. P. 1972. Learned helplessness. *Annu. Rev. Med.* 23:407–412.

Silverman, C. 1968. *The epidemiology of depression*. Baltimore: Johns Hopkins University Press.

Spitz, R. A. 1946. *Anaclitic depression. The Psychoanalytic Study of the Child*, vol. 2. New York: International Universities Press.

Srole, L., T. S. Langner, S. T. Michael, M. K. Opler, and T. A. C. Rennie. 1962. *Mental health in the metropolis*. New York: McGraw-Hill.

Weissman, M. M., G. L. Klerman, E. S. Paykel, B. Prusoff, and B. Hanson. 1974. Treatment effects on the social adjustment of depressed patients. *Arch. Gen. Psychiatry* 30:771–778.

Weissman, M., and J. Myers. 1976. The New Haven community survey 1967–1975: depressive symptoms and diagnosis. Paper presented to the Society for Life History Research in Psychopathology, October 1976, at Fort Worth, Texas.

Wender, P. H. 1967. On necessary and sufficient conditions in psychiatric exploration. *Arch. Gen. Psychiatry* 16:41–47.

Winokur, G., P. Clayton, and T. Reich, 1969. *Manic-depressive illness*. St. Louis: Mosby.

Recommended Reading

Bibring, E. 1954. Psychoanalysis and the dynamic psychotherapies. *J. Am. Psychoanal. Assoc.* 11:745–779.

Mapother, E. 1926. Discussion of manic-depressive psychosis. *Br. Med. J.* 11:872–876.

Menninger, K. 1963. *The vital balance.* New York: Viking Press.

Weissman, M. M., and G. L. Klerman. 1977. Sex differences and the epidemiology of depression. *Arch. Gen. Psychiatry* 34:98–111.

Personality Disorders

CHAPTER 14

Alfred H. Stanton

N OTHING IN PSYCHIATRY involves more controversy and ambiguity than the identification of personality disorders. The reasons are not far to seek. Character, or personality, is a dominant human interest, and diversity and individuality in personality are major values in our pluralistic society. Patients who are the objects of psychiatric attention because of their very "character" may feel attacked at their core, and the psychiatrist trying to "treat" them is likely to be classed with reformers or, worse, brainwashing authoritarians, ready to commit people to hospitals simply because of political or social nonconformity. The fact that the boundaries of the disorders are indefinite seems to confirm the need for wariness.

Nevertheless, "character" has been considered intimately relevant to medicine at least since Hippocrates and Galen. Their belief that diseases arise from excesses of blood, yellow bile, black bile, and phlegm included corresponding types of dispositions—sanguine, choleric, melancholic, and phlegmatic—a classification of temperaments that has lasted longer than any other and is deeply embedded in our common language (see Temkin, 1973).

Like Hippocrates and Galen, Gall and Spurz-heim centuries later based a classification of temperaments on an assumed biological base, introducing the "science" of phrenology. Thirty-seven discreet "organs" in the brain and the associated local enlargements of the skull corresponded atomistically with thirty-seven individual traits—memory, trust, ambition, sexual interest, fidelity, and so on—which they thought could be diagnosed by inspection and palpation (see Davies, 1947, 1955). The serious problems in the critical analysis of character are nowhere more apparent than in the fact that phrenology held sway for decades throughout the nineteenth century. It was developed by the same critical neurologists whose major contributions to neuroanatomy were accurate and definitive.

The Nature of Character

Human behavior, particularly interpersonal behavior, is consistent in style, recognizable over time and from setting to setting, and, to a large extent, characteristic of every person. This stability is central to the concept of character, although moral coloring tends often to enter definitions of character—as in "a man of character." Thus character or personality is a consistent and stable pattern of behavior shown by a person in meeting a variety of challenges and opportunities, consistent over long periods of his life and recognized as special to each person.

The stability is surprisingly high. Studying two-year-old children, Escalona and Heider (1959) predicted their behavior with considerable accuracy; these predictions were checked by others when the children were between five and six (Yarrow and Yarrow, 1964; see also Murphy, 1964). Moss and Kagan (1964) also noted consistency in passivity and dependence in children from age three to age nine and from ten to young adulthood. Other longitudinal studies have generally reported similar consistency when global characteristics were studied, less when more specific traits were analyzed. Even with advancing age, changes have proved to be less than had been expected (Kuhlen, 1964). There is some decline among the elderly in demands on the self for achievement and in social relations ("disengagement"; see Cumming and Henry, 1961), some decreased general level of drive, increased anxiety and caution, and some increase in rigidity of views and habits, but much consistency in character is maintained nonetheless.

Experiences of isolation, concentration camps, and forced indoctrination produce significant changes in behavior, but they are limited almost to the duration of the stimulus situation (Haggard, 1964; Holt, 1964). The major exception is the effect of prolonged enforced living in an environment of interpersonal sterility or anomie, as in some prisons or mental hospitals. This situation seems to produce lasting changes involving apathy, gross restriction of emotional responsiveness, pettiness, and undue preoccupation with immediate concrete interests and routines (Barton, 1959; Gruenberg, 1967).

However, physicians do meet patients whose relatives describe a sudden change in the patient's personality, a change the patient may not recognize or admit. This change is nearly always an indication of potential major illness and requires immediate careful study.

Character or Personality Types

Character is usually thought of as referring simply to a type of person, with no implication of illness or disorder. The character each person thinks himself to have is an integral part of his self-image—accepted, ego-syntonic, an indispensable part of his sense of identity. In spite of each person's sense of his own unique individuality, it is very clear that characters fall into various types and, historically, manifold classifications of character or personality have been described. Although the types usually have no implication of abnormality, they are thought of as maladaptive when the characteristics are extreme. I shall mention only a few of the most commonly cited personality types, restricting my account to those that have won wide acceptance and are associated with abnormality in their extreme forms.

Personality Types and Body Build

Lombroso was the last major contributor to the tradition of atavism and degeneration derived from Morel. Morel believed that mental illness and characterological defects arose from "degeneration," which he defined as deviations from the normal human type that are transmittable by heredity and that deteriorate progressively toward extinction (see Ackerknecht, 1959). Lombroso found physical "stigmata of degeneration" in the bodies of criminals and of the psychiatrically disordered, without realizing that most of the so-called stigmata are widely distributed in the general population. Aside from gross malformations, they included facial or other bodily asymmetry, a low hairline, webbing of the ear pinnae, eyebrows meeting at the midline, extra nipples, congenital naevi, and alterations of the extremities like clubbing of the feet or fingers minor or major in degree. Degeneration was felt to include or lead to impulsiveness, self-centeredness, low moral standards, criminality, vagrancy, and other socially maladaptive characteristics. However, more careful observation showed that, aside from a few unusual syndromes, the association of physical and psychosocial degeneration was illusory.

Kretschmer (1936) described pyknic, athletic, asthenic, and dysplastic body types and correlated them with, respectively, the extroverted (cyclothymic) character, the epileptic and "epileptic personalities," the schizoid personality, and, finally, a miscellaneous ineffective group associated with the dysplastics. His associations were clinically intuitive and suggestive, although they seem to be used less and less.

Sheldon (1940, 1954) developed a new quantitative rating of physique on the presumed basis of endo-, meso-, and ectomorphic builds according to the embryological layers he thought to be predominant. The combinations of these three elements were associated, ultimately unsuccessfully, with three psychological types: endomorph (visceral interests), mesomorph (activity and muscular interests), and ectomorph (intellectual specialization). Sheldon's ratings of physical types were not matched by correspondingly successful measures of character, and there remains today only a general opinion that body build is probably associated with temperament.

Masculine and Feminine Personality

Personality types are clearly related to sex. Sex roles are so full of presuppositions about character that the very terms *feminine* and *masculine* usually refer not to physical sex characteristics but to ways of behaving, dress, etiquette, and socially determined self-conceptions. Conventions regarding masculine and feminine behavior are the focus of attack from both feminist and scientific skeptics. Nonetheless, ideas of gender identity are often of poignant medical pertinence—for instance, with those biological males who feel themselves to be entirely feminine and appeal for surgical intervention to permit them to marry men. The possibility that a trait may have primarily social sanction and not invariant biological roots does not make it less real, and the polarity of sexual traits is as valuable to many as it is threatening to others.

Finding interpersonal characteristics that are solidly anchored to sex has proved remarkably difficult; the field is a treacherous one to investigate. Possibly consistent differences between boy and girl babies in the nursery are reported and then disappear; Maccoby and Jacklin (1974) note that small boys show more anger to other boys than girls do to other girls. Aggression, passivity, receptiveness, directness, and indirectness are often thought to vary between the sexes, but objective confirmation has proved elusive.

Greater verbal skills among women, particularly at grade- and high-school age, have been consistently reported, and a preference for a "global" approach to problems rather than an analytical, differentiated one has been found to characterize women more than men. Witkin et al. (1962) developed a test to differentiate those subjects who determined their position in a dark room primarily from external cues (field-dependent) from those who used internal cues (field-independent). Evidence showed that they were differing personality types, consistent over time and in a number of assessments; women are more field-dependent than men. But the summary finding of this comprehensive review of sex differences in temperament was that, although some clear-cut differences have been found, they are relatively slight when compared with the range of individual differences within each sex. Stein (1969) has discussed the problems in bias and resistance that are found in psychoanalytic discussions of male-female character differences.

Circumstances are similar with character types associated with various sexual deviations. It was long widely believed that homosexual men differed from heterosexual men in a number of characterological dimensions, but when careful systematic canvasses of practicing homosexual men who were not seeing therapists were completed, the differences melted away (Hooker, 1958). Similar close studies of homosexual women have not yet been made. The terms *exhibitionistic, narcissistic, masochistic*, and *sadistic* are used interchangeably both for the particular sexual deviation (the type of activity used to heighten preorgasmic sexual arousal) and for character in general. This usage has been confusing, particularly since some of the character terms have achieved considerable status among psychiatrists—but it remains to be shown whether or not there is in fact any closer relationship between the character type and the sexual deviation that led to its name.

Psychoanalytic Theories of Personality Type

Psychoanalytic theories of character, although appearing early (Freud, 1908), were not the focus of major clinical or theoretical attention until the treatment of patients with serious character disorders became much more common toward the middle of the century (Stein, 1969).

Freud identified traits of orderliness, parsimony, and obstinacy as related to the "assimilation" of anal eroticism in the subject's development; the traits seem to coexist and the "anal character" was established in psychoanalytic theory. Freud later (1917, 1931) added to this observation other characterological consequences of libidinal development, noting the "erotic" character type (dominated by the fear of losing the love of others and therefore dependent upon others), the "obsessional" type (dominated by the fear of his own conscience with, as it were, an internal instead of an external dependence, self-reliance, and conservatism), and the "narcissistic" type (whose main characteristics are self-preservation, activity, aggressiveness, leadership, and opposition to the established state of affairs). Although mixtures of the three are usual and important, the mixture of all of them in equal proportions would make, for Freud, a model of the normal, or ideal, character. Freud anticipated later suggestions with his surmise that each character type might tend to correspond to particular neurotic disorders if the subjects fell ill—the erotic with hysteria, the obsessive with the corresponding neurosis, and the narcissistic with psychotic disorders. Somewhat later the "oral dependent" personality was identified, although it overlapped considerably with Freud's erotic type. The oral dependent character is highly dependent upon others for love and acceptance; often anticipates getting them; and is consequently optimistic, sometimes unrealistically so, oriented toward others and toward pleasing them, and often anxious or even desperate when the source of his security is threatened by disapproval, separation, or his own inner rejection of the source of his security.

The other major classification of personality types derived from early psychoanalytic interest in drives and their control was made by Jung (1918), in his description of extroversion and introversion: "Nature knows two fundamentally different ways of adaptation, which determine the further existence of the living organism; the one is by increased fertility accompanied by a relatively small degree of defensive power and individual conservation; the other is by individ-

ual equipment of manifold means of self-protection, coupled with a relatively insignificant fertility" (p. 331). The extrovert spends himself; the introvert defends himself. Jung elaborates with a description of the contrasting attitudes in thinking, activity, and personal relations between the objective, active, externally oriented extrovert and the subjective, inner-oriented, sensitive introvert. He thought the introvert more prone to schizophrenia (as did Meyer).

Character Disorders

The stable attributes of a person, his character, may be maladaptive, often clearly so. Many cases exist where the borderline between adaptive and maladaptive cannot be precisely identified, but the fact that we have no specific definition of twilight does not eliminate the difference between day and night. All the common psychoneuroses occur in patients with particular types of character; the relationship is so close that the personality disorders are usually given the names of the associated psychoneuroses. The most common ones are discussed here.

The *paranoid personality* is characterized by an alert, touchy, suspicious attitude, mistrust both of others and of self, and sensitivity to slights, to exclusion, and to possible deception. The patient is prone to believe that "something funny" is going on around him, or will be very shortly. He is usually quick to place blame for any unfortunate occurrence elsewhere, partly to ensure that he is not blamed; he has a strong tendency to assign hidden motivations to others, often in the form of "psychoanalytic interpretations." Contemptuous of the "naive" who may challenge these interpretations, the patient can be easily taken in on very slight grounds and tries to defend himself against his own naiveté. In one instance, a man needed to buy a used car when they were in very short supply. After several days of shopping, he reported to his psychiatrist that he did not know if he was ever going to buy one—because of the amount of cheating he expected—although he had to have one. Finally he confessed that, seeing his thirtieth car, he had simply bought it without checking it, afraid otherwise that he might never buy one. In fact, his latent gullibility had been gratified without his recognizing it.

The *cyclothymic personality* is similar to the extrovert: patients are active, assertive, full of initiative, friendly, and outgoing, but often insensitive to others. Uncomfortable with prolonged solitude, they respond to boredom by compulsively finding something to do; as a result, activities and interests may often be superficial, almost impersonal. These periods of activity and optimism may alternate with periods of depression, worry, fear of failure, a sense of hopelessness, futility, or meaninglessness, sometimes strong guilt. Stubbornly and arbitrarily moral, a cyclothymic patient usually conceals this rigidity when active, often by its opposite—an allegiance to "fun," which itself may function as a moral imperative on others ("don't be a wet blanket").

Patients with a *schizoid personality* are shy and socially withdrawn, often to the point of being eccentric. Sensitive to hurt, they tend to assume they are unlike anyone else in unidentified ways, and they often try to solve the problem of this difference by introspection, analysis, and acute observation of others. Closeness, anger, and exposure or other troublesome interpersonal encounters are met by withdrawing, by maintaining social distance, and often by angrily rejecting other people. Solitary thinking tends to produce lavish fantasy, high originality, independence, and often great precision and rigor. Emotional experience tends to be constricted, with annoyance and anxiety more easily experienced and expressed than friendliness, warmth, disappointment, grief, and other feelings. Small talk is very difficult and usually unpleasant. Pleasures are generally muted and tend to be intellectual in type. Private fantasies of entitlement, or ideas of fairness, may be so unrealistic as to suggest grandiose delusions, but true delusions are unlikely.

The *obsessive-compulsive (anancastic) personality*, extremely common, is characterized by usually minor obsessions (worry, preoccupation), primarily verbal in nature, which often involve mildly angry contemplation of "unethical" or nonconformist behavior by others. Patients are inhibited, are concerned about obligations, and tend to expect conformity by others to their own standards of behavior. Their constricted emotional range is similar to that of schizoid personalities but not usually so severe.

The *hysterical personality* is dominated by the urgent need to please others in order to master the fear of being unable to do so. This results in restless activity, dramatization and exaggeration, seductiveness, either social or overtly sexual in manner (often creating disappointment for the other person), and immature and unrealistic dependence upon others (Slavney and McHeigh, 1974).

The person with an *asthenic personality* is concerned about weakness and tiredness, concentrates on his body and his health, and fears exercise and injury. He gives serious attention to diet fads and other health matters. An increasingly common new form is focused upon emotional or mental health and shows great preoccupation with "healthy" relationships with others.

The *passive-aggressive personality*, though poorly demarcated, is primarily characterized by the use of submissive or passive interpersonal techniques as ways of attacking others, usually those on whom the patient is dependent. Withdrawal, disinterest, obstructionism, negativism, procrastination, inefficiency, direct or indirect sabotage, often by errors of omission, mark his actions; in more direct contacts, hurt feelings and lack of initiative are typical. Usually passive techniques are the only significant ways of expressing aggression, although brief temper outbursts may occur.

Inadequate personality is a term encompassing those persons who without any conspicuous lack of ability nevertheless fail, often completely, in fields demanding effort and risk. Sports, school, work, and social and home life are all scenes of their repeated failure and easy giving up or avoidance. Such patients are often relaxed and enjoyable in interpersonal relations, usually avoiding conspicuous trouble, and may possess normal or high intelligence; but the aggravating failures persist, with or without expressions of an intention to reform and do better. With some patients, social competence is grossly deficient and faux pas follows faux pas, but the more usual situation is a graceful withdrawal from full social participation.

Narcissistic Character Disorders

Patients with narcissistic character disorders have come into increasing prominence recently. The classification should be distinguished from the narcissistic personality type described by Freud, although the concepts overlap. The disorder has been recognized and treated as such. The patient is often free of conspicuous symptoms, and the problem may not be identified without rather extensive familiarity with the patient's history and pattern of living. He may be fairly seriously handicapped without recognizing any need to seek advice or treatment. Nevertheless there are signs of serious inadequacy in ego development.

Tolerance for anxiety is low. This condition is often not at all obvious, as in situations of stress, when the person may seem to behave with unusual equanimity. If he does, however, it is because he has developed, in response to the anxiety, ideas of omnipotence, of invulnerability, of special persecution or withdrawal, and, often, of dismissal of the anxiety-provoking person or situation. Each of these responses may prove seriously crippling, but they occur repeatedly even if the person recognizes their cost to him. Impulse control—delay in gratification—is also inadequate both in the degree of tolerable delay and in the amount of organization and flexibility available in the pursuit of goals. Any blocking of his wishes will usually be followed by personalizing the "blame" for what happened to an unusual degree, attributing it either to himself or to others.

Although poor impulse control and low anxiety tolerance are common, nonspecific problems, defects in self-management, in self-esteem, and in the sense of the unity, substantiality, and separateness of the self are more characteristic. Patients with narcissistic character disorders are likely to be successful and to appear normal when their work, personal relations, and activities are superficially examined. A full intellectual awareness of his own particular existence, persisting through time and in various situations, is generally possessed by the patient, but it is unreliable in a number of ways. The patient tends to govern his relations according to a perception of others as like himself (a mirror image),

as a source of satisfaction of his own special needs, or as someone he wants to be like. If the idealized person in his life fails in any of these respects, the patient often responds with enormous contemptuous anger (narcissistic rage); if the other person is lost, the loss is more likely to lead to rage, terror, a sense of going out of existence, or to his rapid replacement by someone else than it is to grief, yearning, or sophisticated efforts to reestablish the relationship.

This narcissistic type of personal relation may appear "normal" for long periods, and indeed some admixture of narcissistic and more objective relations occurs in everyone. People who are limited to primarily narcissistic relations, however, are vulnerable not only to separation and loss, with its threat of catastrophe, but to glimpses of the superficiality of the relationship at such times as selecting gifts (when the knowledge of what the other wants is buried behind the automatic tendency to assume he wants what the giver would want) and at times of special intimacy or significant success with the other (when the response is likely to be primarily in terms of a sense of inadequacy, envy, futility, emptiness, or aggressive triumph, rather than the deeper pleasures possible in a more personal relationship). So much of life seems to have an "as if" character that this name has been given to some narcissistic personalities by Deutsch (1942). Uncertainty about the limits of one's self makes closeness to the other a potential threat—loss of the self through being immersed in the other—so that the relationship must be held fixedly between too great closeness and too great distance. This frozen position is enforced by fear and mistrust not only of the other but of the whole world of other people and of oneself, characterized by constant alertness or frequent tests of the relationship; it is a pattern often sensed by the other as controlling in the extreme.

Self-esteem is maintained only precariously. If successes seem to dissolve into vanity, closeness into threat, and if others are always seen as trying unpredictably to "escape," the usual social reinforcements of self-esteem are no longer effective, and isolation or denial of much of experience becomes necessary. The idealized other person becomes all good, and the bad is attributed to others; any mixture is intolerably threatening. Old ideas and fantasies of omnipotence, omniscience, omnipotentiality, unquestioned entitlement, are rekindled and become essential occasionally; but they must be denied at the same time because they threaten relations with the others who are needed.

All these characteristics hamper treatment in psychotherapy, and their recognition and management by patient and therapist is at best complex, slow, and marked by repeated acceptance of transference fantasies as real by the patient or by frequent efforts to make them real. Thus acting out by rigidly controlling the therapist, by incessant testing, by more or less desperate pleas for special praise or acceptance, by actions eliciting special punishments or abandonment—all are consequences of this type of personality organization. While they appear with special clarity in the psychotherapeutic situation, they are likely to be present in one form or another throughout the patient's life. Treatment, though terribly demanding, can be successful and of such general benefit as to justify the effort; to succeed, however, it must be conducted differently from the treatment of other kinds of psychoneurotic disorders (Kernberg, 1970a; Altman, 1975).

The central problem of the narcissistic personality—the heavy investment of effort to protect self-esteem, self-continuity, and self-cohesiveness—is consistent with a number of different, more superficial ways of living associated with narcissism. Many patients are withdrawn, protecting the omnipotent fantasy by avoiding its open display, but at the cost of inhibition, secret envy, frequent hurt feelings, and poverty in social experience. Others continuously maintain an active exhibitionistic type of life but avoid fully meaningful relations with others—the lonely leader always on display. Some remain persistently self-sacrificing to protect their illusion of moral superiority, but at the cost of depression, spitefulness, and lack of pleasure.

Narcissistic personality disorder is often found in patients with addictions, persistent sexual disorders (including prostitution and promiscuity), or in the poorly described group of professional criminals. Here reliance upon fantasies of omnipotence, or association with the "omnipotent" leader, the assumption of unquestioned en-

titlement, is the outcome of a failure of the ego ideal to develop from childhood narcissistic conceptions of parental promises (Murray, 1964).

Borderline Personality Organization

Recent years have seen the emergence of a new concept of personality disturbance—the borderline patient. The concept gathers together patients previously labeled with a bewildering variety of diagnoses: ambulatory schizophrenia, latent schizophrenia, preschizophrenia, schizophrenic character, abortive schizophrenia, pseudopsychopathic schizophrenia, pseudoneurotic schizophrenia, psychotic character, subclinical schizophrenia, borderland and occult schizophrenia, borderline personality, condition, or syndrome (Gunderson and Singer, 1975). To this list may perhaps be added "spectrum disorder," referring to the schizophrenic spectrum.

Although borderline patients may regress into a transient psychosis under provocation, they are considered to possess a relatively stable and distinctive personality organization (Kernberg, 1967; Grinker, Werble, and Drye, 1968; Gunderson and Singer, 1975). They share many of the characteristics of patients with narcissistic personality disorders but are distinguished by a number of additional pathological characteristics. Transient disturbances of consciousness are not unusual—states of depersonalization, derealization, and dissociation. While reality testing functions, it is not entirely reliable. Accounts of emotionally important events may be reported in a dissociated way (without the patient's full awareness of his account); he may report them convincingly but falsely (usually not as lies but without the patient's significant identification with the event), blurring the reality of what happened and being heavily influenced by the response of his listener. Anger, anxiety, loneliness, and a painful awareness of not having pleasure when it might be expected (anhedonia) are dominant emotions, and impulsive self-injuring actions are common. Sexual contacts are usually superficial and often diverse in character, frequently serving to obtain relief from solitude and its felt dangers more than pleasure or a deeper relation with the partner.

Kernberg's accounts emphasize a typical psy-

chopathology. The person's defensive organization is primarily at a primitive level; he constructs
his self-image from identifications and projections with a successful distinction of self from
others but with an incomplete synthesis of his
own self. As a result, dissociation, idealization,
denial, and primitive forms of projection persist.
The therapist's structured confrontation of the
patient with his defenses usually results in
improvement by establishing more adult perceptions (with a schizophrenic patient, this confrontation may aggravate the regression).

The Antisocial Personality

Still another type of disorder related to narcissistic personality disorders is the antisocial personality, a concept closely related to the older
term *psychopathic personality*. This group of patients is primarily characterized by stubbornly repeated antisocial acts, usually not highly stereotyped as in the impulse disorders (kleptomania,
voyeurism, pyromania, and such) but equally or
more persistent and with no greater appearance
of sensible purpose. The patient's account,
usually displacing blame, denying wrongdoing,
or implying reform, is so poorly constructed, and
addressed to such a skeptical listener, that he
typically cannot expect to be believed; nevertheless, he seems to demand credence and is really,
though superficially, hurt when the listener does
not "trust" him. For such a patient, loyalty is
usually only an aspiration he cannot enact; he
may experience intense feelings of guilt, but that
emotion is fleeting and soon repaired without
basic alterations in behavior (McCord and Mc-
Cord, 1964; Cleckley, 1955). Self-injury is nearly
universal, and, in contrast to those of both borderline patients and narcissistic personalities, the
patient's job or school career generally shows
much less accomplishment than his innate abilities might promise. This patient has been
described as having a "semantic dementia" by
Cleckley (1955); his personal relations, career
identifications, beliefs, and values seem to cry
aloud that he does not understand how others
can take anything seriously. Anxious, lost,
deeply puzzled, he tries unsuccessfully to cope
by bravado and constant activity. Psychotherapy

is exceptionally unpromising, as the following
case illustrates.

John first consulted a psychiatrist at the request of his mother when he was fifteen. He was
the younger by three years of two sons. His
father had died when the patient was eight,
leaving his family reasonably well off but not
wealthy. The mother sought help because of
John's persistent absences from high school, his
association with peers he was afraid of, and an
arrest for the use of amphetamines in large
doses. The arrest led to a suspended sentence
conditional on his consulting a psychiatrist.

At the age of eight he hanged a neighbor's cat
in his attic; he showed no emotion when it was
discovered, except for uneasiness about how his
parents would respond. This first conspicuous
misbehavior was followed by a long series of
increasingly serious deeds, such as imprisoning a
younger boy playmate for about twelve hours.
John was always secretive and never fought or
voluntarily took part in competitive sports with
others of his age. He rarely made serious efforts
to conceal what he had done after it was discovered, although he did lie fluently in getting away
and preparing for the deed. He showed little
emotional response when blamed, as he increasingly was, for all sorts of misdemeanors (even
ones he did not commit). This behavior antedated his father's sudden and unanticipated
death by a few months and changed little with
the loss of his father. His mother, who did not re-
marry, became the authority, bewildered and defeated after a short time. The brother associated
with others of his own age, and John, who had
no close friends or playmates of his own, often
begged to be taken along with the older boys,
although he was always largely uninvolved on
such outings.

He reached high school in spite of growing
troubles with attendance and grades but received
several warnings prior to his arrest. A period of
hospitalization, with intensive psychotherapy,
led to his discharge against advice, although his
physical condition was much improved and his
drug intake had diminished; he had received sedatives instead of amphetamines. He was, however, ineffective, distant, uninvolved with
others, fearful of both peers and adults, inept in
all physical activities, achieving (in spite of
average intelligence) only the most marginal
competence in typing after months of agonizing,
irregular practice and instruction. His achieve-

ment of even minimal standards was the occasion of both surprise and enormous pride to him.

Throughout his hospitalization he had continued to try to find, legally or illegally, barbiturates and amphetamines, alcohol, and other drugs. He escaped repeatedly, making his way to areas of the city where he was approached by homosexual men or prostitutes, never accepted their overtures, and was frequently robbed or exploited in some other way.

Seen ten years later, he was even less able to manage by himself. His mother had died, and John had spent many thousands of dollars pursuing drug kicks and transient dangerous encounters with quasi-criminal homosexual men, though he had rarely had any full sexual contact with men and none with women. With male prostitutes he demanded more sexual favors than they were willing to deliver, and he had been beaten up many times in these encounters. He had been robbed of large amounts of money and threatened with death twice. He still was weakly proud of his typing ability (it had not been tested for many years), acknowledged the wisdom of psychiatric advice he had ignored, and expressed hope that he might be able "this time" to get on the right track. Off and on John was living with his brother and his wife, but he had worn out his welcome and resented his brother's having money when he did not, although he appreciated the brother's reliability in arranging for his care. He disappeared after a few interviews on this occasion. Several years later, he was again in a psychiatric hospital, in a generally similar state.

Although treatment is prolonged, usually stormy, often interrupted and resumed, and always wearing, an unknown but appreciable number of patients ultimately improves. Usually, when improvement does occur, patients become particularly narrow, conventional people, living a life almost the opposite of the disorganized one they had lived before. This partial recovery, and the frequency of death either at their own or at others' hands, are the reasons for the clinical observation that there are few "psychopaths" older than forty.

Types of Neurotic Character

A different group of patients is widely recognized, distinguished from the patients above and from those character types closely associated with particular psychoneuroses. Patients with these neurotic character disorders have a much more natural and effective allegiance to the values and experiences of others, and to social conventions, than patients with narcissistic types of disorder. Although they may show persistent maladaptive symptoms they are never without partial conscious insight and understanding of the social or rational constraints on their actions, even while they may not obey them. Remorse, regret, anxiety, guilt, bewilderment, and social perspective are genuine and always present, even when patients are ineffective in preventing their symptomatic actions. Two different types of neurotic character disorder have been commonly recognized, unfortunately often given the same name. The selection of names here is therefore somewhat arbitrary: impulse disorders and neurotic characters.

Impulse Disorders

Patients with impulse disorders recurrently carry out complex stereotyped actions, usually clearly antisocial, often with a great though obscure excitement and fear of being caught, for reasons they are generally at a loss to explain. Like patients with minor compulsions (which occur again and again and are wildly irrational), the patient knows he is being irrational, can delay the action until an expedient time, is concerned about his "will power," and is secretively defensive of his actions. Most characteristically, the actions are highly repetitive rituals with a foreseen outcome and also, often enough, an unforeseen outcome in that they proceed remorselessly until the patient is caught or made the victim of his impulse. The compulsive gambler, without recognizing his aim, continues to gamble as long as he is winning, until finally he loses everything. The peeping Tom takes greater and greater chances—ostensibly to get a better view but actually until he is seen and recognized.

Like the compulsive person who "cannot" stop touching a doorknob, biting his fingernails, or touching a part of his body, the impulse-disordered patient wonders why he must do the things he does, makes resolutions, notes with despair the risks he is taking, and continues to take them. His actions endanger or at least affect his social life in major ways, and he knows it. In some cases relief or a sense of fulfillment follows the act; occasionally the relief is manifestly sexual, with orgasm. The common symptomatic acts are well known: transvestism, voyeurism, exhibitionism, pyromania, compulsive gambling, polydrug addiction (in contrast to single-drug addiction, usually a more serious disorder), kleptomania, and compulsive spending. The actions are accompanied by an inconspicuous but real neurotic alteration in character, with chronic anxiety beyond the immediate fear of being caught, guilt, fear of losing one's mind, shame, and, usually, inhibition of normal sexual responses. Relief after arrest is common.

Neurotic Characters

In a study of prisoners, Alexander and Staub (1956) identified a special group of patients who were well adjusted in prison but subdued and seemingly full of feelings of guilt. They might try to escape as their release approached, transparently in order to be caught, and even their crimes had been aimed toward detection. The "criminal in search of punishment" is afraid of independence and tends therefore to be a follower, timid and fearful although he often covers his timidity with gruffness and bluster. Alexander followed Freud in describing this mechanism, but he identified the problem as one of a whole character, persistent through the years before and after imprisonment, or often in the absence of correctional experience.

Character Disorders Associated with Physical Disease

Psychosomatic Disorders

Typical character disorders, or types, have been repeatedly associated with such maladies as hypertension, peptic ulcer, breast malignancy, asthma, coronary disease, and intractable eczema. However, some years ago in a major study, the experienced members of the Chicago Psychoanalytic Institute failed to identify matching personalities when they tested the

physical formulations objectively and randomly. This evidence has contributed to greater caution in making characterological associations to illness.

A major remaining character "disorder" associated with physical illness is a well-documented relation between coronary disease and personality type, identified empirically and labeled Type A and Type B by Friedman, Rosenman, and their colleagues (Rosenman et al., 1964, 1970; Jenkins, Friedman, and Rosenman, 1971; Friedman et al., 1974). Type A patients, prone to coronary disease, tend to be hard-driving, competitive, aggressive, impatient, restless, acutely aware of time pressures and responsibilities, dedicated, and ambitious; physically they show muscle tension, including tension in the face muscles, explosive speech, and hyperalertness. Type B patients are not driven in these ways and are much less prone to coronary disease.

Diseases of the Central Nervous System

As in the case of disorders already considered, many individual neurological diseases have been associated with particular types of character. Multiple sclerosis and combined-systems disease are two of many in which the original association has not been confirmed by quantitative analysis or where the confounding influence of institutionalization has not been excluded.

In the case of convulsive disorders, a typical personality has been reported. The personality was believed to be typified by considerable irritability and impressive outbursts of anger, a certain "adhesiveness" or "viscosity" in interaction with others, pedantry, slowed reactions, deepened emotional response, and, most characteristically, excessive religious and moral preoccupation. These characteristics were thought (usually in institutionalized patients) to lead to a progressively serious deterioration in social and intellectual functioning. There was uncertainty about the degree to which this process was attributable to the side effects of the anticonvulsive medication available at the time (phenobarbital and bromides). With the advent of many anticonvulsive medications (both more effective and with fewer side actions), and with greater understanding of the subtypes of epileptic seizure, the relation of convulsive disorders to personality changes has also undergone reassessment.

Several studies have cast doubt on the existence of a characteristic ictal personality altogether, but the triad of irritability, pedantry, and deepened emotionality has survived in association with temporal lobe epilepsy; to them has been added the characteristic of hyposexuality (Blumer, 1975) in contrast to the excessive sexuality and impulsive violence that may characterize seizures. All these characteristics may improve either with the medical control of seizures or, at times, following the occurrence of each seizure.

Genetic Factors

Throughout history there has been an assumption that temperament, character, and psychiatric disorder are biologically inherited, and the interpretation of the theory has been colored by the century in which the view was held. It was not until the development of modern genetics that research tools appeared that may clarify the old controversy usually associated with the discussion of the inheritance of character. Although temperament often seems to run in families, new information about biological inheritance has appeared. Rosenthal and Kety (1968) found a group of "spectrum disorders" vaguely described but corresponding roughly to "borderline patients" or patients with severe "character disorders" who, more frequently than expected, were the biological children of schizophrenic mothers raised in nonschizophrenic adopting families who did not know the psychotic parentage of the adopted child. This study invites clarification of the nature of spectrum disorders.

In 1970, Price and Jacobs described a group of men possessing an XYY chromosome abnormality (an extra male chromosome), who were apparently overrepresented among the inmates of a disciplinary mental hospital in Scotland. Described as unusually tall, victims of severe acne, and of variable but often normal intelligence, the XYY subjects were found to show "extreme instability and irresponsibility, with severe impairment of the ability to consider the consequences of their actions" (p. 31). The

authors concluded that intellectual capacity, sexual instinct, aggressive impulses, and emotional responses were all consistent with immaturity, defective development, or inadequate control and that it was reasonable to consider the disorder more or less directly attributable to the extra Y chromosome. A subsequent but mistaken newspaper report of an extra Y chromosome found in a notorious mass murderer lent an almost hysterical authority to these vigorous conclusions. Although the basic finding has been confirmed in several studies, the behavioral conclusions have been restated somewhat differently by other investigators and not confirmed by still others. The XYY abnormality often exists in normal men who have no known criminal trends. Although impulsivity was reported in the XYY inmate-patients, and although differences from other inmates in defensiveness, sociability, and conceptions of what is acceptable were described, XYY patients have often been less aggressive than the average inmate and usually have committed offenses similar to, or milder than, those committed by other prisoner-patients. Hook's thorough review (1973) makes it clear that the patients (and incidentally also XXY and XXYY Klinefelter's syndrome patients) are overrepresented in these prison-hospital settings, but the identification of characteristic behavioral patterns is only in a preliminary and very tentative stage; no detailed objective descriptions or measurements have been reported.

Change of Character

Although character is, in general, highly stable, it may change abruptly and profoundly. If such an alteration occurs, it may be ignored by the patient's family and not recognized by the patient himself. However, the physician must recognize and interpret such change correctly, since it usually signifies the likelihood of dangerous organic illness. Vascular disease of the brain, Alzheimer's disease, metabolic disorders, heavy metal intoxication, neoplastic disease, and general infectious diseases like general paresis commonly announce their presence by a change in character; profound character change is not likely without them, unless incipient psychosis is present. Rapid, profound alteration in character therefore demands the physician's prompt and serious attention. The character of the patient cannot be ignored in these circumstances without grave danger to his health and even to his life.

References

Ackerknecht, E. H. 1959. *A short history of psychiatry*. New York: Hafner.

Aichorn, A. 1925. *Wayward youth*. New York: Meridian, 1955.

———— 1964. *Delinquency and child guidance, selected papers*. New York: International Universities Press.

Alexander, F., and H. Staub. 1956. *The criminal, the judge and the public: a psychological analysis*. Rev. ed. Glencoe, Ill.: Free Press.

Altman, L. J. 1975. A case of narcissistic personality disorder: the problem of treatment. *Int. J. Psychoanal.* 56:187–195.

American Psychiatric Association. 1968. *Diagnostic and statistical manual of mental disorders*. 2nd ed. Washington, D.C.

Barton, R. 1959. *Institutional neurosis*. Bristol: John Wright.

Blumer, D. 1975. Temporal lobe epilepsy and its psychiatric significance. In *Psychiatric aspects of neurologic disease*, ed. D. F. Benson and D. Blumer. New York: Grune & Stratton.

Cleckley, H. 1955. *The mask of sanity*. St. Louis: Mosby.

Cumming, E., and W. E. Henry. 1961. *Growing old: the process of disengagement*. New York: Basic Books.

Davies, J. 1947. Gall and the phrenological movement. *Bull. Hist. Med.* 21:275–321.

———— 1955. *Phrenology: fad and science*. New Haven: Yale University Press.

Deutsch, H. 1942. Some forms of emotional disturbance and their relationship to schizophrenia. *Psychoanal. Q.* 11:301–321.

Escalona, S., and G. Heider. 1959. *Prediction and outcome*. New York: Basic Books.

Fenichel, O. 1945. *The psychoanalytic theory of neurosis*. New York: Norton.

Freud, S. 1908. Character and anal erotism. In *Standard edition*, ed. J. Strachey. Vol. 9. London: Hogarth Press, 1959.

———— 1917. On transformations of instinct as exemplified in anal erotism. In *Standard edition*, ed. J. Strachey. Vol. 17. London: Hogarth Press, 1955.

———— 1931. Libidinal types. In *Standard edition*, ed. J. Strachey. Vol. 21. London: Hogarth Press, 1961.

Friedman, G. D., H. K. Ury, A. L. Klatsky, and A. B. Siegelaub. 1974. A psychological questionnaire predictive of myocardial infarction: results from the Kaiser-Permanente epidemiologic study of myocardial infarction. *Psychosom. Med.* 36:327–343.

Gant, H. M. 1975. DSM III revisions debated. *Psychiatr. News* 10:16–17, 36.

Grinker, R. R., B. Werble, and R. Drye. 1968. *The borderline syndrome*. New York: Basic Books.

Gruenberg, E. M. 1967. The social breakdown syndrome—some origins. *Am. J. Psychiatry* 123:1481–89.

Gunderson, J. G., and M. T. Singer. 1975. Defining borderline patients: an overview. *Am. J. Psychiatry* 132:1–10.

Haggard, E. A. 1964. Isolation and personality. In *Personality change*, ed. P. Worchel and D. Byrne. New York: Wiley.

Holt, R. R. 1964. Forcible indoctrination and personality change. In *Personality change*, ed. P. Worchel and D. Byrne. New York: Wiley.

Hook, E. B. 1973. Behavioral implications of the human XYY genotype. *Science* 179:139–150.

Hooker, E. 1958. Male homosexuality in the Rorschach. *J. Proj. Tech.* 22:33–54.

Jenkins, C. D., M. Friedman, and R. H. Rosenman. 1971. *The Jenkins activity survey for health prediction*. Chapel Hill: University of North Carolina.

Jung, C. G. 1918. A contribution to the study of psychological types. In *Collected works*, ed. H. Read. Vol. 6. Bollingen Series 20. Princeton: Princeton University Press, 1971.

Kernberg, O. 1967. Borderline personality organization. *J. Am. Psychoanal. Assoc.* 15:641–658.

———— 1968. Treatment of patients with borderline personality organization. *Int. J. Psychiatry* 49:600–619.

———— 1970a. Factors in the psychoanalytic treatment of narcissistic personalities. *J. Am. Psychoanal. Assoc.* 18:51–85.

———— 1970b. A psychoanalytic classification of character pathology. *J. Am. Psychoanal. Assoc.* 18:800–822.

———— 1975. *Borderline conditions and pathological narcissism*. New York: Aronson.

Kohut, H. 1971. *The analysis of the self*. New York: International Universities Press.

Kretschmer, E. 1936. *Physique and character*. London: Miller.

Kuhlen, R. G. 1964. Personality change with age. In *Personality change*, ed. P. Worchel and D. Byrne. New York: Wiley.

Maccoby, E. E., and C. N. Jacklin. 1974. *The psychology of sex difference*. Stanford, Cal.: Stanford University Press.

McCord, W. and J. 1964. *The psychopath*. Princeton, N.J.: Van Nostrand.

Moss, H. A., and J. Kagan. 1964. Report on personality consistency and change from the guidance study. *Vita Humana* 7:127–138.

Murphy, L. B. 1964. Factors in continuity and change in the development of adaptational style in children. *Vita Humana* 7:96–114.

Murray, J. M. 1964. Narcissism and the ego ideal. *J. Am. Psychoanal. Assoc.* 12:477–511.

Price, W. H., and P. A. Jacobs. 1970. The 47, XYY male with special reference to behavior. *Semin. Psychiatry* 2:30–39.

Reich, A. 1960. Pathological forms of self-esteem regulation. *Psychoanal. Study Child* 15:215–232.

Rosenman, R. H., M. Friedman, R. Strauss, M. Wurm, R. Kositchek, W. Hahn, and N. T. Werthessen. 1964. A predictive study of coronary heart disease: the western collaborative group study. *J.A.M.A.* 189:15–26.

———— 1970. Coronary heart disease in the western collaborative group study: a follow-up experience of 4½ years. *J. Chronic Dis.* 23:173–190.

Rosenthal, D., and S. S. Kety. 1968. *The transmission of schizophrenia*. New York: Pergamon.

Sheldon, W. H. 1940. *The varieties of human physique*. New York: Harper.

———— 1954. *Atlas of men: a guide for somatotyping the adult male of all ages*. New York: Harper.

Slavney, P. R., and P. R. McHeigh. 1974. The hysterical personality: a controlled study. *Arch. Gen. Psychiatry* 30:325–329.

Stein, M. H. 1969. The problem of character theory. *J. Am. Psychoanal. Assoc.* 17:675–701.

Stolorow, R. D. 1975. Toward a functional definition of narcissism. *Int. J. Psychoanal.* 56:179–185.

Temkin, O. 1973. *Galenism: rise and decline of a medical philosophy*. Ithaca, N.Y., and London: Cornell University Press.

Witkin, H. A., R. B. Dyk, H. F. Paterson, D. R. Goodenough, and S. A. Karp. 1962. *Psychological differentiation: studies of development*. New York and London: Wiley.

World Health Organization. 1967. *Manual of the international statistical classification of diseases, injuries, and causes of death*. Vol. 1. Geneva.

Yarrow, L. J. and M. R. 1964. Personality continuity and change in the family context. In *Personality change*, ed. P. Worchel and D. Byrne. New York: Wiley.

Organic Mental Disorders

CHAPTER 15

Benjamin Seltzer
Shervert H. Frazier

O RGANIC BRAIN SYNDROME is a general term conventionally used to describe those conditions of impaired function of the nervous system that are manifested by psychiatric symptoms. This concept contrasts with the majority of psychiatric syndromes, called "functional," in which there is no obvious physical cause. In some ways, this distinction is artificial. Behavior can never be divorced from its anatomical substrate in the brain, but neither can it be treated as a pure neurological phenomenon without reference to learning and the environment. Many psychiatric syndromes previously thought to be functional, such as general paresis and the avitaminoses, have been found to be organic in nature. On the other hand, even though increasing evidence points toward a biological basis for schizophrenia and depression, the psychodevelopmental model of these conditions may remain quite valid. Nevertheless, despite these difficulties, it is useful and important from a pragmatic point of view to distinguish "functional" from "organic" psychiatric syndromes. These categories have vastly different prognostic and therapeutic implications. The placement of a patient into the wrong one of these diagnostic alternatives can profoundly influence his subsequent progress.

Organic mental disorders are very common. Although precise data are difficult to find, some authorities estimate that they account for one out of five first admissions to a mental hospital (NIMH, 1966) and also occur frequently in general hospitals (Reding and Daniels, 1964; Lipowski, 1967b). Over 50 percent of geriatric patients in mental hospitals have this diagnosis (Riley and Foner, 1968), and many elderly people in the community also suffer from some degree of organic mental impairment (Broe et al., 1976). As the mean age of the American population rises and more persons reach advanced age, the problems of geriatric psychiatry, including "organic brain syndrome," will inevitably become major medical and social issues.

Considerable confusion surrounds the classification and description of organic mental disorders. These conditions occupy a kind of borderland between psychiatry and neurology, and each field has its own way of viewing these syndromes. According to the *Diagnostic and Statistical Manual* of the American Psychiatric Association (DSM-II), "the organic brain syndrome is a basic mental condition characteristically re- sulting from diffuse impairment of brain tissue function from whatever cause" (p. 22). Its symptoms are impairment of orientation, mem- ory, judgment, and intellectual function and la- bility and shallowness of affect. Although a vari- ety of different pathological processes (such as intracranial infection, brain trauma, and circula- tory disturbance) are recognized as possible causes of an organic brain syndrome, and although appropriate diagnostic names and code numbers are provided for each, this usage never- theless implies that all of these syndromes, regardless of etiology, are more or less variations on the same clinical theme. The classification scheme does make a distinction between "psy- chotic" and "nonpsychotic" organic brain syn- dromes, depending upon the patient's capacity to meet the ordinary demands of life; there is also a distinction between "acute" and "chronic" brain syndromes based on the relative reversi- bility of the condition.

Many difficulties persist in this schema, how- ever, for it fails to take into account the extremely complex, mosaic-like nature of the nervous system. Disease of one portion of the nervous system may give rise to symptoms quite different from those caused by disease in another portion. Different pathological processes do not necessarily affect the nervous system in precisely the same way. Even the so-called diffuse diseases consistently affect specific portions of the ner- vous system. The traditional psychiatric view therefore fails to take into account the wide di- versity of organic mental disorders. Entities such as Alzheimer's disease, Broca's aphasia, and de- lirium tremens have little in common, aside from being diseases of the nervous system. To imply that they are variations of the same common syndrome is misleading. Nor is the distinction between psychotic and nonpsychotic brain syn- dromes particularly helpful, for in some cases these terms merely indicate the severity of the process. Finally, the equation of acute with reversible, and chronic with irreversible, does not hold up under scrutiny. Many brain syn- dromes of acute onset may persist and become chronic while certain chronic conditions are po- tentially treatable.

Since the organic brain syndromes are basi-

cally neurological diseases, and since the psychi- atric nosology has its shortcomings, approaching these conditions from a more strictly neuro- logical point of view may be preferable. This ap- proach requires a somewhat different orientation toward an individual's mental status. Psychia- trists are trained to place special emphasis on the developmental aspects of human psychology. In the formal assessment of the mental status, they focus primarily on the content and process of the patient's thinking, his judgment, reasoning, and ability to evaluate reality. A disturbance of these functions in a person with a normal nervous system may suggest a specific psychiatric diag- nosis. When the possibility of damage to the nervous system exists, however, these findings prove less helpful. Our knowledge of the nervous system is simply too crude to know how to inter- pret, in neurological terms, such complex phe- nomena as thinking and judgment. Patients with organic mental disorders often do have abnor- malities of this nature, but these symptoms do not help to differentiate these patients from those with functional disease, nor to distinguish the different forms of brain disease. Instead, empirical evidence shows that certain other cate- gories of function, such as attention, short- and long-term memory, language, and construc- tional ability (drawing, stick design, and so forth) are far more important in evaluating patients with suspected brain damage. (The rationale for emphasizing these particular categories and the significance of abnormalities in each are pre- sented in chapter 4, "Neural Substrates of Behavior.") The decision that a particular pa- tient's symptoms have an organic etiology, like other diagnostic decisions in medicine, rests on a synthesis of clinical, historical, and laboratory information. No easy formula for the diagnosis of "organicity" can be offered. Coupled with other appropriate data, however, abnormalities of these particular cognitive functions point toward one of the organic syndromes.

Another aspect of the mental status also has different meanings for the psychiatrist and neu- rologist and may create great diagnostic diffi- culty. Abnormalities of affect and behavior are among the most common symptoms of psychiat- ric disease. The majority of cases have no de- monstrable pathological basis and may legitimately be called functional in nature. Under other circumstances, however, damage to the nervous system may cause symptoms very similar, if not identical, to those occurring in functional disorders.

Psychiatrists have long realized that many organic mental disorders are associated with abnormalities of affect and behavior. In fact, accounts of organic brain syndromes in psychiatric textbooks devote considerable space to a description of these changes. The authors sometimes interpret these symptoms as the individual's response to his illness or as an exaggeration of previously existing personality traits. This explanation may often be valid. On the other hand, since the structures affected by brain disease involve precisely those forming the anatomical bases of affect and behavior (see chapter 4, "Neural Substrates of Behavior"), the emotional symptoms of organic mental disorders might equally be considered the direct effect of damage to the nervous system. Nor can we uncritically assume that an individual with brain damage will respond to his surroundings in the same way as an individual whose nervous system is intact. For these reasons, the neurologist is cautious in interpreting the emotional changes of neurological disease and considers some of these changes to be hard evidence for brain disease.

Most of the neurological categories that have been mentioned can be related to some specific portion of the brain. By carefully searching for abnormalities of these functions, one can often pinpoint precisely the site of a lesion. The utility of this approach in determining specific diagnosis and treatment is therefore obvious. However, DSM-II refers primarily to another group of neurological diseases, those less easily localized to a specific portion of the brain—the so-called global or diffuse syndromes. To call these syndromes diffuse, however, may not be completely justified. No pathological process, aside from death, affects all cells in all parts of the nervous system to an equal extent. Alzheimer's disease, for example, usually considered the prototype of diffuse cerebral disease, often has a predilection for the parietal and temporal lobes. Even cerebral anoxia, a gross process that would seem to involve the entire brain, causes a very selective pattern of damage to the nervous system.

Parallel to these specific patterns of anatomical involvement are distinct, recognizable clinical syndromes.

The remainder of this chapter will focus on the nonfocal, diffuse cerebral diseases. Two of the most common and important general syndromes in this category—the acute confusional state and progressive dementia—will receive special attention. A careful appraisal of a patient's mental status will allow for a specific, as well as a general, diagnosis. Certain other common organic mental disorders will also be described, along with the psychiatric aspects of several well-known neurological diseases.

Acute Confusional States

A common phenomenon in clinical medicine is the acute onset of psychiatric symptoms in a patient suffering from a physical illness. Because we assume the mental changes result from metabolic insult to the brain, we sometimes call this syndrome "acute brain syndrome" or "metabolic encephalopathy." The clinical presentation of the syndrome may take several forms, all well known to most psychiatrists and similarly described by most textbooks. Differences appear, however, in naming the syndrome and determining what constitutes the basic, underlying impairment of mental function. *Acute brain syndrome, toxic psychosis, delirium, confusional state,* and *clouding of consciousness* are among the many terms used to denote either the entire syndrome or one of its clinical manifestations. This diversity of usage among texts reflects the clinician's imprecision and inconsistent use of these terms. Furthermore, no fixed agreement exists concerning the very nature of the disorder or the criteria necessary for diagnosis. For some, a clouding of consciousness is the *sine qua non* (Lipowski, 1967a); for others, a global cognitive impairment (Engel and Romano, 1959). Still others require only disorientation and impairment of memory for diagnosis (Woodruff, Goodwin, and Guze, 1974). Many textbooks group all of the different manifestations into one general syndrome (Posner, 1971), while other authors insist on an important distinction between several clinical variants (Adams and Victor, 1974). In the face of this bewildering situation, this chapter adopts the term *acute confusional state* to refer to the broad range of these related conditions; further, we maintain that a selective deficit of attention is the one feature common to all.

Clinical Description

Although there may be considerable variation in other aspects of the clinical presentation, the cardinal derangement in all confusional states is a disorder of attention. This means that the patient cannot focus sufficiently on incoming stimuli to fix them clearly in his mind. He lacks concentration and is easily distracted. Thinking therefore loses its usual clarity and direction. The mildest form may result in merely a certain vagueness or sluggishness of thought processes; in the extreme form, the patient may be incapable of maintaining a coherent stream of thought. Disordered attention may be likened to the state of disconnected mental rambling experienced by many normal individuals just prior to falling asleep.

Observation of a confused patient reveals the many facets of this inability to attend. His conversation has a fragmentary and disjointed quality. He suddenly stops in mid-sentence and fails to complete his thought; seconds later he takes up a totally unrelated idea. Behavior also loses its usual direction toward a goal. The patient is easily distracted; in the course of a medical examination, he may abruptly stop his participation and respond to an irrelevant noise coming from the next bed. Often he misperceives the distracting stimuli; for example, he may mistake a sound in the corridor for a human conversation. Although the patient may be very inattentive to ordinary stimuli in the environment, his attention may sometimes be abnormally riveted by these distractions.

From the foregoing discussion, one may deduce that a confused patient will have difficulty with almost any intellectual operation. Since he cannot consistently attend to his surroundings, he may be disoriented in regard to time and place. Since he cannot adequately register incoming information, he will be incapable of remembering this information after an interval. If, however, he can be momentarily roused to make the effort to concentrate, he may perform these tasks correctly. Therefore, disorientation and memory loss, although commonly found, are not essential to the diagnosis of a confusional state. Rather, they are secondary to the inattention. Other disorders of higher cortical function may also be seen; confused patients frequently misname objects and have a gross disturbance of the ability to write (Chédru and Geschwind, 1972). A severely confused individual may be difficult to test for cognitive function, however, and diagnosis is usually based on direct observation of the patient's inability to attend.

Aside from inattention and distractibility, the clinical picture of confusional state varies considerably. An alteration in consciousness is not an essential feature, and some patients remain fully alert. However, many do show some reduction in the level of consciousness. In some this amounts to nothing more than an unusual quietness or tendency to sleep, but in others there is progression through states of increasing lethargy to torpor, stupor, and coma. In some patients, lethargy alternates with periods of an almost hyperalert vigilance.

In addition to the illusionary misperceptions mentioned above, the patient in an acute confusional state often experiences hallucinations. The hallucinations are usually visual, but they may also be auditory or tactile; no consistency is evident in the content or the duration of the hallucinations.

The emotional tone of an acute confusional state may also vary. Some patients are quiet, apathetic, withdrawn, and unperturbed by hallucinations. This state is sometimes called "simple confusion" or "quiet delirium." Other patients are sweaty, tremulous, anxious, and hyperactive (agitated delirium). These terms are purely descriptive and do not imply a specific etiology. Many patients experience both poles of emotional response during an acute confusional state.

Acute confusional states usually have a fairly sudden onset and occur in the context of some obvious medical illness. They are therefore particularly common in a general hospital. Most confusional states have a tendency to worsen at night; patients may be bright and alert during the day, only to slip into a state of confusion at night. One woman in the early stages of delirium tremens was able to work during the day as a nurse but experienced visual hallucinations when alone in her apartment at night. In some instances the signs of a confusional state may be the first warning of an impending systemic illness. Unfortunately, many physicians recognize only the more flagrant and dramatic forms of the confusional state. Careful assessment of the mental status might, in some circumstances, forestall a medical catastrophe.

Etiology

An acute confusional state is almost always secondary to a pathological process outside of the nervous system. In a few exceptional circumstances, confusion may be caused by a primary disease of the brain. The feature common to most of the conditions causing a confusional state is a derangement of normal body metabolism. This disturbance presumably has an adverse effect on the function of the neuronal cell, but its mechanism or mechanisms are purely speculative. If the metabolic imbalance can be promptly corrected, or the toxin removed, then the confusional state can usually be reversed and the brain undergoes no permanent changes. But if the metabolic derangement is permitted to continue beyond a certain point, the brain may suffer irreparable damage. When such damage occurs, however, the clinical syndrome usually becomes quite different. In place of a confusional state marked by inattention, fixed deficits of cognitive function and behavior now appear (see the discussion of other common neuropsychiatric syndromes later in this chapter). An acute confusional state can therefore be viewed as the fleeting clinical manifestation of a temporary, reversible alteration of brain chemistry and physiology.

A wide variety of pathological processes can cause this alteration in neural function. To enumerate the causes of acute confusional states is to catalogue almost every illness, intoxication, or metabolic disturbance known to exist. Some of the major categories, with important examples of each, are listed below.

Metabolic disorders
  1. hypoxia, hypercarbia (in pulmonary disease, heart disease, anemia)
  2. hypoglycemia, hyperosmolarity
  3. ionic imbalance: sodium, potassium, calcium, magnesium, acid-base
  4. other diseases; hepatic encephalopathy, uremic encephalopathy
  5. vitamin B_1 deficiency (Wernicke's encephalopathy)
  6. endocrine disorders: thyroid, parathyroid, adrenal (rare)
Infections
  1. systemic: pneumonia, typhoid fever, malaria, septicemia
  2. intracranial: meningitis, encephalitis
Postoperative states
Intoxications: alcohol, sedatives, anticholinergics, opiates, stimulants, levodopa, digitalis, heavy metals (rare)
Drug withdrawal states: alcohol, sedatives
Neurological diseases
  1. following seizures
  2. following head trauma
  3. hypertensive encephalopathy
  4. focal disease: right parietal lobe and inferomedial surface of the occipital lobe

Although a few etiologies give a characteristic clinical picture, for the most part these syndromes lack specificity. In most cases reliance must be placed on laboratory data and other manifestations of the disease to make a specific, etiologic diagnosis.

Metabolic disorders. Metabolic disorders are frequent causes of acute confusional states. In fact the term *metabolic encephalopathy* is often used to describe the entire syndrome. Electrolyte disturbance, acid-base imbalance, hypoglycemia, hyperosmolarity, and anemia are among the most common specific etiologies. The endocrinopathies are less frequent and are usually marked by a slowly progressive dementia. Patients with chronic lung disease and congestive heart failure may develop an acute confusional state because of hypoxia and hypercarbia. Another important group of patients are those with serious kidney or liver disease (uremic encephalopathy and hepatic encephalopathy). In these latter states, the inattention of a confusional state may also be associated with seizures and asterixis, a characteristic flapping tremor of the extended hands

(Adams and Foley, 1953). Although classically described in hepatic encephalopathy, asterixis is found with the other metabolic confusional states as well.

Laboratory analysis, together with recognition of the other characteristic signs of the underlying disease, will usually make clear the cause of the encephalopathy. In some patients, however, especially elderly people with multiple medical problems, the metabolic derangement, as recorded by laboratory examination, may be minimal.

Wernicke's encephalopathy is an acute confusional state caused by a deficiency of thiamine (vitamin B_1). In this country, it is found in chronic alcoholics with a grossly inadequate diet. Wernicke's encephalopathy has all the typical features of an acute confusional state, usually of the quiet, apathetic variety, but with the additional finding of eye-movement paralyses (Victor, Adams, and Collins, 1971). If adequately treated, the patient usually improves. If inadequately or belatedly treated, however, the patient may develop a permanent amnestic syndrome (Korsakoff's disease). Wernicke's encephalopathy encompasses the acute stage of inattention. Korsakoff's disease refers to the chronic, fixed deficit of memory.

Infections. Systemic infections associated with a high fever are one of the classical causes of an acute confusional state. Pneumonia, typhoid fever, and malaria are perhaps among the best known, but infection from any agent in any part of the body, if sufficiently severe, may be responsible for some form of the syndrome. Acute infection of the brain and its coverings, such as bacterial meningitis or viral meningoencephalitis, are also major causes of acute confusional states. A patient with fever and a confusional state must have his cerebrospinal fluid examined to exclude this extremely serious diagnostic possibility.

Postoperative states. An acute confusional state may sometimes follow a surgical procedure. Its occurrence can usually be attributed to a combination of metabolic imbalances, anesthetic effects, and infection with fever; it usually subsides when properly treated. A confusional state can be a very serious complication of surgery, however, since an agitated, delirious patient, if unattended, may disconnect intravenous infusions, undo surgical dressings, and tear apart sutures.

In the early days of open-heart surgery, postoperative delirium was a frequent complication. The incidence of this phenomenon is now much reduced, owing to better recognition of its occurrence and improved technique—specifically, less hypotension and less time on bypass (Tufo, Ostfeld, and Shekelle, 1970). A number of writers have emphasized the psychological factors contributing to postcardiotomy delirium and have drawn analogies to the hallucinatory states that can follow prolonged sensory deprivation (Heller and Kornfeld, 1975).

Intoxications. A larger number of different toxins, medicinal agents being perhaps the most significant, may cause acute confusional states. The drug need not be at a toxic level to cause an acute confusional state, particularly if the individual has some physical illness or metabolic derangement at the same time. Some of the most common responsible agents have already been listed. Aside from the state of inattention, common to all such conditions, associated symptoms depend upon the other effects of the offending agent. Sedatives and hypnotics can cause a depression in the level of consciousness in addition to the confusional state. Stimulant drugs can produce a hyperactive, agitated confusion. The anticholinergic agents may cause hallucinations as well as pupillary changes.

Drug withdrawal states. Just as intoxication with many drugs may cause a confusional state, the sudden withdrawal of some of these agents will cause a similar condition. Alcohol is probably the most common offender. Delirium tremens may occur beginning several days (typically three or four) after the cessation of heavy drinking; it occasionally lasts for as long as a week but usually runs its course in two or three days. In the classic case, the patient is sweaty, tremulous, hyperactive and restless. His pulse is quickened, and his pupils are dilated. His head and eyes dart back and forth as they follow his visual hallucinations. His hands pull at the bedclothes as though trying to uncover some hidden object. Hallucinations frequently involve seeing small animals, but the content varies. Some patients remain quietly and unobtrusively confused throughout the entire episode. Alcohol withdrawal is also associated with another type of hallucination, nearly always auditory in nature, but this *acute auditory hallucinosis* invariably occurs in a clear sensorium without confusion, prior to the onset of the delirium tremens, and is much less common than the delirium tremens. Similarly, alcohol withdrawal seizures ("rum fits") always precede the confusional state. Delirium tremens can be a grave medical problem with a mortality rate as high as 15 percent (Victor, 1975). The clinician must therefore recognize the syndrome not only in patients who have some other obvious complication of alcohol but also in individuals who develop a confusional state within the first few days of hospitalization for some other cause.

Confusional states are also found after withdrawal from other agents, particularly barbiturates and the other hypnotic sedatives. A confusional state, strictly defined, is not a characteristic of withdrawal from the narcotic analgesics.

Neurological diseases. As mentioned above, primary disease of the nervous system, sufficient to cause pathological changes in the brain, seldom causes an acute confusional state. One important exception is intracranial infection. A nonspecific confusional state is also seen transiently in individuals who are just regaining consciousness after head trauma or a major motor seizure.

Furthermore, two conditions of strictly focal pathology of the brain may produce a confusional state: (1) infarctions of the inferomedial surface of the occipital lobe (Horenstein, Chamberlain, and Conomoy, 1967), an uncommon condition, and (2) more commonly, certain lesions of the right parietal lobe (Mesulam et al., 1976).

Differential Diagnosis

In most well-developed confusional states, the diagnosis is not difficult. The recent onset of mental symptoms in a patient with recognized medical disease presents few problems. Diffi-culties do arise, however, when the mental changes overshadow the other manifestations of the disease. If the changes are mainly those of a quiet, apathetic sort, they may be missed altogether by an unobservant examiner. If, however, such changes are of the wild, agitated, and combative type, they may be mistaken for a primary psychiatric condition.

Although schizophrenia and manic-depressive psychosis may have an explosive onset and do sometimes cause sudden flare-ups, they usually appear somewhat more slowly and in patients with a history of prior mental disturbance. The sudden onset of a change in thinking and behavior in a person with no history of such features always suggests an acute confusional state rather than a functional psychosis. Differences also exist in the clinical appearance of these syndromes. The abnormal behavior, thinking, and speech of the confused patient have a completely aimless, haphazard, and disjointed nature. By contrast, the abnormal motor activity of a schizophrenic often has a repetitive, stereotyped quality; his abnormal speech may have the same feature. Confused patients are sometimes lethargic and tremulous; their *visual* hallucinations and illusionary misperceptions are unstructured. The schizophrenic is usually alert and his *auditory* hallucinations and delusionary ideas are generally well organized and consistent. Many patients with schizophrenia *can* be formally tested, and the results often show that their memory and other cognitive functions are perfectly intact. Another common finding on mental-status testing of schizophrenics is a great variability in response—some of their responses are completely correct while others are wildly off the mark. The confused patient, on the other hand, may be very difficult to test at all.

An acute manic episode might also be mistaken for an agitated confusional state. Here, again, the history is all-important. In addition, the very strong, consistently euphoric affect of the manic patient can be differentiated from the fragmented, constantly shifting, less consistent affect of the confused patient.

An acute confusional state differs considerably from the state of progressive dementia, and the two syndromes ought not to produce any difficulties in differential diagnosis. An untreated confusional state might, however, eventually lead to a state of fixed cognitive impairment.

To determine the cause of an acute confusional state is essentially an exercise in routine medical diagnosis. The associated signs of systemic illness, together with the findings on laboratory examination, usually provide the answer. Most of the abnormalities can be detected by checking the blood for the usual biochemical parameters and for toxins. Cerebrospinal fluid should be examined in many cases, and this procedure must be undertaken if any possibility of intracranial infection exists. The electroencephalogram usually shows an abnormal tracing in cases of acute confusional state but, aside from certain special cases such as hepatic encephalopathy, can rarely suggest a specific etiology.

Treatment

The treatment of an acute confusional state involves primarily the treatment of the underlying illness. This usually consists of correction of a fluid or electrolyte imbalance, treatment of infection, administration of vitamins, or removal of a toxic agent. In the withdrawal syndromes, the basic principle is to reintoxicate the patient with the same or a similar agent and then allow for a less precipitous withdrawal. Patients with delirium tremens should be well hydrated. Since these patients will usually have been eating improperly during their binges, they must also receive vitamins. Administration of glucose solutions to a patient with only marginal stores of thiamine can precipitate Wernicke's encephalopathy. General nursing measures, such as keeping the room well lighted, avoiding loud noises and unnecessary movement, and constantly reassuring the patient, may help reduce the intensity of the delirium.

Caution should be exercised in the administration of drugs to patients with acute confusional states. Since agents such as the sedatives and hypnotics may only further depress the level of consciousness and worsen a confusional state, they must be used sparingly. In certain cases of extreme agitation and restlessness, however, such as delirium tremens, they may be necessary. Many different sedatives or major tranquilizers might be used, and each has its advocates (Victor, 1975). Paraldehyde, one of the earliest

agents to be developed, remains an effective and safe choice when more modern means of sedation may be contraindicated.

If treated promptly and adequately, an acute confusional state may be completely reversed. Sometimes mental improvement may lag behind recovery from the general disease. If untreated or treated too late, however, acute confusional states have a high incidence of mortality or permanent neurological damage (Guze and Daengsurisri, 1967). The early recognition of an acute confusional state is therefore of extreme importance. This can be easily accomplished if the physician takes the time to assess the mental status of every patient he examines.

Progressive Dementia

Dementia is usually defined as a general deterioration in intellectual abilities due to some disorder of the nervous system. Actually, it involves a disintegration of personality and behavior as well as of intellect. The process of dementia eventually strips an individual of all those qualities that make him uniquely human. Dementia must be distinguished from mental retardation, which implies that an individual never fully acquired all of these attainments, and from such disorders as Korsakoff's disease or aphasia, which primarily affect one category of intellectual function and result from a highly focal insult to the brain.

The dementias form a group of clinical syndromes and not a pathological entity. Although dementia may have many causes and each of the dementing diseases has its own distinctive features, sufficient similarity exists among them to justify grouping them together under the general term *dementia*. The following clinical description therefore represents a composite picture of the syndrome, but adheres most closely to the clinical picture of the primary, or idiopathic, dementias, numerically the most common. In a later section of this chapter, more specific remarks will be made about some of the individual dementing illnesses.

Clinical Description

Dementia usually begins insidiously and progresses slowly; it may be impossible to say precisely when the process began. Occasionally the history suggests a sudden onset, following an injury, medical illness, or emotional upset, but it is likely that these events only serve to call attention to a previously existing process.

Just as the onset is insidious, the first signs of dementia are often elusive and may involve subtle changes in personality and behavior. In the majority of cases, the personality change is toward a certain lack of spontaneity. Patients seem apathetic and withdraw from their family and friends. They prefer to sit quietly by themselves and may lose interest in sexual activity. At this stage, many patients give the impression of being depressed, and some may in fact have true depressive complaints as they vaguely perceive the changes they are undergoing. At this point, the differential diagnosis can be very difficult. The patient with an early dementia may be misdiagnosed as suffering from depression while the elderly individual who is simply depressed may be unfairly consigned to the category of patients with dementia. In some demented patients, however, the personality and mood changes differ. These individuals become unusually expansive and disinhibited and lose their usual sense of the social niceties. Gross errors of judgment may lead to professional and financial embarrassment, and some individuals become involved in sexual misadventures. This particular clinical picture is less common than the quiet, apathetic syndrome and is more apt to occur when there is damage to the frontal lobe.

Along with these changes in personality come signs of intellectual deterioration. The patient has difficulty with any activity that requires new or original thought. Dementia may thus be apparent at an earlier stage in a person whose occupation requires intensive intellectual activity than in someone who faces less rigorous demands. Difficulty with memory is often obvious. The patient will repeat questions over and over again because he cannot remember the answers. He will forget to keep appointments and may forget some of the events of his past life. Some patients try to prevent embarrassment by carrying a notebook that contains some of this information. As the disease progresses, patients frequently become lost, even in familiar surroundings, and may find it impossible to perform such functions as driving an automobile, preparing a meal, or even dressing themselves.

The deterioration progresses slowly but relentlessly. Memory impairment becomes increasingly more apparent, and the patient may fail to recognize even his closest relatives and friends. Speech begins to acquire an empty, stereotyped quality and conveys progressively less meaning. Eventually the patient reaches a pitiable state of mute, almost total withdrawal from the world around him. During this advanced stage patients may be incontinent, and some become hyperactive, loud, and assaultive. Once this stage is reached, death from some intercurrent infection usually follows within months.

On examination, the typical patient with mild to moderate dementia will be fully alert and reasonably attentive. Most patients will be neatly groomed and socially appropriate as they interact with the physician. Patients with the frontal lobe type of syndrome, however, may be sloppy in appearance, and their behavior may not be the same as that previously seen in the patient. At this stage of the disease, patients may have some insight into the nature of their disability and express a degree of subjective depression. With time, however, although the patient may admit to memory and other intellectual problems, he seems less convincingly concerned.

Patients show a deficit in the ability both to learn new information and to remember facts that they knew in the past. The difficulty with memorization is conventionally tested by asking the patient to remember the names of a few unrelated objects or the details of a short, simple story. Once it is certain that the patient has registered the information and understands the task, his attention is distracted by going on to some other part of the examination. Five or ten minutes later, he is asked to recall the objects or the story. Most patients with well-developed dementia will be unable to retain this information. At the conclusion of the interview, they may not be able to remember the name of the examiner or the details of the examination. Memory for past events can be surveyed by asking the patient about his own earlier life or facts of common knowledge, such as the names of major political figures or important dates. The difficulty of the questions must be flexible, based on what is known about the patient's premorbid intellectual ability. Early in the course of the disease, memory loss may be apparent only by a certain hesitancy and uncertainty in response, but as it progresses the patient may have such a severe impairment of memory that he cannot explain how he came to be in the present situation. The result is disorientation regarding time and place. At this point, patients often cannot recollect even the major events of their own lives. Not all memories are equally affected, however, and the more remote events of a person's life are often better remembered than the more recent.

Language is also affected by dementia. Although at first it may seem essentially normal, it later acquires a certain vagueness and imprecision. Long, roundabout phrases may be substituted for specific words, and one can sometimes detect paraphasic errors. On confrontation, a patient may correctly identify a pair of eyeglasses, but the lenses are described as "the inside of the glasses" and the frames as "the outer part." More specific, localizable aphasic disorders, of the type described in chapter 4, "Neural Substrates of Behavior," however, are not a regular feature of dementia. Eventually speech becomes simplified to the point of being merely a collection of clichés and short responses.

One can nearly always demonstrate difficulties with tasks that require the integration of visual and spatial information. Thus a patient may be incapable of copying a simple geometric design such as a cube or of drawing a house or a flower. Patients have inordinate difficulty in arranging matchsticks into a simple figure such as a W. Sometimes the examiner has the opportunity to observe even more striking abnormalities. The patient may struggle desperately in a perplexed, unsuccessful attempt to put his clothes back on, particularly if the sleeve of the shirt or nightgown has been turned inside out. Some patients, particularly those with advanced dementia, may even be uncertain how to manipulate a knife and a fork. Difficulties with calculations, right-left orientation, interpretation of proverbs, and the detection of similarities between related objects may also be observed.

In the final stage of the disease, the patient is often difficult to examine. He is extremely easily distracted and totally inattentive. Patients frequently strike out and resist examination. Speech consists of a few perseverated phrases, or there may be no speech at all. Under those circumstances, cognitive function may be impossible to test.

Etiology

Progressive dementia has a number of different causes, some of which are listed below.

Primary dementias
1. Alzheimer's disease
2. senile dementia
3. Pick's disease
Secondary dementias
1. infections
   a. chronic granulomatous meningitis (tuberculous, fungal)
   b. tertiary neurosyphilis: general paresis
   c. Jakob-Creutzfeldt disease
   d. brain abscess
2. trauma: chronic subdural hematoma
3. toxic and metabolic disturbances
   a. pernicious anemia
   b. folic acid deficiency
   c. hypothyroidism
   d. bromide poisoning
4. circulatory disorders: multiinfarct dementia
5. neoplasms
6. other neurological diseases
   a. Huntington's chorea
   b. Parkinson's disease
   c. Parkinson-dementia complex
   d. multiple sclerosis
   e. cerebellar degenerations
7. normal-pressure hydrocephalus

Basically, the dementias can be divided into two major categories: (1) those in which dementia occurs as part of some other pathological process (the secondary dementias) and (2) those in which dementia is the only major abnormality (the primary dementias). The latter category is by far the most common, and will be discussed in some detail. Some of the more important secondary dementias will also be mentioned.

Primary dementias: presenile and senile dementias. In the majority of cases with the clinical syndrome described above, thorough evaluation will fail to reveal an obvious cause for the dementia, and the clinical course will be one of relentless progression. These idiopathic cases of dementia are arbitrarily called "presenile dementia" or "senile dementia," depending upon whether the onset is before or after the age of sixty.

Presenile dementia—Alzheimer's disease is the most common form—usually begins after the age of forty-five and is said to be more common in women than in men. Occasional families have a very high incidence of Alzheimer's disease (Pratt, 1970), as do individuals who have survived the other complications of Down's syndrome (Olson and Shaw, 1969). Most cases are sporadic, however, and provide no clue to their cause. Of all the illnesses presenting as progressive dementia, Alzheimer's disease comes closest to the clinical description given above. Patients with this syndrome characteristically show the neat, socially appropriate, withdrawn picture in the early stages, possibly because the parietal and temporal lobes are affected earlier than the frontal. Eventually these patients progress through increasing stages of deterioration until death intervenes. The average length of the disease is seven years. Early in its course these patients have no elementary neurological findings, but in the later stage they sometimes develop seizures and have upgoing toes, rigid limbs, and grasp and suck responses. Laboratory investigation is singularly uninformative except for contrast procedures or computer-assisted tomography of the brain, tests that show only cortical atrophy.

Alzheimer's disease has a distinctive neuropathology (Corsellis, 1976). The brain is very small with gross atrophy of the cerebral gyri and, in the later stages, dilation of the ventricular system. The degeneration is particularly prominent in the hippocampus and association areas of the cortex. Primary motor and sensory areas, such as the precentral gyrus or occipital lobe, are relatively preserved. Microscopic examination reveals a loss of cortical neurons and two unique pathological phenomena: (1) neurofibrillary tangles, skeins of filamentous structures within the cell bodies of the neurons, and (2) senile plaques, collections of neuronal debris lying free of the cell bodies in the ground substance of the brain (Terry and Wisniewski, 1975). The quan-

tity of these substances has been more or less correlated with the degree of mental deterioration (Blessed, Tomlinson, and Roth, 1968).

It is not surprising that Alzheimer's disease was described relatively early in the history of modern neurology (around 1906), for the occurrence of progressive dementia in an individual at the prime of life is a very dramatic event. Far more common, however, is the intellectual deterioration that occurs in the elderly. This is so common, in fact, that until recently it scarcely attracted medical attention; intellectual deterioration was considered almost an inevitable consequence of aging. Furthermore, because aging of the individual is commonly associated with arteriosclerosis of the cerebral and general systemic vessels, it was rather uncritically assumed that most cases of senile dementia could be attributed to cerebral arteriosclerosis.

When the brains of elderly demented people are carefully examined, however, no obvious relationship between the degree of dementia and the amount of arteriosclerosis is found (Fisher, 1968). In fact, these brains show precisely the same changes as those seen in Alzheimer's disease (Tomlinson, Blessed, and Roth, 1970). For this reason, the predominant opinion among neurologists is currently that presenile and senile dementia are essentially the same disease, simply appearing at different ages (Katzman and Karasu, 1975). Only future research will tell whether this interpretation is correct. Certainly, from a clinical point of view, distinguishing the syndrome of presenile dementia from that of senile dementia is very difficult. One has the impression, however, that some patients with senile dementia have a more benign course than others and do not deteriorate so markedly. While Alzheimer's disease has a standard, almost invariable course in nearly all patients, senile dementia may be more heterogeneous.

An important related issue is the connection between senile dementia and the psychological changes of "normal," healthy aging. Is senile dementia merely an exaggeration of normal aging, or is it a distinctly different entity? Efforts have been made to distinguish a "benign" from a "malignant" memory loss in old age (Kral, 1962), the former correlated with normal aging and the latter with senile dementia. For the most part, however, we simply do not know enough about the neuropsychological changes attendant upon normal aging to be able to compare them with the changes of senile dementia. At the present time, the operational definition of senile dementia as a deterioration severe enough to prevent an individual from caring for himself must suffice.

Pick's disease is another primary idiopathic dementia that usually begins in the presenium. Most neuropathologists believe that it has distinctive pathological features, characteristically affecting primarily the frontal and temporal lobes (Corsellis, 1976). Some authors believe it can be distinguished clinically from Alzheimer's disease (Robertson, LeRoux, and Brown, 1958), but since Pick's disease is far less common and since neither can be treated, the distinction has no practical significance at the present time.

Secondary dementias: infections. Three infectious causes for the syndrome of progressive dementia will be singled out for discussion. Although none is common, two can be treated and one has considerable theoretical interest.

General paresis (dementia paralytica), a form of tertiary neurosyphilis, was at one time one of the most common and important causes of progressive dementia (Bruetsch, 1975). Today, because of antibiotics, it is very rare. A variety of different clinical presentations were recognized and well described by psychiatrists of the prepenicillin era. One of the most dramatic was a florid, frontal lobe syndrome of euphoric, socially inappropriate extravagance. Some patients with this syndrome were noted for their delusions of grandeur. Others, however, exhibited a more apathetic simple dementia. Patients with general paresis may have a slurred, stuttering form of speech, with repetition of the initial syllables of words. This disturbance can be brought out by asking them to repeat such test phrases as "Methodist Episcopal" or "Royal Irish Constabulary." The handwriting also deteriorates in general paresis, and patients may have seizures. The classical Argyll Robertson pupil, which is small and irregular and reacts to accommodation but not to light, is a variable finding, but nearly all patients with active general paresis have a positive serologic test for syphilis in the blood and spinal

fluid. There is also a cellular reaction in the spinal fluid. General paresis should be treated by a full course of penicillin. Depending upon the stage of the disease, either a reversal or, at least, an arrest of the mental deterioration will occur.

The chronic granulomatous meningitides, tuberculous meningitis and fungal meningitis, may also cause a progressive deterioration of the mental state. Although it is frequently accompanied by low-grade fever, headache, and some reduction in the level of consciousness, there is nothing specific about the mental syndrome. The duration of the process is usually measured in weeks or months. Examination of the cerebrospinal fluid is the only method of establishing the diagnosis with certainty. If untreated with the appropriate antiinfective agents, these conditions are fatal.

Jakob-Creutzfeldt disease is an entity that until recently would have been discussed under the heading of primary dementia. It is now known to be caused by a transmittable agent, presumably a slow virus (Gibbs and Gajdusek, 1969). The clinical picture is somewhat variable but usually characterized by a rapidly progressive dementia, a variety of motor abnormalities, and prominent myoclonic jerks (Fisher, 1960). The electroencephalogram shows a characteristic abnormality. Jakob-Creutzfeldt disease is fatal.

Bacterial meningitis and viral encephalitis usually present acutely. The patient is quite ill and the differential diagnosis lies more properly with the signs of the acute confusional states rather than with those of dementia. The clinical presentation of a brain abscess is similar to that of a brain tumor.

Secondary dementias: trauma. When trauma injures the nervous system it usually has its maximal effect immediately. Neurological deficit then remains stable or improves. Thus most forms of head trauma do not appear as alternatives in the differential diagnosis of progressive dementia. The one notable exception is the chronic subdural hematoma. This extracerebral collection of blood may slowly expand over a prolonged period of time. In many patients, particularly the elderly, the traumatic episode may have been relatively minor and not remembered by the patient or his family. The clinical picture is thus one of idiopathic progressive dementia. The mental state of a patient with a subdural hematoma has no pathognomonic features (Allen, Moore, and Daly, 1940). In fact, because of its diverse manifestations, it remains one of the most treacherous entities in neurological practice. Large or rapidly expanding subdural hematomas, however, usually cause a decrease in the level of consciousness in addition to intellectual deterioration. Focal neurological signs and headache are variable. Subdural hematomas can be readily demonstrated by brain scan, angiography, or computer-assisted tomography. Surgical evacuation may not only reverse the intellectual deterioration but may also save the patient's life. Subdural hematomas are an important consideration in the differential diagnosis of dementia. (Other neuropsychiatric sequelae of brain trauma are discussed in a later section.)

Secondary dementias: toxic and metabolic disturbances. A wide diversity of metabolic disturbances and intoxications have been implicated as causes of dementia. Some of them have been listed earlier in this chapter. Most of these processes present acutely and initially cause a confusional state. Some may cause a more insidious process, however, which resembles progressive dementia. Routine screening for metabolic abnormalities in patients presenting with dementia is therefore wise.

Several specific entities deserve special mention. Pernicious anemia may sometimes present with intellectual deterioration, affective changes, and paranoid thoughts—symptoms that are quite independent of the better-known neurological complication of vitamin B_{12} deficiency, subacute combined degeneration of the spinal cord. The dementia may even precede the megaloblastic anemia (Strachan and Henderson, 1965), so that only an assay of the serum B_{12} level can positively exclude this diagnosis. Folate deficiency may cause a similar syndrome (Strachan and Henderson, 1967). Hypothyroidism may also cause progressive dementia, as well as other psychiatric symptoms; these may occur without the classical stigmata of myxedema (Logothetis, 1963). Chronic drug intoxication or exposure to industrial toxins is another potential cause of dementia. Chronic bromide intoxication was at one time a fairly common cause of reversible mental impairment. The clinician must therefore inquire into these possibilities when examining a patient with dementia.

Secondary dementias: circulatory disorders. Arteriosclerosis is no longer considered an adequate explanation for most cases of senile dementia. Vascular disease usually affects the nervous system by thrombus, embolus, or hemorrhage. These processes occur acutely and cause focal neurological disease. They must not be confused with the progressive, multifaceted intellectual and personality deterioration of dementia. In one group of patients, however, a series of relatively small infarcts over a period of time eventually destroys enough cerebral tissue to cause the clinical syndrome of dementia. This entity, now called multiinfarct dementia (Hachinski, Lassen, and Marshall, 1974), usually occurs in hypertensives with a history of repeated strokes and a steplike deterioration. Patients have a variety of focal neurological signs such as extensor plantar responses, in addition to the mental deterioration, and often exhibit the fleeting laughing and crying spells seen in persons with pseudobulbar palsy (see chapter 4, "Neural Substrates of Behavior"). Treatment of hypertension may stay the course of the disease, and early treatment of asymptomatic individuals with hypertension ought to prevent the appearance of this form of dementia.

Secondary dementias: neoplasms. Tumors of the cranial cavity usually cause focal neurological signs, depending upon their anatomical relation to neural structures. When these signs are prominent, the syndrome should not be confused with progressive dementia. At other times, however, the focal signs may be minor or completely absent, and the predominant symptoms are psychiatric. Such a presentation can be produced by a tumor located anywhere in the cranium, but tumors in certain locations are particularly apt to produce these symptoms. Tumors growing in or near the frontal lobe frequently present with the gradual onset of mental changes. Two rather different syndromes may be seen. One group of patients presents with the classical frontal lobe syndrome of jocular but irritable euphoria; their conversation is punctuated by joking and punning. Although they may know that they have a cerebral tumor, they seem unperturbed by the seriousness of the condition. Other patients, the second group, have quite a different clinical picture, characterized by an extreme apathy, reluctance to speak, and a general slowness to respond. One must remember, however, that although these patients give the impression of being globally demented, their memory and other cognitive functions are often relatively normal. This situation demonstrates that intellectual functions, behavior, and affect may be independent neurological activities, selectively involved by different processes. An apathetic and akinetic syndrome may also be observed in patients with lesions that involve the very core of the central nervous system and block the ventricular pathways, causing an internal hydrocephalus.

Psychiatric symptoms may be produced by cerebral tumors of all pathological descriptions. Some of these tumors, such as a meningioma pressing on the frontal lobe or a colloid cyst obstructing the third ventricle, may be histologically benign. Complete or partial removal, with alleviation of symptoms, is sometimes possible. Brain tumors can be demonstrated by any of the usual neurodiagnostic procedures.

Secondary dementias: other neurological diseases. Dementia is also a feature of a number of well-known neurological diseases such as multiple sclerosis, Huntington's chorea, and Parkinson's disease. In these cases the prominent neurological findings make the diagnosis clear.

Secondary dementias: normal-pressure hydrocephalus. In the past decade attention has been directed to a particular subgroup of demented patients who have hydrocephalus in the presence of normal cerebrospinal fluid pressure (Adams et al., 1965; Benson et al., 1970). These patients have a distinctive syndrome characterized by progressive dementia, urinary incontinence, and a peculiar abnormality of gait. Some patients have a history of meningitis, head trauma, or subarachnoid hemorrhage, but others have an unremarkable history. Pneumoencephalography reveals a dilation of the ventricles, but the injected air fails to fill the cortical sulci. Radioisotope injected into the lumbar subarachnoid space collects within the ventricles of the brain but does not reach that part of the subarachnoid space over the convexity of the brain. There appears then to be an obstruction to the normal flow of cerebrospinal fluid from the ventricles of the brain to its usual site of absorption in the cortical subarachnoid space. Except for cases of trauma, infection, or bleeding, no obvious reason exists for the block in cerebrospinal fluid flow, nor is there an adequate explanation for the lack of elevated spinal fluid pressure. Whatever the cause, some patients improve when the cerebrospinal fluid is shunted, by means of a surgical procedure, to another body cavity such as the atrium of the heart.

The initial hopeful reports of improved mental status following shunting led many physicians to recommend this procedure for a large number of demented patients. Unfortunately, the results have not been uniformly successful, and a reappraisal of the syndrome has followed (Messert and Wannamaker, 1974). Possibly many of the unsuccessful procedures were performed on patients who did not meet all of the criteria for the syndrome. More must be learned about the clinical limits of the syndrome and the indications for surgery. Nevertheless, normal-pressure hydrocephalus remains an important consideration in the differential diagnosis of dementia because of its potential treatment.

Differential Diagnosis

The syndrome of progressive dementia must be differentiated from other neurological processes affecting the mental state and from certain psychiatric conditions. Differentiation from other neurological diseases is usually not difficult if one keeps in mind the definition of dementia as a progressive process, involving deterioration of multiple facets of the intellect. Thus, monosymptomatic disturbances such as aphasias or amnesias, and the acute confusional state, which is relatively sudden in onset and primarily a disturbance of attention, should not be mistaken for dementia.

Distinguishing between depression and dementia is a common and important diagnostic problem. Many demented patients have an apathetic, withdrawn appearance that might easily be mistaken for depression. Some patients in the early stage of dementia do have subjective depressive complaints. The elderly, who are the prime candidates for a dementing illness, are also subject to a high incidence of depression (Post, 1965). Furthermore, some depressed patients are so profoundly dejected that they perform very badly on tests of cognitive function. This "pseudodementia" may then be mistaken for evidence of neurological disease (Kiloh, 1961). To misinterpret depression as dementia can be a serious diagnostic error. Depression, even in the elderly, has a far better prognosis than dementia (Roth, 1955).

Several points may help in the differential diagnosis. Patients with depression may have a past history of affective disturbance or a family history of mental illness. The depressive episode may be fairly sudden in onset and have some obvious temporal relationship to a major emotional upheaval. The clinician must distinguish between the outward appearance of depression and the subjective state of the patient. Many individuals with neurological disease merely look depressed but have little inner feeling of sadness. Even if they admit to being despondent, they seldom produce the self-accusations and strong feelings of guilt expressed by the truly depressed. Although some depressed patients may be so retarded or agitated as to be inaccessible to examination, in most cases of depression the mental status can be formally evaluated. This evaluation often shows that the patient's memory, language, and other intellectual functions are perfectly normal. If the mental status cannot be adequately evaluated, and if there is the possibility of depressive illness, it is better not to make a firm diagnosis than to assume the diagnosis of dementia. Too often the diagnosis of dementia consigns an individual to medical neglect, a particularly unfortunate outcome if the patient has a potentially treatable disease such as depression. Laboratory investigation, a description of which follows, may also be helpful in differential diagnosis if it shows some unequivocal abnormality. Normal results do not positively exclude an organic dementia. Finally, incontinence, if it is present, strongly favors a diagnosis of dementia rather than depression.

Under some circumstances, however, it may be impossible to distinguish dementia from depression with certainty. Usually the subsequent course will make the diagnosis apparent. It is justifiable, nevertheless, at this point, to treat the patient as though he were depressed. In this way, a treatable case of depression will not be missed, and the demented patient may have some temporary, symptomatic relief.

Schizophrenia is a disease that nearly always begins in early adult life, and the patient's history usually serves to differentiate this syndrome from dementia. Patients who are schizophrenic are not, however, immune from developing dementia in late life.

Hysterical pseudodementia (Ganser's syndrome) is a rare syndrome in which an individual's responses on mental status testing may resemble those of a demented patient. Ganser's syndrome is usually sudden in onset, found in young people, and occurs when an individual is facing a life situation of tremendous stress (such as combat or imminent execution). The syndrome may be an unconscious, or a conscious, attempt to gain an advantage or escape responsibility.

Once the decision has been made that an individual does have a progressive dementia, the differential diagnosis is the one presented in the list earlier in this chapter and discussed above. A careful history and thorough mental status examination will often allow the clinician to narrow down the diagnostic possibilities. Even though a primary dementia will usually be the obvious decision, the diagnostic impression should be confirmed by laboratory investigation. Since the primary dementias cannot be treated, every effort should be made to find some treatable cause.

An examination of the blood and cerebrospinal fluid will allow for specific diagnosis of metabolic disturbances, syphilis, and other infections. Electroencephalography and routine skull films are helpful as a supplement to other tests but are in themselves rarely diagnostic. Neuroradiological procedures (brain scan, pneumoencephalography, and cerebral angiography) can establish the diagnosis of neoplasms, subdural hematomas, and vascular disease. In the primary dementias, the contrast procedures will often show cortical atrophy and ventricular dilation (*hydrocephalus ex vacuo*). Isotope encephalography is indicated if the possibility exists of normal-pressure hydrocephalus. Computer-assisted tomography, a recently developed procedure, may eventually come to supplant many of these tests. It has the advantage of being both comprehensive and quite safe. Under exceptional circumstances, a cortical biopsy may be justified.

Psychological testing (see chapter 3, "The Clinical Use of Psychological Tests") is often performed in cases of suspected dementia, particularly in the early and middle stages of the disease. Such tests can provide useful information but, like all laboratory tests, must be viewed in the context of the clinical syndrome and not accepted as a substitute for careful examination.

The question is frequently raised as to which demented patients should undergo this rather extensive diagnostic protocol. The number of demented individuals is so large that an evaluation of all would be a considerable undertaking. Certainly most physicians would agree that a younger individual whose dementia shows atypical features should be thoroughly investigated, but some may demur at studying an elderly individual with a long history of intellectual deterioration. No inflexible rule can be propounded. When one considers the uniformly poor prognosis of untreated dementia and the possibility, however remote, of finding a treatable cause through investigation, then one may be inclined toward a more intensive diagnostic approach.

Treatment

The treatment of dementia depends upon the underlying cause. In the secondary dementias, the specific etiology can be attacked. Therapy can range from prescribing penicillin to performing a neurosurgical procedure.

For the majority of patients with a primary dementia, unfortunately, no specific treatment exists. In the early stages, antidepressants may be indicated to treat depressive complaints. Eventually, use of the major tranquilizers may be needed to control distressing and disruptive behavior. Over the years, various other therapies

have been advanced as specific treatments for dementia. These have included vasodilators, vitamins, and hyperbaric oxygen (Prien, 1972). No evidence has shown that any of these therapies is effective.

In the early stages patients may remain at home, if they are carefully supervised. The family should be thoroughly apprised of the nature of the illness and its likely course. Few demands should be placed on the patient, for he may react in a "catastrophic" way, becoming extremely anxious and agitated when confronted by demands beyond his capabilities. In the later stages, the patient's severe deterioration and behavioral disturbance may place an intolerable strain upon the family. At this point the physician's obligation is primarily to the family, to ease their inconvenience and allay their sense of guilt. Commitment to a hospital may be the only practical alternative.

Other Common Neuropsychiatric Syndromes

The syndromes described in this section fit neither into the category of confusional states nor into that of progressive dementias. Although they may sometimes be the end result of an acute confusional state, they are not marked by inattention. Unlike the syndrome of progressive dementia, they are relatively stable or stationary conditions.

Posttraumatic States

Trauma may cause many different patterns of damage to the nervous system. It is, therefore, the pathological process least likely to cause specific, well-delimited syndromes. The clinical effects of significant head trauma range from a brief loss of consciousness (concussion) to a permanent state of coma and quadriplegia. One feature common to nearly all posttraumatic states, however, is some degree of amnesia (Russell, 1971).

Following an episode of significant head trauma, the patient cannot, of course, remember the period of unconsciousness, nor can he clearly recollect the confusional state that usually occurs just after regaining consciousness. In addition, a period of time prior to the injury is erased from memory. At first this "retrograde amnesia" may be extensive, but with time it usually shrinks to the few seconds or minutes leading up to the accident; this period of time is forever lost from memory. In some patients, however, in whom the trauma was severe, the retrograde amnesia is extremely long (covering years or even decades) and does not improve. This condition is invariably associated with a permanent difficulty in learning new information (anterograde amnesia) and is called a posttraumatic Korsakoff's syndrome. (The term *Korsakoff's syndrome* refers to any organic amnestic disorder of this type, whereas *Korsakoff's disease* refers to a particular amnestic syndrome secondary to thiamine deficiency.)

Head trauma can also cause changes of mood, personality, and behavior. Even after relatively minor injuries such as a concussion, many patients complain of headache, dizziness, fatigue, lack of concentration, and anxiety. In the majority of cases, these complaints are of short duration, but in some they can be remarkably persistent. The nature of this "posttraumatic syndrome," whether the direct result of damage to the brain or complicated by purely emotional factors, remains unknown. On the other hand, many patients with more severe head injuries develop very prominent changes in personality and behavior, which are undoubtedly related to brain damage. Thus a patient with contusions of the frontal lobe may develop all of the characteristics of a typical frontal lobe syndrome. Depending upon the degree of severity, the changes may be permanent.

Deficits in cognitive function, such as aphasia or constructional difficulty, may also be found, either alone or in association with personality changes. Sometimes the changes may be rather subtle but are nonetheless disabling, making it difficult for the patient to return to his usual routine. If the patient shows no gross neurological abnormalities, the unwary physician may underestimate the significance of these difficulties.

Dementia pugilistica (the state of being "punch drunk") is a relatively stable condition of intellectual deterioration and behavioral change found in individuals who have sustained repeated head injuries, usually boxers. Subdural hematoma and normal-pressure hydrocephalus (sometimes a complication of head injury) have been described in the section on progressive dementia.

Postanoxic States

The brain can withstand hypoxia and hypotension for only a very brief period of time before neurological symptoms begin to appear. The first sign of neurological dysfunction is usually an acute confusional state; if hypoxia continues, the patient then loses consciousness. Depending on whether or not adequate circulation and oxygenation are promptly restored, the usual outcome is either complete recovery or death. Some patients, however, survive with residual deficits of cognitive function or behavior. A postanoxic Korsakoff's syndrome is one of the possible results.

Alcohol-Related Syndromes

Prolonged heavy ingestion of alcohol and the associated nutritional deficiencies so commonly found in alcoholics can lead to a variety of different organic disturbances of mental function. Wernicke's encephalopathy, delirium tremens, and acute auditory hallucinosis have already been discussed. Korsakoff's disease, which has frequently been mentioned, is described more fully in chapter 27, "Alcoholism and Drug Dependence." Hepatic encephalopathy and posttraumatic states are other causes of mental impairment in alcoholics.

Marchiafava-Bignami disease is a rare complication of alcoholism. Originally reported in Italian males devoted to red wine, the syndrome is now known to exist in patients of both sexes, all nationalities, and many different beverage preferences. The pathological finding of demyelination of part of the corpus callosum is very striking. The clinical features are less regular; a frontal lobe syndrome, with variable motor signs, seems to be the most constant. The disease is usually considered fatal, but cases with prolonged survival, and even recovery, have also been reported (Leventhal et al., 1965). The clinical limits of this syndrome remain uncertain.

In a fairly large number of individuals, prolonged abuse of alcohol leads to a rather poorly defined state of intellectual deterioration and personality change. Many of these persons continue to make a marginal adjustment and remain in the community. In others, the changes become so prominent that they must spend the rest of their lives in an institution. This is a condition often called "alcoholic deterioration." Whether this is a direct effect of alcohol on the brain, the result of vitamin deficiencies or repeated minor trauma, or a variant of Marchiafava-Bignami disease remains undetermined. There is no specific pathological correlation, except for cortical atrophy, and no complete clinical description of this syndrome.

Encephalitis

Viral encephalitis usually begins rather abruptly with fever, stiff neck, headache, and a lowered level of consciousness. Depending upon the specific etiological agent, some cases are benign, with complete recovery, and others result in death or permanent neurological sequelae. Prominent among the sequelae are deficits in cognitive function and abnormalities of behavior.

Herpes simplex encephalitis is a rare but malignant form that has some features of special psychiatric interest. This disease has a definite predilection for the temporal lobes, and psychiatric symptoms may be among the initial presenting features (Wilson, 1976). If the patient survives, he is often left with a devastating memory deficit as well as striking changes in personality and behavior that may closely mimic some of the functional psychoses.

Psychiatric Aspects of Certain Neurological Diseases

We now consider briefly several important neurological diseases with prominent psychiatric symptoms. The reader is referred to a standard neurology textbook for a more complete description of each entity.

Huntington's Disease

Huntington's disease, or Huntington's chorea, is an autosomal dominant degenerative disease of the nervous system, affecting principally the cerebral cortex and basal ganglia. The usual adult form of the disease begins in the fourth or fifth decade of life and is characterized by brief, quick, aimless movements, called chorea, and mental changes. The psychiatric symptoms sometimes precede the chorea, occasionally by years, so that this entity may present a problem in psychiatric diagnosis.

Changes in affect, personality, and behavior are often the most prominent symptoms. The mood disturbance is usually one of episodic depression, and suicide attempts are frequently reported. A schizophrenialike "delusionary hallucinatory state" has also been described (McHugh and Folstein, 1975). Changes in personality and behavior may take several forms. Some patients become apathetic and sloppily indifferent to their usual activities. Others are irritable, surly, and prone to fits of rage. Paranoid features are also common. The depression and irritability are sometimes considered the result of the patient's foreboding that he is to develop the family affliction. But since the psychiatric symptoms often precede the chorea, and since unaffected siblings—similarly at risk—do not develop these striking changes, it seems more likely that they are part of the disease process itself.

Intellectual deterioration is also a finding in Huntington's chorea. In the early stage, however, this disturbance is more the result of apathy and personality change than specific cognitive deficit. Eventually, memory does become impaired, although language remains relatively unaffected. In the late stage, the patient appears to be a globally demented individual, wracked by ceaseless choreiform movements.

No satisfactory treatment exists for this ultimately fatal disease, although a number of drugs, such as haloperidol, physostigmine, and reserpine, may temporarily alleviate the chorea. In the early stages, the patient's psychiatric symptoms may respond to appropriate psychotropic medications. The family history, the presence of chorea, and the demonstration of caudate nucleus atrophy by neuroradiological procedures establish the diagnosis.

Parkinson's Disease

Parkinson's disease is a common neurological syndrome marked by tremor, rigidity, and akinesia. This results in the classical appearance of expressionless facies, shuffling gait, and "pill rolling" movements of the hands. Most cases of Parkinson's disease are idiopathic. A few patients still alive developed the syndrome as a sequel to the encephalitis lethargica pandemic of the 1920s. Drug-induced parkinsonism is an increasingly more common entity.

The neuropsychiatric aspects of Parkinson's disease are rather complex. Because of rigidity and akinesia, the facial expression is fixed, the body immobile, and speech low-pitched and unintelligible. As a result, the patient often appears depressed or demented. Many patients do experience subjective depression. This is usually interpreted as a response to the limitations of a chronic disease. On the other hand, considering current work on the biochemical basis of both Parkinson's disease and depression (Sourkes, 1976a, 1976b), affective changes may be a basic part of the disease. The presence of depression cannot be established with certainty, however, unless the patient is specifically asked about his subjective mood; facial expression may be misleading.

Although patients with Parkinson's disease sometimes give the impression of intellectual impairment, in the past, intact cognitive function was assumed. Indeed, in his original description in 1817, James Parkinson maintained that "the senses and intellect" were unimpaired. More recent studies, however, show that a fairly large proportion (20 to 50 percent) do have evidence of reduced intellectual capacity (Pollock and Hornabrook 1966; Loranger et al., 1972). The dementia is not necessarily very severe, however, and has no distinctive features.

The effect of levodopa on depression and dementia in Parkinson's disease is an unsettled issue. While many patients seem brighter because of increased mobility, others, paradoxically, become depressed. The ultimate effect of the drug on dementia is also unclear. In some patients, memory impairment may actually get worse. This effect may be due to increased longevity, however (Sweet et al., 1976).

The Parkinson-dementia complex is a syndrome of parkinsonism and mental deterioration found exclusively in the Chamorro people of Guam (Hirano et al., 1961). Curiously, the pathological hallmark of this disease is the neurofibrillary tangle also found in Alzheimer's disease.

Multiple Sclerosis

Multiple sclerosis is a relapsing and remitting disease of the central nervous system, characterized pathologically by plaques of demyelination. The clinical manifestations are diverse and the course variable. The diagnosis is made by the occurrence, at intervals widely separated in time, of neurological symptoms referrable to different sites of the nervous system. The psychiatric manifestations of multiple sclerosis are also diverse. Many patients never develop any notable mental abnormality. Others pass through periods of depression or anxiety as they experience the disabling and unpredictable symptoms of the disease.

A characteristic change, usually seen in the advanced stage, is euphoria. Despite blindness, incontinence, paralysis, and painful spasms, the patient maintains a cheerful mood. This is part of a typical frontal lobe syndrome. Other manifestations are poor judgment, irritability, and lack of insight. The physician, who comes in contact with the patient only briefly, may be impressed by his optimistic good humor. Nursing personnel and close family members, who must constantly bear the brunt of his irascible demands, are more familiar with the other aspects of the personality change. Patients with multiple sclerosis often have brief periods of laughing or crying without any apparent cause. This emotional incontinence is also seen in patients with bilateral lesions of the corticobulbar tracts from reasons other than demyelination (pseudobulbar palsy states), but it is not a true psychological symptom since it does not reflect the subjective mood of the patient.

Intellectual deterioration is usually a rather late finding in multiple sclerosis. Nevertheless, the patient's frontal lobe syndrome may render him incapable of mobilizing his intellectual faculties to any purpose even when they are still intact. Eventually, however, these patients do show a true deficit of memory and other cognitive functions. The characteristic speech disorder of multiple sclerosis is nearly always a dysarthria, however, and not an aphasia.

Organic mental disorders constitute a heterogeneous group of abnormal mental states due to definable diseases of the brain. By evaluating patients in terms of specific neuropsychological functions, such as memory, language, and attention, specific diagnoses can be made and patient management can be planned for both circumscribed and multifaceted disorders.

References

Adams, R. D., C. M. Fisher, S. Hakim, R. Ojemann, and W. Sweet. 1965. Symptomatic occult hydrocephalus with "normal" cerebrospinal fluid pressure: a treatable syndrome. N. Engl. J. Med. 273:117–126.

Adams, R. D., and J. Foley, 1953. The neurological disorder associated with liver disease. Res. Publ. Assoc. Res. Nerv. Ment. Dis. 32:198–237.

Adams, R. D., and M. Victor. 1974. Delirium and other confusional states. In Harrison's principles of internal medicine, ed. M. M. Wintrobe, G. W. Thorn, R. D. Adams, E. Braunwald, K. J. Isselbachev, and R. G. Petersdorf. 7th ed. New York: McGraw-Hill.

Allen, A. M., M. Moore, and B. B. Daly. 1940. Subdural hemorrhage in patients with mental disease. N. Engl. J. Med. 223:324–329.

American Psychiatric Association. 1968. Diagnostic and statistical manual of mental disorders. 2nd ed. Washington, D.C.

Benson, D. F., M. LeMay, D. H. Patten, and A. B. Rubens. 1970. Diagnosis of normal-pressure hydrocephalus. N. Engl. J. Med. 283:609–615.

Blessed, G., B. E. Tomlinson, and M. Roth. 1968. The association between quantitative measures of dementia and degenerative changes in the cerebral grey matter of elderly patients. Br. J. Psychiatry 114:797–811.

Broe, G. A., A. J. Akhtar, G. R. Andrews, F. I. Caird, A. J. J. Gilmore, and W. J. McLennan. 1976. Neurological disorders in the elderly at home. J. Neurol. Neurosurg. Psychiatry 39:362–366.

Bruetsch, W. L. 1975. Neurosyphilitic conditions: general paralysis, general paresis, dementia paralytica. In Organic disorders and psychosomatic medicine, ed. M. F. Reiser. American handbook of psychiatry, vol. 4. New York: Basic Books.

Chédru, F., and N. Geschwind. 1972. Disorders of higher cortical function in acute confusional states. Cortex 8:395–411.

Corsellis, J. A. N. 1976. Ageing and the dementias. In Greenfield's neuropathology, ed. W. Blackwood and J. A. N. Corsellis. 3rd ed. Chicago: Year Book.

Engel, G. L., and J. Romano. 1959. Delirium: a syndrome of cerebral insufficiency. J. Chronic Dis. 9:260–277.

Fisher, C. M. 1960. The clinical picture of Creutzfeldt-Jakob disease. Trans. Am. Neurol. Assoc. 85:147–150.

—— 1968. Dementia and cerebral vascular disease: dementia in cerebral vascular disease. In Cerebral vascular diseases, sixth conference, ed. J. F. Toole, R. G. Siekert, and J. A. Whisnant. New York: Grune & Stratton.

Gibbs, C. J., and D. C. Gajdusek. 1969. Infection as the etiology of spongiform encephalopathy. Science 165:1023–25.

Guze, S. B., and S. Daengsurisri. 1967. Organic brain syndromes: prognostic significance in general medical patients. Arch. Gen. Psychiatry 17:365–366.

Hachinski, V. C., N. A. Lassen, and J. Marshall. 1974. Multi-infarct dementia: a cause of mental deterioration in the elderly. Lancet 2:207–209.

Heller, S. S., and D. S. Kornfeld. 1975. Delirium and related problems. In Organic disorders and psychosomatic medicine, ed. M. F. Reiser. American handbook of psychiatry, vol. 4. New York: Basic Books.

Hirano, A., L. T. Kurland, R. S. Krouth, and S. Lessell. 1961. Parkinsonism-dementia complex, an endemic disease on the island of Guam. I. Clinical features. Brain 84:642–661.

Horenstein, S., W. Chamberlain, and J. Conomoy. 1967. Infarction of the fusiform and calcarine regions: agitated delirium and hemianopia. Trans. Am. Neurol. Assoc. 92:85–89.

Katzman, R., and T. B. Karasu. 1975. Differential diagnosis of dementia. In Neurological and sensory disorders in the elderly, ed. W. S. Fields. New York: Stratton.

Kiloh, L. G. 1961. Pseudodementia. Acta Psychiatr. Scand. 37:336–351.

Kral, V. A. 1962. Senescent forgetfulness: benign and malignant. Can. Med. Assoc. J. 86:257–260.

Leventhal, C. M., J. R. Baringer, B. G. Arnason, and C. M. Fisher. 1965. A case of Marchiafava-Bignami disease with clinical recovery. Trans. Am. Neurol. Assoc. 90:87–91.

Lipowski, Z. J. 1967a. Delirium, clouding of consciousness and confusion. J. Nerv. Ment. Dis. 145:227–255.

—— 1967b. Review of consultation psychiatry and psychosomatic medicine: II. Clinical aspects. Psychosom. Med. 29:201–224.

Logothetis, J. 1963. Psychotic behavior as the initial

indicator of adult myxedema. *J. Nerv. Ment. Dis.* 136:561–568.

Loranger, A. W., H. Goodell, F. H. McDowell, J. E. Lee, and R. D. Sweet. 1972. Intellectual impairment in Parkinson's syndrome. *Brain* 95:405–412.

McHugh, P. R., and M. Folstein. 1975. Psychiatric syndromes of Huntington's chorea: a clinical and phenomenologic study. In *Psychiatric aspects of neurologic disease*, ed. D. F. Benson and D. Blumer. New York: Grune & Stratton.

Messert, B., and B. B. Wannamaker. 1974. Reappraisal of the adult occult hydrocephalus syndrome. *Neurology* 24:224–231.

Mesulam, M.-M., S. G. Waxman, N. Geschwind, and T. D. Sabin. 1976. Acute confusional states with right middle cerebral artery infarction. *J. Neurol. Neurosurg. Psychiatry* 39:84–89.

National Institute of Mental Health. 1966. *Patients in mental institutions, 1964.* Vol. 2. Washington, D.C.: Government Printing Office.

Olson, M. I., and C.-M. Shaw. 1969. Presenile dementia and Alzheimer's disease in mongolism. *Brain* 92:149–156.

Pollock, M., and R. W. Hornabrook. 1966. The prevalence, natural history, and dementia of Parkinson's disease. *Brain* 89:429–448.

Posner, J. B. 1971. Delirium and exogenous metabolic brain disease. In *Cecil-Loeb textbook of medicine*, ed. P. B. Beeson and W. H. McDermott. 13th ed. Philadelphia: Saunders.

Post, F. 1965. *The clinical psychiatry of late life.* Oxford: Pergamon Press.

Pratt, R. T. C. 1970. The genetics of Alzheimer's disease. In *Alzheimer's disease and related conditions*, ed. G. E. W. Wolstenholme and M. O'Connor. London: Churchill.

Prien, R. F. 1972. *Chronic organic brain syndromes: a review of the therapeutic literature with special emphasis on chemotherapy.* Washington, D.C.: Veterans Administration.

Reding, G. R., and R. S. Daniels. 1964. Organic brain syndromes in a general hospital. *Am. J. Psychiatry* 120:800–801.

Riley, M. W., and A. Foner. 1968. *Aging and society.* New York: Russell Sage Foundation.

Robertson, E. E., A. LeRoux, and J. H. Brown. 1958. The clinical differentiation of Pick's disease. *J. Ment. Sci.* 104:1000–24.

Roth, M. 1955. The natural history of mental disorder in old age. *J. Ment. Sci.* 101:281–301.

Russell, W. R. 1971. *The traumatic amnesias.* London: Oxford University Press.

Sourkes, T. L. 1976a. Parkinson's disease and other disorders of the basal ganglia. In *Basic neurochemistry*, ed. G. J. Siegel, R. W. Albers, R. Katz-

man, and B. W. Agranoff. 2nd ed. Boston: Little, Brown.

——— 1976b. Psychopharmacology and biochemical theories of mental disorders. In *Basic neurochemistry*, ed. G. J. Siegel, R. W. Albers, R. Katzman, and B. W. Agranoff. 2nd ed. Boston: Little, Brown.

Strachan, R. W., and J. G. Henderson. 1965. Psychiatric syndromes due to avitaminosis B_{12} with normal blood and marrow. *Q. J. Med.* 34:303–317.

——— 1967. Dementia and folate deficiency. *Q. J. Med.* 36:189–204.

Sweet, R. D., F. H. McDowell, J. S. Feigenson, A. W. Loranger, and H. Goodell. 1976. Mental symptoms in Parkinson's disease during chronic treatment with levodopa. *Neurology* 28:305–310.

Terry, R. D., and H. M. Wisniewski. 1975. Pathology and pathogenesis of dementia. In *Neurological and sensory disorders in the elderly*, ed. W. S. Fields. New York: Stratton.

Tomlinson, B. E., G. Blessed, and M. Roth. 1970. Observations on the brains of demented old people. *J. Neurol. Sci.* 11:205–242.

Tufo, H. M., A. M. Ostfeld, and R. Shekelle. 1970. Central nervous system dysfunction following open-heart surgery. *J.A.M.A.* 212:1333–40.

Victor, M. 1975. Alcoholism. In *Clinical neurology*, ed. A. B. and L. H. Baker. Vol. 2. Hagerstown, Md.: Harper & Row.

Victor, M., R. D. Adams, and G. H. Collins. 1971. *The Wernicke-Korsakoff syndrome.* Philadelphia: Davis.

Wilson, L. G. 1976. Viral encephalopathy mimicking functional psychosis. *Am. J. Psychiatry* 133:165–170.

Woodruff, R. A., D. W. Goodwin, and S. B. Guze. 1974. *Psychiatric diagnosis.* New York: Oxford University Press.

Recommended Reading

Benson, D. F., and D. Blumer, eds. 1975. *Psychiatric aspects of neurologic disease.* New York: Grune & Stratton.

Corsellis, J. A. N. 1962. *Mental illness and the ageing brain.* London: Oxford University Press.

Fox, J. H., J. L. Topel, and M. J. Huckman. 1975. Dementia in the elderly—a search for treatable illnesses. *J. Gerontol.* 30:557–564.

Marsden, C. D., and M. J. G. Harrison. 1972. Outcome of investigation of patients with presenile dementia. *Br. Med. J.* 2.249–252.

Mesulam, M.-M., and N. Geschwind. 1976. Disordered mental states in the postoperative period. *Urol. Clin. North Am.* 3:199–215.

Pearce, J., and E. Miller. 1973. *Clinical aspects of dementia*. London: Baillière, Tindall.

Roth, M. 1971. Classification and etiology in mental disorders of old age. In *Recent developments in psychogeriatrics*, ed. D. W. K. Kay and A. Walk. *Br. J. Psychiatry*, special publication no. 6. Ashford, Kent: Headley.

Slaby, A. E., and R. J. Wyatt. 1974. *Dementia in the presenium*. Springfield, Ill.: Thomas.

Wells, C. E., ed. 1971. *Dementia*. Philadelphia: Davis.

Wolstenholme, G. E. W., and M. O'Connor, eds. 1970. *Alzheimer's disease and related conditions*. London: Churchill.

Psychosomatic Disorders

CHAPTER 16

David V. Sheehan
Thomas P. Hackett

T HE MYSTERIOUS and elusive interrelationship between the mind and the body has fascinated man for centuries. Although awareness that the mind (psyche) could influence dysfunction and disease in the body (soma) dates back to Greek and Roman civilization, the discipline we know today as psychosomatic medicine began only about fifty years ago. For several decades, the field flourished and it appeared that the mind-body enigma would finally be understood. But then, because of inherent difficulties in defining the scope of the field, because of semantic ambiguities, and because early theoretical models proved inadequate, interest began to wane, and some believed psychosomatic medicine to be merely a passing fad. Today, however, major research and clinical development based on modern investigative methods have sparked renewed interest and stimulated a widespread effort to understand the role of psychosomatic factors in physical and emotional illness (Lipowski, 1977).

The American Psychiatric Association, struggling with some of the semantic difficulties, dispensed with the term *psychosomatic* in 1952 and substituted *psychophysiologic autonomic and visceral disorders* in their standard nomencla-ture. In 1968, in the second edition of the *Diagnostic and Statistical Manual of Mental Disorders* (DSM-II), they used "psychophysiologic disorders (physical disorders of presumably psychogenic origin)" and noted that "this group of disorders is characterized by physical symptoms that are caused by emotional factors and involve a single organ system, usually under autonomic nervous system innervation" (p. 46). In the forthcoming third edition (DSM-III), the A. P. A. will introduce still another classification, "psychological factors in physical conditions," which will include "(1) the traditional psychosomatic disorders, (2) any disorder which would have been diagnosed as a psychophysiologic disorder under the criteria of DSMII, and (3) any physical condition in which psychological factors are significant in initiation, exacerbation or perpetuation of the disorder" (Looney, Lipp, and Spitzer, 1977, p. 234). Despite all these efforts to avoid the term, *psychosomatic* persists throughout the recent literature.

Psychosomatic medicine concentrates on the role of psychosocial variables, not in causing disease but in altering individual susceptibility to disease. It may be defined as the study of the reciprocal relationships among sociological, psychological, and biological factors in maintaining health and in influencing the onset and course of disease.

T. S. Kuhn (1962) points out that scientists in any discipline share a group of common assumptions and associated hypotheses, designed to highlight significant questions, which he calls a "paradigm." The key figures in the history of science are men and women whose work epitomizes each paradigm or who first articulate it most clearly. Because this concept of paradigms is useful in viewing the field of psychosomatic medicine, this chapter presents (1) the key theorists in the field of psychosomatic medicine, (2) the principal concepts or hypotheses in the field, and (3) significant research data supporting these hypotheses. In order to reflect the current complexity of the field and the variety of viewpoints within it, we have emphasized carefully designed and rigorously controlled psychophysiological studies. Concepts and studies that lack empirical validation and whose influence has waned are mentioned only because of their historical and heuristic value or because they appear frequently in the literature.

The history of modern psychosomatic medicine may be divided into three phases (Lipowski, 1977). Before 1920 psychosomatic medicine was studied as a branch of philosophy. Generalizations about mind-body relationships were either highly speculative or truisms acknowledging psychosocial influences on health. There was considerable interest in the psychosomatic aspects of hysteria and in its response to ritual psychological interventions, including hypnosis.

From 1920 to 1955, clinical anecdotes and imaginative speculations led to more systematic study in two directions—the psychodynamic and the psychophysiological. The psychodynamic approach was based on psychoanalytic theory and its practitioners relied on psychoanalytic techniques in making observations and developing concepts. Franz Alexander, who formulated many assumptions central to psychosomatic medicine, was the principal proponent of this approach. Although the work of members of this school stimulated much research and gave rise to hopes for more effective treatments, their methodology was weak and the advances they foresaw did not materialize. Disillusionment followed; by

the late 1950s the movement was becoming part of medical history, although it still has a few disciples (Kellner, 1975). During the same period, H. G. Wolff and his coworkers at Cornell University were pursuing another major direction in psychosomatic research, that of psychophysiological studies and epidemiological methods. Accompanied by less fanfare but based on more scientifically rigorous methods, their work has been productive and lasting in its influence (Lipowski, 1977).

The third phase of modern psychosomatic medicine, beginning after 1955, has been characterized by greater rigor in methodology and more emphasis on the study of psychophysiological responses to environmental stimuli. Current psychosomatic theories are increasingly precise, behaviorally oriented, and physiological yet holistic in their focus. Speculative psychologizing and basing sweeping generalizations about somatic symptoms on anecdotal evidence have decreased.

Theories and Schools

Philosophical ideas concerning the effects of the mind, passions, or emotions on the body, and vice versa, influenced medical and psychological thinking in the seventeenth, eighteenth, nineteenth, and even the twentieth centuries. In 1818, J. C. A. Heinroth first coined the term *psychosomatic* when he discussed insomnia. K. W. M. Jacobi (1822) used the term *somatopsychic*, although he favored a somatic orientation. F. Groos integrated these two viewpoints and wrote on both psychic and somatic elements in mental illness.

The emergence of "dynamic" or "philosophical" psychiatry can be traced to 1775, when the physician Franz Anton Mesmer found that he could modify the course of physical symptoms by using magnets and the "animal magnetism" in his own person—that is, that verbal suggestion could produce physiological changes. With the work of Jean Martin Charcot in the 1880s, the technique of hypnosis gained acceptance in medicine. His treatment of hysterical patients demonstrated the role of psychological factors in the genesis of physical symptoms such as hysterical seizures and directly influenced Sigmund Freud.

By 1905, Freud's elaboration of the unconscious provided the most comprehensive explanation to that date of mental and psychosomatic phenomena. In his papers on the psychodynamics of anxiety and conversion hysteria (1894, 1895, 1905), Freud was able to relate the "conversion symptom" to fixations at or regressions to earlier (oral or anal) or later (phallic) levels of emotional development (see chapter 10, "Psychoneurotic Disorders"). He described the symptom as a somatically expressed compromise between a forbidden impulse and the defense against it. If, for example, the wish to kick someone in public is repressed, the drive may find discharge through the symptom of paralysis of a leg. The symptom would thus have a symbolic connection to the wish.

Freud based these "conversion" formulations on a reflex arc model. In response to external or internal stimuli, emotional energy seeks discharge along a reflex arc-like path. During its course along the arc, emotional energy and its memory traces will be either repressed or discharged into action or thought. If discharge into action is not possible, some of the energy is channeled into thought. If this substitution is inadequate, other channels of discharge are sought, or the energy is repressed from consciousness, producing anxiety. If even these measures fail, a compromise resolves the conflict between the repressed unconscious wish and the repressing defensive force. The energy involved in this conflict finds discharge through conversion into a hysterical symptom.

Paralleling the development of Freud's psychological theories to explain physiological disturbances, the work of Sir Charles Scott Sherrington, I. P. Pavlov, Walter B. Cannon, and, later, Hans Selye clarified the neurophysiological mechanisms involved. In 1906, Sherrington demonstrated that even the simplest reflex arc is subject to continuous alteration and even reversal by cognitive influences from the central nervous system. This fact indicated the importance of psychological processes such as learning in the control of behavioral discharge.

Cannon's experimental work (1920, 1932) provided the basic conceptual model for psychosomatic medicine. His most important contribution was his demonstration that chemical factors were involved in mediating emotional and neural changes in distant organs. This finding led him to intense study of adrenal medullary function and the observation that stimulation of sympathetic nerves had effects on distant sensitized smooth muscles and the heart. He discovered an adrenergic transmitter later named sympathin. Cannon emphasized that bodily changes caused by emotional responses to stress prepare the organism defensively for the struggle for existence. He proposed that the adrenal medulla serves an emergency role and that its hormone is liberated in significant quantity only in circumstances of "fight or flight." He believed that the animal's body is prepared neurologically and endocrinologically for either of these responses, with epinephrine playing an important role in activation.

Cannon also outlined a thalamic theory of emotions: emotion is experienced when the discharge of a pattern of excitation in the thalamus is communicated to the cortex. The emotions serve as energizers, and the nervous system is involved in preparing the body for action or in mobilizing emergency functions like flight or aggression ("fight") in response to fear or rage. Emotional tension can thus be conducted by the nervous system to influence the autonomic nervous system and the endocrine system. Chemical mediators (hormones) are released and transported to cardiac muscle, smooth muscle, and other organs to alter activity. If this supply of hormones is excessive or chronic, functional alteration and, finally, structural change occur in tissue. Cannon described homeostasis, a mechanism by which the organism mobilizes itself to maintain a dynamic equilibrium, despite environmental stress, by means of feedback devices.

Selye (1946, 1950) further clarified the body's organized reaction to stress, which he called the general adaptation syndrome. He focused on the pituitary adrenocortical system's response to stress and the role of adrenocorticotrophic hormone (ACTH) as a mediator.

The Psychoanalytic School

Freud's comprehensive theory of the mind, particularly as it interpreted the interrelationship of mind and body, was a major stimulus to further investigation. Most of the key figures of the psychoanalytic movement elaborated on Freud's central ideas and explored the psychological aspects of psychosomatic symptoms in greater detail. Their many contributions are reviewed in Otto Fenichel's comprehensive work *The Psychoanalytic Theory of Neurosis* (1945); a few deserve special mention here because of the significance of their theoretical contributions.

Sandor Ferenczi (1926) used Freud's theories to explain bodily symptoms and dysfunctions generally thought to be outside the individual's control ("involuntary" nervous system). Felix Deutsch (1939), Paul Federn (1940), and Phyllis Greenacre (1952) emphasized that body trauma such as surgery or infection, occurring in the early, impressionable libidinal stages of development, was a significant factor in determining which organ later developed psychosomatic dysfunction.

The work of Freud, Cannon, and the neurophysiological investigators was synthesized in the psychosomatic theories of Flanders Dunbar and Franz Alexander. They did not believe that psychosomatic symptoms necessarily have symbolic meaning related to repressed wishes; rather, in their view, symptoms result from the blocking of emotional expression. Both were directly influenced by Freud and Cannon, and both elaborated on the role of autonomic and hormonal pathways in mediating visceral dysfunction.

Dunbar's *Emotions and Bodily Changes* (1947) organized and clarified all the available scattered observations connecting psychological factors to physical illness. It provided the final stimulus for the founding of the Psychosomatic Society in 1939 and for the recognition of psychosomatic medicine as a distinct, organized branch of medicine. Dunbar was the first investigator systematically to correlate particular "personality profiles" with specific organic illnesses; she proposed that these statistical correlations had predictive value. The "hard-driving executive" personality type is perhaps the most enduring of her profiles. In Dunbar's view, psychosomatic illness results from the overactivity of the autonomic nervous system and endocrine system in their attempts to inhibit discharge of psychological tension. Empirical studies have failed to support this hypothesis.

Alexander's "organ specificity" hypothesis (1939, 1950; Alexander and French, 1948) was based on psychoanalytic theory. Like Freud, he viewed the nervous system as a hydrostatic system in which dammed-up energy flowed down involuntary nervous pathways. He proposed that specific stresses evoke specific unconscious neurotic conflicts ("constellations"), which, in turn, result in specific organic diseases. A stressful stimulus evokes a specific unconscious neurotic conflict, creating anxiety and central arousal, which lead to regression to an earlier psychosexual stage of development. The psychosomatic patient regresses to the stage at which he is "fixated," that is, the stage at which the specific unconscious conflict originated. Later theorists conceded that "ego regression" might be a partial rather than a total regression of the ego.

Alexander also hypothesized that specific emotional reactions are discharged along specific pathways (1950); extreme sadness, for example, is discharged through weeping. Chronic suppression of emotional reaction leads to chronic tension and discharge along the appropriate "specific" autonomic nervous system (ANS) pathways and results in structural change in tissue and, finally, disease. The severity of psychosomatic symptoms depends on the individual's hereditary and constitutional vulnerability to the physiological concomitants of affect ("x factor"). Alexander characterized the fundamental tension involved in psychosomatic disturbance in terms of the conflict between the desire to take in and retain and the desire to give or expel, rather than in terms of Cannon's fight-flight response. Alexander was the first to differentiate between the "motor" symptoms of conversion hysteria and the "vegetative" symptoms of psychophysiological reactions (1939, 1950; Alexander and French, 1948). In conversion hysteria, the symptom may have symbolic significance and defends against anxiety. In vegetative neuroses, the symptoms are not symbolic, nor do they directly defend against anxiety or affect. In fact, the vegetative symptoms are a result of failure of the psychological defenses to protect against arousal of affect. As a result of Alexander's studies (1939, 1947, 1950; Alexander et al., 1961; Alexander and French, 1948), seven psychosomatic disorders—asthma, peptic ulcer, ulcerative colitis, hypertension, thyrotoxicosis, neurodermatitis, and rheumatoid arthritis—were labeled the "holy seven"; psychoanalytic psychotherapy was emphasized in treating these disorders.

The Rochester School

Influenced by Erich Lindemann (1944) at Harvard, George Engel (1955, 1956), William Greene (1954), and A. H. Schmale (Schmale and Iker, 1966) of the Rochester Medical School focused on object loss and the frustration of drives as crucial factors precipitating psychosomatic illness. Failure to complete mourning leads to a state of hopelessness, helplessness, and despair—what Engel called a "giving up/given up" state. In the presence of other predisposing factors, which dictate which organ will be affected, this state contributes to a psychosomatic illness. Engel, Schmale, and Greene postulated that the quality or subjective meaning of a loss is correlated with the onset of illness. They proposed that this complex of factors is neither necessary nor sufficient for the emergence or exacerbation of somatic or psychiatric illness but that it contributes to such illness. The mediating biological mechanisms have not been clarified.

The Cornell School

H. G. Wolff (1950) stressed the adaptive and nonspecific nature of the psychosomatic symptom in coping with stress. As a consequence of his interest in the effects of real-life stress on the patient, he set up experimental situations to resemble as closely as possible stressful situations on the job or in the home. Wolff emphasized the role of the culture in defining how a life stress is perceived, the symbolic meaning of the stress, and how or why particular organs are affected. Stressful environmental stimuli may, for example, evoke conscious emotional responses and a variety of universal, nonspecific physiological responses, including redness, swelling, hypersecretion, and hypermotility. Wolff's ingenious and carefully designed studies quantified variables and focused on the more readily observed conscious factors in stressful situations.

Working together at Cornell, S. Wolf and H. G. Wolff (1947; Wolff and Itase, 1950) developed techniques to measure psychophysiological responses. Studying manifest behaviors and physiological variables as indicators of emotional states, they measured responses during a variety of emotional reactions and pioneered in the use of movies to evoke emotions in subjects and in relating them to galvanic skin response.

The Cornell school is regarded as naturalistic in its orientation and has been widely criticized by the psychoanalytic school as superficial and for failing to acknowledge unconscious motivation. Investigators at Cornell often described psychological coping patterns along psychoanalytic lines, however, and invoked specific psychological events in causing specific psychosomatic symptoms (their studies, for instance, implicated anal character traits in psychosomatic diarrhea).

The Sociocultural School

Margaret Mead (1947) and J. L. Halliday (1946, 1948) were among the first investigators to emphasize disturbances ("illnesses") in society and to describe the ways they precipitate illness in individuals. An individual's symptom, in this view, is an attempt to cope with a sick society. Emphasizing prevention, Mead and Halliday focused on mother-child relationships in different generations and cultures and on the influence of economic stress and altered value systems on the prevalence and incidence of certain disorders.

Richard Rahe and Thomas Holmes at Seattle combined the sociocultural approach with the naturalism of the Cornell school. Their experiments over the past decade (Holmes and Masuda, 1974; Holmes et al., 1957; Rahe, 1973, 1975; Rahe et al., 1970) have clarified the role of a broad spectrum of life changes in precipitating a wide variety of illnesses and symptoms, not merely those hitherto regarded as psychosomatic. Their approach is quantitative, in contrast to the qualitative approach of the Rochester group, although the two approaches are mutually complementary rather than exclusive. Rahe and Holmes demonstrated in controlled studies that crucial, unusual, or unanticipated life events require physical adaptation; the greater the adaptation needed to cope with these changes, the more likely a person is to suffer a physical illness. The Schedule of Recent Experiences (SRE), used to quantify the stress of life changes, is a checklist of forty-three key events requiring various degrees of adaptation (losses, childbirth, catastrophe, success). Each life change is assigned a particular number of life change units (LCUs); the death of a spouse, for example, is rated at 100 LCUs, and a minor violation of the law, 11 LCUs. Within a particular time period, each individual accumulates an LCU score. In prospective studies, Rahe and Holmes found an almost linear relationship between LCU stress scores and the number of illnesses individuals experience. This effect was most marked in the six months following these life events. Although no preponderance of particular illnesses was apparent, nearly all major organ systems and diagnostic categories were found. Thus the more life change units an individual accumulates, the more likely he is to experience illness of all kinds in the subsequent six-month period. Life changes may help predict which individuals are at risk of developing physical and psychiatric symptoms and diseases, but they reveal little about the etiology of any disease (Goldberg and Comstock, 1976). Although these findings may only make the obvious explicit, the clarity and the methodological soundness on which they are based are necessary first steps toward increased rigor in investigating psychosomatic illness. This work must consequently be considered a milestone in psychosomatic research.

The Visceral Learning School

In Russia, I. M. Sechenov provided the impetus for integrating psychology and medicine in *The Reflexes of the Brain* (1863). I. P. Pavlov's studies on the conditioned reflex (1927) led to animal experimentation and finally to classical conditioning of psychosomatic symptoms and diseases. In an important review article, G. Razran (1961) presented the major tenets and findings of "corticovisceral medicine" in the USSR; this overview influenced many of the early workers in the West who were investigating visceral learning in relation to psychosomatic disturbances.

The work of Leo DiCara and Neal Miller (1968a)

in the United States in the 1950s and 1960s demonstrated that the autonomic nervous system could be conditioned within limits. Before the publication of their work, it was widely held that this part of the nervous system was automatic, "unconscious," and quite outside voluntary control. Since the ANS is considered an important mediating mechanism in the genesis of psychosomatic symptoms, the fact that it could be instrumentally conditioned and to some extent brought under voluntary control opened up new possibilities for the treatment and manipulation of such symptoms. DiCara and Miller (1968b) were able instrumentally to condition a variety of specific, autonomically controlled responses in curarized rats—heart rate, vasomotor responses, gastrointestinal motility, urine production, and blood pressure, all conditioned independently of each other and in both directions. This achievement provided a model for the manipulation of the mechanisms of psychosomatic illness by behavioral control. J. Kamiya (1961) noted that subjects could learn to control their electroencephalographic (EEG) activity if given immediate information on their performance (biofeedback); his work was the initial stimulus for the widespread clinical application of and research into biofeedback techniques.

D. Shapiro and his colleagues (1970), influenced by Razran's writings, extended the investigation of how physiological parameters can be influenced and controlled by methods based on learning theory; these methods condition blood pressure changes without concomitant changes in heart rate. The group found, however, that the carry-over outside the laboratory for conditioned lowering of blood pressure was poor. Using operant conditioning, T. Weiss and B. T. Engel (1971) taught patients with premature ventricular contractions to control them by learning to control and decrease heart rate through biofeedback. B. T. Engel and his colleagues (1974) had excellent results with six cases of intractable fecal incontinence using a biofeedback (anal pressure) training device. T. H. Budznyski and his colleagues (1973) have reported on the use of electromyogram (EMG) feedback training, notably with tension headaches. J. D. Sargent, E. E. Green, and E. D. Walters (1970), in a study with less careful controls or follow-up, reported success in treating patients with migraine headaches by conditioning hand-temperature control ("handwarming biofeedback") to abort migraine attacks. In general, the clinical application of these techniques to visceral training has been disappointing, as in the case of blood pressure control. Learned EMG control, however, has several useful applications in psychosomatic medicine, notably in the treatment of muscle tension and paresis, tension headaches, spastic torticollis, and subvocalization.

Major Hypotheses and Concepts

What hypotheses have influenced the investigators whose work we have described? The questions on which these hypotheses have been based may be summarized as follows:

1. Is stress a frequent antecedent of physical illness?

2. Can emotional states and stress alter the course of an illness?

3. Can specific types of stress or specific emotional states cause specific syndromes?

4. If any or all of the above are true, what is the link or mediating mechanism between the perception of stress and the assimilation of its impact on the affected tissue or system?

Several terms and hypotheses are frequently used in discussion of these questions and deserve our attention.

Psychogenesis

Many psychosomatic theories assume that specific psychological factors—personality traits, intrapsychic contents, conflicts, affects, defensive patterns, and memories—cause somatic disease or physiological dysfunction. In I. Galdston's words, the psyche is seen as a "morbific agent" (1955). Within this framework, the first events in a causal chain are emotions, subjective experiences, and cerebral activity that later result in physical, organic, somatic changes. In our view, the major fallacy underlying this hypothesis is that the mind cannot itself initiate such a causal chain; it can only respond to external stimuli and mediate them.

Somatization

In 1908, Wilhelm Stekel first used the term *somatization* to describe "a type of bodily disorder arising from a deep-seated neurotic cause," equating it with Freud's concept of "hysterical somatization conversion" (see Hinsie and Campbell, 1960). Other psychoanalytic theorists have viewed somatization as (1) the means by which personality elements are translated into somatic symptoms; (2) a state of ego regression resulting in failure to neutralize libidinal or aggressive energy, which is then displaced to an organ system, producing a symptom or sign; or (3) a physical outlet for unconscious mental processes. These are interesting but speculative explanations for ill-defined and poorly understood psychophysiological relationships. *Somatization*, however, has some use as a descriptive term for physiological and somatic concomitants of emotion. The term is also used operationally by behavior scientists to describe a host of signs, symptoms, and complicated syndromes commonly accepted as stemming from psychophysiological disturbances—for instances, the vegetative derangements in depressions (insomnia, anorexia, impotence, and lethargy).

Psychosomatic Disease

The concept of psychosomatic disease assumes that there is a distinct group of illnesses of psychogenic etiology and, by extension, that psychological methods have a special place in the treatment of those conditions. This view limited early psychosomatic research by focusing it largely on Franz Alexander's "holy seven" illnesses and has led to speculation about psychological characteristics of psychosomatic patients—as if they existed as a distinct group. Lipowski, however, notes that critical reviews of these conditions "stress multiple etiology, reject dominance of psychogenesis, call for refinement of methodology, and largely cast doubt on the existence of disease specific personality or psychodynamic constellations" (1968, p. 403). The term *psychosomatic disease* is now somewhat archaic, since most investigators and clinicians believe that psychosocial factors influence the onset and course of all illness and are particular to no special group.

The Specificity Hypothesis

The specificity hypothesis was a logical outcome of the concepts of psychogenesis and psychosomatic disorder. Draper (1924, 1935, 1942) and Alvarez (1931) noted the relationships among certain emotions and personality types and certain diseases. Alexander and Dunbar extended these observations with their theories that specific psychopathological events cause specific psychosomatic symptoms. The hypothesis as enunciated by Franz Alexander (1950) is accepted by most analytically oriented psychiatrists and has provided a considerable stimulus to psychosomatic research. Although Alexander mentioned multiple factors in the precipitation of psychosomatic illness, however, he in fact placed more emphasis on psychodynamic than on physiological mechanisms; he overgeneralized in attempting to explain the pathogenesis of disparate syndromes and in providing a unifying psychosomatic hypothesis for these conditions. Studies based on the specificity hypothesis have still provided no conclusive evidence that a specific psychodynamic pattern is either sufficient or necessary in the etiology of psychosomatic illness. Research during the last fifteen years has, in fact, shown that

1. Psychological variables or conflicts are not good predictors of specific psychosomatic illnesses, and vice versa. In fact, a wide range of personality types and conflicts is often seen in psychosomatic illness. The only current evidence for the specificity hypothesis is the relationship between Type A behavior patterns (discussed later in this chapter) and the development of coronary heart disease (Friedman and Rosenman, 1974).

2. A variety of nonspecific stresses can predictably evoke specific "psychosomatic" dysfunctions in animal studies.

3. The same psychological conflicts and variables have been implicated across a broad spectrum of different illnesses.

4. The specificity hypothesis has usually been invoked to explain diseases of unknown etiology; it has not led to any significant therapeutic advances.

Statistical correlations among psychological conflicts, personality traits, and somatic illness are not, in any event, the same as causal factors; much of the research based on the specificity hypothesis has been misleading in its conclusions because of the erroneous equation of correlation and cause.

The Nonspecific Hypothesis

G. F. Mahl (1953; Mahl and Brody, 1954) first formulated the "nonspecific" hypothesis of psychosomatic illness, proposing that a multitude of stresses, rather than a specific psychological stress, are important in the genesis of psychosomatic illness and that heredity, constitution, and conditioning are crucial in determining which organ becomes the site of disease. Mahl identified and studied the physiological concomitants of stress in detail, regarding them as universal and important intervening variables in the genesis of psychosomatic illnesses, so that any stressful event may evoke chronic anxiety. Furthermore, whether the stress is clearly dangerous (an air raid, for example) or psychological (public speaking), the physiological concomitants are similar.

This hypothesis implies that any event that evokes an excessive emotional reaction may precipitate a psychosomatic illness. It does not imply that the psychodynamic factors (such as unconscious conflicts, regression, failure of ego defenses, or disturbed object relations) have any specific effect in precipitating illness. Rather, the crucial factors in determining which organ is affected are constitutional organ vulnerability and, possibly, early "pathological" conditioning. The hypothesis is at least consistent with a current and extensive body of research and clinical data, ranging from Selye's "general adaptation syndrome" research to the work of Holmes and Rahe on life change.

The Individual Response Specificity Hypothesis

R. B. Malmo (1962) and J. I. and B. C. Lacey (1958, 1962; J. Lacey, Smith, and Green, 1955), among others, have proposed that a wide range of stimuli evoke physiological responses specific for the individual and consistent over time. A person who is a "cardiac reactor," for example, may react to different unrelated stresses with palpitations, while a "muscle reactor" may develop frontal (frontalis muscle) headaches in response to the same stresses. Alternately, an individual may be a "cardiac reactor" in one situation and a "gastric reactor" in another. Genetic influences, prior exposure to illness and stress, operant conditioning, personality, and individual coping strategies have all been invoked to explain these enduring psychological and physiological response characteristics and individual susceptibility to disease (Lipowski, 1968, 1977; Miller, 1975; Wittkower, 1974).

This hypothesis differs from the nonspecific hypothesis in not positing an anxiety state as an intervening variable and in allowing for individual differences in physiological response. Unlike the specificity hypothesis, it assumes that a wide range of stimuli and a wide range of psychodynamic factors may account for a specific psychodynamic illness.

R. S. Lazarus (1966) introduced the working concept of coping when he noted that a stimulus can evoke a stress reaction by psychological means only if it is interpreted by the individual as harmful or threatening, so that coping processes are brought into play to minimize potential harm. The way in which the cognitive process evaluates any stimulus depends on factors in the stimulus configuration and within the individual's psychological structure.

Other personality factors that influence coping include current mental set, attitude, and defenses. These have been considered important in predicting whether a person will augment, reduce, or leave unchanged the stressful stimulus. Thomas Hackett and Ned Cassem (1973), for example, have demonstrated the role of optimism (denial of worry) in favoring recovery from myocardial infarction and in predicting a long-term favorable outcome. Similarly, D. A. Hamburg and J. E. Adams (1967) have studied defensive maneuvers other than the classical ego defenses in coping with stress, including information seeking and utilization. R. R. Grinker (1966) emphasizes the role of creativity, productivity, and pride as aids in the acceptance of illness. Current level and pattern of autonomic arousal, psychophysiological state, presence or absence of physical illness, and state of consciousness are other variables that influence the individual's response. Some investigators postulate that emotional states such as anxiety, anger, and depression are important intervening, measurable variables between psychological and somatic events. A widely accepted and well researched example of a multifactorial hypothesis based on individual response specificity is the work of Mirsky (1958) on the etiology of duodenal ulcer. However, as Grinker points out, no specific relationship exists between any single emotional process and a specific disease. Specificity is a tempting and tidy package with little evidence, if any, to support it.

The Body Image Perception Hypothesis

Schilder (1950) has pointed out that body image reflects cognitive and affective attributes and shows some correlation with physiological reactivity. In his view, the development of body image is shaped by social, biological, and psychological factors, and it continues to change. Body image has been used to explain and predict symptom choice in a variety of psychological and psychosomatic conditions. Its importance in anorexia nervosa and obesity has been repeatedly emphasized by Bruch (1962, 1973). Taylor and his colleagues (1966) have posited that patients who benefit most from plastic surgery have the least impaired body image before surgery.

Body image may thus help predict the illness or symptom a person will develop in response to stress. Fisher and Cleveland (1958), for example, used responses in the periphery of ink blot images as a measure of definiteness of perceived body boundaries. They found that patients with definite boundary responses developed symptoms in outer body layers, such as disorders of the skin, muscle, and joints, while patients with indefinite boundary responses developed symptoms in internal organs, such as peptic ulcer. They also found that patients with definite boundary responses adjusted better to physical disability such as amputation. Other research in this area postulates a similar relationship between an individual's body image and his physiological responses. Nichols and Tursky (1967) found that pain tolerance was greater in patients whose responses indicated indefinite body boundaries.

Psychosomatic Syndromes in Major Organ Systems

The following description of psychosomatic syndromes affecting major organ systems focuses primarily on the psychophysiological factors involved. We shall discuss for the most part research designed to test the hypotheses just discussed.

Psychosomatic research design and methodology were heavily influenced by psychoanalytically oriented psychiatry from 1930 to 1960; they have been less rigorous than efforts in disciplines with a more empirical tradition. A large number of reports of successful treatments in the psychosomatic literature are anecdotal and therefore not controlled. Failure to control for the effects of variables that could account for the phenomenon or change under investigation may lead to unreliable interpretations. Since 1960, however, experimental psychologists and physiologists have played an increasingly important role in research in the field; they have emphasized rigorous methodology and empirical data in drawing conclusions.

Franz Alexander (1950) held that psychological factors are "necessary but not sufficient" in the development of psychosomatic disorders—that is, that they are essential factors in precipitating illness but cannot by themselves provoke the onset of the psychosomatic disorder. Other theorists now contend that psychological factors are neither necessary nor sufficient but are primarily an aggravating stress in these conditions.

Gastrointestinal Disorders

The gastrointestinal system has an ancient and intimate relationship with emotions. Diarrhea has plagued troops before battle from the time of Alexander the Great to the present, and duodenal ulcer was one of the first conditions to be linked with life stress. Some historians maintain that William Beaumont, the United States Army physician who viewed the mucosa of Alexis St. Martin through a gastric fistula, was the first American psychosomaticist. From its oral entrance to its anal exit, the gastrointestinal tract can truly be regarded as a psychophysiological *camino real* of emotions.

Anorexia nervosa. As a symptom complex, anorexia nervosa might be more accurately called "psychogenic malnutrition." The condition is found predominantly in women; only 10 percent of patients are men. It occurs in all age groups, but the average age of onset is 21.5 years. Sir William Gull presented the first detailed clinical descriptions in 1874. Stanley Cobb (1943) suggested three factors as prerequisites for a diagnosis of anorexia nervosa: (1) voluntary resistance to eating; (2) conspicuous loss of weight in excess of 20 percent of the premorbid figure; and (3) the presence of amenorrhea in female patients. Many anorexic patients experience no loss of appetite but actively refuse to eat food despite being tormented by hunger pains. Others do lose their appetites, but often this loss is secondary to an increase in blood ketones from starvation. Attempts to lose weight through the use of laxatives or enemas, self-induced vomiting, or secret disposal of food are not uncommon. Many patients are overactive, restless, and full of energy despite cachexia. Amenorrhea is a frequent but not invariable finding in females and may precede or follow malnutrition; in a large percentage of cases, menstruation does not resume until up to three years after recovery of normal eating habits. Mild anemia; constipation; bradycardia; decreases in body temperature, blood pressure, basal metabolic rate, and respiratory rate; dry, scaly, and grayish skin; hypertrichosis; brittle nails; and loose and carious teeth are all frequently found. Mortality rates may reach 15 percent.

Anorexia occurs in patients at all levels of character organization, from the most severely disturbed to the functioning neurotic. According to Bruch (1962), the traits most frequently found include

1. a disturbance of body image with a stubborn lack of concern over emaciation
2. a disturbance in the accuracy of perception of stimuli arising in the body, especially enteroceptive signals indicating nutritional need
3. a pervasive, paralyzing sense of personal ineffectiveness, so that patients experience themselves as acting only on stimuli from outside themselves

Within Bruch's psychoanalytic framework, a wide variety of factors may predispose the individual to this symptom complex. Among the most frequently encountered are parents who had a special preoccupation with food; early dietary problems; phobic dread of food; or personally unpleasant symbolic significance of food.

Every variety of treatment has been successful in certain cases, only to fail utterly in others. The treatment that shows the most promise is behavior therapy (Stunkard, 1972). On the basis of the finding that anorexic patients were more physically mobile than normal controls, Stunkard restricted their walking and made mobility contingent on weight gain, in a systematic, stepwise fashion; predictable weight gain resulted. Similar systematic manipulation of behaviors that precede, accompany, or follow weight loss usually led to weight gain. Some psychotherapeutic approaches, including hypnosis, group therapy, and individual psychoanalysis, have also been helpful but not predictably so.

Obesity and bulimia. Obesity is an excessive accumulation of fat in the storage areas of the body so that the body weight is raised more than 10 percent above the standards for people of the same age, sex, and height. Bulimia ("canine eating") is voracious eating and may be organically caused, as in hyperthyroidism. Although genetic, biochemical, and hypothalamic factors contribute significantly to both conditions, emotional factors have also been assumed to play an important role.

H. I. and H. S. Kaplan (1957) reviewed studies that attempted to isolate an emotional constellation of personality traits specific to obesity and overeating. A variety of conflicts, impulses, symbolic meanings, and dynamics were found to be involved, most of which concerned orality and pathological dependency. Some obese people failed to recognize correctly whether they were hungry or full and could not differentiate between hunger and dysphoric affects perceived viscerally. None of the studies cited, however, found a specific personality type or psychodynamic conflict in obese people. Emotional factors ("stress") appeared significant in two small subgroups of obese people—those with "night-eating syndrome," characterized by morning anorexia, evening hyperphagia, and insomnia; and those with "binge-eating syndrome." Both

groups periodically ingested large quantities of food in a short space of time and were often anxious and self-condemning afterward.

Stunkard (1959) found that obese women denied feeling hunger even when their stomachs showed hunger contractions, demonstrating a deficit in the perception of physiological hunger. In a review of eight studies, he found that manipulating the immediate contiguities and consequences of the patient's eating behavior, after completion of a detailed behavioral analysis, resulted in predictable weight loss.

The "stimulus bound" theory (LeMagnen, 1971) states that in the presence of a stimulus (food), obese people, failing to perceive when they are viscerally satiated, will continue to eat while the stimulus is present. Similarly, in the absence of the stimulus, they may go for long periods without "feeling hungry," even when their stomachs are contracting vigorously. Thus it is the stimulus of the presence of food, rather than hunger or appetite, that causes the person to eat.

Although in several anecdotal reports Bruch has described long-term success for anorexia and obesity using psychoanalytically oriented psychotherapy, controlled studies using psychological treatments for obesity have had disappointing results. Plesset and Shipman (1963), for example, found that obese patients with high levels of anxiety and depression (especially in response to dieting) were unsuccessful in weight reduction and maintenance. Stunkard (1972) has published impressive findings on the use of behavioral techniques in the treatment of obesity, but few such methods have resulted in lasting success over time.

Duodenal ulcer disease. The preeminent symptom of duodenal ulcer is localized epigastric pain. It usually occurs one to three hours after a meal and is relieved by food and alkalies. The pain is often intense late at night, and the condition is frequently chronic, with periodic remissions and exacerbations.

Duodenal ulcer has long been considered a stress-related illness and is accepted as more prevalent in "civilized" nations and in urban areas, especially among administrative and professional males in higher socioeconomic strata. The search for a specific personality profile or conflict in these patients began early. Alvarez (1931) chose the "go-getter" type, while Hartman (1933) described "the man who needs to overcome obstacles" as especially vulnerable.

Working with psychoanalytic techniques at the Chicago Institute of Psychoanalysis, Franz Alexander described an unconscious conflict between dependency and independence in these patients. He posited that it resulted from the persistence of intense unconscious oral-receptive tendencies and their frustration by the adult ego (by shame or pride) or external circumstance. The critical factor was the frustration or oral dependent help-seeking demands for love: "The repressed longing for love is the unconscious psychological stimulus directly connected with the physiological processes leading finally to ulceration" (1950, p. 103). Otto Fenichel (1945) agrees that the peptic ulcer patient is hungry for love. If a constitutional vulnerability exists in the presence of the conflict, an ulcer develops. According to Fenichel, some patients overcompensate for their dependent needs by becoming independent and responsible ("pseudoindependent"); others are openly dependent or demanding. The validity of this hypothesis remains in question. Studies claiming to support it have not been adequately controlled for contaminating variables and have interpreted a wide range of nonspecific stresses as examples of this specific conflict.

Mahl and Karpe (1953) tested the specificity hypothesis in relation to duodenal ulcer in a female analytic patient over time. They found that all the "high acid hours" were also high anxiety hours, while the "low acid hours" were low anxiety hours. Three of the low acid hours were interpreted as expressions of intense dependency cravings and hostility over their frustration. The investigators believed these findings demonstrated that secretion of hydrochloric acid (and vulnerability to peptic ulcer) increased with anxiety, whatever its origin, and not with specific needs (passive, dependent, sexual, or hostile) or their frustration.

G. L. Engel's classic studies of an infant, Monica, with a gastric fistula showed that (1) the rate of HCl secretion was correlated with the infant's behavioral activity; (2) the child became depressed and withdrawn in response to loss, a

mood that was correlated with a marked decrease in HCl secretion; (3) assertive, aggressive behavior, on the other hand, was correlated with an increase in HCl secretion (Engel, Reichsman, and Segal, 1956). Working with hypnotized and nonhypnotized subject, Kehoe and Ironside (1963) showed that HCl secretion was highest when anger was induced and lowest when the subject felt hopeless and helpless.

Outstanding studies were conducted by I. A. Mirsky (1958). Patients with duodenal ulcer were found to have higher levels of pepsinogen in the urine and blood than those free of the disease. Serum pepsinogen was therefore used as an index of gastric secretion. Mirsky compared the serum pepsinogen levels with psychological data in a group of healthy men entering the Army. Data were collected by means of several psychological tests (Rorschach, Saslow questionnaire, Blacky test) and psychoanalytically oriented interviews focusing on styles of interpersonal interaction. All those who developed or had a duodenal ulcer were "hypersecretors," that is, had high serum pepsinogen levels, and also showed evidence of a "psychic conflict relative to passive oral receptive wishes" and developed duodenal ulceration "in response to a meaningful life situation which mobilizes or intensifies their psychic conflict" (p. 297). Neither the high rate of gastric secretion nor the specific pattern of psychodynamic conflict was the single, essential determinant of ulcer formation, but in combination they had good predictive value. In another long-term study, Mirsky (1958) compared the incidence of ulcers in the top 2 percent of hypersecretors with incidence in the lowest 2 percent, all groups having been exposed to the expected variety of inevitable environmental stresses. A large number of hypersecretors developed duodenal ulcers; over a twenty-year period, however, none of the hyposecretors developed an ulcer.

Because the hypothalamus, autonomic pathways, and catecholamine mechanisms are considered important in mediating psychological stress, some of the more significant studies of the psychosomatic aspects of peptic ulcer disease have focused on this neurological link between the original stress and the resulting ulcer. Some investigators have observed the high parasympathetic irritability of the ulcer patient, while

G. B. J. Glass and S. Wolf (1950) have linked oversecretion of HCl to autonomic imbalance—that is, excessive vagal discharge. W. R. Waddell (1956) showed that differences in urinary levels of catecholamines between ulcer and nonulcer patients reflected a difference in sympathetico-adrenal responsiveness. Catecholamines that directly influence gastric secretion may be dependent largely on the influence of the vagal reflex centers and perhaps on the activation of specific hypothalamic areas (Cohen, Bondurant, and Silverman, 1960).

Although psychophysiological studies of duodenal ulcer in human subjects have merit in identifying salient variables, animal studies have become increasingly important in research because they permit even more precise control and study of interacting factors. The use of animals in all areas of psychosomatic research has in fact grown in recent years and has contributed much to our understanding of psychophysiological mechanisms.

H. D. French and his colleagues (1957) applied electrical stimulation to the hypothalamus in a test group of monkeys, comparing them to a control group, and identified the hypothalamus as an important mediator between higher cortical centers and the stomach in the development of gastroduodenal ulcers. In his "executive monkey" experiments, J. V. Brady (1958) demonstrated that the stress of determining whether or not a shock would be received was more damaging to the monkeys' gastric mucosa than the effect of the shock itself.

The loss of ability to predict and maintain control over the environment appears to be one of the important psychological variables contributing to greater susceptibility to ulcer formation. J. M. Weiss (1972) studied the effects of giving immobilized rats varying degrees of control over receiving a shock. He found gastric ulceration was greatest in the helpless, yoked rats who had no control over their environment; the greater the control, the less the ulcer formation. In a series of brilliant, carefully controlled animal studies, Ader (1964, 1965, 1967, 1970, 1971, 1973; Ader et al., 1960) demonstrated that increased vulnerability to developing an ulcer depended on

1. the degree of duration of enforced immobilization of the animal
2. the timing of immobilization during the twenty-four-hour activity cycle so that imposed immobilization is greatest during the peak activity period
3. biological predisposition and sex
4. high inherited plasma pepsinogen levels
5. prenatal influences (offspring more susceptible to ulcer formation if pregnant females handled)
6. various early life experiences and socioenvironmental factors (age of separation from the mother, individual or group housing, amount of preweaning handling, individual or group rearing)
7. the circumstances of facing stress (alone or with other animals)

Other investigators (Sawrey and Sawrey, 1966; Stern et al., 1960) have also demonstrated that vulnerability to ulcer increases when a stress is faced by an animal alone rather than in a group.

Regarding psychological treatment for ulcer patients, Franz Alexander (1946) reported that active, brief, psychoanalytically oriented psychotherapy directed toward resolving the patient's specific emotional conflict could produce marked symptomatic improvement. Orgel (1958) described a follow-up study of peptic ulcer patients treated with psychoanalysis; after ten to twenty-two years, ten cases were symptom-free; five had failed to improve. As with many other studies of treatment described in this chapter, however, the data supplied do not necessarily prove the authors' optimistic conclusions. Failure to control for extraneous factors that might influence outcome and other serious methodological flaws make interpretation of the results difficult. Even when taken at face value, the results reported are less than impressive; other explanations, such as spontaneous remission, may account for the findings. We are not suggesting that these treatments are ineffective but, rather, that no compelling evidence yet exists to demonstrate their effectiveness. Because of its cost and uncertain outcome, some clinicians find it difficult to recommend long-term psychotherapy for ulcer patients. They believe that these specialized psychological treatments may be no more effective for this condition than the simple, ongoing support provided by the internist, surgeon, or other primary-care physician.

Disorders of Eliminative Function

The relationship among anal conflicts, character traits, and the disorders of eliminative function has been widely emphasized. White and Jones (1940), for example proposed that neurotic conflicts caused parasympathetic overactivity, giving rise to the syndrome known as irritable colon. Although many have proposed a correlation between "persistent anal character traits" and this condition, good empirical data are lacking. Stress has also been found to play an important role in aggravating spastic colitis, irritable colon syndrome, and chronic constipation.

Ulcerative colitis primarily affects the mucosa and submucosa of the large intestine. Mucosal congestion and multiple petechial hemorrhages are followed by ulceration; later the intestinal wall is thickened and made rigid by fibrosis, and the lumen is narrowed. The first symptom is usually bright red blood passed from the rectum following defecation; later the stools become more frequent and fluid and contain more mucus and blood. Crampy abdominal pain is a common early symptom.

The importance of emotional factors in ulcerative colitis was first noted by C. D. Murray (1930) and A. J. Sullivan and C. A. Chandler (1932). Erich Lindemann (1945) believed "morbid grief" was the important etiological agent. M. Sperling (1946) attempted to explain colitis by noting the mother-child relationship in a typical ulcerative colitis patient. According to her findings, the mother has a contradictory attitude; she attempts to hold the child in a state of dependency to satisfy her own needs while simultaneously showing strong, unconscious destructive impulses toward the child. Unable to satisfy the mother, the child becomes frustrated, and his increasingly repressed destructive impulses are discharged through bleeding.

Grace, Wolf, and Wolff (1958) felt that a subject overwhelmed by environmental demands develops ulcerative colitis as part of an aggressive, hostile behavior pattern aimed at ridding himself of these demands. G. L. Engel (1954a, 1954b,

1955, 1956, 1958; Engel and Schmale, 1967) believed that a real or fantasied object loss or disturbance in a relationship with a key figure results in a typical depression characterized by helplessness and despair. This depression then leads to the impaired vascularity of the mucosa and submucosa of the colon (presumably mediated by neuroendocrine mechanisms) that is seen in ulcerative colitis. Because the early mother-child relationship is said to be symbiotic, the child's basic needs evoke anxiety, guilt, and shame in the "colitigenic mother." In order to receive security and love, the child relinquishes autonomy over bodily function to his mother. Separation, real or fantasied, is therefore especially traumatic.

Many writers note the anal characteristics and the regressive pregenital emotional organization of ulcerative colitis patients. These patients are seen as strongly and ambivalently dependent on the mother, a state that results in unconscious sadistic, hostile impulses; they are similar in character organization to other patients with eliminative dysfunctions such as spastic colon. Franz Alexander (1950; Alexander and French, 1948) identified two emotional conflicts as precipitants of ulcerative colitis: "(1) the frustration of a need to carry out an obligation whether it is biological, moral, or material . . . and (2) the patient's hopeless attitude about his capacity to accomplish something which requires concentrated expenditure of energy" (Alexander and Flagg, 1965, p. 877).

Similarities in psychological factors between ulcerative colitis and regional ileitis have been noted, but data are insufficient for conclusions. Some evidence does suggest, however, that hereditary or constitutional vulnerability is a factor. J. B. Kirsner (1971) found that 17 percent of the relatives of ulcerative colitis patients had similar symptoms, compared to 4 percent of the relatives of a control group.

In 1961, H. I. Weinstock reviewed follow-up studies of forty ulcerative colitis patients who had been hospitalized and treated with short-term (three-month) psychotherapy. Psychotherapy prevented neither recurrence after discharge nor ileostomy. These patients had no specific personality profiles or conflicts, and they improved during hospitalization regardless of the form of treatment. In a series of joint investigations, G. E. Daniels, J. F. O'Connor, and A. Karush studied psychogenic factors in ulcerative colitis and the effect of psychotherapy on the course of the disease (Daniels, 1948; Daniels et al., 1962; Karush, Hiatt, and Daniels, 1955; Karush et al., 1968, 1969). They concluded that

1. Patients who received psychotherapy in addition to the usual medical regimen had a more favorable somatic and psychological response than a matched control group that did not receive psychotherapy.

2. Patients with depression, paranoia, schizophrenia, lack of a precipitating event, severe ego impairment, strong symbiotic needs, or attitudes of passive helplessness and those who derived secondary gain from the illness had a poorer prognosis than those who possessed a sounder mental apparatus.

3. Longer therapies gave more lasting results, although less intensive psychotherapy helped the majority of patients. "Individuated" patients—those with relatively independent coping strategies—responded well to therapeutic techniques involving interpretation and abreaction (emotional release through recalling painful, repressed experiences), while "symbiotic" patients—those who were more dependent—did better with support, suggestion, and graded abreaction. Improvement was greatest when the therapist's interest, empathy, and optimism were combined with his patient's hopefulness.

The methodological flaws in this series of studies make evaluation of the conclusions difficult. Karush and his colleagues (1968, 1969), for example, supply data to support their conclusions and make correlations among the variables in the studies; they fail, however, to cite correlation coefficients to support them. Furthermore, the small sample on which some of the conclusions are based raises questions of statistical significance and makes interpretation difficult. Because the methodological bases of other studies (Grace, Wolf, and Wolff, 1958; Murray, 1930; Sperling, 1946) are not significantly more rigorous, they add little to clarify the issues. At this time, therefore, no strong evidence demonstrates that the more in-depth psychotherapies are predictably more helpful in decreasing the symptoms of ulcerative colitis than simple sup-

port; however, these supportive psychotherapeutic measures have value in helping the patient cope with the illness itself, its associated emotional problems, and the medical treatment regimen.

Respiratory Disorders

Perhaps because breathlessness so commonly accompanies fear or anxiety, and because sighing occupies a respected niche in the literature of love, the psychosomaticist rarely has difficulty in relating respiratory disturbances to emotions. With the extensive accounts of asthmatic belletrists, the relationship takes on depth and color. The stage is further set by nineteenth-century folklore, which attributes high gifts of the mind to those unfortunates who slowly coughed out their lives with consumption. During the course of a day, all of us can measure our emotional tone by the ease with which we breathe. The breath quickens with delight and becomes a moan in sorrow; it reflects emotion in audible form.

Asthma. Asthma is an allergic condition characterized by bronchospasm that produces expiratory wheezing, prolongation of expiration, and intermittent acute attacks of dyspnea. Symptoms remit spontaneously or with appropriate treatment. Bronchospasm, bronchial edema, and mucous plugs all contribute to the bronchial obstruction and other symptoms and signs of the condition. Hereditary, endocrine, autonomic, allergic, infectious, psychological, and social factors have been implicated in causing the disease, but their interrelationships have not been clarified.

Sir James McKenzie first drew attention to the role of psychological factors in asthma in 1886 when he described "rose asthma," an allergic reaction experienced by a woman when she saw a paper rose under glass. Careful studies using objective personality tests have indicated a wide variation in personality types among asthmatics rather than identifying a single personality type. McDermott and Cobb (1939) studied fifty cases of bronchial asthma and noted that the majority of patients showed compulsive neurotic traits. Franks and Leigh (1959) studied the widely used

Maudsley personality inventory profiles of asthmatic, "psychotic," and normal subjects; those in the asthmatic group were labeled "mildly neurotic," a condition thought to be secondary to the disease itself. Glasberg et al. (1969) found more oral-dependent needs and separation anxiety among asthmatics. In administering several test batteries to sixty-one asthmatics, Knapp, Mathé, and Vachon (1976) noted high scores for dominance and tender-mindeness, evidence of interpersonal adjustment difficulties, and a "field-independent cognitive style"—that is, a thinking pattern independent of the environment in which it operates.

Failure to find a specific "asthmatic" personality type led to attempts to identify a particular unconscious conflict. Although a variety of conflicts has been suggested as causing the disease, no validating consensus exists. Much emphasis, however, has been placed on the unconscious fear of loss of the mother or a mother substitute. Theories frequently cited in the clinical literature relating asthma to this loss include suppressed desire for the mother (E. Weiss, 1922); anticipated rejection by a mother figure because of unacceptable wishes or actions (T. M. French and F. Alexander, 1941); fear of separation from the mother, so that the asthma attack is the symbolic equivalent of a repressed cry for the lost mother or a cry of rage—the mastery of the fear of being left alone therefore governs the asthmatic's life (T. M. French and F. Alexander, 1941); pregenital conversion of a psychological conflict into a learned, symbolically meaningful pulmonary expression (Deutsch, 1951; Fenichel, 1945; and Sperling, 1963); inhibition of free communication with a person on whom the patient depends (F. Alexander and Flagg, 1965).

Important observations on the relationship of psychodynamics to asthma are summarized here.

1. McDermott and Cobb (1939), T. M. French and F. Alexander (1941), and Deutsch (1951) reported that dreams, fantasies, and fears of water or drowning were common and intense in asthmatics; these phenomena may, in their view, be factors in precipitating dyspnea and the build-up of respiratory secretions, which are experienced as drowning.

2. Stein and Ottenberg (1958) and Herbert, Glick, and Black (1967) noted asthmatics' heightened sensitivity to odors and described a perceptual blocking of association to common odors. On the basis of their observations, they proposed that asthma was a physiological defense against odors connected with unconscious, unresolved anal conflicts (perception of and preoccupation with such odors had frequently antedated asthma attacks).

3. Mathé and Knapp (1971) used two types of stress on a control and an asthmatic group. The asthmatic group responded selectively with a decrease in air passage conduction and slowed breathing; they also reported experiencing significantly less anger in response to the provoking stress than did the control group.

4. Block and his coworkers (1964) proposed that the asthmatic population was not homogeneous but was divisible into two groups: those with low allergy test scores and those with high scores. Those with low scores had significantly more psychogenic precipitants of asthma than those with high scores. Purcell, Bernstein, and Bukantz (1961) found more neuroses and child-rearing problems in the mild allergy reactors, who had remissions when away from home. Freeman and his colleagues (1967) noted that the allergic weak reactors were more unhappy and depressed.

Various family studies of asthmatics (Abramson, 1954; Block et al., 1964, 1966; Miller and Baruch, 1948) have been unable to agree on typical maternal characteristics. In some studies, the mother was described as "rejecting" or "engulfing." In others, young asthmatic males perceived their mothers, in retrospect, as rejecting, controlling, or both more frequently than did controls. Minuchin's group (Liebman, Minuchin, and Baker, 1974) proposed that the family dynamic reinforced illness in asthmatic children. Although Knapp and Nemetz (1957) found a high positive correlation between the severity of pulmonary disease and the severity of the personality disturbance (which often preceded the asthma), they found no factor with universal significance in patients' family background.

A wide variety of interventions has been helpful to some asthmatics. Interruption of stressful interactions in the family, even by moving the asthmatic to another environment, is helpful to about 50 percent of patients, particularly those with weak allergy responses. Tricyclic antidepressants have a bronchodilatory effect in animals and humans (Avni and Bruderman, 1969; Mattila and Muittari, 1968). The claim that these drugs' augmentation of catecholamine action and anticholinergic effects is beneficial centrally and peripherally is confirmed by positive results in early clinical trials.

Falliers's controlled study (1970) suggests that hypnosis may have long-term benefits for asthmatics. A. B. Alexander and his colleagues (1972) proposed that relaxation training was helpful in mild cases. In a controlled study, Moore (1967) found that systematic desensitization produced significantly more improvement in peak air flow than simple suggestion and relaxation therapy. Vachon and Rich (1976) suggest biofeedback based on air passage resistance as a possible treatment. The results of Groen and Pelser's group therapy study (1960) and of the family therapy study of Liebman, Minuchin, and Baker (1974) are encouraging about the use of these methods in asthma. Sperling (1963) and Knapp, Mathé, and Vachon (1975) report good results using long-term psychoanalytically oriented psychotherapy with severe asthmatics.

Tuberculosis. Numerous investigators have stressed the role of psychological factors in tuberculosis and its prognosis (Berle, 1948; Derner, 1953; Holmes et al., 1957; Korkes and Lewis, 1955; Merrill, 1953; Sparer, 1956; Wittkower, 1955). Holmes found a significantly higher number of psychosocial stresses in the lives of tubercular patients in the years preceding the onset of the disease than in healthy people's lives. However, no uniform personality type or specific psychodynamic conflict could be identified in any of these studies. The inordinate need for affection observed in the premorbid personalities of tuberculosis patients may have been secondary to the increased number of psychosocial stresses with which they were coping. Using projective psychological tests, Rebner (1957) noted a greater tendency to direct aggression onto themselves among relapsed, hospitalized tuberculosis patients than among members of control groups.

Psychosocial factors, particularly losses, have also been implicated in vulnerability to common colds (Ruddick, 1963; F. Alexander and Flagg, 1965) and to vasomotor rhinitis.

Hyperventilation syndrome. Some individuals express their anxiety under stress in the form of hyperventilation. In most cases, the degree of alarm experienced by these patients is out of proportion to the actual stressful situation. The physiological changes accompanying hyperventilation explain most of its signs and symptoms. After a few seconds of hyperventilation alveolar carbon dioxide levels fall, causing alkalosis. This reaction, in turn, produces cerebral vasoconstriction, which results in a 33-percent decrease in mean cerebral blood flow during active hyperventilation (Kety and Schmidt, 1946) and thus in EEG and behavioral changes. Peripheral vasoconstriction that causes sweating, pallor, and cold in the extremities may be mediated by sympathetic pathways. The alkalosis, or decrease in blood carbonate, causes a drop in ionized calcium that results in paresthesias and sometimes tetany. Narrowing of coronary arteries and electrocardiogram changes (such as lowering of S-T segments, inversion of T waves, and premature ventricular contractions) may accompany hyperventilation.

The physiological effects of hyperventilation can be reduced by having the patient breathe into a paper bag, thus increasing alveolar carbon dioxide. Psychotherapy, minor tranquilizers, and antidepressants have all been helpful in the treatment of this condition. When the syndrome is recurrent, it is most often accompanied by sudden, spontaneous, unexplained panic attacks and other autonomic and somatic manifestations of anxiety. In such cases, both phenelzine and imipramine are significantly superior to placebo in the treatment of this disorder (Sheehan, Ballanger, and Jacobson, 1977).

Skin Disorders

Blushing in shame and blanching with fear are such common experiences in our repertoire of psychophysiological responses that we know from an early age how surely our integument betrays our state of mind. While skin disease is a more complex and elusive blemish than a blush, it is nonetheless thought to be intricately linked with a complex of emotions.

Neurodermatitis. The terms *neurodermatitis* and *eczema* are used synonymously. Eczema is an inflammatory skin reaction usually of allergic etiology. It may be a manifestation of generalized hypersensitivity or a reaction to external and locally applied allergens. The skin lesions are many and varied. They are characterized by erythema, vesicle formation, edema, exudation, and weeping. The condition goes through two phases, wet and dry, and involves the flexures, including the neck and ankles.

In 1891 Brock and Jacket coined the term *neurodermatitis* (see Engels and Wittkower, 1969). They held that emotional factors exerted a greater influence on the skin than on any other organ. The skin was said to reflect conflicts involving exhibitionism, masochism, masturbation, shame, anger, fury, impatience, suppressed weeping, sexual arousal, and the regressive revival of infantile skin eroticism. Blushing was believed to reflect shame and guilt; pallor equalled fear; itching was a sign of impatience; scratching was due to guilt-driven, self-destructive impulses, and so forth. A careful review of the literature from 1937 to the present leads to the following conclusions:

1. A variety of psychosocial stresses and changes, notably loss, antedate the flare-up of skin diseases.

2. There is no general agreement that a specific personality profile or unconscious conflict can be identified in any skin disease.

3. Heredity, conditioning, and other factors are undoubtedly important in causing skin diseases.

Cleveland and Fisher (1956) compared patients with neurodermatitis with three other groups: a group with industrial and accidental skin lesions; patients with rheumatoid arthritis; and those with low back pain. Those in the dermatitis group had a higher degree of masochism, a more negative self-concept, and more defenses against exhibitionism than those in the other groups. Like rheumatoid arthritis patients, they had "high barrier" responses on projective testing, perceiving their body boundaries as

impermeable armor plate that protected them from internal disruption. In 195 cases of primary neurodermatitis (atopic dermatitis), Anderson and Cross (1963) found that the severity of dermatitis and the degree of emotional disturbance were closely related to the distribution of the skin lesions (on the face rather than the hands). It is unclear whether the emotional disturbance or the distribution of the skin lesions was primary. Miller and Jones (1948) and Wittkower (1953), among others, found various disturbances in the child-parent relationships of children with neurodermatitis; these children's dependency, vulnerability to loss, and longing for love were stressed.

Pruritus and urticaria. Pruritus is characterized by the symptom of itching; many investigators have found histories of sexual frustration or inhibited sexual excitement in afflicted patients, particularly in those with pruritus vulvae and pruritus ani. These researchers suggest that the associated scratching is a masturbatory equivalent. Macalpine (1953) noted anal, sexual, exhibitionistic, and homosexual conflicts as well as pregnancy fantasies in a group of males with pruritus ani. According to Wittkower and Edgell (1951), pruritus strikes a balance between pleasure and pain. In seventy-seven of their ninety patients, psychological stresses, particularly losses, had immediately preceded the onset of dermatitis.

Saul and Bernstein (1941), F. Alexander (1950), and others have proposed that urticaria represents suppressed weeping from the skin. Kepecs, Robin, and Brunner (1951) showed that exudation into the skin increases during weeping as well as when weeping is inhibited, disproving Saul and Bernstein's hypothesis.

Psoriasis. A chronic dermatitis, psoriasis is characterized by dry, sharply demarcated plaques covered with layers of silvery scales. When the scales are removed by scraping, multiple fine bleeding points are exposed. The disorder characteristically involves extensor surfaces and flexures and may affect the scalp, but it is rare on the face. Among patients with psoriasis, no specific personality type or conflict constellation has been found. Whether psychological difficulties are primary precipitants or concomitants of pso-riasis is unclear. Individual problems and psy-chosocial changes may precede flare-ups of this condition.

Skin allergies. Smith (1962a, 1962b) identified specific personality traits in patients with allergic disorders, while others found more general traits. Most investigators agree on the patient's vulnerability to loss, dependency, and strong need for love. The work of Mason and Black (1958) and Ikemi, Nakagawa, and Tsukata (1963) has clearly demonstrated the effect of sug-gestion, with or without hypnosis, in the produc-tion and inhibition of an allergic skin response.

Musculoskeletal Disorders

Rheumatism, hoary and venerable in the biogra-phies of men and women from pre-Christian times to the present, is seldom regarded as a psy-chosomatic condition except by the initiated. Stanley Cobb, one of the prime movers of psy-chosomatic medicine in this country, was a victim of rheumatoid arthritis. Although he suf-fered with gentlemanly stoicism and maintained a wry humor, he took pleasure in relating how his badly deformed rheumatic hands hurt far worse on some days than on others, even though he rarely knew why. "Must be deep inside that hurts," he would say, pointing to his head.

A chronic inflammatory disease of the connec-tive tissues, *rheumatoid arthritis* predominantly affects the joints but often involves other sites; it is characterized by morning stiffness in the joints, pain on movement, joint swelling, tissue thickening over a joint, and subcutaneous nod-ules.

Halliday (1937, 1942), Booth (1939), and Johnson, Shapiro, and Alexander (1947) have all noted a marked tendency toward bodily activity and competitive outdoor sports among rheuma-toid patients, especially women. These patients are described as sacrificing themselves masochis-tically in the service of others. These authors see them as "benevolent tyrants" who often overtly reject the "feminine" role and develop strong "masculine" protest reactions. According to Johnson, Shapiro, and Alexander, parental restrictions prevent the child from expressing

frustration freely by random motor discharge. When these prohibitions against aggressive dis-charge are introjected, a "psychological strait jacket" results. In this way an equilibrium is es-tablished between discharge and control of ag-gression. If the discharge of aggression is inhib-ited, the equilibrium is upset. The consequent increase in muscle tone is believed to aggravate or precipitate the arthritis. T. M. French and L. B. Shapiro (1949) have noted that these pa-tients express repressed impulses through their skeletal systems in their dreams; McLaughlin and his colleagues (1950) found that those who recalled their dreams had the best clinical response to treatment with adrenocorticotrophic hormone (ACTH). A variety of parental constel-lations, childhood deprivations, and infantile de-pendency traits are reported by some authors. Most researchers agree that losses and psycho-logical changes frequently precede exacerbations of the disease. There is no good, scientific evi-dence that psychotherapy is any more effective in the treatment of these patients than placebo.

Gynecological and Obstetrical Disorders

Woman's complaints have been targeted as psy-chosomatic for as long as the term has been used—and eons before, we suspect, perhaps be-cause women have been more open and honest in reporting a mood accompanying a symptom. They may also have possessed the insight that mind could make the "mysterious leap" to body and were penalized for this wisdom. Perhaps the nature of the menstrual cycle, with sexual prohi-bitions and concomitant bouts of unusual emo-tional expression at opposite poles, was the cause. Until the recent discovery of hormonal shifts, which probably account for some emo-tional lability, indisposition was often considered capricious or deliberate.

Menstrual disorders. In their classic study corre-lating women's ovarian functions (measured by vaginal smears and temperature charts) with material from their psychoanalysis, Benedek and Rubenstein (1942) found parallel emotional and hormonal cycles. Psychological material re-flected an outward heterosexual interest during the phase of estrogen activity, while a passive-receptive and narcissistic bearing was found in the psychological material during progesterone activity. A depressive attitude existed into menstruation itself, perhaps because of a drop in estrogen and progesterone. Psychological material also revealed regret over failure of pregnancy.

Because menstruation is viewed as an important symbol of femininity, it may precipitate or reactivate related fears and guilt feelings. Among others, Simmel (1932) believed that specific conflicts find special expression through the uterus in the form of dysmenorrhea. Benedek (1950) emphasized the woman's basic reluctance to accept her feminine role as a causal factor in menstrual disorders, while Thompson (1943) identified cultural factors, especially female resentment of masculine dominance, as common in patients with this condition.

Symptoms of *premenstrual tension* include engorgement of the breasts, abdominal bloating and discomfort, mild edema, headaches, nausea, vomiting, and diarrhea. Psychological concomitants include depression, anxiety, irritability, mood swings (weeping and euphoria), and fatigue. Existing personality traits and conflicts may be accentuated and behavior disorders may be exacerbated during the menstrual and premenstrual cycles. Although organic factors, such as hormonal imbalance, are the primary variables in this condition, psychological stress may accentuate latent organic vulnerabilities.

The absence of menstruation (*amenorrhea*) or scanty menstruation (*oligomenorrhea*) usually result from suppression of the hypothalamic influence on the anterior pituitary gland. When the level of luteinizing hormone drops, lowering estrogen production, the ovarian cycle is suppressed. Such reactions appear in response to a variety of psychosocial stresses, such as physical danger, loss, or cessation of an active sexual life; the menstrual cycle frequently returns to normal after sexual relationships are reestablished. A variety of sexual conflicts have been implicated in these conditions but are by no means the universal precipitants.

Amenorrhea may also appear as part of the syndrome of false pregnancy (*pseudocyesis*). In such a case, amenorrhea is accompanied by other signs of pregnancy, such as abdominal distention, breast changes, and weight gain. Pseudocyesis may be the covert expression of a pathological wish for or fear of pregnancy. It may also reflect conflicting attitudes regarding pregnancy and related sexual functions. Benedek (1956), among others, noted the unconscious hostility of some women toward their mothers and toward having children of their own. The resulting guilt feelings precipitate pseudocyesis, which he conceptualized as an attempt to undo these hostile impulses. It may also represent other conflicts: competition with other women, a desire to hold on to a man, or an attempt to fulfill dependency needs or to achieve feminine identity. Pseudocyesis is found in many personality types but most frequently in hysterical or schizophrenic patients.

Menorrhagia and *noncyclic uterine bleeding* usually result from an imbalance in ovarian hormone production around menarche and menopause. They may also occur during or following stress and may accompany depression.

Menopause. Decline of ovarian function causes vasomotor instability and a more labile emotional state. However, many psychosomatic complaints in menopausal women result from anxiety and depression. A highly significant correlation exists between emotional turmoil at menopause and a history of premenstrual depression, dysmenorrhea, and menstrual disorder. Benedek (1959) believed these disturbances reflect a failure to find compensation and sublimated outlets for the loss of reproductive power and the growing independence of children.

Conception and pregnancy. Sterility may at times be functional, due to dystonic fallopian tubes, which prevent the ovum from reaching the uterus, or to supposed psychological suppression of ovulation. A number of studies have shown that the incidence of pregnancy following adoption in women presumed to have been sterile from either psychological or organic causes was no greater than chance pregnancy when no adoption occurred—dispelling the old wives' tale that conception often follows adoption.

Many women suffer an exacerbation of their

neuroses during pregnancy. Others with severe symptoms may become symptom-free and contented. The symbolic meaning of a particular pregnancy is a crucial factor in the way a woman responds to it. Nausea and vomiting, false labor pains, and food idiosyncrasies in pregnancy are poorly understood. Chertok, Mondzain, and Bonnaud (1963) studied hyperemesis gravidarum and concluded that the condition stemmed from an ambivalent attitude toward the child.

Childbirth involves sudden, major psychological and physiological changes. Conflicts in the mother may result in suppression of lactation and in irritability, colic, and feeding problems in the child. Kulka, Walter, and Fry (1966) demonstrated a significant parallel in the EMG and EKG fluctuations between mother and child during their interaction. Blau and his colleagues (1963) conducted a controlled study of the mothers of premature infants. They found that the "premature mothers" had a higher incidence of unwanted pregnancy, showed more negative and hostile attitudes to pregnancy, and were more "immature" than the control group. Their findings suggest that these stresses are important in precipitating premature delivery.

McDonald, Gynther, and Christakos (1963) found significant positive correlations between maternal anxiety and birth weights, length of labor, and obstetrical complications. Personality profiles or traits, specific emotional conflicts, and psychological attitudes are of little value in predicting postpartum psychological disturbances (depression or psychosis), despite anecdotal claims to the contrary. Some investigators report that the incidence of severe depression and psychosis postpartum is the same as at other periods during a woman's life; the woman with a personal or family history of depressive illness is more vulnerable.

Abortion. Ten percent of pregnancies end in spontaneous abortion. Psychological stress is undoubtedly a factor in some of these cases. In a study of habitual aborters, Tupper (1962) found pathological changes in the placentas in which an excess of collagen appeared to be present. He also found antibodies to collagen in the women's serum. These patients also manifested marked autonomic instability and uterine reactivity,

even to minor stimuli. A variety of physiological stresses thus appears to affect uterine circulation and consequent placental detachment. Tupper found that supportive psychotherapy aimed at reducing stress was particularly effective in helping twenty-four out of twenty-five habitual aborters produce live babies.

Metabolic and Endocrine Disorders

Manifestations of these illnesses may seem like symptoms visited upon us by a wrathful, cruel, and whimsical deity; protuberant eyes and overwhelming restlessness; a summer tan that does not fade by Thanksgiving and a sense of fatigue not assuaged by sleep; a moon face and a peculiar deposition of fat between the shoulders ("buffalo obesity"). Signs of these disorders include dwarfism and giantism as well. The curious phenomenon is how much the soma can be distorted by these profound disturbances of metabolism and the endocrine system with relatively little change in mentation.

As investigators have attempted to clarify mechanisms that mediate between psychosocial stimuli and pathological changes, considerable laboratory research has focused on neuroendocrine and neurophysiological mechanisms (Johnson, 1974; Kiely, 1974; Whybrow and Silberfarb, 1974) and on immune mediating mechanisms (Amkraut and Solomon, 1974; Stein, Schiavi, and Camerino, 1976). Mason's work on neuropsychoendocrinology over many years has been notable (see Mason, 1975). He has studied the influence of a variety of psychosocial stimuli, emotional states, and psychological defenses and of developmental history on the patterns of many separate and concurrent hormonal responses.

Thyrotoxicosis. Thyrotoxicosis is a condition marked by hyperplasia and hyperfunction of the thyroid gland tissue, with excessive secretion of thyroid hormones and moderate diffuse enlargement or discrete toxic nodular change in the thyroid gland. Weight loss, diarrhea, polyphagia, eye signs, myasthenia, and myopathy are cardinal features. Anxiety, irritability, emotional lability, and autonomic overactivity are also found. Depression, apathy, euphoria, psychosis, and delirium occur less frequently, sometimes as secondary drug reactions.

In 1803, Caleb Parry reported the acute onset of thyrotoxicosis in a twenty-one-year-old girl after a severe fright. Gibson (1962) noted that sudden severe stress could precipitate the disease in genetically vulnerable people; chronic stress, however, appeared to be more important. Lidz (1954) found emotional precipitants in approximately 80 percent of cases. Although stress is thought to have an effect on thyroid function, the evidence that would confirm this theory is still in dispute. For example, Hetzel, de la Haba, and Hinkle (1952) used stress interviews to produce changes in the protein-bound iodine (PBI) levels of both normal and hyperthyroid subjects. In contrast, F. Alexander and his coworkers (1961) conducted a study using a stressful film with normal and hyperthyroid subjects; they found that hyperthyroid patients reacted to the film with an elevation of ^{131}I uptake (a measure of thyroid activity), while normal patients failed to exhibit such reactivity of the thyroid gland. Kracht and Kracht (1952) produced a "fright thyrotoxicosis" by exposing wild rabbits to a barking dog. The thyroid released its stored hormone quickly, and the animals finally died in a thyroid crisis. These findings revealed that stimulation of the anterior hypothalamus or the median eminence causes a rapid rise of ^{131}I in the thyroid venous blood and may thus indicate one of the neuroendocrine pathways that mediate these stresses. This study, together with Alexander's work on iodine uptake, is important because it begins to identify some intervening neuroendocrine mechanisms between the original stress and the onset of the disease.

Psychoanalytic studies, notably that of Ham, Alexander, and Carmichael (1949), identified specific personality traits and emotional conflicts in hyperthyroid patients; these traits develop in the patients' struggle for self-sufficiency and maturity. In psychodynamic terms, repeated threats to security in early life, such as frustration of dependency needs, lead to a desperate attempt to identify prematurely with one of the parents. This precocious identification is a defense against repetition of early feelings of rejection and frustration. Ensuing pseudo-self-reliant struggles require both the defense of denial and

counterphobic and compulsive attempts to take on what is most feared (independence, for example). In response to stress, patients characteristically struggle toward maturity rather than regressing. If counterphobic defenses against dependency needs break down under stress, hyperthyroidism may be precipitated. Similar specific personality traits and psychodynamic conflicts have been held responsible for a variety of other psychosomatic illnesses, including asthma, duodenal ulcer, and colitis.

Myxedema. Psychological changes in patients with myxedema, a form of hypothyroidism described by Sir William Gull in 1873, range from mania to retardation. Psychosis, confusional states, mental slowing, apathy and depression, impairment of memory and judgment, and excitement and irritability may occur. The incidence of psychiatric complications increases with the duration and severity of the condition; these complications are not necessarily reversible with medical treatment. Although most psychiatric complications of myxedema remit with adequate medical management, additional measures, such as tricyclic antidepressants, may be necessary in the treatment of the severe depression that often complicates the disease.

Parathyroid disease. Psychiatric complications frequently accompany parathyroid disorders. In primary hyperparathyroidism, anxiety, irritability, depression, and confusional states have been found to correlate with the serum calcium level (Schwartz, 1965). Anxiety, depression, agitation, psychosis, confusional states, delirium, and suicidal ideation occur in hypoparathyroidism.

Diabetes mellitus. In his studies of diabetic patients, Cannon (1920) found that fear can cause glycosuria even in normal subjects when liver glycogen is broken down in response to autonomic nervous system activation and epinephrine secretion. Diabetics are more vulnerable than nondiabetics to such changes. Hinkle and Wolf (1949, 1952) showed that stress (induced by interviews), especially stress that produced despair and hopelessness, could cause a ketosis even though the patient had kept strictly to his diet;

clinical acidosis would result if the stress was sustained. Lonely and depressed diabetics may neglect to regulate their diet or insulin requirements purposely to gain help or hospitalization or to attempt suicide. In reviewing the influence of emotional states in diabetes, many authors, notably Lidz (1954), Bruch and Hewlett (1947), and Slawson, Flynn, and Kollar (1963), have found that the onset of diabetes mellitus closely followed stressful experiences, particularly object loss, grief, and depression.

Medical management of diet and insulin is the mainstay of treatment. S. M. Kaplan and his colleagues (1960) found that glycosuria decreased in depressed diabetics treated with imipramine. Psychiatric intervention may thus be indicated in cases of failure to comply with the medical regimen, a frequent occurrence in depressed patients.

Addison's disease. Partial or complete destruction of the adrenal cortex occurs in Addison's disease and results in hormonal deficiencies of varying severity. Clinical features appear only when 90 percent of the gland has been destroyed; they are characterized by pigmentation of the skin and buccal mucosa, muscle wasting, weakness, and atrophic changes in other organs. Other clinical features result either from glucocorticoid, mineralocorticoid, or sex hormone deficiencies. The most prominent psychological findings are apathy and negativism (in 80 percent of cases), depression and irritability (50 percent), and suspiciousness and agitation (17 percent); psychotic states are found in 5 to 10 percent of untreated cases (G. L. Engel and Margolin, 1941). All of these states usually remit when the condition is treated.

Cushing's syndrome. Cushing's syndrome is caused by glucocorticoid excess, hyperplasia of the adrenals, or tumors. It is characterized by central (truncal) obesity, muscle weakness, moon facies, hypertension, atrophy of the skin, hirsutism, hyperglycemia, glucosuria, osteoporosis, and menstrual disorders. Approximately half of the cases produce a wide variety of psychiatric symptoms. Depression and agitation are most frequent; psychosis and euphoria occur rarely. Symptoms remit when the condition is

treated medically or surgically. Lipowski's recent work (1975) shows that psychiatric complications of physical illness are ubiquitous; medical and psychiatric disorders coexist in 25 to 50 percent of the patients in any treatment setting.

Cardiovascular Disorders

Ours is surely the age of the cardiovascular system. If our nineteenth-century forebears were concerned with constipation and indigestion, we outdo them in our concern with dieting, exercising, and tranquilizing ourselves with drugs and alcohol—all in an effort to reduce the strain on our cardiovascular systems. It would be an unusual middle-class, educated American who could not spell out in some detail the doctrine of how stress increases blood pressure, which, in turn, adds to the work of the heart.

We all know that the pulse quickens in response to passion or panic. Cardiovascular changes accompany most emotional reactions as concomitants of the neuroendocrine response to stress. The cardiovascular system may be indirectly influenced by stress through changes in electrolytes, clotting mechanisms, and fat levels. Psychological stress can seriously aggravate existing cardiovascular disease and may precipitate heart rate disturbances, arrhythmias, and syncope, especially in constitutionally vulnerable individuals. Psychological stress is mediated through an imbalance between the sympathetic and the parasympathetic tone of the heart. In psychophysiological studies of public speakers, Taggart, Carruthers, and Somerville (1973) found that this group had EKG changes, tachycardia, and increased levels of triglycerides, free fatty acids, and plasma noradrenaline.

Coronary artery disease. Dunbar, Wolfe, and Rioch (1936) and Gildea (1949) systematically described a coronary prone personality as one with the following characteristics:
1. a great need and respect for authority, yet a childhood conflict with it
2. compulsive, hard-driving traits; a propensity for careful planning and pursuit of one career
3. preference for intellectual activities over physical sports, with few hobbies; faulty identification with the father, leading to insecurity,

compulsive compensatory competitiveness, and particular vulnerability to failure

Miles and his colleagues (1954) were unable to confirm the results of Dunbar and Gildea. Mordkoff and Parsons (1968) reviewed the entire literature on the coronary personality and found no consistent support for any particular personality configuration or for focal conflicts, conscious or unconscious, in this group. They noted lack of control groups in the studies and other methodological discrepancies between clinical and experimental studies, which may account for divergent findings.

In a series of studies, Friedman and Rosenman (Friedman, 1969; Rosenman and Friedman, 1963; Rosenman et al., 1975) have described an overt behavior pattern important in the pathogenesis of coronary artery disease, especially in younger patients. The two groups of subjects on which they reported demonstrated contrasting behavior patterns. The behavior of one group (Type A) included (1) excessive competitive drive; (2) ambitiousness and achievement orientation; (3) a chronic sense of urgency; (4) an inclination to multiple commitments; (5) an immersion in deadlines. This behavior was, however, said to be unrelated to anxiety, fear, worry, or any of the simple neuroses. In contrast, patients with Type B behavior could relax more easily, were less competitive, and were not habitually concerned with meeting deadlines. Type B people might thus be described as not possessing many Type A traits. Physiologically, Type A personalities, in contrast to those in the Type B group, manifested significantly higher serum triglycerides, cholesterol, phospholipids, and low-density lipoprotein lipids. Type A's also had lower ratios of A/B lipoprotein to cholesterol. These differences were not caused by differences in diet, weight, or physical activity between members of the two groups. In addition, Type A subjects showed significantly higher urinary levels of 17-ketosteroids, 17-hydroxycorticosteroids, 5-hydroxyindole, epinephrine, and norepinephrine during working hours than did Type B subjects. In a prospective study, Jenkins and his coworkers (1967, 1968) found that those diagnosed as Type A Personalities had a significantly higher subsequent incidence of first occurrence of coronary artery disease than did Type B personalities.

This coronary personality profile may in fact be exacerbated by environmental stresses rather than based entirely on causative personality factors. Ward and Sheehan (1977) found a strong positive correlation between Type A behavior patterns and high recent life stress scores; the nature of the relationship between these two factors and myocardial infarction will require investigation. In order to demonstrate that Type A personality characteristics alone are important risk factors in coronary artery disease and myocardial infarction, it will be necessary to compare groups of patients of both personality types whose life stress scores are similar. The issue of personality types in coronary heart disease is controversial and is still hotly debated. However, the concept of the coronary prone personality has stimulated considerable continuing research activity, the results of which are already being applied in preventive programs (Friedman and Rosenman, 1974; Jenkins, 1976a, 1976b). Hackett and Cassem (1973) found denial of painful affects and experiences to be a prominent coping mechanism subsequent to myocardial infarction. When cases were followed prospectively, mortality and morbidity were lower in groups of patients who denied worry and were more optimistic.

There is less dispute about the effect of severe loss on mortality from coronary artery disease. The death rate in a sample of 4,000 widowers, during their first six months of bereavement, taken from the National Health Service was found to be 40 per cent higher than the expected rate based on national figures for married men of the same age; coronary artery disease was the principal cause of death (Parkes, Benjamin, and Fitzgerald, 1969).

Essential hypertension. Essential hypertension is characterized by a sustained rise of systemic blood pressure above 140 mm Hg (systolic) and 90 mm Hg (diastolic), for which no cause can be found. A normal subject usually reacts to anxiety with an elevation of systolic blood pressure, a fall in diastolic blood pressure, and a decrease in peripheral resistance. A hypertensive individual responds with an elevation of both systolic and diastolic blood pressure.

Franz Alexander (1939), among others, proposed that the hypertensive patient has chronically inhibited aggressive and sexual impulses. Outwardly, the patient maintains remarkable self-control and is extremely compliant and pleasing to others. Oken (1960) found that patients who inhibited anger had a higher diastolic and a lower systolic blood pressure, at equal levels of anger, than did those who fully expressed anger. However, hostility may be a consequence of elevated blood pressure, or both may be dependent on a third factor, such as central catecholamine metabolism.

Numerous studies have failed to establish a specific personality profile or conflict constellation that distinguishes hypertensives as a group. Most investigators agree, however, that emotional stress accompanying psychosocial changes has a major influence on the clinical course and the likelihood of complications. Evidence on the role of emotional factors in the etiology of hypertension is suggestive but by no means conclusive. Henry (1975; Henry, Meehan, and Stephens, 1967) demonstrated the importance of experimentally induced psychosocial factors, such as overcrowding and disruption of social organization, in inducing hypertension in mice. In an epidemiological study, Cobb and Rose (1973) found a high incidence of hypertension in air traffic controllers. Although clinical studies have reported the effects of biofeedback (Goldman, Kleinman, and Snow, 1975) and relaxation (Stone and De Leo, 1976) techniques in lowering high blood pressure, the evidence that psychotherapy, conditioning, and biofeedback are reliable in treating hypertension is weak. Antihypertensive medication remains the mainstay of treatment.

Congestive heart failure. Hickam, Cargill, and Golden (1948) demonstrated that anxiety imposes a considerable burden on the heart—a stress comparable to that of exertion. If cardiac reserve is inadequate, congestive heart failure may result in a very anxious patient. Chambers and Reiser (1953), for example, found that congestive heart failure was precipitated by emotional stress in 76 percent of their subjects.

Vasodepressor syncope. Fainting, or vasodepressor syncope, occurs with a sudden drop in blood pressure. Romano et al. (1943) and Ro-

mano and Engel (1945) made the following observations:

1. Fear is an important factor, and fainting is more likely to occur when fear must be suppressed.
2. Fainting usually occurs in response to some actual, threatened, or fantasied injury to the body, such as receiving an injection or having blood drawn.
3. The person is usually erect before fainting.
4. The phenomenon may be "contagious" in large groups.
5. Emotional factors allow vasodilation in muscles that are not contracting; in the absence of contraction or compensatory vasoconstriction, blood can pool beyond a critical level, and the result is a drop in blood pressure.

Graham, Kabler, and Lunsford (1961) dispute these psychobiological views and stress the diphasic nature of fainting. Studies on pilots suggest that some emotional states, such as aggression and confidence, increase tolerance to gravitational forces, while others, such as anxiety or hopelessness, decrease tolerance.

Migraine headache. Attacks of migraine headache are periodic and marked by prodromal disturbances (scotoma, paresthesia, speech difficulty) and pain, which is classically unilateral. Photophobia also occurs; the attack often ends with vomiting and may be followed by euphoria. Vasoconstriction produces the premonitory symptoms (prodromi); overcompensatory vasodilation follows and causes pain.

A broad spectrum of personality profiles and specific conflicts has been found in migraine patients. Touraine and Draper (1934) described (1) retarded emotional development; (2) superior intelligence; and (3) loss of dependency. Knopf (1935) characterized the migraine patient as ambitious, reserved, relaxed, dignified, "goody-goody," and lacking a sense of humor. H. G. Wolff (1937) noted compulsive, perfectionistic, ambitious, and competitive traits and an inability to delegate authority. Fromm-Reichmann (1937) described migraine patients as intellectually brilliant people redirecting hostile, envious impulses against the self because of guilt. Selinsky (1939) noted struggle, resentment, anxiety, and compulsive traits in migrainous patients. Repressed rage is the primary factor noted by Lippman (1954). Because these studies failed to use adequate controls, they can be interpreted only with great caution. Most authors agree, however, that emotional stress may lead to an attack in vulnerable individuals.

Medical management is the mainstay of treatment. If psychosocial stress aggravates the condition, psychotherapy may be indicated. Biofeedback has also been used in the control of migraine (Sargent, Green, and Walters, 1970), but it is far from gaining universal acceptance.

Ménière's Disease

The work of Fowler and Zeckel (1953) on Ménière's disease, which is characterized by vertigo, demonstrates the delicate interrelationship among the autonomic nervous system, endocrine factors, and the cerebral cortex in precipitating acute attacks. In response to severe stress, red blood cells clump and stick in the small labyrinthine vessels, producing local disturbances and, eventually, the characteristic structural changes of the advanced stages of the disease.

Hematological Disorders

Diseases of the blood are as likely to be influenced by the emotions as those of any other organ system. As the nature of autoimmunity and its disorders is uncovered, we predict that an abundance of observations will implicate both the formed elements and the plasma of blood in psychophysiological phenomena.

Browne, Mally, and Kane (1960) conducted a three-year psychosocial study of twenty-eight hemophiliac children and their families. They found that psychological factors, notably the anticipation of increased activity and independence, apparently contributed to the timing of spontaneous bleeding episodes. Macht (1952) found that anxiety affects clotting time in blood donors; coagulation time was one to three minutes in the most anxious, three minutes in the moderately anxious, and eight to twelve minutes in the relaxed group. Benedict (1954) found that psychological stress involving object

loss was related to the onset and recurrence of a series of cases of familial spherocytosis, sickle cell anemia, and thrombocytopenic purpura.

Because of the psychological changes that so frequently occur in the later stages of pernicious anemia, many theories associate personality traits and the disease. Lewin (1959), however, found no specific personality traits in ten patients with pernicious anemia. Again, as with many other diseases, depression and recent life change (loss, for example) preceded the onset of the illness, but the severity of the depression was not related to the severity of the illness.

Psychological Factors in Malignant Disease

The relationship between the onset of cancer and emotional disruption can be seen by recalling that cervical carcinoma was known for many years as "widows' disease" because it so often became manifest during bereavement. More recently, Schmale and Iker (1966) were able to predict a positive cervical smear in thirty-six out of fifty-one cases on the basis of the patient's response to a precarious life event with feelings of hopelessness.

Miller and Jones (1948) were the first to stress the role of psychological factors in the development of leukemia. Many subsequent studies have supported this claim. Most, however, are poorly designed, and their results are questionable. Le Shan and Worthington (1956b) identified the cancer patient as a highly dependent personality who lacks autonomy and has little ability to relate to others. Bahnson, Bahnson, and Wardwell (1971) describe denial, strong commitment to social norms, bleakness, depletion, and lack of emotional meaning as prominent in cancer patients. Recent studies of breast and lung cancer patients suggest that such patients have a marked tendency to repress experience or expression of certain emotions, especially anger (Abse et al., 1974; Greer and Morriss, 1975). It is unclear, however, whether this phenomenon is secondary to their illness.

Although object loss, psychosocial change, and depression are repeatedly stressed as precipitating causes (Greene, 1954; Kowal, 1955; Le

Shan and Worthington, 1956a, 1964; Meerloo, 1954; Schmale and Iker, 1966), other investigators (Aleksandrowicz et al., 1964; Bahnson, Bahnson, and Wardwell, 1971) have been unable to confirm this hypothesis in their studies. Greene (1954) found no characteristic personality patterns in longitudinal studies of patients with lymphomas and leukemias.

Riley (1975) found that the latency time for development of mammary carcinoma in mice carrying the Bittner oncogenic virus varied with the stress to which they were subjected. After 400 days, 92 percent of the mice who were stressed or handled excessively had developed tumors, compared with only 7 percent of undisturbed, nonstressed mice. He hypothesized that stress led to increased adrenal cortical activity with consequent T cell deficiency and impairment of the host defense system. This process increased the animals' susceptibility to carcinoma.

Renneker and his colleagues (1963) noted greater self-confidence and ability to express basic drives outwardly among long-term survivors of breast cancer with metastases. Among male patients with terminal cancer, those who appeared calm in the presence of inner anxiety had a poorer medical prognosis (Blumberg, West, and Ellis, 1954). Katz et al. (1970) believe that good ego strength and an ability to express basic drives adaptively are traits that increase host resistance to a wide variety of illnesses, including cancer.

Accident Proneness

Although not specific to any organ system, accident proneness is a true psychosomatic disease. Marbe (1926) found that an individual who has had one accident is more likely to suffer repeated accidents than an accident-free person is to have an initial accident. There is little question that some people are more accident prone than others and that emotional reactions and psychosocial life changes are important factors in this vulnerability.

Dunbar (1943, 1947) recognized accident proneness as a psychological, social, and somatic disease and found individuals in this group to be impulsive, decisive, and resentful toward author-

ity. She saw the accident as an attempt to expiate unconscious guilt by self-punishment; the combination of resentment and guilt was hazardous.

In a carefully controlled study of car accidents, Conger et al. (1957, 1959) noted that accident prone people were (1) less able than others to control hostility; (2) excessively self-centered or excessively socially centered; (3) excessively preoccupied with fantasy or excessively reactive to external stimuli; (4) more fearful of, vulnerable to, and angry about losses than other people; (5) less able than others to tolerate tension. No specific diagnostic character type could be identified.

In a study of accident prone children (Conger and Gaskill, 1967), they found that these children were (1) more anxious than non-accident prone children; (2) more disturbed emotionally; (3) more active before and after birth; (4) earlier to develop motor skills and better coordinated; (5) offspring of less stable, more insecure parents.

The history of psychosomatic medicine reveals much imaginative speculation without the necessary rigorous empirical testing. Many classic studies lack validation and have not been replicated. Only recently has consistently good empirical research with adequate controls been implemented. There is a need for more skepticism and for careful and accurate description of observations rather than the application of unproven theoretical constructs that often distort description. We must be daring in what we attempt, but cautious in what we claim.

In 1921 Bertrand Russell wrote:

Philosophy, from the earliest times, has made greater claims and achieved fewer results than any other branch of learning. The one and only condition I believe, which is necessary in order to secure for philosophy in the near future an achievement surpassing all that has hitherto been accomplished by philosophers, is the creation of a school of men of scientific training and philosophical interests, unhampered by the tradition past and not misled by the literary methods of those who copy the ancients in all except their merits.

These remarks apply to both the past and the future of psychosomatic medicine.

References

Abramson, H. A. 1954. Evaluation of maternal rejection theory in allergy. *Ann. Allergy* 12:129–140.

Abse, D. W., N. M. Wilkins, R. L. van de Castle, W. D. Buxton, J.-P. Demars, R. S. Brown, and L. G. Kirschner. 1974. Personality and behavioral characteristics of lung cancer patients. *J. Psychosom. Res.* 18:101–113.

Ader, R. 1964. Gastric erosions in the rat: effects of immobilization at different points in the activity cycle. *Science* 145:406–407.

—— 1965. Effects of early experience and differential housing on behavior susceptibility to gastric erosions in the rat. *J. Comp. and Physiol. Psychol.* 60:233–238.

—— 1967. Behavior and physiological rhythms and the development of gastric erosions in the rat. *Psychosom. Med.* 29:345–353.

—— 1970. Effects of early experience and differential housing on the susceptibility to gastric erosions in lesion susceptible rats. *Psychosom. Med.* 32:568–580.

—— 1971. Experimentally induced gastric lesions. Results and implications of studies in animals. In *Duodenal ulcer*, ed. H. Weiner. Advances in Psychosomatic Medicine, vol. 6. Basel: Karger.

—— 1973. Early experience and susceptibility to disease: the case of gastric erosions. In *Ethology and development*, ed. S. A. Barnett. Clinics in Developmental Medicine no. 47. Philadelphia: Lippincott.

Ader, R., R. Tatum, and C. C. Beels. 1960. Social factors affecting emotionality and resistance to disease in animals: age of separation from the mother and susceptibility to gastric ulcers in the rat. *J. Comp. and Physiol. Psychol.* 53:446–454.

Aleksandrowicz, J., A. Brozak, K. Kaczanowski, A. Kepinski, and A. Zurowska. 1964. Psychological and anthropological analysis of leukemia patients. In *Psychosomatic aspects of neoplastic disease*, ed. D. Kisser and L. L. Le Shan. Philadelphia: Lippincott.

Alexander, A. B., D. R. Miklich, and H. Hershkoff. 1972. The immediate effects of systematic relaxation training on peak expiratory flow rates in asthmatic children. *Psychosom. Med.* 34:388–394.

Alexander, F. 1939. Emotional factors in essential hypertension. *Psychosom. Med.* 1:173–179.

—— 1946. Training principles in psychosomatic medicine. *Am. J. Orthopsychiatry* 16:410–412.

—— 1947. Treatment of a case of peptic ulcer and personality disorder. *Psychosom. Med.* 9:320–330.

—— 1950. *Psychosomatic medicine: its principles and applications*. New York: Norton.

Alexander, F., and W. Flagg. 1965. The psychosomatic approach. In *Handbook of clinical psychology*, ed. B. B. Wolman. New York: McGraw-Hill.

Alexander, F., G. W. Flagg, S. Foster, T. Clemens, and W. Blahd. 1961. Experimental studies of emotional stress. I. Hyperthyroidism. *Psychosom. Med.* 23:104–114.

Alexander, F., and T. French. 1948. *Studies in psychosomatic medicine*. New York: Ronald Press.

Alvarez, W. C. 1931. *Nervous indigestion*. New York: Hoeber.

American Psychiatric Association. 1968. *Diagnostic and statistical manual of mental disorders*. 2nd ed. Washington, D.C.

Amkraut, H., and G. F. Solomon. 1974. From the symbolic stimulus to the pathophysiologic response: immune mechanisms. *Int. J. Psychiatry Med.* 5:541–563.

Anderson, P. C., and T. N. Cross. 1963. Body cathexis and neurodermatitis. *Compr. Psychiatry* 4:40–46.

Avni, J., and I. Bruderman. 1969. The effect of amitriptyline on pulmonary ventilation and the mechanics of breathing. *Psychopharmacologia* 14:184–192.

Bahnson, C. B., M. B. Bahnson, and W. I. Wardwell. 1971. A psychological study of cancer patients. *Psychosom. Med.* 23:466–467.

Benedek, T. 1950. The functions of the sexual apparatus and their disturbances. In *Psychosomatic Medicine*, ed. F. Alexander. New York: Norton.

—— 1956. Psychological aspects of mothering. *Am. J. Orthopsychiatry* 26:272–278.

—— 1959. Sexual functions in women. In *American handbook of psychiatry*, ed. S. Arieti. New York: Basic Books.

Benedek, T., and B. B. Rubenstein. 1942. The sexual cycle in women. *Psychosom. Med.* monogr. series vol. 3, nos. 1,2.

Benedict, R. 1954. Psychosomatic correlations in certain blood dyscrasias. *Psychosom. Med.* 16, no. 1:41–46.

Berle, B. B. 1948. Emotional factors and tuberculosis: a critical review of the literature. *Psychosom. Med.* 10:366–373.

Blau, M. D., B. Slaff, K. Easton, J. Welkowitz, J. Springarn, and J. Cohen. 1963. The psychogenic etiology of premature births. *Psychosom. Med.* 25:201–211.

Block, J. H., E. Harvey, P. H. Jenning, and E. Simpson. 1966. Clinicians' conceptions of the asthmatogenic mother. *Arch. Gen. Psychiatry* 15:610–618.

Block, J. H., P. H. Jenning, E. Harvey, and E. Simpson. 1964. Interaction between allergic potential and psychopathology in childhood. *Psychosom. Med.* 26:307–320.

Blumberg, E. M., P. M. West, and F. W. Ellis. 1954. A possible relationship between psychological factors and human cancer. *Psychosom. Med.* 16:277–286.

Booth, G. C. 1939. The psychological approach in therapy in chronic arthritis. *Rheumatism* 1:48–59.

Brady, J. V. 1958. Ulcers in "executive monkeys." *Sci. Am.* 199:95–104.

Browne, W. J., M. Mally, and R. P. Kane. 1960. Psychosocial aspects of hemophilia: a study of twenty-eight hemophiliac children and their families. *Am. J. Orthopsychiatry* 30:730–740.

Bruch, H. 1962. Perceptual and conceptual disturbances in anorexia nervosa. *Psychosom. Med.* 24, no. 2:187–194.

——— 1973. *Eating disorders: obesity, anorexia nervosa and the person within.* New York: Basic Books.

Bruch, H., and I. Hewlett. 1947. Psychologic aspects of the medical management of diabetes in children. *Psychosom. Med.* 9:205–209.

Budznyski, T. H., J. M. Stoyva, C. S. Adler, and D. J. Mullaney. 1973. EMG biofeedback and tension headache: a controlled outcome study. *Psychosom. Med.* 35, no. 6:484–496.

Cannon, W. B. 1920. *Bodily changes in pain, hunger, fear and rage.* 2nd ed. New York: Appleton.

——— 1932. *The wisdom of the body.* New York: Norton.

Chambers, W. N., and M. F. Reiser. 1953. Emotional stress in the precipitation of congestive heart failure. *Psychosom. Med.* 15:38–60.

Chertok, L., M. L. Mondzain, and M. Bonnaud. 1963. Vomiting and the wish to have a child. *Psychosom. Med.* 25:13–18.

Cleveland, S. E., and S. Fisher. 1956. Psychological factors in the neurodermatoses. *Psychosom. Med.* 18, no. 3:209–220.

Cobb, S. 1943. *Borderlands of psychiatry.* Cambridge, Mass.: Harvard University Press.

Cobb, S., and R. M. Rose. 1973. Hypertension, peptic ulcer and diabetes in air traffic controllers. *J.A.M.A.* 224:489–492.

Cohen, S. I., S. Bondurant, and A. J. Silverman. 1960. Psychophysiological influences on peripheral venous tone. *Psychosom. Med.* 22, no. 2:106–117.

Conger, J. J., and H. S. Gaskill. 1967. Accident proneness. In *Comprehensive textbook of psychiatry*, ed. A. M. Freedman and H. I. Kaplan. Baltimore: Williams & Wilkins.

Conger, J. J., H. S. Gaskill, D. D. Glad, L. Hassel, R. V. Rainey, W. L. Sawrey, and E. S. Turrell. 1959. Psychological and psychophysiological factors in motor vehicle accidents. *J.A.M.A.* 169:1581–87.

Conger, J. J., H. S. Gaskill, D. D. Glad, R. V. Rainey, W. L. Sawrey, and E. S. Turrell. 1957. Personal and interpersonal factors in motor vehicle accidents. *Am. J. Psychiatry* 113:1069–74.

Daniels, G. E. 1948. Psychiatric factors in ulcerative colitis. *Gastroenterology* 10:59–62.

Daniels, G. E., J. F. O'Connor, A. Karush, L. Moses, C. A. Flood, and M. Lepore. 1962. Three decades in the observation and treatment of ulcerative colitis. *Psychosom. Med.* 24, no. 1:85–93.

Derner, G. F. 1953. *Aspects of the psychology of the Tuberculous.* New York: Hoeber.

Deutsch, F. 1939. *The production of somatic disease by emotional disturbance.* Baltimore: Williams & Wilkins.

——— 1951. Thus speaks the body. *Acta Med. Orient.* 10:67.

DiCara, L. V., and N. E. Miller. 1968a. Changes in heart rate instrumentally learned by curarized rats as avoidance responses. *J. Comp. Physiol. Psychol.* 65:8–12.

——— 1968b. Instrumental learning of systolic blood pressure responses by curarized rats: dissociation of cardiac and vascular changes. *Psychosom. Med.* 30:484–494.

Draper, G. 1924. *Human constitution: a consideration of its relationship to disease.* Philadelphia: Saunders.

——— 1935. The common denominator of disease. *Am. J. Med. Sci.* 190:545–558.

——— 1942. The emotional component of the ulcer susceptible constitution. *Ann. Intern. Med.* 16:633–658.

Dunbar, F. 1943. *Psychosomatic diagnosis.* New York: Harper, Hoeber.

——— 1947. *Emotions and bodily changes.* 3rd ed. New York: Columbia University Press.

Dunbar, H. F., T. P. Wolfe, and J. M. Rioch. 1936. Psychiatric aspects of medical problems: psychic component of disease process (including convalescence) in cardiac, diabetic and fracture patients. *Am. J. Psychiatry* 93:649–679.

Engel, B. T., P. Nikoomanesh, and M. M. Schuster. 1974. Operant conditioning of rectosphincteric responses in the treatment of fecal incontinence. *N. Engl. J. Med.* 290:646–649.

Engel, G. L. 1954a. Studies of ulcerative colitis, I. Clinical data bearing on the nature of the somatic process. *Psychosom. Med.* 16:496–501.

——— 1954b. Studies of ulcerative colitis, II. The nature of the somatic processes and the adequacy of psychosomatic hypotheses. *Am. J. Med.* 16:416–433.

——— 1955. Studies of ulcerative colitis, III. The nature of the psychological processes. *Am. J. Med.* 19:231–256.

——— 1956. Studies of ulcerative colitis, IV. The significance of headaches. *Psychosom. Med.* 18, no. 4:334–346.

——— 1958. Studies of ulcerative colitis, V. Psychological aspects and their implications for treatment. *Am. J. Dig. Dis.* 3:315–337.

Engel, G. L., and S. G. Margolin. 1941. Neuropsychiatric disturbances of Addison's disease and the role of impaired carbohydrate metabolism in production of abnormal cerebral function. *Arch. Neurol. Psychiatr.* 45:881–883.

Engel, G. L., F. Reichsman, and H. L. Segal. 1956. A study of an infant with a gastric fistula, I. Behavior and the rate of total hydrochloric acid secretion. *Psychosom. Med.* 18:374–398.

Engel, G. L., and A. H. Schmale. 1967. Psychoanalytic theory of somatic disorder: conversion, specificity, and the disease onset situation. *J. Am. Psychoanal. Assoc.* 15:344–365.

Engels, W. D., and E. D. Wittkower. 1969. Allergic and skin disorders. In *Comprehensive textbook of psychiatry*, ed. A. M. Freedman and H. I. Kaplan. Baltimore: Williams & Wilkins.

Falliers, C. J. 1970. Treatment of asthma in a residential center—a fifteen-year study. *Ann. Allergy* 28:513–521.

Federn, P. 1940. The determination of hysteria versus obsessional neurosis. *Psychoanal. Rev.* 27:265–276.

Fenichel, O. 1945. *The psychoanalytic theory of neurosis.* New York: Norton.

Ferenczi, S. 1926. *Further contribution to the theory and technique of psychoanalysis.* London: Hogarth Press.

Fisher, S., and S. E. Cleveland. 1958. *Body image and personality.* New York: Van Nostrand.

Fowler, E. P., Jr., and A. Zeckel. 1953. Psychophysiological factors in Ménière's disease. *Psychosom. Med.* 15:127–139.

Franks, C. M., and D. Leigh. 1959. The theoretical and experimental application of a conditioning model to a consideration of bronchial asthma in men. *J. Psychosom. Res.* 4:88–98.

Freeman, E. H., F. J. Gorman, M. T. Singer, M. T. Affelder, and B. F. Feingold. 1967. Personality variables and allergic skin reactions: a cross-validation study. *Psychosom. Med.* 29:312–332.

French, H. D., R. W. Porter, E. B. Cavanaugh, and R. L. Longmire. 1957. Experimental gastroduodenal lesions induced by stimulation of the brain. *Psychosom. Med.* 19, no. 3:209–220.

French, T. M., and F. Alexander. 1941. Psychogenic factors in bronchial asthma. *Psychosom. Med.* monograph series 4, vol. 2, nos. 1, 2.

French, T. M., and L. B. Shapiro. 1949. The use of dream analysis in psychosomatic research. *Psychosom. Med.* 11:110–112.

Freud, S. 1894. The neuro-psychoses of defence. In *Standard edition*, ed. J. Strachey. Vol. 3. London: Hogarth Press, 1962.

——— 1895. Studies in hysteria. In *Standard edition*, ed. J. Strachey. Vol. 2. London: Hogarth Press, 1955.

——— 1905. Fragment of an analysis of a case of hysteria. In *Standard edition*, ed. J. Strachey. Vol. 7. London: Hogarth Press, 1953.

Friedman, M. 1969. Pathogenesis of coronary heart disease. New York: McGraw-Hill.

Friedman, M., and R. H. Rosenman. 1974. *Type A behavior and your heart.* New York: Knopf.

Fromm-Reichmann, F. 1937. Contribution to the psychogenesis of migraine. *Psychoanal. Rev.* 24:26–33.

Galdston, I. 1955. Psychosomatic medicine. *Arch. Neurol.* 74:441–450.

Gibson, J. G. 1962. Emotions and the thyroid glands: a critical appraisal. *J. Psychosom. Res.* 6:93–116.

Gildea, E. F. 1949. Special features of personality which are common to certain psychosomatic disorders. *Psychosom. Med.* 11:273–281.

Glasberg, H. M., P. M. Bromberg, M. Stein, and T. J. Luparello. 1969. A personality study of asthmatic patients. *J. Psychosom. Res.* 13:197–204.

Glass, G. B. J., and S. Wolf. 1950. Hormonal mechanisms in nervous mechanism of gastric acid secretion in humans. *Proc. Soc. Exp. Biol. Med.* 73:535–537.

Goldberg, E. L., and G. W. Comstock. 1976. Life events and subsequent illness. *Am. J. Epidemiol.* 104:146–158.

Goldman, H., K. M. Kleinman, and M. Y. Snow. 1975. Relationship between essential hypertension and cognitive functioning: effects of biofeedback. *Psychophysiology* 12:569–573.

Grace, W. J., S. Wolf, and H. G. Wolff. 1958. *The human colon.* New York: Harper, Hoeber.

Graham, D. T., J. D. Kabler, and L. Lunsford, Jr. 1961. Vasovagal fainting: a diphasic response. *Psychosom. Med.* 23, no. 6:493–507.

Greenacre, P. 1952. Pregenital patterning. *Int. J. Psychoanal.* 33:410–415.

Greene, W. A., Jr., 1954. Psychological factors and reticuloendothelial disease: preliminary observations on a group of males with lymphomas and leukemias. *Psychosom. Med.* 16:220–230.

Greer, S., and T. Morriss. 1975. Psychologic attributes of women who develop breast cancer: a controlled study. *J. Psychosom. Res.* 19:147–153.

Grinker, R. R. 1966. The psychosomatic aspects of anxiety. In *Anxiety and behavior*, ed. C. D. Spielberger. New York: Academic Press.

Groen, J. J., and H. E. Pelser. 1960. Experience with,

and results of, group psychotherapy in patients with bronchial asthma. *J. Psychosom. Res.* 4:191–205.

Gull, W. W. 1874. Anorexia nervosa (apepsia hysterica, anorexia hysterica). *Trans. Clin. Soc. London* 7:22–28.

Hackett, T. P., and N. H. Cassem. 1973. Psychological effects of acute coronary care. In *Textbook of coronary care*, ed. L. E. Meltzer. Amsterdam: Excerpta Medica.

Halliday, J. L. 1937. Psychological factors in rheumatism: preliminary study. *Br. Med. J.* 1:213.

—— 1942. Psychological aspects of rheumatoid arthritis. *Proc. R. Soc. Med.* 35:455–457.

—— 1946. Epidemiology and the psychosomatic affections: a study in social medicine. *Lancet* 2:185–191.

—— 1948. *Psychosocial medicine: a study of the sick society*. New York: Norton.

Ham, G. C., F. G. Alexander, and H. T. Carmichael. 1949. Dynamic aspects of personality features and reactions characteristic of patients with Graves' disease. *Res. Publ. Assoc. Res. Nerv. Ment. Dis.* 29:451–457.

Hamburg, D. A., and J. E. Adams. 1967. A perspective on coping behavior. *Arch. Gen. Psychiatry* 17:277–284.

Hartman, H. R. 1933. Neurogenic factors in peptic ulcer. *Med. Clin. North Am.* 16:1357–69.

Henry, H. P. 1975. The induction of acute and chronic cardiovascular disease in animals by psychosocial stimulation. *Int. J. Psychiatry Med.* 6:145–158.

Henry, J. P., J. P. Meehan, and P. M. Stephens. 1967. Use of psychosocial stimuli to induce prolonged systolic hypertension in mice. *Psychosom. Med.* 29:408–432.

Herbert, M., R. Glick, and H. Black. 1967. Olfactory precipitation of bronchial asthma. *J. Psychosom. Res.* 11:195–202.

Hetzel, B. S., D. S. de la Haba, and L. E. Hinkle. 1952. Rapid changes in plasma PBI in euthyroid and hyperthyroid subjects. *Trans. Am. Goiter Assoc.* Springfield, Ill.: Thomas.

Hickam, J. B., W. H. Cargill, and A. Golden. 1948. Cardiovascular reactions to emotional stimuli, effect on the cardiac output, arteriovenous oxygen difference, arterial pressure, and peripheral resistance. *J. Clin. Invest.* 27:290–298.

Hinkle, L. E., Jr., and S. Wolf. 1949. Experimental study of life situations, emotions, and the occurrence of acidosis in a juvenile diabetic. *Am. J. Med. Sci.* 217:130–135.

—— 1952. Summary of experimental evidence relating life stresses to diabetes mellitus. *J. Mt. Sinai Hosp.* 19:537–570.

Hinsie, L. E., and R. J. Campbell. 1960. *Psychiatric dictionary*. 3rd ed. New York: Oxford.

Holmes, T. H., N. G. Hawkins, C. E. Bowerman, E. R. Clarke, and J. R. Joffe, Jr. 1957. Psychosocial and psychophysiologic studies of tuberculosis. *Psychosom. Med.* 19:134–143.

Holmes, T. H., and M. Masuda. 1974. Life change and illness susceptibility. In *Stressful life events: their nature and effects*, ed. B. S. and B. P. Dohrenwend. New York: Wiley.

Ikemi, Y., S. Nakagawa, and Y. Tsukata. 1963. Psychosomatic study of so-called allergic disorders. *Jap. J. Med. Prog.* 50:451.

Jacobi, K. W. M. 1822. Sammlungen fur du Heilkunde der Gemathskrankheiten. 3 vols. Elberfeld: Schoman.

Jenkins, C. D. 1976a. Psychologic and social risk factors for coronary disease. *N. Engl. J. Med.* 294:987–994.

—— 1976b. Recent evidence supporting psychologic and social risk factors for coronary disease. *N. Engl. J. Med.* 294:1033–38.

Jenkins, C. D., R. H. Rosenman, and M. Friedman. 1967. Development of an objective psychological test for the determination of the coronary-prone behavior pattern of employed men. *J. Chronic Dis.* 20:371–379.

—— 1968. Replicability of rating the coronary-prone behavior pattern. *Br. J. Prev. Soc. Med.* 22:16–22.

Johnson, A. N., L. B. Shapiro, and F. Alexander. 1947. A preliminary report on a psychosomatic study of rheumatoid arthritis. *Psychosom. Med.* 9:295–300.

Johnson, L. C. 1974. Psychophysiological research: aims and methods. *Int. J. Psychiatry Med.* 5:565–573.

Kamiya, J. 1961. Behavioral, subjective and physiological aspects of drowsiness and sleep. In *Functions of varied experience*, ed. D. W. Fiske and S. R. Maddi. Homewood, Ill.: Dorsey.

Kaplan, H. I. and H. S. 1957. A psychosomatic concept. *Am. J. Psychother.* 11:16–38.

Kaplan, S. M., J. W. Mass, J. M. Dixley, and W. D. Ross. 1960. Use of imipramine in diabetes. *J.A.M.A.* 174:511–517.

Karush, A., G. E. Daniels, J. F. O'Connor, and L. O. Stern. 1968. The response to psychotherapy in chronic ulcerative colitis. I. Pretreatment factors. *Psychosom. Med.* 30:255–276.

—— 1969. The response to psychotherapy in chronic ulcerative colitis. II. Factors arising from the therapeutic situation. *Psychosom. Med.* 31:201–226.

Karush, A., R. B. Hiatt, and G. E. Daniels. 1955. Psychophysiological correlation in ulcerative colitis. *Psychosom. Med.* 17:36–56.

Katz, J. L., H. Weiner, T. F. Gallagher, and L. Hellman. 1970. Stress, distress and ego defenses: the psychoendocrine response to impending tumor. *Arch. Gen. Psychiatry* 23:131–142.

Kehoe, M., and W. Ironside. 1963. Studies on the experimental evocation of depressive responses using hypnosis. II. The influence of depressive responses upon the secretion of gastric acid. *Psychosom. Med.* 25:403–419.

Kellner, R. 1975. Psychotherapy in psychosomatic disorders. *Arch. Gen. Psychiatry* 32:1021–28.

Kepecs, J. G., M. Robin, and M. J. Brunner. 1951. The relationship of certain emotional states and transudation into the skin. *Psychosom. Med.* 13:10–17.

Kety, S. S., and C. F. Schmidt. 1946. The effect of active and passive hyperventilation on cerebral blood flow, cerebral oxygen consumption, cardiac output and blood pressure of normal young men. *J. Clin. Invest.* 25:107.

Kiely, W. F. 1974. From the symbolic stimulus to the pathophysiological response: neurophysiological mechanisms. *Int. J. Psychiatry Med.* 5:517–529.

Kirsner, J. B. 1971. Ulcerative colitis: mysterious, multiplex, and menacing. *J. Chronic Dis.* 23:681–684.

Knapp, P. H., A. A. Mathé, and L. Vachon. 1976. Psychosomatic aspects of bronchial asthma. In *Bronchial asthma, its nature and management,* ed. E. B. Weis and M. S. Segal. Boston: Little, Brown.

Knapp, P. H., and S. J. Nemetz. 1957. Sources of tension in bronchial asthma. *Psychosom. Med.* 19:466–485.

Knopf, O. 1935. Preliminary report on personality studies in 30 migraine patients. *J. Nerv. Ment. Dis.* 82:270, 400.

Korkes, L., and N. D. C. Lewis. 1955. An analysis of the relationship between psychological patterns and outcome in pulmonary tuberculosis. *J. Nerv. Ment. Dis.* 122:524–563.

Kowal, S. J. 1955. Emotions as a cause of disease. *Psychoanal. Rev.* 42:217–227.

Kracht, J. and V. 1952. Histopathology and therapy of the shock thyrotoxicosis in the wild rabbit. *Virchows Arch.* [*Pathol. Anat.*] 321:238–274.

Kuhn, T. S. 1962. *The structure of scientific revolutions,* Chicago: University of Chicago Press.

Kulka, A. N., R. D. Walter, and C. Fry. 1966. Mother-infant interaction as measured by simultaneous recording of physiological processes. *J. Am. Acad. Child Psychiatry* 5:496–503.

Lacey, J. I. and B. C. 1958. Verification and extension of the principle of autonomic response-stereotype. *Am. J. Psychol.* 71:50–73.

—— 1962. The law of initial value in the longitudinal study of autonomic constitution: reproducibility of autonomic responses and response patterns over a four-year interval. *Ann. N.Y. Acad. Sci.* 98:1257–90.

Lacey, J. I., R. Smith, and A. Green. 1955. Use of conditioned autonomic responses in the study of anxiety. *Psychosom. Med.* 17:208–217.

Lazarus, R. S. 1966. *Psychological stress and the coping process.* New York: McGraw-Hill.

LeMagnen, J. 1971. Advances in studies on the physiological control and regulation of food intake. *Prog. Physiol. Psychol.* 4:203–261.

Le Shan, L. 1964. Some observations on the problem of mobilizing the patient's will to live. In *Psychosomatic aspects of neoplastic disease,* ed. D. M. Kissen and L. L. Le Shan. Philadelphia: Lippincott.

Le Shan, L., and R. E. Worthington. 1956a. Loss of cathexis as a common psychodynamic characteristic of cancer patients. An attempt at statistical validation of a clinical hypothesis. *Psychol. Rep.* 2:183–193.

—— 1956b. Personality as a factor in the pathogenesis of cancer: a review. *Br. J. Med. Psychol.* 29:49–56.

Lewin, K. K. 1959. Role of depression in the production of illness in pernicious anemia. *Psychosom. Med.* 21:23–27.

Lidz, T. 1954. The thyroid. In *Recent developments in psychosomatic medicine,* ed. E. D. Wittkower and R. Cleghorn. Philadelphia: Lippincott.

Liebman, R., S. Minuchin, and L. Baker. 1974. The use of structural family therapy in the treatment of intractable asthma. *Am. J. Psychiatry* 131, no. 5:535–540.

Lindemann, E. 1944. Symptomatology and management of acute grief. *Am. J. Psychiatry* 101:141–148.

—— 1945. Psychiatric problems in conservative treatment of ulcerative colitis. *Arch. Neurol. Psychiatr.* 53:322–324.

Lipowski, Z. J. 1968. Review of consultation psychiatry and psychosomatic medicine. 3. Theoretical issues. *Psychosom. Med.* 30:395–422.

—— 1975. Psychiatry of somatic diseases: epidemiology, pathogenesis, classification. *Compr. Psychiatry* 16:105–124.

—— 1977. Psychosomatic medicine in the seventies: an overview. *Am. J. Psychiatry* 134, no. 3:233–244.

Lippman, C. W. 1954. Recurrent dreams in migraine: an aid to diagnosis. *J. Nerv. Ment. Dis.* 120:273–276.

Looney, J. G., M. R. Lipp, and R. L. Spitzer. 1977.

New classification of psychophysiologic disorders. In *Scientific proceedings of the 130th annual meeting of the American Psychiatric Association*. Washington, D.C.

Macalpine, I. 1953. Pruritus ani. *Psychosom. Med.* 15:499–508.

Macht, D. I. 1952. Influence of some drugs and of emotions on blood coagulation. *J.A.M.A.* 148: 265–270.

Mahl, G. F. 1953. Physiological changes during chronic fear. *Ann. N.Y. Acad. Sci.* 56:240–249.

Mahl, G. F., and E. B. Brody. 1954. Chronic anxiety symptomatology, experimental stress and HCl secretion. *Arch. Neurol. Psychiatr.* 71:314–325.

Mahl, G. F., and R. Karpe. 1953. Emotions and hydrochloric acid secretion during psychoanalytic hours. *Psychosom. Med.* 15:312–327.

Malmo, R. B. 1962. Activation. In *Experimental foundations of clinical psychology*, ed. A. J. Bachrach. New York: Basic Books.

Marbe, K. 1926. Praktische Psychologie der Ungälle und Bitriebschaden. Munich and Berlin: Oldenbourg.

Mason, A. A., and S. Black. 1958. Allergic skin responses abolished under treatment of asthma and hayfever by hypnosis. *Lancet* 1, no. 7026:877–880.

Mason, J. W. 1975. Emotion as reflected in patterns of endocrine integration. In *Emotions—their parameters and measurement*, ed. L. Levi. New York: Raven Press.

Mathé, A. A., and P. H. Knapp. 1971. Emotional and adrenal reactions to stress in bronchial asthma. *Psychosom. Med.* 33:323–340.

Mattila, M. J., and A. Muittari. 1968. Modification by imipramine of the bronchodilator responses to isoprenaline in asthmatic patients. *Ann. Med. Intern. Fenn.* 57:185–187.

McDermott, N. T., and S. Cobb. 1939. A psychiatric survey of 50 cases of bronchial asthma. *Psychosom. Med.* 1:203–244.

McDonald, R. L., M. D. Gynther, and A. C. Christakos. 1963. Relations between maternal anxiety and obstetric complications. *Psychosom. Med.* 25, no. 4:357–363.

McKenzie, J. N. 1886. The production of "rose asthma" by an artificial rose. *Am. J. Med. Sci.* 91:45–57.

McLaughlin, S. T., R. N. Zabarenko, P. B. Diana, and B. Quinn. 1950. Emotional reaction of rheumatoid arthritis to ACTH. *Psychosom. Med.* 15: 187–199.

Mead, M. 1947. The concept of culture and the psychosomatic approach. *Psychiatry* 10:57–76.

Meerloo, J. A. M. 1954. Psychological implications of malignant growth: a survey of hypotheses. *Br. J. Med. Psychol.* 27:210–215.

Merrill, B. R. 1953. Some psychosomatic aspects of pulmonary tuberculosis. *J. Nerv. Ment. Dis.* 117: 9–28.

Miles, H. H. W., S. Waldfogel, E. L. Barrabee, and S. Cobb. 1954. Psychosomatic study of 46 young men with coronary artery disease. *Psychosom. Med.* 16, no. 6:455–477.

Miller, F. R., and H. W. Jones. 1948. The possibility of precipitating the leukemic state by emotional factors. *Blood* 3:880–884.

Miller, H., and D. W. Baruch. 1948. Psychosomatic studies of children with allergic manifestations: I. Maternal rejection: a study of sixty-three cases. *Psychosom. Med.* 10:275–278.

Miller, N. E. 1975. Application of learning and biofeedback to psychiatry and medicine. In *Comprehensive textbook of psychiatry*, ed. A. M. Freedman, H. I. Kaplan, and B. J. Sadock. Vol. 1. 2nd ed. Baltimore: Williams & Wilkins.

Mirsky, I. A. 1958. Physiologic, psychologic, and social determinants in the etiology of peptic ulcer. *Am. J. Dig. Dis.* 3:285–313.

Moore, N. 1967. Behavior therapy in bronchial asthma—a controlled study. *J. Psychosom. Res.* 9:257–277.

Mordkoff, A., and D. Parsons. 1968. The coronary personality: a critique. *Int. J. Psychiatry* 5:413–426.

Murray, C. D. 1930. Psychogenic factors in the etiology of ulcerative colitis and bloody diarrhea. *Am. J. Med. Sci.* 180:239–248.

Nichols, D. C., and B. Tursky. 1967. Body image, anxiety and tolerance for experimental pain. *Psychosom. Med.* 29, no. 3:103–110.

Oken, D. 1960. An experimental study of suppressed anger and blood pressure. *Arch. Gen. Psychiatry* 2:441–456.

Orgel, S. Z. 1958. Effect of psychoanalysis on the course of peptic ulcer. *Psychosom. Med.* 20, no. 2:117–123.

Parkes, C. M., B. Benjamin, and R. G. Fitzgerald. 1969. Broken heart: a statistical study of increased mortality among widowers. *Br. Med. J.* 1:740–743.

Pavlov, I. P. 1927. *Conditioned reflexes*. London: Oxford University Press.

Plesset, M. R., and W. G. Shipman. 1963. Anxiety and depression in obese dieters. *Arch. Gen. Psychiatry* 8:530–535.

Purcell, K., L. Bernstein, and S. Bukantz. 1961. A preliminary comparison of rapidly remitting and persistently "steroid-dependent" asthmatic children. *Psychosom. Med.* 23:305–310.

Rahe, R. H. 1973. Subjects' recent life changes and

their near future illness reports. *Ann. Clin. Res.* 4:1–16.

—— 1975. Epidemiological studies of life change and illness. *Int. J. Psychiatry Med.* 6:133–146.

Rahe, R. H., J. L. Mahan, Jr., and R. J. Arthur. 1970. Prediction of near-future health change from subjects' preceding life changes. *J. Psychosom. Res.* 14:401–406.

Razran, G. 1961. The observable unconscious and the inferable conscious in current Soviet psychophysiology: interoceptive conditioning, somatic conditioning and the orienting reflex. *Psychol. Rev.* 68:81–147.

Rebner, I. 1957. "Role of personality as a factor in relapse." Ph.D. dissertation, University of Montreal.

Renneker, R., R. Cutler, J. Hora, D. Bacon, G. Bradley, J. Kearney, and M. Cutler. 1963. Psychoanalytic explorations of emotional correlates of cancer of the breast. *Psychosom. Med.* 25, no. 2:106–123.

Riley, V. 1975. Mouse mammary tumors: alteration of incidence as apparent function of stress. *Science* 189:465–467.

Romano, J., and G. L. Engel. 1945. Studies of syncope. III. The differentiation between vasodepressor syncope and hysterical fainting. *Psychosom. Med.* 7:3–15.

Romano, J., G. L. Engel, J. P. Wells, E. B. Ferris, H. W. Ryder, and M. A. Blankenhorn. 1943. Syncopal reactions during simulated exposure to high altitude in decompression chamber. *War. Med.* 4:475–489.

Rosenman, R. H., R. J. Brand, D. Jenkins, M. Friedman, R. Straus, and H. Wurm. 1975. Coronary heart disease in the western collaborative group study. *J.A.M.A.* 223, no. 8:872–877.

Rosenman, R. H., and M. Friedman. 1963. Behavior patterns, blood lipids, and coronary heart disease. *J.A.M.A.* 184:934–938.

Ruddick, B. 1963. Colds and respiratory introjection. *Int. J. Psychoanal.* 44:178–190.

Russell, B. 1921. *The analysis of mind.* London: Allen and Unwin.

Sargent, J. D., E. E. Green, and E. D. Walters. 1970. The use of autogenic feedback training in a pilot study of migraine and tension headaches. *Headache* 12:120–124.

Saul, L. J., and C. Bernstein. 1941. The emotional settings of some attacks of urticaria. *Psychosom. Med.* 3:349–369.

Sawrey, J. M. and W. L. 1966. Age, weight and social effects on ulceration rate in rats. *J. Comp. Physiol. Psychol.* 61:464–466.

Schilder, P. 1950. *The image and appearance of the human body.* New York: International Universities Press.

Schmale, A. H., Jr., and H. P. Iker. 1966. The affect of hopelessness and the development of cancer. I: Identification of uterine cervical cancer in women with atypical cytology. *Psychosom. Med.* 28: 714–721.

Schwartz, T. B., ed. 1965. *Year book of endocrinology 1964–65.* Chicago: Year Book.

Sechenov, I. M. 1863. *The reflexes of the brain.* Cambridge, Mass.: M.I.T. Press, 1965.

Selinsky, H. 1939. Psychological study of the migrainous syndrome. *Bull. N.Y. Acad. Med.* 15: 757–763.

Selye, H. 1946. The general adaptation syndrome and the diseases of adaptation. *J. Clin. Endocrinol. Metab.* 6:117–230.

—— 1950. *Physiology and pathology of exposure to stress.* Montreal: Acta Press.

Shapiro, D., B. Tursky, and G. E. Schwartz. 1970. Differentiation of heart rate and systolic blood pressure in man by operant conditioning. *Psychosom. Med.* 32:417–423.

Sheehan, D. V., J. Ballanger, and G. Jacobson. 1977. The treatment of endogenous anxiety with somatic, hysterical and phobic symptoms—a double blind placebo-controlled comparison of phenelzine and imipramine. Paper presented to the 6th International Congress of the World Psychiatric Association, September 1977, Honolulu.

Sherrington, C. 1906. *The integrative action of the nervous system.* New Haven: Yale University Press.

Simmel, E. 1932. The psychogenesis of organic disturbances and their psychoanalytic treatment. *Psychoanal. Q.* 1:166–170.

Slawson, P. F., W. R. Flynn, and E. J. Kollar. 1963. Psychological factors associated with the onset of diabetes mellitus. *J.A.M.A.* 185:166–170.

Smith, R. E. 1962a. An MMPI profile of allergy. *Psychosom. Med.* 24:203–209.

—— 1962b. An MMPI profile of allergy. II. Conscious conflict. *Psychosom. Med.* 24:543–553.

Sparer, J. 1956. Personality, stress, and tuberculosis. New York: International Universities Press.

Sperling, M. 1946. Psychoanalytic study of ulcerative colitis in children. *Psychoanal. Q.* 15:302–329.

—— 1963. A psychoanalytic study of bronchial asthma in children. In *The asthmatic child,* ed. H. I. Schneer. New York: Harper & Row.

Stein, M., and P. Ottenberg. 1958. The role of odors in asthma. *Psychosom. Med.* 20:60–65.

Stein, M., R. C. Schiavi, and M. Camerino. 1976. Influence of brain and behavior on the immune system. *Science* 191:435–440.

Stern, J. A., G. Winokur, A. Eisenstein, R. Taylor, and M. Sly. 1960. The effect of group vs. individual housing on behavior and physiological responses to stress in the albino rat. *J. Psychosom. Res.* 4:185–190.

Stone, R. A., and J. De Leo. 1976. Psychotherapeutic control of hypertension. *N. Engl. J. Med.* 294:80–84.

Stunkard, A. 1959. Obesity and the denial of hunger. *Psychosom. Med.* 21, no. 4:281–290.

——— 1972. New therapies for the eating disorders. *Arch. Gen. Psychiatry* 26, no. 5:391–399.

Sullivan, A. J., and C. A. Chandler. 1932. Ulcerative colitis of psychogenic origin. *Yale J. Biol. Med.* 4:779–796.

Taggart, P., M. Carruthers, and W. Somerville. 1973. Electrocardiogram, plasma catecholamines and lipids, and their modification by oxyprenolol when speaking before an audience. *Lancet* 2:341–346.

Taylor, B. W., E. M. Litin, and T. J. Litzow. 1966. Psychiatric considerations in cosmetic surgery. *Mayo Clin. Proc.* 41:608–623.

Thompson, C. 1943. "Penis envy" in women. *Psychiatry* 6:123–125.

Touraine, G. A., and G. Draper. 1934. The migrainous patient. *J. Nerv. Ment. Dis.* 80:1–23, 183–204.

Tupper, W. R. C. 1962. Psychosomatic aspects of spontaneous and habitual abortion. In *Psychosomatic obstetrics, gynecology, and endocrinology*, ed. W. S. Kroger. Springfield, Ill.: Thomas.

Vachon, L., and E. S. Rich, Jr. 1976. Visceral learning and asthma. *Psychosom. Med.* 38, no. 2:122–130.

Waddell, W. R. 1956. The physiologic significance of retained antral tissue after partial gastrectomy. *Ann. Surg.* 143:520–553.

Ward, H. W., and D. V. Sheehan. 1977. "Life change and achievement motivation correlates of JAS type A behavior pattern score in coronary heart disease patients."

Weinstock, H. I. 1961. Psychotherapy in severe ulcerative colitis: its ineffectiveness in preventing surgical measures and recurrences. *Arch. Gen. Psychiatry* 4:509–512.

Weiss, E. 1922. Psychoanalyse eines Falles von nervösem Asthma. *Int. Z. Psychoanal.*, 8:440–455.

Weiss, J. M. 1972. Influence of psychological variables on stress-induced pathology. In *Physiology, Emotion, and Psychosomatic Illness*, ed. R. Porter and J. Knight. Ciba Foundation Symposium 8. New York: Associated Scientific Publishers.

Weiss, T., and B. T. Engel. 1971. Operant conditioning of heart rate in patients with premature ventricular contractions. *Psychosom. Med.* 33:301–321.

White, B. V., and C. M. Jones. 1940. Mucous colitis. *Ann. Intern. Med.* 14:854–872.

Whybrow, P. C., and P. M. Silberfarb. 1974. Neuroendocrine mediating mechanisms: from the symbolic stimulus to the physiological response. *Int. J. Psychiatry Med.* 5:531–539.

Wittkower, E. D. 1953. Studies of the personalities of patients suffering from urticaria. *Psychosom. Med.* 15:116–126.

——— 1955. *A psychiatrist looks at tuberculosis.* 2nd ed. London: National Association for the Prevention of Tuberculosis.

——— 1974. Historical perspective of contemporary psychosomatic medicine. *Int. J. Psychiatry Med.* 5:309–319.

Wittkower, E. D., and P. G. Edgell. 1951. Eczema: a psychosomatic study. *Arch. Dermatol. Syphilol.* 63:207–219.

Wolf, S., and H. G. Wolff. 1947. *Human gastric function.* New York: Oxford University Press.

Wolff, H. G. 1937. Personality features and reactions of subjects with migraine. *Arch. Neurol. Psychiatr.* 34:895–921.

——— 1950. Life stress and bodily disease—a formulation. In *Life stress and bodily disease*, ed. H. G. Wolff and C. C. Itase. Baltimore: Williams & Wilkins.

Wolff, H. G., and C. C. Itase, eds. 1950. *Life stress and bodily disease.* Baltimore: Williams & Wilkins.

Recommended Reading

Alexander, F. G., and S. T. Selasnick. 1966. *The history of psychiatry.* New York: Harper & Row.

Bliss, E. L., and C. H. H. Branch. 1960. *Anorexia nervosa.* New York: Harper & Row, Hoeber.

Grinker, R. R. 1961. *Psychosomatic research.* New York: Norton.

Margolin, S. G. 1951. The behavior of the stomach during psychoanalysis: a contribution to the theory of verifying psychoanalytic data. *Psychoanal. Q.* 20:349–373.

Reiser, M. F., and H. Bakst. 1959. Psychology of cardiovascular disorders. In *American handbook of psychiatry*, ed. S. Arieti. Vol. 1. New York: Basic Books.

Rosenman, R. H., C. D. Jenkins, M. Friedman, and R. W. Bortner. 1968. Is there a coronary-prone personality? *Int. J. Psychiatry* 5:427–429.

Shapiro, A. P. 1960. Psychophysiological mechanisms in hypertensive vascular disease. *Ann. Intern. Med.* 53:64–83.

Skinner, B. F. 1953. *Science and human behavior.* New York: Macmillan.

Principles of Treatment and Management

The Psychotherapies: Individual, Family, and Group

CHAPTER 17

William W. Meissner
Armand M. Nicholi, Jr.

I N 1895, the Viennese physician Josef Breuer described an incident in his treatment of a young woman suffering from a number of severe physical and emotional symptoms.

It was in the summer during a period of extreme heat and the patient was suffering very badly from thirst; for, without being able to account for it in any way, she suddenly found it impossible to drink. She would take up the glass of water that she longed for, but, as soon as it touched her lips she would push it away like someone suffering from hydrophobia . . . This had lasted for some six weeks, when one day during hypnosis she grumbled about her English "lady-companion," whom she did not care for, and went on to describe with every sign of disgust how she had once gone into this lady's room and how her little dog—horrid creature!—had drunk out of a glass there. The patient had said nothing, as she had wanted to be polite. After giving further energetic expression to the anger she had held back, she asked for something to drink, drank a large quantity of water without any difficulty, and awoke from her hypnosis with the glass at her lips; and thereupon the disturbance vanished never to return. (Breuer and Freud, 1895, pp. 34–35)

From this first recorded observation of the actual, permanent removal of a hysterical symptom solely through verbal communication between patient and physician, Breuer went on to make the momentous discovery that both physical and psychological symptoms could effectively be removed when the patient, under hypnosis, verbalized thoughts and feelings related to them. His now famous patient Anna O. described his method of treatment as "the talking cure"; his observations set the stage for Freud's investigations leading to the discovery of psychoanalysis and the formulation of the technical and theoretical concepts underlying the major forms of psychotherapy practiced today.

Psychotherapy may be defined simply as "the treatment of mental and emotional disorders based primarily on verbal and nonverbal communication with the patient" (American Psychiatric Association, 1975, p. 130). This broad definition encompasses a wide variety of therapies that differ in intensity and duration—from hypnosis, Gestalt therapy, reality therapy, logotherapy, and transactional analysis to supportive therapy, brief psychotherapy, psychoanalysis, group therapy, marital therapy, and psychodrama.

Although many types of psychotherapy are practiced today, this chapter will discuss only the most widely used and most representative forms. Classical psychoanalysis and psychoanalytic psychotherapy, for example, are two closely related types of therapy that use psychoanalytic concepts and techniques to modify human behavior. Because of its extremely limited application, however, classical psychoanalysis will be discussed only to differentiate it from the more widely used psychoanalytic psychotherapy. This form of therapy is applicable to the whole continuum of emotional disorders, including the neuroses, the personality disorders, and the reconstituted psychoses (those in patients no longer overtly psychotic). Behavior therapy, another form of psychotherapy, will be discussed in a later chapter (see chapter 19, "Behavior Therapy and Behavioral Psychotherapy").

To evaluate and treat patients with emotional disorders, the clinician must be well grounded not only in the various forms of psychopathology but also in the major forms of psychotherapy. Only then can he direct the patient to that form of therapy most effective in treating his disorder. Psychotherapy is a serious undertaking with enormous potential for harm as well as for healing. It must therefore be practiced only by a professional with some understanding of the limits of his training and experience. An inexperienced therapist ought always to conduct therapy under the supervision of an experienced clinician.

Principles of Psychotherapy

This section focuses on the principles and parameters of several forms of psychotherapy. Disregarding the specific techniques of therapy—techniques mastered best through closely supervised work with individual patients—we will consider those dimensions of the therapeutic process common to all forms of psychotherapy: (1) the relationship between diagnosis and the most suitable form of therapy; (2) the therapeutic relationship; (3) regression; (4) resistance; (5) therapeutic objectives; and (6) the ethical issues embedded in the therapeutic experience.

Relationship to Diagnosis

Diagnosis plays an important role in all aspects of the therapeutic process. The therapist's diagnostic impression guides him not only in determining the most suitable form of treatment during the initial evaluation but also in the spe-

cific, delicate, moment-to-moment interactions with a patient throughout the course of therapy. Last but not least, diagnosis helps both therapist and patient decide when therapy must end. That decision requires a diagnostic evaluation of the extent to which therapeutic goals have been achieved and the degree to which changes in the patient represent an enduring achievement that will not undergo dissolution after treatment stops.

Because no one form of therapy is appropriate for all patients, the therapist must make important diagnostic distinctions in deciding on the most effective form of treatment. Though his decision may leave room for discussion and difference of opinion, this basic principle holds: any scientific approach to the treatment of emotional disorders must be based on detailed knowledge of the efficacy of specific forms of therapy for specific forms of psychopathology.

The therapist must decide which patients are capable of sustaining and profiting from particular forms of therapy. In addition, psychotherapy, even given the broad range of its forms and modalities, is inappropriate for some patients. Such patients may be treated by a variety of somatic therapies and management techniques. Ideally, the majority of these patients can be brought to a point at which psychotherapy becomes useful and appropriate.

Although the therapist begins to develop his diagnostic impression during the initial evaluation of the patient, he continues to refine and modify this impression as long as therapy continues. The accuracy and sensitivity of the therapist's diagnosis contributes in some measure to his therapeutic effectiveness. In establishing his diagnosis the clinician avoids simply attaching a diagnostic label to the patient by dropping him into the appropriate category from the American Psychiatric Association's *Diagnostic and Statistical Manual of Mental Disorders* (DSM-II). Not only do few patients fit these categories, but this limited and crude but all too popular method of assessing illness contributes little of practical therapeutic value. Diagnosis, in a more pertinent and refined sense and in the hands of a skilled clinician, empathically captures the patient's inner world and results in increased understanding of the patient's conflicts, anxieties, affectations, strengths, and aspirations. Throughout the therapeutic process, therefore, the therapist refines his diagnosis by observing and assessing the patient's accessibility, his level of anxiety or depression, his defenses, and his readiness for therapeutic intervention.

The skilled clinician recognizes that during the course of therapy the patient's inner world undergoes constant modification. Recognizing and evaluating these changes helps the therapist determine the dosage and timing of his therapeutic intervention. Because these factors are always critical, the therapist's capacity to evaluate the patient's state of mind accurately is largely responsible for his effectiveness. He must therefore be able to evaluate the quality, nature, and intensity of the patient-therapist relationship. This capacity, though important in all phases of therapy, is particularly significant during the final stages, when therapeutic goals must be evaluated and the all-important mutual decision made to terminate. Thus the diagnostic process contributes to all stages of therapy, from the initial evaluation, through the sometimes long and tedious phase of alleviating symptoms and resolving conflicts, to the decision to bring therapy to a close.

The Therapeutic Relationship

Psychotherapy adheres to the medical model both in its emphasis on diagnosis and in the significant position it gives to the relationship between therapist and patient. It differs from the general medical approach, however, in that the therapist-patient relationship becomes the primary factor in the treatment. The quality and nature of the relationship can enhance or severely impair effective therapeutic intervention. Thus the skilled therapist makes specific interventions only in terms of his evaluation of the overall dynamics of his relationship with his patient. Two significant aspects of the therapeutic relationship are the therapeutic alliance and the transference. Although these processes are at work in all psychotherapy, they are particularly important in individual forms of therapy.

The therapeutic alliance. The therapeutic alliance (see chapter 1, "The Therapist-Patient Relationship") involves primarily the conscious (or preconscious), rational, and nonneurotic aspects of the relationship between patient and therapist. It is based on their explicit or implicit agreement to work together toward a mutually desired objective, the improvement and maturation of the patient.

As the therapist attempts to form an alliance with the more responsible and mature aspects of the patient's ego, a therapeutic split occurs on both sides of this alliance. In the patient, a split occurs between the observing part of his ego and those parts of his ego caught up in neurotic conflict. In the therapist, a split occurs between ego functions involved in the therapeutic process and those caught up in his own neurotic conflicts, which may cause the therapist to respond with enormous anxiety to unconscious impulses within the patient. Thus an effective alliance occurs ideally between the more responsible aspects of the egos of both the therapist and the patient.

The therapeutic alliance makes it possible for the therapist to make specific interventions even when they arouse considerable anxiety in the patient. It also sustains the patient's capacity to accept and to integrate these interventions. (An intervention is an action by the therapist—such as confrontation or clarification, both discussed in a later section—that tends to increase a patient's self-awareness or to influence his behavior.) In addition, the therapeutic alliance provides a stable basis allowing both parties to experience, observe, and overcome barriers to the therapeutic process that may arise in either patient or therapist. For example, the therapeutic alliance helps the process of therapy weather the patient's negative, hostile, or distrustful feelings, especially when such feelings stem from the negative transference. The same holds true for distortions and disturbances arising within the therapist, especially those stemming from unresolved unconscious conflicts (see chapter 1, "The Therapist-Patient Relationship"). The therapeutic alliance therefore helps keep the therapeutic relationship intact and helps resolve stresses, distortions, and forces that would otherwise destroy it.

To decide on the method of therapy most appropriate for a given patient, the therapist must closely observe and carefully assess the patient's capacity to establish a therapeutic alliance. If the patient has generally been able to form healthy, trusting, mutually satisfying relationships, he probably has the capacity to establish an effective alliance. Conversely, a patient with a limited ability to establish trusting relationships may have a limited capacity to form an effective therapeutic alliance. This limited capacity may reflect an impairment in early one-to-one relationships, particularly at the level of trust-generating and autonomous interaction with the mother. The firmness or solidity of the therapeutic alliance determines in large measure the patient's tolerance for therapeutic regression and for the relative passivity of the therapist. In severely disturbed patients with minimal capacity for alliance, the therapist must pay particular attention to the vicissitudes of the alliance and constantly support and reinforce it. The skilled therapist will therefore tend to use supportive therapy with these patients because they usually tolerate the induced regression of more insight-oriented approaches poorly.

Transference. The second aspect of the therapeutic relationship is the transference, the process of experiencing, toward a person in the present, patterns of feeling and behavior that originated in the past (see chapter 1, "The Therapist-Patient Relationship"). This unconscious process results in a repetition of attitudes, fantasies, and affects originally experienced in early relationships—primarily with parents but also with other family members such as siblings or grandparents or extrafamilial figures such as teachers or doctors. Transference occurs in all human relationships, more intensely in proportion to their duration and emotional significance. Because therapy often extends over a long period of time and because it deals with strong emotions, the therapeutic relationship provides a natural matrix for the development of transference feelings.

Transference feelings may appear at any time during the therapeutic process; they become more intense and create more resistance as therapy progresses. The patient experiences transference feelings in proportion to the degree of regression he undergoes. Because transference occurs unconsciously and because transference feelings have such a peculiar vitality and forcefulness, the patient often mistakes them for real love or anger. As regression continues, the trans-

ference feelings may increase in intensity to the point where they interfere with therapeutic progress. The patient may experience strong erotic feelings toward the therapist, which may interfere with effective therapy. Or he may experience intensely hostile feelings toward the therapist and prematurely break off therapy.

Transference feelings may be so intensely focused on the therapist that they give rise to a *transference neurosis*, a condition in which early neurotic feelings and reactions make up the bulk of the patient's feelings toward the therapist; in this state, the original childhood conflicts between instinctual drives and the defenses against them are reactivated. The transference neurosis provides a powerful therapeutic tool, since the therapist can help the patient to observe his transference feelings and neurotic conflicts as they manifest themselves in the therapist-patient relationship. The intensity and unique vividness of these feelings make them useful for demonstration and interpretation. The transference neurosis, however, also provides the most powerful resistance to the therapeutic process because it involves long-standing, unresolved conflicts and feelings that are more intense and more highly charged emotionally than those usually involved in transference.

Transference feelings, particularly the transference neurosis, provide powerful resistance insofar as the patient seeks to keep the therapeutic interaction solely on a transference basis rather than on the basis of effective analysis leading to change. The resistance arises primarily from the patient's wish to use the transference as a source of gratification, as when a female patient prefers to regard transferred sexual and loving feelings toward a male therapist as real and clings to them rather than face the painful work of understanding and working through that is required by the therapeutic process.

The therapist must be aware of another important aspect of the therapeutic relationship, namely, his own feelings of countertransference. *Countertransference* (see chapter 1, "The Therapist-Patient Relationship") is the displacement onto the patient of attitudes and feelings derived from the therapist's earlier life experiences; these intense, often inappropriate feelings may arise from unresolved, unconscious conflicts in the therapist and may cloud his understanding and responsiveness. On the other hand, he may, if aware of these countertransference feelings, use them for valuable clues to the latent meaning of the patient's behavior, thoughts, or feelings. In this way, the therapist may use his own unconscious as an instrument in establishing contact with the patient's unconscious.

Although transference feelings occur in all forms of psychotherapy, the skilled therapist handles transference phenomena according to the patient's diagnosis and the particular form of therapy used. With some patients the therapist will foster the development and expression of transference feelings, while with others he will minimize or avoid them. In general, the therapist will foster the development and expression of transference feelings when he feels that this will not disturb the patient's capacity to distinguish reality from fantasy (the reality of the therapeutic relationship from the fantasy relationship implied in the transference), when he feels sure of a strong enough therapeutic alliance against which to test out the transference elements, and, finally, when he has sufficient time to help the patient work through and resolve the transference involvement. These conditions are optimally present in the psychoanalytic situation. They may also be found to lesser degrees in other, briefer or more superficial forms of therapy. Many patients are either not capable of forming a transference neurosis or have difficulty in maintaining a therapeutic alliance. Forms of therapy that do not rely on the mobilization and working through of transference may therefore be more appropriate for these patients.

If the therapist chooses to focus on transference feelings, he realizes that only a firm therapeutic alliance enables the patient to gain enough distance from his transference feelings to identify them, recognize their source, and integrate the therapist's interpretation of them. Through these interpretations, the patient gradually recognizes the distinction between transference feelings and real feelings toward the therapist. He recognizes that transference feelings come from an earlier time in his life, realizes that they are inappropriate to his present life situation, and begins to see the therapist in a less distorted form.

In determining the most appropriate form of therapy for a given patient, the therapist must assess the patient's capacity to tolerate transference feelings while maintaining an effective therapeutic alliance. By working through these transference feelings, the patient will work through and resolve his underlying neurotic conflicts. In terms of diagnosis, patients with neuroses, neurotic characters, and some narcissistic characters may be capable of this form of intense therapeutic work. It is less likely that patients with more primitive forms of personality organization—the forms of borderline and psychotic pathology in which ego defects are prominent and ego strengths are impaired—would benefit from this sort of transference-based treatment. For such patients, therapy can be modified and directed more toward maintaining a consistent alliance and dealing with the ongoing, present-day context of the patient's experience.

Regression

Another prominent feature of psychotherapy is regression, the tendency of a patient to return to earlier, more childish or infantile patterns of thinking, feeling, and functioning. This phenomenon may be observed outside the treatment situation in the series of progressions and regressions of normal child development. A child may revert to bed-wetting or lose bowel control when hospitalized or under stress. Regression may also be observed in adults during play, during certain kinds of creative activity, or during physical illness that causes a person to become clinging and excessively demanding. Regression may be constructive and therapeutic or obstructive and pathological. Therapeutic regression emerges as part of the therapeutic process and provides the therapist with a vehicle for demonstrating important data from the patient's past in an unusually clear and convincing way.

Pathological regression, on the other hand, has a destructive influence on therapy and results when the regression appears too rapidly or is too intense or too prolonged. This kind of regression overwhelms the patient and interferes with his ability to understand and meaningfully to integrate insights gained from observing regression patterns. Because it interferes with his capacity for self-observation, pathological regression makes it difficult for the patient to work effectively with the therapist. Pathological regression may be seen in neurotic patients who are overwhelmed with anxiety and express the fear that they are becoming too dependent and losing all control over their thoughts and feelings. Extreme forms of pathological regression may be seen in psychotic patients who use primary process thinking and who become incontinent or play with feces.

The therapist may encourage or facilitate regression in patients undergoing psychoanalytically oriented psychotherapy or psychoanalysis by using an office setting that offers minimum sensory stimulation, by assuming the passive role, by encouraging the patient to focus entirely on himself, by instructing the patient to express all thoughts, fantasies, and feelings regardless of how foolish or childish they sound, and by various other techniques common to the more intensive forms of individual psychotherapy. As regressive phenomena emerge, the patient may develop a childlike dependence on the therapist, demand to be held or taken care of, speak in a whiny, childlike tone, or experience temporary changes in body image. He may say that he feels like a small child and as he leaves the office express surprise that he is as tall as the therapist. How the patient reacts and relates to the therapist during this phase of therapy provides important data from early life experiences for understanding and reworking conflicts.

As a critical part of his diagnostic task, the therapist must assess the patient's capacity to tolerate therapeutic regression and determine to what degree this regression can be induced. The quality of the therapeutic alliance and the patient's inner resources determine in large measure his capacity to tolerate regression and to meaningfully integrate the data such regression provides. When regression is already a significant part of the patient's pathological picture, further regression is undesirable and the therapist must minimize it. If regression threatens a patient's ability to discriminate between fantasy and reality, or if it generates overwhelming anxieties, the regression will be unproductive and possibly harmful. Therapeutic regression is more likely to be fruitful if it rests within the limits of

the patient's capacity to maintain ego functioning and a working therapeutic alliance. A carefully induced therapeutic regression fosters the emergence of transference feelings and the development of transference neurosis. (This in turn confronts the therapist with perhaps the most powerful source of resistance—indicating that even therapeutic regression has both positive and negative features.)

The degree to which regression can be safely induced is always a difficult question for the therapist. Even in neurotic patients with substantial ego strength, the therapist may find it necessary to induce deep regression, to the level of early primary relationships. Some clinicians also believe that deep regressions may be attempted in borderline or psychotic patients if carried out in fairly intensive therapy extending over many months or years. Even in these patients, however, such regressions rarely prove effective without the prior attainment of some degree of significant therapeutic alliance. The question of whether the regressive aspects of therapy should be maximized or minimized and to what degree depends on diagnostic criteria and continues to generate discussion and controversy among therapists.

Resistance

Resistance comprises all those elements and forces within the patient, both conscious and unconscious, that oppose the treatment process. The therapist encounters resistance in all forms of therapy, but particularly in individual psychotherapies. Despite the patient's wish for treatment, he possesses internal forces that oppose therapeutic progress. The therapeutic process tends to shift the patient's inner psychic equilibrium and to create anxiety in him. Through resistance, he mobilizes his defensive resources to diminish anxiety and maintain internal equilibrium. Because the therapist provokes this disequilibrium, the patient unconsciously blames the therapist and the therapy for the anxiety he suffers. Consequently his mobilized defenses act to resist or oppose the therapeutic process.

In all forms of individual psychotherapy the therapist must make a critical decision: should he leave the patient's resistances intact or attempt to reduce them? If he attempts to reduce these resistances by bringing them into awareness in certain patients, his efforts may arouse extreme anxiety and induce excessive regression. When this happens, he must change direction, at least temporarily, and leave the patient's defensive organization intact. In better integrated and better functioning patients, where his efforts do not have these untoward effects, the therapist must undermine resistance in order to promote therapeutic regression, unmask deeper material, and help the patient attain additional insight. In considering the patient's resistances, therefore, the therapist must be sensitive to the patient's capacity for dealing with and resolving the resistance without being overwhelmed. The therapist's respect for the patient's defenses and resistances is especially important in the initial phase of therapy, particularly in establishing a secure therapeutic alliance. If the patient observes this sensitive respect from the therapist, he may be more willing to form an alliance. If the patient's resistance precludes the formation of an alliance, however, the therapist may have no choice but to deal with the resistance at the outset by confrontation or interpretation (discussed in a later section). When to support the patient's defenses and when to confront and attempt to resolve them are questions that challenge the diagnostic skills and empathic sensitivity of every therapist.

The working through of the patient's resistances not only increases the availability of unconscious content but also fosters therapeutic regression. As the potential for regression increases, resistance increases correspondingly. Therapeutic regression stirs up considerable anxiety against which the patient must defend himself. In relatively intense and long-term psychotherapy, the increasing regression facilitates transference and its correlative transference resistances. Transference resistance occurs when the patient displaces feelings from figures of the past onto the therapist and obstructs therapeutic progress by undermining the therapeutic alliance and interfering with effective therapeutic intervention.

The therapeutic alliance may be undermined by positive or negative transference resistance. As discussed in chapter 1, "The Therapist-Patient Relationship," positive transference resistance may create in the patient such a desire to please the therapist that he refuses to expose his conflicts, and negative transference resistance may cause the therapist to appear hostile and persecuting, so that the patient no longer sees his interventions as helpful. Transference resistance is the most powerful form of unconscious resistance. The working through and resolution of such resistance are essential for permanent therapeutic benefit to the patient and often form the central issues to be worked through in intensive psychoanalytically oriented psychotherapy.

Therapeutic Objectives

Progress in therapy is difficult to assess if either therapist or patient does not have clearly in mind the goals they hope to achieve. Therapeutic objectives are therefore an important factor in the therapeutic interaction. They must be correlated with the diagnosis and motivation of the patient, the motivation of the therapist, and other practical considerations. Therapeutic objectives must be arrived at by mutual agreement between patient and therapist, never by a unilateral decision.

Therapeutic objectives may range from narrowly focused and short-term goals, such as symptom relief or crisis resolution, to long-term objectives such as profound characterological change and resolution of the patient's basic conflicts—or, more realistically, a reduction in the intensity of these conflicts. In some cases, the goal may be merely to provide a supportive relationship, to sustain the patient during a particular crisis or period of stress. Supportive efforts may be limited in time or may extend over a long period, particularly with patients whose capacity for therapeutic work and for adequate functioning without a sustaining therapeutic relationship is limited. Certain fragile personalities function relatively well when provided with a supportive substitute ego in the therapist.

Goals set at the beginning of therapy may of course be modified or replaced by new ones as therapy progresses. Patients, for example, often come into treatment because of an acute crisis or an exacerbation of symptoms that they resolve after a short period of therapy. During the therapeutic work, however, they uncover a deeper personality dysfunction or conflict, which they decide must also be resolved. This decision leads therapist and patient to reassess and refocus the therapeutic objectives to longer-term and more extensive personality change. In regard to therapeutic goals, Winnicott (1965) distinguishes management from treatment. In the management of patients, he suggests that the goal is to do as little as possible in dealing with the patient's difficulties; in treatment, however, he suggests that the goal is to accomplish as much as possible for and with the patient. Management involves a limited, short-term objective, while treatment involves a more extensive long-term goal.

When setting therapeutic objectives with the patient, the therapist must consider a number of determinants. First, the patient's diagnosis limits the kind and extent of therapy prescribed. Since diagnosis is an ongoing process, the therapeutic objectives are similarly open and modifiable. Second, the patient's motivation must be considered. For many patients the achievement of symptomatic relief or the resolution of an immediate crisis is the sole objective. The therapist's zeal must therefore be tempered by an awareness of the patient's motivation and therapeutic needs.

In setting therapeutic goals, the therapist must also consider his own motivation. Unless he is interested in treating a particular patient, his lack of motivation can undermine the effectiveness of treatment. Other considerations include financial resources (the patient may not be able to afford extensive or intensive treatment with a private therapist but may qualify for such treatment at a community psychiatric clinic with scaled fees) as well as available therapy time and the limits of the therapist's skills. The effect of the patient's financial circumstances on therapeutic objectives is becoming an increasingly important problem with the increase in prepaid treatment plans and forms of third-party payment.

In summary, the therapeutic objectives must be established early in therapy by mutual agreement between patient and therapist and must be reviewed and modified throughout the course of therapy. In this way, the therapist and patient can decide which old goals are no longer feasible, choose new goals on the basis of what has been uncovered during the therapeutic process, assess overall therapeutic progress, and establish the best time to terminate.

Ethical Issues

The basic issues of confidentiality and responsibility pervade the whole realm of psychotherapy and are particularly important in individual psychotherapy. Confidentiality is an essential part of the therapeutic contract and of an effective therapeutic alliance. Consequently, the therapist must resist intrusions into the privacy of the therapeutic relationship from a variety of sources, including family members, institutions, civil authorities, and—quite pressingly and increasingly —third-party insurance carriers. In the limited space of this chapter, we make no attempt to resolve all the complex issues of confidentiality but simply indicate that it is an area of significant conflicting interests and that infringement of confidentiality unavoidably undermines the therapeutic alliance.

The second important ethical issue is responsibility, specifically the therapist's responsibility to the patient, spelled out in the therapeutic contract, an informal verbal agreement to work together within the confines of the therapist-patient relationship toward the therapeutic goals, and enacted in the therapeutic alliance. In all psychotherapy, the therapist's ultimate commitment to the welfare of his patient governs and directs his therapeutic interventions toward what he understands to be ultimately in the patient's best interests. This principle implies that the therapist always uses his best therapeutic skills to promote and accomplish for his patient the most effective course of treatment.

The patient's participation in the therapeutic alliance also involves a specific responsibility. He is obliged to participate productively, work cooperatively with the therapist, come to appointments on time, and involve himself in the therapeutic work. Failure to accept these responsibilities breaches the therapeutic contract and impedes therapeutic progress.

In summary, these ethical dimensions of the therapeutic relationship cannot be compromised without undermining the therapeutic alliance and thereby the effectiveness of therapy.

Individual Psychotherapies

Psychoanalytic Psychotherapy

Psychoanalytic psychotherapy, a form of individual psychotherapy, derives its theory from the psychoanalytic model. Psychoanalytic psychotherapy must therefore be adequately distinguished from other forms of individual psychotherapy such as classical psychoanalysis, on the one hand, and more limited and supportive psychotherapy, on the other.

In general, psychoanalysis strives for the most intense and all-encompassing resolution of the patient's conflicts and revision of his personality structure. Psychoanalytic psychotherapy, on the other hand, aims at symptom resolution and the adaptive functioning of the patient; it undertakes less profound structural and personality modifications. Psychoanalytic psychotherapy is usually carried on face to face, rather than with the use of the psychoanalytic couch. (There exists today, however, a tendency to use the couch less even in psychoanalysis.) In psychoanalytic psychotherapy, the therapist is more active, allowing a smaller time lapse prior to his interventions. The analyst, on the other hand, employs indefinite delay to foster the maximum tolerable regression and the emergence of unconscious conflict. While analysis focuses primarily on the relationship between analyst and patient, psychoanalytic psychotherapy focuses primarily on the patient's life situation and secondarily on the therapeutic relationship. Consequently, the relationship between therapist and patient in psychoanalytic psychotherapy has more definite boundaries and is usually less intense than in the analytic situation.

Psychoanalytic psychotherapy, an insight-oriented therapy, must be distinguished from more supportive psychotherapies, therapies more concerned with bolstering ego defenses and minimizing regression and anxiety. Supportive psychotherapy will be discussed later in this chapter.

Indications. Criteria for patients optimally suited for psychoanalytic psychotherapy parallel those for psychoanalysis itself. Some clinicians believe that patients who adequately meet these criteria would benefit maximally from classical psycho-analysis, but others disagree. Consequently, the question of whether psychoanalytic psychotherapy or psychoanalysis is more suitable for a given patient is not only a difficult matter of clinical judgment but also often open to discussion.

The criteria of analyzability include (1) the capacity for a therapeutic alliance—that is, a reasonably well-integrated ego and some ability to relate effectively, (2) sufficient resourcefulness for effective therapeutic work, (3) the capacity to sustain therapeutic regression and to master the resulting anxiety, (4) the capacity to form a transference neurosis, and, finally, (5) the capacity to maintain the distinction between fantasy and reality. Patients can be effectively treated in psychoanalytic psychotherapy if they demonstrate some degree of these characteristics; consequently, this form of psychotherapy can play an effective role in treating the whole range of psychopathology.

Certain distinctions must be made in the application of psychoanalytic psychotherapy. The patients best suited to this method are those suffering from neurotic conflicts and symptom complexes, from reactive conditions (particularly depression), and from the whole realm of non-psychotic character disorders. It is also the treatment of choice for patients with borderline personalities, though the management of these patients' regressive episodes may require a blending of supportive therapeutic techniques with those of insight-oriented psychotherapy. Although these cases require occasional modification of therapeutic technique, the basic objectives of the analytically oriented approach remain in force.

This form of psychotherapy has little or no place in the management of acute psychotic regression, but it certainly has a place in the treatment of more compensated psychotic patients who have the capacity for long-term intensive treatment. Once again, the analytic approach must be significantly modified to include more supportive elements, especially during severe and repeated regressive episodes. These modifications will be discussed in the section on supportive psychotherapy.

Techniques. The techniques of psychoanalytic psychotherapy are derived from the model of psychoanalysis. The primary technique, *free association*, requires the patient to express his thoughts freely, to say all that comes to mind without selectiveness or modification and without concern about whether the thoughts are relevant or appropriate. Free association necessitates a considerable degree of passivity on the part of the therapist and encourages a significant degree of regression in the patient. The more active the therapist, the more he deters the patient's efforts to associate.

Free association requires a peculiar split in the patient's ego functioning. Part of the patient's mind drifts to allow unconscious thoughts to rise to consciousness, while another part collaborates with the therapist in the evaluation and assessment of these thoughts. The capacity to drift into regression and to work within the therapeutic alliance, required by free association, varies considerably among patients. With patients who cannot sustain regression without undue anxiety, the therapist must assume a more active therapeutic stance.

Among the major therapeutic techniques, the therapist's capacity to listen meaningfully and constructively is indispensable (see chapter 1, "The Therapist-Patient Relationship"). Observation of the patient's behavior and attention to what he means, as well as to what he says, provides the foundation for therapeutic understanding. In insight-oriented therapy, the therapist listens not only to the patient's manifest content but also to the latent unconscious meanings underlying the manifest content. Furthermore, the empathic listening attitude of the therapist fosters therapeutic regression and thus aids in the emergence of transference.

Another important element in the psychotherapeutic approach is the therapist's attention to alliance building. The importance of the therapeutic alliance to the success of psychotherapy has already been discussed. A good therapeutic alliance depends on the establishment and continual reinforcement of a therapeutic contract with the patient, the appropriate degree of activity on the part of the therapist, and, finally, the therapist's ability to convey to the patient empathic understanding of what the patient is feeling and experiencing.

If the therapeutic contract is broken, if the therapist fails to convey empathy, or if the therapist is excessively passive at certain critical stages of the therapy, the therapeutic alliance may become unraveled and therapy disrupted. In working with unstable personalities, the therapist may have to adopt a supportive stance in order to stabilize the patient's ego resources and minimize the regression and the intensity of anxiety. Though regressive episodes may help stabilize the alliance, particularly with borderline patients, they run the obvious risk of increasing the patient's dependence. However, the therapist must frequently allow this dependence to develop in such patients as a side effect of facilitating the alliance. Such dependence may never be totally resolved but may become a focus of later therapeutic concern.

Questions are a significant part of the therapist's technique; they may be used to acquire information or to focus the patient's attention on a specific issue. Appropriate, sensitive, tactful questions facilitate the patient's understanding and insight, underline the mutual concern with the patient's problem, and support and reinforce the therapeutic alliance. Inappropriate, insensitive, and excessively challenging questions increase the patient's anxiety, arouse a sense of frustration and inadequacy in him, and consequently undermine the therapeutic alliance.

The skilled therapist develops techniques of questioning that reflect sensitivity to what the patient feels and facilitate the patient's efforts at free association. For example, a patient may describe a pattern of behavior, conclude, "I don't know why I do that," and then become silent. Or, because the patient's conflicts are in large measure unconscious, he may reply to questions he or the therapist raises by saying, "I don't know." The skilled therapist will avoid meeting silence with silence here and will not usually attempt to provide a possible answer for the patient. More often he will encourage the patient to explore the issue by free association and thus help the patient discover answers for himself.

The therapist's sensitivity to the patient's specific needs determines how a question is asked. "How long have you had difficulty responding sexually?" may be considerably easier for some patients to deal with than "How long have you been frigid?" "What led to your changing jobs this time?" may sound less judgmental to a highly sensitive patient than "Why did you get fired again?" Asking questions in terms of "what" and "how" will usually yield more information than questions about "why." These subtle differences in the way a therapist couches his questions help make the difference between a refined approach and an unskilled one.

The therapist may also seek *clarification* of ambiguities by asking questions. Or he may repeat something the patient has said or done as a way of prompting further consideration or associations. Clarifications may thus serve as a mild form of confrontation or even interpretation and may bring the particular issues with which the patient struggles into sharp focus.

In *confrontation*, the therapist directs the patient's attention to a behavior or issue of which both are aware and which the patient has been avoiding. Confrontations usually occur more frequently in psychotherapy than in classical psychoanalysis. They generally relate to the patient's conscious thought or real situations. When carried out from the perspective of a solid therapeutic alliance, confrontations help the patient stand aside and observe his own thoughts and actions.

Confrontations may help the therapist deal with setting limits to the patient's tendency to act out, with the patient's resistances, with crises arising within or outside of therapy, or with disruptions of the therapeutic alliance. (The therapist must be particularly attentive to his own countertransference distortion or difficulties.) Confrontation may therefore help the therapist with therapeutic stalemates, misuse of treatment, attempts to manipulate, attempts to seduce or attack the therapist, serious misconceptions about treatment, and persistent defenses and resistances that threaten to subvert the therapeutic process.

Perhaps the most important therapeutic tool is the therapist's use of *interpretation*. Interpretations are verbal interventions that help the patient become aware of previously repressed material in a meaningful and affectively significant way. The interpretation brings into conscious awareness and intellectually illuminates an area of conflict that has previously been repressed. Interpretation is therefore the pri-

mary tool of insight-oriented psychotherapy. Interpretations may be either dynamic or genetic. Dynamic interpretations focus on the current operation of psychic forces and motivations, while genetic interpretations focus on connections between past and present emotional reactions and experiences.

The therapist often uses interpretation to combat the patient's resistance, to make the patient aware of his efforts to block the work of treatment. Through interpretation, the therapist brings into focus the unconscious meanings and genetic roots of resistance. Resistances are overdetermined, in that they rest on multiple unconscious fantasies; only by bringing these fantasies into consciousness and specifically dealing with them can the therapist help the patient overcome the resistance. Frequently the fantasies underlying specific resistances merge with those underlying the neurotic symptoms, so that the therapist's attempt to resolve defenses also provides him with insight into the unconscious roots of the patient's illness.

Thus the therapist's interpretation of resistance, the uncovering of unconscious motivations and their genetic origins, is an essential part of the therapeutic process. Interpretations that fail to touch on the specific life experiences and concrete fantasies of the patient tend to be ineffective and diffuse. A common error in psychoanalytic psychotherapy is moving too quickly to the interpretation of unconscious content. The therapist must first prepare the way by helping the patient to deal with and overcome his defenses. Otherwise the therapist's interpretation may precipitate excessive anxiety or regression and thus undermine the treatment process.

The therapist also uses interpretation to deal with transference. The patient's real feelings toward the therapist must be distinguished from transference feelings, those displaced from earlier relationships. While the patient's real feelings may form an important area for discussion, clarification, and resolution in therapy, transference feelings serve as the primary focus for interpretation. Where the transference elements emerge with sufficient clarity and force, they provide significant insight into basic conflicts and their origins. But insights derived from transference must always be integrated with the patient's current real-life difficulties and their resolution.

One of the most difficult tasks confronting the therapist is determining the right time to make an interpretation. His ability to sense the right moment to make a specific interpretation and to make that interpretation with appropriate intensity and depth requires a combination of training, intuition, and experience. This ability in large measure determines his effectiveness in conducting insight-oriented therapy, and the skilled therapist seeks to refine this ability throughout his professional life.

The most appropriate time to make an interpretation is when the patient has brought sufficient unconscious material into awareness and accomplished sufficient work with the therapist to be on the verge of arriving at the interpretation himself. At this point, a simple question from the therapist will suffice to help the patient make his own interpretation. A properly timed interpretation will often strike the patient with enormous emotional impact and clarity—he will suddenly see and understand an aspect of his life or a specific pattern of behavior that has puzzled him for years. Such therapeutic experiences are among the most gratifying for both patient and therapist. When an interpretation has the proper timing and depth, the patient will not only be able to accept it enthusiastically but will be able to confirm and integrate it with past and current experiences both within and outside of therapy.

Premature interpretations heighten the patient's resistance and in one way or another impair the unfolding of further unconscious material. Erroneous interpretations, which no therapist can entirely avoid, may not necessarily impede therapy. If, however, they reflect the therapist's countertransference feelings, they may intensify the patient's resistance and undermine the therapeutic alliance. Incomplete or inexact interpretations may be less damaging if stated in a conjectural tone or as tentative hypotheses offered for the patient's consideration. In this way they may serve as a first step toward a more complete interpretation. The therapist may state, for example, "I wonder if there is any relationship between your inability to tolerate your roommate and the long-standing conflicts you described with your brother?"

The therapist must guard against superficial and general interpretations that fail to reach an adequate and therapeutically appropriate depth. He must also avoid interpretations that explore unconscious material before the patient is prepared to deal with it. Such inappropriate probing often reflects the therapist's own unresolved voyeurism or seductiveness and may stem from countertransference difficulties. Deep interpretation of unconscious material must take place gradually and only after the patient has been adequately prepared. This preparation increases the patient's capacity to accept and to integrate such interpretations.

The therapist may also use *reconstruction*, a technique closely related to interpretation. In reconstruction, the therapist attempts to correlate, understand, and tie together for the patient forgotten, repressed, but psychologically significant early-life experiences. The patient's free associations, behavior, dreams, and transference reactions may suggest traces of these experiences. The therapist bases his reconstruction not only on the patient's overt material but also on the significant aspects that appear to be missing from it; he attempts through further exploration to attain fuller understanding of the patient's symptoms and conflicts by filling in the gaps. Like interpretation, reconstruction may be a gradual process. The therapist may repeat the reconstruction, gradually making it more complete as he gains access to more material. This repetition supplies the basis for still more complete reconstruction and deeper understanding.

Once a patient gains insight through his free associations and through interpretation or other therapeutic intervention, his therapeutic work has only begun. Insight alone seldom produces significant changes. Rather, it must undergo a laborious process called "working through," which constitutes the bulk of psychotherapeutic work. In working through, the insight—that is, the particular unconscious conflict brought to consciousness—and all of its ramifications must be explored, extended, and tested again and again. By tracing the conflict back to its origins and exploring its past and current manifestations in all aspects of the patient's life, the patient and therapist overcome the resistances to the insight and the patient learns to accept, integrate, and understand it both intellectually and emotionally. The process of working through helps reduce the intensity of the conflict, giving the patient increased control over it and thus effecting significant change. Thus change depends not only on insight but on the working through of that insight and, perhaps most important, on the continual exertion of the patient's will to change.

In psychoanalytic psychotherapy, the therapist explores the patient's transference feelings with him, especially when these feelings impede therapy by acting as resistance and when they reflect regression and the emergence of the transference neurosis. When this neurosis emerges with sufficient clarity and force, the patient's basic conflicts are often focused in dramatic ways in relation to the therapist and thus provide opportunity for the patient to gain basic insights into his conflicts and progressively to work them through. Resolution of these basic conflicts in the context of transference is one of the major objectives of the therapy. Success in gaining this particular objective depends on the nature of the patient's psychopathology and his inherent capacity for the therapeutic work.

Outcome. The outcome of psychoanalytic psychotherapy must be measured against the therapeutic objectives. Psychoanalytic psychotherapy implies that the therapist undertakes to accomplish as much with the patient as is possible within obvious limitations. As a long-term, intensive, insight-oriented form of psychotherapy, psychoanalytic psychotherapy aims at fundamental changes in the patient's adaptive functioning and personality organization.

Realistic considerations may of course require the therapist and the patient to settle for more modest objectives. Frequently, patients find themselves significantly less motivated to continue the therapy after achieving relief of symptoms. The time the therapist has available to work with the patient may be limited, or the patient may be forced to move to another city within a particular time span. The decision that sufficient work has been done within the limitations for therapy to be brought to a close must be arrived at by patient and therapist together.

In general, the ideal course of therapy would achieve the following aims: (1) removal or improvement of symptoms; (2) resolution or reduction in the intensity of basic conflicts; (3) resolution of the patient's therapeutic dependence, allowing him greater autonomy and increased self-esteem; and (4) an adequate degree of adaptive and mature functioning. These criteria must often be modified and less than optimal goals accepted. When compromise occurs, both therapist and patient must be aware that their settling for modified objectives may result in difficulties for the patient later on and necessitate additional therapeutic work.

Assessment. Attempts to assess psychoanalytic psychotherapy have had an unfortunate history. Eysenck's critique (1965) suggested that the effects of therapeutic intervention on patients differed little from normal life experience without treatment. He reported that roughly a third of patients improved, another third got worse, and another third showed little or no change. Subsequent investigators, however, have questioned Eysenck's data and conclusions.

Assessment based on more careful studies, with particular attention to patient selection and outcome criteria (the guidelines used to measure therapeutic change) that do justice to the complexity of the human personality and the psychotherapeutic process, lead to a much more optimistic conclusion. Such studies suggest that psychoanalytic psychotherapy, properly utilized, is the most effective form of therapeutic intervention for specific groups of patients. A recent Menninger Clinic study (Kernberg et al., 1972) indicates that for borderline patients purely supportive treatment is relatively ineffective and that an insight-oriented approach based on working through the transference relationship (with supplemental hospitalization) is most effective. Thus support is increasing for the position that psychoanalytic psychotherapy is the optimal treatment for patients with neurotic disorders and conflicts and for patients with borderline personality organization.

Other extensive studies indicate a more limited applicability of psychotherapy in the treatment of psychosis (Grinspoon, Ewalt, and Shader, 1972; May, 1968). The use of drugs, particularly the phenothiazines, seems to be more effective than psychotherapy in most psychotic patients. But even in this area, a select group of patients appears to respond more positively to drugs in combination with group or individual psychotherapy.

Additional research is required to provide specific criteria for selecting patients who will respond positively to psychotherapeutic intervention. Current trends suggest that particular types of patients respond best to particular psychotherapeutic techniques. Attempts to extend our psychotherapeutic skills beyond the realm of their appropriate application is counterproductive.

Supportive Psychotherapy

Supportive psychotherapy is a form of psychotherapy that reinforces the patient's defenses and helps him to suppress and control disturbing thoughts and feelings by such measures as reassurance, suggestion, inspiration, and persuasion. Unlike psychoanalytic psychotherapy, supportive therapy focuses primarily on present difficulties and avoids probing into the past or the unconscious. It is limited in therapeutic objectives rather than in duration. The specific indications for this therapy can be considered in terms of the patient's current situation or in terms of his specific diagnosis.

Indications. Situationally, a therapist can use supportive psychotherapy most effectively when a patient experiences acute stress and turmoil or when a patient with psychotic potential goes into acute decompensation (that is, deteriorates and becomes overtly psychotic). Thus the therapist uses supportive psychotherapy primarily in dealing with life crises or regressive episodes. The death of a loved one, divorce, illness, the loss of a job, or a developmental crisis may precipitate such episodes. Supportive psychotherapy is the therapist's response to the patient's acute disorganization and inability to cope with such crises, to master anxiety, and to maintain effective functioning under great emotional turmoil. Such crises may occur frequently in extremely fragile patients.

In diagnostic terms, the therapist can provide supportive therapy to psychotic patients and, intermittently, to borderline patients; he will rarely use this approach with patients who have neurotic difficulties or character disorders. With fragile and disorganized patients, a supportive involvement may be the most that can be accomplished and such patients may be seen at intervals over extended periods of time.

Techniques. While a therapist using insight-oriented approaches fosters regression by undermining patients' resistances and probes the unconscious by deep intervention, the therapist using supportive treatment moves in the opposite direction. He minimizes the intensity of therapeutic involvement by limiting the frequency and duration of patient visits. He also attempts to minimize the patient's regressive tendency, to stabilize and maintain the patient's functioning defensive structure, and to contain the patient's sometimes overwhelming anxiety within manageable limits.

In supportive therapy, therefore, the therapist uses reassurance and supportive reinforcement to reduce anxiety and assumes an active therapeutic stance to promote a sense of alliance and helpfulness and to minimize regression. In this way the therapist offers himself as a constant and readily available support with whom the patient may achieve a stable and therapeutically consistent relationship. However, he avoids premature reassurance, which the patient may interpret as a lack of understanding of the severity of his illness and the intensity of his suffering.

In supportive therapy, the therapist may also use extrapsychotherapeutic means to achieve these ends. He is more likely than in insight therapy to use medication as a means of calming the patient. He is willing to use hospitalization to help the patient control his behavior and to remove him from excessive stimulation contributing to the crisis or regressive stress. The therapist regards medication or hospitalization as a protective device that acts as a buffer between the patient and overwhelming anxiety and turmoil. He may offer the patient advice, supply him with information, or educate him explicitly in regard to aspects of his life and experience.

In general, the therapeutic stance of the therapist in the supportive relationship is relatively active. He offers himself to the patient as a supportive, friendly, protective, and constant object and adopts a firmly but gently authoritarian attitude. He tolerates the patient's needs for dependency and attachment instead of attempting to explore and change them. The quality of the alliance, therefore, differs considerably from that in psychoanalytic psychotherapy.

In the supportive context, the therapist offers the patient a surrogate ego he can depend upon. Though conflicts over dependency may develop even in patients who need such a relationship, the advisability of attempting to modify the patient's dependence toward increasing self-reliance remains controversial. Usually the prolonged course of supportive psychotherapy leads to a gradual decrease in the frequency of therapeutic sessions with a gradual weakening in the intensity of the therapeutic relationship, but the ties of dependency to the supportive therapist are generally left relatively intact. These ties may remain strong even when therapeutic contacts are spaced out over months or years.

In a supportive relationship the therapist focuses on the patient's current life experience—his contacts, relationships, stresses, emotions, disappointments, hopes, and gratifications. The therapist seeks to mobilize the patient's available resources to deal with these aspects of his ongoing experience and to manage the difficulties he encounters in a more effective and adaptive manner.

Outcome. The therapeutic objectives of supportive psychotherapy must necessarily be modest, but modesty by no means implies simplicity or ease of achievement. Supportive therapy aims at the reconstitution and stabilization of the patient's functioning. This process may require short-term involvement or a relationship extending over considerable periods of time.

Frequently, however, the supportive approach achieves in a relatively short time its primary objective of returning the patient to a more effective, predecompensation level of functioning. Once the goal is achieved, the usefulness of merely supportive therapy is limited, and the therapist may move to a more insight-oriented approach. He must gradually change his techniques to those of psychoanalytic psychotherapy while constantly testing the patient's capacity to sustain this type of treatment.

Even so, the therapist must be ready to respond to transient regressive episodes or de-compensations, which the shift to insight-oriented therapy may precipitate. In working with more regressed psychotic patients, the therapist may encounter great resistance to the acceptance of responsibility and relinquishment of dependence on the therapist that such a change in approach necessitates.

Assessment. Although supportive psychotherapy may serve as an effective, short-term holding action, it may also be the optimal treatment modality over an extended period. A therapist will find it most useful in the management of disruptive turmoil or regressive episodes and in the regressive phases of more insight-oriented treatment.

The Menninger study (Kernberg et al., 1972) indicate that in the treatment of borderline patients and some others, supportive therapy increases the effectiveness of insight-oriented approaches. Supportive measures were most effective in the reconstitution of acutely decompensated patients, particularly in the hospital setting. Within this context, when the supportive measures have achieved their objectives, hospitalization is no longer necessary. It must then be decided whether such patients will benefit from further therapeutic intervention.

Many such patients profit immeasurably from an insight-oriented approach, which examines the origins and causes of their acute decompensation. Other patients, however, languish in a continuing state of dependence and disorganization, which prevents them from entering into further therapy. For these patients, a continuing supportive relationship, together with the resources of psychopharmacology and hospital facilities, will help maintain adequate stabilization and a modest level of functioning in the outside world.

Brief Psychotherapy

Brief psychotherapy is a limited, insight-oriented type of therapy, limited both in its objectives and in the number of patient visits. It can be distinguished from psychoanalytic psychotherapy, where greater emphasis is placed on the role of profound insight, and also from supportive psychotherapy with its reduced emphasis on the role of insight.

Indications. In brief psychotherapy, the therapist uses fundamental psychodynamic principles to help the patient achieve limited insight into a specifically defined area of emotional conflict. Consequently, this form of therapy works best with patients whose level of functioning is relatively effective except for the specific area of conflict in their presenting complaint. Brief psychotherapy requires the capacity to relate to the therapist in a cooperative and productive manner (alliance), the ability to share pertinent feelings with the therapist, the capacity for insight, and, above all, a basic motivation to achieve insight.

Sifneos's studies of brief psychotherapy (1972) indicate that motivation is the primary predictor of successful outcome. The therapist uses brief psychotherapy, therefore, as a form of crisis intervention (see chapter 22, "Patient Management"). By helping the patient gain greater insight into a specific area of acute emotional turmoil, the therapist enables him to mobilize his ego capacities in the service of resolving this area of conflict.

Techniques. Brief psychotherapy is time-limited, and the therapist and patient set the limits either in reference to the attainment of specific therapeutic goals or in terms of a specific number of visits. Ideally, the therapist seeks an optimal time span to achieve limited objectives. The patient's initial positive transference motivates him to work toward the therapeutic objectives, but this positive transference must be achieved before the emergence of transference neurosis. Transference neurosis develops gradually over time, but its emergence alters the treatment in the direction of transference issues. The early period of transference motivates the patient to work through specific conflict areas without the deeper involvement of the transference neurosis. The therapist should be wary of patients who expect magical cures in the specified, limited number of clinic visits.

Brief psychotherapy is also explicitly focused—that is, it concentrates on immediate areas of emotional conflict. The separation of a manageable area of conflict from deeper and more extensive areas of conflict is often technically difficult. Frequently a number of interrelated conflicts exist at different psychic levels. But brief psychotherapy strives to avoid deeper characterological issues, particularly those involving dependency needs. It therefore specifically avoids early dependent needs and problems with passivity, which can create entanglements and lead to complications during treatment.

Thus in brief psychotherapy the therapist attempts to be reality-oriented, to focus on the patient's current life conflicts without emphasizing past experience. This limited focus does not exclude all aspects of the patient's past experience, however, because acquired patterns of reaction may play a significant role in current conflicts. Patients may tend to give a characteristic meaning to a variety of everyday experiences. Such a bias may, for example, take the form of imagining themselves to be totally controlled by or to have total control over the environment. These attitudes reflect a variety of underlying, unconscious determinants and often lead to a single predominant and repetitive pattern of ordering and responding to stimuli. Insight into such patterns contributes significantly to the patient's ability to deal with current difficulties.

Brief psychotherapy may also be defined as a problem-solving process, but one in which the therapist helps the patient mobilize his own resources to deal with the problem rather than solving it, as in insight-oriented therapy. This definition helps to structure the therapy. The task-orientation keeps the objective clearly in mind and emphasizes attainment of a solution within a short time.

The problem-solving process has several phases. The first is *perceptual organization*, during which the therapist helps bring a definable conflict into focus. During this phase, the therapist may also evaluate the patient's capacity for reorganization and reordering. In the second phase, *perceptual reorganization*, the therapist attempts to reorder conscious material by clarification and occasional confrontation. He connects newly uncovered thoughts and feelings to the structure of the defined conflict. The patient's resistances limit this reordering and uncovering. A phase of *transference interpretation* may follow, in which the therapist uses the patient's previously achieved insights and feelings toward him to give a more emotionally vivid and experiential context to the patient's new insights into the conflicts. In the final phase of *termination and integration*, if the therapist has been correct in his interpretation, the patient will begin to work through his problem with an accompanying decrease of symptoms.

Outcome. In brief psychotherapy, the therapist seeks to reduce the presenting distress and bring symptomatic relief to the patient. The therapist's goal of helping the patient gain insight into an explicitly defined area of conflict removes brief psychotherapy from the realm of transference cure, which by definition is achieved without insight (see chapter 1, "The Therapist-Patient Relationship"). The insight gained helps mobilize the patient's resources to master the disturbing anxiety and to resolve the conflict.

Assessment. Brief psychotherapy was developed and has been used most effectively in outpatient clinics, particularly when offered to selected groups of patients best able to profit from it. Partly because of the increasing role of third-party insurance plans with benefits covering only a limited number of outpatient visits, brief psychotherapy is an increasingly significant form of treatment. Such pragmatic and extrinsic considerations aside, however, the limited objectives of brief psychotherapy may or may not satisfy the patient's needs. The option of more extensive psychotherapeutic work should be left open to the patient when he demonstrates the need and the capacity for it. In a significant number of properly selected and well-motivated patients, however, brief psychotherapy may be all that is required.

Group Psychotherapies

The group approach to psychotherapy has grown rapidly over the last fifty years and has become a major focus of psychiatric interest and experience. With our knowledge of group processes playing an increasing role in understanding contemporary life and with increasing pressures on the psychiatric profession to treat greater numbers of patients, group therapy takes on particular significance and utility. Material in this section is intended for potential group therapists as well as for those evaluating or referring patients for group therapy.

While individual psychotherapy involves the interaction between two parties, the therapist and the patient, group psychotherapy involves combinations of individuals occupying the patient or the therapist roles. The typical configuration is that of a single therapist or leader and a number of patients (usually six to eight) participating in a single group process. Variants on this basic configuration include multiple therapists and smaller or larger groups. Thus in group therapy there may be one or more cotherapists, and in family therapy there may be one or more therapists and one or more families.

We will discuss basic principles underlying group therapy and then focus on intensive group therapy, family therapy, and psychodrama.

Patient Selection

Opinions regarding patient selection for group therapy have changed as therapists' experience with the group process has deepened and broadened. Like all other forms of therapy, group therapy is better suited to some patients than to others; like their counterparts in individual psychotherapy, group therapists consider relatively healthy, neurotic, nonnarcissistic patients who function well to be ideal for the group process.

At one time group therapists considered certain patients poor treatment risks for the group approach, including severe psychoneurotics, psychotics, patients with organic difficulties, patients with psychosomatic problems, depressed patients, narcissistic patients, and paranoid patients. With increasing experience, however, therapists have realized that all of these patients can be approached effectively through some form of group therapy but that patients with more severe pathology require variations in approach and technique.

The therapist must carefully select his patients for group therapy. Before recommending a patient for this therapy, the therapist should give him an adequate diagnostic appraisal. The therapist must consider the patient's presenting problem, his history, his pathology, and his suitability for joining the particular group under consideration. Because patients often interact with the group in patterns predetermined by previous family involvements, the therapist may also find it helpful to explore the patient's important interpersonal involvements, specifically those within his family of origin.

The decision to treat patients in a group rather than in individual therapy is not always clear-cut. In general, patients capable of forming a workable transference and sustaining the difficult work of therapy deserve that opportunity in a one-to-one context. But such patients often do well in groups. Patients who have difficulty with inappropriate interpersonal relationships, who tend to act out feelings, or who may develop a transference that would excessively complicate individual therapy can be treated effectively in groups. By the same token, certain narcissistic patients may be excessively disruptive to the group effort or may find it overly difficult to become a functioning member of the group. Such patients may do better in individual therapy. In addition, patients may have a preference for or against group treatment, and this preference must also enter into the therapist's decision. Even so, referral to group treatment may be made simply on the grounds that no other form of treatment is available.

Group Organization

How large a group should be, how long and how frequently it should meet, and how homogeneous the members should be are important issues that must be considered in establishing a therapy group. Though no ironclad rules prevail, the therapist determines these specific parameters only after deciding on the nature, purpose, and function of the group.

The size of a group relates inversely to the intensity of the therapeutic interaction. In intensive, analytically oriented group therapy, for example, the optimal number of group members is seven or eight. Increasing the number above eight dilutes the intensity of group interaction, and decreasing the number below seven heightens the intensity of interaction with the leader and undercuts the effectiveness of the group process. However, if groups are less exploratory and more supportive or problem-oriented, larger numbers can be involved effectively.

The organization and function of a group determine the frequency and duration of meetings. More frequent meetings increase the intensity of the interaction among members and correspondingly deepen the level of responsiveness among members and between members and the leader. Though most groups meet once weekly, the number of meetings may be altered according to group purposes.

The duration of meetings also affects the intensity of the members' interaction, since the group process requires adequate time to develop. Yet excessively long meetings may encourage the group not to concentrate on serious issues. In general, an hour is considered the minimum time required for the group to accomplish some work; two hours has been found to be excessively long. The ideal length for group meetings falls somewhere in the middle ground, from an hour and a quarter to an hour and a half. The group itself may decide how often and how long to meet. Groups have their own style and pacing, and, within limits, the members may feel that they need more time or can work more effectively with less time.

Groups may be homogeneous or heterogeneous in terms of patients' age, educational level, race, sex, and diagnosis. Therapy groups appear to do better when they are heterogeneous and balanced. The group ought not to be too heavily weighted with members of one sex, with schizophrenic or borderline patients, or with patients significantly removed in age from the rest of the group. There are exceptions to this rule of thumb, however. Disturbed adolescents, geriatric patients, acute psychotics, alcoholics, and patients with serious physical handicaps often work more effectively in homogeneous groups.

The group may operate in an open or closed fashion. A closed group comprises patients selected to work together within a limited time frame. The termination date may be preset or determined as the group proceeds, but the group works together toward its termination. Though members may be replaced if they drop out in the early phases of therapy, the group is gradually closed to new members during the later phases. Open groups accept and terminate patients continually in the course of the group process, so that termination becomes an issue for individual patients rather than for the group itself. An open group will have a continual turnover of members, while the group itself may persist for many years.

Each type of structure has advantages. The closed group allows for a greater intensity of group interaction, deeper involvement in the group process, and the opportunity to work through the process of termination more thoroughly. Closed groups also have the advantage when the availability of the therapist is limited to a specified period of time. The open group, on the other hand, can develop an ongoing group process and can make the benefits of group experience and insight available to incoming patients.

The Group Process

Three basic phases characterize the life of a group, bring specific issues into focus, and dominate group interaction. In the initial stage, the patient is concerned with the question of inclusion, whether he will be accepted and will become a part of the group. He no longer functions as an isolated individual but is gradually incorporated into the body of the group. The dominant issues are membership and giving and receiving or, in more analytic terms, concerns about narcissism and symbiotic longing. In the second phase, questions of power and autonomy preoccupy the patient. Can the patient function as an independent person within the group, and can he maintain autonomy in the face of the leader's presumed power? Is power focused in the leader or distributed and shared among the group members? In the third phase of group interaction, the issues of equality and sharing influence group members' acceptance of each other as individuals, the expression of real affection and support, and the capacity for mature and healthy mutuality. This equality promotes and sustains the autonomy of each group member. These three phases can be considered to parallel traditional analytic concepts of oral, anal, and genital development.

Group formation is the process by which a number of individuals becomes an effectively functioning group. Group life gradually generates a therapeutic context in which patients can resolve their underlying conflicts and work toward maturity and self-sustaining autonomy.

The nature of this evolution may vary among groups or may fluctuate in intensity as the group develops. However, the group leader must constantly keep this evolution in focus as he attempts to understand and respond to the flow of events in the group interaction.

The Role of the Leader

The group therapist or leader plays a central role in the process of group development, even though his role varies considerably within different kinds of groups. Where the leader adopts a more active and manipulative stance, the group consolidates around the leader so that effective therapeutic action occurs between the leader and the members. An active leader diminishes the level of anxiety within the group but also generates expectations and transference difficulties. A less active leader, on the other hand, raises the level of group anxiety and forces the group to consolidate itself, often against the leader. The more passive stance of the leader thus fosters the evolution of the group itself as a therapeutic instrument and brings more sharply into focus patterns of interaction and individual distortions that contribute to the group process and reflect the individual and collective pathologies. Thus the locus of therapeutic action lies more between members than between members and the leader.

The role of the leader is particularly significant in the initial phases of group formation. His position vis-à-vis the group determines whether the initial issues of inclusion and acceptance will be focused around the leader or within the group itself. In either case, the leader sets the course for the group's further development and evolution.

Throughout the life of the group, its particular characteristics, the specific phase of its development, and the personality and theoretical orientation of the leader will help to define his role. Within the group, however, the therapist must maintain a flexible stance, varying his interaction and responsiveness in terms of the ongoing activity of the group and the apparent needs of the members. He must avoid a preselected, fixed, theoretically determined role. Groups that have developed a considerable degree of solidarity have less need of therapeutic activity from the leader. Unstable and more fragmented groups, however, may require greater activity from the leader to maintain cohesiveness and to facilitate group efforts.

Nonetheless, the leader's character traits—exhibitionism, narcissism, tendencies toward omnipotence, or need for control—may exert a powerful influence on his style. The therapist must therefore be as alert to problems of countertransference as he would be in individual psychotherapy. Out of another set of neurotic conflicts and needs—such as excessive passivity or fear of appearing less than perfect—therapists may also err in the direction of withdrawal from the group process, isolation, or failure to intervene directly and actively when required.

Even within a group, each member's psychodynamics and personality are unique. The ultimate effectiveness of the group leader depends on his capacity to detect and respond to the members' varying needs and, through appropriate intervention, to facilitate the working of the group process. The therapist must deal actively with patients' tendencies to regress, particularly in the case of psychotic or borderline patients, and their tendencies to act out, either within or outside of the group. A member may, for example, threaten to assault another physically within the group meeting, or two members may carry out a destructive relationship outside the group. The skillful therapist, however, acts to mobilize group resources to deal with such problems rather than dealing with members on an individual basis himself, a tactic that can undermine group efforts and frustrate the group process. The underlying intent of disruptive events in the group is often precisely such an undermining of group work, and the therapist must avoid aiding this unconsciously determined activity.

A number of styles characterize the patterns of interaction of groups. At one end of a continuum of patterns of member-to-member and leader-to-member interactions is the analytic approach, in which the leader adopts a relatively inactive role and encourages the evolution of the group process. In this process, the group gradually consolidates and gains a degree of cohesiveness, and the material brought to the group interaction gradually deepens from a superficial level to more basic conflicts. These conflicts then become available for corrective action, either by the ongoing group interaction or by interpretation by the leader.

The other extreme of interaction patterns is the existential approach. Here the therapist no longer stands aside as a separate leader but engages as much as possible in the group interaction as a member among members. In this participatory approach, the therapist shares his own feelings, attitudes, and countertransference difficulties with the group, along with observations stemming from his own greater experience of group phenomena.

The transactional approach stands midway between these extremes. The leader focuses on the current pattern of interactions among group members and between the leader and group members. Though the leader acts as a participating member of the group, the focus remains on the transactional aspects of the group process and he makes no attempt to delve into the patients' past experiences or the elements of underlying conflict or transference distortion.

One cannot predetermine whether one style will be more advisable or more therapeutically effective. Different leaders feel comfortable with different styles and, as a general principle, work more effectively with the style most comfortable for them and best suited to their own personalities. The group leader, however, must recognize the role countertransference may play in his choice of style and must be open to using other modalities of interaction to achieve therapeutic results. In addition, the most suitable style or modality may vary from group to group, depending on the group's purposes and organization.

While therapy groups most often have a number of patients and a single group leader, groups may also have multiple therapists. Male and female cotherapists may provide advantages for some groups. This arrangement diversifies the skills and personality dispositions contributed by the leaders to the group process and facilitates the emergence of transference patterns derived from earlier family interactions. Their transference reactions may be split between male and female therapist in such a way that the pattern becomes more easily discernible and more readily available for interpretation. The interaction between therapists can also be useful in providing a model for male-female interaction and perhaps a healthier source of identification than the patients' original models. In heterosexual groups, with inevitable male-female conflicts and significant transference distortions, this combination of therapists may be particularly helpful.

Also important are the so-called leaderless groups—not only those in which the leader abstains from exercising leadership but also those specifically organized to function without any designated leader. Such groups have been called "self-help groups" and have proved of some usefulness to individuals manifesting high levels of resistance to any form of authoritative or expert leadership. Self-help groups of drug addicts have been particularly effective. Leaderless groups may also provide a mutually supportive context for interaction among alcoholics or the elderly.

In addition, groups with a leader may occasionally meet without the leader, when the leader cannot be present. Such occasional leaderless meetings may foster expression of feelings and attitudes about the leader and stimulate aspects of group interaction that might not otherwise have surfaced. It is important that the group review and analyze such leaderless sessions subsequently with the leader present.

Group versus Individual Psychotherapy

Group psychotherapy has advantages that differ from those of individual psychotherapy. Both forms of treatment encompass a wide variety of approaches, levels of intensity, and applicability. They differ, however, in that in general the group experience does not expose basic conflicts and subtle forms of defense in as great a depth as individual insight-oriented psychotherapy nor work them through with the same degree of thoroughness. The group process, however, adds a different dimension to the patient's therapeutic experience, one unavailable through individual psychotherapy alone.

Although the group process does not induce a transference neurosis, as do more analytically oriented forms of individual psychotherapy, it nonetheless mobilizes a variety of transference phenomena. Consequently, the emphasis in group work shifts from the resolution of individual patients' nuclear neurotic conflicts to the study of group dynamics and the understanding of disturbances in interpersonal relationships. The development of more effective ways of relating interpersonally and the influence of corrective emotional experiences within the group compensate for the loss of depth in the patient material.

Ethical Issues

The primary ethical issues in group therapy are confidentiality and responsibility, already discussed in regard to psychotherapy as a whole. As in individual therapy, the therapist must maintain the confidentiality of the group work; he must ensure that communications within the group remain privileged and are not discussed with persons outside of the group. Obviously the members must share this responsibility; their capacity for maintaining confidentiality is directly related to how well they function as a group. Group members may tend to discuss issues raised in the group with spouses, friends, or other individuals; the therapist must make clear that such discussion undermines the sense of trust and cohesiveness essential to the group's functioning.

In a more general sense, responsibility for the group and for the smooth functioning of the group process is shared by the leader and the members. The leader's primary responsibility is to facilitate the group process and to maximize its benefits for individual patients. As the group evolves, members gradually accept responsibility for the functioning of the group and the welfare of its members. Patients' social interaction with each other outside of the group sessions raises an important question of responsibility. Such activity is often a form of acting out and therefore an undermining of group cohesiveness. As a general rule, the group leader should minimize his own social contact with individual patients outside of the group. Where appropriate, extragroup contacts should be worked back into the fabric of the group process by discussing them during the group sessions.

In the rapidly expanding field of group therapy, the ethical aspects of the treatment situation, particularly the responsibility incumbent on those who assume the position of group leader, cannot be sufficiently emphasized. Failure to do so has often resulted in group techniques deleterious to the patients. Situations in which patients' defenses have been overwhelmed, with subsequent breakdown, in which inappropriate techniques have been applied, with countertherapeutic effects, or in which patients are forced into compromised positions of emotional or physical exposure or manipulation can be counted among such ethically questionable results.

Intensive Group Therapy

Intensive group therapy adheres to a more analytic model and usually involves fairly small, heterogeneous groups of seven or eight members. In intensive group work, the leader assumes a relatively passive stance. He allows material and patterns of interaction to develop more fully within the group before intervening. The leader oversees the group process, allows it to emerge, and intervenes only to focus the group's attention on specific issues and on patterns of group interaction that might otherwise escape notice.

The leader's unwillingness to give answers, solve problems, or adopt an active position vis-à-vis the group turns the initiative back to the members and forces them to deal with specific questions and anxieties. Thus the group is encouraged to use its own resources and to mold itself into a functioning, cohesive unit. In the beginning, the group members work against and in spite of the leader rather than in submission to or collaboration with him.

Indications. Intensive group therapy may be useful for a broad spectrum of patients with neurotic and characterological problems, as well as for patients with a more borderline personality organization. Reasonably well-compensated psychotic patients also may benefit from such groups, but it is advisable to limit their number to one or two in any given group. Psychotic patients' sensitivity to unconscious issues may facilitate the group work, but the presence of too many such patients can be disorganizing and disruptive. The tendency for such patients to regress can be tolerated and responded to by the healthier resources of other group members, but only within limits.

Group process. Cohesion is the sense of mutual belonging and participation that members of a group experience when sharing common goals. This feeling does not occur automatically but must be achieved. By gaining cohesiveness, the group becomes a functioning organization capable of therapeutic work. As cohesiveness evolves, members recognize that they share personality traits, defenses, conflicts, and problems, and a sense of common effort emerges. A degree of regression is induced and encourages sharing of more personal, painful, and often more primitive material. When the group reaches an optimal degree of cohesion, it can accomplish the most effective therapeutic work; at this time the group also becomes most responsive to the interventions and interpretations of the leader. The cohesiveness of the group creates an accepting and empathic emotional atmosphere that makes possible significant identifications with the leader and with healthier aspects of other members. It is out of the matrix of the group that individual patients must work to separate themselves as individuals, thus gaining greater maturity and autonomy.

Conflicts in the group setting differ from those in other forms of psychotherapy only in that they are expressed in a more externalized form in relationship to other group members. Patients may split ambivalent feelings and assign them to different members of the group at different times. The leader must identify and be sensitive to underlying conflicts and to the way a patient displays them in the group interaction.

Intensive groups tend to experience regression. The regression deepens as the group work progresses. Often the most significant changes occur only after the group as a whole reaches an adequate level of regression. The depth of material manifested by group members (from earlier developmental levels), the degree of mutual projection, and the tendency for primary process forms of expression and organization to dominate the group interaction all reflect the depth of regression.

The basic assumptions reflect the unconscious dynamics in the emotional (non-task-oriented) level of the group interaction. The basic assumptions of *fight-flight*, *pairing*, and *dependency* reflect the underlying trends toward regression in the group. Fight may appear as hostility, antagonism, or escape from the group; flight may take the form of running away from stress, by joking, disrupting the meeting, daydreaming, intellectualizing, or incoherent rambling. Pairing behavior may include two members' making private remarks to one another or one member's reaching out continually to another with expressions of warmth, approval, and agreement. Dependency may be manifest in behavior that elicits aid from the leader or other members or that appeals to tradition, experts, or events from prior periods of group interaction.

The group always engages in some degree of work (task-directed effort) and inevitably strains one or another part of the group system. This strain may give rise to conflict, tension, anxiety, ambiguity, and confusion. Problems of orientation, evaluation, and control relate primarily to the work area; problems of decision, tension management, and integration relate to the emotional area. Emotionality is an inner-directed, unlearned pattern of group response to its unconscious needs to maintain itself as a group under the strain caused by forces external or internal to the group. The basic assumptions (described above) are the patterns of group emotionality that dominate the group interaction.

Group transference phenomena have the same origins and significance as transference in any other setting. In a heterogeneous group, however, the transference manifests itself in different ways. Group members displace transference feelings onto the leader or leaders, especially when male and female cotherapists serve as the bearers of parental images. Feelings and attitudes may, however, be displaced onto other group members. Indeed, the variety of group members provides many transference opportunities. Patients may transfer elements from other significant figures in their lives, such as siblings or spouses, onto others in the group. Frequently aspects of the family configuration or even the entire pattern can be identified in the patient's reaction to the group. A frequent manifestation of transference is "sibling rivalry" with other group members for the attention or interest of the group leader.

Acting out is the expression by a patient of his conflicts and fantasies in behavior outside the group session instead of in words within the group session. For example, a patient may express hostile feelings toward another member by calling him on the phone and objecting to his taking sides during a group session. Acting out impedes group inquiry and understanding. Psychopathic or borderline patients with a poor tolerance for inner tension have the greatest tendency to act out. The group's capacity to control this tendency is proportional to its degree of cohesion. Patients may act out as a way of drawing the leader into a controlling, limit-setting position. More often than not, the leader can call upon group resources for limit setting, but on occasion the leader must take the responsibility himself in order to prevent excessive destructiveness. On the other hand, the leader must distinguish acting out from the patient's attempts to seek a greater degree of autonomy and mastery.

"Acting in" is the expression of a patient's conflicts within the group in actions instead of in words. One patient, for example, may physically assault another. This nonverbal behavioral reenactment of the patient's conflicts can have a severely disorganizing effect on the group and can be extremely destructive to group interaction.

Resistance is as critical in group therapy as in any other form of therapy and may be focused in terms of the group's basic assumptions. Group resistance may be expressed by all or some of the group members; it may take the form of prolonged silences, periods of dependency on and overvaluation of the leader, or hostility toward and attacks on the leader.

Defensive patterns may arise in connection with events in the group history such as interruptions for vacations, introduction of new members, termination or departure of longer-term members, and expressions of countertransference difficulties by the group leader. These resistances must be clarified, interpreted, and to some extent worked through before the underlying emotions, conflicts, and fantasies can be examined. The emergence of group resistance is a specific indication for more active confrontation and interpretation by the leader. In group work, as in other forms of therapy, the rigidity of resistances impedes the therapeutic process. The leader may inadvertently reinforce group resistances by playing into the unconscious needs and defensive structure of the members. Thus the group resistance often represents the sum total of the mutually reinforcing resistances of the group members.

The group process called working through mobilizes elements in the group to deal with such resistances and defenses and gradually modify them over time. This success of working through depends on the ability of various group members to recognize transference distortions and to help other members abandon such neurotic involvements. The working through and deepening of the material, in order to make basic conflicts available for modification, distinguish intensive group therapy from other more superficial reality-based or supportive group approaches.

Termination systematically brings to a close the patient's involvement in the group. It occurs when he has achieved certain predetermined goals. Consequently, termination must be carefully distinguished from premature flight, which occurs when the individual feels compelled to flee the group because of anxiety he cannot master.

In an open group, where individual members terminate at different times, the usual criteria for termination of therapy apply. The decision to leave the group depends largely on the patient's continuing motivation and his felt need for treatment, but the final decision to terminate is an appropriate subject for group discussion. Successful termination in such groups can raise group morale and contributes substantially to other members' sense of accomplishment and self-esteem. Premature departures from the group, however, may represent failures of the group process and, by implication, failure of the other members to deal effectively with the difficulties of the patient who has left the group.

In the closed group, the criteria for termination depend on the level of development of the group process. The therapist must assess whether the group has become an effectively functioning therapeutic matrix allowing free and easy communication, whether the members of the group have achieved some sense of individuation and autonomy, whether the patients

function on the basis of reality rather than fantasy, whether narcissistic and dependency needs have been resolved or reduced, and whether the patients' life difficulties outside of the group have improved. Though the therapist should regard these criteria as optimal and never achieved fully, he can expect significant progress to be made toward them.

During termination, a significant process both for individual patients and for the group as a whole, the critical issues of attachment, autonomy, and dependence must be worked through and resolved. In this final stage of the group, the basis for the stabilization and integration of the patient's emerging autonomy take place. Termination must always be discussed at length within the group and a consensus reached whenever possible.

Assessment. Intensive group therapy, properly conducted and given sufficient time to deal with the members' basic conflicts, has proved its clinical worth. The therapeutic results compare favorably with results of individual psychotherapy. Although group therapy may not work through basic issues with as much thoroughness and depth as individual approaches, the value of group approaches has been amply substantiated.

It must be remembered that even symptomatic improvement in patients suffering from symptom neuroses (as opposed to character neuroses) often takes considerable time and an intense group experience, sometimes over the course of years. Deeply embedded characterological problems require even more extensive therapeutic efforts. When patients can be kept involved in the group process and when the group process develops properly with competent leadership, significant therapeutic gains can be expected, specifically a decrease in the intensity of inner conflicts and greater degree of control over them.

Family Therapy

Indications. Family therapy as a form of group therapy has evolved over the last quarter-century. Family therapy is usually possible only with children, adolescents, or young adult patients and its advisability depends on the degree of family involvement with the patient as well as the availability of the family to participate. This approach is indicated when a patient's difficulties reflect ongoing relationships with the family, particularly a family with identifiable psychopathology in other members. The approach and aims of family therapy are similar to those of group therapy, except that the family is a natural, preformed group that has a significant psychological history before coming to treatment. The same is not true of group therapy, where the group is newly formed of strangers.

Generally the therapist encounters difficulties keeping the father and the patient's siblings in the therapeutic situation. Frequently one parent will, behind the scenes, pressure the rest of the family into treatment, intensifying resistance in these family members. In a typical pattern, the father and other family members attend a few sessions, and then begin to find excuses not to come, ultimately leaving the therapist with the patient and the patient's mother. Family therapy is optimally conducted with all of the family members present but can continue reasonably effectively with a fragment of the family.

The therapy is more effective if all family members participate because they are all involved to varying degrees in the family emotional interaction and thus contribute in their separate ways to the family pathology. Even if only one member of the family is available for treatment, however, the effect on the family can be indirectly continued through that member.

Group process. The family differs from other therapeutic groups in that it is a natural rather than an artificial grouping, bound together by marriage, blood, and a history spanning a number of years. Moreover, the family naturally includes members of both sexes and at least two generations. Consequently certain aspects of the group process—such as regression and conflict—are relatively well developed and articulated at the beginning of therapy and play a role in the therapy process.

The family may be looked at from a number of perspectives. Perhaps the most important concept is that of the family emotional system, or the level of emotional organization of the family group. In this view, each member contributes a proportion of unconscious, unresolved affective material to the emotional interaction within the family. Thus, a system emerges involving specific family members in varying degrees and exercising powerful emotional influences between and among family members. A set of interlocking projections and introjections (see chapter 9, "The Dynamic Bases of Psychopathology") characterizes this system, lends a specific quality to family interactions, and defines and articulates each family member's sense of self. In a pathological family, for example, the parents may project undesirable or conflictual aspects of their personalities onto the child, who then internalizes (introjects) these elements and makes them a part of his own growing personality. Thus a mother may project her feelings of inferiority and lack of value onto her daughter; the daughter is seen and treated as inferior and devalued and comes to experience herself as inferior and devalued.

Within the family emotional system, some members manifest a relative lack of self-differentiation, leaving them more susceptible to conflicting emotional influences derived from other parts of the family system. Thus the child's emerging sense of self may be powerfully influenced by unexpressed but nonetheless active projections from other members of the family who have unresolved conflicts. The family therapist must define this unconsciously functioning family system and examine the resulting pattern of projections and introjections, the related distortions, and the patterns of behavioral interaction among family members.

The family system may also be conceptualized in terms of homeostatic principles. This system works to preserve an equilibrium; any disturbance in the balance of forces activates counterforces that reduce the disequilibrium and bring the system back into balance. These forces preserve the delicate balance among family members in the emotional system.

Often during the course of therapy, as a result of therapeutic intervention, one of the family members will attempt to define a more coherent sense of self and free himself from entanglement in the family emotional system. Such an attempt elicits powerful counterpressures from other family members to defeat this bid for autonomy and to return the deviant member to his proper place within the system. The presence of these powerful forces underlie family rigidity, impede the patient's bid for greater emotional maturity, and serve as the basic rationale for family therapy as opposed to other forms of therapy.

At another level, family therapists have focused on patterns of transactional interaction among family members. Transactions are communications at many levels transmitted by verbal, nonverbal, affective, behavioral, or gestural means. These transactional patterns are extremely important and also serve as indicators of underlying affective involvements. At this level one can identify such important transactional mechanisms as double binding, pseudomutuality, and pseudohostility. In a double bind there are conflicting communications, usually between the parents and the child. One message is explicit and verbal; the other, contradictory message is implicit and nonverbal. A parent may thus tell the child to grow up and be more independent while withdrawing affection and approval when the child behaves in a more independent, adult manner. In pseudomutuality the appearance of a sense of relationship is maintained to cover underlying conflicts, tensions, and lack of real relationship. Conversely, in pseudohostility the appearance of hostility masks the underlying anxiety related to intimacy and the sharing of affection. Such mechanisms serve to blur real differences among family members, prevent the achievement of real individuality by any of them, and obscure any potentiality for real relationship between family members.

The most prominent emotional constellation is the emotional triad—the smallest stable emotional relationship system. The two-person, or dyadic, system is relatively unstable insofar as communication between the partners becomes open and meaningful or tends to break down, leading to disruption of the dyad. The three members involved in the triad work to preserve the integrity of the triad. If two of the members move toward each other and establish a more open communication, this prompts the third member to interrupt this communication and to attempt to establish a closer involvement with one or other of the two. Within the triad, the sense of emotional integrity and cohesiveness of the self depends upon the involvement and emotional communication from the others. In the opposite direction, when the level of tension and anxiety rises between any pair, they work to escape the tension in the dyad by shifting forces within the triad to involve the third member.

Within a family system, there may be stable or shifting patterns of triadic involvement involving different family members at different times. The triadic patterns repeat themselves over and over again through the family history. One of the most characteristic involves the "emotional divorce" between mother and father, in which the father is forced into the passive, weak position, leaving the mother to hold the more aggressive, dominating, and forceful (sometimes castrating) position. The child caught up in this interaction as the third member may become chronically infantilized and dependent on the mother. If the father and mother become more emotionally involved, the child is shunted to the side and must recreate the emotional divorce to reestablish his dependent relationship with the mother. Therapeutic intervention must identify these triadic involvements and allow the members to disengage and to achieve a higher level of self-differentiation.

Techniques. Family therapy is conducted with as many of the family members as possible and involves treatment of more than one member of the family simultaneously in the same session. This includes both parents, their children, and any other significant figure in the family interaction who is able to participate effectively in the therapy. There may be one or more therapists. A male and a female cotherapist may provide sex-differentiated role models. One of the major difficulties in family work is that the therapist must constantly keep in focus the family process and relate to the family as a functioning unit, rather than to individual members.

Family dynamics create constant pressures on the therapist to become involved in the preestablished family emotional configurations and to take sides. Frequently the therapist tries to stand aside from the interaction and to facilitate the communication between members of the family. Gradually helping the family to become aware of underlying emotional configurations allows for a loosening of triadic configurations and opens up the potentialities for further growth. The therapist contributes to this process by supporting attempts by individuals to gain a more autonomous stance.

One variation of family therapy is *multiple family-group therapy*, with more than one family group meeting together with one or more therapists. This approach broadens the base of interaction and communication. Members of the other families uninvolved in the emotional system of any given family are better able to make astute observations and freer to communicate those observations.

Another modality of family treatment is *couples therapy*. A single couple or a group of couples may meet with one or more therapists. These groups focus on present patterns of interaction with only occasional reference to genetic determinants. The elucidation of projective distortions and the opening of channels of communication contribute to the resolution of problems. An important aspect of couples work is the way in which the marriage partners interact to elicit undesirable responses. Through the group process, for example, a wife may discover how her own behavior and projective distortions elicit or contribute to her husband's ill treatment of her. These patterns are often mutual and reciprocally reinforcing. Progressive pathological interaction between spouses can be clarified, understood, and interrupted in this type of therapy.

Assessment. The whole area of family therapy is new and experimental. Because it rests on theories about which there is little consensus, evaluation is difficult at this time. Specific controlled and careful outcome studies have not yet been done. Clinical experience, however, suggests that family therapy is an extremely fruitful modality of treatment in selected cases. It is often useful in a short-term setting to deal with specific problems and to open channels of communication within a family. It may be used in conjunction with other forms of therapy—most often with individual therapy for one or more of the family members. Such combined approaches may promote therapeutic work but may also create complications and difficulties (see the discussion, later in this chapter, of combined therapies).

Psychodrama

Psychodrama is a form of group therapy in which patients act out roles and characterizations in dramatic form on a stage. It encourages patients to act out inner tensions, conflicts, and feelings. The emphasis is on spontaneity and uninhibited expression of feelings, thoughts, and attitudes. In a dramatic setting, patients take specific roles and act them out. The roles include director, actor, auxiliary ego, and protagonist. The specific techniques are role playing, role reversal, soliloquy, and the use of doubles and mirrors to express, through auxiliary egos, parts of the patient that he cannot express himself. The auxiliary ego is usually a staff member trained to act out different roles so as to intensify the patient's emotional reaction. He may represent some important figure in the patient's life, or he may express the patient's hidden impulses, wishes, and attitudes or unacceptable parts of the patient's self.

Psychodrama, a technique not broadly utilized or generally accepted, stands at one end of the spectrum of group therapy approaches, among those that rely on spontaneity and expressiveness. Such expressive, supportive, inspirational group approaches seem to have beneficial short-term effects. They enable patients to feel better and often to modify specific pathological behaviors. However, the long-term effects and the persistence of change wrought through such approaches remain questionable.

We must distinguish the use of "acting out" in psychodrama from "acting out" in psychoanalysis. Acting out in the psychoanalytic sense is the expression of unconscious conflicts through activity rather than by recall and verbalization. This nonverbal expression works against the therapeutic need to experience and analyze conflicts to gain greater insight. Acting out in the analytic context is a form of resistance that expresses in behavior the rigid and repetitive qualities of the unconscious.

In psychodrama, acting out through dramatic performance is a vehicle for making more conscious, and thus more available, the unconscious, repressed aspects of the patient's personality, his conflicts, wishes, feelings, and attitudes. For those patients whose capacities for verbalization are minimal or for whom verbal expression is difficult, dramatizing and acting out may be effective. Often therapeutic breakthroughs can be achieved this way. Psychodramatic techniques may have specific applicability when other therapeutic modalities have proved unsuccessful in reaching the patient. They may also be used to open up untouched areas of the patient's experience for further exploration. The development of firm guidelines for the use of psychodrama will depend on future experience and systematic evaluation.

Combined Therapies

Combined therapies integrate group or family therapy with individual psychotherapy. Clinical opinion varies from the belief that combined approaches should never be used to the belief that they should always be used. There are no clear indications for combined approaches, and at this point the decision to use them with a given patient is a matter of clinical judgment. Patients in individual therapy may benefit from the multiplicity of transference opportunities and social interactions provided by a group. Similarly, certain group patients may deepen their level of insight and working through in supplemental individual sessions.

The technical aspects of combined approaches will depend on whether the therapist and the group leader are the same individual or two different individuals. Where the therapist is also the group leader, transference intensifications may increase the patient's resistance; they may also have a clarifying effect. Another problem is that the increased individual attention may intensify the patient's narcissism and wish for intimacy with the therapist.

Where the therapist and group leader are different individuals, other kinds of transference difficulties arise. A splitting of the transference may sometimes occur so that the patient's negative feelings focus on one therapist and his positive feelings on the other. The patient may externalize conflicts by provoking disagreement between therapists who then make conflicting

recommendations to the patient. Therapeutic success depends in large measure on effective collaboration between the therapists and on their capacity to resolve personality differences. Where a therapist's narcissism or interpersonal difficulties contaminate the therapeutic collaboration, combined therapy will flounder. Disparities between therapists invite acting out behavior. The therapists must establish clear guidelines and fully agree on the respective areas of therapeutic responsibility.

Combined therapies have not been sufficiently used or studied to permit a sound appraisal. Evaluations up to this point have been unsystematic and anecdotal. In this as in all other areas of therapy, the selection of patients for whom a particular therapeutic approach will be appropriate poses a challenging problem for future evaluation.

The foregoing discussion of psychotherapeutic approaches used in modern psychiatry embraces a wide range of individual and group treatment modalities. The account is synthetic and condensed and does not allow us to consider many of the refinements or nuances of these approaches; neither have we the space here to include a variety of more or less experimental approaches to human behavior that lie closer to the fringe of psychiatric interest. Rather, we have focused our attention on the main modalities of psychotherapeutic intervention.

Our discussion has emphasized the importance of the role of careful and accurate diagnosis, both in the primary decision about what form of therapy will be undertaken to help the patient with his difficulties and in guiding the course of ongoing therapy. Discriminating the type of therapeutic approach that is appropriate for a given patient depends on the therapist's diagnostic skill; the same is true for continuing assessments of whether that therapy is in fact helping the patient and should be continued or, on the other hand, whether it needs to be modified, interrupted, or stopped.

The therapist-in-training should master one therapeutic approach to the best of his ability; as experience, necessity, or interest dictates, he should then begin to enlarge the range of his therapeutic skills by learning and working in other modalities. Two important results of his training should be an awareness of his own therapeutic limitations and the realization that a given therapist cannot and should not be expected to deal with all kinds of patients with all kinds of therapeutic modalities. Not only therapists but therapeutic modalities as well have inherent limitations. If a therapist masters a therapeutic technique, he learns and gains considerable respect for its limitations.

Forms of intensive, long-term, and anxiety-producing therapy—the model for which is psychoanalysis—cannot be usefully undertaken by many patients. They require a degree of ego strength that will allow the patient's ego to continue functioning adequately in performing the work of the analysis even in the face of the analytic regression. Patients whose tolerance for regression is poor, and whose capacity to maintain discriminating and synthetic ego functions in spite of such regression is compromised, obviously run the risk of an ego regression in such therapy and should not be subjected to it. The range of individual psychotherapy, however, is quite broad, and meaningful therapeutic work (with proper adaptation of the therapeutic approach to the patient's needs) can be done in nearly the full range of psychopathology. In acutely decompensated or psychotic patients, the therapy may need to be interrupted or combined with a variety of supportive and management techniques that help the patient to get through the period of acute psychosis and ideally enable him to return to the therapeutic work. With patients who cannot tolerate or use the therapy situation or whose motivation is inadequate for them to do any meaningful work within therapy, it is better not to undertake therapy and to utilize whatever other management approaches can be employed to help the patient deal with his difficulties.

Although psychiatrists in general have gained a great deal of knowledge and experience in treating various forms of psychopathology, much of this information remains impressionistic, intuitive, or anecdotal. Only in the last few years—with extensive and careful studies, particularly outcome studies of various forms of psychotherapeutic intervention, using appropriate techniques of patient selection, control groups,

and outcome evaluation—have we begun to collect hard data to reinforce and often correct our clinical impressions. However difficult and problematic such research may be, it offers us a solid hope that psychotherapeutic efforts will gain an increasingly firm and scientifically validated foothold in the armamentarium of psychiatric interventions.

References

American Psychiatric Association. 1968. *Diagnostic and statistical manual of mental disorders*. 2nd ed. Washington, D.C.

——— 1975. *A psychiatric glossary*. Washington, D.C.

Breuer, J., and S. Freud. 1895. Studies on hysteria. In *Standard edition*, ed. J. Strachey. Vol. 2. London: Hogarth Press, 1955.

Eysenck, H. J. 1965. The effects of psychotherapy. *Int. J. Psychiatry* 1:99–144.

Grinspoon, L., J. R. Ewalt, and R. I. Shader. 1972. *Schizophrenia: pharmacotherapy and psychotherapy*. Baltimore: Williams & Wilkins.

Kernberg, O. F., E. D. Burstein, L. Coyne, A. Applebaum, L. Horwitz, and H. Voth. 1972. Psychotherapy and psychoanalysis. *Bull. Menninger Clin.* 36:1–275.

May, P. R. A. 1968. *Treatment of schizophrenia*. New York: Science House.

Sifneos, P. E. 1972. *Short-term psychotherapy and emotional crisis*. Cambridge, Mass.: Harvard University Press.

Winnicott, D. W. 1965. *The maturational processes and the facilitating environment*. New York: International Universities Press.

Recommended Reading

Ackerman, N. W., ed. 1958. *The psychodynamics of family life*. New York: Basic Books.

———, ed. 1970. *Family process*. New York: Basic Books.

Adler, G., and P. G. Myerson, eds. 1973. *Confrontation in psychotherapy*. New York: Science House.

Balint, M., P. Ornstein, and E. Balint. 1972. *Focal psychotherapy: an example of applied psychoanalysis*. Philadelphia: Lippincott.

Balsam, R. M. and A. 1974. *Becoming a psychotherapist: a clinical primer*. Boston: Little, Brown.

Bergin, A. E., and H. H. Strupp. 1972. *Changing frontiers in the science of psychotherapy*. Chicago: Aldine-Atherton.

Berne, E. 1966. *Principles of group treatment*. New York: Oxford University Press.

Bion, W. R. 1961. *Experiences in groups*. London: Tavistock.

Boszormenyi-Nagy, I., and J. L. Framo, eds. 1965. *Intensive family therapy*. New York: Harper & Row.

Bruch, H. 1974. *Learning psychotherapy*. Cambridge, Mass.: Harvard University Press.

Dewald, P. 1970. *Psychotherapy: a dynamic approach*. 2nd ed. New York: Basic Books.

Fenichel, O. 1941. *Problems of psychoanalytic technique*. Albany, N.Y.: *Psychoanal. Q.*

Foulkes, S. H. 1965. *Therapeutic group analysis*. New York: International Universities Press.

Foulkes, S. H., and E. J. Anthony. 1965. *Group Psychotherapy: the psychoanalytic approach*. 2nd ed. Baltimore: Penguin.

Frank, J. D. 1961. *Persuasion and healing: a comparative study of psychotherapy*. Baltimore: Johns Hopkins University Press.

Fromm-Reichmann, F. 1950. *Principles of intensive psychotherapy*. Chicago: University of Chicago Press.

Greenson, R. R. 1967. *The technique and practice of psychoanalysis*. Vol. 1. New York: International Universities Press.

Haley, J. 1963. *Strategies of psychotherapy*. New York: Grune & Stratton.

Haley, J., and L. Hoffman. 1967. *Techniques of family therapy*. New York: Basic Books.

Kaplan, H. I., and B. J. Sadock, eds. 1971. *Comprehensive group psychotherapy*. Baltimore: Williams & Wilkins.

Langs, R. J. 1973. *The technique of psychoanalytic psychotherapy*. Vol. 1. New York: Aronson.

—— 1974. *The technique of psychoanalytic psychotherapy*. Vol. 2. New York: Aronson.

——1976a. *The bipersonal field*. New York: Aronson.

——1976b. *The therapeutic interaction*. 2 vols. New York: Aronson.

Lidz, T., S. Fleck, and A. R. Cornelison. 1965. *Schizophrenia and the family*. New York: International Universities Press.

Malan, D. H. 1963. *A study of brief psychotherapy*. Philadelphia: Lippincott.

Mann, J. 1973. *Time-limited psychotherapy*. Cambridge, Mass.: Harvard University Press.

Paul, I. H. 1973. *Letters to Simon: on the conduct of psychotherapy*. New York: International Universities Press.

Powdermaker, F., and J. D. Frank. 1953. *Group psychotherapy*. Cambridge, Mass.: Harvard University Press.

Slavson, S. 1964. *A textbook on analytic group psychotherapy*. New York: International Universities Press.

Toman, W. 1969. *Family constellation*. New York: Springer-Verlag.

Wallerstein, R. S. 1975. *Psychotherapy and psychoanalysis: theory, practice, research*. New York: International Universities Press.

Wolf, A., and E. K. Schwartz. 1962. *Psychoanalysis in groups*. New York: Grune & Stratton.

Yalom, I. 1975. *The theory and practice of group psychotherapy*. 2nd ed. New York: Basic Books.

Zuk, G., and I. Boszormenyi-Nagy, eds. 1967. *Family therapy and disturbed families*. Palo Alto, Cal.: Science & Behavior Books.

Chemotherapy

CHAPTER 18

Ross J. Baldessarini

THROUGHOUT the recorded history of medicine, attempts have been made to utilize chemical or medicinal means to modify abnormal behavior and emotional pain. Alcohol and opiates have been used for centuries, not only by physicians and healers but also spontaneously for their soothing or mind-altering effects. Stimulant and hallucinogenic plant products have also been a part of folk practices for centuries. More recently, man has applied modern technology, first to "rediscovering" and purifying many natural products and later to synthesizing and manufacturing their active principles or structural variants with desired effects. Throughout the discussion that follows, the classes of chemicals used for their "psychotropic" effects (altering feelings, thinking, and behavior) will be referred to by the somewhat awkward terms *antipsychotic*, *antidepressant*, and *antianxiety* agents. This system of terminology grows out of the "allopathic" tradition of modern scientific medicine based on treatment by drugs producing effects opposite or antagonistic to those of a given illness. It has been estimated that perhaps 10 percent of the American population uses psychotropic agents by prescription.

The modern era of psychopharmacology has been dated from 1949, when the antimanic effects of the lithium ion were discovered, or 1952, when reserpine was isolated and chlorpromazine and the monoamine oxidase inhibitor iproniazid were introduced into Western medicine. Also in the early 1950s, the antidepressant monoamine oxidase (MAO) inhibitors and, soon thereafter, the tricyclic antidepressant agents were introduced. Meprobamate was introduced in 1954, and chlordiazepoxide was being developed before 1960. Thus by the end of the 1950s psychiatry had available therapeutic agents for the major psychoses, including schizophrenia, mania, and severe depression, and for more minor neurotic disorders. Remarkably few new kinds of psychotherapeutic agents have appeared since that time. The past twenty years have been marked by an accumulation of structural analogues of the earlier agents (which are more similar than different) and by considerable gains in understanding the biological and clinical actions of the drugs and their appropriate use.

The impact of the modern psychopharmaceuticals on the practice of psychiatry in the 1950s and 1960s has been compared with the impact of antibiotics on medicine. Quantitatively, the utilization of chlorpromazine compares well with that of penicillin: in the first decade of its availability this antipsychotic drug was given to approximately 50 million patients, and about 10,000 scientific papers were written about it. In the 1970s, the tens of millions of prescriptions for psychoactive agents account for almost 20 percent of all prescriptions, a fact that underscores the revolutionary impact of these drugs on clinical as well as theoretical psychiatry.

Prior to the 1950s, most severely disturbed psychiatric patients were managed in relatively isolated, secluded, private or public institutions, usually with locked doors, barred windows, and other physical restraints. The few medical means of managing them included the use of barbiturates, bromides, narcotics, and anticholinergic drugs such as scopolamine for sedation, as well as soothing baths and wet packs, "shock" therapies with insulin or convulsant drugs, and, later, electrically induced convulsions and neurosurgical techniques including prefrontal leukotomy. Since that time, most of those forms of treatment, except for electroconvulsive therapy (ECT), have virtually disappeared. Most locked doors have opened; patients and psychiatric treatment facilities themselves have been returned to "the community," to general hospitals, and to open day hospitals, or to hospital-based or local outpatient clinics. To conclude that the availability of modern drugs has been solely responsible for these changes would be a gross exaggeration. During the same period, changes in the management of psychiatric patients were also beginning; these included the use of group and milieu techniques, an appreciation of the untoward regressive effects of institutions upon behavior, and a strongly increased social consciousness throughout medicine, particularly in community psychiatry. A fair conclusion would be that these social and administrative changes and the new drugs had mutually facilitating and enabling effects.

Statistics that confirm the important impact of the antipsychotic and antidepressant drugs on hospital practice include the observation that in the United States the number of hospitalized psychiatric patients reached a peak of close to 0.6 million in 1955, with an initially rapid and now slower downward trend since that time (about 0.2 million in 1974), despite a net increase in the total population. This change has resulted not only from beneficial effects of the modern drugs but also from policy decisions to alter the pattern of health care delivery. Rates of new admissions and of readmissions have not kept pace with the potentially misleading decline in the prevalence of hospitalization; in certain categories, especially among the very young and the very old, new admission rates have increased since the 1950s. Although a number of patients who might formerly have been hospitalized are now kept "in the community," often under conditions of marginal or inadequate adjustment causing considerable distress to their families, certainly a large proportion of patients formerly kept in hospitals for many months are now capable of returning to useful and productive lives in weeks or even days thanks to both the current philosophy of care and the effects of modern chemotherapy (more information on these topics is available in chapter 29, "Psychiatric Epidemiology").

A number of very serious problems remain, despite the striking improvements in our ability to manage patients with psychotic mental illnesses. While many acute episodes of psychosis can be interrupted or shortened with modern therapies, and while highly disturbed and regressed behavior is now relatively infrequent even in public mental institutions, available chemotherapies have severe shortcomings. These include limitations of efficacy and problems of toxicity. Many chronic and difficult schizophrenic patients do not respond well to antipsychotic drugs. In such cases, the temptation to "do something" by continuing to use medications indefinitely at some risk of potentially irreversible neurological side effects should be resisted. The antidepressant drugs are not only relatively toxic, potentially lethal, and used in a population at high suicidal risk, but they are also slow and clinically unsatisfactory drugs; their efficacy in comparison to placebo is not always obvious.

The difficulties and expense of developing new drugs call for increased cooperation among the pharmaceutical industry, federal regulatory agencies, and academic psychopharmacologists, particularly since the rate of development of significantly new and better agents has slowed in the past decade, while the shortcomings of existing agents (toxicity of antipsychotic agents and toxicity and ineffectiveness of antidepressants) have become increasingly evident.

Antipsychotic Agents

The category of antipsychotic agents includes a number of compounds proven effective in the management of a broad range of psychotic symptoms and particularly useful in the treatment of schizophrenia and mania. Nearly all of the currently available agents produce a variety of neurological effects in animals and in patients, and considerable speculation has focused on whether the neurological effects of these drugs on the control of movement are necessary or even desirable. Some psychopharmacologists have been sufficiently struck by the regular association between antipsychotic and extrapyramidal effects (such as parkinsonism, dystonias, and dyskinesias) to suggest the term *neuroleptic* (producing signs of neurological disorder) for this class of drugs, a usage common in Europe.

Pharmacology

The earliest antipsychotic drugs were the phenothiazines and the *Rauwolfia* alkaloids (1952–53), although the usefulness of lithium salts for the management of excited or manic patients had been described earlier (1949). The first antipsychotic phenothiazine, chlorpromazine, was developed in France. Chlorpromazine was first tried clinically in 1951 as a preanesthetic sedative by the French surgeon Laborit, who described some of its peculiar effects on behavior ("artificial hibernation"), including a retention of consciousness associated with striking indifference to the surroundings. In 1951–52 in Paris, several psychiatrists noted the ability of the new agent to increase the efficacy of barbiturates to sedate manic and other psychotic patients. In 1952–53, Delay and Deniker reported a more extensive experience with the use of the new agent alone in psychiatric patients in Paris. The drug was used as early as 1954 in the United States but its unique usefulness in psychosis was not at first appreciated, although it was used as an antiemetic, sedative, and hypothermic agent.

Nearly twenty phenothiazines have reached the stage of clinical application since the introduction of chlorpromazine; they include several subtypes that differ in the chemical structure of the side-chain moiety (table 18.1, fig. 18.1). The terminal amine group may have straight carbon-chain substituents (*aliphatic* or *aminoalkyl* phenothiazines, such as chlorpromazine, promazine, and triflupromazine), or it may incorporate the amino nitrogen atom into a cyclic structure, as in the *piperidine* derivatives (such as thioridazine and mesoridazine) and the potent *piperazine* derivatives (such as trifluoperazine, perphenazine, and fluphenazine). The tricyclic core of the molecules was also altered, without loss of antipsychotic effects, and the *thioxanthenes* became the first nonphenothiazine antipsychotic agents. The thioxanthenes also include aliphatic types (such as chlorprothixene) and several potent piperazines (such as thiothixene). Further experimentation with the tricyclic structure has resulted in other structural variants of the phenothiazines, notably the still-experimental *acridanes*, which have a nitrogen atom in the central ring but no sulfur atom.

In Belgium in 1959, Janssen, while experimenting with a series of derivatives of meperidine (Demerol) in search of a better analgesic agent, developed the *butyrophenones*, which can also be called *phenylbutylpiperidines* (fig. 18.2). The only butyrophenone in regular clinical psychiatric use in the United States as an antipsychotic agent at present is haloperidol. Droperidol (Inapsine), another butyrophenone, is available as an anesthetic agent, although it can also be used in psychiatric emergencies. The butyrophenones share with the piperazine phenothiazines high potency and a strong tendency to affect the extrapyramidal motor system, but the butyrophenones have considerably less tendency to produce sedation, hypotension, and anticholinergic effects.

Several new compounds structurally related to the butyrophenones are undergoing clinical study at the present time. They include the *diphenylbutylpiperidines*, such as pimozide, penfluridol, and fluspirilene (see fig. 18.2). These compounds are interesting because pimozide is

TABLE 18.1. Equivalent doses of commonly used antipsychotic agents, by chemical type.

Generic name	Trade name[a]	Approximate dose (mg/day)[b]
Phenothiazines		
Aliphatic		
Chlorpromazine	Thorazine, etc. (generic)	100
Triflupromazine	Vesprin	30
Piperidine		
Mesoridazine	Serentil	50
Piperacetazine	Quide	12
Thioridazine	Mellaril	95
Piperazine		
Acetophenazine	Tindal	20
Butaperazine	Repoise	12
Carphenazine	Proketazine	25
Fluphenazine	Prolixin, Permitil	2[c]
Perphenazine	Trilafon	10
Trifluoperazine	Stelazine	5
Thioxanthenes		
Aliphatic		
Chlorprothixene	Taractan	65
Piperazine		
Thiothixene	Navane	5
Dibenzazepines		
Loxapine	Loxitane, Daxolin	15
Clozapine	(Leponex, experimental)	60
Butyrophenones		
Haloperidol	Haldol	2
Diphenylbutylpiperidines		
Pimozide	(Orap, experimental)	0.3–0.5
Penfluridol	(experimental)	2 (1 week dose)[c]
Fluspirilene	(experimental)	—
Indolones		
Molindone	Moban	10
Rauwolfia alkaloids		
Reserpine	Serpasil, etc. (generic)	1–2

[a] Trade names in parentheses are not yet licensed in the U.S. The commercial preparations are available as soluble salts (most are hydrochlorides; Loxitane or Daxolin is a succinate; Repoise is a maleate). Other agents that are not commonly employed now or are less effective are not included, e.g., mepazine (Pacatal), promazine (Sparine), prochlorperazine (Compazine). A recent survey of the cost of antipsychotic agents indicated that the least expensive preparations (less than $20 for a typical one-month supply) were: Permitil < Moban < Thorazine < Stelazine < Prolixin < Taractan < Prolixin decanoate < Repoise.

[b] Data are summarized as averages from several sources, some of which vary greatly. These numbers are only an approximate guide, and dosage for each patient must be established by the clinical response. In switching from high doses of one agent to a dissimilar one, it is well to proceed gradually over several days to decrease the risk of side effects from the newly introduced drug.

[c] Injectable fluphenazine esters are used in doses of 25–100 mg every 1–4 weeks. Long-lasting diphenylbutylpiperidines can be used once weekly; penfluridol can be used as 2 percent of a *weekly* dose of chlorpromazine (i.e., 40 mg/week can replace 2100 mg/week of chlorpromazine).

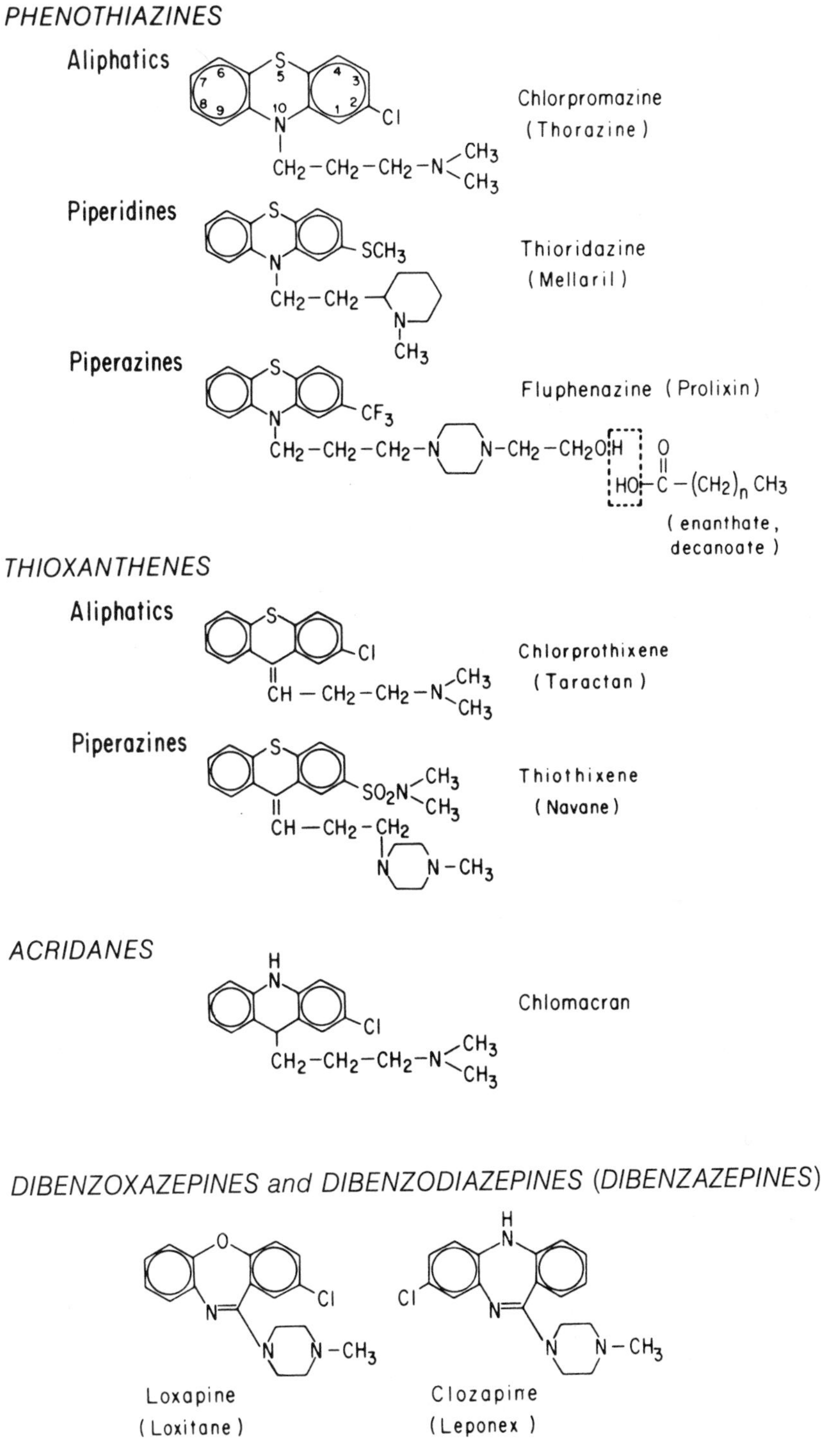

FIGURE 18.1. Tricyclic antipsychotic agents.

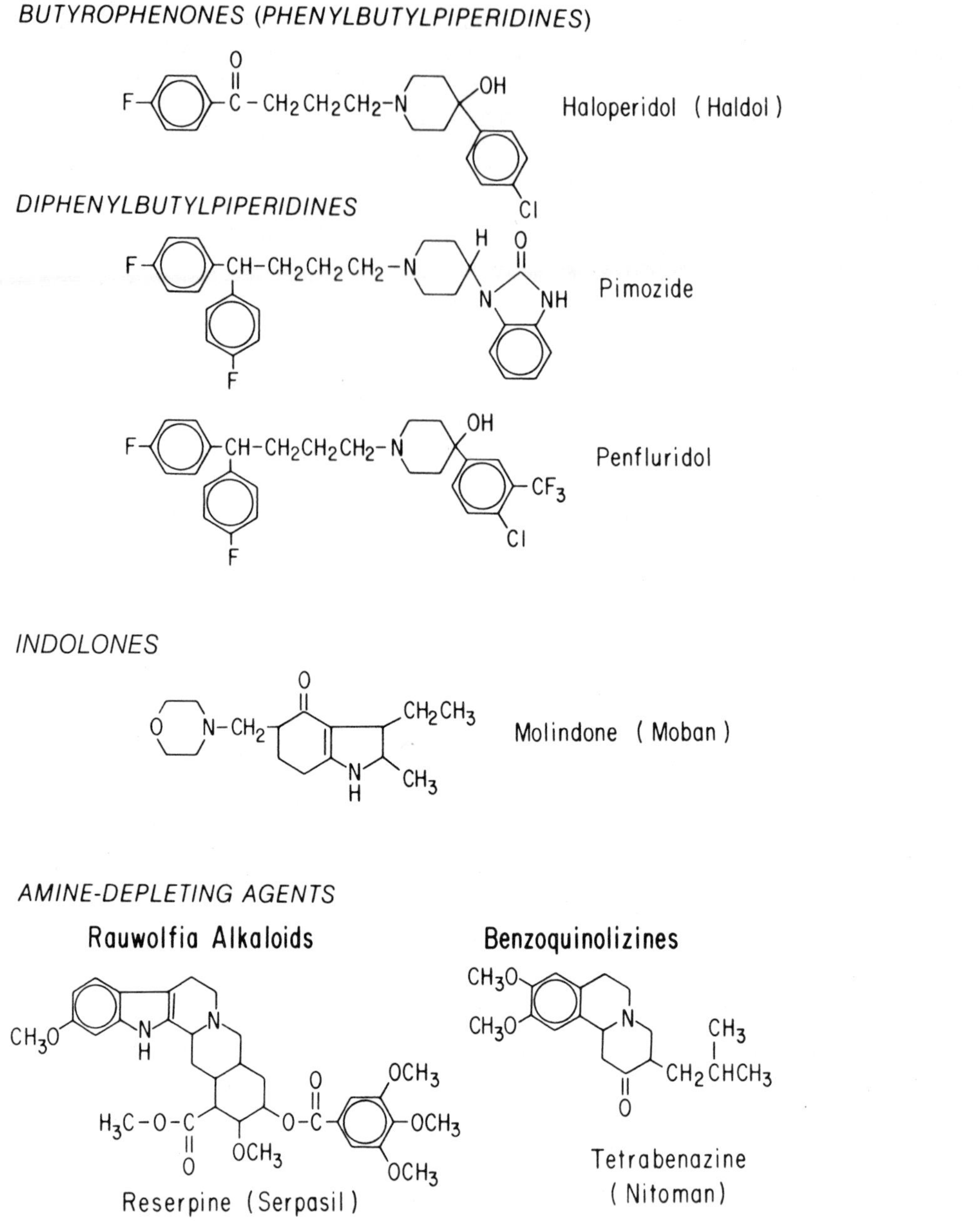

BUTYROPHENONES (PHENYLBUTYLPIPERIDINES)

Haloperidol (Haldol)

DIPHENYLBUTYLPIPERIDINES

Pimozide

Penfluridol

INDOLONES

Molindone (Moban)

AMINE-DEPLETING AGENTS

Rauwolfia Alkaloids

Reserpine (Serpasil)

Benzoquinolizines

Tetrabenazine (Nitoman)

FIGURE 18.2. Other antipsychotic agents.

one of the most potent neuroleptic agents known, and its effects on central catecholamine mechanisms are quite selective for dopamine receptors. In addition, penfluridol and fluspirilene have a prolonged duration of action, lasting about a week, even after oral administration. The only other long-acting antipsychotic agents are long-chain aliphatic fatty-acid esters of fluphenazine

(the enanthate or the decanoate), which are useful in the management of chronically psychotic outpatients who are unreliable in taking oral medications, as their effects last from one to four weeks after a depot injection in oil.

Another class of antipsychotic compounds of potentially great importance are the piperazine derivatives of *dibenzazepine* tricyclic molecules, such as clozapine (see fig. 18.1), or their structural analogues (the recently released dibenzoxazepine, loxapine, with an oxygen atom instead of a second nitrogen atom in the central ring, and metiapine, a dibenzo*thi*azepine with a sulfur atom replacing the same nitrogen atom). Clozapine has particular theoretical and practical importance as it is reported to lack the neurological (neuroleptic) actions of other antipsychotic agents in animals and in patients. This finding supports the hope that other drugs can be developed that retain the desired antipsychotic effects without producing extrapyramidal reactions.

A number of other types of molecules with demonstrated antipsychotic effects include indole derivatives, *indolones*, like oxypertine and the recently approved molindone (see fig. 18.2). A large number of other agents has been partially evaluated but none is yet available commercially.

In addition to these agents, several alkaloids derived originally from the Indian snakeroot plant (*Rauwolfia serpentina*) and later synthesized, notably reserpine, rescinnamine, and deserpidine, are known to have antipsychotic actions; for a short time in the early 1950s there was considerable interest in their clinical effects. A number of entirely synthetic polycyclic compounds, such as tetrabenazine (fig. 18.2) and benzquinamide, share with the Rauwolfia alkaloids the ability to deplete amine stores from cells containing catecholamines and indoleamines, particularly in the brain. This amine depletion probably contributes to the autonomic and central depressant effects of these agents. While all of these amine-depleting agents have some antipsychotic efficacy, they did not produce clinical benefits equal to those of the phenothiazines in controlled comparisons. This limited efficacy and their considerable side effects (especially sedation, hypotension, and marked vagal dominance in the gut), together with a tendency to induce depression, have led to their virtual abandonment for the treatment of psychotic illness. It is, however, worth knowing that reserpine, in much higher doses (5–10 mg/day or more) than used for the treatment of hypertension, can be utilized if side effects or allergic reactions preclude the use of other antipsychotic drugs.

The antipsychotic drugs' mechanism of action is not completely understood. Their phar-

macological actions at the level of the reticular formation, hypothalamus, and limbic system of the brain appear to correlate well with their behavioral and clinical effects, while other effects at the hypothalamus and basal ganglia seem to account for many of the autonomic and neurological side effects of these agents. At the neuronal level, an important effect of these drugs is the blockade of central neurotransmission mediated by dopamine. Many of these local actions are probably mediated by the actions of the drugs on neuronal membranes, although the precise local chemical changes remain obscure.

Clinical Use

One of the most difficult problems for a physician is choosing from the bewildering variety of antipsychotic compounds now available. The most important generalization that will help simplify the problem is that antipsychotic drugs are remarkably similar in their main effects and overall efficacy. The available controlled clinical trials of many drugs do not yet permit a rational selection of a class of agents, much less a particular drug, for a specific type of psychotic patient, nor does a rational basis for combining different antipsychotic agents now exist. On the other hand, it is reasonable to try a number of agents serially, in adequate and increasing doses (or even by injection and for periods of several weeks or months), to give an individual patient who responds poorly to an initial medication the benefit of any doubt. Moreover, all drugs may not be equally effective for a given patient, and it is unwise to change to another antipsychotic agent when one drug seems to be working well. It is important to realize, however, that a very common reason for apparent failure of treatment is reluctance to take the medication prescribed.

Because there are clear differences in the incidence of side effects with different classes of antipsychotic agents, the selection of a drug for an individual patient can rationally be made on the basis of side effects. While the *potency* (effect per milligram) of antipsychotic agents can vary by more than a hundredfold (see table 18.1), the overall clinical *efficacy* for most agents, as determined in controlled comparisons of large numbers of cases of schizophrenia, is remarkably similar, provided that adequate doses were used (at least the equivalent of 300–400 mg of chlorpromazine a day). Similar data based on large numbers of systematic comparisons are unfortunately not available for other forms of psychosis, although the same generalization appears clinically to be valid for most types of psychotic illness.

A few notable exceptions to this rule have been found. For example, in about 60 percent of controlled studies, promazine (Sparine) and mepazine (Pacatal) were no better than a placebo, and reserpine failed to produce results better than placebo in about a third of its trials. Furthermore, since prochlorperazine (Compazine) failed in about 22 percent of comparisons with placebo and is associated with a high risk of acute dystonic reactions, it cannot be recommended as an antipsychotic agent. Molindone is not consistently as effective as other antipsychotic drugs, although it offers the advantage of chemical dissimilarity to other agents for cases of dangerous sensitivity reactions; among newer agents, chemical uniqueness is also provided by loxapine. Nearly every other antipsychotic agent in common use produced better results than placebo in at least 80–90 percent of comparisons. Although in 17 percent of 66 controlled studies chlorpromazine failed to be more effective than placebo, these results cannot be taken as important evidence against its efficacy, since they include a number of older studies in which relatively small doses of the drug, now known to be inadequate, were given. Moreover, in at least 97 studies that have made direct comparisons of antipsychotic agents in schizophrenia, no agent was demonstrated to be more effective than chlorpromazine. In a large NIMH-VA cooperative study (Caffey et al., 1970), comparing a phenothiazine with a placebo, 75 percent of schizophrenic patients improved within six weeks and only 5 percent became clinically worse, while of those given a placebo only 25 percent were improved and 50 percent were unchanged or worse. Ordinary sedatives such as phenobarbital have consistently failed to produce better results with psychotic patients than an inactive placebo.

Clinical folklore based on anecdotal experience and perhaps on a misinterpretation of the significance of certain side effects has led to the widespread but probably erroneous impression that the high-potency agents (particularly the piperazine phenothiazines and the butyrophenones) are somehow more "incisive" in their ability to interrupt florid psychotic symptoms, or that the same agents are uniquely beneficial for withdrawn and apathetic schizophrenics due to putative "activating" effects. Few firm data derived from controlled clinical trials support these concepts. While no scientific support for these practices exists, there is also no reason *not* to select the more potent antipsychotic agents for floridly psychotic or withdrawn patients. Attempts to tailor therapy to the individual patient's requirements are also reasonable. These can include trying a different type of agent, experimenting with higher doses than usually recommended in a hospital setting for limited periods of time if little progress is observed within several weeks, and making clinical use of differences in side effects among the various drugs. The selection of appropriate dosages can be facilitated by a table of therapeutically equivalent doses (see table 18.1). The phenothiazines with low potency tend to have greater sedative side effects (and more tendency to produce hypotension in the initial phase of treatment) and thus are reasonable choices for very agitated and sleepless patients. Administering most or all of a daily dose at bedtime for patients with insomnia or for those troubled by sedation during the day is also reasonable. This practice is safest after an initial period of adaptation to gradually increasing, divided daily doses. The relatively slow clearance rates of the antipsychotic agents permit this practice, as well as the occasional omission of doses for several days or sometimes several weeks, later in the course of prolonged maintenance therapy, without appreciable loss of antipsychotic effect. Prolonged periods without medication are not likely to be tolerated until after at least several months of treatment, possibly because the drug gradually saturates tissue pools that turn over slowly.

With the possible exception of elderly and infirm senile patients, demonstration of consistent antipsychotic effects at doses less than the equivalent of 300–400 mg of chlorpromazine a day is difficult. Furthermore, antipsychotic drugs in low doses are not particularly good antianxiety agents and have too much risk of side effects to indicate their routine use in the management of ordinary or neurotic anxiety. The selectivity of the clinical actions of antipsychotic agents, in contrast to sedatives and antianxiety agents, fails to support the older idea that antipsychotic drugs were simply "tranquilizers." Moreover, the ability of antipsychotic drugs to interrupt specific features of psychotic illnesses, including delusions and hallucinations, often with a gradual disappearance of thought disorder, strongly suggests that the terms *tranquilizer* and *major tranquilizer* should be abandoned.

While the term *antischizophrenic* has been suggested as a synonym for "antipsychotic" agents, this usage misrepresents the fact that antipsychotic agents are useful for a number of severe psychiatric illnesses, including schizophrenia, mania, agitated psychotic depression, paranoid disorders, involutional and senile psychoses, some aspects of organic dementia and acute brain syndromes, and reactions to hallucinogens such as amphetamine (although benzodiazepines are more often used for reactions to hallucinogens other than amphetamines). Moreover, the antipsychotic effects are most readily observed in acute and florid cases of psychotic excitement with considerable psychotic anxiety and agitation. It is possible (but hard to prove or disprove) that the effects on thinking and social behavior are secondary to the reduction of these aspects of psychotic affect. The main clinical consideration is that psychosis should not be treated with sedatives (except for rapid sedation in emergencies) or antianxiety agents, nor should antipsychotic agents ordinarily be used to treat anxiety. The target symptoms that consistently benefit from antipsychotic drugs include combativeness, tension, hyperactivity, hostility, negativism, hallucinations, acute delusions, insomnia, poor self-care, anorexia, and sometimes seclusiveness; improvement in insight, judgment, memory, and orientation, however, is less likely.

In addition to acuteness and excitation, other predictors of favorable response to antipsychotic drugs include lack of an insidious, prolonged onset or a long chronic history; history of a relatively healthy premorbid adjustment and social, educational, and professional accomplishment; lack of previous psychotic breakdown; and prior favorable responses to similar medications or other physical treatments.

Abundant evidence now shows that the currently available antipsychotic drugs are effective in treating psychosis. As we have seen, controlled studies using more than 300 mg of chlorpromazine a day, or equivalent doses of other antipsychotic drugs, have consistently demonstrated their efficacy, for the most part in patients within the schizophrenic diagnostic spectrum. These results have led to the current impression that failure to treat relatively acute exacerbations of psychoses, including chronic forms of schizophrenia, with antipsychotic medications in adequate doses is irresponsible. In many cases of truly chronic "poor prognosis" schizophrenia, the benefits of indefinite chemotherapy become increasingly difficult to demonstrate as the duration of treatment and illness increase. Moreover, the sometimes modest benefits are harder to justify against the risks involved, particularly the possibility of potentially irreversible neurological sequelae, notably tardive dyskinesia, and subtle impairment of the higher cortical functions and psychomotor skills. Unfortunately, the best data are based on relatively short periods of maintenance support with the antipsychotic agents. They suggest an appreciable relapse rate following recovery from an acute psychotic illness or exacerbation of schizophrenia when active medication is discontinued immediately upon discharge from hospital. Interestingly, relapse is unusual within the first few weeks after discontinuation of medication and is most likely to occur between the second and sixth months. For this reason, the usual practice is to continue antipsychotic medications for several months or even a year or longer after the period of initial improvement. The reasons for this pattern of relapse are obscure but may include the gradual removal of medication that accumulated in the initial weeks of treatment.

In managing patients with psychotic illnesses over many years, the conduct of a medication regimen requires considerable clinical judgment and flexibility toward the changing clinical needs of the patient. The safest guideline is to use the least medication for the shortest time necessary to obtain the desired results, with occasional attempts to reduce dosage or to omit medication for at least a few days at a time, or even for weeks or months, watching closely for early signs of psychotic relapse that signal the need for more medication. Only rarely will a patient require a rigidly fixed dose of medication indefinitely.

A more complicated question is whether other forms of treatment contribute importantly to the management of chronic schizophrenic psychoses. Unfortunately, the evaluation of the role of psychotherapies in schizophrenia has been much less rigorous than that of the chemotherapies. However, some information is available, based on comparisons of chemotherapy and other psychosocial forms of treatment, including work at the Massachusetts Mental Health Center (Grinspoon, Ewalt, and Shader, 1972) and the extensive studies of May in California (1968). These studies concluded that the presence or absence of an antipsychotic agent made a marked difference in the clinical outcome in schizophrenia, while supportive milieu treatment and rehabilitation efforts or intensive psychotherapy, even when conducted by experienced therapists, contributed very little and were largely ineffective when used without medication. In a similar study of nearly 400 chronic schizophrenics, Hogarty and his colleagues (1973) evaluated the rate of relapse after a year of treatment and found that only 26 percent of the patients treated with chlorpromazine plus supportive psychotherapy relapsed (and perhaps 10 percent in that category did not take the medication regularly), while 63 percent treated with identical support plus placebo relapsed; withholding psychotherapy, that is, using drug treatment alone, increased the relapse rates by only another 10 percent.

The importance of psychotherapy in the treatment of schizophrenia remains a controversial topic and one that is still heavily influenced by traditions and schools of thought and practice rather than by scientific evaluation. Clearly, dynamic and psychoanalytic psychotherapy has contributed a great deal to our appreciation of the psychotic experience and to hypotheses about intrapsychic dynamics and the possible

influences of early and current life experiences on the course of schizophrenia. Moreover, some analytic therapists have invested enormous efforts in the treatment of small numbers of chronic schizophrenics with encouraging but anecdotal results. A fair consensus exists among psychotherapists that probing and uncovering techniques are contraindicated in the psychotherapy of schizophrenia. Even though its efficacy is not rigorously demonstrated, many psychiatrists include supportive and rehabilitative efforts with medications in their work with chronically psychotic patients on both clinical and humanitarian grounds. On the other hand, the still prevalent hypothesis that thorough and lasting change in schizophrenia can only be gained by prolonged, intensive, and expensive attempts to bring about characterological change must be judged as unproven at the present time. Moreover, the idea that medications are merely palliative or even capable of depriving patients of a positive or "growth-promoting" experience of "working through" the psychosis in psychotherapy can no longer be supported. Psychosis is painful and its early termination or alleviation should be the desired and appropriate goal of management. Moreover, a confused and incoherent patient is not an optimal candidate for rational verbal psychotherapy, and evidence suggests that the antipsychotic agents can facilitate the relationship and verbal interchanges between patient and therapist (Grinspoon, Ewalt, and Shader, 1972).

A recent source of suspicion and criticism of the use of medication in schizophrenia has come from the suggestions of some overly zealous community-oriented professionals and certain "antipsychiatrists" critical of the "medical model" of schizophrenia as a disease. They have asserted that medications are used by agents of an oppressive society (medically trained psychiatrists) to control eccentric or sensitive persons or to force upon them a medical label for what is really a unique or idiosyncratic life style or highly personal point of view. Finally, it can be stated categorically that the use of "orthomolecular" or "megavitamin" treatments for chronic psychosis has not been demonstrated to have anything to offer (Lipton, 1973).

Toxicity and Side Effects

The most important point to clarify concerning the systemic toxicity and side effects of the antipsychotic agents is that they are in general among the safest drugs available in medicine. This safety in no small measure accounts for their enormous popularity and widespread use. The overall incidence of important systemic side effects during the short-term use of these drugs is a few percent, although effects that are more annoying than dangerous regularly occur. These side effects include peculiar feelings of heaviness or sluggishness, weakness or faintness, and a variety of mild anticholinergic autonomic effects, including dry mouth and blurred vision.

Among the most common side effects are those involving movements and posture, presumably mediated by the effects of the antipsychotic agents on the extrapyramidal motor system. For example, the common drug-induced parkinson syndrome may reflect the ability of the antipsychotic agents to block the actions of dopamine as a synaptic neurotransmitter in the caudate nucleus of the brain, much as spontane-

ously occurring parkinsonism reflects the selective degeneration of the nigrostriatal dopamine-mediated pathway to the caudate nucleus. Several discrete extrapyramidal syndromes are associated with the use of neuroleptic antipsychotic agents, including acute dystonias, parkinsonism and motor restlessness (akathisia), late or tardive dyskinesia, and unusual reactions such as withdrawal dyskinesias and catatonia. Except for parkinsonism, the pathophysiological bases of these reactions are not clear.

The *acute dystonias* occur within the first few days of treatment and are most common with the more potent agents, especially the piperazine phenothiazines and haloperidol. Seen somewhat more frequently in younger male patients, they involve moderate or dramatic and distressing tonic contractions of the muscles of the neck, mouth, and tongue and may include the axial-postural muscle groups in opisthotonos; oculo-gyric crisis also occurs. The main problem with this syndrome is to recognize it and not to ascribe it to a seizure disorder, tetany, or tetanus or, as too commonly happens, to call it "hysterical." When the diagnosis is considered, the

TABLE 18.2 Equivalent doses of antiparkinson agents.

Generic name	Trade name	Dose range (mg/day)[a]
Amantadine	Symmetrel	100–300
Benztropine	Cogentin	1–6
Biperiden	Akineton	2–6
Diphenhydramine	Benadryl	25–100
Ethopropazine	Parsidol	50
Orphenadrine	Disipal, Norflex	300
Procyclidine	Kemadrin	6–20
Trihexyphenidyl	Artane, etc. (generic)	5–15

[a] These agents are commonly prescribed orally three times a day to provide the total daily adult doses stated. Benztropine (2 mg) and diphenhydramine (25–50 mg) are commonly used intramuscularly or intravenously to reverse acute dystonic reactions to antipsychotic agents. Amantadine has recently been used to treat drug-induced parkinsonism and catatonia; it is relatively expensive. Diphenhydramine and orphenadrine are antihistaminic and anticholinergic; ethopropazine is a strongly anticholinergic phenothiazine; the other agents are atropinelike. Most are available as soluble hydrochlorides.

treatment by parenteral injection of an antiparkinson agent can be dramatically effective (see table 18.2). Two popular agents to counteract this side effect are diphenhydramine (Benadryl, 25–50 mg intramuscularly or 25 mg intravenously) and benztropine mesylate (Cogentin, 2 mg intravenously), although positive results have also been obtained with agents as dissimilar as sedatives and anxiolytic (antianxiety) agents such as diazepam (Valium) and stimulants such as caffeine. If dystonic reactions recur frequently, calcium metabolism should be evaluated.

The syndrome of *drug-induced parkinsonism* (which should *not* be called "pseudoparkinsonism") is strikingly similar to other forms of the condition, except that tremor is less prominent, and includes bradykinesia and rigidity, stooped posture, festinating gait and masklike inexpressive facies, and sometimes drooling. The onset of the syndrome is usually after the first week of treatment and within the first month. Although no "tolerance" to these drugs' antipsychotic effects develops, some degree of tolerance to their extrapyramidal effects is evident, since the motor signs usually fade away over two or three months, leading to a decreasing requirement for antiparkinson medications.

The proper place of antiparkinson medications in the management of antipsychotic chemotherapy remains somewhat controversial. As a general practice, use of antiparkinson medications "prophylactically" before manifestation of extrapyramidal side effects is not necessary, although these agents are sometimes used in this way. Continued use of these agents for longer than two or three months at constant dosage is less reasonable. A number of practical and theoretical reasons support the recommendation to use the lowest effective doses of antiparkinson drugs for the shortest possible time: dystonic crises and severe parkinson reactions are not routinely expected; treatment can easily be initiated when it is indicated; tolerance to the early extrapyramidal effects of antipsychotic drugs is usual; and the potent anticholinergic properties of antiparkinson agents can induce toxic brain syndromes that are not always immediately recognized in psychotic patients. Moreover, evidence exists that anticholinergic agents can di-

minish the intestinal absorption of antipsychotic medications, and preliminary evidence suggests that they may partially interfere with antipsychotic effectiveness. There are also good evidence that anticholinergic agents can worsen many cases of tardive dyskinesia and some theoretical reasons to suspect that they might contribute to the risk of developing it.

Among the antiparkinson agents, those most widely used to treat drug-induced parkinsonism are the anticholinergic and antihistaminic agents (table 18.2). Amantadine (Symmetrel) may also be useful; it has almost no anticholinergic activity and may be less toxic than other antiparkinson agents. Although the dopamine agonists, amphetamine and L-dopa, can be used in spontaneous forms of parkinsonism, their tendency to induce agitation and psychotic exacerbation contraindicates their use with psychotic patients. The use of antiparkinson agents can also be minimized or avoided by lowering the dose of the antipsychotic drug or by changing to one with less potential for inducing extrapyramidal reactions. As a general rule, antipsychotic agents with higher potency induce dystonic reactions and parkinsonism with greater frequency than less potent agents (table 18.1), while the less potent agents tend to induce sedation and autonomic effects more frequently. Moreover, agents with low potency and relatively strong central anticholinergic actions, notably thioridazine (Mellaril), are particularly unlikely to induce extrapyramidal effects.

The other important early motoric symptom that occurs along with or slightly later than parkinsonism is the sometimes highly distressing motor restlessness, fidgeting, pacing, "restless legs," and drive to move about known as *akathisia* (or acathisia, but *not* "akathesia" or "akisthesia"). This syndrome is frequently dismissed as a sign of increasing psychotic anxiety or agitation and inappropriately treated by increasing the dose of the antipsychotic drug. The reaction can sometimes be managed by reducing the dose of antipsychotic medication or by changing to a different agent. Antiparkinson drugs may have a beneficial effect, as do anxiolytic agents with muscle-relaxing properties such as diazepam (Valium). Unfortunately, many cases respond poorly to treatment and a clinical decision must be made, weighing the distress of the akathisia against the need for antipsychotic medication.

Among the less frequent reactions to antipsychotic agents are *catatonic reactions* and *"withdrawal dyskinesias."* Severe akinetic and catatonic reactions and mutism have been associated with high doses of potent antipsychotic agents such as fluphenazine or haloperidol, particularly in those patients with previous extrapyramidal reactions including bradykinesia and rigidity. Sometimes such reactions look more like malignant, acute forms of parkinsonism. The use of intravenous amobarbital (Amytal) is not helpful in differentiating this reaction from catatonic schizophrenia, as psychotic thinking may or may not be expressed. The temptation will be to give even higher doses of the offending antipsychotic agent, although improvement usually follows *reduction* of its dosage.

Some evidence exists that antiparkinson agents, including amantadine (Symmetrel), may also be of value. The recently popular attempt to treat schizophrenic patients poorly responsive to usual oral doses of antipsychotic drugs with parenteral medication or with "megadoses" of potent agents (up to hundreds of milligrams of haloperidol or fluphenazine), somewhat surprisingly, has been reported not to be attended by an impressive increase in the incidence of acute extrapyramidal reactions. On the other hand, the abrupt withdrawal of such doses of drug is very frequently complicated by the development of acute choreoathetotic reactions, similar in appearance to tardive dyskinesia but usually lasting for only a few days. Similar reactions have been described after the abrupt discontinuation of usual doses of antipsychotic agents in children and young adults. Hypothetically, these reactions might represent a rebound functional increase in the activity of previously inhibited dopaminergic mechanisms in the basal ganglia.

A late-appearing extrapyramidal syndrome is leading to a reappraisal of the value of uninterrupted and indefinitely prolonged antipsychotic chemotherapy of chronic psychosis; it is called *tardive* (late) *dyskinesia*. This syndrome was reported as early as 1959 and is being recognized more frequently now. It consists of involuntary or semivoluntary movements of a choreiform tic-like nature, sometimes with an athetotic or dystonic component; it classically involves the tongue, facial, and neck muscles but often affects the extremities and muscles controlling posture and sometimes those involved in breathing. The earliest sign of tardive dyskinesia may be subtle vermiform movements of the surface of the tongue or the floor of the mouth. Although "oral-buccal-masticatory" movements are commonly considered the most classical form of the syndrome and are especially common in older patients, abnormalities of posture and at least mild choreiform movements of the fingers and toes are not unusual. Younger patients often have impressive involvement of the extremities and trunk. There is some evidence that senility or underlying organic brain damage may predispose to this syndrome, and spontaneous pouting, sucking, and tongue-thrusting movements are not uncommon in senile brain disease. These are further reasons for using smaller doses of antipsychotic agents in elderly patients, who may also be unusually sensitive to their cardiovascular effects.

Drug-related tardive dyskinesia can occur in otherwise healthy young patients and even in those who do not have a chronic psychosis. Although some forms of the syndrome might be mistaken for the peculiar stereotyped movements seen in some chronic schizophrenics, the movements of tardive dyskinesia are much less voluntary and purposeful and more classically choreoathetotic. The movements in tardive dyskinesia generally become much worse on withdrawal of the antipsychotic medication, and they can be *temporarily* suppressed by administering higher doses of the offending agent or other potent antipsychotic agents as well as the amine-depleting agents reserpine and tetrabenazine or other antidopamine agents. The leading current hypothesis is that the syndrome may represent a functional overactivity of dopamine as a neurotransmitter in the central nervous system (CNS), possibly arising with attempts to compensate for the chronic blockade of dopaminergic mechanisms produced by the antipsychotic drugs. Since the syndrome may be irreversible or may last for many months after withdrawal of the antipsychotic agents, other irreversible neurotoxic effects on central neurons seem probable; the current neuropathological information on this question remains equivocal.

While the syndrome of tardive dyskinesia has been said to be more unsightly than subjectively distressing and is claimed to be a relatively trivial matter in most cases, this view is not correct. The syndrome, though painless, can be quite embarrassing and distressing, especially in outpatients who function relatively well. In some cases, the patient's skills in feeding and self-care, as well as in vocational manual dexterity, can be badly impaired, and severe cases can be as disabling as Huntington's disease. A thorough neurological evaluation of cases of tardive dyskinesia will include a vigorous attempt to exclude other forms of choreiform disease such as Huntington's disease, rheumatic chorea, Wilson's disease, and other rare toxic or degenerative dyskinetic syndromes. The incidence of the syndrome has varied among epidemiological studies from a few percent to as much as 40–50 percent of patients maintained on antipsychotic medications for many years. The syndrome rarely develops in less time than a few months, and there is some evidence that if antipsychotic agents are withdrawn early, the signs of tardive dyskinesia may fade within a period of months.

The treatment of tardive dyskinesia is highly unsatisfactory; antiparkinson agents usually worsen the condition. The most effective short-term treatment is to suppress the manifestations of the disorder with any potent antipsychotic or amine-depleting agent, but this approach usually requires increasing doses of the suppressing agent, fails eventually, and may contribute further to the underlying problem. On the other hand, there is currently no evidence that continued suppression of the symptoms results in their eventual worsening. Perhaps the best means of dealing with the problem, as the search for "nonneuroleptic" antipsychotic agents continues, is to seek to avoid it by the thoughtful and conservative use of antipsychotic medications in low but effective doses, and only as indicated by *objectively discernible and clinically responsive* signs of improvement in psychotic disorders of thought, mood, or behavior.

Some evidence indicates that low-potency phenothiazines may increase the incidence of *seizures* in epileptic patients, although the pi-perazines and haloperidol may have somewhat less tendency to do this. Usually a clinical decision must be made to balance the need for antipsychotic medication and the control of seizures with anticonvulsants, the dosage of which may need to be increased.

Antipsychotic agents have also been associated with severe "*hypothalamic crises,*" marked by hyperthermia, sweating, drooling, tachycardia, dyspnea, seizures, and unstable blood pressure. Milder forms of the same symptoms sometimes accompany severe extrapyramidal toxicity of antipsychotic drugs. Similar reactions and rare instances of unexplained (presumably cardiac) "sudden death" have been ascribed to the tricyclic antidepressants as well as to antipsychotic agents.

A remarkable characteristic of antipsychotic agents, in contrast to most other central nervous system depressants, is that their lethality and potential for inducing deep and prolonged coma and respiratory depression are quite limited. Thus they have a very high *therapeutic index* (ratio of toxic or lethal dose to effective dose). Their lethal dose in humans is not known; patients have survived acute ingestions of many grams of these agents, and it is virtually impossible to commit suicide by an acute overdosage of an antipsychotic agent. On the other hand, since ingestions are often mixed, it is essential to consider the presence of potentially more lethal and treatable forms of acute intoxication, including those due to barbiturates or to agents with important central anticholinergic activity, such as the tricyclic antidepressants and the common antiparkinson agents. For the latter forms of intoxication, dialysis can be used to remove barbiturates; it is not possible to remove antipsychotic agents or antidepressants by dialysis due to their strong binding to protein and lipids. The central anticholinesterase agent, physostigmine (or eserine, Antilirium) can be used to treat the central anticholinergic (atropinelike) syndrome (see table 18.5). Physostigmine can also have beneficial effects in some cases of intoxication with an antipsychotic agent alone, especially thioridazine, a particularly anticholinergic phenothiazine. The attempt to induce vomiting after overdoses of antipsychotic agents may be unsuccessful due to their antiemetic effects. One practical result of the limited acute toxicity and addiction potential of the antipsychotic agents is that large quantities of the drugs can be prescribed with relative impunity, even for patients with impaired judgment and impulse control.

The peripheral *anticholinergic actions* of most antipsychotic agents are modest and are usually limited to annoying symptoms such as dry mouth and blurred vision, although ileus and urinary retention can occur, particularly in older patients. One should worry about the chance of precipitating an acute attack of glaucoma with any agent with anticholinergic activity, but even with antidepressant drugs, this event is rare and is usually associated with "narrow angle" glaucoma, itself unusual. Acute glaucoma is an emergency calling for immediate ophthalmological treatment. Chronic glaucoma can almost always be managed with cholinomimetic eye drops, even while anticholinergic psychotropic agents are used. Cholinergic agents in eye drops (such as pilocarpine nitrate, 1-percent ophthalmic solution) to overcome cycloplegia, or in a mouthwash or orally (in daily doses of 5–15 mg of neostigmine, or 5–10 mg of pilocarpine) to increase salivation, can be tried, but they have not been particularly helpful in countering side effects of the antipsychotic or antidepressant agents; 75 mg/day of bethanechol (Urecholine) may be useful.

A number of other *ophthalmological problems* may occur with the antipsychotic agents. The most serious is an irreversible degenerative pigmentary retinopathy due to large doses of thioridazine (above 900 mg/day). In addition, prolonged high doses of low-potency phenothiazines and thioxanthenes have been associated with the deposit of drug substances and pigment in the cornea and lens, as well as in the skin. Deposits in the eye can be visualized best with a slitlamp, rarely impair vision appreciably, and slowly disappear over many months after withdrawal of the medication. Although penicillamine and other agents have been advocated to hasten the removal of phenothiazines from the eye or skin, there is little evidence that they help appreciably. Skin reactions include photosensitivity early in treatment and, later, a blue gray discoloration, usually associated with prolonged high doses of chlorpromazine. Maculopapular rashes occur on occasion, and there is some risk

of contact dermatitis among nurses handling solutions of antipsychotic agents.

The risk of severe *cardiovascular toxicity* due to antipsychotic agents is not high. Although frank hypotension is not often encountered, orthostatic hypotension can be a problem, especially with the less potent phenothiazines and in elderly patients. The hypotensive effects of these agents are quite idiosyncratic and poorly correlated with doses; thus the common ritual of giving small test doses of intramuscular medication to patients newly treated with phenothiazines is poorly founded. An important practical reason for avoiding large intramuscular doses, especially of the less potent agents, is that they are painful and may lead to elevated levels of transaminases or lactic dehydrogenase due to local necrosis (and *not* to liver damage). If severe hypotension does develop, it can usually be managed by bed rest, elastic stockings, and elevation of the legs. If a vasoactive agent is required, the rational choice is a purely alpha-adrenergic pressor amine such as metaraminol (Aramine) to reverse the modest alpha-antagonistic effects of phenothiazines; rarely will the more potent agent *l*-norepinephrine (Levophed) be required. Beta-agonistic cardiac stimulants such as epinephrine or isoproterenol (Isuprel) will contribute to pooling of blood in the splanchnic and peripheral areas to worsen the hypotension and are thus contraindicated. The effects of antipsychotic agents on blood pressure are unpredictable, and they carry a slight risk of increasing the vulnerability to potentially lethal ventricular cardiac arrhythmias (a much more serious problem with the tricyclic antidepressants), as well as of potential drug interactions (see table 18.6). It is therefore preferable to omit the medication for a day or two prior to electroconvulsive therapy (ECT) with barbiturate anesthesia and prior to surgery whenever possible. Haloperidol, the potent piperazine phenothiazines, and molindone may be relatively safe for cardiac patients and less likely to interact badly with digitalis and other cardiovascular and diuretic agents.

Other annoying side effects of antipsychotic agents include presumably *autonomic* or *hypothalamic effects* such as changes in appetite, weight gain, fluid retention, breast enlargement and engorgement (in males as well as females) and even galactorrhea, changes in libido, and ejaculatory incompetence in males. These effects are most often associated with the less potent phenothiazines and particularly with thioridazine (Mellaril). Thioridazine has even been advocated as an adjunct in the treatment of premature ejaculation.

Finally, although there has been a great deal of concern about jaundice and agranulocytosis due to antipsychotic agents, these problems are in fact encountered infrequently. The *jaundice* is almost always an allergic cholestatic type and is usually transient. It was formerly observed more commonly than it is today, particularly in association with chlorpromazine, and may be less frequent now (incidence not more than 2 percent) due to the increased purity of the drug. It usually appears within the first month of treatment. Frank *agranulocytosis* is rare (incidence less than 0.01 percent) and has a peak incidence within the first two months of treatment, particularly in older females. Agranulocytosis is a potentially catastrophic and often rapidly developing medical emergency with a high mortality rate. It can rarely be predicted from occasional routine white blood cell counts and must be suspected and promptly evaluated in cases of malaise, fever, or sore throat that occur early in the course of antipsychotic chemotherapy. Leukocyte counts, frequently repeated in the first two months of treatment, may reveal a downward trend, predicting agranulocytosis, although early, moderate, nonprogressive reductions in white blood cell counts are not unusual. For these reasons, some hematologists now advise weekly leukocyte counts for at least eight weeks. A number of defensive rituals of little value have developed in the medical management of prolonged use of antipsychotic agents, including occasional routine "liver function tests" and "blood counts," which contribute little except a false sense of security and possibly some decreased risk of the accusation of malpractice. Such laboratory tests cannot substitute for an alert and clinically well-informed physician.

The question of the safety of antipsychotic agents in *pregnancy and lactation* is still poorly resolved. These agents do pass the blood-placenta barrier as well as the blood-brain barrier and are to some extent secreted in human milk; they can induce a mild degree of sedation followed by motoric excitement in the newborn. There is no evidence, however, that they are responsible for an increased incidence of fetal malformations. Nevertheless, the current consensus is that the use of antipsychotic agents should be avoided insofar as possible in pregnancy and lactation, certainly in the first trimester of pregnancy. On the other hand, clinical judgment must be exercised in cases where the indications for medication or psychiatric hospitalization are compelling.

Summary

The availability of modern, effective, and safe antipsychotic drugs has contributed to an almost revolutionary change in the pattern of delivery of psychiatric care. These agents have supported and reinforced the recent melioristic expectations of hospital and community psychiatry. Most psychotic patients can be managed in open psychiatric hospitals or in general hospitals, and the duration of hospitalization has been markedly reduced. Many psychotic patients can be maintained at home, and many incipient attacks of acute psychosis can be managed by psychiatrists or primary care physicians without the need for hospitalization. A large number of antipsychotic drugs exists, and most are also more or less neurotoxic or "neuroleptic."

Although there are many chemical types of antipsychotic drugs, they are pharmacologically more similar than different, partly as a result of the method of predicting the antipsychotic activity of new agents by their essentially neurological actions in animals. The main shortcoming of the available antipsychotic agents is their regular tendency to produce acute and sometimes long-lasting or even irreversible forms of neurological disorder of the extrapyramidal motor system. A second shortcoming of antipsychotic drugs is that their efficacy is easiest to demonstrate in patients with acute illnesses with the best prognosis; an increasing frequency of disappointing results is encountered, however, as the duration of chronic psychosis, and particularly "process" schizophrenia, lengthens. Better agents are being sought that would produce antipsychotic effects with minimal neurological toxicity.

Lithium Salts

Although antipsychotic drugs are used in the treatment of mania, the lithium ion is a unique agent with considerable selectivity in the treatment of mania. Lithium is greatly inferior to the antipsychotic agents, however, in the treatment of other forms of psychosis, particularly schizophrenia. It may have beneficial effects on certain acute psychoses, sometimes called "acute schizophrenic reactions," in which an affective component is very prominent and some of which may represent atypical forms of mania. Lithium salts also have a unique place in the long-term maintenance of patients with a variety of severe recurrent mood disorders. The differential effectiveness of antipsychotic agents and lithium salts has led to a much needed reawakening of interest in the careful differentiation of acute psychoses and reconsideration of a tendency in American psychiatry to use the term *schizophrenia* inappropriately, almost as a synonym for *psychosis*.

Cade in Australia gave animals a lithium salt, noted a quieting effect, and decided to try lithium clinically as a sedative. In 1949, he reported several striking anecdotes of responses among severely disturbed manic patients. This report led to an intense investigation of the biology and clinical actions of lithium salts in Europe in the 1950s and 1960s. The results of several studies led to the early acceptance of lithium into European and English psychiatric practice as a highly effective and safe treatment for manic-depressive illness, both for the treatment of acute mania and for reducing the frequency and severity of recurrent mania and depression. Lithium salts were not accepted into American practice until 1970 for a number of reasons. One was strong skepticism among American physicians about the safety of lithium salts, following reports in 1949–50 of several cases of severe intoxication and even of death among medically ill patients using large uncontrolled amounts of lithium chloride as a salt substitute while on a sodium-restricted regimen for cardiac or renal failure. We now know that sodium restriction and diuresis increase the retention and toxicity of the

lithium ion markedly and that lithium salts cannot be used safely in gram quantities without careful monitoring of blood levels. In addition, lithium has a very narrow margin of safety (low therapeutic index; see table 18.3). Another factor contributing to the slowness of development of lithium therapy was lack of commercial interest in this inexpensive, unpatentable mineral and, consequently, lack of industrial support to demonstrate the efficacy and safety of its use. Before lithium was accepted into American psychiatric practice, an overwhelming amount of evidence was accumulated to support its usefulness and safety. Experimentation is currently underway to evaluate the possibility that other metal ions might have useful behavioral effects; cesium can produce behavioral quieting in animals, and rubidium has many characteristics similar to those of potassium and can produce behavioral stimulation in animals. Rubidium has already been given to humans safely and has some apparent stimulatory or antidepressant activity.

Pharmacology

Lithium is usually administered as 300-mg tablets or capsules of the dibasic carbonate salt, Li_2CO_3 (as the generic substance or as the commercially available preparations Eskalith, Lithane, or Lithonate). Lithium is readily absorbed after oral administration (injectable forms are not used), and it is easily measured by techniques used to assay sodium and potassium. Unlike sodium and potassium ions, lithium lacks a preferential distribution across cell membranes. Lithium ion is eliminated almost entirely by renal excretion. As with sodium, 70–80 percent of the lithium ion, which readily passes into the glomerular filtrate, is reabsorbed in the proximal renal tubules, with almost no absorption of lithium in the distal renal tubules. Sodium diuresis and deficiency of sodium tend to increase the retention of lithium and hence to increase its toxicity. The average half-life of lithium in the body varies somewhat with age, from about 18 to 36 hours. It is not possible to increase the rate of removal of lithium by the administration of most saluretic drugs; the thiazide diuretics or spironolactone, by preferential removal of sodium, may even increase lithium retention and toxicity. The use of lithium in patients with salt restriction or sodium wasting requires extra caution in monitoring blood levels of lithium and avoiding intoxication. Fluid loading, solute-induced diuresis (as with mannitol), and theophylline can all contribute to some increased renal excretion of lithium in cases of intoxication, and dialysis techniques are very effective in serious cases of overdosage.

The mechanism of action of lithium ion in affective disorders is still not clearly defined, although several interesting aspects of its effects have been pointed out. Most of the attention has been directed to the effects of lithium on electrolyte balance across membranes, including neurons. Although lithium might help to correct a reported tendency for intracellular sodium concentration to increase in severe affective disorders, the detailed mechanisms by which lithium might thus exert a beneficial or mood-stabilizing effect are not clear. Moreover, the basic concept that the distribution of sodium is abnormal in mania and severe depression is not well established. Considerable evidence supports the view that lithium in clinically attainable concentrations can exert antagonistic actions at synapses mediated by catecholamines in the brain (see fig. 18.4). These actions include inhibition of the release of norepinephrine and dopamine, as well as weak actions on the uptake (increases) and retention (decreases) of catecholamine neurotransmitters in presynaptic nerve terminals. Lithium ion interferes with the ability of some hormones to stimulate adenylate cyclase, which is believed to be an important component of the receptor mechanism of several hormones, including the catecholamines. These findings accord well with the popular hypothesis that catecholamines may be functionally overactive in the brain in mania, but they do not help to explain the reported mood-normalizing actions of the lithium ion in recurrent depressive illnesses.

Clinical Use

Lithium carbonate was not licensed for the treatment of mania in the United States until 1970. Since considerable fear about its toxic potentialities still exists, it has only gradually been accepted into general psychiatric practice outside of teaching centers. A recent estimate is that only about 50,000 patients are receiving this agent, while perhaps a million or more Americans with severe recurrent mood disorders could be so treated.

A large number of controlled studies demonstrate the efficacy of lithium carbonate in hypomania and acute mania, with improvement rates typically of 70–80 percent in ten to fourteen days. Considerable evidence also indicates that this agent has significant prophylactic utility in preventing recurrent attacks of mania and of manic and depressive episodes in bipolar affective disorders. In a recent review of eight controlled studies of the prophylactic effects of lithium, the overall relapse rate was 68 percent among 274 patients given a placebo and only 23 percent among 271 patients maintained on a lithium salt (Davis, 1975). The initial indication for which lithium carbonate was licensed was the treatment of mania per se, although at the present time the prolonged use of lithium for prevention of recurrent mania and of bipolar disorders is also a widely accepted practice. The evidence for the utility of lithium salts in the treatment of unipolar recurrent depressive disease is still incomplete, and support for the usefulness of lithium as a primary treatment for depressive illnesses is weak and inconsistent.

One of the problems in evaluating lithium's spectrum of utility in psychiatric illness is the differential diagnosis of the psychoses and the severe mood disorders. While lithium salts are a poor treatment for schizophrenia, some evidence suggests that they may have beneficial effects in some atypical forms of acute psychosis, particularly in "schizoaffective schizophrenia," and in dysphoric or paranoid forms of mania, which can be as florid as an acute exacerbation of a schizophrenic illness (Gershon and Shopsin, 1975). There is also a growing impression that many cases that superficially appear as unipolar recurrent depression are found, on close investigation, to have episodes of moderate euphoria and increased energy, activity, and productivity.

One other important aspect of lithium carbonate is that even though its usefulness in acute mania is solidly based on experimental evidence, the response to lithium by itself is, in fact, usually impractically slow. The addition of an antipsychotic agent within the first few days of treatment is usually necessary to bring about prompt behavioral control of frank mania, particularly in a general hospital or an open psychiatric unit. More promising is the evidence that lithium therapy may serve to diminish the rate and severity of recurrences of mood disorders.

While some hesitation to use lithium therapy remains, the principles of its use are really quite simple (table 18.3). In most cases, treatment will be started with an episode of acute mania or hypomania. Although a tendency to avoid initiating treatment in depressed manic-depressive patients has developed, no evidence exists that this is necessary. If lithium is started mainly for its prophylactic actions in a period of normal mood, or if its use is to be continued indefinitely after an acute attack of mania, two important guidelines should be followed. First, the indications should be convincing and, second, the patient should be reliable enough to follow the required medical regimen. Thus infrequent episodes of even severe mania or depression separated by several years, or relatively frequent episodes of milder abnormalities of mood, require clinical judgment to balance the inconvenience and risk of the treatment against the indications for it. Very impulsive or suicidal patients are not good candidates for the sustained use of lithium treatment on an outpatient basis, since the ingestion of even a few days' supply of lithium car-

bonate can be highly toxic or even lethal. One advantage of lithium in prophylactic treatment is that many bipolar or recurrent manic patients who are reluctant to be inhibited by antipsychotic agents or to engage in prolonged contact with a psychiatrist or psychotherapist will accept the almost imperceptible subjective effects of lithium and will comply with medical supervision and blood tests.

When lithium treatment is initiated in hypomania or mania, it is usual to hospitalize the patient, although treatment can sometimes be started on an outpatient basis. Initial medical evaluation should include a physical examination and laboratory tests of renal, electrolyte, and thyroid function, fasting blood sugar, complete blood count, and electrocardiogram (EKG). While lithium has been used safely and successfully in cases of severe cardiovascular and renal disease, these conditions require close monitoring of electrolyte balance and excellent medical consultation. The requirements for repeated laboratory and medical evaluations are not clearly established, but sound practice calls for reevaluation of renal, electrolyte, cardiac, and thyroid functions and general medical status at least once or twice a year.

When administration of lithium carbonate is started in manic patients, the initial dose is usually 600 or 900 mg/day, in divided oral doses

TABLE 18.3. Principles of the use of lithium ion.

Indications

- Acute hypomanic and manic episodes
- Recurrent manias, bipolar illness, and perhaps depressions

Acute treatment

- Slow action as plasma Li^+ reaches 1.2–1.6 mEq/liter
- Usually add antipsychotic agent during early phase of treatment
- Monitor serum level and watch closely for toxic signs
- Expect toxicity at 2–3 and lethality above 5–7 mEq/liter

"Maintenance" treatment

- May add antidepressants, ECT, or antipsychotics as needed
- Plasma levels 0.8–1.2 mEq/liter
- Monitor serum levels infrequently
- Li^+ retention and toxicity increased if Na^+ decreased: with sweating, diarrhea, diuresis (including postpartum diuresis); and on resolution of mania
- Watch skin, thyroid, renal function

(table 18.3). The goal is to increase the dose gradually over several days to attain blood levels above 1.0 mEq/liter (ideally between 1.2 and 1.6 mEq/liter); although blood levels as high as 2.0 mEq/liter have been accepted, this is probably an unnecessarily risky general practice. Rapid increases in the dose and blood level of lithium ion often produce gastrointestinal distress, which can usually be avoided by increasing the dose gradually and by using the medication three or four times a day with or just after a meal. The required final oral dose to attain the desired blood level varies considerably; younger and larger patients require larger doses. Typically, doses range between 1200 and 3600 mg/day for manic patients.

The most important principle in the use of lithium is that with this drug, unlike every other medication used in psychiatry, the oral dose is not an adequate guideline; the proper maintenance of blood concentrations of the agent is crucial. Because of the short half-life of the lithium ion in the body, blood levels vary markedly over the twenty-four-hour cycle; therefore, doses must be divided and blood levels assayed according to a strict protocol. The accepted convention defines appropriate blood levels as those measured eight to twelve hours after the final dose of the day and prior to the first morning dose. In the first few days of lithium therapy in manic patients, blood assays should be obtained daily and then every other day. An antipsychotic drug will probably be required in the first week of treatment. While electroconvulsive therapy was formerly common in the treatment of mania, its usefulness has never been properly established scientifically; with the availability of antipsychotic agents, ECT is rarely necessary in the treatment of mania. Once the appropriate dose of lithium carbonate is known, it can be continued until the mania begins to abate; at this point, risk of change in the fluid and electrolyte balance occurs, as well as increased chance of lithium intoxication, calling for gradual reductions in the dose toward a "maintenance" blood concentration of about 1.0 mEq/liter.

For prophylaxis after discharge from hospital, blood levels of 0.8–1.2 mEq/liter are adequate and safe. Usually each patient has a stable requirement of the total daily dose to obtain the desired blood level of lithium (typically between 600 and 1500 and most often 900 mg/day), although considerable variation occurs among patients. After a few weekly blood assays to establish the appropriate maintenance dose for the individual patient, blood assays can be performed infrequently, perhaps monthly or even less often, with random and unannounced blood samples taken as a check on the reliability of the patient's use of the drug. Normally salt supplements are not necessary, but the maintenance of a normal sodium intake and output is important. Patients have been maintained on stable doses of lithium carbonate between episodes of mania or depression for many years without problems.

Toxicity and Side Effects

The most common problems associated with the use of lithium salts are mild or occasionally distressing nausea, vomiting, and diarrhea, usually when doses are increased rapidly. Effects on the nervous system, including lightheadedness, may also be felt, but typically the subjective effects of lithium are minimal and patients rarely complain of feeling "medicated" or mentally dull. A fine resting tremor is common and is of no particular importance, although a clear increase in tremor or unsteady handwriting can be an important early clue to incipient intoxication. The most important means of detecting serious intoxication early are the clinical signs, and blood assays should be considered only as secondary and confirmatory. When signs of intoxication are noted, the intake of lithium should be decreased or stopped without waiting for the results of a blood lithium assay.

Early signs of *intoxication* include increasing tremor, weakness, ataxia, giddiness, drowsiness, slurred speech, blurred vision, and tinnitus. More severe intoxication includes increased neuromuscular irritability, increased deep tendon reflexes, nystagmus, and increasing lethargy and stupor leading to frank coma, sometimes with generalized seizures. Extrapyramidal reactions are rare with ordinary doses of lithium, but choreoathetosis can occur with severe intoxication. The electroencephalogram (EEG) ordinarily reveals generalized slowing, with a prominent activity at 4–6 Hz (cycles per second), even without toxic levels of lithium. Toxicity can be expected at blood levels of 2–4 mEq/liter, and levels much above 5 mEq/liter may be fatal. In acute lithium overdoses, the usual causes of death are the secondary complications of coma, including pneumonia and shock. A small number of cases of uncertain significance have been reported that raise the question of whether the combination of lithium in high doses with haloperidol may produce severe forms of irreversible and even fatal CNS intoxication, although this combination has been used safely throughout the world for many years and continues to be used. It is particularly important to watch for subtle forms of organic mental disorder (delirium) in elderly patients receiving prolonged lithium treatment.

Cardiovascular problems are unusual in patients given controlled quantities of lithium salts. Hypotension and arrhythmias are rare, although electrocardiographic changes can occur. With doses that are likely to be encountered clinically, the most typical changes are similar to those associated with hypokalemia, even though blood levels of potassium are almost always normal. These changes include flattening and even inversion of the T waves; effects are dose-dependent and reversible and probably have little pathophysiological significance. In experimental animals, extraordinarily high concentrations of lithium (above 10 mEq/liter) have been reported to produce changes resembling those of hyperkalemia, including high, peaked T waves, T-wave inversions, depressed S-T segment, widened QRS complex, and evidence of atrioventricular dissociation and conduction blockade. Depressed or absent P waves and atrial fibrillation and standstill with independent ventricular responses also occur.

Severe *renal tubular damage* due to lithium had been a concern, mainly because pathological changes were reported in early cases of gross overdosage with lithium chloride in patients with preexisting circulatory and renal disease. Renal tubular damage in the rat was also reported, but these findings are difficult to relate to the clinical situation since the studies involved toxic doses of lithium salts. A much more likely clinical problem is nephrogenic diabetes insipidus resulting in the intake of many liters of water per day and the output of huge quantities of very dilute urine. This syndrome is now believed to be due to the ability of lithium ion to interfere with the activity of antidiuretic hormone (ADH) on the renal tubules, either preventing its access to the membrane receptor site or blocking the response of an ADH-sensitive adenylate cyclase. This syndrome is usually managed conservatively by reducing the intake of lithium or by completely discontinuing its use. When there are compelling indications to continue the use of lithium, the syndrome often responds paradoxically to thiazide diuretics, as do other forms of nephrogenic diabetes insipidus; this treatment might be considered after appropriate medical consultation.

Another metabolic abnormality is the development of *goiter* in patients receiving ordinary doses of lithium salts for prolonged periods. Patients almost always remain euthyroid or slightly hypothyroid, although the circulating levels of thyroid-stimulating hormone (TSH) may increase, resulting in a form of benign, diffuse nontoxic goiter. There is experimental evidence of lithium's ability to interfere with thyroid metabolism at several points, including the iodination and release of iodinated tyrosine, and some evidence of its interference with the actions of thyroxin on target tissues, much as the actions of ADH seem to be impaired (Gershon and Shopsin, 1975). Again, there is no serious danger from the goiter, but judgment must be exercised, with the help of endocrinological consultation, as to whether to continue the treatment with lithium. Rarely will significant functional hypothyroidism or frank myxedema occur, although in many cases thyroxin leads to regression of the goiter and the maintenance of a euthyroid status while lithium therapy is pursued.

Other toxic effects of lithium include the occasional development of localized edema and eruptions or even ulcerations of the *skin*. Antihistaminic agents help the rashes, and for the rare skin ulcers, topical steroids are useful. Hepatic and bone marrow toxicity are rarely associated with lithium therapy, although mild elevations of the leukocyte count in the peripheral blood of uncertain significance are not unusual.

A great deal of concern surrounds the use of lithium in *pregnancy and lactation*, partly based on evidence in experimental animals that very high doses of lithium are associated with fetal wastage and anomalies of the central nervous system. Together with other alterations in fluid and electrolyte metabolism in pregnancy, lithium clearance increases; with the diuresis after delivery, there may be an increased retention of lithium and increased risk of intoxication. Fetal distress may occur when lithium is used near term, and hypotonia and listlessness may follow hyperkinesis in the newborn infants of mothers taking lithium. A small number of reports of human fetal anomalies associated with the use of lithium in pregnancy exist, together with sufficient circumstantial evidence concerning the potential fetal toxicity of lithium to urge avoidance of its use in the early months of pregnancy, to advise caution and discontinuation of lithium before term, and to permit the use of lithium in pregnancy only for the most urgent indications.*

Summary

Lithium ion provides a useful and specific form of chemotherapy for manic and hypomanic episodes, although its clinical actions may be delayed for a week or more, requiring the use of an antipsychotic agent in the initial period to control the behavior of very disturbed patients. The main limitation of lithium is its narrow therapeutic index and requirement of close medical supervision. The most promising aspect of the use of lithium is its prophylactic effectiveness in reducing the frequency and severity of manic and depressive attacks in manic-depressive illness.

Antidepressant Agents

Until the 1950s, the medical treatment of depression included the amphetamines for psychomotor retardation and the barbiturates for agitation. Although stimulants are still occasionally used for cases of mild, short-term neurotic depression, there is little reason to use these medications in most cases of depression. Their use in severe depression is not indicated and may even worsen agitation and psychosis. In the late 1940s,

structural analogues of nicotinic acid used in the treatment of tuberculosis, especially the hydrazine compound *iproniazid* (Marsilid), were found to have euphoriant or mood-elevating and behaviorally activating properties in some patients. In the early 1950s, iproniazid was reported to have useful antidepressant properties in psychiatric patients, and it was found to be a potent and irreversible inhibitor of the amine-catabolizing enzyme, monoamine oxidase (MAO). Since that time other hydrazine compounds and nonhydrazines with MAO-inhibiting properties have been introduced into psychiatric practice; they will be discussed below. A few years later, the second important and now dominant class of antidepressants, *tricyclic antidepressant compounds*, was introduced.

The "tricyclic" compounds have two benzene rings joined through a central seven-member ring (fig. 18.3). The original compound of this class, imipramine (Tofranil) was developed and tested clinically in schizophrenics because its preclinical properties and structure were superficially similar to those of the phenothiazines. In one of the initial clinical trials of the new drug, Kuhn found in 1957–58 that it had little antipsychotic efficacy but had mood-elevating and behavior-activating properties (Klerman and Cole, 1965). Since that time, imipramine and other structurally related tricyclic agents have been repeatedly demonstrated to be effective in several types of depression in controlled comparisons with either a placebo or a stimulant. Although these clinical effects have not always been easily demonstrable in contrast to most trials of the antipsychotic agents, and despite considerable toxicity and side effects of this class of drugs, they have become by far the most popular and common medical treatment for depressions of all kinds, particularly severe depressions.

Pharmacology

The pharmacological effects of the MAO inhibitors and tricyclic antidepressants have given the most important support to the "amine hypotheses of affective disorders," which suggest that depression is associated with a relative lack of activity of certain amine neurotransmitters known to occur in the brain, most probably

---

* All experiences with lithium in pregnancy should be reported to the research registry established for this purpose at Langley Porter Psychiatric Institute in San Francisco.

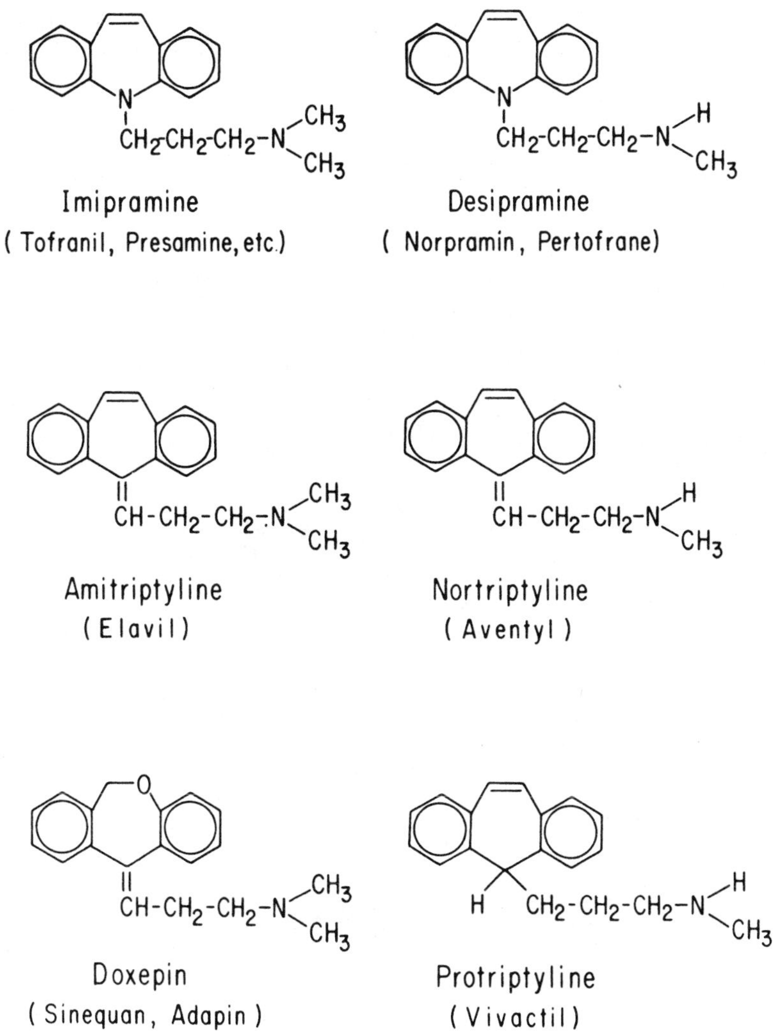

FIGURE 18.3. Tricyclic antidepressants.

norepinephrine and dopamine (the "catechol-amine hypothesis"), while mania may be an expression of an overactivity of these amines. Furthermore, other amines, including acetylcholine and perhaps serotonin, may modify the effects of diminished catecholamine neurotransmission. The interactions of MAO inhibitors and tricyclic antidepressants with the sympathomimetic and behavioral-activating amines are summarized in figure 18.4.

The MAO inhibitors block the inactivation of amines with "direct" effects (acting on adrenergic receptors) and "indirect" effects (acting through the release of norepinephrine) by the

catabolic enzyme MAO, and so potentiate their actions. The tricyclic agents block the neuronal uptake of amines into the presynaptic nerve ending; this process is crucial for the *inactivation* of *direct* sympathomimetic amines such as norepinephrine and for the *activity* of *indirect*, or catecholamine-releasing, sympathomimetic amines, such as tyramine, which must first enter the sympathetic nerve endings to act. The tricyclic antidepressant compounds are also much more potent *anticholinergic* agents than their antipsychotic analogues. The central anticholinergic effect may contribute to their antidepressant actions.

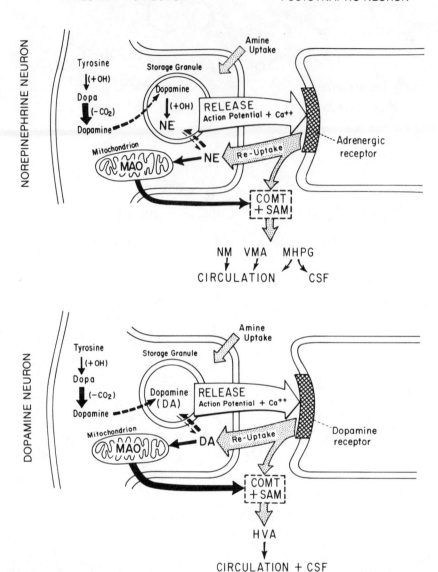

FIGURE 18.4. Central catecholamine-mediated synapses. Many psychopharmaceuticals have important actions at the norepinephrine synapse (above) and the dopamine synapse (below). Antipsychotic agents block release of dopamine (*DA*) and dopamine receptors in the limbic system (possibly accounting for their antipsychotic effect) and corpus striatum (extrapyramidal effects); they also have some antagonistic effects at norepinephrine (*NE*) receptors (sedation?). Reserpine blocks intraneuronal storage. Tricyclic antidepressants mainly block uptake of amines and reuptake of norepinephrine; monoamine oxidase (*MAO*) inhibitors block inactivation of many amines. Lithium salts block release of norepinephrine and dopamine and may also block norepinephrine receptors. Stimulants increase release of norepinephrine and dopamine, block their reuptake, and have a weak anti-monoamine oxidase effect. *COMT*, catechol-O-methyltransferase; *Dopa*, dihydroxyphenylalanine; *HVA*, homovanillic acid; *VMA*, vanillylmandelic acid; *MHPG*, 3-methoxy-4-hydroxyphenylethyleneglycol; *NM*, normetanephrine; *SAM*, S-adenosyl-L-methionine.

Clinical Use

The diversity of conditions subsumed under the generic term *depression* and the inconsistency with which clinicians and investigators categorize depressions make evaluation of the treatment of depression difficult. Regardless of the scheme of categorization followed, it is generally agreed that depressions vary in severity. The more severe forms include those referred to as "endogenous," "psychotic," "manic-depressive," "involutional," "agitated," or "vital," depending on the clinical form of the illness and the patient's history. In contrast, the less severe forms are said to be "minor," "reactive," "neurotic," "situational," or "anxious" depressions. While the prognosis for less severe depressions is better, demonstrations of the efficacy of medical treatments are much clearer for the more serious depressions with more pronounced "biological" symptoms such as anorexia, insomnia, loss of drive and sexual interest, and diurnal change. The lesser depressive illnesses tend to recover more rapidly, to remit spontaneously, and to respond to psychotherapy or to sedatives, antianxiety medications, or stimulants, as well as to nonspecific treatments including placebos, about as well as to tricyclic antidepressants. A difficulty in evaluating medical treatments of depression is that spontaneous remission rates for unselected depressions are about 20–25 percent within the first four to six weeks and exceed 50 percent within a few months, even for more severe depressions. Moreover, a placebo will increase the remission rates of acute depression to about 40–50 percent in the first month or two.

The tricyclic antidepressants have their clearest effects in the more serious depressions, for which their performance in controlled clinical trials has been fairly consistent, although not dramatic. The best performance of the drugs has been documented in trials that attempted to exclude the less severe depressions, that used adequate doses of medication (more than 100 mg/day of imipramine or the equivalent of another agent), and that persisted for at least a month. In controlled trials for a mixture of depressive syndromes of varying severity, overall improvement rates with tricyclic antidepressants have been about 70 percent, in contrast to about 40 percent

with a placebo; that is, only an additional 30 percent of patients with significant depressive illnesses responded to the active medication. A few who respond poorly to a tricyclic agent respond satisfactorily to an MAO inhibitor, and about half of those who respond poorly to a tricyclic agent respond to ECT. While ECT has consistently outperformed MAO inhibitors or tricyclic antidepressants, the overall gain is only on the order of 10–20 percent.

Among the specific antidepressants, more similarities than differences in overall effectiveness are seen. The tricyclic antidepressants (see fig. 18.3, table 18.4) have performed better than MAO inhibitors, with the possible exception of tranylcypromine (Parnate), which has amphetaminelike properties as well as ability to inhibit MAO and which has produced results about equal to those of imipramine in a small number of comparisons. Among the tricyclic antidepressants, amitriptyline (Elavil) has produced somewhat better overall results than other tricyclic agents. While a demethylated congener of amitriptyline, protriptyline (Vivactil) is more potent than either amitriptyline or nortriptyline, its overall efficacy is no greater than that of the other tricyclic antidepressants. Amitriptyline produces somewhat more sedation (at least initially) than most other antidepressants, and the demethylated antidepressants generally produce less and may even have early stimulating actions; protriptyline may produce the least sedation. Amitriptyline has more potent anticholinergic activity than other tricyclic antidepressants, and desmethylimipramine (desipramine), the least, with other agents clustering between them. This consideration suggests that desipramine may be a more rational choice for elderly patients at high risk of anticholinergic brain syndrome or of cardiac toxicity, although its greater safety has not been demonstrated clinically. Doxepin (Sinequan) has acquired an undeserved reputation as having special antianxiety or mixed antipsychotic and antidepressant qualities and as having little ability to inhibit uptake into noradrenergic neurons. The suggestion that doxepin does not block the uptake and hence the antihypertensive actions of the postganglionic sympathetic blocking agent guanethidine (Ismelin) is not correct, although this antihypertensive agent may be

TABLE 18.4. Equivalent doses of tricyclic antidepressants.

Generic name	Trade name	Dose range (mg/day)[a]
Amitriptyline	Elavil, etc. (generic)	50–300
Desipramine[b]	Norpramin, Pertofrane	75–200
Doxepin	Adapin, Sinequan	75–300
Imipramine	Tofranil, etc. (generic)	50–300
Nortriptyline[b]	Aventyl	50–100
Protriptyline[b]	Vivactil	15–60

[a] Although the ratio of a severely toxic or lethal dose to a typical daily dose (approximate therapeutic index) may be as high as 10 to 30, five to ten days' supply is a safer amount to dispense. Doses above 250 mg of amitriptyline, or the equivalent of other agents, are best reserved for inpatients. Daily doses are initially divided into two or three portions, but total doses of 150 mg or less can later be given at bedtime for convenience. Amitriptyline is available in combination with perphenazine (Etrafon, Triavil). Most commercial preparations are soluble hydrochlorides. Imipramine is also available as the slower-acting pamoate (Tofranil-PM) that can be given in the same daily dose as the hydrochloride, in one or two portions, but it is more expensive and probably not safer than giving the hydrochloride twice a day or at bedtime. The usually effective dose is 150–200 mg of imipramine hydrochloride (or the equivalent of another agent) achieved over several days; smaller doses are used in children and elderly patients. In changing agents it is wise to make the conversion *gradually* over several days to avoid intoxication.

[b] Demethylated agents.

at least partially effective for the first two or three weeks of treatment with doxepin. The main conclusion based on these various comparisons is similar to that for the antipsychotic agents. Thus, while differences in the overall efficacy of the various tricyclic antidepressants are not easy to document, subtleties based on potencies and the relative chances for various side effects or drug interactions do exist.

The possibility of predicting responses to a specific antidepressant by a metabolic test has been suggested. Thus initially high excretion of the urinary metabolite of norepinephrine MHPG (see fig. 18.4) may correlate with a favorable response to amitriptyline, while lower levels of MHPG seem to predict a favorable response to imipramine. These differences do not simply correlate with "agitated" versus "psychomotorically retarded" depressions.

While the metabolic approach to predicting responses to chemotherapy is potentially very important, chemical tests of this kind are not yet applicable to routine clinical use. The possibility that an initial activating response to amphetamine might be a useful predictive index of response to a tricyclic antidepressant or to ECT has also been suggested. A somewhat more promising metabolic approach is to select optimal agents and doses based on blood levels of the antidepressant drug or its metabolites, as estimated by powerful and selective chemical methods such as gas-liquid chromatography. In some academic centers, particularly in Europe, this approach is being applied clinically almost routinely. The results of such monitoring suggest that poor clinical response may be associated with blood levels that are excessively high or too low (Åsberg, 1974).

In the selection of a specific agent for a specific case of depression, antipsychotic drugs must also be considered. In comparisons of tricyclic antidepressants and antipsychotic agents in groups of relatively unselected cases of serious depression, the overall benefits of the two types of agents have been about the same. In one of the earliest studies, thioridazine was used, leading to its exaggerated reputation as a specific agent for severe or psychotic depression. In fact, any antipsychotic agent performs about as well as any antidepressant in such unselected comparisons (although comparisons of the same agents in schizophrenic patients reveal poor results or even worsening of psychosis with antidepressants). The "trick" involved in the comparison of antipsychotic and antidepressant agents is that the types of depressive syndromes specifically helped by the two agents are different. Antipsychotic agents are most helpful in cases of psychotic or involutional depression with a great deal of agitation and guilty or morbid rumination of delusional proportions, while tricyclic antidepressants are selectively useful for more motorically retarded depressions, as manic-depressive depressions usually are. Tricyclic antidepressants can even increase agitation in some cases of psychotic depression, and the addition or even exclusive use of an antipsychotic agent in the first few days or weeks of the treatment of such an illness can bring about more rapid benefits than a tricyclic antidepressant alone.

It is not true that antidepressant agents are so stimulating and behaviorally activating as to worsen the insomnia that typically accompanies serious depressions. Antidepressants even facilitate the deeper phases of sleep that are usually decreased in adult depression. On the other hand, the use of imipramine in the management of childhood enuresis has been reported to be associated with a partial suppression of deeper phases of sleep. The vulnerability of bipolar manic-depressive patients to "switching" from "retarded" depression to mania is increased in the course of treatment with a tricyclic antidepressant. Conversely, the use of antipsychotic agents in mania has occasionally been complicated by the rapid switch from mania to depression.

In schizophrenic illnesses, the place of antidepressant agents is not clearly defined. Administration of at least moderate doses of antidepressants has been tried in withdrawn or apathetic schizophrenics, usually without clear benefits, and the antidepressants have been added to the treatment of more clearly depressive phases of schizophrenic or schizoaffective illnesses. These practices are not without risk, however, since stimulants, MAO inhibitors, and tricyclic antidepressants can increase or induce agitation, delusions, and hallucinations in schizophrenic and other psychotic patients, and occasionally antidepressants have been associated with the "uncovering of latent psychosis" in patients with schizoid, hysterical, paranoid, or "borderline" character traits. Moreover, there is a risk of compounding a functional psychosis with an anticholinergic, toxic organic psychosis, particularly with daily doses of antidepressants above 200 mg of imipramine or the equivalent of another antidepressant, and with even lower doses if an antipsychotic agent and an anticholinergic antiparkinson agent are also being used.

The clinical use of antidepressant agents varies with the type of illness being treated. An elaborate medical evaluation before starting treatment is usually not necessary in younger and healthy individuals, but a good appreciation of the cardiovascular, cerebrovascular, gastrointestinal, urinary, and ophthalmological status of elderly depressed patients, who are at greater risk of toxic effects of the antidepressants, is well advised. Usually treatment is started with moderate doses of the tricyclic agents in outpatients or elderly patients; an initial daily dose as small as 25 mg/day of imipramine is an extreme, and 50–75 mg/day is typical. The amount is usually increased by 25 or 50 mg every day or two to doses of 100–150 mg/day of imipramine or the equivalent of another agent (see table 18.4). With inpatients, it is more common to start with 100–150 mg and to reach doses of 150–200 mg/day quickly. Doses above 200 or 250 mg/day of imipramine or its equivalent are associated with increased risks of toxic effects, including cardiovascular toxicity and psychotic agitation and confusion, and are best reserved for carefully supervised hospitalized patients, preferably after a trial of two or three weeks at 150–200 mg/day.

In severe depression and in cases of refusal of

food and oral medications, an injectable form of imipramine or amitriptyline can be used (initially, 100 mg/day in divided doses, intramuscularly), although the efficacy or speed will probably not be increased in that way. If psychosis or severe agitation is present, it is usually necessary to add an antipsychotic agent. There is little reason to add a hypnotic medication for sleep. If agitation and suicide risk are high, several unilateral ECTs can be given while waiting for the effects of the antidepressant. Although ECT can be administered safely while antidepressants are being used, it is wise to omit the first dose of antidepressant on the morning of ECT and to use pre-ECT anticholinergic agents (to minimize secretions and vagal effects on the heart) sparingly if at all. Although it might seem to be a good idea, it is not usual to give a stimulant in the first few days of hospitalization while awaiting the antidepressant effects of a tricyclic agent, due to the meager benefits of amphetamine and like agents and added risks of inducing agitation and hypertension.

An important feature of all antidepressant agents is their delay in clinical onset of antidepressant effect, typically at least a week, and sometimes up to three weeks. The failure of objective improvement in activity, sleep, appetite, mood, or social interest within a week is an unfavorable prognostic sign, suggesting that the final result will be unsatisfactory. If the objective response is poor (the patient is usually the last to acknowledge improvement) after four or five weeks of adequate doses of a tricyclic antidepressant, and if there is not even slight improvement in two or three weeks, there is little likelihood that changing to another agent or increasing doses above 300 mg of imipramine or its equivalent will help. At that point, the two main choices are to try an MAO inhibitor or ECT, and there is little reason not to go directly to ECT, as it is the most likely to have additional benefit. With outpatients, a period in hospital at that point may also provide additional nonspecific benefits. If an MAO inhibitor is used, for example in a patient who refuses ECT, it is safest to allow at least a week (and, better, two weeks) for the tricyclic agent to be metabolized and excreted before adding the MAO inhibitor, in order to avoid the rare but potentially

catastrophic drug interactions that may occur, including hyperpyrexia and convulsions.

The half-lives of tricyclic agents are long enough so that using the bulk of a day's dose at bedtime for convenience and to combat insomnia is a reasonable practice. For outpatients, these results can also be achieved by the use of the more slowly released pamoate salt of imipramine (Tofranil-PM), of which the daily dose is the same as for the more usual soluble hydrochloride salt. This preparation is more expensive and does not offer a clear advantage over ordinary imipramine hydrochloride, now available as a less expensive generic drug (Tofranil, Imavate, Presamine, SK-Pramine, and others). However, when large doses of an antidepressant are being used (above the equivalent of 150 mg/day of imipramine), it is probably safer to use divided doses to minimize anticholinergic and cardiotoxic actions of the drugs.

Due to the potentially severe toxicity and limited margin of safety of all antidepressant agents, dispensing more than a week's supply to a depressed and possibly suicidal outpatient is unwise. The risk of suicide may increase with initial improvement, since activity usually increases before mood elevation. Another aspect of the safe use of antidepressant agents is that a change from one agent to another, even at an equivalent dose, should be made gradually, preferably using increasing divided doses over several days. The expense of antidepressant agents can be minimized by prescribing the generic agents, and the largest unit dose available (50-mg tablets, for instance, rather than two 25-mg tablets). After appreciable clinical improvement of a severe depressive illness has been achieved with a tricyclic antidepressant agent, it is usual to continue the treatment at 100–150 mg/day of imipramine or its equivalent for several months, and perhaps up to a year for a more severe illness or in patients with a prior history of frequently recurrent depression. Doses as low as 75 mg/day in this phase of treatment are less effective in preventing relapses.

A similar chemotherapy regimen is followed by patients treated initially with ECT. This approach has evolved from clinical experience and many reports of relapse after partial treatment of depressions. The exact duration of the treatment depends on the individual patient's response, ability to resume normal responsibilities, premorbid personality, ongoing stresses and life situation, and the duration, rate of recurrence, and response to treatment of prior depressions. The sustained use of tricyclic agents in unipolar manic-depressive illness can be as useful as lithium is in preventing or diminishing unipolar or bipolar illnesses, although the safety of this practice is not yet fully established. The usefulness of indefinitely continued treatment of outpatients with "chronic characterological depressions" is not clear, although this treatment is occasionally prescribed.

Attempts have been made to increase the efficacy or the rapidity of onset of antidepressant agents. Thyroid status may alter the efficacy of antidepressants, and thyroid function should be evaluated in patients who fail to respond to adequate doses of an antidepressant within about a month. The addition of thyroid hormone (for instance, 25 μg of l-triiodothyronine, Cytomel) even to euthyroid patients might improve the response to tricyclic antidepressants in some female patients, although this approach increases the risk of cardiac toxicity in patients at high risk (such as the elderly or those with prior myocardial infarction). Thyroid-stimulating hormone (TSH) may have a similar effect, and hypothalamic thyrotropin-releasing factor (TRF) may itself have mood-elevating and even antidepressant effects when given intravenously, although these effects have not been replicated consistently. While the search continues for more effective and safer antidepressant therapies, the cornerstones of the medical therapy of severe depressive illness are the tricyclic antidepressants and ECT.

Tricyclic antidepressants have been used for conditions other than depression. The usefulness of MAO inhibitors and tricyclic agents in certain phobic neuroses has been reported. These agents and ECT are occasionally helpful in pain syndromes that might represent "depressive equivalents," as well as in migraine and narcolepsy. Several disorders of children, including enuresis, school phobias, and a variety of "nervous habits," have been treated with antidepressants, especially with doses of imipramine of 25–75 mg/day an hour or more before bedtime.

Toxicity and Side Effects

The agents used in the treatment of mood disorders (tricyclic antidepressants, MAO inhibitors, and lithium salts) are much more toxic in acute overdosage than the antipsychotic agents and unfortunately must be given to patients at increased risk of attempting suicide. The most common toxic side effects of the tricyclic antidepressants are extensions of their pharmacological activities. These include anticholinergic actions leading to dry mouth, sweating, and ophthalmological effects. The latter include variable but usually mild mydriatic effects and often some degree of cycloplegia, leading to blurred near vision due to the impairment of accommodation. These problems are more annoying than dangerous and can usually be managed by simple means, including candy or mouthwashes and reading lenses. There is also a risk of inducing acute glaucoma, as discussed previously in regard to the antipsychotic agents; this risk is greater with tricyclic antidepressants. Cholinergic eye drops, mouthwashes, or systemic medications have been tried for these various symptoms but are usually not very helpful. Moreover, some degree of tolerance to these side effects normally develops. (The overuse of candy for dry mouth can lead to monilial infections.)

More *serious antivagal effects* of this highly anticholinergic class of agents include paralytic ileus and urinary retention; thus extra caution is necessary in elderly patients and men with prostatism, and urgent medical intervention is required when these conditions develop. Treatment of these problems includes eliminating or reducing the dose of antidepressant, giving cholinergic smooth-muscle stimulants such as bethanechol (Urecholine, 2.5 or 5.0 mg, subcutaneously as needed). When severe inhibition of gastrointestinal or urinary function occurs with even small doses of antidepressants, it may be necessary to change the treatment to ECT or an MAO inhibitor. Among the tricyclic agents, desipramine is less antimuscarinic, while amitriptyline is the most potently anticholinergic (about 5 percent as potent as atropine, but given in doses more than 100 times greater than atropine).

A serious consequence of the anticholinergic and direct quinidinelike cardiac depressant effects of the tricyclic antidepressants is their *cardiac toxicity*. Tachycardia and arrhythmias are not unusual and are to be expected in cases of acute overdosage. EKG changes include tachycardia, prolongation of the Q-T interval, and flattening of the T waves. Decreased strength of contraction (negative inotropic effect) often occurs, and there is some risk of syncope. Postural hypotension is not unusual, although the mechanisms underlying this effect are not clear. Some beneficial effects have been reported with the use of steroids for postural hypotension due to tricyclic antidepressants or MAO inhibitors when more conservative management did not suffice. Because there is an increased risk of malignant ventricular arrhythmias, cardiac arrest, and congestive heart failure with the tricyclic antidepressants, they must be used in lower doses and with great caution in elderly patients at risk for myocardial infarction and stroke. An important consideration in choosing the treatment for serious depression in elderly or infirm patients is that with its modern modifications, ECT is probably as safe as if not safer than the antidepressant drugs. The mortality rate with the tricyclic agents is comparable to that of ECT and may even be higher if overdoses are included; certainly the morbidity rate with the drugs is considerable, especially if minor as well as more serious toxic effects and overdosages are taken into account.

The untoward effects of tricyclic antidepressants on the *central nervous system* include mild dizziness and lightheadedness, insomnia and restlessness, or fatigue and somnolence. Fine and occasionally gross resting tremors are common and may respond to diazepam (Valium). Extrapyramidal syndromes are rare, possibly due to the powerful anticholinergic actions of these drugs, which are sufficient to induce antiparkinson effects. They must be used with caution by patients receiving anticholinergic antiparkinson medications and would be expected to worsen choreas, including tardive dyskinesia. Some risk exists of provoking or worsening agitation and psychosis in patients with other psychotic or unstable characterological conditions in addition to depression, and large doses of tricyclic antidepressants can induce a toxic organic psychosis resembling that due to atropine poi-

soning (table 18.5). This toxic state is not always easy to diagnose in severely depressed patients who are already agitated and psychotic. Seizures and the worsening of epilepsy have also been associated with the antidepressants.

Various skin reactions have been described, and an allergic-obstructive type of jaundice occasionally occurs early in the course of treatment. Agranulocytosis is rare. There may be a tendency to gain weight, as well as occasional hypoglycemic effects of the tricyclic agents.

In contrast to the antipsychotic agents, the tricyclic antidepressants are highly toxic when taken in large *overdoses*, and they are an increasingly common choice in suicide attempts by increasingly younger patients. Acute doses above 1000 mg are almost always very toxic, but doses as low as a few hundred milligrams, especially of amitriptyline, have been severely toxic in adults as well as children. Acute doses in excess of 2000 mg can be fatal. The monomethylated ("nor" or "desmethyl") derivatives may be slightly less toxic than the parent compounds. Due to the relatively low therapeutic index (margin of safety) of all tricyclic antidepressants, it is unwise to dispense more than a week's supply of medication, and certainly never more than 1000 mg of imipramine or the equivalent of another agent (see table 18.4). Large overdoses of the antidepressants commonly induce signs of *anticholinergic poisoning* early: with restless agitation, confusion, disorientation, perhaps seizures and hyperthermia, dry, sometimes flushed skin, tachycardia, sluggish and at least moderately dilated pupils, decreased bowel sounds, and often acute urinary retention (table 18.5); later, severe central nervous system depression and coma (rarely lasting more than twenty-four hours) sometimes result. The early toxic effects are probably due to peripheral and central anticholinergic and antivagal actions of these potent muscarinic blocking agents. The cardiac toxicity can be particularly dangerous and may include severe depression of myocardial conduction, with various forms of heart block, atrial fibrillation and more malignant ventricular arrhythmias or cardiac arrest. A peculiarity of tricyclic poisoning is that the risk of cardiac arrhythmia continues for a week or more after the initial brain syndrome has cleared considerably. Many of the agents commonly em-

TABLE 18.5. Anticholinergic and cholinergic excess
syndromes.

Anticholinergic syndrome

Causes
   Acute overdose or excessive prescription of medications with antimuscarinic properties, especially in combination: tricyclic antidepressants, most antiparkinson agents, some antipsychotics (especially thioridazine), many
proprietary sedative-hypnotics, many antispasmodic preparations, several plants (e.g., Jimson weed, some mush-
rooms).

Neuropsychiatric signs
   Anxiety; agitation; restless, purposeless overactivity; delirium; disorientation; impairment of immediate and
recent memory; dysarthria; hallucinations; myoclonus; seizures.

Systemic signs
   Tachycardia and arrhythmias; large, sluggish pupils; scleral injection; flushed, warm, dry skin; increased temperature; decreased mucosal secretions; urinary retention; reduced bowel motility.

Treatment
   Adults (initial or test dose): 1–2 mg physostigmine salicylate, intramuscularly, or *slowly* intravenously; repeat
as needed after at least 15–30 minutes.
   Children: 0.5–1.0 mg physostigmine salicylate, as for adults (neostigmine, pyridostigmine, etc., do not enter
the CNS).

Physostigmine-induced cholinergic excess

Neuropsychiatric
   Confusion, seizures, nausea and vomiting, myoclonus, hallucinations, often after a period of initial CNS improvement when physostigmine is given to treat the anticholinergic syndrome.

Systemic signs
   Bradycardia, miosis, increased mucosal secretions, copious bronchial secretions, dyspnea, tears, sweating,
diarrhea, abdominal colic, biliary colic, urinary frequency or urgency.

Treatment or prevention
   Atropine sulfate—CNS and systemic actions: 0.5 mg per mg of physostigmine, intramuscularly or subcutane-
ously.
   Methscopolamine bromide (Pamine)—no CNS action: 0.5 mg per mg of physostigmine, intramuscularly.
   Glycopyrrolate (Robinul)—no CNS action: 0.1–0.2 mg per mg of physostigmine, intramuscularly.

---

ployed to manage ventricular arrhythmias can lead to further conduction blockade and cardiac depression. Electrical defibrillation, conversion, and cardiac pacing may be necessary. All cases of moderate to severe tricyclic poisoning should ideally be managed in a medical intensive care unit, with constant cardiac monitoring, excellent medical and cardiological supervision, and immediately available defibrillating and resuscitation equipment. Continued cardiac monitoring is also wise for several days after the initial recovery of consciousness and orientation.

Removal of these agents by dialysis techniques is impossible, and forced diuresis adds little and may contribute to cardiac failure. Furthermore, while many cardiac drugs, including digitalis, are contraindicated or dangerous, both cardiac and central nervous system manifestations of anticholinergic poisoning may be treated successfully with reversible anticholinesterase agents; see table 18.5 (Granacher and Baldessarini, 1975). Neostigmine (Prostigmin) and pyridostigmine (Mestinon) have been used successfully in the management of the cardiac effects of a number of atropinelike agents, including tricyclic antidepressants and antiparkinson agents. However, these anticholinesterase drugs are charged quaternary ammonium compounds that poorly penetrate the blood-brain barrier, and *only physostigmine* or eserine (Antilirium) has both

TABLE 18.6. Interactions of psychopharmaceuticals with other agents.[a]

Agent	Neuroleptic antipsychotics	Tricyclic antidepressants	MAO inhibitors
Alcohol, anxiolytics, antihistamines	More sedation	More sedation and anticholinergic effects	More sedation, decreased metabolism
Anesthetics	Potentiation of hypotension	Cardiac arrhythmias(?)	Potentiation
Barbiturates	More sedation, increased metabolism of neuroleptics	More sedation and anticholinergic effects, increased metabolism of antidepressant	More sedation, decreased metabolism of MAO inhibitors
Narcotics, especially meperidine	Potentiation	Some potentiation	Dangerous CNS depression or excitation and fever
Anticonvulsants	Decreased effectiveness	Decreased effectiveness	CNS depression
Anticholinergics, antiparkinson agents, spasmolytics	Unpredictable, decreased absorption of neuroleptics	Mutual potentiation, more anticholinergic effects	Potentiation, CNS intoxication, decreased metabolism of MAO inhibitors
L-dopa	Mutual antagonism	Decreased absorption	Possible hypertension
Stimulants, anorexics	Mutual antagonism, decreased metabolism of neuroleptics	Potentiation, hypertension, decreased metabolism of tricyclics	CNS excitation, hypertension, fever
Reserpine	Some mutual potentiation	Acute hypertension, later some inhibition, arrhythmias(?)	Paradoxical hypertension and acute CNS excitation
Alpha-methyldopa	Mutual potentiation	Possible antagonism	Paradoxical hypertension
Alpha-methyltyrosine	Possible potentiation of antipsychotics, sedation	—	—
Guanethidine, bethanidine, debrisoquine	Some antagonism and withdrawal hypotension	Antagonism, severe withdrawal hypotension	Potentiation, acute hypertension with guanethidine
Hypotensive diuretics	More hypotension	—	More hypotension
Hypotensive smooth muscle relaxants (e.g., hydralazine)	More hypotension	—	More hypotension
Any agent with MAO-inhibiting action (e.g., Eutonyl, Furoxone, Matulane)	Potentiation, hypotension or hypertension and extrapyramidal symptoms	Seizures, hyperpyrexia	Additive toxicity
Alpha-adrenergic agonists (e.g., norepinephrine, phenylephrine)	Decreased effectiveness	Potentiation	Potentiation
Clonidine (Catapres)	Potentiation (?)	Antagonism (mechanism unknown)	Potentiation (?)
Indirect sympathomimes (e.g., tyramine in food)	Some antagonism	Antagonism	Hypertension, CNS excitation, stroke
Alpha-adrenergic blockers (e.g., phentolamine, phenoxybenzamine)	Potentiation, hypotension	Antagonism	Antagonism
Beta-adrenergic agonists (e.g., epinephrine, isoproterenol)	Hypotension	Potentiation	Potentiation
Beta-adrenergic blockers (e.g., propranolol)	Hypotension	Antagonism	Antagonism acutely, potentiation later
Anticoagulants (e.g., coumarins and indanediones)	Potentiation, decreased metabolism (withdrawal bleeding)	Minimal potentiation	Probable potentiation

[a] Unless otherwise stated, effects are those of the psychopharmaceutical on actions of the medical agents in the first column. Dash indicates no effect known; question mark indicates no effects clearly demonstrated, but should be suspected.

TABLE 18.6. (continued)

Agent	Neuroleptic antipsychotics	Tricyclic antidepressants	MAO inhibitors
Cardiac agents (e.g., quinidine, digitalis)	Possible potentiation	Possible potentiation	?
Steroids	—	Unpredictable	?
Insulin and oral hypo-glycemics	Potentiation or inhibition	Unpredictable, possible potentiation	Potentiation
Oral alkalis (e.g., Amphojel) and resins (e.g., Cholestyramine, Questran)	Absorption of neuroleptics decreased	Absorption of tricyclics decreased	?

central and peripheral cholinergic activity. Physostigmine therefore represents the treatment of choice in the management of intoxications with agents possessing significant anticholinergic activity. Principles of its use are outlined in table 18.5.

Other aspects of the pharmacology of the tricyclics should also be appreciated in the management of their overdoses. For example, the ability of these compounds to potentiate directly sympathomimetic amines such as norepinephrine complicates the use of such pressor substances in the management of hypotension and shock in tricyclic poisoning. Furthermore, tricyclic antidepressant agents potentiate and prolong the actions of barbiturates, probably through competition for hepatic microsomal enzymes, which are particularly important in inactivating the shorter-acting barbiturates. Diazepam (Valium) is probably a safe anticonvulsant in this situation and is not likely to induce respiratory depression.

The tricyclic agents have many *interactions with other drugs* (table 18.6). They increase the CNS depression due to alcohol, barbiturates, and other sedatives as well as antipsychotic agents and anticonvulsants. Barbiturates and glutethimide (Doriden), much more than the benzodiazepines, also induce hepatic microsomal enzymes required for the metabolism of the tricyclic agents, possibly decreasing their efficacy. The seizure threshold may be lowered, calling for increased doses of anticonvulsants. The effects of any anticholinergic agent, including antiparkinson drugs, will be additively in-

creased due to the antimuscarinic activity of the tricyclic antidepressants, and the combination has a risk of inducing a toxic confusional brain syndrome, agitation, and sometimes hyperpyrexia. Antipsychotic agents are contraindicated in cases of toxic agitation in overdoses of tricyclic antidepressants due to their own moderate anticholinergic actions.

A difficult combination to manage satisfactorily is *depression and hypertension*. Antihypertensive agents, possibly due to their central antiadrenergic properties, are associated with depression. This association may occur unpredictably at any point in the treatment of hypertension and is most common in patients with a prior history of depression. It has most frequently been reported with reserpine (Serpasil) and other Rauwolfia alkaloids, and occasionally also with α-methyldopa (Aldomet). Guanethidine is one of the few antihypertensive agents with little CNS activity; it has rarely been associated with depression. Due to a blockade of the uptake of guanethidine into postganglionic sympathetic nerve fibers, however, treatment of hypertension with this agent in patients who are also depressed is usually made unsuccessful by the addition of any of the currently available tricyclic antidepressants (and to some extent the phenothiazines as well, but less so haloperidol or molindone). The antihypertensive effects of other agents, including reserpine and the Veratrum alkaloids, can also be diminished by the tricyclic antidepressants. The use of diuretics with tricyclic antidepressants for the management of hypertension in depressed patients is safe, although even moderate hyponatremia may induce depressant effects. While it is also possible to treat hypertension with large doses of a beta-adrenergic blocking agent—such as propranolol (Inderal)—combined with the vascular smooth-muscle relaxant hydralazine (Apresoline), high doses of the former can produce central sedative effects and may induce clinical depression; hydralazine has occasionally induced toxic psychoses. However, this combination of antihypertensive agents with tricyclic antidepressants has not yet been evaluated. One other approach to the management of depression with hypertension might be to take advantage of the hypotensive effects of MAO inhibitors, and particularly the nonhydrazine pargyline (Eutonyl), which was initially withdrawn as an antidepressant due to its hypotensive effects and later relicensed as an antihypertensive agent. However, this use of pargyline has not yet been adequately evaluated; moreover, it must be used *alone* due to the risk of potentially severe toxic interactions of an MAO inhibitor and tricyclic antidepressant marked by hypertension, seizures, and hyperthermia.

The safety of antidepressant drugs in *pregnancy and lactation* has not been established. They pass the placental barrier and can be se-creted in low levels in human milk. In severe prepartum and postpartum depression, ECT can be used safely.

Stimulants and MAO Inhibitors

Inhibitors of the enzyme monoamine oxidase (fig. 18.5, table 18.7) are historically important, as they have had a major impact on the medical treatment of depression and on biological theories attempting to relate brain metabolism to psychiatric illness. In recent years, the MAO inhibitors have had limited use because of their unsuccessful competition with the tricyclic agents, which are superior antidepressants, and because of their toxic effects. The MAO inhibitors are severely toxic on acute overdosage and have the potential to induce a large number of unwanted and even dangerous interactions with other drugs, chemicals, hormones, and metabolic conditions (see table 18.6).

In controlled trials of the currently available MAO inhibitors, their efficacy has been consistently inferior to that of ECT and the tricyclic antidepressants. The exception to these rather dismal results has been the amphetaminelike nonhydrazine MAO inhibitor, tranylcypromine

TABLE 18.7. MAO inhibitors and stimulants, equivalent doses and approximate therapeutic index.

Generic name	Trade name	Dose range (mg/day)	Ratio of lethal to daily dose[a]
MAO inhibitors[b]			
Isocarboxazid	Marplan[c]	10–30	10–15
Phenelzine	Nardil[c]	30–75	5–10
Tranylcypromine	Parnate[d]	10–30	6
Stimulants			
d-Amphetamine	Dexedrine, etc. (generic)	10–20	10–50
Methylphenidate	Ritalin	20–30	10–50

[a] The ratio of lethal to daily doses (approximate therapeutic index) is an estimate, based on reports of severe intoxication and lethality in adults, and suggests the number of days' supply that may be dispensed safely; ratios for children are two to five times lower.
[b] Other MAO inhibitors have been used but are no longer marketed (Catron, Marplan, Marsilid, Monase, Niamid) or are not used in psychiatry (Eutonyl, Eutron, Furoxone, Matulane).
[c] The effectiveness of the recommended doses of Marplan or of low doses of Nardil (45 mg/day) compared to placebo is not certain.
[d] Not recommended over age 60 or in cardiac patients.

(Parnate), which has outperformed a placebo in at least three out of four studies and was found equal to imipramine in antidepressant efficacy in three out of three; in addition, phenelzine (Nardil) has done well recently when used at doses in excess of 50 mg/day. Although most antidepressants and MAO inhibitors require one to three weeks to produce beneficial effects, tranylcypromine may act within a few days, possibly due to its amphetaminelike stimulant actions.

At the present time, the main indication for the use of MAO inhibitors is as a second choice when a vigorous trial of a tricyclic antidepressant has produced unsatisfactory results. Even this can be done only at the expense of a further delay of at least seven to ten days after stopping the tricyclic agent to permit its metabolism and excretion and to avoid rare but potentially severe interactions with MAO inhibitors. It is usually better to hospitalize patients and to add ECT for cases of serious depressions responding poorly after several weeks of adequate doses of a tricyclic agent. If an MAO inhibitor is to be used, at the present time tranylcypromine appears to be the most effective agent and the most rapid in the onset of clinical effects and termination of chemical effect; it is also the most toxic on acute overdosage. An additional reason to consider tranylcypromine as an initial therapy for severe depression is that it lacks the severe anticholinergic and potentially cardiotoxic effects of the tricyclic agents, thus offering a theoretical advantage in elderly patients with heart disease, provided that contact with sympathomimetic agents can be scrupulously avoided and that hypotension does not complicate the treatment.

Some psychiatrists have claimed special effects of the MAO inhibitors in certain states, not necessarily depressions, that are marked by neurotic anxiety and phobia, although tricyclic antidepressants may also have similar effects. This use of MAO inhibitors is particularly popular in England, where MAO inhibitors and tricyclic antidepressants are sometimes combined, although the combination of MAO inhibitors or stimulants with tricyclic antidepressants cannot be recommended as a safe practice.

When MAO inhibitors are used clinically, a number of *toxic effects* may be encountered. *Hypotensive effects*, typically orthostatic hypoten-

sion, are usually a relatively minor problem. This may be due to the gradual accumulation in sympathetic nerve endings of amines lacking direct sympathomimetic activity at the expense of the normal synaptic transmitter, norepinephrine (the "false transmitter" hypothesis). The hypotension may become worrisome in patients at high risk of heart attack or stroke. Severe *parenchymal hepatotoxic reactions* also occur infrequently, although they are more serious than the biliary stasis associated with the antipsychotic and tricyclic antidepressant agents. This toxicity is serious enough to justify frequent, perhaps weekly, determinations of serum bilirubin and transaminase activities and to contraindicate the use of MAO inhibitors in patients with chronic liver disease, for whom *small* doses of tricyclic antidepressants can be given cautiously. Manifestations of CNS *toxicity* of MAO inhibitors include agitation, insomnia, and toxic psychoses, as well as the provocation of previously quiescent functional psychoses.

The most serious toxic effect of the MAO inhibitors is their ability to provoke *acute hypertensive crises*, sometimes associated with hyperpyrexia, seizures, intracranial bleeding, and cardiovascular collapse. These catastrophic reactions are fortunately rare and can best be avoided by the scrupulous avoidance of medications, foods, and beverages containing appreciable quantities of sympathomimetic amines, especially those produced by fermentation, such as wine, beer, and cheeses. The reaction has been associated classically with tyramine, a common byproduct of bacterial fermentation. Since more than 10 mg of tyramine is required to produce hypertension, the most likely foods are the cheeses and certain yeast products used as food supplements; the most likely MAO inhibitor is tranylcypromine. In addition, a large number of prescription drugs and proprietary medications contain sympathomimetic agents or other compounds that can induce untoward reactions in the presence of MAO inhibitor (see table 18.6). These medications include any of the amphetamines or other sympathomimetric phenylalkylamines: Benzedrine, Dexedrine, methamphetamine (Desoxyn), ephedrine, norephedrine, and phenylephrine (Neo-Synephrine), some of which occur in proprietary cold and sinus medications and decongestant inhalers. Because L-dopa and α-methyldopa (Aldomet) can be converted to sympathomimetic amines, they must also be avoided. Patients with pheochromocytoma or carcinoid syndrome should not receive an MAO inhibitor. Moreover, the combination of an MAO inhibitor with the acute amine-releasing effects of reserpine or other catecholamine releasing agents, including guanethidine, can induce paradoxical hypertensive reactions and central excitation. If such a hypertensive reaction is encountered, specific treatment is the immediate but slow intravenous injection of a potent alpha-adrenergic blocking agent, such as phentolamine (Regitine) in doses of 5 mg as needed. In an emergency, if a specific alpha-blocking agent is not available, parenteral injections of chlorpromazine (Thorazine, in doses of 50–100 mg intramuscularly) can be used while appropriate medical treatment is arranged.

MAO inhibitors have also produced unwanted *interactions with other medications* (table 18.6). Typically, they potentiate many central depressants, including the barbiturates, "minor tranquilizers," phenothiazines, antihistamines, narcotic analgesics, and alcohol. Meperidine in particular has been associated with severe reactions that are not well understood pharmacologically but have included reactions resembling overdoses of a narcotic, including coma, as well as states of extreme excitement, seizures, and fever. Narcotics should never be used for headache in patients taking an MAO inhibitor, and the headache requires immediate evaluation of blood pressure. MAO inhibitors require particular caution in the management of surgical anesthesia and should be avoided for at least several days prior to surgery. The combination of an MAO inhibitor and a tricyclic antidepressant can induce central excitation, seizures, hyperpyrexia, and death in addition to hypertensive crises, especially if parenteral or high doses of the tricyclic agents are used. The demethylated tricyclic antidepressants are particularly potent blockers of norepinephrine uptake and so may produce hypertension with an MAO inhibitor. Potentiation of anticholinergic or antiparkinson agents, oral hypoglycemics, and insulin can also be anticipated. MAO inhibitors in combination with salt-losing diuretic agents have induced

HYDRAZINE

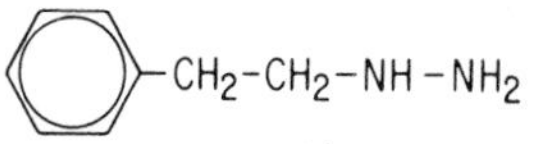

Phenelzine (Nardil)

NON-HYDRAZINE

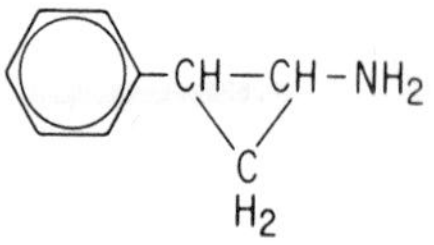

Tranylcypromine (Parnate)

FIGURE 18.5. Monoamine oxidase inhibitors.

severe hypotension. Some drugs other than antidepressants have MAO-inhibiting effects. These include the antihypertensive agent pargyline (Eutonyl), the nitrofuran antibiotics such as furazolidone (Furoxone), and a cancer chemotherapy agent, procarbazine (Matulane).

Stimulant drugs, especially the amphetamines, were formerly used in the attempt to treat depression, often in combination with barbiturates for anxiety and agitation. The most common stimulants now in use include the amphetamines—d,l-amphetamine (Benzedrine), d-amphetamine (Dexedrine), and methamphetamine (Methedrine, Desoxyn, and others)—and methylphenidate (Ritalin); see figure 18.6, table 18.7. These agents produce peripheral and central sympathomimetic effects, potentiate the availability and activity of catecholamines, and produce strong cortical arousal, probably through brainstem mechanisms mediated by the ascending reticular activating system. They usually induce behavioral-activating or euphoriant effects, but in some subjects they may occasionally induce somnolence or dysphoria. Their cortical arousal actions seem to underlie their usefulness in the management of the rare neurological syndrome narcolepsy (for which antidepressants are also helpful), and may contribute to their usefulness in the childhood syndrome known as hyperactivity or "minimal brain dysfunction," for which good evidence is available based on controlled studies. Stimulants also have some short-lasting anorexic effects but are not useful for weight control, except for their placebo effect, after the initial few days of dieting. Similarly, they have consistently

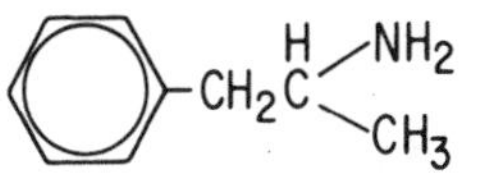

Amphetamine (Benzedrine, Dexedrine)

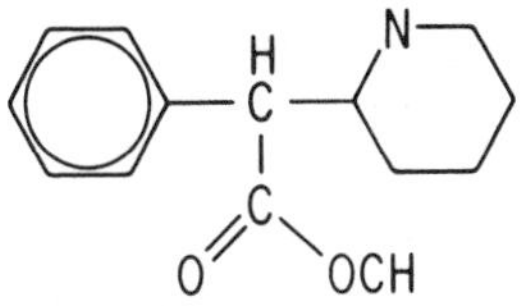

Methylphenidate (Ritalin)

FIGURE 18.6. Stimulants.

been found to be ineffective antidepressants in controlled studies. Stimulants as well as the catecholamine precursor L-dopa, which has been tried as an experimental therapy for depression, may even induce or increase psychotic agitation in severe depression. Claims are sometimes made that stimulants have something to offer in the management of short-lived neurotic forms of depressive illness, although this is a questionable indication for which psychosocial interventions are usually appropriate.

Thus current indications for the use of amphetamines in medical practice are very limited. Moreover, there is a considerable risk of abuse of this class of agents. Although the risk of true physiological addiction is often exaggerated, some dysphoria and depression of mood ("crashing") commonly follow the abrupt discontinuation of high doses of amphetamines. In very high and prolonged doses, stimulants can induce a paranoid psychosis, responsive to antipsychotic drugs, and in lower doses they can induce psychotic exacerbations in schizophrenic patients. Since they are ineffective antidepressants and poor anorexic agents, it is remarkable that their production and prescription continue at high rates.

Summary

The modern chemotherapy of depression is based on the use of a series of structural analogues of the phenothiazines. In contrast to the largely antiadrenergic antipsychotic agents, "tricyclic" antidepressants potentiate the actions of catecholamines and have strong antimuscarinic effects. The latter actions contribute to their annoying and more serious atropinelike effects on the eye, salivary glands, heart, gut, bladder, and central nervous system. It is unfortunate that the drugs used for patients at increased risk of suicide are so toxic and potentially lethal.

While antidepressant effects of the tricyclic antidepressants have been demonstrated in controlled clinical trials among outpatients as well as inpatients, their efficacy is more impressive for the more severe forms of depression. For milder forms of the syndrome, their effects are not much better than those of antianxiety agents, a placebo, or other nonspecific treatments, nor are they impressively better than psychotherapy. Even in serious depressions, the antidepressant drugs are usually not effective for a week or more, and the rate of relapse is high unless patients are maintained on the medications for at least several months. In severe cases of depression, more consistent and more rapid effects are obtained with ECT, which should still be used in the treatment of many acute, severe psychotic depressions, with acutely suicidal patients, and when the tricyclic antidepressants fail to work within a month or so, as happens in as many as 30 percent of severe depressions.

The antipsychotic agents are also useful in the treatment of agitated and psychotic forms of depression. The MAO inhibitors are now largely of historical interest; with the exception of tranylcypromine, they are inferior antidepressants and their use is complicated by the many restrictions required by their toxic interactions with other agents. Stimulants have little if any place in the treatment of serious depressive illnesses. Several experimental chemotherapies for depression have been investigated, including hormones and precursors of biogenic amines, but have not resulted in useful treatments.

Due to the limited efficacy, slowness, and toxicity of the currently available agents, the search for better antidepressants must be pursued more vigorously. Nothing fundamentally new has occurred in the treatment of depression since the introduction of ECT in the 1930s and of the MAO inhibitors and imipramine in the 1950s.

Antianxiety Agents

No ideal generic term for this class of agents has yet been found. The use of the synonyms "antianxiety," "anxiolytic," or "tranquilizer" to some degree represents wishful thinking, based on a long search for drugs that are specific for anxiety and distinctly different from the general anesthetics, sedatives, and hypnotics. Antianxiety agents have been of interest to physicians throughout the history of medicine. Early in this century, the main antianxiety agents were the bromides, along with ethanol and its structural analogues, paraldehyde and chloral hydrate. Then the barbiturates became the standard sedatives and hypnotics. More recently, propanediols were introduced, leading in the 1950s to the production of meprobamate (Miltown, Equanil), shown to be useful in anxious patients in 1957.

The search for safer antianxiety agents lacking the potentially lethal central depressant, respiratory depressant, and addicting properties of all of the previously mentioned sedative-hypnotic tranquilizing agents led to the development of the benzodiazepines (see figure 18.7, table 18.8). Chloridazepoxide (Librium) was introduced in 1960 and found to have potent taming effects in animals and anticonvulsant, skeletal-muscle relaxant, and sedative-antianxiety effects in humans. The popularity of the benzodiazepines is illustrated by the fact that chlordiazepoxide (Librium) and diazepam (Valium) have been among the top three most-prescribed drugs of all kinds, at rates approaching 100 million prescriptions a year in the United States and a cost of about 500 million dollars. Another benzodiazepine, flurazepam (Dalmane), is one of the safest and most popular sedative-hypnotics. The benzodiazepines have useful antianxiety effects and are relatively safe.

Pharmacology

The agents used for anxiety and mild dysphoria all depress the CNS, approximately in proportion to the dose. Milder central depression can provide clinically useful antianxiety effects more or less separable from frank sedation. Many of the agents have anticonvulsant actions and muscle-relaxant properties. Larger amounts of sedatives produce a toxic brain syndrome, resulting eventually in coma, respiratory depression, and death. All of the sedative-tranquilizers, including the benzodiazepines, have a greater or lesser tendency to be required in increasing doses due to tolerance, and to produce psychological dependence and addiction. A trend in the development of these agents has been a gradual improvement of the therapeutic index, with consequent separation of antianxiety and sedative effects, and a lessening of the addictive potential, notably with the benzodiazepines. Other characteristics of most of the sedative-antianxiety agents are that they have relatively little effect on autonomic functions, with the exceptions of the antihistamines, diphenhydramine (Benadryl) and hydroxyzine (Atarax, Vistaril), and on the extrapyramidal system. The sedative-tranquilizers have no useful antipsychotic activity.

The barbiturates, especially phenobarbital, continue to be used by some physicians for the management of neurotic anxiety and dysphoria. Phenobarbital is a long-acting barbiturate and has a considerable degree of renal excretion (20–30 percent) independent of its hepatic metabolism, in contrast to the shorter-acting barbiturates, which are more rapidly metabolized by hepatic enzymatic activity. The limited euphoria associated with phenobarbital decreases its potential for abuse; its prolonged duration of action reduces its ability to produce severe withdrawal reactions but complicates the management of acute overdoses. Phenobarbital can "induce" the synthesis and activity of hepatic microsomal enzymes to increase its own rate of metabolism. Although this effect is not an important factor in tolerance to the barbiturates, it can have important consequences for the actions of other drugs and hormones, including increased inactivation of dihydroxycoumarin and steroids, and increased production of porphyrins (see table 18.6).

The propanediols are also metabolized mainly by hepatic microsomal oxidases, and meprobamate induces these enzymes. Since it is more rapidly excreted than phenobarbital, the increased rate of oxidation of meprobamate can contribute to its tolerance. Tybamate is even more rapidly metabolized and excreted than meprobamate, decreasing its useful duration of ac-

SEDATIVE-ANTIANXIETY AGENTS

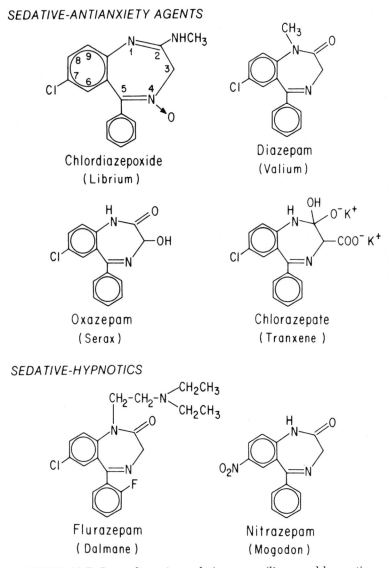

FIGURE 18.7. Benzodiazepine sedative-tranquilizers and hypnotics.

tion but also reducing the probability of addiction, since much less drug accumulates in tissue. Addiction to meprobamate occurs after prolonged use of doses not much greater than the upper limits of recommended doses.

The benzodiazepines (fig. 18.7, table 18.8) are extraordinarily popular, although they are similar in many respects to previously available sedatives, including the barbiturates and the propanediols. Thus the benzodiazepines have rather widespread and diffuse inhibitory effects in the central nervous system and important anticon-

vulsant as well as muscle-relaxant activity, partly mediated by inhibitory effects on reflex activity. The benzodiazepines and nearly all of the sedatives produce slow-wave and low-voltage fast (beta) activity in the EEG. Nevertheless, the benzodiazepines have characteristics that separate them from the barbiturates, and that are partially shared by the propanediols. These include depressant actions in the limbic system at lower doses than their more generalized depressant effects on the cerebral cortex and the reticular activating system. This partial selectivity correlates with taming effects in animals, the relatively selective suppression of conditioned (especially "avoidance" behaviors) more than unconditioned responses, and with their clinical antianxiety effect and relative lack of sedation in comparison with older sedatives.

The sedative-tranquilizers (except the antihistamines) exhibit "cross-tolerance," or the ability of one to produce tolerance to the effects of the others. It follows that withdrawal of addicting doses of any of these agents can be accomplished by the use of gradually diminishing doses of any one of them, as is commonly done with a barbiturate (see table 18.9). The benzodiazepines are less likely than other sedatives (except antihistamines) to produce dangerous withdrawal syndromes. The danger of severe coma, respiratory depression, and death following an acute overdose of a benzodiazepine is also less than after a comparable multiple of the average daily dose of a barbiturate, propanediol, or other sedative. One way of summarizing the unique characteristics of the benzodiazepines is to point out that their dose-response relationships are much "flatter" than those of the barbiturates and nonbarbiturate sedatives (but less gradual than the antipsychotic agents), so that doubling the dose produces much less sedation than occurs with the other sedatives.

Benzodiazepines (see fig. 18.7) differ in several important ways. Diazepam (Valium) is particularly rapidly absorbed after oral administration and induces euphoria and acute intoxication, which contribute to its popularity as a drug of abuse. Diazepam is also particularly lipophilic and undergoes relatively prolonged elimination. Flurazepam (Dalmane) and nitrazepam (Mogodon) are much more like sedatives than the other benzodiazepines in that their "antianxiety" or behavior-inhibiting effects occur at doses close to those that induce ataxia and somnolence, limiting their usefulness to hypnotic effects. Development of tolerance to sedation by flurazepam is much less than for other hypnotics. Although the benzodiazepines can lead to the induction of hepatic enzymes, this mechanism does not seem to contribute appreciably to the tolerance that develops, nor do they have enough effect to increase the rate of inactivation (and to increase the required dose) of other drugs such as the coumarin anticoagulants or the anti-depressants, as the barbiturates and glutethimide have been reported to do (see table 18.6). A number of other experimental treatments of anxiety are being investigated. These include the use of beta-adrenergic blocking agents that prevent many of the peripheral autonomic expressions of anxiety and stress.

Clinical Use

None of the sedative-tranquilizer group of antianxiety drugs is useful as a primary therapeutic agent in severe psychiatric illness, although these drugs have occasional specialized applications in patients with disturbances that will be described below. The main usefulness of the antianxiety agents is in the *short-term treatment* of relatively transient forms of anxiety, fear, and tension. They are also widely used as preoperative sedatives and in the management of short-lived, painful syndromes and psychosomatic and other illnesses with unexplained physical manifestations. Benzodiazepines have been claimed to have some immediate euphoriant and antianxiety effects in moderately severe anxious neurotic depressions and to be of some benefit during the delayed onset of action of an antidepressant. Tolerance to the antianxiety, euphoriant, and sedative effects of all of the sedative-tranquilizers leads to a loss of their effectiveness over time and an increased risk of dependency, abuse, and addiction. These agents are more often used in general medicine than in psychiatry.

Many psychiatrists believe that prolonged or characterological nonpsychotic disorders involving anxiety and dysphoria are better treated with psychotherapy and limit antianxiety agents to brief use in the less common, more acute, short-lived, and usually reactive forms of neurotic illness. Psychotherapists are often particularly disinclined to rely on the antianxiety agents, since the descriptive characteristics of patients who tend to respond well to antianxiety agents are different from those of patients who are usually considered good candidates for the rational and verbal psychotherapies. Favorable patient response has been associated with relatively low socioeconomic class, lack of psychological sophistication, and inability to express unhappiness verbally in terms of intrapsychic or interpersonal conflict; a more favorable response also tends to occur in patients with passive and almost magical expectations of the physician. An enthusiastic, charismatic presentation of the medication and its sedative effects by the physician also seems to help. Patients who are more active, vigorous and extroverted tend to dislike the sedative effects of antianxiety agents and may even become more uncomfortable taking them.

The broad and loosely defined applications of antianxiety agents and the high rate of favorable responses to a placebo in many of these conditions (30–60 percent of subjects) increases the difficulty of demonstrating significant benefits from an active drug (Rickels, 1968); moreover, the short-lived reactive forms of anxiety eventually improve spontaneously. The main conclusions from reviews of drug trials are that sedative-tranquilizing agents have appreciable and fairly consistent antianxiety effects beyond a placebo effect and that demonstration of the superiority of one agent or class over another is extremely difficult, leaving one to select a specific agent on the basis of considerations other than its demonstrated superiority in a given condition.

For routine use in the treatment of neurotic anxiety, the short-acting barbiturates and non-barbiturate sedatives produce excessive sedation and have unacceptably high addiction potential and lethality. *Barbiturates* (as well as diazepam or the highly sedating butyrophenone droperidol) are occasionally used in emergencies to produce rapid sedation in psychotic, manic, or enraged patients, especially in addition to a sedating antipsychotic agent such as chlorpromazine. Amobarbital (Amytal and generic) is still given intravenously to facilitate the differential diagnosis of catatonic behavior or to uncover highly defended thoughts or feelings in diagnostic or abreactive therapeutic interview techniques. Moreover, the long-acting barbiturate phenobarbital has come out about as well as any of the more modern anxiolytic agents in most drug comparisons, and it is far less expensive.

The *propanediols*, which seemed to be very promising in the 1950s, are now known to be no better than the barbiturates, and meprobamate carries an unacceptable risk of addiction and of fatality on overdosage. The addicting dose of meprobamate in fact overlaps the therapeutic range. Physical signs of withdrawal can follow the discontinuation of doses as low as 1200 mg/day; severe withdrawal with seizures can be expected at doses above 3200 mg/day, while the therapeutic range is 1200–2400 mg/day. A newer propanediol, tybamate, is much less likely to produce addiction, but its comparisons with barbiturates and the benzodiazepines have shown it to be an inferior antianxiety agent.

The *benzodiazepines* (fig. 18.7, table 18.8) are

TABLE 18.8. Tranquilizing sedatives used for anxiety: benzodiazepines.

Generic name	Trade name	Dose range (mg/day)	Ratio of lethal to daily dose[a]
Sedative-tranquilizers			
Chlordiazepoxide	Librium, generic	15–100[b]	10
Chlorazepate	Tranxene	15–60	5
Diazepam	Valium	6–40	20
Oxazepam	Serax	30–120	?
Sedative-hypnotics			
Flurazepam	Dalmane	15–30 (at bedtime)	10
Nitrazepam	(Mogodon)	unavailable in U.S.	?

[a] The human lethal dose of the benzodiazepines is poorly established but exceeds a week's supply of ordinary doses. Rare fatalities have been reported after 700–1000 mg of Librium or Valium.
[b] Up to 400 mg may be used in delirium tremens.

popular because their effects in anxiety are consistently superior to a placebo and because they are relatively safe agents, with relatively low risk of addiction or suicide. Diazepam (Valium) has become the most popular benzodiazepine in the 1970s. Unfortunately, the rapid activity of diazepam and its tendency to induce euphoria have also made it a popular drug of abuse, and its prolonged duration of action and affinity for lipid and protein suggest that overdoses of diazepam might be somewhat more dangerous than those of other benzodiazepines. Oxazepam (Serax) is the most rapidly metabolized and cleared benzodiazepine; it has no active metabolites or tendency to accumulate in tissue, suggesting that it might be relatively safer for use in elderly patients or those with impaired hepatic function. Oxazepam is also the most potent anticonvulsant of this group of drugs. Flurazepam (Dalmane) and nitrazepam (Mogodon, not available in the United States) are more potent in their sedative effects than the other benzodiazepines and are recommended only for nighttime sedation and sleep. They are probably less likely to produce tolerance than other hypnotics. Their lethality on overdosage and potential for abuse and addiction appear to be no greater than for other benzodiazepines and much less than with the short-acting barbiturates and nonbarbiturate hypnotic-sedatives, although this is not yet clearly established. The benzodiazepines are relatively expensive.

Toxicity and Side Effects

For all sedatives, the most commonly encountered problem is daytime sedation, with drowsiness, decreased mental acuity, some decrease in coordination and occupational productivity, and increased risk of accidents, particularly when sedatives are combined with alcohol. Autonomic and extrapyramidal side effects are not usually encountered with the sedatives. Liver damage and blood dyscrasias are rare. Interactions with other medications occur (see table 18.6), particularly with the barbiturates, but only rarely with the benzodiazepines.

It would be a mistake to conclude that the benzodiazepines are totally innocuous. Overdoses have led to death in rare cases with doses equiva-

lent to about two weeks' supply. The common use of high doses of chlordiazepoxide and diazepam in the treatment of alcoholic withdrawal and the use of diazepam intravenously to control seizures or cardiac arrhythmias are occasionally complicated by apnea or cardiac arrest. Some patients become dysphoric, agitated, angry, or otherwise "disinhibited" while taking benzodiazepines. This effect resembles that of alcohol, and while most commonly ascribed to chlordiazepoxide, it is not unique to that agent. Rarely, frank rage reactions have been observed.

The most serious problems of sedatives are related to their tendency to produce *tolerance* and physiological *addiction*, in addition to psychological dependence. Moreover, they are lethal in acute overdoses in varying degrees. The phenomenon of tolerance to both the antianxiety and the sedative effects of sedatives can contribute to innocent self-medication in increasing doses. Rapid intoxication and euphoria with the short-acting barbiturates, most of the nonbarbiturate sedative-hypnotics, and most impressively with diazepam among the benzodiazepines contribute to their abuse and to a brisk black market in these agents. Physicians can deal with the problems associated with sedative-tranquilizing agents by selecting those with least potential for abuse, addiction, and lethality and by using the drugs for clear indications and for short periods of time. Patients with a previous history of abuse of other sedatives or alcohol and with other dyssocial or impulsive traits should be treated with this class of agents very cautiously. In general, the use of sedative-tranquilizers in patients with character disorders and more characterological forms of neurosis is unlikely to be helpful except in acute exacerbations of turmoil or anticipatory anxiety and is likely to lead to abuse.

The production of physical addiction to sedatives varies with the daily dose of drug and duration of its use. Meprobamate is highly addicting. With short-acting barbiturates, signs and symptoms of withdrawal can be expected after the intake of about four to five times the usual daily dose for more than a month, and severe withdrawal reactions, with hypotension, seizures, delirium tremens, and hallucinosis, can be expected to occur two or three days after discontinuation of prolonged dosage more than five times the ordinary daily dose, and certainly above ten times this dose. The withdrawal syndrome is strikingly similar to that associated with alcohol.

Withdrawal from addiction to barbiturates and other sedatives is a serious and life-threatening medical problem, in contrast to withdrawal from narcotics, which is unpleasant but almost never fatal. Special measures to be taken in managing sedative withdrawal are outlined in table 18.9. Physical dependence on the benzodiazepines has been studied most extensively with the oldest agents of that group, chlordiazepoxide and diazepam. Addiction is not likely unless abuses reach at least ten, or more likely twenty, times the usual daily dose and continue for several months. This pattern in part reflects the pro-longed half-life of these agents, much as the long-acting barbiturate phenobarbital infrequently leads to physical dependence and a withdrawal syndrome. Furthermore, the onset of a withdrawal syndrome with the benzodiazepines, glutethimide (Doriden), and phenobarbital is considerably later than with either the short-acting barbiturates and sedatives (two to three days) or alcohol (three to five days); it is usually seen at four to eight days but sometimes as long as two weeks after withdrawal. Even when a withdrawal syndrome is encountered after abuse of the benzodiazepines, it is likely to be of only moderate intensity and is rarely associated with seizures.

The benzodiazepines have a comfortable margin of safety in comparison with other sedatives. Nevertheless, although it is commonly said

TABLE 18.9. Principles of withdrawal in addiction to barbiturates and other sedatives.

1. A short-acting barbiturate (e.g., pentobarbital, Nembutal) has similar actions ("cross-tolerance") to most of the sedative-tranquilizers except the antihistamines (which rarely produce addiction) and can be used to withdraw from nonbarbiturates as well as from all barbiturates, greatly simplifying the technique.

2. Withdrawal from barbiturate-type addiction (in contrast to opioid addiction) is a medically serious undertaking, best done in hospital and carried out *slowly* (especially with phenobarbital, glutethimide, and the benzodiazepines, although the withdrawal syndrome with benzodiazepines is rarely severe).

3. Estimate the amount of pentobarbital required to protect against withdrawal symptoms after initial intoxication has cleared by giving sufficient doses (usually 200–400 mg, preferably orally) at 4–6 hour intervals to induce *mild* intoxication (drowsiness, slurred speech, ataxia, incoordination, nystagmus) within an hour of each dose and to avoid prominent withdrawal symptoms (tremulousness and hypotension 4–6 hours after each dose). In a 24-hour period 800–2400 mg are typically required; up to 400 mg of pentobarbital a day can be discontinued abruptly.

4. Stabilization continues for two to three days for most barbiturates and nonbarbiturate sedatives. The daily dose is given in four to six portions. Because of their tendency to produce severe withdrawal symptoms a week or more after withdrawal, a stabilization period of seven to ten days is recommended for phenobarbital and glutethimide and following abuse of the benzodiazepines in very large doses.

5. Withdraw over approximately ten to twenty days by removing not more than 100 mg of pentobarbital a day and *only* after stabilization is attained (mild intoxication and minimal withdrawal signs during a twenty-four-hour period) and maintained for the recommended number of days. If withdrawal signs develop, stop withdrawal until the signs disappear and resume at 50 mg/day.

6. As an alternative to step 5, some experts recommend substituting phenobarbital (long-acting), 30 mg for each 100 mg of pentobarbital during the stabilization period and withdrawing it at the rate of 30 mg/day.

7. The short-acting barbiturates are not useful in the management of withdrawal from opiates. Even though there is cross-tolerance between alcohol and barbiturates, detoxification of alcoholics is usually accomplished with benzodiazepines (chlordiazepoxide or diazepam). Addiction to meprobamate is often overcome by slow withdrawal of the offending agent by the same principles outlined above.

that committing suicide with a benzodiazepine is virtually impossible, most deliberate overdoses involve more than one agent, typically whatever the victim has at hand, and can present complicated and difficult toxicological problems. Recommendation of a specific number of days' supply of a benzodiazepine that can be dispensed safely is difficult; rare deaths have been reported following the acute ingestion of 600–1000 mg of chlordiazepoxide or diazepam, and there are reports of survival of doses of more than 2000 mg. With other sedatives and hypnotics, as a general rule, the acute ingestion of ten days' supply at once will regularly produce severe intoxication and may be lethal, and the ingestion of twenty times the daily or hypnotic dose is very likely to be fatal. Thus even though fatality is less likely and more unpredictable with acute overdoses of the benzodiazepines, dispensing more than perhaps two weeks' supply of a benzodiazepine, or a week's supply of other sedatives, is unwise.

The safety of the sedative-tranquilizers in *pregnancy* has not been established. Little compelling evidence indicates that the benzodiazepines are teratogenic, although a possible association between cleft lips or palate and the use of diazepam in the first trimester has recently been suspected. The barbiturates can alter fetal hepatic metabolism and should be avoided. Meprobamate has been claimed to be safe in pregnancy but physiological dependence of the fetus on it or on the barbiturates and nonbarbiturate sedatives can be expected.

Summary

Anxiety and dysphoria are ubiquitous human experiences. They are most effectively and appropriately treated with chemotherapy when they represent acute and severe symptoms of neurotic psychiatric illness or reactive or anticipatory features of medical or surgical illness. Antianxiety medications should be used for brief periods of time both because of their tendency to induce tolerance to their antianxiety and sedative effects and because of the risk of psychological dependence and even physical addiction to most sedatives. Their routine and sustained use for psychiatric patients with characterological

disorders is of questionable value and increases risk of abuse.

The history of psychopharmacology has been marked by the partially successful search for more effective and less toxic antianxiety agents, and has included the replacement of alcohol and the bromides by the barbiturates in the early twentieth century and the later addition of nonbarbiturate sedatives, including the propanediols. All of these agents are severely toxic and potentially lethal when taken acutely in doses above twenty times the normal daily dose and physically addicting when used for several months at doses only a few times above the usual daily doses. Their withdrawal can be managed by the substitution of a short-acting barbiturate and its *slow* withdrawal over two or more weeks. Since the 1960s, the benzodiazepines have become the most useful antianxiety agents, with the widest margin of safety and a limited potential for addiction. Sociological studies suggest that the "metapharmacological" aspects of anxiolytic agents, including personal characteristics of patients and their physicians, contribute to the clinical results obtained with antianxiety agents, the efficacy of which depends at least partly on suggestion and placebo effects.

The preceding summary of the various categories of psychotropic agents in current clinical use indicates that effective and relatively safe medical treatments are now available for most of the major psychiatric illnesses. Their usefulness is most apparent in the more acute and severe forms of psychiatric illness. Unfortunately, many persistent forms of psychosis, neurosis, and character disorder respond less well to chemotherapeutic interventions. Even in those syndromes that are responsive to medications, the most efficient and humane use of medical therapies in psychiatry, as in any medical specialty, requires a careful balance of applied medical technology and attention to the patient as an individual and a member of a social network—aspects of psychiatric care that are emphasized in other chapters of this book.

Psychopharmacology has had important influences on the development of modern psychiatry; many of these were discussed in the introduction to this chapter. To reiterate, the availability of agents that have impressive beneficial or deleterious effects on mental activity, mood, and behavior has led to an increased interest in the biological and medical aspects of psychiatry since the 1950s—aspects that had lost some influence due to the prominence in twentieth century American psychiatry of psychosocial and particularly psychoanalytic theories and techniques. In addition, the development of psychopharmacology has interacted with other hopeful and positive approaches to psychiatric illness that have evolved in the post-World War II era; the result has been a continuing atmosphere of optimism about the treatability and rehabilitation of many severely ill psychiatric patients.

References

Åsberg, M. 1974. Plasma nortriptyline levels—relationship to clinical effects. *Clin. Pharmacol. Ther.* 16:215–229.

Cade, J. F. J. 1949. Lithium salts in the treatment of psychotic excitement. *Med. J. Aust.* 36:349–352.

Caffey, E. M., S. C. Karin, L. E. Hollister, and A. D. Pokorny. 1970. *Drug treatment in psychiatry*. Washington, D.C.: Veterans Administration.

Davis, J. M. 1975. Overview: maintenance therapy in psychiatry. *Am. J. Psychiatry* 133:1–13.

Delay, J., P. Deniker, and J. Harl. 1952. Utilisation therapeutique psychiatrique d'une phenothiazine d'action centrale elective (4560 RP). *Ann. Med. Psychol.* 110:112–117.

Gershon, S., and B. Shopsin. 1975. *Lithium: its role in psychiatric research and treatment*. New York: Plenum Press.

Granacher, R. P., and R. J. Baldessarini. 1975. Physostigmine: its use in acute anticholinergic syndrome with antidepressant and antiparkinson drugs. *Arch. Gen. Psychiatry* 32:375–380.

Grinspoon, L., J. R. Ewalt, and R. I. Shader. 1972. *Schizophrenia: pharmacotherapy and psychotherapy*. Baltimore: Williams & Wilkins.

Hogarty, G. E., S. C. Goldberg, and the Collaborative Study Group. 1973. Drugs and sociotherapy in the aftercare of schizophrenic patients. *Arch. Gen. Psychiatry* 28:54–62.

Klerman, G. L., and J. O. Cole. 1965. Clinical pharmacology of imipramine and related antidepressant compounds. *Pharmacol. Rev.* 17:101–141.

Lipton, M. A., et al. 1973. *Megavitamin and orthomolecular theory in psychiatry*. Task Force report no. 7. Washington, D.C.: American Psychiatric Association.

May, P. R. A. 1968. *Treatment of schizophrenia: a comparative study of five treatment methods*. New York: Science House.

Rickels, K. 1968. *Nonspecific factors in drug therapy*. Springfield, Ill.: Thomas.

Recommended Reading

Appleton, W. S., and J. M. Davis. 1973. *Practical clinical psychopharmacology*. New York: Medcom Press.

Baldessarini, R. J. 1975. Biogenic amine hypotheses in affective disorders. In *The nature and treatment of depression*, ed. F. F. Flach and S. C. Draghi. New York: Wiley.

Baldessarini, R. J. 1977. *Chemotherapy in psychiatry*. Cambridge, Mass.: Harvard University Press.

Ban, T. A. 1969. *Psychopharmacology*. Baltimore: Williams & Wilkins.

———— 1975. Drug interactions with psychoactive drugs. *Dis. Nerv. Syst.* 36:164–166.

Clark, W. G., and J. del Giudice, eds. 1970. *Principles of psychopharmacology*. New York: Academic Press.

Cole, J. O., and J. M. Davis. 1969. Antipsychotic drugs. In *The schizophrenic syndrome*, ed. L. Bellak and L. Loeb. New York: Grune & Stratton.

Efron, D. H., ed. 1968. *Psychopharmacology: a review of progress: 1957–1967*. Public Health Service publication no. 1836. Washington, D.C.: Government Printing Office.

Forrest, I. S., C. J. Carr, and E. Usdin, eds. 1974. *Phenothiazines and structurally related drugs*. New York: Raven Press.

Garattini, S., E. Mussini, and L. O. Randall, eds. 1973. *The benzodiazepines*. New York: Raven Press.

Gattozzi, A. A. 1970. *Lithium in the treatment of mood disorders*. U.S. National Clearinghouse for Mental Health Information (NIMH), publication no. 5033. Washington, D.C.: Government Printing Office.

Glassman, A. H., and J. M. Perel. 1973. The clinical pharmacology of imipramine. *Arch. Gen. Psychiatry* 28:649–653.

Greenblatt, D. J., and R. I. Shader. 1974. *Benzodiazepines in clinical practice*. New York: Raven Press.

Hollister, L. E. 1973. *Clinical use of psychotherapeutic drugs*. Springfield, Ill.: Thomas.

Klein, D. F., and J. M. Davis. 1969. *Diagnosis and*

drug treatment of psychiatric disorders. Baltimore: Williams & Wilkins.

Kline, N. S., S. F. Alexander, and A. Chamberlain. 1974. *Psychotropic drugs: a manual for emergency management of overdosage*. Oradell, N.J.: Medical Economics.

Morris, J. B., and A. T. Beck. 1974. The efficacy of antidepressant drugs. *Arch. Gen. Psychiatry* 30:667–674.

Muller, C. 1972. The overmedicated society. *Science* 176:488–492.

Rech, R. H., and K. E. Moore, eds. 1971. *An introduction to psychopharmacology*. New York: Raven Press.

Schildkraut, J. J. 1970. *Neuropsychopharmacology and the affective disorders*. Boston: Little, Brown.

Shader, R. I., ed. 1972. *Psychiatric complications of medical drugs*. New York: Raven Press.

Shader, R. I., and A. DiMascio, eds. 1970. *Psychotropic drug side-effects*. Baltimore: Williams & Wilkins.

Sudilovsky, A., S. Gershon, and B. Beer, eds. 1975. *Predictability in psychopharmacology: preclinical and clinical correlations*. New York: Raven Press.

Swazey, J. P. 1974. *Chlorpromazine in psychiatry*. Cambridge, Mass.: M.I.T. Press.

Valzelli, L. 1973. *Psychopharmacology: an introduction to experimental and clinical principles*. Flushing, N.Y.: Spectrum.

Behavior Therapy and Behavioral Psychotherapy

CHAPTER 19

Lee Birk

BEHAVIOR THERAPY may be defined as the array of clinical concepts and therapeutic procedures that have been systematically developed from the experimental observation and modification of animal and human behavior. In its most sophisticated clinical form, behavior therapy is not limited to simple motor reflex learning, or even to the whole range of learned external behaviors mediated by skeletal muscles —from crude and simple actions (like bar pressing) to subtle and complex behavioral sequences, or "chained responses" (like parallel skiing, violin playing, or sculpting). Rather, as with other psychotherapeutic approaches, behavior therapy includes and even emphasizes techniques for modifying those problematic and difficult-to-measure internal responses that we call feelings and thoughts.

What Distinguishes Behavior Therapy from Other Therapies?

Although behavior therapy as a significant clinical enterprise is less than two decades old, the scientific origins of behavior therapy go back more than fifty years, to Pavlov (1928, 1941) and Thorndike (1898) and even before. In 1920,

Watson and Rayner reported their classic experiment with the eleven-month-old infant Albert, demonstrating that a "phobia" could be created by classical conditioning and that it obeyed familiar principles of stimulus generalization; this term refers to the experimentally observed fact that stimuli very similar to a conditioned stimulus will elicit the same conditioned response, although in a progressively weaker form, as the stimulus used becomes less and less similar to the one used in the original conditioning. Watson later sparked widespread enthusiasm and criticism by advocating a radical, sweeping, and rather simplistic form of "behaviorism," claiming to explain not only all phobias but all of human personality by simple stimulus-response (S-R) bonds. As early as 1924, Mary Cover Jones successfully treated phobias in children by a behavioral method, which we would now call *in vivo* systematic desensitization, using eating as a competitive response. In addition, W. Horsley Gantt (1944, 1953) working in the Pavlovian Laboratory in Adolf Meyer's department at Johns Hopkins Medical School during the 1930s, 1940s, and 1950s, almost singlehandedly (and just barely) kept alive in this country the ideal of a behavioral approach to psychiatry.

It was not until the late 1950s, however, that—almost simultaneously and on three continents—three major research traditions began to coalesce into a set of clinically useful ideas and methods, as opposed to ideals and laboratory hypotheses. The first consisted of the work of Wolpe, Lazarus, and Rachman (Wolpe, 1958), which began in South Africa and was later transplanted to the United States. In their early work they emphasized competitive response or "counter-conditioning" treatment strategies. The second, beginning in the United States, was the research of Skinner and his students, especially Ogden Lindsley (Lindsley and Skinner, 1954), in operant conditioning, which emphasized precise analysis and contingency control of the clinical situation. The third tradition, the importance of which has been underestimated, was the work of M. B. Shapiro (1961) and his colleagues, especially Isaac Marks (1972, 1976), at the Maudsley Hospital in London; this work emphasized the value of treating the single psychiatric case as an experiment in itself. In this respect, they are following in the footsteps of Claude Bernard in medicine.

Throughout the 1960s, behavior therapy grew prodigiously into a fully recognized and at times almost oversold approach to treatment problems in clinical psychiatry. Early in 1970, the American Psychiatric Association chartered a task force to evaluate the achievements and potential of the behavioral approach. In mid-1973 this task force published its report, *Behavior Therapy in Psychiatry*. The report's summary conclusion was this: "The work of the Task Force has reaffirmed our belief that behavior therapy and behavioral principles employed in the analysis of clinical phenomena have reached a stage of development where they now unquestionably have much to offer informed clinicians in the service of modern clinical and social psychiatry" (Birk et al., 1973, p. 64).

Beginning in the late 1960s and early 1970s, a number of researchers and clinicians (Goldiamond and Dryud, 1968; Birk, 1968, 1970, 1972; Sloane, 1969; Marmor, 1971; Feather and Rhoads, 1972; Rhoads and Feather, 1974) wrote about the use of behavior therapy together with a psychodynamic approach. Most recently, Birk and Brinkley-Birk (1974, 1975) have proposed a conceptual synthesis of behavioral and psychoana-

lytic elements, proposing that such synthesis permits the development of therapeutic strategies more efficacious than either approach alone.

Insistence on the Observable

What distinguishes behavior therapy and behavioral psychotherapy from other therapies is an unusual insistence on observable phenomena, as opposed to inferred processes, in guiding diagnosis and treatment. Historically, this very significant difference between behavioral and dynamic psychotherapies arises from the rootedness of the behavioral therapies in experimental scientific method. When behavior therapists work toward modifying feelings or behaviors, they adopt a rigorous standard for evidence for evaluating the phenomena in question; that is, they insist on having some way to observe, validate, and at least crudely quantify those feelings (internal behaviors) that are being treated as the target symptom. The purest of behaviorists would insist on some method of direct observation and actual measurement. An example of direct observation would be the use of an electromyogram (EMG) to monitor precise levels of tension in the frontalis muscle.

Such precise electromyographic measurement of a feeling and its electronic translation into a moment-to-moment, quantitative, and highly accurate auditory display to the patient—in the form of a series of small clicks varying in frequency per minute—constitute the basis for a highly effective and efficient behavioral method for the treatment of tension headache. On the other hand, less pure behaviorists—the majority of clinical behavior therapists—are willing to address much more difficult-to-measure behaviors, such as unwelcome sexual or aggressive impulses, acute feelings of depression, or repetitive obsessional thoughts. In the latter cases, no available analogue for the electromyogram has yet been developed. The behavioral clinician must therefore either define these phenomena as out of his purview and job description because of the impossibility of their direct observation and measurement or lower his epistemological standards and be willing to accept and work with self-report data. There are and can be no other alternatives because impulses and thoughts are, by their very nature, purely subjective and private events, never directly observable in themselves nor subject to external validation.

Indirect Methods of Observation

By collaborating with patients toward a precise specification of what constitutes a systematic response, and by asking patients actually to tally their own subjective perception of the occurrence of these responses, one can obtain highly useful data. For instance, a patient who habitually pulls out his eyebrows, bites his fingernails, or smokes and is motivated to break the habit can be asked to keep a careful day-by-day record on index cards of particular impulses to pull, bite, or smoke, together with whether or not the covert impulse (O) was translated into an overt behavior (X). The following is a sample of what a self-report data sheet might look like. The notation [O → X] indicates that the patient reported he not only felt an impulse but actually translated this impulse into an overt, directly observable response.

	7:00 A.M.—alarm went off
[O]	7:05 A.M.—felt edgy; didn't feel like getting up
[O → X]	7:25 A.M.—after shaving, tried to call office; line busy; thought of conference scheduled for 10:00 A.M.
[O]	9:10 A.M.—hurrying to read mail; thought again of conference
[O → X]	9:25 A.M.—asked secretary to call regional director long distance; felt upset waiting for call to come through
[O → X]	9:40 A.M.—preparing data for meeting; felt pressured and worried about conference
[O]	9:50 A.M.—looked at watch; left for conference

Having patients keep records of this kind, tallying the occurrence and the precise timing of impulses, overt behaviors, and their thoughts and feelings at the time, generates a fairly accurate frequency record of target internal behaviors.* It

---

* The valid point can be made, of course, that when a patient records or tallies one of his own responses, this record keeping in itself influences the behavior being monitored, producing an inevitable and built-in distortion, secondary to the measurement process. This effect is quite analogous to the Heisenberg uncertainty principle in physics. Despite this inherent distortion, the clinical value of carefully collected self-report data can be enormous.

also provides both the patient and the therapist with a large amount of useful clinical information about the precise external and internal conditions under which the target behavior occurs. The target behavior is the particular, carefully specified element of the patient's total behavioral repertoire being treated as the chief complaint, the modification of which helps the patient's life situation. In many cases, the target behavior is obvious (head banging, for example). In other instances, subtle behavioral analysis is necessary to refine a vague complaint, such as "shyness," into the separate and complex behavioral components that it comprises. Avoidance of eye contact, a soft speaking voice, and submissive body postures are almost always involved in shyness. In addition, however, many other very subtle and idiosyncratic observable responses must be recognized and addressed if a particular shy individual is to be helped optimally.

In the sample self-report data sheet, the response seems to occur following frustrating external stimuli (busy telephone line) and internal stimuli (worry about conference). The clinical utility of records like this one is generally astonishing to both patients and fledgling behavior therapists. In most cases, the patient simply is not aware of the situational and thematic details revealed by such tally records and could never provide such a rich history, even with very extended retrospective history taking. After being collected in this way, these contextual data surrounding symptom occurrence are used in a continuing, ever-broadening behavioral analysis: a precise specification of the variables that influence the frequency of the target behavior. For example, from the tally the patient and the therapist may conclude inductively that the patient feels like biting his nails when he is frustrated and angry and that he has in his current behavioral repertoire no apparent alternative to nail biting that would be an effective outlet for these feelings. If a history of underassertiveness (or inappropriate assertiveness) corroborates the lack of a more adaptive response functionally equivalent to nail biting, such a tally might indicate that assertive training should also be a part of a comprehensive behavioral approach to the patient's presenting problem, in order to help him learn appropriate self-assertion as an alternative response to nail biting.

In addition to the typically voluminous index-card tally, the raw data thus accumulated should be periodically summarized quite concisely in the form of an ongoing, day-to-day trends graph. Usually the therapist does this together with the patient, at least in the beginning. If the therapist treats graph making with genuine enthusiasm, regarding it as a cooperative, mutual, and social task in which patient and therapist share, he reinforces the patient's labors in collecting accurate and complete data. Since the data should include notations about subjective, internal responses (private events), only the patient himself *can* collect a complete record, and it is therefore very important that the therapist attend carefully to his own behavior so as to influence optimally the patient's data-collection behavior. The therapist must elicit this behavior, shape it toward completeness and relevance, and maintain it through continued reinforcement.

Figure 19.1 shows a small segment of an actual graph constructed with a severely obsessional

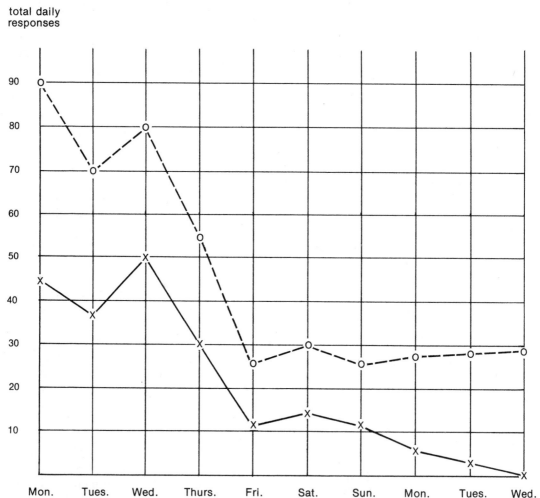

FIGURE 19.1. Sample trends graph constructed with an obsessional patient. Impulses toward avoidance behavior are indicated by the Os and actual avoidance behaviors by Xs. This patient expected that inhibiting actual avoidance behaviors would increase the frequency of impulses, that is, that line O-O-O would rise as line X-X-X fell. In fact he was wrong and the behavioral analysis of his problem was correct: his impulses toward avoidance *decreased* as he voluntarily inhibited actual avoidance behaviors.

patient. Here the target behavioral symptom was any irrational avoidance behavior associated with the patient's profound fear of cancer, which he viewed delusionally as an illness to which he was uniquely susceptible. Thus the patient felt he could not safely touch doorknobs, money, a bar of soap, his own clothes, and many, many other items without elaborate precautionary rituals. He used wax paper to grasp a doorknob, kicked doors shut with his shoe, and routinely discarded soap he had used only once and refused to touch it, even in order to throw it away. The graph summarizes a period in the treatment during which the patient was asked to make earnest efforts not to reinforce all these impulses to avoid imagined contamination by allowing himself to engage in actual avoidance behaviors. The patient was most reluctant to do this because, a priori, he felt that if he were to inhibit actual avoidance behaviors, he would feel in more danger of cancer, leading to more fear, and therefore would actually increase the frequency of avoidance impulses. In this false expectation he had failed to recognize that his high level of fearful thoughts was in part being reinforced and maintained by his high level of overt avoidance responses, inasmuch as avoidance behaviors served temporarily to reduce the patient's high level of anxiety.

This sample graph illustrates some typical patterns: (1) the number of subjective impulses exceeds the number of overt behavioral responses, and (2) the number of impulses does not diminish to zero (by extinction) until well after the number of overt behavioral responses has reached zero and remained at zero for some time. A common example of the latter phenomenon is that of the reformed heavy smoker who may have to wait months or even years before he not only never smokes but rarely experiences a compelling urge to smoke. A more experimental example, and one with ubiquitous and pivotally important clinical analogues, is the experimentally observed much greater resistance to extinction of cardiac-conditioned reflexes, in comparison to motor-conditioned reflexes. One example of a simple cardiac-conditioned reflex is the occurrence of a marked tachycardia in response to an auditory signal that was originally a neutral stimulus but that, after repeated pairing of the

signal tone with a painful electric shock, comes through learning to have the effect of producing a sharp increase in heart rate in response to the tone alone. Gantt (1953), who first observed this phenomenon experimentally in dogs, called it "schizokinesis" and reported a ratio of 100:1 or more in terms of the number of learning trials required to produce extinction of the "cardiac CR" (the cardiac component of a conditioned reflex) in comparison with "motor CR" (the muscular component). If the reader will allow himself a brief lapse into the imprecision of anthropomorphic thinking, he will understand that since the cardiac CR is a response to a conditioned tone that signals an impending electric shock, it may be thought of as part of the dog's "feeling" about the coming shock, as well as part of his "impulse" to flex—that is, withdraw—the forepaw that is about to receive the shock.

Epistemological Levels in Behavior Therapy

Internal medicine has reached its present relatively advanced level through precise and careful observation of normal physiological processes, of the effects of various disease processes on them, and, finally, of the modifications of physiological and disease processes by drugs or other treatments. In medicine, the day-to-day management of cases that are especially difficult diagnostically or therapeutically remains very much rooted in the careful collection of relevant data on the individual case. Yet in medicine, experience indicates that always relying on a full battery of expensive, time-consuming diagnostic tests can be monumentally inefficient and certainly not in the patient's interest. Often definitive treatment may be recommended without such elaborate assessment on the basis of the clinician's knowledge of the high probability of a fully successful outcome.

In a parallel manner, experienced behavior therapists may offer apparently simple cases presumptive treatment directly, without collecting detailed base-line data. In such cases, often only an hour or two of consultation before presumptive treatment begins is necessary. Prime examples here would be the use of assertive training with individuals who have complaints referrable to being habitually meek or sporadically explosive or both and the use of systematic desensitization for people with unrealistic and maladaptive fears. The point here is that behavior therapists should be, and are, quite pragmatic and empirical. Although the behavior therapist will always want to have a clear and specific behavioral base line before beginning treatment, it is often not clinically necessary to ask the patient to spend several weeks assembling a large stack of index cards tallying the target behavior —his chief complaint, behaviorally analyzed— before treatment is begun. In many puzzling or difficult cases, however, or in situations where specific research goals make this necessary, such an investment of time and energy is clearly warranted and worthwhile.

Epistemologically, then, in behavior therapy, as in internal medicine, there is often no substitute for the detailed study of the individual case; this study may be vital for the development of enough understanding to permit a favorable clinical outcome, or it may be important for the scientific advancement of the field as a whole. This is an area where accumulated clinical wisdom, mature scientific balance, and a proper ethical concern for the patient and the immediacy of his problem ideally should lead to well-balanced, cost-effective judgments. Many times placing the patient's welfare first will dictate prompt initiation of presumptive treatment. When this is the case, lofty ideas of behavioral science should not be used to rationalize an obsessionally meticulous approach to helping people with life problems.

Behavioral Analysis

An adequate behavioral analysis is the *sine qua non* of effective behavior therapy. While the behavior therapist will not in every case spend several weeks collecting a detailed behavioral base line before he begins his efforts at modification, he should *in every case* arrive at a functionally sound behavioral analysis before beginning treatment. That is, he should know precisely what the presenting, problematic behaviors are: how frequently and under what circumstances (stimulus conditions) they occur; what factors and persons may be operating to reinforce and

maintain them; what factors and persons may be operating to punish nascent, more adaptive behaviors that might otherwise emerge as satisfactory alternatives to the problematic behaviors; and what effective behaviors the patient has in his current repertoire that might be used as a competing response system or as reinforcing stimuli for more adaptive behavioral patterns. Gaining an overall, contextual view, not just of the problematic behaviors but of the patient's life as a whole, is also necessary. Information regarding the original sources of the problematic behaviors in terms of their learned origins is also helpful in designing a program of treatment. Therapeutic outcome will be much improved if the therapist is incessantly curious about how, when, why, and from whom the patient learned his present behaviors, including both the presenting problematic behaviors and any persistent idiosyncratic attitudes (habitual cognitive sets) the patient seems to live by. If possible, a thorough behavioral evaluation should include interviewing at least briefly the important people in the patient's life, usually together with him and in various combinations, in order to observe directly how each person affects his behavior.

Behavior therapy is an applied clinical discipline and thus always involves two related steps: (1) conducting a behavioral analysis (described above) and (2) carrying out a program of treatment based on this analysis. The first step is by far the more difficult of the two, requiring much clinical experience, skill, and sophistication, a good grasp of learning theory, and enough patience and persistence to track down all the relevant environmental determinants of the presenting symptom. *If the behavioral analysis is wrong or incomplete, a positive outcome from treatment cannot be expected.*

A preliminary behavioral analysis is always made before formal treatment begins and is then progressively refined and modified as more and more is learned about the patient, his environment, and his responses to ongoing events, including the treatment itself. (In sex therapy especially, the patient's response to the treatment recommendations is a very important primary source of clinical data; see chapter 20, "Sex Therapy.")

Indications for Behavior Therapy

In general, any patient who complains of a discrete symptom—such as a specific fear, compulsion, obsession, psychosomatic symptom, or behavioral deficit—deserves at least an evaluation for behavior therapy. An evaluation is even more emphatically indicated if a careful history suggests that external stimuli trigger the symptom or significantly influence its frequency or intensity. Patients with multiple symptoms can also be treated behaviorally, sometimes by more than one technique. On the other hand, the experienced behavior therapist will be aware of patients with "migratory complaints" and problems where no clear correlations can be discovered between particular antecedent stimulus situations and particular maladaptive responses. This latter type of patient is usually better treated in psychotherapy and best treated in behavioral psychotherapy. Some of these patients apparently have a psychotic core and thus are responding to shifting and chaotic internal stimuli, while others may be constantly creating new symptoms because of the presence of strong guilt or anger as an acquired idiosyncratic drive state. For either of these groups of patients, behavioral psychotherapy affords a much fuller opportunity for a subtle and sophisticated behavioral analysis. A broad, thorough, psychodynamically sophisticated behavioral analysis is the crucial factor for maximizing favorable outcome because it clarifies why, for example, a patient who would ordinarily be expected to be punished by a certain event is, in fact, reinforced (masochistically) by it.

The following specific disorders are eminently treatable behaviorally: the full range of phobias, simple and complex; obsessive-compulsive neuroses, even severe ones; facial and other tics, including torticollis and Gilles de la Tourette's syndrome;* stuttering, tension headache, migraine headache, and Raynaud's disease; "impotence," "frigidity," vaginismus, premature ejaculation, ejaculatory incompetence, genital psychoanesthesia. There is no justification for failing to refer people with any one of these problems for specific behaviorally oriented therapy.

* Drug therapy (with haloperidol) is also very important in the treatment of this syndrome.

In addition, behavior therapy may be the treatment of choice for eliminating a wide range of maladaptive habits: hair and eyebrow pulling; pathological scratching; nail biting; exhibitionism; ego-dystonic transvestism or fetishism; head banging and other self-destructive behaviors in children; intractable hiccuping, sneezing, or vomiting; and difficult voiding, to cite a few. Behavioral techniques may also be used to help people control or eliminate smoking, drinking, or overeating behaviors. For such habit problems, in selected cases with high hypnotizability and unambivalent motivation, treatment by hypnosis may be more efficient than behavior therapy. For frank alcoholism and obesity, behavior therapy should be combined with behavioral psychotherapy, which in turn typically involves both group and family work.

Finally, behavioral techniques can and should be used to ameliorate symptoms of mental retardation, hospitalism, and childhood and adult psychoses. No attempt will be made in this brief chapter to describe the myriad of specific techniques used for all these extremely wide-ranging problems. Rather, the section that follows will be devoted to a consideration of the major categories of core techniques of behavior therapy, those that every psychiatrist must know in order to make appropriate and sophisticated referrals. For the first three techniques discussed—systematic desensitization, assertive training, and sex therapy—most psychiatrists now in training should find it worthwhile to seek out enough supervised clinical experience using behavioral techniques to be able to use these methods with competence and confidence in their own future practices.

Core Behavioral Techniques

If therapists learning these techniques—systematic desensitization, assertive training, and sex therapy—view them as a collection of pre-specified procedures, these three "core" techniques will seem to have very little in common with each other, and therapeutic outcome will necessarily suffer. In all three techniques the therapist must pay specific attention to the behavior to be changed, to its antecedents, and to the consequences of that behavior. Thus for each of the three core techniques the therapist must devote his attention to three key questions: First, what is the behavior to be changed (the target behavior)? Second, what are the stimuli leading to the behavior? Third, what are the events that follow the behavior, serving either to reinforce or to punish it?

Systematic Desensitization

Developed almost twenty years ago by Joseph Wolpe and popularized courageously (if at times provocatively) by him against a strong tide of opposition from psychoanalytically oriented therapists, systematic desensitization is one of the most important and commonly employed behavioral treatment techniques. For years much of the psychiatric community reacted against behavioral treatment with a fervor now recognizable as an artifact of tradition and a priori theorizing rather than as a corollary of empirically established fact. Literally dozens of studies have now demonstrated the usefulness of systematic desensitization in the treatment of maladaptive fears, as well as its greater efficacy and efficiency in comparison with traditional psychotherapy (Wolpe et al., 1973). In contrast to the situation ten to fifteen years ago, current psychoanalytic literature emphasizes theoretical "integration" of the accepted effectiveness of systematic desensitization—and of behavior therapy as a whole—rather than attempting to demonstrate how it cannot and does not work, or how it inevitably leads to "symptom substitution." In fact, no solid evidence exists that symptom substitution, as earlier conceived, occurs at all.

Wolpe developed his now famous method for human patients after making a crucial observation during his earlier work on the experimental induction of neurotic behavior in cats. He discovered that when cats with experimentally induced "phobias" could be induced to engage in a competitive response (eating) in a series of rooms progressively more similar to the one in which they had developed a conditioned fear response, the experimenter could progressively reduce and eventually eliminate the "experimental neurosis"—that is, the experimentally induced (learned) fear responses. Before such "therapy,"

the cats were demonstrably "neurotic" all the time, in a constant fear state with no apparent stimulus, and showing crouching, piloerection, and even fear-induced defecation with only slight provocation. Quite predictably, however, following the principle of stimulus generalization, they showed the most fear in the room where the original traumatic conditioning had occurred. After "therapy" they were free of all these anxiety symptoms, even in the original chamber. Wolpe constructed an elaborate theory permeated with rather abstruse concepts from Hullian learning theory to explain why this worked. The theory also involved borrowing a legitimate neurophysiological term from Sherrington—*"reciprocal inhibition"*—to refer to the fact that a competitive response (in this case, eating) served to block the neural connection between the sensory perception of the conditioned fear stimuli and the conditioned anxiety responses, thus paving the way for a restoration of normal behavior. Wolpe was struck by the stimulus generalization aspects of experimental neuroses: the closer the stimulus properties of a given room were to those of the room in which the original traumatic learning took place, the more intense was the phobic response to that room. From this he developed the idea of pairing a competitive response with a hierarchy of progressively more intense and difficult conditioned stimulus situations.

This, in brief, is systematic desensitization: using a competitive response (such as eating, relaxation, sexual arousal, or animated conversation) to inhibit a *previously learned anxiety response* (such as fear of heights or closed spaces or *phobias* about snakes, spiders, or boats*) through an ascending hierarchy of progressively more intense, fear-producing stimulus situations.

Although Wolpe pioneered in the development of desensitization techniques, he was not the solitary inventor of systematic desensitization any more than Freud was the solitary discoverer of the unconscious. Watson and Rayner

---

* *Learned fears* may be very intense and even severe, sometimes (rarely) even crippling, but they do not involve a learned association between an external stimulus and an unsolved and unconscious or partially unconscious personal conflict, as do *phobias* (see chapter 9, "The Dynamic Bases of Psychopathology," and chapter 10, "Psychoneurotic Disorders").

(1920) described an experimentally induced fear and Jones (1924) employed processes essentially similar to desensitization thirty years before Wolpe developed and popularized this type of treatment strategy.

In classical systematic desensitization, the patient is taught a method of muscluar relaxation that will function later as the competitive response. Hypnosis may be used as an aid in learning relaxation, but it is not a necessary part of the process. Furthermore, desensitization can be accomplished in cases where the patient cannot be hypnotized. Beyond this, hypnosis may add an element of apparent magic and may thus increase the patient's tendency to relate to the behavior therapist in a dependent, childlike way rather than working with him collaboratively as an adult. Such regressive side effects of hypnosis are especially troublesome if the patient is receiving systematic desensitization adjunctively while also working in the context of a more wide-ranging psychotherapy, since the latter depends in part on new learning mediated by the patient's recognition and understanding of transference feelings. The use of biofeedback in relaxation training, on the other hand, is not a problem in this way; it has been shown to be a valuable aid, both in learning relaxation and in monitoring the actual level of muscular relaxation as treatment proceeds.

Although individual preferences vary, many behavior therapists use what is known as a modified Jacobson technique in teaching relaxation (Jacobson, 1938), a technique based on the principle of contrasting effects. The patient is asked to clench one fist tightly, his right if he is right-handed, while carefully leaving the other at rest. With his fist still tightly clenched, he is then asked to pay careful attention to all those places in his forearm and hand that feel tight, tense, and uncomfortable. Next he is instructed to begin slowly to "let go," *gradually* to let all the tension created earlier to ebb away. Then he is instructed to try to let go still more, each time he breathes out, even though he thinks he has let go completely. Each time he breathes out, the suggestion of greater relaxation is amplified by the therapist's saying quietly, "Let go," simultaneously with each rhythmic relaxation of the respiratory muscles. After a minute or so of this

procedure, the patient is asked to describe the sensations in his right hand as opposed to those in his left. Typically the patient is struck by the marked difference between his two hands; the right is usually described as feeling "relaxed, warm, and pleasantly heavy" in comparison with the left.

From this point on, teaching relaxation by first teaching contraction and strong tension involves working through all the major muscle groups of the body in a similar fashion. These groups include even the frontalis and platysma muscles, as well as the muscles of the tongue. It is important for the therapist to develop an orderly system for dealing with all the major muscle groups. One convenient way is to demonstrate each exercise by actually doing it with the patient. In this way, the therapist is reminded of any muscle group he has omitted because he himself will feel continued tension in those muscles. Also, of course, this method harnesses the additional advantages of *modeling*—the tendency of higher organisms to acquire complex or difficult responses more efficiently and rapidly when, as a part of their learning process, they can observe and imitate another organism that has already fully learned the desired response. Such participation by the therapist enhances learning and quickly reduces the patient's initial embarrassment at assuming some of the ungraceful postures that are required.

Once the patient becomes familiar with the form of the exercises, the amount that each muscle group is deliberately tensed—in order to help the patient learn relaxation as a contrasting response—is gradually and progressively decreased, using a "stimulus-fading" method, until the patient has the capacity to relax each bodily muscle group at will without having to employ any preceding increase in muscle tension. The patient is asked to practice this for twenty to thirty minutes twice a day at home and to pay special attention to determining what muscle group he himself uses especially heavily as a channel for tension; he is then asked to work particularly hard on mastering the voluntary relaxation of that muscle group. (Many patients can state at the outset which muscle group will be most difficult for them to relax, while others discover which group is most tense during the exercises.) This initial work in learning relaxation should require not more than two to six office visits plus practice at home.

During the initial sessions, in addition to learning relaxation, the patient is asked to construct and bring in a hierarchy of hypothetical stimulus situations that he has reason to believe would cause him to experience increasingly intense fear. The lowest level of such a hierarchy would be a peaceful, affectively neutral scene, and just above that a mild scene with some attenuated and distant elements of what the patient fears most, and so on through progressively graded steps. At the top of the hierarchy, the pinnacle scene should elicit a maximally intense fear response. For example, two separate general themes are common in flight phobias: the fear of being closed in and the fear of crashing or falling out of the sky to one's death. Still other themes may be relevant and crucial for success, such as fear of making a spectacle of oneself, fear of being thought a coward, and so forth. Hierarchies must reflect *all* the themes that underlie a particular phobia in a particular patient.

A patient who sought treatment because of severe sleep-onset insomnia was found to have an underlying fear of dying, which made him avoid sleep. He had undergone a surgical operation in which he was convinced he was going to die, and during a wartime situation he had been exposed to battlefields littered with dismembered dead and dying men. Near the bottom of his hierarchy were activities like "driving past a hospital" and "getting ready to go to bed at night." At the very top was his imagining "being locked in a morgue overnight, surrounded by dozens of dead bodies . . . and having to stay there alone until morning." This patient, who had a fourteen-year history of severe insomnia, with substantial weight loss, frequent viral infections, and—since they increased his fear—a paradoxical wakeful response to sedatives, made a full and lasting recovery in only seven hours of treatment by systematic desensitization.

The treatment would have failed, however, if each of the themes of death, dying, hospitals, dead bodies, and confinement had not been included in the hierarchies.

Usually the patient is asked to rate each scene on the hierarchy in terms of its anticipated potential to evoke anxiety, in units called subjective

units of distress (SUDs). The peaceful scene at the bottom of the hierarchy can be set at zero, representing the maximum freedom from anxiety the patient ever feels, and the most terrifying one at the very top at 100, representing the maximum anxiety the patient ever feels. For those scenes in between, the patient assigns a numerical level that he believes approximates the fear-producing potential of the particular scene relative to the others. Although SUD scale "measurements" are only crudely quantitative and are dependent on self-report, this method has obvious clinical advantages. It should, for example, protect the therapist from unwittingly working with a hierarchy containing huge gaps, where the supposedly graded steps might, for example, be rated by the patient in terms of SUDs in this way:

. 2 . . 5 . . . 9 . . . . . .16. . . . .

. . . .

. . . . .95. . . . .

SUD ratings should also be combined with more direct and physiological measures of fear, such as heart rate, and for research purposes with measures like the palmar sweat test. (Although the latter is too cumbersome for routine use, it supplies sound quantitative data).

Once the hierarchy has been constructed and the patient has learned relaxation (to serve as a competitive response), the therapist helps the patient remain relaxed while the patient vividly imagines each of the scenes. Step by step, the therapist presents each scene in the hierarchy while the patient continues to combat anxiety elicited by the imagined scene with deliberate deep relaxation. The patient uses a digital signaling system, usually the brief raising of the index finger, to indicate an uncomfortable high level of anxiety. The therapist should supplement this information by direct observation of the patient's breathing, facial expression, and vascular state. It can be supplemented also by EMG feedback. If the patient signals a high degree of anxiety, he may be asked to imagine an already practiced scene and work up again to the difficult scenes. When a scene evokes very little anxiety, the therapist goes on to the next step in the hierarchy.

As treatment proceeds, it is absolutely imperative for the therapist to encourage (to the point of insistence) real-life degrees of exposure to the phobic stimulus situation that the patient has already mastered in the imagined situation. On the other hand, the therapist should not encourage the patient to tackle tasks he is not yet prepared for, as this will lead predictably to failure and reinforce the link between fear-conditioned stimuli and fear responses. If an overload of intense fear stimuli elicits anxiety responses so strong that they overwhelm and undermine the intended, competitive response (relaxation), the phobic response will obviously be strengthened.

Although Wolpe's contribution of systematic desensitization to behavior therapy (Wolpe, 1958) was a great one, and although his was an unprecedentedly parsimonious view of neurotic processes and of psychotherapy, the most recent experience and research, especially that of Marks (1972, 1976), indicates very clearly the need for a further refinement of theory and practice in the direction of still greater parsimony. Some recent studies show that the prior teaching of relaxation as a competitive response may not be crucial for success in systematic desensitization. This is an area still being explored in controlled studies, however. Recent research has indicated statistically that neither prior relaxation training nor the use of carefully graded hierarchies is crucial for success in systematic desensitization. This fact, however, is not tantamount to proof that they are without clinical value in all cases, and accepting it as proof would be going far beyond the data now available. Perhaps imaginal desensitization will eventually prove to be required only in those cases where the resistance to *in vivo* desensitization procedures is sufficient to warrant initial treatment of a less threatening sort. The same can be said for the construction of carefully graded hierarchies, and even for the use of imaginal scenes at all. This leaves undisputed only the effectiveness of systematic exposure *in vivo* to feared but realistically harmless stimuli. In classical systematic desensitization, this sort of exposure was simply expected to occur—and was gently encouraged —as an auxiliary process in the treatment. In recent years, so-called *in vivo* desensitization— utilizing actual exposure to effect real-life extinction experiences—has been adopted increasingly as an exclusive treatment of phobias.

Generally, *in vivo* methods seem to be superior in efficiency to imaginal ones, although in particular cases it may be crucial to teach relaxation and employ imagined scenes prior to any *in vivo* exposure. An imaginal form of desensitization has been described here in detail because of its historical significance, because of its current wide use, and because it still is the treatment of choice in particular cases where it may be impossible to go directly to *in vivo* exposure.

It may be that the classic form of desensitization introduced by Wolpe for use with human patients served, at times quite usefully, merely as a complex persuasive maneuver to get phobic patients to undergo real-life extinction experiences, which previously (typically for phobic patients) they had strenuously avoided.* The future of desensitization, as well as its most sophisticated and efficient use in the present, seems to lie in emphasizing sheer *in vivo* exposure to feared but realistically harmless stimuli and in deemphasizing, whenever possible, all the other components—relaxation, hierarchical subtleties, and imaginal rehearsal.

My own strong preference has for years been to use *in vivo* desensitization whenever feasible; not only is this treatment procedure usually faster, but, in addition, it provides more directly observable data. Moreover, the classic imaginal form of desensitization, with its emphasis on the therapist's teaching the patient to be thoroughly relaxed, followed by the therapist's taking the responsibility for actively and vividly describing a series of scenes that the patient is to imagine while remaining totally passive and relaxed, may tend to foster undue dependency. (A further potential disadvantage is the possibility that the whole procedure may counterproductively activate sexual feelings toward the therapist.) In contrast, *in vivo* desensitization not only does not encourage the patient to adopt a dependent and childlike stance with respect to the therapist but actually requires him to exercise courage and adult responsibility. Thus, in working with an agoraphobic patient, for example, I commonly begin immediately, even in the first hour, by going outside with the patient and requesting that he—or more usually she†—walk as far as

---

* The original desensitization procedure used by Wolpe to treat his experimentally neurotic cats was, of course, an *in vivo* desensitization technique, employing actual exposure to rooms increasingly similar to the one where the experimental neurosis was learned.

† Most agoraphobic patients are female.

possible away from me. Such an active, real-life approach, early in the treatment, communicates that the goal of therapy is behavioral change and that the patient and the therapist together are responsible for working actively to maximize such change. In an *in vivo* approach, each feared response performed by a phobic patient constitutes a real-life "extinction trial," because, realistically, no feared consequences follow the response. (*Extinction* refers to the process in which a learned or conditioned response—in this case a fear response—is repeated over and over without reinforcement or punishment and so eventually returns to its preconditioning base line of intensity.) In the case of an unrealistic fear treated by exposure *in vivo*, this would mean that the fear response would eventually become zero or nearly zero.

By actually accompanying patients on some of their assigned extinction trials, the therapist will find that he falls heir to an important source of self-report data: in this situation of induced stress, the patient often produces a flood of thematically relevant, associatively rich material that can be used to discover and to help the patient understand how and why he learned the particular fear now undergoing extinction by *in vivo* desensitization. Thus *in vivo* desensitization usually generates useful cognitions, which can be used to facilitate the change process. Dynamically trained therapists will recognize this phenomenon as a form of structuring the "working through" of insights *before* those insights actually develop. The behavior therapist thus gives strategic primacy to what dynamic therapists call "working through," and uses it to facilitate useful insight, rather than working toward insight with the vague hope that, once acquired, such insight will one day be actualized and worked through as real change.

Before this discussion of systematic desensitization concludes, a few words should be said about the dangers inherent in the fact that this technique has been naively and destructively oversold. First, there is the annoying tendency, which occurs even among some otherwise sophisticated psychiatrists, to equate systematic desensitization with behavior therapy as a whole—a fallacy analogous to equating internal medicine not just with antibiotics but with a partic-

ular brand of one of the tetracyclines. Second, this field is rife with novices whose behavioral enthusiasm exceeds their clinical wisdom, and these inexperienced practitioners are capable of indiscriminately using a rote desensitization paradigm with almost any kind of patient or any type of clinical situation, sometimes with very bad results. Thus patients with ungrieved losses or violently unstable marriages, among other problems, may be run through mindless hierarchies that contribute more to the problem than to its solution.

Systematic desensitization is only one of a number of particular techniques for the reduction or elimination of maladaptive fears. *If there is no fear*—if the main problem is unresolved grief, guilt, or anger—*then desensitization is not appropriate*. Furthermore, not every patient who comes labeled—even self-labeled—as having a phobia really has one. Many patients experience obsessional symptoms as phobias or have institutionalized avoidances that are maintained by a web of social reinforcement ("secondary gain") rather than by real fear. Before embarking on a course of desensitization, it is therefore important to ask specifically about autonomic signs of fear, about the thematic elements of the phobic situation, and about the social consequences of the phobic behavior. When the patient attempts to approach the phobic stimulus, does his heart beat fast? Does it pound? Does he sweat, or do his palms become moist? Does someone else routinely offer comfort and reassurance or assume responsibility during the period of phobic avoidance? Finally, before embarking on a course of imaginal desensitization, the therapist must ascertain that the patient is capable both of visualizing scenes at will and of experiencing palpable fear in response to an imagined representation of the phobic stimulus.

Two other procedures should be mentioned along with desensitization because they are also extinction-based fear reduction procedures. One is *flooding*—an abbreviation of "stimulus flooding" (Marks, 1972). Its aim is to saturate, or flood, the phobic patient with maximally fear-producing stimuli without permitting him to terminate the stimuli or to escape. Obviously then, flooding is a "cold turkey," forced extinction situation—one that can be very rapidly effective, but that is for most purposes unnecessarily unpleasant and that has the potential to do real harm. If the patient should manage to escape the flooding situation before his fear responses have begun to subside, the procedure will actually operate to make the original fear worse.

The second procedure, *response prevention* (Mills et al., 1973), is much like flooding but depends on the fact that anxiety regularly issues in a behavioral response. It is used with patients who have severe obsessive-compulsive rituals like hand washing. These rituals typically occur after the patient encounters some external stimulus, such as a doorknob. Often, however, only a thought that he regards as bad or dirty or dangerous is sufficient to produce the ritual response. Subjectively, the particular ritual is apparently intended magically to undo or neutralize the contact that has just occurred. Even if the patient "knows" intellectually that the ritual is superstitious, it still has the capacity to reduce temporarily a very high level of anxiety and thus is maintained by negative reinforcement—the temporary reduction of an ongoing aversive drive (in this case, high anxiety). In response prevention, the patient is forced to undergo extinction of his rituals and his obsessional fears through eliminating the possibility of his making the ritualized response. For example, if his problem is hand washing, the handles are taken off the water faucets, and the water is turned off except during brief and narrowly defined periods each day. The patient is therefore compelled to learn viscerally, not just intellectually, that the ritual is superfluous to his real safety. In behavioral terms, his avoidance responses, previously maintained by negative reinforcement, are forced to undergo extinction.

Assertive Training

In assertive training, strong self-assertion is used as a competitive response to inhibit conditioned anxiety and fear in a way that parallels conceptually the use of relaxation in systematic desensitization. The reader will understand this intuitively if he recalls instances in which he has experienced the rapid dissipation of strong premonitory anxiety by actually beginning an activity. Thus one may be very nervous before giving a lecture or a dramatic performance or before an examination, but this anxiety usually diminishes sharply when the actual performance begins. The crucial factor here is that assertion as an active performance begins to serve successfully as a competitive response capable of inhibiting the anxiety that previously existed unopposed, provided one learns to experiment with *strong* self-assertion.

Clinically, assertive training is a technique for individuals who chronically fail to stand up for their own rights in a firm, effective, and appropriate way. Patients who can profit from it are not limited to meek Caspar Milquetoast types. It is equally indicated for patients who "hold it all in" as long as they can and then explode in a self-defeating rage. It is also extremely useful, especially when combined with group therapy, for many patients with chronic, unremitting depression, the manifest affect of which is helplessness. It is in fact helpful in some form to a very wide spectrum of people who are situationally underassertive—people who can be effectively assertive with strangers, or even with their bosses, but not with their spouses, for example. (In the latter case, assertive training should be combined with some form of couple therapy.) Other people can secure their rights and can express anger appropriately and without great difficulty, but they may be almost paralyzed by inhibition and embarrassment when they attempt to express warmth, liking, and affection toward another person. In this case, modified assertive training techniques may be used, sometimes called "training in emotional freedom" (Lazarus, 1971). This technique is usually most effective if done at least partly *in vivo*, in group therapy. In this natural social setting, genuinely warm feelings and modeling can facilitate new learning and its subsequent generalization to the extratherapeutic situation; in addition, modeling helps group patients to learn to express warm feelings. In other cases, patients may have striking deficits of particular social skills, such as introducing themselves, saying hello, or making or responding to social invitations. These patients may be helped with a variant of assertive training, which is often called "social skills training."

All types of assertive training techniques rely

centrally on *behavioral shaping*. Behavioral shaping refers to the process in which successive approximation is used to condition a complex desired response. First, the organism is reinforced for any response that is in the direction of the desired response (or even any response that vaguely resembles the first phase of a complex desired response); next, the criterion for reinforcement is slowly, steadily, and progressively raised. An animal analogue would be teaching the response "three turns to the right." First any rightward-turning or rightward-looking response is reinforced; then, by successive approximation, rightward movement of the shoulder girdle, then the pelvic girdle, then the legs, is required as a criterion for reinforcement. After one full turn is learned, the criterion for reinforcement is progressively raised still further, until finally the organism performs the exact response desired. In this way, organisms can be taught very complex responses that they literally could never learn by simple respondent conditioning.

In the description of assertive training technique that follows, however, the focus is purposely on the more classical dyadic mode of pure assertive training, for persons unable to express anger or secure their own rights, as opposed to training in emotional freedom or social skills training. Thus the discussion emphasizes frank behavioral shaping through role rehearsal, role reversal, and modeling.

As Wolpe pointed out (1958), certain types of questions are invaluable in determining the need for assertive training, for example:

"Suppose you are waiting in a line for theatre tickets and someone cuts in front of you. What would you do?"

A patient starkly in need of assertive training might well say something like this:

"Well, inside I'd be knotted up, burning. It would probably spoil my whole evening, and the knot in my stomach would still be there when I went to bed that night, but I wouldn't say anything—because I wouldn't want to make a scene."

Other valuable screening questions are

"Suppose you go to a department store and buy a sweater, then later after leaving the store you discover it has a hole in it. What would you do?"

"Suppose you go to a restaurant and want a quiet table in a darkish corner where you can talk, but the hostess seats you at a table right in the center of the room, bustling with people, light, and noise. What would you do?"

"Suppose a friend [some patients are assertive enough with strangers, but not with friends] borrows ten dollars from you and promises to pay you back the next day at lunch. The next day lunch comes and goes but nothing happens. What would you do?"

"Suppose your husband or wife does or says something at your expense, something you regard as clearly unfair. What would you do?"

In addition to the dyadic interview, potentiated by these screening questions, if possible, it is advisable and provides a much richer source of reliable data to create and to utilize fully all reasonable opportunities for directly observing *in vivo* the patient's assertive and other social behaviors. What is he like in the waiting room, with the other people there? How does he deal with the secretary or receptionist? How does he behave in a joint interview situation with his wife? What is he like with the whole family? How does he react in a group? These points of course all anticipate discussion of behavioral psychotherapy as a process of *in vivo* observation and behavioral shaping. However, in many cases, classical, single-goal-oriented behavior therapy techniques are used most effectively when they arise from or are embedded in the context of a more broadly ranging behavioral psychotherapy. The latter permits enough direct observation of social behaviors to effect a more accurate behavioral diagnosis, reflecting subtleties of the life situation that the patient cannot report fully because he does not yet recognize and understand them.

If a clear diagnosis can be made of a broad or a narrow deficit in assertive behavior by using any or all of these kinds of probes, then assertive training would be useful and is indicated. Not only do early treatment sessions typically remove all doubt as to the relevance of enhancing assertive responses, but they usually lead to a spontaneous outpouring of diverse social situations in the patient's actual life in which he feels stymied and frustrated because of his difficulty with assertive responses. Treatment begins with a further probe for recent actual situations in the patient's ongoing life when he did not assert himself optimally. These situations are then discussed in detail, together with the patient's and the therapist's ideas as to what specific responses might have been more effective. Before the end of the hour, the patient is asked to be alert during the coming week to similar situations requiring assertive behavior and to note how he responds to them. In the next session the therapist asks the patient about these situations—what he actually said and did, and what the outcome was. The patient is then asked, "If you had it all to do over again, how would you handle it, what actually would you say?" Usually the therapist can make at least a few suggestions that improve further on the patient's own initial attempt at redesigning a response that the patient would regard as ideal. He can also help by giving his reasons for preferring a particular version, and, either then or later, he can also help by role-playing or modeling a desirable response, like an actor.

In behavioral psychotherapy, in an ongoing therapy group for example, the therapist can accomplish much the same thing, almost in passing, by first asking the patient what he *did* say and what he *now* thinks he might better have said, and then by volunteering what he himself might have done ("If that had happened to me, I think I might have said . . .").

In the more structured, classical version of assertive training, the patient is asked repeatedly to role-play such troublesome situations, each time trying to respond in a more nearly ideal way. After each attempt, the patient is offered a gentle critique of his assertive "act." The therapist points out soft and apologetic tones, or overly belligerent ones, and notes for the patient diffident postures, lack of direct, sustained eye contact, and telltale hesitations. The therapist can use mimicry effectively here if he is skillful at ensuring that the patient realizes that this use of mimicry is never derisive but is, rather, intended for his benefit and his own therapeutic goals. Then the therapist asks the patient to try again—"*Much* louder and stronger this time, and without the apologetic gestures." This role-

playing is repeated as many times as necessary, with constantly responsive gestural feedback (reinforcement and punishment). The gestural feedback offered during the performance is in the form of frowns, fortissimo gestures, "O.K." signs, and affirmative nods. In his criticism the therapist should be constructive and good-natured, and humor may at times be used to advantage if it is clearly shared with the patient. In any event, the core idea is to use behavioral shaping (successive approximation) to produce eventually an assertive performance that has been enhanced in content, directness, volume, and tone. In this final, enhanced performance, residual signs of apologetic diversions and hesitations or of sagging emphasis, either verbally or nonverbally, should not appear.

To achieve this result, role reversal is at times employed; in role reversal the patient is asked to play the role of his oppressor, while the therapist plays the patient's role. This reversal affords further opportunities for the therapist to use modeling; in this way he can demonstrate the possibility of formulating a strong, confident, assertive response, regardless of what his adversary says. Thus learning proceeds through a mixture of instruction, coaching, modeling, role rehearsal, role reversal, and behavioral shaping, all with the aim of bringing easy assertive responses into the patient's repertoire.

Since the strongest part of this technique is the behavioral shaping component, it is very important never to praise or otherwise reinforce diminished assertive performances. It can be tempting to offer encouragement to a disheartened patient on his fifth or seventh attempt to master a role-played assertive situation, but if, as often happens, he does less well on his fifth try than he did on the previous one, he must be bluntly told so. Praise—as distinct from reassurance or encouragement—is only useful after a performance that successively approximates the agreed-upon goal.* Anticipatory role-playing of situations and confrontations that are expected or needed may

* Praise should never directly follow (that is, be contingent upon) a diminished assertive performance. Between trials the patient may need encouragement or reassurance, but if this is needed and offered it should by all means be done noncontingently.

also help the patient prepare for the week to come.

As in systematic desensitization, the patient should be urged to try out his newly practiced skills in real life, especially when his skill seems great enough to master the particular hierarchical level of difficulty represented by the actual situation. He should not be forced prematurely into precipitating assertive situations that are still clearly too difficult in terms of his skill or confidence level. Such precipitation will only be counterproductive, because it will very likely result in a confrontation with an employer or relative or friend in which the patient's nascent assertive repertoire will be punished, not reinforced. Such an outcome would operate to confirm the patient's pretreatment conviction that no assertion is the only safe stance for him.

In the very first few sessions it is usually necessary to deal with the patient's objections that "this is all so artificial." This objective is usually best accomplished by reassuring patients that their new assertiveness will seem artificial to them at first but that as they continue to use and profit from the use of assertive behaviors, assertiveness will in time not only seem quite natural but actually become part of them. Thus, eventually, they will find themselves quite naturally using assertive behaviors that at first seemed to require great effort and forethought. After three to five sessions of learning progressively more assertive behavior, patients become (appropriately) very excited about increasing assertiveness in their expressive styles because they begin to grasp the potential for enhancing the quality of their lives. Thus the need to convince patients of the value of assertive training, despite its "artificiality," is usually short-lived; the patient soon begins to bring to the sessions a tried and definite enthusiasm.

Sex Therapy

Because of its immense clinical importance, and also because of the appreciable differences in treatment strategy, depending on which of the six basic sexual dysfunctions is being treated, sex therapy is presented separately in detail in chapter 20, "Sex Therapy." The purpose of this discussion of core behavioral techniques is to place sex therapy as a whole in perspective as a set of techniques that should properly be considered as one of the behaviorally based therapies—both because it involves the brief treatment of specific focal symptoms and because the workings of specific sex therapy techniques can best be understood and guided by reference to a learning theory model.

It is important, however, in locating these techniques among the behaviorally based therapies to acknowledge the great debt that sex therapy, and all of psychiatry, owes first to Kinsey, more recently to Masters and Johnson, and most recently to Kaplan, for opening the field of sexual functioning first to scientific inquiry, and now to direct therapeutic influence. None of these pioneers has been a behavior therapist. In addition to providing the first accurate, scientific description of the basic physiology of sexual arousal, intercourse, and orgasm, Masters and Johnson made a great therapeutic advance by emphasizing direct work with both members of a couple when one or both partners were sexually dysfunctional. On the other hand, as early as 1958, Wolpe, a behavior therapist, wrote about the treatment of impotence and frigidity and advocated the use of sexual arousal itself as a competitive response.

Almost all of the techniques developed in the pioneering work of Masters and Johnson and of Kaplan depend on a single, unifying principle: cultivating sensual pleasure and gradual sexual arousal, and, in a carefully graded way, pairing these responses with sexual situations that ordinarily would have elicited degrees of guilt, shame, worry, or anxiety sufficient to inhibit sexual arousal and pleasure.

Thus, shorn of all complexity and the art of how to do it, sex therapy works through a series of successful, confidence-restoring, hierarchically graded sexual experiences. In effect, this is the method of systematic desensitization, using sexual arousal (rather than relaxation) as a response competitive with anxiety. The only two exceptions are the Semans squeeze technique for premature ejaculation, which, in learning theory terms, clearly functions as a punishment, and the Kegel exercises for weakened pubococcygeal muscles (the muscles subserving female orgasm).

Other Behavioral Techniques

The concepts and facts derived from studies of operant conditioning are really central to all clinical work in behavior therapy and behavioral psychotherapy. In fact, no therapist or analyst can ever be in the same room with any patient, or exchange words, looks, nods or gestures, without operant conditioning's being involved. Both patient and therapist, aware of it or not, will be reinforcing some responses and punishing other responses in the behavior of the other person. Operant conditioning is nevertheless discussed within the category of "other behavioral therapies" because in its pure form it is not one of the most commonly used or "core" behavior therapies.

Operant Methods

The principles of operant conditioning seem alarmingly (and deceptively) simple. *Punishment* is defined as anything that decreases the frequency of the response immediately preceding it—spanking a dog immediately after he jumps up on a person, for example. A more clinical example, and one to avoid, especially in dealing with underassertive patients, is that of a therapist exploding with anger immediately after the patient criticizes him. A therapeutically useful example, drawn from the practice of couple therapy, may be seen when a therapist makes a strong negative interpretation immediately after a spouse asserts some infantile entitled "right" with respect to his marital partner. It is often strategically important, in clinical practice, to use punishment not just after a maladaptive response but actually during such a response; such punishment interrupts the full response, which is part of a complex chain of maladaptive behavior.

Positive reinforcement is anything that increases the frequency of the response immediately preceding it, such as delivering a bit of food or water to an experimental animal immediately after the response of bar pressing. A more clinical example is that of expressing interest or making an affectively positive interpretation immediately after a habitually meek person expresses some annoyance.

Negative reinforcement refers to the temporary interruption of an ongoing negative stimulus, which serves to reinforce (increase the frequency of) the immediately preceding response. Functionally, then, the stimulus used is an aversive one. A simple example would be putting on sunglasses in bright light; this response removes the mildly aversive stimulus of glaring brightness and therefore negatively reinforces the response of putting on the sunglasses. In a laboratory example, an experimental animal in a room with a shock-grid floor might turn the shock off for five seconds each time it pressed a bar. In this way, the response of bar pressing would be negatively reinforced. A clinical example, drawn from work with severely disturbed phobic-obsessional patients, is the therapist's continuously and purposefully violating the patient's magical safety rituals (an aversive stimulus for the patient) and then ceasing to do this immediately after the patient himself makes some response in which he atypically confronts one of his fears directly. Such a strategy is rarely needed, but when it is, there may be no real substitute for it; it can literally be lifesaving.

Neither past general experience nor a priori judgments establish whether a given stimulus is in fact reinforcing or punishing; this varies from person to person and must always be established empirically. Fully confident specification of reinforcers and punishers thus requires a number of observed trials. On the other hand, an increase or decrease in frequency can be effected by a single application of a reward or punishment. This is called "one-trial learning" or, if the consequence is punishing, "traumatic learning."

Operant methods capitalize on all these principles to change behavior in desirable ways. Largely because of the negative views of Skinner (1953) on the use of aversive stimuli, particularly for punishment, and because of Skinner's association with the word *operant*, it is in fact true that most people referring to operant methods in behavior therapy are talking about systematically using positive reinforcement to increase desirable behaviors. Aversive stimuli may, however, be used beneficially after a response, to decrease the frequency of that response (punishment); or they may be used as ongoing negative stimuli, the temporary cessation of which, contingent on a particular response, can be used to increase the frequency of that response (negative reinforcement). Aversive techniques are therefore customarily categorized separately from operant methods, even though punishment is as much a part of operant conditioning theory as is reinforcement.

It is part of the fundamental pragmatism and empiricism of behaviorism that no stimulus is assumed to be "positive" or "negative"; rather, stimuli can be judged to be reinforcing or punishing only by observed trials. This is important clinically because for some schizophrenic patients, for example, the stimulus of a smile or a friendly hello is in fact punishing and because some stimuli that are punishing for most people are reinforcing for some guilty or masochistic patients.

Habitual or high-frequency behaviors can serve as reinforcers if they are made to follow and be contingent on low-frequency behaviors; this is known as the Premack principle. For example, a person who habitually watches television as a high-frequency behavior but rarely exercises can effectively increase the frequency of his exercising behavior if he permits himself to watch television only after a period of exercising. The Premack principle is extremely useful clinically in designing made-to-order behavioral programs for self-control and for correcting maladaptive deficits of particular behaviors.

The most important use of an operant strategy—and this *does* include the use of punishment—is in behavioral psychotherapy, where the use of punishment, positive reinforcement, and behavioral shaping of problematic behaviors can be directly modified, *in vivo*, within a natural social setting. The next most important use is within assertive training, as has already been described. A third common and very important application is to hospital ward-management situations, as noted in the American Psychiatric Association's task force report:

The problem in developing a successful ward management program based on operant methods is to find a reinforcer of wide applicability, one that can follow immediately the behavior it is designed to reinforce . . . One solution is to use a *conditioned reinforcer*, a "token," to bridge the delay between the occurrence of the desired response and the availability of the in-

nately reinforcing stimulus, and to provide a money-like currency that can then be exchanged for a variety of items and activities, according to the patient's choice . . . The "token" economy system is unlike many ward management systems that tend to encourage patient dependency. It is basically a work-payment incentive system. As such, it strengthens behaviors compatible with those in the society at large, such as regular performance on a job, self-care, maintenance of one's living quarters . . . Operant principles employed via token economies are powerful agents of behavior change. Of perhaps as great importance is the fact that nonprofessional personnel are the actual agents of therapeutic change in a token system. (Birk et al., 1973, pp. 11–12)

Use of such token reinforcement systems has thus been quite demonstrably effective in improving the behavior of the patients within institutions, in terms of self-care and personal hygiene behaviors, patient socialization, and in-hospital work performance, and in reducing extreme or bizarre behavior.

On the other hand the issue of how to use token programs more effectively to facilitate the return of some patients to extrainstitutional environments has not been worked out. The ideal token program of the future should include a range of extrainstitutional three-quarter-, half-, and quarter-way houses to which the patient might go after he has improved within a full-time institution. Theoretically, then, patients who improve in a token economy program should not be expected to do without it abruptly when discharged; rather, transition should occur by a series of gradual steps, analogous to laboratory stimulus-fading procedures. In this way, some patients at least should be able to make a series of successful smaller transitions and eventually be able to retain useful behaviors acquired through token reinforcement—with only natural adult reinforcement processes maintaining the new behaviors. (Most of us take a bath because we look, smell, and feel clean afterward, not because we get a lollipop or a token for it; the patient who learns bath taking through token reinforcement should ideally reach the same level of self-maintenance.)

Token systems to implement operant methods of behavior therapy are also being used effectively in classrooms with disadvantaged, hyperactive, retarded, and emotionally disturbed children, and most important, to improve self-help skills in retardates.

The most effective way to eliminate inappropriate or maladaptive behavior appears to be to punish it, while at the same time reinforcing some desired alternative behavior. Thus punishment has an important place in behavior therapy, and even more so in behavioral psychotherapy. The importance of the technique should never become an excuse for the therapist to be vindictive or sadistic, but if a therapist cannot use punishment consciously and well when needed, he is, in my own view, an inadequate and even reckless therapist, analogous to an internist who can give antidotes but cannot induce vomiting, or a surgeon who can give blood but cannot tie off bleeders. In behavioral psychotherapy, especially in behavioral couple therapy, such a deficit in the therapist's behavioral repertoire is glaring and serious indeed.

Any therapist using punishment in any form—from disinterested facial expressions and affectively negative interpretations to aversive conditioning—should know that the most he can expect from punishment is a period of response suppression. Punishment does not produce extinction and therefore does not ordinarily produce a permanent elimination of a response. It should therefore almost always be employed together with reinforcement of some new, desired behavior. In some cases, strong punishments may produce long-lasting suppressions of responses, but not true extinction (Holland and Skinner, 1961).

Punishment used in this way serves to interrupt and block the old stereotyped maladaptive behavior; because of the concomitant reinforcement of a new behavior, the change that occurs is permanent. (Pure punishment would produce only temporary response suppression, plus a storm of autonomic reactivity.)

Classical Aversive Techniques

Although the most subtle and most important uses of punishment are in behavioral psychotherapy rather than in classical behavior therapy, mention of its uses in the latter area is necessary.

The use of punishment with, for example, a brief, noninjurious but painful electric shock in order to treat dangerous self-destructive behaviors in children can avoid mutilation, as in tongue or finger biting, or even death, as in head banging. Similarly, I have used aversive conditioning as part of the treatment for a long-standing and stubborn smoking habit in a patient in danger of losing his fingers from Buerger's disease. With consenting nonpsychotic adults, such as the man with the smoking problem, it is important to emphasize the collaborative quality of the treatment, so that the patient feels the shock sessions as something the therapist is doing *with* him, not *to* him.

Much early disenchantment with the use of aversive conditioning in alcoholism and addiction came from very poorly executed behavior therapy. Insufficient attention was paid to the need for precise time and contingency control of the punishing stimulus. Virtually all of the early work done with apomorphine and other drugs suffers from this disqualifying defect. Unlike nausea-producing drugs, electric shock has sharp and precisely controllable onset-offset properties. And much of even the more recent work with aversive conditioning has not placed sufficient emphasis on the need for the concomitant reinforcement of an alternative new response.

One of the better done and more promising recent innovations is that of Lovibond (1970), who has treated alcoholism not by punishing all drinking but by using measured, high levels of blood alcohol as the target behavior to be reduced by aversive (shock) conditioning. Lovibond's method has the added advantage that the patient and his spouse together choose the criterion blood-alcohol level to be used for him by watching a videotape of the patient's increasingly disorganized behavior as he purposely gets drunk while periodically having his blood-alcohol level measured. Certainly for most cases such an aversive treatment strategy should be used only in conjunction with other therapy. The therapist should combine it with assertive training if the patient can express anger only when slightly drunk, for example, or with sex therapy if the patient requires five or six drinks to make him feel sexually free, and so on.

Biofeedback

Biofeedback can be defined as the use of monitoring instruments (usually electrical) to detect and amplify internal physiological processes within the body in order to make this ordinarily inaccessible internal information available to the individual and, literally, to feed it back to him in some form. Thus, for example, through biofeedback, a patient with a tension headache (one caused by abnormal levels of tension or contraction in the frontalis or occipitalis muscles of the head) ordinarily knows only that the front or the back of his head hurts or doesn't hurt. With biofeedback he can know precisely from moment to moment what is the level of tension (contraction) in his frontalis and occipitalis muscles by two different means: (1) through the use of an electromyogram to detect activity in those muscles and (2) through an amplification and display system by means of which he can "hear" the level of muscular activity as a series of small clicks spaced in time as a function of the level of tension or "see" the level of tension by reading a dial.

The clinical importance of utilizing such organ-specific artificial feedback is that, with continued exposure and practice (biofeedback training), individuals can apparently learn to bring under partial conscious control particular bodily functions that are not ordinarily subject to conscious control (like heart rate and blood pressure) or that are ordinarily under only minimal conscious control (like tension in the frontalis and occipitalis muscles). Currently, the most important and common clinical application is in the treatment of headache syndromes.

Like other psychosomatic disorders, tension headache begins with life stress and touches upon unsolved inner conflicts. The familiar psychophysiological paradigm is this:

life stress and unsolved inner conflicts →
physical symptoms.

For psychophysiological headache syndromes —including both tension headache and migraine headache—suppressed or poorly recognized anger (latent anger responses) are typically at the heart of the matter. Psychotherapy, emphasizing insight and the cognitive uncovering of such anger and the reasons for it, can deal with one part of the problem. Assertive training, the behavior therapy procedure in which the patient learns to express his angry feelings more directly and effectively (once he recognizes them), can also help. These measures are ways of dealing with the left or input side of the psychophysiological paradigm; biofeedback is a way of dealing with the right or output side of that paradigm—the side that, for tension headache patients, means that they have increased levels of tension in the occipitalis and frontalis muscles and resultant pain.

Whatever the external life stress or the inner conflict may be, this phenomenon of increased occipitalis and frontalis muscle tension, for tension headache patients, is the final common pathway of life stress. Thus the patient can learn to become aware through biofeedback of the quantitative level of tension in the muscles of his head and can learn to reduce that level in order to relieve the pain of headache or to abort a headache in the making. Biofeedback training also can facilitate cognitive learning about the triggering stimuli for such psychosomatic reactions, thus facilitating the work of concomitant psychotherapy and assertive training as they are used to deal with the input side of the psychophysiological equation.

In the treatment of the complex neurovascular migraine syndrome by biofeedback, the headache itself is treated as the target symptom. The headache is apparently secondary to a situation of excessive sympathetic outflow resulting finally in painfully pulsating and distended extracranial arteries. Thus hand warming (possible only with decreased sympathetic outflow) is used as a target physiological response, and temperature feedback is used to achieve this. Temperature feedback also may be used to alleviate the vascular insufficiency symptoms of Raynaud's disease.

EMG feedback is useful in the treatment of tics, in relaxation training, in monitoring the course of imaginal desensitization, in the treatment of sleep-onset insomnia, and in stroke rehabilitation. Some useful biofeedback procedures are in use in treating (and studying) cardiac arrhythmias, and research is continuing on biofeedback for hypertension. In addition, biofeedback procedures still in the early stages of development and trial are being used in the treatment of asthma, colitis, ulcer, and even epilepsy.

Behavioral Psychotherapy: A Process of In Vivo Observation and Operant Shaping

Behavioral psychotherapy can be defined as psychotherapy guided in its major aims and strategies and in its moment-to-moment execution by direct observation of the relevant social systems and by the principles of learning theory. It is impossible to function as a skilled behavioral psychotherapist without acquiring an almost unthinking mastery of learning theory as it applies to clinical situations. Thus one cannot be a behavioral psychotherapist without first becoming an accomplished and experienced behavior therapist, just as one cannot be a ski racer without first becoming a skier. In classical behavior therapy, the therapist has the luxury of dealing with a single problem, or at most with a few well-defined problems, using well-defined techniques like assertive training, systematic desensitization, biofeedback, and aversive conditioning to help him achieve his aims, once he has articulated a satisfactory behavioral analysis. In the most difficult problems treated by classical behavior therapists, it is of course true that the therapist must actually invent and continually modify as necessary a composite treatment technique, based on a detailed and continuing behavioral base-line study, in order to solve complex individual problems of behavioral engineering.

In behavioral psychotherapy, on the other hand, the patient comes because of complaints and dissatisfactions that initially at least are much more vague, ill defined, multiple, and amorphous. Or he may complain about others: he cannot get along with his wife or make good relationships with people, and he has no idea, or only the vaguest ideas, what *in his own habitual behavior* contributes to this problem. Thus the initial behavioral analysis, which in simple, classical behavior therapy may require an hour or two of interviewing, or in complex behavior therapy a week or two of index-card data-gathering, may require twenty, forty, or more hours of direct observation of the patient's actual functioning within a natural social system—pref-

erably the very social system in which he experiences his amorphous dissatisfaction, or a replica of it. Typically, with varying emphases depending on the nature of the case,* he is seen in several different social settings—for example, in couple therapy, in family therapy with his parents or in-laws, and also with his children, as well as in therapy with a group of his peers. In my own work with couples, I arrange to see both members of the couple not just triadically with the spouse but also dyadically without the spouse, as well as with the spouse in a group of peers (spouse-pairs) and without the spouse in a same-sexed group of peers. This variety of groupings is accomplished by seeing the couple for initial diagnostic visits first together, then separately, then together again. Real treatment then begins in a three-way group setting; several different couples come regularly on the same afternoon or morning and meet sequentially in three separate meetings all on the same day. In the first meeting all the women (wives) are together as a group; in the second, all the men (husbands) are together as a group (for fairness and balance, the men and women alternate week by week in terms of the order of meetings); in the third meeting, all the spouse-pairs (couples) are together as a group.

The full details of how one employs a learning model in group, family, and couple therapy are clearly beyond the scope of this chapter, or of any single chapter. The important features to be stressed here, in this abbreviated treatment of behavioral psychotherapy, as distinct from classical behavior therapy, are: (1) the deliberate combination of elements of a psychoanalytic or psychodynamic approach with a behavioral approach in order to enhance the therapeutic power of the former, the breadth of the latter, and the therapist's overall effectiveness (Birk and Brinkley-Birk, 1974) and (2) the use of direct observation within the relevant natural social systems to enhance precise, comprehensive, and relevant behavioral analysis and to improve both the results of treatment and the range of human life problems that can be usefully approached

---

* The "case" in fact becomes not an individual but a whole social system—a couple plus their children, plus their families of origin in family therapy, for instance.

using a natural science methodology (Birk and Brinkley-Birk, 1975).

Use of a natural science methodology—second-nature for laboratory-trained behaviorists—leads to direct therapeutic power, power to produce *direct* behavioral changes that can revolutionize the way a couple communicates, the way a family deals with grief or anger, or the way one person in a group relates to another. The directness of these methods is emphasized here because with them insight is not a necessary precursor of far-reaching change. Insight also helps but may at times lag behind direct behavioral change. In couple and family therapy formats, the therapist actually observes directly the social systems in which the patient experiences his difficulty, however amorphously. In a group therapy format, however, the group is not at first a natural social group. Like a jury, a therapy group is an assemblage of somewhat randomly chosen peers, which eventually becomes a natural social group by working together. And, as in therapy within a couple or family format, in group therapy an individual can learn, and a therapist can directly observe, not only that a patient's behavior is socially isolating, hostile, provocative, seductive, or maladaptive but *precisely* what about it is so, and how it can be usefully modified.

Thus the behavioral psychotherapist operates by using direct observation within a relevant social system (almost always several different social systems) and uses this unique vantage point to forge an increasingly refined, subtle, and comprehensive behavioral analysis. As the therapist becomes sure of elements of the problem, such as a subtle pattern of sulky underassertiveness limited to relations with the spouse or an inability to make eye contact with opposite-sexed peers, he shares this information with the patient and the group. The therapist's observations and formulations are refined and validated—or revised—by the group as a whole. Once this refinement is accomplished, the therapist must establish a specific treatment contract to which the patient subscribes. The therapist can then begin direct use of operant methods to modify the contributory problematic behaviors. These operant methods, as has been stated earlier, do include punishment in the form of interrupting the old

behavior with negative interpretations, but they also always employ simultaneous positive reinforcement of a more acceptable and effective alternative behavior to the one being punished.

In behavioral psychotherapy the therapist consciously uses behavioral shaping or successively raising the criterion level for reinforcing a response to a progressively higher level. Put another way, behavioral shaping is a technique of successive approximation in which the desired new behavior occurs in full bloom only near the end of the shaping process. In pursuing therapeutic goals through behavioral shaping, the therapist functions as a punisher, as a reinforcer, and also as a catalytic source of "discriminative stimuli" signaling the availability of reinforcement if a response is emitted. In using discriminative stimuli to catalyze new behaviors, the therapist also consciously uses the principle of stimulus fading—gradually doing less and less to discourage (punish) the old behaviors and to encourage the new behaviors (by direct reinforcement or by supplying discriminative stimuli).

When therapeutic goals are reached, the behavioral psychotherapist strives for phased and very gradual termination, still following the principle of stimulus fading. Thus the behavioral psychotherapy patient or couple frequently progresses from weekly meetings to biweekly meetings to monthly meetings, to quarterly meetings, to a follow-up visit in about a year.

All this emphasis on the principle of stimulus fading increases the durability of the new behavioral patterns learned, and this durability is essentially equivalent to the probability that the new behavior will maintain itself *with natural consequences only following it*. The new behavior will of course maintain itself naturally only if it truly "works better" than the old behavior and brings more reinforcement from the world at large.

In work of this kind the behavioral psychotherapist is often assisted by group process: other group (or family) members, by identification and by modeling, typically adopt some version of the therapist's reinforcement-and-punishment stance with respect to individuals within the group. Thus, after some considerable shared experience, the therapist himself may supply only a minimal discriminative stimulus, and another group member may provide the reinforcement.

In addition to consciously using reinforcement, punishment, discriminative stimuli, modeling, and stimulus fading, the behavioral psychotherapist systematically employs stimulus generalization in the service of therapeutic goals. In a behaviorally oriented therapy group, patients typically see each other socially, in various combinations outside the group and in places and situations outside those of the usual therapy meeting. All of this of course promotes the transfer of newly learned behaviors to the larger life situation and accelerates the useful breakdown of patients' destructively rigid but all too common compartmentalizations of "therapy behavior" and "life behavior."

The Impact of Behavioral Science and Behavior Therapy on Psychiatry

Psychiatry is, or should be, an art. But it should be an art based on the application of scientific methodology to human life problems, as well as on the relevant, always expanding findings of its multiple root sciences—experimental psychology and learning theory; the brain sciences, including neuroanatomy, neurophysiology, neurochemistry, and neuropharmacology; genetics; anthropology and nonhuman primate studies, to name only some of the most important. In this list of root sciences, none is more important than learning theory, though I believe others are equally important. Yet the average psychiatrist, including those still in training, has had very little education in basic behavioral science.

It is now belatedly obvious that those planning to be psychotherapists of any type need to prepare themselves with basic science courses in conditioning and learning; those courses should include supervised laboratory experience with animal learning processes, including extinction, punishment, stimulus generalization, behavioral shaping, and stimulus fading. Those who intend to specialize in behavior therapy, and especially in behavioral psychotherapy, should have particularly thorough backgrounds in the basic sciences underlying this field. Like other clinicians, of course, they should also have long, broad, and adequately supervised experience across a large

range of diagnoses, cultural settings, types of patients and problems, and therapeutic modalities. Specifically, they should know how and when to use phenothiazines, lithium, tricyclic antidepressants, or monoamine oxidase inhibiting drugs; when to consider organic treatments like electroconvulsive therapy; and when to arrange for special neurological study or tests, such as electroencephalography to look for psychomotor seizures. In addition, they should know enough about themselves psychoanalytically to understand their own countertransference reactions. Most of these broad requirements for the education of a therapist, listed here in some detail, can be met with relative ease; there is however cause for deep concern about the current existence of a great gap—indeed, a stark empty hole—in the basic behavioral science preparation of most therapists-to-be.

A parallel gap, more obvious though less serious, appears in clinical behavioral education, where a virtual absence of well-trained behavior therapists exists on the teaching faculties of even the very best psychiatric residency training programs. And there are even fewer departments with experienced behavior therapists who also are medically trained. This clinical gap probably cannot be fully remedied until the basic science gap is reduced. And, even if this occurred, the teaching efforts of those found to fill the clinical gap would bear only five to ten percent of the fruit possible if these teachers were able to work with residents already armed with an adequate education in basic behavioral science.

In summary, behavioral science has already added to the practice of psychiatry a multiplicity of treatment techniques of established clinical value. Beyond this, the field seems to be on the threshold of a new and perhaps even greater contribution through the further development of behavioral psychotherapy. This field, true to its natural science origins, relies on direct observation, *in vivo*, of the social systems relevant to the problems of individuals and uses this unique vantage point for precise behavioral analysis and subsequent therapy using operant social learning techniques. The natural science origins of these behavioral contributions represent one stream among many confluent ones, all of which clamor for a renewed appreciation of the basic science foundations of modern psychiatry.

One of the contributions that is more particular to behavior therapy is what I regard as the proper recapture of major professional responsibility for outcome in psychiatry. I do not doubt the validity of the phenomenon of unconscious "resistance"; it should not, however, be used as a large, all-purpose shield to ward off blame when the patient undergoes years of therapy yet makes very little progress or actually becomes worse. Behavior therapists generally accept what I consider to be a rather appropriately large share of responsibility for clinical outcome because when they do something that doesn't "work" clinically, the reason tends to be looked for not in patient resistance but in terms of one or more of the following:

1. an inadequate (incomplete or wrong) behavioral analysis
2. poor execution of well-designed therapy, based on an adequate behavioral analysis
3. an inappropriate choice of treatment method, as in clinical situations where behavior therapy in itself is quite ineffective—acute psychosis, or temporal lobe epilepsy masquerading as a simple learned eating disorder, for example
4. insufficient therapeutic leverage, instances in which the therapist could not or simply did not get adequate control of the significance reinforcers and punishers in the patient's life

The fact that this field requires full acceptance of this kind of professional responsibility is a large part of what makes working within it both exhilarating and a constant learning experience in itself.

References

Birk, L. 1968. Social reinforcement in psychotherapy. *Cond. Reflex* 3:116–123.

—— 1970. Behavior therapy—integration with dynamic psychiatry. *Behav. Ther.* 1, no. 4:522–526.

—— 1972. Psychoanalytic omniscience and behavioral omnipotence: current trends in psychotherapy. *Semin. Psychiatry* 4, no. 2:113–120. New York: Grune & Stratton.

—— 1974. Intensive group therapy: an effective behavioral-psychoanalytic method. *Am. J. Psychiatry* 131, no. 1:11–16.

Birk, L., and A. Brinkley-Birk. 1974. Psychoanalysis and behavior therapy. *Am. J. Psychiatry* 131, no. 5:499–510.

—— 1975. The learning therapies. In *Overview of the psychotherapies*, ed. G. Usdin. New York: Brunner/Mazel.

Birk, L., S. Stolz, J. P. Brady, J. V. Brady, A. Lazarus, J. Lynch, A. Rosenthal, W. D. Skelton, J. Stevens, and E. Thomas. 1973. *Behavior therapy in psychiatry*. American Psychiatric Association task force report. Washington, D.C.

Feather, V. W., and J. M. Rhoads, 1972. Psychodynamic behavior therapy. *Arch. Gen. Psychiatry* 26:503–511.

Gantt, W. A. H. 1944. *Experimental basis for neurotic behavior*. New York: Harper and Brothers.

—— 1953. Principles of nervous breakdown in schizokinesis and autokinesis. *Ann. N.Y. Acad. Sci.* 56:143–163.

Goldiamond, I., and J. E. Dryud. 1968. Some applications and implications of behavioral analysis for psychotherapy. In *Proceedings of the annual conference on research in psychotherapy*. Vol. 3. Washington, D.C.: American Psychological Association.

Holland, J., and B. F. Skinner. 1961. *The experimental analysis of behavior*. New York: McGraw-Hill.

Jacobson, E. 1938. *Progressive relaxation*. Chicago: University of Chicago Press.

Jones, M. C. 1924. The elimination of children's fears. *J. Exp. Psychol.* 7:382–390.

Lazarus, A. A. 1971. *Behavior therapy and beyond*. New York: McGraw-Hill.

Lindsley, O. R., and B. F. Skinner. 1954. A method for the experimental analysis of behavior of psychotic patients. *Am. Psychol.* 9:419–420.

Lovibond, S. H. 1970. Aversive control of behavior. *Behav. Ther.* 1:80–91.

Marks, I. M. 1972. Perspective on flooding. *Semin. Psychiatry* 4, no. 2:129–138. New York: Grune & Stratton.

—— 1976. The current status of behavioral psychotherapy. *Am. J. Psychiatry* 133, no. 3:253–261.

Marmor, J. 1971. Dynamic psychotherapy and behavior therapy. *Arch. Gen. Psychiatry* 24:22–28.

Mills, H. L., W. S. Agras, D. H. Barlow, and J. R. Mills. 1973. Compulsive rituals treated by response prevention. *Arch. Gen. Psychiatry* 28:524–529.

Pavlov, I. P. 1928. *Lectures on conditioned reflexes*. Edited by W. A. H. Gantt. Vol. 1. New York: International Publishers.

—— 1941. *Lectures on conditioned reflexes*. Edited by W. A. H. Gantt. Vol. 2. New York: International Publishers.

Rhoads, J. M., and V. W. Feather. 1974. Application of psychodynamics to behavior therapy. *Am. J. Psychiatry* 131:17–20.

Shapiro, M. B. 1961. The single case in fundamental clinical psychological research. *Br. J. Med. Psychol.* 34:255–262.

Skinner, B. F. 1953. *Science and human behavior*. New York: Macmillan.

Sloane, R. B. 1969. The converging paths of behavior therapy and psychotherapy. *Int. J. Psychiatry* 7, no. 7:493–503.

Thorndike, E. L. 1898. *Animal intelligence: an experimental study of the associated processes in animals*. New York: Macmillan.

Watson, J. B., and R. Rayner. 1920. Conditioned emotional reactions. *J. Exp. Psychol.* 3:1–14.

Wolpe, J. 1958. *Psychotherapy by reciprocal inhibition*. Stanford: Stanford University Press.

Wolpe, J., J. P. Brady, M. Serber, W. S. Agras, and R. P. Liberman. 1973. The current status of systematic desensitization. *Am. J. Psychiatry* 130:961–965.

Recommended Reading

Agras, W. S. 1972. *Behavior modification, principles and clinical applications*. Boston: Little, Brown.

Ayllon, T., and N. H. Azrin. 1965. The measurement and reinforcement of behavior of psychotics. *J. Exp. Anal. Behav.* 8:357–383.

—— 1968. *The Token Economy*. New York: Appleton-Century-Crofts.

Ayllon, T., and E. Haughton. 1964. Modification of systematic verbal behavior of mental patients. *Behav. Res. Ther.* 2:87–97.

Bandura, A. 1969. *Principles of behavior modification*. New York: Holt, Rinehart and Winston.

Bandura, A., and R. H. Walters. 1963. *Social learning and personality development*. New York: Holt, Rinehart and Winston.

Beck, A. 1970. Cognitive therapy: nature and relation to behavior therapy. *Behav. Ther.* 1:184–200.

Birk, L. 1973. Psychoanalysis and behavioral analysis: natural resonance and complementarity. *Int. J. Psychiatry* 11, no. 2:160–166.

Birk, L., ed. 1973. *Biofeedback: behavioral medicine—The clinical uses of biofeedback in medicine and psychiatry*. New York: Grune & Stratton.

Brady, J. P. 1971. Metronome-conditioned speech retraining for stuttering. *Behav. Ther.* 2:129–150.

Crisp, A. H. 1966. "Transference," "symptom emergence" and "social repercussion" in behavior therapy: a study of fifty-four treated patients. *Br. J. Med. Psychol.* 39:179–196.

Ferster, C. B. 1972. Clinical reinforcement. *Semin. Psychiatry* 4, no. 2:101–111. New York: Grune & Stratton.

—— 1973. A functional analysis of depression. *Am. Psychol.* 28:857–870.

Goldfried, M. R., and G. C. Davison. 1976. *Clinical behavior therapy*. New York: Holt, Rinehart and Winston.

Guttmacher, J., and L. Birk. 1971. Group therapy: what specific therapeutic advantages? *Compr. Psychiatry* 12, no. 6:546–556.

Harris, A. H., and J. V. Brady. 1973. Instrumental (operant) conditioning of visceral and autonomic functions. *Semin. Psychiatry* 5, no. 4:365–376. New York: Grune & Stratton.

Kanfer, F., and H. Phillips. 1970. *Learning foundations of behavior therapy*. New York: Wiley.

Leitenberg, H. 1976. *Handbook of behavior modification and behavior therapy*. Englewood Cliffs, N.J.: Prentice-Hall.

Liberman, R. P. 1972a. Behavioral methods in group and family therapy. *Semin. Psychiatry* 4, no. 2:145–156. New York: Grune & Stratton.

—— 1972b. *A guide to behavioral analysis and therapy*. New York: Pergamon Press.

Liberman, R. P., and D. E. Raskin. 1971. Depression: a behavioral formulation. *Arch. Gen. Psychiatry* 24:515–523.

Mowrer, O. H. and W. M. 1938. Enuresis—a method for its study and treatment. *Am. J. Orthopsychiatry* 8:436–459.

Rachman, S., R. Hodgson, and I. M. Marks. 1971. Treatment of chronic obsessive-compulsive neurosis. *Behav. Res. Ther.* 9:237–247.

Risley, T. R. 1968. The effects and side effects of punishing the autistic behaviors of a deviant child. *J. Appl. Behav. Anal.* 1:21–34.

Saslow, G. 1975. Application of behavior therapy. In *Overview of the psychotherapies*, ed. G. Usdin. New York: Brunner/Mazel.

Seligman, M. E. P. 1974. Depression and learned helplessness. In *The psychology of depression*, ed. R. J. Friedman and M. M. Katz. Washington, D.C.: Wiley, Halsted Press.

Seligman, M. E. P., S. F. Maier, and R. L. Solomon. 1971. Unpredictable and uncontrollable aversive events. In *Aversive conditioning and learning*, ed. F. R. Brush. New York: Academic Press.

Skinner, B. F. 1938. *The behavior of organisms*. New York: Appleton-Century.

Strobel, C. F., and B. C. Glueck. 1973. Biofeedback treatment in medicine and psychiatry: an ultimate placebo? *Semin. Psychiatry* 5, no. 4:379–393. New York: Grune & Stratton.

Walton, D., and M. D. Mather. 1964. The application of learning principles to the treatment of obsessive-compulsive states in the acute and chronic phases of illness. In *Experiments in behavior therapy*, ed. H. J. Eysenck. New York: Macmillan.

Wolpe, J., and A. A. Lazarus. 1966. *Behavior therapy techniques.* Oxford: Pergamon Press.

Yates, A. J. 1970. *Behavior therapy*. New York: Wiley.

—— 1975. *Theory and practice in behavior therapy.* New York: Wiley.

Sex Therapy: A Behavioral Approach

CHAPTER 20

Ann W. Birk

S ex therapy is a short-term, behaviorally based psychotherapy, limited in its objectives, empirical and eclectic in its methods, and narrowly circumscribed in its focus. It is the treatment of choice for male and female sexual dysfunctions that are clearly psychosomatic in nature, and it can be a useful adjunctive therapy for organic sexual disorders. It has also proved effective in the clarification and resolution of sexual problems that reflect a more broadly based conflict within the marital relationship.

The sexual dysfunctions are commonly agreed to be erectile dysfunction (impotence), premature ejaculation, and ejaculatory incompetence (retarded ejaculation) in the male, and general sexual dysfunction (frigidity), orgasmic dysfunction, and vaginismus in the female. The primary objective of sex therapy is alleviation of the chief complaint (target symptom) in the sexually dysfunctional individual or couple and, concomitantly, the extension of sexual adequacy over a broader range of sexual situations. Although symptom relief defines the goal of sex therapy, the focus of treatment in each case is the specific pathogenic mechanism or set of mechanisms that operates immediately and directly to prevent full and pleasurable sexual functioning. Pre-cise identification of these inhibitory factors is the first stage of sex therapy; systematic modification of these factors and concurrent maximization of arousal-promoting factors constitutes the second stage. In practice this combination of psychotherapeutic and behavioral methods blends insight, interpretation, clarification, and behavioral shaping—the latter effected by the assignment of corrective experiential tasks.

Short History

The theoretical and clinical foundations of sex therapy are a product of two separate historical traditions. The first is identified with the systematic study of human sexuality undertaken first by Kinsey and significantly advanced by Masters and Johnson. The second is represented by the research of Pavlov, Wolpe, and others on the experimental conditioning of animal behavior.

The research of Kinsey and Masters and Johnson has contributed directly to the evolution of a science of human sexuality. The Kinsey reports on male and female sexual behavior, published in the late 1940s and early 1950s, remain significant studies; the approach, however, was exclusively sociological. Human sexuality was not investigated as a psychophysiological phenomenon until the establishment of a laboratory for sexual research at Washington University Medical School in 1954. This laboratory was co-directed by the gynecologist William Masters and his research associate, Virginia Johnson. Data collected from the laboratory study of the normal sexual responses of men and women were compiled and published in 1966 in the landmark volume by Masters and Johnson, *Human Sexual Response*. A second volume by Masters and Johnson, *Human Sexual Inadequacy*, followed in 1970 and laid the technical foundations for the treatment of sexual dysfunction. Since 1970, a notable addition to the research-oriented studies of Masters and Johnson has been the clinical work of Helen Singer Kaplan, described in *The New Sex Therapy* (1974).

Although the standard treatment techniques that have come to be associated with sex therapy were developed, tested, and publicized by Masters and Johnson and Kaplan, there was no explicit agreement among them concerning the nature and scope of a theoretical structure linking these specific techniques. The behavioral tradition provides a potential, albeit still unacknowledged, model for understanding and evaluating the established therapeutic techniques as well as extending and increasing their effectiveness.

It has long been recognized within the behavioral tradition that a manipulation of key environmental variables is sufficient to alter animal behavior, even to disrupt those response patterns that are said to be instinctive. Insofar as the sexual response of animals, or indeed of humans, is a natural response, ordinarily reinforced and maintained by environmental stimuli and a strong internal drive, it is usually self-sustaining. Pavlov, Wolpe, and others, however, established experimentally that the sexual response is no less susceptible to conditioning than other sorts of animal or human behaviors; in fact, the sexual response in animals and humans has been demonstrated to be particularly easy to disrupt and inhibit. This fact fits with the observed high incidence of sexual maladaptation even in people without other psychiatric problems. If, for example, a strong aversive stimulus is paired with sexual behavior or attempted sexual behavior, a disruption of the normal sexual response typi-

cally occurs and can persist even after the aversive stimulus is withdrawn. Wolpe (1958) found that reactivation of the normal response is possible by manipulating the environmental variables to emphasize arousal-producing or arousal-promoting factors and to minimize aversive stimuli competitive with, or antagonistic to, normal sexual behavior.

Wolpe extended and adapted this conditioning process generally to the treatment of phobic avoidance behavior in humans, a technique he called psychotherapy by reciprocal inhibition. As a therapeutic strategy, reciprocal inhibition involved systematic pairing of two mutually inhibiting responses: relaxation and fear, for example, or sexual arousal and anxiety, where careful structuring of the therapeutic experience guaranteed that the desired response would be present to a degree sufficient to inhibit the phobic or anxious response. Behavioral theory developed from the work of Wolpe and others provides a well-established model and methodology for altering human behavior—for maximizing and reinforcing desired responses and for inhibiting or punishing neurotic or undesired responses. Sex therapy relies implicitly on behavioral principles, for it is a learning process contingent on the successful mastery of a graduated series of experiential tasks.

Basic Principles

Sexual problem is a loose label that has come to be applied to a poorly defined group of symptoms ranging from extreme, crippling sexual dysfunctions, both organic and psychosomatic, through middle-range sexual inhibitions, to the hostile, provocative sexual behaviors characteristic of a dyadic power struggle. The term is also frequently used to describe variants of the sexual response, pathological variants as well as those approaching normalcy. The mere existence of a sexual problem is not, therefore, sufficient to warrant treatment in the behaviorally based sex therapy program described in this chapter.

Indications and Contraindications

The type of therapy described here is specifically and primarily indicated for psychosomatic sexual dysfunctions and for middle-range sexual inhibitions. If the cause of the impaired response appears to be primarily organic, on the other hand, sex therapy may still be undertaken either as an adjustment-oriented treatment adjunctive to appropriate medical or pharmacological management or as a therapeutic regimen designed to maximize the functional aspects of the impaired response and to promote pleasure-enhancing adaptations.

For the so-called sexual variations such as homosexuality, fetishism, and unusual sexual object choices or practices, sex therapy is generally not indicated, unless it is used in combination with, or as an adjunct to, more traditional forms of psychotherapy or behavior therapy. It may be used as an exclusive treatment format for any of these sexual variations only if the variation represents a sexual adaptation to an otherwise alienated or dysfunctional response. For example, a man who is situationally impotent with his wife and all other heterosexual partners may develop a compulsive masturbatory-exhibitionistic behavior. In this case, alleviation of the situational impotence is likely to effect a secondary therapeutic benefit automatically, namely, elimination of the compulsive sexual behavior. It is an unusual case, however, that does not require adjunctive psychotherapy.

Finally, sexual problems exist that are neither sexual dysfunctions nor sexual variations. These problems are the result of a destructive interpersonal power struggle in which sex is used as a means of asserting control, securing leverage, expressing anger, or undermining the partner. For this type of sexual problem, sex therapy may be used initially in order to expose the latent (unacknowledged) destructiveness of the couple's sexual and nonsexual interaction and to precipitate later resolution of the dyadic conflict in some other more appropriate therapeutic format.

The Sexual Response: Normal and Dysfunctional

The human sexual response is a highly organized, orderly biochemical and physiological process that prepares the otherwise quiescent reproductive organs for sexual union with a mate. In order for such a union to occur, a profound alteration in the shape and function of the reproductive organs of each sex is required. The first

stage of the sexual response, *excitement*, is characterized in both sexes by genital vasocongestion, that is, reflex dilation and engorgement of the blood vessels in the penis and in the circumvaginal erectile tissue. Secretion of genital lubricants, especially important in the female response, occurs concomitantly during this stage.

The second stage, *plateau*, is marked by the attainment of peak vasocongestion in male and female, a state preparatory to orgasmic discharge. In the male, the testicles are swollen and drawn into a position near the perineal floor. In the female, the circumvaginal tissues reach the limit of their vascular distention. Together with the highly tensed pubococcygeal and perineal muscles, these swollen erectile tissues constitute the female's "orgasmic platform."

The third stage, *orgasm*, is analogous in male and female. It is characterized by involuntary, regular contractions of the bulbar muscles in the male and of the circumvaginal muscles in the female. Male orgasm is actually biphasic; the bulbar contractions composing the highly pleasurable, ejaculatory component of orgasm are immediately preceded by regular, involuntary contractions of the urethra and the perineal muscles. These first-stage contractions are experienced as urgent, premonitory pulsations and are called the emission phase of orgasm. If this first phase is impaired, orgasm occurs without seminal emission. If the subsequent ejaculatory or bulbar phase is impaired, seminal fluid is released, but without force and without orgasmic pleasure.

Following orgasm is *resolution*, a stage marked by gradual return to the body's unaroused, basal state. At any point during resolution, the female response is capable of complete reactivation. The male response, however, requires a variable interval of recovery, the so-called refractory period, before it can be reactivated in its entirety.

Although the human sexual response appears to be an orderly physiological process involving a nexus of apparently interdependent stages, experimental and clinical evidence now suggests that the response is in reality two discrete processes, vasocongestion and orgasm. Genital vasocongestion is primarily a vascular process. Although this stage usually precedes orgasm in the normal response, orgasm can occur in the presence of only minimal genital vasocongestion. Orgasm, on the other hand, involves the reflex discharge of tension in the bulbar muscles of the male and in the circumvaginal muscles in the female. Although orgasm is usually associated with a high degree of genital vasocongestion, the latter is not a necessary or sufficient condition for orgasm. The six common sexual dysfunctions are thus clinically distinct pathological entities. Erectile dysfunction in the male and general sexual dysfunction in the female are disorders specific to the vasocongestive process. Orgasm can occur in the presence of vasocongestive failure for either sex. Premature ejaculation and ejaculatory incompetence in the male and orgasmic dysfunction in the female are sexual disorders specific to the orgasmic phase of the response. Normal vasocongestive function can coexist with orgasmic dysfunction. Vaginismus is a disorder associated with neither vasocongestion nor orgasm; it is a conditioned, involuntary contraction of the circumvaginal muscles in response to the perceived threat of vaginal penetration. A woman with severe vaginismus may be fully responsive to sexual stimuli exclusive of those with phobic significance for her. The presence of one sexual dysfunction does not necessarily imply the presence of another, but it is not unusual to find them together—erectile dysfunction combined with premature ejaculation or ejaculatory incompetence in the male, or orgasmic dysfunction concurrent with general sexual dysfunction or vaginismus in the female.

Causes of Sexual Dysfunction: Remote and Immediate

Requisite to full sexual adequacy in male and female is a healthy reproductive system, anatomically intact and free from neurological, hormonal, and vascular defects. Factors adversely affecting any element in this intricate biological network can disrupt a significant portion of the physiological processes regulating the sexual and reproductive capacities. Pathogenic factors are of two types: organic and psychosocial. The organic factors, such as disease, trauma, anatomical anomaly, drugs, and obesity, are capable

of preventing or compromising sexual function, but with appropriate medical and behavioral-psychotherapeutic management the destructive influence of some organic conditions is reversible. While the nature and extent of the organic factors affecting human sexuality are still only incompletely understood, psychosocial factors nonetheless represent a vastly more significant set of causes underlying sexual dysfunction.

Theoretically, two broad categories of psychosocial factors adversely affect sexual adequacy: (1) the original, remote conditions or factors predisposing to the acquisition of a sexual dysfunction and (2) the immediate factors or conditions systematically maintaining the dysfunction. In the first category are developmental, cultural, constitutional, and psychological forces thought to influence the genesis of adult sexual inadequacy by determining long-range sexual expectations, attitudes, and values. One set of remote, antecedent factors affecting adult sexuality results from a repressive developmental atmosphere including strongly inhibitory familial, social, religious, or cultural forces. A second group is experiential in nature; sexual traumas such as incest, rape, or early aversive experiences (including sexual failures, embarrassing exposures, unwanted pregnancies, and pregnancy scares) generate an expectation of continuing anxiety-provoking, pleasureless sexual experiences. A third type of factor exists in a generally destructive interpersonal atmosphere antagonistic to the development of a warm, supportive, mutually rewarding sexual relationship. A fourth set of remote determinants of sexual inadequacy is psychological to the extent that neurotic features of the personality, such as a chronic depressive, negativistic outlook, hysterical seductiveness, chronic pathological passivity, oedipal anxiety, and other neurotic conflicts, prevent the development of a healthy attitude toward adult sexual interaction.

The categories of remote and immediate causes are only operationally distinct, although the distinction is essential (Kaplan, 1974). The remote causes are defined by their relative distance from the sexual experience itself; the immediate causes, by their direct and immediate operation within the sexual context. The immediate determinants of sexual inadequacy are those conditions maintaining dysfunction in the form of ineffective sexual behavior or obstruction in the awareness or perception of sexual stimulation. Ignorance, misinformation, inexperience, a poor feedback system, and the abdication of responsibility for personal sexual satisfaction are examples of factors limiting the effectiveness or sufficiency of sexual stimulation. Obstruction in the awareness of sexual stimulation is distinct from ineffective sexual behavior in that adequate physical stimulation is not sufficient for normal sexual function in the presence of distracting intrapsychic activity. Persistent feelings of guilt, anxiety, shame, conflict, or hostility, obsessive monitoring, and self-fulfilling negative expectations are examples of psychic mechanisms competitive with the awareness of sexual stimulation and sensation.

Adequate sexual behavior and function are contingent on the elimination of the immediate pathogenic causes. While the remote determinants of sexual inadequacy may manifest themselves as or be reflected in the immediate determinants, it is the set of immediate causes operating directly within the sexual experience that constitutes the primary focus of sex therapy. It is sometimes possible, in the course of therapy, to isolate and identify the specific immediate pathogenic mechanisms, such as anxiety, shame, or hostility, that translate remote factors such as an early repressive history or oedipal anxiety into ongoing erectile dysfunction or some other sexual dysfunction in adulthood. When such identification cannot be made, however, the remote conditions predisposing to adult sexual inadequacy must generally remain peripheral to the behaviorally based treatment of sexual disorder. It cannot be emphasized too strongly that treatment of sexual dysfunction that proceeds by attempted analysis and resolution of deep-seated psychopathology is often not an appropriate approach to the restoration of sexual adequacy.

Treatment of Sexual Dysfunction

Two stages are involved in the treatment of sexual dysfunction: (1) patient history and behavioral analysis, which involve establishing a base line for existing sexual function and specifying the variables that seem to promote or inhibit sexual function, and (2) therapy, which works toward the elimination of maladaptive factors competitive with sexual adequacy and the restoration of confidence and expectation of ongoing sexual competence.

History and Behavioral Analysis

Human sexuality is more than the sum of discrete sexual events; it is a physical capacity as well as a composite of the attitudes, motivations, expectations, and self-evaluation each person brings to and abstracts from sexual and nonsexual experience. Taking a history, therefore, involves eliciting information and forming impressions from a number of different perspectives: medical, psychiatric, marital, and sexual. The medical history should focus on medical health in general and on accidents, trauma, use of drugs or alcohol, stress and fatigue levels, possible diabetes or other illness, and the possibility of vaginal infection in particular. In some cases, particularly when the history is one of unremitting dysfunction as opposed to situational dysfunction, referral for a medical, gynecological or urological, and neurological examination is an essential diagnostic step. Psychiatric history should include an inventory of each partner's current emotional status and information about developmental, familial, social, and religious backgrounds. Marital history should involve an assessment of the general quality of the relationship—the level and degree of openness in communication; the extent to which fun, pleasure, and mutual satisfaction are valued; and the amount of interpersonal affection, warmth, and responsiveness. In addition, the marital evaluation should include a comparison of the quality of the present relationship with its own best times and with previous relationships of both partners. The sexual history for each individual should include information about maturation and the response to it, acquisition of and reaction to information about sex and reproduction, early sexual experiences, and all previous sexual or potentially sexual relationships. It is customary during the diagnostic phase of sex therapy both to interview the couple together and to interview each partner separately. It is not unusual to acquire more relevant material from the individuals when seen separately than when they are interviewed as a couple.

Resolution of a sexual dysfunction or inhibition depends not only on effective treatment but also on a precise formulation of the intrapsychic and interpersonal dynamics involved and an accurate analysis of current symptomatic and nonsymptomatic sexual patterns. Although the working formulation of a case evolves as treatment proceeds, a tentative hypothesis about the remote or deep-seated causes of the current dysfunction should be made by the end of the formal history-taking stage. The second diagnostic step is critical to a successful treatment outcome: accurate analysis of the symptomatic and nonsymptomatic sexual patterns. This analysis should include a general evaluation of the quality and frequency of sexual contact (including masturbation), the sexual expectations and attitudes of each partner, the significance of sex and of the particular sexual problem for each partner, feelings about conception and contraception, and the actual mode of contraception employed. It is essential, in particular, to elicit a detailed description of what happens before, during, and after a typical sexual interaction—the situations, devices, partners, feelings, fantasies, or activities that produce pleasure, emotional ease, and sexual arousal, as well as those that produce discomfort, anxiety, or sexual failure. At the conclusion of this second diagnostic stage, a pretreatment base line of existing sexual adequacy should have been established and a determination made of the factors adversely affecting the sexual response of either person and of those reliably enhancing the sexual response. It is customary to formulate the base line as a hierarchy of situations in which the lowest levels are defined as those that elicit the maximal available function of the untreated response, and the highest levels, as those that elicit maximal dysfunction. The specific conditions adversely affecting the sexual response —anger, guilt, shame, obsessive monitoring of the sexual interaction, negative expectations, poor communication, ineffective stimulation, overcompliance of one partner, withholding, hostile or undermining sexual behavior—are the immediate determinants of sexual dysfunc-

tion and define the target of the behavioral strategies. Issues relative to the remote determinants of sexual dysfunction are likely to surface during the course of treatment and therefore compose at least part of the material discussed during therapy sessions, but they are not directly accessible to behavioral shaping—conditioning by manipulation of the key variables—during the performance of experiential tasks.

Therapy for Sexual Dysfunction

Although the course and strategy of treatment programs for the sexually dysfunctional individual or couple vary according to the individuals involved and the type of dysfunction treated, a few basic principles and concepts underlie the different treatment formats.

Six common sexual dysfunctions have been delineated. Four represent an insufficient or inhibited sexual response: erectile dysfunction and ejaculatory incompetence in the male and general sexual dysfunction and orgasmic dysfunction in the female. Treatment for each of these four dysfunctions conforms in general to the behavioral model for systematic *in vivo* desensitization. Treatment by this method involves step-by-step mastery of a graduated series of therapeutic exercises constructed and assigned by the therapist. These exercises typically follow a hierarchical scheme in which the lowest levels are relatively easy tasks that should elicit no elements of the target sexual symptom. Some early therapeutic exercises of this sort have come to be known as "sensate focus exercises," since they foster a focused, undistracted awareness of sensual pleasure resulting from gentle caressing or massage by the partner. It is customary to proscribe genital stimulation, intercourse, and other activities leading to high levels of sexual arousal during the early phase of treatment in order to interrupt the maladaptive sexual pattern. This interruption allows a new, unsymptomatic pattern to emerge as the product of each successive therapeutic experience. As sensual pleasure and sexual arousal begin to be experienced regularly in association with undemanding, unthreatening sexual situations, pleasure and arousal begin to act as natural, reliable responses inhibiting the previously conditioned feelings of guilt, shame, embarrassment, anxiety, or alienation, thus reducing the tendency to monitor, undermine, or otherwise suppress the positive aspects of the experience. Liberated from the previous burden of inhibitory psychic mechanisms, the sexual response is gradually encouraged to emerge and flourish in safe, structured situations without pressure and without goals. It is essential at every step on the treatment hierarchy to assign a therapeutic task only if a high probability of success is associated with it. A task that is too advanced has probable failure implicit in it and risks activating sexual defenses and reinforcing feelings of inadequacy, thus confirming an already negative sexual self-image. The experiential tasks will have a positive therapeutic value only if the behavioral recommendations are exactly tailored to each individual case and are responsive to personal preferences and values.

Although treatment programs for the four dysfunctions characterized by an insufficiency or inhibition in response conform to a general desensitization scheme, there are variations in the treatment plans specific to each of these four dysfunctions.

Erectile dysfunction. Treatment for erectile dysfunction begins with the assignment of exercises commensurate with the established base-line levels of sexual function, almost always at the level of the sensate focus exercises with all forms of genital stimulation temporarily proscribed. Nondemand genital stimulation is gradually introduced when it is obvious to the therapist that this will not produce anxiety, symptomatic behavior, and expectations of failure. The optimal therapeutic exercise at this stage of treatment is a "cycling" exercise in which arousal is brought to a moderate, nonthreatening level and then allowed purposely and naturally to subside. The stimulation is repeated and continued through several cycles with ejaculation an option not necessarily either recommended or proscribed. Two important benefits result from introducing genital stimulation in the form of cycling. First, the sexual response is shaped away from being a rapid, linear progression from nonarousal through orgasm; instead, the response is shaped toward approximating the more natural, more mutual situation in which arousal is an un-

hurried, non-goal-oriented building of erotic tension. In addition, cycling promotes the development and refinement of uninhibited awareness of subtle shifts in sensation and arousal and, with repetition, instills a confidence that high levels of arousal will return even after repeated loss of erection. The therapist might also recommend the use of fantasy, erotic literature, or movies —whatever helps to produce the desired response until erection can be elicited easily and the individual is no longer dependent on a narrowly circumscribed mode of stimulation. Once erectile function is restored with direct manual stimulation by the partner, vaginal containment exercises and finally intercourse are gradually introduced. Progress through the graduated series of exercises is contingent upon continued positive experiences. It may be necessary to repeat experiential tasks, or to drop back in the hierarchical series to a less threatening activity, if it appears that a particular exercise either produces the symptom or arouses an uncomfortably high level of tension, anxiety, or discouragement. It is important that erotic stimuli be allowed to increase in intensity only so long as pleasure, sexual arousal, and nonsymptomatic behavior keep pace. At the point where inhibition or other distractions threaten the effectiveness of a sexual exercise, the behavioral components of the situation should be modified until progress through the experiences can be resumed.

Ejaculatory incompetence. Treatment for ejaculatory incompetence conforms to a general hierarchical desensitization scheme in which the lowest levels of the hierarchy are defined as those pretreatment situations in which the male patient is least symptomatic and the highest levels are defined as those situations in which he either cannot ejaculate at all or experiences the most difficulty. The most common pretreatment base line for this condition is one in which ejaculation occurs most easily in response to a rough form of self-stimulation and usually does not occur easily, if at all, in response to intravaginal stimulation. A stimulus-fading approach is adopted for ejaculatory incompetence whereby the strongest and most reliable stimulus situation for ejaculation is initially prescribed. Subsequent tasks include a combination of the conditions in which ejaculation routinely and easily occurs with increasing proportions of the more difficult, less reliable stimulus situations. In a typical case, stimulus fading would involve assigning self-stimulation to the point of ejaculation with stimulation by the partner (first manual, then intravaginal) introduced at the point of ejaculation, then near the point of ejaculation, and gradually farther and farther from the point of ejaculation. Treatment is completed when ejaculation is no longer exclusively dependent on the original, pretreatment stimulus situation.

General sexual dysfunction. Therapy for general sexual dysfunction, as with erectile dysfunction, follows a relatively straightforward desensitization hierarchy, beginning with nongenital sensate focus exercises, through simple genital pleasuring and quiet intravaginal containment, to nondemand intercourse. Progress through this series of structured exercises is contingent on continued positive, nonsymptomatic experiences. Since this dysfunction is frequently, although not necessarily, correlated with orgasmic dysfunction, it may be easier to treat the latter first, since therapy typically involves self-stimulation early in treatment and adds heterosexual or dyadic exercises later. Self-stimulation may be less threatening to the woman with general sexual dysfunction than heterosexual activities, even when those are carefully structured and circumscribed.

Orgasmic dysfunction. Unlike the dysfunctions just discussed—in which the condition is rarely, if ever, absolute—orgasmic dysfunction can be complete for many women; that is, they have never experienced orgasm under any circumstances. The immediate goal of therapy in the case of an absolute orgasmic dysfunction is to help the woman experience one orgasm. This is usually achieved during self-stimulation exercises involving week-by-week encouragement and reassurance from the therapist, perseverance on the part of the woman, and, not uncommonly, the adjunctive use of a stimulating device, erotic literature, or fantasies. Once orgasm has been achieved, therapy follows a stimulus-fading approach in which the woman learns to respond with orgasm to a broader range of stimulation

modes; treatment at this point is essentially the same for women who were anorgasmic (had an absolute dysfunction), for women who were situationally dysfunctional, and for women with general sexual dysfunction. Heterosexual exercises are assigned beginning with simple massage, followed by genital stimulation in the form of cycling, and proceeding through the levels of intravaginal containment and intercourse. It may be necessary to recommend incorporating more direct-stimulation techniques in the exercises involving penetration and intercourse until these adjunctive measures are no longer required.

The two other dysfunctions, premature ejaculation and vaginismus, are characterized by an excessive or uncontrolled response to sexual stimuli. Therapy for these dysfunctions conforms to a treatment format different from the *in vivo* desensitization model underlying the therapy programs described for erectile dysfunction, ejaculatory incompetence, general sexual dysfunction, and orgasmic dysfunction.

Premature ejaculation. This dysfunction involves regular, reflex, uncontrolled ejaculation in response to erotic stimulation. Although ejaculation for different men with this dysfunction may occur over a range of stimulus situations, from anticipation of a date to vaginal penetration or intense and prolonged intravaginal stimulation, usually the condition is defined neither by timing nor by situation but, rather, by the uncontrolled, reflex quality of the ejaculatory response. Treatment involves "punishing" or reducing the frequency of the premature urge to ejaculate by consistently and immediately following its occurrence with a negative consequence administered by the partner in the form of either a gentle but firm squeeze to the glans penis or the abrupt cessation of arousing stimulation. In a typical case, the first therapeutic exercises are designed to elicit the urge to ejaculate (but not ejaculation itself) in response to moderately intense stimulation—usually manual stimulation by the partner. When the urge to ejaculate is first sensed, it is immediately followed by either the squeeze or the abrupt cessation of stimulation; both techniques are usually sufficient to inhibit ejaculation. Stimulation is then resumed until the ejaculatory urge recurs. The sequence of stimulation, ejaculatory urge, and punishment is usually recommended as a series of three or four cycles per therapeutic experience. As the frequency of uncontrolled ejaculatory urges declines in moderately intense sexual situations, the therapeutic experiences are structured to include more intensely arousing stimulation modes, culminating in intravaginal stimulation. As uninterrupted stimulation becomes possible at higher levels of arousal, it serves to reinforce a nonejaculatory adaptation. With consistent application of this stimulation-punishment method, the interval between early arousal and ejaculation is significantly and permanently lengthened, and the urge to ejaculate is rendered more controllable.

A prerequisite to the success of this technique is that the man with premature ejaculation learn to recognize the premonitory signals of ejaculation so that the squeeze can be applied before ejaculation occurs. In itself this is an indispensable element in the resolution of the problem, since it implies learning to focus awareness on a pattern of sexual sensation and to overcome or minimize the effects of inhibitory or distracting feelings.

Vaginismus. Vaginismus is an uncontrolled phobic response to the perceived threat of vaginal penetration, which takes the form of spastic closure of the vaginal introitus: the circumvaginal muscles undergo repeated, prolonged contraction in the presence of threatening stimuli. Treatment for vaginismus is a modified "flooding" technique, that is, controlled exposure to the phobic stimulus (vaginal penetration) through a graded hierarchy of actual stimulus situations. Proceeding through the hierarchy to effective resolution involves a combination of three elements:

1. Vaginal containment of progressively larger objects. These objects should be of a size and type that guarantee successful containment during the initial attempts. It is imperative both that early containment exercises be successful and that the penetrating objects be allowed to remain in place until a reasonable level of physical and emotional comfort can be reached and sus-

tained. Otherwise, early failure or premature removal operate to reinforce fear and avoidance, seriously aggravating the problem and heightening the likelihood of failure in subsequent trials.

2. Mastering the technique of voluntary contraction and relaxation of the pubococcygeal and perineal muscles, the so-called Kegel technique or exercises. Once learned, these exercises should be employed to induce muscle fatigue prior to containment attempts. This drastically reduces the chance that vaginal spasm will result in an unsuccessful (and destructive) attempt at an extinction experience. Extinction of the phobic symptom can occur only under conditions of nonreinforcement.

3. Inducement of general relaxation or sexual arousal during penetration exercises, in order to oppose the phobic anxiety which produces spastic closure of the vaginal introitus.

In addition to modifying the pathogenic components in the sexual behaviors of dysfunctional individuals or couples, the assigned experiential tasks also serve to restructure sexual expectations, goals, and patterns of communication. Couples learn to substitute sensuous, pleasure-producing behaviors and mutuality for alienation and the often narrow, demanding, goal-oriented sexual behaviors associated with and contributing to the symptoms of sexual inadequacy. Open and frank communication of sexual needs and reactions is encouraged; it is the mainstay of a satisfactory sexual relationship. As a result of both the behavioral tasks and the office therapy sessions, couples learn to employ direct and unambiguous means rather than covert, negative, or ambivalent signaling to convey a sexual message, and they are encouraged to adopt a responsible, confident, unpressured attitude toward sex, stifling any residual impulses to criticize, undermine, and thwart the partner or otherwise foment pressure and alienation.

Psychotherapy

In-office psychotherapy sessions serve several functions. They provide an opportunity to review the results of assigned behavioral tasks; to supply information, encouragement, and advice where necessary; to interrupt by direct clarification, interpretation, or suggestion any signs of countertherapeutic progress-watching, intellectualizing, responsibility-shifting, or avoidance; to reinforce and affirm the positive, mutual, pleasure-maximizing elements in the reported experiences; and to explore and discuss issues relevant to the remote determinants of the sexual symptoms.

Management of resistance to change on the part of one or both individuals is almost always necessary at some point during treatment sessions. Resistance usually takes the form of a negative reaction to the assigned therapeutic tasks. Negative reactions may include the report of finding little or no time for the assigned tasks or experiencing either no sensation or frank discomfort during the pleasurizing sessions: the expression of continued anxiety, hostility, or fear of rejection by the partner; or the disclosure of previously unadmitted feelings of discouragement, pessimism, fear, or disappointment about therapy and about the marital relationship.

Management of the resistance to the extent, and only to the extent, that it is directly impeding the progress of therapy is essential for a favorable outcome. Sometimes reassurance, interpretation, or clarification by the therapist is sufficient to remove the immediate, acknowledged obstacle to continued progress. More often, a restructuring of the behavioral tasks is required in order to reduce anxiety and remove the resistance-promoting conditions. Occasionally, however, actual interruption of the behavioral procedures is warranted in order to focus attention on destructive aspects of the marital relationship or to probe the deeper sources of intrapsychic discomfort. In very rare instances, persistent expressions of fear, disgust, pessimism, or hostility may be sufficiently intense to require a radical shift of gears in the treatment or even termination of therapy altogether. When sex therapy uncovers deep-seated, intractable marital hostility or severe psychopathology, it is imperative to terminate focused sexual therapy and deal with the immediate problem, rather than running the risk of reinforcing strongly negative attitudes about sex by insisting on continued performance of prescribed sexual tasks.

Issues in the Clinical Practice of Sex Therapy

Unlike the more traditional forms of psychotherapy, the practice of sex therapy has no well-established format. Procedural differences specific to different sex therapy treatment centers have formed around four issues: (1) the use of dual-sex cotherapy teams versus single therapists; (2) the conditions under which patients will be accepted for treatment; (3) the frequency of sessions and duration of treatment; (4) the use of conjoint sexological examination or actual observation of the dysfunctional couple during behavioral exercises and direct sexual involvement between therapists and patients. A brief description of the key points in these issues follows.

1. Masters and Johnson began their work as a team and continue to argue the merits of the dual-sex cotherapist approach over those of the single therapist. Their point is that each sex requires a representative in sex therapy much like the proverbial "friend in court." Evidence indicates, however, that one experienced psychotherapist who is trained to work with couples and is comfortable with and knowledgeable about sexual matters germane to each sex can be just as effective in most cases as the dual-sex team. There are some difficult cases, especially those in which same-sex modeling effects play a significant therapeutic role, in which two therapists are essential, but a precise understanding of the dynamics and obstacles in each individual case should be sufficient to dictate the correct choice and assignment of therapist or therapist team. An inflexible position on this issue can be unnecessarily expensive, inefficient, and sometimes countertherapeutic.

2. Agreement exists among most sex therapists that the optimal candidates for therapy are young, heterosexual, married couples with monosymptomatic sexual dysfunction uncomplicated by either personal psychopathology or interpersonal pathology. Many sex therapy clinics therefore screen out single individuals, unmarried couples, older persons, homosexuals, and couples who show significant marital discord or psychiatric disturbance. There is evidence, how-

ever, that a flexible and individualized approach to the practice of sex therapy produces better results than a rigid screening procedure. When sex therapy is undertaken for appropriate cases, it can be very effective for some individuals (heterosexual or homosexual), for some unmarried couples (heterosexual or homosexual), for teenagers, for couples in their later years, and, indeed, for couples with profound interpersonal conflicts or personal intrapsychic pathology. When sex therapy is not effective, the individual or couple will, at the very least, gain a better understanding of the real source of conflict and an enlightened motivation to seek a more appropriate form of therapy. Judgments about the long-range efficacy of sex therapy for those seeking help for a sexual problem are more accurate and effective when they are made on the basis of empirical data gathered from and with the participation of the individual or couple in question than when they are made from statistical generalizations.

3. Although sex therapy is by nature and objective a short-term therapy, a practical variation exists in the frequency of meetings and duration of treatment. Masters and Johnson, for example, formalized the two-week, six- or seven-meeting-per-week approach. Others have adopted a less intensive format that involves brief but open-ended therapy with meetings once or twice a week. There are obvious advantages to both approaches. The intensive, two-week treatment program demands high motivation, full attention, and a sharp focus, and it can take advantage of a rapidly building momentum. The less intensive approach, that is, weekly or semiweekly meetings, necessitates achievement of symptom resolution within the ongoing life context—a difficult objective but usually more enduring in the long run than a noncontextual treatment of sexual inadequacy.

4. The issue of a therapist's direct involvement with the sexual examination or behavior of his patients is a highly controversial one. Some therapists routinely conduct a preliminary conjoint sexological exam, for both medical and educational reasons, and some employ direct observation of the sexual behavior of their patients as a diagnostic and therapeutic aid. There is no obvi-

ous clinical reason for any direct intervention of this sort, and even less for any sexual involvement with patients. When a medical exam proves necessary, referral to an outside physician is sufficient for diagnostic purposes.

The Patient-Therapist Relationship

At some point in the course of any therapy, including sex therapy, it is predictable that feelings about the therapist will develop. In sex therapy, these feelings frequently have a sexual orientation, taking the form of attraction, curiosity, or competitiveness. The latter sometimes manifests itself as overcompliance in following recommendations or as active resistance to the therapist's suggestions. When such feelings become evident, they should be acknowledged and handled matter-of-factly in an open, gentle, pointedly nonjudgmental discussion. At the very least, verbal acknowledgment of the feelings, followed by the therapist's interpretation and clarification, can lead to a more permissive attitude toward sexuality and to a clearer self-understanding. In some cases, such discussion can resolve a stalemate in therapy or contribute to a more completely integrated sexual identity.

Feelings that the therapist develops about the patient should be explored until the source and reason for the feelings can be identified. In any case, the relationship between therapist and patient should, and typically does, act as a vehicle for therapeutic change and not as an obstacle to the achievement of treatment goals.

Other Sexual Problems

Variations on the major dysfunctions occur that result from genuine inhibition but do not necessarily involve actual impairment of sexual function. These include genital psychoanesthesia (lack of sensation), a phobic response to specific areas or modes of stimulation, and unusually low levels of libido with no conspicuous malfunction of the sexual response. In general, sexual problems of this sort can be managed by a combination of psychotherapy and in vivo desensitization. A significant subcategory of sexual problems, however, is not derived from inhibition, fear, or anxiety and involves no actual dysfunction; these problems stem from and reflect a seriously destructive interpersonal situation. The sexual problem in these cases is usually the result of a marital power struggle, in which sex is used as a source of leverage. In cases where the couple can acknowledge only that a sexual problem exists, beginning therapy with the behavioral recommendation of simple, mutually pleasurable tasks is frequently the quickest and most effective way to expose the interpersonal conflict. Resistance usually appears almost immediately in these cases; one partner may, for example, express more discomfort than an innocent pleasurizing session seems to warrant. Many individuals within this type of relationship need some form of external, empirical validation of its destructiveness before they can acknowledge to each other the real issues underlying their sexual problem. A shift to a more appropriate set of therapeutic objectives is thus facilitated by providing the couple with an opportunity to act out and discuss the power struggle in a safe, therapeutic forum. With its strong experiential emphasis, sex therapy provides an opportunity for direct interpersonal confrontation that other forms of marital therapy do not.

Sex therapy is a short-term, behaviorally based psychotherapy for the treatment of psychosocial sexual dysfunction. It operates to enhance and maximize the existing level of sexual competence and simultaneously to eliminate the negative contingencies previously undermining sexual function. Therapy is usually terminated on the basis of two indicators: (1) when relief from the sexual symptom has been achieved and full sexual function restored or achieved anew and (2) when sexual attitudes and expectations have been restructured to reflect and complement this change. In other words, individuals are ready to stop treatment not just when they can function sexually but when they know they can function.

A final word should be said regarding sex therapy and its inherent limitations. That it is a particularly effective therapy is not in doubt; outcome figures confirm the favorable claims made on behalf of its behavioral-psychotherapeutic approach. Although it can rebuild and restructure a sexual relationship, however, it cannot supply the other key ingredient in an enduring human union—love. Some couples may develop an intensely satisfying sexual relationship within a loveless marriage; in other couples, severe sexual dysfunction may exist with love, warmth, and generosity. It is not always the case that love and sexual compatibility coexist, or that the presence of one is automatic assurance of the other.

References

Kaplan, H. S. 1974. *The new sex therapy: active treatment of sexual dysfunctions*. New York: Brunner/Mazel.

Masters, W. H., and V. E. Johnson. 1966. *Human sexual response*. Boston: Little, Brown.

—— 1970. *Human sexual inadequacy*. Boston: Little, Brown.

Wolpe, J. 1958. *Psychotherapy by reciprocal inhibition*. Stanford, Cal.: Stanford University Press.

Recommended Reading

Hartman, W. E., and M. A. Fithian. 1972. *Treatment of sexual dysfunction: a bio-psycho-social approach*. Long Beach, Cal.: Center for Marital and Sexual Studies.

Kaplan, H. S. 1975. *The illustrated manual of sex therapy*. New York: Quadrangle Press.

Kaplan, H. S., C. J. Sager, and H. A. Lear, eds. *Journal of Sex and Marital Therapy*.

Kinsey, A. C., W. B. Pomeroy, and C. E. Martin. 1948. *Sexual behavior in the human male*. Philadelphia: Saunders.

Kinsey, A. C., W. B. Pomeroy, C. E. Martin, and P. H. Gebhard. 1953. *Sexual behavior in the human female*. Philadelphia: Saunders.

Medical aspects of human sexuality. New York: Hospital Publications.

Sexual medicine today. Insert, *Med. Trib.*

Electroconvulsive Therapy

CHAPTER 21

Carl Salzman

T HE USE of electrical shock as a healing procedure is not new to man. Bioelectric discharges from torpedo fish and electric eels were recognized as early as 2750 B.C., and in A.D. 46 Scribonius Largus introduced the electrical powers of the torpedo fish into clinical medicine as a cure for headache and gout. Electric fish served as the source of curative bioelectricity until 1745, when the Leyden jar, an early collector and condenser of electricity, was invented.

Modern electroconvulsive therapy is derived from the use of chemically induced seizures as a curative process. Weikardt, in 1798, used camphor to produce epileptic convulsions as a treatment for mental illness. During the nineteenth century, electricity was used to treat all forms of disordered behavior, as well as hysteria, melancholia, and neurasthenia. Toward the end of the century, electrodes were often applied to the head, although the convulsions that sometimes ensued were considered undesirable complications.

Early in the twentieth century, Sakel introduced insulin and von Meduna used pentylenetetrazol (Metrazol) to produce seizures as a treatment for schizophrenia. These workers believed,

as did many psychiatrists at the turn of the century, that epilepsy and schizophrenia could not coexist in the same body; schizophrenia could be cured, therefore, by driving it out with medically induced therapeutic seizures. The use of electricity rather than chemicals to produce seizures as a treatment for schizophrenia was introduced by Cerletti and Bini in Rome in 1938.

Although clinical improvement in some patients with schizophrenia was noted, early electroconvulsive therapy (ECT) tended to produce fractures of the dorsal spine because of violent muscle contractions of the back during the seizures. In addition, the treatments terrified patients. The synthesis of succinylcholine in 1941, however, made it possible to modify the strength of the peripheral seizure activity, thus reducing the probability of fracture. About the same time, general anesthesia began to be used with succinylcholine, and this refinement effectively eliminated patients' terror. It soon became apparent that only central nervous system (CNS) seizure activity, and not peripheral systems seizure, was necessary for the clinical effect of ECT. Atropine, 0.6 mg to 1 mg, was introduced as an additional pretreatment medication to block the marked vagal stimulating properties of ECT in order to avoid potentially serious cardiac complications.

During the early years, ECT produced equivocal results as a treatment for schizophrenia. As experience with this procedure grew, however, it became clear that ECT was an extremely useful treatment for affective illness, particularly severe depression. With the introduction of antipsychotic drugs during the 1950s and 1960s, ECT declined as a treatment for schizophrenia but remained an effective treatment for depression. Today ECT is used primarily in treating severe affective illness. Although ECT is effective in treating catatonic excitement and states, its efficacy in treating other symptoms of schizophrenia is still under investigation.

Prior to 1957, one electrode was routinely placed over each temporal area of the scalp. During the late 1940s and early 1950s, effects of ECT on different cortical lobes were studied by the application of electrodes to other parts of the scalp. When electrodes were applied only over the nondominant temporal hemisphere, ECT produced less postseizure confusion and memory loss. Furthermore, recent evidence suggests that such unilateral electrode placement to the nondominant hemisphere produces a therapeutic response equivalent to bilaterally administered ECT.

Today ECT usually consists of the application of a unilateral stimulus to the nondominant temporal scalp of a patient who has received pretreatment atropine, succinylcholine, and a general anesthetic. The seizure induced lasts between 5 and 20 seconds, with a brief postictal state. Within 15 to 60 minutes, the patient is able to resume activity and, in some cases, return to work. The most frequent immediate side effect is a headache, which responds to aspirin, and occasional muscle aches from the succinylcholine. Memory loss and confusion are proportional to the number and frequency of the treatments and are described more fully later in this chapter.

Recently a procedure known as multiple-monitored ECT has been described in which the patient is given several ECTs monitored by electroencephalogram (EEG) in one session, during which peripheral seizures are completely blocked with large succinylcholine doses (Abrams, 1974). In some centers, this technique is being used with increased frequency (Blachly, 1976).

Effects of ECT

The passage through brain tissue of an electric current of sufficient strength to induce a seizure is an event of considerable somatic significance. The transient neurochemical, neurophysiological, cardiovascular, and endocrinological alterations that may result from ECT are listed below.

Neurological
1. immediate loss of consciousness
2. loss of superficial and deep tendon reflexes
3. flattening of EEG activity followed by slow waves with a gradual return to normal; reappearance of alpha waves when consciousness is regained; resumption of an approximately normal state in most cases within 5 to 30 minutes after the last seizure, the frontal regions resuming normal rhythm more slowly than other regions
4. postictal automatisms and involuntary movements in some cases
5. no discernible correlation among clinical improvement, degree of mental confusion, and changes in brain metabolism or blood flow

Neuropathological
1. increase in blood-brain barrier permeability, and capillary leakage in the central nervous system
2. increase in spinal fluid nucleic acids, nucleases, and deaminases
3. increased extracellular brain fluid, decreased electrolyte concentration, and cerebral edema with distention of perivascular space (all changes transitory)
4. no proven cellular destruction
5. moderate cerebral oxygen drop and very marked cerebral blood flow decrease immediately post-ECT
6. decrease in total brain norepinephrine with an increase in neuronal discharge onto receptor sites; increased synthesis and therefore (presumably) increased utilization of norepinephrine
7. increased dopamine and serotonin turnover

Cardiovascular
1. brief asystole with application of current
2. bradycardia during the tonic phase, tachycardia in the clonic, and arrythmias of several minutes' duration in the postconvulsive period; tachycardia from 120 to 150 per minute
3. brief blood pressure decrease during the early tonic phase followed by marked rises (about 50 mm Hg) above the control level during the late tonic phase and throughout the clonic phase (blood pressure rise increased by atropine)
4. blood pressure effects independent of the peripheral convulsion and centrally stimulated

Endocrine and autonomic nervous system
1. increase of 75 percent in plasma epinephrine levels immediately after the seizure, subsiding in about 10 minutes; rise of about 40 percent in plasma norepinephrine concentration with a slower decline to normal
2. uniform rise in plasma 17-hydroxycorticosteroid levels and eosinopenia
3. water retention
4. menstrual cessation or irregularities in some women
5. transitory increases in plasma glucose and plasma protein; sodium, potassium, and chloride; calcium and phosphorus; cholesterol and free fatty acids; blood urea nitrogen (BUN) and nonprotein nitrogen (NPN); carbon dioxide; uric acid; lymphocytes and neutrophils

Sleep and REM time
1. decreased but not completely absent rapid eye movement (REM) sleep
2. decrease in number of eye movements in REM sleep, presumably indicating a change by ECT in the pontine reticular system

No direct information is available regarding the production of permanent brain damage following ECT. Anatomical studies have been inconclusive. Recent evidence (Essman, 1974) suggests that ECT inhibits RNA synthesis in the brain, although other work suggests no detectable or marked changes in protein concentration in rat brains following ECT.

Two recent studies (Goldman, Gomer, and Templer, 1972; Templer, Ruff, and Armstrong, 1973), however, provide inferential data suggesting that ECT causes permanent functional brain damage. In each study, chronic schizophrenic patients who had forty or more ECT treatments over the course of their lives were matched with schizophrenic patients who had experienced no ECT. The ECT-treated patients showed significantly inferior performance on the Bender-Gestalt perceptual-motor performance task. These results suggested the possibility of permanent brain damage, although the presence of preexisting organic disease in this group of chronic schizophrenic patients could not be ruled out.

Psychiatric Syndromes Indicating ECT

A variety of psychiatric symptoms has been reported to respond to ECT; specific indications for its use include severe affective disorders, particularly psychotic depression, and catatonic schizophrenic states.

Affective Disorders: Depression

Severe depression is the primary indication for ECT. Recurrent unipolar depressions, the depression of bipolar affective illness, involutional depressions, postpartum depressions, and severe depressions of later life all respond well to ECT. Among the depressive symptoms that predict a good response to ECT are early morning awakening, anorexia and weight loss, constipation, decreased sexual urges and functioning, low self-esteem, feelings of worthlessness, a sense of helplessness and hopelessness, preoccupation with guilt, thoughts or acts of self-destruction, and delusions of somatic dysfunction. The vegetative signs of depression, insomnia and anorexia, are often the first to respond to ECT, before a change in mood occurs. Improved grooming and social behavior follow as the depressive mood begins to lift; feelings of helplessness, hopelessness, and worthlessness diminish, and suicidal preoccupation disappears.

Among severe depressives, at least two types customarily respond well to ECT. One is the motorically retarded, mute, anergic, and withdrawn patient; the other is the patient who is agitated or who obsessively ruminates over guilt. Patients whose depression is of psychotic proportions, with delusions of somatic dysfunction (the erroneous conviction that part of the body is absent, diseased, or malfunctioning), or with delusions of persecution based on overwhelming guilt and need for punishment, also respond well to ECT. Mild depressions that accompany the frustrations, losses, and disappointments of everyday life are *not* indications for ECT.

Since the introduction of antidepressant medications, several research studies have appeared comparing ECT with drugs in the treatment of severe depression. In one study, for example, 76 percent of patients with depression who received ECT showed a marked improvement, and another 16 percent showed a mild or moderate improvement (Greenblatt, Grosser, and Wechsler, 1964). These improvements were substantially higher than those for tricyclic or monoamine oxidase inhibitor antidepressants, and higher than those for placebo. In differentiating various depressions according to diagnosis, depressed patients with manic-depressive disease or with involutional psychotic reactions who received ECT showed 78-percent and 85-percent marked improvement rates, respectively; these rates were much higher than the improvement rate with drug treatments or with placebo. ECT was less successful than other treatments, including placebo, for psychoneurotic depressive reactions.

Clinical observers have noted the high relapse rate among depressed patients who are treated with ECT (Seager and Bird, 1962). Whether this is due to the recurrent nature of the illness or to the transient therapeutic effect of ECT is uncertain. Nevertheless, these observations have prompted research utilizing antidepressant drugs in combination with ECT to prevent relapse. In the few such studies published to date, imipramine and amitriptyline have been found useful in reducing the relapse rate, although the drugs have not improved the therapeutic outcome of ECT (Abrams, 1975).

In summary, ECT is clearly indicated for the severely depressed patient. It has been found to be the most effective treatment, particularly if the patient is psychotic, and may in fact be life-saving by decreasing suicidal preoccupation or by relieving the serious physical consequences of the vegetative components of depression. Again, ECT should not be considered for neurotic or reactive depressions, or for mood fluctuations of normal daily life.

Affective Disorders: Mania

ECT has been clinically observed to control hyperexcitable states that result from a variety of causes, such as mania, catatonic excitement, and agitated depressions. Although now supplanted by lithium, ECT is occasionally used to control the hypermotility of manic patients during the early phase of drug therapy, before clinically effective blood levels of lithium are attained. The combined use of lithium and ECT is not contraindicated if renal and cardiac functions are adequate.

Schizophrenia

ECT as a treatment for schizophrenia is more controversial than its use in affective illnesses. Prior to the development of antipsychotic drugs, convulsive therapies including ECT were among the primary treatments for schizophrenia. In patients suffering from acute psychotic turmoil and in younger patients experiencing their first episode of psychosis, ECT was found to terminate or diminish the psychotic symptoms rapidly; patients who exhibited either catatonic excitement or catatonic stupor also responded particularly well to ECT. Patients who had been schizophrenic for many years, however, rarely responded.

In a review of clinical efforts (Alexander, 1944), 83 percent of schizophrenic patients were reported to be "successfully" treated with ECT. However, ECT-treated schizophrenic patients observed over several years required more readmissions than patients not treated with ECT. Unfortunately, none of the research used control groups, defined diagnostic criteria, or described outcome measures. Other reviewers have concluded that ECT, like other treatments, is useful in any "good prognosis" case, but that the overall efficacy of ECT in schizophrenia is doubtful.

With the introduction of phenothiazine derivatives in the 1950s and 1960s, ECT treatment of schizophrenia declined. Early comparative studies suggested that chlorpromazine and ECT produced equivalent remission rates, although the drug-treated patients remained fewer days in the hospital (Langsley, Enterline, and Hickerson, 1951); patient preference was clearly in favor of chlorpromazine. As newer antipsychotic compounds were introduced and research and clinical observations regarding their efficacy increased, the role of ECT in schizophrenia diminished. Most clinical experience began to suggest that ECT was not the primary treatment modality for schizophrenia, except for catatonic excitements and stupors.

Recently, however, a carefully controlled study of the treatment of schizophrenic patients judged to be treatable (May, 1968), utilizing a variety of treatment modalities including pharmacotherapy, psychotherapy, ECT, and milieu therapy, has reported the following results: antipsychotic drugs produced the greatest diminution of psychotic symptoms; ECT produced better results than psychotherapy without drugs and a more effective outcome than milieu therapy alone. Drugs with or without psychotherapy were thus found to be the best treatment, and the study concluded that "ECT cannot be considered to be desirable as an alternative or serious rival to ataraxic drugs alone or to psychotherapy plus drugs" (p. 267). In a five-year follow-up of patients in this study, however, ECT-treated patients had, as a group, fewer hospital readmissions than did the patients who received any other treatment. The authors concluded that ECT was equal to or better than drug treatment for the patients in this study (May and Tuma, 1976).

Subsequent reports have supported the therapeutic efficacy of ECT in combination with antipsychotic medications (Weinstein and Fischer, 1971; Turek, 1973). Although combination of treatments appears to be a successful regimen for schizophrenic symptoms and is more efficacious than either treatment alone, more carefully controlled studies are necessary in order to replicate these observations.

In summary, the literature describing ECT for the treatment of schizophrenic symptoms is con-troversial. There is consensus, however, that ECT is very useful in catatonic syndromes and not very useful in chronic schizophrenia. Further controlled research and clinical observations are needed to ascertain whether or not ECT is useful for the large group of young, acute schizophrenic patients. Most authors agree that an occasional patient who has not done well on other therapies may show marked improvement following ECT, although no theoretical explanation for such results is available.

Other Syndromes

ECT, like many other treatment procedures, has been used with some success in a wide variety of psychopathological and medical conditions, including asthma, chronic tension states, anorexia nervosa, characterological anxiety states, toxic psychosis, obsessive-compulsive syndromes, pellagra-associated akinesias, psychoses that sometimes accompany general paresis, thalamic pain, and trigeminal neuralgia. Some clinicians have used ECT for psychiatric patients whose overt behavior was erroneously thought to be masking a depression. Alcoholism and drug addictions, in particular, have been treated with ECT using this rationale. Reports of these uses are clinical and anecdotal; at this time, controlled empirical studies supporting such uses of ECT do not exist. A single case study suggests that ECT may be therapeutic in the resolution of pathological grief reactions and does not interfere with the psychotherapeutic work of mourning (Lynn and Racy, 1969).

Again, most of these treatment successes have been isolated cases or small-sample clinical observations, obtained under noncontrol conditions. The data are therefore insufficient to support a general statement regarding the usefulness of ECT in patients suffering from these conditions.

Syndromes Contraindicating ECT

Psychiatric Contraindications

Patients with character disorders do not tend to improve with ECT. Borderline personality disorders, pseudoneurotic schizophrenia, and sociopathic personality disorders also do poorly. Hysterical symptoms, anxiety reactions, and obsessive-compulsive symptoms are not alleviated by ECT, and in some cases they may worsen. Addictions, sexual deviations, and perversions also remain unaffected by the treatment.

Medical Contraindications and Risks

Although modern ECT may be safely administered to a wide variety of patients, specific physical contraindications for its use must be kept in mind. Since ECT transiently elevates cerebrospinal fluid pressure, any space-occupying lesion or preexisting increased intracranial pressure is an absolute contraindication for ECT. A recent myocardial infarction also precludes ECT, since arrythmias may occur during the seizure and may precipitate another infarction. When the electrocardiogram and cardiac enzymes stabilize, ECT may be administered, but with caution. Vertebral osteoporosis or healed vertebral fractures are not absolute contraindications for ECT, but particular care must be taken to ensure adequate muscle relaxation so that the seizure will not exacerbate existing spinal pathology.

General anesthesia risks apply to patients treated with modified ECT. When a patient has a barbiturate allergy, or a personal or family history of acute intermittent porphyria, intravenous diazepam may be substituted for succinylcholine as an anesthetic. Some patients may have an absence or relative deficiency of serum pseudocholinesterase secondary to liver disease, malnutrition, or congenital deficiency. Since this enzyme hydrolyzes succinylcholine, its absence necessitates the use of a different muscle relaxant.

Previous exposure to anticholinesterase agents, such as the organophosphorus inhibitor echothiophate (used to control glaucoma), can also lower serum pseudocholinesterase levels. Under such circumstances, use of succinylcholine is contraindicated until adequate serum pseudocholinesterase levels can be attained.

Memory Loss and Unilateral ECT

Bitemporal ECT produces an anterograde and retrograde amnesia that usually becomes apparent after three to four treatments and that increases with the number and frequency of ECT treatments. Anterograde amnesia is characterized by an inability to acquire new information (particularly proper names) and starts from the time the procedure is begun. Retrograde memory loss also starts from the time of the first ECT treatment and often encompasses recent events of the patient's life, including the precipitating events which led the patient to seek treatment. In such cases, the patient may leave ECT not understanding the reason for the treatments or hospitalization. Although parts of the memory loss are occasionally permanent, most patients find that their memory and the ability to acquire new information return in 4 to 6 weeks if they have had between 5 and 15 treatments in a series. Patients who receive larger series of ECT may have greater residual memory loss. After the conclusion of an ECT series, some patients do not remember details of their hospitalization, although they fully remember events before and after the ECT series. In contrast, other patients are able to function at work on the same day that they have had an ECT treatment. Memory loss that includes areas of psychological conflict may also be observed. It is unclear whether such memory loss is due solely to ECT or partly to conflict repression.

Theoretically, the amnesia produced by ECT is due to the passage of electricity near or through the dominant temporal lobe. Empirical observations beginning in the 1940s have suggested that memory loss is diminished if the electroconvulsive stimulus is applied to the nondominant (usually right) temporal surface of the scalp. Although there has been consensus regarding the decrease in memory loss when unilateral treatment is compared with bilateral, the clinical efficacy of the two types of treatment has been the subject of considerable debate. Recent reviews of the literature and controlled clinical studies (Fleminger et al., 1970; Stromgren, 1973) have concluded that in severe endogenous depression, unilateral nondominant treatment is as efficient as bilateral treatments.

Theories of ECT

Although ECT has been a psychiatric treatment since 1938, it has remained solely an "empirical" procedure, that is, the causes of its efficacy are incompletely understood. Clinical work as well as placebo-controlled studies (MacDonald et al., 1966) provide abundant evidence indicating the necessity for a cortical seizure to occur in order to obtain a therapeutic response. Peripheral clonic seizure movements have been found unnecessary; placebo ECT (the entire procedure minus the cortical convulsion) has likewise been found to produce no therapeutic effect. In a recent review of ECT theories, Miller (1968) concludes that the experimental data regarding this procedure are so poor that more careful exploration of factors upon which ECT effect depends must be undertaken.

Several psychoanalytic theories exist explaining the efficacy of ECT. Some suggest that the procedure provides an "age regression" to infantile developmental stages and that as the patient recovers from this regression, corrective growth results. Others have posited that the patient's felt need to expiate unconscious guilt leads to the fantasy or interpretation of ECT as punitive atonement; with the ECT procedure as the enactment of punishment for past sins (real or imagined), guilt is thus assuaged and, in this view, provides the basis for improvement. Some psychological theories, particularly learning theories, trace the efficacy of ECT to the therapeutic effect of amnesia for precipitating traumatic events, a line of thought resembling the repression model. Others consider ECT an "aversive stimulus" for the extinction of maladaptive behaviors.

A recent group of neurobiologically oriented researchers entertain the hypothesis that ECT, in some manner, alters amine metabolism in the central nervous system. Many workers have found an increase in serotonin levels following ECT. Other observers have noted a decrease in norepinephrine immediately following a single ECT treatment (although an increase in norepinephrine and its metabolites has been observed after a series of treatments as well). In any case, this evidence suggests a persistent increase in norepinephrine turnover. Increased dopamine levels have also been observed following ECT. According to Kety (1974), the increase in CNS amines presumably promotes synaptic activity beneficial to affectively ill patients. Among the various theories that attempt to account for the efficacy of ECT, the biochemical amine hypotheses seem most plausible, since alterations in catecholamine function are increasingly thought to influence affective illness.

Ethical Considerations

It is axiomatic that treating physicians should prescribe ECT only for valid clinical reasons and should use the minimum number of treatments necessary for therapeutic effect. Nevertheless, serious ethical questions have recently been raised about ECT as a mode of psychiatric treatment. Most of these concerns involve the potential for severe neurological damage that may follow treatment and the concern that whatever clinical benefit is derived may be far outweighed by such an attendant hazard.

Recent concern has also been voiced regarding the use of ECT as an instrument of political or social repression. Those who see government- or state-supported psychiatric institutions as agents of a repressive society are not likely to be persuaded that the calming effect of ECT in the hyperexcited or violent patient is being used for therapeutic purposes only.

Discussions of the potential abuse of ECT crystallize around the patient's right to refuse ECT. Although few would argue with a patient's right to refuse any treatment, psychiatrists may feel an ethical dilemma when confronted with a protesting patient whose life is at risk and whose refusal of ECT stems from the delusions of a psychotic depression. The patient's right to be treated with ECT must therefore also be considered. Since ECT has demonstrated efficacy in severe depression and may even be lifesaving in some circumstances, how can the treating physician ethically withhold the treatment? It has been suggested (Beresford, 1971) that since ECT is a proven effective and relatively safe procedure, patients involuntarily hospitalized for psychotic depressions might contend that the hospital was negligent in omitting it as a medically indicated and effective treatment.

Difficult ethical dilemmas are also associated with providing sufficient information to satisfy informed-consent requirements to a patient who wishes to give permission for ECT, and considerable debate has ensued as to how much information about ECT leads to truly informed consent. Is it ethical to provide information that may frighten a patient who would respond to the treatment and whose condition will, in all likelihood, worsen if it remains untreated? Psychiatrists also have the responsibility to inform the patient of the hazards of a severe depression that cannot be treated by any other means.

An even more difficult question involves the capacity of a severely ill patient to absorb enough information to be "informed" at all about ECT, regardless of the amount of information offered. To varying degrees, psychotically depressed patients may be incapable of fully appreciating what they are being told, and may be equally incapable of making an appropriate decision on the basis of such information.

In addition to these concerns about the use of ECT, questions have been raised within the psychiatric profession, as well as by the lay public, regarding the injudicious use of ECT. Examples of such misuse include conferring of affective disorder diagnoses to qualify otherwise inappropriate patients for ECT. Its use in children and adolescents is similarly not a standard clinical procedure and must not be done routinely. There is concern about the use of more than the standard number of ECT treatments in a series, that is, more than 12 to 20. Massachusetts, for example, has passed a law to limit the number of ECT treatments in a 12-month period to 35 in an effort to eliminate overuse.

It is necessary, therefore, to enunciate clearly the legitimate principles of ECT administration. As a clinical procedure, ECT is of considerable use in the treatment of affective illness, particularly severe depression. It also may offer symptomatic relief in certain life-threatening conditions such as suicidal preoccupation, hyperexcitable states, and fulminating catatonia. For patients suffering severe physiological sequelae of an affective illness, such as anorexia or prolonged insomnia, the symptomatic relief may also be lifesaving. There is, of course, no legitimate use of ECT for people who choose to voice opposition to established political or social authority. ECT should be given only as a voluntary procedure, with informed consent as determined by acceptable medical or legal guidelines. When increased risks are anticipated due to concurrent medical pathology, the patient must be informed of such risks. The potential for memory loss must be dis-

cussed with the patient in advance, although it is reasonable to reassure the patient that memory loss is transient in most cases. If a nonvoluntary or protesting patient must be treated, it should be only as a lifesaving procedure and only with the approval of the local court; the patient must be represented by independent counsel at any court hearing involving ECT.

It is more difficult to establish the correct number of ECT treatments to be administered for particular clinical conditions. The usual range of treatments does not exceed 20, although in rare instances, more may be required. For patients whose condition may require more than the standard number of treatments, an evaluation by a psychiatrist from another institution should be made. Children and adolescents should have an independent evaluation by a board-certified child psychiatrist before any ECT can be administered.

If the overuse and misuse of ECT can be eliminated full attention can then be directed to clinical research and its results, as well as to some of the more complex ethical problems that accompany legitimate ECT use. It is hoped that increased cooperation among medical and legal professionals in the fields of clinical psychiatry, research, and civil liberties, together with all other concerned citizens, will lead to more effective guidelines for the protection of patients' rights and health.

References

Abrams, R. 1974. Multiple ECT: what have we learned? In *Psychobiology of convulsive therapy*, ed. M. Fink, S. S. Kety, J. McGaugh, and T. A. Williams. Washington, D.C.: Winston.

—— 1975. ECT and psychotropic drugs. In *Rational psychopharmacotherapy and the right to treatment*, ed. F. J. Ayd, Jr. Baltimore: Ayd Medical Communications.

Alexander, G. H. 1944. "Shock" therapies: a method of more accurate estimation of their therapeutic efficacy. *J. Nerv. Ment. Dis.* 99:992–924.

Beresford, H. R. 1971. Legal issues relating to electroconvulsive therapy. *Arch. Gen. Psychiatry* 25:100–102.

Blachly, P. H. 1976. New developments in electroconvulsive therapy. *Dis. Nerv. Syst.* 37:356–358.

Essman, W. B. 1974. Effects of electroconvulsive shock on cerebral protein synthesis. In *Psychobi-*

ology of convulsive therapy, ed. M. Fink, S. S. Kety, J. McGaugh, and T. A. Williams. Washington, D.C.: Winston.

Fleminger, J. J., D. J. Horne, N. P. U. Nair, and P. N. Nott. 1970. Differential effect of unilateral and bilateral ECT. *Am. J. Psychiatry* 127:430–436.

Goldman, H., F. E. Gomer, and D. I. Templer. 1972. Long-term effects of electroconvulsive therapy upon memory and perceptual motor performance. *J. Clin. Psychol.* 28:32–34.

Greenblatt, M., G. H. Grosser, and H. Wechsler. 1964. Differential response of hospitalized depressed patients to somatic therapy. *Am. J. Psychiatry* 116:935–943.

Kety, S. S. 1974. Biochemical and neurochemical effects of electroconvulsive shock. In *Psychobiology of convulsive therapy*, ed. M. Fink, S. S. Kety, J. McGaugh, and T. A. Williams. Washington, D.C.: Winston.

Langsley, D. G., J. D. Enterline, and G. X. Hickerson. 1951. A comparison of chlorpromazine and ECT in treatment of acute schizophrenic and manic patients. *Arch. Neurol. Psychiatry* 81:384–391.

Lynn, E. J., and J. Racy. 1969. Resolution of pathological grief after electroconvulsive therapy. *J. Nerv. Ment. Dis.* 148:165–169.

MacDonald, I. M., M. Perkins, G. Marjerrison, and M. Podilsky. 1966. A controlled comparison of amitryptyline and electroconvulsive therapy in the treatment of depression. *Am. J. Psychiatry* 122:1427–31.

May, P. R. A. 1968. *Treatment of schizophrenia*. New York: Science House.

May, P. R. A., and A. H. Tuma. 1976. A follow-up study of the results of treatment of schizophrenia: hospital stay and readmission. In *Evaluation of psychological therapies*, ed. R. L. Spitzer and D. F. Klein. Baltimore: Johns Hopkins University Press.

Miller, E. 1968. Psychological theories of ECT. *Int. J. Psychiatry* 5:154–165.

Murillo, L. G., and J. E. Exner. 1973. The effects of regressive ECT with process schizophrenics. *Am. J. Psychiatry* 130:269–272.

Salzman, C., R. I. Shader, D. A. Scott, and W. Binstock. 1970. Interviewer anger and patient dropout in walk-in clinic. *Compr. Psychiatry* 11:267–273.

Seager, C. P., and R. L. Bird. 1962. Imipramine with electrical treatment in depression—a controlled trial. *J. Ment. Sci.* 108:704–707.

Stromgren, L. S. 1973. Unilateral versus bilateral electroconvulsive therapy. *Acta Psychiatr. Scand.* 240:5–65.

Templer, D. I., C. F. Ruff, and G. Armstrong. 1973. Cognitive functioning and degree of psychosis in schizophrenics given many electroconvulsive treatments. *Br. J. Psychiatry* 123:441–443.

Turek, I. S. 1973. Combined use of ECT and psychotropic drugs: antidepressive and antipsychotics. *Compr. Psychiatry* 14:495–502.

Weinstein, M. R., and A. Fischer. 1971. Combined treatment with ECT and antipsychotic drugs in schizophrenia. *Dis. Nerv. Syst.* 32:801–809.

Recommended Reading

Holmberg, G. 1963. Biological aspects of electroconvulsive therapy. *Int. Rev. Neurobiol.* 5:389–412.

Kalinowsky, L. B., and P. H. Hoch. 1961. *Somatic treatment in psychiatry*. New York: Grune & Stratton.

Salzman, C. 1975. Electroconvulsive therapy. In *A manual of psychiatric therapeutics: practical psychopharmacology and psychiatry*, ed. R.I. Shader. Boston: Little, Brown.

Sanford, J. L. 1966. Electric and convulsive treatments in psychiatry. *Dis. Nerv. Syst.* 27:333–337.

Squire, L. R. 1975. Memory functions six to nine months after electroconvulsive therapy. *Arch. Gen. Psychiatry* 32:1557–64.

A Note on Psychosurgery / T. Corwin Fleming

O PERATIONS on the human brain designed to treat mental illness began in 1956 when Moniz described the results of cutting the prefrontal tracts in a series of patients. Various operations on the frontal lobes were subse- quently performed, including cortical undercutting, cortex removal, and fiber cutting under direct vision or blindly through the orbits. These operations were carried out on thousands of mentally ill patients of all descriptions, and two general problems soon arose. First, undesirable immediate side effects occurred—confusion, apathy, incontinence, and loss of inhibition—as well as delayed sequelae such as seizures, personality changes, and loss of intellect. These problems could be minimized by cutting only the inferomedial fibers in the frontal lobes and by using more selective techniques such as radioactive-isotope implantation or radiofrequency lesions. Alternatively, lesions were made in other areas of the part of the brain that is thought to be involved with emotion—the limbic lobe. Thus, operations on the cingulum, cingulate gyrus, and substantia inominata were said to have effects similar to the original prefrontal lobotomy. It is not clear, however, that any one surgical site or technique is superior to others. In general, current surgical techniques are claimed to have largely eliminated deleterious side effects.

The second problem that arose during the early days of psychosurgery was that not all patients obtained relief from their mental illness. It gradually became clear that one symptom that predicted a favorable clinical response was a feeling of "tortured self-concern." Diagnostically, patients who were chronically depressed or suffered from an obsessive-compulsive neurosis responded best to the procedure. Another factor contributing to a good outcome was the ability of the patient's family to participate in his rehabilitation after discharge. Unfavorable prognostic factors were hysteria, thought disorder, sociopathic behavior, and organic brain syndrome. Youth, lack of temporary response to prior treatment, and chronic illness were also considered to be adverse prognostic factors.

Today patients who are selected for psychosurgery generally have disabling mental illness, have had adequate trials of all other treatment modalities, and have a poor prognosis for spontaneous recovery. The results of surgery with modern techniques on such selected cases vary with the series but, in general, more than 50 percent of patients show a major improvement and few are made worse by the procedure. Those patients who fail to respond may improve after a second, more extensive operation.

At the present time, psychosurgery is performed infrequently in the United States; most current work is being carried out in England. One of the many reasons for this situation is the lack of controlled prospective studies demonstrating the efficacy and safety of psychosurgery. It has been suggested that the most feasible way to evaluate the procedure is to undertake such operations in a research setting where effort is made to set up a control population. It is premature to eliminate psychosurgery totally without this further research.

Recommended Reading

Freeman, W., and J. W. Watts. 1950. *Psychosurgery*. Springfield, Ill.: Thomas.

Greenblatt, M., F. Arnot, and H. C. Solomon. 1950. *Studies in lobotomy*. New York: Grune & Stratton.

Moniz, E. 1956. How I succeeded in performing the prefrontal lobotomy. In *The great physiodynamic therapies in psychiatry*, ed. A. M. Sackler. New York: Hoeber-Harper.

Sweet, W. H. 1973. Treatment of medically intractable mental disease by limited frontal leucotomy—justifiable? *N. Engl. J. Med.* 289:1117–25.

Tucker, W. I. 1966. Indications for modified leukotomy. *Lahey Clin. Found. Bull.* 15:131–139.

Patient Management

CHAPTER 22

Peter E. Sifneos

T HIS CHAPTER focuses on the management of the psychiatric patient, with special emphasis on psychiatric emergencies and the concept of psychological crisis. When a crisis is viewed as a point along a continuum of mental processes, both the factors responsible for the development of the crisis and the formation of patient symptoms are elucidated. Knowledge of the events precipitating the emergency thus facilitates patient management, enabling the clinician to steer a course through the emergency.

Psychological Crisis and Symptom Formation

A psychological crisis is a painful internal state that occurs when an individual attempts to cope with stressful environmental or internal stimuli. It may be a positive or a negative turning point, depending on the effectiveness of the individual's psychological resources and adaptive mechanisms.

Any undesirable internal or environmental situation may evoke stress in a patient. The death of a loved one—probably the most serious environmental hazard—and other losses such as the end of a relationship, the loss of a job, financial failure, or medical illness may result in a crisis. When these situations produce maladaptive reactions, they cause temporary incapacitation. In addition to these obviously difficult events, seemingly minor problems that create little discomfort for one person may have serious consequences for another.

The mechanisms used to deal with stressful events determine the outcome of a psychological crisis. If the individual adapts, he usually overcomes the crisis and may even attain a more effective level of psychological functioning. If, on the other hand, his mechanisms are maladaptive, his anxiety may increase, and his need to alleviate the anxiety becomes imperative. At this point, he may develop symptoms or behavior patterns that temporarily stabilize the situation. Although symptom formation may establish a new equilibrium, the resulting level of functioning is far from optimal. Thus one can view psychiatric symptom formation as a compromise between the pressures exerted on the individual by outside forces and the maladaptive reactions or defense mechanisms the patient utilizes to deal with them. This process results in a restriction of the patient's freedom to act. When symptoms fail to stabilize the situation quickly, the crisis intensifies, the patient calls upon further reactions to manage it, and increasingly serious symptoms usually appear, resulting in a further general restriction of the patient's freedom and often creating a psychiatric emergency.

The Psychiatric Evaluation

The *sine qua non* for the proper management of the patient in a psychological crisis is a careful evaluation (see chapter 2, "History and Mental Status"). Thus before taking specific action to help the patient return to a state of emotional equilibrium, the doctor asks two fundamental questions during the initial interview: what is the etiology of the patient's problem, and what kind of intervention best suits his particular needs—that is, does the patient have sufficient ego strength to withstand a probing psychotherapeutic approach, or are his needs best served by a supportive approach?

Determination of the appropriate approach to treatment depends on the useful (though admittedly oversimplified) separation of patients into two major categories: those who possess and those who lack sufficient ego resources (Sifneos, 1967). The first category comprises individuals suffering from mild neurotic difficulties with circumscribed symptoms and interpersonal disturbances of limited severity, as in the following example:

After graduating from college, a twenty-three-year-old woman returned to live with her parents while she looked for a job. She became anxious and experienced an intensification of her anxiety (a psychological crisis) after an argument with her mother. An intelligent and independent young woman who had been a good student and had several close friends, she interacted easily with the interviewer, expressing great interest in understanding the nature of her difficulties. During the evaluation she discovered that her anxiety resulted from persistent fantasies concerning her mother's death. She associated these fantasies with a wish to live alone with her father, whose favorite she had always been and with whom she had had an unusually close relationship as a child. After a few therapeutic sessions her anxiety subsided, and the conflicts that precipitated the crisis were less intense.

This patient, like other articulate, flexible, and psychologically sophisticated patients, responded well to short-term dynamic psychotherapy aimed at resolving the conflicts underlying the immediate psychological crisis. In certain situations, patients with similar strengths suffer from monosymptomatic phobias that can be treated rapidly and successfully by behavioral techniques (see chapter 19, "Behavior Therapy and Behavioral Psychotherapy") or by hypnosis.

The second category of patients—those who lack ego resources—comprises severely neurotic, borderline, or psychotic patients whose psychological assets are restricted as a result of genetic, biological, or early developmental disturbances. Both their symptoms and their interpersonal difficulties seriously incapacitate them, and they deal with their crises in a maladaptive way. Some patients suffering from psychosomatic illnesses may also be included in this category.

A passive, dependent, unemployed thirty-two-year-old man who lived with his mother and whose father had died when he was six years old became upset and withdrawn after his mother's death. He had a history of alcoholism and lacked close relationships. The medication prescribed by his family doctor did not help; unable to deal with his crisis, he became depressed, and soon afterwards he contemplated suicide. When examined at the emergency unit of the hospital, he was withdrawn and uncommunicative. He was admitted to the psychiatric unit for further observation and treatment. Because he lacked the capacity to handle his crisis adaptively, he needed hospitalization and long-term therapy.

To determine into which of these two categories a patient most appropriately falls, the psychiatrist must have a clear picture of the patient's psychological development and current psychodynamic functioning. To gain this perspective, he depends on the most reliable tool in his armamentarium—a thorough psychiatric history.

Taking the History

A thorough history (see chapter 2, "History and Mental Status") from infancy to the onset of the present crisis must be based on two principles. The first principle calls for gathering information according to a chronological scheme. Thus the clinician should ask about the patient's earliest memories as well as about the family atmosphere during his early life and the particular forms of interaction with parents and siblings; information about early peer relationships, performance at school, and dealings with teachers and details concerning puberty, adolescence, and educational achievements should be gathered systematically. These historical data will elucidate the circumstances of the patient's adult life, his marriage, his current interpersonal relations and work performance, and the nature of his presenting problem. The therapist may thus observe patterns of behavior that have developed from early childhood, have repeated themselves throughout the patient's life, and interfere with the patient's functioning.

The second principle of history taking calls for the use of both open-ended and forced-choice questions. Open-ended questions may elicit overelaborate descriptions and details that flood the evaluator with irrelevant information and waste valuable interviewing time. Simple yes or no answers, on the other hand, give an impoverished picture of the patient's psychological life. Thus both open-ended and forced-choice questions must be used judiciously by the evaluator to obtain necessary details. The details of the patient's history, when organized according to his psychodynamics and current adaptive mechanisms, will provide a relatively complete picture of his life patterns and will help the therapist formulate a plan for resolving the crisis. Over time, the therapist's clinical experience will refine his selection of appropriate questions with a wide spectrum of patients and situations.

Psychiatric Emergencies

Instances occur when psychiatric symptoms fail to stabilize the crisis situation. At such times, the patient's psychological state may deteriorate rapidly and confront the evaluator with a psychiatric emergency.

The patient experiences the emergency as an unexpected, acutely painful state; he is unable to overcome it and to return to his previous state of emotional equilibrium. The clinician—and not the patient himself or his family or friends—is best able to evaluate the presenting problems and decide whether or not they constitute a psychiatric emergency.

Psychiatric emergencies are characterized by grossly abnormal behavior of four main types: (1) self-destructive behavior; (2) destructive and sometimes homicidal behavior directed toward others (seen in some patients in acute psychotic, paranoid, manic, or depressive states, in certain patients with chronic brain syndromes, and in those in postconvulsive states); (3) severe deliria or intoxications caused by drugs or alcohol; (4) panic states resulting from latent homosexual, hysterical, or hypochondriacal reactions (Wayne, 1966).

These psychiatric emergencies result from the patient's use of maladaptive reactions in a desperate attempt to overcome a deepening psychological crisis and to regain his earlier state of psychological equilibrium. Because such efforts usually fail, the patient becomes enmeshed in a progressively more restrictive psychological net. Under these circumstances, the patient frequently considers an attempt at suicide to be the only action open to him.

The Suicidal Patient

Because it occurs so frequently, attempted suicide has been discussed extensively not only by psychiatrists (see chapter 28, "Treating the Person Confronting Death") but also by internists, sociologists, anthropologists, public health officials, lawyers, criminologists, novelists, and philosophers. Although efforts to classify suicidal patients according to specific diagnostic criteria or to differentiate suicide from attempted suicide may be superficially helpful, these efforts add little to our understanding of causal factors underlying suicidal behavior. These factors involve each patient's particular adaptational modes and reactions to extreme psychological stress. In the case of attempted suicide, two additional factors must be kept in mind: first, the patient's conscious and unconscious intentions and, second, the method used in the attempt.

Intent and method are usually closely associated with the patient's immediate, predominating feelings, the events precipitating the attempt, and the patient's psychological conflicts over his wish to live or die. Extensive inquiry into these factors helps the evaluator understand the psychodynamics of the suicide attempt.

Three categories of suicidal patients are defined by the wish to live or die: those in whom wishes for life predominate, those who have ambivalent feelings regarding death and life, and those in whom death wishes predominate. In reference to the latter group, Hendin (1967) believes that patients may view death as retaliatory abandonment, retroflex murder, a reunion, self-punishment, or rebirth; before the suicide attempt some patients feel that they have already died emotionally.

The most common situations creating a crisis concern loss—not only of a loved one but also of property, a job, or health. These experiences, in turn, may arouse morbid feelings of hostility and hopelessness. A particular event can then result in a crushing loss of self-esteem. Unable to cope with such feelings, the patient sees the desperate act of suicide as the only solution. Thus patients suffering from psychotic or neurotic depression and from various psychotic episodes account for the majority of suicide attempts.

Effective management of the patient who threatens or attempts suicide depends on the accurate assessment of suicidal intent. First and foremost, the therapist must establish rapport with the patient and try to understand the various factors involved in the development of the crisis. A severely suicidal or depressed patient should be hospitalized in order to protect him from himself and to see that he receives proper therapy. Despite all precautions, however, a patient strongly determined to kill himself will usually succeed. Communicating to the patient that the therapist takes his threats seriously and is concerned, sympathetic, and genuinely interested may be the first step in helping him overcome his despair and his unwillingness to continue living.

The problems with both actually and potentially suicidal patients are many, and evaluation and treatment of these patients severely test the psychiatrist's skill. Except for patients who have lost contact with reality, each adult human being is responsible for his own life. The therapist who feels omnipotent and believes that the patient cannot survive without him often mismanages the suicidal patient.

The therapist preoccupied with criticism he may receive from his colleagues if his patient attempts suicide may also precipitate a downward course in the patient's illness. First, the therapist's insecurity will be communicated to the patient, who may respond with manipulative behavior, and, second, the therapist may fail to take the calculated risks necessary to reverse the patient's self-destructive patterns. The therapist must take the patient's communications or subtle messages of despair seriously. If, for example, a patient mentions the possibility of suicide casually during an interview and then dismisses the statement as not serious, the therapist should pursue the subject and inquire more closely into the patient's suicidal thoughts; he must explore this subject until he is convinced that the patient has no intention of destroying himself. He must ask, therefore, whether the patient has thought of the method he would use to kill himself. If the patient answers in the affirmative, further information should be obtained. For example, the therapist should ask whether the patient has managed to procure the means to carry out his plan. Does he have barbiturates on hand? How many pills? Does he have a gun? Is it loaded? Such explicit questions can help the psychiatrist evaluate the seriousness of the patient's intent. If he does not do so, the results may be tragic.

A seriously depressed nineteen-year-old college student was admitted to the hospital after attempting suicide. She was an orphan who had spent her childhood with her maternal grandmother, whom she detested. She had recently ended a relationship with a boy friend who had forced her to have sexual intercourse, and she described the experience as painful. To avoid her feelings, she dissociated herself from the sexual act by fantasizing that she was sitting on the sofa watching her boy friend have intercourse with her. The resident in charge of her care soon left for a different service, and the patient was assigned to a new doctor. During the first interview with her new therapist, the patient's depression appeared to have lifted; she described feeling better and asked whether she could be discharged. The new resident agreed and gave her an appointment for an outpatient visit for the following week. She kept this appointment but again appeared to be seriously depressed and asked to be readmitted to the hospital. The resident hesitated because of the shortage of beds. She insisted that she should be readmitted, however, and he reluctantly gave in. At this point she seemed to become suddenly preoccupied and said that she wanted to visit her mother's grave before returning for admission the following day. Smiling vaguely, she added that she needed to obtain a toothbrush and a pair of pajamas before returning to the hospital. The doctor agreed, indicating that a bed would be ready for her the following day. The patient failed to return. She was found hanged in her grandmother's basement.

Sudden changes in mood, sudden decisions, or quick solutions to problems also merit careful attention, for they are often overlooked.

A seventy-two-year-old businessman with a history of several episodes of severe depression became depressed following financial reverses in the stock market. He was treated by a psychiatrist on an outpatient basis twice a week, but his mood remained unchanged. He talked about suicide as a solution for his financial difficulties but reassured the therapist that he would never take such action. The therapist accepted this statement and failed to inquire further about his concrete plans. In the next-to-last interview, the patient looked very depressed, withdrawn, and preoccupied. Alarmed by his appearance, the therapist suggested hospitalization. The patient refused, however, and the therapist did not press him further but made an appointment with him for the following day; the patient promised to return. He did in fact come back, and a marked change seemed to have taken place overnight. He was smiling and said he had worked all night putting his financial affairs in order. He claimed to feel much better and added, "Doctor, it seems as if a big weight had been removed. Now I feel relieved." The therapist, pleased by this apparent change, commented accordingly. The patient smiled as he was leaving and said, "So you think that I am really improving, doctor?" The patient shot himself in his apartment, leaving a note saying that no one had understood the complexity of his problems and that he considered suicide the best way out. The doctor had misunderstood the implication of the "smiling depression" and misinterpreted the patient's statement about straightening out his financial affairs. He had indeed done so, but only in preparation for his death.

Physicians, colleagues, or well-known people admitted as suicidal patients may also present management problems. To accord special privileges to these patients, such as relaxing suicide precautions and permitting them access to potentially lethal tools like razor blades or belts as a way of making their hospital stays more tolerable courts unnecessary risk. The status of a patient must never interfere with sound clinical judgment; once the recommendation for hospitalization or suicide precautions has been made, it must be scrupulously carried out, regardless of the patient's social or professional standing.

Another complication in management may arise from the ingestion of alcohol, which may, in combination with other drugs such as barbiturates, create a lethal mixture for the patient. In addition, whether or not the patient's stomach contains food determines in large measure the immediate management of a suicidal patient who has ingested drugs and may determine whether or not the patient survives.

Some patients attempt suicide in a desperate effort to manipulate people in their environment. "Manipulative suicide" may be effective when the patient succeeds in obtaining everything he wants; it may be effective only for a limited time; it may satisfy the patient but be unrealistic, when success occurs only in the patient's imagination; or, finally, it may be ineffective, when it fails in both reality and fantasy (Sifneos, 1966).

Perhaps more than all other psychiatric emergencies, manipulative suicide taxes the physician's ingenuity and patience. The manipulative patient strives to rearrange the environment in order to continue living as he desires and to achieve his ends by controlling another person. Because suicide manipulators wish for life rather than death, they often give the impression that their attempts are less than serious. When the mode used does not appear particularly lethal, the doctor may dismiss the attempt as a gesture and make no serious effort to investigate it; this failure may prove disastrous. Manipulative intent should be assessed carefully, since the seriousness of the attempt can not be judged merely on the basis of the method used. For example, the use of aspirin may be considered a less than serious method of committing suicide, yet it may cause fatal hemorrhaging in a patient hypersensitive to salicylates. A patient with no intention of dying, who ingests a drug to manipulate another person, may kill himself with an unintentional overdose. Furthermore, if a patient who seriously contemplates suicide takes aspirin and the attempt fails, this attempt may be labeled a gesture. He may then make a second, successful attempt using a different method. The therapist must not assume that a patient is knowledgeable about pharmacology and anatomy or that he knows precisely which drugs or dosages are lethal.

Suicide manipulators are often in a state of great emotional turmoil, with poor judgment and poor impulse control. Failure to admit these patients to the hospital is, in my opinion, a serious mistake. Hospitalization provides the patient with some security against further suicide attempts as well as an opportunity to gain perspective on his manipulative behavior.

Even when hospitalized, however, suicide manipulators prove difficult to manage. They are not usually interested in understanding the psychological factors underlying their attempt but are, rather, "action-oriented"; if their manipulation results in obtaining what they wish from another person, they see little reason to question the meaning of such "successful" behavior. Thus these patients tend to continue their behavior, and subsequent attempts may eventually cause death—particularly if they employ a previously untried method. Manipulation is integral to the character structure of these patients, and they try to manipulate everyone around them, including the psychiatrist. The psychiatrist must therefore make it clear to the patient that he understands these manipulative tendencies, that he considers them destructive, that he will not respond to them, and that he will help the patient to overcome them.

The psychiatrist must also be aware of the negative countertransference feelings that manipulative patients often evoke, as well as the anger they arouse among ward personnel. He must guard against these negative feelings' prompting him to discharge the patient prematurely.

The Assaultive Patient

As a general rule, assaultive patients should be admitted to a hospital with adequate psychiatric facilities (Ewalt, 1967); the protective atmosphere of the hospital provides the ideal environment for their proper management. Because an overwhelming fear usually lies close to the surface of an angry, destructive, or paranoid patient, the therapist must try to ascertain what the patient fears, what motivates his assaultive behavior, and what will win his cooperation.

Answers to these questions, important as they may be, do not necessarily suggest how to handle a dangerous patient. The psychiatrist's behavior during such a critical situation depends to a great extent on his own state of mind. He may understandably feel anxious or fearful. Acknowledging his fears to himself and remaining as calm as possible despite them are paramount to good management of the assaultive patient. Such an attitude will invariably reassure the patient, who often imagines that his destructive urges will terrify the doctor as they have terrified him and others with whom he has had contact. Mechanically restraining such patients may confirm their fears and should therefore be considered only as a last resort.

On occasion, the therapist may react to his own fears by becoming angry and punitive. Although the therapist may deny such feelings, the sensitive patient may perceive what lies behind such denials. This recognition may cause the patient to panic, to become convinced that everyone is lying to him, and to feel trapped. It is usually such situations that provoke an attack upon a doctor, an attack that may cost the doctor his life.

The therapist should consider using physical restraints, however, in managing unpredictable and impulsive patients suffering from acute brain syndrome, "episodic dyscontrol," catatonic excitement, or confusion following an epileptic seizure. If chemical restraints are required, they should be used to sedate the patient quickly. All furnishings except a mattress should be removed from the patient's room. Excessively excitable or manic patients, on the other hand, though hyperactive, can generally be convinced to cooperate without use of physical restraints. They usually respond well to haloperidol for their immediate management and to lithium carbonate for long-term prophylaxis.

The Delirious Patient

The treatment of drug intoxications and delirium tremens due to alcohol withdrawal requires the immediate use of appropriate sedation, with good nursing care. During acute episodes, phenothiazines may be used intramuscularly to calm the patient rapidly. In the case of delirium tremens, many clinicians consider the treatment of choice to be paraldehyde in combination with chlorpromazine several times a day. Morphine is contraindicated, and sedating alcoholic or drug-intoxicated patients with barbiturates may lead to irreversible coma and death. (See chapter 27, "Alcoholism and Drug Dependence.") A delirious patient may wander around and injure himself on a psychiatric ward as well as in an intensive care unit or on a surgical postoperative ward. Every effort should therefore be made to warn ward personnel to observe such patients closely.

Drug intoxication occurs frequently, and the onset of a psychotic episode following the ingestion of LSD, mescaline, bromides, or even alcohol is familiar to psychiatric emergency staff. With recent increases in the consumption of drugs and alcohol by young people, attention should be paid to distinguishing drug intoxication from acute adolescent turmoil and temper tantrums. Before making a diagnosis, the therapist must establish rapport with the young patient, a task that may not be easy because of the mistrust and suspiciousness exhibited by some adolescents toward adults. The tendency of young people to view the doctor as allied with their parents or the police may complicate the situation. Impartiality, firmness, and respect for individual rights, whether the patient is young or old, rational or irrational, are always helpful in bringing a psychiatric emergency under control.

The Acutely Anxious Patient

Acute anxiety or panic states and hysterical or hypochondriacal reactions should also be considered psychiatric emergencies. At times such panic states are associated with acute paranoid episodes, particularly in the case of latent homosexual patients. Individuals living in close quarters—in college dormitories, camps, or Army barracks—who harbor latent homosexual wishes may, as a result of casual comments concerning their appearance or a friendly pat on the back, suddenly develop acute anxiety, indistinguishable at times from a psychotic break. Similar occurrences in hypochondriacal individuals

may result from a minor sickness or a casual remark by a physician that convinces the patient he is seriously or incurably ill. Acute anxiety may also complicate hysterical reactions and be expressed in a variety of symptoms. The principles of management delineated for psychiatric emergencies in general apply to the panic states as well.

Management Guidelines for Psychiatric Emergencies

Psychiatric emergencies may occur in an outpatient clinic, an office setting, or an inpatient facility and present a variety of problems that require particular management procedures.

Obtaining an adequate history. Although an understandable temptation exists to deal with a psychiatric emergency by taking immediate action, the therapist must make every effort to resist doing so until he has full knowledge of the factors responsible for the crisis. Insufficient knowledge, regardless of the urgency of the situation, may create difficulties.

It may be difficult for the evaluator to obtain necessary information from a secretive, suspicious, or negativistic patient. If, for example, the therapist is told of an assault by the patient on a member of the patient's family, he cannot disregard such information, even if the patient refuses to talk about it. On the other hand, to accept as fact what may be mere fantasy will interfere irreparably with the establishment of the therapist-patient relationship. If a clear picture of the difficulties does not emerge, and if all attempts to collect pertinent information from the patient fail, the clinician must rely on the patient's mental status; the judicious use of tranquilizers or antidepressants may help mollify the patient and eventually to clarify the situation.

A twenty-nine-year-old woman, brought to the hospital by two older sisters who claimed that she had always been suspicious, had recently complained that people were trying to kill her; the day she came to the emergency floor of the hospital, she had accused one sister of putting rat poison in her soup and had then attacked the sister with a knife. The patient complained of being chronically tired and agreed to being hospitalized for "a rest" but vehemently denied her sisters' accusations. While on the ward she refused to talk and became reclusive and progressively more irritable. After all efforts at obtaining information had been exhausted and her diagnostic picture remained unclear, she was placed on chlorpromazine to help establish the diagnosis. A few days later she appeared more relaxed and volunteered that she was feeling better. Soon afterwards, she stated that she no longer heard voices accusing her sisters of being agents of the devil who were going to torture her and poison her food. The medication had helped to bring into the open her psychotic thought processes, thus confirming her sisters' story.

On the other hand, less disturbed exhibitionistic or hysterical patients may be given medication too precipitately. Reducing their anxiety may interfere with their motivation to understand their difficulties and lead to their leaving the hospital against medical advice.

Hospitalizing the patient. On occasion, the doctor may be forced to stand firm with a patient who refuses to be hospitalized. The patient's refusal and his vehement objections often signify an attempt to deny his wishes to be taken care of. If the psychiatrist is firm in presenting his decision to hospitalize the patient in order to provide him with protection and treatment, the patient will usually agree with a sigh of relief, despite previous protestations.

Anticipating impulsive behavior. At times a highly anxious patient may insult or threaten to assault ward personnel. Serious complications may result if staff members respond to such challenges. With potentially assaultive patients, the therapist should avoid direct confrontation and strive to obtain cooperation by persuasive means. He should take care to avoid laying hands on or even touching a potentially explosive and impulsive catatonic, paranoid, or panicky latent homosexual patient. Failure to anticipate impulsive acting out by such patients may result in destructive behavior that could otherwise have been avoided.

Diagnosing medical illness. Problems may arise when the physical complaints of a hypochondriacal patient are lightly dismissed. The clinician should take care to rule out the existence of medical illness. For example, the electrical activity of the brain in patients suffering from episodic dyscontrol, a syndrome of periodic violent or unpredictable assaults, should always be examined. At times such patients have lesions of the temporal lobe, the limbic system, or other parts of the brain and may be treated successfully with appropriate medication.

Because violent behavior arises from a variety of factors—including the absence of a drug to which the patient is addicted, encephalitis, or a psychotic illness—failure to diagnose the underlying cause will result in inappropriate management. On occasion, physical illnesses such as encephalitis, meningitis, or brain tumors may be obscured by heavy alcohol intake or the ingestion of drugs, thereby complicating the diagnosis.

A muscular, six-foot, 200-pound, thirty-five-year-old truck driver suffering from meningitis was brought to the emergency ward in a state of acute intoxication. He appeared cooperative during his physical examination, but, when a consulting neurologist decided to perform a lumbar puncture, the patient became suspicious and hostile. When forced to submit to this procedure, he exploded. He raved, threatened the doctor, and finally wrenched a steel bar from the bed and struck at everything in sight. The lumbar puncture needle was still *in situ* when he was finally subdued and sedated. The next day, after eighteen hours of deep sleep, he was docile and apologetic for his destructive activity, even though he could recall few details of what happened. Once he had recovered from the effects of the alcohol, his meningitis was diagnosed and treated.

Investigating patient fears. Violence may also result from overwhelming fear or from a feeling of being trapped. Thus the therapist should seek to ascertain the cause of the patient's fear and avoid responding to the surface anger. Reassurance aimed at eliminating the fear usually helps calm the patient, whereas questions concerning his angry feelings may confirm for the patient that the therapist, like everyone else, does not really understand him and may reinforce his conviction that his case is hopeless. Such a state of desperation may in turn precipitate an assault or a suicide attempt.

Being decisive in emergencies. Finally, patients with manipulative tendencies, psychopathic behavior, an excessive tendency to lie, or passive-aggressive features may arouse hostility on the part of the staff, who then may pressure the psychiatrist to set firm limits. The doctor should decide the best course of management and communicate his plan firmly to both the patient and the medical staff. If he vacillates between his own opinion and those of colleagues, he will succeed in giving double messages, which invariably create difficulties with the patient and the ward staff.

Evaluation of Masked Dependency Needs

The discussion of patient management thus far has emphasized particular techniques for meeting psychiatric emergencies. Crucial decisions, however, must also be made in the management of less seriously disturbed patients, and guidelines set forth concerning their care.

Patients with hysterical character traits (see chapter 10, "Psychoneurotic Disorders," and chapter 14, "Personality Disorders"), for example, may create serious problems in management and treatment. Although these traits occur in both sexes, they occur most frequently in women, often in women of unusual physical attractiveness. Such patients tend to sexualize relationships and to be provocative in their dress, speech, and gestures. Usually, however, they harbor a deep-seated fear of close physical contact and have had a lifelong history of seriously disturbed interpersonal relationships. Their lack of sexual gratification often leads to extremely vivid fantasies that may, in turn, lead them to fabricate events and to have false convictions about the motives of others. Their highly suggestible, overly dramatic, and easily excitable behavior is characterized by excessive dependence and attention-seeking gestures. Dramatic outbursts and seductive behavior thus usually express dependency needs rather than sexual needs.

The early history of these patients often includes the loss of a parent through death or desertion, leaving them feeling lonely and unloved. As children they developed coquettish mannerisms and temper tantrums in a desperate attempt to please or to gain attention. These early experiences relate directly to the overwhelming need for attention and affection these patients manifest in adult life.

Hysterical patients prove difficult to manage because of their tendency to be provocative toward ward personnel and therapists. If the therapist fails to recognize the intense dependency needs beneath the patient's provocative speech and behavior and focuses solely on its sexual content, he may precipitate panic and destructive acting out in the patient. In addition, he will encourage a cycle wherein the patient gains attention but feels that it has been given only because of her physical attractiveness. This perception, in turn, leads to feelings of emptiness and depression, to a need for increased attention, and to further exhibitionism—a continuing, frustrating cycle of sexual acting out followed by unmet dependency needs and despair.

Treatment of these patients can prove as difficult as their management on a ward, and an impasse in therapy may warrant transfer to another therapist. A therapist of the same sex may prove helpful. Although such a therapeutic alliance may reveal covert homosexual longings, unresolved maternal conflicts more often emerge.

A twenty-two-year-old woman was admitted to the hospital, after drinking heavily, with the complaint that she had been abducted by a group of men who had assaulted her sexually. Although she described this as a terrifying experience, she appeared to be aloof and indifferent to what had happened to her. An only child, she had been strongly attached to her father, an alcoholic who died when she was seven. She described her mother as cold and distant and her life as a child and an adult as devoid of close friendships. After graduation from high school, she worked intermittently as a secretary and a model and, during the years immediately prior to her hospitalization, started to drink excessively. During sessions with her therapist in the hospital, she spoke of exciting, "fantastic" episodes in her life. Her dress and behavior tended to be sexually provocative, and when the therapist attempted to discuss reasons for this behavior, she strove to please him by describing a number of sexual escapades in great detail. Her behavior, however, not only failed to improve but actually deteriorated. She began to have pseudo-fainting spells, falling to the floor where she would be readily observed, picked up, and carried back to her room. During a ward conference, a decision was made to transfer her to a female therapist who was advised to treat her firmly, to avoid discussing sexual behavior, and to focus on the patient's dependent, ambivalent feelings toward her mother. The ward personnel were instructed to refrain from picking her up when she "fainted" and to allow her to recover. The female therapist's firm but sympathetic attitude effected rapid change; the patient's exhibitionistic behavior ceased, and her preoccupation with sexual escapades changed to concern with more relevant issues. Later she admitted that she had not been raped and had, in fact, never experienced sexual intercourse. She volunteered that ever since her father's death she had disliked and mistrusted men. Her therapy progressed smoothly from then on.

Crisis Intervention and Brief Psychotherapy

Many psychiatrists still believe that psychotherapeutic techniques of short duration are either second-best to long-term psychotherapy or unnecessary. Convincing evidence, however, indicates that short-term psychotherapeutic interventions are often appropriate (Adler and Myerson, 1973; Malan, 1975, 1976a, 1976b; Mann, 1973); they are the treatment of choice for certain well-integrated patients with circumscribed but nonetheless incapacitating difficulties (see chapter 17, "The Psychotherapies").

The therapist cannot often apply the technical principles used in long-term psychotherapy to short-term treatment. Many therapists, for example, adhere rigidly to the general rule of avoiding the patient's transference feelings in long-term therapy unless they appear as resistance during the psychotherapeutic session. In short-term therapy, the opposite holds true; failure to utilize transference feelings, which are often predominant during the early phase of short-term therapy, may prolong treatment unnecessarily. On the other hand, the therapist should be mindful that the explicitness and depth appropriate in the investigation of transference issues differs according to the severity of different patients' illness. With more seriously disturbed patients, the primary aim is support;

with less seriously disturbed patients, insight and understanding of psychological conflicts (Sifneos, 1972).

With relatively healthy neurotic patients, the therapist's support and advice is only minimally beneficial and often contraindicated; it may give the patient the impression that his therapist has failed to understand him and considers him sicker than he really is. Such an attitude may convince the patient to stop psychotherapy or to look for a new therapist.

Short-term psychotherapy and crisis intervention both focus on a specific, acute issue or problem. Investigation of long-standing, pregenital characterological conflicts, such as dependency needs or passive tendencies, may confuse the aims of this approach and prolong treatment. Failure to terminate therapy when the immediate issue has been solved may also cause problems. Termination should be discussed openly with the patient, but time need not usually be spent dealing with the patient's feelings of loss, as in long-term psychotherapy with patients suffering from more severe conflicts.

Thus diagnostic distinctions must be made in considering what type of psychotherapeutic intervention is indicated for various types of patients. Short-term therapy is primarily indicated for basically healthy individuals, while longer-term psychotherapy or other interventions are appropriate for individuals with long-standing, severe conflicts. The proper match-up of therapeutic approach and patient group thus requires particular attention to the characteristics and requirements of each.

Psychological crises arise when patients are unable to cope with internal or external stress. In managing such patients—whether or not a psychiatric emergency exists—the clinician must attempt to understand the factors leading to the crisis by establishing rapport, even with a seriously disturbed or dangerous patient, and by obtaining a careful history of the development of the patient's psychological difficulties. This understanding, combined with an awareness of the genetic and psychodynamic aspects of the patient's conflicts, forms the basis for determining appropriate treatment and proper management for the psychiatric patient.

References

Adler, G., and P. G. Myerson. 1973. *Confrontation in psychotherapy*. New York: Science House.

Ewalt, J. R. 1967. Other psychiatric emergencies. In *Comprehensive textbook of psychiatry*, ed. A. M. Freedman and H. I. Kaplan. Baltimore: Williams & Wilkins.

Hendin, H. 1967. Suicide. In *Comprehensive textbook of psychiatry*, ed. A. M. Freedman and H. I. Kaplan. Baltimore: Williams & Wilkins.

Malan, D. H. 1975. *A study of brief psychotherapy*. New York: Plenum.

—— 1976a. *The frontier of brief psychotherapy*. New York: Plenum.

—— 1976b. *Toward the validation of dynamic psychotherapy*. New York: Plenum.

Mann, J. 1973. *Time-limited psychotherapy*. Cambridge, Mass.: Harvard University Press.

Sifneos, P. E. 1966. Manipulative suicide. *Psychiatr. Q.* 40:523–537.

—— 1967. Two different kinds of psychotherapy of short duration. *Am. J. Psychiatry* 123, no. 9:1069–75.

—— 1972. *Short-term psychotherapy and emotional crisis*. Cambridge, Mass.: Harvard University Press.

Wayne, G. J. 1966. The psychiatric emergency: an overview. In *Emergency psychiatry and brief therapy*, ed. G. J. Wayne and R. R. Koegler. *Int. Psychiatry Clin.* 3, no. 4:3–8. Boston: Little, Brown.

Special Populations

The Child

CHAPTER 23

Elinor Weeks
John E. Mack

P SYCHIATRIC ATTENTION to children in America started in the courts in the 1890s with concern for juvenile delinquents and gradually expanded to meet the needs of other children. The early history of psychiatric services to children reflects their orientation toward the delinquent. At the turn of the century, judges in Colorado and Illinois encouraged the development of psychiatric services in juvenile court clinics to investigate antisocial acts. Illinois set up the first juvenile court in 1899, and in 1909 William Healy opened the Chicago Juvenile Psychopathic Clinic. Healy deemphasized heredity, organ impairment, and neurological deficit as causes of juvenile delinquency. The Judge Baker Foundation in Boston, named for Judge Harvey H. Baker, opened in 1917 to study the psychiatric problems of juvenile delinquency.

Prior to the twentieth century, care for children generally meant institutional care. During the nineteenth century, institutions for children needing care for various reasons sprang up. Girls were often sent to industrial schools and boys to military schools; the more serious offenders were sent to state institutions. In 1863 Massachusetts established the first Board of Charities and Corrections (Department of Public Welfare) with responsibility for "dependent, defective, and delinquent children." By 1897, similar agencies existed in sixteen states.

At the beginning of the twentieth century, services for children began to proliferate and their scope and direction to widen. Between 1910 and 1920 foster homes, probation officers, and special classes in public schools were established, each with a different role in relation to children. The federal Children's Bureau, established in 1912, encouraged legislation in maternal and child health programs, aid to dependent children, and child welfare services.

Beginning in the 1920s the child guidance clinics extended psychiatric services to children other than delinquents, pioneering in the early multidisciplinary use of social work, child psychiatry, criminology, education, and psychology to diagnose and treat emotionally disturbed children. Through this approach, the combined influences of family, school, and neighborhood in the life of the child were considered. Douglas A. Thom established the Habit Clinic in Boston in 1921; by 1931, there were 232 child guidance and habit clinics in America.

Child psychiatry in the 1920s, influenced by Anna Freud's application of psychoanalytic theory to child psychopathology and the use of play therapy, moved toward becoming a distinct field. Although Sigmund Freud concentrated on adult pathology and did not have children in his clinical practice, he nevertheless laid the groundwork for the development of child psychiatry in his emphasis on the crucial nature of childhood experience in the emotional lives of both children and adults.

Child psychiatric services now include diagnostic, therapeutic, and emergency interventions offered privately and through clinics and comprehensive mental health centers. Various infant, child, and adolescent services are provided through guidance and court clinics, in general and psychiatric hospitals, in schools, and in other community agencies. Infants often receive help through child development projects that work with the mother-infant pair; preschoolers, through programs for the emotionally disturbed; and school-age children, through psychiatric centers and consultation to schools, private psychotherapy, and, occasionally, psychoanalysis. As the field of child psychiatry has matured, additional modalities such as family therapy and behavior therapy have been introduced (see chapter 17, "The Psychotherapies," and chapter 19, "Behavior Therapy and Behavioral Psychotherapy").

Normal Child Development

The developmental timetable of the human infant and child is more extended than that of other species. The newborn's reflex systems permit, at a brainstem level, automatic functions such as breathing, sucking, swallowing, circulation, and temperature regulation. Although recent research and observations in the field of child development demonstrate that infants vary in individual temperament, sleep and waking cycles, and demand feeding schedules, the mother-infant dyad remains essential for the child's emotional development. Infants cry when hungry, soiled, or uncomfortable, and the mother often interprets the nuances of their cries. The child without consistent mothering (that is, the long-term availability of a specific person or persons and relatively uniform patterns of responsiveness in that person) may become severely withdrawn (anaclitic depression)

and even die (Spitz and Wolf, 1946). Infants in all societies are totally dependent during the first months of life on the mother or a maternal substitute for feeding, changing after soiling, clothing, protection, and loving. Children can survive physically without the care of one specific person, but prolonged deprivation of consistent mothering in infancy results in impaired emotional development in which later human relationships suffer.

In the discussion of childhood development that follows, reference to comments about mothering are more frequent than references to fathering because the majority of studies of parenting to date concern the mother rather than the father. The father's importance both as a caring parent and as a responsible person who serves the child as a model for identification should not, however, be underestimated.

The mother-infant relationship begins during the prenatal period, and just as the mother's physical well-being affects the growth of the fetus, her attitudes toward the unborn child may well affect her later relationship with the infant. The successful delivery of a breathing, reacting infant is a significant psychological experience for both parents, and the parents of an unhealthy or physically defective baby may feel deeply troubled. As a result of a mother's anxiety and disappointment, she may react to such an infant with extremes of overprotection or rejection.

Continuous change and growth are fundamental characteristics of child development. From conception to adulthood, major changes occur in the body, in relationships within and outside the family, in language and cognitive development, in adaptation and control of aggression, in sexuality, and in the capacity to understand and live with one's feelings in relationship to external reality. If a child fails to receive physical comfort, love, and attention during infancy, he may be hampered in motor abilities, verbal skills, and interpersonal relationships.

Theories of Development

Concepts derived from psychoanalysis so pervade modern child psychiatry that their origins are not always readily apparent. Child psychoanalysts have described the normal developmental sequences that occur in sexuality, aggression, reality testing, conscience formation, and aspects of ego functioning. In 1936, in *The Ego and the Mechanisms of Defense*, Anna Freud described the normal psychological defensive modes by which children cope with the outside world. These defenses, when inappropriately mobilized, may hamper the individual and may themselves contribute to psychopathology. Classical psychoanalysis stresses the roles played by sexuality and aggression in human development and the formation of three basic components of psychic organization—the drive-focused id, the reality-oriented ego, and the conscience-forming superego.

Psychoanalytic theory describes oral, anal, phallic, oedipal, latency, and preadolescent stages of psychosexual development, each period having erotic and aggressive characteristics. The oral stage (birth to 1 year) focuses on the mouth and is a time during which issues of trust and dependency begin to be negotiated. During the anal stage (1 to 3 years), anal sphincter control is learned and separation-individuation and autonomy begin. The sexual organs become the focus of the child's interest in the phallic phase (3 to 5 years), and during these years, which also make up the oedipal period, intense wishes to possess exclusively the parent of the opposite sex and take the place of the parent of the same sex lead to inevitable disappointment and conflicts. During latency (5 to 12 years), the child's interests focus on learning, intellectual development, and the formation of peer relationships; sexuality is largely repressed. Contemporary observations of children indicate that the "going underground" of sexuality and aggression (from which the term *latency* is derived) is less common than was thought in Freud's time, perhaps in part as a result of the greater freedom now allowed children. Preadolescence sees shifts in body growth, anticipated sexuality, and beginning moves toward heterosexuality.

Various later theories of child development, such as those of Melanie Klein and Erik Erikson, are derived from and modify classical psychoanalytic theory. Klein formulated a theory of child development that attributes to children a more accelerated developmental timetable than does classical Freudian theory. In the 1940s the Kleinian and Freudian schools became firmly established in London as rival camps. Erik Erikson's theory of development categorizes behavioral complexes or ego modes that accompany the classical Freudian stages of libido development. His "epigenetic" stages in childhood include basic trust versus basic mistrust (birth to 1 year), autonomy versus shame and doubt (1 to 3 years), initiative versus guilt (3 to 5 years), industry versus inferiority (5 years to adolescence), and identity versus role confusion (adolescence to adulthood). Erikson emphasizes the importance of the individual's attaining a sense of identity to achieve optimal growth and fulfillment with regard to self and others (1959).

Other theorists stress aspects of cognitive development. Jean Piaget in particular has intensively studied the development of the child's perceptual and sensorimotor systems and has described four periods of cognitive growth and development: the sensorimotor period (birth to 2 years), the preoperational period (2 to 7 years), the stage of concrete operations (7 to 11 years), and the stage of formal operations (11 years through adulthood). (See chapter 8, "Theories of Personality," for a fuller discussion of Freudian, Kleinian, Eriksonian, and Piagetian concepts of development.)

Developmental Achievement

Beginning in infancy, the child moves along a continuum of developmental phases or stages, each characterized by certain typical achievements. Parents have reported that the newborn smiles from the first day of life, but the first smile with social, communicative meaning comes within the first two months of life. By the age of 2 months, the infant can use his eyes to focus on nearby things. At 3 months, the baby is social, enjoying the company of other people. Parents may encourage the infant to use his hands by giving him small toys for exploration and may help the child's verbal development by talking and singing.

Motor ability is fundamental to child development. Neurological development of the body contributes to the advancing ability to crawl, sit, and finally walk upright. From 4 to 7 months, an infant with normal brain growth uses his hands to explore the environment through feeling, holding, and dropping items. Children walk with support at 9 to 12 months, then alone at 12 to 15 months of age. The time from the child's use of single words (9 to 18 months) to his use of complete sentences (18 to 24 months) varies with the individual. In the toddler stage (18 to 36 months), a child learns to ambulate with a characteristically unsteady, vigorous gait. The toddler's enhanced motor skills enable him to widen the scope of his explorations of the surrounding environment. From infancy to nursery school age, the child is expected to learn to delay gratification, to separate from his mother, to go to the toilet, to dress himself to some degree, to learn language and to speak, to feed himself, and to have some control over his behavior.

The changes in the child from 1 to 3 years are perhaps the most remarkable in the human life span. By the age of 3 a child usually has mastered the concept of I-you and has developed his basic gender identity—a core sense of being male or female. The 2-year-old insists during the third year on becoming more autonomous, frequently demanding his own way and tolerating poorly any frustration of his wishes. Easy tiring and the inability to tolerate much sharing with others highlight this period. If the parents, who remain central protective figures, do not understand these idiosyncrasies, they may feel anxious, angry, or rejected. The child's normal exploration and curiosity contribute to the high incidence of accidents and ingestions in this age group.

From age 3 to 5, the preschool period, the child gains further bodily mastery and his imaginative play increases. The child uses play and fantasy to explore the outside world, to master its complex demands, and to express his increasingly rich inner life. In play the child tends to explore his identification with the parent of the same sex and often shows a wish to follow in that parent's occupational footsteps.

The child often expresses a wish for exclusive rights to the parent of the opposite sex when both parents are available. It is not unusual to hear a boy in the 3-to-5 age period state that he will marry his mother, or a girl say she will marry her father and receive a baby from him. A child normally resolves this triangular (oedipal) conflict by accepting his failure to obtain the desired parent and by identifying with the parent of the same sex as a role model. Conscience formation and the development of guilt feelings begin during this period.

Preschool-age children experience many terrifying dreams, fears, and transient difficulties in separating from loved ones, especially parents. They often feel omnipotent and magically in control of their environment and can be quite self-centered. Normally, however, a concern for others and an ability to share also begin to develop during this period.

Primary school age is a period of heightened learning, the mastery of many tasks, and the development of work patterns. Positive feelings toward teachers enhance the enjoyment of learning. Close, sustained friendships evolve. The boy often has one or more male friends and usually treats girls as taboo, although social acceptance of heterosexual friendship seems to be increasing among primary-school-age children. The boy may distance himself from the mother, resisting close physical contact like kissing and hugging. The girl often has a single best friend, seeks closeness to her mother to further establish her identity as a female, and is less ambivalent toward boys than they are toward her. Traditionally, girls were seen as mother's helpers who learned from her or from other women about cooking, sewing, and caring for the house. With the influence of the women's liberation movement and other contemporary changes in the status of women, girls have been developing occupational horizons similar to those of boys. It is too early to tell how these cultural shifts will be manifested in child development.

Preadolescent or prepubescent girls often have one specific best girl friend, a love of animals (often horses), and a growing recognition of body changes anticipating womanhood. In preadolescence and early adolescence, boys increasingly identify with masculine figures—fathers, uncles, and grandfathers—in work, play, athletic, and vocational activities.

Loss and Mourning in Childhood

Throughout the course of a child's development, he may be exposed to separation, trauma, illness, and death, and to a variety of strange, anxiety-producing environments and situations. The individual child's capacity to deal with these threats is a function of his age, developmental stage, and ego strength. In facing separation and divorce, the child's constant hope is for reparation and reunion. In experiencing and mourning a death, however, the essential element concerns coping with its finality.

Separation and Divorce

Parental separation, divorce, and abandonment inevitably affect children deeply, resulting in feelings of deprivation, guilt, and loneliness. The child's experience of the loss, especially his perception of his own role in the event, can variously affect self-esteem, future work, and interpersonal relationships and identifications; the impact of the experience depends on the stage of the individual child's development, the nature and degree of contact with the noncustodial parent, and the sensitivity of the parents in listening to and appreciating the child's feelings about the change.

The child psychiatrist may be of service in counseling parents—with or without seeing the child—before, at the time of, or after a separation and divorce so that they can help their child recognize and deal with his feelings of loss and responsibility. If a child reveals distress through spoken and behavioral clues or bodily symptoms, the child psychiatrist may help in evaluating the problem and, if necessary, arrange for appropriate counseling or treatment.

A child's normal relationship to both parents varies at different stages of development. In separation and divorce, the child's feelings toward the parent with whom he remains may be intensified by the absence of the modulating influence of the other parent.

Wallerstein and Kelly (1975) observed thirty-four 2½- to 6-year-old children both at the time of their parents' separation and one year afterward and noted a variety of emotionally disturbed responses to the direct stress of parental separation and divorce. Nearly half of the total sample of preschool children showed developmental deviations within a year after the parents' separation. The 2½- to 3¾-year-olds demonstrated pri-

marily sustained "neediness" and a range of developmental regressions and aggressive difficulties. The disturbances ceased if consistent or substitute parenting was provided. The 3¾- to 4¾-year-old age group experienced symptoms reflecting depression, guilt, and feelings of discontinuity with their environments. The 5- to 6-year-old children showed less vulnerability to developmental problems—perhaps because of the establishment of relationships outside the home. Susceptible girls overromanticized their attachment to their fathers, reflecting unrealistic sexualized and rescue fantasies. Some children demonstrated learning difficulties. The children followed had shown no major emotional problems prior to their parents' separation.

The period from 3 to 6 years is characterized by expressions of antagonism toward the parent of the same sex with unconscious and at times conscious wishes for an exclusive relationship with the parent of the opposite sex. These feelings may be intensified and their expression made more explicit when the child's parents are separated. For example, after a holiday visit with her father, a 5-year-old girl told her mother that she really would prefer to live with him. The mother was devastated until she realized that this feeling toward the father was appropriate for the child's age. In the case of older children, community ties, especially established peer relationships, may be important determinants of the child's preferences and should be considered in making recommendations about where and with whom he should live.

A 9-year-old boy and 12-year-old girl informed their mother—with whom they had had mainly normal developmental struggles—that they would prefer to live with their father, who had remained in their original home community. She felt totally rejected. However, when she realized their need for the geographical continuity of their old home environment and their old friends, she could permit them to move back with their father. The mother accepted the new situation as an alternative in the best interest of her children. She maintained frequent contact and was open to a change in their living situation whenever advisable.

Divorce and separation, although generally upsetting for children, may be less distressing or

may even be welcome when the child has suffered from intense conflicts in the family and believes he will be better off with one of the parents
out of the home. Obvious examples are situations in which one parent has been physically
abusive to the other or to children because of alcoholism, drug abuse, or mental illness.

Discussing the child's concerns realistically
and imparting objective information about divorce can help children to feel less isolated and
lonely. A comment commonly heard from children—"We are divorced"—reflects the identification of many children with the parents' divorced status. The burden of self-blame from
feelings that their wishes or behavior brought
about the separation can be dispelled by appropriate discussion of feelings and factual explanations geared to a child's individual capacity to
understand. The saddest situation occurs when
the child feels and is completely abandoned; "I
have no daddy" is not an uncommon expression.
If the absent parent cannot be available, then
that reality and the child's feelings about it can
be discussed and possibilities sought for the substitution of other persons—relatives, counselors,
or family friends—for the missing parent. Some
children, with help from the available parent and
other adults (including at times a professional),
can grow to understand that they are not the
cause of the parent's absence and even eventually come to appreciate the parents' problems.

Children without knowledge of the truth about
the absent parent may create extraordinary tales
to explain his absence and play out incredible
and exciting reunions and rescue operations.
One early adolescent girl, for example, reported
that her father (whom she had never seen)
would come to the door, whereupon her mother
would "drop dead"; her stepfather and half sister would then cry as she left with her father for a
foreign country in his private plane. Her father,
a foreigner, was in reality totally unavailable to
her, and her longing eventually led her into running away from home and into severely self-
destructive delinquency.

Children with a geographically distant parent
may successfully maintain contact through
letters and occasional visits if consistent and
loving concern and attachment are communicated. It is the parents' responsibility when

the children are young to establish regular times
for visiting. When this cannot be arranged, it
may need to be enforced by the courts.

In child guidance work, helping parents to
focus on their own feelings about their failed
marriage and to appreciate their children's separate existence is essential. Divorced parents vary
in their relationships with one another and in relation to their children from attitudes of complete flexibility and cooperation to such extremes
of antagonism and hostility that communication
becomes possible only through lawyers. Some
parents wish the other parent to be literally banished from the child's life. In extreme cases, in-
terstate and even international kidnapping of
children by the noncustodial parents has occurred. Parents may devalue the other parent in
front of the child or verbally attack the child by
insidious comparison with the hated ex-spouse.
Similarly, frustrated parents may use the threat
that the child will be abandoned to the ex-spouse
as a form of punishment or control. In all these
instances the child psychiatrist or counselor can
be of help in enabling parents to understand the
ways in which they are displacing onto the child
conflicted feelings that derive from the failed
marriage.

If a child is unwanted, if parents married because of a pregnancy or other compelling circumstances, or if a child was conceived to hold
together an incompatible marriage, the child
may later reap accusations from parents for actions over which he had no control. Again, depending on their openness to education, parents
can be helped to see their child's needs rather
than focusing purely on their own. In the following example, the child's confused identity stems
from the mother's denial of his need for accurate
knowledge concerning his paternity.

A 5-year-old boy was seen for reevaluation because of problems with aggression in nursery
school. He had been seen at the age of 2 when
his parents failed to recognize his independent
behavior as developmentally normal. Shortly
after an unsuccessful attempt to complete a diagnostic evaluation at that time, the mother divorced, remarried, and changed her child's sur-
name. The child was not told that his father had
left the area and that his stepfather had adopted
him. At the time of the reevaluation, the boy

wrote his first name and the initial of his adopted name. When asked his name, he replied, "Mark Nobody." The therapist told the mother that she thought her son was confused about his paternity and name. The mother stated she had never sensed his confusion but admitted she had discouraged any discussion of the matter. The therapist advised her to share the truth with the boy about his two fathers.

A stepparent may have real difficulties in dealing with ambivalent feelings about not being the natural parent and in coping with the anger, disappointment, and rivalry shown by many stepchildren. Patience, caring, and consistency on the part of both parents, however, can help the stepparent-child relationship develop into an important and mutually satisfying bond.

The needs and vulnerabilities of the child and the family in circumstances of divorce and separation are critical, complex, and ever-increasing. Greater consideration of these issues in both mental health and legal circles is needed to cope more effectively and humanely with the immediate problems of these situations, as well as to prevent future problems arising from neglectful or insensitive mishandling of the initial wrenching experience.

Death and Mourning

According to Furman (1964), a mature individual's capacity to mourn involves an acceptance of the reality of loss, a perspective of time, the ability to perceive oneself as separate from other people, and the capacity to sustain painful feelings. The anger experienced at the dead person for "deserting" through death is often extremely difficult to accept, especially for those who are intolerant of their own angry or aggressive feelings. It is also important to be at least somewhat comfortable with one's own aggression and able to tolerate aggressive thoughts and feelings without excessive guilt in order to come to terms with the loss of loved persons. In addition, in order to give up the lost person emotionally, the individual needs to be able to transfer affection and love to someone else and to accept love in return (Nagera, 1970).

The development of these capacities begins in childhood. Children may react to the death of significant persons with modes different from the prolonged grief and mourning of adults. Depending upon their stage of emotional development, children may, instead, respond to their underlying distress with anxious, aggressive, regressive, or troubled behavior.

By 1960 profound conceptual differences and considerable confusion had developed in the literature concerning mourning in children. The discrepancies resulted primarily from the interpretation of clinical observations in the light of differing theoretical assumptions, often coupled with a failure to define precisely the ways in which children react to loss and separation at various developmental stages. For Bowlby (1960), "mourning" is possible from 6 months on, and he states that early childhood grief has many parallels in adult mourning. Furman (1964) states that even 2- to 3-year-olds can acknowledge death and should be included in the family sharing of loss experiences and that children at age $3\frac{1}{2}$ to 4 have a capacity for mourning. Anna Freud (1960) feels that true mourning does not occur until the child accepts death as a reality and gives up the lost person. Other theorists believe that mourning in the adult sense does not occur until adolescence, when the child has developed the capacity to detach himself emotionally from the parent.

The needs of a child who has experienced loss differ according to his developmental stage. If an infant loses his mother, a new caretaker is necessary for the maintenance of life and the fulfillment of basic needs. If a substitute mother is provided, the infant will be exposed to new sensory experiences different from those of the mother, even though the child is not yet aware of his separate existence from others. After a child is a year old, he can specifically identify the caretaking or mothering person and experiences severe pain when prolonged separation occurs. Overt affect, however, may not reflect a child's true feelings. Most small children deny that they are troubled or unhappy; even in the 6-to-12 age group, youngsters may behave gleefully or excitedly or become excessively active to mask the expression of sad feelings. Adolescents are capable of understanding death, but even they tend to avoid mourning in the adult sense.

All children search for replacements for loved

persons they have lost and may persist in holding on to magical fantasies of reunion with a person who has died or left in order to avoid feelings of loss. The lack of long periods of manifest grief in children may create misunderstanding in families, especially when children wish soon after a loss to pursue their normal play activities. Parents can help their children to deal with loss through realistic education concerning the realities of death. Anna Freud believes that questions about death can be answered directly when asked even by a young child (Nagera, 1970). It is often easier for the child to come to terms with death if his first encounter with it is not too emotionally charged, as in the case of the death of an animal (especially one other than a treasured pet).

Realistic and judicious sharing of familial, societal, and religious aspects of mourning (services, wakes, burials) can help to reinforce the reality of the loss while simultaneously providing supportive and empathetic experiences within the family and community. Feinberg (1970) points out that family discussions that allow the expression of ideas and feelings about separation, loss, and death can be helpful to children. When loss of a parent or separation due to the child's or parent's hospitalization occurs, consistent caring from familiar adults is important to prevent additional emotional trauma.

Many adults (including professionals) may fail to deal with painful situations that concern children because of their own unresolved feelings regarding death and stigma and the poignant sadness of a child's grief. Some pediatricians, for example, may for these reasons avoid any discussion of feelings toward illness, body disfiguration, or death on a children's cancer ward. Nurses and religious individuals may at times be more able than the physician to listen to and talk with children about death. It is helpful to spell out specifically for children that death and anesthesia are different from sleep. Caring persons may unintentionally precipitate a sleep phobia by telling a child that the dead appear to sleep and that anesthesia is "like sleep."

The value of therapeutic intervention in a time of loss is illustrated in the following case:

In a family of eight children, ranging in age from 4 to 12, the loss of two grandparents oc-

curred during the same period. The paternal grandmother had been ill with terminal cancer for months, and at family meetings the children had asked questions and expressed sadness about her illness. Unexpectedly, the maternal grandfather also became ill during this period and died just twenty-four hours after the grandmother. At a home visit soon after the grandfather's death, the therapist was asked by the oldest child to attend the wakes; the parents had only planned to include the eldest in the funeral proceedings. The therapist recommended that all the children attend both wakes and that the older ones also attend the funerals and burials; the parents agreed to follow this recommendation. After the grandmother's wake, the 4-year-old spoke of the color of her grandmother's dress, several of the older children cried, and one child spoke of missing the grandfather more than the grandmother because he had already had a chance to say good-bye to the grandmother. All of the children and the parents were able to talk with the therapist and among themselves about the varied reactions of people outside of the family, and the therapeutic relationship was strengthened by the therapist's attendance at the wakes. None of the children developed untoward behavioral symptoms following the deaths.

Dislocations of children and separation from parents due to divorce, separation, moves, illness, imprisonment, and death, as well as psychological removal of a parent through alcoholism, illness, drug abuse, or severe emotional illness, are emotionally significant and can be traumatic for children. Children may feel responsible for not having prevented these tragedies and troubles, especially if adults around them have been unable to talk openly and realistically about disturbing or painful changes in the family. With highly emotional matters such as death, sex, and religion, it may be wise for the therapist to gain parental agreement concerning his approach to the material involved. For example, a religious parent may wish to explain death to a child in a fashion quite different from that of someone with other religious, agnostic, or atheistic ideas.

Realistic education of children before they experience the deaths of loved persons and animals and preparation for unavoidable separations due to parents working away from home during the day, a child's hospitalizations, and the experience of beginning school can be helpful to verbal children. All children can be aided by discussions and by caring and loving support at times of stress and increased vulnerability.

The Diagnostic Assessment of the Child and His Family

The purpose of the diagnostic evaluation of a child is to obtain a systematic and comprehensive view of his strengths, vulnerabilities, and psychopathology in order to be able to offer appropriate help. From the beginning, the diagnostic evaluation of a child differs from that of an adult. Parents, siblings, teachers, pediatricians, and court officials most frequently request help for the child. Unlike the adult, the child, except in middle or late adolescence, rarely asks for aid directly. The parents or other guardians usually accompany the child to the clinic or psychiatrist's office.

An individual mental health professional or a multidisciplinary team consisting of members of several professions (social work, teaching, nursing, pediatrics, clinical psychology, and psychiatry) may perform the evaluation and are responsible to the parent or other guardian. Other persons involved in the child's life are often contacted, such as other family members, the school principal, guidance counselors, or probation officers, a practice not usually employed in adult outpatient evaluations. Problems of fire setting, suicidal and homicidal intent, drug abuse, delinquency, and running away are generally shared with the responsible parent or legal guardian when the patient is felt to be in emotional difficulty or jeopardy. Issues related to pregnancy or abortion are not necessarily shared with parents, especially in the case of older adolescents who wish to take responsibility for their own decisions.

Multiple diagnostic sessions are more often required in child psychiatry than in adult work, both to gain the trust of the child and to accumulate the material needed for an assessment of him and his family. The more the parents and the child understand about the diagnostic process, the more smoothly it flows. A family interview in the office or home may give insight into family interactions and psychodynamics. The evaluation may also include a school visit to talk with the teacher and to observe the child in the classroom or on the playground. Parents are interviewed because they are biologically and emotionally connected with the child and are most knowledgeable about the child's life; sharing photograph albums, developmental data from a baby book, health records, school reports, and childhood artwork may provide additional helpful information.

Exclusion from the child's play sessions may increase parental anxiety about the evaluation, and lack of sufficient feedback may cause parents to terminate the diagnostic workup before it is completed. Some diagnosticians find it valuable to report impressions during the course of the evaluation. Others can allay parents' anxiety by explaining that impressions and recommendations will be given at the final conference.

History

A basic requirement of a full diagnostic workup is a complete family portrait encompassing at least three generations. The parents' histories reflect their own childhood experiences and can point to repetitive generational patterns. A family history includes information about the mother, maternal grandparents, and maternal siblings and about the father and his parents and siblings. The mother's history includes her age, health, background, places of residence, religion, original family constellation, schooling, work history, interests, date of marriage, separation, and divorce, contraceptive information (if indicated), hospitalizations, prior psychiatric and social service contacts, and the nature of her relationship with the patient currently and in the past. The father's history is analogous with the addition of military history, which reveals moves and separations. History of alcoholism, drug abuse, or contacts with legal institutions for either or both parents should be included when appropriate. Grandparents may, through their presence, illnesses, and deaths, be highly meaningful persons to children. Data about siblings is also important. Knowledge of siblings' history of psychiatric treatment or contact with mental health personnel, special schooling, and other counseling is also helpful. A description of the home, with a floor plan showing who sleeps where and with whom, is often valuable. Exploration of parental financial history may be pertinent to billing, referral for financial assistance, or the understanding of conflicts in the family over money.

The diagnostician tries to assess from the parents' descriptions what the child was like during the various developmental phases—infancy, toddler, preschool, primary school, and adolescence. He inquires about the mother's pregnancy, labor, and delivery, the neonatal period, and the child's early developmental milestones (walking, talking, toilet training). The purpose of learning about development is twofold: first, to discover if the child has matured normally and, second, to gain knowledge about the child's interactions and relationships with the mother, father, siblings, and other significant figures.

The existence of particular symptoms can be discovered by asking specifically about fears, tics, obsessions, hypochondriasis, head banging, and nightmares. Frequently such symptoms may be mentioned among the initial presenting problems.

Questions focusing on issues of self-control, aggression, passivity, compulsions, and phobias are helpful in learning about the totality of the child's behavior. Information about friends of both sexes, best friends, group relationships in childhood, and evidence of early sexual curiosity and explorations should be obtained, although a parent will often withhold information he considers embarrassing concerning a particular symptom or aspect of the child's development. A history of thumb-sucking, rocking, masturbation, and of the parents' attitudes toward these autoerotic behaviors should be elicited.

A child's avocations, such as sports, collecting, music, dancing, and art, reflect a capacity for enjoyment. Parents or other legal guardians may report observing sadness, happiness, crying, and anger and can also give information about the rarer instances of suicidal acting out, running away, attempts to hurt others, or unusual thoughts or behavior. Questions about the parents' hopes for the child's future may reveal their unconscious wishes toward the child and may clarify puzzling aspects of problems with which the child appears burdened. Questions about schooling include place, age of the child at

various grades, repetitions, academic records, relationships with teachers and peers, and the child's reaction when separated from the home. Whether or not the primary-school-age child, as well as the teen-ager, has been delinquent or has been to court may also be significant.

In taking a medical history from a parent or pediatrician, the diagnostician receives information on sensitive subjects like enuresis (bedwetting), encopresis (fecal retention and soiling), menarche or pregnancy in girls, or the onset of puberty in boys. The interviewer may also wish to inquire about hospitalizations, accidents, allergies, medications, infectious diseases, drug and alcohol use, or the disturbance of any other bodily system that might have psychological or emotional significance.

When questions arise regarding neurological or other organic difficulties, the child is referred to the appropriate specialist. Children are referred to a pediatric neurologist when there is concern about petit mal, other types of seizure, localizing signs, or any findings that may indicate a central nervous system disorder. Occasionally a child with sudden aggressive outbursts or odd behavioral patterns may be suffering from temporal lobe seizures. Children who are hyperkinetic, have perceptual motor problems, or demonstrate marked learning disabilities should routinely have a neurological consultation. A pediatric neurologist conducts the neurological examination, using EEG, scans, and skull X rays as indicated.

Numerous appropriate referrals for help originate with the teacher. Because teachers spend long periods of time with children outside the family matrix, they can have intimate knowledge of a child's cognitive skills, peer relationships, responses to authority, and personality traits. A visit to the school and a conference with the teacher and principal are often illuminating. Frequently teachers also have insights into the family dynamics from years of contact with the child, parents, and siblings. Sometimes the child will demonstrate emotional disturbance in the classroom of which the parents are unaware or which they deny.

Social agencies, such as the local welfare department, adoption agencies, child welfare agencies, hospitals, and summer camps often contribute significant material about a child and his family. Information can often be obtained in writing after a parent has signed a release.

The Examining Interview

In the initial examining interview the child should understand who the interviewer is, and by the end of the first session he should have some idea, in terms he can appreciate, of why he is being seen. Many children are afraid of doctors because they associate them with physical examinations, pills, needles, and other procedures. They may be helped with this anxiety if they are told that the doctor is a "talking doctor" or a "worry doctor." The interviewer should note how the child separated from the parent, the qualities of the relationship established with the interviewer, and the child's range of activity and affective expressions.

Examining tools for younger children, who often tell their stories through play, may include puppets, clay, paints, and crayons. The older child (especially the preadolescent) may prefer to sit and talk. A combination of single questions and simple comments usually aid the flow of the child's communication, and an attitude of open and attentive or even seemingly naive or bewildered curiosity may be helpful in encouraging a child to confide his thoughts. During the sessions the interviewer is aware of the child's use of denial, avoidance, repression, and projection to keep away from troubling subjects and needs to be sensitive to the child's often limited ability to tolerate disturbing feelings. The interviewer should be careful not to threaten a child's precarious self-regard but also needs to feel secure in setting appropriate limits—defining the boundaries of behavior—in the session.

If the child is trusting, able, and willing, good use can often be made of ordinary conversation. Children may be more spontaneous than adults and sometimes share openly their worries and concerns. If a child is shy, verbal techniques to help him feel more comfortable are often helpful. Questions about three wishes a child would choose to have granted or what animal he would most or least like to be are often amusing to him, and the answers are informative to the interviewer.

Unlike adults who use conversation, younger children may communicate their emotional conflicts and feelings only indirectly, through play. Space and materials for play are thus needed in performing the diagnostic evaluation. A play area need not be elaborate. Children may begin by playing alone and then gradually give the examiner an opportunity to join them. The diagnostician tries to enable the child to express his thoughts and feelings with a minimum of leading or imposition of the examiner's own ideas. Sometimes complex, symbolic, and creative, the play may clarify to varying degrees what is troubling the child. Generally all productions (paintings and drawings) are left with the diagnostician as part of the work done together, although the diagnostician may wish in special instances to let the child take something with him.

If a child is unable to play or to talk because of physical or emotional illness, the diagnostician may need to talk to the child without his answering verbally, or talk with a parent who is also present. Children are frequently observed in their own environment—home, school, playground, neighborhood, or, if hospitalized, on the hospital ward.

Psychological testing is a useful tool to help in the diagnosis of organ impairment; to distinguish among neuroses, character disorders, and psychoses; to gain a fuller understanding of personality structure, psychodynamics, inner conflicts, deficits in reality testing, and defensive structure; and to evaluate intellectual achievement. They may also help determine various aspects of ego functioning, as well as degree and quality of perceptual-motor, cognitive, affective, or integrative function. Without testing, a longer time might be expended clinically by a child psychiatrist or psychologist in order to obtain a definitive diagnosis. Many more tests are available and utilized for testing children than for testing adults; they are frequently multipurpose and multifaceted (see chapter 3, "The Clinical Use of Psychological Tests").

Intelligence tests have been challenged in recent years as requiring concepts and vocabulary used more commonly by white, middle-class children, placing children of other racial and socioeconomic backgrounds at a disadvantage. If intelligence tests depend too heavily on the acquired, learned skills of the dominant cultural group, they are likely to underestimate significantly the intellectual endowment or potential of minority group members.

Emotional Disorders of Childhood

Ideally a child matures in an intact, loving family that provides him with adequate care, as well as with teaching and limit setting to deal realistically with the complexities of the outside world. The goal of all childrearing is to help the child develop the capacity to exist independently, to work, to enjoy recreational activities, and to experience satisfying human relationships. Emotional disorders in childhood may result from physical abnormalities, inadequate parenting, or any disturbing relationships or traumatic events that interfere with the development of these capacities.

Central nervous system abnormalities may cause perceptual, sensory, verbal, and motor difficulties. Physical handicaps may interfere with normal ambulation, sphincter control, and exploration of the environment, while physical illnesses may inhibit normal childhood activities in school and at play. Disturbances in parent-child relationships, or other disruptions within the family or in the outer world, may cause emotional disorders of varying duration and severity, depending upon the phase of development and the child's relative success in mastering earlier developmental tasks. Transient psychopathological reactions occur inevitably in response to traumatic events, or in the course of normal development.

A Developmental View of Childhood Psychopathology

Pathology may be conceptualized in a variety of ways. Anna Freud, in *Normality and Pathology in Childhood* (1965), utilized the concept of developmental lines; examples include "from dependency to emotional self-reliance," "toward bodily independence," "from egocentricity to companionship," and "from play to work." These lines are useful in conceptualizing areas of major change from childhood to adulthood, with pathology resulting from failure to negotiate the

transitions among them. Concepts of normality and abnormality may thus be understood in relation to behaviors and achievements expected within given developmental periods.

Infancy period. In early infancy difficulties may be related to congenital physical abnormalities. Neurological diseases may be temporary or, in some instances, chronic or ultimately fatal. The rare cases of infantile autism, failure to thrive, and anaclitic depression may reflect discord in the maternal-infant relationship, but the presence of central nervous system pathology must be looked for carefully.

Problem areas for parents of infants may also occur that are routinely discussed with pediatricians and, if available, child development specialists. Difficulties associated with feeding, waking, soiling, play, and activity may concern parents in the course of their infant's growth and development or as the family adjusts to a major change.

Toddler period. Children who are physically ill between the ages of 1 and 3 may not be able to master the normal developmental tasks of beginning acquisition of speech, ambulation, and toileting. Landmarks of normal speech, social, personal, and motor development have been delineated and may be utilized for comparison purposes when considering normality and abnormality. The eating, sleep, and motor disturbances that occur in early childhood, such as decreased appetite or sleep, restlessness, and refusal to walk, may be transient, persistent, or regressive (that is, demonstrating the loss of developmental accomplishments already mastered). Therapeutic attention in the severe developmental disorders may concentrate on helping the mother and father with basic parenting problems. The parents may be guided in promoting development through the use of appropriate play items, talking with the child, and providing close physical contact. Depressed parents may withdraw from their children with a resulting withdrawal on the part of the children. In these cases, a parent may need help with his own emotional difficulties. The significance of fathers in parenting is receiving increasing attention in mental health and judicial spheres.

Preschool period. The child who develops normally during the preschool years (3 to 6) demonstrates remarkable progress motorically, intellectually, and in speech and sphincter control. Selma Fraiberg (1959) referred to this period as the "magic years" because of the remarkable opening up of the imagination that occurs. Various fears and phobias are also common during this period, but most of them subside with normal maturation and the child's development of a clearer sense of reality. In the United States, most children of preschool age attend nursery school or have some experience playing with other children their own age. Abnormalities observed may include difficulty relating to peers, problems with the management of aggressive impulses, early symptoms of learning disability, accident proneness, childhood forms of depression, and, rarely, psychosis.

The world of the preschool child is still centered on the mother and the father but enlarges to include other family members, the school, the neighborhood, and childhood friends. The 2-year-old's normal refusal to do what others wish may continue abnormally in these years in the form of severe temper tantrums. Problems may be transient and reactive to environmental stresses or more lasting, resulting in fixed defensive and characterological patterns. Psychopathology at this age does not, however, necessarily lead to permanent symptoms or to established disorders in later life. Symptoms may shift. The untreated encopretic child may, for example, stop soiling but develop sexual deviations such as voyeurism or exhibitionism in later life. Interestingly, no correlation has been established between specific emotional disorders in childhood and the development of particular forms of mental illness in later adult life.

One of the first cases in the literature from this age group is the example of the phobic neurosis in a preschool boy (Little Hans) described in Freud's "Analysis of a Phobia in a Five-Year-Old Boy" (1909). The child, reacting to his feelings of jealousy toward his newborn sister and to his father's relationship to his mother, developed a phobia of horses. The horses represented a displacement of his image of his father, from whom he feared punishment for his unacceptable aggressive wishes. Through Freud's guidance, the

father was able to assist the child with his conflicts and help him to recover from his phobia.

School-age period. The school-age child (6 to 12) is involved with his family, school, and friends. The most frequent psychiatric problems during this period occur in learning, school attendance (school phobia with problems separating from home), aggressive acting out (such as fire setting and stealing), and childhood forms of reactive depression over family stresses or events.

Since boys have problems related to aggressive impulses and behavior more frequently than girls during this period, they are more often referred for psychiatric evaluation. Suicidal threats, gestures, and attempts can occur in children as young as 5, but serious suicidal attempts are rare prior to puberty.

Diagnostic Aspects of Childhood Emotional Disorders

The Group for the Advancement of Psychiatry (G.A.P.) report *Psychopathological Disorders of Childhood* (1966), formulated by the Committee on Child Psychiatry, lists ten categories of childhood disturbances and is helpful because of its description of symptoms and its consideration of pathology in relation to concepts of normality and health. Many of the diagnostic terms and descriptions that follow are drawn from this categorization. In addition, other commonly used diagnoses, such as borderline conditions, hyperactivity, depression, learning disabilities, and physical handicaps are also described.

Psychophysiological disorders. In child psychiatric centers, especially those associated with general hospitals, children are often referred for psychiatric evaluation of psychophysiological disorders such as asthma, peptic ulcer, and enuresis, in which hereditary, allergic, and emotional sources of pathology may intertwine. A team approach in which a pediatrician, nurse, social worker, and psychiatrist collaborate in helping to understand the etiology of the symptoms and to alleviate or decrease them has proven to be most useful.

For example, chronic asthmatic children may, in addition to the allergic and infectious components of the illness, have emotional precipitants such as acute stress, disappointments, or loss of family members. Increased bronchoconstriction and occasional cyanosis may occur with emotional stress. Therapeutic interventions include individual psychotherapy and parental and family guidance, together with medical management aimed at symptomatic relief. Children can learn how their thoughts and emotions may relate to their symptoms and thereby gain some capacity to control, minimize, and even prevent attacks.

A particularly close or even smothering mother-child relationship is common in cases of asthma; the mother's difficulty in permitting the child to become independent and autonomous seems to be central to the psychopathology. However, it is not often clear to what extent the form of the mother-child attachment is the result of the child's disorder rather than its cause.

Developmental disorders. Abnormalities in development may arise from a lag in maturation or other deviation. As Rexford and Van Amerongen have noted (1974), difficulties may occur in specific functions or abilities in the motor, speech, sensory, cognitive, social, psychosexual, and affective areas, or they may involve the total integrative capacities of the personality. Several mothers formerly addicted to heroin complained of clinging, swearing, demanding behavior, and temper tantrums persisting since age 2 in their 5-year-old children. These indications of developmental lag or failure to mature were related to familial disorganization that included inconsistent limit setting, numerous moves, multiple parenting situations, and separations from the mother.

Psychoneurotic disorders. Psychoneurotic disorders arise from internal conflicts involving sexual and aggressive impulses that are kept from consciousness by psychological defense mechanisms. Although the conflicts that produce neuroses may originate in the preschool years, the disorder may not be apparent until the primary school period or later. The G.A.P. report on diagnosis in child psychiatry provides seven subdivisions of psychoneurosis. Each of these neuroses has individual characteristics and utilizes mechanisms of defense, summarized by

Anna Freud in 1936 as denial, projection, regression, repression, isolation, introjection, reaction formation, undoing, sublimation, and turning against the self.

Each of the psychoneurotic disorders is related to unconscious conflicts. The anxiety type of psychoneurotic disorder is characterized by diffuse anxiety. A phobia (anxiety hysteria) involves the displacement of elements of unconscious conflict onto external persons, places, animals, and situations. The conversion type (conversion hysteria) is a disorder in which unconscious conflict and symbolization lead to immobilization or other impairment of a particular body part. In dissociative states—another form of hysteria—depersonalization or a sense of separation of the self from its surroundings occurs. In obsessive-compulsive neurosis repetitive, uncontrollable, and sometimes contradictory thoughts and ritualistic acts seem to force themselves upon the sufferer. In adolescents with a depressive type of psychoneurotic disorder, body activities such as sleeping and eating may be disturbed, and feelings of self-deprecation and guilt occur, usually related to unacceptable negative feelings toward a loved person.

Personality disorders. In personality disorders, the patient does not feel conflicted about his troubled or troubling behavior. The G.A.P. report on diagnosis of childhood disorders proposes nine classifications of personality disorders: compulsive, hysterical, anxious, overly dependent, oppositional, overly inhibited, overly independent, isolated, and mistrustful personalities. Subdivisions include the tension-discharge disorders (impulse-ridden and neurotic personality disorders), sociosyntonic personality disorder, and sexual deviation. Personality disorders are often difficult to treat because the child may be unaware of intrapsychic pain, tends to blame others, and denies or is not conscious of responsibility for his difficulties with other people.

Sociopathic and delinquent disorders. The sociopathic and delinquent disorders—really subclasses within the group of personality disorders—are characterized by socially unacceptable behavior, especially poorly controlled aggressive and sexual impulses or self-protective aggressive reactions to various fears. These behavioral disorders reflect conflict between the child and his environment and cause stress for both society and the individual patient. Society is burdened by the child's destructive attacks on persons and property and at the same time is responsible for rehabilitating him. Patients with these disorders act in ways that are to some degree ego-syntonic, and they do not, for that reason, feel guilty or show other signs of internal conflict when they steal, cheat, or commit other antisocial acts.

Proper diagnosis of the underlying pathology determines the selection of the appropriate treatment approach. It is important never to infer the nature of the psychiatric problem from the presenting complaint or symptom alone. For example, a child may be referred for aggressive behavior when the actual problem is an underlying depression.

A school nurse referred a boy, age 8, after she discovered he had attempted to strangle another child. The mother and child were seen immediately. The boy was alert, well oriented, and described how his friend had provoked him by hitting him; he then choked his friend in self-defense, without any wish to hurt him. The patient's father had died of cancer several months prior to the referral and the mother, who was severely depressed, had been unable to tell the children that their father was permanently gone. The family was seen together as a unit and treatment focused on the unresolved grief reaction over the father's death. The depression had made the boy more sensitive to provocation, resulting in his excessive aggressiveness.

Presenting symptoms are often misleading, as seen in the following case.

An adolescent boy, who had been indulged and favored after having febrile seizures and surgery for a congenital urinary tract abnormality in the toddler period, was considered by his family to be retarded and therefore unable to function in a regular school system. Psychological testing, however, distinguished between what had been thought to be retardation and the boy's refusal to apply himself intellectually. Although not in fact retarded, he was preoccupied with fantasies of violence, feared abandonment, and lied to his family and therapist about antisocial sexual acting out. His passivity and

stubbornness, which had been confused with retardation, were linked to his preoccupation with his violent fantasy life; preoccupation with these aggressive fantasies critically hampered his ability to work in school. He also expected others to wait on him, as his parents had done throughout childhood. The boy was treated in a residential setting where the teachers insisted that he complete his work and where he was expected to abide by the residential rules. In psychotherapy he was helped to understand the roots of his violent fantasies, linked to past surgery, and to learn to take responsibility for caring for himself.

During treatment the child or adolescent may experience emotional distress as he becomes less able to ward off painful memories and disappointments and uses defense mechanisms of denial or blaming of others or resorts to impulsive and immediately gratifying activity. The patient is helped to tolerate, appreciate, respect, acknowledge, and live with his feelings and thoughts and to control maladaptive behavior through the resolution of conflicts in therapy and through the help provided by the therapist's empathy, understanding, and example.

Depression in childhood. Depression, in the sense that the term is used to define and describe depressive illness in adult life, is not found in children, although the adult syndrome of early morning waking, weight loss, inability to work, and self-degradation may be seen in late adolescents. Children, however, may nevertheless defend themselves against sadness and feelings of loss. They may manifest a form of depression or reaction to loss by withdrawal, running away, refusal to eat, fears, and generalized unhappiness with complaints of bodily distress. Very young children subject to severe maternal deprivation may at first protest the separation from the mothering person but then become apathetic and show decreased interest in sporadic substitute caretakers. If the deprivation is protracted, immobility and even death may result, a syndrome Spitz and Wolf (1946) term *anaclitic depression.* Older children may have delinquent or other behavior problems, psychosomatic reactions, or poor achievement in school when depression is an underlying problem. The depressed child, rather than crying or expressing sadness directly, may act out other feeling states, such as destructive anger, sullenness, or even a kind of tense cheerfulness.

An 8-year-old boy with a severe cyanotic congenital cardiac abnormality requiring multiple cardiac operations faced still another surgical procedure but denied his fear of the surgery. In his violent play, however, every doll and animal was injured or died in accidents. In psychotherapy sessions prior to surgery, the therapist helped him master his fear by symbolically repairing the injuries he had inflicted in play. The therapist realistically discussed with him the approaching surgery, which also helped allay his fears.

A number of child therapists have noted how often aggressive behavior is used to cover underlying feelings of sadness.

The mother of an 8-year-old boy complained of his aggressive outbursts at home. In a diagnostic play session, he let a rubber rhinoceros break into a store without knocking and also spoke of missing his father, whom his mother said was away in the Army. The mother had not revealed to her social worker, therapist, or son that the father was in prison for breaking and entering, although the boy's play revealed unconscious suspicion if not knowledge of the actual events. Treatment included having the mother tell her son the truth about his father's criminal activity. This information contributed to the cessation of the boy's aggressive outbursts and to his recognition and expression of his sad feelings, particularly those related to missing his father.

Psychotic disorders. The psychotic child fails to test reality appropriately, manifests bizarre behavior, has severe disturbances in human relationships, and shows developmental deviations and impairment in such basic ego functions as thinking and impulse control. A psychotic disorder may include symptoms of withdrawal or extreme apathy, preoccupation with fantasy, disordered thought processes, speech disturbance, extreme anxiety, worries about the body with distorted perception of the body image, severe fears, and suicidal and homicidal activity. The psychotic disorders of childhood have been subdivided into early infantile autism, symbiotic infantile psychosis, and other forms often called

childhood schizophrenia because of their resemblance to schizophrenic illness in adults.

Leo Kanner (1948) identified the following characteristics of infantile autism: aloneness, impoverished communication, obsessive repetition and request for sameness in activity, and fascination with inanimate things rather than with people. Although autistic withdrawal may not be manifest until the fourth year or later, it has been hypothesized by Margaret Mahler and others that autism is the result of the infant's failure to move beyond a normal autistic phase (birth to 3 months) to a symbiotic phase of development (3 to 12 months) in which beginning recognition and distinguishing of other people occurs. In the case of symbiotic psychosis, a somewhat later developmental fixation in the symbiotic phase and a failure of the child to progress to the phase of separation-individuation (12 to 36 months) is seen. Childhood forms of schizophrenia may lack Bleuler's secondary symptoms of delusions, hallucinations, illusions, and severe motor abnormalities, such as catatonic withdrawal or excitement states; adult subcategories of paranoid and catatonic schizophrenia are generally not used by child psychiatrists. Childhood forms of psychosis, especially when chronic, may evolve into disorders resembling severe adult forms of schizophrenia.

The onset of childhood psychosis may be insidious or appear quite abrupt. Adults may have been unaware of a process that had been developing in the child for several months or even years. No typical or classical presentation exists, and the course of the illness varies with diagnosis, ego strengths gained prior to onset, and treatment. Childhood psychosis has a poorer long-term prognosis than other childhood disorders. Treatment modalities include psychotherapy, psychoactive drugs, intensive work with parents, behavior modification techniques, therapeutic nursery school experiences or special classes, and, at times, inpatient hospital and residential care.

Brain syndromes and retardation. Brain syndromes result from pathology of the central nervous system and are manifested by impairments of affect, "judgment, discrimination, learning, memory, and other cognitive functions," according to the G.A.P. classification (p. 263). In addition, children may have accompanying neurotic, psychotic, and behavioral difficulties. Team approaches involving neurologists, pediatricians, psychologists, psychiatrists, and experts in retardation can help brain-damaged children and their families. Retarded children are likely to be handicapped by secondary emotional disturbances (see chapter 26, "Mental Retardation").

A retarded young man, age 26, experienced all the wishes of a young adolescent boy for female companionship. He developed the delusion that a young woman who had in fact rejected him was actually in his presence. The stress of being unloved exacerbated a seizure disorder from which he also suffered. The patient received help from his therapist in testing by verbal clarification the reality of his situation and in sharing his feelings; his parents felt less frustrated once they were helped to understand the regressed nature of his basically adolescent fixation.

Hyperactivity. Hyperactivity has a variety of causes, some known (including organic and social factors) and some obscure; it has been recognized by psychiatrists as a clinical entity since the 1950s. Renshaw (1974) discusses hyperactivity as a syndrome or collection of behavioral manifestations that may include marked sleep disturbances, short attention span, extreme excitability, poor impulse control and concentration, destructiveness, and disturbed interpersonal relationships. Hyperactive or "hyperkinetic" children, as they are often called, have been recognized as early as $1\frac{1}{2}$ years of age. Most often parents or teachers report the syndrome between the ages of 5 and 7, when classroom expectations place new stresses on the child. The incidence in the population is about 6 to 10 percent before the age of 10, and boys are diagnosed as hyperactive four times as often as girls.

Treatment of hyperactivity includes therapy for the child, casework with the parents, and, at times, special classes with a large teacher-to-pupil ratio. Hyperactive children frequently respond well to treatment with stimulants (amphetamines and methylphenidate) prior to puberty. With pharmacological treatment, children may sleep better, be neater, and concentrate on

and complete work more easily. Bed-wetting, if present, may also disappear with drug treatment. Therapeutic dosage varies with the individual patient and is usually administered morning, noon, and late afternoon. Many parents are anxious about the use of these drugs because in recent years amphetamines have been associated with drug abuse and methylphenidate (Ritalin) with growth retardation. Side effects of amphetamines, especially loss of appetite and sleeplessness in the child, may cause initial or continual concern among parents and physician. In addition, some schools have been said to use these drugs on children without appropriate evaluation or prior parental involvement, as social strait jackets.

The prognosis for hyperactivity is hopeful if secondary difficulties with family, peer relationships, and school are not too severe prior to diagnosis and treatment. Perhaps the most unfortunate cases of hyperactivity are those in which the child is institutionalized with an erroneous psychiatric diagnosis and then given inappropriate drug therapy or other improper treatment.

Disorders of handicapped children. Children with physical handicaps such as blindness, cerebral palsy, and congenital cardiac disease are more vulnerable to emotional disturbances, especially to those associated with impaired self-esteem, because of the burden their handicaps impose on the course of their development. Freeman (1968) has pointed out that children with handicaps differ in their responses to life stresses and human contacts, depending on the specific nature of the handicap, age at onset, severity, duration, and course and type of medical treatment. Researchers have not been able to establish a clear relationship between a particular physical handicap and a specific personality pattern or developmental deviation. The handicapped child may find it difficult to make friends or to feel accepted in the family because of his problems with poor self-regard, defensive aggression, fears, separation from the care-taking person, and regressive behavior.

Borderline children. The "borderline" child as described by Rosenfeld and Sprince (1963, 1965) characteristically has extreme anxiety, problems in reality testing, poor impulse control, odd behavior, an abnormal relationship with the mother and other persons, and excessive aggressiveness or marked withdrawal. Child psychiatry has not generally accepted this diagnosis because of its lack of specificity. In treating borderline children the therapist should be more active than in his work with the neurotic and should concentrate on setting limits, preventing destructive behavior, and helping the child form a sustained positive therapeutic attachment as well as give up the pathological use of primitive defenses such as denial, displacement, projection, and introjection.

Learning disabilities. Learning disabilities, like hyperactivity, have a variety of causes; societal and organic factors are clearly recognized, while other factors are obscure. In the United States, professionals working with children have recognized learning disabilities since the latter part of the nineteenth century. Morgan described "congenital word-blindness" in 1896, and in 1917 Augusta Bronner wrote *The Psychology of Speech Abilities and Disabilities*, detailing children's difficulties with reading, speech, and spelling.

A child is diagnosed as having a learning disability when he is unable to learn in the classroom because of difficulties in perceiving, integrating, retaining, or transmitting words and information. The problem may result from visual or auditory perceptual difficulty. Children with learning disabilities may be two or more years behind the level expected for age and grade, and these discrepancies need not be associated with low intelligence, physical abnormalities, or inadequate schooling. Emotional abnormalities, school failure, inability to make friends or personal rejection by peers at school, and the frustration and disappointment shown by teachers and by adults at home exacerbate learning disabilities.

Learning disabilities are widespread, with a higher statistical incidence in boys than in girls. Early detection and prevention are of major consequence for the individual child's future. Some states require that all children with emotional and retardation problems affecting their learning receive a multidisciplinary assessment with recommendation for remedial work and reevaluation periodically. Laws also provide for screening young children entering the school system for learning disabilities and retardation.

Parents sometimes bring children to the psychiatrist's office for symptoms and behavior that are secondary to their difficulty in learning.

One adolescent was referred to the therapist with the complaint that he stole clothing from schoolmates who did well academically. He reported years of cheating and not telling his family about his inability to sequence letters, to comprehend and organize on exams, and to write papers. Psychological testing to ascertain the cause of the learning disability, followed by psychotherapy to help him to accept and grasp the ways his emotions contributed to his failure to learn adequately, enabled the boy to improve his capacity to learn and perform in school.

School failure, truancy, delinquency, and, ultimately, unemployment and poverty may result from disabilities in learning.

As part of the diagnostic workup, psychological testing may help distinguish abnormalities in visual and auditory perception and in intellectual functioning. A neurological examination helps identify learning difficulties related to organ impairment. Treatment focuses on a multidisciplinary approach using specialized educational services, psychotherapy, drug therapy for accompanying hyperactivity, if present, and behavior modification with positive reinforcement of certain desired behavior.

The Psychiatric Treatment of Children

The psychiatric treatment of children aims to relieve symptoms, reduce the level of disturbing behavior, resolve conflict, and improve the child's relationships in the family, at school, and with peers. A variety of treatment modalities are available, including individual, group, and family psychotherapy; psychotropic medication; psychiatric hospitalization (intense psychiatric milieu with psychiatrists present at the hospital facility); therapeutic residential care (structured environment with outside consulting psychiatrist); and behavior modification. The therapist uses empathy, knowledge, and objectivity as tools to aid the patient. The treatment of children almost always involves working with the parents—especially the mother, although fathers are becoming increasingly involved in the treatment plan.

The psychiatric treatment of children takes place in a variety of settings—guidance clinics, hospital offices or wards, schoolrooms, therapeutic nurseries, homes, neighborhood facilities, court clinics, therapeutic summer camps, and residential treatment centers. As in the diagnostic evaluation, the therapist may find it useful to have a play area with equipment that permits young children self-expression. The therapist needs to know the cultural, social, ethnic, and racial aspects of a child's family background and environment; treating a child without an understanding of these factors may lead to inappropriate approaches. Many first-generation children seen in treatment facilities for children experience emotional difficulties as a result of their position between the old world of the parents and the new world of their school and neighborhood.

Prevention through prenatal intervention may be of value, although results are difficult to document. Pregnant women frequently benefit, especially when pregnant for the first time, from discussing their concerns, hopes, and fears about pregnancy and parenthood with an obstetrician, nurse, social worker, or pediatrician. General hospitals sometimes offer social service consultation to all pregnant women in the prenatal clinic. Skillful intervention may help mothers with unresolved conflicts to avoid the recapitulation of their own disturbing problems, left over from their earlier life experience, in their children.

Individual psychotherapy with children may be short-term or long-term; in selected cases, psychoanalysis may be indicated. Short-term therapy (up to about sixteen sessions) is used when a specific therapeutic goal is set and the therapist anticipates that the child will benefit from a limited period of treatment. Short-term therapy may be most useful when the child's disorder is a reaction to a personally disturbing life event, such as the death of a parent or a sibling. Longer periods of therapy are indicated in the treatment of symptom neuroses, character disorders, psychosomatic problems, and psychoses. Some children, especially those with poor peer relationships, benefit from taking part in groups

with several children of nearly the same age. In such "activity groups," primary-school-age children are able to express their conflicts in work and play situations, and they may be the treatment of choice for older but less verbal or more action-oriented children. In groups, the child's peers serve as therapeutic helpers to the adult therapist through constructive examples in behavior and by providing useful comments. Psychoanalysis of children is more intensive than psychotherapy, entailing a greater investment of time and money by the family over a period of many months and even years; it may include as many as four or five treatment sessions per week. The process also involves a more systematic analysis of the child's conflicts and, in classical treatment, the working through of transference issues.

When a child is treated individually or in a group, a therapist nearly always sees the mother and father concomitantly. The mental health professional who sees the parents may treat the child as well, or one or more colleagues may work with family members separately. Parents often need help in understanding feelings of guilt, assisting the child on a day-to-day basis, and, ultimately, comprehending their own contributions to the child's difficulties. In particular, they need to understand how their own unresolved conflicts have had an impact on their child. The mother of an encopretic child, for example, felt she was responsible for her 7-year-old boy's illness because she had gone to work for about a year when he was 2 to 3 years old. The caseworker helped the mother express her feelings of guilt and sense of responsibility, while the child was taught by verbal discussion to respond to body sensations related to defecating, leading to cessation of his encopresis.

Family therapy may increase the family's ability to share mutual feelings and concerns. In addition, in this treatment mode the child is not singled out as the sole focus—a circumstance that can create additional stress. The therapist selects family therapy for those cases in which the child's difficulties reflect major family problems or in which therapeutic change can best be achieved by shifts in the manner in which the family as a whole deals with its dilemmas. Therapists should use family therapy only when they are skilled and comfortable with it and believe in its effectiveness.

Behavioral therapy utilizes specific rewards or the anticipation of them to alter symptomatic behavior. To produce modification of behavior in retarded children and in some disturbed children, the therapist uses positive and negative reinforcement by granting and withholding rewards. Conflicts underlying the disturbed behavior are not affected by this treatment.

Drugs are used markedly less in children than in adults. Chlorpromazine and thioridazine are sometimes used to treat primary-school-age children diagnosed as suffering from childhood forms of psychosis (Eveloff, 1970). In the case of children in withdrawn states, especially autism, trifluoperazine and thioridazine may be helpful in reducing anxiety and decreasing disorganized thought processes. Extrapyramidal dystonic reactions and increased risk of seizures (in patients with seizures) are difficulties with which the physician should be familiar before prescribing phenothiazines. Imipramine is at times an effective adjunct in treating enuresis because its action permits increased bladder capacity; however, the physician must be alert to the numerous possible neurological, anticholinergic, allergic, and gastrointestinal symptoms and side effects that may result from its use. Amphetamines and methylphenidate may be useful prior to puberty in helping the hyperactive child control his behavior and increase his attention span.

Children are admitted to residential treatment centers when they are unable to remain in the home environment or when it is thought that treatment will progress more rapidly and smoothly if the child is away from the home. Usually such centers provide a highly supervised and structured therapeutic, educational, and living setting for the delinquent, as well as for children from preschool age through adolescence with other behavioral and emotional problems; individual psychotherapy may or may not be a regular part of the program. The length of treatment in residential centers varies with the nature of the child's disturbance and needs and the availability of educational, therapeutic, and vocational services.

Nursery and day care centers in the United States are used by mothers who work or who wish their children to have a peer experience before going to kindergarten. Special nursery school programs also exist for treating emotionally disturbed or retarded children. The psychiatrist who acts as consultant to a therapeutic nursery school must collaborate closely with teachers to help the disturbed child. Concomitant work with parents strengthens the therapeutic program.

Child Psychiatric Emergencies

Child psychiatric emergencies vary in their urgency from situations that present an immediate threat to life to problems that are more gradual in their destructive impact on the patient and his family. Suicide, homicide, fire setting, running away, sexual assaultiveness, school phobia, child abuse, incest, and refusal of children to cooperate with life-sustaining medical procedures are considered the principal problems requiring immediate attention and action for their prompt resolution. Drug and alcohol abuse, usually considered adult problems, may pose a direct threat to the well-being or life of children. When any of these conditions is encountered or suspected, an intervention is indicated and should be initiated, if possible, the same day, and followed by a complete diagnostic evaluation and therapeutic steps. Treatment of emergencies may require hospitalization, especially in cases involving suicide and homicide.

Suicide. Actual suicide or severe suicide attempts are rare in preadolescent children, although the expression of suicidal ideas or self-destructive behavior requires a psychiatric examination to ascertain the seriousness of the intention and the presence of psychotic delusions or unusual thoughts, and to protect the child, through hospitalization if necessary. Suicidal action may be impulsive or may have been contemplated over a period of time. Usually it accompanies low self-esteem, a history of losses, a depressed mood, and troubled relationships within the child's family.

Children from troubled homes who have followed the directions of an inner voice to ingest a poison or to jump out of a window are examples of unusual cases requiring psychiatric hospitalization. Determining the fine line between ideas or wishes and the actual inability to avoid acting on suicidal thoughts requires a skillful and experienced psychiatric examiner. As with adults, previous suicide attempts and the seriousness of the suicidal method contemplated must be considered; hanging, fire, jumping from heights, or using a gun are especially ominous and may, though not always, indicate a more dangerous problem than those that prompt overdosing or wrist cutting. The examining physician's sense of anxiety and concern is frequently a helpful barometer when coupled with accumulated clinical experience.

A suicide may result from extreme tensions that have built up within a family. For example, a 14-year-old boy who shot himself had been one of many children. One severely retarded sister drained the entire family's patience and time, and the boy and his other siblings refrained from bringing friends home because of their embarrassment about their sister's condition. Their recreation was minimal because of the time expended in continually supervising their sister. The boy had failed to warn his parents of the unhappiness that had apparently led to his death, and his parents chose to view the death as accidental.

Homicide. Although retarded and psychotic children have been known to commit aggressive acts resulting in the death of a close family member or peer, murder is rarely committed by preadolescent children. Statements indicative of murderous intent must be treated seriously and swiftly, as should those about suicidal intent, in order to determine the severity of the expressed thought and to protect persons who might be threatened.

Fire setting. Most people are fascinated by fire, and learning constructive uses for and control of fire is part of normal maturation. Fire setting has multiple causes. Children who set fires are often neglected, unsupervised, angry, victims of aggression, or overstimulated. Young children may experiment with setting fires without knowing how to manage them. Teen-agers have been found to set fires in response to cumulative anger caused by such circumstances as physical assault,

familial rejection, and removal to foster homes. The history of one group of adolescent firesetters revealed that each of their fathers had either been a fireman or was in some way vocationally involved with fire, suggesting a strong element of identification among the determinants of fire setting (Macht and Mack, 1968).

Running away. Children's running away may be considered an emergency when the child places himself in a life-threatening situation.

A 12-year-old girl ran away from home repeatedly with the encouragement of several of her friends. Although she denied she was in danger, walking at night along lonely, deserted city streets, she betrayed knowledge of her danger by not taking her dog along because she was fearful for his safety. After several emergency psychiatric visits following episodes of running away, it became apparent that she really missed her absent father, who lived far away and whom she had not seen for five years. The therapist encouraged her to call her father on the telephone. She agreed, called him, and then announced she would no longer run away because she wanted to be home when her father came for the visit he had promised during the phone conversation.

Child abuse. Physical injury and neglect of children may take the form of starvation or dehydration, beatings, burnings, and other bodily insults resulting at times in severe physical harm and including fractures, subdural hematomas, burns, scars, and ruptured spleens. Abuse of children in America is currently more openly acknowledged than previously, and child services and agencies—social, pediatric, and legal—are more active now in aiding abusive parents, protecting children, and intervening legally at times to remove children from danger. Adults who hurt children were usually themselves subjected to physical abuse as children. Self-help parent organizations analogous to Alcoholics Anonymous have been formed for parents who struggle with the impulse to injure a child. Therapeutic programs to help young parents understand their feelings so that they will not need to repeat familial abusive patterns toward their own children are also proving valuable. Many states require that professions caring for children and their families report any suspicion of child abuse.

School phobia. School is children's work. If a child fails to attend school, his education may be jeopardized. There are two distinct types of school phobia. The first is that of the child beginning school, especially in the first grade. The first day of school may itself present a crisis for a child and his mother because of her feeling that she is losing her child to the world outside the family. For the young child, school phobia usually involves fears, conscious and unconscious, that something may happen to his mother while he is absent from home. The mother may respond by covertly or even openly encouraging the child to remain home. School phobia becomes an emergency when the child (especially in the early school years) refuses or is absolutely unable to attend school. Attempts to separate the child from the mother or to force him into the classroom may cause marked anxiety bordering on panic. Nevertheless, a firm approach with both parents and child is often reassuring and helpful in enabling the child to return to school. In the second type of school phobia, adolescents may "hook" school because of severe anxiety or panic concerning real or imagined threat to themselves or to family members. Close work with the school is of course essential for the therapist in helping a child and his parents to overcome a school phobia.

Incest. Children occasionally arrive in emergency rooms with a history of sexual assault by a family member. Instances of intercourse between fathers and daughters are less rare than those between mothers and sons. It is important to understand in cases of overt incest how provocative or emotionally involved the child is in the sexual relationship with a parent or sibling; it is often equally important to differentiate the patient's fantasy from the actuality of his life experience. In working with cases of incest, the therapist must also establish whether the parent or parents wish to interrupt what has begun. Children may, out of fear or love for a parent, refuse to explore their feelings in cases of incest, or even admit to what is taking place. Mental health professionals will often wish in cases of incest, as in those of child abuse, to avail themselves of legal counsel in planning a therapeutic

approach, as interruption of the deviant relationship by legal intervention is often necessary to protect the child.

Aiding the Uncooperative Pediatric Patient

Small children are often combative and uncooperative with medical procedures in order to avoid what they fear will be a violation or injury to their bodies. The child psychiatrist may be able to help a totally uncooperative child who is able to talk about his concerns to accept painful medical treatment.

A child who resisted intravenous therapy for osteomyelitis was helped to understand her worries and fears through play therapy; she was helped to see that she required intravenous antibiotics for her "sore" bone and subsequently became cooperative, docile, and passive in accepting care. The play had consisted of the child's pretending to be the doctor and administering many needles to her doll (the play patient). The therapist asked questions and then explained various hospital procedures as the young girl reenacted in play what she herself had experienced. None of this play was initiated by the therapist; she had only to provide play materials and then listen closely in order to help the child become acquainted with medical procedures necessary for her treatment and to reduce anxiety.

Adequate preparation for elective procedures and brief explanations when emergency procedures are necessary can help a child change dramatically from a combative and resistant patient to a cooperative one.

Child Psychiatry in the Community

Child guidance centers in the United States have provided multidisciplinary services for children for over fifty years. Since the 1960s federal, state, and locally funded centers have established specialized services for children; by 1971 four hundred local programs were in operation. Services offered in comprehensive community mental health centers include therapeutic nursery programs, retardation services, consultation to pediatric units, and outpatient treatment.

Some cities have nurse practitioners based in neighborhood schools who offer medical care to children and are able to identify emotional difficulties early in their course and make referrals to mental health treatment facilities. Direct service and psychiatric consultation have also reached neighborhoods in recent years through satellite clinics, multiservice centers, settlement houses, community recreational centers, and local public and private schools.

Neighborhood facilities for partial hospitalization and inpatient psychiatric care for children are in short supply because of low demand for such services, except by the relatively few parents of children in need. In many states, children requiring inpatient psychiatric care are hospitalized miles away from their homes, friends, neighbors, and local schools.

Psychiatric Consultation

The role of the psychiatric consultant varies with the type of agency, need, and his own flexibility. He may be looked to for definitive help in decision making and for direct or follow-up treatment, or he may be asked only to provide suggestions to other caregivers. The consultant may or may not personally examine the child or talk with the family. When a mental health professional consults, he is a guest of the agency rather than the primary care provider. A skillful consultant will ascertain whether the problems about which he is asked relate directly to a case being considered or reflect a problem within the agency itself. This process often involves listening to the needs of the agency as well as those of the patient or client. Since a psychiatric consultant frequently works in an agency for a specific number of hours over an extended period of time, often for many years, he has the opportunity to develop a close collaborative relationship with the agency, its staff and the community (see chapter 30, "Community Psychiatry").

Child psychiatry as a subspecialty of psychiatry contributes a developmental approach to the field of psychiatry as a whole. With knowledge of the developmental stages of childhood, the psychiatrist seeing adults can better understand both the normal and the pathological events and occurrences of specific developmental stages in the patient's past. An adult's capacity to love and be loved, sexual identification, educational, work, and avocational interests, and defense mechanisms all reflect patterns of intrapsychic and interpersonal childhood development within a particular family matrix. The preventive possibilities and ramifications implied by the structural foundations of this approach can provide ever increasing momentum for knowledge, alleviation of stress, and actualization of human potential throughout continuing life cycles.

References

Bowlby, J. 1960. Grief and mourning in infancy and early childhood. *Psychoanal. Study Child* 15:9–52.

Erikson, E. 1959. Growth and crises of the healthy personality. In *Identity and the life cycle. Psychol. Issues* monograph no. 1. New York: International Universities Press.

Eveloff, H. 1970. Pediatric psychopharmacology. In *Principles of psychopharmacology*, ed. W. G. Clark and J. del Giudice. New York: Academic Press.

Feinberg, D. 1970. Preventive therapy with siblings of a dying child. *J. Am. Acad. Child Psychiatry* 9:644–668.

Fraiberg, S. 1959. *The magic years*. New York: Scribner's.

Freeman, R. 1968. Emotional reactions of handicapped children. In *Annual progress in child psychiatry and child development*, ed. S. Chess and A. Thomas. New York: Brunner/Mazel.

Freud, A. 1936. *The ego and the mechanisms of defense*. New York: International Universities Press, 1970.

———— 1960. Discussion of Dr. John Bowlby's paper. *Psychoanal. Study Child* 15:53–62.

———— 1965. *Normality and pathology in childhood: assessments of development*. New York: International Universities Press.

Freud, S. 1909. Analysis of a phobia in a five-year-old boy. In *Standard edition*, ed. J. Strachey. Vol. 10. London: Hogarth Press, 1955.

Furman, R. 1964. Death and the young child: some preliminary considerations. *Psychoanal. Study Child* 19:321–333.

Group for the Advancement of Psychiatry. 1966. *Psychopathological disorders of childhood: theoretical considerations and a proposed classification*. Vol. 6, report no. 62. New York: Mental Health Materials Center.

Kanner, L. 1948. Early infantile autism. *Am. J. Orthopsychiatry* 19:416–426.

Macht, L. B., and J. E. Mack. 1968. The firesetter syndrome. *Psychiatry* 31:277–288.

Nagera, H. 1970. Children's reactions to the death of important objects: a developmental approach. *Psychoanal. Study Child* 25:360–400.

Renshaw, D. 1974. *The hyperactive child*. Chicago: Hall.

Rexford, E., and S. Van Amerongen. 1974. Psychological disorders of the grade school years. In *American handbook of psychiatry*, ed. S. Arieti and G. Caplan. New York: Basic Books.

Rosenfeld, S., and M. Sprince. 1963. An attempt to formulate the meaning of the concept "borderline." *Psychoanal. Study Child* 18:603–635.

——— 1965. Some thoughts on the technical handling of borderline children. *Psychoanal. Study Child* 20:495–517.

Spitz, R. A. 1945. Hospitalism: an inquiry into the genesis of psychiatric conditions in early childhood. *Psychoanal. Study Child* 1:53–74.

Spitz, R. A., and K. M. Wolf. 1946. Anaclitic depression: an inquiry into the genesis of psychiatric conditions in early childhood, II. *Psychoanal. Study Child* 2:313–342.

Wallerstein, J. S., and J. B. Kelly. 1975. The effects of parental divorce: experiences of the preschool child. *J. Am. Acad. Child Psychiatry* 14:601–616.

Recommended Reading

Baldwin, A. 1968. *Theories of child development*. New York: Wiley.

Blos, P. 1962. *On adolescence: a psychoanalytic interpretation*. New York: Free Press.

Bremner, R., ed. 1970. *Children and youth in America: a documentary history*. Vol. 2. Cambridge, Mass.: Harvard University Press.

Chess, S., and A. Thomas, eds. 1968–1974. *Annual progress in child psychiatry and child development*. New York: Brunner/Mazel.

Deutsch, H. 1944. *The psychology of women*. Vol. 1. New York: Grune & Stratton.

Erikson, E. 1963. *Childhood and society*. New York: Norton.

Furman, R., and A. Katan. 1969. *The therapeutic nursery school*. New York: International Universities Press.

Gesell, A., H. Halverson, H. Thompson, F. Ilg, B. Castner, L. Ames, and C. Amathuda. 1940. *The first five years of life: a guide to the study of the preschool child*. New York: Harper and Brothers.

Gesell, A., R. Ilg, L. Ames, and G. Bullis. 1946. *The child from five to ten*. New York: Harper and Brothers.

Gesell, A., R. Ilg, L. Ames, and J. Rodell. 1974. *Infant and child in the culture today*. New York: Harper & Row.

Glasscote, R., M. Fishman, M. Sonis, and L. Cass. 1972. *Children and mental health centers*. Washington, D.C.: Joint Information Service of the American Psychiatric Association and the National Association for Mental Health.

Kessler, J. 1966. *Psychopathology of childhood*. Englewood Cliffs, N.J.: Prentice-Hall.

Lewis, M., A. Solnit, M. Stark, I. Gabrielson, and E. Klatskin. 1966. An exploration study of accidental ingestions of poison in young children. *J. Am. Acad. Child Psychiatry* 5:255–271.

MacDonald, M. 1965. The psychiatric evaluation of children. *J. Am. Acad. Child Psychiatry* 4:569–612.

Mahler, M. S., and M. Furer. 1970. *Human symbiosis and the vicissitudes of individuation. Infantile Psychoses*, vol. 1. New York: International Universities Press.

Proskauer, S. 1969. Some technical issues in time-limited psychotherapy with children. *J. Am. Acad. Child Psychiatry* 8:154–169.

——— 1971. Focused time-limited psychotherapy in children. *J. Am. Acad. Child Psychiatry* 10:619–639.

Provence, S., and R. Lipton. 1967. *Infants in institutions*. New York: International Universities Press.

Wolman, B. 1972. *Manual of child psychopathology*. New York: McGraw-Hill.

The Adolescent

CHAPTER 24

Armand M. Nicholi, Jr.

ADOLESCENCE is the most confusing, challenging, frustrating, and fascinating phase of human development. This description holds true, unfortunately, not only for those living through adolescence and their immediate families but also for clinicians attempting to understand its complexity and to diagnose and treat its pathological manifestations.

Adolescence plays a profoundly significant role in the life of the individual and in society as a whole. For the individual, the normal maturational processes occurring during adolescence involve the organization, synthesis, and crystallization of personality traits and qualities that ultimately constitute adult character structure. Furthermore, because of changing biological and sociological factors, adolescence now constitutes an increasingly large percentage of the average life cycle. If, as some authorities believe, adolescence begins with the onset of puberty and ends with the attainment of emotional and economic independence, then an individual may spend ten to fifteen years in this phase between childhood and adulthood. For society as a whole, adolescence exerts a strong influence in establishing the tone of our particular culture. Currently, adolescent dress, hair style, language, and music

have a marked impact on the adult world, apparently influencing adult life styles more than they are influenced by them.

This chapter will consider (1) the definition of adolescence; (2) the current state of our knowledge about adolescence; (3) normal adolescence: early, middle, and late phases; (4) pathology of adolescence: general considerations, recent research, epidemiology, and adjustment reactions of adolescence; and (5) the treatment of adolescents.

Definition

The 1975 edition of the American Psychiatric Association's *Psychiatric Glossary* defines adolescence as "a chronological period beginning with the physical and emotional processes leading to sexual and psychosocial maturity and ending at an ill-defined time when the individual achieves independence and social productivity. The period is associated with rapid physical, psychological and social changes" (p. 48). If the enormously complex experience we call adolescence can be defined at all, this definition is perhaps as satisfactory as any. It encompasses all those definitions that focus entirely on the biological as-

519

pects—"the period between puberty and maturity," for example, from *Dorland's Medical Dictionary*—as well as those that focus solely on the psychological aspects—such as "the psychological stage in personality and character development that follows the latency phase of childhood" (Josselyn, 1974, p. 382).

The modern concept of adolescence does not appear in the literature on child rearing until the late nineteenth century (Demos and Demos, 1969). However, it was not until the early twentieth century that G. Stanley Hall first introduced the term and formally recognized adolescence as a separate stage of human development (1904). One year later, Freud published *Three Essays on the Theory of Sexuality* (1905). In this work, he mentions "the transformations of puberty" and explains a number of features of the adolescent process. By introducing his then shocking notion that children have sexual feelings, he altered our understanding of adolescence. Before his publication of this work, puberty and adolescence were thought to mark the beginning of an individual's sex life. From that time on, adolescence was no longer considered the beginning of sexuality but merely the bridge from a sexuality that began at birth to that found in the adult.

Current Knowledge

Although the duration and influence of adolescence appears to be increasing steadily, our knowledge of this stage of development remains sketchy and rudimentary. Making up perhaps 15 to 20 percent of the average life span, adolescence characteristically receives less than 1 percent of the space in most modern textbooks on psychiatry. The *Diagnostic and Statistical Manual of Mental Disorders* of the American Psychiatric Association (DSM-II) devotes about three lines exclusively to this topic.

In addition to being sketchy, our knowledge of adolescence remains confusing and controversial. There appear to be as many definitions of adolescence as authors writing about it. Even the boundaries of adolescence—that is, when it begins and when it ends—remain unclear. Some say adolescence begins with puberty, the onset of menarche in the girl and the equivalent changes

in the boy (Anthony, 1974). Others say it begins as early as two or more years before the onset of puberty and includes all the physical and hormonal changes that immediately precede puberty (Josselyn, 1974). The upper boundary of adolescence remains even more vague. Clinicians and investigators define the end of adolescence in ambiguous and confusing ways, not in biological terms, as with its beginning, but in psychological and social terms. Adolescence ends when the individual "consolidates his identity as an adult," "achieves independence," "adopts an adult social role," "attains autonomy," "finds a nonincestuous love object," "marries and assumes a full-time work responsibility," "achieves an adult-adult relationship with the family," and so forth. If we look carefully at these criteria, we see that adolescence can end at eighteen years of age or continue throughout life.

Our picture of the exact nature of adolescence, of what is normal and what is abnormal, is also unclear. Some clinicians and investigators view the whole of adolescence as a period of acute and sustained upheaval. They believe such turbulence is not only healthy but necessary and inevitable; conversely, they believe the absence of intense turmoil to be unhealthy. This view, first expounded by G. Stanley Hall (1904) more than a half-century ago and embraced since then by most psychoanalytic observers, has been perhaps most forcefully stated by Anna Freud. Describing the adolescent, she mentions "his anxieties, the height of elation and depth of despair, the quickly rising enthusiasms, the utter hopelessness, the burning—or at other times sterile—intellectual and philosophical preoccupations, the yearning for freedom, the sense of loneliness, the feeling of oppression by the parents, the impotent rages or active hates directed against the adult world, the erotic crushes—whether homosexually or heterosexually directed—the suicidal fantasies, etc." (1958, p. 260). She then asserts that these "upheavals" reflect normal maturational processes, necessary for the integration of "adult sexuality into . . . the individual's personality" (p. 264). The constant upheavals of adolescence "are no more than the external indications that such internal adjustments are in progress" (p.

264). Furthermore, she asserts that the absence of outer evidence of inner unrest in the form of intense moodiness and rebelliousness "signifies a delay of normal development and is, as such, a sign to be taken seriously" (pp. 264–265). She suspects the untroubled, considerate, and cooperative adolescent of having built up excessive defenses against his drive activities, of having been crippled by this process, and, perhaps more than any other, of being in need of therapeutic help. This view of the intrinsic nature of adolescence, which implies that the "craziness" of adolescence is normal and its absence abnormal, has influenced our understanding of and therapeutic approach to this age group for decades.

Recent research has questioned the validity of this view. During the past decade, large-scale longitudinal studies of adolescence have raised serious questions about the inevitability of intense upheaval in the adolescent (Weiner, 1970). Studies by Douvan and Adelson of 3,500 adolescents (1966) and by Offer and his colleagues of two other large samples of adolescents in public high schools (Offer and Offer, 1968; Offer, 1969; Offer, Marcus, and Offer, 1970) found the incidence of turmoil and severe crisis to be unusually low. They observed the overwhelming majority of these adolescents to be relatively free of the dramatic conflicts described in the psychoanalytic literature as part of the normal adolescent process. The researchers found relationships with parents to be "stable, consistent, and empathic" (Offer, 1969, p. 223). These adolescents came, by and large, from traditional families and stable communities. Using the guidelines and resources of their parents to help them adapt to internal and external pressures, they tended to be less dependent on peers for guidance and approval. And although they manifested mild forms of rebelliousness, primarily between the ages of twelve and fourteen, these episodes could in no way be interpreted as serious disturbances. These and other large survey studies of normal adolescents have led clinicians and researchers to realize that the traditional view of adolescence as a highly disturbed state is at best a vast overstatement; at worst, a gross distortion. Perhaps this traditional view reflects the danger of making wide generalizations from a relatively few case histories of disturbed individuals.

If our view of the normal process of adolescence has been unclear, so have our views of pathology and treatment. Modern dynamic psychiatry has not yet established a useful theoretical formulation of adolescence nor evolved an effective therapeutic approach. Attempts to fit adolescence into classical psychoanalytic theory —to see it as a recapitulation of infancy (E. Jones, 1922) or a reactivation of the Oedipus complex (Spiegel, 1951)—have proved disappointing. Anna Freud (1958), after reviewing the many theoretical contributions to the literature of adolescence, states that our knowledge remains unsatisfactory and our analytical approach to treatment disappointing. However, Erikson's concepts of identity crises, identity diffusion, and psychosocial moratorium (1968) have been an exception and have proved helpful clinically—especially in understanding and working with late adolescents.

Clinicians have found it difficult to agree on when an adolescent needs treatment. If one considers normal adolescence to be continual upheaval, then one will have difficulty distinguishing transient episodes that merely reflect the normal processes of maturation from states of deep-seated and persistent psychopathology. "The adolescent manifestations come close to symptom formation of the neurotic, psychotic, or social disorder," writes Anna Freud, "and merge almost imperceptibly into . . . almost all the mental illnesses. Consequently, the differential diagnosis between the adolescent upsets and true pathology becomes a difficult task" (1958, p. 267). Some theorists have felt that the normal upheavals of adolescence were so similar to any number of severe illnesses that they could be diagnosed only in retrospect. If the disturbance resolved itself in time, one could consider it a normal manifestation of adolescence. This view has led some clinicians to a rather casual approach to the treatment of the disturbed adolescent and has often led to less than happy relationships between psychiatry and the adolescent's family.

Normal Adolescence

To understand pathology, one must have a clear concept of normality. Because of the long-standing difficulty in distinguishing the normal from the pathological manifestations of adolescence, this section will focus considerable attention on the various phases of normal adolescence. Emphasis will be placed on internal and external stresses that may contribute to adolescent disorder and on aspects of behavior that may reflect adolescent psychopathology.

Early Adolescence

Because the emotional development of the early adolescent involves coming to terms with the virtual explosion of biological changes occurring in his body, these changes will be considered in some detail. Striking changes of face, limbs, and trunk, the increase of gonadal hormones, and the appearance of primary and secondary sex characteristics evoke a degree of bewilderment in the child.

These physical changes begin to make their appearance as early as two years before the onset of puberty (the term is derived from the Latin *puber*, meaning adult). This period immediately before puberty will be considered here as part of early adolescence, although many authorities refer to it as "preadolescence" or "pubescence."

In the girl, preparatory changes may begin at ten or eleven years of age, sometimes as early as eight or nine. Estrogen levels increase and specific feminine characteristics begin to appear. The breasts begin to develop, and the areolae and nipples increase in size and pigmentation. Breast development may be the first sign of impending puberty, and the breasts may reach full size before menarche. The pelvis widens and layers of subcutaneous fat alter the contours of the body. First pubic and then axillary hair appear. In the boy, the initial physical changes appear about one year after the cells of the testes begin to secrete testosterone. The shoulders broaden, the genitals enlarge slightly, and the voice begins to deepen as the larynx increases in size (Wolstenholme and O'Connor, 1967). The boy usually remains leaner and more angular than the girl. Pubic, axillary, facial, and chest hair gradually appear in that order.

In both sexes, a growth spurt occurs just prior to puberty. The limbs and neck grow more rapidly than the head and trunk and produce the long-legged, awkward look of a young colt so typical of this age. In addition, the pores of the skin increase in size, the sebaceous glands become more active, and acne makes its first unwelcome appearance. One side of the body may change more rapidly and more fully than the other (Stone and Church, 1968), adding to the child's bewilderment.

The beginning of the menstrual flow (menarche) and the occurrence of seminal emissions mark the actual onset of puberty in girls and boys, respectively. For reasons not yet fully ascertained, the onset of puberty has been occurring at an increasingly early average age. For the past hundred years, the average age of menarche, for example, has been dropping by about four months every ten years (Tanner, 1962). The average age for the onset of menses was 16.5 years in 1860; it is currently 12.5 years. The onset of puberty in boys generally occurs about two years later than in girls and manifests the same trend toward earlier onset (Blizzard et al., 1970). This change has been attributed to better nutrition, though other factors may also play a role. The trend toward earlier onset of puberty has.psychological significance because it thrusts the extensive emotional adjustments of this phase of development on a child considerably younger than the adolescent of a century ago.

The emotional adjustments demanded of the early adolescent have led researchers and clinicians to consider puberty a crisis period within the life cycle. Even when a young child has been sufficiently informed beforehand concerning the changes taking place in his body, these changes may still produce wonder about what is happening and apprehension about the possible outcome. The adolescent's body changes so rapidly that he feels strange and awkward in it, as though it belonged to someone else. Relatives who have not seen him for a while may often comment on how much he has grown, intensifying his feelings of awkwardness and self-consciousness. Studies of this age group show that the majority are preoccupied and markedly dissatisfied with their bodies (Frazier and Lisonbee, 1950). The early adolescent may spend long hours looking into a mirror and wondering what he will look like in the future.

In addition to physical changes, the early adolescent begins to acquire new capacities for thinking and reasoning that, in a sense, contribute to his stress. A part of the cognitive revolution that Piaget (1958) describes in young adolescents, whom he calls preadolescents, is the ability to think beyond the present and to worry about the future. In the years preceding this phase, the child's thinking is more concrete and focuses primarily on the present and on external reality. As he approaches puberty, he develops the capacity to think more abstractly, to be more reflective and self-critical, to think not only of the present but of the past, and to think systematically. He may become more introspective and begin a rich fantasy life. He may become acutely aware of the passage of time and of his own mortality. Questions of meaning and destiny may cause him to think seriously about philosophical and religious issues.

All in all, the physical changes of early adolescence evoke mixed feelings—the excitement of growing up is tempered by apprehension about what this growth involves and occasional yearnings for the relative security of childhood. The young adolescent may display unusually mature thought and behavior one moment and regress to the behavior of a young child the next. Sometimes he may deal with his fears and other uncomfortable feelings by becoming defensive, irritable, and secretive. At this age, he may confide only in a close chum, who often replaces the larger group he played with earlier.

Sullivan considers this "chumship" characteristic of the years immediately preceding puberty and necessary for developing the capacity for interpersonal intimacy. Earlier, the child's relationships are essentially exploitative, based solely on fulfilling his own needs. At this age, the nature of his relationships changes from what Sullivan calls cooperation, competition, and compromise to collaboration in reciprocally meeting others' needs. A special sensitivity toward the needs of others develops and provides the basis for the capacity to form real love relationships later on. Sullivan believes the experience of seeing oneself through the eyes of others helps correct false notions about oneself and not only facilitates emotional growth but actually prevents emotional illness. This period of "chumship," Sullivan wrote in 1953, is incredibly impor-

tant in saving many handicapped people from serious mental disorder that might otherwise be mentable. And Anthony emphasizes that every therapist working with his age group should keep in mind Sullivan's concept of "chumship" as the "essential therapeutic ingredient" (1974, p. 379).

The "gang" at this period usually consists of groups of two interacting with other groups of two. Sometimes the group may consist of three, with one of the three acting as the leader and model for the other two. Sullivan also considers this type of interaction vitally important to development, because it promotes for the first time what he calls "consensual validation of personal worth." The child often shares anxieties or other problems with the group and receives support from them. Sullivan believes this intimate communication between chums helps correct self-deception and leftover egocentricisms, especially those of the child who may have been on the fringes of larger childhood social groups 1953. This pairing phenomenon has, in addition to its remedial and growth aspects, potential for trauma. The close intimate relationship with a chum carries with it the possibility of rejection, ostracism, and consequent loneliness. The breakup of these early relationships can be exceedingly painful. Anthony states that "it is in this era that loneliness reaches its full significance and goes on relatively unchanged for the rest of life" (1974, p. 380). The defenses marshaled against loneliness at this age determine in some measure how the individual will conduct his relationships throughout his life.

The physical changes of early adolescence may begin at any point in a wide range of times, and their onset appears to relate to specific personality characteristics in the adolescent that may extend to adult life. M. C. Jones (1965) has studied the impact of early and late maturing in both boys and girls over a number of years. Her evidence indicates that early onset of pubertal changes results in distinct advantages for boys but distinct disadvantages for girls. At the peak of growth, the early-maturing girls are taller than both the other girls and the boys, and this difference apparently adds to their self-consciousness. Adolescent boys who mature early are found to be physically stronger and more athletic, whereas late maturers are less masculine and more childish. The late maturers were treated by both peers and adults as immature. When the researchers studied these same boys at seventeen years of age, they found the early maturers to be more competent, less dependent, more popular, more responsible, and better athletes. Both peers and adults considered them more attractive. The late-maturing boys showed more personal and social difficulties, prolonged dependency, more rebelliousness, and deep feelings of rejection by their peers throughout adolescence. On the other hand, the early-maturing girls were found to be submissive, listless, and lacking in poise. Such girls had little influence on the group and seldom attained a high degree of popularity, prestige, or leadership. The researchers found late-maturing girls relatively more confident, outgoing, and assured than the early-maturing girls.

One other possible relationship of biological change to personality concerns the relationship of hormones to mood. Some investigators believe that hostility, irritability, depression, and other signs of emotional lability may be more than a reaction to radical changes in physical appearance (Hamburg, 1974). A significant increase in the level of gonadal hormones may be directly related to altered moods during early adolescence. The relationship of mood to changes in the level of such hormones has been well researched during other phases of life, especially during pregnancy and menopause (Lunde and Hamburg, 1972).

In addition to the extensive biological changes occurring in the early adolescent, certain environmental and social changes add external stress, especially the change from elementary to junior high school. During perhaps the most psychologically inauspicious age, the early adolescent has imposed on him the burden of adjusting to the strange environment of a new school—new and older peers, new teachers, new and imposing buildings, and a more demanding curriculum. At a time in life when he most needs the support of a stable and familiar environment, he is thrust into an unfamiliar one. (Unfortunately, many children are sent away to boarding school at this age, an event that some look back on as one of the most traumatic experiences of their lives.) The need for stable boundaries when both inner and outer worlds appear to be changing and unstable motivates the early adolescent to test his environment frequently, to probe its limits—not so much to defy them as to find out where they are and consequently to find out where he is, to help define himself. Poorly defined boundaries often increase his anxiety. For this reason a parent or teacher who allows the early adolescent (even one who may be constantly pushing for fewer restrictions) the same freedom and permissiveness afforded an older adolescent will often produce considerable anxiety, if not outright hostility, in the younger child. This reaction accounts in part for the seventh and eighth grades' reputation as the most difficult to teach and as those with the highest teacher turnover—as in the following case:

The headmaster of a private girls' school called in a psychiatrist to help solve an unusual behavior problem between a particular seventh-grade teacher and her class of twelve- to thirteen-year-old girls. With this teacher, the girls would yell, throw erasers and chalk, spill ink over the teacher's desk, and write obscene and insulting remarks about the teacher. As the semester wore on, the class became more and more out of control, subsiding only when the teacher fled the classroom in tears. With another teacher they liked and respected, this same class would sit absolutely quiet and absorbed in their work. The psychiatrist's discussions with the teacher having difficulty and with several students revealed that early in the semester the students began to test the limits set by their teachers. This particular teacher, however, had taught college students and had also had some difficulty accepting and exercising authority; she told the girls that she considered their behavior childish and "ignored it, hoping it would go away." Her failure to set firm limits and her inability to effect external control of their impulses intensified the anxiety the girls were experiencing as a result of their phase of development. They projected the intolerance and contempt they felt toward their own insecurity onto the teacher whom they perceived, like themselves, as weak and insecure. Such feelings would ordinarily be reserved for a vulnerable peer. The girls said of the unfortunate teacher, "She was too soft. We never knew when to stop," and of the other teacher, whom they admired, "She liked us and joked with us, but she always made it clear how far to go. You always knew where you stood."

In summary, early adolescence is a period of rapid physical change that marks the end of childhood and the beginning of adulthood. The young adolescent experiences an intensification of impulses, develops a strong attitude of defensiveness, establishes a new intimacy with one or two peers of the same sex, and manifests a new and extended capacity for critical and abstract thought.

Middle Adolescence

Middle adolescence comprises approximately the years from fifteen to eighteen, the period the average individual spends in high school. With the exception of a few large-scale studies of normal high school students, investigations have given this phase relatively little attention. Psychologically, a relative inner tranquility prevails during these years.

In mid-adolescence the individual must come to terms with his new body image and with his sexual identity. The recognition and acceptance of what the boy perceives as features of masculinity and the girl as features of femininity contribute to a mature identity. If an individual does not adequately fulfill cultural stereotypes because of slow physical development or genetic and family variations, he may suffer negative feelings about his body. Since few individuals fit the stereotype completely, some degree of dissatisfaction with the body occurs frequently. Studies of high school students show that a large percentage expressed dissatisfaction with one physical trait or another—their weight, height, voice, or complexion—though dissatisfaction occurs less frequently than in junior high school students, that is, in early adolescents (Frazier and Lisonbee, 1950).

The first serious effort to separate from parents usually occurs in mid-adolescence. This attempt may evoke feelings of loss and mourning and contribute to brief episodes of moodiness and irritability. Parents may also react to threatened separation in diverse and subtle ways that make separation more difficult. Feelings of loneliness and isolation may give rise to overin-

dulgence in food or long periods of idleness alternating with self-denial and intense work. The influence of parents begins to wane at this age, and peer influence takes on increased significance. Recent studies have shown that the transition from parental influence to peer-group influence is occurring at an increasingly early age in the United States (Bronfenbrenner, 1970). Thus parents no longer serve as models and guides to behavior to the same extent they did a generation ago. Because the peer group is often in conflict with parental values, an adolescent today finds it difficult to ascertain what behavior is expected of him and thus suffers a kind of culture shock within his own culture.

The adolescent will attempt to cope with the confusion, loneliness, and isolation he feels by establishing relationships with adults and peers outside of the family for the support, guidance, and identification he previously received from his parents. Intense attachments or "crushes" may be formed with teachers, coaches, or older students, and not infrequently, in fantasy, with celebrities. The adolescent's tenuous identity often makes him feel uncomfortable, however, when a relationship with a firmly established identity becomes too close. Thus close adult relationships may change rapidly, not only because they arouse anxiety in the adolescent but also because they reactivate yearnings and unresolved conflicts with parents. The need to establish independence and a clear inner definition may cause the adolescent to devalue his parents in an effort to make separation from them easier. Relationships with parents and other adults may therefore alternate between great emotional warmth and cooperation and open defiance and rebelliousness.

Relationships with peers of the same sex take on special significance during these years, providing support needed for establishing independence from the family. Acceptance by the peer group is enormously important, and the individual will take great pains to conform to the musical taste, language, dress, and other customs of adolescent culture. This culture changes rapidly, and what is acceptable one year may be looked on with disdain the next. Long hours on the telephone with close friends may consume a large segment of the day and help fill the void caused by loneliness and isolation. Activities with peers in athletic and other organizations also help overcome a sense of not belonging. Considerable sexual energy may be sublimated in athletic activities, with an unusual willingness to engage in demanding training schedules. From this particular age group, therefore, may come world-class athletes, especially in sports such as gymnastics and swimming.

In mid-adolescence, emotional energy previously invested in the parents now finds a source outside the family. Though the adolescent yearns for close relationships, he may find them difficult to tolerate. Considerable time and energy may be spent daydreaming of someone who has been observed at a distance and idolized. The adolescent may reach out tentatively toward members of the opposite sex. When a friendship with such a person develops and dating begins, disillusionment often sets in quickly and another distant person is idolized. This pattern protects the adolescent from commitments for which he is not yet ready emotionally. The telephone, so popular with this age group, allows a degree of intimacy without concomitant physical closeness, which the adolescent may find threatening. The breakup of a relationship with a member of the opposite sex, tenuous though it may have been, may nevertheless prove exceedingly painful and cause a major emotional crisis.

Sexual impulses, intensified during puberty, remain intense during this phase of adolescence. Permissiveness, the lack of moral guidelines, the sexually stimulating aspects of the mass media, and other dimensions of today's society make control of these impulses particularly difficult for the modern adolescent. Here again he finds himself in conflict—a part of him desiring sexual intimacy and another part fearing it, feeling emotionally unready for it, and sometimes seeing such expression as contrary to parental values. How the adolescent handles these conflicting internal and external demands determines in large measure his future character structure. His ability to attain impulse control will determine the extent of this control as an adult (Blos, 1968). Character has been defined as "the habitual mode of bringing into harmony the tasks presented by internal demands and by the external

world" (Fenichel, 1945, p. 467). It has been observed that most adolescents are unprepared psychologically for coitus (Group for the Advancement of Psychiatry, 1968) and that the new sexual freedom has a destructive effect on adolescents' ability to sublimate sexual impulses and establish a mature character structure (Deutsch, 1967; Nicholi, 1974b). Sublimation and control of impulses have become particularly difficult in a society that no longer considers the sublimation of sexual and aggressive impulses to be one of its civilizing tasks. An increasing number of young people seek psychiatric help because of inability to control impulses, in marked contrast to the inhibition of impulses that characterized clinical problems among the young in the past.

As the mid-adolescent enters late adolescence he confronts the difficult task of leaving home, of choosing a college or finding a job, and of finding among the billions of people on earth someone with whom to share his life. He must make the difficult shift from responsibility to an outside parent to responsibility for himself—a change that makes failure harder to tolerate. Finally, he must cope with subtle maneuvers by his parents to keep him dependent and thus to avoid the pain of loss.

Late Adolescence

Late adolescence is an indefinite span of time beginning at approximately eighteen years of age and extending well into the twenties. How far it extends varies with each individual and depends on how long he takes to accomplish the psychological tasks required to permit him to feel comfortable assuming an adult role in society. Some individuals struggle with these adolescent tasks throughout their lives.

By focusing on a particular late-adolescent life style popular within a small group of young people during the last decade, Keniston (1970) has attempted to delineate a new and separate stage of development called "youth." Most investigators, however, consider this phase simply a variant of late adolescence (Hamburg, 1974).

Late adolescence begins for a large majority of individuals upon graduation from high school. Whether they obtain a job or go to college, they enter a phase dedicated primarily to the task of defining who they are and establishing some notion of what they want to become.

Erikson has focused considerable attention on late adolescence and has contributed concepts that have proved especially helpful in understanding its complexities. He considers the period of prolonged adolescence—the time most individuals in our society spend in college or job training—as a "psychosocial moratorium," a period of delay in human development. During this time, "through free role experimentation [the individual] may find a niche in some section of his society, a niche which is firmly defined and yet seems to be uniquely made for him" (1968, p. 156). Erikson sees this delay as necessary for the sexually mature adolescent to catch up with himself psychologically and socially —that is, to develop a "psychosocial capacity for intimacy" and a "psychosocial readiness for parenthood" (p. 156). Until he has some understanding of who he is, some concept of how others see him, the adolescent will not be ready to make the types of commitment to career and to a mate demanded by the adult world. "When maturing in his physical capacity for procreation," Erikson writes, "the human youth is as yet unable either to love in that binding manner which only two persons with reasonably formed identities can offer each other, or to care consistently enough to sustain parenthood. The two sexes, of course, differ greatly in these respects and so do individuals" (p. 242). The singular task that the late adolescent must therefore complete, before entering adulthood, is to establish a unique identity of his own. Erikson's concepts of "ego identity," "identity crisis," and "identity confusion" shed light on the adolescent's struggle toward self-definition and maturity.

Erikson first used the term *identity crisis* to describe the condition he observed in veterans of the Second World War who experienced the loss of a "sense of personal sameness and historical continuity" (p. 17). He called this a loss of "ego identity" because it involved impairment of functions attributed to the ego. He then observed the same state of confusion in severely disturbed young people, noting that at this age the condition was acute and usually transient in nature.

He concluded eventually that an identity crisis occurred as a part of all normal adolescent development. The severity of the crisis determined whether it warranted psychiatric attention.

The clinical picture of severe, acute identity diffusion includes an inability to make decisions, a sense of isolation, a feeling of inner emptiness, an inability to establish satisfying relationships, a distorted concept of time, a sense of urgency, and a marked inability to work or concentrate. Sometimes the identity confusion finds expression in what Erikson calls a "negative identity." Here the adolescent takes on a role presented to him as most undesirable or dangerous. Sometimes the negative identity may be a reaction to excessive demands of overly ambitious parents. A parent with deep-seated conflicts may unconsciously foster a negative identity by continuously reminding the adolescent to avoid behavior he would not otherwise even consider or by subtly rewarding such behavior with increased attention. A mother with an unconscious need to behave promiscuously may subtly encourage her daughter in this direction by excessive warnings against it. Erikson describes a mother with an alcoholic brother who responded selectively to those traits in her son that seemed to point toward the son's following in his uncle's footsteps.

Adolescent Behavior Patterns

The concept of identity provides a framework for understanding many aspects of both normal and pathological adolescent behavior. The following discussion focuses briefly on a few salient features of this behavior as experienced by adolescents entering the last quarter of the twentieth century.

Drugs. During the past decade, ingestion of drugs for nonmedical reasons has become a common adolescent experience. A 1973 survey of illicit drug use indicates that 40.9 percent of adolescents take drugs in some form (Gelineau, Johnson, and Pearsall, 1973). Until the 1970s, drug use occurred primarily in late adolescence, and studies focused on patterns of use among college students (Mizner, Barter, and Werme, 1970; Rouse and Ewing, 1973; Walters, Goethals, and Pope, 1972). Several of these studies showed a majority of college students to be involved to different degrees with a variety of drugs.

Though enormous public concern over drug use resulted in the appointment of presidential committees and the passage of legislation to cope with the problem, its causes and the extent of drug use among the young remain unclear. Research findings have been complex and at times misleading. One study, for example, may show a marked decrease in drug use in a particular age group; another, a marked increase.

On the basis of research conducted with college students, Nicholi describes finding "a complex, constantly changing pattern of drug use" wherein different drugs become popular at different times and among different age groups (1974a, p. 224). Evidence indicates that, although during the 1970s older college students have been turning away from drugs, overall usage among adolescents has risen, with increasing numbers of younger adolescents involved. A considerably larger percentage of entering college freshmen have already used drugs and their involvement has in many cases begun as early as junior high school. Early involvement occurs primarily with marijuana usage; the hallucinogenic drugs do not usually enter the picture until college. A later study among high school and junior high school students by Hamburg, Kraemer, and Jahnke supports these findings. These investigators have reported that drug and alcohol use among younger students is substantial and increasing and that they found a substantial amount of drug use among junior high school students (1975). They also found a relationship between age and use of certain drugs; the median age of first use was 13.1 years for hard liquor, 13.8 years for marijuana, and over 17 years for hallucinogenic drugs, stimulants, depressants, and narcotics.

What motivates the adolescent to take drugs? Does the immense popularity of drugs among adolescents reflect an increase in psychopathology? Or is drug use merely a currently popular mode of finding new experiences and participating in a life style that differs from and defies the establishment? A number of studies have compared drug users with nonusers in reference to psychological functioning and psychiatric impairment. A study of college students by Robbins et al. found drug users to be more "moody, anxious, impulsive, and rebellious" than a control sample of nonusers (1970, p. 1748). Other studies have shown users to have "relatively poor social adjustment" (Mirin et al., 1971, p. 1134), "passive life styles and low purpose in life" (Shean and Fechtmann, 1971, p. 112), and "hysterical-obsessive personality traits" (Zinberg and Weil, 1970, p. 119). Harmatz, Shader, and Salzman (1972) tested large numbers of marijuana users and nonusers for manifest psychiatric symptomatology and found significantly more impairment among the users. This difference became more pronounced when the marijuana users also used other drugs for nonprescriptive purposes.

In an attempt to explore the psychological reasons that young people, many of whom placed a high premium on intellectual functioning, took drugs that are potentially dangerous to the mind, Nicholi (1974a) investigated a sample of college students who had ingested LSD. This study attempted to ascertain who influenced students in the initial ingestion of the drug and to determine the emotional factors that motivated its continued use. Findings include the following: The initial experience with LSD results from the influence of a peer who reports pleasurable reactions to the use of the drug. The influence of a roommate or friend carries considerably more weight than newspaper articles read about the dangers of the drug or rumors about other students who have had unhappy experiences. A strong relationship exists between the specific emotional conflicts of these students and the claims made for the drug by its proponents. In the minds of the students, promises about what the drug can do for them far outweigh the risk. A few of the needs the students feel the drug can meet are helping them feel love for others and overcome a sense of loneliness, making them productive and creative, making them more socially and sexually effective, and filling a moral and spiritual void. However, "the failure of the drug [LSD] to meet these expectations plus its inconsistency in producing the desired mood alteration has led to a gradual decline in its use" (p. 225). As the use of LSD has decreased, the use of marijuana and alcohol has increased.

During the past fifteen years, drug use has become widespread among adolescents in this country. To understand the normal and pathological manifestations of this age group better, the clinician must be alert to constantly changing patterns in the use of drugs during the various phases of adolescence.

Sexuality. Throughout adolescence the individual struggles with an acute sense of not belonging. No longer a child and not yet an adult, he often feels that he is an outsider and that no one needs or wants him. The late adolescent who leaves the familiar surroundings of home for the strange environment of a college or a job often feels adrift and struggles with a profound sense of loneliness and longing. This feeling in turn intensifies his need or "hunger" for a close relationship, especially with someone of the opposite sex. This need motivates him to reach out for such a relationship—tentatively at first but, depending on the individual, with increasing persistence. The self-centeredness and the pervasive sense of inadequacy of early and middle adolescence gradually lessen and make more tolerable the risk of possible rejection inherent in reaching out for this closeness. In establishing these early relationships, the adolescent tends to idealize and overestimate new friends, to experience sudden intense episodes of "falling in love," to become suddenly disenchanted, and to change to new involvements. Though these heterosexual relationships of middle and late adolescence may be whimsical, capricious, and short-lived, they may nevertheless involve deep emotional involvement, and their termination may cause some of the most painful feelings an individual encounters.

For many adolescents today, the sexual freedom of our culture exacerbates a conflict-ridden issue. Because of the early onset of puberty, the adolescent is biologically ready for coitus at a considerably earlier age than his counterpart of a century ago. Yet his psychological and social readiness is considerably delayed. Many factors account for this delay, not the least being that the long years of education required to prepare for most careers today prolong emotional and financial dependence on the family and make early marriage difficult. In addition, the adolescent has been reared in a permissive society. In this society the mass media, for purposes of exploitation, tend to keep sexual impulses at a high pitch and to encourage their free expression. The adolescent, especially the older adolescent, has an intense need not only for sexual expression but also for guidelines on how best to conduct this aspect of his social life. As part of his struggle for identity, he seeks a moral framework for his life and desires to know not only what behavior is expected of him but also what behavior is in his best interests. When he turns to the adult world, he often finds more confusion than enlightenment. Even when he turns to the medical profession, he may receive conflicting messages. The problem of sexual ethics within the profession itself is an issue of increasing concern (see chapter 1, "The Therapist-Patient Relationship"), and the professional literature on adolescence may prove more confusing than helpful. For example, the Group for the Advancement of Psychiatry's *Normal Adolescence* (1968) raises the question of whether premarital intercourse fosters healthy psychological development in the adolescent. In answering this question, the authors attempt objectively to present "two major and opposing points of view" and state that the answer "finally has to be formulated in terms of the maturity of a given adolescent boy or girl" (p. 86). They state, however, that those who express concern over sexual permissiveness in adolescence derive their thinking "more from fear of sexual impulses and guilt over sexuality than from careful observation and study" (p. 87). The authors also speak of traditional sexual standards that discourage intercourse outside of marriage as "a set of taboos and prohibitions which historically may have been appropriate but today seem inappropriate in the light of medical scientific advance" (p. 85). Modern medicine, the authors imply, has made invalid the concerns upon which these standards were probably based—"concerns about venereal disease, illegitimate pregnancy and its destructive impact on the family" (p. 85). Even the more unsophisticated adolescents, however, realize that these concerns not only remain extremely relevant today but present a greater problem to our society than at any time in the past. This kind of information has made many adolescents feel disillusioned and misled by proponents of the new sexual permissiveness and confused as to where to turn for reliable guidelines on how to conduct their lives.

Deutsch believes this new sexual freedom has failed to keep its many promises. She states that young people caught up in this new freedom "suffer from emotional deprivation and a kind of deadening, as a result of their so-called free and unlimited sexual excitement" and that "the spasmodic search for methods by which to increase the pleasure of the sexual experience indicates unmistakably that the sexual freedom of our adolescents does not provide the ecstatic element that is inherent—or should be—in one of the most gratifying of human experiences" (1967, p. 102). She goes on to say, "The inadequacy . . . of the sexual experience as such is expressed not only in their needs for drugs but also in the increasing interest they show in sexual perversions" (p. 102). Deutsch refers to the new sexual freedom as creating "a psychological disaster" (p. 102) and interfering with "the development of real tender feelings of love and enchantment" (p. 103). She also refers to the "social and personal catastrophe of illegitimate motherhood" among young girls (p. 106) and expresses the fear that this phenomenon will increase. Her fears are confirmed by statistics that show over a half-million teenage pregnancies for 1974, with a quarter of a million terminating in abortion. That 50 percent of teenage marriages end in divorce within five years makes these findings no less disturbing. Deutsch points out that teenage pregnancies are "compulsive" and that sexual instruction and modern contraceptives will do little to prevent them.

Many who have worked closely with adolescents over the past decade have realized that the new sexual freedom has by no means led to greater pleasure, freedom, and openness, more meaningful relationships between the sexes, or exhilarating relief from stifling inhibitions. Clinical experience has shown that the new permissiveness has often led to empty relationships, feelings of self-contempt and worthlessness, an epidemic of venereal disease, and a rapid increase in unwanted pregnancies. Clinicians working with college students began commenting on these effects as early as ten years ago. They have noted that students caught up in this new sexual freedom found it "unsatisfying and meaningless" (Halleck, 1967, p. 642). In a more recent study of normal college students (those not under the care of a psychiatrist), Nicholi (1974b) found that, although their sexual behavior by and large appeared to be a desperate attempt to overcome a profound sense of loneliness, they described their sexual relationships as less than satisfactory and as providing little of the emotional closeness they desired. They described pervasive feelings of guilt and haunting concerns that they were using others and being used as "sexual objects." These students' experiences underscore Freud's observation that, when sexual freedom is unrestricted, "love [becomes] worthless and life empty" (S. Freud, 1912, p. 188). The disillusionment of late adolescence with this sphere of their lives as well as with drugs has contributed to the recent religious preoccupation among youth, especially the trend toward traditional religious faith. Though the basic Judeo-Christian morality conflicts strongly with their past behavior and current mores, they find the clear-cut boundaries it imposes less confusing than no boundaries at all and more helpful in relating to members of the opposite sex as "persons rather than sexual objects" (Nicholi, 1974b).

Like drugs, sexual behavior may be an expression of severe inner conflict. Halleck (1967) has shown a relationship between promiscuity and the presence of severe emotional conflicts among college students seeking psychiatric help.

Cars and motorcycles. No discussion of adolescence would be complete without mention of the significant role the motor vehicle often plays in the modern adolescent life style. Erikson notes that "the most widespread expression of the discontented search of youth as well as of its native exuberance is the craving for locomotion" (1968, pp. 243–244). He writes that "the motor engine, of course, is the very heart and symbol of our technology, and its mastery the aim and aspiration of much of modern youth. In connection with immature youth, however, it must be understood that [the] motor car . . . offers to those so inclined passive locomotion with an intoxicating delusion of being intensely active . . . While vastly inflating a sense of motor omnipotence, the need for active locomotion often remains unfulfilled."

For the adolescent seeking a clear inner definition, the car or the motorcycle may assume intense symbolic meaning with many levels of emotional appeal. The adolescent's preoccupation with a car's external appearance—the constant taking apart and rebuilding, painting, and modifying its appearance and sound—often reflects the bodily dissatisfaction so characteristic of this age group.

The motor vehicle may be used to satisfy inner needs and to work out inner conflicts. Through the motor vehicle, the adolescent may express anger, defiance, power, mobility, and independence from the adult world. The automobile often provides not only an image of great speed and power but the appearance of a self-contained, enclosed world allowing for the expression of feelings he would otherwise be unable to express. The automobile also provides privacy for dating and intimacy.

The motor vehicle, like drugs and sexual behavior, may be a means of expressing severe inner conflict. This fact may explain in part why motor vehicle accidents are the leading cause of death in late adolescence. Although a vast number of studies has focused on the emotional and psychological causes of automobile accidents in the general population, few have focused solely on the adolescent, even though adolescent deaths constitute a large percentage of motor vehicle fatalities. One study on the motorcycle, illustrates how adolescent pathology expresses itself via a motor vehicle and contributes to injury and death. The motorcycle is a particularly good vehicle for understanding this phenomenon; although the number of adolescents who drive motorcycles is only one-tenth the number who drive automobiles, the motorcycle accounts for twice as many injuries as automobiles. It is sixteen times more dangerous than the automobile and causes five times as many deaths per mile (Cracchiolo, Blazina, and MacKinnon, 1968).

Nicholi (1970) presents findings of an in-depth study of a group of patients manifesting unusual emotional investment in the motorcycle, all of whom were accident prone and had experienced one or more serious motorcycle accidents. The motorcycle intruded into their daily activities, their repetitive dreams, and their conscious and unconscious fantasies. Among these patients, the striking similarity of the symbolic meaning of the motorcycle, the tendency to use the vehicle as both an adaptive and a defensive means of dealing with emotional conflict, and the remarkable number of other shared characteristics led to the designation of the clinical disorder from which they suffered as "the motorcycle syndrome." The essential features of this syndrome are the following: (1) an unusual preoccupation with the motorcycle; (2) a history of accident proneness extending to early childhood; (3) persistent fear of bodily injury; (4) a distant conflict-ridden relationship with the father and a strong identification with the mother; (5) extreme passivity and an inability to compete; (6) a defective self-image; (7) poor impulse control; (8) fear of and counterphobic involvement with aggressive girls; and (9) impotence and intense homosexual concerns.

These patients experienced a serious ego defect stemming from a distant and difficult father-son relationship. A tenuous masculine identification led them to perceive the motorcycle as an essential part of their body image. The motorcycle served to strengthen a fragile ego. The conscious attraction to and fear of the motorcycle was found to parallel unconscious conflicts relating to an ambivalence toward expression of what the patient considered the masculine part of himself. The relationship of the vehicle to these unconscious conflicts compounded the adolescent's anxiety, increased his tension, lessened his control, and made him more susceptible to accidents. In these adolescents, the motorcycle served as an extension of what the patient considered his masculine self—the assertive, active, aggressive, competitive parts of his psychological make-up. Each of the patients showed a lifelong avoidance of and tenuous identification with a highly competent and critical father that left them inhibited and unable to exercise the assertive components of their emotional make-up effectively. When the adolescent felt weak, the motorcycle gave him strength; when passive, a "sense of doing something and getting somewhere" (p. 594); when effeminate, a feeling of virility; when impotent, a sense of potency and power; when withdrawn, a sense of assertion and thrusting forward. These positive feelings, however, were never free from the haunting awareness of danger.

The motorcycle was found to serve both a helpful and a harmful function—that is, it is used both adaptively and defensively. Helpful or adaptive functions involve attracting attention, giving a feeling of strength, and improving, if only transiently, the patient's inner definition. The cycle helped him express the more assertive, more active part of himself—the part that, having been inhibited and paralyzed, could not otherwise find expression.

The maladaptive use of the cycle involves replacing constructive use of time with relatively unconstructive activity. Charging through the streets on a motorcycle gives the adolescent a sense of moving ahead, of doing, and of exerting himself; but it is finally a false sense and a poor substitute for concentrated effort. Racing a motorcycle into the middle of the night relieves the anxiety of rejection or failure, but it effects little change in the conditions causing the anxiety. A fast, noisy, breathtaking ride tends to relieve apprehension over exams, but it helps little in preparing for them. The cycle simulates sexual feeling and even helps the adolescent approach a girl, but it contributes little to forming a meaningful relationship with her. The cycle helps express anger, but the destructive tendencies of these adolescents made a machine that can travel 125 miles an hour a less than adaptive means of doing so.

In addition to these maladaptive aspects, the patients' conscious fears of the motorcycle —often based on a realistic awareness of its dangers—reactivated unconscious fears, intensified anxiety, and lessened their control of the vehicle. The psychological factors made the motorcycle especially dangerous to these young people and contributed to the high rate of serious accidents among them.

The Pathology of Adolescence

Confusion surrounding the pathology of adolescence has led to frequent diagnostic errors in the past and, overall, to a less than completely successful therapeutic experience with this age group. Many factors have contributed to this confusion. First, some forms of adolescent turmoil do indeed mimic severe pathology, though not as frequently as was once believed. This similarity has sometimes led the clinician to diagnose a serious disorder one day only to be confronted with a completely recovered patient the next or to dismiss as transient turmoil what later proves to be a persistent, serious disorder. Second, adolescence does not fit the classical psychodynamic theoretical concepts, which have therefore contributed relatively little to our understanding of either its normal state or its pathology. After trying unsuccessfully to fit the data into a preexisting theoretical framework, investigators attempted to modify the theory to fit the data. Some of these efforts—Erikson's concepts, for instance—have proved helpful. Third, treatment of the adolescent has often been programmed for failure before it begins. The adolescent, frequently referred for treatment against his will by the parent with whom he is most in conflict, tends to see the therapist as an ally of the parent and as part of the adult world he is rebelling against. Struggling for autonomy, he finds enforced treatment a threat and often reacts to the treatment situation and the therapist with resistance if not open hostility. Partly out of confusion and misconception and partly out of frustration, some theoreticians have tended to view psychiatric symptoms in adolescence as part of the normal maturational process, and some have even suggested that the adolescent not be treated at all.

Recent research—spurred in part by the widespread unrest and drug use of the 1960s—has gradually changed these concepts of pathology. Large-scale studies of both normal and emotionally disturbed adolescents have called into serious question the traditional concept that intense upheaval mimicking all degrees of psychopathology is universally experienced in adolescence. On the contrary, studies have revealed that the vast majority of adolescents experience relatively little turmoil and few manifest psychiatric symptoms. Though some rebelliousness, especially in early adolescent boys, and episodes of moodiness and irritability occur frequently, these episodes are short-lived and in no way approach sufficient intensity to be considered pathological.

Recent studies have made untenable the conviction long embraced by psychiatrists "that the upholding of a steady equilibrium during the adolescent process is in itself abnormal" (A. Freud, 1958, p. 267) or that adolescence involves by definition structural upheavals that may resemble any of the serious adult disorders. These studies have also led clinicians to pay closer attention to psychiatric symptoms when they do occur in the adolescent. Psychiatrists no longer quickly dismiss symptoms as transient manifestations of the normal adolescent process without first assessing them carefully. Masterson's studies (1967) have shown that severe psychiatric disorder in adolescence usually does not disappear with time. If left untreated or incompletely treated, most of these disorders tend to persist and become psychiatric disorders of adulthood.

Although clinicians have expressed the need for epidemiological studies of adolescence (Henderson, Krupinski, and Stoller, 1971), no comprehensive study covering all of adolescence has yet been conducted. One epidemiological investigation of college students (Nicholi, 1967) found

TABLE 24.1. Secondary diagnoses of psychiatric dropouts. (From Nicholi, 1967. Copyright 1967, the American Psychiatric Association. Reprinted by permission.)

Category	Number	Percentage
Manic-depressive reaction	7	1.3
Psychotic depressive reaction	3	0.5
Schizophrenic reaction	29	5.3
Anxiety reaction	56	10.1
Dissociative reaction	2	0.4
Conversion reaction	2	0.4
Phobic reaction	1	0.2
Obsessive-compulsive reaction	13	2.4
Depressive reaction	122	22.1
Inadequate personality	6	1.1
Schizoid personality	36	6.5
Cyclothymic personality	6	1.1
Paranoid personality	3	0.5
Passive-aggressive personality	34	6.2
Compulsive personality	6	1.1
Sexual deviation	16	2.9
Emotionally unstable personality	15	2.7
Adjustment reaction of adolescence	130	23.6
Miscellaneous	64	11.6

that 10 percent of the undergraduate population suffered emotional conflicts sufficiently severe to prompt them to consult a psychiatrist during their undergraduate experience. Among 551 students who left college for psychiatric reasons, this study reports the following diagnostic categories: 35.7 percent (196 students) with a diagnosis of neurotic disorder; 23.6 percent (130 students) with a diagnosis of transient situational disorder; 22.1 percent (122 students) with a diagnosis of character disorder; 7.1 percent (39 students) with psychotic disorders; and 11.6 percent (64 students) with miscellaneous other diagnoses. For the prevalence of more specific illnesses, see table 24.1. By far the most prevalent of disorders among these students were adjustment reactions of adolescence (23.6 percent) and depression (22.1 percent). A little over 5 percent of these students suffered from various forms of schizophrenia. On the basis of this sample—one that may to some degree represent all phases of adolescence—the pathology afflicting the adolescent runs nearly the entire gamut experienced by adults. The exception, of course, is that vaguely defined conglomeration of symptoms referred to as "adjustment reaction of adolescence."

Adjustment Reaction of Adolescence

Because the diagnostic category of adolescent adjustment reactions occurs most frequently and is the most difficult to diagnose with certainty, it will be useful to focus primarily on describing its features and discussing its differentiation from the other common disorders of this age group. For a further discussion of pathology, the reader is referred to other chapters on the clinical syndromes.

The term *adjustment reaction of adolescence* is listed in the DSM-II as one of the transient situational disturbances—"those transient disorders of any severity (including those of psychotic proportion) that occur in individuals without any apparent underlying mental disorders and that represent an acute reaction to overwhelming environmental stress." As examples of its symptoms, the manual lists "irritability and depression associated with school failure and manifested by temper outbursts, brooding and discouragement" (A.P.A., 1968, p. 49).

Clinical features. The outstanding clinical feature of this disturbance is a gradual or acute change in behavior indicating that the adolescent is having difficulty coping with internal or external stress. Its manifestations therefore vary with each phase of adolescence and with the stresses peculiar to that phase. In early adolescence, for example, the inability to cope may manifest itself in a marked increase in the open expression of aggression and defiance. Anger may lie close to the surface, and the slightest frustration or irritation may provoke an angry outburst or temper tantrum characteristic of a younger child. The intensity of such outbursts appears inappropriate to the precipitating circumstances. Defiance may be directed against all authority —parents, older siblings, teachers, coaches, or police—or it may be expressed in delinquent behavior within groups, where the risk of an untoward reaction from parents or other authority is lessened. The stresses characteristic of this early phase (discussed earlier in detail) include the biological changes of puberty, the increased peer pressure to be popular socially and to compete athletically, and increased academic demands and family responsibilities that necessitate giving up time previously spent in play.

In addition to aggressive, acting-out behavior, the early adolescent may react to stress by becoming excessively passive and withdrawing from his usual interests and activity. He may manifest clinical signs and symptoms of adult depression. The breakup of an early adolescent "chumship" or the failure to make an athletic team or to attain academic goals can result in withdrawal, loss of self-esteem, moodiness, chronic fatigue, and feelings of anxiety and depression. Hyperactive behavior with great bursts of energy may alternate with periods of passivity and withdrawal. Suicide gestures, as a cry for help, are not uncommon reactions to stress during this phase.

In middle adolescence, regressive behavior, severe anxiety, or episodes of depression result from demands made to establish heterosexual relationships, to become independent of parents, or to make decisions about what college to attend. The breakup of a romantic relationship may precipitate a crisis of apathy and withdrawal; filling out applications for college or for a job and making plans to leave home permanently may evoke acute anxiety and fears of growing old, of parents dying, of being abandoned, or of being unprepared to face the outside world. Feelings of depersonalization may occur and be expressed in terms of strange sensations within the body. During this phase, strong attachment to a friend of the same sex may evoke doubts about sexual identity. The fear of sexual inadequacy and the need to test masculinity or femininity may lead to sexual experience for which the individual is emotionally unprepared and which may therefore result in anxiety, guilt, despondency, and feelings of worthlessness and self-contempt; these feelings may interfere with the adolescent's functioning and require psychiatric help.

In late adolescence the stresses that precipitate adjustment reactions involve primarily those processes concerned with forming an identity pattern, finding an answer to the questions "Who am I?" and "What am I to become?" The late adolescent may experience considerable stress moving from a home where he has received recognition, comfort, and security to a college or university environment where no one seems to be aware of his existence. The solitude of study may intensify loneliness—perhaps the most painful and intolerable of all human feelings. A highly competitive academic environment may create an underlying atmosphere of apprehension about the possibility of failure and about work that appears never to be done.

Other factors may also cause stress in the late adolescent. The pressure to choose a career, to make a lifelong commitment to vocation, may overwhelm the adolescent. He often lacks not only a clear idea of his interests and abilities but also firsthand knowledge of what specific career choices involve. The inability to sustain a close relationship with someone of the opposite sex may also precipitate a crisis. As the late adolescent completes college, the internal and external pressure to find a mate intensifies, and the termination of a relationship may precipitate feelings of failure and inadequacy.

Many late adolescents today also find the moral confusion of our particular culture stressful. They complain of the absence of a moral frame of reference within which to conduct their lives and experience confusion and turmoil in attempting to live without moral guidelines. Others complain of a "vague restlessness" and confusion about the meaning of their college experience specifically and their lives generally. They often become preoccupied with questions of purpose and destiny and acutely concerned with the passage of time, aging, and death. The twentieth or twenty-first birthday often precipitates a mild crisis, perhaps because the former signifies leaving one's teens and the security of childhood, while the latter signifies entering adulthood with a burden of responsibilities and "impossible decisions." Late adolescents speak despairingly of feeling old, of having accomplished little in their lives, and, as students, of living a parasitical existence (Nicholi, 1974b). Distance from family, loneliness, a sense of moral and spiritual void, and dissatisfaction with themselves and their relationships precipitate a crisis with anxiety, intense turmoil, despondency, and other symptoms. Because these symptoms usually disappear once the internal or external stress lessens, they constitute the clinical features of an adjustment reaction of adolescence.

Mental status. Examination of a patient experiencing an adjustment reaction of adolescence may reveal a variety of signs and symptoms but no single pathognomonic feature. With an early adolescent, whose parents may refer him for evaluation against his will, the therapist may encounter considerable hostility and uncooperativeness. The patient may appear solemn and answer questions in monosyllables or with a shrug of his shoulders. Older adolescents are usually more cooperative, especially if they have been referred by a peer, older friend, or advisor. The adolescent often appears restless, irritable, and apprehensive. He may have difficulty talking because of dryness of the mouth. The patient may look sad, withdrawn, and extremely tired; these signs may appear separately or along with those described earlier. He may have dark shadows under his eyes, may appear frightened and confused, and may complain of difficulty concentrating. He may describe an acute sense of not belonging and manifest an inability to keep track of time. In addition to the frequent findings of confusion, anxiety, and depression,

the examiner may find signs and symptoms that mimic those of any of the adult emotional disorders.

Etiology. Adolescent adjustment reactions, like other adolescent disorders, may be conceptualized within different frameworks. For example, all adolescent psychopathology may be considered to result from attempts on the part of the individual to establish an identity, a clear inner definition of himself. Adjustment reactions of adolescence may therefore all be considered manifestations of an identity crisis. Erikson's concepts of identity diffusion, negative identity, and psychosocial moratorium are helpful, especially in understanding adjustment reactions occurring in late adolescence. Other theoreticians, however, have tended to conceptualize the causes of adolescent psychopathology within the framework of ego defenses against strong dependent feelings toward the parents (A. Freud, 1958). The particular defenses used determine the specific form of psychopathology. For example, the adolescent may react to anxiety induced by his dependence with flight to parent substitutes outside the family. This defense by displacement of feelings may lead to relationships with adults similar in age to the parents but opposite in all other respects, with persons between the adolescent's and the parents' generations who represent ideals, or with "gangs" of contemporaries. These gang relationships may lead to acting-out behavior that brings the adolescent into conflict with school and other authorities.

In addition, the adolescent may defend against his feelings toward his parents by turning them into their opposites—love into hate, dependency into rebellion, admiration into derision. Denial and reaction formation (see chapter 9, "The Dynamic Bases of Psychopathology") are the common defenses used here. The clinical picture shows a hostile adolescent in open and compulsive rebellion against his parents.

Still another common defense is the withdrawal of feelings from the parents and their investment in the self. This process may result in inflated ideas of the self, in fantasies of unlimited power, or in hypochondriacal sensations; alternatively, the adolescent may react by regressive changes in all parts of his personality. Defense by regression may result in a lapse in ego functioning, in difficulty distinguishing between the internal and external worlds, and in a severe state of confusion and turmoil. Defenses against the intensification of impulses that the adolescent experiences may result in adolescent asceticism, a state in which the adolescent denies himself all pleasures, even food and sleep, and lives a spartan existence for brief periods of time. Eating disorders, withdrawal, and other symptoms may result.

Differential diagnosis. The identification of adjustment reactions of adolescence presents one of the most difficult of all diagnostic problems. Unfortunately, this diagnosis has often been used as a "wastepaper basket," including all adolescent problems not understood by the examiner. Because an adolescent adjustment reaction may simulate or occur simultaneously with other psychiatric disorders, the adolescent must be observed over a period of time and assessed carefully.

In making this diagnosis, the clinician must keep in mind that the symptoms—primarily anxiety, confusion, and despondency—are reactions to internal or external stress; once this stress is reduced or eliminated, the symptoms will usually disappear and the patient will return to normal. If the symptoms are severe and seriously interfere with the patient's functioning, they may, if untreated, persist and develop into an adult psychiatric disorder.

The differential diagnosis must include consideration of all of the major psychiatric disorders whose symptoms will become clear when the adolescent is observed over a period of time. It may be particularly difficult to distinguish between severe adjustment reactions and schizophrenia. A history of psychological trauma in early childhood may indicate the more serious pathology. Nicholi and Watt (1977), for example, have demonstrated a statistically significant higher incidence of parental death in the childhoods of adolescent schizophrenics than in those of other adolescent psychiatric patients and of normal adolescent controls. Childhood bereavement, this study concluded, though not specific in its pathogenic influence, was a contributing etiological factor in schizophrenia.

When the adolescent suffers from schizophrenia, the symptoms of this disorder (see chapter 11, "Schizophrenic Reactions") will become evident over time. Grinker and Holzman (1973) found that one-third of hospitalized adolescents eventually given the diagnosis of schizophrenia presented no diagnostic difficulty. The other two-thirds presented a clinical picture of adolescent reaction; however, the reactions produced unusually severe chaos and turmoil, so severe that they were considered to be of psychotic proportions. Close observation of these patients revealed the underlying schizophrenic process.

Personality disorders must also be differentiated from adolescent adjustment reactions. A careful history will reveal lifelong patterns of behavior that interfere with a patient's functioning; the type of personality disorder will depend on the particular patterns present (see chapter 14, "Personality Disorders"). The various psychoneurotic disorders must also be considered in the differential diagnosis. As previously mentioned, an adolescent suffering from a specific neurotic disorder will generally manifest the symptoms of that disorder (see chapter 10, "Psychoneurotic Disorders"). The onset of these symptoms can be traced to early conflicts. If an adolescent crisis occurs in an individual with such an underlying disorder, the crisis may precipitate or exacerbate the illness.

Adolescent depression. In evaluating the adolescent, the examiner must be alert to the presence of depression and the accompanying risk of suicide. In recent years the suicide rate among adolescents shows the greatest rise of any age group, and suicide is currently one of the leading causes of adolescent death (Jacobizner, 1965). Despite these statistics, depression among adolescents has been a neglected area of study, partly, perhaps, because in the past many clinicians have seriously doubted the existence of real depression in adolescence and therefore of any real danger of suicide. Recent studies of suicide and epidemiological studies of late adolescence, however, show depression to be one of the most common disorders afflicting this age group.

Depression in adolescence may be a transient, situational reaction or it may be a long-standing, severe, crippling disorder with all of the signs and symptoms of depression in the adult. Manic-depressive psychoses, however, are believed to be extremely rare in early adolescence. Furthermore, the clinical picture of adult depression may not appear before the age of fourteen years. Depression in an adolescent of any age, however, may express itself in ways that make diagnosis extremely difficult. A young adolescent may appear bored, listless, or restless, avoid being alone, and find it difficult to become absorbed in any activity. Sometimes depression expresses itself in alcohol or drug abuse, in sexual promiscuity, in antisocial acting out, in careless automobile and motorcycle driving, or in poor academic performance.

The way internal and external stress can combine forces to effect depression in an adolescent has been illustrated in the study of students who drop out of college for psychiatric reasons. As mentioned earlier, research has indicated that depression is by far the most frequent and most significant causal factor in the decision to leave college (Nicholi, 1967). The types of depression among these dropouts (and perhaps most of the depressions in this age group) appeared not to be related to object loss and therefore were not best understood within traditional concepts. These students' depression seemed to be related more closely to a discrepancy between the actual state of the self, on the one hand, and the ideal state of well-being, on the other. The awareness, gradual or abrupt, of this discrepancy resulted in the clinical picture frequently observed in the dropout: feelings of lassitude, inadequacy, and hopelessness, low self-esteem, and inability to study.

Many of the adolescents in this study were intellectually talented. Their concept of the ideal self was based on both fact and fantasy. The fantasy frequently centered on the need to be perfect—"When I saw that I couldn't get an A, I no longer felt like trying." The concept of the ideal self was based on previous academic success; the home and the secondary school environment once provided maximum positive feedback for that success. The fantasy, the success, and the narcissistic feedback helped defend against strong feelings of inadequacy and deep-seated doubt about intellectual competence. The college environment, on the other hand, provided a minimum of positive feedback. An array of awesome professors and highly competitive classmates threatened the student; the college became no less threatening when it provided him with his first less than perfect grade. The self-image that once provided satisfaction and a feeling of well-being was replaced by an image creating profound inner turmoil. Stress became so intense that the adolescent, striving to maintain or regain a state of well-being, saw no alternative to leaving college.

Treatment. The mild adjustment reactions of adolescence usually respond well to short-term supportive measures and to steps directed toward alleviating or eliminating the precipitating stress. In the young adolescent, reassuring the patient, the parents, and teachers or other adults caught up in the patient's turmoil will not only contribute to resolving the turmoil but will also help the adults to be more tolerant of the patient during the process of resolution. In more severe adjustment reactions, more intensive therapy may be indicated.

Therapy with Adolescents: Principles and Techniques

The basic principles discussed in chapter 1, "The Therapist-Patient Relationship," and chapter 17, "The Psychotherapies," apply to psychotherapy with the adolescent. They need, however, to be modified according to the age of the adolescent and the particular disorder being treated. Opinion about treatment differs widely; some therapists believe the adolescent should be treated with the most intense and carefully modified analysis, while others feel he should not be treated at all (Anthony, 1969). Several general rules hold; in spite of differences of opinion: (1) the younger the adolescent, the more the basic principles of therapy for adults must be modified and the more flexible must be the approach of the therapist; (2) regardless of the age of the adolescent, therapy ought to be carried out face to face; (3) therapy should be focused primarily on the patient's current functioning, his testing of reality, and his current relationships and on conscious and preconscious material; it should concentrate relatively little on unconscious material; (4) interpretation should be used sparingly, support given through suggestion, and change effected through clarification and confrontation; and (5) a process of integration and synthesis should predominate over one of dissection and analysis. A mutual sharing of feelings between therapist and patient may often prove helpful, as will focusing on issues of self-esteem and responsibility.

Certain technical problems arise in therapy with adolescents. The first and most difficult task confronting the therapist is to establish initial rapport and to help the patient recognize his need for help, if such a need exists. With the young adolescent, an introductory phase of therapy is usually necessary before a working relationship can be established. With any adolescent, especially the younger one, the establishment of this relationship may prove extremely difficult. The adolescent seldom sees his need for help and is usually brought to the doctor against his will; in addition, he is usually brought by his parents, those most involved in his anger, defiance, and turmoil. If the therapist is a friend of the parents, the therapeutic effort, if not doomed to failure, will at best meet with considerable resistance. The young adolescent often feels the therapist is part of an adult conspiracy and approaches the whole therapeutic situation with a suspiciousness that sometimes borders on paranoia. It helps, therefore, to deal with the patient as directly as possible and not through his parents. Treating the adolescent like a human being with rights and privileges of his own will help. If the parents call for an appointment, the doctor can ask to speak with the patient, work out a convenient time with him, and let him make transportation arrangements with his parents. It is also best to see the adolescent —even the very young adolescent—first alone and then to ask him for permission to speak with the parents. Because the adolescent has an intense fear of becoming dependent on the therapist, asking his permission to speak with his

parents gives him some sense of control over what is happening. If he requests the therapist not to speak with his parents, the therapist will fare better if he honors this request for at least the first session or two. If the therapist believes interviews with the parents are necessary—and many therapists in the case of young adolescents think such an interview mandatory—the therapist can work through the issue with the adolescent over a period of time, helping him to see why such interviews might eventually be helpful to him.

An adolescent who is acting out can also present difficult technical problems. Some therapists have found it helpful to set limits firmly in a nonpunitive manner (Bergen, 1964). The adolescent will often perceive such limits as an expression of friendly concern. The limits will usually lessen anxiety in the patient and perhaps in the therapist as well. Often adolescents have difficulty controlling their impulses and are relieved to receive control from outside.

Adolescents often have difficulty recognizing their need for help, regardless of how obvious this need may be to teachers, parents, or advisors. If asked why he has come to see the doctor, the adolescent may quote the referring source but quickly disagree. If the therapist then explores this area in detail with the patient, the adolescent may come to understand how his difficulties have interfered with his living his life as he wishes and thus come to recognize his need for help. Sometimes this area will be too charged emotionally for him to discuss it with the therapist until an element of trust has been established. The therapist may have to backtrack in such a case to find some less emotionally charged area to explore—perhaps some interest the patient has in common with the therapist. If such a subject can be found, a silent patient may quite spontaneously begin talking with considerable enthusiasm and the difficult task of beginning a relationship will have taken a significant step forward.

The older adolescent presents fewer technical difficulties, and the therapist can usually proceed as he would with an adult. He will usually find it helpful, however, to be more directive and, because of the fragile self-esteem of most adolescents, considerably more supportive during the initial contact than he would be with an adult patient. Because the older adolescent usually recognizes his need for help and comes on his own initiative, he is generally more strongly motivated than the younger adolescent. For these reasons, treatment has been more readily available to the older adolescent than to younger ones, and until recently he has been the subject of considerably more attention from investigators.

Group therapy has been found to be effective with some adolescents. Because of their fragile self-image, however, the involvement of some younger adolescents in a group of peers who obviously need help may confirm their fears about their own inadequacy, and they may refuse to cooperate. Group therapy has been found to be effective for adolescents whose problems manifest themselves primarily in current interpersonal difficulties, who show a pattern of withdrawal and isolation, or who become involved in gangs bound together by destructive behavior. For example, an adolescent may be involved in a gang only because of its delinquent behavior or its involvement with drugs.

During the past few years, family therapy has begun to play an important part in the treatment of adolescent problems. Therapists have realized that adolescent turmoil and other symptoms may often be a direct reflection of disturbed family functioning. In examining the adolescent, some therapists now also assess the family, with the result that the family may be treated as a unit or particular members of the family may be directed toward individual therapy. Problems considered especially amenable to family therapy include adolescent school phobias and certain borderline and schizophrenic disorders.

Adolescence, barely recognized by the profession at the beginning of the century, has generated sufficient interest during the past decade to have become a subspecialty of psychiatry. The growth of knowledge about this stage of life has been slow and marked by controversy and misconceptions. With recent research now beginning to focus more on this age group, we have begun to attain a new theoretical and clinical

understanding of the adolescent that is not only rapidly changing our concepts of normality and pathology but also forging a more hopeful and more efficacious approach to treatment.

References

American Psychiatric Association. 1968. *Diagnostic and statistical manual of mental disorders.* 2nd ed. Washington, D.C.

—— 1975. *A psychiatric glossary.* Washington, D.C.

Anthony, E. J. 1969. The reaction of adults to adolescents and their behavior. In *Adolescence: psychosocial perspectives,* ed. G. Caplan and S. Lebovici. New York: Basic Books.

—— 1974. The juvenile and preadolescent periods of the human life cycle. In *American handbook of psychiatry,* ed. S. Arieti. Vol. 1. 2nd ed. New York: Basic Books.

Bergen, M. E. 1964. Some observations in maturational factors in young children and adolescents. *Psychoanal. Study Child* 19:275–286.

Blizzard, R., A. Johanson, H. Guyda, A. Baghdassarian, S. Raiti, and C. Migeon. 1970. Recent developments in the study of gonadotrophin secretion in adolescence. In *Adolescent endocrinology,* ed. F. Heald and W. Hung. New York: Appleton-Century-Crofts.

Blos, P. 1968. Character formation in adolescence. *Psychoanal. Study Child* 23:245–263.

Bronfenbrenner, U. 1970. *Two worlds of childhood.* New York: Simon and Schuster.

Cracchiolo, A., M. E. Blazina, and D. S. MacKinnon. 1968. The high price of the economical motorbike. *J.A.M.A.* 204:175–176.

Demos, J. and V. 1969. Adolescence in historical perspective. *J. Marriage Fam.* 31:632–638.

Deutsch, H. 1967. *Selected problems of adolescence.* New York: International Universities Press.

Douvan, E., and J. Adelson. 1966. *The adolescent experience.* New York: Wiley.

Erikson, E. H. 1968. *Identity: youth and crisis.* New York: Norton.

Fenichel, O. 1945. *The psychoanalytic theory of the neurosis.* New York: Norton.

Frazier, A., and L. K. Lisonbee. 1950. Adolescent concerns with physique. *School Rev.* 58:397–405.

Freud, A. 1958. Adolescence. *Psychoanal. Study Child* 13:255–278.

Freud, S. 1905. Three essays on the theory of sexuality. In *Standard edition,* ed. J. Strachey. Vol. 7. London: Hogarth Press, 1953.

——— 1912. On the universal tendency to debasement in the sphere of love. In *Standard edition*, ed. J. Strachey. Vol. 11. London: Hogarth Press, 1961.

Gelineau, V., M. Johnson, and D. Pearsall. 1973. A survey of adolescent drug use patterns. *Mass. J. Ment. Health* 3, no. 2:30–40.

Grinker, R. R., Sr., and P. S. Holzman. 1973. Schizophrenic pathology in young adults. *Arch. Gen Psychiatry* 28:168–175.

Group for the Advancement of Psychiatry. 1968. *Normal adolescence*. New York: Scribner's.

Hall, G. S. 1904. *Adolescence: its psychology and its relations to physiology, anthropology, sociology, sex, crime, religion and education*. New York: Appleton.

Halleck, S. L. 1967. Psychiatric treatment of the alienated college student. *Am. J. Psychiatry* 124, no. 5:642–650.

Hamburg, B. A. 1974. Coping in early adolescence. In *American handbook of psychiatry*, ed. S. Arieti. Vol. 2. 2nd ed. New York: Basic Books.

Hamburg, B. A., H. C. Kraemer, and W. Jahnke. 1975. A hierarchy of drug use in adolescence: behavioral and attitudinal correlates of substantial drug use. *Am. J. Psychiatry* 132, no. 11:1155–61.

Harmatz, J., S. Shader, and C. Salzman. 1972. Marijuana users and nonusers. *Arch. Gen. Psychiatry* 26:108–112.

Henderson, A. S., J. Krupinski, and A. Stoller. 1971. Epidemiological aspects of adolescent psychiatry. In *Modern perspectives in adolescent psychiatry*, ed. J. C. Howells. New York: Brunner/Mazel.

Jacobizner, H. 1965. Attempted suicides in adolescence. *J.A.M.A.* 191:101–105.

Jones, E. 1922. Some problems of adolescence. In *Papers on psychoanalysis*. 5th ed. London: Balliére, Tindall & Cox, 1948.

Jones, M. C. 1965. Psychological correlates of somatic development. *Child Dev.* 36:899–911.

Josselyn, I. M. 1974. Adolescence. In *American handbook of psychiatry*, ed. S. Arieti. Vol. 1. 2nd ed. New York: Basic Books.

Keniston, K. 1970. Youth: a "new" stage of life. *Am. Scholar* 39:631–654.

Lunde, D., and D. Hamburg. 1972. Techniques for assessing the effects of sex hormones on affect, arousal, and aggression in humans. In *Recent progress in hormone research*, ed. A. B. Astwood, vol. 28. New York: Academic Press.

Masterson, J. F., Jr. 1967. *The psychiatric dilemma of adolescence*. Boston: Little, Brown.

Mirin, S., L. Shapiro, R. Meyer, R. Pillard, and S. Fisher. 1971. Casual versus heavy use of marijuana: a redefinition of the marijuana problem. *Am. J. Psychiatry* 127:1134–40.

Mizner, G. L., J. T. Barter, and P. H. Werme. 1970. Patterns of drug use among college students: a preliminary report. *Am. J. Psychiatry* 127:15–25.

Nicholi, A. M., Jr. 1967. Harvard dropouts: some psychiatric findings. *Am. J. Psychiatry* 124:105–112.

——— 1970. The motorcycle syndrome. *Am. J. Psychiatry*. 126:1588–95.

——— 1974a. Emotional determinants of LSD ingestion among college students. *J. Am. Coll. Health Assoc.* 22:223–225.

——— 1974b. A new dimension of the youth culture. *Am. J. Psychiatry* 131:396–400.

Nicholi, A. M., II, and N. F. Watt. 1977. The death of a parent in the etiology of schizophrenia. *Am. J. Psychiatry*, in press.

Offer, D. 1969. *The psychological world of the teenager: a study of normal adolescent boys*. New York: Basic Books.

Offer, D., D. Marcus, and J. L. Offer. 1970. A longitudinal study of normal adolescent boys. *Am. J. Psychiatry* 126:917–924.

Offer, D. and J. L. 1968. Profiles of normal adolescent girls. *Arch. Gen. Psychiatry* 19:513–522.

Piaget, J. 1958. *The growth of logical thinking from childhood to adolescence*. New York: Basic Books.

Robbins, E., L. Robbins, W. Frosch, and M. Stern. 1970. College student drug use. *Am. J. Psychiatry* 126:1743–51.

Rouse, R. A. and J. A. Ewing. 1973. Marijuana and other drug use by women college students: associated risk taking and coping activities. *Am. J. Psychiatry* 130:486–491.

Shean, G., and F. Fechtmann. 1971. Purpose in life scores of student marijuana users. *J. Clin. Psychol.* 27:112–113.

Spiegel, L. A. 1951. A review of contributions to a psychoanalytic theory of adolescence. *Psychoanal. Study Child* 6:375–393.

Stone, L. J., and J. Church. 1968. *Childhood and adolescence*. New York: Random House.

Sullivan, H. S. 1953. *The collected works of Harry Stack Sullivan*. Vol. 1. New York: Norton.

Tanner, J. M. 1962. *Growth at adolescence*. 2nd ed. Oxford: Blackwell.

Walters, P., G. Goethals, and H. Pope. 1972. Drug use and life style among 500 college undergraduates. *Arch. Gen. Psychiatry* 26:92–96.

Weiner, I. B. 1970. *Psychological disturbance in adolescence*. New York: Wiley.

Wolstenholme, G. E. W., and M. O'Connor. 1967. *Endocrinology of the testis*. Boston: Little, Brown.

Zinberg, N., and A. Weil. 1970. A comparison of marijuana users and nonusers. *Nature* 22:119–123.

The Elderly Person

CHAPTER 25

Martin A. Berezin

T HE NUMBER of old people in the United States has increased remarkably since the turn of the century. In 1900, 3 million people were over age sixty-five, representing 3 percent of the total population. Currently that figure has risen to twenty-two million, approximately 10 percent of the population. Decreased infant mortality throughout these decades has permitted more people to reach old age and, along with public health measures and "miracle drugs," has been one of the primary causes for this striking increase.

What Is "Old"?

Notions of what "old age" is and when it begins need clarification. Not many years ago old age began at forty. This age limit has now risen and sixty-five is accepted as the beginning of old age. Within the socioeconomic context of our culture, the selection of age sixty-five is correlated with retirement and Social Security—based on the precedent of legislation enacted in Germany under Bismarck in 1883, providing old age and death benefits for persons sixty-five years of age and over. Occupation may also determine what is old. An athlete such as a basketball player may

be considered old at thirty, while farmers, physicians, legislators, scholars, and politicians may go on working into their eighth or ninth decades.

Myths and Misconceptions

Certain physical and cognitive changes are concomitants of aging, defining additional dimensions of being "old." These altered states alone are not pathological and should be considered the natural results of the aging process. I make this statement because of the frequent misconception that old age is a process of disorder and disease. In fact, the commonly held image of infirmity, feebleness, second childhood, memory loss, and uselessness overlooks the fact that most people age comfortably and in good health. Statistics demonstrate that of the 22 million people over age sixty-five, fewer than 5 percent require custodial care (von Mering and Weninger, 1959). Misconceived stereotypes of the aged as defective and ill reflect a prevalent cultural gerontophobia, deriving from a value system that prizes youth, action, and achievement and attaches stigma to inaction and lowered achievement. Butler refers to a "form of bigotry we now tend to overlook: age discrimination or age-ism, prejudice by one age group toward other age groups" (1969, p. 243). Bunzel defines gerontophobia as "the unreasonable fear and/or irrational hatred of older people by society and by themselves" (1972, p. 116). Another contribution to gerontophobia arises from the fact that most studies of old people have used hospital and nursing home residents as their subjects, probably because this population is most easily and conveniently available. However, the use of this population for study has encouraged the equation of old age with illness.

Altered States in Old Age

What age-specific physical and cognitive changes are normal concomitants of the aging process? Berezin and Stotsky (1970) found the following to be among them:
1. decreased basal metabolic rate
2. reduced oxygen uptake in the brain due to insufficient cerebral circulation
3. reduced visual acuity
4. reduced auditory acuity, especially for higher frequencies
5. decreased sensitivity to taste and smell
6. decreased sensitivity to pain and vibration
7. increased susceptibility to changes in temperature
8. digestive problems, including difficulties in elimination, as well as upper gastrointestinal tract symptoms
9. increased decay and loss of teeth
10. loss or graying of hair
11. drying, thinning, wrinkling of skin, increased pigmentation and loss of skin turgor
12. loss of muscle tone and atrophic changes in muscle
13. skeletal changes due to osteoporosis
14. decreased kidney function
15. decreased cardiac output
16. loss of elasticity of connective tissue
17. loss of neurons within the central nervous system

The significance of these physical changes lies in the fact that they are experienced as loss and may act as stress, precipitating idiosyncratic psychological reactions.

Alterations other than somatic changes impinge on the aging person. Perhaps the most significant impact is that of loss. Not only do losses occur in terms of the physical body, but important emotional losses in terms of significant people and love objects—spouse, children, friends, relatives, associates, and colleagues—are also sustained.

In addition to the somatic changes and the loss of love objects, still other conditions mark an age as geriatric. One of the more dramatic occupational changes is retirement. The issue of retirement is frequently publicized, for it has produced a considerable amount of agonizing on the part of the young as well as the old. Reactions to retirement are quite varied, ranging from a total incapacity to retire, sometimes manifested in early death, to the polar opposite in which retirement is successful and pleasant. A significant factor producing problems of retirement is the highly prized work ethic of our cultural value system. Without work, without occupation, many older people feel demeaned and suffer a loss of self-esteem and self-respect.

Attitudes toward retirement are changing. There is now a more positive awareness that the leisure time that accompanies retirement is important in itself. The capacity to enjoy leisure time cannot be learned suddenly after reaching old age but must be encouraged and learned early as a way of life. It appears that society has come to recognize that the strict adherence to and worship of a work ethic is undesirable and may become psychologically harmful. One aspect of the recent manifestations of unrest and rebellion among young people, with denigration of many "establishment" and materialistic values, is, in my opinion, the expression of a weakening of the rigidity of the traditional work ethic and an increasing appreciation of the positive value of other activities. However, the current "old" in our society remain the prime victims of this ethic.

Psychodynamics

The age-specific conditions that mark those designated as elderly are descriptive and phenomenological. While important in their own right, they remain sterile observations until they are understood in psychodynamic terms. The significance of each event, somatically or extrasomatically, must be appreciated on an individual basis. Each change must be viewed within the framework of the individual's personality structure—which enables us to appreciate the differing responses to each condition. The range of responses may vary from mature coping to complete psychological breakdown.

Timelessness of Drives

Coping operations—defensive and adaptive ego mechanisms—are established very early and, once established, persist throughout life. Equally timeless are the manifestations of the instinctual life, from which drives, wishes, and motivations arise. The old person yearns for, needs, and desires the same satisfactions, gratifications, and pleasures as do young people. There may be a quantitative difference in such needs but not a qualitative difference.

The timelessness of drives is demonstrated in studies of sex and old age (Berezin, 1969). These studies further dispel many myths and misconceptions about sex during this period of life. There is, however, a cultural prejudice against the expression of sexual desires and activities in old age, seen in the assumption that what is considered to be virility at twenty-five becomes lechery at sixty-five.

The prejudice extends to the notion that old age should be sexless. An important root of this prejudice is the persistence of early oedipal reactions of children who cling tenaciously to their conviction that parents are sexless. Claman tells the story of Sam Levenson, the schoolteacher and homespun philosopher of television fame, who once said, "When I first found out how babies were born, I couldn't believe it! To think that my mother and father would do such a thing!" After reflection, he added, "My father—maybe, but my mother—never!" (Claman et al., 1966, p. 207). This persistent attitude is a cultural prejudice and serves as a basis for certain countertransference resistances on the part of researchers and therapists.

As a consequence of this early oedipal attitude, elderly people themselves view their own sexual desires, fantasies, and feelings negatively. The result is a self-fulfilling prophecy as young people become older: elderly people feel guilt and shame about their sexual desires. The fact remains, however, that older people are "vitally interested, terribly confused, and hunger eagerly for information about the norms of sexuality in the geriatric age population" (Feigenbaum, Lowenthal, and Trier, 1967, p. 2).

In study after study, one important fact emerges—the discovery that sexual behavior in the elderly corresponds to their individual sex life when they were younger; those who were active when young will be active when old, and those who were inactive when young will be inactive when old. It becomes clear then that old age as a variable affecting sex life does not play as significant a role as is commonly assumed.

Elderly people are capable of an active sex life in their eighties and nineties, provided they are healthy and have an available partner. That sex desires do not disappear is evidenced by the fact that when sexual intercourse is not available, masturbation is used by both men and women as a substitute (Berezin, 1975). Kinsey and his associates (1953) describe one woman in her nineties who masturbated to orgasm regularly.

Despite the publicity given to aphrodisiacs and hormones for the elderly, these preparations are essentially useless, except perhaps in their placebo effect. Masters and Johnson, referring to elderly females, state that "elevation of sexual responsiveness rarely results directly from the administration of estrogen or estrogen-like products" (1966, p. 242).

Many studies on sex and the aged do not evaluate significant accompanying conditions, a deplorable omission. Physical sexual activities cannot tell the whole story. What is omitted is love, affection, tenderness, and interpersonal relationships, factors that should be part of the study of the total psychosexual picture. A greater understanding of the significance of the psychosexual life in the elderly will enable those who are involved in their treatment and management to assess the total personality organization more accurately.

Timelessness of Life Style

The ego-adaptive and defensive operations established early in childhood continue to be used for the remainder of the individual's life. These ego operations, which vary in quality and quantity from person to person, produce the individual variations among people that may be called character style. Style does not change throughout life. It has been said that when a person becomes old, he is the same as he has always been, only more so.

While new ego operations may not be available, under the impact of severe trauma or stress, a given ego defense may become exaggerated in an effort to cope. For example, an individual who has customarily used the mechanism of projection throughout life and who is later confronted with more stress than he can cope with may develop a shift, by exaggeration, from projection to paranoid states. In other people, similarly, overcompensated aggression is used in the service of denying passivity; under stress, this overcompensation may fail, giving rise to an exaggerated passivity, to the distress of the individual as well as others. This last phenomenon occurred in an active, hard-working business executive when faced with retirement. He became passive and extremely dependent, and he frequently complained about his condition in a whining, childlike way. His wife remarked on how different he seemed to be, that he had (in her words) "changed from a tiger to a pussycat."

An example of a lifetime fixation and the persistence of a stage of libidinal organization—in this case, orality—is seen in a woman patient of seventy-five, who was preoccupied all her life with the need for narcissistic supplies. She had been diagnosed years earlier as having an "oral narcissistic character disorder" and as a woman whose defensive abilities were quite fragile. At age seventy-six, as though to confirm absolutely this diagnosis, she wrote this poem.

> Am I a Man-Eater
> Fat or thin, short or tall
> You must think I love them all.
> If they are kind—if they are nice
> If some have the proper spice
> I could cook them in a stew
> With a sauce—and mustard too
> And tenderize to be sure—
> They'll be better—than a cure.
> (Berezin, 1972, pp. 1486–87)

This poem leaves little room for doubt as to the accuracy of the diagnosis of her orality.

Organic Mental Disorders

Organic mental disorders are of a special diagnostic interest in geriatrics, for the incidence of such conditions increases markedly with age. While the diagnosis may not be as evident today as it was a generation ago, "organic brain syndrome" is still often used incorrectly and is sometimes a "wastebasket" diagnosis, which fulfills even more the expectations engendered by gerontophobia. In other words, to label an aged person incorrectly with such a diagnosis betrays a sense of medical helplessness and becomes a way of disposing of rather than confronting a problem. Unfortunately, once established, the diagnosis discourages the search for a more refined and accurate appraisal of the presenting condition. Not all old people who are apathetic and dull and who have some degree of recent memory defect are necessarily suffering from organic mental disorders. A differential diagnostic approach should include evaluating depression, obsessive-compulsive character disorders, and loneliness syndromes (Berezin et al., 1974). A further refinement would include a quantitative analysis of the coexistence of such disorders. Obviously, without such a sharpened diagnostic evaluation, proper management of the patient and his family becomes impossible.

The significance of recent memory defects is under consideration. Traditionally, it has been assumed and stated in many textbooks that recent memory defects are pathognomonic of organic mental disorder. Although such memory defects do come about as a result of organic brain disease, recent memory defects may nevertheless be traceable to other causes, such as depression and apathy. More important, while memory defects due to organic cause may be irreversible, those due to emotional or psychological causes may be reversible, a feature that demands careful evaluation.

Another misconception lingers with respect to organic mental disorders. Often the diagnosis applied to brain disorders is arteriosclerotic disease. In fact, while the diagnosis may be valid, it does not occur with the frequency attributed to it. There is "a much less frequent association of arteriosclerosis with dementia. Much more often the classical changes of Alzheimer's disease or its senile counterpart are demonstrable without significant vascular disease" (Berry, 1975, p. 60). Alzheimer's disease has for a long time been labeled as presenile dementia and is still so labeled in many textbooks. Histopathological studies, however, show that Alzheimer cellular changes occur in advanced senile dementias as well as in the so-called presenile conditions.

Unfortunately, it is often difficult to establish an early diagnosis of organic brain changes. The diagnosis can be made essentially only by clinical evaluation. The early signs and symptoms may be so subtle as to be overlooked altogether, so that, for example, a mild or occasional memory lapse may not be noted, especially by nonprofessional family members and friends. Furthermore, by the time a diagnosis is established by clinical evaluation, the disorder is generally quite far advanced. Only retrospectively can one determine that early signs and symptoms may have been significant and their subtlety overlooked. At present, no method of establishing the diagnosis at an early stage in the disorder exists.

With respect to those organic mental disorders that are arteriosclerotic in origin, the early work of Rothschild (1942) demonstrates (by autopsy) that no correlation exists between the amount of brain tissue damage and the amount of behavioral manifestations; severe behavior disorders may show minimal organic brain change, while massive brain changes may accompany very mild behavior disorders.

Finally, for the most part, patients with organic brain changes require custodial care either by families or in institutions. Treatment with hyperbaric oxygen or injections with hormones, procaine, or other substances are still controversial and under continuous study. Thus far, such studies have failed to demonstrate any significant value or consistency of replication (Eisner, 1975).

Nonorganic Psychiatric Disorders

The nonorganic psychiatric conditions found in the aged may be divided into two general categories: (1) those conditions in old age that represent the recurrence of a lifelong psychiatric disorder, such as manic-depressive psychosis or schizophrenia, and (2) those disorders that ap-

pear for the first time after the age of sixty-five (Blau and Berezin, 1975). These two categories are roughly equally divided with respect to incidence when measured by psychiatric hospitalization statistics.[*]

In those cases where psychiatric disorder occurs for the first time after the age of sixty-five, a review of the life history of the individual inevitably demonstrates the existence of a lifelong behavior pattern that has been fragile in some respect and that now, under stress, is no longer capable of sustaining its equilibrium.

Functional psychiatric disorders in the aged are essentially the same as those encountered in younger age groups. Diagnosis, however, is often complicated by the presence of varying degrees of organic brain damage. The coexistence of organic and nonorganic psychiatric disorders must be considered in establishing a diagnosis in any geriatric patient.

With respect to psychiatric disorders in the elderly, the important people in the patient's life, especially the spouse and children, are particularly involved. The elderly person is usually less able than a younger one to care for himself or to take the necessary steps to obtain care and treatment. What follows is a role reversal in which the child cares for the parent, as opposed to the earlier period when the parent cared for the child. Family involvement is a special feature of illness in the aged, and family members may suffer more than the patient, especially if the patient is confused because of organic brain changes. The patient may actually have little if any subjective suffering. Often the management of the geriatric patient focuses not on the patient himself but on the family, who may need support from physicians, social workers, and hospital or nursing home personnel.

A misconception prevails that families "dump" their elderly into a custodial care facility in order to be rid of the problem. The facts are otherwise. Family members not only do not dump old people but in fact tend to hold on too long to a sick, disabled elderly parent to the detriment of both the family and the patient. The current opinion among gerontologists is that it makes little sense for family and patient to wait too long for an el-

[*] C. Tibbitts, 1976: personal communication.

derly person to go to a nursing home or to retire gracefully to a comfortable area. Goldfarb states: "It doesn't make any sense *not* to take advantage of protection that is available" at a time when an elderly person can best utilize various facilities (1973, p. 5).

I will return later to some implications of the relationship between the elderly patient and those in the family and environment who tend to them (or who try to manage the total situation).

Therapy

The treatment of psychiatric illness in the aged varies as much as does treatment in the younger age population. Two of the major forms of treatment are psychotherapeutic and psychopharmacological.

Psychotherapy

The prevalence of gerontophobia should not cause us to overlook psychotherapy as an available and effective treatment modality for the elderly. (The term *psychotherapy* as used here refers to a one-to-one relationship between the therapist and the patient.) It includes, but does not necessarily confine itself to, exploration of the unconscious with the hope of achieving insight and resolution of some conflicts; psychoanalytically oriented psychotherapy is thus practical and feasible for many geriatric patients. According to Bibring's classification (1954), psychotherapy may also include clarification, suggestion, manipulation, and abreaction.

Of particular significance in psychotherapy is the awareness of special transference-countertransference issues. Usually a therapist, often a psychiatric resident, will be younger than the elderly patient. To begin with, a young psychiatrist may feel uneasy in treating someone old enough to be his parent or grandparent. This countertransference issue can be a block to good therapy because the uneasiness is transmitted to the patient, who reacts in turn. With increased experience, therapists come to appreciate that transference may not represent reality (Nunberg, 1951) and that the elderly patient is not guided by his calendar age. In fact, rather than viewing the young psychiatrist as a child figure,

much evidence supports the opposite: the elderly patient may see him as a peer or even as a parental figure (da Silva, 1967; Berezin and Fern, 1967; Hauser, 1968; Brooks, 1969; Zarsky and Blau, 1970).

A number of writers (Goldfarb, 1962, 1969; Weinberg, 1957; Pfeiffer, 1971) have long advocated the use of psychotherapy for the elderly. There are psychiatric disorders in the elderly in which individual psychotherapy is the therapy of choice; the therapist may be a psychiatrist or a paramedic, such as a trained social worker or a clinical psychologist. In addition to individual psychotherapy, more recently the increased use of group psychotherapy has demonstrated its value (Linden, 1953, 1971; Liederman and Liederman, 1967; Goldfarb, 1971).

Psychopharmacology

Psychopharmacology as a mode of therapy for the aged occupies a valuable position, but because of possible complications it must be used judiciously. Davis has written that "(1) the elderly are often more prone to certain drug side effects, and (2) the probability of drug-drug interactions is increased because patients are more likely to be taking medication for other ailments. In addition, the geriatric patient may be taking proprietary medications purchased without prescription." Davis also suggests that "since mental functioning is reduced by sedative hypnotics, the highly medicated elderly patient may often benefit from the elimination of these drugs from his treatment program . . . It is helpful to obtain a drug-free baseline state by halting all current medication" (1974, p. 145).

Lipsitt (1974) echoes similar caveats and emphasizes the need for vigilance, prudence, knowledge, and questioning in the use of all pharmaceutical agents in all geriatric patients.

Salzman and Shader also point out the difficulties in the problem area of drug use: "Research problems that are of primary concern in the evaluation of drug effect in the elderly include biologic variability, age, gender, dose, toxicity, polypharmacy, placebo effect, initial severity of symptoms, capacity to respond to drugs, and the unique problems of rating drug effect" (1974, p. 166).

The various agents used in psychopharmacological therapy have a relatively short history. Such agents are usually classified as antidepressant, antipsychotic, antianxiety, or sedative. New drugs appear and older ones are phased out. Furthermore, research and clinical experience add to our knowledge of contraindications and new side effects (see chapter 18, "Chemotherapy," for a discussion of individual agents). Suffice it to say that the clinician must keep himself informed of a constantly changing ebb and flow of psychopharmacological agents.

Death and Dying

It is commonly assumed that as a person ages he becomes more preoccupied with ideas of his own death and that old people are fearful and anxious about this matter. On the contrary, it is rare for old people to be afraid of approaching death. Such imputations about fearfulness among the aged usually arise from the projections of younger people. Old people do not ignore the fact of approaching death, but they do not commonly have pathological reactions to it. Usually the concern is not about dying but about how death may come, whether it will be sudden or lingering, with or without pain, or whether one will be a burden to others. (For further discussion of the dying elderly person, see chapter 28, "Treating the Person Confronting Death.")

On the other hand, the family may suffer more than the aged person himself about the facts of death and dying. The state of dying and loss affects people involved with the patient, such as spouse, children, siblings, relatives, friends, and colleagues. These "environmental people" are required to cope with painful and poignant situations over which they have no control. Once a diagnosis is made, the final steps toward death and loss are progressive and irreversible. The awareness of irreversibility produces a feeling of helplessness, and it is this helplessness that can be the worst disease of all. What is especially difficult for friends and relatives is that full mourning cannot occur until the loss itself becomes final, and without mourning a final resolution of grief is impossible.

The concept of "partial grief" (Berezin, 1970) describes this situation in which an unresolved grief state is precipitated by a partial rather than a total loss. Partial losses need not have a direct connection to death itself but may be observed in situations that suggest the beginning of the "end of the road," or in others such as retirement or birthdays in advanced years. Partial losses can occur at fiftieth wedding anniversaries as well as on other significant anniversaries. Family members in such circumstances are reminded, consciously or unconsciously, that a previous identity in a person has changed and time ahead is more finite.

The unresolved grief seen in partial grief states unfortunately may lead to regressive positions, aggressive and hostile outbursts, projection, and depression. Sometimes the treating physician is confronted by family members who make impossible demands for lifesaving measures (or the opposite), or he may observe previously friendly siblings becoming more quarrelsome and fighting among themselves. Such manifestations are consistent with the family's sense of helplessness and their inability to cope with what may in fact be an impossible situation in a sick or dying relative or friend.

When irrational behavior occurs in such states of partial grief, a family conference with the psychiatrist (or other treating person) acting as a neutral, understanding, objective, and knowledgeable resource has been found useful. In such a conference, the family is confronted with the reality of the situation and the prognosis is openly discussed. The reactions, especially feelings of helplessness, are reviewed, and the need for unity within the family is stressed. The appeal is both to the realities of the aged person's situation and to the awareness of the uncomfortable struggles among those who grieve.

The importance of the individual's intrapsychic and psychosexual history in his ability to negotiate the geriatric stage in the life cycle has been stressed throughout this chapter. In addition, a number of issues less specific to the individual elderly patient are important in the variety of reactions to old age—among them social attitudes toward old age, restrictions on useful activity among the elderly, and the frequent separation of the old from the rest of the population. Because these issues involve the medical sphere in which increasing numbers of elderly people seek assistance, they are important considerations for psychiatrists as well as for other medical caregivers.

As already noted, physical complaints may be exacerbated by the societal role accorded the elderly, a role that often leads to isolation and subsequent feelings of loneliness and abandonment. Psychosocial factors can contribute to both physical and psychiatric disturbances and may complicate the distinctions between the two. One type of problem often presents a clinical picture resembling the other, and their effects may be mutually reinforcing. Reports of previously diagnosed "brain syndrome," for instance, are in many cases now recognized as severe depression. This blurred line is likely to grow even less distinct as the numbers of elderly people in our population grow. An awareness of psychosocial factors is therefore crucial to an understanding of the elderly; these factors deserve serious attention in their care and management.

References

Berezin, M. A. 1969. Sex and old age: a review of the literature. *J. Geriatr. Psychiatry* 2:131–149.

—— 1970. Partial grief in family members and others who care for the elderly patient. *J. Geriatr. Psychiatry* 4:53–64.

—— 1972. Psychodynamic considerations of aging and the aged: an overview. *Am. J. Psychiatry* 128:1483–91.

—— 1975. Masturbation and old age. In *Masturbation—from infancy to senescence*, ed. I. M. Marcus and J. J. Francis. New York: International Universities Press.

Berezin, M. A., and D. J. Fern. 1967. Persistence of early emotional problems in a seventy-year-old woman. *J. Geriatr. Psychiatry* 1:45–60.

Berezin, M. A., and B. A. Stotsky. 1970. The geriatric patient. In *The practice of community mental health*, ed. H. Grunebaum. Boston: Little, Brown.

Berezin, M. A., et al. 1974. Symposium on the concept and phenomenology of depression, with special reference to the aged. *J. Geriatr. Psychiatry* 7:3–83.

Berry, R. G. 1975. Pathology of dementia. In *Modern perspectives in the psychiatry of old age*, ed. J. G. Howells. New York: Brunner/Mazel.

Bibring, E. 1954. Psychoanalysis and the dynamic psychotherapies. *J. Am. Psychoanal. Assoc.* 2:745–770.

Blau, D., and M. A. Berezin, 1975. Neuroses and character disorders. In *Modern perspectives in the psychiatry of old age*, ed. J. G. Howells. New York: Brunner/Mazel.

Brooks, L. 1969. A case of eroticized transference in a 73-year-old woman. *J. Geriatr. Psychiatry* 2:150–162.

Bunzel, J. H. 1972. Note on the history of a concept—gerontophobia. *Gerontologist* 12:116, 203.

Butler, R. N. 1969. Age-ism: another form of bigotry. *Gerontologist* 9:243–246.

Claman, A. D., D. Schwartz, R. A. H. Kinch, and N. B. Hirt. 1966. Introduction to panel discussion: sexual difficulties after 50. *Can. Med. Assoc. J.* 94:207–217.

da Silva, G. 1967. The loneliness and death of an old man: three years' psychotherapy of an eighty-one-year-old depressed patient. *J. Geriatr. Psychiatry* 1:5–27.

Davis, J. M. 1974. Psychopharmacology in the aged: use of psychotropic drugs in geriatric patients. *J. Geriatr. Psychiatry* 7:145–159.

Eisner, D. A. 1975. Can hyperbaric oxygenation improve cognitive functioning in the organically impaired elderly? *J. Geriatr. Psychiatry* 8:173–188.

Feigenbaum, E. M., M. F. Lowenthal, and M. L. Trier. 1967. Aged are confused and hungry for sex information. *Geriatr. Focus* 5, no. 20:2.

Goldfarb, A. I. 1962. The psychotherapy of elderly patients. In *Medical and clinical aspects of aging*, ed. H. T. Blumenthal. New York: Columbia University Press.

—— 1969. The psychodynamics of dependency and the search for aid. In *The dependencies of old people*, ed. R. A. Kalish. Ann Arbor: University of Michigan Institute of Gerontology.

—— 1971. Group therapy with the old and aged. In *Comprehensive group psychotherapy*, ed. H. I. Kaplan and B. J. Sadock. Baltimore: Williams & Wilkins.

—— 1973. *Managing the disturbed elderly patient in family practice: when to consider institutional care*. McNeil Laboratories interview series, no 3. Fort Washington, Pa.

Hauser, S. T. 1968. The psychotherapy of a depressed aged woman. *J. Geriatr. Psychiatry* 2:62–87.

Kinsey, A. C., W. B. Pomeroy, C. E. Martin, and P. H. Gebhard. 1953. *Sexual behavior in the human female*. Philadelphia: Saunders.

Liederman, P. C. and V. R. 1967. Group therapy: an approach to problems of geriatric outpatients. *Curr. Psychiatr. Ther.* 7:179–185.

Linden, M. E. 1953. Group psychotherapy with institutionalized senile women: study in gerontologic human relations. *Int. J. Group Psychother.* 3:150–170.

———— 1971. Geriatrics. In *The fields of group psycho-therapy*, ed. S. R. Slavson. New York: Schocken Books.

Lipsitt, D. R. 1974. Psychopharmacology in the aged: discussion. *J. Geriatr. Psychiatry* 7:160–164.

Masters, W. H., and V. E. Johnson. 1966. *Human sexual response*. Boston: Little, Brown.

Nunberg, H. 1951. Transference and reality. *Int. J. Psychoanal.* 32:1–9.

Pfeiffer, E. 1971. Psychotherapy with elderly patients. Paper presented at the 24th annual meeting of the Gerontological Society, Houston.

Rothschild, D. 1942. Neuropathologic changes in arteriosclerotic psychoses and their psychiatric significance. *Arch. Neurol. Psychiatr.* 48:417–436.

Salzman, C., and R. I. Shader. 1974. Psychopharma-cology in the aged: research considerations in geriatric psychopharmacology. *J. Geriatr. Psychiatry* 7:165–184.

von Mering, O., and F. L. Weninger. 1959. Social-cultural background of the aging individual. In *Handbook of aging and the individual*, ed. J. E. Birren. Chicago: University of Chicago Press.

Weinberg, J. 1957. Psychotherapy of the aged. In *Progress in psychotherapy, anxiety, and therapy*, ed. J. H. Masserman and J. L. Moreno. Vol. 2 New York: Grune & Stratton.

Zarsky, E. L., and D. Blau. 1970. The understanding and management of narcissistic regression and dependency in an elderly woman observed over an extended period of time. *J. Geriatr. Psychiatry* 3:160–176.

Mental Retardation

CHAPTER 26

Norman R. Bernstein

A NY DISCUSSION of the psychiatric profession's role in relation to the field of mental subnormality raises several issues of emphasis and involvement. Many factors reveal a professional disengagement despite ever increasing amounts of new data in the field.

Most demographers claim that approximately three children in every hundred are retarded. Six million children and adults in this country are designated as mentally retarded. Although the number of retarded and mentally handicapped individuals in the United States continues to be about three times the number of schizophrenics, the number of psychiatrists who give a significant amount of time to this field remains less than 1 percent. Psychiatrists generally are not interested in and do not use the broad range of knowledge or treatment techniques available when confronted with these patients.

Lack of meaningful links between facts and specialty classifications contributes to this disinterest. Chapters on mental retardation, for example, are generally paired with those on child psychiatry because retardation occurs in the early years of personality development, but, in fact, most retarded people in the world are not children, and their behavior is not that of psychiatrically disturbed children. The perspective of the psychiatrist is further distorted by his nosology, which categorizes retardation as a separate entity. Actually, however, retardation coexists with all of the known psychiatric categories and the condition is in fact likely to predispose those who suffer from it to psychiatric disorders (Kirman, 1975).

Implicit in many of these facts is a pervasive prejudice held by psychiatrists concerning the importance of intellect in human functioning, exemplified by Kessler (1966), who states that "the one . . . common denominator [of the retarded] is slowness to learn." The definition found in the American Psychiatric Association's *Diagnostic and Statistical Manual of Mental Disorders* in current use (DSM-II) states: "Mental retardation refers to subnormal general intellectual functioning which originates during the developmental period and is associated with impairment of either learning and social adjustment or maturation or both" (p. 14). Emphasis in the United States tends to be on the use of the IQ as the main criterion of developmental retardation, although the development of adaptive behavior is also impaired, and the condition includes problems of cognitive styles, learning, and social adjustment. We tend to think of mental retardation as a unitary entity. In reality it is a complex, multifaceted problem besetting millions of handicapped people who suffer in different degrees and whose problems are caused by a variety of agents. Perhaps, then, the most crucial focus for change in this field lies in attitudes of professionals rather than in an array of new data.

Intelligence

Even though we assume that a fundamental aspect of mental retardation is lowered intelligence, we have difficulty defining the nature of intelligence. Robinson and Robinson (1965, p. 3) state that despite "vast expenditures of private and public funds for studies connected with education and development, the confusion about the nature of intelligence still exists; indeed, the concept is almost as obscure now as it was many years ago. Paradoxically, greater and greater efforts are being made to develop information about intelligence, although few can agree on a definition of what they consider intelligence to be." They state, further, that intelligence is currently viewed not as a concrete entity but as a "trait or complex of traits grouped by theoreticians to describe a class of behaviors which may be broadly labeled intelligent" (p. 10). They feel that in practical as well as theoretical terms, the concept of intelligence must be treated in relation to other facets of personality, and they point out that those involved with test design have focused specifically on mental mechanisms and abstract ability, as distinct from knowledge. Wechsler's well-known test of intelligence, for example, emphasizes factual information and the ability to reason abstractly. Robinson and Robinson comment:

Intelligence refers to the whole class of cognitive behaviors which reflect an individual's capacity to solve problems with insight, to adapt himself to new situations, to think abstractly, and to profit from his experience. The concept is an invention which corresponds roughly to "cognitive capacity" . . . Intelligence furthermore is an elastic concept which describes quite different sorts of behavior at different life stages. It is thus a forever emerging capacity which differs both in quality and in breadth with the individual's age and experience as well as with his constitution. (p. 15)

Together with Bruner (1971), they affirm that any adequate discussion of the concept of intelligence must be involved with the issues of development and maturation in the individual.

Great emphasis is placed on the use of intelligence tests alone to categorize individuals as mentally retarded. The American Psychiatric Association, for example, groups people according to five measured intelligence levels, although they make it clear that other information about the behavior and adaptive functioning of the child should be considered in assessing the degree of retardation. The numbers on IQ tests do not manifest any magical precision. Reverence for mathematics as the language of science should not blind us to the limits of test accuracy nor make us fix people permanently by some numerical value (Heaton-Ward, 1975). The following categories are the most widely used in DSM-II:

Borderline retardation: an IQ between 68 and 83. These people can become independent citizens with the proper training and occasional help.

Mildly retarded: an IQ between 52 and 67. The mildly retarded need special education but are capable of working at unskilled jobs.

Moderately retarded: an IQ between 36 and 51. The moderately retarded person should be able to learn to communicate but is unsuitable for education in a school; he can work in a sheltered environment but needs permanent guidance and supervision.

Severe retardation: those with IQ test scores between 25 and 39 on the Wechsler and between 20 and 35 on the Stanford-Binet. The severely retarded person can learn to feed, wash, and dress himself under supervision, but even as an adult he needs complete supervision.

Profound retardation: those persons whose IQs score below 25 on the Wechsler Scale and below 20 on the Stanford-Binet; these people will require nursing care and feeding all their lives.

These are all rough categories. Because temperament, personality, training, environmental conditions, and emotional adjustment affect all of them and determine adaptation for most people, test scores should always be used with other information to determine retardation. Rutter et al. (1969) have suggested a triaxial classification for all children that would include behavior, IQ, and etiology as factors in the assessment of mental capacity.

The Broader Meaning of Mental Deficit

In attempting to designate people as retarded—as distinct from normal individuals, mentally ill persons with psychiatric diseases, or those suffering cultural handicaps—different authors have used a variety of approaches. Doll's definition (1941) involved six qualities of retardation: (1) social incompetence, (2) mental subnormality, (3) developmental arrest, (4) continued manifestation at maturity, (5) constitutional origin, and (6) incurability. Current cultural and social studies, however, are changing the viewpoints of the experts so that constitutional origin is no longer accepted as a necessary characteristic of retardation. Furthermore, the fact that IQ has been shown to rise in many different situations indicates that many cases of mild retardation are far from incurable. Some authors have stressed the fact that our language and system of psychological testing are most appropriate for the assessment of middle-class individuals, and biases have recently become more apparent. Kanner takes up the issue in a different way, pointing out that some individuals would be retarded in any cultural setting but that others can successfully perform uncomplicated jobs and function in particular settings without stigma. He states: "In our midst, their shortcomings, which would remain unrecognized and therefore nonexistent in the awareness of a more primitive cultural body, appear as soon as scholastic curricula demand competition in spelling, history, geography, long division, etc. It is preferable to speak of such people as intellectually inadequate rather than mentally deficient" (1957, p. 71). Masland, Sarason, and Gladwin conclude that "a diagnosis of mental deficiency or retardation is compounded in our culture of medical, psychological, social and cultural considerations (implicit or explicit), and a setting in which the relevance of any one of these is different will produce a different distribution of individuals identified as subnormal by the members of the society under study" (1958, p. 282).

The effort to distinguish mental deficiency

from mental disease involves many professionals in controversy. Because of competition among caretakers of the retarded, special issues arise in categorizing the problems inherent in differences between deficiency and disease. If mental retardation is considered a disease, then it falls within the province of doctors, who treat diseases. If it is considered a social problem, it should be viewed in the context of social subsystems, that is, courts, services, and welfare agencies. And if it is an educational issue, then it becomes the responsibility of teachers, administrators, and state and local governments. Obviously it is the responsibility of all professional groups to use the best skill and knowledge available in helping the retarded and not to allow themselves to be manacled by terminology. Toward this end, Gunzberg writes, "A mental *handicap* is not a mental illness; it is mostly an unfortunate state to which one is born, just as one might be born with a club foot or a hunched back. On the other hand, a mental *disorder* or mental *disease* usually develops in someone who has previously achieved normal mental functioning. The various terms synonymous with mental defect, such as mental retardation or mental subnormality, should not therefore be confused with the terms used to describe psychotic and neurotic disorders" (1968, p. 8). While he is making one point well, Gunzberg is scanting another, which will be stressed later—that is, that a child born with normal endowment in a severely deprived environment might very well become functionally retarded and that children labeled as retarded may later function at higher IQ levels (Skodak and Skeels, 1949). Perhaps it is useful to think of the retarded as particular children who have particular vulnerabilities in the area of cognitive functioning and whose cultural and social backgrounds may disable them. Heber notes in the manual of the American Association on Mental Deficiency: "An individual may meet the criteria of mental retardation at one time and not at another. A person may change status as a result of changes in social standards, or conditions, or as a result of changes in efficiency of intellectual functioning, with level of efficiency always being determined in relation to the behavioral standards and norms of the individual's chronological age group" (1959, p. 4). Kessler (1966) adds that current thinking views mental retardation as a symptom rather than a diagnostic entity and that retardation should not imply a specific causation.

Physical Factors in Mental Deficiency

In considering the variety of causative factors involved in mental retardation, Jordan suggests that "our language shapes our thinking so that we think of some mechanism intruding into the course of normal development . . . we usually expect to find some single agent involved and its role is contributory. Thus, in polio we have identified a particular biological agent which acts directly on an otherwise normal body" (1966, p. 154). Many different causes of mental retardation exist; they are generally separated into those that are genetic or hereditary and those that are environmental. Kirman (1975) notes that there are hundreds of discrete genetically determined syndromes which produce mental defect by interference with cerebral development or function. However, because at least half of all retarded persons demonstrate no physiological defect or genetic problem, other investigators, such as Eisenberg (1968), have stressed that sociogenic factors are at least as fundamental as hereditary factors in causing defective intellectual functioning. Although much valid current thinking attributes most retardation to social causes, this does not negate the fact that hereditary factors account for a large part of the existing population of the retarded.

Not only do many different causes of mental deficiency exist, but the condition manifests itself to varying degrees. In part, this variation reflects the normal distribution of intelligence according to a bell-shaped curve, in which 3 percent of the population have very low intellectual endowment, while, at the other end, a similar group of individuals show intelligence quotients above 144.

Organic Causes

Among the many different groups of retarded individuals, one of the most common and well known is that group manifesting Down's syn-

drome, or mongolism, which affects about 10 percent of the children found in institutions for the retarded. This disease was first described a hundred years ago and is notable for the Oriental shape of the eye, the palpebral fissures, and a fold at the inner corner of the eye (from which the term *mongolism* is derived; despite the misnomer, this syndrome is not related to race and occurs in Negro, Caucasian, and Oriental children). In addition, looseness of muscular tone, abundant skin around the neck, high cheekbones, and a protruding tongue are generally seen; hands tend to be broad and thick and to have one thick line instead of the several creases that demarcate the normal palm, while the fingers are usually short and curve inward.

These symptoms are related to clearly demonstrated chromosomal abnormalities, although variations occur in the nature of these abnormalities and in the severity of the disease. At one time, children with mongolism died before puberty; now, with better care, they are living to adulthood. Three basic etiological groups have been established: those with three of chromosome number 21 (trisomy); those in whom chromosome combinations of both normal and trisomic cells are found in different tissues (mosaicism); and those in whom a fusion of two chromosomes, mostly numbers 15 and 21, is found. Overall, these patients have extra chromosomal material, bearing forty-seven instead of the normal forty-six human chromosomes, and the different combinations of this genetic material derange a variety of developing tissues. Some abnormal genetic material may be borne by parents free of the syndrome. In addition to hereditary factors, however, advanced childbearing age increases the likelihood that a child will be born with mongolism.

Children with Down's syndrome tend to have IQs under 50, though there are many exceptions, attested to by *The World of Nigel Hunt*, written by a boy in England with this condition (1967), and Seagoe's *Yesterday Was Tuesday All Day All Night* (1964). The general characterization of these children as lovable and docile, calm and cheerful, is not altogether accurate. Although they will not be very troublesome if left alone with no demands placed upon them, when pressured to learn, to perform on a higher level, or to behave in more mature social ways, they will begin to show irritability and some of the negativism, truculence, and reluctance seen in many children who are being "trained."* Menolascino (1968) and other authorities have restudied mongoloid children and found that because they are large in number and show many of the visible marks of being defective, they are therefore prone to become receptacles of many of the clichés about the retarded. Many thousands of children, however, regardless of low intelligence, are not all likely to manifest the same personality, style of learning, or level of intelligence.

Prenatal Conditions

During the period of fetal formation during pregnancy, a number of conditions may produce retarded children. Best known among these is German measles, or rubella, a viral disease normally not of great consequence in childhood. Occurrence in women during the first trimester of pregnancy, however, carries considerable likelihood that the unborn child will suffer central nervous system damage and consequent mental retardation.

Malnourished women tend to have smaller children than healthy women and to have premature children more often. Recent evidence indicates that insufficient amino acids for proper brain cell development, due to protein-deficient diets during pregnancy, are a cause of mental retardation. In addition to dietary deficiencies, poor people are also likely to suffer from inadequate medical and obstetrical care, a lack that increases the danger of mental retardation.

Noxious agents can also contribute to mental retardation. Several years ago the drug thalidomide, given to pregnant women, was found to cause deformed and retarded babies; it has since been withdrawn. Other agents produce similar effects, but most of these are now prohibited. X rays of the mother's abdomen were given more commonly in the past to judge the size and position of the fetus, but this practice, too, has been found to be damaging to developing tissues

* Special educators make the distinction between the "educable" retarded—those with IQs of 50 or above—and the "trainable"—those with IQs between 20 and 50.

and has, for the most part, been discontinued. At the present time, we are becoming increasingly aware of the possibly harmful role played by biochemical agents such as food additives.

Conditions of Birth

Children injured by trauma to the brain during delivery or those who do not receive sufficient oxygen during this period may suffer internal bleeding. Death of brain tissue may result, leading to many defects in cerebral functioning and to mental retardation.

Children born prematurely may also suffer from mental retardation. An infant with a birth weight of under 2300 grams tends to have less fully formed organs and to have gone through labor in a much more rapid manner than larger newborns. A premature infant is particularly vulnerable to being damaged during the process of labor and is also more likely to have central nervous system damage—both because tissues are incompletely formed and because the infant may not be able to make the shift from being a dependent organism within the mother to being a self-sustaining, breathing system after birth. Almost one-quarter of children born with cerebral palsy have birth weights under 2500 grams. Neurological damage and retardation accompanied by electroencephalogram (EEG) abnormalities are more common in inverse ratio to birth weight.

The purpose of listing these categories is not to present all of the physical causes of mental retardation but merely to indicate the principal physical sources for defect and to mention the various ways in which intellectual function can be altered.

The following is a classification of physical causes of retardation in current medical usage (adapted from DSM-II):

Following infection and intoxication
  1. cytomegalic inclusion body diseases, congenital
  2. rubella, congenital
  3. syphilis, congenital
  4. toxoplasmosis, congenital
  5. encephalopathy associated with other prenatal infections

6. encephalopathy due to postnatal cerebral infection
7. encephalopathy, congenital, associated with maternal intoxications
8. bilirubin encephalopathy (Kernicterus)
9. postimmunization encephalopathy
10. encephalopathy, other, due to intoxication

Following trauma or physical agent
1. encephalopathy due to prenatal injury
2. encephalopathy due to mechanical injury at birth
3. encephalopathy due to asphyxia at birth
4. encephalopathy due to postnatal injury

With disorders of metabolism, growth, or nutrition
1. cerebral lipoidosis, infantile (Tay-Sachs disease)
2. cerebral lipoidosis, late infantile (Bielschowsky's disease)
3. cerebral lipoidosis, juvenile (Spielmeyer-Vogt disease)
4. cerebral lipoidosis, late juvenile (Kuf's disease)
5. lipid histiocytosis of kerasin type (Gaucher's disease)
6. lipid histiocytosis of phosphatide type (Niemann-Pick's disease)
7. phenylketonuria
8. hepatolenticular degeneration (Wilson's disease)
9. porphyria
10. galactosemia
11. glucogenosis (Von Gierk's disease)
12. hypoglycemosis

Associated with gross brain disease (postnatal)
1. neurofibromatosis (von Recklinghausen's disease)
2. trigeminal cerebral angiomatosis (Sturge-Weber-Dimitri's disease)
3. tuberous sclerosis (Epiloia, Bourneville's disease)
4. intracranial neoplasm, other
5. encephalopathy associated with diffuse sclerosis of the brain
   a. acute infantile diffuse sclerosis (Krabbe's disease)
   b. diffuse chronic infantile sclerosis (Merzbacher-Pelizaeus disease)

c. infantile metachromatic leukodystrophy (Greenfield's disease)
d. juvenile metachromatic leukodystrophy (Scholz's disease)
e. progressive subcortical encephalopathy (Schilder's disease)
f. spinal sclerosis (Friedreich's ataxia)
6. encephalopathy, other, due to unknown or uncertain cause with the structural reactions manifest

Associated with diseases and conditions due to unknown prenatal influence
1. anencephaly (including hemianencephaly)
2. malformations of the gyri
3. porencephaly, congenital
4. multiple-congenital anomalies of the brain
5. other cerebral defects, congenital
   a. craniostenosis
   b. hydrocephalus, congenital
   c. hypertelorism (Greig's disease)
   d. macrocephaly (Megalencephaly)
   e. microcephaly, primary
   f. Laurence-Moon-Biedl syndrome

With chromosomal abnormality
1. autosomal trisomy of group G (Trisomy 21, Langdon-Down disease, mongolism)
2. autosomal trisomy of group E
3. autosomal trisomy of group D
4. sex chromosome anomalies
5. abnormal number of chromosomes
6. abnormal shape of chromosomes

In referring to this list, readers should bear in mind that all the syndromes presented can occur in mild or severe forms so that the diagnosis of one of them does not necessarily determine the level of intellectual functioning. However, a general correlation exists between more profound retardation and the presence of organic features; children who have suffered demonstrable brain damage, with definitive, visible loss of brain tissue, are more likely than others to have severe forms of mental retardation.

Social Causes of Mental Deficit

Of the nearly 150,000 children born each year in this country who are expected to be retarded, the majority will have mild mental retardation with no evidence of organic brain damage. In fact, of the 6,000,000 retarded individuals in this country, 85 percent, or 5,220,000 are mildly retarded; about 400,000 are moderately retarded, while about 75,000 are profoundly and severely retarded. As Cytryn and Lourie point out, the group of over 5,220,000 retarded individuals making up the vast majority "can be educated to a limited extent and are potentially able to adjust, at least marginally, to the demands of society and to employment. This group comes predominantly from the lower socio-economic strata of our society, and it is believed that many of its members are retarded due to *environmental deprivation*. The lower socio-economic groups also supply a disproportionately large number of the moderately and severely retarded" (1975, p. 1160). Hurley (1968) writes about the danger of assuming prematurely and without sufficient proof that retardation is hereditary in origin. He points out that the hereditary determinant should be scientifically substantiated before it is assumed. Further, although he feels that about 15 percent of all cases of mental retardation are due to genetic causes, he notes that any such figure remains a guess. He stresses that the high prevalence of mental retardation among the poor is unrelated to the intellectual endowment of this class and points out that a high percentage of these groups are retarded in function rather than lacking in endowment.

This is, of course, a very important restatement of the basic concept that in all biological development an innate factor is needed, which is then stimulated to function by the environment. Development of each function of the body will vary according to the surrounding environment. If, for example, a child is brought up in the dark, or reared in isolated circumstances, he will be less "intelligent" when measured by the conventional social and academic standards. If a child is brought up in a minority group in the midst of severe poverty, he will hear a different grammatical language; he will be less well fed; he will get less medical care, less attention, and fewer opportunities to focus on intellectually stimulating objects and activities.

Bowlby's worldwide survey for the World Health Organization (1951) demonstrates the crucial role of proper nurture, care, and environmental stimuli among children brought up in institutions. In contrast, Kushlick reports:

Mild subnormality appears to be a temporary incapacity characterized mainly by educational difficulties experienced at school . . . There is now evidence which suggests that mild subnormality in the absence of abnormal neurological signs, epilepsy, electroencephalographic abnormalities, biochemical abnormalities, chromosomal abnormalities, or sensory defects occurs only among the lower classes. Indeed there is evidence that almost no children of higher social class parents have IQ scores of less than 80 unless they have one of the pathological processes mentioned above. (1968, pp. 380–381)

The Growth and Development of Retarded Children

When a child is born mildly retarded, he may show some signs of the condition at birth. If, however, no physical abnormalities are apparent, as is the case with the majority of these children, the parents will not note anything remarkable. A typical course of development is one in which the parents find that the child is an easy baby to manage. They may find the child a bit quiet and undemonstrative, but often they remark that "this has been the easiest baby." The child will tend to go through all the normal stages of development slowly. He is likely to play with his fingers, to follow objects, and to reach for people in a "lazy" manner. Children normally sit up at about the age of six months; the retarded child may not sit until ten or eleven months. This may still not be very alarming to the parents because he eats and sleeps in a smooth and rhythmic way. The same casualness may be manifested in the child's approach to crawling and trying to walk, and he may not seem to bother to make the effort, so that instead of being interested in standing, and tottering about at one year, he is still playfully sitting. Not walking is considered normal until about seventeen months; the retarded child may begin around this time, or he may not walk until the age of two or later. Whereas speech comes to the normal child around the age of two, with phrases, responsive sounds, and the beginning of sentences, the retardate will be slow in this area and may not say anything significant until age three or even four. With the delay in these functions, most parents are quite worried and are likely to seek professional help, but what is amiss may still not be clear.

Traditional views have reinforced the notion that if a child is backward because of mental retardation, he will be uniformly backward in all developmental and intellectual functions. This is assumed to contrast with psychiatrically ill children, who may be especially musically or mathematically talented, for example, but who may also have reading difficulties and be primitively dependent. In a similar fashion, retarded children show different levels of functioning in different areas. The developmental style of the retarded child, however, is usually delayed and less energetic than that of normal children. Toilet training is slower, partly because the speech and communication pattern is absent and because the child may not get the sense of what is being taught to him as readily as another child; he may also enjoy mouthing and smearing more than other children.

According to Erikson's developmental scheme, the first psychological phase is the oral phase, stressing the mouth as the area for making contact with the world—for exploring and tasting, as well as for incorporating the food that is essential to life. As Erikson states (1950), the first mutual regulation between child and mother —the child's pattern of accepting things and the mother's or culture's way of giving them—occurs in this phase. He posits that the child's basic sense of trust evolves at this point. It is also in this oral phase of development that the child is most profoundly helpless and dependent upon the care-taking abilities of the mother or parenting person. In humans, this period of total dependency is greater than in other animals, and in the retarded child it is further prolonged.

Normally, the child progresses further in his musculoskeletal development as he separates himself from other individuals, gets up and starts moving around, and explores the world around him for himself. The child learns to submit to certain rules of the world about his bowel products, while becoming more competent in his adventures in the world. Erikson describes the second basic conflict in the life of the child as autonomy versus shame and doubt—one of the basic issues for the child to resolve in his development. The normal child may tussle and squabble over being trained on the toilet, but he proceeds exuberantly with learning this and other things simultaneously. For the retarded child, the evolution is slower, the tendency toward mouthing is greater, and dependency is more salient.

The speech of the retarded child is poor, and this alters his conceptualization of the world. Because language development is one of the great organizers of the mind and of intellectual functioning, it is almost impossible to separate thoughts about concepts and objects from our words for these concepts and objects. The delay in word usage by people of subnormal intellect is both the sign of their handicap and a cause of further handicapping. Earle (1961) wrote that in the subnormal, weakness and simplicity in biological and psychic development tend to be inherent. This observation overlaps with that of Webster (1963) that retarded children observed in nursery schools tend to be more apathetic, to play with less initiative, to sit more quietly with a toy, and to be more self-involved or mildly autistic than others. They can be roused, but they require more stimulation to become involved than children of normal intelligence.

As the child develops, he begins to look around more, to play with other children, and to be dealt with by them according to their aggressiveness, physical skill, and temperament. A pecking order is established in the nursery, and it is clear that the retarded child is different. By this time parents have usually taken the child to a variety of specialists, sometimes as many as eleven or twelve pediatricians, neurologists, psychologists, endocrinologists, or child psychiatrists, either searching for a diagnosis or trying to have the diagnosis of mental retardation changed to something they can tolerate more readily.

For almost all parents, the news of a retarded child is a terrible blow. It has been described by Olshansky (1962) as "chronic sorrow," the continuing sorrow of a parent who feels he has lost his hopes of perfection and a "complete" child. Stages of shock and realization and recognition are involved in this sorrow, each one of which will influence the way a child is handled as he grows up. Some parents overprotect and do not stimulate the child to use the abilities he has. Others are so depressed that they cannot do much for the child. In still others, the sadness is interwoven with a kind of impotent rage toward the world. Many parents are angry at the retarded child, though they try to cover this up, hating to admit feelings of anger toward a helpless child. Most try to do their best in spite of their personal sense of loss and sadness, but some become cool and distant and withdraw from the retardate the sustained warmth and stimulation that he requires even more than other children. Some parents try to quash their own sadness and embark on brisk programs, pushing the children relentlessly toward speech training, toilet training, nursery school, exercises, and a host of other "stimulating" activities. If they push too hard, they overwhelm a vulnerable child and tend to make him withdraw even further. Fathers are usually most able to distance themselves from the grief of bearing a retarded child, plunging into their work and leaving most of the intimate child care to mothers. In later years, however, fathers feel the impact more.

The child at no point develops totally on his own or within himself, and each developmental step attempted by any child occurs in a particular environmental matrix. We are progressively more aware of the influence of temperament —the endowed reactive style—on the interplay between mothers and children. Some mothers are particularly good with aggressive children and love the challenge; others can feel comfortable only with "easy" children who have smooth rhythms. These factors set up resonances between mothers and children that alter the style of development. The mother's tolerance for the slowness of a retarded child and her ability to identify with him will aid in the effective use of his capacities during his more protracted developmental course.

During the oedipal phase, both male and female children become aware of their sexual organs and begin to explore them as part of their evolution of self-concept in relation to both parents. For Erikson, issues of assertiveness and possessiveness are paramount during this phase. For all children, this phase of development occurs over several years of life, and the patterns and ideas, the fantasies, the pokings, the teasing words, the explorations, and the fears are all parts of a larger fabric. The subnormal child will tend to move through this phase of psychological

development later than other children and to bear with him the aggregate attitudes of his slowed maturation; his speech is still meager, often marked by an impediment, and he still shows a greater-than-usual dependence upon his parents for care.

The oral and anal phases have been handled differently by the retardate than by other children, determining how he handles later phases of development. He tends to be more fearful, more guilty, and more excited and bemused by the new and mysterious questions of sexual differences, his own genitals, the ways in which boys and girls differ, and where babies originate. By this time, he is also likely to have been made aware that these aspects of life will be different for him. Parents often feel that their retarded children should be protected from sexuality, or have it hidden. These feelings arise partly out of sympathy, from the sense that their children will not be likely to marry and have normal sexual lives, and partly out of fear that the retarded, with their limited control and comprehension, will either be taken advantage of sexually (if they are girls) or be sexually aggressive (if they are boys). Parental concerns about these matters begin early and sink in deeply, with the result that the child who most needs instruction and calm support is likely to get silence, abrupt instructions, and anxious lectures from parents who handle these matters more effectively with their other children. Consequently the child is more likely to inhibit questioning, to keep his confused thoughts to himself, and to act as if he doesn't notice the things that are going on around him. This is strikingly true in children growing up in schools for the retarded, where all of the inhibiting pressures tend to be more stark, no matter how well-intentioned the organization of the institution.

The social context in which all developmental changes occur shapes them. Hurley (1968) points out that for the poor, constant awareness of their own abject status and the failure it implies lead to embarrassed withdrawal and isolation within society. This observation also applies to the retarded child, who is taught by his sociofamilial context—his sister who is ashamed of him, his mother who feels burdened by him, his father who may feel put off and annoyed by him. He comes to feel that people look at him differently, particularly if he has the clothes, or the "look," or the haircut, or any of the organic signs that people associate with retardation. By the time a child gets to school, where he may be placed in a special class or a special position in a regular class, he is aware of his special status and will generally handle this by inhibition. While authors describe hyperactivity as a part of the retarded child's repertoire, this finding may not be valid in view of the enormous overflow of energy in normal children, who also show varied jerking, twitching, and squirming movements. This behavior generally decreases with age in all children, and the retarded tend to be quiet when older. Whether this diminution is part of a maturational process or whether children are beaten into submission by social circumstances remains questionable.

In spite of this attempt to outline a "normative" development in abnormal individuals, it is clear that, in Kessler's words, "the term 'mentally retarded' embraces a range of patients, from the totally helpless child in the crib to the child whose handicap is apparent only in school. In addition to this variation in the degree and type of handicap, causes of the retardation vary, and so do physical and personality characteristics associated with it . . . Mentally retarded children are as different from one another as are children of normal or superior intelligence" (1966, p. 166). Heber declares in regard to the personality of the retarded:

The extreme paucity of experimental data bearing on the relationship between personality variables and behavior efficiency of the retarded person is indeed remarkable in view of the generally acknowledged importance of personality factors in problem-solving. Textbooks are replete with statements describing the retarded as passive, anxious, impulsive, rigid, suggestible, lacking in persistence, immature, and withdrawn, and as having a low frustration tolerance and an unrealistic self-concept and level of aspiration. Yet not one of these purported attributes can be either substantiated or refuted on the basis of available research data. (1964, p. 169)

Problems of Language and Learning Style

One area in which the retarded appear to have consistent difficulties is that of verbal expression.

Spradlin (1963) concludes, after surveying a number of studies in the language problems of the retarded, that most of the children in institutions have speech defects. In both private and public day schools, a high incidence of speech defects is also found; articulation and voice problems constituted the highest percentage of speech difficulties (this is also true for normal children). However, the whole gamut of speech problems is found among retarded children and adults—mutism, delayed onset of speech, disorders of articulation, phonation problems, and stuttering. Failures of comprehension and symbolization also occur.

Hurley (1968) has pointed to the high correlation of verbal ability with other aspects of cognitive functioning. In the home of the poor family, for example, where too many people crowd into too few rooms, the noise level is usually unbearable; television, phonograph, and radio are regularly heard. For the infant, this constant din is noxious and unintelligible. In order to survive, a child must deaden his mind to sound and learn inattention; the child does not distinguish between relevant and irrelevant sounds. This presents problems in school when he hears the teacher as inattentively as he hears the sounds he has habitually turned off outside the classroom. Because retardation and poverty are so often related, an environment of deprivation compounds speech and language difficulties.

Earle (1961) sees subnormality as more basic than simplemindedness or low intelligence; he sees it, rather, as biological weakness manifest as failure of neurophysiological development and general inability to respond effectively to the environment. Earle believes that developmental failure or weakness may be due to immaturity, emotional disturbances, personality inhibition, or even to prolonged institutional residence. Proponents of the social causes theory of mental retardation feel, however, that his views apply only to the profoundly retarded. Arguments persist as to how much intellectual defect is innate and how much derives from the quality of life.

Another position, well demonstrated by Zigler (1967), Perry (1974), and others, has gained continuing support. This view holds that many of the reported differences between retardates and normal children of the same age are the result of motivational and emotional differences that reflect differences in environmental histories. Zigler acknowledges the importance of lower intelligence but states that "many of the effects of institutionalization may be constant, regardless of the person's intelligence level" (p. 296). A person with low intelligence experiencing life events and challenges develops particular behavior patterns skewed by his retardation; these responses differ greatly from those of a person with greater intellectual endowment. An obvious example of this difference is the greater amount of failure that the retardate typically experiences. If the retardate could somehow be guaranteed a history of greater success, we would expect his behavior to be more nearly normal, regardless of his intellectual level. Zigler found that deprived retarded children are desperate to have some relationship with a supportive adult. He found that, in learning situations, they will strive to follow instructions that will keep them in contact with this adult, an observation that certainly agrees with that often made about the retarded seeking attention and affection. Social deprivation, however, can also make the retardate fearful, wary, mistrustful, and evasive with strangers.

Zigler further suggests that such negative reactions explain some behavior that had previously been claimed to be part of the cognitive rigidity of the subnormal. For example, after an institutionalized retardate's wariness has been allayed, he becomes more responsive than the normal individual to social reinforcement. In addition, retardates will persist at tasks they are learning because of ties to teachers with whom they have achieved a positive relationship. Zigler notes that the many failures experienced by retardates produce a cognitive style of problem solving characterized by "outer-directedness": the retarded child distrusts his own solutions to problems and seeks guidance from others. This, Zigler believes, explains the suggestibility so frequently described in the retarded child. "Evidence has now been presented indicating that, relative to normals of the same mental age, the retarded child is more sensitive to verbal cues from an adult, is more imitative of the behavior of adults and of his peers, and does more visual scanning" (p. 297). Zigler feels that retardates hunger more in a problem-solving situation for praise and encouragement and care much less about being correct or meeting challenges than middle-class children of normal intellect. It has become clear that children with slowed and handicapped learning have personal needs and the understandable yearnings of a stigmatized minority. Retarded children want appreciation and affection, and, if these are supplied, they can utilize their learning capacities more fully than has been previously appreciated. Many classroom behavior problems can be helped by meeting these needs.

In regard to school, Berlin notes in discussing consultation and special education that "most teachers who work with both the educable and the trainable groups complain that their primary stumbling block is the negativistic, stubborn, hyperactive, hostile, destructive, and sometimes assaultive behavior of these children. Occasionally they express concern about the less frequently encountered, very apathetic, listless, and withdrawn students" (1966, p. 281). He goes on to describe how to deal with these issues in school and points out the gratification of teachers in seeing improvements. These children and their families respond to counseling from teachers, psychologists, and psychiatrists, and also to psychotherapy in selected cases. The underlying psychodynamics is not basically different from that found in the emotional disturbances of other types of people.

By the time the retardate reaches adolescence, he has learned his defective role. He knows where he stands with his family, in his group, and in the general society. In spite of this, an interesting phenomenon occurs: people of inadequate means who are expected to fail in society appear to manage relatively well once they escape from the school system. Tarjan (1966) points out that instead of the estimated 3 percent of the population referred to earlier in this chapter as retarded, only 1 percent is visible in the community. The fact that income levels for the mildly retarded approach those of normal individuals signifies that many retarded persons learn to function well in the community. Charles (1953) has shown that many who had been considered mentally retarded during their school years succeed in leading independent lives in adulthood. If social independence and gainful employment are viewed as contraindications of mental retardation, we must conclude that the diagnosis of mental retardation in childhood does not necessarily determine retardation in adult life.

Despite organic handicaps, conceptual defects, poverty, social stigma, family ambivalence, and personal shame, and counter to the social attitude and those of the bureaucracies of schools and the community, enormous numbers of retardates seem to transcend the problem; they disappear into general society. If they evade the problems of filling out an income tax return and are not stigmatized by their draft boards, they are hard to find and difficult to follow up; 95 percent live outside of institutions. Large numbers of mentally handicapped children in school in fact make an adaptation to the larger world, even if they have considerable trouble and need extra support.

The Role of the Psychiatrist and Psychiatry

The role of the psychiatrist covers a broad spectrum of problems and opportunities in relation to the complexities and misperceptions surrounding the retardate's physical, emotional, and social reality. It is difficult to discuss this role without noting that it is controversial. Although only about 1 percent of the psychiatrists in this country spend a majority of their time with the retarded, most psychiatrists are called upon at some time to diagnose, evaluate, treat, or refer patients who have problems of retardation. The clearest early functions for the psychiatrist are clinical: to make the most practical evaluation of crucial personality factors, specifying evidence of major or minor emotional dysfunction or psychopathology, and to devise programs for therapeutic intervention. Commitment—to issues of increased research in such areas as intelligence and adaptive behavior; attitude change, among professionals as well as other citizens; and social advocacy—is a prevailing need, providing the foundation for the functions of the professional focusing on care of the retarded.

Examination and Diagnosis

The competently trained psychiatrist need not rely on special training to perform the necessary examination of the retarded. Arriving at a diagnosis from the results of psychological tests alone, or deducing the diagnosis from a combination of perinatal and postnatal history and neurological and IQ assessments, has unfortunately been common. While the latter approach is doubtless important in many of the more marked cases, for that large proportion of cases in which the patient is mildly retarded (85 percent of retardates) or is borderline and has no physical defects, the skills of the clinical psychiatrist should be employed along the same lines as for psychiatric assessment of normal adult and child evaluation.

Several special caveats should be entered. The examiner must try not to foreclose his diagnosis at the outset. The focus must be on personality assessment, pondering what kind of coping style and mental mechanisms are being used and how the adaptation of the individual is failing or succeeding within his circumstances. The role of the family, the school, and the community should be sharply defined in separating the presenting complaint from the psychiatric diagnosis. Most frequently the problems that bring the patient with mental retardation to the psychiatrist are related to the stigma of mental deficiency and the fear of what the patient's defects may produce, as well as to the desire for information about how to handle psychiatric problems. The need for resources to help the family and the patient is widespread. The real request may be for a new training school referral, a special day activity program for the child, home training help, or a sheltered workshop for the adult patient. To fulfill the role of diagnostician and referral agent, the psychiatrist must be able to find and communicate with the educational authorities, social workers, and psychologists in the community where the patient will live.

For diagnosis in cases where cognitive defect is suspected, it is important to define the role of the examiner clearly for the patient. This entails more explanation than would be necessary with other adults or children and differs from the problem of the paranoid or suspicious patient. The retarded patient needs to be told clearly and in simple language why he is being examined, and who the doctor is. The retarded patient is frequently correct in believing that he is being handled administratively or punitively because this is the reality of many of his experiences. He also needs to be told in the simplest language and the most supportive way possible what he should expect. It is also important that the attitude of the interviewer be both cordial and instructive. This approach may be at some variance with the usual psychiatric training technique of not over-structuring what is told to the patient, but the distinction is necessary and the difference in this style of interviewing is useful in communicating with these patients and their families.

The purpose is to define the context for the retarded patient. In addition, a more specific effort should be made to elicit verbal responses from him. If handled supportively and sensitively, and if given the opportunity, the retarded person with an IQ above 40 can verbalize many feelings—a goal that should be sought in all assessments.

One of the most common pitfalls in dealing with adult retardates, who may come to the interview behaving in peculiar ways or wearing bizarre jewelry or clothing, is to misdiagnose them as simple schizophrenics. In fact they are fixated and childlike and are ready to describe their relationships to their "toys" in words that are quite distinct in meaning and intention from the special symbolism found in schizophrenic symptomatology.

Psychopharmacology

Pressure to provide services for large numbers of patients leads to the selection of treatment methods that require the least time and effort. While there are some indications for prescribing drugs for the retarded, misuse is more evident. The use of psychoactive agents should be based only upon specific psychiatric indication. Phenothiazines, for example, most appropriately and effectively used as antipsychotic agents, have been widely used to tranquilize retarded persons in situations where better management and milder medications would work. Roger Freeman (1970) comments that management of behavior disturbances in special schools and institutions can only be helped to a limited degree by the use of tranquilizers. Drugs may easily be misused, circumventing a more basic understanding of the

significance of the disturbed behavior within a developmental and environmental context. Quieting patients with drugs may allay parents' and physicians' anxiety and distract attention from developing rehabilitative programs; in this instance, drugs are used as "chemical strait jackets." Finally, drugs are frequently prescribed in inappropriate dosages for inadequate periods of time.

The most crucial feature to be borne in mind is the specific indication of the medications. Pharmacological agents that are useful with other psychiatric patient populations are useful with the retarded also. These are not agents that are intended to cure specific forms of retardation, such as antileading agents or hormonal treatments for cretinism; rather they can be a useful element in the psychiatrist's ability to manage and alter psychological malfunction (see chapter 18, "Chemotherapy," for a fuller treatment of the subject of psychopharmacology). The field of mental retardation suffers from the same lack of standardization of drug-level usage found in the field of child psychiatry.

Genetic Counseling

Recently a vogue for giving genetic information to parents of the retarded has developed. Whether genetic counseling comes from a pediatrician, a neurologist, a psychologist, a geneticist, or a family doctor, it frequently needs to be tempered by psychological knowledge of parents' grief. Diagnosis should of course be precise and statistics should be correct. What is too often lacking, however, is the crucial awareness that parents cannot absorb factual knowledge well, that they must go through a grief reaction, and that this bereavement usually takes about six weeks to run its course.

The various assessments of what people learn regarding retardation from genetic counseling indicate both the difficulty and slowness with which parents absorb the facts and the importance of establishing a relationship with them in order to impart these data. In this area the psychiatrist can be helpful both to families and to his colleagues in offering such counseling, and he can usefully apply his knowledge about the conflicting feelings of parents—the anger interwoven with grief at having a retarded child, and the fluctuations in their attitudes toward care-taking professionals.

Therapeutic Modalities

A little-attended but important body of data (Bernstein, 1970) indicates the usefulness of formal psychiatric approaches to the retarded. All the modalities and techniques of treatment can be used with both adults and children if the structure of the personality problem and its association with cognitive defect are clearly defined. Schizophrenia, depression, anxiety, conversion states, and the multitude of hypochondriacal complaints and phobic symptoms can be approached in group and individual therapies involving support, clarification, manipulation of the environment, and drugs. The special need is to understand the setting in which the therapist will work, because the therapist is likely to be working with an institution, a sheltered workshop, an association for retarded citizens, the family, and sometimes with educators or psychologists who want to apply behavior-modification measures simultaneously. Behavior modification has had enormous utility with the retarded, and while psychiatrists are becoming more informed about this, the professionals applying this technique with the retarded are usually nonmedical. Effective treatment requires defining as sharply as possible the areas and target symptoms to be treated. Assessing the distribution and appropriateness of care is especially necessary to define treatment roles when, for example, a teacher or psychologist is handling a patient with behavior modification at the same time that a psychiatrist is employing a psychodynamic approach to the same patient.

The Psychiatrist and Advocacy

Many of the functions of the psychiatrist with the retarded involve problems of institutional care and administration, physical rehabilitation, special education, or guardianship, and issues of legal concern over testamentary capacity and competence. The legal handicaps of the retarded are many and vary among jurisdictions with regard to rights to marry, make contracts, appear in court, own property, or be sterilized; these issues must be approached according to the prevailing regulations. All of them entail intricate problems and can only be touched upon by saying that the psychiatrist has an opportunity to function as an agent both for his patients and for general betterment of care for the retarded if he sees these aspects of his role clearly. Effective psychiatric consultation demands clear and specific knowledge of the social matrix in which the retardate's problems occur. The retarded in our society are poor and disliked, and their facilities are meager. In order for clinical work to benefit these patients and their families, the doctor must have a realistic idea of therapeutic possibilities and limitations.

The field of retardation comprises a whole galaxy of dilemmas and challenges. We have problems defining intelligence and mental retardation. We need more knowledge of neurophysiological and genetic factors, as well as of the nature of learning and teaching. There is also a clear necessity for social action, as Hurley makes poignantly clear:

The major obstacles to the social change that would eliminate mental retardation are prejudice and ignorance of the real nature of poverty . . . The term "cultural deprivation" is a euphemism. It suggests that the only difference between the poor child and his wealthier counterpart is a trip to a museum or a zoo . . . "The family is the first and most basic institution in our society for developing the child's potential, in all its many aspects: emotional, intellectual, moral and spiritual, as well as physical and social. Other influences do not even enter the child's life until after the first highly formative years." (1968, pp. 55–56)

The process of family life among the poor is largely an accommodation to low socioeconomic status, which helps explain the higher prevalence of mental retardation (or, more correctly, "environmental deprivation") within this segment of the population. Because the household is the complete world of the child for a long period of time, the quality of life in that world is crucial. If all the child's senses are not stimulated adequately from birth, his intellectual potential will suffer.

Our understanding of the complex phenomena of retardation will increase to the extent that all the relevant etiological factors—psychosocial, genetic, and constitutional—as well as their psychodynamic concomitants are approached multilaterally, each acknowledged with respect to the others. Thus, rather than being a field irrelevant to the interests of the psychiatrist, mental retardation provides as yet unexplored opportunities for research in personality theory and for treatment and management of stigmatized individuals, as well as for expanding the skills of the individual clinician.

References

American Psychiatric Association. 1968. *Diagnostic and statistical manual of mental disorders*. 2nd ed. Washington, D.C.

Berlin, I. N. 1966. Consultation and special education. In *Prevention and treatment of mental retardation*, ed. I. Philips. New York: Basic Books.

Bernstein, N. R., ed. 1970. *Diminished people: problems and care of the mentally retarded*. Boston: Little, Brown.

Bowlby, J. 1951. *Maternal care and mental health*. World Health Organization monograph no. 2. Geneva.

Bruner, J. 1971. *Toward a theory of instruction*. Cambridge, Mass.: Harvard University Press.

Charles, D. C. 1953. Ability and accomplishment of persons earlier judged mentally deficient. *Genet. Psychol. Monogr.* 47:3–71.

Cytryn, L., and R. Lourie. 1975. Mental retardation. In *Comprehensive textbook of psychiatry*, ed. A. N. Freedman, H. I. Kaplan, and B. J. Sadock. Vol. 1. Baltimore: Williams & Wilkins.

Doll, E. A. 1941. The essentials of an inclusive concept of mental deficiency. *Am. J. Ment. Defic.* 46:214–219.

Earle, C. J. C. 1961. *Subnormal personalities: their clinical investigation and assessment*. London: Baillière, Tindall, & Cox.

Eisenberg, L. 1968. The social development of human intelligence. Paper presented at the 7th International Congress of Mental Health, August 1968, London.

Erikson, E. H. 1950. *Childhood and society*. New York: Norton.

Freeman, R. 1970. Use of psychoactive drugs for intellectually handicapped children. In *Diminished people: problems and care of the mentally retarded*, ed. N. R. Bernstein. Boston: Little, Brown.

Gunzburg, H. C. 1968. *Social competence and mental handicap*. London: Ballière, Tindall, & Cox.

Heaton-Ward, W. A. 1975. *Mental subnormality*. Bristol: John Wright.

Heber, R. 1959. A manual on terminology and classification in mental retardation. Monograph supplement to *Am. J. Ment. Defic.* 64, no. 2.

—— 1964. Personality in mental retardation. In *Mental retardation: a review of research*, ed. H. A. Stevens and R. Heber. Chicago: University of Chicago Press.

Hunt, N. 1967. *The world of Nigel Hunt*. London: Garrett-Helix.

Hurley, R. L. 1968. *Poverty and mental retardation: a causal relationship*. New York: Vintage Books.

Jordan, T. E. 1966. *The mentally retarded*. 2nd ed. Columbus, Ohio: Merrill.

Kanner, L. 1957. *Child Psychiatry*. 3rd ed. Springfield, Ill.: Thomas.

Kessler, J. 1966. *Psychopathology of childhood*. Englewood Cliffs, N.J.: Prentice-Hall.

Kirman, B. 1975. *Mental handicap: a brief guide*. London: Staples.

Kushlick, A. 1968. Social problems of mental subnormality. In *Foundations of child psychiatry*, ed. E. Miller. London: Pergamon Press.

Masland, R. L., S. B. Sarason, and J. Gladwin. 1958. *Mental subnormality: biological, psychological, and cultural factors*. New York: Basic Books.

Menolascino, F. 1968. Emotional disturbances in mentally retarded children: diagnostic and treatment aspects. *Arch. Gen. Psychiatry* 19:456–464.

Olshansky, S. 1962. Chronic sorrow: a response to having a mentally defective child. *Soc. Casework*, 43:191–194.

Perry, N. 1974. *Teaching the mentally retarded child*. New York: Columbia University Press.

Robinson, H. B. and N. M. 1965. *The mentally retarded child: a psychological approach*. New York: McGraw-Hill.

Rutter, M., S. Lebovici, L. Eisenberg, A. V. Sneznevskij, R. Sadoun, E. Brooke, and T. Y. Lin. 1969. A triaxial classification of mental disorders in childhood: an international study. *J. Child Psychol. Psychiatry* 10:41–61.

Seagoe, M. 1964. *Yesterday was Tuesday all day all night*. Boston: Little, Brown.

Skodak, M., and H. M. Skeels. 1949. A final follow-up study of 100 adopted children. *J. Genet. Psychol.* 75:85–125.

Spradlin, J. 1963. Language and communication of mental defectives. In *Handbook of mental deficiency*, ed. N. R. Ellis. New York: McGraw-Hill.

Tarjan, G. 1966. Mental retardation: implications for

the future. In *Prevention and treatment of mental retardation*, ed. I. Philips. New York: Basic Books.

Webster, T. 1963. Problems of emotional development in young retarded children. *Am. J. Psychiatry* 120:37–43.

Zigler, F. 1967. Familial mental retardation: a continuing dilemma. *Science* 155:292–298.

Recommended Reading

Bagdikian, B. H. 1966. *In the midst of plenty*. Boston: Beacon Press.

Bellak, L., and M. Hurvich. 1969. A systematic study of ego functions. *J. Nerv. Ment. Dis.* 148, no. 6:569–585.

Bernstein, N. R. 1970. The subnormal. In *The practice of community mental health*, ed. H. Grunebaum. Boston: Little, Brown.

Bernstein, N. R., and F. J. Menolascino. 1970. Apparent and relative mental retardation: their challenges to psychiatric treatment. In *Psychiatric approaches to mental retardation*, ed. F. J. Menolascino. New York: Basic Books.

Bernstein, N. R., and J. O. Rice. 1972. Psychiatric consultation in a school for the retarded. *Am. J. Ment. Defic.* 76:718–725.

Cruickshank, W. M., ed. 1971. *Psychology of exceptional children and youth*. Englewood Cliffs, N.J.: Prentice-Hall.

de la Cruz, F., and G. LaVeck, eds. 1973. *Human sexuality and the mentally retarded*. New York: Brunner/Mazel.

Edgerton, R. 1967. *The cloak of competence*. Berkeley: University of California Press.

Gardner, W. I. 1971. *Behavior modification in mental retardation*. Chicago: Aldine.

Heber, R. 1961. Modifications in the manual on terminology and classification in mental retardation. Monograph supplement to *Am. J. Ment. Defic.* 64, no. 7.

Kanner, L. 1967. *A history of the care and study of the mentally retarded*. Springfield, Ill.: Thomas.

Katz, E. 1968. *The retarded adult in the community*. Springfield, Ill.: Thomas.

Kirman, B. 1965. The etiology of mental subnormality. In *Modern perspectives in child psychiatry*, ed. J. G. Howells. London: Oliver and Boyd.

Mercer, J. 1973. *Labeling the mentally retarded*. Berkeley: University of California Press.

Philips, I., ed. 1966. *Prevention and treatment of mental retardation*. New York: Basic Books.

Poser, C. M. 1969. *Mental retardation: diagnosis and treatment*. New York: Hoeber.

Sarason, S., and J. Doris. 1969. *Psychological problems in mental deficiency*. New York: Harper & Row.

Alcoholism and Drug Dependence

CHAPTER 27

George E. Vaillant

GENERALIZATIONS about drug dependence must be made cautiously. Not only are there many different drugs of abuse, but also there are no truly dangerous drugs, only people who use drugs dangerously. For this reason, some clinicians have said there are as many different addictions as there are people. Since physicians must appreciate patterns of illness as well as individual idiosyncracies, this chapter will make generalizations about drug dependence; no individual will fit exactly into the patterns offered.

Since the difference between self-detrimental drug use and socially disapproved drug use is often unclear, definitions are important. In 1969, the World Health Organization has offered standard definitions of drug abuse, drug dependence, physical dependence, and tolerance. The term *drug abuse* refers to excessive drug use, inconsistent with acceptable medical practice. *Drug dependence* refers to a state, psychic or physical, of interaction between human and drug characterized by a compulsion to take the drug on either a continuous or a periodic basis, to experience its psychic effects or to avoid the discomfort of its absence. *Tolerance* is an altered physiological state brought on by continuous use of a drug and resulting in a declining effect of a given dose. *Physical dependence* is an altered physiological state brought on by continued use and resulting in physiological symptoms on withdrawal. *Psychic dependence* is an often used but nonspecific term that refers to drug dependence without demonstrated physical dependence.

No single formula fits all drugs. For example, drug dependence on cigarettes results in little tolerance or physical dependence but marked psychic dependence. Heroin abuse produces far more tolerance than alcohol, but physical dependence on alcohol leads to withdrawal symptoms more severe than those of withdrawal from heroin. Although amphetamines, marijuana, and lysergic acid diethylamide (LSD) all lead to tolerance and drug abuse, they have not been convincingly demonstrated to produce physical dependence. The effects of several commonly abused drugs are summarized in table 27.1.

Defining Alcoholism

Alcoholism is the most ignored public health problem in America but a treatable one. It affects from 5 to 10 percent of the adult population, including 20 to 40 percent of all adult pa-

TABLE 27.1 Effects of commonly abused drugs (0 = no effects; + = mild effects; ++ = marked effects).

Drug	Tolerance	Psychic dependence	Physical dependence
Alcohol	+	++	++
Amphetamines	++	++	0?
Barbiturates	++	++	++
Caffeine	+	+	0
Chlordiazepoxide	++	++	+
Cocaine	+	++	0
LSD	++	+	0
Marijuana	+	+	0
Nicotine	+	++	+
Opiates	++	++	++

tients admitted to general medical and surgical wards. In American males aged twenty-five to forty-four, alcoholism plays a major role in the four leading causes of death: accidents, homicide, suicide, and alcoholic cirrhosis.

The World Health Organization definition of *alcohol dependence* is when the consumption of alcohol by an individual exceeds the limits that are accepted by his culture or when it injures his health or social relationships (1969). Clearly, however, one can become dependent without necessarily violating some social norms and injure health without becoming dependent. The American Psychiatric Association's *Diagnostic and Statistical Manual* (DSM-II) breaks down alcoholism into the categories of episodic excessive drinking, habitual excessive drinking, and alcohol addiction. Jellinek (1960) has divided alcoholic drinking into the following categories: *alpha*, alcohol abuse for relief of psychic distress (such as depression); *beta*, physical damage from alcohol without dependence (as in hepatic cirrhosis); *delta*, inability to abstain rather than loss of control (the two-liter-a-day wine drinker, for instance, rather than the "lost weekender"); *epsilon*, temporally spaced, "bender" drinking; and *gamma*, alcohol abuse with tolerance, physical dependence, and loss of control. Clearly, over time all four of Jellinek's other types may progress to *gamma*-type drinking.

Intoxication is often defined, especially in relation to driving offenses, as a blood alcohol concentration exceeding 100–150 mg per 100 ml of blood. Depending on body weight and rate of gastrointestinal absorption, this blood level reflects recent ingestion of 4 to 8 ounces of whiskey, 1 to 2 quarts of beer, or a 26-ounce bottle of wine.

All the above definitions are more useful as epidemiological pigeonholes than as guides to treatment. The critical clinical issue is whether the user should alter his alcohol consumption and, if so, whether the user can no longer exert voluntary control over alcohol ingestion and will thus require more than good advice. In other words, sporadic, deliberate intoxication and voluntary heavy drinking must be distinguished from the illness or "disease" of alcoholism, wherein the individual cannot consistently exert control over alcohol ingestion. Subjectively, the question becomes whether the user drinks when he wishes to refrain or continues drinking past the point at which he had earlier decided to stop. Objectively, alcohol use becomes "abuse" or an illness when alcohol ingestion impairs an individual's social relationships, health, job efficiency, or ability to avoid legal difficulties.

Defining Polydrug Abuse

Conventionally, drug abusers are classified by the drug of abuse. However, although many alcoholics will only abuse alcohol, individuals who at one point in time abuse hallucinogens or barbiturates or amphetamines may, over a life-time, abuse a variety of drugs. For example, perhaps three-quarters of opiate abusers will also at some other time abuse barbiturates or alcohol. In this chapter, therefore, specific types of drug abuse will be subsumed under the single label *polydrug abuse*. For a more detailed discussion of the clinical features and the mental status resulting from the abuse of specific drugs, the reader is referred to three relatively comprehensive references: Glatt, 1974; Brecher, 1972; and Goodman and Gilman, 1970.

Polydrug abusers constitute about 1 to 2 percent of the population. Although most alcohol abusers will not be relabeled polydrug abusers, most polydrug abusers will at some point in their lives abuse alcohol. Polydrug abusers tend to use those drugs that are available and in fashion and that exert subjective effects that they appreciate. For example, at age twelve, a polydrug abuser tends to use inhalants and cigarettes because they are available. Seeking some means of enhancing emotional response, some schizoid individuals say they prefer amphetamines and lysergic acid. Some depressed individuals who fear loss of control and their own violence choose opiates over alcohol and sedatives. Other depressed, inhibited individuals seeking loss of control will tend to use so-called sedatives like barbiturates and alcohol in preference to other drugs, but it is important to keep in mind that individuals and drug fashions change over time.

The terms *sedative* and *stimulant* are misnomers. A basic principle of psychopharmacology is that drug effect depends upon the user's environment and activity pattern as much as on the pharmacology of the drug. For example, the "sedative" alcohol makes sitting still difficult if we are studying, it stimulates us when we dance, and it facilitates combat if we are provoked. In contrast, the "stimulant" amphetamine helps us to study, calms hyperactive children in a classroom, and at all but the highest doses may reduce the likelihood of physical combat.

Etiology of Alcoholism and Polydrug Abuse

Both alcoholism and drug abuse are as multidetermined and as unpredictable as whether an individual will develop tuberculosis, become a violin player, or move to a large city. At the very least, eight broad etiological factors affect alcoholism and polydrug abuse, and all these factors interact with each other and with the host. The nature of the factors contributing to alcoholism and polydrug abuse has direct bearing on their treatment.

First, availability is important. In Vietnam, when cheap, pure heroin was readily available, its abuse increased; people who work near alcohol (such as waiters and bartenders) have high rates of alcoholism. If patterns of drug abuse are profoundly affected by supply, however, effective social manipulation of supply is complex. In Scandinavian countries, altering contingencies affecting each drink (by increasing the price of alcohol) has reduced alcohol abuse; putting emetics into airplane glue has made that form of inhalant less desirable for use by teen-agers. In the United States, however, legal prohibition of alcohol did little to affect the rate of alcoholism, Draconian prison terms have not deterred importation or use of heroin, and putting warning signs on packages has not reduced cigarette sales. Only social experiment can determine which legal or economic controls will effectively alter availability.

A second factor affecting drug abuse is whether the drug is slow- or fast-acting. The capacity of a drug to alter consciousness rapidly increases its potential for abuse. Here again, alcoholism and polydrug abuse are similar. Rapidly absorbed, concentrated spirits like vodka and gin are more likely to lead to drug dependence than diluted alcohol in the more slowly absorbed fermented beers and wines. Similarly, the use of fast-acting pentobarbital or intravenous heroin is more likely to result in dependence than the use of slower-acting phenobarbital or oral methadone.

A third factor is whether use of a drug produces pharmacological tolerance and physical dependence. Certainly one of the factors maintaining alcohol and heroin abuse is the discomfort of the withdrawal symptoms. Once physical dependence is established, conditioning—both Pavlovian (instrumental) and Skinnerian (operant)—plays a dominant role in the maintenance of addiction. For example, a wide variety of familiar stimuli will evoke conditioned withdrawal symptoms in a long abstinent heroin addict, and some addicts report that they can get high just from a needle inserted in their arms (instrumental conditioning). Other individuals become habituated to the stereotyped but repeatedly reinforced "hustling" behavior that becomes the daily rhythm of a heroin addict (operant conditioning).

Genetic background is a fourth factor that affects alcoholism but has not yet been shown to affect polydrug abuse. The child of an alcoholic, adopted at birth into a nonalcoholic family, is at greater risk of developing alcoholism than the child of a nonalcoholic adopted into a nonalcoholic family. Individuals whose ethnic background is Japanese or Chinese exhibit more flushing and report more physical discomfort after ingesting moderate amounts of alcohol than Caucasians. Perhaps similar differences in response to alcohol within ethnic groups are important factors in the development of alcoholism.

A fifth factor affecting abuse is culture. If the culture provides clear guidelines for nonabusive drug use, be it peyote, opium, or wine, abuse is less likely. For example, Italians and Jews allow children to drink but strongly prohibit drunkenness in anyone; they enjoy low rates of alcoholism. In contrast, cultures that frown on children drinking but that accept drunkenness (such as Irish and Anglo-Saxon) have higher rates of alcoholism. Culture also determines whether prohibition of use will be effective. For example, as long as only doctors said that "speed kills," intravenous amphetamine use continued to increase. As soon as peers began to caution users about intravenous use, abuse declined. Culturally homogeneous Mormon universities can successfully forbid Coca-Cola and coffee, but prohibitions of heroin in culturally fragmented urban high schools are ignored. Conceptually, such social controls must be distinguished from the legal controls discussed previously.

A sixth factor, childhood environment, seems to differentiate the alcoholic from the polydrug abuser. Since alcoholics often justify their addiction by recalling childhood unhappiness, retrospective studies have implicated poor nurture as a cause of alcoholism. However, prospective studies that have followed nondelinquent teenagers into middle life do not find dramatic differences between the childhoods of alcoholics and nonalcoholics. On the other hand, childhood environment plays an important role in polydrug abuse. Heroin addicts have unhappier childhoods than their socioeconomically matched nonaddicted peers. Using painstaking prospective techniques, S. and E. Glueck (1968) demonstrated that a noncohesive home environment, a neglectful mother, or a neglectful or punitive father predicts future juvenile delinquency by age five or six. Statistically, delinquents misuse all drugs both earlier and more often than their socioeconomic peers. If other drugs are not available, perhaps 40 percent of adjudicated juvenile delinquents will develop alcoholism as adults.

The seventh factor, personality, also plays a more important role in the genesis of polydrug abuse than in that of alcoholism. Although authorities have often agreed that alcoholics are premorbidly passive, sociopathic, dependent, unaggressive, depressed, mother-dominated, and often latently homosexual, no prospective study of alcoholics has confirmed this profile. In fact, prospective studies reveal that the prealcoholic person appears quite average or even more aggressive, independent, and heterosexually oriented than his peers. However, chronic alcohol intoxication produces dependency and irresponsibility directed toward the very individuals that the alcoholic most loves. As a result, over time, alcohol abusers become lonely and depressed and appear antisocial.

In the United States the personality of the polydrug abuser is not easily distinguished from that of the sociopath. However, during the special circumstances of the war in Vietnam, as many as 40 percent of enlisted men in Vietnam (that is, of a relatively normal sample) at one time or another abused heroin. After their return to the United States, only about 5 percent of Vietnam heroin abusers continued to use opiates. This fact sharply differentiates a normal population from individuals who become dependent on heroin in the United States, of whom only 5 percent will achieve stable remission after a single treatment experience. Significantly, factors predicting persistent heroin dependence in veterans after return to America did not include the amount of heroin used in Vietnam, ethnicity, or social class. Rather, important factors were whether or not the individual completed high school, had had a criminal record, or had also abused amphetamines and barbiturates (that is, was a polydrug abuser) in Vietnam.

From the limited data available, polydrug abusers who become abstinent demonstrate more severely impaired personalities than do abstinent alcohol abusers. For example, Alcoholics Anonymous, an organization run by abstinent alcoholics, is a remarkably stable, benign, and successful organization. By contrast, self-help organizations for drug addicts (with a few notable exceptions like Synanon) have been fragile, often dissolving or evolving into sadistic, autocratic communities.

The eighth factor, symptom relief, also differentiates alcoholism from polydrug abuse. Nicotine, alcohol, and barbiturates provide little real relief from psychological distress. Despite his psychic dependence on cigarettes, a heavy cigarette smoker often acknowledges that he enjoys few of his thirty to forty daily cigarettes. The alcoholic is less honest and may maintain that he drinks to combat loneliness, anxiety, and depression. However, videotapes made before, during, and after alcoholic drinking demonstrate what experienced workers and sober alcoholics have known for some time, namely, that from an objective viewpoint, chronic use of alcohol makes people more withdrawn, less self-confident, more depressed, and often even more anxious.

In contrast, amphetamines and opiates do provide real symptom relief. Opiates effectively curb hunger and anger and soothe almost every aspect of suffering. Individuals on methadone maintenance are often able to lead more stable lives than when abstinent. For a brief period, amphetamines and cocaine are truly mood-elevating.

These etiological differences between the alcoholic and the polydrug abuser lead to an important conclusion. Due to poor childhood nurture, emotional distress, and sociopathic behavior, the polydrug abuser has always been lonely and seeks an effective anodyne. In contrast, the nondelinquent alcoholic becomes socially isolated as the result of abuse of a drug that produces loneliness and sociopathy rather than re-

lief of emotional pain. While this generalization is not true for every individual, it focuses attention on the reason why alcoholism may be conceptualized as a disease and why the primary purpose of treatment must be to facilitate abstinence, not to relieve alleged underlying disorders such as depression and anxiety. Polydrug abuse, however, is usually a symptom of underlying psychosocial difficulties. Unless these difficulties are addressed, the removal of one drug results in substitution of another.

Treatment of Alcoholism

Diagnosis is the first step in treatment, but it is most difficult, and more than half the alcoholics seen by physicians go undiagnosed. This lack of recognition exists because different social groups regard alcohol abuse so differently, because individual use patterns differ so widely, because the alcoholic's denial is so convincing, because many physicians recognize only stereotypes of alcoholic drinkers, and because alcoholics are adept at concealing overt signs of intoxication.

The clinician must learn to conceive of alcoholism as a "disease" that causes depression, marital breakup, and unemployment, not a symptom that results from such distressing events. In other words, to decide if a person is drinking alcoholically, it is important to ask, "Was your use of alcohol one of the reasons that your wife left you?" rather than merely accepting the patient's explanation ("I did not drink really heavily until my wife left").

No single symptom is sufficient, and the diagnosis of alcoholism can be reached only after the considered integration of evidence from all available sources. The interviewer must appreciate that individuals drinking alcoholically are very frightened by what is happening to them and cannot be relied on to divulge their symptoms freely.

A series of questions has been devised that can identify most people with alcoholism: Has the user tried to stop drinking to prove he still can or changed brands or otherwise tried to limit his drinking? Has he begun to sneak drinks or become more irritable when people comment on his drinking? Does he regret what he says or does after drinking? Has the user experienced blackouts (memory lapses while intoxicated)? Do his hands shake the morning after, or does he drink in the morning to steady himself after the night before? The individual who answers yes to more than one or two of the above questions is very likely to be an alcoholic. Contrary to popular belief, a red nose, alcohol on the breath, frequent drunkenness, and solitary drinking are not good indices of alcoholism.

Once the diagnosis of alcoholism is made, it must be communicated to the patient. Alcoholism distorts the family equilibrium, and the resulting denial can reach extraordinary proportions. It is usually helpful to discuss the problem with the whole family together. Supporting the family in gentle confrontation is effective and ensures that all members receive the same message. In discussing alcoholism, it is important to "keep it simple." Due to the associated guilt, alcoholism is an emotionally laden subject; also, immediately following detoxification, most alcoholics suffer from a mild dementia ("wet brain") that may not fully clear for six months. Thus all instructions must be simple, unambiguous, and focused on alcohol as the primary problem.

Whether or not to consider alcoholism a disease provokes controversy among clinicians. Nevertheless, it is important to explain to patients that their alcoholism, like a disease, has a life of its own and is not a moral or psychological problem. Repeated relapses that injure an alcoholic's loved ones generate enormous guilt and confusion. The ensuing shame further enhances denial. Thus experience has shown that the concept of disease facilitates acceptance of illness and treatment. It does not serve to excuse continued alcohol abuse, nor does it imply helplessness on the part of the patient or the doctor.

Only when doctor, family, and patient are agreed that the patient has an illness that requires treatment can effective long-term treatment begin. Such treatment includes four components: (1) offering the patient an effective, nonchemical substitute for alcohol, (2) reminding him continuously that even one drink can lead to relapse, (3) repairing the social and medical damage that he has experienced, and (4) restoring self-esteem. Alcoholics Anonymous or its reasonable facsimile offers the simplest way of providing all four. First, the continuous hope, the

gentle peer support, and the exposure to truly successful people in AA provide a substitute for drinking and for the lost drinking companions. Second, not only do AA meetings go on daily, especially on weekends and holidays, but they also single-mindedly underscore the special ways that alcoholics delude themselves. Thus AA allows the alcoholic, often unconsciously driven to relapse, to remain conscious of this danger. Third, belonging to a group of caring individuals who have found solutions to the typical problems that beset the newly sober alcoholic alleviates loneliness. Fourth, the opportunity to identify with helpers who once were equally disabled and then to help others to stay sober enhances self-worth.

Prolonged hospitalization provides the first three components but ignores the fourth. Psychotherapy and tranquilizing drugs provide the first component, but ignore the second and fourth. For example, providing the anxious alcoholic with tranquilizers will give temporary relief of anxiety, but over the long term such prescription reinforces the notion that relief of distress is pharmacological, not human; pharmacotherapy may serve to facilitate the chain of conditioned responses that leads to picking up a drink at the next point of crisis. Psychotherapy is limited both because alcoholics trying to stay sober often need help at odd hours and because their low self-esteem is worsened by depending on nonalcoholic individuals. Disulfiram (Antabuse) and similar compounds that produce illness if alcohol is ingested are reminders not to drink but take away a cherished addiction without providing anything in return.

In counseling alcoholic patients, there are some useful guidelines. The first is that once a clinician is sure that the use of alcohol puts the user out of control, he should not try to prescribe good advice and controlled drinking. An analogous situation is the futility of advising a two-pack-a-day smoker to cut down to five cigarettes. Obviously, the nondependent individual whose drinking is truly reactive or merely excessive for good health may be helped by good advice about moderation and by a little education about the physical consequences of heavy drinking.

Unfortunately, the clinician cannot simply refer the alcohol-dependent person to Alcoholics Anonymous, any more than he could refer someone to a church or a hobby club. People need to be introduced to AA, either by the physician or by a member. Few go to their first meeting by themselves. However, AA is a "program of attraction"; compulsory attendance in Alcoholics Anonymous is rarely beneficial. In recommending AA, clinicians should remember that regular attendance at meetings may be as unpleasant and painful a prospect as applying iodine to a cut; meetings should not be described as enjoyable. Until a patient can accept AA, other forms of combined treatment—such as, group therapy and a halfway house and disulfiram (0.25 gm per day) and vocational rehabilitation—must be devised to provide the four therapeutic components outlined above.

The clinician must remember that the treatment of alcoholism asks the patient to give up forever a substance that he truly, albeit ambivalently, values and loves. For that reason, abstinence should be prescribed one day at a time; proclamations that the individual may never again take a drink should be avoided. Threats of death or chronic illness are rarely effective.

Lastly, clinicians are often unable to disguise their disappointment and resentment when their patients, seemingly willfully, relapse. Thus clinicians should take the first "step" of Alcoholics Anonymous seriously and admit their own "powerlessness over alcohol." To take an alcoholic's drinking personally, to see it as part of resistance or transference or as evidence of poor motivation, is to miss the point. Experienced workers in the field of alcoholism recognize that they are incapable of judging what is adequate motivation and that relapse to or remission from alcoholism is still a mystery. In alcoholism, as in much of medicine, we dress the wound; the individual's own resources heal it.

Alcoholism affects the entire family. In the past, because social workers and psychiatrists have viewed alcoholism as symptom and not disease, they have sometimes unwittingly implied that the spouse is the cause of the alcoholic's illness and needs treatment. Such an approach is rarely productive. The alcoholic's relatives will gain more strength and comfort if they understand that their relative cannot control his drinking and that no one understands the cause. Relatives can obtain help in many ways. Al-Anon

is a self-help organization in which the spouses of alcoholics assist each other in understanding the "disease," learn how not to interfere with the recovery process, and, most important, discover how to get help for themselves. Alateen is a self-help organization in which troubled adolescents in alcoholic families help each other to understand their painful home life. Professional family counseling can also be very effective.

In treating alcoholic intoxication and withdrawal, the physician must take an active role. Intoxication is manifested by slurred speech, nystagmus, motor incoordination, hyporeflexia, and a fluctuating mental state between somnolence and rowdiness. It is usually effectively treated with bed rest. Extreme excitement or violence may be controlled with 5 mg haloperidol intramuscularly.

Unless properly treated, the withdrawal syndrome of someone physically dependent on alcohol is profoundly uncomfortable and may result in convulsions and delirium tremens. Accurate diagnosis and proper treatment of the withdrawal syndrome is therefore important. Physiological withdrawal usually begins 6 to 24 hours after heavy drinking has stopped and is best identified by the following signs: sweating, hyperreflexia, increasing tachycardia, confusion, agitation, hyperventilation, and elevation of systolic blood pressure. Patients may be in withdrawal and still have alcohol on their breath. Conversely, surgical patients, due to preoperative and postoperative medication, may not develop withdrawal until a week after admission.

A safe and effective treatment for alcohol withdrawal is the administration of large doses of chlordiazepoxide—usually 100 mg every two to four hours (up to 300 mg) until symptomatic relief is obtained. As a guide for additional medication, signs of withdrawal as outlined above, not subjective complaints or tremulousness, are the most reliable. If in the first 24 hours more than 400 mg of chlordiazepoxide is required, 50 mg of oral chlorpromazine should be added to each 100-mg dose of chlordiazepoxide. Since chlordiazepoxide has an effective half-life of 24 to 48 hours, once initial control of symptoms is achieved, tapering of the drug will be achieved largely by the body's own slow metabolism of the drug. Thus, on the second day, the first day's dose of chlordiazepoxide can usually be cut in half or by two-thirds. Little further medication is required after the third day. Inflexible regimens (such as 50 mg of chlordiazepoxide every six hours) can result in undermedication during the most dangerous stage of withdrawal and overmedication by the fourth day. (Some physicians prefer paraldehyde or chloral hydrate; these drugs are shorter-acting but not quite as safe.) If benzodiazepines are contraindicated, magnesium sulfate and phenobarbital are usually effective in relieving the withdrawal state.

Major complications associated with withdrawal are seizures, mild dementia, delirium tremens, and hallucinosis. During the first 24 hours of withdrawal, a complicating hypomagnesemia can occur which contributes to a lowered seizure threshold and should be treated. Should withdrawal seizures ("rum fits") occur, they may be treated symptomatically; vitamins and routine administration of phenytoin (Dilantin) are not effective. However, if the patient is taking maintenance Dilantin before the onset of withdrawal, it should be continued. If daily Dilantin is begun during the withdrawal period, to prevent seizures in a patient with a past history of repeated seizures, a loading dose should be administered parenterally (about a gram of Dilantin in 500 cc of 5-percent dextrose and water administered over 1 to 4 hours will usually suffice).

For a few days to weeks after their last drink, patients who had been drinking heavily will exhibit a mild dementia or "wet brain." This condition can be distinguished from the memory defect of Korsakoff's psychosis because in mild dementia the memory and orientation defects are relieved by offering the patient clues. If the obtunded state following withdrawal does not progressively improve, or if it worsens, the possibility of an unsuspected subdural hematoma should be vigorously investigated.

Clinically, delirium tremens resembles most other acute deliria (see chapter 15, "Organic Mental Disorders"). The major difference is that delirium tremens is a hypermetabolic state, and dangers of hyperpyrexia, dehydration, electrolyte imbalance, and mortality (up to 15 percent) are great. Delirium tremens usually occurs 50 to 100 hours after cessation of heavy drinking and should always be treated on the acute medical service of a general hospital. It can be differen-

tiated from severe withdrawal by the profound disorientation, markedly increased sweating, terror, and, of course, hallucinations and delusions. Adequate management includes close "flow sheet" monitoring of autonomic and metabolic function by the physician. Phenothiazines, rather than chlordiazepoxide, should be used to control the hyperactivity and excitement of delirium tremens. Although chlordiazepoxide prevents delirium tremens by allowing the patient to taper physical dependence slowly, it is relatively ineffective in controlling delirium and psychosis once they are present. Up to 100 mg of chlorpromazine intramuscularly every hour may be required to control the patient so that he is not dangerous to himself or others and so that his other problems may be treated.

Alcoholic hallucinosis may occur independently of delirium and if so, like seizures, it is most evident in the first 24 to 48 hours after the cessation of drinking. Hallucinations may be visual, auditory, or both. In unusual cases, auditory hallucinosis may persist for weeks or months after withdrawal and is often resistant to phenothiazines. Such chronic hallucinations are usually derogatory, accusatory, repetitive, and unusually concise. Although they occur in a clear, oriented sensorium, whether the condition is related to schizophrenia remains uncertain.

Once detoxification is complete, insomnia and anxiety may persist for weeks to months, but in treating these symptoms, the administration of minor tranquilizers and sleeping pills can rarely be justified. Such drugs only stimulate the alcoholic's fantasy that intoxication solves everything.

In addition to conditions associated with withdrawal, other complications of alcoholism occur. Some chronic alcoholics present with Wernicke-Korsakoff's psychosis, presumably due to thiamine deficiency. Wernicke's encephalopathy is of acute onset and potentially fatal. It is manifested by confusion, memory loss, apathy, and confabulation; physical signs include impaired gait, coma, and weakness of extraocular movements, especially of lateral gaze. It should be treated immediately in the emergency room with 100 mg of intramuscular thiamine. The coma and ocular findings may clear in minutes. Care should be given to administer the thiamine before intravenous glucose is administered; cellular metabolism of the glucose infusion will put increased demands on already depleted brain thiamine and further impair neuronal function.

If the patient survives the Wernicke's encephalopathy, the residual state, Korsakoff's psychosis, is characterized by marked disorientation and memory loss. The memory deficit is characterized by marked confabulation and a characteristic lack of insight regarding the memory loss. The neuropathological changes of Wernicke-Korsakoff's psychosis are characterized by hemorrhages and neuronal loss in the mamillary bodies and in the gray matter adjacent to the third and fourth ventricles. Over a six-month to two-year period, full recovery may occur in 25 percent of cases, and an additional 50 percent will improve significantly. Although vitamin supplementation is not needed, an adequate diet is essential. Thus Korsakoff's psychosis is one of the few psychiatric conditions that actually improve on prolonged, involuntary hospitalization. The relatives of a patient who has been incapacitated by Korsakoff's psychosis should be advised that improvement may continue for at least a year.

Alcohol abuse is a complicating factor in roughly half of all completed suicides, attempted suicides, murders, and fatal automobile accidents. Thus it is important to assess the suicide potential of many patients with alcoholism. Alcoholism, however, is a far more common cause of depression than depression is of alcoholism. Treating a suicidal patient for his underlying alcoholism may thus often be more effective than treating his overt depression.

Other serious medical complications of chronic alcoholism include acute and chronic liver damage, hepatic encephalopathy, polyneuritis, cerebellar degeneration, subdural hematoma, gastritis, chronic pulmonary infection (especially tuberculosis), hypoglycemia, various anemias, labile hypertension, pancreatitis, esophageal varices, duodenal ulcer, and cardiomyopathy. For the management of these conditions, the reader is referred to medical texts.

Treatment of Polydrug Abuse

Since polydrug abuse is symptomatic of underlying social or personality disorders and because various drugs may be involved, the treatment of polydrug abuse is complex. (For a detailed discussion of withdrawal from individual drugs, the reader is referred to texts such as Glatt, 1974; Brecher, 1972; and Goodman and Gilman, 1970.)

Although chronic abuse of amphetamine, cocaine, lysergic acid, and marijuana results in distress and sometimes psychosis, it does not produce physical dependence. Thus the withdrawal of patients from these drugs requires only symptomatic relief and psychological support.

Withdrawal from dependence on heroin or other opiates should be attempted on an inpatient basis in a strictly drug-free environment; opiate detoxification is rarely successful on an outpatient basis. On the first day of withdrawal, physiologically dependent heroin addicts rarely require more than 40 mg of methadone (a long-acting opiate) in divided oral doses. The dose of methadone may then be reduced by 5 mg a day in most cases. In terms of discomfort and medical danger, opiate withdrawal has been compared to a one-week bout with influenza. The more immune the staff is to manipulation and game playing by addicts, the smoother the addict's own withdrawal will be.

Withdrawal from barbiturates, meprobamate, and most prescription sleeping pills may produce status epilepticus and prolonged delirium. Individuals dependent on these drugs should be withdrawn in a general hospital with careful pharmacological tapering. The magnitude of barbiturate dependence may be crudely assessed by giving a patient who has been without barbiturates for a few hours 200 mg of oral pentobarbital. If after an hour the individual is sleepy and manifests nystagmus, the likelihood of pharmacological dependence is small. If in one hour the individual is fully alert and without nystagmus, physical dependence is present. A typical withdrawal regimen is 800 mg of pentobarbital in divided doses during the first 24 hours, with subsequent tapering by 50 mg a day. Signs of undermedication include a positive glabellar reflex, a pulse increase from a supine to erect position of greater than 15 beats a minute, hyperreflexia, twitching, sweating, agitation, and vomiting. In cases of combined alcohol and barbiturate (or other sedative) dependence, pentobarbital for the first 24 hours, followed by tapered doses of phenobarbital, appears to be a satisfactory regimen.

Contrary to common belief, physical dependence on diazepam (Valium) and chlordiaze-poxide (Librium) does occur. Because these compounds are long-acting, withdrawal signs may not be seen for a week and may persist for two weeks or more. If the support of a hospital treatment milieu is provided, medication during withdrawal is rarely necessary.

Since polydrug abuse, like delinquent behavior, is symptomatic of underlying problems, detoxification plays only a small role in the treatment of addiction. Youths steal cars or use heroin not just because their friends do or because it is fun but because they lack psychosocial alternatives. Unfortunately, society's approaches to both delinquency and polydrug abuse are inadequate and have more to do with politics or philosophical bias than with scientific data.

Polydrug abuse can rarely be effectively treated with a single treatment modality. Drug abuse must be replaced with effective alternatives. For example, since narcotics are used in part for symptomatic relief, pure opiate antagonists are rarely effective. In contrast, methadone prevents the euphoric effect of "illegal" heroin but is also an active opiate that can both tranquilize the addict and "addict" him to a treatment program; ideally such a program will include vocational rehabilitation, group therapy, and medical care. Methadone has been effective in reducing crime and social disability. Many opiate users have also given up narcotics through either short-term or long-term substitution of alcohol.

Like the alcoholic, the polydrug abuser must ultimately substitute people for drugs. However, unlike alcoholics, polydrug abusers rarely obtain help and comfort if their families of origin and spouses are included in treatment; this is because their original families are often more socially disorganized. Rather than returning to parents or former spouses, polydrug abusers are helped by finding respectful employers, new loved ones, and more tolerant families (like those in halfway houses).

Polydrug abuse, especially opiate abuse, dominates and provides a structure for the addict's daily existence. Treatment, therefore, must provide an alternative structure for living. Neither prolonged imprisonment nor drug legalization is an effective alternative; neither prepares the individual for community living. Similarly, by

themselves, psychotherapy programs that involve at most only an hour or two of the addict's day are rarely useful.

Treating the addict either as a patient or as a criminal is usually futile. It is harmful, on the one hand, to excuse him from limits in time present or, on the other, to punish him too severely for past misdeeds. All of the above reactions decrease self-esteem and make less mature modes of adaptation more likely. Rather, programs should try to facilitate individual maturation. It is often helpful to ask the addict—with peer support—to condemn the drugs and self-deception that he once enjoyed, but such reaction formation is a potentially unstable solution. The army, participation in a community drug program with a sheltered workshop, ideological movements, and employment enforced through parole all provide effective community structures that help a polydrug user reorganize his life. Settings that eventually allow the drug abuser to help peers altruistically, such as employment in drug rehabilitation programs or Synanon, are most effective.

In the treatment of polydrug abuse, coercion plays an unpredictable role for four reasons. First, in masochistic personalities, self-destructive behavior may actually relieve mental discomfort, and so punishment may accomplish little. Second, only certain punishments will work. For example, long prison sentences per se do little to promote subsequent community abstinence, but prolonged parole, which mandates regular employment, is comparatively effective. Third, if coercion is to be successful, the penalties must be enforced and not exist only in the statute books. Thus, if parole is enforced, it is far more effective than unenforced civil commitment laws. Fourth, for reasons not fully understood, coercion must be socially acceptable. Prohibition of alcohol or marijuana has proved quite useless, but efforts to remove intravenous amphetamines and certain hallucinogens from the illegal market have received more community support.

Finally, the fact that polydrug abusers are similar to delinquents limits the number of useful treatment alternatives. Often delinquents have received too little early supervision from both parents; such individuals cannot subsequently be ordered to do something that they do not know how to do. We can, for example, pass laws against truancy but not against illiteracy. Thus although Synanon and Alcoholics Anonymous both involve social coercion, they are effective not just because they require abstinence and provide limits but also because they offer training in alternatives to addiction. They give as well as take away.

A basic theme throughout this chapter has been that drugs are an ineffective substitute for people. Any treatment that promotes supportive group membership in a drug-free environment is a far more effective means of treating drug addiction than efforts to provide psychological insights or better drugs.

References

American Psychiatric Association. 1968. *Diagnostic and statistical manual of mental disorders*. 2nd ed. Washington, D.C.

Brecher, E. M., and editors of *Consumer Reports*. 1972. *Licit and illicit drugs*. New York: Consumers Union.

Glueck, S. and E. 1950. *Unraveling juvenile delinquency*. New York: Commonwealth Fund.

———— 1968. *Delinquents and nondelinquents in perspective*. Cambridge, Mass.: Harvard University Press.

Glatt, M. M. 1974. *A guide to addiction and its treatment*. New York: Wiley.

Goodman, L. S., and A. Gilman, eds. 1970. *The pharmacological basis of therapeutics*. 4th ed. New York: Macmillan.

Jellinek, E. M. 1960. *Disease concept of alcoholism*. New Haven: College and University Press.

World Health Organization. 1969. Sixteenth report of the WHO Expert Committee on Drug Dependence. Technical report series no. 407. Geneva.

Recommended Reading

Bourne, P. G., and R. Fox, eds. 1973. *Alcoholism: progress in research and treatment*. New York and London: Academic Press.

Chein, I., D. L. Gerard, R. S. Lee, and E. Rosenfeld. 1964. *The Road to H*. New York: Basic Books.

Goodwin, D. W., F. Schulsinger, L. Hermansen, S. B. Guze, and G. Winokur. 1973. Alcohol problems in adoptees raised apart from alcoholic biological parents. *Arch. Gen. Psychiatry* 28:238–243.

Jones, M. C. 1968. Personality correlates and antecedents of drinking patterns in adult males. *J. Consult. Clin. Psychol.* 32:2–12.

Mello, N. K., and J. H. Mendelson, eds. 1971. *Recent advances in studies of alcoholism*. Washington, D.C.: Government Printing Office.

Meyer, R. E. 1972. *Guide to drug rehabilitation: a public health approach*. Boston: Beacon Press.

Robbins, L. N. 1974. *The Vietnam drug user returns*. Special Action Office monograph series A, no. 2. Washington, D.C.: Government Printing Office.

Sellers, E. M., and H. Kalant. 1976. Alcohol intoxication and withdrawal. *N. Engl. J. Med.* 294:757–762.

Tamerin, J. S., and J. H. Mendelson. 1969. The psychodynamics of chronic inebriation: observations of alcoholics during the process of drinking in an experimental group setting. *Am. J. Psychiatry* 125: 886–899.

Unterberger, H., and L. DiCicco. 1973. Planning alcoholism services. *Contemp. Drug. Probl.*, winter: 697–716.

Vaillant, G. E. 1966. A twelve-year follow-up of New York narcotic addicts: IV. Some characteristics and determinants of abstinence. *Am. J. Psychiatry* 123:573–584.

Victor, M., R. D. Adams, and G. H. Collins. 1971. *The Wernicke-Korsakoff syndrome*. Philadelphia: Davis.

Wikler, A. 1973. Dynamics of drug dependence: implications of a conditioning theory for research and treatment. *Arch. Gen. Psychiatry* 28:611–616.

Treating the Person Confronting Death

CHAPTER 28

Ned H. Cassem

ELP the dying patient? Can one realistically hope to improve the lot of a thirty-five-year-old mother dying of cancer by making her feel better? Feel better about what? At the bedside of the dying, the professional may feel overwhelmed by dread of the encounter or by the presumptuousness of his expectation to help. Yet because the dying have no less right to help than the living, their difficulties and needs require specific attention.

Thanatology is the science or study of death. Broadly conceived, it includes the study of dying as a psychophysiological process, the care of the dying person, including both adults and children, and the care of persons who seek death by suicide. The nondying directly affected by death—the bereaved and the care-giving personnel—are included, as are healthy persons whose lives are disrupted by irrational fears of death.

Psychiatric interest in the concrete problems of the dying is a recent phenomenon. Freud's agonizing seventeen-year struggle against oral cancer (Jones, 1957) is never reflected in his writings, even in those about death. Gifford (1969) has provided a historical review of psychoanalytic theories about death and also reports on the few individuals who became involved in empirical studies of the subject. In 1915 Freud, introducing his notion that the unconscious has no representation of death, explored unconscious convictions of immortality. In 1923, before he linked death and aggression in theory, Freud presented evidence that conscious fears of death represent underlying fears of helplessness, physical injury, or abandonment. In depressive states, on the other hand, fears of punishment, castration, rejection, or desertion may represent fears of death.

The first analyst to investigate the dying themselves was Deutsch in 1933. Little further work was done in the field until Eissler's publication in 1955 signaled an era of empirical interest in dying patients. Beginning with the work of Feifel (1959) and Saunders (1959), significant contributions—from Weisman and Hackett (1961; Hackett and Weisman, 1962), LeShan and LeShan (1961), Hinton (1967), Glaser and Strauss (1965), and several others—multiplied until 1969, when Kübler-Ross's now classic work evoked worldwide interest in the emotional concerns of the dying. The observations and recommendations that follow are based on the work of these investigators as well as my own (Cassem and Stewart, 1975).

The Psychophysiological Process of Dying

Dying is a process that keeps the body near the forefront of the mind. Having contracted a disease that may eventually cut him down (like heart disease) or devour him (like cancer), the patient interprets or even anticipates bodily changes as ominous. Symptoms are likely to produce fear when present, but fear is often present long before their arrival. The body, once regarded as a friend, may seem more like a dormant adversary, programmed for betrayal. Dying persons, even before disintegration begins, fear many things; loss of autonomy, disfigurement, being a burden, becoming physically repulsive, letting the family down, facing the unknown, and many other concerns are commonly expressed. When all fears were compared for frequency in one sample of cancer patients (Saunders, 1959), the three that topped the list were abandonment by others, pain, and shortness of breath. These fears were expressed before the patients were symptomatic; they felt that as their illness progressed, family and hospital staff would gradually avoid them, their conditions would become increasingly painful, or the illness would encroach on breathing capacity and suffocate them.

Because physicians and families also worry about what will happen to the dying person, it is helpful to know which difficulties are, in fact, the most distressing when the patient is terminal. When Saunders (1959) documented the exact incidence of practical problems in terminal cancer at St. Joseph's Hospital in London, she found that the three most common complaints were nausea and vomiting, shortness of breath, and dysphagia. It was striking that pain did not appear high on the problem list; with proper medication, about 90 percent of her patients remained pain-free. Largely because of her efforts, avoidance of dying patients decreased at St. Joseph's, but one can expect to find it in most chronic hospitals or nursing homes. Nausea and dyspnea are psychophysiological experiences in which the patient is usually miserable. Relief of these and other troublesome symptoms helps restore peace of mind.

Just as there are familiar physical reactions, like nausea, to a fatal illness, familiar reactions of the mind also occur. To describe the psychological process that begins with getting the news about illness and ends in death, Kübler-Ross (1969) presented a framework of five stages experienced by the dying person. In the first stage, *shock and denial*, the patient says, "No, not me." He may simply be numb and appear completely unaware of the bad news, disagree with the diagnosis, or remain oblivious to its implications. Denial may persist for moments or pervade the rest of the person's life. More characteristically, it fluctuates, waxing and waning over the course of the illness. In the stage characterized by *anger*, the patient says, "Why me?" Angry outbursts may be directed toward hospital menus, treatment regimens, physicians, families, life in general, or God. Past life may be reviewed, usually with inability to find oneself at fault for hygienic or moral reasons. A sense of unfairness, frustration, and helplessness generate a normal sense of outrage that may turn into periods of bitterness. In the stage termed *bargaining*, the patient says, "Yes, it is me, but . . ." and puts a condition on acceptance, such that he hopes or plans for something that can mitigate disappointment. A characteristic hope would be that life be extended until a special event occurs, such as a wedding, birth, or graduation. In the stage referred to as *depression*, the patient confronts the sadness of the reality: "Yes, it is me." He may do a good deal of weeping, be intermittently withdrawn and uncommunicative, brood, and be weighed down by the full impact of his condition. Despair and suicide are common preoccupations during this time. The final stage, *acceptance*, is conceptualized as a state reached through emotional work, so that losses are mourned and the end is anticipated with a degree of quiet expectation. It is seen as a restful, albeit weary time, almost devoid of feeling.

The notion of stages is by no means new and is not restricted to dying. As a dynamic process, dying is a special case of loss and the stages represent a dynamic model of emotional adaptation to any physical or emotional loss. Despite its theoretical validity, the concept of the stages is often misused. A common misapplication of the concept in caring for dying patients is the attempt to help an individual through the stages one after the other. It is more accurate and therapeutically more practical to regard them as normal reactions to any loss. They may be present simultaneously, disappear and reappear, or occur in any order. Responding to the emotional distress of the dying often reduces their physical distress. Pain in particular diminishes when a patient is helped to feel understood, less anxious, and less alone.

In fact, some investigators have introduced experimental psychological measures to combat illness directly. In work as yet unpublished, Simonton and Simonton (1974) use relaxation techniques patterned after Jacobson (1938) to induce remission or even cure in cancer patients. Once the patient is relaxed or in a modified trance, suggestions are made that he picture his white cells and immune mechanisms mobilized in concentrated attack upon his malignancy. The results are anecdotal and await controlled replication. The rationale is much the same as that suggested by Surman et al. (1973), who demonstrated the effectiveness of hypnosis in the removal of warts—that is, that a person may be able to influence his immune defense systems.

Care and Management of the Dying Adult

Questions far outnumber answers wherever the dying are cared for. Many controversies remain unresolved. The investigators mentioned earlier have outlined objectives in the care of the terminally ill that the physician can consider from the time treatment begins. Because the patient's bedside can be an uncomfortable place for the physician, several practical considerations for management are added in support of the goals.

Goals of Treatment

Deutsch (1933) observed in his clinical sample of dying patients that the decline in vital processes is accompanied by a parallel decline in the intensity of instinctual aggressive-erotic drives. Fear of dying is reduced as the pressures of inner instinctual demands decline. The illness can be viewed by the patient as a hostile attack from an outside enemy or as a punishment for being bad (interpreted by Deutsch as inflicted from within by a harsh superego). Since the patient can worsen his predicament by reacting with increasing hostility toward outside objects or with self-punitive actions to offset experienced guilt, Deutsch's therapeutic objective is a "settlement of differences." The ideal stage is reached when all guilt and aggression are balanced, permitting the patient a guilt-free "regression" to the love relationships of childhood and infancy. Deutsch judges this regression impossible without conflict under other circumstances because of the incestuous nature of the earlier relationships, but he infers that guilt is atoned for by the knowledge of imminent death. One could also infer that the patient's relationship to the therapist would fall under the same protective mantle. For Eissler (1955), therapeutic success depends on the psychiatrist's ability to share the patient's primitive beliefs in immortality and indestructibility. In addition, sharing the dying patient's defenses and developing intense admiration for his inner strength, beauty, intelligence, courage, and honesty are the main forces in the psychiatrist's supportive relationship with the patient. Kübler-Ross (1969) speaks of the unfinished business of the dying—reconciliations, resolution of conflicts, and pursuit of specific remaining hopes. For Saunders (1969), the aim is to keep the person feeling like himself as long as possible. In her view, dying is also a "coming together time" when family and staff are encouraged to help one another share the burden of the terminal illness. LeShan and LeShan (1959), choosing deliberately not to emphasize dying (the minor problem in their views), explore aggressively with patients what they wish to accomplish in living (the major problem). Weisman and Hackett (1961) have coined the term *appropriate death*, for which Weisman (1972) delineates the following conditions: the person should be relatively pain-free; should operate on as effective a level as possible within the limits of his disability; should recognize and resolve residual conflicts; should satisfy those remaining wishes consistent with his present plight and ego ideal; and should be able to yield control to others in whom he has confidence.

Perhaps more important than any other principle in caring for the dying is that the treatment be unique and individualized. This goal can only be accomplished by getting to know the patient, responding to his needs and interests, proceeding at his pace, and allowing him to shape the manner in which those in attendance behave. There is no one "best" way to die.

Treatment Recommendations

Most of what is known about dying patients comes from them. All investigators have emphasized the reversal of expertise manifest in care of the dying. In this field patients are the teachers; those who take care of them can only try to learn. Over the years, observations made by patients on various aspects of their management have helped in the recognition of the following eight essential features in the care and management of the dying patient (Cassem and Stewart, 1975).

Competence. In an era when some discussions of the dying patient seem to suggest that "love" excuses most other faults in the therapeutic relationship, encouraging the misconception that competence in physicians and nurses is of secondary importance for dying patients would be unfortunate. Competence is reassuring, and when one's life or comfort depends on it, personality considerations become secondary. Being good at what one does brings emotional as well as scientific benefits to the patient. No matter how charming physicians, nurses, or I.V. technicians may be, for example, the approach of the person who is most skillful at venipuncture brings the greatest relief to an anxious patient.

Concern. Of all attributes in physicians and nurses, none is more highly valued by terminal patients than compassion. Although they may never convey it precisely by words, some physicians and nurses impart to the patient that they are genuinely touched by his predicament. A striking example came from a mother's description of her dying son's pediatrician: "You know, that doctor loves Michael." Compassion is a quality that cannot be feigned. Although universally praised as a quality for a health professional, compassion extracts a cost usually overlooked in his training. The price of compassion is conveyed by the two Latin roots, *con* and *passio*, to "suffer with" another person. One must be touched by the tragedy of the patient in a literal way, a process that occurs through experiential identification with the dying person. This process of empathy, when evoked by a person facing death or tragic disability, ordinarily produces uncomfortable, burdensome feelings, and internal resistance to it can arise defensively. Who can bear the thought of dying at twenty? It is therefore understandable that professionals do not encourage discussion of such a topic by the individual facing it. In addition to guarding against the development of compassion, students are sometimes advised to avoid "involvement" with a patient. When a patient gets upset, hasty exits or evasions are thus more likely. On the other hand, few things infuriate patients more than contrived involvement; even an inability to answer direct questions may be excused when it stems from genuine discomfort on the physician's part. One woman, even though she wanted more information about how much longer she could expect to survive with stage IV Hodgkin's disease, preferred to ask her physician as few questions as possible. "Whenever I try to ask him about this, he looks very pained and becomes very hesitant. I don't want to rub it in. After all, he really likes me."

What are the emotional traumas a compassionate nurse or physician is required to sustain? They can be summarized by the "stages" the terminal patient goes through. Since the stages describe the emotional process in the terminal patient, it is only logical that they call forth similar reactions in a sympathetic observer. As physician and patient view the patient's predicament together, the physician, depending on his sensitivity, is likely to experience shock, denial, outrage, hope, and devastation. Involvement —"real" involvement—is not only unavoidable but necessary in the therapeutic encounter. Patients recognize it instantly. As a hematologist percussed the right side of his twenty-nine-year-old patient's chest, his discovery of dullness and the recurrent pleural effusion it signaled brought the realization that a remission had come to an abrupt end. "Oh, shit," he muttered. Then, realizing what he had said, he added hastily, "Oh, excuse me, Bill." "That's all right," the young man replied. "It's nice to know you care."

Comfort. With the terminal patient, comfort has a technology all its own. "Comfort measures" should not indicate that less attention is paid to the patient's needs. In fact, comforting a terminally ill person requires meticulous devotion to a myriad of details. Certain things are basic, like narcotic medication to relieve pain. The most common mistake is inadequate dosage or frequency of medication. For example, even though the duration of action of meperidine hydrochloride (Demerol) is three hours, it is common to find orders written for administration every four hours. Pain medication orders for patients with continuous pain are too often written "p.r.n.," which can demean the patient by forcing him to beg for medication. The goal of narcotic administration is pain relief with a dosage and frequency adequate to dispel pain and prevent its return. The fear, often covert, of addiction is not justified by experience. Fewer than 1 percent of hospitalized medical patients treated for pain with narcotics develop a serious problem of addiction (Marks and Sachar, 1973); actual addiction in terminal patients has not been described. Some comfort measures are dramatic, such as pressor infusions to ward off pulmonary edema, while others are simple, like providing fresh air and light in the room.

The ingenuity of skillful, thoughtful caregivers can be taxed in bringing comfort to the terminal patient. Attention to detail demands systematic vigilance by physicians and nurses. An excellent example is mouth care for terminal patients. While most people appreciate the comfort of fresh taste and breath, few could imagine that an entire book *The Terminal Patient: Oral Care,* could be written on this topic (Kutscher, Schoenberg, and Carr, 1973). Yet the mouth is the instrument by which one speaks, tastes, chews, drinks, sucks, bites, and grins. Its care involves the face, teeth, dentures, tongue, gums, lips, and larynx. Pain, dryness, infection, odor, secretions, drooling, hemorrhage, nutrition—these problems can be complicated and cause

much discomfort. This book details myriad technical aspects of comfort and suggestions for its realization, such as isotonic saline and 20-percent Karo mouth washes for stomatitis and potassium chloride rinses for dry mouth; a reminder that dumping syndrome may result because the tip of the nasogastric tube has slipped into the duodenum; and a note that pain in the jaw may be associated with vincristine.

The principles of drug use apply to patients living on borrowed time as they do to patients living under more fortunate circumstances. Alcohol can be used to great advantage for those patients who want it and can profit from its effects. Tranquilizers and antidepressants should be used when symptoms of anxiety and vegetative symptoms of depression distress the dying patient.

Psychedelic drugs were first used for dying patients by Kast (1966) and have been studied extensively at the Maryland State Psychiatric Research Center since 1955 (Kurland et al., 1973). In the hands of the latter investigators, lysergic acid diethylamide (LSD) or dipropyltryptamine (DPT) was an adjunct to brief courses of intense psychotherapy. Cancer patients were selected who were experiencing pain, depression, anxiety, and psychological isolation associated with staff feelings of frustration and inadequacy. After an average interval of 10 hours of psychotherapy, a single psychedelic session was introduced whose full duration averaged 20.2 hours. Flowers and stereophonic classical music were provided on the day of treatment, and after the patient's return to his usual state of consciousness, significant persons (spouse, children, parents, friends) were invited to share the final period of the psychedelic session. All but 6 of 41 ratings for depression, anxiety, pain, fear of death, isolation, and difficulty of management showed significant changes. According to global index ratings, 36 percent were dramatically improved; 36 percent, moderately improved; and 19 percent, unimproved. Only 8.3 percent were worse. No changes were made in the amount of narcotics consumed before and after psychedelic therapy (Kurland et al., 1973). In 1973, Goldberg, Malitz, and Kutscher edited a book on the use of psychopharmacological agents for the terminally ill. Of great promise is the recent demonstration by

Sallen, Zinberg, and Frei (1975) of the anti-emetic efficacy of oral cannabis for patients receiving cancer chemotherapy. Relief of nausea induced by the agents has hitherto been extremely difficult.

Communication. Talking with the dying is a highly overrated skill. The wish to find the "right thing" to say is a well-meaning but misguided hope among persons who actually do or want to work with terminal patients. Practically every empirical study has emphasized the ability to listen over the ability to say something. Saunders summed it up best when she said, "The real question is not 'What do you tell your patients?' but rather 'What do you let your patients tell you?'" (1969, p. 59). Most people have a strong inner resistance to letting dying patients speak their minds. If a patient presumed to be three months from death says, "My plan was to buy a new [automobile] in six months, but I guess I won't have to worry about that now," a poor listener will say nothing or "Right. Don't worry about it." A better listener might say, "Why do you say that?" or "What do you mean?"

Communication is more than listening. Getting to know the patient as a person is essential. Learning about significant areas of the patient's life, such as family, work, or schooling, and chatting about common interests represent the most natural if not the only ways the patient has of coming to feel known. After a seventy-nine-year-old man of keen intellect and wit had been interviewed before a group of hospital staff, one of the staff said, "Before the interview tonight I just thought of him as another old man on the ward in pain." Nothing esoteric is necessary to talk to a dying person. Like anybody else, he gets his sense of self-respect in the presence of others from a feeling that they value him for what he has done and for his personal qualities. Allowing the dying person to tell his own story helps build a balanced relationship. The effort spent getting to know him does him more psychological good than trying to guess how he will cope with death.

The physician can help dissolve communication barriers for other staff members by showing them the uniqueness of each patient. Comments like "This man has thirty-four grandchildren" or "This woman was an RAF fighter pilot" (both describing actual patients) convey

information that can help staff find something to talk about with the patients. Awkwardness subsides when patients seem like real people and not merely "a breast CA" or some other disease. This rescue from anonymity is essential to prevent a sense of isolation. Communication is more than verbal. A pat on the arm, a wave, a wink, or a grin communicates important reassurances, as do careful backrubs and physical examinations.

Patients occasionally complain about professional and lay visitors who appear more interested in the phenomenon of dying than in the patients as individuals. A woman in her early fifties, with breast cancer metastatic to bone, brain, lungs, and liver, entered the hospital for a course of chemotherapy. During her entire six-week stay she was irascible, argumentative, and even abusive to the staff. She responded extremely well to treatment, experienced a substantial remission, and left the hospital. She later told her oncologist, apologizing for her behavior, "I know that I was impossible. But every single nurse who came into my room wanted to talk to me about death. I came there to get help, not to die, and it drove me up a wall." A wise caution is to take conversational cues from the patient whenever possible.

Children. Investigators have unanimously concluded that the visits of children are likely to bring as much consolation and relief to the terminally ill as any other intervention. A useful rule of thumb in determining whether a particular child should visit a dying patient is to ask the child whether he wants to visit. No better criterion has been found.

Family cohesion and integration. A burden shared is a burden made lighter. Families must be assisted in supporting one another, although this process requires the effort of getting to know family members as well as the patient. Conversely, when the patient is permitted to support his family, the feeling of being a burden is mitigated. The often difficult work of bringing the family together for support, reconciliations, and improved relations can prevent disruption when death of the patient initiates the work of bereavement. The opportunity to be present at death should be offered to family members, as well as the alternative of being informed about it while waiting for the news at home. Flexibility is the rule, with the wishes of the family and patient paramount. After death, family members should be offered the chance (but never pressured) to see the body before it is taken to the morgue. Parkes (1972) has documented the critical importance to grief work of seeing the body of the dead person.

Cheerfulness. Dying people have no more relish for sour and somber faces than anybody else. Anyone with a gentle and appropriate sense of humor can bring considerable relief to all parties involved. "What do they think this is?" said one patient of his visitors. "They file past here with flowers and long faces like they were coming to my wake." Patients with a good sense of humor don't enjoy unresponsive audiences either. It is their wit that softens many a difficult incident. Said one elderly man with a tremor, after an embarrassing loss of sphincter control, "This is enough to give anybody Parkinson's disease!" Wit is not an end in itself. As in all forms of conversation, the listener should take the cue from the patient. Forced or inappropriate mirth can increase a sick person's feelings of distance and isolation.

Consistency and perseverance. Progressive isolation is a realistic fear of the dying person. A physician or nurse who regularly visits the sickroom provides tangible proof of continued support and concern. Saunders (1969) emphasizes that the quality of time is far more important than the quantity. A brief visit is far better than no visit at all, and patients may not be able to tolerate prolonged visiting. Patients are quick to identify those who show interest at first but gradually disappear from the scene. Staying power requires hearing out complaints. Praising one of her nurses, one 69-year-old woman with advanced cancer said, "She takes all my guff, and I give her plenty. Most people just pass my room, but if she has even a couple of minutes, she'll stop and actually listen to what I have to say. Some days I couldn't get through without her."

Breaking Bad News

Because so many reactions to the news of diagnosis are possible, having some plan of action in

mind ahead of time that will permit the greatest variation and freedom of response is helpful. The following approach is suggested. Begin by sitting down with the patient in a private place. Standing while conveying bad news is regarded by patients as unkind and an expression of wanting to leave as quickly as possible. Inform him that when all the tests are completed, the physician will sit down with him again. Spouse and family can be included in the discussion of findings and treatment. As that day approaches, the patient should again be warned. This warning permits those patients who wish no information, or minimal information, to say so.

If the findings are unpleasant—as in the case of a biopsy positive for malignancy—how can they best be conveyed? A good opening statement is one that is (1) rehearsed so that it can be delivered calmly; (2) brief—three sentences or less; (3) designed to encourage further dialogue; and (4) reassuring of continued attention and care. A typical delivery might go as follows: "The tests confirmed that your tumor is malignant [the bad news]. I have therefore asked the surgeon [or radiotherapist or oncologist] to come by to speak with you, examine you, and make his recommendations for treatment [we will do something about it]. As things proceed, I will be by to talk with you about them and about how we should proceed [I will stand by you]." Silence and quiet observation for a few moments will yield valuable information about the patient, his emotional reactions, how he deals with the facts from the start. While observing, the doctor can decide how best to continue the discussion, but sitting with the patient for a period of time is an essential part of this initial encounter with a grim reality that both patient and physician will continue to confront together, possibly for a very long time.

Telling the Truth

Without honesty human relationships are destined for shipwreck. If truthfulness and trust are so obviously interdependent, why does so much conspiracy exist to avoid truth with the dying? The paradoxical fact is that for the terminally ill, the need for both honesty and avoidance of the truth can be intense. Sir William Osler is reputed to have said, "A patient has no more right to all the facts in my head than he does to all the medications in my bag." Perhaps a routine blood smear has just revealed that its owner has acute myelogenous leukemia. If he is twenty-five, married, and the father of two small children, should he be told the diagnosis? Is the answer obvious? What if he had sustained two prior psychotic breaks with less serious illnesses? What if his wife says he once said that he never wanted to know if he had a malignancy?

Most empirical studies in which patients were asked whether or not they should be told the truth about malignancy indicated overwhelming desire for the truth. When 740 patients in a cancer detection clinic were asked (prior to diagnosis) if they should be told their diagnosis, 99 percent said they should be told (Kelly and Friesen, 1950). Another group in this same clinic was asked after the diagnosis was established and 89 percent of them replied affirmatively, as did 82 percent of another group who had been examined and found free of malignancy. Gilbertsen and Wangensteen (1962) asked the same questions of 298 survivors of surgery for gastric, colon, and rectal cancers and found that 82 percent said they should be told the truth. The same authors approached 92 patients with advanced cancer, judged by their physicians to be preterminal, and were told by 79 percent that they should be told their diagnosis.

How many don't want the truth or regard it as harmful? Effects of blunt truth telling have been empirically studied in both England and the United States. Aitken-Swan and Easson (1959) were told by 7 percent of 231 patients explicitly informed of their diagnoses that the frankness of the consultant was resented. Gilbertsen and Wangensteen (1962) observed that 4 percent of a sample of surgical patients became emotionally upset at the time they were told and appeared to remain so throughout the course of their illness. Gerlé, Lunden, and Sandblom (1960) studied 101 patients; members of one group were told, along with their families, the frank truth about their diagnoses, while with the other group an effort was made to maintain a conspiracy of silence between family and physician, excluding the patient from discussion of the diagnosis. Initially greater emotional upset appeared in the group in which patient and family were told together, but

the authors observed in follow-up that the emotional difficulties in the families of those patients "shielded" from the truth far outweighed those that occurred when patient and family were told the diagnosis simultaneously. In general, empirical studies do not support the myth that truth is not desired by the terminally ill or harms those to whom it is given. Honesty sustains the relationship with a dying person rather than retarding it. The following example is drawn from Hackett and Weisman, 1962:

A housewife of 57 with metastatic breast cancer, now far advanced, was seen in consultation. She reported a persistent headache, which she attributed to nervous tension, and asked why she should be nervous. Turning the question back to her, the physician was told, "I am nervous because I have lost sixty pounds in a year, the priest comes to see me twice a week, which he never did before, and my mother-in-law is nicer to me even though I am meaner to her. Wouldn't this make you nervous?" The physician replied, "You mean you think you're dying." "That's right, I do," she answered. He paused and said quietly, "You are." She smiled and said, "Well, I've finally broken the sound barrier; someone's finally told me the truth."

Not all patients can be dealt with so directly. A nuclear physicist greeted his surgeon on the day following exploratory laparotomy with the words, "Lie to me, Steve." Individual variations in willingness to hear the initial diagnosis are extreme. And diagnosis is entirely different from prognosis. Many patients have said they were grateful to their physician for telling them they had a malignancy. Very few, however, react positively to being told they are dying. My own experience indicates that "Do I have cancer?" is a not uncommon question, while "Am I dying?" is a rare one. The latter question is more common among patients who are dying rapidly, such as those in cardiogenic shock.

Honest communication of the diagnosis (or of any truth) by no means precludes later avoidance or even denial of the truth. In two studies cited above in which patients had been told their diagnoses outright (including the words *cancer* or *malignancy*), they were asked three weeks later what they had been told. Nineteen percent of one sample (Aitken-Swan and Easson, 1959) and

20 percent of the other (Gilbertsen and Wangensteen, 1962) denied that their condition was cancer or malignant. Likewise, Croog, Shapiro, and Levine (1971) interviewed 345 men three weeks after myocardial infarction and were told by 20 percent that they had not had a heart attack; all had been explicitly told their diagnoses. For a person to function effectively, truth's piercing voice must occasionally be muted or even excluded from awareness. I once spoke on four successive days with a man who had a widely spread bone cancer. On the first day, he said he didn't know what he had and didn't like to ask questions; on the second, that he was "riddled with cancer"; on the third, that he didn't really know what ailed him; and on the fourth, that even though nobody likes to die, that was now the lot that fell to him.

Truth telling is no panacea. Communicating a diagnosis honestly, though difficult, is easier than the labors that lie ahead. Telling the truth is merely a way to begin, but since it is an open and honest way, it provides a firm basis on which to build a relationship of trust.

The Role of Religious Faith and Value Systems

Investigation of the relationship between religious faith and attitudes toward death has been hampered by differences in methodology. Lester (1972b) and Feifel (1974) have reviewed much of the conflicting literature on the relation between religious faith and fear of death. Other research has tried to clarify the way belief systems function within the individual. Allport (1958) contrasted an "extrinsic" religious orientation, in which religion is mainly a means to social status, security, or relief from guilt, with an "intrinsic" religious orientation, where values appear to be internalized and subscribed to as ends in themselves. Feagin (1964) provides a useful twenty-one-item questionnaire for distinguishing the two types of believers. Experimental work (Magni, 1972) and clinical experience indicate that an extrinsic value system, without internalization, seems to offer no assistance in coping with a fatal illness. A religious commitment that is intrinsic, on the other hand, appears to offer a

good deal of stability and strength to those who possess it.

Many patients are grateful for the chance to express their own thoughts about their faith. If a patient has religious convictions, a useful question can be asked during discussion of the illness: "Where do you think God stands in all this?" followed by "Do you see your illness as imposed on you by God? Why? What sort of a being do you picture God to be?" Answers can be scrutinized for feelings of guilt and for the quality of relationship the individual describes with God.

Belief in an afterlife is another useful area for questioning and helps in assessing tolerance of doubt, an important quality of mature belief. In general, those persons who possess a sense of the presence of God, of being cared for or watched over, are more likely to manifest tranquillity in their struggle with terminal illness. In 1974 Kübler-Ross wrote: "Before I started working with dying patients, I did not believe in a life after death. I now do believe in a life after death without a shadow of a doubt" (p. 167). When M. G. Michaelson reviewed Kübler-Ross's book along with several others on death and dying, he quoted the above passage and added, "Damned if I know what's going on here, but it does seem that everyone who's gone into the subject comes out believing in something crazy. Life after death, transformation, destiny, belief . . . These are the words of hard-nosed scientists fresh from their investigations" (1974, p. 6). Careful investigation of religious faith in the dying needs to be pursued.

Care of the Dying Child and His Parents

Fatally ill children pose poignant and difficult problems for their parents and caregivers. Easson (1970) and Spinetta (1974) have reviewed contributions to the understanding of these issues in a field that needs more empirical study. Any approach to helping a dying child and his family must be based on the understanding of the child's attitudes toward death.

The most common adult misconception is that children cannot comprehend the meaning of death. Even teen-agers are often treated as though they did not understand mortality. Anthony (1940) and Nagy (1948) were the first to study empirically the development of the death concept in children. Table 28.1 summarizes the development of this comprehension in healthy children. Three phases characterize the gradual understanding of the death concept. Children five or younger regard death as reversible, comparable to a journey or sleep. Six months after the death of her father, a three-year-old girl asked, "Mommy, will Daddy be home for Christmas?" Because of the inability of children in this age group to grasp the finality of death, I recommend that parents not compare death to sleep, natural as that is, because of the likelihood that a sick child with this association will be afraid to go to sleep at night. (This fear is a common feature of very sick adults troubled by specifically nocturnal insomnia. The fear is often unconscious and its treatment is difficult.) Between the ages of five or six and nine or ten, the child personifies death as a ghost or bogyman who comes to transport the dying person away. The causation is seen as external ("Who killed him?"). At this stage death becomes a definite fact of life, although it is common for the child to

regard it as remote—as something that happens only to the very old. The two most abstract elements in the concept of death, irreversibility and universality, are incorporated later. Comprehension of these elements is regarded as marking a complete grasp of the essential notions of the death concept. Acquisition of the concept of irreversibility marks the third and final phase in concept development and appeared after age nine in Nagy's (1948) study. Steiner (1965) and Portz (1972) discovered its appearance at ages seven and eight, respectively. Grasp of death's universality has been found as early as age eight and a half by Peck (1966), though other studies set it at nine or later, and Steiner (1965) found its mean age of onset in her sample to be eleven. The significance of these studies is great: the average child has a complete understanding of the essential notion of death between the ages of eight and eleven. Of course, a child's comprehension can be quite threatening to adults. Michele, age eleven and dying of a brain tumor, said, "My parents won't tell me anything, but I know. I've got a tumor, people die of it . . . Of

TABLE 28.1. Concepts of death in healthy children.

Concept	Age	Investigator
Reversible	3–5	Anthony, 1940; Nagy, 1948
Similar to sleep, journey, departure	3–5	Anthony, 1940; Nagy, 1948; and most others
Due to violence	3–5	Rochlin, 1965; Natterson and Knudson, 1960
Personified	6–10	Nagy, 1948
Externally caused	5–9	Anthony, 1940; Nagy, 1948; Natterson and Knudson, 1960; Safier, 1964
Fact of life	5–9	Most investigators
Inevitable	5–9	Most investigators
	3–5	Rochlin, 1965
Irreversible	9+	Nagy, 1948
	8	Portz, 1972
	7	Steiner, 1965
Universal	9+	Nagy, 1948
	8+	Anthony, 1940
	11	Steiner, 1965
	$8\frac{1}{2}$	Peck, 1966

course I know that I won't get better. Children do sometimes die; I'm going to die too" (Raimbault, 1972).

What fears accompany the growth of this comprehension of death in children? Table 28.2 presents a summary of fears specific to the phases of conceptual development outlined above. Children five or younger dread separation from parents. Minimizing the threat of death for them requires specific attention to maintaining contact with parents and reassuring the child about the return of a parent who must leave for short periods. One important application of this principle is the inclusion of children in all death rituals, such as wakes, funerals, *shivah*, and burial. Parents who fail to do so risk frightening the child far more by separating him from his family at a time when death has already caused one separation in the family. No child is too small to be included. As with visitation of the sick or dying, the child should be allowed to go unless he requests not to; he is usually a better judge of the situation than the parent.

Between the ages of six and ten, the child normally develops fears of bodily injury and mutilation, particularly as the victim of aggressive actions. The use of dolls in describing surgical procedures to children in this age group is an effective method of neutralizing some of their fears. This is also the age in which parental discipline becomes formalized in the child's primitive conscience, where "good" acts deserve reward and "bad ones," punishment. The child, now very vulnerable to feelings of guilt, is likely to regard death or illness as a punishment for being "bad." Accordingly, children of this age should be re-

TABLE 28.2. Specific fears associated with death in children and adolescents.

Age	Fears
Up to 4–5	Separation
6–10	Aggression; mutilation; guilt; loneliness
10+	Own death; abandonment
Adolescence	Shame

minded explicitly that illness does not befall them or their siblings because they were bad children. Similarly, all exhortations that imply guilt should be avoided, such as "If you are a good boy and take your medicine, nothing will happen to you." Finally, loneliness is listed here because it is, unfortunately, often experienced by fatally ill children. From around the age of ten on, the concerns of children can be strikingly adult (as noted in the case of Michele, above). They wonder what their own death will be like, particularly whether it will be painful, and, even more, whether they will be left to face it alone when it comes.

Shame is listed as a special concern of the adolescent to emphasize how embarrassed and self-conscious the pubescent youngster can be with a new and rapidly changing body. To have this body threatened or disfigured by a fatal illness can result in feelings of intense shame, even repulsiveness, for the adolescent. All of these age-specific concerns should be assumed to be present to some degree in ill children and great care given to their alleviation.

Like healthy children, fatally ill children understand the meaning of death and are usually aware of their own predicament. Waechter (1972) studied four groups of sixteen children, aged six to ten: those with a fatal illness, those with a chronic but nonfatal illness, those with an acute brief illness, and those with no illness (healthy group). The anxiety scale scores, as well as the derived-fear scores, from the Thematic Apperception Test (TAT) of the fatally ill children were significantly higher than those of all other groups and demonstrated that the most anxiety was expressed by those children for whom death was the predicted outcome. The projective tests revealed significantly more specific concern about death among the fatally ill children. Moreover, every child in this latter diagnostic category (100 percent) used death imagery at least once in his responses to the protocol. Images of loneliness in this group also significantly exceeded those expressed by the other three groups. The main character in the stories of the fatally ill children died or was assigned a negative future significantly more often than in the other children's stories. Many parents had gone to great lengths to ensure that the diagnosis was never mentioned to the child and the illness never discussed with him. Waechter's study also demonstrated that the less opportunity the child had to discuss the illness at home, the higher his score on the general anxiety scale was. Avoiding talk about the illness appeared to indicate to the child that it was too terrible to discuss.

Even more difficult than discussing the illness with a dying child is the problem of remaining in his presence. What truth is there in the accusation that we avoid and isolate the dying child? What is the child's perception of this? To study these questions, Spinetta, Rigler, and Karon (1974) compared twenty-five children hospitalized for the first time with a diagnosis of leukemia and twenty-five hospitalized for a chronic, nonfatal illness; all children were aged six to ten. In an ingenious design, the experimenters used a three-dimensional hospital-room replica, scaled so that 1 inch equaled 1 foot. Using a child-patient doll matched for sex and race with the child, they presented sequentially father, mother, nurse, and doctor dolls with the instruction, "Here comes the nurse; put her where she usually stands." Distance from the child-patient doll was recorded in centimeters in each case. On the first admission, the twenty-five leukemic children placed the figures significantly farther away than did the control group of chronically ill children. The experiment was repeated with subsequent admissions. While the distance of placement increased for both groups in the subsequent admission, the leukemic children increased the distance significantly more than did the chronically ill, lending strong support to the hypothesis that the child's sense of isolation grows stronger as he nears death. The implication of these empirical studies is clear. Effective care of the dying child must focus both on helping the child communicate his concerns and on helping the parents (and staff) deal with the personal fears that lead them to avoid or isolate the child.

Management of the dying child is an individualized matter, understood best by the parents. The days that can be lived normally will be most enjoyable to the child, and for these days overindulgence may be just as damaging as neglect. Although professionals should not tell parents how to take care of their children, supplying

them with a list of specific concerns, like the one in table 28.2, is helpful. Discovering the child's specific fear is a basic objective. One ten-year-old girl with leukemia, who had done well emotionally up to the time her chemotherapy began to produce hair loss, went to bed in her room and did not come out. Promises of getting a wig proved of no help, but when she learned that the hair loss was an effect of medication, she promptly resumed her normal activities. She had associated loss of hair with death, and when her hair began to fall out, she thought she was dying. Children need encouragement to express and discuss specific fears of this kind (Toch, 1964; Yudkin, 1967; Evans, 1968; Easson, 1970).

What does one tell a child about death or prognosis? Experienced pediatricians are too wise to answer this in any simple way, although most tend to shield the child from labels like "leukemia" or "cancer," and all are wisely careful to avoid predicting when the child will die. However, the discomfort over what to say to the child about illness and death is often a primary obstacle for the parents and the medical caregivers. This uncertainty, coupled with the strong desire not to harm the child or make his predicament any worse, is a major obstacle to allowing the child to express specific fears. Children's questions are often blunt and alarming. "What is death like?" "Am I going to have a coffin?" "Are you and Daddy going to come to visit me when I'm in the grave?" are all questions that have been asked by children under ten. The most helpful technique in dealing with these confrontations is to ask for the child's own answer to the question. Thus "What do you think it's like?" "What do you want done?" "What would you like us to do?" would be helpful initial responses to the three sample questions. Only in this manner can the adult learn more specifically what is on the child's mind. The boy who asked the first question said he thought that in death a bogyman would come to take him away. Later he said he thought death would hurt. His mother was able to comfort him on both points. The seven-year-old girl who asked the second question said she wanted to choose the colors of the casket, while the seven-year-old girl who asked the third question said that she wanted visitors at the grave and promptly changed the subject to what kind of company she might have in heaven. Although it is painful and difficult to take children seriously, letting them say what is on their minds best guarantees understanding them and finding ways to comfort them. Imagined fears are almost always worse than reality, and astonishing equanimity has been seen in children who are confident that they will not be left alone, attacked, or regarded as bad.

Kübler-Ross has enlightened many about the symbolic language in a child's drawings. The same symbolism can be seen in dolls or other play objects. Sometimes children will talk about drawings, especially if the drawings, not the child, are made the focus of discussion by asking what the child in the drawing thinks, not what the artist thinks. One child who had undergone six major abdominal operations in five months introduced me to a grape named Joe. When I asked where his head was, she told me one pole of the grape was his navel, and in response to the repeated question said that the other pole represented his anus. When I asked what it was like for Joe to be contained between navel and anus, she replied with a smile, "Oh, it's not so bad, most of the time." She then declined to discuss Joe further. Some children will not discuss their drawings or play objects at all, and some are so eloquent that little need be added. Nonverbal communication can be more important at tense moments for the child. Children are reassured by being touched, hugged, or rocked (Kennell, Slyter, and Klaus, 1970), especially if the person doing it is relaxed and accepting. Various authors have pointed out the child's interest in toys, dolls, furry animals, and television; these absorbing objects do not lose their appeal when a child is sick.

Any support given to the parents will greatly benefit the child. While parents will find some understanding of the material presented above very helpful, they have their own needs. From the time they learn of the diagnosis, each may assume that the other will not be able to tolerate the tragedy of their child's illness and both will attempt to minimize any display of weakness and sometimes of any emotion at all. Often numb at first, parents may at times be filled with a sense of injustice or outrage. Repeatedly asking themselves whether they should have noted the illness earlier or acted on the symptoms sooner, and aware that they may have minimized the symptoms even to the extent of regarding them as trivial, emotional, or psychosomatic, the parents may have considerable feelings of guilt. Allowing them to explore and state these concerns is essential. Suicidal thoughts are probably the rule rather than the exception during the child's illness, particularly in the mind of the mother. These thoughts ("When Julie goes, I'm next") can be alarming but are far less threatening if expressed.

While helping parents to maintain as normal a life routine for the sick child's siblings as possible, it is necessary to remember that the well children in the family may become objects of unwitting resentment, another feeling whose emergence can cause considerable distress even in a parent who in no way acts it out. "Why couldn't it be Joe instead of Julie?" is a spontaneous feeling that may cause a parent to experience acute guilt and shame, sometimes for years. If allowed to verbalize such feelings, parents should be reminded that feelings are completely different from actions. Another source of parental discomfort is the need to seek further consultation about treatment for their fatally ill child. The death of another child on the same hospital floor, particularly if afflicted by the same illness, is likely to devastate the parents of a child who is enjoying a remission.

If parents request reading material to help deal with their healthy children, Jackson (1965) and Grollman (1967) are recommended; three useful texts have been designed to be read directly to children after a death has occurred: Grollman, 1970; Harris, 1965; and Stein, 1974. In some cities, organizations exist in which parents of children who are dying or have died support one another; these include the Society for the Compassionate Friends (Stevens, 1973), Candlelighters, and One Day at a Time.

Who cares for the caregiver? Physicians, nurses, social workers, and chaplains who work with dying children have all been asked how they tolerate it. Two major difficulties must be overcome. First, how does one steer a course between incapacitating emotional overinvolvement and callous, detached withdrawal? Schowalter (1970) observes that pediatric house officers who are parents themselves find the horror of a dying child more real than do those who are not parents, but they also tend to have more empathy and work better with the parents than their single peers. He finds a tendency in all house officers studied to avoid getting emotionally involved with dying children. The second dilemma of health workers in this setting is how to obtain gratification from fighting a losing battle. Although they may actually deny that it is a losing battle for some period of time (and this denial can be useful), the ultimate reality remains. An interest in and respect for the child and his parents can be developed through encounters with them that provide gratification. This process, of course, implies emotional investment in the child and his parents. Parents of dying children frequently admitted, although with embarrassment, that the desire to see a physician, nurse, or other member of the hospital personnel motivates their hospital visiting more than just seeing their own child. These encounters with parents as well as with the children provide the staff with specific feedback about their importance, effectiveness, and helpfulness in the situation. Flexibility is important. In a survey of pediatricians' attitudes toward the care of fatally ill children, Weiner (1970) notes that as pediatricians get older they develop more flexible attitudes toward parental visiting hours and parental participation in actual child care. Another issue that parents need to discuss with physicians and staff is whether the child should die in the hospital or at home.

Mechanisms to ensure and promote growth in the ability of hospital personnel to take care of dying children and their parents should include formal training. As helpful as that may be, however, other mechanisms are necessary to optimize staff performance and morale in the treatment setting itself, whether inpatient or outpatient. Schowalter (1970) advocates a multidisciplinary team meeting, including pediatric house officers, child psychiatry fellows, nurses, social workers, chaplains, medical and nursing students, and others who work in the setting. Such meetings are conducted by a staff child psychiatrist and senior pediatrician. In similar situations, nurses and house officers have stressed the need for a liaison person to deal with the parents and children directly because both are more likely to feel uncomfortable with the parents. Inviting a parent to a group meeting, either a multidisciplinary or a nursing group, can provide a model for allowing parents to discuss their concerns. Group members can also be invited to express their own feelings about children and parents and to arrive at specific management plans through sharing reactions and observations (Cassem and Hackett, 1975). Where parents' groups exist, the opportunity for staff members to visit maintains contact and provides a chance to see how parents cope with often incomprehensible tragedy.

Care and Management of the Suicidal Person

Death casts its shadow not only on the terminally ill but also on individuals determined or tempted to hasten its arrival. Care of the suicidal person represents a frequent health challenge. The tenth leading cause of death, suicide is known to claim from 22,000 to 25,000 lives annually, although the actual death toll (with many suicides disguised as accidents) may be about twice this number (Schneidman, 1975). For white males aged fifteen to nineteen it ranks second, and for physicians under forty it ranks first among causes of death. In the United States the recorded overall suicide rate is 10 to 12 per 100,000, placing this country midway in international suicide rates listed by the World Health Organization (1968). Japan, Austria, Denmark, Sweden, West Germany, and Hungary have rates higher than 20 per 100,000, while Italy, Spain, New Zealand, and Ireland have rates of 6 per 100,000 or less. For every completed suicide about eight attempts occur. Those who are widowed, divorced, or single kill themselves significantly more often than married people. In the United States, urban and rural dwellers are at equal risk, in contrast to Europe, where risk is greater in urban areas. The suicide rate among blacks, one-third that of whites two decades ago, is now more nearly equal, especially in urban areas. Protestants outrank Jews and Catholics among completed suicides. Half of American male suicides accomplish the act by firearms, a means used by one-fourth of women. More than one-third of female and about one-fifth of male victims use poisonous agents (including gas) to bring death. Hanging or strangulation is chosen by about one-fifth of both men and women.

The Psychodynamics of the Suicidal Person

Self-destruction was seen by Freud (1917, 1920) as murder of an introjected love object toward whom the victim felt ambivalent. Schneidman (1975) reports that this classic and controversial theory stemmed from a statement by Wilhelm Stekel at a Vienna meeting in 1910 that no one killed himself unless he had either wanted to kill another person or wished another's death. Freud's initial conclusions stemmed from his work with depression, in which his discovery of hostility directed inward led to the prominence of aggression in his theory of the dynamics of melancholia. Not all depressed patients, however, engage in suicidal behavior, nor is the suicide attempter always depressed. Zilboorg (1938) points out that some suicidal patients have the unconscious conviction that they are immortal and will not die. In addition to hostility, he found an absence of the capacity to love others in suicidal patients (1937). Rado (1956) has added the concept of expiation: suicide atones for past wrongs and becomes a way of recapturing the love of a lost or estranged object. Menninger's *Man Against Himself* (1938) extends the traditional psychoanalytic concept of self-directed aggression to include other self-destructive behaviors that stop short of suicide, classifying them as chronic (asceticism, martyrdom, neurotic invalidism, alcohol addiction, antisocial behavior, psychosis); focal (mutilation, multiple surgical procedures, malingering, accident-proneness); and organic or psychological (masochism, sadism —with both self-punitive and erotic features). Despite the prominence of self-destructive behavior in everyday life, the relationships between such behavior and depression are not uncontroversial. In a series of careful empirical studies, for example, Beck (1967) was not able to confirm the presence of internalized aggression in depressed patients.

What most appropriately characterizes the state of mind of the person most likely to complete suicide? In addition to hostility, the withdrawal of social support—typified by sudden or intensified estrangement—places a person at much greater risk. Anniversaries of losses and holidays may rewaken all the original, keen feelings of abandonment, loneliness, fury, guilt, defectiveness, isolation, and hopelessness in the individual and increase his proneness to take his life. Beck (1963) stresses that suicidal behavior is most likely when a person perceives his predicament as untenable or hopeless. As psychoanalytic theories of narcissism and ego development expand, self-destruction is coming to be viewed as an effort to restore the balance of wounded self-esteem. Weisman (1971) points out that death itself may not be the wish of the completed suicide victim but that his wish to die signals his conviction that "his potential for being someone who matters has been exhausted" (p. 230). Rochlin (1973), in a creative replacement of the "death instinct" theory, points out that suicide itself, like other forms of aggressive action, serves to restore bruised or shattered self-esteem. Self-inflicted death is, then, a preferred solution to and an honorable way out of the person's crisis of self-esteem, in which hopelessness and helplessness are not only the key subjective features for the individual but also the chief clues for the observer that suicide is about to occur.

Clinical Evaluation of Suicide Risk

In a thorough review of the literature of suicide prevention, Litman (1966) concluded that, despite decades of interest and prolific writing on the topic, scientific study had barely begun. Six years later, Lester (1972a) could find no evidence that suicide prevention affected the suicide rate. Yet prevention depends on the accurate identification of the individual most likely to kill himself. Litman et al. (1974) suggest that the criticism of intervention programs may in part reflect a failure to differentiate between the acutely suicidal person, who is perhaps actually being rescued, and the chronically suicidal person, who, because of a somewhat lower profile, eludes detection and becomes the program "failure."

Depression should always alert the clinician to his duty to assess suicide risk (Fawcett, 1972;

Murphy, 1975b). A mental checklist should include age (men's suicide rates peak in the eighties; women's, between fifty-five and sixty-five); sex (men complete suicides about three times as often as women, while women attempt it two to three times as often as men); alcoholism; absence or recent disappearance of "fight," distress, or strong feeling (sudden calm in a previously suicidal person may stem from a definite resolve to die); refusal to accept help immediately; and prior experience as a psychiatric inpatient.

If the person has already made an attempt, its degree of lethality predicts the danger of a subsequent attempt. To assess this factor, the "risk-rescue" criteria of Weisman and Worden (1972) should be used. Information regarding the degree of risk (method used, degree of impairment of consciousness when rescued, extent of injury, time required in hospital to reverse the effects, intensity of treatment required) and the rescue circumstances (remoteness from help, type of rescuer, probability of discovery, accessibility to rescue, and delay between attempt and rescue) can be established in a careful history. Serious physical illness can increase suicide risk but does not diminish the importance of the foregoing points of assessment; it is the attitude toward the illness that requires explanation. Low tolerance for pain, excessive demands or complaints, and a perception of lack of attention and support from the hospital staff are danger signals in the assessment of suicide potential (Farberow, Schneidman, and Leonard, 1963).

Recently Reich and Kelly (1976) analyzed seventeen suicides in 70,404 consecutive general hospital admissions; the only two without a psychiatric diagnosis were cancer patients. The most significant warning of impending suicide was some sort of rupture in the patient's relationship with hospital staff, ranging from angry accusations and complaints to the perception (in the two cancer patients) that the staff was giving up on them.

Psychometric scales for assessment of suicide risk are available (Beck, Schuyler, and Herman, 1974; Zung, 1974). Beck, Kovacs, and Weisman (1975) provide a promising beacon to guide the physician in his search among so many variables. In a rigorous investigation of 384 suicide attempters, employing scales to measure hopelessness, suicide intention, and depression, this group demonstrates that hopelessness is the key variable linking depression to suicidal behavior. Therefore, encouraging physicians to focus on this particular clue may lead to new gains in suicide prevention.

Finally, one should always ask directly whether the person is considering suicide. Excellent evidence exists that a suicidal patient will admit his intentions to a physician if asked (Delong and Robins, 1961).

Contrary to popular belief, the physician is more likely than any other individual or agency to encounter the completed suicide victim shortly before his death. Analyzing all successful suicides in St. Louis County in 1968–69, Murphy (1975a, 1975b) discovered that 81 percent had been under the care of a physician within six months prior to suicide. By contrast, suicide prevention centers had contact with no more than 2 to 6 percent of the suicidal patients in their localities (Weiner, 1969; Barraclough and Shea, 1970; Sawyer, Sudak, and Hall, 1972). More soberingly, Murphy (1975a) documents that 91 percent of overdose suicide victims had been under the recent care of a physician (compared with 71 percent of controls), and in over half the cases, the physician had supplied by prescription the complete means for suicide.

Treating the Suicidal Person

Self-esteem or self-respect is the most basic psychic condition to be guarded if life is to continue. Therefore the restoration and maintenance of the individual's narcissistic equilibrium is the aim of the therapist confronted by a person tempted to destroy himself. Certain practical features of this relationship can be summarized from Schneidman (1975) and others.

1. The therapist should stand as an ally for the life of the individual and in a calm and gentle but firm and unequivocal way make clear that his role is direct and active, including intervention to prevent suicidal behavior when the person makes this known. This intervention may include sending the police to the patient's home, depriving him of the means of suicide (pills or weapons), or hospitalizing him by involuntary

commitment. This approach is justified by those situations where suicidal communication is a cry for help (Farberow and Schneidman, 1965) and must be accompanied by equally forthright reminders to the patient of the therapist's drastic limitations—that he is only rarely able to control another's behavior; that responsibility for behavior belongs to its initiator; that unconscious hopes for someone else to stop the execution of a plan are very often disappointed, and that without the patient's actually cooperating (at least unconsciously), the therapist could not prevent or reverse a single suicide attempt.

2. This active relationship requires a delicate but deliberate violation of the usual confidences of the therapeutic relationship. Self-destructive plans are never to be held in confidence when their disclosure may prevent the death of the patient. It is not the plan that prompts action from the therapist (he can be content to hear in confidence innumerable variations) but the emergence of indications that execution of plans is likely.

3. Repeated monitoring of suicidal potential is an important feature of working with an actively suicidal patient. Suicidal intent, the extent of hopelessness, and events on the patient's "calendar," such as anniversaries of losses and most holiday seasons, require direct questioning for proper assessment.

4. Despite his status as an ally for life, the therapist must also have the capacity to hear out carefully and to tolerate the feelings of despair, desperation, anguish, rage, loneliness, emptiness, and meaninglessness articulated by the suicidal person. The patient needs to know that the therapist takes him seriously and understands. This understanding may require the therapist to explore the patient's darkest feelings of despair—a taxing empathetic task.

5. Reduction of social isolation and withdrawal is essential. Active advice and encouragement may be required, as well as family, couple, or group treatment. Self-esteem develops through relationships with others, and introjection of a benign and supportive love object is an essential feature of ego development. A shortage of such love objects is often so prominent in the lives of suicidal patients that replacement of bad introjects may seem (and some say theoretically is)

impossible. These persons are skilled at distorting interpersonal relationships and evoking rejection. For this reason the therapist's investment in and respect for them may mark the first and only relationship in which they can begin to eliminate distorting perceptions of all relationships.

6. Relationships, work, hobbies, and other individualistic activities enhance and maintain self-esteem. Community agencies may help the patient renew or initiate such activities.

7. Coexisting psychiatric disorders must be treated. Suicide does not respect diagnostic categories. Potential for completed suicide, while representing an escape from an intolerable, hopeless crisis of self-esteem, must be dealt with in a manner appropriate to the psychopathology of the individual. Thus with the suicidal schizophrenic, reality testing, increased medication, and even ECT may be essential to prevent death. With the borderline patient or narcissistic personality, one is likely to spend even more time than usual interpreting negative transference or rehearsing the typical sequence of behaviors outlined by Adler (1973): highly idealized expectation, followed by inevitable disappointment and reactive rage, culminating in self-destructive behavior. Similar considerations for depression, anxiety, and other conditions must be made. If the patient has no psychiatric illness, as in the case of patients with cancer or dependence on chronic hemodialysis, attention to factors that can restore self-esteem and respect are also paramount.

8. Finally, the therapist himself must at times seek support or consultation when treating a patient with potential for completing suicide. Of all the difficulties encountered, the most troublesome is almost surely the countertransference hatred that suicidal patients often evoke in their caregivers (Maltzberger and Buie, 1974). When hostility is prominent in the patient, hypercritical, devaluating, scornful rage may be directed at the therapist for long periods of time. Then the patient's feelings as well as the therapist's own reactions can make treatment seem like an ordeal.

Treating a suicidal person can be quite anxiety-provoking for the therapist. The need to balance consideration for the patient's safety with the goal that he live his life independently in his own world reminds us how limited the therapist's powers are—that is, they are no stronger than the patient's desire to make use of help. The therapist who appreciates his ultimate inability to stop the person who really wants to kill himself is far more likely to be effective in restoring the person's sense of self-esteem and wholeness. Respect for independence, like investment in a patient's well-being, is itself therapeutic. Clarifying these limitations with the patient helps convey respect for his autonomy and reminds the therapist that a completed suicide can occur despite complete fulfillment of his responsibility. Both are thereby better enabled to see that the risks of their mutual encounter are worth taking.

Care of the Bereaved

Heberden, listing the causes of death in London in 1657, assigned tenth rank to "griefe." Four centuries later, Engel (1961) argued eloquently that grief should be classified as a disease because of its massive impact on normal function, the suffering it involves, and the predictable symptomatology associated with it. Parkes's *Bereavement* (1972) represents the most comprehensive contemporary summary of the empirical factors associated with the entire process. *Bereavement* refers to the process of accommodation to a specific loss, including anticipatory grief and mourning (Weisman, 1974); *grief* denotes the conscious impact of loss on an individual; *mourning* is the reactive process of coping with the loss.

How can one distinguish normal from abnormal grief? In his pioneer work with survivors of the Cocoanut Grove fire, Lindemann (1944) describes pathognomonic features of normal grief: (1) somatic distress, marked by sighing respiration, exhaustion, and digestive symptoms of all kinds (C. S. Lewis wrote in 1961, after the death of his wife: "No one ever told me that grief felt so much like fear. I am not afraid, but the sensation is like being afraid. The same fluttering in the stomach, the same restlessness, the yawning. I keep on swallowing," p. 7); (2) preoccupation with the image of the deceased, a slight sense of unreality, a feeling of increased emo-

tional distance from others, and such an intense focus on the deceased person that the grief-stricken may believe themselves in danger of insanity; (3) preoccupation with feelings of guilt; (4) hostile reactions, irritability, and a disconcerting loss of warm feelings toward other people; and (5) a disruption or disorganization of normal patterns of conduct.

In abnormal grief reactions, Lindemann found that the postponement of the experience or the absence of grief is usually associated with much more difficulty during bereavement. Parkes (1972) observes that hysterical or extreme reactions to loss (such as prolonged screaming and shouting, repeated fainting, and conversion paralysis) carry a prognostic significance as bad as the absence of grief. Cultural norms must of course be consulted to determine what is extreme in expressing grief. Lindemann (1944) lists nine signs of abnormality, which he calls "distorted reactions": (1) overactivity without a sense of loss; (2) the acquisition of symptoms belonging to the last illness of the deceased, presenting as conversion (hysterical) or hypochondriacal complaints; (3) a recognized medical disease, such as ulcerative colitis, rheumatoid arthritis, or asthma (although Lindemann linked these diseases to the group of psychosomatic conditions recognized at the time, subsequent investigations have shown that after the death of a loved one, survivors are at a significantly increased risk of death and illness); (4) alteration in relationships to friends and relatives, with progressive social isolation; (5) furious hostility against specific persons, resembling a truly paranoid reaction; (6) such suppression of hostility that affectivity and conduct resemble a schizophrenic picture, with masklike appearance, formal, stilted, robotlike movements, and no emotional expressiveness; (7) lasting loss of patterns of social interaction, with absence of decisiveness and initiative; (8) behavior that is socially and economically destructive, such as giving away belongings, making foolish business deals, or performing other self-punitive actions with no realization of internal feelings of guilt; and (9) overt agitated depression. It is important to note that Lindemann was impressed by the rarity of these manifestations of abnormal grief among the families of the Cocoanut Grove victims. Clayton, Desmarais, and Winokur (1968) and Clayton (1974), in extensive investigations of bereaved persons, have firmly established in follow-up how well most bereaved persons recover. At three months after the loss, Clayton found that four out of five patients were improved, and only 4 percent were worse. Rees and Lutkins (1967) have shown that widows and widowers have a significantly increased death rate for their age category in the first year following the death of their spouses. Holmes and Rahe (1967) have demonstrated that loss in many forms increases the risk of illness. Contrary to Rees and Lutkins' data, Clayton failed to find an increase of morbidity among a sample of bereaved persons in the St. Louis area.

How long does bereavement take? A parent who recently joined a parents' group after the death of his child asked this question. Another parent replied, "My son died thirty years ago, so I don't know yet," eloquently expressing the way grief can remain while behavior returns to normal. Treatment of the abnormal reactions is of primary importance.

The Process of Mourning

While many schemes are useful in conceptualizing mourning, that of Bowlby (1961) is classic.

1. In the first phase, the survivor is preoccupied with the lost person. In accord with animal models of loss, this time is characterized by searching and protest. The behaviors may seem bizarre yet are entirely normal. One boy of fourteen lost his best friend from nephritis. For three months thereafter he carried on prolonged conversations with his departed friend, with the conviction not only that his questions and discussion of future plans were heard but that his friend was present. Vivid hallucinatory experiences of the deceased person occur in about 50 percent of bereavement reactions (Rees, 1970). A mother who lost her twenty-year-old daughter repeatedly found herself in the girl's room. She wore the girl's clothes and on occasion put on the girl's nightclothes and lay in her bed striving for some sort of meeting with her. The German artist Kollwitz described working on a monument for her younger son who was killed in October 1914. Two years later she noted in her diary, "There's a drawing made, a mother letting her dead son slide into her arms. I could do a hundred similar drawings but still can't seem to come any closer to him. *I'm still searching for him*, as if it were in the very work itself that I had to find him" (Parkes, 1972, p. 39; italics added). Children of Israeli soldiers missing in action have been observed repeatedly to lose objects, complain loudly and tearfully about the losses, and, suddenly finding the object, carry it about on display, urging adults in the family to rejoice with them in the discovery; in one case the object was a picture of the missing father.* It is important for an observer to recall that even apparently bizarre behavior in a bereaved person may represent the searching or protest phase of the mourning process.

2. The second phase described by Bowlby is one of disorganization, a preoccupation with the pain of the experience, characterized at times by turmoil or even despair. One father, two years after the loss of his ten-year-old son, told a group: "It hurts. I could tell you all about how you'd feel going through the whole thing, but I could never tell you about the emptiness that comes . . . afterward. That hurts more than anything—at times it aches." C. S. Lewis noted after the death of his wife, "Her absence is like the sky, spread over everything" (1961, p. 13). The pointlessness of life and the reasonableness of suicide are common in the minds of the bereaved in this period. Social interaction seems impossible, and yet solitude is intolerable. "I want others to be about me," Lewis observed. "I dread the moments when the house is empty. If only they would talk to one another and not to me" (p. 7).

3. Finally, a phase of reorganization occurs in which normal functioning and behavior are restored. Reversals during this time are the rule, and the reappearance of the earlier two phases should be expected. During the reorganization process, the bereaved person is caught off guard by memories and repeated realizations of the pain of loss. A widow, at the ringing of a phone, may be devastated by the sudden realization that her husband will never phone her again. Returning to scenes or sights shared with the deceased is a common occasion of grief and an

---

* Reported by M. Rosenbaum at Psychiatric Grand Rounds, Massachusetts General Hospital, Boston, Massachusetts, in 1975.

opportunity to further the process of mourning. Death after a long illness, for example, may seem acceptable to a survivor because it terminates the pain and debilitation of the lost person. But return to a scene that recalls the lost person in a healthy state may precipitate new feelings and make the death entirely unacceptable. One widow used to carry the picture of her husband as he looked at his worst. When she felt sad she would take the picture out and look at it, "to remind myself that he couldn't be expected to go on."

Psychologically, death represents the rupture of the survivor's attachment to the lost person—a bond heavily laden with feelings, conveniently oversimplified as those of love and those of hate. For example, a wife dies. Because of her the husband felt loved, better, stronger, whole; her death comes as a personal blow, even to his own self-esteem ("narcissistic injury"). He now feels smaller, weaker, fragmented. He may feel cheated, angry, and desirous of lashing out. For all his hostile feelings toward her he now feels guilt, probably in proportion to his negative feelings ("I might have been angry, but I wouldn't have wished this for her in a million years"). In the classic view of Freud (1917), the libido invested in the lost object, through the process of mourning, was freed to allow the survivor to invest feeling in new love objects. Despite impressions given by some theorists, investment in the lost person is not forsaken. Rather, a progressive clarification of the attachment seems to occur, until both positive and negative feelings toward the dead person are restored to a realistic balance and the lost one is viewed with more perspective. In this clarification process, the survivor puts in perspective his own role and value in the relationship, thereby restoring his own damaged self-esteem.

Being Helpful to Those in Mourning

No less than the dying, mourners are outcasts of society. Their presence is painful to many who surround them, and efforts to silence, impede, or stop mourning are common. Most societies and subcultures have rituals for beginning the process of mourning, such as wakes or *shivah*,

funerals, and burial services. These rituals have significant values (see Cassem, 1976): (1) They provide an occasion for the gathering of the social network of support that surrounds the family unit. (2) Those gathered activate important memories about the deceased, sometimes providing the bereaved with information and relationships not previously known. (3) Tributes paid to the dead person emphasize both his worth and the fact that he is worth the pain and stress of grieving. (4) Family units may be drawn closer together. (5) Rituals permit expression of sorrow, set some limits on grieving, and provide legitimate outlets for expressing positive feelings. (6) Rituals reemphasize the reality that the deceased person is dead and gone, often by providing a view of the body (failure to see the dead body generally retards grieving). (7) The funeral permits other people in the community to pay their respects and initiate their own grieving. (8) Death rituals for the community provide occasions to grieve for losses unrelated to the deceased, a chance to continue unfinished mourning. (9) Rosenblatt (1975) presents cross-cultural evidence from seventy-eight societies that overt expressions of anger following a death are less common where ritualists deal with the body up to and during burial. (10) Because the bereaved generally remember nonverbal expressions of concern and affection more clearly than verbal expressions, rituals provide the formal occasion to bring others into the mourners' presence.

The task of the mourner is threefold: first, to experience and reflect upon his feelings toward the lost object during life and the feelings evoked by death; second, to review the history of the attachment; and third, to examine his own wounds, attend to their healing, and confront the task of continuing without the lost object. To help the bereaved, one need only facilitate the three parts in this process.

Allowing the bereaved to express feelings is essential. The most important part of this process is to avoid the maneuvers that nullify grieving. Clichés ("It's God's will"), self-evident but irrelevant reassurances ("After all, you've got three other children"), and outright exhortations to stop grieving ("Life must go on") should be carefully avoided. Some acquaintance with the nature of mourning is helpful, because many of the expressions of pain or seemingly aberrant behavior are necessary elements in the searching-disorganization-reorganization process. Tolerance of reversals from cheerful to grief-stricken feelings during the reorganization phase is essential.

Presence means more than words. Above all, the friend who can remain calm and quiet in the presence of a weeping or angry or bitter mourner is highly valued. Embarrassment only increases the discomfort of the grieving person. A touch can be worth a thousand words, as can moist eyes or a quiet tear. Friends who arrive at the home of the bereaved with food, or offer to take the children on an outing, or make some other tangible gesture do more than those who ask to be called if anything is needed.

Sharing memories may help complete the memories of the deceased. The bereaved may be helped by looking through old photograph albums or collections of letters as they try to put the lost person into perspective. Persevering patience over the long haul is essential. Many acquaintances disappear after the funeral and burial rituals. Those who can continue to visit make a great difference. Letters or notes are valued by mourners. Anniversaries are key foci in the grieving trajectory. Special attention to the bereaved on that day is part of the most basic care of mourners.

Return to activity is usually an essential feature of the recovery process, both because it brings the mourner back into contact with concerned fellow workers and because the therapeutic effects of work on self-esteem help repair the narcissistic injury of the loss. Most bereaved persons benefit from returning to work within three to six weeks after the death of a loved one. Self-help groups continue to be among the most effective modalities for permitting expression of emotion, demonstrating that bereavement and its feelings are universal and supplying the compassion and respect necessary for rebuilding self-esteem. The prototype for these groups is the widow-to-widow program (Silverman et al., 1974).

Reading can sometimes help bereaved persons. Often the most consoling books are stories of persons sustaining tragic losses, such as Anne Morrow Lindbergh's (1973) or C. S. Lewis's (1961). Edgar Jackson's *You and Your Grief* (1966), written for the bereaved family, provides helpful directives.

Sudden Death

Death with time to prepare is difficult enough, but sudden death inflicts a unique trauma on the survivors. Death on arrival at the hospital, stillbirth, sudden infant death, accidental or traumatic death, sudden cardiac arrest, death during or after surgery, murder, suicide—each carries its own set of horrors for the survivors, and in them the shock of death is dramatically intensified. Guilt is likely to be a much more serious problem because of the total absence of any preparation or opportunity to "do things right." Where violence and disfigurement are present, these feelings will be even further intensified.

General rules for dealing with the bereaved apply here, with certain specific emphases.

1. The chance to view the body, even when mutilated, should be offered to the family members. If severe mutilation is present, the family should be very carefully warned; they should be told that the body is disfigured and that they may wish not to view it but may do so if they desire. In addition, a chance to do something for the body can at times be very helpful to a survivor who has had no chance to do anything. Some funeral directors offer parents of children who have died suddenly the opportunity to wash and prepare the child's body for burial or to help in this procedure; most parents accept and benefit greatly from this opportunity. The need to view the body is greater when death is sudden.

2. Patience with the prolonged numbness or shock of the family is an essential feature of their care.

3. Physical needs can be attended to and may be the only avenue of communication. Leading the family to a quiet room, providing comfortable seats, bringing coffee, and other little acts of kindness performed in a compassionate and quiet way are helpful.

4. The numb survivor may also benefit from very gentle questions that help to review the last hours of the deceased. This review starts the

searching process and leads to areas where guilt is present. What happened? Were there any prodromal symptoms? Any premonitions? Who saw him last? Families who do not wish to explore these crucial questions at the time should not be pushed.

Later issues are very similar to those mentioned above. The questions of guilt are usually more agonizing. The day may be relived thousands of times. In certain cases of sudden death, specific conflicts should be kept in mind. Parents stricken by a sudden infant death should receive all the available standard information on this syndrome, in which careful explanations emphasize that the causes are unknown and the usual self-accusations about what could have been done are groundless. Survivors of a murder victim often experience retaliatory murderous fury (sometimes unconsciously). Fear of not being able to control vindictive aggression can amount to panic in some individuals, with an inability to identify the feeling. Survivors of a suicide victim are often the victims of an angry gesture and frequently must cope with their own hatred of the victim.

The main handicap for professionals is lack of an opportunity to develop a relationship with the survivors prior to the death of the victim. It is a time when close friends and relatives need to be mobilized.

Anticipatory Grief

Lindemann (1944) uses the term *anticipatory grief* to refer to a special case of separation in which death is assumed and later found to be untrue—a husband missing in action in World War II, for example. Having gone through the phases of grief, the mourner in this situation can be at a disadvantage if the lost person returns, for the grief work may have been done so well that she finds herself freed of her attachment to the love object and unready to receive him back. Since that time, the term has come to signify the reaction experienced in the face of an impending loss. Sudden death provides no opportunity for anticipatory grief. On the other hand, Parkes (1970) points out that most of the widows he has studied knew in advance that they would lose a husband. Aldrich (1974) notes several differences between anticipatory and conventional grief. First, anticipatory grief is shared by both the patient or victim and the family, whereas conventional grief is experienced by the bereaved alone. Second, anticipatory grief has a distinct end point in the physical loss of death, whereas conventional grief may be prolonged for years. Third, the pattern of the two types may be different, with anticipatory grief often accelerating as death nears and conventional grief beginning at a high level of intensity and gradually decelerating. Fourth, hostile feelings toward the (about-to-be) lost person differ in the two states. If the lost person is still alive, as in anticipatory grief, the survivor's negative feelings tend to be experienced as more dangerous. Fifth, hope can accompany anticipatory grief in a way that it cannot once death has occurred. Finally, the question arises whether anticipatory grief can make conventional grief unnecessary or whether the work of mourning be accomplished before death occurs. It is a fact that where anticipatory grief is possible, the intensity of the feelings of loss may actually decelerate as death draws nearer. In this case, death itself is viewed as increasingly acceptable. On the other hand, Aldrich notes that the sample of Cocoanut Grove bereaved appeared to accomplish their mourning more quickly than did the sample of Parkes's widows (1970). No evidence can as yet satisfactorily answer the question of whether unexpected loss requires longer grieving than an anticipated loss.

Weisman (1974) reminds us of the importance of viewing grief and love as mirror images of each other. Each enhances the other. Rochlin (1965) has argued in detail that the powerful dynamic impetus produced by our losses is indispensable to emotional maturation. Mourning can lead to some of man's highest achievements as well as result in many pathological states when delayed or unresolved.

Difficulties of Caregivers

Cultural taboos spare no one from their subtle pressures. The "American way of not dying" (Paul Ramsey's phrase) pervades the population. Even in the major arenas where death now occurs—general hospitals, nursing homes, and chronic-care facilities—staff members may become uncomfortable at the mere mention of death. Health professionals who attend the dying are not immune to bedside discomfort. Glaser and Strauss (1965), in a careful study of nurses on a general hospital floor, documented that the sicker the patient was and the closer he was to death, the less time the staff spent with him. This relationship was true even though the more seriously ill patients were located closer to the nursing station. Despite a consensus that dying persons fear abandonment, avoidance of them is the rule rather than the exception.

Why does the doctor tend to avoid some dying patients or, if he does not avoid them, remain quite ill at ease in their presence? Encounters with dying persons generally represent either a personal threat to the professional or a threat to his relationships. A personal threat can arise from exposure to serious disability or dying. "There is to be no mention of the word *death* here" can represent a denial that death will ever claim the doctor. The surgeon who says, "There can be no such order as 'DNR' [Do Not Resuscitate]," may be denying that failure is possible in the struggle against death. Avoidance of paralyzed or disfigured patients may protect the physician from the realization that the same fate could befall him. As mentioned earlier, absorbing and responding to a dying person's plight is very difficult; compassion can impose a heavy burden on the sympathetic professional. "I don't think I can take another story like the one I just heard" expresses a familiar and realistic worry.

A dying person poses a threat to the professional's own human attachments. First of all, the doctor is reminded that death means loss of the relationship with the patient himself, and of all the investment and caring that has gone into it. Secondly, imminent loss of a patient reminds the professional of his own past losses and of threatened ones. Care of a dying woman, for example, can recall the death (real or feared) of a mother, sister, or spouse. Wounds of an incompletely grieved loss are reopened. Losses in one's life are not discrete; they are cumulative. Those who care for the dying sustain repeated bereavement.

Because of the repeated stresses posed by these threats, professionals develop defenses. One course is to avoid involvement with patients in order to minimize personal loss or discomfort.

This is the probable source of fixed "styles" of relating to patients. For example, the physician who follows the initial communication of the diagnosis to the patient with a standardized, nonstop monologue detailing diagnosis, treatment, and course of the disease is not trying to baffle, overwhelm, or lose the patient altogether but rather to minimize his own anxiety by handling every initial "bad news" session the same way. Intellectualization, discussing the dying person mainly as an interesting "problem" or "case," functions protectively as well. Some professionals say of the patient that he "can't take it," which is often a projection of their own fear. Further examples would illustrate other defense mechanisms; what is important is that physician discomfort and avoidance arise mainly from instincts of self-defense rather than from any desire to alienate or harm the patient.

Criticism of physicians tends to be widespread and can generate unfortunate hostilities. A common accusation is that doctors are more afraid of death than other people and entered medicine for that reason. Sophisticated critics refer to Feifel's 1965 study of physician attitudes toward death, which shows that physicians spent significantly less time in conscious thought about death than did two control groups of other professionals. Feifel et al. (1967) have also demonstrated more fearfulness of death in medical students than in two control samples. Patient dissatisfaction with doctors' communication patterns, their avoidance mechanisms, and their manner in the sickroom compounds the alienation of dying patient and physician.

In response to such criticism some physicians have become defensive or even hostile themselves. When forced to assume the adversary role, the doctor is at a distinct disadvantage. The physician as well as those who work with him might be helped by keeping certain reflections in mind. Although everyone is fascinated with death, physicians grapple with it more frequently than others and are sought out by those who wish to prevent or postpone it. Conflict or discomfort in the presence of death is intensified by the combination of two factors: frequent exposure and high responsibility. The findings of Feifel et al. (1967) may also be accounted for by the increased exposure of medical students to death and to the widespread belief of the population that the physician is the last barrier against it. Natural disappointment that a terminally ill person cannot be saved can lead to resentment. As one who could not reverse the illness, the doctor may become the object of some or all of the family's resentment and blame. Finally, those who accuse doctors of inability to communicate with dying patients seem to forget that everyone has difficulties in this regard, including the patients' families.

What can be done to decrease the defensiveness of the physician? In addition to enjoying the exercise of greater responsibility in helping prevent or postpone death, doctors pay for this privilege by stronger feelings of failure and guilt when their hopes and the patient's are disappointed. Colleagues or coworkers of an oncologist who is particularly gruff will accomplish much more with a sympathetic approach than with a hostile one—"It must be difficult to work with patients whose illnesses always have such poor odds for cure or recovery." Or one might say to the surgeon after an untimely failure, "It's been a tough day, but you did everything you could." Such sympathetic comments have the greatest likelihood of turning tense situations into mutually supportive ones. Finally, more systematic efforts need be undertaken to help health personnel who work on the front lines deal with their own feelings about suffering, disappointment, failure, and death. Ideally this process should begin early in training, so that the repeated exposure to traumatic experiences can be accompanied by emotional growth with its major features, compassion and equanimity.

Fear of Death in Nondying Persons

In 1915, after Freud's original statement that death has no representation in the unconscious, an oversimplified interpretation of psychoanalytic theory tended to translate fear of death as fear of castration. In fact Fenichel, interpreting Freud, stated, "It is questionable whether there is any such thing as a normal fear of death; actually the idea of one's own death is subjectively inconceivable, and therefore probably every fear of death covers other unconscious ideas" (1945), pp. 208–209). Contemporary literature emphasizes the opposite—that fear of death motivates a large portion of every human's behavior, generating multiple activities aimed at avoiding or denying mortality (Becker, 1973). Meyer (1975) has explored the relationship of many neurotic anxieties to underlying fears of death. The tendency to diagnose the neurosis of our era as thanatophobia conveys erroneously that no one faces death with equanimity. Sheps (1957) has actually asserted that a terminal patient who failed to show marked anxiety was denying fear of death. Weisman (1972) points out the "tendentious fallacy" involved here, reminding us that acceptance of death without denial is not only a possible but a frequent occurrence. When suspecting a neurotic fear of death, the clinician should explore for guilt, masochism, and dependency, with close attention to the social function of the symptom (death fear).

Death is often viewed as the ultimate punishment. Hostile and erotic feelings or deeds are usually what the patient believes have earned this fate. One year after marriage, for instance, a young woman experienced the onset of panic states in which she thought death was imminent. Work with her revealed these attacks were immediately preceded by an impulse to seek a sexual relationship with a man other than her husband. When panic-stricken, however, she was unable to leave the house. Her panic state actually protected her from acting out her impulse, serving a useful psychic function.

Masochistically inclined persons may also speak of a horror of death. Prolonged, detailed, florid, or melodramatic descriptions of pain and suffering are clues to the masochistic trait. For example, a middle-aged woman with a diagnosis of terminal carcinoma was admitted to a chronic hospital to die. She spoke at great length of her imminent demise, the repeated and terrible tragedies throughout her entire life, and her fear of death. One physician, skeptical of the diagnosis, investigated further. Thorough workup revealed no trace of malignancy; on receiving the news of misdiagnosis, the patient became profoundly depressed at the prospect of discharge. Although her voiced fears also brought her attention (secondary gain), she clearly talked of misery with enthusiasm (primary gain).

For other individuals, a specific death neurosis, such as cardiac neurosis, which preoccupies them with the possibility of sudden death, becomes the justification for a regressive withdrawal to infantile dependency. Cardiac disease (or a heart attack) can be an honorable excuse for abandoning adult responsibilities. These patients' frequent verbal reminders that sudden death is only hours or moments away permits them to tyrannize their families—"Don't stay home on my account; of course, I may not be here when you return." Here the expression of fear functions to justify the patient's helplessness, while maintaining nearly complete control of his family's services. The problems of living are so complicated and overwhelming for some persons that preoccupation with death becomes a welcome diversion. Ruminating about death is easier than shouldering the burdens of life.

When the shadow of death indicates that life is now measured, life and time become more precious. Deeper meanings and clearer priorities often emerge for the dying person, who can no longer afford to postpone opportunities. He must make the most of his time. Those who care for persons confronting death or its consequences share the opportunity to examine what makes a life meaningful. Sharing burdens, insights, and support, patient and professional are given a chance to absorb and pursue these discoveries together.

References

Adler, G. 1973. Hospital treatment of borderline patients. *Am. J. Psychiatry* 130:32–35.

Aitken-Swan, J., and E. C. Easson. 1959. Reactions of cancer patients on being told their diagnosis. *Br. Med. J.* 1:779–783.

Aldrich, C. K. 1974. Some dynamics of anticipatory grief. In *Anticipatory grief*, ed. B. Schoenberg, A. C. Carr, A. H. Kutscher, D. Peretz, and I. Goldberg. New York: Columbia University Press.

Allport, G. 1958. *The nature of prejudice*. New York: Doubleday.

Anthony, S. 1940. *The child's discovery of death*. New York: Harcourt, Brace.

Barraclough, B. M., and M. Shea. 1970. Suicide and samaritan clients. *Lancet* 2:868–870.

Beck, A. T. 1963. Thinking and depression: I. Idiosyn-cratic content and cognitive distortions. *Arch. Gen. Psychiatry* 9:324–335.

——— 1967. *Depression: clinical, experimental, and theoretical aspects*. New York: Harper & Row, Hoeber Medical Division.

Beck, A. T., M. Kovacs, and A. Weisman. 1975. Hopelessness and suicidal behavior. *J.A.M.A.* 234:1146–49.

Beck, A. T., D. Schuyler, and I. Herman. 1974. Development of suicidal intent scales. In *The prediction of suicide*, ed. A. T. Beck, H. L. P. Resnik, and D. J. Lettieri. Bowie, Md.: Charles Press.

Becker, E. 1973. *The denial of death*. New York: Free Press.

Bowlby, J. 1961. Processes of mourning. *Int. J. Psychoanal.* 42:317–340.

Cassem, N. H. 1976. The first three steps beyond the grave. In *Acute grief and the funeral*, ed. V. R. Pine, A. H. Kutscher, D. Peretz, R. C. Slater, R. De-Bellis, R. J. Volk, and D. J. Cherico. Springfield, Ill.: Thomas.

Cassem, N. H., and T. P. Hackett. 1975. Stress on the nurse and therapist in the intensive care unit and the coronary care unit. *Heart Lung* 4:252–259.

Cassem, N. H., and R. S. Stewart. 1975. Management and care of the dying patient. *Int. J. Psychiatry Med.* 6:293–304.

Clayton, P. J. 1974. Mortality and morbidity in the first year of widowhood. *Arch. Gen. Psychiatry* 30:747–750.

Clayton, P. J., L. Desmarais, and G. Winokur. 1968. A study of normal bereavement. *Am. J. Psychiatry* 125:168–178.

Croog, S. H., D. S. Shapiro, and S. Levine. 1971. Denial among male heart patients. *Psychosom. Med.* 33:385–397.

Delong, W., and E. Robins. 1961. The communication of suicidal intent prior to psychiatric hospitalization: a study of 87 patients. *Am. J. Psychiatry* 117:695–705.

Deutsch, F. 1933. Euthanasia, a clinical study. *Psychoanal. Q.* 5:347–368.

Easson, W. M. 1970. *The dying child*. Springfield, Ill.: Thomas.

Eissler, K. 1955. *The psychiatrist and the dying patient*. New York: International Universities Press.

Engel, G. L. 1961. Is grief a disease? *Psychosom. Med.* 23:18–22.

Evans, A. E. 1968. If a child must die. *N. Engl. J. Med.* 278:138–142.

Farberow, N. L., and E. S. Schneidman, eds. 1965. *The cry for help*. New York: McGraw-Hill.

Farberow, N. L., E. S. Schneidman, and C. V. Leonard. 1963. Suicide among general medical and surgical hospital patients with malignant neoplasms. *Med. Bull. Veterans Admin.* MB-9:1–11.

Fawcett, J. 1972. Suicidal depression and physical illness. *J.A.M.A.* 219:1303–06.

Feagin, J. R. 1964. Prejudice and religious types: a focused study of Southern fundamentalists. *J. Sci. Study Religion* 4:3–13.

Feifel, H. 1965. The function of attitudes toward death. In *Death and dying: attitudes of patient and doctor. Group Adv. Psychiatry* symp. 11, 5:633–641.

—— 1974. Religious conviction and fear of death among the healthy and the terminally ill. *J. Sci. Study Religion* 31:353–360.

Feifel, H., ed. 1959. *The meaning of death.* New York: McGraw-Hill.

Feifel, H., S. Hanson, R. Jones, and L. Edwards. 1967. Physicians consider death. In *Proceedings of the 75th Annual Convention of the American Psychological Association,* ed. E. Vinacke et al. Vol. 2.

Fenichel, O. 1945. *The psychoanalytic theory of neuroses.* New York: Norton.

Freud, S. 1915. Thoughts for the times on war and death. In *Standard edition,* ed. J. Strachey. Vol. 14. London: Hogarth Press, 1957.

—— 1917. Mourning and melancholia. In *Standard edition,* ed. J. Strachey. Vol. 14. London: Hogarth Press, 1949.

—— 1920. Beyond the pleasure principle. In *Standard edition,* ed. J. Strachey. Vol. 18. London: Hogarth Press, 1955.

—— 1923. The ego and the id. In *Standard edition,* ed. J. Strachey. Vol. 19. London: Hogarth Press, 1961.

Gerlé, B., G. Lunden, and P. Sandblom. 1960. The patient with inoperable cancer from the psychiatric and social standpoints. *Cancer* 13:1206–17.

Gifford, S. 1969. Some psychoanalytic theories about death: a selective historical review. *Ann. N.Y. Acad. Sci.* 164:638–668.

Gilbertsen, V. A., and O. H. Wangensteen. 1962. Should the doctor tell the patient that the disease is cancer? In *The physician and the total care of the cancer patient.* New York: American Cancer Society.

Glaser, B. G., and A. L. Strauss. 1965. *Awareness of dying.* Chicago: Aldine.

Goldberg, I. K., S. Malitz, and A. H. Kutscher, eds. 1973. *Psychopharmacologic agents for the terminally ill and bereaved.* New York: Columbia University Press.

Grollman, E. A. 1970. *Talking about death.* Boston: Beacon Press.

Grollman, E. A., ed. 1967. *Explaining death to children.* Boston: Beacon Press.

Hackett, T. P., and A. D. Weisman. 1962. The treatment of the dying. *Curr. Psychiatr. Ther.* 2:121–126.

Harris, A. 1965. *Why did he die?* Minneapolis: Lerner.

Hinton, J. 1967. *Dying.* Baltimore: Penguin Books.

Holmes, T. H., and R. H. Rahe. 1967. The social readjustment rating scale. *J. Psychosom. Res.* 11:213–218.

Jackson, E. N. 1965. *Telling a child about death.* New York: Channel Press.

—— 1966. *You and your grief.* New York: Channel Press.

Jacobson, E. 1938. *Progressive relaxation.* Chicago: University of Chicago Press.

Jones, E. 1957. *The life and work of Sigmund Freud.* Vol. 3. New York: Basic Books.

Kast, E. C. 1966. LSD and the dying patient. *Chicago Med. Sch. Q.* 26:80–87.

Kelly, W. D., and S. R. Friesen. 1950. Do cancer patients want to be told? *Surgery* 27:822–826.

Kennell, J. H., H. Slyter, and M. H. Klaus. 1970. The mourning response of parents to the death of a newborn infant. *N. Engl. J. Med.* 283:344–349.

Kübler-Ross, E. 1969. *On death and dying.* New York: Macmillan.

—— 1974. *Questions and answers on death and dying.* New York: Macmillan.

Kurland, A. A., S. Grof, W. N. Pahnke, and L. E. Goodman. 1973. Psychedelic drug-assisted psychotherapy in patients with terminal cancer. In *Psychopharmacologic agents for the terminally ill and bereaved,* ed. I. K. Goldberg, S. Malitz, and A. H. Kutscher. New York: Columbia University Press.

Kutscher, A. H., B. Schoenberg, and A. C. Carr. 1973. *The terminal patient: oral care.* New York: Columbia University Press.

LeShan, L. and E. 1961. Psychotherapy and the patient with a limited life span. *Psychiatry* 24:318–323.

Lester, D. 1972a. The myth of suicide prevention. *Compr. Psychiatry* 13:555–560.

—— 1972b. Religious behaviors and attitudes toward death. In *Death and presence,* ed. A. Godin. Brussels: Lumen Vitae Press.

Lewis, C. S. 1961. *A grief observed.* Greenwich, Conn.: Seabury Press.

Lindbergh, A. M. 1973. *Hour of gold, hour of lead.* New York: Harcourt, Brace.

Lindemann, E. 1944. Symptomatology and management of acute grief. *Am. J. Psychiatry* 101:141–148.

Litman, R. E. 1966. The prevention of suicide. In *Current psychiatric therapies,* ed. J. H. Masserman. Vol. 6. New York: Grune & Stratton.

Litman, R. E., N. L. Farbérow, C. I. Wold, and T. R. Brown. 1974. Prediction models of suicidal behaviors. In *The prediction of suicide,* ed. A. T. Beck,

H. L. P. Resnik, and D. J. Lettieri. Bowie, Md.: Charles Press.

Magni, K. G. 1972. The fear of death. In *Death and presence*, ed. A. Godin. Brussels: Lumen Vitae Press.

Maltzberger, J. T., and D. H. Buie. 1974. Countertransference hate in treatment of suicidal patients. *Arch. Gen. Psychiatry* 30:625–633.

Marks, R. M., and E. J. Sachar. 1973. Undertreatment of medical inpatients with narcotic analgesics. *Ann. Intern. Med.* 78:173–181.

Menninger, K. A. 1938. *Man against himself*. New York: Harcourt, Brace.

Meyer, J. E. 1975. *Death and neurosis*. New York: International Universities Press.

Michaelson, M. G. 1974. Death as a friendly onion. *New York Times Book Review*, 21 July 1974, pp. 6–8.

Murphy, G. E. 1975a. The physician's responsibility for suicide. I. An error of commission. *Ann. Intern. Med.* 82:301–304.

—— 1975b. The physician's responsibility for suicide. II. Errors of omission. *Ann. Intern. Med.* 82:305–309.

Nagy, M. H. 1948. The child's view of death. *J. Genet. Psychol.* 73:3–27.

Natterson, J. M., and A. G. Knudson. 1960. Observations concerning fear of death in fatally ill children and their mothers. *Psychosom. Med.* 22:456–465.

Parkes, C. M. 1970. The first year of bereavement: a longitudinal study of the reaction of London widows to the death of their husbands. *Psychiatry* 33: 444–467.

—— 1972. *Bereavement: studies of grief in adult life*. New York: International Universities Press.

Peck, R. 1966. "The development of the concept of death in selected male children." Doctoral dissertation, New York University.

Portz, A. 1972. The child's sense of death. In *Death and presence*, ed. A. Godin. Brussels: Lumen Vitae Press.

Rado, S. 1956. *Psychoanalysis of behavior*. New York: Grune & Stratton.

Raimbault, G. 1972. Listening to sick children. In *Death and presence*, ed. A. Godin. Brussels: Lumen Vitae Press.

Rees, W. D. 1970. "The hallucinatory and paranormal reactions of bereavement." M.D. thesis.

Rees, W. D., and S. G. Lutkins. 1967. Mortality of bereavement. *Br. Med. J.* 4:13–16.

Reich, P., and M. J. Kelly. 1976. Suicide attempts by hospitalized medical and surgical patients. *N. Engl. J. Med.* 294:298–301.

Rochlin, G. 1965. *Griefs and discontents: the forces of change*. Boston: Little, Brown.

—— 1967. How younger children view death in themselves. In *Explaining death to children*, ed. E. A. Grollman. Boston: Beacon Press.

—— 1973. *Man's aggression*. Boston: Gambit.

Rosenblatt, P. C. 1975. Uses of ethnography in understanding grief and mourning. In *Bereavement: its psychosocial aspects*, ed. B. Schoenberg, I. Gerber, A. Wiener, A. H. Kutscher, D. Peretz, and A. C. Carr. New York: Columbia University Press.

Safier, G. 1964. A study in relationships between the life and death concepts in children. *J. Genet. Psychol.* 105:283–294.

Sallen, S. E., N. E. Zinberg, and E. Frei, III. 1975. Antiemetic effect of delta-9-tetrahydro-cannabinol in patients receiving cancer chemotherapy. *N. Engl. J. Med.* 293:795–797.

Saunders, C. 1959. Care of the dying: the problem of euthanasia, 1–6. *Nurs. Times* 55:960–961, 994–995, 1031–32, 1067–69, 1091–92, 1129–30.

—— 1969. The moment of truth: care of the dying person. In *Death and dying*, ed. L. Pearson. Cleveland: Case Western Reserve University Press.

Sawyer, J. B., H. S. Sudak, and S. R. Hall. 1972. A follow-up study of 53 suicides known to a suicide prevention center. *Life-Threatening Behav.* 2:227–238.

Schneidman, E. S. 1975. Suicide. In *Comprehensive textbook of psychiatry*, ed. A. M. Freedman, H. I. Kaplan, and B. J. Sadock. Vol. 2. 2nd ed. Baltimore: Williams & Wilkins.

Schowalter, J. E. 1970. Death and the pediatric house officer. *J. Pediatr.* 76:706–710.

Sheps, J. 1957. Management of fear in chronic disease. *J. Am. Geriatr. Soc.* 5:793–797.

Silverman, P., D. MacKenzie, M. Pettipas, and E. Wilson, eds. 1974. *Helping each other in widowhood*. New York: Health Sciences.

Simonton, O. C. and S. 1974. Management of the emotional aspects of malignancy. Paper presented at the symposium New Dimensions of Habilitation for the Handicapped, held by the Florida Department of Health and Rehabilitative Services, 14–15 June 1974, at the University of Florida–Gainsville.

Spinetta, J. J. 1974. The dying child's awareness of death: a review. *Psychol. Bull.* 81:256–260.

Spinetta, J. J., D. Rigler, and M. Karon. 1974. Personal space as a measure of a dying child's sense of isolation. *J. Consult. Clin. Psychol.* 42:751–756.

Stein, S. B. 1974. *About dying: a book for parents and children*. New York: Walker.

Steiner, G. 1965. "Children's concepts of life and death: a developmental study." Doctoral dissertation, Columbia University.

Stevens, S. 1973. *Death comes home*. New York: Morehouse-Barlow.

Surman, O. S., J. K. Gottlieb, T. P. Hackett, and E. L. Silverberg. 1973. Hypnosis in the treatment of warts. *Arch. Gen. Psychiatry* 28:439–441.

Toch, R. 1964. Management of the child with a fatal disease. *Clin. Pediatr.* 3:418–427.

Waechter, E. 1972. Children's reaction to fatal illness. In *Death and presence*, ed. A. Godin. Brussels: Lumen Vitae Press.

Weiner, I. W. 1969. The effectiveness of a suicide prevention program. *M.H.* 53:357–363.

Weiner, J. M. 1970. Attitudes of pediatricians toward the care of fatally ill children. *J. Pediatr.* 76:700–705.

Weisman, A. D. 1971. Is suicide a disease? *Life-Threatening Behav.* 1:219–231.

———— 1972. *On dying and denying*. New York: Behavioral Publications.

———— 1974. Is mourning necessary? In *Anticipatory grief*, ed. B. Schoenberg, A. C. Carr, A. H. Kutscher, D. Peretz, and I. K. Goldberg. New York: Columbia University Press.

Weisman, A. D., and T. P. Hackett. 1961. Predilection to death: death and dying as a psychiatric problem. *Psychosom. Med.* 23:232–256.

Weisman, A. D., and W. J. Worden. 1972. Risk-rescue rating in suicide assessment. *Arch. Gen. Psychiatry* 26:553–560.

World Health Organization. 1968. *The prevention of suicide*. Geneva.

Yudkin, S. 1967. Children and death. *Lancet* 1:37–41.

Zilboorg, G. 1937. Considerations on suicide, with particular reference to that of the young. *Am. J. Orthopsychiatry* 7:15–31.

———— 1938. The sense of immortality. *Psychoanal. Q.* 7:171–199.

Zung, W. W. K. 1974. Index of potential suicide (IPS): a rating scale for suicide prevention. In *The prediction of suicide*, ed. A. T. Beck, H. L. P. Resnick, and D. J. Lettieri. Bowie, Md.: Charles Press.

PART SIX

Psychiatry and Society

Psychiatric Epidemiology

CHAPTER 29

Morton Beiser

P SYCHIATRIC EPIDEMIOLOGY is the study of mental illness and mental health in whole populations. Whereas biochemists and neurophysiologists are concerned with microscopic aspects of human behavior, and clinicians, with similarities and differences among individuals and small groups, psychiatric epidemiologists address their attention to macroscopic questions such as how society and culture affect mental health.

Orientation to the Field

Two current definitions of epidemiology—one narrow and one broad—suggest the evolving nature of the field and also hint at the kinds of changes taking place within it. Webster's definition of epidemiology as "a medical specialty treating of epidemics" is a narrow one. When the field was still new, its practitioners were almost exclusively concerned with the study of sudden outbreaks of disease in populations (the classical definition of "epidemic"), and this limited definition would have been acceptable. Today, many

The research for this chapter was accomplished while the author was a Macy Faculty Scholar, 1974–75.

epidemiologists still study epidemic illnesses with the goal of identifying factors relating to their onset and persistence. Once these factors are identified, control may become possible, either by ameliorating conditions that produce illness or by enhancing those that promote resistance.

An event known as the Broad Street Pump Incident provides one the of the most famous examples of an epidemiological inquiry giving rise to an effective public health program. An outbreak of cholera in the Golden Square area of London in August and September of 1848 prompted John Snow to study the pattern and distribution of the disease (Snow, 1855). By means of a carefully constructed map on which he plotted the distribution of cases, Snow was able to demonstrate that the outbreak had a geographical center—a common water pump in London's Broad Street. Next, Snow noted that two groups —first, the inmates of an institution and, second, employees of a brewery—did not develop illnesses according to the epidemic pattern, even though they were in the heart of the epidemic area. Each group had its own wells, and the brewery employees probably did not drink water at work since they were allowed a daily ration of their product. The first observation raised a strong suspicion about the source of contamination, and the second provided enough confirmation to lead to a dismantling of the Broad Street pump. The epidemic was brought under control (but there is no documentation about the effect, if any, of this experience on English views regarding temperance).

This example demonstrates two salient characteristics of the field. First, Snow formulated his ideas about the spread of cholera before the specific microorganism, *Vibrio cholerae*, had been identified. (Pasteur's great work leading to the germ theory of disease was not to begin for another decade.) Despite this limitation, Snow was able to recommend effective action. In actual practice, this pattern is not unusual. Epidemiological inquiry usually produces data about association among variables, rather than a definitive understanding of process. Though only partial knowledge, the data may nonetheless suggest methods of control. Second, Snow's studies were not "pure" science. They were carried out in order to control a threatening health situation. A strong element of applied science thus also characterizes epidemiology.

In recent years, epidemics in the usual sense of the term have become less common, at least in industrialized societies. Rather, the "diseases of civilization," such as cancer and arteriosclerotic heart disease, have come to demand more attention by medical scientists, and this new sociomedical priority has had its effect on epidemiology. Not only have the boundaries of the field broadened to include a focus on chronic illness, but a major conceptual shift has taken place regarding the nature of illness.

For a number of years, the field of epidemiology was dominated by the notion that each disease had one overwhelming cause. This model, based on the discovery of the role of microorganisms in disease, gained a great deal of popularity; many infectious illnesses did become treatable once the causal bacteria and viruses could be isolated. Success, however, was by no means universal; not every illness behaved as the model predicted it should. In tuberculosis, one of the notable examples, mycobacteria could indeed be identified, but relating them to what happened clinically was difficult. First of all, some individuals were apparently infected but did not become ill. Furthermore, people who contracted the disease showed widely varying clinical courses: some died, some recovered, and some had a prolonged course of remissions and exacerbations. Because tuberculosis and other conditions did not fit neatly with the single-cause theory, a number of scientists began to reemphasize the importance of host and environmental factors in illness. The concept that illnesses have a "multifactorial etiology" was gradually (and in some quarters, grudgingly) accepted as a replacement for the notion of a single, overwhelming cause.

Modern epidemiology has been influenced by these two developments—an interest in chronic illnesses and a search for multiple etiological factors. Webster's definition of the field does not take these developments into account. A broader definition is needed to describe the field more accurately. Epidemiology is a field of inquiry dealing with the health and disease of populations and groups in relation to their environment and ways of living.

The Special Case of Psychiatric Epidemiology

The field of psychiatric epidemiology is still very young. While men have been concerned about mental aberrations since ancient times, the systematic counting of episodes of illness with a view toward their control is largely a twentieth-century phenomenon. As usual, however, some of the great figures were ahead of their time. Esquirol, for example, counted hospital admissions in Paris from 1786 to 1836 and found a fourfold increase in patients, which he attributed to an improvement in facilities. Maudsley (1872) estimated that the number of mental patients in England doubled from 1840 to 1870 and suggested that the increase in numbers was caused by the Lunacy Acts passed during that period (particularly those of 1845, 1853, and 1861). The acts ensured more complete registration of mentally ill patients. They also made better care for the hospitalized mentally ill possible; because of this, patients lived longer and the numbers of "insane" on the hospital rolls increased.

Epidemics of mental disorder. The earliest publications on the epidemiology of mental disorders dealt with reactions sweeping through populations in a manner reminiscent of epidemics of infectious illness. One classic example concerns an epidemic that beset southern Italy during the seventeenth century. An uncontrollable urge to dance, called tarantism, purportedly resulted from the bite of a tarantula but more probably was a psychological reaction occurring on a mass basis. The incident left its mark in music as the tarantella, a form of very fast dance. Some observers have suggested that phenomena as apparently diverse as tarantism, the medieval outbreaks of flagellation, the mass possession of the nuns of the Ursuline Convent of London (Lewis, 1967), and, in our own day, the unusual group behavior of sects such as the snake handlers in the southern United States (La Barre, 1969) are forms of collective emotional upset.

"Epidemics" of unusual behavior are by no means confined to history or exotic peoples. Kerckhoff and Back, in a work called *The June Bug* (1968), present an excellent study of an epidemic of illness in a clothing mill in the southern United States. The illness, characterized by nausea, vague pains, and fainting, was widely attributed to the bite of an insect in a shipment of cloth from a foreign country. During the week in June when the illness reached its peak, almost half the employees experienced symptoms; some were hospitalized, and the operations of the mill nearly ground to a halt. Then, as suddenly as it had begun, the episode was over. Subsequent investigations by medical and public health experts turned up no unusual bugs or any other physical factors to explain this strange occurrence.

In their discussion of the case, the authors use the term *hysterical contagion* as an explanatory concept. They suggest that psychological tension among the employees, due partially to conditions on the job and partially to conflicts between job and home, provided the starting point for the reaction. Fear, inspired by rumors about a strange bug, became "contagious" in this atmosphere and the result was a raging, if short-lived, epidemic. Kerckhoff and Back sug-

gest that the net effect was a sort of "psychological strike" during which people managed to get temporary respite from stress and to retaliate against an unsympathetic management.

Tarantism, possession on a large scale, and the June Bug all present features that seem analogous to a true epidemic. To carry the analogy too far, however, would be a mistake. It is not at all clear, for instance, that any of these behaviors should be called an illness. Nor is it clear how a formulation such as behavioral "contagion" helps us to understand the actual process. For although people with psychiatric disturbances may affect the behavior of others, only rarely do they do so by infecting them.

These cases, though undeniably fascinating and colorful, form only a minor part of the field of psychiatric epidemiology. The bread-and-butter subjects of psychiatry—the psychoses, neuroses, psychosomatic conditions, and character disorders—have also been studied, but generally within the framework of the epidemiology of chronic illnesses.

Psychiatric disorder in a chronic illness framework. As late as the 1900s, the successive domination of psychiatry by the organic and then by the psychoanalytic schools of thought impeded the development of psychiatric epidemiology. Both organic psychiatry and psychoanalysis were characterized by a preoccupation with the individual rather than with the larger society and by an interest in a disease model, positing a basic underlying process accounting for any symptoms a patient displays. Within an organic framework, this process could be traced to an anatomical abnormality; for the psychoanalysts, it was traceable to instinctual aberrations.

Before the field of psychiatric epidemiology could mature, an adequate clinical and theoretical base had to be established, including at least three elements: (1) the idea that mental health was a public health problem as well as a clinical problem; (2) the notion that symptoms and behaviors could be studied in their own right without any a priori assumptions about underlying internal processes; and (3) recognition that contemporary experience could exert a profound influence, even on adult personality. (The last point had been convincingly demonstrated during the late eighteenth and early nineteenth centuries—the era of Pinel, Chiarugi, and the Tukes—but was too quickly forgotten.)

These three themes were introduced and developed at various times and in various places during the early part of the twentieth century. Within the psychoanalytic "inner circle" itself, Alfred Adler (1911) began to stress the importance of social forces on personality and challenged the supremacy of instinctual theory. His theoretical convictions eventually led to a rupture with Freud in 1911. At about the same time, Adolf Meyer was teaching a new generation of clinicians and researchers in the United States that the family and community played a powerful role in the genesis of illness. Meyer also challenged the notion that psychological symptoms were traceable to an underlying disease; he preferred to think of symptoms as faulty reaction patterns and recommended that they be studied in their own right (Meyer, 1958).

Child psychology and juvenile delinquency in particular were subjects of great interest during this period. In 1922, William Healy published the results of a six-year study in which he demonstrated a relationship between delinquency and socioeconomic factors and discredited the theory of defective genes or degeneracy as root causes. In related fields, men like sociologist Émile Durkheim and social psychologist George Herbert Mead made important theoretical contributions in areas relating disturbance to social psychological factors and phenomena. The introduction of intelligence testing provided the hope that similar types of instruments could be developed to measure psychological disorder on a mass basis.

The golden age of psychiatric epidemiology, at least in the United States, was finally ushered in by a major social event—World War II. In part, expansion of the field occurred because wartime conditions provided an unusual opportunity to observe large groups of healthy military and civilian populations reacting to situations that could never be simulated in more normal times. Some of the findings were unexpected. For example, several countries under direct enemy attack reported a reduction in the rate of hospitalization for psychoses among civilian populations, sug-

gesting that changes in community process affect individual chances of becoming ill with a psychosis (Hemphill, 1941; Hopkins, 1943).

Observations of soldiers under combat conditions also yielded important clinical insights. World War I introduced the term *shellshock* to clinical practice. From its original connotation of physiological upset due to actual brain damage, it changed over the years to mean, in a vague way, a reaction to the emotional stress of combat (Adrian, 1959). By the time of World War II, this theme developed more fully into concepts like Kardiner and Spiegel's "traumatic neuroses of war" (1947).

Another development, whose effect was at first less immediately apparent than theoretical modification or clinical advance, had far-reaching consequences. During the war, the selective service rejected 850,000 men as unfit because of their psychiatric problems. When discharge records were reviewed, the findings were again shocking: 43 percent of all medical discharges during World War II were for psychiatric reasons (Mora, 1959).

After the war, mental hospital and psychiatric wards of veterans' hospitals were crowded. An ominous statistic began to circulate: one out of every two hospital beds in the country was occupied by a psychiatric patient. In sum, psychiatric disorder no longer meant just a few hopeless cases. It had clearly deprived the nation of manpower at a time when it was urgently needed, and it was soon to become a drain on the postwar economy. Mental health had become a public health problem.

Working Definitions in Epidemiology

Before presenting an overview of some of the major works in psychiatric epidemiology, a review of frequently used epidemiological terms is necessary to provide some of the conceptual parameters within which studies are formulated. While the terms presented are found in the general epidemiological literature, the examples have been chosen to illustrate the application of these concepts to psychiatric phenomena.

In one way or another, all epidemiological studies are concerned with rates of occurrence of patterns of health and illness. *Prevalence* is one of the most widely used of these measures. The prevalence of a disease is its frequency at a particular time. During a given day of the year, for example, if one counted one hundred cases of depression in a community of one thousand people, the prevalence rate would be ten percent. *Incidence* refers to the number of new cases of an illness arising during a particular time period. Let us suppose that, one year later, we studied the same community and found that ten people who had not been ill at the time of the original survey had developed a depression during the year. Since 10 out of 1,000 people developed new illnesses during the time period, the incidence would be established as 1 percent. The higher the incidence of an illness, the higher will be the prevalence.

The other factor limiting prevalence rates is the *duration* of an illness. A disease like influenza may have a very high incidence rate. In our sample community, every one of the thousand inhabitants could experience at least one episode during the course of a year. A prevalence figure for any given day of the year might be low in spite of this because the recovery period from influenza is short enough that relatively few cases accumulate over a period of time. Depression, on the other hand, tends to persist. Thus, even though the incidence of depression may be quite low, prevalence rates may be high because people with the condition accumulate and a population count at any point in time will reveal a higher proportion of cases. Thus a change in prevalence may result from (1) a change in incidence; (2) a change in duration; or (3) a change in both incidence and duration.

Besides recovery, the only other way a "case" of illness will disappear from a population is through death. Highly fatal illnesses, then, might show low prevalence rates while cases of chronic illness would once again tend to accumulate. (For a more extended treatment of measurements of disease frequency, see a basic text, such as McMahon, Pugh, and Ipsen, 1960.)

The terms *true prevalence* and *treated prevalence* are also sometimes encountered. Treated prevalence refers to the number of cases of a disease at a particular time as estimated by the number of cases then in treatment. For example, one may try to estimate the prevalence of schizophrenia in a community from the number of patients hospitalized for this condition on a given day. This method, however, has obvious limitations. People may suffer from a disorder, particularly one that is psychiatric in nature, and never come into treatment; they may live too far from a treatment facility, they may be too defensive to seek treatment, or they may not see the treatment being offered as relevant to their problem. In addition, administrators may decide, for various reasons, to limit the admission of certain categories of patients to certain facilities. All of these factors distort the true picture of illness in a community.

Most treatment data cannot be used to study the cause of an illness because separating out the forces that cause an individual to become ill from those that serve to identify him as a patient is impossible. In order to overcome this limitation, studies of true prevalence have been attempted. Typically, such studies involve field surveys of entire populations or of representative samples. People included in the study population are examined and rated according to some predetermined criterion of illness, regardless of whether or not they have been in formal treatment. Examples of such studies (described later in this chapter) include those of Lin and his colleagues in Taiwan, the work of Essen-Möller and Hagnell in Sweden, Leighton's Stirling County survey, and the Midtown project carried out by Rennie and Srole. As might be expected, the rates for disorder that these studies reveal are far higher than those based on even the most comprehensive approach to treated prevalence.

Treatment data reveal relatively little about the extent of psychiatric illness, but they tell us a great deal about how a society views the care and treatment of mental patients. One way in which society removes people whose behavior it cannot or refuses to tolerate is to hospitalize them. Social judgments about the limits of tolerable behavior are not fixed; they vary over time, changing to conform to prevailing ideologies about what is expected of individuals and about the responsibility of the community to its members. Furthermore, evidence suggests that people exhibiting the same behaviors may receive different kinds of treatment, according to factors such as social position, which should be extraneous to these decisions. Treatment data, in short, act as a commentary on the society that generates them; when understood in this way, they are extremely valuable.

Morton Kramer of the National Institute of Mental Health has contributed many important studies of treated prevalence in which frequent references to *resident patient rates* are made. Kramer defines resident patients as "all those patients present in the hospital on a given day plus all those on short-term leave with the expectation that they would return within seven days" (Kramer et al., 1972, p. 19). The resident patient rate is simply a ratio, with the number of resident patients forming the numerator and the population at risk, the denominator. The resident patient rate for the entire country is the number of resident patients divided by the total population. One can also apply this concept to a subpopulation. For example, the resident rate of never-married men is the number of resident patients in this category divided by the number of men who have never been married in the general population; in comparison with other groups, the resident patient rate for this particular subpopulation is high.

Treated incidence and *true incidence* bear the same relationship to each other as do treated and true prevalence. True incidence studies are very rare, partly because ascertaining when a psychiatric disorder begins is difficult. Studies using treatment figures sidestep this issue entirely or make an implicit assumption that the time between the onset of an illness and entry into treatment does not vary much from case to case. Since the assumption is at best dubious, treated incidence data must be interpreted with caution.

Review of Some Major Studies

Epidemiological studies may be classified in many ways, for example, by dividing them into categories according to method—such as true prevalence versus treated prevalence. In practice, however, the choice of a particular method, such as a survey of treatment records versus a community survey, is not arbitrary; the method is dictated by the purpose of the study. For the following discussion of some of the major works in the field, a classification system that reflects

this pragmatic orientation seems appropriate. Six categories will be described, based on a list of uses for epidemiology suggested by Morris (1957): those that aim (1) to study historical trends; (2) to aid in planning and evaluating services; (3) to fill out the clinical picture of an illness; (4) to make a community diagnosis; (5) to study etiology; and (6) to help in developing classifications of illnesses.

Studying Historical Trends

One recurring question in psychiatry is whether the rate of mental illness is increasing or decreasing. Goldhamer and Marshall (1953) studied mental hospital admission rates in Massachusetts over the century from 1840 to 1940. On the basis of these data they concluded that the incidence of severe mental illnesses among young adults had not changed during that period, but they did note a relative increase in the number of old people with diagnoses of senile psychosis. The latter data raise a new question. Has the incidence of senile psychosis really risen, or are we, in contemporary America, more prone to hospitalize older people than were our forebears a century ago?

Goldhamer and Marshall's study is sometimes cited as evidence that the popular notion that the increasing complexity of modern life "drives people crazy" is invalid. What if, however, the effects of social stress showed up more strongly in forms other than hospitalizable illnesses, as neuroses and psychosomatic disturbances, for example, rather than as frank psychoses?

A study by Tsung-Yi Lin in Taiwan bears on this point. Lin surveyed several communities in Taiwan in the years between 1946 and 1948 and then resurveyed them, using the same techniques, fifteen years later (Lin, 1953; Lin et al., 1969). The rate for mental illnesses had almost doubled for all illnesses other than psychosis; the prevalence of psychosis showed no change or possibly even a slight drop. Had Lin studied only psychosis, his results would have looked very much like those of Goldhamer and Marshall. In fact, Lin demonstrated that the rates for minor mental disorders did vary over time, perhaps reflecting the stress of social and political upheavals in Taiwan's recent history. True prevalence data like Lin's, which can be used to study trends over time, are very rare.

Planning and Evaluating Services

We are fond of claiming that a virtual revolution in mental health care and treatment has occurred over the past twenty-five years. What kind of commentary can epidemiology offer?

First of all, we have seen significant changes in mental hospital statistics, the most obvious and dramatic of these being a decrease in total number of patients. Kramer and his colleagues (1972) report that from 1946 to 1955 the resident patient population of state and county mental hospitals had been increasing at a rate just under 2 percent per year. In 1955 an all-time peak figure of 558,922 inpatients was reached. Since that time, the numbers have steadily declined, and they are now about half what they were in 1955 (Greenblatt and Glazier, 1975).

Also, since 1955 tranquilizers have come into wide use. While assigning total credit for these changes to the spread of chemotherapy is tempting, other important developments took place as well, each of which made its contribution. Beginning in the 1950s, for example, nursing homes became increasingly popular alternatives to mental hospitals as a way of caring for the elderly mentally ill. At the present time, these nursing homes probably house more geriatric psychiatric patients than all psychiatric facilities combined (Kramer, 1970).

Another factor accounting for the decline in inpatient rates is the virtual disappearance of some types of patients who had formerly made up a large proportion of the chronic population of mental hospitals. In the 1930s and 1940s, patients with general paresis and other syphilitic diseases of the central nervous system formed a significant part of the caseload of psychiatric inpatients. The following decades witnessed the development of penicillin therapy and improved public health practices, both of which made possible the prevention of tertiary syphilis. As the remaining old patients died off in the hospitals, with no new ones taking their places, the resident population decreased.

Secular changes in the larger society have had their effect as well. The earlier decades of this century were characterized by large-scale immigration, urbanization, and industrialization in America, each of which contributed to high rates of hospitalization. The pace of all three has slackened considerably since the immediate postwar years.

The use of mental hospitals has declined, but other facilities, such as mental health clinics and psychiatric units in general hospitals, have expanded. One might expect that the availability of these new services would serve to reduce mental hospital admissions, but the facts do not bear out this prediction. Even though hospital populations are declining, the number of first admissions and readmissions is increasing. The only logical inference one can draw from this is that the new network of supportive mental health services makes it easier to plan for earlier discharge and in this way militates against a rise in the inpatient census (Orlinski and D'Elia, 1964).

Tranquilizers, of course, also make planning for earlier discharge easier, and this fact confounds the problem of sorting out the respective contributions of chemotherapy and of community mental health programs. Some data from Great Britain are helpful and interesting in this respect. In that country, where administrative reform in mental health and development of community alternatives began before they did in the United States, hospital populations were on the decrease before tranquilizer therapy was introduced.

Reducing the number of hospitalized patients is one of the major goals of the community mental health center movement. In fact, a careful reading of President Kennedy's famous February 1963 Congressional address on this topic suggests that he felt this to be the major goal of the movement. In mental health circles, however, providing care for formerly hospitalized patients was considered only part of a larger and more ambitious program of reform. Among other emphases, the idea that mental health services should be allocated on the basis of need and not restricted, as they had been in the past, by factors such as geography, education, or income became paramount (Joint Commission on Mental Illness and Health, 1961; Yolles, 1968).

Hollingshead and Redlich's study, *Social Class and Mental Illness* (1958), played a role in stimulating this ideology. The authors surveyed all psychiatric treatment facilities, both public and private, in New Haven in 1950 and found that treatment was unequally distributed among the population, varying with the social class of patients. Psychotherapy was offered far more often to socially advantaged groups, whereas patients from low socioeconomic background were more likely to be treated by physical methods such as electroconvulsive therapy and drugs or by directive treatment.

Ten years later, Meyer and Bean (1968) followed the progress of patients who had been included in the New Haven study and found that social class was related to result. Patients from lower-class backgrounds were more likely still to be in hospitals years afterward, whereas upper-class patients were more likely to have recovered or to be in outpatient therapy. The implications were clear. The quantity and quality of mental health services were not being determined solely on the basis of need but were being influenced by supposedly irrelevant factors like social position.

When the National Institute of Mental Health (NIMH) assumed responsibility for enacting the Community Mental Health Center program, it produced a set of guidelines, prominent among which was the directive that new mental health services be developed on the basis of need. Individual states were empowered to determine their own priorities for mental health funding, but NIMH set standards by requiring epidemiological data as a justification for programs and as an index of need (Osterweil, 1967).

Most of the data used to assess need or to evaluate the effectiveness of programs relate, as might be expected, to patients in treatment. The data demonstrate that mental health services have proliferated over the past decade and that they are being used by more people. They also show that treatment resources are still not distributed in a flexible, nondiscriminatory fashion on the basis of need. For instance, different patterns of care for white and nonwhite patients are apparent (Kramer et al., 1972; Willie, Kramer, and Brown, 1974), and children do not receive a proportional share of the mental health dollar, even though they are the fastest growing segment of the population (Joint Commission on Mental Health of Children, 1970).

In addition to making possible the study of trends, treatment data can be useful for planning services. For example, the finding that the elderly made up such a large proportion of the mental hospital population stimulated the expanded use of nursing homes as an alternative. (Although this change leads to a reduction in mental hospital census figures, whether or not care for the elderly improves is a matter that desperately needs to be evaluated.) At best, though, these data can only reveal who has used the services in the past. This information, in turn, may give a distorted picture of who actually requires services in the general community. A team of research workers in North Carolina, for example, conducted a survey of true prevalence on a community-wide basis (Edgerton, Bentz, and Hollister, 1970). They identified the groups at highest risk for mental disorder and most in need of services as nonwhite, nonmarried, poorly educated, and elderly people living in rural areas. The typical client of a mental health clinic, on the other hand, was a white mother or child from a middle-class background.

Treatment data can only be used for evaluation with a good deal of reservation about their meaning. If a patient disappears from the treatment rolls, does this signify that he has been cured? Or, on the other hand, has he passed into another system of care, such as a nursing home or a welfare agency?

The *case register*, originally developed by Brooke in Great Britain, provides a partial solution for some of these problems. A case register is a central file in which all people with mental disorders in a community are identified. Cumulative statistical records are maintained for each person regarding his contacts with psychiatric services and other systems in the community. These data can help to show how patients move among medical, social, and educational facilities, and they can be used to document such factors as the overlap of services, whether any segments of the population are using services disproportionately, and where service gaps exist. While unquestionably a valuable tool, a case register raises a number of ethical and legal questions concerning the confidentiality of records and the protection of individual privacy that must be resolved before it can receive widespread acceptance.

Evaluation efforts have been relatively scant in the mental health field. The main problem is not lack of adequate methodology. It is grounded in more fundamental issues, such as the universal human difficulty in specifying goals and relating them to achievement and in allowing our efforts to be examined by an outsider (or, worse yet, a computer).

Although evaluation often reveals shortcomings such as those briefly dealt with in this section, the aim of program evaluation is not to condemn but, rather, to produce guidelines for charting future directions and priorities. Without this kind of internal stimulation, feedback, and logically directed evolution, the mental health movement runs the risk of drifting into obscurity on a sea of rhetoric and good intentions.

Filling Out the Clinical Picture of an Illness

Although a considerable amount is known about the outcome of major psychiatric disorders, relatively few studies have been conducted of the evolution and course of neuroses and psychosomatic illnesses. These conditions consume a great deal of clinical time and effort, a fact that makes the relative lack of interest in their clinical course disturbing. Knowledge concerning how much effect treatment has on these disorders is necessary. Without base-line descriptions of what happens to these conditions in the natural course of human events, however, such an evaluation becomes impossible.

Several longitudinal studies have been made using two major data sources: patients who had been placed on waiting lists for therapy (Saslow and Peters, 1956; Wallace and White, 1959; Barron and Leary, 1955) and community samples of people with disorders who had never contacted treatment agencies (Beiser, 1976). Results have been fairly consistent; anywhere from one-third to one-half of patients with minor disorders experience a remission within three to five years. People who recover from symptoms without treatment differ from those who do not by (1) being better able to form interpersonal relationships; (2) showing more evidence of group affiliations; (3) being more economically advantaged; and (4) showing fewer characterological problems. For example, people who are diagnosed

as "hysterical," as "antisocial," or as having a "character disorder" are less apt to recover than those diagnosed as having neurotic conditions. The fact that these are some of the very factors by which people are selected as "good candidates" for psychotherapy raises some interesting questions about how to assess the effects of such therapy.

Making a Community Diagnosis

The studies whose purpose focuses on community diagnosis deal with two related questions. First, how much mental disorder is there in the community? And, second, are there groups at special risk of developing disorders?

How much mental disorder? The earliest estimates for rates of mental illness were based on the numbers of cases hospitalized during a given time period. Even as a measure of treated incidence and prevalence, these measures fell short because they did not cover all the possible places where a person with psychiatric problems might go for treatment.

The study of Hollingshead and Redlich (1958), still the most comprehensive treated prevalence survey ever done, revealed that 808 persons per 100,000 in the population of New Haven (slightly less than 1 percent) were in some form of psychiatric treatment. These figures can be compared with some recent national data, with interesting results. In 1966, 1.2 percent of the population of the United States were patients in mental hospitals, psychiatric services of general hospitals, or outpatient psychiatric clinics. Estimates place another million people in some form of private therapy in this country (Kramer et al., 1972). In all, then, somewhere between 1.5 and 2 percent of the population was in some form of contact with mental health services fifteen to twenty years after completion of the New Haven study.

Several early publications have suggested that even the most comprehensive treated prevalence figures underestimate the number of cases one would find in a general community survey (Cohen and Fairbank, 1938; Cohen, Fairbank, and Greene, 1939; Lemkau, Tietze, and Cooper, 1942; Roth and Luton, 1943; Bremer, 1951; Lin, 1953). Still, North Americans were unprepared for the staggering findings of two studies done here in the early 1950s. These have become well known as the Stirling County and Midtown studies.

The Stirling County study, directed by Alexander H. Leighton, took place in a rural, bicultural (Acadian-Catholic and English-Protestant) county in Nova Scotia (Leighton, 1959; Hughes et al., 1960; D. Leighton et al., 1963).* A sample of 1,010 subjects, representing the total population of men and women above the age of eighteen, was drawn. Nonpsychiatrists conducted structured interviews that provided data on bodily symptoms, disturbed feeling states, difficulties in life adjustment, and various social and biographical information. Local general practitioners were interviewed for ancillary health and social information about each subject.

Once these data had been collected, a team of psychiatrists examined each person's protocol and assigned several types of mental health ratings: (1) a listing of all the symptom complexes displayed, if any; (2) an overall rating of "caseness," that is, the person was considered a case of psychiatric disorder if the psychiatrists felt that, given the number and pattern of his symptom complexes, he probably was suffering a diagnosable psychiatric disorder; (3) a typology rating based on a subject's caseness rating, plus the amount of impairment he suffered in everyday life as a result of his disorder.

The Midtown study, initiated and originally directed by Thomas A. C. Rennie (and after his death by Alexander H. Leighton), followed the same general outline (Srole et al., 1962; Langner and Michael, 1963).† A representative sample (1,660) of the adult population of Midtown Manhattan was interviewed. Whereas in the Stirling

County study the sample was drawn from all people over the age of eighteen, the Midtown study focused on people aged twenty to fifty-nine. Supplemental information about each person was gathered by checking through hospital, clinic, and social agency records. Psychiatrists assessed the data and made several ratings, including (1) a listing of symptom complexes (as in the system used in the Stirling study) and (2) an overall mental health rating somewhat like the Stirling typology ratings.

These two studies have been widely quoted and widely compared. In view of the popularity they have enjoyed and because it seems unlikely that surveys of this magnitude and complexity will be undertaken very often, discussion of the results in some detail seems merited.

Both studies address the problem of how much disorder exists in the community, and both do it at several different levels. In each study, a respondent is rated as showing as many symptom patterns as seem appropriate. The vast majority of these patterns are minor and transient, such as having an upset stomach from emotional causes or going through a period of feeling weepy and blue. The fact that a person reports having, or having had, one or more of these reactions does not qualify him as a "case."

Caseness and *typology* in the Stirling system and *mental health rating* in the Midtown study are global judgments arrived at by a clinical process that takes into account the nature and severity of a person's symptom patterns, the appropriateness of these symptoms to the situation, and other clinical judgments. At the global level, 23.4 percent of the Midtown sample were judged to have serious symptoms and impairment; only 18.5 percent were considered completely well. Almost one-third of the Stirling sample had a psychiatric disorder (caseness rating); 20 percent had a disorder that was interfering with their lives to the extent that they were thought to need clinical attention (typology rating); only 17 percent were judged free from disorder.

Both the Midtown and Stirling County studies conclude that roughly one-fifth of the population requires psychiatric services at any one time, a figure at least ten to fifteen times greater than the number of persons actually seen in hospitals

---

* The report on the Stirling County study fills three volumes. Volume 1 presents the frame of reference; volume 2, the social science background, and volume 3, methodology and findings. Chapter 13 of the final volume is a useful summary of findings and theory; specialists and nonspecialists alike may find it helpful to begin their study of the volumes with this chapter.

† In the report on the famous Midtown study, volume 1 emphasizes theory and methods as well as findings, and volume 2 begins with a very useful summary of the findings presented in Volume 1; after introducing more findings, the authors of volume 2 synthesize the information and raise hypotheses for future research.

and mental health clinics during the course of a year. The prevalence of symptom patterns found in each of these studies is presented in table 29.1. Comparisons between the two studies are a little difficult. Some are presented here, both because they are interesting and in order to demonstrate that one must be aware of the methods and definitions used in a particular study before making interpretations.

More than half the residents of each area had psychophysiological disturbances, most commonly involving the gastrointestinal tract. Many people also had psychoneurotic symptoms, but since the two studies employed different categories, comparisons between them are difficult.

More schizophrenics were found in Midtown, but this cannot be taken as proof of the popular notion that urban living drives people mad. Schizophrenics are one category of marginal people who tend to drift into the central areas of large cities where they can find cheap lodging and anonymity (Dunham, 1965). Public facilities like mental health clinics tend to be located in or

near downtown areas and this is probably another feature explaining the concentration of psychotic people in Midtown. People who need treatment on a continuing basis tend to locate close to areas where it is accessible (Kohn, 1968).

The differential rates for mental deficiency and brain syndrome are probably spurious. The Stirling psychiatrists had more information available to judge mental deficiency and this probably accounts for the higher rates. The percentage of people with brain syndromes derives from a sampling issue: no people above the age of fifty-nine were sampled in Midtown, thus eliminating the group at highest risk for having organic mental disorders, particularly senility.

The differences between the two studies for sexual deviant rates, on the other hand, are probably actual. In fact, since there were no community informants in Midtown, as there were in Stirling (and this is the most likely source for such information), one would speculate that the Midtown figures are an underestimate and that the differences between the two are even

TABLE 29.1. Prevalence of symptom patterns in Stirling County, 1952, and in Midtown Manhattan, 1953. (Adapted from D. Leighton et al., 1963, table 3-1, pp. 74–75; and Langner and Michael, 1963, table 15.2, p. 407.)

Symptom pattern	Percentage of sample with symptom pattern[a]	
	Stirling	Midtown
Psychophysiological	59.5	51.7
Psychoneurotic		
Anxiety	10.0	15.1
Depression	7.2	23.6
Other	41.1	(no corresponding category)
Mixed anxiety	(no corresponding category)	70.8
Alcoholic	3.5	4.6
Psychotic		
Schizophrenia	0.5	4.9
Affective psychosis	0.3	0.3
Mentally deficient	4.8	2.5
Brain syndrome or senile	2.3[b]	1.2
Epileptic	0.2	0.4
Sexually deviant	0.0	1.0

[a] Percentages total more than 100 because each respondent may have had more than one symptom pattern.

[b] The original table indicates 2.5 percent for this category; cases of epilepsy have been subtracted out here and assigned to a separate category.

larger than they seem. This difference is difficult to interpret. Do people with sexual deviations find it easier to "come out of the closet" in the more liberal atmosphere of Midtown? Or, on the other hand, do people whose sexual preferences do not follow the norm tend to leave the conservative environment of small towns and rural areas in search of a more flexible and open life style in big cities?

Studies of true prevalence are uncommon. Investigations of the true incidence of mental disorders in populations are rarer still. One exception is a long-range study conducted by Erik Essen-Möller (1966) and Ollie Hagnell (1966) in Sweden.* In 1947, four psychiatrists examined and made mental health ratings on virtually all the residents (2,250) of a small rural parish in Sweden, which was given the code name of Lundby. Ten years later, one psychiatrist interviewed and rated all the survivors and obtained extensive data on nearly all those who had died. The incidence of mental disorder could then be calculated for the group who had shown no disturbance up to and including the time they were initially examined in 1947. About 11 percent of the men and 20 percent of the women developed a mental illness for the first time between 1947 and 1957.

The estimated cumulated risk up to age sixty was 43.4 percent for men and 73.0 percent for women. In other words, by the time they reached age sixty, almost half of the men and three-quarters of the women of Lundby would have experienced at least one episode of mental disturbance. Most of these episodes were mild and of comparatively short duration (less than four months). When he considered only serious disturbance, Hagnell found a considerable difference in his figures; about 8 percent of men and 15 percent of the women could expect to suffer an impairing mental disorder by the age of sixty.

Who is at risk? The epidemiologist may begin his investigations with a question about how many

* The works employ a terminology that is confusing for North American readers; perhaps for this reason, they are not widely known here. Nevertheless, they are important studies of true prevalence and true incidence of psychiatric disorders.

people suffer from a disorder, but his interest soon turns to why certain groups seem to develop more than their share while others remain relatively untouched. He has then embarked on a search for cause. An important intermediate step is necessary between establishing crude prevalence rates and studying etiology; this stage involves characterizing high- and low-risk groups. Once these characterizations have been made, hypotheses about cause are often generated, which can then be investigated by other means.

Many investigations have been carried out with the aim of determining who is at risk for developing disorder. Despite their diversity, the studies have yielded some common findings that suggest that—for any individual—the type of person he is, his environment, and his particular life experiences are factors influencing his mental health.

Age is related to mental health. Most studies conducted in the Western world suggest two peak periods of risk for developing disorder. The first is between the ages of twenty-five and forty-five; after this age, there is a plateau, and then another peak occurs after age sixty. The first peak, the one for young adults, is associated with the development of neuroses and other minor mental disorders that may not require hospitalization. The peak after sixty is different. It brings with it not only an increase in psychiatric symptoms but a definitely greater chance of being hospitalized, usually with a diagnosis like psychosis of the senium. It might be concluded that a person faces two major periods of stress during his adult life—first, at about the time he is establishing himself occupationally and in a family, and, second, when the productive years, at least as this society defines them, are over. Old age brings with it organic brain changes that account for some of what is observed as mental disorder. However, this pattern of increased prevalence in later years does not take place in cultures where age confers a different status (Murphy, 1959; A. Leighton et al., 1963), suggesting that the process is at least partially social.

In the United States, more men than women are admitted to mental hospitals. Paradoxically, the resident patient rate for women is higher, because women in hospitals tend to live longer than men in hospitals, just as they do when not hospitalized. In true prevalence studies, women have appeared as having more psychoneurotic and psychosomatic disorders than men, whereas men have higher rates of alcoholism and personality disorder. Some people have interpreted these rates to mean that the style of expressing discomfort is different for the two sexes, that is, that women tend to be more in touch with their feelings and to suffer inwardly, while men express their discomfort through action.

Mental health and marital status are related in an interesting way. Rates of illness are higher for never-married, separated, divorced, and widowed people than they are for married people. The figures are quite dramatic. In 1969, for instance, one in every 85 separated or divorced people in the United States was admitted to a state or county hospital. Never-married men are another high-risk group, although never-married women are not (Morrell, 1974; Seiler and Summers, 1974). Interpreting these data is not easy. Marriage may protect people from developing disorder; on the other hand, mental illness may prevent one from marrying or precipitate a divorce.

The same kinds of considerations apply to another important variable—social class. Findings have been remarkably consistent; social class, usually measured by some combination of one's occupation, education, and financial status, bears an inverse relationship to mental health (Dohrenwend and Dohrenwend, 1969). In other words, the lower one's social standing, the higher the risk of developing a psychiatric disorder. One of the most widely debated questions in psychiatric epidemiology is whether this relationship is based on social selection or social causation. Advocates of the social selection hypothesis argue that people with mental illnesses (at least, severe mental illnesses like schizophrenia) get poorer educations and poorer jobs and drift downward in the social-class scale (Dunham, 1965). According to the theory of social causation, people from disadvantaged social groups fall prey to mental illness because they are likely to suffer childhood deprivations and traumata that leave them more vulnerable in later life (Beiser, 1972, 1973) and because they are blocked from attaining significant goals as adults (Leigh-

ton, 1959). This argument is really another variant of the "nature-nurture" controversy that runs through all of psychiatry. In this case, so much evidence exists for both sides that it seems logical to conclude that both social selection and social causation are operative.

The demonstration that social class and mental health are related provided a point of entree for social scientists into what had hitherto been a medically dominated specialty. The notion of cause that most social scientists bring to this field, however, is not simply that lack of money makes people mentally ill. The theory is more complex. Poverty is seen as being associated with a set of other conditions and a life style that result in many kinds of deprivations for individuals unfortunate enough to be caught up in them. The anthropologist Oscar Lewis, for example, introduced the term *the culture of poverty* to connote a whole way of life involving blocked opportunity, lack of material comfort, a shortage of resources, and a cycle of self-defeating behaviors, all of which characterized the urban slums he studied (Lewis, 1961).

Lewis's concept of the culture of poverty is similar to what Alexander Leighton and his colleagues termed *sociocultural disintegration*. In this frame of reference, the total community is looked at as a quasi-organism functioning as a system of interrelated parts. When a breakdown in the functioning of the system occurs, the needs of the people living in the community are compromised and mental illness may result. Indicators that a community is not functioning properly or has disintegrated include broken homes, few and weak interpersonal associations, inadequate leadership, few recreational activities, hostility, and inadequate communication. In this frame of reference, poverty per se is not the direct cause of mental illness. Poverty, rather, tends to be associated with sociocultural disintegration, and it is the latter that exerts the causal influence.

In addition to attributes like age and sex and position in the social structure, the risk of mental disorder seems to be associated with another category of factors that I shall call "life experiences," of which bereavement is a prototypical example. People who have lost a loved one have more psychosomatic disorders and more neurotic problems and show more suicidal behavior than their nonbereaved counterparts in the general population. They also have a higher risk of dying themselves. Since cardiac complications are a frequent cause of these unusual deaths, at least one group of workers calls this the "broken heart syndrome" (Parkes and Brown, 1972). The greatest risk occurs when the death has been sudden, following an accident, for example, or untimely, as in the death of a child, which is more upsetting for survivors than the death of an elderly person (Parkes, 1972).

The specific nature of a stress may be less important than the sheer number of stressful experiences a person has. The Midtown study (Srole et al., 1962; Langner and Michael, 1963) showed that the more adverse circumstances one faced in childhood, the greater the risk of developing disorder as an adult. Adults are at greater risk for developing psychosomatic and neurotic illness after periods of cumulative stress (Wolff, 1950; Rahe, McKean, and Arthur, 1967). Stating this may seem a bit like documenting the obvious, since common sense would suggest the same thing. However, evidence is less than overwhelming that this knowledge has had an impact on clinical theory or practice.

Studying Etiology

A detailed description of some of the important research of Benjamin Pasamanick permits us to examine two different approaches to the study of cause in epidemiology, the case history and the cohort methods. (For a discussion of genetics and the etiology of mental disturbances, see chapter 6, "Genetic and Biochemical Aspects of Schizophrenia," chapter 11, "Schizophrenic Reactions," and chapter 13, "Affective Disorders.") Pasamanick's work began with an observation that prematurity and complications of pregnancy are often associated with fetal death, usually on the basis of brain damage (Pasamanick, 1961). He reasoned that a fraction of infants might be injured in this way but would not die; rather, in later life they would have conditions like cerebral palsy, epilepsy, and organically based mental deficiency. Still others might develop behavioral problems because their subclinical brain damage would render them less able to handle stress.

In his early studies, Pasamanick followed a typical case history method. He chose a sample of children with mental subnormality and a comparison group of children who were as closely matched as possible, except that they had normal intelligence. Comparison of the clinical histories of both groups showed that the subnormal children were more likely to have been born prematurely than the controls, that their mothers had suffered more complications during pregnancy, and that more abnormalities had developed in the neonatal period. These findings constitute one level of support for a concept Pasamanick refers to as the "continuum of reproductive casualty." According to this concept, abnormalities of pregnancy may result in a variety of outcomes, ranging from fetal death, at one end of the spectrum, to various behavioral abnormalities due to slight brain damage, at the other.

Case history studies have limitations, however. The investigator has no control over the quality and quantity of data gathered, since it has been completed by other people before he begins his research. Cohort studies offer more control over the data and more precision. Pasamanick followed his original studies with a cohort study of 500 premature babies (Knobloch and Pasamanick, 1966). He also selected a control group—babies born in the same hospitals as the prematures with the same socioeconomic backgrounds. At forty weeks of age, the premature babies had more neurological abnormalities and showed more cases of retarded development, which is what he had predicted.

Pasamanick also showed that complications of pregnancy occur more commonly in lower-class groups than in all others. Thus, the continuum of reproductive casualty may be a factor contributing to the higher rate of mental disorders among the socioeconomically disadvantaged.

Epidemiology also has something to say about the effects on children of being separated from their parents, a topic that has received a considerable amount of clinical attention. Two British investigators, Douglas and Blomfeld (1958), studied a national sample of 5,386 children born during one week in 1946. By the time the cohort had reached age five, a considerable number had been separated from their parents for more than a few days. The group of children who had experienced separations had more behavioral problems than those who had not. Social class again exerted an effect. Lower-class children experienced more separations and more upsetting kinds of separations. When upper-class parents were away for a few days, they were likely to have gone on vacation, leaving the child with a housekeeper or relative in his own home. A typical lower-class separation, however, took place because the mother or father became ill; during the period of illness the child was sent to live with someone else, whom he might or might not have known beforehand.

Other studies, involving older children, suggest that parental deprivation in early life is associated with the later development of aggressive and antisocial behavior (Bowlby, 1944; Provence and Lipton, 1962; Wardle, 1961; Wardrup, 1967) and difficulties in peer relationships (Lynn and Sawrey, 1959) but not neurotic symptoms.

Developing Classifications

The study of epidemiology requires some system for classifying people into groups. One method is simply to separate people with an illness from people without an illness, categories usually based on some sort of clinical judgment. After a study has been completed, the investigators may find that their data suggest a way to improve the original classification scheme. A survey team in New York City, for example, asked a sample of normal adults whether or not they had a variety of psychosomatic and neurotic symptoms (Benfari et al., 1974). During the analysis of the data, the investigators found it impossible to group the symptoms into clear-cut diagnostic categories like depression and anxiety. In fact, symptoms assumed to belong exclusively to one diagnostic category were more likely to be reported together with a list of complaints coming from other supposedly exclusive categories. These findings suggested that traditional clinical categories need to be revised, since they do not always reflect the way symptoms actually occur in nature.

People may also be grouped according to whether or not they have undergone a particular experience loosely considered to be the cause of an illness. Pasamanick's work, for example,

viewed in conjunction with clinical experience, suggests that particular subgroups of learning difficulties, conduct disturbances, and perhaps some neurotic problems encountered in childhood might form a category such as "minimal brain damage" that could be useful in research. A research worker familiar with this category and the hypothesis that underlies it—that adverse prenatal experience may be associated with some form of organic deficit—might raise further questions about how a common deficit finds expression in a variety of behaviors, such as how other aspects of a child's personality mediate the expression of a deficit or how socioenvironmental forces act to uncover, suppress, or compensate for organic deficit.

All learning difficulties are clearly not the result of brain damage; however, some difficulties in learning may demonstrate a common linkage with organically based conduct disturbances and neurotic problems. Others may arise primarily because children grow up in nonstimulating environments or because they attend bad schools. Separating the two and investigating each not only seems more satisfying logically but may also suggest new approaches in unexplored areas. Far from adding up to a dry exercise in classification, establishing commonalities among phenomena that are usually considered to be different may stimulate new questions for research and suggest innovations in therapy and prevention.

The first kind of categorization described above, classifying by signs, symptoms, and other characteristics of an illness, is sometimes called "grouping by manifestational criteria." The second, classifying by means of a similar experience, is called "grouping by experiential criteria" (McMahon, Pugh, and Ipsen, 1960).

Psychiatric epidemiology includes the study of collective emotional reactions resembling classical epidemics and, more important, phenomena like neuroses and psychosomatic disorders that can be seen as types of chronic illness. Six uses of psychiatric epidemiology are suggested, all of which, in fact, are variations on a common theme—how epidemiology can help in preventing and controlling illness. Epidemiological investigation does not result in a detailed understanding of the process of an illness; however, it often produces partial insights that can suggest ways to control and prevent disorder in a population.

Many of the studies reviewed in this chapter point to ways in which the medical care-giving system could be changed in order to improve mental health. Attention to maternal and prenatal care should be a high priority. Different patterns of outreach to high-risk groups, such as the elderly and the recently bereaved, should become the concern of psychiatric facilities, particularly community mental health centers. Provisions must be made to ensure that everyone has equal access to facilities, including currently underserviced and poorly serviced groups, such as children, the elderly, and racial minorities.

The care-giving system is only one part of the total fabric of a community. Studies reviewed in this chapter point to other subsystems that might be influenced in order to help improve people's lives.

The approaches suggested here are really hunches based on the partial knowledge gained through research of various kinds. Some might prove to be as misguided as the closing of public swimming pools to control polio in the days before the virus was isolated. Given the mental health needs of our society, however, this is a necessary risk. Practitioners and policy makers cannot afford to wait for definitive answers; they must use the partial knowledge they have at hand as effectively as they can. We must hope that a wise use of information already in our possession will lead to more Broad Street pumps in medical practice, particularly in mental health.

References

Adler, A. 1911. *Neurotic constitution*. New York: Moffat.

Adrian, E. D. 1959. Our concern for the mind. *Br. Med. J.* 2:78–81.

Barron, F., and T. Leary. 1955. Changes in psychoneurotic patients with and without psychotherapy. *J. Consult. Psychol.* 19:239–245.

Beiser, M. 1972. The etiology of mental disorders: sociocultural aspects. In *Manual of child psychopathology*, ed. B. B. Wolman. New York: McGraw-Hill.

—— 1973. Poverty, social disintegration, and personality. In *Interaction: readings in human psychology*, ed. K. O. Doyle. London: Heath.

—— 1976. Personal and social factors associated with the remission of psychiatric symptoms. *Arch. Gen. Psychiatry* 33, no. 8:941–947.

Benfari, R. C., M. Beiser, A. H. Leighton, J. M. Murphy, and C. M. Mertens. 1974. The manifestation of types of psychological states in an urban sample. *J. Clin. Psychol.* 30, no. 4:471–483.

Bowlby, J. 1944. Forty-four juvenile thieves: their characters and home life. *Int. J. Psychoanal.* 25:19–53.

Bremer, J. 1951. A social psychiatric investigation of a small community in northern Norway. *Acta Psychiatr. Scand.* Suppl. 62.

Cohen, B. M., and R. Fairbank. 1938. Statistical contributions from the mental hygiene study of the eastern health district. *Am. J. Psychiatry* 94:1377–95.

Cohen, B. M., R. Fairbank, and E. Greene. 1939. Statistical contributions from the eastern health district of Baltimore. III. Personality disorder in the eastern health district. *Hum. Biol.* 11:112–129.

Dohrenwend, B. P. and B. S. 1969. *Social status and psychological disorder*. New York: Wiley.

Douglas, J. W. B., and J. M. Blomfeld. 1958. *Children under five*. London: Allen and Unwin.

Dunham, H. W. 1965. *Community and schizophrenia: an epidemiological analysis*. Detroit: Wayne State University Press.

Edgerton, J. W., W. K. Bentz, and W. G. Hollister. 1970. Demographic factors and responses to stress among rural people. *Am. J. Public Health* 60, no. 6:1065–71.

Essen-Möller, E. 1966. Individual traits and morbidity in a Swedish rural population. *Acta Psychiatr. Scand.* suppl. 100.

Goldhamer, H., and A. Marshall. 1953. *Psychosis and civilization*. Glencoe, Ill.: Free Press.

Greenblatt, M., and E. Glazier. 1975. The phasing out of mental hospitals in the United States. *Am. J. Psychiatry* 132, no. 11:1135–40.

Hagnell, O. 1966. *A prospective study of the incidence of mental disorder*. New York: Humanities Press.

Healy, W. 1922. *The individual delinquent: a textbook of diagnosis and prognosis*. Boston: Little, Brown.

Hemphill, R. E. 1941. Importance of first year of war in mental disease. *Bristol Med. Chir. J.* 58:11–18.

Hollingshead, A., and F. C. Redlich. 1958. *Social class and mental illness*. New York: Wiley.

Hopkins, F. 1943. Decrease in admissions to mental observation wards during war. *Br. Med. J.* 1:358.

Hughes, C. C., M. Tremblay, R. N. Rapoport, and

A. H. Leighton. 1960. *People of cove and woodlot*. The Stirling County Study, vol. 2. New York: Basic Books.

Joint Commission on Mental Health of Children. 1970. *Crisis in child mental health: challenge for the 1970's*. New York: Harper & Row.

Joint Commission on Mental Illness and Health. 1961. *Action for mental health: final report*. New York: Basic Books.

Kardiner, A., and H. Spiegel. 1947. *War stress and neurotic illness*. New York: Hoeber.

Kerckhoff, A. C., and K. W. Back. 1968. *The June bug*, New York: Appleton-Century-Crofts.

Knobloch, H., and B. Pasamanick. 1966. Prospective studies on the epidemiology of reproductive casuality: methods, findings and some implications. *Merrill-Palmer Q.* 12:7–26.

Kohn, M. L. 1968. Social class and schizophrenia: a critical review. In *Transmission of schizophrenia*, ed. D. Rosenthal and S. Kety. Oxford: Pergamon Press.

Kramer, M. 1970. Problems in psychiatric epidemiology. *Proc. R. Soc. Med.* 63: no. 6:553–562.

Kramer, M., E. S. Pollack, R. W. Redick, and B. Z. Locke. 1972. *Mental disorders/suicide*. Cambridge, Mass.: Harvard University Press.

La Barre, W. 1969. *They shall take up serpents*. New York: Schocken.

Langner, T. S., and S. T. Michael, 1963. *Life stress and mental health*. Thomas A. C. Rennie Series in Social Psychiatry, vol. 2. New York: Free Press of Glencoe.

Leighton, A. H. 1959. *My name is legion*. The Stirling County Study, vol. 1. New York: Basic Books.

Leighton, A. H., T. A. Lambo, C. C. Hughes, D. C. Leighton, J. M. Murphy, and D. B. Macklin. 1963. *Psychiatric disorder among the Yoruba*. Ithaca, N.Y.: Cornell University Press.

Leighton, D. C., J. S. Harding, D. B. Macklin, A. M. MacMillan, and A. H. Leighton. 1963. *The character of danger*. The Stirling County Study, vol. 3. New York: Basic Books.

Lemkau, P., C. Tietze, and M. Cooper. 1942. Mental hygiene problems in an urban district. *Ment. Hygiene* 26:100–119.

Lewis, A. 1967. Ebb and flow in social psychiatry. In *The state of psychiatry*. New York: Science House.

Lewis, O. 1961. *The children of Sánchez*. New York: Random House.

Lin, T. Y. 1953. A study of the incidence of mental disorder in Chinese and other cultures. *Psychiatry* 16:141–148.

Lin, T. Y., H. Rin, E. K. Yeh, C. C. Hsu, and H. M. Chu. 1969. Mental disorders in Taiwan, fifteen years later: a preliminary report. In *Mental health research in Asia and the Pacific*, ed. W. Caudill and T. Y. Lin. Honolulu: East-West Center Press.

Lynn, D. B., and W. L. Sawrey. 1959. The effects of father absence on Norwegian boys and girls. *J. Abnorm. Soc. Psychol.* 59:258–262.

Maudsley, H. 1872. Is insanity on the increase? *Br. Med. J.* 36:36–39.

McMahon, B., T. F. Pugh, and J. Ipsen. 1960. *Epidemiologic methods*. Boston: Little, Brown.

Meyer, A. 1958. *Psychobiology. A science of man*. Springfield, Ill.: Thomas.

Meyer, J., and L. Bean. 1968. *A decade later. A follow-up study of social class and mental illness*. New York: Wiley.

Mora, G. 1959. Recent American psychiatric developments. In *American handbook of psychiatry*, ed. S. Arieti. vol. 1. New York: Basic Books.

Morrell, L. 1974. "Calculating the odds of becoming a psychiatric patient." Epidemiological findings for the public sector of U.S. Mental Health Services.

Morris, J. N. 1957. *Uses of epidemiology*. Edinburgh: Livingstone.

Murphy, H. B. M. 1959. Culture and mental disorder in Singapore. In *Culture and mental health*, ed. M. K. Opler. New York: Macmillan.

Orlinski, N., and E. D'Elia. 1964. Rehospitalization of the schizophrenic patient. *Arch. Gen. Psychiatry* 10:47–54.

Osterweil, J. 1967. Applications of epidemiological findings to community mental health planning. *Psychiatr. Res. Rep. Am. Psychiatr. Assoc.* 22:249–258.

Parkes, C. M. 1972. *Bereavement: studies of grief in adult life*. New York: International Universities Press.

Parkes, C. M., and R. J. Brown. 1972. Health after bereavement: controlled study of young Boston widows and widowers. *Psychol. Med.*, 34:449–461.

Pasamanick, B. 1961. Epidemiologic studies in the complications of pregnancy and the birth process. In *Prevention of mental disorders in children*, ed. G. Caplan. New York: Basic Books.

Provence, S., and R. Lipton. 1962. *Infants in institutions*. New York: International Universities Press.

Rahe, H., J. D. McKean, Jr., and R. J. Arthur. 1967. A longitudinal study of life changes and illness patterns. *J. Psychosom. Res.* 10:355–366.

Roth, W. F., and F. B. Luton. 1943. The mental hygiene program in Tennessee. *Am. J. Psychiatry* 99:662–675.

Saslow, G., and D. D. Peters. 1956. A follow-up study of untreated patients with various disorders. *Psychiatr. Q.* 30:283–302.

Seiler, L. H., and G. F. Summers. 1974. Towards an

interpretation of items used in field studies of mental illness. *Soc. Sci. Med.* 8:459–467.

Snow, J. 1855. On the mode of communication of cholera. In *Snow on cholera*. New York: The Commonwealth Fund, 1936.

Srole, L., T. S. Langner, S. T. Michael, M. K. Opler, and T. A. C. Rennie. 1962. *Mental health in the metropolis.* Thomas A. C. Rennie Series in Social Psychiatry, vol. 1. New York: McGraw-Hill.

Wallace, H. E. R., and M. B. H. White. 1959. Natural history of psychoneurosis. *Br. Med. Q.* 1:144–148.

Wardle, C. J. 1961. Two generations of broken homes in the genesis of conduct and behavior disorders in childhood. *Br. Med. J.* 11:349–354.

Wardrup, K. R. H. 1967. Delinquent teenage types. *Br. J. Crim.* 714:371–380.

Willie, C. V., B. Kramer, and B. S. Brown, eds. 1974. *Racism and mental health.* Pittsburgh: University of Pittsburgh Press.

Wolff, H. G. 1950. Life situations, emotions and bodily disease. In *Feelings and Emotions*, ed. M. L. Reymert. New York: McGraw-Hill.

Yolles, S. F. 1968. The comprehensive national mental health program: an evaluation. In *Comprehensive mental health*, ed. L. M. Roberts, N. S. Greenfield, and M. H. Miller. Madison: University of Wisconsin Press.

Community Psychiatry

CHAPTER 30

Lee B. Macht

C OMMUNITY PSYCHIATRY has become increasingly important as a field of practice, teaching, and research during the past fifteen years. The term *community psychiatry* is now used in at least two major ways. First, it refers to any clinical practice that occurs outside a hospital and in this way refers to a context or setting for work. Second, it refers to the focus of this growing subspecialty on a population, not only on the individual, a focus that affects organization and care-giving practice—within a community agency, community mental health center, community residence, or governmental agency. It also describes techniques and theories focusing on an entire population or subparts of a population, in contrast to those focusing on individuals or even groups; clinical work in this regard extends from aiding an individual with a depression to considering other members of the population who might be vulnerable to forces producing the same syndrome. An attempt is thus made in community psychiatry to examine factors in the environment impinging on the individual and to work with other individuals and populations who are particularly vulnerable or "at risk." As a corollary, an emphasis on prevention and on the promotion of mental health is maintained.

The field is also concerned with a range of etiological factors from the genetic through the psychological and social, encompassing both service and research dimensions. It includes social psychiatry in its study of social forces in the etiology of disorder and the promotion of health and its relation to social and cultural dimensions in treatment and prevention activities. It also utilizes epidemiological methods in program planning and in understanding population dynamics and population-centered issues (see chapter 29, "Psychiatric Epidemiology"). The close association of the term *community psychiatry* with the terms *preventive* and *public health psychiatry* often leads to synonymity—ideally of accomplishment as well as intent. The term *community mental health* is used synonymously with *community psychiatry* and reflects the interdisciplinary nature of the field (the latter term is used more frequently in this chapter because the subject of this book is psychiatry). Many of the major contributions in the development of this field, however, have come from the work of those in allied endeavors—social work, psychology, nursing, public health, sociology, social anthropology —and indigenous community workers.

Thus the community psychiatrist provides treatment services within the family, neighborhood, or larger social system. He considers ways in which the person defined as the patient represents the problems of a population with similar difficulties. In seeing a kindergarten child with a school phobia, for example, the community psychiatrist both treats that child and considers the issue of separation in all children entering the school; he devises ways of working with the school and its staff to assist all of these children in order both to treat the disorder and to prevent its clinical occurrence. He is concerned, furthermore, with the ways in which the school can promote psychological growth and mental health. Thus both community mental health and community psychiatry involve similar dimensions of practice and conceptualization.

History of Community Psychiatry

American psychiatry began in the community when Benjamin Rush opened the first psychiatric unit in the Pennsylvania Hospital, a community general hospital, in 1765. The era of "moral treatment" in American psychiatric hospitals (Bockoven, 1963) in the 1830s and 1840s was characterized by humane treatment utilizing many milieu therapy techniques in small hospitals operated by superintendents with a genuine community orientation; cure rates were similar to today's, returning nearly 90 percent of the patients admitted to their own communities. Nineteenth-century American psychiatry had a clear community focus, including community and parent education (R. Caplan, 1969).

The rise of moral treatment grew in the sociocultural context of an emphasis on individualism, and its subsequent decline in the post-Civil War period was related to a contravening series of issues. These included a growing concern for a "scientific medicine," arising from an interest in cellular pathology that brought with it the myth of the incurability of mental illness. In addition, the inspired leaders of the moral treatment movement slowly died and did not train a cadre of successors, while an economic recession made the cost of adequate treatment services a critical issue.

Large waves of immigrants during the latter decades of the nineteenth century helped to swell the size of hospital populations, rendering them less and less therapeutic. By the 1870s and 1880s, this combination of forces produced a decline in the early, interpersonal and humanistic phase of American psychiatry—an enlightened era of critical importance to our understanding of the development and continuation of community mental health.

Despite the relatively primitive nature of psychiatry as a science during the nineteenth century, some basic principles related to community psychiatry had evolved. Edward Jarvis, in his report "Insanity and Idiocy in Massachusetts: Report of the Commission on Lunacy" (1855), clearly demonstrated that state hospitals were used most by people living in the surrounding areas or on the transportation routes to the hospitals. This observation had major implications for the twentieth-century movement to place services closer to the communities in which people live and work. The second half of the nineteenth century also saw a wave of reform frequently associated with Dorothea Dix's attempts to improve services and hospitals for the mentally ill.

The beginning of the twentieth century witnessed increased emphasis on work in the community with the development of psychopathic or receiving hospitals in the community, notably those in Boston and Colorado. Early in this century Adolf Meyer called for services of a collaborative nature in the community as part of the social fabric of the "district." He also advocated the use of family physicians in psychiatric work and coined the term *mental hygiene* (1915).

The citizens' movement, which was to evolve into community participation and control by the 1960s, began as early as 1908 when Clifford Beers's *A Mind That Found Itself* was published and he founded the National Committee for Mental Hygiene. This development led to the mental hygiene movement that extended the concern of psychiatry to "all aspects of human existence."

The development of both "satellite" and child guidance clinics in the 1920s and the evolution of ambulatory programs increased the community focus of mental health services. Experience in military psychiatry during both world wars demonstrated the importance of treating people as close to their social networks as possible and of returning them rapidly to their usual social milieu. Experience in general-hospital psychiatry during those years also led to the development of consultation techniques. Furthermore, the professions of social work and psychiatry were coming closer together, particularly on issues of prevention.

The post-World War II era saw a burgeoning of training and service programs and the beginning of federal support for mental health. In 1946, the passage of the National Mental Health Act provided training and research funds and grants in aid to the states for clinic and treatment facilities. The National Institute of Mental Health (NIMH) began its work in 1949, and in 1955 the Congress passed the Mental Health Study Act, establishing a Joint Commission on Mental Illness and Health. This commission was charged with analyzing and reevaluating the human and economic problems of mental illness and making "realistic recommendations" for action. Its report, *Action for Mental Health* (1961), dealt with many issues in community psychiatry, including the use of a variety of caregivers and prevention in mental health. It focused on plans for improving mental hospitals and on early and adequate treatment of the mentally ill.

In 1963 Congress passed the Community Mental Health Centers Act, which authorized appropriations for construction and staffing of comprehensive community mental health centers on the basis of a federal-state matching formula. Some 425 centers have become operational throughout the country, although 2,000 were originally planned. A parallel development in the 1960s was the formation of psychiatric services within governmental agencies such as the Peace Corps and the Office of Economic Opportunity. At the same time, mental health services developed as integral aspects of comprehensive neighborhood health centers, and citizen participation increased markedly during this era.

Although the term *deinstitutionalization* became popular in the 1970s, state hospital populations had in fact begun to decline as early as 1955 due to advances in psychopharmacology, social psychiatry, psychotherapy, and community psychiatry. Bertram Brown, then director of NIMH, stated that in 1971 only 43 percent of patient encounters, nationally, were inpatient (in contrast to 77 percent in 1955); 19 percent of care took place in inpatient services (49 percent in 1955); and outpatient services accounted for 42 percent of patient encounters (23 percent in 1955).

Other aspects of the field began to develop in the 1940s with Erich Lindemann's studies of acute grief during the tragic Cocoanut Grove fire in Boston. Crisis theory and crisis intervention developed further during the 1960s in the work of Lindemann, Caplan, Parod, and others. Mental health consultation techniques, first developed in the 1930s, evolved further through the work of Caplan and others during the 1950s and 1960s. The 1960s also saw considerable development in the field of community health (with mental health as an integral part), and the 1970s are witnessing the development of comprehensive human services that integrate a variety of services, including mental health, public health, public welfare, youth services, and corrections. At least twenty-six state governments now have human service or human resources departments. The late 1960s and the 1970s also produced further decentralization of a range of mental health services to neighborhoods and the development of neighborhood psychiatry. These efforts are all products of the history just outlined and of the increasing need to broaden the scope of mental health to provide services to people in the community.

Conceptual Aspects of Community Psychiatry

As a basis for understanding community psychiatry, the following section will present theoretical issues encompassing the range of interrelationships among individuals, population groups, and societal subsystems. Subsequent sections of this presentation build upon these conceptual dimensions as they relate to technical and programmatic concerns.

Interrelationship of Individual and Social Systems

A crucial issue in community psychiatry is the attempt to conceptualize the interrelationship of individual dynamics and those of larger systems. The individual is seen as affected in his functioning by family, significant others, neighborhood, and social institutions, as well as by broad social conditions, systems, and issues. In turn, individual development, psychodynamics, and ego structure affect these systems. Both the individual and the society therefore affect and are affected by each other, each with its own dynamics and laws of operation.

General systems theory, group dynamics, and social psychology provide conceptual bases for understanding these interactions, and ego psychology serves as the mediating framework between the individual and his surroundings. In addition, the impact of social reality upon the individual has increasingly been recognized within the psychiatric field, and new attempts are being made to understand this complex field of forces and then to decide where best to intervene—at the level of the individual, the family, the neighborhood, the social institution, or the community.

A chronic schizophrenic patient living in a housing project, for example, experiences an exacerbation of auditory, persecutory hallucinations and is subsequently seen at a neighborhood health center. Investigation reveals a wave of violence and unrest in the project following the removal of rent control, with other residents also upset, symptomatic, and feeling helpless and enraged. In this situation, the community psychiatrist has two prime considerations: (1) the impact of this reality on the individual (who comes as the patient) and (2) the degree to which he can treat that individual patient or provide support for the whole population similarly affected. The latter may involve contacting the housing authority, organizing tenant groups, or working with other caregivers to effect change; each of these possible courses in turn addresses different technical dimensions. In any given case, the mode of intervention depends on the level chosen and the interrelations of individual and social forces at that particular level.

Prevention

The concept of prevention, a major concern of community psychiatry, operates on three levels, primary, secondary, and tertiary. Primary prevention can occur only in the community and focuses on diminishing the incidence of new cases in a population over a defined time period by counteracting the forces that produce illness. Primary prevention programs focus on reducing the risk for the vulnerable population as a whole, and the individual's situation is seen as representing the issues confronting an entire group. Thus when a Job Corps psychiatrist sees a youngster in acute turmoil as a result of leaving home and entering a Job Corps center, his work focuses on two dimensions of the situation simultaneously: on the particular youngster's separation and adjustment problems and on his status as representative of all youngsters entering the Corps who need support and assistance with these concerns; the second dimension may require that the psychiatrist attempt to develop large-scale interventions to assist all Corps members in this situation. Although the content and structure of these broad interventions derive from clinical understanding, the aim of the community psychiatrist is to translate this understanding into preventive activities on a larger scale.

Primary prevention has two major emphases in mental health. First, the long-term approach concerns the provision of those supplies—nutritional, physical, emotional, and social—that keep people healthy. The second focuses on intervention in life crises in order to produce healthy resolution that strengthens personality and fosters development (a topic discussed in greater detail in the section on crisis intervention and support systems). The worker who participates in programs designed to provide stimulation and increased human interaction to infants, as in early mother-child intervention programs, is working in the first domain of primary prevention, while the worker who designs a program of support for new immigrants or other groups experiencing life crises is working in the second.

Secondary prevention refers to those activities that reduce the disability rate due to a disorder by lowering the prevalence of established cases in a population at risk at a certain point in time. Prevalence includes both new and old cases of the disorder and the population at risk includes all members of the population who might, under certain circumstances, suffer from the disorder. Secondary prevention, as reflected in reduced prevalence, usually involves shortening the duration of disability through early case identification and improved treatment. Primary prevention also clearly involves lowering prevalence by reducing the rate (or incidence) of new cases. In secondary prevention, however, the rate of old cases is also lowered by reducing the length of illness. Thus any treatment or early case-identification programs contribute to secondary prevention through their impact on the population at risk. Programming in this area involves complex dilemmas in planning and setting priorities. Screening programs of various sorts have been attempted, and services have been developed within "front-line" agencies in the community, such as schools, neighborhood centers, and general hospitals, in order to facilitate early diagnosis, referral, and treatment. In this sense, each of these programs contributes to the secondary prevention effort.

Tertiary prevention refers to efforts designed to reduce the rate of "residual defect," or lowered capacity of ego function, that can continue in occupational and social spheres after the acute phase of the disorder. These programs are designed to reduce disability through large-scale rehabilitative efforts to return people to their highest potential for social and work functioning as rapidly as possible. Such efforts as the development of aftercare networks, community residences, alternatives to hospitalization, rehabilitation and work programs, and community education may effect tertiary prevention.

Support Systems

A support system is a group or social aggregate providing the individual or individuals with physical, emotional or psychological, and social input or supplies. It is a network of few or many persons who relate to the individual and buffer, reinforce, or nurture him. The support system gives the individual personalized attention in his own terms; its activity may be ongoing, short-term, or time-limited. Support systems fulfill at least three functions: (1) mobilization of psychological capacities and inner resources and promotion of mastery; (2) sharing of real-life tasks; and (3) provision of extra material supplies, guidance, and information. In our society one sees many examples of spontaneous support systems, frequently modeled on the extended family.

Individuals in these natural community groupings of nonprofessionals have frequently encountered and dealt with similar difficulties; reciprocity and mutual identification therefore exist and are reinforced.

More organized nonprofessional support systems, or self-help groups, such as Alcoholics Anonymous and religious organizations, also serve in these capacities. In addition, professionals—acting either alone or in association with citizen or community groups—can at times develop new support systems such as those established for employees in mental hospitals, the Peace Corps, VISTA, and the Job Corps, early parent support groups, and endeavors like the Harvard Widow-to-Widow Project (which has now been replicated in many communities).

Support systems are a major focus for both service and research in community psychiatry. They relate to all three levels of prevention by intervening in the long-term provision of supplies as well as during periods of crisis (primary prevention); by providing a potent means of early case identification and at times treatment (secondary prevention); and by significantly reducing residual disability (tertiary prevention). Support systems are based on a belief in the reciprocal relationship between the individual and larger social systems. They reflect a community approach involving large population groups, frequently directed toward vulnerable or high-risk populations but clearly also having major impact on the psychology, development, and functioning of individual participants (G. Caplan, 1974).

Crisis Theory and Crisis Intervention

Another important set of conceptual issues in community psychiatry is the focus for the development of crisis theory and stems from the early work of Erich Lindemann on acute grief (1944), that of Kaplan and Mason on premature birth as a family crisis (1960), and the theoretical work of Erik Erikson on developmental and life cycle crises (1950). As noted in chapter 29, "Psychiatric Epidemiology," one important aspect of crisis work is the identification of high-risk populations.

According to crisis theory (Caplan, Macht,

and Wolf, 1969), a person usually behaves in a fairly consistent and predictable manner; he has emotional ups and downs, but on the whole his psychological functioning maintains a state of equilibrium. This equilibrium is attained during growth and development as an individual acquires a repertoire of coping and problem-solving mechanisms; he knows what to expect in his usual life situation and, when faced with a problem, he can deal with it in a reasonably satisfactory manner and in a relatively short period of time. When he faces an unclear or unexpected situation, his psychological equilibrium is upset as he wrestles with the problem, but usually his repertoire of problem-solving techniques is sufficient to arrive at a satisfactory solution in a relatively short time and to return to his previous equilibrium. Thus, while a person can expect vicissitudes, both personal and situational, in his life, these represent minor deviations from his normal state and do not change his psychic equilibrium enough to cause him to experience a crisis.

At times, however, a person experiences more severe and protracted upsets in his psychological equilibrium. On such occasions his usual psychic state is disrupted for several days or weeks, and he shows signs of cognitive disorder—mainly confusion and bewilderment—as well as of emotional upset, tension, anxiety, depression, shame, guilt, or hostility. These periods of crisis usually resolve themselves spontaneously and the individual returns to a steady state of psychological functioning. To be a useful concept, *crisis* must be defined as an upset in equilibrium that is unusual for a particular person. In general, an arbitrary measure of crises as periods of upset in an individual's steady state that last at least several days has been useful; for obscure reasons, most crises studied have not lasted longer than four to six weeks.

Clear transitional periods occur during an individual's development and account for a considerable proportion of the life crises he experiences. These developmental crises, arising from the processes of personality development, are expectable and predictable in the life cycle and have been described by several authors, most prominently Erik Erikson (1950), as an inherent part of a typical individual's psychosocial and psychological development. The social structure and its expectations for individual development and familial and social adaptation further contribute to the fact and nature of anticipated crises, as well as to the manner in which they are sanctioned. Adolescence is the prime example of such an expected life crisis, involving changes in physiology, individual psychological development, and social role expectations.

In addition to the predictable developmental crises, any individual manifests unexpected upsets in psychological equilibrium, apparently in response to accidental life happenings. Like the developmental crises, these accidental crises occur most frequently at transitional periods; quite often a difference is noted when an individual's personality pattern after the crisis is compared with his state preceding its onset. Personality change may, therefore, take place during any crisis, whether developmental or accidental. Thus an individual's established coping mechanisms may change in the course of a crisis as adaptation occurs, and he may actually come to function at a higher developmental level as a result. Adolescence may be considered a paradigm for this process. An individual may be dependent upon parents and elders prior to this developmental crisis; as a result of the upheaval of the crisis, however, he may separate, become independent, master separation issues anew, and progress toward adulthood and maturity. Similarly, in accidental crises, new adaptation and coping mechanisms may evolve and provide evidence of developmental advances in terms of ego functions, defense mechanisms, and adaptive and problem-solving capacities. While coping mechanisms are not called into question in terms of their adaptive value in the usual progress of one's life, during crises and their resolution such mechanisms are constantly being challenged, and adaptive change may even be required for survival.

Crisis theory is based on the assumptions that life holds both the opportunity for healthy personality development and the hazard of unhealthy personality change and that such changes take place during crisis periods. Thus it is important to learn as much as possible about factors determining whether a change during a crisis period will be healthy or unhealthy, as well as about how intervention may ensure a healthy outcome. A series of studies over the past twenty to twenty-five years has elucidated some of the phenomena of crises.

A crisis appears to be precipitated by unexpected or temporarily insurmountable problems that overtax the individual's current repertoire of problem-solving methods. The situation precipitating a crisis must be perceived by the individual himself as confusing or problematic. An individual's past experience strongly colors his perceptions of and responses to such situations; cultural systems, values, and traditions further define whether a particular situation is problematic or not. Objectively identical situations may precipitate a crisis in one individual but not in another. In any particular culture, on the other hand, certain situations are likely to precipitate crises in a significantly large proportion of the population. In most cultures, for example, adolescence is a crisis period requiring new individual adaptations to social role imperatives required for adulthood. In Western society, retirement is a similar, culturally defined crisis period, requiring individual adaptation to a particular, culturally determined time period. Thus the culture may define a transitional period that may then be experienced by the individual as a crisis, calling into play new adaptive and coping mechanisms and bringing about the potential for individual change and growth.

Situations that provoke crises are of three main types: (1) they may involve the threatened loss of an important source of need satisfaction, whether psychosocial, sociocultural, or physical; (2) they may involve an actual loss; or (3) they may involve situations of challenge, that is, of increased opportunity for need satisfaction associated with increased demands upon the individual.

Confrontation by a seemingly insoluble but inescapable, novel problem that is nevertheless of great importance produces the upset in equilibrium—the hallmark of crisis. In addition, the essential aspect of the crisis period itself is the series of attempts by the individual to work out new methods of internal adjustment or external adaptation in order to cope with the psychological tasks involved and to defend against the rise of tension and the pressures of anxiety, depression, and other unpleasant emotional side effects of disequilibrium.

Crisis resolution involves the individual in the discovery of new coping responses, new ways of dealing with psychological tasks, and possibly new relations with his external social milieu; this involves an addition to his previous problem-solving repertoire and to his adaptive patterns. A person may make effective or ineffective adjustments and adaptations in such a situation. An effective choice will enable him to deal with the problems that precipitated the crisis in the world of reality as defined by his culture; the additions to his problem-solving repertoire are then considered healthy, because he has learned to deal in an effective way with a type of situation that was previously beyond his problem-solving capacity. On the other hand, relying on magical explanations during a crisis or dealing with the problem by avoiding it indicates that a person has been overwhelmed by the problem. Regression or alienation from immediate surroundings may allow the individual to separate himself from a reality that is too much to bear; such coping responses are considered psychologically unhealthy. The individual thus regresses, possibly developing a neurosis or psychosis or emerging with an increased potential for such breakdowns in the future, should some fresh crisis-inducing situation occur.

During the crisis, the choice between alternative paths represents the outcome of a complicated system of forces. Among the most important are forces in the personality of the individual. From this point of view, personality is conceived of as the current representation of patterns of behavior that have crystallized during the individual's entire past life in relation to biological, psychological, and sociocultural factors. Particularly crucial are an individual's choices of problem-solving techniques, gradually accumulated as a result of repeated learning experiences, and his capacity to persevere in problem-solving despite frustration and confusion. The current state of ego strength of the individual, which can be associated with his general state of fatigue or freshness and physical health, also affects his response to a crisis, as does the current meaning of the problematic situation in relation to his past experience—particularly the intensity of symbolic links with the past and the degree to which the current situation stimulates revival of old conflicts. Further significant factors in determining the individual's response are his current psychosocial and sociocultural interactions with his social milieu. In this connection, great importance is attached to the support of the individual's ego strengths by "significant others" and also to the active collaboration of these people with the individual in order to accomplish the adaptive tasks involved in the crisis situation.

In certain extreme cases, the outcome of the crisis will be so strongly influenced by powerful forces in one or another of these areas that it will be predetermined. The fundamental premise of crisis theory, however, is that in most situations, predicting the outcome of the crisis by an analysis of the antecedent factors is impossible. The outcome will, instead, be determined by the actual interplay of forces during the crisis situation itself. The forces associated with the present behavior of "significant others" toward the individual are of prime importance, and their help and support may tip the balance toward either mental health or illness. As an individual's tension rises during a crisis, his motivation to seek help from others increases, and the signs of manifest distress have a critical effect on the people around him, who usually are stimulated to come to his aid.

In addition to an increased motivation to seek help from the social group, the individual in crisis shows an increased susceptibility to influence—a matter of supreme importance from a preventive psychiatric point of view. By deploying helping services to deal with individuals in crisis, a small amount of effort can lead to a maximum lasting response. Crisis theory and intervention have thus become important in community psychiatry, and crisis intervention programs have been developed in community mental health centers to provide short-term treatment in these situations. Programs of a broader-based nature have been developed as well. One example is widow-to-widow counseling, wherein people who have experienced loss of a spouse provide support for the newly widowed. Job Corps and Peace Corps "crisis of arrival" programs, wherein newly arrived participants receive supportive services, are also examples of broad-scale crisis intervention. Experience indicates that such efforts do stabilize individual adjustment and promote psychological growth (Macht and Scherl, 1974).

The significant others to whom a person in crisis turns for help, and whose behavior at such times may tip the balance of his psychological forces toward or away from healthy problem solving, may be individuals such as family and friends, to whom he is linked as sources of gratification of his fundamental needs. They may also include professional and nonprofessional community caregivers—the community's agents in providing help for those in need. (The help that can be given to someone in crisis by a care-giving agency is called *preventive intervention* and is dealt with briefly later in this chapter.)

Relating Services to Needs

Another conceptual issue in the field focuses on relating services to needs and developing ways of meeting people's needs in the most comprehensive and relevant manner possible. Surveys, need assessments, and citizen participation serve as means of obtaining input. Emphasis on learning how people define their own problems and priorities and how they decide where to turn for outside assistance has increased. Experience has frequently shown that for many people mental health services, as narrowly defined, are low in priority when compared with jobs, housing, welfare, education, and even general health services. To be relevant to the need within a community, mental health services must perforce be built into other care-giving systems.

Technical Aspects of Community Psychiatry

A population-centered approach to psychiatric problems must be concerned with the technical aspects of the field—those techniques developed to further community psychiatric goals. These techniques aim at focusing on populations, either directly or through other caregivers to whom the mental health professional is consultant or teacher, and providing direct clinical services within community settings.

Mental Health Consultation

Consultation provides a method for the mental health professional to assist another worker (frequently from a related human services field or from the field of education) to function more effectively with individual clients, groups, or programs related to human behavior or development. This technique has major significance as a population-centered approach, since by working with a variety of other caregivers, a mental health specialist potentially has a real, albeit indirect, impact on large numbers of people. Mental health consultation is based on an egalitarian relationship, compared with the more hierarchical relationship in supervision. It evolves over time between consultant and consultee, with the person seeking consultation (consultee) retaining responsibility for the client he is trying to assist or for the program administrators who have sought the consultation. The process includes establishing a consultation contract, forming a relationship, assessing the problem, delivering the consultation message, establishing an educational process, and ameliorating interpersonal issues of a work-related nature. It can be performed in individual or group settings, and it frequently blends, in practice, with education and skill training. Consultation is categorized according to four main types, depending upon the focus and purpose of the consultation.

Client-centered case consultation. This approach derives from the consultation model in which the specialist sees a patient referred by a generalist. The goal is to assist the consultee to find the most effective way to help his client or patient by evaluating the client's problems, frequently through direct clinical assessment by the consultant. A secondary goal is education that will enable the consultee to deal with similar problems on his own in the future.

Consultee-centered case consultation. In this form, the stimulus for consultation comes from a problem raised by the client or patient, but the primary purpose is to assist the consultee to function more effectively. The focus is thus on the consultee and on assisting him to deal with similar problems in the future; assessment of the

client's situation is secondary. The consultant's job is to assess and remedy the consultee's work difficulty, which may arise from lack of knowledge, skill, confidence, or objectivity or from some focal personal or interpersonal difficulty that impedes effective work with the client.

Program-centered administrative consultation. Here, as with client-centered case consultation, the primary focus in program-centered administrative consultation is on the program (analogous in this context to the client) and upon its nature, content, or organization. Assisting consultees to be more effective program administrators in the future is secondary. The consultant assesses the program's goals, operation, and management and makes suggestions for changes in structure, content, or function. When the problem with the program involves the functioning of the consultee, the consultation blends into consultee-centered administrative type.

Consultee-centered administrative consultation. In this type of consultation, the primary focus is on helping the consultee become a more effective program administrator. It is similar to consultee-centered case consultation in that it is primarily aimed at assessing and remedying the consultee's difficulties involving knowledge, skill, confidence, direction, or interpersonal relations. This assessment is undertaken in order to assist the consultee in areas of his current or future work that affect the operation of the program and its staff and participants.

Each of these forms of consultation can affect large groups of people, but the latter two are considered to have the greatest potential impact on community mental health because they affect programs related to the mental health of large populations. As with any categorization, this schema should be viewed as flexible because, in practice, the various forms of mental health consultation blend into one another.

One detailed and subtle technique, "theme interference reduction" (G. Caplan, 1964, 1970), holds particular prominence in the field of consultation. It is an indirect method employed when the consultee's work difficulty is caused by lack of objectivity due to an aspect of his own personality and functioning of which he is unaware. Origins of the interfering theme or inner issue are not explored with this technique; rather, the unconscious issue is dealt with in a displaced, nonpersonal fashion. Because of his own life issues, the consultee in this situation generally has a preconceived notion about the client that leads him to believe a poor outcome is inevitable. The consultant assists the consultee in exploring positive alternatives so that the negative prophecy is not fulfilled. The interfering theme is thereby weakened so that, in future situations, a reduction of tension and pessimism will decrease the possibility that the consultee will repetitively enact his own theme in his work with clients or programs.

Mental Health Education

As a form of public education, mental health education attempts both to provide information and to alter attitudes and behavior. It aims at individual as well as social change in its efforts to alter attitudes and promote better adaptation, with a major emphasis on small groups, particularly discussion models, and on the use of mass media. Many programs in this field are located in schools, focusing on teachers, students, and parents and involving content ranging from sex education to drugs, alcohol, and interpersonal relations. The national Job Corps program, for example, developed a series of health education modules, including such mental health topics as drugs, sex, alcohol, and "getting along with others." Specific content came from actual experience of Corps members and from an attitude survey in which they participated. The goals of the program were to provide information as well as to develop new attitudes. Rather than using a lecture format, each module was developed for small group discussion and teaching, and a variety of workers at local Job Corps centers were trained as group discussion leaders. The content of the modules consisted of short episodes drawn from life and related to particular topics; discussion, rather than sensitivity training as such, was the vehicle for learning and changing. Many school systems and other organizations have developed similar courses.

Other programs aim at increasing the skills of generalists who work with people in areas related to mental health by training them in a variety of areas such as interviewing techniques, family work, and therapy concerning death and dying. Other efforts are geared toward parent education and the needs of special groups such as clergy and welfare workers.

Some view anticipatory guidance as a mental health education strategy. This technique has been compared with immunization or inoculation in physical medicine and is an attempt to assist people to anticipate the reality, content, and emotional impact of a predictable life crisis. Its goal is to minimize the impact of the crisis so that, rather than being overwhelmed, the individual can develop new problem-solving capacities and adaptive coping mechanisms. This goal is accomplished by working with individuals or groups to explore in advance what the crisis will be like and by examining both cognitive and affective issues related to it. Anticipatory guidance relies upon anticipation as a high-level ego function and can be a useful preventive technique.

Large-scale attempts at anticipatory guidance have been carried out by the Peace Corps and the Job Corps. Peace Corps volunteers, as part of their training prior to going overseas, read a pamphlet entitled "Adjusting Overseas" (see G. Caplan, 1964) and are then involved in small group discussions focusing on practical and emotional concerns of adjustment raised by placement in a foreign country. Similarly, Job Corps trainees, prior to leaving for centers, participate in a program of anticipatory guidance including individual and group discussions, films and slides of centers, and conversations with returned graduates of the program (Macht and Scherl, 1974). The Job Corps also developed an emotional support program for newly arrived members at centers and evolved a program of anticipatory guidance to assist with other predictable crisis periods.

Crisis Intervention

The technical aspects of crisis intervention involve both anticipatory guidance and support —assisting people in dealing with specific, focal emotional and reality issues and helping them to find new adaptive and problem-solving techniques. Its impact derives from the willingness that many people feel to become involved with helpers during times of crisis. Such situations thus present the opportunity to foster a healthy rather than a maladaptive outcome and to assist the individual in developing coping mechanisms for use in handling future crises. This mode of intervention grows from experience in helping people deal with loss and bereavement as a life crisis and has importance in community psychiatry because of its relative economy and preventive potential and because it can be used across a broad population base—both by training and utilizing a variety of community caregivers and by developing and implementing support systems. These significant others have their greatest impact on the individual during the time when the tension of the crisis is approaching its climax.

Collaboration, Coordination, and Cooperation

As community mental health programs evolve, three techniques—collaboration, coordination, and cooperation—become increasingly important. In collaboration, whether work is focused on a client or on the development and operation of a program, two or more people work together to solve a common problem and share responsibility for the process and outcome. They may, as the result of discussion and joint planning, arrive at joint decisions and carry out action together—in marked contrast to consultation, where the consultant acts only as an advisor and the consultee alone carries out the action. In coordination, two or more people providing services to a client or program inform each other of their activities and attempt to synchronize their actions and develop ways of preventing unconstructive overlap, duplication, or counterproductive action as they work to provide separate but related services. In activities involving cooperation, two or more people assist each other in providing a service to a client or program. Each might provide different services, but they work together in a common venture to enhance each other's contribution. Each of these functions has its own complex techniques, and each is crucial in developing and operating community pro-

grams where a variety of agencies and workers are involved with a client or program.

Community Organization, Development, and Action

Community organization allows intervention to take place when the community as a social system is of concern through its impact on its individual members. In part, this mode of intervention grew from Alexander Leighton's Stirling County study (1959) and his concept of "sociocultural disintegration." Debate has ensued about the role of the mental health worker in the social network and the legitimacy of active participation as a professional function. Frequently, however, consultation and program development do involve community organization.

The sociologist Eduard Lindemann (1921) outlined steps in community organization and action that still apply today.
1. expression of community need
2. spreading awareness of need within the community
3. making the leadership of the community recognize the need
4. presentation of solutions
5. conflict of solutions
6. investigation of solutions with expert assistance
7. open discussion
8. emergence of a practicable solution
9. compromise on the basis of tentative progress
In his discussion of community dynamics and mental health, Klein (1968) elaborates further on the basic processes involved in community organization. These activities frequently have an impact on mental health because they counteract sociocultural disintegration by providing personal solutions. Community participation thus functions as an important type of intervention and has become an integral aspect of community health and mental health.

The development of any community mental health program involves considerable organization in setting up and working with the community board of a mental health center, neighborhood health center, or health systems agency. This work may in fact be a paradigm for community organization in a variety of different areas. It includes identifying citizen leaders with a commitment to particular concerns and working with them to identify needs, to plan and implement services, and to arrive at a viable partnership of professionals and laymen in the interest of patients and the development of services. These endeavors fuse professional expertise with citizen knowledge of the reality of people's needs and life styles. They are particularly successful when the needs are recognized by the community or neighborhood and can be articulated by its formal or informal representatives.

Citizen and consumer groups have become increasingly important in mental health and retardation, and their input can educate professionals and make services more relevant and culturally syntonic. Professionals have only recently developed new ways of working effectively with consumers as coequal partners.

The development of viable professional-citizen partnerships involves mutual learning and change, the evolution of a group process, and the satisfactory resolution of control issues by all parties. Such a partnership aids immeasurably in making services relevant to the community's needs and enhances the growth and development of individual participants and community alike.

Clinical Practice in Community Settings

The context of a community program for clinical practice brings certain technical and program issues clearly to the fore: provision of a range of therapeutic modalities, limited resources and relatively unlimited needs, responsibility for the entire population of an area or program, relevance to the needs of the people to be served, sociocultural and economic factors, and the interrelationship of reality and intrapsychic conflict. Teamwork in the treatment of individuals, families, and social networks becomes a major practical concern.

Translating Clinical Experience and Research into Programs

A major technical area in community psychiatry is program development, the attempt to translate what is known about clinical care and people's needs into service programs capable of reaching large numbers of consumers. This translation involves the general areas of needs assessment (including the ways people define their own needs for outside assistance); psychiatric epidemiology; information and data-system input; translation of psychological and sociopsychological understanding into programs and systems of care; and input from legislative, judicial, and executive bodies, citizen groups, and the mass media. Frequently gaps in existing services at the community level are filled by the development of formal and informal support systems and are addressed by consumer and citizen advocacy.

Programmatic Aspects of Community Psychiatry

The major conceptual and technical issues discussed so far are expressed in various programs that form the basis of the service aspect of community psychiatry. The programs are thus vehicles for the implementation of these conceptual and technical issues; in considering each of these program areas, this discussion will focus on direct service aspects in the community, as well as on the range of consultation, education, collaboration, and community-organization activities. Furthermore, we will examine briefly how the three levels of prevention and the population-centered approach are developed through different kinds of programs.

Community Mental Health Centers

Inaugurated in 1963, community mental health centers resulted from a mandate to provide accessible, comprehensive (preventive, diagnostic, therapeutic, and rehabilitative) care with continuity of services based in the community. As both a clinical and a public health approach to delivering services, centers usually involve active community participation by citizens as center board members, volunteers, and workers. The three levels of prevention are emphasized, along with a commitment to serve a specific community and to be responsible for the mental health care of its entire population. In a number of localities the mental health center also provides services for the mentally retarded. Centers are funded by federal-state matching grants, state, local, and private funds, contracts, and third-party reimbursements. A trend toward the latter, as well as toward the operation of centers as private health corporations, is apparent.

Basic to such programs is the definition of the community to be served. The federal Community Mental Health Center Program designates so-called catchment areas (expressing the center's function of gathering in all those who need care) of 75,000 to 200,000 people from a geographically defined region. Considerable discussion has ensued as to whether or not this concept can reflect "real communities," as people define where they live and come from; some have felt that in urban areas, neighborhoods, and rural areas, counties or towns are more useful population bases than the more arbitrarily defined catchments.

The original federal definition of the community mental health center includes five essential services: inpatient care, partial hospitalization (day or night care), outpatient care, twenty-four-hour emergency services, and community consultation and education. Inpatient care delivered at a central mental health facility or in a community general hospital has tended to be short-term or, less frequently, to last for an intermediate time period with admissions averaging several weeks to months (although some admissions may be for days and some up to a year). Emphasis is on rapid reintegration into the community, and patients move flexibly, depending on their clinical situation, between services—from inpatient to partial (day or night) care with continuity of caretakers and involvement of family and community caregivers. Emergency services at one designated place in the community, for example, may provide both diagnosis and treatment. Consultation and education as major preventive thrusts are perhaps the most innovative aspects of the program, employing techniques described earlier to work with clergy, teachers, police, and other community workers. For example, the school consultant working with administrators to reduce stress in the school is involved with primary prevention. When he assists teachers in identifying disturbed students, he is involved with early case identification or secondary prevention. When he works

with both teachers and administrators to develop techniques and programs for classroom management of disturbed children from the community, he is developing rehabilitative or training programs to ameliorate the residual effects of mental illness, thus working toward tertiary prevention.

Several patterns have evolved, including that of the primary center and more decentralized programs, with numerous sites in the community and affiliations with a wide variety of health, social service, and educational agencies. Different centers emphasize different services, depending on local need and organization. Typical patterns have not emerged, but the most frequent basic model is the "multiple-agency center," involving at least two participants, a general hospital and a mental health outpatient clinic (either of which may be publicly supported or nonprofit corporations). Local initiative is encouraged in planning, management, and citizen participation.

In addition to the original five essential services, many centers provide specialized diagnostic programs (for mental retardation, for example); services for the seriously and chronically ill, such as state hospital units serving the community; precare and aftercare for state hospital patients; rehabilitation services; community alternatives to hospitalization (halfway houses, group homes, cooperative apartments, as well as nursing home placement, back-up, and consultation services); training programs (for professional and nonprofessional staff and students, for instance); and research and evaluation of program utilization, impact, and cost. Further specialized services for children and the elderly and programs for treatment, prevention, and rehabilitation in the areas of alcoholism and drug abuse are now also considered essential. In fact, the Community Mental Health Centers Amendments of 1975 require all of the above services for federally funded centers. In addition, these amendments also require coordination with other human services systems, satellite centers, and services for ethnic minorities. All are essential if the center is to be truly comprehensive.

A major issue is the responsibility of the center and the community in caring for its most severely ill and handicapped members, primarily state hospital and psychotic patients from the area, as well as the mentally retarded and geriatric populations. Community alternatives to state and private hospitalization are receiving a new emphasis, and some centers have evolved into comprehensive human service agencies, coordinating and integrating other health and social services needed by the center's clients. Recently, some workers have come to feel that community mental health centers represent a transitional form of service delivery as we move toward more truly community-based programs wherein mental health is integrated with other community human services agencies. Under these circumstances, the specialized mental health center or hospital provides back-up services and is linked to the community through staff and program.

Alternative Counseling Centers

During the 1960s, alternative counseling centers, hot lines, and halfway houses arose side by side with the burgeoning mental health establishment (community mental health centers and hospitals). Originally these services arose to serve disenfranchised young people who had "dropped out," and they addressed what were felt to be the ills of established clinics, bureaucracies, and therapies. Although initially viewed as alternative helping organizations, many have themselves evolved into small community mental health centers, and they survive, flourish, and are synthesizing their initial innovative ideals with more traditional aspects of service delivery. Staffed primarily by paraprofessionals, occasionally with professional consultation and back-up, these centers provide short-term and group counseling services to many people who would not use other aspects of the delivery system. Literally hundreds have developed across the country; Holleb and Abrams (1975) describe their development, philosophy, functioning, and future.

Neighborhood Psychiatry

A number of workers (Macht, Scherl, and Sharfstein, 1976) have defined neighborhood psychiatry—a new aspect of the community psychiatry field—as mental health work within a defined geographic, psychosocial, and sociopolitical area or neighborhood. It includes mental health practice within a particular facility or facilities, such as neighborhood health and multiservice centers, as well as with neighborhood organizations and networks.

Neighborhood work is related to but distinctly different from work within a community mental health center. Current practice includes direct clinical services for children and adults, consultation and collaboration with other caregivers, and development of work with social networks in the neighborhood. Thus, the whole range of community psychiatry techniques is utilized; efforts originally viewed as "outreach" or "satellite centers," however, are increasingly seen as primary or front-line services.

Several patterns of practice have emerged, including solo neighborhood mental health services—where mental health workers operate directly in the neighborhood or from a storefront, mobile van, or other neighborhood base—and mental health services within comprehensive neighborhood health and human service centers. In the latter programs, several patterns of mental health workers' liaison with broader neighborhood health and social service programs have emerged. In one, the mental health worker provides consultation but no direct service to primary caregivers. In the second pattern, the mental health service operates in isolation within a neighborhood health center—that is, a mental health clinic exists within a more comprehensive neighborhood service center but has little or no integration with other services. In a third, the mental health service is an integral part of a comprehensive health center, and mental health workers become members of the overall staff and integral partners on comprehensive care teams. A final pattern consists of the mental health service as an integral part of a comprehensive center or program, with a mental health worker in a position of executive responsibility within the organization. In this model, the mental health worker has overall clinical and planning authority within the comprehensive center and works to integrate a range of services including mental health.

With each of these patterns (save that of pure consultation), a wide range of direct and indirect techniques may be used by the clinician, including consultation, education, coordination, collaboration, and cooperation. In addition, the opportunity exists to work with neighborhood residents and with social networks and environmental factors.

Neighborhood practice is similar to work in a community mental health center but shows distinct differences, bringing with it a keener sense of the patient's life space and style and of the internal and external forces operating within the social field. It also most clearly highlights the importance of a variety of care-giving systems in solving people's problems and presents the practical need to integrate services. Furthermore, the clinician who practices in a neighborhood gains unique experience from working on the patient's own "turf." He can thus appreciate the strengths, talents, and struggles of people living in the neighborhood, opening new vistas for clinical and preventive work, as well as for theoretical understanding. Equally important for the mental health worker in neighborhood practice is the opportunity to share more fully in the life experience of his patients. This area may also provide greater opportunity for focusing on population issues in the planning and delivery of services.

Psychiatry in Nonhealth Agencies

Mental health intervention in nonhealth agencies includes work with schools, preschool programs, work, welfare, and religious organizations, legal services, prisons, courts, and police. Various techniques are used in each of these areas to provide direct services, especially crisis intervention and a variety of consultation and education efforts. Some agencies have integrated psychiatry into their structure, the psychiatrist serving as a responsible executive within the organization. Three levels of prevention are incorporated, but primary prevention is emphasized and the program of the agency becomes a focus for mental health intervention in addition to serving its primary purpose. A work program may, for example, provide job-skill training but also intervene in problems of self-esteem, mastery, interpersonal relations, identity, and independence and autonomy.

Because nonhealth agencies work with people where they define what is relevant in their own

lives, they can reach increasing numbers of people who do not utilize formal mental health services. These large-scale programs serve wider populations, and mental health services within these agencies further the population-centered approach of community psychiatry.

Self-Help Programs

As a programmatic expression of support systems, self-help programs such as Alcoholics Anonymous and Synanon have achieved increased importance. Although psychiatrists and others function as consultants and at times as program developers in these efforts, such professionals must be aware of the need to allow the self-help group its own autonomy and not to disrupt its natural processes. Investigators view these endeavors as an important new aspect of community psychiatry, capable of population-centered approaches at times of crisis and of enduring intervention, with the potential for reaching an entire population around relevant life issues (G. Caplan, 1974). As formal and informal networks within the community, these programs can address problems that have been neglected by the formal mental health system. Like nonhealth agencies, they do not define people as patients, a practice that can have negative implications for identity.

Community Alternatives to Institutionalization

The development of halfway houses, group homes, and cooperative apartments for the mentally ill and retarded is based on the view that these community-based alternatives to large institutions can prevent chronicity and institutionalism and can lead to more normal lives for their clients (Lamb, 1976). These kinds of programs have steadily increased as the large state mental hospitals and schools for the retarded have been phased out, although concern has arisen in some areas about the quality of care and community acceptance. In order to function well, such programs require professional back-up, support, and consultation; ideally, they bring community psychiatry directly into contact with clinical, social, philosophical, and ethical concerns about the quality of life.

Psychiatry in Governmental Agencies

An important area for community psychiatry has been work within governmental agencies at all levels—international, federal, state, and local. In addition to working as administrators of mental health and retardation programs, community psychiatrists in government agencies have used consultation, collaboration, and policy-making techniques in a variety of settings, ranging from the League of Nations to such federal agencies as the Health, Education and Welfare, Labor, and State Departments, the Federal Aviation Agency, the military, the Peace Corps, and the Office of Economic Opportunity. Probably best known have been programs that provided direct and indirect services in the latter three organizations. At state and local levels, psychiatrists have begun to work within comprehensive human services and education departments, school systems, and correction departments, functioning both as consultants and as executives.

Psychiatry and Comprehensive Health and Human Services

Further development in the field of community psychiatry occurs in the new area of its connections with comprehensive health and human services programs (Scherl, 1977), where the emphasis is on the integration of mental health with other services already described. As problems are defined in broader health and human terms, new services are brought to bear on life dilemmas, leading to the development of coordinated service systems. In many local and state programs, integration of mental health with services for the retarded, public health, corrections, youth services, and welfare has been increasingly emphasized in planning, monitoring, and actual provision of services. This emphasis requires further development of community psychiatry techniques, especially collaboration, coordination, and cooperation, and some workers recognize this aspect of the field as a major ongoing need (Scherl and Macht, 1977). Federal legislation for comprehensive health planning determines this direction, as does the development of human services departments in twenty-six states and the evolution of comprehensive health and multiservice centers in urban neighborhoods, small towns, and rural areas.

Training for Community Psychiatry

Training in the field of community psychiatry has involved both generalists and specialists, and training programs in community settings have proliferated; in some, training at all levels is fully community-oriented rather than institution-based. Specialist training has in the past been intended for advanced students in specialized community psychiatry training programs. The trend, however, is clearly toward multidisciplinary community training early in the career of students, as well as toward in-service, continuing education, and retraining efforts. In addition to traditional education in clinical practice and basic sciences, major elements of community psychiatry curricula include the social and behavioral sciences, public health, community mental health techniques, administration, planning, community organization and development, and research in community mental health.

Research and Evaluation

Although a detailed review of research in the field is beyond the scope of this chapter, it is possible to highlight specific studies that illustrate significant research directions. The work of Leighton, Srole, and Hollingshead and Redlich has had a major impact on the development of community psychiatry and is described more fully in chapter 29, "Psychiatric Epidemiology." Numerous studies have been conducted in the conceptual, technical, and program areas described in this chapter, some of which will be described here.

The Sociopsychological Interface

The work of Levinson and Gallagher (1964) demonstrates the complexity of the processes of individual and social interaction and includes studies of "patienthood" and of various workers in the field. Levinson's studies of leadership functions in collaboration with Klerman (1967, 1969) and with Hodgson, Levinson, and Zaleznik (1965) and the work of Macht (1977) further delineated problematic role issues requiring psychological work to integrate various aspects of individual and social dynamics. The work of Erikson (1950) and Hartmann (1964) pointed to related issues and to the ego as the individual's integrating agency. Other workers have dealt with social forces and individual psychology in many different domains, from psychohistory to social psychology and cultural anthropology.

Crisis Theory and Crisis Intervention

The work of Lindemann on acute grief (1944) and of Kaplan and Mason on premature birth (1960) served to define crisis theory and the dimensions of crises. Studies of engagement, marriage, and bereavement further explored this area, while studies by English and Colmen with Peace Corps volunteers (1966) and by Macht and Scherl with Job Corps trainees (1974) defined predictable life crises in the careers of participants in various programs and suggested preventive intervention in these situations.

Mental Health Consultation

Research in this area has dealt with the development of a typology of consultation as well as with such factors as program analysis, the consultee, and the purpose and duration of consultation. Iscoe et al. (1967) showed, for example, in a study of school consultation, that teachers felt consultants were most helpful in facilitating understanding of children's problems, conveying greater knowledge of human behavior, and confirming the teacher's own judgments and least helpful in such areas as enhancing communication with principals. Basically these are not evaluative studies; rather, they describe aspects of consultation practice, including roles, functions, selection, characteristics of consultants and consultees, and problems for which consultation is sought. In Aiken's study of consultation to a family service agency (1957), a case-centered focus predominated. Macht,

Scherl, and English, in a study of Job Corps psychiatric consultation (1968), found that problems in which consultants were involved included individual case-focused situations, development of programs, such as group living, and general program functions, such as limit setting and communication.

Studies of the consultation process have included work on the perceptions, attitudes, and opinions of the participants, as well as analyses of actual behavior during the consultation. Outcome studies on consultation have examined changes in the consultee and the system, as well as the effect of consultation on the client. In these areas, Teitelbaum (1961) found that teachers who were part of a consultation program, for example, attained more confidence and professional growth than those who did not receive consultation. Dorsey, Matsunga, and Bauman demonstrated in their study of consultation to public health nurses (1964) that the greatest effects derived from work with patients, early case identification, improved understanding, and changed attitudes. In a "quasi-experimental" study, Iscoe et al. (1967) found no statistical evidence that consultation produced changes in teachers' mental health orientation. Several studies have attempted to evaluate its impact on clients, with varying conclusions. Chapman (1966) found some positive effects of consultation to unit commanding officers (military performance satisfactory or improved in two-thirds of cases). Hunter and Ratcliff (1968) showed that the distribution of client outcome (better, same, worse) on observed interpersonal behavior was similar for direct-service and case-centered consultation in a community mental health center. Bolman et al. (1969) found no significant changes in college students in a dormitory with a consultation program to counselors and house fellows compared with those in a dormitory without such consultation. Eisenberg (1958) found that a combination of direct service and consultation to a welfare department produced significantly greater improvement in those children whose case-workers had participated in consultation about the child's treatment plan.

Research in this area reflects complexities in practice and research methodology similar to those in psychotherapy research. There have been little replication and few in-depth, controlled studies, and difficulties have been compounded by the broad and at times poorly defined goals of consultation.

Mental Health Program Evaluation

Evaluation research has studied the description, utilization, effectiveness, cost, and outcome of programs and has encountered significant problems with community and professional acceptance, resources, use of control groups and experimental design, determining program objectives, and assessing factors leading to success. Program description studies, as well as studies of client satisfaction and expert judgment, have achieved the highest level of sophistication, using such indices as admission and recidivism rates. Such studies have predominated thus far in the literature. For example, reports by Macht et al. (1969) and Macht (1975) of mental health in antipoverty programs and neighborhood health centers demonstrate various models, as do those of Levenson (1972), Whittington (1972), and Glasscote and his colleagues (1964, 1969) on community mental health centers. Borus et al. (1975) and Borus (1976) describe program models and discuss linkage issues in neighborhood mental health; these reports also describe the use of mental health staff in neighborhood health centers and present some qualitative evaluation data. Other descriptive program studies are included in Macht, Scherl, and Sharfstein (1977).

An excellent example of comparative and outcome studies is the report by Pasamanick, Scarpitti, and Dinitz (1967), who studied hospitalization rates of schizophrenics treated at home by public health nurses with and without medication, revealing the home care-drug combination to be most effective. Other specific studies in this area include that of Zwerling and Wilder (1964), whose investigation of day treatment demonstrates its efficiency and effectiveness. Straker (1968) studied brief psychotherapy and found it reduced dropouts and eliminated waiting lists. Follette and Cummings (1967) studied medical utilization in a prepaid group practice of patients who had received brief psychotherapy and in a similar group who had not and found a significant

reduction in medical care utilization in the former. Grad and Sainsbury (1966) studied the impact on suicide and hospitalization rates of a community program in Chichester, England, and found suicide rates unchanged and hospitalization rates significantly reduced with the advent of the community service, compared with a town with no community-based service, where rates for both remained the same; however, significant problems with families of patients treated at home were also found.

The work of Brown et al. (1966) raises questions as to whether comprehensive community-based services reduce hospital readmissions. Several studies demonstrate that community care is feasible even for chronic psychiatric patients, but other studies show just as clearly that large numbers of chronic psychotics are unable to exist outside an institutional setting. Further significant questions are raised by the studies of Anthony (1969, 1970) and by Arnhoff's commentary (1975), as well as by others, regarding the impact upon children in families where psychotic parents are treated at home. These are high-risk situations for the development of major mental illness in children, although etiological factors are complex. Anthony's research, for example, shows that in a group of forty-three such children from urban areas, about 15 percent will develop a psychosis; 40 percent will become juvenile delinquents; and the remainder will be normal, with a 10 percent subgroup who are "superior, creative people." Issues of timing of the parents' illness and of home versus hospital treatment are complex and incompletely understood at present. Arnhoff raises serious questions about the social consequences of mental health policy in this area.

Mental health program evaluation, although critical to maximally effective program development, is at present a developing field and must include formal and informal evaluation as we move toward a science of service delivery. Klerman (1974) has reviewed some recent studies and highlighted several areas for greater scrutiny. First, "catchmenting" as an administrative, planning, and coordinating mechanism produces a rational system of coordinated care that increases utilization of local services; initially it appears to increase hospitalization rates as untreated persons receive services. Other studies (Tischler et al., 1972; Goldblatt et al., 1973) have found that it also results in fewer dropouts, improved crisis intervention accessibility, and consumer satisfaction. Second, community alternatives to mental hospitalization require further study. Several studies document the efficiency of intensive treatment, early discharge, and community treatment in preventing chronicity, but few data exist regarding optimal duration of hospitalization or the quality of life of discharged patients in the community; some reports have caused concern about the marginal existence of many former hospital patients and the extent to which patterns of chronicity are reestablished in the community. Third, evidence from the national experience with community mental health centers shows that only 10 percent of staff time is spent in consultation and education, and in many programs it is far less. The impact of this work upon primary prevention is yet to be established. In a slightly different vein, Beck and Long (1977) present a conceptual schema and protocols for single and cross-program comparative evaluation studies.

Dilemmas and Potential

During the past fifteen to twenty years, several dilemmas in the field of community psychiatry have become apparent. Many people believe that the community mental health movement "oversold" itself early in its development and made promises it could not possibly keep, especially in the area of prevention, in the focus on improving the quality of life, and in the implication that community-based services would be less expensive than traditional, institution-based services. This assertion is yet to be clearly proven.

Many dilemmas were raised for practitioners who had never functioned outside of hospital or office settings when they moved into complex community arenas. Frequently, they were ill prepared by background, experience, training, or personality for this work. When greeted by resistance, they were easily rebuffed and frustrated and retreated to safer asylums. It was difficult to recognize that social change, or even acceptance

of mental health consultants, might take as long as individual change, that it was even more complex and that it came with difficulty, at times with shock, and in some cases not at all.

Reliance on federal initiative and funding for this "bold new approach," often to the detriment of local initiative and commitment, occurred too frequently. As federal dollars dwindled, community mental health continued to flourish only where local communities and some states had themselves recognized the need for effective services as a high priority, especially during times of economic recession. With the eventual advent of national health insurance, the clear need to include mental health services is apparent; some proposals now favor service delivery through community mental health centers, neighborhood health centers, or health maintenance organizations. Deciding which services to cover and what models to use will require sustained technical and negotiating efforts.

Many agencies, especially early in the history of community mental health development, did not know how to make use of mental health consultants (and consultants, in turn, did not always understand what the agencies and nonprofessional support systems had done and could do independently.) Perception of delicate balances was needed—balances between what consultants could offer and what agencies needed and wanted, between a consultant's limitations and the fragile nature of the equilibrium in many agencies. Also, most agencies and communities needed and wanted mental health workers who would provide clinical care and not act only as consultants. The pure consultation model clearly proved inadequate for many mental health workers; direct service gave them credibility and legitimacy when working with other agencies and caregivers. Crucial dilemmas of coordination and priorities for direct service, compared with consultation and education, emerged in which both might be important in a community or agency. Funding for the indirect services continues to be problematic because they are not currently reimbursable.

A curious dilemma arose regarding federal and state definitions of "communities." "Catchment areas" tended to impose artificial boundaries in order to meet population-base requirements. Many advanced community programs have now begun to decentralize services to more natural areas, such as neighborhoods and towns, leading, in part, to the development of neighborhood psychiatry.

One of the most serious problems in the field has been the tendency of community psychiatry, until recently, to neglect the most seriously ill in the population. There are now signs of a new interest in the former mental hospital patient and in the retarded. If the responsibility for their care is not met, community psychiatry will surely suffer and may be in great jeopardy.

One of the major areas of real impact has been in children's services. In part, community psychiatry is related to the child guidance movement and similarly views the familial and social context of the child as crucial to development. The long trend toward community-based child mental health services, including prevention, will continue and will require innovative linkages with community care of the severely mentally ill and retarded, possibly through a focus on high-risk groups of children such as those with chronically psychotic, depressed, or alcoholic parents.

In recent years, education and training in community psychiatry have suffered severe cuts in federal appropriations, raising issues of survival. Even where local communities have built or maintained an interest in community mental health, the limited numbers of trained practitioners constrain optimal program efficacy. Community psychiatry is not so easily learned after formal training ends as some once thought. The number of good training programs is small, faculties limited, and committed and dedicated students less available than they once were. Research and evaluation in the field have also been curtailed by limited funds and lack of trained personnel; these limitations have naturally impeded progress, especially in the area of prevention.

Community psychiatry belongs to no one discipline. Within this truly interdisciplinary field, new and complex relationships have developed among several related but previously disparate professions and paraprofessional groups. Each has unique contributions to make, and each has

had to define its own uniqueness while searching for common conceptual and practical bases. Issues of status and equity have, at times, proved difficult to address and are still not fully resolved; the need for new ways of working together and for mutual understanding and trust continues. Collaboration has been problematic, albeit enriching, and is compounded by the rapid influx of paraprofessionals into the field. They have proved their ability to perform many mental health functions (in some settings more usefully than professionals), but they need training, support, and back-up, as well as equitable career ladders and opportunities.

A further issue has been collaboration between citizens, or consumers, and providers—an area fraught with difficulty, usually over the issue of control. As true working partnerships have evolved in some places, this problem has faded, but continued work is necessary for further progress. As difficult as such collaboration has been at times, positive results enhance services and promote growth and development of citizens and professionals alike. In the health field, this development has been most advanced in community mental health, and this area can serve as a beacon light to illumine the hazards and the opportunities for those who follow.

Community psychiatry reflects dominant views, forces, and attitudes in the larger society. Like moral treatment, it arose in a period of heightened social concern and commitment to individual and humanistic values. Events of the 1960s reflected these concerns nationally, and if community psychiatry is in decline due to a shift in the values that motivated its development, those values, which are common to much of modern psychiatry, may also be in jeopardy.

What may be emerging in the 1970s and for the future, however, is not so much a declining field as a more sober and mature one that knows both the exhilaration and the limitations of its childhood and adolescence. The emergence of a broader community health and primary care interest can include and build upon the experience of community mental health. Many communities across the country are demanding increased community services, and we are now able to treat many patients in community programs rather than in institutions. However, many also now recognize the need for both institutional and community services, programmatically linked in order to meet the total needs of any community. The days of the either-or view may be ending.

We are now also on the brink of developing preventive approaches, particularly early in life, and recognize more of the side effects of community psychiatry development in relation to issues of prevention, such as the impact on children of chronically disturbed parents treated in the community; the goal is not to decrease such care for these individuals but to develop preventive programs for their offspring.

As community psychiatry evolves and is incorporated into the mainstream of psychiatric practice, teaching, and research, issues of the quality of life (including housing, education, racism, violence, and poverty) become crucial psychiatric concerns in dealing with patients, former patients, and nonpatients. The complex interrelations of an individual's intrapsychic functioning and current sociocultural situation are the matrix for further integration of community and clinical psychiatry in order to provide a fuller understanding of the total person.

One of the great strengths of community psychiatry has been its emphasis on service delivery—bringing therapeutic advances to people where they are, in a way that is relevant to their lives, and in a manner that increases utilization. Low-income groups and minorities need this type of delivery, as do the chronically mentally ill. Regardless of future breakthroughs, the issue of how to bring what we know and discover to the people who need it will remain of prime concern and will inevitably involve community practice of some sort. Finally, community psychiatry embodies principles of responsibility for the mental health of a whole population. Although questions about how best to meet this challenge persist, community psychiatry has furthered the ongoing social responsibility of medicine and all the helping professions for the entire community.

Rather than dissolving in gloom over its future, community psychiatry and its practitioners must enter the adulthood of the field rededicated to its values, sobered by its past, and committed to its ongoing ideals of the highest quality in service, teaching, and research in order to reach its still largely untapped potential.

References

Aiken, D. 1957. "Psychiatric consultation in the family agency." Doctoral dissertation, University of Chicago.

Anthony, E. J. 1969. The developmental precursors of adult schizophrenia. In *The transmission of schizophrenia*, ed. D. Rosenthal and S. Kety. Long Island City, N.Y.: Parthenon Press.

——— 1970. A clinical evaluation of children with psychotic parents. In *Annual progress in child psychiatry and child development*, ed. S. Chess and A. Thomas. New York: Brunner/Mazel.

Arnhoff, F. 1975. Social consequences of policy toward mental illness. *Science* 188:1277–81.

Beck, J. C., and J. Long. 1977. Evaluation of mental health services in a neighborhood center. In *Neighborhood psychiatry*, ed. L. B. Macht, D. J. Scherl, and S. S. Sharfstein. Lexington, Mass.: D. C. Heath, Lexington Books.

Beers, C. W. 1908. *A mind that found itself*. Garden City, N.Y.: Doubleday.

Bockoven, J. S. 1963. *Moral treatment in American psychiatry*. New York: Springer.

Bolman, W. M., S. L. Halleck, D. G. Rice, and J. L. Ryan. 1969. An unintended side-effect in a community psychiatric program. *Arch. Gen. Psychiatry* 20:508–513.

Borus, J. F. 1976. Neighborhood health centers as providers of primary mental-health care. *N. Engl. J. Med.* 295:140–145.

Borus, J. F., L. A. Janowitch, F. Kieffer, R. G. Morrill, L. Reich, E. Simone, and L. Towle. 1975. Coordination of mental health services at the neighborhood level. *Am. J. Psychiatry* 132:1177–81.

Brown, B. 1973. Keynote address presented at "Mental Health Services for the '70s: Neighborhood Psychiatry," a conference held 7–9 June 1973, at the Massachusetts Institute of Technology, Cambridge, Mass.

Brown, G. W., M. Bone, B. Dalison, and J. K. Wing. 1966. *Schizophrenia and social care*. London: Oxford University Press.

Caplan, G. 1964. *Principles of preventive psychiatry*. New York: Basic Books.

——— 1970. *The theory and practice of mental health consultation*. New York: Basic Books.

———— 1974. *Support systems and community mental health: Lectures on concept development*. New York: Behavioral Publications.

Caplan, G., L. B. Macht, and A. B. Wolf. 1969. *Manual for mental health professionals participating in the Job Corps program*. Washington, D.C.: Office of Economic Opportunity.

Caplan, R. B. 1969. *Psychiatry and the community in nineteenth-century America*. New York: Basic Books.

Chapman, R. F. 1966. Group mental health consultation—report of a military field program. *Milit. Med.* 131, no. 1:30–35.

Cobb, S., and E. Lindemann. 1943. Neuropsychiatric observations after the Cocoanut Grove fire. *Ann. Surg.* 117:814–824.

Dorsey, J. R., G. Matsunga, and G. Bauman. 1964. Training public health nurses in mental health. *Arch. Gen. Psychiatry* 11, no. 2:214–222.

Eisenberg, L. 1958. An evaluation of psychiatric consultation services for a public agency. *Am. J. Public Health* 48:742–749.

English, J. T., and J. G. Colmen. 1966. Psychological adjustment patterns of Peace Corps volunteers. *Psychiatr. Opinion* 3:29–35. Erikson, E. H. 1950. *Childhood and society*. New York: Norton.

Erickson, E. H. 1950. *Childhood and society*. New York: Norton.

Follette, W., and N. A. Cummings. 1967. Psychiatric services and medical utilization in a prepaid health plan setting. *Med. Care* 5:25–35.

Glasscote, R., D. Sanders, H. M. Fortenzer, and A. R. Foley, eds. 1964. *The community mental health center: an analysis of existing models*. Washington, D.C.: American Psychiatric Association.

Glasscote, R., J. N. Sussex, E. Cumming, and L. H. Smith. 1969. *The community mental health center: an interim appraisal*. Washington, D.C.: Joint Information Service.

Goldblatt, P. B., R. M. Berberian, B. Goldberg, G. L. Klerman, G. Tischler, and H. Zonana. 1973. Catchmenting and the delivery of mental health services. *Arch. Gen. Psychiatry* 28:478–482.

Grad, J., and P. Sainsbury. 1966. Evaluating the community psychiatric service in Chichester: results. In *Evaluating the effectiveness of mental health services*, ed. E. M. Gruenberg. New York: Milbank Memorial Fund.

Hartmann, H. 1964. *Essays on ego psychology: selected problems in psychoanalytic theory*. New York: International Universities Press.

Holleb, G. P., and W. H. Abrams. 1975. *Alternatives in community mental health*. Boston: Beacon Press.

Hollingshead, A. B., and F. C. Redlich. 1958. *Social class and mental illness*. New York: Wiley.

Hodgson, R. C., D. J. Levinson, and A. Zaleznik. 1965. *The executive role constellation: an analysis of personality and role relations in management*. Boston: Harvard University Graduate School of Business Administration, Division of Research.

Hunter, W. F., and A. W. Ratcliff. 1968. The range mental health center: evaluation of a community oriented mental health consultation program in northern Minnesota. *Community Ment. Health J.* 4, no. 3:260–267.

Iscoe, I., J. Pierce-Jones, S. T. Friedman, and L. McGehearty. 1967. Some strategies in mental health consultation: a brief description of a project and some preliminary results. In *Emergent approaches to mental health problems*, ed. E. L. Cowen, E. A. Gardner, and M. Zax. New York: Appleton-Century-Crofts.

Jarvis, E. 1855. *Insanity and idiocy in Massachusetts: report of the commission on lunacy*. Cambridge, Mass.: Harvard University Press, 1971.

Joint Commission on Mental Illness and Health. 1961. *Action for mental health*. New York: Basic Books.

Kaplan, D. M., and E. A. Mason. 1960. Maternal reactions to premature birth viewed as an acute emotional disorder. *Am. J. Orthopsychiatry* 30: 539–550.

Klein, D. C. 1968. *Community dynamics and mental health*. New York: Wiley.

Klerman, G. L. 1974. Current evaluation research on mental health services. *Am. J. Psychiatry* 131:783–787.

Klerman, G. L., and D. J. Levinson. 1969. Becoming the director: promotion as a phase in personal-professional development. *Psychiatry* 32:411–427.

Lamb, H. R. 1976. *Community survival for long-term patients*. San Francisco: Jossey-Bass.

Leighton, A. 1959. *My name is legion*. New York: Basic Books.

Levenson, A. 1972. The community mental health centers program. In *Handbook of community mental health*, ed. S. E. Golann and C. Eisdorfer. New York: Appleton-Century-Crofts.

Levinson, D. J., and E. B. Gallagher. 1964. *Patienthood in the mental hospital*. Boston: Houghton Mifflin.

Levinson, D. J., and G. L. Klerman. 1967. The clinician-executive: some problematic issues for the psychiatrist in mental health organizations. *Psychiatry* 30:3–15.

Levinson, D. J., J. Merrifield, and K. Berg. 1967. Becoming a patient. *Arch. Gen. Psychiatry* 17:385–406.

Lindemann, E. 1944. Symptomatology and management of acute grief. *Am. J. Psychiatry* 101, no. 1:141–148.

Lindemann, E. C. 1921. *The community—an introduction to the study of community leadership and organization*. New York: Association Press.

Macht, L. B. 1975. Beyond the mental health center: planning for a community of neighborhoods. *Psychiatr. Ann.* 5, no. 7:56–69.

_____ 1977. Reflections on the psychiatrist as commissioner: a special case of the clinician-executive. *Psychiatr. Opinion*, in press.

Macht, L. B., and D. J. Scherl. 1974. Adjustment phases and mental health intervention among Job Corps trainees. *Psychiatry* 37, no. 3:229–240.

Macht, L. B., D. J. Scherl, W. J. Bicknell, and J. T. English. 1969. Job Corps as a community mental health challenge. *Am. J. Orthopsychiatry* 39, no. 3:504–511.

Macht, L. B., D. J. Scherl, and J. T. English. 1968. Psychiatric consultation: the Job Corps experience. *Am. J. Psychiatry* 124, no. 8:1092–1100.

Macht, L. B., D. J. Scherl, and S. S. Sharfstein, eds. 1977. *Neighborhood psychiatry*. Lexington, Mass.: D. C. Heath, Lexington Books.

Meyer, A. 1915. Where should we attack the problem of the prevention of mental defect and mental disease? In *The collected papers of Adolph Meyer*, ed. E. E. Winters. Baltimore: Johns Hopkins University Press, 1952.

Pasamanick, B., F. R. Scarpitti, and S. Dinitz. 1967. *Schizophrenics in the community*. New York: Appleton-Century-Crofts.

Scherl, D. J. 1977. Reorganization of the human services and the practice of neighborhood psychiatry. In *Neighborhood psychiatry*, ed. L. B. Macht, D. J. Scherl, and S. S. Sharfstein. Lexington, Mass.: D. C. Heath, Lexington Books.

Scherl, D. J., and L. B. Macht. 1977. "Repetition compulsion: are comprehensive human services the next community mental health fad?"

Srole, L., T. S. Langner, S. T. Michael, M. K. Opler, and T. A. C. Rennie. 1962. *Mental health in the metropolis: the midtown Manhattan study*. Series in Social Psychiatry, ed. T. A. C. Rennie, vol. 1. New York: McGraw-Hill.

Straker, M. 1968. Brief psychotherapy in an outpatient clinic: evolution and evaluation. *Am. J. Psychiatry* 124:1219–26.

Teitelbaum, D. I. 1961. "An evaluation of an experimental program of assistance for newly appointed teachers in certain elementary schools of New York City." Doctoral dissertation, New York University.

Tischler, G. L., J. Heinisz, J. K. Myers, and V. G. Garrison. 1972. Catchmenting and the rise of mental health services. *Arch. Gen. Psychiatry* 27:389–392.

Whittington, H. G. 1972. *Clinical practice in community mental health centers*. New York: International Universities Press.

Zwerling, J., and J. F. Wilder. 1964. An evaluation of the applicability of the day hospital in treatment of acutely disturbed patients. *Isr. Ann. Psychiatry* 2:162–185.

Recommended Reading

Bellak, L., and H. Barten, eds. 1975. *Progress in community mental health*. Vol. 3. New York: Brunner/Mazel.

Golann, S. E., and C. Eisdorfer, eds. 1972. *Handbook of community mental health*. New York: Appleton-Century-Crofts.

Grunebaum, H., ed. 1970. *The practice of community mental health*. Boston: Little, Brown.

Task Force on Community Mental Health Program Components. 1975. *Developing community mental health programs: a resource manual*. Boston: United Community Planning Corporation.

Psychiatry and the Law

CHAPTER 31

Alan A. Stone

F ORENSIC PSYCHIATRY, once an arcane subject of minimal interest to the psychiatric profession, has become a crucial focus of concern during the past two decades. Unfortunately, it is not a subject that is readily understood and assimilated. Indeed, the relationship between psychiatry and law is much more complicated and intricate than most psychiatrists appreciate. In fact, there are a number of distinct legal problems that bear on psychiatry or that require psychiatric information. These areas of interaction include those listed below; many of them are discussed in detail in this chapter.

1. civil commitment proceedings
2. the insanity defense
3. competency to stand trial
4. sexual psychopath laws
5. contractual capacity
6. testamentary capacity
7. confidentiality
8. tort law
9. the juvenile courts
10. family law
11. court clinic
12. correctional institutions

Each of these interfaces of law and psychiatry includes narrow legal tests, traditional doctrines, and jurisprudential concepts unique to that area. The history of the relationship between law and psychiatry reflects a failure to appreciate fully these discrete areas and the distinctions among them. There is no single area of interrelationship in which generalizable legal principles can be formulated and then applied to the others. For example, the substantive concept *insanity*, which is itself a totally ambiguous term, has been inappropriately equated with psychosis and applied as a unitary standard by psychiatrists to evaluate criminal responsibility, competency to stand trial, civil commitment, contractual capacity, and testamentary capacity.

This kind of confusion has made its way into supposedly authoritative documents such as the last American Psychiatric Association *Psychiatric Glossary*, which defined insanity as "a vague legal term for psychosis, now obsolete in psychiatric usage. Generally connotes: (a) a mental incompetence, (b) inability to distinguish 'right from wrong' and/or (c) a condition that interferes with the individual's ability to care for himself or that constitutes a danger to himself or others" (1969, p.49). Such a definition, equating insanity and psychosis and thus offering a single psychiatric standard for the solution of the different and complex legal tests, perpetuates the mistakes and ambiguity alluded to above. (The most recent glossary has corrected this error.) The fault, however, does not rest entirely on the shoulders of psychiatry; the law has been equally guilty of ambiguity and imprecision. On those rare occasions when a psychiatrist does consult a statute, it is often at least a hundred years old and may contain terms like *insanity*, *lunacy*, and *idiocy*, which are vague and confusing and provide no simple or clear guidance.

The Building Blocks of Law

In order to understand, or at least appreciate, the complexity of the relationship between law and psychiatry, it is useful to understand the six building blocks of law itself: (1) statutes, (2) the Constitution, (3) common law, (4) criminal versus civil law, (5) the adversary system, and (6) case law (Berman, 1971). The best approach to that appreciation is to examine these features as they appear in a case. I have chosen *State ex rel. Hawks* v. *Lazaro* (1974), which has the advantage of being typical of the current ferment in law and psychiatry. Ronald Lee Hawks was committed to the Huntington State Hospital in West Virginia for an indeterminate period. He was diagnosed by psychiatrists as both mentally ill and mentally retarded.

1. Hawks was committed under a *statute* that sets out the standards and the procedures to be followed for civil commitment. Such statutes enacted in the state legislature form a major but not the sole ingredient of law. Obviously it is incumbent on every psychiatrist to familiarize himself with at least the statutory standard for civil commitment in his state and with procedures with which he must comply or in which he must participate.

2. Hawks, through his lawyer, appealed to the Supreme Court of West Virginia, claiming that the procedures set forth in the statute had not been faithfully carried out and that, furthermore, those procedures were unconstitutional. The *Federal Constitution* is, of course, a major component of law with which all statutes must comply. (A further complication is that each state also has its own constitution.) Hawks, in this case, claimed that due process of law as con-

templated in the Constitution and its amendments had been violated. This due process argument has been invoked again and again in recent major cases in law and psychiatry. Essentially, it is a demand that procedures be fair, and fairness demands a variety of constitutional protections for the person whose liberty is at stake.

3. The court, in deciding whether Hawks had obtained due process of law under these statutes, confronted a long-standing tradition—the doctrine of *parens patriae* (father of his country)—whose origin goes back to the years of Edward I in England. Essentially, it allowed the kings of England to stand in the role of parent to members of the nobility who were found to be "idiots or lunatics." The doctrine's original intent was to protect property and not persons.

This English doctrine, transformed over centuries of judicial interpretation, has been accepted together with many others into what is called the *American common law*. The common law is a composite of such ancient traditional doctrines and judicial opinions reformulated and accepted as part of the fabric of jurisprudence. One way to think about the common law is as the distillate of centuries of judicial opinions and analysis. The doctrine of *parens patriae* has come in modern times to stand for the broad proposition that the state can act in what it takes to be the best interest of the citizen who is incapacitated or a minor. In practice, the doctrine of *parens patriae* has been even further expanded to allow state intervention on behalf of any citizen whether incapacitated or not—for example, to enjoin pollution to protect the interests of citizens. It has served for more than a century as the legal rationale for a variety of state interventions. Under this rationale, a distinction arose that held that when the state acted presumably to help under *parens patriae*, its interventions into the lives of its citizens need not be guided by the same standards of procedural fairness as are applicable in a criminal trial where the state acts to punish. In the latter case, the criminal defendant is allowed, for example, to confront his accusers and to insist that proof be beyond a reasonable doubt.

4. A further procedural distinction is signified by the fact that the involuntary hospitalization of Ronald Lee Hawks was carried out under a set of

what are called *civil statutes* rather than criminal statutes. A central feature of the current ferment in law and psychiatry is the rejection of the moral legitimacy of the doctrine of *parens patriae* in an attempt to provide the potential patient with all of the same rights as an alleged criminal. That challenge is exactly what happened in the Hawks case. The consequences of such reform will be discussed below. Here, however, I shall describe one of those rights that the courts have said is the guarantor of all other rights, namely, the right to legal counsel.

5. The hallmark of the Anglo-American system of law is its adversary nature. This struggle is repugnant to most psychiatrists, particularly when they testify in court and are subjected to sharp and sometimes hostile cross-examination. But the *adversary system* is the very foundation of our legal system. It affords every person brought before the court a champion who represents his client zealously within the bounds of the law. The defense attorney and the prosecutor confront each other in an attempt to present the facts and the law on their sides as powerfully as possible. In the process they also confront each other's "expert" witnesses in a manner bearing little relationship to a scientific search for truth.

Before psychiatrists condemn the adversary system because of what it does to them they should consider its unique advantage: it is the key to invoking all the other rights that allow the individual to defend himself against the power of the state before any lawful tribunal. Furthermore, one might contrast the Anglo-American adversary procedure with the Continental inquisitorial system, in which the judge, rather than being an impartial presiding officer, participates in the investigation. As the legal Canons of Ethics state, "An adversary presentation counters the natural human tendency to judge too swiftly in terms of the familiar that which is not yet fully known: the advocate, by his zealous preparation and presentation of facts and law, enables the tribunal to come to the hearing with an open and neutral mind and to render impartial judgments" (American Bar Association, 1969, § EC 7-19, p. 26).

6. The Supreme Court of West Virginia in deciding the Hawks case ruled on a number of important questions; these rulings thenceforth are the case law in West Virginia. The importance and impact of case law in regard to *Hawks* is illustrated by the court's deciding, among other things, that henceforth in West Virginia, an alleged patient (a) must be present at his commitment hearing; (b) must be allowed to confront and cross-examine witnesses (including psychiatrists); and (c) must have a lawyer who is his zealous advocate within the bounds of ethics. The *Hawks* decision therefore controls every subsequent civil commitment in West Virginia. It forces civil commitment to follow the forms and procedures of the criminal courts in many respects. That, of course, will mean great expense for the state in terms of lawyers', judges', and psychiatrists' time, if civil commitment is to continue at any appreciable rate. If psychiatrists are in court testifying, they cannot be in the hospital treating patients. Thus, inevitably, this decision, which is typical of a trend, alters not just the law but the provision of mental health care in a variety of ways. The constraints posed by such procedural reform have produced a drastic decline in involuntary confinement throughout the United States.

This description of the building blocks of law is by no means complete, but it does give some sense of the law's complexity. Although the interfaces between law and psychiatry have always been more complicated than was appreciated, a new level of complexity has been imposed by a series of sweeping constitutional decisions. The psychiatrist should therefore assume that any simple or brief assertions about psychiatry and law are to be accepted with caution. Much of what follows here can only point the way. (Further specifics may be found in Stone, 1975.)

Civil Commitment

Each state has its own standards and procedures for voluntary and involuntary entry into mental hospitals, and the psychiatrist must, as noted above, familiarize himself with the specifics in his state. Many states are in the process of radical revision of their mental health codes; the general direction of this revision is indicated in the Hawks case. The "alleged" patient's constitutional rights are being given articulated legal

protection, the length of confinement is specified with periodic review, and objective legal
standards must be met before involuntary confinement is permitted.

Prior to recent revisions in state mental health
codes, four different legal standards for civil
commitment were in wide usage; the patient had
to be mentally ill and (a) dangerous to others, (b)
dangerous to himself, (c) gravely disabled, or (d)
in need of treatment. The last of these is the
clearest instance of the "medical model" of civil
commitment. It allowed mental illness to be the
sole criterion for involuntary confinement. Radical criticism of diagnostic concepts, together
with a growing emphasis on the civil rights of
the mentally ill and disabled, has led reform-
oriented courts and legislatures to repudiate this
and similar "subjective" standards.

The current focus of the courts and legislation
is on the standard of dangerousness, which is
supposedly "objective"—that is, dangerousness
to self or others. In reality, since dangerousness
involves a prediction of future behavior, its application to individual cases creates insurmountable
problems. How imminent must the danger be?
How serious? How probable? What person or actuarial device can assess these "objective" variables? Although some psychiatrists still claim to
be able to predict dangerous behavior, the great
weight of opinion is to the contrary. Often, in
the immediate context of a clinical emergency
where all the situational variables are clear, the
psychiatrist will have a sense that a patient is
dangerous. At a court hearing several days later,
however, the context for prediction has changed
and prediction is much more difficult. Even if
some predictive capacity exists, it is unlikely that
any expert could assert that his judgment was
valid by a court's standard of "beyond a reasonable doubt" or "clear and convincing proof."

The growing emphasis on dangerousness does
not, however, avoid the problem of diagnostic
labels. All civil commitment statutes in fact contain two criteria—mental illness and dangerousness. Many psychiatrists define mental illness
as psychosis and neurosis, thus excluding the
majority of persons who are dangerous to
society, such as psychopaths and individuals
with personality disorders. Since the vast majority of those who have traditionally been con-

sidered mentally ill are not dangerous, it is unclear who is the proper target of such statutes.
One can only conclude that these new standards, when rigidly applied using the procedures
described in the Hawks case, will markedly reduce the number of persons involuntarily confined in mental health facilities. Statistical evidence documents this trend throughout the
country.

Another question remains: When are these difficult standards to be applied and by whom? The
courts have increasingly held that where liberty
is at stake, due process of law requires an adversary hearing before a judge at which the patient
is present and represented by counsel. The time
at which the hearing must be held and the procedures employed differ in the different jurisdictions. It is quite probable that in order to meet
due process those hearings must be held within a
very few days of admission and must provide
many of the same procedural steps as does a
criminal trial. The admitting psychiatrist may
have to testify and be cross-examined in the patient's presence as to diagnosis and evidence for
dangerousness to self or others. At least two federal jurisdictions now require the examining psychiatrist to warn the patient in advance of any interview that information revealed may be used to
commit the patient.

Since some of the courts have held that no
treatment (such as drugs or electroconvulsive
therapy) can be given until such a legal hearing
has validated the patient's commitment, the psychiatrist must know the law in his state or risk
legal sanctions if he treats without such judicial
authority. (Psychotropic drugs as restraint but
not as treatment have been allowed under
emergency conditions.) Similar risks exist if the
psychiatrist at any time treats Christian Scientists, or others who oppose medical treatment
on religious grounds, against their will.

Although the above discussion focuses on
the standard of danger to self and others, most
jurisdictions have retained a standard similar to
"gravely disabled." That standard has, however,
been interpreted very narrowly as the inability to
take care of one's basic needs such as food and
shelter.

Read broadly, all of the legal developments in
civil commitment suggest both a distrust of psy-

chiatry and a growing repudiation of the traditional legal doctrine of *parens patriae*. Not all states have gone this far in revising civil commitment; some allow brief confinement with minimal procedural safeguards. Only if commitment is to be prolonged will the full panoply of court procedures be invoked. There is a real possibility, however, that such statutes will be found unconstitutional and that every potential patient will be legally entitled not only to an early hearing of the type described but to a speedy jury trial as well.

The Right to Treatment

The purpose of involuntary confinement of citizens who are not judged by courts to be criminals is obviously some form of treatment or rehabilitation. Unfortunately, many of the facilities in which such citizens are involuntarily confined provide inadequate treatment. The sometimes tragic conditions in these institutions were generally ignored by the courts until the 1960s.

The first important case recognizing that civil commitment followed by neglect was a problem of clear constitutional significance was *Wyatt* v. *Stickney* (1971). In this case the judge held that "to deprive any citizen of his or her liberty upon the altruistic theory that the confinement is for humane and therapeutic reasons and then fail to provide adequate treatment violates the very fundamentals of due process" (325 F. Supp. 781), a decision that had sweeping implications. Similar cases have since been decided in other categories of noncriminal confinement, such as mental retardation and juvenile detention. The importance of *Wyatt* v. *Stickney* and its legal offspring is that they are class action suits—suits brought on behalf of all patients involuntarily confined in one or more hospitals in the jurisdiction. If a state is to comply, it presumably must upgrade treatment to meet standards set by the court.

However, the right to treatment as it has been formulated in the courts exists only if a person is involuntarily confined. It is a *quid pro quo* theory that deprivation of liberty must be balanced by adequate treatment. Consequently, it is possible for a state to comply by discharging patients rather than appropriating the funds and resources to treat the mentally ill and disabled.

Many patients are confined in state institutions because no other place is available. The legal status of such persons as the severely mentally retarded, chronic process schizophrenics, and those designated as senile psychotic is irrelevant for all practical purposes. Such patients have no home to go to and no other institution may be willing to accept them. Can the right to treatment help such patients? One federal judge has held that such patients are at least entitled not to be exposed to harmful conditions and on that basis has ordered sweeping improvements in an institution for the mentally retarded. Other courts are working toward negotiated settlements to improve conditions without setting the standards themselves.

Thus far the right-to-treatment suits have not produced all of the sweeping reforms hoped for by their advocates. Too often the results have been precipitate deinstitutionalization without adequate discharge planning or appropriate aftercare. The most recent right-to-treatment suits have been resolved by consent decrees, in which the plaintiffs and the defendants have worked out mutually acceptable plans to improve the system of mental health care. Some of these plans have included provisions for community-based care, in an attempt to anticipate the problems of rapid deinstitutionalization.

In *O'Connor* v. *Donaldson*, the Supreme Court avoided giving its imprimatur to the right to treatment. It did hold that if a patient is not dangerous to himself or to others, is able to survive outside the hospital, and is not getting treatment, he must be released. A psychiatrist who continues to confine a patient involuntarily in such a situation may be liable for monetary damages for violating the patient's civil rights.

The Right to Refuse Treatment

Along with the growing concern about adequate treatment has come a parallel concern about imposing treatment on unwilling subjects. There are a variety of legal problems involved. How shall it be determined whether a patient is competent to accept or refuse treatment? What is informed consent and how is it obtained in the case of a patient whose mental condition is the basis of his hospitalization? What are the malpractice implications of withholding treatment because the patient who is disturbed withholds consent? What kind of psychiatric emergency justifies imposing treatment without consent? How much must one disclose to a psychiatric patient about the potential side effects of a given treatment, a disclosure that may itself cause profound anxiety? Unfortunately all of these questions are becoming increasingly worrisome, but the courts have not yet given clear answers or directions to the psychiatrist.

Informed consent is thought to involve three aspects. First, it must be voluntarily given; no coercion, explicit or implicit, may be involved. Second, it must be knowing, including an awareness of possible side effects; even rare complications should be explained to the patient. (However, if it is a question of malpractice, most states require only that the doctor tell the patient what other doctors tell their patients.) Third, the patient must have the mental capacity to give consent. When he does not have the capacity to give consent voluntarily and knowingly, the usual practice has been to obtain that consent from the closest relative or a court-appointed guardian. Such substituted consent procedures are now being challenged, and it is appropriate for every inpatient facility to develop a patients' rights committee with lay participation to establish reviewable standards and procedures of informed consent and to consult federal and state consent procedures now being promulgated.

Some states have initiated regulation of particular psychiatric treatments such as electroconvulsive therapy, psychosurgery, and aversive therapy. These statutes, regulations, or court decrees may impose special consent procedures, and the psychiatrist who utilizes such treatments must be aware of them. Recently, psychiatrists in the Alabama state mental hospital system were charged with criminal and civil contempt for failure to follow the legal procedures for ECT set out in the *Wyatt* v. *Stickney* decision, the major right-to-treatment case. The judge leaned over backward not to punish the psychiatrists.

A long tradition of work therapy exists in institutional psychiatry, based on the assumptions that such work is rehabilitative and contributes to the sense of community. It is also true that work therapy has provided a source of free labor in large, financially strapped institutions. A 1973 decision held that all such labor that the institution would otherwise pay for must be paid for if done by patients (*Souder* v. *Brennan*, 1973). This requirement included all maintenance work, patient care, and kitchen and dining room chores. The *Souder* decision was unexpectedly overturned by the Supreme Court in 1976 on the basis of considerations that have nothing to do with the issues involved in patient labor. Therefore, unless states have already initiated regulations under which patients should be paid, they are apparently under no constitutional obligation to do so.

The Psychiatrist's Role in the Courts

Psychiatric testimony in the criminal courts is more often than not an embarrassment to the profession for several reasons. First, when clinical judgment is exposed to the adversary process, it is out of context and inevitably distorted. Second, the opposition has an obligation to make the most of this distortion and any other weaknesses as well. Third, psychiatric testimony is usually resorted to when there is no question that the defendant has done the thing alleged, in which case it is invoked as an alternative to traditional justice. Finally, many psychiatrists who testify are ignorant about the relevant law and ill prepared to offer pertinent testimony.

The Insanity Defense

Most standard psychiatric textbooks give primary emphasis in their consideration of law and psychiatry to the insanity defense. This defense is, however, of little practical consequence; it is rarely invoked and then rarely successful in most jurisdictions. Its major interest is moral, philosophical, and theoretical. The arguments struggled over on the battlefields of the insanity defense reflect the contradiction between the law's enduring free-will theory of the morality of action and psychiatry's deterministic theories of its causes.

Such considerations, although of profound interest to anyone concerned with the great theories of mind and behavior, cannot be discussed here in any reasonably concise fashion. The interested reader should consult Goldstein's *The Insanity Defense* (1967).

The insanity defense is a test of criminal responsibility and varies in different jurisdictions. The principal tests are as follows:

The M'Naghten Test (Daniel M'Naghten's Case, 1843)

[E]very man is to be presumed to be sane, and . . . to establish a defense on the ground of insanity, it must be clearly proved that, at the time of the committing of the act, the party accused was labouring under such a defect of reason, from disease of the mind, as not to know the nature and quality of the act he was doing; or if he did know it, that he did not know he was doing what was wrong. (10 C. & F. 210–211, 8 Eng. Rep. 722–723)

This is now the sole test in fewer than half the states, but is one of the standards in most jurisdictions. Critics feel that it places too great an emphasis on cognitive capacity.

The Irresistible Impulse Test

1. *Parsons* v. *State*, 1887

Did he know right from wrong, as applied to the particular act in question? . . . If he did have such knowledge, he may nevertheless not be legally responsible if the two following conditions concur: (1) If, by reason of the duress of such mental disease, he had so far lost the power to choose between the right and wrong, and to avoid doing the act in question, as that his free agency was at the time destroyed; (2) and if, at the same time, the alleged crime was so connected with such mental disease, in the relation of cause and effect, as to have been the product of it solely. (2 So. 866–867)

Most jurisdictions drop the key word "solely" from this formulation.

2. The Federal Rule (*Davis* v. *United States*, 1897)

[The accused is to be classed as insane if] though conscious of [the nature of his act] and able to distinguish right from wrong . . . yet his will, by which I mean the governing power of his mind, has been otherwise than voluntarily so completely destroyed that his actions are not subject to it, but are beyond his control. (165 U.S. 378)

The irresistible impulse test is nowhere relied on as the sole test, and has been rejected by twenty-two states, England, and Canada. However, it is used in conjunction with the M'Naghten test in an increasing number of jurisdictions, now about fifteen. Goldstein (1967), in his scholarly treatise, argues that such a test is most compatible with psychodynamic ego psychology.

The Durham Test (Durham v. United States, 1954)

[A]n accused is not criminally responsible if his unlawful act was the product of mental disease or mental defect . . . We use "disease" in the sense of a condition which is considered capable of either improving or deteriorating. We use "defect" in the sense of a condition which is not considered capable of either improving or deteriorating, and which may be either congenital, or the result of injury, or the residual effect of a physical or mental disease. (214 F.2d 874–875)

The Durham rule, which originated in the Court of Appeals for the District of Columbia, has since been specifically rejected there (*United States* v. *Brawner*, 1972). It has, however, been adopted by statute in Maine and the Virgin Islands. The New Hampshire test most resembles Durham, but its basic intent is to allow the jury to formulate the insanity standard. The failure of Durham is the subject of considerable legal literature.

The ALI Test (American Law Institute, 1962)

1. A person is not responsible for criminal conduct if at the time of such conduct as a result of mental disease or defect he lacks substantial capacity either to appreciate the criminality of his conduct or to conform his conduct to the requirements of law.
2. As noted in the Article, the terms "mental disease or defect" do not include an abnormality manifested only by repeated criminal or otherwise antisocial conduct. (§4.01)

As of 1971, the ALI Test had been adopted by statute in seven states and by decision in three more. On the federal level, six circuit courts of appeal have adopted the test as is, and two others have made minor modifications. Paragraph 2 is specifically intended to exclude the psychopath or sociopath.

In addition to psychiatric testimony pertinent to these various tests, some courts allow psychiatrists to testify as to whether the defendant had the requisite premeditation or malice for the specific crime charged.

Competency to Stand Trial

The law of the United States as interpreted by the Supreme Court (*Pate* v. *Robinson*, 1966) requires the defense attorney, the prosecutor, and the judge to raise the issue of mental illness whenever they believe that the defendant may be ill and that such illness may interfere with his capacity to participate in a trial. Unfortunately, the law has no threshold that must be reached before such inquiry into the mental capacity of the defendant is required. Furthermore, if after a trial is concluded evidence is brought forward indicating that the defendant was incompetent, a new trial will be ordered. It should also be noted that a court can preclude the possibility of bail by requiring a competency examination and committing the defendant to a mental health facility.

The competency question, in terms of both numbers and consequences, is the most important mental health inquiry pursued in the criminal law system. Psychiatrists have failed to recognize this fact and have further confused the test of competency with the test of criminal responsibility (the insanity defense).

The test of competency is set by statute and may be worded differently in different jurisdictions. Essentially it is a two-pronged test involving the capacity to consult with one's lawyer and to understand the proceedings against one. The Supreme Court's formulation, applicable in federal courts, is that the test must be whether the defendant has sufficient present ability to consult with counsel with a reasonable degree of rational understanding and whether he has a rational as well as a factual understanding of the proceedings against him.

Since lawyers vary, and proceedings as well, this is not an objective or fixed standard. Much less capacity may be needed to understand a misdemeanor charge, such as public drunkenness, than a complicated tax fraud proceeding. Unfortunately, psychiatrists have not recognized these distinctions and the courts have provided little supervision or guidance. The result has been the prolonged confinement of thousands of defendants who have never had their day in court, some of whom may well have been competent, given the crimes with which they were charged. The Supreme Court, recognizing this abuse,

held in *Jackson* v. *Indiana* (1972) that the confinement of alleged incompetents be limited to a reasonable time. If such defendants cannot be restored to competency in a foreseeable period of therapy, they must be treated like any other allegedly mentally ill person and either civilly committed or released.

When a psychiatrist is asked to evaluate competency to stand trial, he should perform a thorough mental status examination. Based on that examination and standard considerations (orientation, sensorium, memory, thought disorder, affect, conation) he should form a clinical impression of the patient in traditional psychiatric terms. At that point it is appropriate to consult one of the available checklists for competency. The Group for the Advancement of Psychiatry (1974) has compiled the following checklist; the defendant should have the ability to

1. understand his current legal situation
2. understand the charges against him
3. understand the facts relevant to his case
4. understand the legal issues and procedures in his case
5. understand legal defenses available in his behalf
6. understand the dispositions, pleas, and penalties possible
7. appraise the likely outcomes
8. appraise the roles of defense counsel, the prosecuting attorney, the judge, the jury, the witnesses, and the defendant
9. identify and locate witnesses
10. relate to defense counsel
11. trust and communicate relevantly with his counsel
12. comprehend instructions and advice
13. make decisions after receiving advice
14. maintain a collaborative relationship with his attorney and help plan legal strategy
15. follow testimony for contradictions or errors
16. testify relevantly and be cross-examined if necessary
17. challenge prosecution witnesses
18. tolerate stress at the trial and while awaiting trial
19. refrain from irrational and unmanageable behavior during the trial
20. disclose pertinent facts surrounding the alleged offense

21. protect himself and utilize the legal safeguards available to him

The psychiatrist should try to evaluate each of these factors; indeed, they may be the basis for a structured interview. Although some forensic experts disagree, the majority recommend that the psychiatrist not offer a personal conclusion on the ultimate question of competency unless requested to do so by the court. It is the court's role to decide that question, and it is the role of the psychiatrist to supply the relevant information. The Group for the Advancement of Psychiatry's Report on *Misuse of Psychiatry in the Criminal Courts* (1974) provides a detailed account of the further intricacies of procedures and the role of the psychiatrist.

The Fifth Amendment

The examination of defendants by psychiatrists in connection with a criminal trial creates the possibility of self-incrimination. Although the psychiatrist cannot testify to directly incriminating evidence revealed to him by the patient in the course of such an examination, the psychiatrist's reports and opinions often affect the fate of the defendant. For example, psychiatric reports inadmissible as testimony may find their way into the presentencing report. Informal communication between psychiatrist and prosecutor may influence prosecutorial discretion in the decision to press charges or the level of charges at which plea bargaining begins.

Some states have allowed defendants to refuse an examination by a psychiatrist for the state on the basis of the Fifth Amendment, while others have allowed lawyers and psychiatrists for the defense to be present. Other complex legal compromises, such as making taped psychiatric testimony available to the prosecution psychiatrist, have also been negotiated.

The psychiatrist in this situation confronts ethical, legal, and practical problems. Ethically, it seems appropriate for the examining psychiatrist to make known at the outset the fact that he does not have a traditional therapeutic relationship in which the defendant can be assured of confidentiality. Legally, the psychiatrist should, in my view, insist that the court instruct him as to the specific goals and purposes of the exami-

nation and whether any *Miranda*-type warning ("Anything you tell me may be used against you") is required. The burden should be on the judge to clarify and set these legal constraints. Practically speaking, there is no question that such warnings, and the possible presence of a lawyer invoking the Fifth Amendment in his client's behalf, will affect the quality and completeness of the psychiatric evaluation. Although I have serious reservations about the value of such evaluations, I see no alternative that protects the rights of the defendant as such rights are defined by the criminal justice system.

Juvenile Courts

The juvenile courts were established in the United States at the turn of the century as the most explicit instance of the doctrine of *parens patriae*. Because the presumed goal was to rehabilitate rather than punish juveniles, the same concessions regarding constitutional rights were made as those in the area of civil commitment. Unfortunately, due to grossly inadequate institutional resources, the goal of rehabilitation has rarely been accomplished. The Supreme Court took note of this inadequacy in the famous *Gault* case, but rather than rectifying the inadequacies in the rehabilitative system, the Court imposed some of the procedural safeguards available in criminal courts. The practical result was to make it somewhat more difficult to enter the juvenile "rehabilitation" system. Nonetheless, given the rising rates of criminal behavior in minors, the juvenile facilities of many states are overwhelmed. Right-to-treatment litigation in this area has already been successfully brought in one federal jurisdiction. The decision limits corporal punishment and places constraints on the use of psychoactive drugs, but how the standards of positive care and treatment will be established for juveniles remains problematic.

Psychiatrists who testify in juvenile courts will often find the proceedings informal by comparison with criminal trials. Judges will welcome any alternative disposition, such as day care, halfway houses, and outpatient therapy. Most judges recognize the inadequacies of juvenile facilities like state training schools and thus are reluctant to confine any but the most egregious offenders.

Since access to mental health resources is one of the court's major alternatives, the psychiatrist who testifies as to disposition in fact controls an important community resource. This consideration is important because if psychiatrists rely on traditional prognostic and treatment considerations, they may well screen out minority children. If, for example, in an inner city context, psychiatrists give access to treatment to intelligent, verbal children with interested and intact families, their individual decisions may well result in the exclusion of minority children from treatment.

Although radical critics of the psychiatrist's role in legal proceedings emphasize the stigmatizing implications of psychiatric diagnosis, in practice the real concern is quite the contrary. In the juvenile courts and in the lower criminal courts, the psychiatric alternative is often preferable to jail or prison. Psychiatrists may find no easy way to resolve such problems, but they should at least be aware of them.

The juvenile courts in different jurisdictions have different statutes and procedures. Broadly speaking, four groups of children may come before such courts: First, children who are neglected or abused—medical testimony may be required as to temporary or permanent termination of parental rights. Second, abandoned children—the court may simply act to authorize some custodial arrangement. Third, children in need of supervision—this group includes runaways and truants—that is, children whose acts, if done by an adult, would not be a crime. The problems of such children are often attributable to family psychodynamics. Unfortunately, when such cases come before the court in an adversary fashion, the conflicts and tensions in the family are often exacerbated. A variety of legal and psychiatric criticisms have been leveled against the use of the courts to deal with such problems. Finally, delinquent children—this group comprises children who have committed acts that would be designated as crimes if performed by adults.

Sexual Psychopath Statutes

Many states have a variety of noncriminal procedures for the indefinite confinement of persons thought to be both criminal and mentally ill. The majority of these procedures aim at deviant sexual behavior that is dangerous to the community. The avowed goals of "sexual psychopath" statutes are to provide treatment and to offer society greater protection through an indeterminate sentence limited by cure. Like other procedures for civil rather than criminal confinement, this type of statute is now being attacked on all sides. The constitutional due process arguments previously noted have been raised; in addition, the sex psychopath statutes are challenged as unconstitutionally vague.

Putting the legal arguments to one side, there is considerable psychiatric uncertainty about the reliability and validity of the diagnostic entity "sexual psychopath." There are, in addition, all of the problems already noted of predicting which so-called sexual psychopath will be dangerous. Finally, it is clear that the treatment of persons so labeled is difficult at best and few states have allocated the resources necessary to undertake such treatment.

Given these legal and psychiatric difficulties, considerable sentiment now exists for the abolition of civil commitment of the "sexually dangerous" in favor of standard criminal procedures. Ironically, one of the arguments against abolition is the danger of prison life for the sexual psychopath. Heterosexual and homosexual pedophiles are often singled out as victims of serious physical assaults and sexual abuse within prison.

Maryland has a civil procedure directed at the dangerous recidivist. It does not focus solely on sexual crimes; rather, it embraces a broader category, the defective delinquent, whose dangerous criminal behavior is presumably complicated by or associated with some mental disability. This civil procedure has withstood repeated constitutional challenge. In the process, however, its application has been hedged with procedural restraints. Of special interest is the requirement that rehabilitation and treatment in Maryland utilize a graded tier system that seems to embody the principles of behavior modification. As inmates adapt to the routines and accept the available programs, they move up to better living conditions with fewer restraints.

Claims have been made that Maryland's is an effective treatment milieu. Whatever the merit of such claims may be, a new problem has arisen with the graded tier method. Constitutional arguments have been advanced against behavior modification, particularly when aversive techniques are used, when initial living conditions constitute cruel and unusual punishment, or when the inmate does not voluntarily consent to such treatment. Judging from this and other examples, we seem rapidly to be approaching the point at which most behavior-modification treatment methods for antisocial behavior will be deemed unconstitutional by the courts. The Maryland legislature, responding in part to these considerations, has recently elected to do away with the state institution dealing with defective delinquents.

Testamentary Capacity

The test of competency to stand trial is not a unitary, bright-line test. Rather, it seems to depend on the complexity of the proceeding and the nature of the lawyer-client relationship. That analysis is consonant with the current trend in law, which tries to articulate different kinds of legal competency and to assert that incompetency in terms of one legal function does not necessarily mean incompetency in terms of all. This trend parallels the reforms in civil commitment in its rejection of the proposition that once a person has been found "mentally ill" or "insane" or "psychotic," that person is therefore incompetent for all legal purposes. The reformers argue that each aspect of competency should be determined on the narrow legal standards applicable to the specific legal function. Thus competence to vote, to contract, to marry, and to make a will would be separately delineated.

As noted in the beginning of this chapter, legal functions can be fully understood only in the context of the doctrines, common law, and statutes specific to that area of law. Here I shall discuss only competency to make a will—testamentary capacity. The courts have formulated a standard, that is, case law, which has met the test of time: it has been in use at least a century, it is almost universally accepted, and, not surprisingly, it emphasizes cognitive capacity. According to Brakel and Rock (1971), the court requires that the testator:

A. Know, without prompting, the nature and extent of the property of which he is about to dispose.
B. Know the nature of the act which he is about to perform.
C. Know the names and identity of persons who are to be the objects of his bounty.
D. Know his relation toward them.
E. Have sufficient mind and memory to understand all of these facts.
F. Appreciate the relations of these factors to one another.
G. Recollect the decision which he has formed.
(p. 305).

Often the psychiatrist, when testifying as to testamentary capacity, will be asked a series of hypothetical questions incorporating the foregoing requirements—for example, "Assuming that Mr. Jones had advanced arteriosclerosis and episodes of confusion, would it be possible for him to know . . . "

Wills are likely to be challenged long after they have been made and only after the testator is dead. The reliability and validity of psychiatric testimony under those conditions can surely be questioned. Since wills are usually drawn up by lawyers, the language contained therein will give little indication of the testator's cognitive capacity. Thus, unless detailed psychiatric evaluations contemporaneous with the creation of the will are available, the psychiatrist is forced to deal with inferences based on secondary sources.

Psychiatric Malpractice

For most of this century, psychiatric malpractice has been a minimal problem when compared with malpractice in medicine, surgery, and the other specialties. Since insurance carriers place the psychiatrist in the same risk rate category as the general practitioner, the psychiatric profession helped to subsidize its colleagues for a long time. Recently, however, there has been a significant increase in claims of psychiatric malpractice, and rates for psychiatric malpractice insurance have begun to escalate.

Dawidoff defines psychiatric malpractice as follows: "Malpractice is a special remedial category designed to regulate professional misfeasance. Its attributes are the measurement of lack of skill and care by a physician in a doctor-patient relationship against a professionally proved standard of community practice. It involves damages caused the patient by the acts of a psychiatrist" (1973, p. 15).

Practically speaking, it is difficult to demonstrate that a psychotherapist failed to meet the community standard of care. The few successful suits related to psychotherapy involve egregious behavior such as exploiting patients sexually, revealing damaging information gained during treatment, or assaulting patients physically.

Malpractice suits are more likely to occur when innovative therapy, electroconvulsive therapy, and psychotropic drugs are involved. In the case of such drugs, failure to use care in prescribing, to follow proper indications or restrictions on use, or to warn of hazardous side effects and complications of usage are all possible grounds for malpractice. Given the rather high incidence of tardive dyskinesia and the failure of most psychiatrists to inform their patients of the risks, one can anticipate many malpractice claims.

One important malpractice issue is suicide. The logic of the courts' thinking in these cases goes to the issue of whether the doctor or the hospital could have foreseen the risk. If a doctor thought a patient was suicidal and did not take adequate precautions, he will be generally held liable. Thus, if a patient's record indicates that on admission it was thought that suicidal tendencies were present but no suicide precautions were ordered, there will be liability. On the other hand, "an ingenious patient harboring a steady purpose to take his own life cannot always be thwarted" (*Hirsh* v. *State*, 1960; 168 N.E. 2d 372). Obviously, the adequacy of suicide precautions is always debatable after the fact, but the courts have not asked the impossible. Nonetheless, no clear rule emerges from the appellate cases on suicide. The courts seem willing to consider the facts in each situation and determine retrospectively whether there has been negligence.

There is a general trend in the courts to ask, in malpractice suits, whether patients were fully informed about a proposed treatment. The doctor has a duty to be candid and to disclose the risks of a recommended treatment or risk malpractice if damage arises from an undisclosed risk. Some of the insurance carriers who offer malpractice insurance to psychiatrists can provide specific information about informed consent and other precautions to avoid malpractice. In some instances this service is available without charge to the insured psychiatrist.

Confidentiality

Confidentiality is one of the most crucial considerations in the enterprise of psychiatry and yet few practitioners seem to recognize the legal and ethical constraints imposed on confidentiality. *The Principles of Medical Ethics with Annotations Especially Applicable to Psychiatry* states:

A physician may not reveal the confidences entrusted to him in the course of medical attendance, or the deficiencies he may observe in the character of patients, unless he is required to do so by law or unless it becomes necessary in order to protect the welfare of the individual or of the community.

. . . When the psychiatrist is ordered by the court to reveal the confidences entrusted to him by patients he may comply or he may ethically hold the right to dissent within the framework of the law. When the psychiatrist is in doubt, the right of the patient to confidentiality and, by extension, to unimpaired treatment, should be given priority. The psychiatrist should reserve the right to raise the question of adequate need for disclosure. In the event that the necessity for legal disclosure is demonstrated by the court, the psychiatrist may request the right to disclosure of only that information which is relevant to the legal question at hand. (American Psychiatric Association, 1973, p. 1063).

The Canons reflect the kind of problem that arose in the *Lifschutz* case (1970). California requires anyone who wishes to sue in a damage action to waive all doctor-patient privileges. This allows the defendants' lawyers to interrogate all doctors who may at any time have treated the person suing, presumably to get the best possible evidence about the measure of damages. Psychiatrists understandably are distressed about this intrusion on confidentiality. They argue that such laws are contrary to public policy in that they discourage patients who need psychiatric treatment from obtaining it and that such patients, if they do seek psychiatric help under such circumstances, may be inhibited from making the kind of free, total disclosure necessary for psychotherapy. They also argue that patients cannot knowledgeably waive the privilege because they cannot know the ways in which the psychiatrist has construed the material. Another concern is that the patient's mental health may be adversely affected by the psychiatrist's testimony.

The California courts have not been insensitive to such arguments and have attempted to distinguish between diagnostic considerations and broader psychodynamic formulations as suggested in the Canons of Ethics. They have suggested that detailed personal information may be withheld. This distinction is difficult to maintain in practice, and new litigation is in process at this writing that seeks to exempt psychiatric testimony further.

It is important to recognize the strong pressures for all available psychiatric testimony in these situations. Juries have begun to award substantial sums for psychic trauma on the basis of psychiatric testimony favorable to the plaintiff; when such large amounts are at stake, courts naturally want the best evidence. Nonetheless, the Canons of Ethics properly urge the psychiatrist at least to resist an initial subpoena. The psychiatrist may find it possible to consult with the court and state his reasons for objecting to giving testimony, but he has no legal right to resist a direct order from the court. At that point the psychiatrist risks being held in contempt.

Some states have a doctor-patient privilege, and some have a specific psychiatrist- or psychotherapist-patient privilege. Since the different state statutes have varying provisions, the psychiatrist should know what limitations exist in his particular jurisdiction. Such a privilege is created by the legislature, and no case law exists suggesting that this privilege is protected by the Constitution. Furthermore, as the California cases illustrate, the privilege is the patient's to waive and not the doctor's (but see below).

There are many other contexts outside the courtroom where, in order to obtain some benefit, a patient must either acknowledge a psychotherapeutic relationship or waive the confidentiality of that relationship in part or in toto. The A.P.A.'s "Principles of Medical Ethics" again gives good and useful advice.

The continuing duty of the psychiatrist to protect the patient includes fully apprising him of the connotations of waiving the privilege of privacy. This may become an issue when the patient is being investigated

by a government agency, is applying for a position, or is involved in legal action. The same principles apply to the release of information concerning treatment to medical departments of government agencies, business organizations, labor unions, and insurance companies. Information gained in confidence about patients seen in student health services should not be released without the student's explicit permission.
. . . The ethical responsibility of maintaining confidentiality holds equally for the consultations in which the patient may not have been present and in which the consultee was not a physician. In such instances, the physician consultant should alert the consultee to his duty of confidentiality.
Ethically the psychiatrist may disclose only that information which is immediately relevant to a given situation. He should avoid offering speculation as fact. Sensitive information such as an individual's sexual orientation or fantasy material is usually unnecessary. (p. 1063)

Situations arise in which the psychiatrist "in order to protect the welfare of the individual or of the community" may wish to reveal confidences—for example, to initiate involuntary civil commitment. On this question, the Canons give no guidance whatsoever as to what kind of danger is sufficient. A decision in a recent California case, *Tarasoff* v. *Regents of the University of California* (1976), held that "psychotherapists" have a duty to protect the public and that this duty may require them to reveal confidences and to warn a third party who is endangered by a patient. That decision, although limited to California, creates a most unfortunate precedent. This new liability places psychotherapists' interests in conflict with those of their patients. Given the problem of false positives in predicting dangerous behavior, there is the unfortunate consequence that psychotherapists may reveal the confidences of unnecessarily large numbers of patients to avoid the risk of damage suits. If psychotherapists feel obliged to advise patients in advance of this legal duty, the result may well be the suppression of important therapeutic material. Fortunately, no other state has yet adopted this imprudent legal requirement.

The confidentiality of psychiatric records in hospitals also poses difficult problems. The trend is to allow patients access to their medical and psychiatric records. Such records may, however, contain information from third parties—relatives and referring doctors, for example—given with the expectation of confidentiality. There is currently so much legislation and litigation on the subject of access to hospital records that no clear direction can be given. The so-called Buckley Amendment giving parents access to school files, including medical and psychiatric records, has caused great consternation and legal confusion that may take years to unravel. There are many other aspects of confidentiality that cannot be discussed here.

It is obvious that the area of law and psychiatry is in a state of flux and ferment. New law is being made every day. Courts have taken upon themselves not only the task of protecting the rights of the mentally disabled but also that of regulating the institutions in which patients are treated. The psychiatrist will find the law intruding on everyday practice, and the future will bring more rather than less intrusion. The psychiatrist has no choice but to become familiar with the important junctures of law and psychiatry. A new generation of forensic psychiatrists, schooled in the broad constitutional questions that have added so much complexity to the field, must be developed. Most important, psychiatrists must develop working relationships with lawyers who are sensitive to the special problems attendant on the provision of mental health care and who recognize the reality of mental illness.

References

American Bar Association. 1969. Code of professional responsibility and causes of judicial ethics. Chicago.

American Law Institute Model Penal Code. 1962. Proposed Office Draft §4.01.

American Psychiatric Association. 1973. The princi-ples of medical ethics with annotations especially applicable to psychiatry. Am. J. Psychiatry 130: 1057–64.

——— 1969. Psychiatric glossary. 3rd ed. Washington, D.C.

Berman, Harold. 1971. Talks on American law. Rev. ed. New York: Vintage Books.

Brakel, S., and R. Rock. 1971. The mentally disabled and the law. Chicago: University of Chicago Press.

Davis v. United States, 165 U.S. 373 (1897).

Dawidoff, D. L. 1973. The malpractice of psychiatrists. Springfield, Ill.: Thomas.

Durham v. United States, 214 F.2d 862 (D.C. Cir. Ct. 1954).

In re Gault, 387 U.S. 1 (1967).

Goldstein, A. 1967. The insanity defense. New Haven: Yale University Press.

Group for the Advancement of Psychiatry. 1974. Misuse of psychiatry in the criminal courts: competency to stand trial. Report no. 89. New York.

Hirsh v. State, 168 N.E.2d 372 (1960).

Jackson v. Indiana, 406 U.S. 715 (1972).

In re Lifschutz, 467 P.2d 557 (1970).

Daniel M'Naughten's Case, 10 C. & F. 200, 8 Eng. Rep. 718 (1843).

O'Connor v. Donaldson, 95 S. Ct. 2486 (1975).

Parsons v. State, 2 So. 854 (Ala. 1887).

Pate v. Robinson 383 U.S. 375 (1966).

Souder v. Brennan, 42 U.S.L.W. 2271 (D.D.C., Nov. 14, 1973), 367 F. Supp. 808 (D.D.C. 1973).

State ex rel Hawks v. Lazaro, 202 S.E.2d 109 (1974).

Stone, A. A. 1975. Mental health and law: a system in transition. Washington, D.C.: Government Printing Office.

Tarasoff v. Regents of the University of California, 551 P. 2d 334, 131 Cal. Rptr. 14 (1976).

United States v. Brawner, 471 F.2d 969 (D.C. Cir. Ct. 1972).

Wyatt v. Stickney, 325 F. Supp. 781 (M.D. Ala. 1971), enforced 344 F. Supp. 373 and 344 F. Supp. 387 (M.D. Ala. 1972), aff'd sub nom. Wyatt v. Aderholt, 503 F.2d 1305.

Index

Psychoneurosis: and psychoneurotic disorders, 173–196; "mixed," 173, 177; psychodynamics of, 174–177

Psychopathic deviate: on MMPI scale, 47

Psychopathology: personality theories and, 115–145; dynamic bases of, 147–171; psychoneurotic disorders, 173–196; unitary view of, 201–202, 205; Menninger's concept of, 202; and Meyer's theory of "psychobiology," 261; of children, 495–517; and nonorganic psychiatric disorders of elderly, 545–546.

Psychopharmaceuticals. *See* Drug therapy; Drugs; Pharmacology

Psychophysiological disorders of children, 507–508

Psychosis: schizophreniform, 68, 201, 231; toxic, 99, 100, 215, 246–247, 275, 299, 339, 340, 341, 398, 413, 416, 420, 421, 475; sleep deprivation and, 109; Freud's view of, 130, 265; classified by Kraepelin, 200, 207, 213, 243–244; -vulnerable individual, 206, 232–233, 251; redefinitions of, 209, 265; affective, 216; depressive, 216, 269; and prepsychotic behavior, 218–219, 220–221, 222; as alternative to pain, 220; and psychotic insight, 222; family views of, 231; "transference," 232; paranoid, precipitation of, 249–250, 423; and psychotic-neurotic dichotomy in etiology of depression, 260, 261, 262, 263, 265–267; and psychotic depression, 262, 265–267; and "psychotic" vs. "nonpsychotic" organic brain syndromes, 298; therapy for, 365, 369–370, 374, 378, 385, 439, 510, 513, 514; and violent behavior, 488; in children, 507, 510; senile, increase in, 614; insanity equated with, 651; Korsakoff's, *see* Koraskoff, S. S.

Psychosocial crises. *See* Crisis

Psychosomatic disorders, 617; and history taking, 29; sleep and, 111; Franz Alexander's theories of, 128, 320; and schizophrenia, 203, 226; depression and, 256, 277; personality and, 292, 328–345; nomenclature, classification, and definition of, 319–320; and history of modern psychosomatic medicine, 320–325; "holy seven," 322–323, 325; major hypotheses and concepts of, 325–327, syndromes of, in major organ systems, 328–345; women and, 328, 337–338, 621; psychotherapy for, 333, 334–335, 452; biofeedback and, 335, 343, 344, 452–453; bereavement and, 596. *See also* Accident; Gastrointestinal disorders; Musculoskeletal disorders; Respiratory disorders; Skin disorders

Psychosurgery, 72, 388, 479–480; legal regulation of, 656

Psychotherapy, approaches to: referral for, 29, 38–39; supervision of, 39,

358, 439; "active," 127; as "corrective experience," 128, 228, 229; failures in and nonresponse to, 131, 201, 360, 361–362: client-centered, 138, 376, 635; magnetic, 149; insight-oriented, 175, 360, 365–372, 377; behavioral, 203–204, 439, 446, 447, 450, 451, 453–455; individuation in, 233, 333; milieu, 234–235, 628; psychoanalytic, vs. classical psychoanalysis, 357–358, 365–370, 383, 385; and principles of, 358–364; and termination of, 358, 364, 369, 373, 374, 380, 384, 468, 470, 490; and therapeutic objectives, 363–364, 369; and assessment of, 369–370, 373; supportive, 370–371; analytic, 376; transactional, 376, 382; dual-sex cotherapist, 376–377, 382, 468; vs. drug therapy, 423, 426–427; and praise in, 447

Psychotherapy, basic techniques: abreaction, 227, 228, 229, 333, 427, 547; suggestion, 228, 333, 547; manipulation, 228, 229, 547; clarification, 228, 359, 367, 372, 468, 538, 547; interpretation, 228, 333, 363, 367–368, 372–373, 468, 538; confrontation, 229, 290, 359, 363, 367, 372, 488, 538; reconstruction, 368; "working through," 368–369, 380, 444, 513, 538

Psychotherapy, brief, 371–373, 490, 644. *See also* Crisis

Psychotherapy for children and adolescents, 380–382, 503, 505, 509, 510, 512, 513–517, 539; team approach in, 507–508, 511; consultation in, 517; and mental retardation, 561

Psychotherapy, combined, 384–385; with hospitalization, 369, 370, 371, 388, 402, 484; with drugs, *see* Drug therapy

Psychotherapy, family, 227, 234, 251, 276; couple/marital, 278, 383, 445, 449, 453–454; children/adolescents and 380–382, 513, 539; in alcoholism, 572, 573; and suicidal person, 595

Psychotherapy, group, 224, 233–234, 251, 278, 329, 373–377, 445, 447, 453–454; vs. individual, 278, 374, 377, 546; for alcoholism, 374, 377, 571, 572–573; intensive, 378–380; psychodrama, 379, 383–384; children/adolescents and, 513, 539; for suicidal person, 595

Psychotherapy for specific disorders/conditions: neuroses, 177–178, 181, 185, 187–188, 191; depression, depressive neurosis, manic-depressives, 193, 196, 269, 272, 276–279, 445, 473; hypochondriasis, 196; paranoia, 230, 250–251; psychosomatic disorders, 333, 334–335, 452; during pregnancy, 339, 513; "migratory complaints," 439; sexual dysfunction, 467–468; geriatric, 546; alcoholism, 572; for dying adult, 581–582; for suicidal person, 594–596; schizo-

phrenia, *see* Schizophrenia

Puberty. *See* Adolescence and preadolescence; Menarche

Pugh, T. F., 613, 623

Punishment: unconscious need for, 122, 196, 474; and socialization of children, 143–144; in therapy, 227, 447, 449, 450–451, 454, 466–467, 477, 486, 576; anticipated, 232; "criminal in search of," 292; self-, and accident-proneness, 345; and masochism, 439, 576; defined, 449; social coercion as, 576–577; death as, 589, 602

Punning, 33. *See also* Speech

Purcell, K., 334

Puységur, A. M. J. C. de, 149

Pyromania, 33, 290, 292, 514, 515

Rabies: symptoms and treatment, 70

Rabin, A. I., 46

Rabiner, E. L., 234

Rachman, S., 434

Racism. *See* Cultural factors

Racy J., 475

Rado, S., 272, 593

Rafferty, J. E., 45

Rage: of paranoid schizophrenic, 34; rabies and, 70; brain pathology and, 71; defense mechanisms against, 204, 214, 220, 344; narcissistic, 288; repression of, in migraine, 344; assertive training and, 445; and temper tantrums, 487, 507, 533, 534; of suicidal person, 595

Rahe, R. H., 323, 324, 326, 597, 622

Raimbault, G., 589

Ramsey, Paul, 600

Rank, Otto, 126

Ranson, S. W., 63

Ranvier, nodes of, 61. *See also* Neuron

Rao, S., 208

Rapaport, David, 43, 123, 133, 144

Rapport. *See* Therapist-patient relationship

Ratcliff, A. W., 643

Rauwolfia. *See* Reserpine (Serpasil)

Raymond, F., 178

Raynaud's disease, 439, 452

Rayner, R., 433, 440

Razran, G., 324

Reaction formation, 158–159, 190, 508, 535; counterdependence, 158, 159, 162

Reading impairment. *See* Alexia

Reality: and transference/countertransference, 9–12, 15–16, 361; testing, 44, 265, 266, 289, 512, 595; fantasy vs., 128, 170, 171, 201, 213; ego vs., and psychosis or neurosis, 130, 165, 167, 190, 220, 221, 229, 248, 265; child's perception of, 167, 510, 512; and derealization, 195, 289; manic patients and, 259. *See also* Denial

Rebner, I., 335

Reciprocal inhibition. *See* Inhibition